Encyclopedia of
HUMAN
DEVELOPMENT

These three volumes are dedicated in the hope that the knowledge gained by exploring the topics within these pages can be used to make the world a better, safer, and more peaceful place to live in—and to those lost, from the class of 1964, Weequahic High School, and that interesting and memorable weekend in October of 2004.

Encyclopedia of HUMAN DEVELOPMENT

Editor
Neil J. Salkind
University of Kansas

Associate Editor
Lewis Margolis
University of North Carolina

Managing Editors
Kimberly DeRuyck and Kristin Rasmussen
University of Kansas

Volume 3

A SAGE Reference Publication

SAGE Publications
Thousand Oaks ■ London ■ New Delhi

For information:

Sage Publications, Inc.
2455 Teller Road
Thousand Oaks, California 91320
E-mail: order@sagepub.com

Sage Publications Ltd.
1 Oliver's Yard
55 City Road
London EC1Y 1SP
United Kingdom

Sage Publications India Pvt. Ltd.
B-42, Panchsheel Enclave
Post Box 4109
New Delhi 110 017 India

Printed in the United States of America

Library of Congress Cataloging-in-Publication data

Encyclopedia of human development / Neil J. Salkind, editor.
    p. cm.
Includes bibliographical references and index.
ISBN 1-4129-0475-7 (cloth : alk. paper)
    1. Social evolution—Encyclopedias. 2. Human evolution—Encyclopedias. 3. Developmental psychology—Encyclopedias. 4. Human behavior—Encyclopedias. I. Salkind, Neil J.
HM626.E53 2006
155'.03—dc22

2005008606

05   06   07   08   09   10   9   8   7   6   5   4   3   2   1

Acquiring Editor:	Jim Brace-Thompson
Editorial Assistant:	Karen Ehrmann
Project Editor:	Tracy Alpern
Proofreaders:	Dennis Webb
	Libby Larson
	Theresa Kay
Typesetter:	C&M Digitals (P) Ltd.
Indexer:	Pamela Van Huss
Cover Designer:	Michelle Kenny

Contents

Editorial Board

List of Entries

Reader's Guide

ABUSE

Battered Child Syndrome
Battered Woman Syndrome
Child Abuse
Child Neglect
Elder Abuse
Elder Neglect
Elder Maltreatment
Incest
Rape
Sexual Abuse

ADOLESCENCE

Adolescence
Dating
Delinquency
Gangs
Juvenile Delinquency
Storm and Stress
Teenage Pregnancy

AGING AND OLDER DEVELOPMENT

Activities of Daily Living (ADLs)
Advance Directives
Age Discrimination
Ageism
Aging
Aging Parents
Aging Well
Assisted Living
Average Life Expectancy
Baltimore Longitudinal Study on Aging
Berkeley/Oakland Longitudinal Studies
Chronological Age

Dementia
Elder Abuse
Elder Maltreatment
Elder Neglect
Generation Gap
Gerontology
Older Adulthood
Stroke
Theories of Aging
Very Old Age
Widowhood and Widowerhood
Wisdom

BIOGRAPHIES

Adler, Alfred
Ainsworth, Mary Salter
Ames, Louise
Apgar, Virginia
Bandura, Albert
Barker, Roger
Baumrind, Diane
Bayley, Nancy
Binet, Alfred
Bowlby, John
Brazelton, T. Berry
Bronfenbrenner, Urie
Brown, Roger
Bruner, Jerome
Chomsky, Noam
Darwin, Charles
Erikson, Erik
Flavell, John
Freud, Sigmund
Gardner, Howard
Gesell, Arnold
Gilligan, Carol

Magical Thinking
Metacognition
Moral Development
Object Permanence
Preoperational Thought
Primary Circular Reactions
Scaffolding
Schema
Sensory Development
Social Cognition
Stages of Development
Stages of Moral Development
Theory of Mind
Zone of Proximal Development (ZPD)

DEATH AND DYING

Assisted Suicide
Bereavement
Bereavement Overload
Brain Death
Death
Death with Dignity
Dying
Euthanasia
Funerals
Hospice
Infanticide
Mortality
National Hospice Study
Palliative Care
Parasuicide
Right-to-Die Movement
Stages of Dying

EARLY CHILDHOOD DEVELOPMENT AND EDUCATION

Abecedarian Research Project
Child Care/Day Care
Early Childhood
Early Intervention Programs
Failure to Thrive
Head Start
Kindergarten Readiness
Mozart Effect
NICHD Child Care Study
Noble Savage
Nursery (Preschool)
Perry Preschool Program
Preschool Years

Reggio Emilia Childhood Program
Resiliency
Toddlerhood
Toilet Training

EDUCATION

After-School Programs
Charter Schools
Competence Versus Performance
Distance Learning
Giftedness
Grade Retention
Higher Education
Individualized Education Programs (IEP)
Literacy
Montessori Method
Motivation
National Assessment of Educational Progress (NAEP)
National Center for Educational Statistics
Reading
SAT
School
School Dropouts
School Readiness
School Years
Sex Education

FAMILIES, FAMILY DEVELOPMENT, AND PARENTING

Adoption
Authoritarian Parenting Style
Authoritative Parenting Style
Child Custody
Child Rearing
Childlessness
Common Law Marriage
Congregate Housing
Corporal Punishment
Cosleeping Arrangements
Deadbeat Dads
Discipline
Divorce
Divorce Mediation
Domestic Violence
Dual-Earner Households
Empty Nest
Extended Family
Family Size
Fathers

Foster Care
Gay Marriages
Glass Ceiling
Grandparents
Intergenerational Relationships
Interracial Marriages
Joint Custody
Kibbutzim
Marital Equity
Marriage
Only Children
Orphans
Parent-Child Interaction
Parent-Child Relationships
Parent Training
Parenting
Parents Anonymous
Permissive Parenting Style
Poverty
Siblings
Single-Parent Family
Single Parents
Spanking
Stepfamilies
Surrogate Mothers

GENETICS/GENETIC TESTING

Alleles
Chromosomes
Fragile X Syndrome
Human Genome Project
Phenotype

HEALTH AND WELL-BEING

Abortion
Acquired Immune Deficiency Syndrome (AIDS)
Acupuncture
Addiction
Allergy
Alzheimer's Disease
Anemia
Apnea
Arteriosclerosis
Asthma
Breast Cancer
Cancer
Cardiovascular Disease
Chronic Fatigue Syndrome

Chronic Illness
Congestive Heart Failure
Creutzfeldt-Jakob Disease
Cystic Fibrosis
Deafness
Diabetes
Dieting
Disasters
Endocrine Disruptors
Epilepsy
Estrogen
Firearms
Health Insurance
Hemophilia
High Blood Pressure (Hypertension)
Homicide
Human Immunodeficiency Virus (HIV)
Huntington's Chorea
Hydrocephalus
Immune System
Inborn Errors of Metabolism
Incontinence
Infectious Diseases
Ionizing Radiation
Klinefelter's Syndrome
Lead Poisoning
Lesch-Nyhan Syndrome
Malnutrition
Methylmercury
Multiple Sclerosis
Noise
Nutrition
Obesity
Osteoarthritis
Osteoporosis
Polychlorinated Biphenyls (PCB)
Positron Emission Tomography (PET)
Preventive Medicine
Prostate Cancer
Reflexes
Rett Syndrome
Rh Factor
Rheumatoid Arthritis
Rubella (German Measles)
Sexually Transmitted Diseases (STDs)
Structural and Functional Brain Imaging
T Cells
Tay Sachs Disease
Teratogen
Testosterone

Thalassemia
Thalidomide
Tourette's Syndrome
Toxoplasmosis
Vaccination
Vitamin Deficiency
Weight
Well-Baby Checkup

INTELLIGENCE, ABILITY, AND APTITUDE

Aptitude
Aptitude Tests
Crystallized Intelligence
Developmental Quotient
Emotional Intelligence
Fluid Intelligence
Intellectual Decline
Intelligence
IQ Tests
Mental Age
Multiple Intelligences
Wechsler Adult Intelligence Scale (WAIS)
Wechsler Intelligence Scale for Children (WISC)

LANGUAGE AND COMMUNICATIONS

American Sign Language (ASL)
Babbling
Baby Talk
Bilingualism
Echolalia
English as a Second Language (ESL)
Language Acquisition Device
Language Development
Mean Length Utterance
Phonics
Phonological Awareness
Private Speech
Second Languages
Semantic Development
Stuttering
Universal Grammar
Whole Language

LAWS AND POLICIES

Americans with Disabilities Act (ADA)
Children with Special Health Care Needs (CSHCN)
Children's Rights
Courtroom Testimony

Inclusion/Mainstreaming
Individuals with Disabilities Education Act (IDEA)
Medicare
Older Americans Act
Public Policy
Social Security

LEARNING AND MEMORY

Amnesia
Classical Conditioning
Dyslexia
Extinction
False Memories
Inhibitory Control
Learning
Learning Disabilities
Long-Term Memory
Memory Failure
Operant Conditioning
Problem Solving
Punishment
Reinforcement
Retention
Short-Term Memory

MENTAL HEALTH, MENTAL DISORDERS, AND SPECIAL GROUPS

Anorexia Nervosa
Antisocial Behavior
Anxiety Disorders
Asperger Syndrome
Attention Deficit Hyperactivity Disorder (ADHD)
Autism
Binge Drinking
Binge Eating
Bulimia Nervosa
Cluster Suicide
Comorbidity
Conduct Disorder
Depression
Developmental Disabilities
Developmental Psychopathology
Down Syndrome
Eating Disorders
Generalized Anxiety Disorder
Independent Living
Mental Retardation
Mood Disorders

Catholicism
Ethnic Cleansing
Ethnic Identity
Hate Crimes
Hispanic Americans
Holocaust
Immigrants
Islam
Judaism
Native Americans
Religion

SEXUALITY AND SEX

Bisexuality
Contraception
Erectile Dysfunction
Extramarital Sex
Heterosexuality
Homosexuality
Intimacy
Kinsey Institute
Lesbians

SOCIAL DEVELOPMENT AND SOCIAL BEHAVIOR

Aggression
Altruism
Androgyny
Attitude
Bar/Bat Mitzvah
Bullying
Career Development
Cohabitation
Conflict
Cooperative Learning
Cooperative Play
Cross-Cultural Development
Disgust
Emerging Adulthood
Empathy
Friendship
Gender Differences
Gender Identity
Gender Role Development
Gilligan's Theory of Feminine Morality
Later Adulthood
Learned Helplessness
Locus of Control

Loneliness
Mentor
Midlife Crisis
Moral Reasoning
Neighborhoods
Peer Pressure
Peers
Pets
Prosocial Behavior
Psychosocial Development
Quinceañera
Self-Fulfilling Prophecy
Sex Differences
Smiling
Social Class
Social Development
Socioeconomic Status
Strange Situation
Stress
Symbolic Play
Television
Video Games
Violence
Volunteering
Work

STATISTICS, RESEARCH METHODS, AND MEASUREMENT

Case Study
Cohort
Correlation
Criterion Referenced Tests
Cross-Sectional Research
Dependent Variable
Diagnostic and Statistical Manual of Mental Disorders
Ethical Standards of Research
Experiment
Experimental Group
Experimental Method
Framingham Study
Generalizability
Hypothesis
Internet
Longitudinal Research
Meta-Analysis
Naturalistic Observation
New York Longitudinal Study (NYLS)
Norm-Referenced Tests
Normal Curve (Bell Curve)
Norms

Observational Learning
Qualitative Methods
Quantitative Methods
Quasi-Experimental Design
Reliability
Sampling
Scientific Method
Seattle Longitudinal Study
Standardized Testing
Statistical Significance
Twin Studies
Validity
Visual Cliff

SUBSTANCE ABUSE

Alcoholics Anonymous
Alcoholism
Amphetamines
Cocaine
Crack Baby Syndrome
Drug Abuse
Drunk Driving
Gateway Drug
Marijuana
Methadone

THEORIES AND IDEAS ABOUT DEVELOPMENT

Applied Behavior Analysis
Conscience

Continuity and Discontinuity in Development
Critical Period
Deferred Imitation
Development
Developmental Direction
Ecological Theory
Ego
Ego Development
Electra and Oedipal Complexes
Ethology
Id
Imitation
Imprinting
Nature–Nurture
Psychoanalytic Theory
Reciprocal Determinism
Self-Efficacy
Sensitive Period
Separation Anxiety
Sociobiology
Superego
Tabula Rasa
Theories of Development
Utopianism

P

Phobias

You gain strength, courage and confidence by every experience in which you really stop to look fear in the face. You are able to say to yourself, "I have lived through this horror. I can take the next thing that comes along." You must do the thing you think you cannot do.

—Eleanor Roosevelt

PAIN

Pain affects more than 50 million Americans yearly, accounting for more than 80% of all visits to physicians and costing more than $70 billion annually in health care and lost productivity. Life without pain would be difficult. Pain serves as a warning device to signal potential tissue damage. It serves a recuperative function that promotes healing. Pain provides low-level feedback about the functioning of our bodily systems. We use this pain to make minor adjustments, such as shifting body weight when sitting long periods. Pain is the symptom that is most likely to lead us to seek treatment. The International Association for the Study of Pain defines pain as an unpleasant experience associated with actual or potential tissue damage to a person's body. The degree to which pain is felt depends on how it is interpreted, and how it is interpreted is influenced by the context in which it is experienced.

Pain is defined as acute or chronic. Acute pain lasts for 6 months or less and results from a specific injury that produces tissue damage. Typically, it disappears when the tissue damage is repaired. Chronic pain is defined by the International Association for the Study of Pain as pain without apparent biological value that has persisted beyond the normal tissue healing time. It occurs in 10.1% to 55.2% of the population. Although it typically begins with an acute episode, it does not decrease with treatment and the passage of time.

Theories of pain must define how we sense pain, or the physical components of the delivery of pain, and how we perceive pain, or how we interpret the sensations our bodies receive. The earliest theories of pain argued that pain is due to nerve impulses produced by an injury and transmitted directly to a pain center in the brain. This specificity model proposed specific sensory receptors responsible for the transmission of different types of sensations. Pain, in this model, is proportional to the extent of the injury. Other theorists argued for a pattern theory of pain, whereby pain sensations result from the transmission of patterns of stimulation at the peripheral nerve endings. The gate theory, developed by Ronald Melzak, a Canadian psychologist, and Patrick Wall, a British neuroscientist, integrates both specificity and pattern theory and begins to explain the importance of psychological factors in the pain experience. Melzak and Wall argue for an attention mechanism whereby nerve impulses are influenced in the spinal cord by other nerve cells that act like gates, either preventing the impulses from getting through or facilitating their passage to the brain.

One manner in which the brain controls pain is through endogenous opioids—narcotic-like substances produced within the body. Wall argues that the brain's involvement is more complex than simply the production of endogenous opioids; rather, pain is a sequence of events that begins when an injury generates an announcement of its presence in the sensory nerves, followed by the attention mechanism selecting the incoming message as worthy of entry, and finally, the brain generating the sensation of pain. Classic theory argues that the brain analyzes the sensory input to determine what has happened and presents the answer as a pure sensation. Wall, on the other hand, proposes that the brain analyzes the input in terms of what action is appropriate. When any of the three components is missing—sensation, attention, or motor planning—pain does not occur.

Psychologist Dennis C. Turk focuses on a cognitive-behavioral model that incorporates anticipation, avoidance, and reinforcement. The critical factor for the cognitive-behavioral model is that people learn to predict events and to respond with appropriate reactions. People with pain have negative expectations about their ability to control certain motor skills, such as walking or bending, without pain and tend to believe they have limited ability to exert any control over their pain.

Treatment of pain is varied and often multimodal. Pharmacological control is the first line of defense. The American Pain Society indicates that it is possible to manage pain adequately in patients, including substance abusers, with life-threatening illness and to do so safely and responsibly using narcotics. Surgical treatment involves cutting the pain fibers at various points in the body, so that pain sensations no longer can be conducted. The effects are often short-lived and may worsen the pain because the treatment damages the nervous system.

Some treatments focus on sensory control of pain. One of the oldest known techniques of pain control is counterirritation, whereby pain is inhibited in one part of the body by stimulating another area. Another sensory control method is the use of exercise. Although at one time it was felt that the less activity, the better, current treatment philosophy emphasizes exercise. A third method of sensory control is acupuncture. In acupuncture treatment, long, thin needles are inserted into points on the body thought to influence areas in which a patient is experiencing pain. It is effective against some forms of pain, both chronic and acute. However, it exacerbates other forms of pain, again both chronic and acute.

Numerous treatments emphasize patient control of pain. One, biofeedback, comprises a wide variety of techniques that provide biophysiological feedback about bodily processes. Another method of patient control is relaxation. Teaching patients relaxation techniques helps them deal more effectively with stress and anxiety, which may indirectly reduce pain. Relaxation also may affect pain directly by relaxing muscles or diverting blood flow. A third method of patient control is hypnosis. Although the exact mechanism by which it works is not clear, hypnosis is effective for the management of some types of acute pain. A fourth method is distraction, which involves turning one's attention away from pain by focusing on other things or by engaging in vigorous activity. Although useful for low-level acute pain, patients with chronic pain cannot distract themselves indefinitely. Finally, guided imagery, in which patients conjure up a picture that they hold in their mind during the painful experience, has been used to control some acute pain and discomfort.

When all other treatments fail for patients with chronic pain, pain management programs may be used. These are interdisciplinary programs, bringing together all that is known about pain control. Patients are carefully evaluated with respect to their pain and pain behaviors. This is followed by an individualized treatment plan based on the profile of the patient's pain and how it has affected his or her life. Pain management programs include several common features, such as patient education about the nature of their illness, training in measures to reduce pain, and group therapy to help patients gain control of their emotional responses. Many programs include family therapy that focuses on the inadvertent reinforcement of pain behaviors by the family. Finally, relapse prevention is an important component to these programs. Studies indicate that these interventions reduce reports of pain disability and psychological distress.

The pain associated with some terminal illnesses is reported by many patients as the most feared component of the illness. For these patients, palliative care is appropriate. Palliative care is similar to hospice care but continues supportive measures such as blood transfusions and tube feedings. Palliative care is more appropriate than hospice care for children. In addition, palliative care is appropriate for children with a wide range of conditions, even when a cure remains a possibility. Bruce Himelstein and colleagues have outlined four types of conditions for which pediatric palliative care is appropriate. The first type includes conditions for which curative treatment is possible but may fail, such as, advanced or progressive cancer. The second includes conditions requiring intensive long-term treatment aimed at maintaining the quality of life, such as human immunodeficiency virus infection. The next type includes progressive conditions in which treatment is exclusively palliative after diagnosis, such as progressive metabolic disorders. Finally, the fourth includes conditions involving severe, non-progressive disability, causing extreme vulnerability to health complications, such as severe cerebral palsy with recurrent infection.

Himelstein and colleagues also address the five essential elements of pediatric palliative care. In the physical dimension, the primary objective is to identify the patient's pain or other symptoms. In the psychosocial dimension, the objectives focus on identifying the fears and concerns of the both the child and the family, understanding what the child knows about death and how he or she copes with such issues, and identifying resources to help in the grieving process. The spiritual dimension involves performing an assessment of the child's hopes, dreams, and values. The Advance Care Planning–Illness Trajectory dimension helps the family decision makers clarify goals for the child's care and addresses the concerns of the family as the end of the child's life nears. Finally, the dimension of practical concerns deals with issues of coordination of the health care team, preferences for location of care, the child's functional status, and financial issues associated with the child's illness.

Our knowledge of pain and effective treatment of it are limited. Research in recent years has expanded our understanding of the dynamics of pain and has helped us focus on methods to treat or alleviate its effects. Future research should broaden our knowledge of this area.

—*Virginia Norris*

Further Readings and References

Himelstein, B. P., Hilden, J. M., Boldt, A. M., & Weissman, D. (2004). Medical progress: Pediatric palliative care. *New England Journal of Medicine, 350,* 1752–1762.

Institute of Medicine of the National Academies. (2003). *When children die: Improving palliative and end-of-life care for children and their families.* Washington, DC: National Academies Press.

Jacobsen, P. B., & Breitbart, W. (2002). Managing pain in chronic illness. In Chesney, M. A., & Antoni, M. H. (Eds.), *Innovative approaches to health psychology: Prevention and treatment lessons from AIDS* (pp. 219–234). Washington, DC: American Psychological Association.

John C. Liebeskind History of Pain Collection. (1998). *Relief of pain and suffering.* Retrieved from http://www.library.ucla.edu/libraries/biomed/his/painexhibit/index.html

McGrath, P. J., Finley, G. A., & Ritchie, J. (1994). *Pain, pain, go away: Helping children with pain.* Retrieved from http://is.dal.ca/~pedpain/ppga/ppga.html

Morris, D. B. (2001, November). Ethnicity and pain. *Pain Clinical Updates, IX*(4).

National Institute of Arthritis and Musculoskeletal and Skin Disorders. (2003, March). *NIAMS pain research: An overview.* Retrieved from http://www.niams.nih.gov/hi/topics/pain/pain.htm

Taylor, S. E. (2003). *Health psychology* (5th ed.). Boston: McGraw-Hill.

Turk, D. C. (2001). Physiological and psychological bases of pain. In A. Baum, T. A. Revenson, & J. E. Singer (Eds.), *Handbook of health psychology* (pp. 117–137). Mahwah, NJ: Erlbaum.

Wall, P. D. (2000). *Pain: The science of suffering.* New York: Columbia University Press.

PALLIATIVE CARE

Since its introduction into medical practice during the 1960s and 1970s in the United States, the United Kingdom, and Canada, palliative care has been defined and practiced in various, and often differing, ways. At its inception, it focused on relief of suffering and care of the adult patient dying from incurable cancer. Over time, the definition and practice have come to focus on improving quality of life and alleviating suffering for both pediatric and adult patients within a wider diagnostic spectrum.

Broadly construed, palliative care refers to care that seeks to prevent, ease, or reduce symptoms without curing the underlying disease or disorder. In this sense, palliative care is not restricted to dying patients or to patients enrolled in hospice programs. Following this general definition, the 1997 Institute of Medicine (IOM) report on improving care at the end of life cites palliative care as an important adjunct to life-prolonging therapies as well as to those who live with chronic illnesses, chronic pain, or other symptoms. The National Hospice and Palliative Care Organization extended this definition in 2003 to include the management of distressing symptoms, provision of respite, and care that begins at diagnosis and continues through death and bereavement.

In contrast are definitions of palliative care that are more restrictive. For example, the 1990 World Health Organization (WHO) definition is specific to care of patients whose disease cannot be cured. Other sources similarly describe palliative care as the management of patients with advanced and progressive disease.

Thus, there is lack of agreement among health care professionals about what palliative care is, who should receive it, when it begins, and when it ends. Indeed, the term is often used interchangeably with terms such as *supportive care, comfort care, hospice care,* and *end-of-life care.* Moreover, some health care professionals continue to associate palliative care with cancer and believe there is a clear line between the ending of cure-oriented care and the beginning of palliative care. In this view, palliative care requires that patients give up treatments aimed at cure, such as radiation or chemotherapy. Others believe the transition between cure and care is more gradual and less definitive. In this view, palliative care complements therapies aimed at curing disease or prolonging life. In addition, it can help patients and families navigate the changing goals of care in the face of progressive illness and the necessity of a wider range of palliative interventions to satisfy increasingly complex care needs. Over time, priority of care shifts away from cure and toward focus on the dying process. Emphasized are end-of-life decision making, care that supports physical comfort, and a death that is consistent with the values and expressed desires of the patient. In this model, the aim is symptom relief and comfort for patients, regardless of their place on the illness continuum.

Despite lack of consensus about the range of palliative care, there is general agreement about its goals. These include a total approach to care provided by an interdisciplinary team, focus on prevention and relief of suffering, and promotion of quality of life. Major concerns include pain and symptom management; giving patients and families the information needed to participate in decisions about care; advance care planning; psychosocial, spiritual, and practical support; coordination of care, including arranging for expert help and services in the community; and remaining sensitive to personal, cultural, and religious values, beliefs, and practices of patients and families.

Consideration of the palliative care needs of children (including both neonatal and pediatric care) has received heightened attention in recent years. Although preparing for a child's death is met with complex emotions by parents, experts believe that the implementation of palliative care strategies at the time of a life-threatening diagnosis can improve the care of those who survive and those who die. However, the 2002 IOM report highlights that children are unique in terms of anatomy, physiology, and psychosocial and cognitive development. As such, specific decisions about palliative care must be adapted to each child's level of development. Moreover, the child's status as a minor necessitates parent involvement in palliative care planning.

Meeting the goals of palliative care requires the coordinated involvement of multiple disciplines, although various settings may have different ways of organizing and staffing care teams. In addition to the attending physician, nurses and social workers are considered key members of an effective palliative care team. Teams may also include psychologists; chaplains; physical, occupational, or speech therapists; home health aides; a bereavement coordinator; trained volunteers; and child life specialists. The patient and his or her family, as well as any others involved in caring for the patient, are considered integral members of the care team as well as the focal point of the caring process.

The practice of palliative care varies widely throughout the United States. The most frequent sites for adult palliative care delivery include hospitals, nursing homes, home care as part of a hospice program, home care without hospice, and inpatient hospices. Some hospitals and nursing homes provide inpatient palliative care units, whereas others provide palliative care through consulting teams or through one or more designated individuals who may be called on for consultation or assistance with palliative care. However, according to the 1997 IOM report, many hospitals and nursing homes have neither an identifiable inpatient palliative care team, nor individual personnel with clearly designated palliative care expertise. Hospices are organizations specifically intended for provision of palliative care to dying patients and those close to them. However, patients who have palliative care needs but who do not qualify for hospice care may be challenged in finding resources. Moreover, the availability of pediatric home hospice care is sparse, though rising.

Palliative care has become an area of special expertise within medicine, nursing, social work, pharmacy, chaplaincy, and other disciplines. The United Kingdom recognized palliative medicine as a medical specialty in 1987, followed by Australia, New Zealand, and Canada. An effort to win specialty recognition in the United States is under consideration. However, many agree that every health care professional that deals directly with seriously ill and dying patients and their families needs a basic grounding and demonstrated core competencies in palliative care. Fortunately, numerous professional societies (e.g., American Academy of Hospice and Palliative Medicine) and organizations (e.g., Last Acts Partnership, Initiative for Pediatric Palliative Care), journals (e.g., *Journal of Pain and Symptom Management*), meetings and conferences, academic centers (e.g., Duke University Institute on Care at the End of Life), and experts in palliative care continue to direct more attention to improved practice, research, and education in the field.

—*Melanie J. Bonner, A. Bebe Guill,
and Megan Brown*

See also Death, Death with Dignity

Further Readings and References

American Board of Internal Medicine. (1996). *Caring for the dying: Identification of and promotion of physician competency. Educational research documents.* Philadelphia: Author.

Armstrong-Dailey, A., & Zarbcok, S. (Eds.). (2001). *Hospice care for children.* New York: Oxford University Press.

Goldman, A. (1996). Home care of the dying child. *Journal of Palliative Care, 12,* 16–19.

Himelstein, B. P., Hilden, J. M., Boldt, A. M., & Weissman, D. (2004). Pediatric palliative care. *New England Journal of Medicine, 350,* 1752–1762.

Institute of Medicine, Committee on Palliative and End-of-Life Care for Children and Their Families (M. J. Field & R. E. Behrman, Eds.). (2002). *When children die: Improving palliative and end-of-life care for children and their families.* Washington, DC: National Academies Press.

Lynn, J., Schuster, J. L., & Kabacenell, A. (2000). *Improving care for the end of life: A sourcebook for health care managers and clinicians.* Oxford, UK: Oxford University Press.

National Hospice and Palliative Care Organization, http://www.nhpco.org

Rushton, C. H. (2001). Pediatric palliative care: Coming of age. In M. Z. Solomon, A. L. Romer, K. S. Heller, & D. E. Weissman (Eds.), *Innovations in end-of-life care: Practical strategies and international perspectives, Vol. 2.* (pp. 167–170). Larchmont, NY: Mary Ann Liebert.

Wolfe, J., Grier, H. E., Klar, N., Levin, S. B., Ellenbogen, J. M., Salem-Schatz, S., et al. (2000). Symptoms and suffering at the end of life in children with cancer. *New England Journal of Medicine, 342,* 326–333.

PANIC DISORDER

According to the current diagnostic definition, panic disorder is diagnosed when (1) there are recurrent unexpected panic attacks, and (2) at least one of the attacks is followed by persistent worry about future attacks, implications of an attack, and a change in behavior due to the attack (i.e., impaired interpersonal functioning). A panic attack is defined as a discrete event that involves intense fear and several physiological reactions such as palpitations, sweating, dizziness, shortness of breath (sometimes experienced as "a band around the chest"), trembling, numbness or tingling in the extremities, and nausea. In addition to these acute physiological reactions, panic attacks often include derealization (feeling that the world or situation is not real) or depersonalization (described as a detached feeling, or that one is outside oneself watching a movie). Finally, during a panic attack, individuals often report feeling that they might die or lose control (physically or mentally).

Panic disorder, characterized by panic attacks occurring regularly or a persistent fear of future panic attacks, has two subtypes. One subtype is panic disorder with agoraphobia (PDA). Individuals with PDA not only have a persistent fear of future panic attacks but also avoid different places or situations out of a concern that another attack may occur. In severe cases, the range of places and situations avoided is so extensive that the sufferer cannot leave the home. Some individuals with PDA may be able to go places when accompanied by someone they trust will successfully care for them should they have a panic attack in public. The other subtype is panic disorder without history of agoraphobia (PD). Sufferers of PD may be apprehensive of having a panic attack in public but do not exhibit the widespread avoidance of public places, with the consequent limitations in mobility, typical of individuals with PDA. PDA and PD have equal prevalence rates of about 3.5%, according to the National Comorbidity Survey.

PREVALENCE AND ETIOLOGICAL FACTORS

Biological studies of the hereditability of panic disorder, either with or without agoraphobia, have not conclusively determined that the disorder is genetically transmitted. Instead, and consistent with models of other anxiety disorders, it has been suggested that a genetic vulnerability exists that potentiates the development of the disorder.

An important aspect of PD and PDA involves the differential gender distribution of the disorders. Although PD is generally higher in women than in men, the gender differences in PDA are striking. Estimates of the differences are as high as 5:1 ratio of females to males with PDA, and with women typically experiencing more severe symptoms. It is generally true for all anxiety disorders that there is a higher prevalence in women than in men, but this gender difference is even more pronounced in the case of PD and PDA.

One dominant model of the etiology of panic involves what has been termed the *false-suffocation alarm,* whereby the individual has an increased sensitivity to carbon dioxide in the environment. When there is an increase in carbon dioxide that would otherwise be undetectable to most individuals, the PD sufferer has an automatic alarm that alerts him or her to the possibility of suffocation. However, because other people in the same situation are both unaware and unaffected by the increased carbon dioxide, the panic sensation of feeling unable to catch one's breath and the associated anxiety appear uncued. Providing direct experimental evidence for the false-suffocation alarm model is complicated by the fact that increased carbon dioxide in the blood brings about physiological responses such as increases in respiratory and heart rates. Therefore, it is difficult to separate whether anxiety associated with a panic attack is due to an increased sensitivity to elevated levels of carbon dioxide in the blood or the misinterpretation of bodily symptoms (e.g., increased respiratory and heart rates).

The problem of misinterpretation of bodily symptoms leads to another major model used to explain panic disorder, namely the dispositional trait of *anxiety sensitivity*. This construct describes the propensity to attribute risk or potential harm to variations in bodily sensations. Someone with elevated anxiety sensitivity is considered at risk for PD or at least has a higher likelihood of experiencing panic attacks. The design of the Anxiety Sensitivity Index reflects the common concerns articulated by PD sufferers. Specifically, three factors have been identified from this measure: fear of cardiovascular symptoms, fear of publicly observable symptoms, and fear of loss of cognitive control. Taken in turn, fear of cardiovascular symptoms is observed in many PD sufferers, who sometimes seek reassurance that they are not having a heart attack by visiting the emergency room during a panic attack. The PD sufferer also dreads the shame and embarrassment of having a panic attack in public where others may witness him or her being overwhelmed and incapacitated. Finally, fear of loss of cognitive control is evident by the all too common complaint among PD sufferers that during a panic attack, they feel they will "go crazy" or lose their minds.

When considered in conjunction with the aforementioned false-suffocation fear hypothesis, anxiety sensitivity is a useful predictor of responses to biological challenge tests. One method is the hyperventilation challenge, in which an attempt is made to replicate panic sensations in the laboratory. It has been found that participants, who have no history of panic but have elevated anxiety sensitivity, tend to experience increased anxiety when instructed to hyperventilate.

TREATMENT OF PANIC DISORDER WITH OR WITHOUT AGORAPHOBIA

Despite the similarities between PD and PDA, treatment outcome for these disorders has been quite different. Treatment for PD alone is reliant on a combination of cognitive and behavioral therapy. Cognitive therapy for PD challenges the threat appraisals associated with physical sensations. These catastrophic misinterpretations of the body's feedback are considered central to the maintenance of PD according to cognitive theorists. Altering these misinterpretations leads, then, to decreases in panic severity.

Although the cognitive approach to therapy has gained prominence and has been proved effective, behavioral therapy is another important component of treatment for PD. Specifically, exposure to interoceptive cues (anxiety-provoking bodily sensations) is necessary for the alleviation of panic symptoms. For example, if a PD sufferer were primarily concerned about heart palpitations, then interoceptive cue exposure would focus on increasing heart rate during the session as part of the exposure treatment. Carefully regulated exposure to the anxiety-provoking sensations results in decreased levels of anxiety elicited when exposed to the same internal cues, feelings of mastery, and an erosion of the confidence in catastrophic predictions based on physical sensations. For example, a panic sufferer may be asked to experience dizziness during a treatment session in order to gain mastery over a sensation commonly associated with panic attacks. A detailed discussion of interceptive cue exposure can be found in Barlow (2002). When this approach is used in conjunction with exposure for situations that are avoided, then the range of mobility is improved in PDA sufferers, although this is more difficult than in PD.

Although the outcome for both cognitive and behavioral interventions for PD has been generally favorable, outcome results in the treatment of PDA have been less positive. Cognitive behavioral therapy for PDA also focuses on challenging the catastrophic misinterpretations of interoceptive cues and providing exposure to these anxiety-producing bodily sensations. However, agoraphobia also requires exposure to situational cues that give rise to anxiety and the risk for panic attacks. The literature suggests that often PDA sufferers do not achieve the level of mobility that matches the outcome goal typically set by therapists. In treating individuals with PDA, it is often necessary to make home visits or extend the duration of sessions in order to ensure a complete return to baseline levels of anxiety during the exposure session. Furthermore, extensive homework assignments for continued exposure are essential to positive outcome for PDA. This includes activities designed to specifically increase mobility, with the same goal of increased mastery over both the environment and anxiety that is experienced in the face of possibly experiencing a panic attack.

—*Dean McKay and Kevin McKiernan*

Further Readings and References

American Psychiatric Association. (2000). *Diagnostic and Statistical Manual of Mental Disorders* (4th ed., text revision). Washington, DC: Author.

Anxiety Network International, http://www.anxietynetwork.com/pdhome.html

Anxiety and Panic, http://www.anxietypanic.com/

Arntz, A. (2002). Cognitive therapy versus interoceptive exposure as treatment of panic disorder without agoraphobia. *Behaviour Research and Therapy, 40*, 325–341.

Barlow, D. H. (2002). *Anxiety and its disorders: The nature and treatment of anxiety and panic* (2nd ed.). New York: Guilford.

Bekker, M. H. J. (1996). Agoraphobia and gender: A review. *Clinical Psychology Review, 16*, 129–142.

Clark, D. M. (1986). A cognitive approach to panic. *Behaviour Research and Therapy, 24*, 461–470.

Craske, M. G. (2003). *Origins of phobias and anxiety disorders: Why more women than men?* Amsterdam: Elsevier.

Craske, M. G., Rachman, S., & Tallman, K. (1986). Mobility, cognitions and panic. *Journal of Psychopathology and Behavioral Assessment, 8*, 199–210.

Keisjers, G. P. J., Hoogduin, C. A. L., & Schaap, C. P. D. R. (1994). Prognostic factors in the behavioral treatment of panic disorder with and without agoraphobia. *Behavior Therapy, 25*, 689–708.

Kessler, R. C., McGonagle, K. A., Zhao, S., Nelson, C. B., Hughes, M., Eshleman, S., et al. (1994). Lifetime and 12-month prevalence of DSM-III-R psychiatric disorders in the United States: Results from the National Comorbidity Survey. *Archives of General Psychiatry, 51*, 8–19.

Ley, R. (1985). Blood, breath, and fears: A hyperventilation theory of panic attacks and agoraphobia. *Clinical Psychology Review, 5*, 271–285.

McNally, R. J. (1994). *Panic disorder: A critical analysis.* New York: Guilford.

McNally, R. J., & Eke, M. (1996). Anxiety sensitivity, suffocation fear, and breath-holding duration as predictors of response to carbon dioxide challenge. *Journal of Abnormal Psychology, 105*, 146–149.

National Institute of Mental Health Panic Disorder, http://www.anxietynetwork.com/pdhome.html

National Institute of Mental Health Therapy Advisor (for Panic Disorder and Panic Disorder with Agoraphobia), http://www.therapyadvisor.com

Peterson, R. A., & Reiss, S. (1992). *Anxiety Sensitivity Index revised manual.* Worthington, OH: International Diagnostic Systems Publishing.

Reiss, S., & McNally, R. J. (1985). The expectancy model of fear. In S. Reiss & R. R. Bootzin (Eds.), *Theoretical issues in behavior therapy* (pp. 107–121). New York: Academic Press.

PARASUICIDE

Parasuicide describes any nonlethal, deliberate self-harm behavior. Linehan further divides parasuicide into the categories of suicide attempts not completed with intent to die, ambivalent suicide attempts with unclear intent to die, and nonsuicidal self-injury. This definition is controversial, however, because some believe that deliberate self-harm behavior should only be considered parasuicide if there is no intent to die. The debate is complicated by the reality that it is often difficult to determine the intentions of people who engage in self-harm. Because of varying definitions of parasuicide and the diversity of locations in which it has been studied, lifetime prevalence rates vary widely from 1% to 6% of the population.

Parasuicidal behaviors range from the most frequently used method of self-poisoning by drug or alcohol overdose to using cutting or piercing instruments on oneself. Parasuicidal behaviors occasionally include methods that are typically more lethal, such as hanging, drowning, consuming potentially dangerous chemicals, jumping from high places, or using guns.

Generally, rates of parasuicidality appear to be higher for females than males. Among females, the highest rates are for 15- to 24-year-olds. Males are at the highest risk between the ages of 25 and 34 years. Racial-ethnic differences have been found among U.S. adolescents, with suicide attempts made by 10% of European American females, 10% of African American females, 8% of African American males, and 5% of European American males. There have not been any comparable studies done recently on adults in the United States. However, ethnic differences have been found in European studies, with young Asian women being at highest risk.

Parasuicidal behavior has been found to predict future parasuicidal behavior as well as completed suicides. As many as 50% of completed suicides have been preceded by parasuicidal behavior. Other generally agreed on risk factors for parasuicide include having a mental disorder (especially borderline personality disorder or depression), substance use, childhood sexual abuse, unemployment, having recently changed living situations, being single or divorced, being female, and being younger. Additional risk factors currently being studied include loneliness, deficits in problem solving, deficits in interpersonal relations and skills, comorbidity, and sexual orientation. A risk factor specific to the elderly is having an acute or chronic physical illness. Experiencing problems at school is an additional risk factor for adolescents. Factors thought to protect against parasuicidality are family closeness, social support, and possibly religiosity.

Treatment for individuals with parasuicidal behaviors should start with a comprehensive assessment of both current parasuicidal ideation and a history of parasuicidal behaviors using clinical interviews and relevant measures. In addition, known and potential risk factors should also be assessed. Assessment should lead to a determination of risk for additional parasuicidal behavior or suicide. Because of the heterogeneity among people who engage in parasuicidal behavior, there is no established treatment procedure to follow once initial assessment and case conceptualization have been completed. However, several interventions have received some empirical support: cognitive-behavioral problem-solving therapy, medication management with flupenthixol decanoate, home visitation to ensure treatment compliance, psychodynamic interpersonal therapy, and dialectical behavior therapy for people with borderline personality disorder. Additional research is needed to determine which treatments are most effective depending on the client's age, culture, and precipitating problems or diagnoses.

—*Marc S. Karver and Nicole Caporino*

See also Assisted Suicide, Cluster Suicide

Further Readings and References

Comtois, K. (2002). A review of interventions to reduce the prevalence of parasuicide. *Psychiatric Services, 53*(9), 1138–1144.

DeLeo, D., Scocco, P., Marietta, P., Schmidtke, A., Bille-Brahe, U., Kerkhof, A. J. F. M., et al. (1999). Physical illness and parasuicide: Evidence from the European parasuicide study interview schedule (EPSIS/WHO-EURO). *International Journal of Psychiatry in Medicine, 29*(2), 149–163.

Fergusson, D. M., Beautrais, A. L., & Horwood, L. J. (2003). Vulnerability and resiliency to suicidal behaviors in young people. *Psychological Medicine, 33,* 61–73.

Gratz, K. L. (2003). Risk factors for and functions of deliberate self-harm: An empirical and conceptual review. *Clinical Psychology: Science & Practice, 10*(2), 192–205.

Joe, S., & Marcus, S. C. (2003). Datapoints: Trends by race and gender in suicide attempts among U.S. adolescents, 1991–2001. *Psychiatric Services, 54*(4), 454.

Linehan, M. (1986). Suicidal people: One population or two? *Annals of the New York Academy of Sciences, 487,* 16–33.

Michel, K., Ballinari, P., Bille-Brahe, U., Bjerke, T., Crepet, P., De Leo, D., et al. (2000). Methods used for parasuicide: Results of the WHO/EURO Multicentre Study on Parasuicide. *Social Psychiatry & Psychiatric Epidemiology, 35*(4), 156–163.

Neeleman, J., Wilson-Jones, C., & Wessely, S. (2001). Ethnic density and deliberate self harm; a small area study in south east London. *Journal of Epidemiology & Community Health, 55*(2), 85–90.

Stewart, S. E., Manion, I. G., & Davidson, S. (2002). Emergency management of the adolescent suicide attemptor: A review of the literature. *Journal of Adolescent Health, 30*(5), 312–325.

Welch, S. S. (2001). A review of the literature on the epidemiology of parasuicide in the general population. *Psychiatric Services, 52*(3), 368–375.

PARENT-CHILD INTERACTION

Throughout the life span, parent-child interaction is an important context for development. Bronfenbrenner's ecological approach to human development describes behavior as unfolding within a nested and interactive set of systems and levels ranging from several microsystems (family, peers, neighborhood) to the macrosystem (broad societal norms and attitudes). Although development clearly occurs within all of these multiple systems and contexts, the family context is one of the most proximal and often the most influential of these systems.

THEORETICAL OVERVIEW

Current research has focused our attention on the quality of parent-child interaction as a critical component in understanding cognitive and social-emotional pathways for children and youth. Parents' unique ways of responding to a child's fundamental needs—and the child's corresponding expectations—are evident in infancy, resulting in interaction patterns that remain generally stable throughout a child's journey into adulthood. Parent-child interaction style is determined by many factors, including parental and child characteristics and propensities, situational factors (such as social class and support systems), and cultural and societal norms.

Many theorists believe that the best way to understand the influence of parent-child interaction on development is to examine the child's development in the context of the parent's behavior. Beginning during infancy and continuing through toddlerhood, children develop the capacity for self-regulation and self-control, and they internalize the standards, rules, and expectations of their family situations. During this time, a child must learn to manage frustrations and excitement, delay gratification, and accept disappointment. With increasingly sophisticated motor skills, children are able to engage with their environments on their own and to negotiate early social relations. Understanding and responding to the views of others, coping with interpersonal tensions, and having the capacity to enjoy play partners are some of the challenging developmental tasks of early childhood.

Diverse theoretical frameworks address how children develop the aforementioned skills as they interact with their primary caregivers. Attachment theory, as well as other psychodynamic and psychosocial views, suggests that self-regulatory processes emerge as early as infancy from the parent-child system. These theories focus on the parent's responsiveness to the child—the degree to which the parent successfully interprets and responds to the child's cues. A parent who promptly picks up and soothes a crying baby or who stops a stimulating game when the child turns away would be described as responsive, synchronous, or attune to the child's cues. A parent who disrupts a child's appropriate attempts at play to assert his or her own agenda or who ignores (or misinterprets) a child in distress might be described as poorly attuned to the child's cues.

Through interactions with the parent, the child's view of self and the world is created. Consistent, responsive interactions with a primary caregiver help the child form a stable core of self-regulatory abilities. If parents provide a reassuring base from which the child can explore and engage the world, following the child's cues and remaining emotionally available yet respectful of the child's autonomy, the child will develop confidence to approach new tasks and resilience in the face of frustration. If a parent is unable to interpret the cues of the child or feels threatened by or responds punitively to the child's growing autonomy, a child's sense of self in relation to his or her world becomes unsure, because the child grows to believe that his or her efforts to communicate needs to the parent will fail. Thus, a child's self-confidence evolves from the confidence the child experienced in the early parent-child relationship. Feelings of security and predictability in the attachment relationship result in the child's self-reliance and the capacity to seek out relations with others who are caring. From this perspective, the parent-child interaction serves as a "working model" that influences interpersonal expectations, as well as affective and behavioral responses to future relationships.

Although parent-child interaction style is often discussed as a unidirectional variable—that is, going from parent to child—anyone who has spent time with children knows that children influence parents as well. For this reason, many researchers have discussed the notion of "goodness of fit," to describe the importance of a parent's ability to adjust his or her own behavior to the child's unique personality in predicting a child's positive outcomes. Although this sort of adjustment represents an aspect of parental responsiveness to the child's behavior, explicitly acknowledging the contribution of the child to the interaction is an important contribution of the goodness-of-fit literature.

The notion of "relationship schemas," derived from the social cognition literature, provides a similar perspective using different language. Cognitive schemas emerge through repeated experience with the primary relationship in a child's life. These "schemas" or "roadmaps" serve as guides to future relationships that can be activated automatically or unconsciously. In addition, relationship schemas include affective and motivational components. Thus, the parent-child interaction contributes to the development of internal roadmaps, which results in schema-consistent motives and behavioral routines. According to this view, a child will engage in behavioral responses and be motivated in ways that are consistent with existing habits of interacting informed by early parent-child interactions.

EMPIRICAL BACKGROUND

Much of research with young children and families has supported these theoretical views. Children who have early relationships marked by responsive and sensitive care tend to have greater attention control in preschool and do better academically, socially, and emotionally in elementary school than children whose interactions with primary caregivers are inconsistent, overstimulating, or punitive. Maternal sensitivity—being responsive in the ways discussed earlier—has consistently been documented as a strong predictor of positive developmental outcomes for young children. Specifically, young children with a history of secure attachment relationships with their parents have skills to become efficient learners and productive social individuals. Children reared by responsive parents are self-reliant in school, delay gratification, are curious, and manage stressful situations well. Similarly, in

social situations, children with secure attachment histories function effectively and develop peer relationships characterized by emotional closeness, empathy, and positive affect.

Patterns of parent-child interaction remain influential through a child's progress toward adulthood. For example, during middle childhood, parent-child interaction style continues to influence the development of the child's self-system, including self-esteem and cognitive competence. As a child's freedom increases and more time is spent with peer groups, parental monitoring becomes a critical issue for both the parent and the child. Interactions characterized by warmth, responsiveness, and respect result in effective monitoring, which guides the child appropriately while accepting and appreciating his or her newly emerging skills and interests.

The quality of parent-child interaction continues to influence positive outcomes during adolescence, although relationships may be strained by increased differentiation between the parent and the emerging adult. As a result of the vast developmental changes that occur at this time, youth seek independence through a variety of venues in many different forms. For example, changes in cognitive functioning may support a "confrontational" style for many youth. Even so, warm and responsive parenting is associated with self-esteem, identity formation (e.g., making choices regarding career paths, sexuality, and religious identification), prosocial behavior, and effective parent-adolescent communication. Furthermore, adolescents who have interactions with parents that are responsive are less likely to be depressed or anxious or to experience a variety of behavior problems. As youth transition into the world of young adulthood with increasing demands and interests, patterns of parent-child interaction will become modified as issues of supervision, authority, and trust are negotiated.

The relevance of parent-child relationships in adulthood and later years has become increasingly more salient as demographic changes in mortality, morbidity, marriage, and fertility have altered the structure of the family in later life. Overall, aging parents continue to provide support to their offspring in ways that are influenced by different factors, including the birth of a grandchild, living distance between parent and child, and parental resources. Likewise, adult children who provide care for their aging parents are often confronted by unique issues of the "sandwich generation," caught between their responsibilities to their parents and the demands of their young children and their careers. Although research in this particular area is limited, reports suggest that the quality of earlier parent-child interaction contributes to the ways parents and their adult children resolve the challenges during this time.

FACTORS INFLUENCING THE PARENT-CHILD INTERACTION

The ways in which the parent-child relationship changes over time reflect how the unique developmental challenges of various stages of life—for both parent and child—affect parent-child interaction style. Other variables that influence parent-child interaction style include stressors such as poverty, mental illness, and substance abuse. Mothers who are depressed, for example, are less responsive to their babies' cues. Very low-income parents have been documented to utter far fewer positive statements and far more negative statements to their children than middle-class parents—a characteristic that is most likely associated with the constraints of poverty but that nonetheless has an impact on the parent-child relationship. Parental education, which is commonly linked with socioeconomic class, also affects parenting behavior. Mothers with higher education are more sensitive to their children's cues as well as more engaged with them. Parenting patterns are also influenced by culture. Choices such as how parents care for infants, the degree to which parents encourage infant exploration, how nurturing and restrictive parents are, and which behaviors parents emphasize and value are determined by the familial cultural belief system.

—*LaRue Allen, Jennifer Astuto,*
and Anita Sethi

Further Readings and References

Chess, S., & Thomas, A. (1996). Temperament: Theory and practice. *Basic principles into practice series: Vol. 12.* Philadelphia: Bruner/Mazel.

Cox, M. J., & Harter, K. S. (2003). Parent-child relationships. In M. H. Bornstein, L. Davidson, C. L. M., Keyes, & K. A. Moore (Eds.), *Well being: Positive development across the life course.* Mahwah, NJ: Erlbaum.

Harkness, S., & Super, C. M. (2002). Culture and parenting. In M. H. Bornstein (Ed.), *Handbook of parenting: Vol. 2. Biology and ecology of parenting* (2nd ed.). Mahwah, NJ: Erlbaum.

Hart, B., & Risley, T. (2002). *Meaningful differences in the everyday experience of young American children.* Baltimore: Brookes.

Shonkoff, J. P., & Phillips, D. A. (2000). Nurturing relationships. *From neurons to neighborhoods.* Washington, DC: National Academies Press. Retrieved from http://www.nap.edu/books/0309069882/html

Sroufe, L. A. (1990). An organizational perspective on the self. In D. Cicchetti & M. Beeghly (Eds.), *Transitions from infancy to childhood: The self.* Chicago: University of Chicago Press.

Zarit, S. H., & Eggebeen, D. J. (2002). Parent-child relationships in adulthood and later years. In M. H. Bornstein (Ed.), *Handbook of parenting: Vol. 2. Children and parenting* (2nd ed.). Mahwah, NJ: Erlbaum.

Zero to Three, for parents, http://www.zerotothree.org/ztt_parents.html

PARENT-CHILD RELATIONSHIPS

The relationship between a parent and child evolves over time through the course of specific developmental periods. The major periods of parent-child relationship development are (1) new parents and young children, (2) early childhood, (3) middle childhood, and (4) adolescent. Although there is a large diversity in family types (e.g., single-parent, same-sex parents), this entry will mainly focus on two-parent heterosexual families.

NEW PARENTS AND YOUNG CHILDREN (AGES 0–3)

The birth of a child is a time of great adjustment for new parents. For example, new parents will need to adjust quickly to having an infant in their lives who depends on them for all its physical and emotional needs. The first few weeks after a child's birth can be especially trying as parents make adjustments in their lives to establish the routines of infant care. One of the initial major decisions new parents must make is the type of child care for their infant. Some families can financially afford to have one parent stay home, typically the mother, and assume child care duties, whereas many families cannot. Out-of-home child care presents many challenges for new parents, including financial, work scheduling, and choosing among the type of care providers available in their local area. In general, research indicates that nonparental care is not harmful to the developing relationship between the mother and infant. However, parents should actively evaluate the quality of care provided by various child care agencies before selecting one for their infant.

The initial transition to parenthood can be stressful and challenging to the existing marital relationship. If the marital relationship was strong before having a child, then new parents typically find more support in their relationship after the baby is born. Couples who can realistically anticipate what changes will occur to their lives (e.g., new responsibilities) before having a baby are generally more satisfied in their lives after the child is born. In general, couples who have more supportive and satisfying marital relationships are better able to manage the challenges following the birth of a child.

During the first 18 months of life, Erik Erikson suggests that it is very important for the infant to develop a sense of trust with parents and the environment. This initial development of trust is generally referred to as *parent-child attachment*. Attachment refers to the bond an infant makes to the parent (most typically the mother) in the early years of life and provides a basic foundation for future development of the child. Healthy parent-child attachments are generally related to better developmental outcomes for the child across the life span and are developed through the consistent, supportive, and caring interaction with a parent.

As the child becomes a toddler, the relationship with parents begins to change in certain ways. Toddlers increasingly become more mobile and are usually quite interested in exploring their environment. Also, toddlers experiment with the emerging use of language and communicating with others in the environment. Erikson suggests that toddlers (ages 18 months–3 years) struggle between their developing sense of autonomy and the need for others to take care of them. For example, the toddler is developing new ways to initiate interaction in the environment (e.g., walking, talking) while still very dependent on the parents for many things (e.g., food, toileting). Toilet training typically takes place between the ages of 2 and 3 and, when mastered, provides the toddler with more autonomy regarding this bodily function compared with prior dependence on a parent for diaper changing. It is important that parents provide high levels of nurturance and support for their children during this period of development.

EARLY CHILDHOOD (AGES 3–6)

Erikson suggests that children between the ages of 3 and 6 are more assertive in initiating activities with others and exploring their environments. Children at this age should be encouraged by their parents to show initiative and curiosity about their world and others around them. They are also discovering such things as responsibility for their own behavior and the impact their behavior has on others, while being socialized into the family (e.g., rules). In addition, this is a typical time for children to be socialized into learning environments, such as preschool settings.

In early childhood, some children may be placed in preschool, whereas others may remain at home with a parent. Similar to nonparental types of care at younger ages, the quality of a preschool program and its staff is important for parents to consider. Children enrolled in preschool programs will have opportunities to become socialized with structured learning environments and interact with peers. In general, children can benefit developmentally from attending a preschool program; however, the quality of the specific program should be assessed by parents before placement.

MIDDLE CHILDHOOD (AGES 6–12)

School entry is a major transition for children and parents at the beginning of the middle childhood years. The child adapts to the demands of the school environment while the parents adjust to having their child in school for a large part of the day. Children learn central academic skills, such as reading, writing, and mathematics. They are also socialized into their school environments and develop a greater set of social skills with others outside of their family. According to Erikson, the skills and attitudes children learn during this period of development contribute to their ability to interact with multiple people (e.g., teachers, peers) across environments. The more success children have at acquiring the skills of this period, the more successful they will continue to be in their later development. In general, it is important that parents establish and maintain a collaborative relationship with their child's teacher and school in order to support their development in this setting.

The parenting roles will likely shift as the child enters school. For example, at earlier ages, children need more physical assistance from their parents to accomplish things in their environment and assist them with decision making. During this period, children depend on their parents less for many things as their physical and cognitive skills become more developed. Parents need to provide children with more psychological support, such as reassurance, boosts to self-esteem, and positive verbal reinforcement so that they develop a positive sense of self. For example, when children encounter novel and challenging situations, they look to their parents for reassurance, guidance, and praise for successful mastery of tasks. This is also a period when many primary caretakers (e.g., mothers) are more likely to enter the workforce, which can produce positive benefits as well as challenges for the particular parent and the family.

ADOLESCENCE (AGES 12–18)

The beginning of this period is associated with puberty, and this process marks the physical transition from child to adolescent. Puberty is a time of physical and psychological change for the adolescent and involves the development of the primary (e.g., development of sexual organs, pubic hair growth) and secondary (e.g., changes in voice, body hair growth) sexual characteristics. During this time, psychological changes in adolescents are also common and generally include things such as increased need for isolation from others, increased display of the range of emotions (e.g., anger, crying), increased sensitivity to and discomfort with physical changes in the body, and decreases in self-confidence. Erickson suggests that adolescents between the ages of 12 and 18 experience a struggle between identity and role confusion. For example, adolescents struggle with the changes produced by the process of puberty while trying to make sense of them and develop a secure identity. In addition, the peer group becomes more influential for the adolescent during this period.

Adolescence also signals a change for parents and how they relate to their children. For example, many parents find that earlier parenting practices do not work well for adolescents because they are making more choices and seeking more independence in their lives compared with younger children. Parents may also be surprised about the need for independence asserted by adolescents as they attempt to develop their own identities and gain more experience making choices in their lives. In general, parents find that adolescents increasingly want to be included in decision making that influences their lives. Parents can supportively include adolescents when making relevant family decisions and provide the structure to teach them how to make good decisions in their lives.

SUMMARY

The relationship between parent and child changes over time in accordance with the natural development of the child. Four major periods in child development are related to significant changes in the parent-child relationship: (1) new parents and young children, (2) early childhood, (3) middle childhood, and (4) adolescence. During each of these periods, the child works to accomplish specific developmental tasks while the parents strive to provide parenting practices that meet the needs of their growing child.

—*Jason J. Burrow-Sanchez*
and Robert March

See also Parent-Child Interaction

Further Readings and References

Ainsworth, M. S. (1979). Infant-mother attachment. *American Psychologist, 34*, 932–937.

Bigner, J. J. (2002). *Parent-child relations: An introduction to parenting.* Upper Saddle River, NJ: Merrill/Prentice Hall.

Bowlby, J. (1969). *Attachment and loss: Vol. 1. Attachment.* New York: Basic Books.

Cox, M. J., Burchinal, M., Taylor, L. C., Frosch, C., Goldman, B., & Kanoy, K. (2004). The transition to parenting: Continuity and change in early parenting behavior and attitudes. In R. D. Conger, F. O. Lorenz, & K. A. S. Wickrama (Eds.), *Continuity and change in family relations: Theory, methods, and empirical findings* (pp. 201–239). Mahwah, NJ: Erlbaum.

Erikson, E. (1963). *Childhood and society* (2nd ed.). New York: W. W. Norton.

Henry, S., & Peterson, G. W. (1995). Adolescent social competence, parental qualities, and parental satisfaction. *American Journal of Orthopsychiatry, 65*, 249–262.

Hoffman, L. (1989). Effects of maternal employment in the two-parent family. *American Psychologist, 44*, 283–293.

KidsHealth, http://www.kidshealth.org/

Merenstein, G., Kaplan, D., & Rosenburg, A. (1997). *Handbook of pediatrics* (18th ed.). Stamford, CT: Appleton & Lange.

National Institute of Child Health and Human Development. (1997). The effects of infant care on infant-mother attachment security: Results of the NICHD study of early child care. *Child Development, 68*, 860–879.

National Network for Child Care, http://www.nncc.org/

Noack, P., & Buhl, H. M. (2004). Child-parent relationships. In F. R. Lang & K. L. Fingerman (Eds.), *Growing together:*

Personal relationships across the lifespan (pp. 45–75). New York: Cambridge University Press.

Waters, E., Merrick, S., Treboux, D., Crowell, J., & Albersheim, L. (2000). Attachment security in infancy and early adulthood: A twenty-year longitudinal study. *Child Development, 71*, 684–689.

PARENT TRAINING

Parent training (PT) is an umbrella term for several related behavioral interventions designed to help parents address child noncompliance and disruptive behaviors. Unlike many therapeutic interventions for children, in which a therapist and a child work to resolve issues, in PT, parents are taught to be the primary "therapists" who implement changes in their own behavior or in the environment to influence changes in the child's behavior. Most PT programs focus on teaching specific behavioral techniques that parents can use across settings. Specifically, parents learn techniques to increase the value of their instructions, methods of positively reinforcing appropriate behaviors, and methods of decreasing reinforcement of inappropriate child behaviors.

THEORETICAL FOUNDATIONS

Constance Hanf is widely considered the "grandparent" of most current PT programs, applying operant behavioral principles to parent-child interactions in the 1960s. Hanf recognized that parental attention could serve as a strong reinforcer of child behavior. Thus, her model of PT included a component of child-directed play, to allow parents to practice attending to (i.e., socially reinforcing) the child's appropriate behaviors. In addition to helping parents increase their attention to nondeviant behaviors, this component also helped increase the salience (i.e., reward value) of parental communication. Another significant component of Hanf's PT program was teaching parents to reduce environmental reinforcement of inappropriate behaviors. Modern versions of this principle include "ignoring" and "time-out" procedures.

PT's evolution over the past 50 years has resulted in the development of a number of different programs designed to improve child compliance and parent-child interactions. Although programs vary in the applications and techniques used, all PT programs currently supported by empirical research maintain their emphasis on behavioral principles. Because of this, the programs discussed below are reviewed in terms of their unique components.

PARENT TRAINING PROGRAMS

Helping the Noncompliant Child

This intervention teaches parents to manage noncompliance in 3- to 8-year-olds by helping parents communicate behavioral expectations clearly and provide appropriate consequences for child behavior (McMahon & Forehand, 1984, 2003). As with other PT programs, this program emphasizes implementation of basic behavioral principles combined with a child-directed focus to improve the salience of parental commands as well as the parent-child relationship. McMahon and Forehand emphasize contingent attention and implementing practice time during the week so that parents can further develop their attending and rewarding skills in the home environment.

This treatment program has been the focus of much empirical research and has been nationally recognized as a best practice for family-based treatment. In two longitudinal investigations, treated families were functioning similar to the ("normal") comparison sample 4.5 and 10 years after the intervention.

Parents and Adolescents: Living Together

Patterson and Forgatch's (1987) program combines behavioral principles with social learning theory, extends the typical approach of managing behavior in young children to discuss how to manage problematic *adolescent* behaviors. Patterson and Forgatch focus on teaching families to balance self-interest with a sense of responsibility and to develop the necessary skills to form lasting relationships. In addition to specific behavioral skills, they also center on the role of parent modeling to help children and adolescents learn to respond appropriately to those around them.

Parent-Child Interaction Therapy

Parent-child interaction therapy (PCIT) is a short-term, evidence-based intervention designed for families with children between the ages of 2 and 6 experiencing a range of behavioral, emotional, and family problems (Eyberg & Robinson, 1982). Two main phases define PCIT with child-directed interaction (CDI) as the initial focus and parent-directed interaction (PDI) implemented once the primary phase has been mastered. This PT program combines basic behavioral principles with a stress on more traditional play therapy techniques and problem-solving skills. PCIT places a strong emphasis on changing parent-child interaction patterns, thus incorporating elements of developmental psychology, attachment theory, and social learning theory. This program identifies characteristics in both the parent and the child as well as environmental factors that influence the parent-child relationship and behavior management.

Several studies have been conducted examining the efficacy of PCIT. Research has indicated that PCIT results in both clinically and statistically significant improvements in the interactional style of parents and children and in the behavior problems of children at home and at school. Parents also report high levels of satisfaction with the content and process of PCIT and more confidence in their abilities to manage their children's behavior. Longitudinal studies have found that parents who completed PCIT continued to report significant changes in their children's behavior 3 to 6 years after completing treatment.

Psychosocial Treatment for Attention Deficit Hyperactivity Disorder

Recent developments for managing attention deficit hyperactivity disorder (ADHD) have focused on the integration of PT (Barkley, 2002). Treatment techniques consist of training parents in general behavioral principles such as applying reinforcement or punishment after appropriate and inappropriate behaviors. The PT program relies primarily on a token economy wherein reinforcement procedures involve praise or tokens (e.g., poker chips, stickers). Punishment involves the loss of tokens or time-out from reinforcement such as parental attention. This treatment's rationale is that parents benefit from using more explicit, systematic, and external forms of presenting rules and instructions to children with ADHD. Although this PT program focuses primarily on behavioral principles, it does incorporate skills for developing more positive parental attention and encouraging parents to attend to children's compliance and independent play. By providing more positive attention to children while they are following directions and playing independently, parents reinforce more appropriate

behaviors. This also helps to foster more positive parent-child interactions.

Only a few studies have been conducted examining the efficacy of PT in children with ADHD. Studies indicated that at a 1-year follow-up reevaluation after treatment, those families that received PT were no longer different from the control group, and the child's school behavior was rated by teachers as significantly better than before treatment.

Incredible Years Parents Training Series

The Incredible Years program is based on the theory that ineffective parenting, family factors, school risk factors, and peer and community risk factors influence the development of child conduct problems (Webster-Stratton & Reid, 2003). The Incredible Years Training Series targets parents, teachers, and children ages 2 to 8. The parent program focuses on promoting parent competencies and strengthening families by increasing parents' positive parenting and self-confidence while replacing critical and violent discipline with more positive strategies such as ignoring, logical and natural consequences, and problem solving. The Parent Training Series has two parts, BASIC and ADVANCE, which center on enhancing positive parent-child relationships, teaching nonviolent discipline techniques, and addressing parents' personal and interpersonal risk factors.

Empirical research on this program has shown significant improvement in parental attitudes and parent-child interactions while significantly reducing parents' reliance on violent and critical discipline and child conduct problems. Research has also demonstrated a significant improvement in parental communication, problem-solving, and collaboration skills when compared with parents who did not complete the ADVANCE program.

Parent Management Training for Conduct Disorder

The Parent Management Training (PMT) program combines cognitive problem-solving skills training with parent management training (Kazdin, 2003). In PMT, parents are trained to alter their children's behavior at home. Parents learn specific procedures to alter interactions with their children, to promote prosocial behavior, and to decrease inappropriate behavior. The theory behind this program is that coercive interactions between parents and children reinforce aggressive child behavior. Additionally, many parents use punitive practices and commands that escalate problem behavior and ignore prosocial behavior. As with the other PT programs, PMT focuses on behavioral principles to reinforce positive behaviors. Parents are also trained to identify, observe, and define problem behaviors in new ways while developing and using a token economy system. Empirical studies have found PMT to produce reliable and significant reductions in antisocial behavior while increasing prosocial behavior.

CULTURAL DIVERSITY IN PARENT TRAINING

Although extensive empirical research has found success for PT programs, recent explorations of the literature have revealed a paucity of research examining cultural diversity and PT. PT programs often address family variables to increase program effectiveness, but most programs do not address cultural variables that affect parents' and children's views of appropriate behavior and discipline. Because research has not examined cultural variables and PT, clinicians remain uninformed about whether parenting programs should be modified for different cultural groups. Success in changing parent behaviors must consider parents' cultural backgrounds because parenting practices are influenced by cultural values about appropriate parenting and appropriate child behavior. Thus, future research in this area is essential to determine which aspects of PT programs are successful across cultures and which areas must be tailored to address cultural differences.

CONCLUSIONS

Although the PT programs discussed here are only a few of the many PT programs available, research consistently has indicated that parent involvement in treatment is related to long-term results of minimized behavioral concerns, even several months and years after the cessation of treatment. More empirically supported treatments are placing a focus on PT to help children maintain therapeutic skills across environments.

—*Margaret M. Richards*
and Ric G. Steele

Further Readings and References

Barkley, R. A. (2002). Psychosocial treatments for attention-deficit/hyperactivity disorder in children. *Journal of Clinical Psychiatry, 63,* 36–43.

Eyberg, S. M., & Robinson, E. A. (1982). Parent-child interaction training: Effects on family functioning. *Journal of Clinical Child Psychology, 11,* 130–137.

Forehand, R., & Kotchick, B. A. (1996). Cultural diversity: A wake-up call for parent training. *Behavior Therapy, 27,* 187–206.

Foote, R.C., Schuhmann, E. M., Jones, M. L., & Eyberg, S. M. (1998). Parent-child interaction therapy: A guide for clinicians. *Clinical Child Psychology and Psychiatry, 3,* 361–373.

Hood, K. K., & Eyberg, S. M. (2003). Outcomes of parent-child interaction therapy: Mothers' reports of maintenance three to six years after treatment. *Journal of Clinical Child and Adolescent Psychology, 32,* 419–429.

Kazdin, A. E. (2003). Problem-solving skills training and parent management training for conduct disorder. In A. E. Kazdin & J. R. Weisz (Eds.), *Evidence-based psychotherapies for children and adolescents* (pp. 241–262). New York: Guilford.

McMahon, R. J., & Forehand, R. (1984). Parent training for the noncompliant child: Treatment outcome, generalization and adjunctive therapy procedures. In R. F. Dangel & R. A. Polster (Eds.), *Behavioral parent training: Issues in research and practice.* New York: Guilford.

McMahon, R. J., & Forehand, R. L. (2003). *Helping the noncompliant child: Family based treatment for oppositional behavior* (2nd ed.). New York: Guilford.

Patterson, G., & Forgatch, M. (1987). *Parents and adolescents: Living together.* Eugene, OR: Castalia.

Webster-Stratton, C., & Reid, M. J. (2003). The Incredible Years Parents, Teachers, and Children training series: A multifaceted treatment approach for young children with conduct problems. In A. E. Kazdin & J. R. Weisz (Eds.), *Evidence-based psychotherapies for children and adolescents.* (pp. 224–240). New York: Guilford.

PARENTING

"It is the entrusted and abiding task of parents to prepare their offspring for the physical, psychosocial, and economic conditions in which they will eventually fare and, it is hoped, flourish." This statement made by Dr. Marc Bornstein, an expert on child development and parenting processes, captures the essence of parenting. At its most basic level, parenting is the process of providing protection and care to children in order to ensure their survival; more ideally, parenting inspires and maximizes the child's potential.

SIGNIFICANCE OF PARENTING

The long-standing assumption that parents assert a direct, deterministic, and powerful influence on their children through the process of socialization has permeated research and theory on human development as well as most cultural belief systems. If children turn out well, it is to the parents' credit; if they turn out badly, it is the parents' fault. Recently, this assumption has been challenged by researchers who highlight the role of biological influences on children's development. Behavioral genetic studies, for example, show that adopted children are more like their biological parents than their adoptive parents on basic characteristics such as personality, intelligence, and mental health. Additionally, some scholars have criticized the emphasis on parenting by asserting that other factors, such as peer relationships, exert a strong influence on development.

Researchers who study the significance of parenting emphasize several issues. First, in biologically related families, genetic and socialization influences are difficult to separate. For example, a child who is musically talented may have inherited that tendency from parents who are also musically gifted. Those same parents would be likely to highlight music at home, making it difficult to determine whether the musical child is a product of genetics, the environment, or (most likely) both working together. If instead that child were adopted by parents who were not musically inclined, the expression of that talent may take a different form or may be actively suppressed. Thus, genetic predispositions (strengths and vulnerabilities) are often modified through experiences created by parents.

Second, the stream of influence between parents and children is bidirectional rather than unidirectional (e.g., from parent to child). A parent who is impatient may cause an infant to react with distress, but an infant who is constitutionally prone to distress also may elicit impatience from the parent. Regardless of who has initiated the chain of events, parents and children often become locked into escalating cycles of action and reaction, in this case distress and impatience. Nonetheless, because parents are more mature and experienced than children, they play a stronger role in establishing the initial interaction patterns and can more effectively induce change by altering their responses (e.g., responding with patience to the distressed infant).

Finally, parents play a significant role in shaping children's environments and thus children's exposure to other factors that influence development, such as peer relationships. For example, parents are more likely than children to make decisions about the neighborhood in which the family resides, the schools that children attend, and many of the activities in which young children engage, and in these ways expose children to certain peers and not others. Additionally, children are more likely to select friends who have similar interests and values, which are rooted primarily in early family experiences. Even broad contextual factors such as poverty and culture are mediated by parents, who, in Bornstein's words, are the "final common pathway to children's development and stature, adjustment and success."

In summary, although past research has likely overstated the deterministic role of parents, scholars continue to document the important ways parents contribute to their children's development. Contemporary thinking on the significance of parenting embraces both nature and nurture, and an important agenda for future research is to study further how parents' socialization efforts interact with children's genetic heritage as well as with other contextual influences to explain the complexities of human development.

CHANGING FACES OF PARENTS

Parents constitute a more diverse group of people than ever before in history. Today's parents may be biologically related, adoptive, foster, or stepparents; they may be single individuals or gay or lesbian couples. First-time biological mothers range in age from younger than 15 to older than 50, with fathers potentially having a greater age span; and grandparents are described as one of the fastest growing segments of the parenting population. In many cultures, siblings take on parenting responsibilities, and in many nations, an increasing number of children spend a substantial portion of time being cared for by professional care providers. Today, only about 35% of children in the United States live in what used to be the traditional household: a household comprising two parents, with one who stays home full-time.

Table 1 presents general demographic information concerning family structure in the United States. This information provides a snapshot of living conditions but does not capture changes in family circumstances that characterize many children's early years. As indicated, 69% of all U.S. children reside in two-parent homes, with at least one biological or adoptive parent. This picture is qualified by race: 81% of children identified as Asian or Pacific Islander live in two-parent homes, compared with only 38% of children identified as black: non-Hispanic. Additionally, these numbers do not identify children whose households have been disrupted by divorce; researchers estimate

Table 1 U.S. Demographic Information (in Thousands) of Family Structure by Race/Ethnic Background

Race[1]	All Races	White: Non-Hispanic	Black: Non-Hispanic	Hispanic	Other: Non-Hispanic
Total population under 18	72,321	44,235	11,170	12,817	4,099
Family Structure					
Two-parent (bio/adopt/step)[2]	49,666 (69%)	34,011 (77%)	4,264 (38%)	8,338 (65%)	3,053 (74%)
Mother-only[3]	16,473 (23%)	7,124 (16%)	5,400 (48%)	3,212 (25%)	737 (18%)
Father-only[3]	3,297 (5%)	1,926 (4%)	595 (5%)	641 (5%)	135 (3%)
Neither parent	2,885 (4%)	1,174 (3%)	911 (8%)	626 (5%)	175 (4%)
Grandparent	1,273 (2%)	541 (1%)	487 (4%)	196 (2%)	50 (1%)
Other relative	802 (1%)	230 (1%)	255 (2%)	257 (2%)	59 (1%)
Non-relative	575 (1%)	301 (1%)	75 (1%)	141 (1%)	58 (1%)
Foster care	235 (<1%)	101 (<1%)	94 (1%)	32 (<1%)	8 (<1%)
Number in poverty[4]	12,133 (16.7%)	4,090 (9.4%)	3,817 (31.5%)	3,782 (28.6%)	NA

SOURCE: March 2002 Current Population Survey from 2000 U.S. Census.

1. U.S. Census groups people by ethnicity (Hispanic/Non-Hispanic) and by race, noting that those of Hispanic descent can be of any race. Space limitations preclude a complete representation of all groups included in the census.
2. Two-parent families include at least one biological or adoptive parent but may also include one stepparent.
3. Mother-only and Father-only also include households in which mother is cohabiting (11% of total) or father is cohabiting (33% of total).
4. Poverty estimates, including raw numbers and percentages, were drawn from *Poverty in the United States: 2002* issued by the U.S. Census (2003).

that nearly half of all marriages end in divorce and that 50% to 60% of all children will live, even temporarily, in households headed by a single parent. Researchers also estimate that one third of all children, at some point, will live in a stepfamily, most likely one composed of a biological mother and stepfather.

A number of recent trends reflect the changing faces of parents. Many people are waiting longer to have children; according to 2002 U.S. birth data, a woman's average age at first birth was 25.1 (a historic high), compared with 21.4 in 1970. Births to unmarried women also reached a high in 2002 of 1,365,966; however, the rate of teen births has declined (30% over the past decade) to an all-time low. For young black teens, the birth rate has declined by 50% since 1990. In the past several decades, assisted reproductive technologies (ARTs) have undergone rapid development, and each year, a growing number of children are born using these technologies. Data from a 1995 report on family growth in the United States indicated that about 2% of women had used an infertility service within that year; another 13% reported having used an infertility service at some time in their lives. In 2001, 107,587 ART cycles were reported resulting in 29,344 (27%) live births and 40,687 babies. Finally, changes in legislation have allowed a more diverse group of people to adopt children. Whereas in the past, agencies routinely screened out applicants who did not meet specific criteria (e.g., economic), today's adoptive parents include those with varying socioeconomic means, older and single individuals, and gay and lesbian individuals or couples.

PARENTING THROUGH THE STAGES OF DEVELOPMENT

The developmental tasks most salient to children change as they mature. For example, an important developmental issue for an infant is attachment, whereas a salient task for a toddler is individuation. Table 2 highlights some of the most significant developmental issues at each stage and the complementary parenting support for optimal development in these areas.

Parenting is at its greatest level of intensity during infancy and toddlerhood. In the first few years of life, children depend entirely on their caregivers, who determine most of their children's experiences. Caregivers decide, for example, whether an infant is held, talked to, or ignored and in what kinds of activities the toddler will engage. Because of the enormous flexibility of the human nervous system during the early years, this period offers unparalleled opportunities for learning and development, which are best supported by an enriched but not pressured environment. Further, although some theorists argue that later experiences can completely alter children's developmental pathways, many assert that the experiences over the first few years of life lay the foundation on which the rest of development builds. Like compounding interest, the investment that warm, engaged, and sensitive caregivers make during the early years pays huge dividends as the secure, self-confident child moves forward.

In the first few months of life, parenting focuses on the provision of basic care, ideally from a warm and responsive caregiver. The caregiver's sensitivity to the child's cues helps the child learn basic regulation and predicts the child's attachment security, which becomes organized toward the end of the first year. In the second year of life, the utterly dependent infant becomes the passionately autonomous toddler, inviting increasing opportunities for discipline (discussed later). Early and middle childhood bring new challenges as children move further out into the world. School adjustment and peer relationships become central, and here, too, children benefit from parents who are involved and supportive.

Adolescence, once characterized as a time of "storm and stress," is now viewed as a period of dynamic change but one that most children (75%–80%) navigate successfully. This period was once also characterized by a severing of ties between parents and their children; contemporary studies show that adolescents benefit from maintaining close and connected relationships with their parents even as they move toward greater independence. Dr. Lynn Ponton, a psychiatrist who specializes in adolescent development, noted that risk taking is a normal part of the important exploration in which teens engage. Parents play a critical role by encouraging their children to take positive risks, such as trying out for a sports team, running for a position in student government, or working on a special project. Adolescents engaged in challenging but positive endeavors are less likely to be drawn to negative risk taking, such as alcohol and drug use.

In summary, children across all stages of development benefit from parents who are warm, engaged, and responsive to their changing needs. Although the time spent in direct contact and interaction with children lessens as children grow older, parental involvement, guidance, support, and monitoring remain important. This may be especially true during adolescence, when parents play a crucial role in helping children to cross the bridge into adulthood.

PARENTING STYLES AND CHILD OUTCOMES

Dr. Diana Baumrind, a psychologist at the University of California at Berkeley, has produced some of the most well-known research on parenting styles. Baumrind's early work highlighted various dimensions of parenting, such as control and nurturance, that were especially important in predicting children's functioning. Subsequent research has focused on two global dimensions: *responsiveness* and *demandingness*. Parents high in responsiveness are attuned and sensitive to their children's cues. Responsiveness also includes warmth, reciprocity, clear communication, and attachment. Parents high in demandingness monitor their children, set limits, enforce rules, use consistent and contingent discipline, and make maturity demands. Taken together, these two dimensions create four parenting styles: *authoritative* (high demandingness, high responsiveness), *authoritarian* (high demandingness, low responsiveness), *rejecting/neglecting* (low demandingness,

Table 2   Developmental Tasks and Parenting Support

Stage of Development	*Developmental Tasks and Attainments*	*Parent's Role to Support Optimal Development*
Infancy	Physiological and behavioral regulation and organization	Sensitive, responsive care contingent upon infant's cues
	Interactional synchrony	Attunement
	Secure attachment	Secure base/safe haven
Toddlerhood and Early Childhood	Sense of autonomous self and sense of efficacy	Encouragement of exploration within safe, supervised environment
	Beginning of independent functioning	Secure base/safe haven; offering acceptable choices
	Developing sense of right and wrong; compliance; impulse control	Positive, consistent discipline; modeling appropriate behavior; coordinated and cooperative interactions
	Development of conscience; empathy toward others	Treating child with empathy; communicating other's perspective
	Movement into wider social group (e.g., peers)	Facilitating opportunities for social interactions beyond immediate family
	Gender identity	Accurate, age-appropriate information
Middle Childhood	Greater level of independence; movement into wider world	Monitoring risks; equipping children with safety skills; providing support
	Greater self-regulation and self-control; cooperation; responsibility-taking	Positive discipline; induction; open communication; co-regulation between parent and child; monitoring
	Successful school adaptation and transitions	Parent-teacher communication; parent involvement; emphasis on learning vs. performance
	Peer acceptance; close friendships; peer group membership	Facilitation of positive peer skills; awareness of and monitoring of peers
	More complex self/other understanding, incl. sex-role identification	Acceptance of child; tolerance for/celebration of diversity
	Self-confidence	Encouragement of and support for mastery
Adolescence/Young Adulthood	Successful navigation of puberty; body image	Support and guidance; avoidance of teasing
	Greater autonomy and self-governance; self-regulation	Increasing opportunities for autonomy; emotional connectedness
	Positive vs. negative risk-taking	Encouragement and facilitation of positive risk-taking; open communication
	Thoughtful vs. impulsive decision making and problem solving	Increasing opportunities for decision making; direct guidance around decision making and problem solving
	Identity exploration and consolidation	Support around identity issues; patience with exploration
	Peer relationships	Direct and indirect monitoring
	Dating and romantic involvements, incl. sexual experiences	Direct guidance and support, especially around risks and rejection/breakups
	Occupational plans	Encouragement for exploration; facilitating opportunities

SOURCE: Based on Cummings, E. M., Davies, P. T., Campbell, S. B. In *Developmental Psychopathology and Family Process: Theory, Research, and Clinical Intervention* © 2000 New York: Guilford (pp. 200–250).

NOTES: Development is dynamic and cumulative; successful navigation of early issues (e.g., secure attachment) supports later development (e.g., self-confidence). Likewise, although responsive parenting adjusts in specific ways to new developmental issues, certain parenting characteristics (e.g., responsiveness, involvement) facilitate development at all phases. Finally, the parent-child relationship is bi-directional and transactional; supportive parenting encourages optimal development, which further encourages supportive parenting.

low responsiveness), and *permissive/indulgent* (low demandingness, high responsiveness). Children who have authoritative parents tend to show the best outcomes (e.g., school success, good peer skills, high self-esteem). This is generally true across ages, ethnicities, social strata, and many cultures. In contrast, children who have rejecting/neglecting parents tend to show the worst outcomes (e.g., delinquency, drug use, problems with peers and in school).

Dr. John Gottman, an expert on marriage and family processes, identified four parenting styles by focusing on how parents handled their children's emotional states, especially negative emotions such as distress and anger. The *dismissing* parent disregards the child's emotions, may disengage from the emotional child or ridicule the child, and wants the negative emotions to disappear quickly. The *disapproving* parent is similar to the dismissing parent but is more judgmental and critical about the child's emotions and may punish the emotional child. Both styles are related to children who have difficulty trusting, understanding, and regulating their emotions. In contrast, the *laissez-faire* parent freely accepts the child's emotional states and may offer comfort but provides little guidance to help the emotional child solve problems. Children with laissez-faire parents have difficulty regulating their emotions, becoming, for example, overwhelmed by emotional states. Finally, the *emotion coach* is accepting and sensitive with an emotional child, respects the child's emotions without telling the child how to feel, and sees emotional moments as opportunities for nurturant parenting and teaching problem solving. Not surprisingly, children of emotion coaches have the best outcomes: they learn to trust and regulate their emotions and to solve problems. Being emotionally savvy, they get along better with peers and have higher self-esteem.

A third approach to parenting comes out of attachment theory, one of today's prominent theories on social and emotional development. Dr. John Bowlby, a clinical psychologist and the "father" of attachment theory, asserted that children develop deep emotional bonds (attachments) to important caregivers over the first few years of life. These attachment relationships, once essential for survival, form the basis for the child's emerging sense of self and relationship style. Children with secure attachments have parents who are sensitive and responsive to the child's attachment-related needs (e.g., holding the distressed child) but who also are supportive of the child's autonomy; children with anxious attachments have parents who are less sensitive, who may be rejecting of the child's needs for intimacy and attachment, or who thwart the child's developing autonomy. Secure children show the best outcomes in virtually every area of development. For example, they have higher self-esteem and get along better with other people, including peers and teachers; they are more persistent on cognitive tasks such as problem solving and know how and when to seek assistance. As adults, individuals who are secure about attachment issues are more likely to provide a secure base for their own children.

Taken together, these various approaches communicate important things about optimal parenting. Not surprisingly, children seem to do best when parents are warm and engaged, when parents are sensitive and responsive to children's needs, and when parents help children to understand and effectively cope with their emotions. Also important are that parents monitor their children, maintain age-appropriate expectations, set and enforce reasonable limits, use consistent discipline (see later discussion), and support the development of healthy autonomy. When thinking about parenting styles, it is important to remember that other factors like the child's temperament, sex, and social context interact with parenting. For example, children reared in dangerous environments may benefit from more restrictiveness on the part of the parent. Additionally, certain child characteristics (e.g., reactive, rebellious) may elicit certain parenting responses (e.g., tighter control).

DISCIPLINE PRACTICES

Discipline and punishment are often confused. Discipline comes from the Latin word, *disciplina*, meaning instruction, training, or knowledge, whereas punishment comes from the word, *poena*, meaning penalty. Discipline, then, includes techniques parents use to teach children desirable behavior, whereas punishment involves a punitive action designed to eliminate undesirable behavior. Scientists of human development agree that discipline is an important ingredient in optimal parenting; there is less agreement on the role of punishment.

The American Academy of Pediatrics has identified three components of effective discipline: a loving parent-child relationship, positive reinforcement to increase good behavior, and strategies for eliminating negative behavior. They strongly discourage the use of physical punishment, and endorse, instead, the use of time-out or the removal of privileges for eliminating negative behavior.

Physical punishment, such as spanking, especially if used frequently, administered harshly, or used by parents who are also low in warmth and responsiveness, is related to negative child outcomes such as aggression and depression. In fact, children who are spanked frequently typically show worse, not better, behavior over time. Additionally, many forms of punishment are unlikely to correct misbehavior in the long term, even though they may control the behavior in the short term.

In contrast, positive forms of discipline are related to better outcomes over the long term, such as self-regulation, self-esteem, and the internalization of appropriate standards of behavior. Child guidance experts offer a number of suggestions for positive discipline, including setting up the environment for success (e.g., removing off-limit temptations, childproofing); setting clear limits and stating these positively (e.g., "please walk" instead of "don't run"); attending to, praising, and modeling good behavior; providing explanations so that children understand why compliance is important; and using natural and logical consequences to correct negative behavior. Induction, which involves making children aware of the consequences of their actions on others, is especially effective for internalization and self-regulation. For example, a group of children throwing water balloons at cars would be less likely to repeat that behavior in the future if the parent helped them to understand the possible consequences of their actions (e.g., causing a car crash) than if the parent responded by yelling, hitting, or using other forms of punishment.

In summary, although punishment may gain immediate compliance in the short term, positive discipline techniques are more effective in helping children learn to manage their own behavior. Such self-management becomes crucial, especially as children move forward into unsupervised environments. Experts on child guidance emphasize that discipline works best within the context of a loving, supportive, and compassionate relationship and that the most effective disciplinarian is firm but also kind at the same time.

WHY PARENTS PARENT IN THE WAYS THEY DO

Why does parenting seem so effortless for some but full of challenges for others? Why are some parents sensitive, responsive, and emotionally engaged with their children, whereas others are aloof, neglectful, or even abusive? Answers to these questions are complex: parenting is multiply determined by numerous factors existing within and between the parent and child, within the immediate context in which the parent and child are embedded, and within the broader social and cultural context.

At the most basic level are the parent and child. As noted earlier, children actively contribute to the parent-child relationship. Parents treat bold children differently than they treat reserved children, and they treat bold boys differently than they treat bold girls. Further, children, themselves, are likely to respond to parenting differently based on their own, unique characteristics. For example, gentle discipline that de-emphasizes power is effective with temperamentally inhibited children. However, uninhibited children benefit most from cooperative strategies that motivate them to identify with their parents. Parents, themselves, bring numerous factors to the caregiving role, including their physical and mental state and wellness (e.g., mood, depression), basic personality, cognitive processes (e.g., attitudes, beliefs, expectations), level of maturity and experience with children, capacities for self-awareness and reflection, and own caregiving history (discussed later). What may be especially important in how parents and children respond to each other is the "goodness of fit," that is, how the unique characteristics and needs of a child mesh with the internal and external resources of the parent.

Parents and children are embedded in a broader context of "family," potentially including other children, a partner, and extended family. The quality of the relationship with one's partner is especially influential. Both mothers and fathers benefit from having supportive relationships with a partner, and parents with that support tend to be warmer and more responsive to their children. Conflict, especially that which is unresolved and chronic, undermines parenting; interventions that bolster the partner relationship are likely to enhance parenting as well. Certainly, being a single parent invites multiple layers of stress, ranging from having no one with whom to share the daily responsibilities of parenting to managing overwhelming economic concerns. Extended family can provide important support to single parents.

Community and social factors, including the parents' world of work, the quality of the neighborhood, the social supports available, and general economic conditions also affect parenting. Parents who enjoy safe communities, stable and fulfilling jobs, and a reasonable standard of living tend to focus more physical and emotional resources on their children. Parents living in impoverished, dangerous environments are likely to approach parenting differently, by being more restrictive and by demanding more immediate compliance, for example. Economic hardship, in particular, exerts a heavy toll on parents and children. The stress engendered by economic adversity is related to numerous problems, such as depression, anxiety, illness, and maladaptive coping (e.g., alcohol use), all of which compromise parenting. In general, as environmental conditions become more extreme, parenting becomes more disrupted. For example, in places where child mortality is high, parents show little investment in children they are not sure will survive.

At the outermost level are cultural influences, which often exert a nonconscious impact on parenting. That is, parents are likely to perpetuate the patterns and habits of their own culture with minimal awareness and reflection. Cultural prescriptions dictate specific parenting practices, such as where children sleep and how to discipline, as well as more global ideas, such as whether children are socialized toward compliance or self-assertion.

In summary, no single factor can completely explain why people parent in the ways they do. Positive factors at each layer (e.g., child with easy temperament, loving family history, stable finances) enhance parenting, whereas negative factors (e.g., child with challenging temperament, abusive history, poverty) present risks. The combined and cumulative picture provides the most complete explanation for differences among parents—why, for example, one parent is responsive while another is neglectful or abusive.

INTERGENERATIONAL PARENTING PATTERNS

Although parenting is influenced by numerous factors at varying levels (discussed earlier), some of the central qualities of parenting can be predicted from the parent's childhood history and how the parent remembers and reflects on that history. Major disruptions in parenting, such as child abuse, are predictably related to similar problems identified in the parent's own childhood; but even subtle differences among parents, such as comfort with intimacy, are associated

with childhood experiences. These intergenerational influences are powerful and often nonconscious; indeed, many parents find themselves repeating intergenerational patterns that they vowed to break.

Although they are powerful, intergenerational cycles are by no means inevitable. The key to breaking negative patterns is to bring to conscious awareness what is nonconscious and to reflect before reacting. Also important is to resolve early negative experiences. For example, parents who have experienced abusive caregiving in their own childhoods are better able to provide optimal care for their children when they are aware that the abuse occurred, can thoughtfully reflect on how the abuse has affected their adult personality and their reactions to their children, and can come to some resolution about their abusive past. In contrast, parents who dismiss the impact of early experiences or who are overwhelmed by hostility and anger about those experiences are at high risk for perpetuating negative cycles. Clinical case studies indicate that the psychological work involved in the processes of awareness, reflection, and resolution is difficult and painful and that it often takes great courage to face one's past. Engaging in some type of therapeutic intervention can provide the support necessary to complete this work.

CONCLUSION

Most people become parents at some time in their lives and regard parenting as one of life's most important yet challenging endeavors. Parenting invokes people's deepest emotions, from great joy to debilitating fear to powerful rage. To be sure, no parent is perfect, and virtually all parents experience times of self-doubt and struggle. When parenting is more painful than joyful, when families are trapped in hurtful cycles, or when parents feel as though they are losing control, intervention is important. Although the United States lags behind other developed nations in the provision of formalized resources to parents, support is available to parents through public and private agencies. Many community health centers sponsor resource and crisis lines where parents can get immediate assistance or referrals to other services. Numerous Web sites also offer connections to expert guidance and to other parents; sometimes simply feeling connected to others who struggle with similar issues can provide relief. Getting help is the mark of a courageous and committed parent; with support, all parents can create positive change from which they and their children will benefit.

—*Molly Kretchmar-Hendricks*

See also Authoritative Parenting Style; Baumrind, Diana; Bowlby, John; Parent-Child Interaction

Further Readings and References

American Academy of Pediatrics. (1998). Guidance for effective discipline. *Pediatrics, 101,* 723–728.

Borkowski, J. G., Ramey, S. L., & Bristol-Power, M. (Eds.). (2002). *Parenting and the child's world: Influences on academic, intellectual, and social-emotional development.* Mahwah, NJ: Erlbaum.

Bornstein, M. H. (Ed.). (2002). *The handbook of parenting.* Mahwah, NJ: Erlbaum.

Collins, W. A., Maccoby, E. E., Steinberg, L., Hetherington, E. M., & Bornstein, M. H. (2000). Contemporary research on parenting: The case for nature and nurture. *American Psychologist, 55,* 218–232.

Cummings, E. M., Davies, P. T., & Campbell, S. B. (2000). New directions in the study of parenting and child development. In *Developmental psychopathology and family process: Theory, research, and clinical implications* (pp. 200–250). New York: Guilford.

Gottman, J., & DeClaire, J. (1997). *The heart of parenting: How to raise an emotionally intelligent child.* New York: Simon & Schuster.

Karen, R. (1994). *Becoming attached.* New York: Warner.

Nelson, J. (1987). *Positive discipline.* New York: Ballantine.

Parenthood, http://parenthoodweb.com

Parenting.Org, http://www.parenting.org

Parent Soup, http://parentsoup.com

Ponton, L. E. (1997). *The romance of risk: Why teenagers do the things they do.* New York: Basic Books.

Seigel, D. J., & Martzell, M. (2003). *Parenting from the inside out: How a deeper self-understanding can help you raise children who thrive.* New York: Tarcher/Putnam.

U.S. Census Bureau. (2003, September). *Poverty in the United States: 2002.* Washington, DC: Authors.

PARENTS ANONYMOUS

Parents Anonymous Inc., one of the largest, international child abuse prevention organizations, is committed to strengthening families through mutual support and parent leadership. Through a network of accredited organizations, parents, and volunteers, Parents Anonymous has developed and implemented a variety of strategies for ensuring positive outcomes for families, including groups for parents and children, advocacy, public education, research, training, and technical assistance.

In 1969, Jolly K. was a single mother concerned about her own parenting ability and seeking to provide a safe and supportive home for her family. Hoping to find an alternative to traditional therapy that frustrated Jolly K., she partnered with her social worker and launched an innovative strategy for supporting families and preventing child abuse—the Parents Anonymous Group. This group provided a unique opportunity for parents with similar problems to share their concerns, explore solutions, and support each others' desire to change. The positive experiences of those first Parents Anonymous group members gave rise to a national movement based on shared parent leadership and mutual support.

Today, Parents Anonymous defines its mission as a commitment to three specific goals: (1) strengthen families and build strong communities, (2) achieve meaningful parent leadership and shared leadership, and (3) lead the field of child abuse and neglect. Furthermore, Parents Anonymous was founded on four guiding principles that today form the basis for all of its activities and services:

- Meaningful parent leadership shapes families, services, and communities.
- Effective mutual support creates a sense of community and belongingness.
- Successful shared leadership between parents and professionals strengthens families and improves services.
- Long-term personal growth occurs through transforming attitudes, learning new behaviors, and building on strengths.

Based on these principles, Parents Anonymous has developed a myriad of activities and services. For example, Parents Anonymous Inc., the national organization, provides training, technical assistance, advocacy, research, and other forms of support for a national network of accredited state and regional organizations working to promote parent leadership and support initiatives in local areas. Additionally, the Parents Anonymous Parent Leadership program, a network of parent leaders from local organizations, provides training and technical assistance for professionals and parents and participates in public education, outreach, and advocacy efforts promoting leadership.

Every year, about 100,000 parents and their children seek help and support from the community-based Parents Anonymous Adult Groups and Children's Program. These groups, held all across the country, meet weekly for 2 hours and are free of charge to participants. Adult Groups are open to any adult concerned about his or her parenting abilities (e.g., grandparents, foster parents, stepparents, and older siblings), regardless of the age of their children, and take place within a variety of settings (e.g., Head Start centers, prisons, battered women's shelters, and family resource centers). Co-led by one elected parent leader and one volunteer professional facilitator, the Adult Groups do not prescribe to a specific procedure. Rather, groups share a set of values based on the organization's guiding principles and the belief that all aspects of parents' life can affect the parent-child relationship. Frequently discussed issues include parenting stress, communication, discipline, child development, and child-rearing attitudes.

While parents attend the Adult Groups, their children may participate in the Parents Anonymous Children's Program held at a corresponding time and location. The Children's Program provides a supportive, safe environment for children of all ages to gain positive social skills, improve their problem-solving abilities, and increase their self-esteem. The curriculum-based program engages children in a variety of developmentally appropriate, hands-on activities designed to stimulate social and emotional development. As a complement to the Adult Group, the Children's Program aims to support positive family changes by ensuring that children's needs are met and by providing an opportunity for children to learn from one another.

—*Amy L. Madigan*

Further Readings and References

Parents Anonymous. (2002). *Program bulletin: The model for parent education.* Claremont, CA: Author. Retrieved from http://www.parentsanonymous.org/paTEST/publications1/ProgBulletin.pdf

Parents Anonymous Inc., http://www.parentsanonymous.org

Rafael, T. (1995). *Perspectives on the Parents Anonymous National Network: 1994 Database survey analysis.* Claremont, CA: Parents Anonymous.

Rafael, T., & Pion-Berlin, L. (1999). *Parents Anonymous: Strengthening families.* Washington, DC: Office of Juvenile Justice and Delinquency Prevention.

PEER PRESSURE

Peer relationships are important for the socialization of children and adolescents Peer groups are important for the development of a sense of well-being. Affiliating with peers is a key developmental task of adolescence, leading to a sense of identity and psychological independence from parents.

Along with the benefits of peer group membership come drawbacks. The effects of peer pressure have for decades been a focus of research. Peer pressure is the channel through which peer group norms are communicated and group cohesion is strengthened when peers convince each other to conform to the norms of the group. However, problems arise when the pressures adolescents exert on each other encourage behaviors that are dangerous, unhealthy, or illegal. Much research attention during the past 20 years has been focused on shedding light on issues of peer influence for negative behaviors, such as identifying peer, self-, and parent-related variables that contribute to the peer influence process. This research has demonstrated the risks associated with peer pressure.

Adolescents are often under significant pressure to strive to become "popular" or a member of the "popular" crowd. These high-status groups, the social goal-states of many adolescents, frequently are characterized by a subculture of norms and values that contradict adult expectations. Although the culture of these "popular" crowds is often also distinctly at variance with adolescents' own beliefs and behaviors, they seek to become part of these crowds anyway. Ethnographic studies have provided evidence that attaining high peer status is a primary goal for many adolescents and that some youth will employ any means necessary to do so. "Popular" adolescents often are the context in which processes of peer influence for antisocial and risk-taking behaviors take place.

TOWARD A DEFINITION OF PEER INFLUENCE

Beginning in the 1960s, researchers have sought to measure the processes by which youth influence, and conform to, the behavior of peers. Early experimental research focused on conformity to peer group behavior, similar to Asch's line-judging studies with adults. The phrase *peer pressure* was coined in the 1980s to explain the new rise in antisocial behavior by adolescents, and prompted more ecologically valid field studies of influence and conformity in school settings.

An important distinction is made between *peer pressure*, or the direct attempts by peers to instigate or prevent behaviors, and *peer influence*, or the indirect social influence of peer behaviors that occur naturally as part of a peer group's norms. Early studies of peer influence in adolescence were based on social psychological theories, such as Sherif's reference group theory. In a classic experiment modeled after Asch's paradigm, researchers established consensus among a group of confederates and measured target adolescents' conformity to the group norm. Although no direct pressure was applied, the normative response of the reference group was sufficient to change the targets' behavior.

In other studies, peer influence has been defined as occurring within the context of interactions with peers whose opinions and influences are clearly present and with whom the individual identifies. Such an indirect, noncoercive view of influence has been implicitly adopted by researchers who see influence as simply the behaviors of the target's close friends or peer group. Others have defined influence as the difference between the frequency of level of a target's self-reported behaviors and the levels of the same behaviors reported by the target's friends or best friend. These researchers measured peer influence as an indirect phenomenon involving no actual act of pressure or coercion on the part of peers.

More *direct, coercive* conceptualizations of peer influence have also been used but are less common. Researchers have sometimes defined peer influence in terms of direct attempts by peers to change, instigate, or prevent specific behaviors. Some researchers have defined direct influence as the strength and valence of peers' reactions to certain behaviors. Others have focused on verbal encouragement by peers to engage or not engage in certain activities. Some researchers even have conceptualized peer pressure simply as the frequency of being offered drugs, alcohol, or cigarettes by peers. Finally, given the important role of parents and peers in the transition to adolescence, definitions of influence that emphasize choosing peer-sanctioned over parent-sanctioned behaviors have also been used.

MEASURING AND CONCEPTUALIZING PEER INFLUENCE

Experimental Methods

Asch's line-judging paradigm to measure conformity sparked interest in the idea of conformity to

group norms and provided a promising method by which to investigate the process in children and adolescents. Studies of influence and conformity in this tradition focused on moral reasoning, stimulus ambiguity, and the attractiveness of the influencer. These studies confirmed that influence and conformity occurred in young populations and that the construct was valid for developmental research.

Hypothetical Vignettes

More recent studies have moved away from experiments to assessments that allow influence research to be conducted within the peer context, such as the school environment. Hypothetical vignettes have been used to obtain information about participants' most likely reaction to a given situation or provocation. Vignettes have also been used to ask adolescents to make a choice between peer-sanctioned activities and parent-sanctioned activities. Others used vignettes to assess children's responses to peer pressure for positive, negative, and neutral behaviors. Children were asked to indicate their likely course of action (e.g., join friends in the activity vs. do something else) as well as the certainty that they would respond in that way. In research using hypothetical vignettes, developmental changes in susceptibility to peer influence have been found, as well as gender differences, with boys conforming to peer pressure for antisocial behavior more than girls.

Similar measures have been used again as an index of adolescents' conformity dispositions to study the relative contributions of conformity dispositions and perceived peer pressure to positive and negative behaviors. Both contributed significantly to the prediction of misconduct and antisocial behavior. Researchers studying the social pressure to smoke in adolescence also have used vignettes to measure the motivation behind smoking. The vignettes varied with respect to the composition of the group imposing influence (e.g., one friend vs. several friends), the nature of the relationship between the target and the group (friends vs. strangers), and whether or not the group was already smoking or if the target would have to initiate the smoking.

Comparisons of Target and Peer Behavior

The most common method of studying peer influence consists of comparisons between the self-reported behaviors of adolescents and the behavior of their best friends or peer group members. This method has been used frequently in studies of antisocial or health-risk-taking behaviors. Some studies have compared adolescents' self-reported behaviors to their perceptions of their friends' behaviors or approval of those behaviors. Others have compared adolescents' self-reported behaviors with their friends' self-reported behaviors.

Similarity between adolescents' behavior and that of their friends or peers does not prove conclusively that influence has taken place, especially if the target participants themselves report the peer behaviors. Using target perceptions of peer behavior will inflate the estimation of influence because adolescents overestimate how similar their peers are to themselves. Similarity in peer behavior may also be attributable to friend selection rather than peer influence, or the process of choosing one's friends based on existing similarities and shared interests. Careful analyses are needed to separate selection from actual influence.

Self-Report Questionnaires

Self-reports of perceived peer pressure have been used in studies of the relative predictions of self-reported peer pressure (direct influence) and friends' behavior (indirect influence) on the occurrence of high-risk behaviors. Varies studies have found that self-reports of direct pressure predict drug use in middle adolescence. Other studies found that these measures predicted cigarette smoking and drug use over and above the effects of conformity, stressful life events, or parental influence. These measures assess what adolescents perceive as influence rather than assuming influence that may actually be due to friendship selection.

Brown and colleagues developed the Peer Pressure Inventory (PPI) to measure perceived pressure in five areas: involvement in social activities, misconduct, conformity to peer norms, involvement in school, and involvement with family. The PPI showed that perceived pressure to engage in misconduct increased with age for boys and girls. Santor and colleagues developed a peer pressure scale to distinguish peer pressure, general conformity (e.g., to authority figures and parents), and the need to be popular. Improving or maintaining one's social status is a key goal for many adolescents. More research is needed to examine the link between conforming to peer pressure and changes in popularity or peer status.

CONCLUSION

More than 30 years of experimental and field research has shown that the influence of peers is a robust predictor of behavioral patterns in childhood and adolescence. Peers' direct and indirect influences are at the core of high-risk behaviors such as smoking, alcohol and drug use, and promiscuous sexual activity. The importance of the study of peer influence is evident.

—*Antonius H. N. Cillessen*
and Lara Mayeux

See also Peers, Social Development

Further Readings and References

Borden, L. M., Donnermeyer, J. F., & Scheer, S. D. (2001). The influence of extra-curricular activities and peer influence on substance use. *Adolescent and Family Health, 2,* 12–19.

Kung, E. M., & Farrell, A. D. (2000). The role of parents in early adolescent substance abuse: An examination of mediating and moderating effects. *Journal of Child and Family Studies, 9,* 509–528.

Mounts, N. S., & Steinberg, L. (1995). An ecological analysis of peer influence on adolescent grade point average and drug use. *Developmental Psychology, 31,* 915–922.

Nemours Foundation. (n.d.). *Dealing with peer pressure.* Retrieved from http://kidshealth.org/kid/feeling/friend/peer_pressure.html

Peer Pressure, http://library.thinkquest.org/3354/Resource_Center/Virtual_Library/Peer_Pressure/peer.htm

Santor, D. A., Messervey, D., & Kusumakar, V. (2000). Measuring peer pressure, popularity, and conformity in adolescent boys and girls: Predicting school performance, sexual attitudes, and substance use. *Journal of Youth and Adolescence, 29,* 163–182.

The Substance Abuse and Mental Health Services Administration's National Mental Health Information Center. (n.d.). *Preparing youth for peer pressure.* Retrieved from http://www.mentalhealth.org/publications/allpubs/CA-0047/default.asp

Urberg, K. A. (1999). Some thoughts on studying the influence of peers on children and adolescents. *Merrill-Palmer Quarterly, 45,* 1–12.

PEERS

During the first year or so of life, parents are the people with whom infants spend most of their time in social interaction. Even during infancy and toddlerhood, however, children are capable of forming intimate, lasting relationships with peers, as psychologist

Carolee Howes has discovered. As children grow older, peers take on a larger and larger role in children's social lives until adolescence, when teenagers spend more time with peers than they do with their parents. What we see then is a gradual transition from parents having primary importance in children's lives, at least in terms of the time spent with them, to peers taking on the more significant role by adolescence.

Researchers have sometimes disagreed about the role that parents and peers play in terms of influence in children's lives. Judith Rich Harris' provocative paper on peer relationships stimulated considerable controversy because she suggested that peers, and not parents, are the primary socialization agents of children. The general consensus, though, is that the relationship that both children and adolescents have with their parents is extremely important and affects the quality of peer relationships in various ways throughout development. Certainly by adolescence, however, peers may come to exert a potent influence on development. Issues such as cliques and crowds, conformity and peer pressure, popularity and leadership, and the role of peers in choices that adolescents make about issues such as drug and alcohol use and sexual behavior all have the potential to drastically affect adolescents' lives, often well into adulthood.

PEER RELATIONSHIPS IN INFANCY AND TODDLERHOOD

Social interactions between babies are relatively rare, compared with interactions between older children, and in most cases are orchestrated by nearby adults. In addition, infants are fairly limited in their ability to engage in social interaction with other infants. However, babies who are placed in close physical proximity to peers will look at, smile at, vocalize toward, and reach out for these other babies. By 6 months of age, babies smile and babble at peers in much the same way as they do with parents. They also begin to engage in reciprocal interactions with one another.

Toward the end of the first year and into the second year, children's increased mobility allows them, in a group environment, to seek out interaction with peers on their own initiative. And, as Carolee Howes has demonstrated, toddlers are capable of selecting particular children with whom they wish to interact. In addition, children's developing verbal skills allow them to move beyond nonverbal means of communication and

to begin using language to express wants and needs and to engage in turn-taking. However, these interactions often involve imitation, rather than some truly coordinated play activity, like playing a game. Also, sustained interaction is rare. Most of children's peer interactions during infancy and toddlerhood take the form of watching other children or playing in parallel with others. Mildred Parten's classic 1932 study of children's social interactions during play demonstrates the progression from nonsocial to social involvement during the first few years of life.

Parten analyzed styles of social play and proposed a three-step sequence for the development of this kind of play. The first level is nonsocial activity, which Parten found was the most common type of play for children younger than 2. This involves unoccupied or onlooker behavior, in which the child might be watching another child but not participating or engaged in what is going on. Nonsocial activity also includes solitary play, in which a child is engaged in some activity alone.

Between the ages of 2 and 3, children begin to engage in parallel play. In this type of play, children play near each other, sometimes even side by side. They often play with similar materials, but do not interact or try to influence one another's behavior.

Then, between the ages of 3 and 6, children engage in associative play and cooperative play. Associative play is similar to parallel play, in that children play near each other with similar materials. However, at this stage they do interact—so they may exchange toys or comment on other's behavior. Cooperative play is the most advanced type of play in Parten's classification system. Here, both children are oriented toward a common goal. They may be acting out a make-believe theme or working together to complete some activity.

Further research on play has shown that as children get older, they do add these higher forms of play to the earlier forms. However, they still can engage in all of these types of play, depending on the situation. For example, as children get older, they acquire associative or cooperative styles of play, but still sometimes engage in solitary or parallel types of play as well.

PEER INTERACTION DURING EARLY CHILDHOOD

The third and fourth years of life mark significant changes in children's peer relationships. As described earlier, Parten's work indicates that children become capable of much more sophisticated kinds of peer interactions than they were in infancy and toddlerhood. Children are much more likely to engage now in cooperative play, a type of play in which children work together to decide what the topic or theme of their play will be (e.g., playing "house," building with blocks, putting together a puzzle). This type of play is much more complex and involved than parallel play, owing in part to the obvious change in the level of social involvement, but also to the child's growing cognitive abilities. The ability to engage in dramatic play, for example, involves a number of social-cognitive skills such as perspective taking and knowledge of other minds (known as "theory of mind"), as well as language skills that allow children to engage in complex verbal descriptions of the dramatic play theme and exchanges of dialogue as children carry out the theme of the play.

In general, we see children's increasing cognitive maturity being reflected in their play. Another way that types of play have been conceptualized is in terms of cognitive maturity being displayed. During infancy and toddlerhood, children's play is primarily functional or sensorimotor, involving simple, repetitive motor movements. Children may engage in activities such as running in circles, rolling a toy car back and forth, or kneading a ball of clay.

During early childhood, children begin to engage in constructive or mastery play. This type of play involves creating or constructing, such as making a house out of toy blocks, drawing a picture, or putting a puzzle together. At this age, children also show a greater interest in pretend or dramatic play. Here, children are using objects to substitute for pretend objects (e.g., pretending that a block is an airplane, or acting out everyday and imaginary roles. By middle childhood, children are able to play games with prearranged rules, such as board or card games, or organized sports such as baseball or soccer.

During early childhood, children also begin to spend greater amounts of time with peers. In addition, this time is often spent at the child's request, rather than the parent's. Children also become more selective about whom they wish to play with. Eleanor Maccoby, one of the leading researchers on gender differences in children, has found that children tend to split into same-sex peer groups during early childhood, a pattern that continues until adolescence with

few exceptions. Maccoby and other researchers have also found that there are gender differences in both the types of children's play and in their verbal interactions during play. Boys are more likely to play outdoors, in larger groups. Girls are more likely to play indoors, in smaller groups or in dyads. When negotiating conflicts, girls are more likely to try to defuse or mitigate conflicts by using strategies like clarifying the other person's feelings, changing the topic, or offering compromises. Boys, on the other hand, are more likely to use direct commands, threats, or physical force to persuade.

When children interact with friends, these interactions also have unique characteristics. Children spend more time with their friends than they do with children who they do not name as friends. Judy Dunn has found that children resolve conflicts differently with friends; they tend to be more forgiving of a friend than of another peer or a sibling. Dunn has also found that friends often show a high degree of caring and intimacy toward one another.

Children also show signs of distress when they lose a friend. In Howes' research with toddlers, she found that when children were separated from a friend because of a change in the day care arrangements, children who lost friends suffered some negative consequences. They had a harder time entering peer groups, engaged in less advanced forms of play, and were rated as more hesitant by teachers.

Friends also show differences in the types of play they engage in. Children who have close friends tend to use more advanced forms of play, such as cooperative and pretend or dramatic play, than children who do not have long-term, close friendships. There are certain skills that children develop when they interact with friends that allow them to use these more advanced types of play. In the context of friendships, children develop the ability to make their wants and needs clear to the other person and to make clarifications when necessary. They also develop listening and perspective-taking skills and have a better understanding of what the other child's role or contribution to the play will be. There is a higher degree of reciprocity between friends, such that when a friend makes a positive gesture or comment, children are more likely to respond positively in kind. Friends seem to agree more than they disagree, and as previously discussed, they are able to manage those disagreements effectively when they do occur.

PEER INTERACTION DURING MIDDLE CHILDHOOD

Once children reach middle childhood, both the nature of children's relationships with peers and their understanding of those relationships become more intimate and complex. When preschool children are asked about the nature of friendship, for example, they typically describe who their friends are in terms of shared activities (e.g., "Mandy's my friend because we play dolls together"). By middle childhood, children realize that friends are people who have spent time together, know each other well, and share common interests. In middle childhood, one of the most important qualities of friendship is trust. A child at this age might say that they are friends with someone because that person "keeps all my secrets. We care about each other and we like to do the same things." Children at this age also understand that friendship is an ongoing commitment, one that doesn't end because of day-to-day disagreements. Advances in children's cognitive skills are partly responsible for their changing conceptions of friendship. Children are more capable of perspective-taking now than they were in early childhood, so they are more aware of others' thoughts and feelings. As they develop more awareness of others' points of view, they are better able to understand the personal interest and characteristics that they share with friends. In addition, they are more aware of the long-term nature of the friendship and thus are more likely to negotiate with friends in cases of disagreement to preserve the relationship.

Friends and relationships within the peer group are obviously much more important to children now than in preschool. Another aspect of social relationships that becomes an issue during middle childhood is children's status within the peer group—whether they are popular or not. Sociometric techniques are measures that have been used to learn what children's peer status is. These techniques may involve asking children to nominate peers they like or don't like, or children may be asked to rank-order every child in the peer group from those they like most to those they like least. These measures yield five categories of acceptance: (1) average, (2) popular, (3) neglected, (4) controversial, and (5) rejected. Children's peer status tends to be well correlated with the types of behavior they display toward their peers.

Some children are rated average in terms of peer status. These children are liked by some children and disliked by others. However, they do not receive high numbers of either positive or negative rankings from their peers.

Popular children are well liked by their peers. They tend to engage in cooperative, friendly social behavior. These children are good perspective takers and are more sensitive to the thoughts and feelings of others. For example, they are likely to ask for an explanation when they do not understand another child's reaction. They also provide their own rationales or suggestions in cases of disagreements with peers. When popular children want to enter an ongoing play activity, they fit themselves into the flow of the play rather than disrupting the play or simply standing by and watching. They are typically viewed as kind and trustworthy and often take on leadership roles within the peer group.

Neglected children seem to go largely unnoticed by their peer groups. These children are less talkative and less socially active than average, but are not less socially skilled than most children. They do seem to enjoy spending time alone in solitary activities. They don't report feeling very lonely or unhappy and simply seem to be less visible to their classmates than other children.

Controversial children tend to receive either strongly positive or strongly negative reactions from their peers. These children can be hostile and aggressive, but they can also engage in positive, prosocial behaviors. These extreme types of behavior are very salient to classmates, and these children are often regarded as leaders, even though some kids dislike them. Because they have positive qualities, they tend not to be excluded socially—they usually are relatively happy and comfortable with their peer relationships.

Rejected children have been the focus of a great deal of the research on peer status, primarily because they are viewed as the group of children most at risk for negative developmental outcomes. Children who are rejected are actively disliked by their peers. These children report feeling unhappy and alienated from their peer group. In addition, rejected children are more likely to do poorly in school or to drop out of school altogether, and they are at higher risk for aggressive, antisocial, and delinquent behavior and for substance abuse problems.

There are two subtypes of rejected children. Rejected-aggressive children have high rates of conflict and are described as hostile by their peers. These children also tend be inattentive, impulsive, and hyperactive. They are also more likely to interpret others' intentions as hostile and to blame others for their social problems. The second category is rejected-withdrawn children. There are fewer children in this subtype than in the rejected-aggressive subtype. These children are more socially withdrawn. They are viewed by their peers as awkward, passive, and socially incompetent. Rejected-withdrawn children report that they feel very lonely and are often concerned for their personal safety. Research studies indicated that they are more at risk for victimization by their peers.

Rejected children seem to have difficulty thinking about or deciding how to enter social situations effectively. For example, a rejected child (or a child at risk for becoming rejected) is more likely to think another child is being hostile, such as interpreting a request for something (e.g., a pencil in class) as a demand. If the rejected (or at-risk) child then responds with hostility, and the other child does likewise, then an argument may result. Over time, these kinds of interactions can lead other children to either begin to experience rejection or to continue to be rejected if the cycle was begun at some earlier point in time. Some intervention programs have tried to train rejected children to observe their peers more carefully and to think about their peers' behavior and intentions in more detail before responding.

PEER INTERACTION DURING ADOLESCENCE

Peer relationships also undergo certain changes during adolescence. One of the biggest changes is the amount of time spend with peers. One estimate is that not counting time spent in class in school, teenagers spend about 22 hours per week with their friends—often more time than they spend with their families. Typically, adolescents enjoy the time they spend with friends more than many other activities. They feel that they share a common bond with friends that they don't share with parents or siblings during this period of development.

The characteristics of teenagers' friendships are similar in certain ways to those of school-age children, but also reflect the changing cognitive capabilities of the adolescent. Adolescents choose friends with similar interests, but also individuals with similar aptitudes, values, and beliefs. A clique is a relatively small peer group that interacts on a frequent basis. These are groups based on friendship, and members are usually of the same sex and race. A crowd is larger group that shares certain characteristics but may or may not interact consistently. Crowds are often designated based on stereotyped perceptions rather than on similarities in actual traits and characteristics. Some common crowds include jocks, brains or nerds, druggies, and popular and unpopular groups.

In the context of friendship, another important quality in adolescence is the support that friends give one another. That support becomes even more important during adolescence than in earlier years. The intimacy that adolescents develop with friends is one of the major paths to identity formation. Adolescents share their most personal feelings and values and beliefs with their friends. This is part of what helps them define themselves and explore their identities. At younger ages, intimacy is important, but a self-disclosure by one child is often responded to by another child saying "Oh yeah, me too." Adolescents are more likely to discuss at length the nature of their feelings and how to resolve issues and problems in their lives. Friendships therefore provide an important source of social and emotional support but also play a pivotal role in helping the adolescent define his or her own identity.

Adolescents discuss different issues with friends than they do with parents. Issues related to their future, such as education and career plans, are discussed with both parents and friends. However, adolescents typically consider their parents' opinions to be more important when making decisions about these things than the opinions of their friends.

Teenagers typically discuss issues like social events, hobbies, clothes, dating, sex, and drug use with their friends, rather than with their parents. They are also more likely to be influenced by friends on these issues and to discuss problems in these areas with friends than with parents. Conformity, or peer pressure, represents the tendency of adolescents to imitate or be influenced by their peers as a means of acceptance. Conformity peaks in adolescence and is highest for activities central to peer culture—dress, appearance, social activities, and dating. Thus, an adolescent is more likely than a younger child or young adult to go along with what their peers are doing, whether that be playing in a band, trying out for the football team, shoplifting, or trying drugs for the first time.

Substance Use in Adolescence

Some of the biggest decisions adolescents must make, with regard to drug use and sex, may be greatly influenced by peers and influenced very little by parents. With respect to drug use, adolescents who become involved with substance use typically have friends who do the same.

A federal survey on children's well-being provides recent statistics regarding adolescent drug use. Some of these statistics include the following:

- In 1999, 8% of 8th graders, 16% of 10th graders, and 23% of 12th graders reported smoking cigarettes daily in the previous 30 days.
- In 1999, heavy drinking remained unchanged from 1998, with 31% of 12th graders, 26% of 10th graders, and 15% of 8th graders reporting heavy drinking (i.e., having at least five drinks in a row in the previous 2 weeks).
- The percentage of 8th, 10th, and 12th graders reporting illicit drug use in the past 30 days remained unchanged between 1998 and 1999. In 1999, 26% of 12th graders reported using illicit drugs in the previous 30 days, as did 22% of 10th graders and 12% of 8th graders.
- The percentage of students in each grade level reporting illicit drug use in the past 30 days increased substantially between 1992 and 1996—from 14% to 25% for 12th graders, from 11% to 23% for 10th graders, and from 7% to 15% for 8th graders. Since 1996, rates have remained stable or have decreased.

Most of the drugs adolescents use are legal—tobacco or alcohol, for example. Most adolescents have tried both of these drugs, but the percentage of adolescents using these drugs on a regular basis is a minority. About half of all high school seniors have tried marijuana, and about 25% report using it on a regular basis. The percentage of adolescents who have used other illegal drugs is much smaller—about 10%. However, alcohol and marijuana are considered to be gateway drugs—drugs that open the door for adolescents to start using more serious illegal drugs like cocaine or LSD. Adolescents who begin drinking or smoking marijuana before 9th grade may be especially at risk. Excessive drug use during adolescence is also related to higher rates of both risky sexual behaviors and antisocial behaviors. These adolescents are also more likely to be in poor health, to be depressed, and to drop out of high school.

Adolescents who develop substance abuse problems are more likely to come from families with high rates of conflict and hostility or from families that engage in very little communication and affection.

In addition, these adolescents are more likely to have problems with anger and impulsive behavior and to have difficulties in school. Peers are another influence—as has been discussed, adolescents are paying attention to what their peers do; and the opinions of peers become more important at this age. Adolescents are therefore likely to seek out peers who share their attitudes toward substance use.

Prevention programs designed to lower the rates of substance use and abuse in adolescents show varying degrees of success. Some programs are based on improving the individual's coping and decision-making skills. These programs involve showing adolescents how to assess risks and how to make decisions, taking responsibility for one's own behavior, and developing coping skills to deal with anxiety or conflicts with other people. However, these programs have been much less successful than programs that also target the family and community. Systemic interventions that attempt to change the environment of the adolescent are more likely to succeed because the adolescent is not alone in the struggle to avoid drug use.

Sexual Relationships and Adolescent Pregnancy

Adolescents are engaging in a new type of peer relationship—the heterosexual or homosexual peer relationship. Heterosexual adolescents who have avoided much interaction with members of the opposite sex as children start to show an interest in developing friendships and dating relationships with members of the opposite sex during adolescence. Most adolescents start to show interest in dating around age 12 or 13, and most have begun to date by the age of 16 or 17. Dating serves a number of functions; it can be a path to selecting a mate—dating helps you find out what kind of person you would eventually like to marry; social function—something that is fun to do and that gives you the chance to get to know a person of the opposite sex and what they are like; status—attractiveness is one of the first things adolescents consider when deciding whom to date; and sexual gratification—sex drive is kicking in as result of sex hormones, and dating is way that adolescents become involved in sexual behavior.

A small percentage (probably between 1% and 10%) of adolescents describe themselves as homosexual, and between 10% and 25% of adolescents have had a sexual experience with a member of the same sex. However, homosexual adolescents face a number of obstacles. They may be unsure about their sexual orientation, and many have heterosexual relationships as well as homosexual ones. It may be difficult to find same-sex dating partners who are willing to have a public relationship. These adolescents also face the possibility of rejection, harassment, or even physical assault by others. Homosexual teenagers have higher rates of both depression and suicide than their heterosexual counterparts. Once they reach early adulthood, however, most are able to come to terms with their sexual orientation.

When adolescents are confronted with making decisions about dating and sex, they often rely more on friends than parents as a source of information and influence. Peers, unfortunately, do not always provide correct or thorough facts about sex. In addition, adolescents are just starting to develop formal operational reasoning, which means they are just starting to think about all of the possible consequences for their behavior. Adolescents tend to focus on the immediate situation instead of the long-term consequences of their behavior. So, they may think mostly about what the sexual experience will be like, and not the possibility of becoming pregnant or getting a sexually transmitted disease. Adolescents also assess their own personal risk incorrectly and may see themselves as personally invincible against the risks associated with unprotected sex. American teenagers are less likely than teenagers in other industrialized countries to use birth control, and even when they do, they are less likely to use effective methods.

About 1 million teenagers become pregnant every year in the United States (although only about half actually give birth). This rate is much higher than for other industrialized countries. This difference seems to be connected to Americans' attitudes toward premarital sex. Sex education is much less common in the United States than in other countries. In addition, programs in the United States are more likely than in other countries to focus on abstinence or delaying intercourse as methods of birth control. However, sex education programs seem to have little effect on whether or not adolescents choose to engage in sexual activity.

Babies of adolescent mothers are at risk for a number of problems during pregnancy and childbirth. They are more likely to be born prematurely, to be of low birth weight, or both. They are also more likely to die within the first year. Adolescent mothers are more likely to drop out of school and are less likely to catch up on their education later compared with women who waited to have children. As a result, adolescent parents are more likely to have low-paying, low-status jobs or to be unemployed. As for their children, they are more likely to have poorer cognitive and social functioning in school. They are more likely to have learning and adjustment problems in adolescence, including problems with delinquency, dropping out, and drug use. They are also more likely to become teenage parents themselves.

So what can be done to reduce the rates of adolescent pregnancy? One approach that shows some promise combines providing information regarding sex and pregnancy in schools with access to community health care services that offer contraception. However, parents often object to such programs, and at best they are helpful only for those adolescents who take advantage of them. As with drug education programs, interventions that target the family and community as well as the individual are most likely to be successful.

SUMMARY

Peer relationships are one of the most influential in children's lives. Peers may be friends or foes, may support us or attack us, and may lead us toward more optimal or less optimal developmental outcomes. In most cases, peers help us learn to play, to develop intimacy, to know ourselves, and to make decisions that will shape the rest of our lives.

—Heather A. Holmes-Lonergan

See also Peer Pressure, Social Development

Further Readings and References

Brown, B. B., & Klute, C. (2003). Friendships, cliques, and crowds. In G. R. Adams & M. D. Berzonsky (Eds.), *Blackwell handbook of adolescence* (pp. 330–348). Malden, MA: Blackwell.

Coie, J. D., Dodge, K. A., & Coppotelli, H. (1982). Dimensions and types of social status: A cross-age perspective. *Developmental Psychology, 18,* 557–570.

Dunn, J. (1988). *The beginnings of social understanding.* Cambridge, MA: Harvard University Press.

Federal Interagency Forum on Child and Family Statistics. (n.d.). *America's children: Key national indicators of well-being.* Available from http://childstats.gov

Harris, J. R. (1995). Where is the child's environment? A group socialization theory of development. *Psychological Bulletin, 102,* 458–489.

Hartup, W. W., & Laursen, B. (1991). Relationships as developmental contexts. In R. Cohen & A. W. Siegel (Eds.), *Context and development* (pp. 253–279). Hillsdale, NJ: Erlbaum.

Howes, C. (1996). The earliest friendships. In W. M. Bukowski, A. F. Newcomb, & W. W. Hartup (Eds.), *The company they keep: Friendship in childhood and adolescence* (pp. 66–86). Cambridge, UK: Cambridge University Press.

Maccoby, E. E. (1998). *The two sexes: Growing up apart, coming together.* Cambridge, MA: Belknap Press.

Parten, M. (1932). Social participation among preschool children. *Journal of Abnormal and Social Psychology, 27,* 243–269.

Rubin, K. H., Fein, G. G., & Vandenberg, B. (1983). Play. In E. M. Hetherington (Ed.), *Handbook of child psychology: Vol. 4. Socialization, personality, and social development* (4th ed., pp. 693–744). New York: Wiley.

Steinberg, L. (2002). *Adolescence.* Boston: McGraw-Hill.

PERMISSIVE PARENTING STYLE

"Parenting styles" are simply one way to think about and classify the many differences from family to family in how parents go about rearing their children. Diana Baumrind, in the early 1970s, formulated a categorization scheme for parenting styles that is still used today. Parenting style is determined by an analysis of where along a continuum of two parenting dimensions a person falls—warmth and control. Warmth is the degree to which parents are understanding, compassionate, and responsive to their children's physiological and psychological needs. Control is the degree to which parents are involved in regulating children's behavior through the provision of goals, expectations, behavioral standards or rules, and discipline and authority. Parenting that incorporates high levels of warmth and high levels of control is classified as authoritative. Parenting characterized by high control and low warmth is labeled authoritarian. Parenting that reflects low levels of warmth and low levels of control is often called neglectful. And finally, the topic of this entry, parenting that involves a high level of warmth and affection but low levels of control, is considered permissive (or indulgent) parenting.

Permissive parents tend to let their children make their own decisions while providing little direction and few boundaries. These parents also tend to provide minimal or inconsistent discipline when their children misbehave. These parents often have relationships with their children that resemble friendships, with little authority being held by the parents. Although this style of parenting provides much love and nurturance, it calls for children and adolescents to make many decisions about the structure and goals of their lives and their behavior, decisions that youngsters are often not mature enough to make.

Although this entry discusses parents in terms of categories or types, parents labeled as permissive are not necessarily permissive all of the time—there is certainly variability in parenting depending on the situation, but this situational variability is centered around an "on-average" permissive style. Different children can also elicit different parenting practices. The parent-child dynamic is highly transactional, such that the parent influences the child and the child influences the parent. One style might work best with a certain child, whereas a different style might be good for another.

Permissive parenting, on the whole, is not associated with positive outcomes for children, mostly because research shows that children need a fair amount of structure, rules, and boundaries. Children from very permissive homes often have poor behavioral self-control and tend to be disobedient, impulsive, and aggressive compared with children from authoritative and authoritarian families. Lacking appropriate parental guidance, children raised permissively tend to have trouble understanding what behaviors and responses are appropriate. Permissive parenting has also been linked with children's poorer performance in school compared with the other parenting styles. Lack of structure and consistent discipline at home often lead children to exhibit behavior problems in the classroom that also get in the way of academic progress. Adolescents who have been reared in a very permissive manner are more likely than others to engage a variety of at-risk behaviors, such as drug and alcohol use and sexual promiscuity.

Although deficits in child behavioral control and academics have been associated with permissive parenting, children of permissive parents tend to have relatively high self-confidence, are generally sociable individuals with many friends, and tend to have warm relationships with their parents and others, at least compared with children of authoritarian parents. The lesson learned is that children need more than just love to develop to their full potential. Children benefit greatly from parents setting appropriate limits as well.

—*Beau Abar and Adam Winsler*

See also Baumrind, Diana; Parent-Child Interaction

Further Readings and References

Bornstein, M. H. (Ed.). (2002). *Handbook of parenting.* Mahwah, NJ: Erlbaum.

Bornstein, M. H., & Bradley, R. H. (Eds.). (2003). *Socioeconomic status, parenting, and child development.* Mahwah, NJ: Erlbaum.

Darling, N. (1999). *Parenting style and its correlates.* Retrieved from http://www.athealth.com/Practitioner/ceduc/parentingstyles.html

PERRY PRESCHOOL PROGRAM

THE HIGH/SCOPE PERRY PRESCHOOL STUDY

The High/Scope Perry Preschool Study began in Ypsilanti, Michigan, in 1962. The study assesses the effects of preschool education on low-income African American children considered at high risk for school failure. The preschool program was operated by the local public schools. The program director was the school district's special education director, David Weikart, who subsequently founded the High/Scope Educational Research Foundation to continue the longitudinal study.

The program provided classes 2½ hours per day, 5 days per week for 30 weeks per year. Groups of 20 to 25 children were assigned to four public school teachers. Teachers also made weekly home visits. The curriculum emphasized active learning. Children planned and reviewed their educational activities daily. Substantial class time was devoted to a balance of teacher-directed and child-initiated activities.

Children entered the study at age 3, with the exception of one cohort who began the first year at age 4. One hundred twenty-eight children were randomly assigned to the preschool program or to a control group with minor exceptions (e.g., younger siblings were assigned to the same group as the first child in a family to enter the study). All children entered public kindergarten at age 5. Data on intelligence quotient (IQ), achievement, and behavior were collected every year from ages 3 to 11, and additional data collections took place at ages 14, 15, 19, 27, and 40. Social and economic outcomes assessed include education, employment, earnings, crime, social services assistance, and family formation.

Key Results

Preschool children experienced a boost in IQ during the preschool years and up to age 7. Effects on achievement and school progress were more durable. The preschool group had higher achievement test scores at age 14, higher high school grade point averages (2.09 vs. 1.68), lower rates of classification as mentally impaired (15% vs. 34%), and higher high school graduation rates (71% vs. 54%). At age 27, they had fewer arrests, were more likely to own a home (36% vs. 13%), had higher monthly earnings, and were less likely to have used social assistance as adults (59% vs. 80%). Many of these effects translate into economic benefits that include cost savings to society and financial benefits to participants. Despite home visitations and the collection of a wide range of family outcome measures, no direct effects were found on parents or the home environment. Benefit-cost analysis finds that the program returned at least $9 for every $1 invested in the program (discounted at 3%), or an internal rate of return of about 16%.

Implications

The Perry study was among the first to demonstrate the effects of intensive preschool education on disadvantaged children over the life course. The study is limited by the small sample size, specifics of the population served, program design, time, and locale. However, many studies have replicated the short-term results, and several have produced similar long-term results. Among these is the Abecedarian Project, another randomized trial in which an intensive birth-to-5 education was found to produce very large long-term educational gains for disadvantaged children.

—W. Steven Barnett and Leonard N. Masse

See also Abecedarian Research Project, Early Intervention Programs

Further Readings and References

Barnett, W. S. (1992). Benefits of compensatory preschool education. *Journal of Human Resources, 27*(2), 279–312.

Campbell, F. A., Ramey, C. T., Pungello, E. P., Sparling, J., & Miller-Johnson, S. (2002). Early childhood education: Young adult outcomes from the Abecedarian Project. *Applied Developmental Science, 6*(1), 42–57.

High/Scope Educational Research Foundation, http://www.highscope.org

National Institute for Early Education Research, http://nieer.org

Schweinhart, L. J., & Weikart, D.P. (2002). The Perry Preschool Project: Significant benefits. *Journal of At-Risk Issues, 8*(1), 5–8.

PERVASIVE DEVELOPMENTAL DISORDERS

The broad diagnostic category of pervasive developmental disorders (PDDs), now often called autistic spectrum disorders (ASDs), encompasses several related yet distinct disorders, including autistic disorder, childhood disintegrative disorder, Rett's disorder, Asperger's disorder, and pervasive developmental disorder, not otherwise specified. The ASDs are characterized by significant and pervasive impairments in several areas, including social interaction skills, communication abilities, and the presence of restricted and repetitive behaviors, interests, or activities. These impairments are atypical relative to the individual's developmental level, usually appear early in life, and are often associated with mental retardation.

AUTISTIC DISORDER (AUTISM)

Autism is characterized by significant impairments in social interaction and communication as well as restricted and stereotypic patterns of behavior, interests, and activities (e.g., resistance to change, repetitive nonfunctional motor mannerisms, and preoccupation with parts of objects). Additionally, unusual responses to the environment (e.g., insensitivity to pain, over-reactivity or under-reactivity to noise) may be present. Social deficits include impairments in the use of multiple nonverbal communicative behaviors (e.g., eye contact, use of gestures), reduced awareness of others, inability to form appropriate relationships, failure to spontaneously share enjoyment and experiences, and lack of social and emotional reciprocity (e.g., not actively participating in social games; not noticing another's distress).

Language comprehension is significantly impaired (sometimes worse than expression) in people with autism, and nearly half are never able to communicate verbally. Those with verbal skills often have odd intonation, reverse pronouns, make up terms (neologisms), rarely use idioms correctly, and may repeat phrases heard on previous occasions (echolalia). Individuals without functional spoken language can benefit from training in the use of sign language, picture exchange, or other forms of augmentative communication (e.g., computers). Pretend play, imitation, and joint attention (seeking attention for the purpose of sharing interest or pleasure) are also impaired.

Both the cognitive deficits and behavioral sequelae of autism can range from mild to severe. Some individuals engage in disruptive behaviors, including self-injury, aggression, and property destruction. Most adults with autism require varying degrees of caregiver support throughout their lives; only a minority of autistic adults achieve independent living. The two most common predictors of better outcome in people with autism are higher intelligence quotient (IQ) and greater functional language.

Recent prevalence estimates range as high as 60 in 10,000 individuals. The disorder is four to five times more common in males, although females are more likely to exhibit more severe mental retardation. Because there is a genetic component in the development of autism, there is an increased risk (3%–10%) for the disorder in siblings of affected people and an even higher risk for partial forms of the disorder appearing in siblings. Although several environmental factors, such as toxins and vaccination, have been suggested to cause autism, there is no evidence supporting this. Neuropathological and neurochemical studies suggest a wide range of possible abnormalities, with the most consistent evidence focusing on the serotonin system (neurochemically) and the limbic system (anatomically).

CHILDHOOD DISINTEGRATIVE DISORDER

Childhood disintegrative disorder (CDD) is probably the rarest and least understood of the ASDs. CDD occurs when a child develops typically for at least 2 years before experiencing a marked overall decline in previously learned skills. Some early signs that may be present before skill regression include irritability, anxiety, increased activity, and a loss of interest in the environment. The decline in skills occurs before the age of 10 (usually between the ages of 3 and 4) and results in significant impairment in the areas of play skills, language, social skills, and adaptive behavior. Additionally, children with CDD may develop stereotypies (nonfunctional repetitive motor or vocal behaviors) and restricted interests. Many individuals with CDD exhibit disruptive behaviors, including aggression and self-injury. The overall presentation of children after regression is nearly indistinguishable from children with autism, and the prognosis is usually poor. Children usually function in the severely mentally retarded range and are at higher risk for developing seizures. Often, subtle neurological impairments and abnormalities are present.

Although a specific cause has not been found, it appears as though CDD occurs as the result of damage to the developing brain. Prevalence data are lacking, although CDD may be underdiagnosed because of the symptom overlap with other ASDs, including Rett's syndrome and autism, as well as degenerative neurological disorders. It is important to conduct a thorough medical and neurological examination to rule out other causes of the developmental regression. This is especially important when regression occurs at a later age (e.g., after age 5). Additionally, individuals with CDD should be monitored closely for seizure disorders. Epidemiological data are limited, but recent data suggest that CDD is more common in males. CDD is a lifelong condition, although the loss of skills usually stabilizes, and some limited improvement occurs.

RETT'S DISORDER

Rett's disorder (also called Rett's syndrome) is a severe neurodevelopmental disorder primarily affecting females that impairs all aspects of development. It causes severe to profound mental retardation, severe communication impairment, loss of functional hand use and other physical disabilities, and impaired social skills, as well as medical problems such as seizures, feeding difficulties, cardiac abnormalities, scoliosis, and autonomic nervous system dysfunction. With an estimated prevalence of 1 in 10,000 to 15,000 female births, it is among the most common causes of mental retardation in young girls. A major research advance came in 1999 when a specific genetic abnormality was identified in most girls with Rett's syndrome. This gene *(MECP2)* encodes for a protein that plays a role in the regulation of gene expression and is found on the Xq28 region of the X chromosome.

Rett's syndrome is unique among the ASDs in that stages of illness progression have been delineated. The first stage begins after a period of typical development that generally lasts between 6 and 18 months. During Stage 1 (early-onset stagnation), deceleration of head growth and reduced interest in playing become apparent. In addition, the appearance of odd hand-waving behaviors and reductions in eye contact and language abilities may be observed. Severe regression occurs in Stage 2 (developmental regression), which occurs between 1 and 4 years of age. In this stage, the characteristic hand-washing or hand-wringing behaviors result in a loss of hand skills;

gross motor impairment and clumsiness are present; the ability to speak is lost; and the capacity to understand language is seriously impaired. Furthermore, cognitive abilities deteriorate, breathing is often irregular, seizure activity often begins, and episodes of laughing during the night may occur. It is during this stage that symptoms may mimic those of autistic disorder, and thus differential diagnosis can be challenging.

The onset of stage 3 (pseudostationary period) is variable. During this time, skills do not deteriorate as much, and the girls begin to interact more with their environments. Although not able to communicate verbally, many with Rett's syndrome are able to make basic communicative efforts using eye gaze and intense staring. Gross motor skills continue to deteriorate, seizures are common, and this period usually lasts years to decades. Stage 4 (late motor deterioration) is typified by complete loss of the ability to walk and increased physical rigidity. Severe scoliosis and progressive muscle wasting are characteristic, and most individuals must use wheelchairs by adulthood. However, seizure activity tends to decrease, the deterioration of cognitive abilities stabilizes, and contact with others improves.

ASPERGER'S DISORDER

Asperger's disorder (or Asperger's syndrome) is characterized by significant and long-standing impairments in social interaction, restricted and repetitive activities and interests, and stereotyped behaviors. Unlike individuals with other ASDs, those with Asperger's syndrome do not display clinically significant delays in language or cognitive development. Because of typical (or nearly typical) cognitive and language development, Asperger's syndrome is often not diagnosed until the late preschool or early elementary school years when social deficits become more apparent. People with Asperger's have narrow interests (e.g., clocks, hotels, or train schedules) with which they are single-mindedly preoccupied to the exclusion of other developmentally appropriate activities. These restricted interests often interfere with social and academic development. For example, individuals with Asperger's often attempt to engage others in conversation related to these stereotyped interests without regard for the other's interest in the topic.

Individuals with Asperger's syndrome generally excel in academic subjects that entail rote memorization but tend to fare more poorly in tasks requiring flexible thinking, creativity, and higher-order cognitive processes such as abstract thinking. Similarly, these individuals tend to apply social rules in a rote manner and evidence a strict adherence to routines. Anecdotally, people with Asperger's syndrome are clumsy or physically awkward and often have difficulty with tasks that require fine motor abilities such as writing.

People with Asperger's often have a distinctive vocal quality characterized by overly formal speech, atypical prosody, and reduced use of gestures. Furthermore, these individuals have difficulty interpreting nonverbal cues (e.g., diverted gaze as indicative of loss of interest) and the more subtle nuances of language. Additionally, an overly literal interpretation of language that results in a lack of understanding of idioms, common expressions, and the like is generally found. Appropriate pragmatic language skills (e.g., eye contact, body proximity during conversation, and appropriate social greetings) are often lacking. Together, these impairments result in social difficulties, peer rejection, and alienation. People with Asperger's are typically aware of their social deficits and may make unsuccessful efforts at social contact, which can result in distress and elevate risk for the development of affective disorders such as depression.

Asperger's syndrome is diagnosed at least five times more frequently in males, and there is often a family history of social difficulties or other ASDs. As Asperger's syndrome has come to be more widely recognized among clinicians and parents, controversy has arisen surrounding accurate and appropriate diagnosis. Some professionals tend to loosely apply diagnostic criteria, and many in the field think that this condition may be overdiagnosed. Thus, reliable prevalence data are currently unavailable. In addition, questions exist regarding how Asperger's fits into the autism spectrum and whether it is actually distinct from high-functioning autism (HFA). Differential diagnosis is complicated by the fact that there is symptom overlap with other disorders (e.g., schizoid and schizotypal personality disorders, nonverbal learning disability, and attention deficit hyperactivity disorder), although there are separate and unique diagnostic criteria that should differentiate Asperger's from these other conditions.

A better prognosis is associated with Asperger's than with the other ASDs because these individuals do not have the cognitive impairments or communication deficits that are associated with autistic disorder, Rett's disorder, and childhood disintegrative disorder. People with Asperger's syndrome may be able to pursue careers related to their restricted interests, although they often fail to achieve occupational status commensurate with their level of cognitive and academic functioning.

PERVASIVE DEVELOPMENTAL DISORDER, NOT OTHERWISE SPECIFIED

A diagnosis of pervasive developmental disorder, not otherwise specified (PDD-NOS) is indicated in individuals presenting with significant impairments in social interactive skills in conjunction with one or both of the following: (1) verbal or nonverbal communication deficits; and (2) stereotyped behavior, interests, or activities. This category includes "atypical autism," or symptom presentations that do not meet full diagnostic criteria for autistic disorder. Clinically, the PDD-NOS diagnosis is often applied rather liberally and inappropriately in cases in which a diagnosis of various behavior disorders, mental retardation, autistic disorder, or one of the other ASDs would be more appropriate.

TREATMENT INTERVENTIONS

Interventions include the use of applied behavior analysis to teach academic, self-care, and adaptive skills and to reduce disruptive behavior. People with autism learn best when skills are broken down into small steps, when provided with many opportunities to practice skills, and when success is rewarded. They may need additional assistance in generalizing skills to different environments. Children with ASDs benefit from structured interactions with their typically developing peers. In individuals without functional spoken language, the use of alternative communication methods such as sign language or picture systems, including the Picture Exchange Communication System (or PECS), is recommended. For some people with autism, medications may be beneficial in reducing disruptive behaviors and stereotypy; improving attention, mood, and sleep; and reducing anxiety and depression, although they are generally considered not to address the core social and communication symptoms. In addition, parents and physicians should be aware of the higher risk of seizure disorders in this population. Parents and professionals should also be cautious when considering unproven interventions. Because the PDDs are severe and not well understood, myriad nontraditional treatments have been introduced, including chelation, facilitated communication, special diets, and secretin. The effectiveness of these interventions is questionable, and some may be harmful.

—Hilary C. Boorstein, Deborah A. Fein, and Leandra B. Wilson

Further Readings and References

Autism Society of America, http://autism-society.org

Families for Early Autism Treatment, http://feat.org

Family Village: A Global Community of Disability Related Resources, http://familyvillage.wisc.edu

Holmes, D. L. (1998). *Autism through the lifespan: The Eden model.* Bethesda, MD: Woodbine House.

International Rett Syndrome Association, http://rettsyndrome.org

Online Asperger Syndrome Information and Support, http://udel.edu/bkirby/asperger

Powers, M. D. (Ed.). (2000). *Children with autism: A parents' guide* (2nd ed.). Bethesda, MD: Woodbine House.

Powers, M. D., & Poland, J. (2002). *Asperger syndrome and your child: A parent's guide.* New York: HarperResource.

Rett Syndrome Research Foundation, http://rsrf.org

Siegel, B. (1996). *The world of the autistic child: Understanding and treating autistic spectrum disorders.* New York: Oxford University Press.

Strock, M. (2004). *Autism spectrum disorders (pervasive developmental disorders).* NIH publication no. NIH-04-5511. Bethesda, MD: National Institute of Mental Health.

PESTICIDES

Pesticides are chemicals used to eliminate animals or plants that are hazards to crops, homes, or health. Rodenticides, herbicides, insecticides, and fungicides all have potential toxicity to nontarget organisms. All pesticides are an acute poisoning hazard, but rodenticides pose the highest risk for children because they are often placed where they are readily accessible.

Most people in industrialized countries are exposed to insecticide, herbicide, and fungicide residues in food, air, and dust. Because children consume more food per body weight and have a higher respiration rate than adults, they are likely to absorb larger amounts of pesticides per body weight compared with adults. Children from families in which at least one member works in agriculture have higher pesticide exposure

than comparison groups. Farm workers may carry home residues on their clothing, bodies, and vehicles. Where families live in close proximity to fields, exposure can occur from drift from spraying operations in the fields. Urban areas with substandard housing also have high pesticide application rates and high human exposure. In contrast, children from families that eat predominately certified organically grown foods have the lowest pesticide exposure of any segment of the population.

As yet there have been no prospective longitudinal studies of the behavioral effects of pesticides on either children's development or the processes of aging. However, nicotine was formerly used as a pesticide, and its mode of action in the nervous system has similarities to some currently used insecticides. Longitudinal studies show that children whose mothers smoked while pregnant score lower on tests of verbal skills, show higher activity levels, perform worse on tests of attention, show higher rates of aggression as adolescents, and have a higher risk for violent criminal acts in adulthood. These findings raise the importance of carrying out longitudinal prospective studies of pesticide exposure, given the similarities in the mechanisms of nicotine and some insecticides.

Cross-sectional studies of the behavioral effects of pesticides on humans have been of limited scope. In a farming community of heavy year-round pesticide use in Mexico, children showed deficits in fine motor coordination, long-term memory, physical stamina, and the Draw-a-Person Test compared with children from an adjacent area without heavy pesticide application. Pesticide applicators score worse on vocabulary tests and report more subjective symptoms such as memory and mood problems, fatigue, irritability, and headaches compared with nonapplicators of similar education and background.

Most insecticides disrupt aspects of neurotransmission. Some neurotransmitters function as gene signaling chemicals during brain development. Therefore, altering the concentrations of neurotransmitters can have serious effects on brain development. Knowledge about the effects of early pesticide exposure on brain development comes from animal research using higher dosages than those to which most people are exposed. Nevertheless, findings show important effects on the development of the mammalian nervous system. For example, dichlorodiphenyltrichloroethane (DDT, a pesticide that is now banned from use in the United States and other industrialized nations) administered early in life can permanently alter the development of the cortex in rodents. DDT also resulted in delayed walking, rearing, and lower overall motor activity. When given to rats early in development, methyl parathion, an organophosphorus pesticide commonly used in farming, caused worse performance on spatial memory tests, reduced the number of cholinergic receptors in the brain, and produced lesions in the hippocampus, an area of the brain that influences memory. Administering chlorpyrifos, also an organophosphorus pesticide, to pregnant rats yielded offspring that showed worse righting reflexes, delayed cliff avoidance, and fewer cholinergic receptors in the brain. Extrapolating from studies of rodents to humans requires many assumptions—hence the need for human epidemiological studies of pesticide effects remains.

—*Colleen F. Moore*

Further Readings and References

Eriksson, P., & Talts, U. (2000). Neonatal exposure to neurotoxic pesticides increases adult susceptibility: A review of current findings. *Neurotoxicology, 21*(1–2), 37–48.

Moore, C. F. (2003). *Silent scourge: Children, pollution, and why scientists disagree.* New York: Oxford University Press.

National Academy of Sciences. (1993). *Pesticides in the diets of infants and children.* Washington, DC: National Academies Press.

U.S. Environmental Protection Agency. (n.d.). *Pesticides.* Retrieved from http://www.epa.gov/pesticides/

U.S. National Library of Medicine. (n.d.). *Pesticides.* Retrieved from http://www.nlm.nih.gov/medlineplus/pesticides.html

PETS

Archeological findings indicate that animals have coexisted with humans and played significant roles in their lives for thousands of years. The first cohabiter was the wolf (*Canis lupus*), the predecessor of the domestic dog. Next came horses, asses, camels, water buffalo, alpaca, llama, turkey, guinea pig, cats, and domestic fowl. The Greeks purchased toys for their pets and embalmed their dead cats to bury them later with the owner. The English monarchs James I, Charles I, Charles II, and James II were avid dog keepers. The Chinese Emperor Ling named his dogs as senior officials of the court, whereas the rulers of the Ming dynasty honored cats. Later, the Manchurian LCh'ing dynasty named the Pekingese dog as the preferred pet, and it was common for women to breastfeed puppies along with their children. The Japanese and Koreans were passionate about dogs. Shogun Tsunayoshi was frequently referred to as the Dog Shogun because of his obsession with them.

When Hernandez arrived in Mexico, he found raccoons living with people. Raccoons were also favorites of California Indians. North American Indians kept moose, young bison, calves, wolves, and bears. The West Indies and Jamaican people kept dogs similar to Maltese lap dogs. Just as Manchurian women did, Jamaican women breast-fed dogs and children at the same time. Likewise, South America Indian mothers suckled dogs, monkeys, opossum-rats, deer, and birds along with their own children.

PSYCHOLOGICAL AND PHYSICAL BENEFITS OF PETS

Pets have been shown to reduce loneliness in young women, elderly people, and homeless individuals and also to reduce stress. Pets also increase social interactions among elderly individuals. People with pets experience reduced risk for heart disease, lower blood pressure and heart rates, and increased survival rates after an illness. Australian cardiologists found that pet owners had lower blood fat levels and lower cholesterol, triglycerides, and blood pressure. Watching aquariums filled with fish results in reduced anxiety, stress, and blood pressure.

Equine-assisted therapy has been used successfully to rehabilitate various disorders, including language, physical, emotional, and social. Hippotherapy, the term applied to the use of horses for physically disabled people such as quadriplegics and multiple sclerosis patients, develops better muscle coordination. Emotionally disabled individuals experience increased self-confidence by mastering riding skills.

THERAPEUTIC ROLE OF PETS

Children

Boris Levinson, a child psychologist, noticed that children with emotional problems were more willing to interact with his dog Jingles than himself. He built on this wordless interaction by joining in the game and directing his attention to the dog rather than the child. Once able to trust the dog, the child was in a better psychological position to transfer trust to a human adult. Based on these findings, the effects of pets on emotionally disabled and mentally retarded adolescents in a special education classroom were examined. After weekly visits over 4 months, the students exhibited reduced aggression and increased interaction among their peers.

Adults

Mentally disabled individuals in institutional settings benefited from interaction with pets. After spending time with an animal in therapy sessions, walking outside on the hospital grounds, and interacting in the ward, the patients who did not respond to conventional treatment became less withdrawn, showed improved communication, and reported feeling happier because of their association with the animals. The presence of birds in a psychiatric hospital resulted in significantly lower hostility scores, increased feeling of safety, and more openness among the patients.

When dogs accompany their human companions on walks, their presence increases the probability of social interactions with others. Furthermore, dogs provide a social reference for friendly gestures and communication.

Prisons

Correctional facilities have found that animals enhance the social interactions of inmates, reduce fighting, and eliminate suicide attempts. Inmates in Virginia who were given birds, fish, and small mammals as pets had significantly lower blood pressure when talking to the pet as opposed to talking to people. The Mansfield (Ohio) Correctional Institution matched inmates with a "death row dog" (dogs that were 1 day away from euthanasia at local animal shelters). The inmate was given the responsibility of training the dog and preparing it for adoption. After working with the dogs, the men reported increased compassion for others, decreased anxiety, improved social interactions, and a greater motivation to complete high school. Women inmates at the Lexington (Oklahoma) Correctional Complex and in Gig Harbor, Washington, adopt dogs from animal shelters and train them for elderly and handicapped citizens. The women report improved attitudes, better self-images, and increased caring for others. Three women inmates at the South Australian Department of Correctional Services were given complete responsibility for the care and training of nine dogs. They indicated that the program enhanced their self-esteem, increased calmness and happiness, and lessened aggression and aggravation.

CHILDREN AND PETS

Pets teach responsibility and reproduction to children. They are also important play partners during middle childhood. Second- and fifth-grade children in the United States described their pets as playmates. German fourth graders played, talked with, and showed daily affection toward their pets. Playing with pets provides a safe environment for children to experiment with their own cognitive exploration and development. For example, children practice language and problem-solving skills on the pets before extending them to their peers. Children between the ages of 9 and 12 years exhibit higher self-esteem as a result of the playmate status of the pet. In addition, pets teach young children how to take care of another living being. Boys have been shown to learn important nurturing skills by interacting with their pets.

Ninety-nine percent of veterinary clients talk to their dogs and cats, whereas eighty percent admit to talking to their pets in the same manner as they talk to other humans. About 70 percent of horse-owning adolescents report telling their horse their problems during the course of grooming it in the solitary confinement of the barn. Eighty-four percent of Scottish children reported that they talked to their pets, and 65 percent believed the pets comprehended the meaning of the conversation. Fifteen percent of Swedish elderly people considered their pet their most significant social contact.

CHOOSING A PET

Animals besides dogs and cats make good pets; gerbils, parakeets, chickens, iguanas, fish, and rabbits are among those animals kept as pets. The important aspect of choosing a pet is determining both the animal's and the human's welfare. The pet owner must be able to provide proper nutrition, veterinary services, and appropriate shelter for the animal.

PET LOSS AND GRIEF

Humans throughout history have grieved over the death of pets. For example, early Egyptians shaved their eyebrows when their cats died, whereas early Romans built tombs to honor their dead pets. More recently, nearly 90% of all veterinary clients exhibited symptoms of grief on the day of a pet's death. Most of the symptoms, such as moderate depression and crying, lasted a week following the death. On the day of the death, pet owners report uncontrollable crying as the most often experienced behavior. After the loss of a pet, most people experience grief, denial, a sense of loss, numbness, and anger. Friends have been found to be more important sources of support than family members.

After natural disasters, many people lose pets. During the largest tornadoes in Oklahoma history in May 1999, many families lost all of their pets and livestock. Those with a close attachment to their pets reported feeling a greater loss than those with low to moderate attachments. In addition, the grief was often more intense in the older owners and those owners who lived alone or with other adults. Although most people adopt another animal after the death of a beloved pet, they also report that they view all pets as individuals and, like children, irreplaceable.

Germans are extremely adamant about honoring the lives of all pets. For instance, residents and visitors alike are required to pay for any animal killed by their automobile. In addition, the local veterinarian estimates the potential number of future offspring the animal could have produced, and the individual must pay monetary damages for these unborn offspring.

—*Sherril M. Stone*

Further Readings and References

Beck, A. M., & Katcher, A. H. (1996). *Between pets and people: The importance of animal companionship.* West Lafayette, IN: Purdue University Press.

Delta Society, http://deltasociety.org/

Friedmann, E., Katcher, A. H., Lynch, J. J., & Thomas, S. A. (1980). Animal companions and one-year survival of patients after discharge from a coronary care unit. *Public Health Reports, 95,* 307–312.

Kidd, A. H., & Kidd, R. M. (1985). Children's attitudes toward their pets. *Psychological Reports, 57,* 15–31.

Leland, L., Kirsch, J., & Stone, S. M. (2004). *The effects of pets on elderly citizens' blood pressure and heart rate.* Kansas City, MO: Great Plains Research Conference.

Levinson, B. M. (1969). *Pet-oriented child psychotherapy.* Springfield, IL: Charles C Thomas.

Melson, G. F., & Fogle, A. (1989). Children's ideas about animal young and their care: A reassessment of gender differences in the development of nurturance. *Anthrozoos, 2,* 265–273.

Michigan State University College of Nursing, http://nursing.msu.edu/habi/

Netting, F., Wilson, C., & New J. (1987). The human-animal bond: Implications for practice. *Social Work, 32,* 60–64.

Pet-Me Pets Therapeutic Animals, http://www.petmepets.org

Serpell, J. A. (1996). *In the company of animals: A study of human-animal relationships.* Cambridge, UK: Cambridge University Press.

Stone, S. M., & Pittman, S. (2003). *Therapy pets in special education classes.* Research Day for Regional Universities, University of Central Oklahoma, Edmond, OK.

Zasloff, R. L., & Kidd, A. H. (1994). Loneliness and pet ownership among single women. *Psychological Reports, 75,* 747–752.

PHENOTYPE

A phenotype is any distinctive structural or functional trait or set of characteristics expressed by an organism. Structure may be observed at any level, including external or internal gross anatomy and organ or tissue histology. Function may be observed at the level of cell biology, tissue biochemistry, organ physiology, or behavior of the whole organism. Phenotypes are used to define and classify individuals and groups in scientific studies and medical practice.

A phenotype may be a single observable characteristic or trait, or it may refer to a combination of traits. Diseases, syndromes, and malformations are clinical phenotypes. Examples of laboratory phenotypes include serum protein electrophoretic patterns, enzyme activities, and metabolite levels. An electrophysiologic response to nerve stimulation could be considered a clinical or laboratory phenotype. A pattern of gene expression detected on a DNA microarray would be a molecular phenotype.

Phenotypes result from interactions involving products of gene expression, the environment, and chance. Sickle cell disease is an autosomal recessive disease phenotype, but sickling of red cells is an autosomal dominant laboratory phenotype caused by deprivation of oxygen on a microscope slide. The disease phenotype of emphysema can be caused by the combination of a genetic predisposition such as alpha-1-antitrypsin deficiency and an environmental exposure such as smoking. Skin cancer is caused by both familial predisposition and sun exposure. A striking example of environmental influence on a structural phenotype is the phenomenon called temperature-dependent sex determination. Atlantic sea turtle gender is determined by ambient temperature during the midportion of incubation. Females are produced at warmer temperatures, whereas male hatchlings are more prevalent in cooler temperatures. When the temperature is in the range of 28° and 30°C, the sex ratio is approximately 1:1.

Chance is involved in the expression of phenotypes. Kurnit and colleagues used computer modeling to show that concepts such as "reduced penetrance" and "multifactorial inheritance" can be accounted for by chance. Their stochastic, probabilistic model demonstrated that incomplete penetrance of phenotypic expression can be due to genes that *predispose* an organism to develop a trait, but do not always cause an abnormal phenotype.

Major clinical features have significant medical, surgical, functional, or cosmetic consequences, whereas *minor* clinical features do not have important detrimental implications. Minor features can be important in defining phenotypes. Iris Lisch nodules are of no functional significance to a patient, but they are specific for the diagnosis of neurofibromatosis type I and provide an important marker for affected individuals. Some recognizable phenotypes such as Down syndrome are defined by their pattern of minor features rather than major features.

Phenotypic traits such as height, blood pressure, head circumference, and intelligence quotient (IQ) are *continuous*. They can be quantified, with measurements distributed in a continuous fashion across a population. Conversion of continuous traits into *discontinuous* ones can be achieved by defining a "threshold." For the examples above, thresholds could be used to define phenotypes of short or tall stature, low blood pressure or hypertension, microcephaly or macrocephaly, and mental retardation or genius status.

Accurate phenotype definition and delineation is important in gene-mapping studies. In fact, what we currently refer to as gene mapping is actually *phenotype mapping*, with the identification of new gene loci merely a by-product of our current ignorance about the human genome. Even after all loci in the human genome have been identified, there will still remain huge gaps in our knowledge about correlations between genotypes and phenotypes.

Mapping studies may be aided by the use of *endophenotypes* or *subphenotypes*, biological markers that characterize complex or poorly defined syndromic phenotypes. These may be presymptomatic risk factors. For example, brain magnetic resonance imaging findings or physiologic test responses characteristic of psychiatric disease may be used in family studies to identify presymptomatic relatives who carry the same genetic predisposition.

Mapping studies may also use broadened phenotypes for conditions that are usually nonfamilial. For example, instead of studying the genetics of autism using only subjects with an established diagnosis, investigators have benefited by also including relatives with related neuropsychiatric traits.

The term *phenotypic heterogeneity* can be used to refer to the phenomenon wherein disparate clinical phenotypes are produced by alleles at a single gene locus. Numerous examples of this now exist in the human genome, where disorders previously thought to be different entities are caused by mutations at the same locus.

—*Arthur S. Aylsworth*

Further Readings and References

Aylsworth, A. S. (2005). Clinical genetics and phenotype definition. In J. L. Hains & M. A. Pericak-Vance (Eds.), *Genetic analysis of complex disease* (2nd ed.). New York: Wiley-Liss.

Jorde, L. B. (Ed.). (2005). *Encyclopedia of genetics, genomics, proteomics, and bioinformatics: Vol. 1. Genetics.* New York: Wiley.

Kurnit, D. M., Layton, W. M., & Matthysse, S. (1987). Genetics, chance, and morphogenesis. *American Journal of Human Genetics, 41,* 979–995.

McKusick-Nathans Institute for Genetic Medicine, Johns Hopkins University, & National Center for Biotechnology Information, National Library of Medicine. (2000). *Online mendelian inheritance in man (OMIM).* Retrieved from http://www.ncbi.nlm.nih.gov/omim/

PHENYLKETONURIA (PKU)

Phenylketonuria (PKU) is an inherited metabolic disorder in which the amino acid phenylalanine cannot be broken down by the body. As a result, unhealthy levels of phenylalanine accumulate, causing a variety of problems, including mental retardation.

Fortunately, doctors can test for PKU at birth, and the negative effects can be prevented with a diet low in phenylalanine.

About 1 of every 10,000 babies is born with PKU. PKU is most common in whites of Northern European ancestry. It occurs less frequently in babies of African and Asian descent. PKU occurs in infants who inherited two copies (one from each parent) of a mutated gene for phenylalanine hydroxylase *(PAH)*. The mutated *PAH* gene, which is found on chromosome 12, is carried by about 1 in 50 people. If two carriers have a child, there is a 25% chance that they will have a child with PKU. If the inherited *PAH* genes are mutated but in different ways, a mild form of PKU may develop.

PAH is responsible for metabolizing phenylalanine in the body. Specifically, after a person eats a food containing phenylalanine, *PAH* turns the phenylalanine into another amino acid, tyrosine (which is used by the body for a variety of purposes). The genetic mutation associated with PKU causes the body to produce insufficient amounts of *PAH* or none at all. As a result, phenylalanine cannot be metabolized, and dangerously high levels build up in the blood and brain. These high levels lead to the signs and symptoms associated with PKU.

Newborns with PKU do not show obvious signs of high phenylalanine levels. However, within a few months, the symptoms are apparent. PKU causes irreversible brain damage, resulting in a variety of problems, including mental retardation, seizures, microcephaly (small head size), stunted growth, hyperactivity, and behavioral problems. Children with the mild version of PKU show similar symptoms, but they tend to be less severe.

Fortunately, the symptoms of PKU are preventable. Infants who are born in a hospital are tested for PKU before they go home (babies born outside of the hospital should be tested as soon as possible after birth). Once detected, prevention of the symptoms can be accomplished through dietary restrictions. Some phenylalanine is necessary for proper growth and functioning; however, the special diet of phenylketonurics (people with PKU) limits intake of phenylalanine to about 10% the normal amount. Phenylalanine is found in high quantities in protein-rich foods, including breast milk, dairy products, beans, eggs, meat, and fish; therefore, people with PKU have to avoid these substances entirely. The artificial sweetener aspartame also contains high quantities of phenylalanine and

must be avoided; for this reason, diet soda bottles and cans include a warning to phenylketonurics that the product contains phenylalanine. Many other substances contain smaller quantities of phenylalanine and may be consumed by people with PKU, as long as the recommended daily amount is not exceeded. In addition to the dietary restrictions, phenylketonurics typically have to drink a high-protein, phenylalanine-free formula that provides many of the essential nutrients that the person would otherwise be lacking.

For newborns with PKU, a diet low in phenylalanine is necessary to prevent brain damage; the restricted diet is particularly important in the first few years of life. After successful treatment for PKU early in life, some adults choose to go off of their special diet. However, most doctors today recommend sticking with the diet for life. It is particularly important for women with PKU to maintain a restricted diet during the childbearing years. High phenylalanine during pregnancy (known as maternal PKU) increases the risk for miscarriage and produces irreversible brain damage in 90% of newborns. Because the child often does not inherit PKU, a special diet after birth does nothing to reduce or prevent symptoms.

Since Asbjorn Folling first described PKU in 1934, researchers have learned a lot about this disorder. Recently, experiments have used mice models of PKU to find better treatments. Researchers hope to eventually find a way to prevent the genetic mutation that causes phenylketonuria.

—Kristine M. Jacquin

Further Readings and References

Batshaw, M. L. (1997). PKU and other inborn errors of metabolism. In M. L. Batshaw (Ed.), *Children with disabilities* (4th ed., pp. 389–404). Baltimore: Paul H. Brookes.

Howlin, P., & Udwin, O. (Eds.). (2002). *Outcomes in neurodevelopmental and genetic disorders.* New York: Cambridge University Press.

Mayo Foundation for Medical Education and Research. (2004). *Phenylketonuria.* Retrieved from http://www.mayo clinic.com/invoke.cfm?id=DS00514

National Center for Biotechnology Information. (2003). Phenylketonuria. *Genes and disease* (section 234). Bethesda, MD: National Library of Medicine. Retrieved from http://www.ncbi.nlm.nih.gov/books/bv.fcgi?call= bv.View..ShowSection&rid=gnd.section.234

National Institute of Child Health and Human Development. (1991). *Education of students with phenylketonuria (PKU).*

Information for teachers, administrators and other school personnel (Report No. NIH-92-3318). Bethesda, MD: Author. (ERIC Document Reproduction Service No. ED402717)

Waisbren, S. E. (1999). Phenylketonuria. In S. Goldstein & C. R. Reynolds (Eds.), *Handbook of neurodevelopmental and genetic disorders in children* (pp. 433–458). New York: Guilford.

Welsh, M., & Pennington, B. (2000). Phenylketonuria. In K. O. Yeates, M. D. Ris, & H. G. Taylor (Eds.), *Pediatric neuropsychology: Research, theory, and practice. The science and practice of neuropsychology: A Guilford series* (pp. 275–299). New York: Guilford.

PHOBIAS

Phobias represent a part of the anxiety disorders spectrum in which the primary symptoms include physiological arousal, cognitive appraisal of impending harm, and avoidance of discrete stimuli and situations associated with the stimuli. Although there are numerous popular descriptors for phobias (i.e., arachnophobia for fear of spiders), the technical term in the *Diagnostic and Statistical Manual of Mental Disorders (DSM)* lists all phobias under the label of *specific phobia*. Within this diagnosis, there are five subtypes: animal, natural environment, blood-injection-injury, situational, and other. Blood-injury-injection phobia is the only subtype with lowered psychophysiological arousal when confronted with the stimuli, leading to increased risk for fainting and loss of muscle tension.

CAUSE AND PREVALENCE

There is no widely agreed on cause of phobias. However, most theorists have agreed that the origins of phobias are based on cognitive and behavioral principles. On the one hand, aversive learning experiences with the phobic stimuli have been considered an important factor in the development of phobias (as is frequently the case in fear of choking, for example). Yet there are many cases of phobia that have no etiological cause that can be readily identified (i.e., blood-injury-injection phobia). A recent theory that addresses this inconsistency is the nonassociative account of phobias. Essentially, this theory posits that individuals who are dispositionally prone to certain phobias may have environmental contingencies that more readily lead to the development of phobias, whereas in the absence of maintaining factors, phobias do not persist. Poulton and Menzies (2002) describe, as an illustration, the finding that most individuals with a fear of water demonstrated extreme anxiety for water at very early ages. In the absence of any learning history that would support this fear (indeed, it would be expected that very young children would have low apprehension regarding water), this is considered supportive, at least in part, for a nonassociative account.

It is estimated that about 11% of the population meet criteria for a specific phobia, as defined by the *DSM*. However, "despite the fact that specific phobia is a common, treatable, and well-understood condition, people with specific phobia rarely present for treatment" (Antony & Barlow, 2002, p. 380). One reasonable explanation is that most phobias do not lead to functional impairment. For example, in most situations, spider phobia does not lead to problems in living or sufficient distress that the sufferer would require treatment.

Although most individuals with specific phobias do not seek treatment for these problems per se, when treatment is initiated, there is a high success rate. Efficacious treatment for specific phobias primarily involves behavioral therapy, typically involving graded exposure in vivo to the stimuli. In some instances, exposure *in imagery* may be used as an additional means of reducing fear, or as a means of initiating treatment on the way to live exposure. For some types of phobias, effective outcome has been obtained in a single prolonged session (i.e., injection phobia). In some cases, it has been observed that adding cognitive therapy (e.g., positive self-statements or challenges to maladaptive beliefs) contributed to efficacy and enhanced long-term outcome.

Although the efficacy of cognitive and behavioral treatment has been established for phobias, some phobias are difficult to treat with exposure in vivo because of logistical constraints. For example, fear of flying ultimately requires taking a flight. The disadvantages of this involve cost, scheduling, and lack of control over the rate of exposure by the therapist. As a means of circumventing this problem, virtual reality treatment has been developed to address the problem of exposure for phobic stimuli that are difficult to treat with in vivo exposure methods. This form of treatment has been found effective for fear of flying and acrophobia.

—Dean McKay and Steven D. Tsao

Further Readings and References

American Psychiatric Association. (2000). *Diagnostic and statistical manual of mental disorders* (4th ed., text rev.). Washington, DC: Author.

Antony, M. M., & Barlow, D. H. (2002). Specific phobias. In D. H. Barlow (Ed.), *Anxiety and its disorders* (2nd ed., pp. 380–417). New York: Guilford.

Craske, M. G. (1999). *Anxiety disorders: Psychological approaches to theory and treatment.* Boulder, CO: Westview.

Eaton, W. W., Dryman, A., & Weissman, M. M. (1991). Panic and phobia. In L. N. Robins & D. A. Regier (Eds.), *Psychiatric disorders in America: The epidemiological catchment area study.* New York: Free Press.

Emmelkamp, P. M. J., Krijn, M., Hulsbosch, A. M., de Vries, S., Schuemie, M. J., & van der Mast, C. A. P. G. (2002). Virtual reality treatment versus exposure in vivo: A comparative evaluation in acrophobia. *Behaviour Research and Therapy, 40,* 509–516.

Kessler, R. C., McGonagle, K. A., Zhao, S., Nelson, C. B., Hughes, M., Eshleman, S., et al. (1994). Lifetime and 12-month prevalence of DSM-III-R psychiatric disorders in the United States: Results from the National Comorbidity Survey. *Archives of General Psychiatry, 51,* 8–19.

Maltby, N., Kirsch, I., Mayers, M., & Allen, G. J. (2002). Virtual reality exposure therapy for the treatment of fear of flying: A controlled investigation. *Journal of Consulting and Clinical Psychology, 70,* 1112–1118.

McNally, R. J. (1994). Atypical phobias. In G. C. L. Davey (Ed.), *Phobias: A handbook of theory, research, and treatment* (pp. 183–199). Chichester, UK: Wiley.

MedlinePlus. (2005). *Phobias.* Retrieved from http://www.nlm.nih.gov/medlineplus/phobias.html

Öst, L. G., & Hellstrom, K. (1994). In G. C. L. Davey (Ed.), *Phobias: A handbook of theory, research, and treatment* (pp. 63–80). Chichester, UK: Wiley.

Öst, L. G., Hellstrom, K., & Kaver, A. (1992). One versus five sessions of exposure in the treatment of injection phobia. *Behavior Therapy, 23,* 263–282.

Öst, L. G., Sterner, U., & Lindahl, I. L. (1984). Physiological responses in blood phobics. *Behaviour Research and Therapy, 22,* 109–117.

Phobia List, http://www.phobialist.com/

Poulton, R., & Menzies, R. G. (2002). Non-associative fear acquisition: A review of the evidence from retrospective and longitudinal research. *Behaviour Research and Therapy, 40,* 127–149.

Royal College of Psychiatrists. (n.d.). *Anxiety and phobias.* Retrieved from http://www.rcpsych.ac.uk/info/anxpho.htm

PHONICS

Phonics is a method of reading instruction that focuses on teaching students the sounds associated with letters and letter combinations. For example, when kindergartners are taught that the letter *c* says /c/ as in candy, *a* says /a/ as in apple, and *t* says /t/ as in tiger, and are later prompted to blend the sounds /c/ /a/ /t/ into "cat," they are learning to read with phonics. Because phonics unlocks word identification and a cascade of associated benefits, including fluency, spelling improvement, and comprehension, it has become, in recent years, the focus of important school improvement efforts in the United States and elsewhere.

RESEARCH AND RECOMMENDATIONS

Reading researchers have conducted countless studies to assess the usefulness of phonics and to identify teaching methods that are most efficient. Comprehensive meta-analyses have revealed that systematic, explicit phonics instruction produces the most significant benefits for students in kindergarten through sixth grade and for children having difficulty learning to read. Here are several important findings about phonics, along with recommendations for instruction.

Phonemic Awareness Is Essential

Learners who have the ability to hear and understand that words are composed of discrete, separate sounds are said to be *phonemically aware* and are ready for phonics. Without phonemic awareness skills, students are likely to struggle with their phonics lessons. To identify those in need of remediation, primary teachers should carefully assess their students' phoneme awareness skills. Oral rhyming, syllable tapping, sound segmentation games, sound substitution, and sound blending serve to develop phoneme awareness. A learner who can listen to the word "hug" and segment the word orally into its component sounds, /h/ /u/ /g/, has mastered phoneme segmentation and is likely to benefit from phonics instruction and be successful in learning how to read.

Good Phonics Instruction Is Explicit

Phonics instruction must be *explicit*—taught directly, actively, and clearly—and practiced until the content is mastered. Reading programs that focus on implicit or discovery methods of learning are less efficient, especially for children at risk for reading difficulties. Programs aligned with incidental or embedded phonics approaches, the so-called *look-and-say* or whole-word method, basal (controlled vocabulary) approaches, worksheets-only methods (without active teaching), or the Whole Language ideology of reading and literacy instruction typically lack systematic teaching of letter-sound associations. Most students require explicit instruction in sound-symbol correspondences of the alphabet letters and letter combinations; they do best when their teachers use active direct instruction methods.

Effective Phonics Instruction Is Systematic

It does not work well to skip around in the phonics curriculum and teach, for example, the phonogram *ing* one day, prefixes the next day, and the sound for the letter *s* the third day. Beneficial phonics instruction must be systematic, orderly, and sequential. In general, teachers who teach systematically follow a phonics content sequence that progresses from easy to more difficult. Commercial phonics programs usually design instructional sequences similar to the one offered here.

Sequence of Phonics Skills by Grade Level

Pre-Kindergarten

- Phonemic awareness skills (sound segmentation, etc.)
- Alphabet recognition, especially recognition of the lowercase letters (using ABC books, ABC songs, and engaging, fun letter-play activities)
- Sound-symbol correspondence of alphabet letters, short vowels (*a, e, i, o, u*) plus consonants (using puppets, alliterative stories, letter-sound pictures, multisensory, direct instruction, and visual-vocal participation.
- Letter formation practice

Kindergarten

- Phonemic awareness skills (e.g., sound segmentation)
- Short vowels (*a, e, i, o, u*) plus consonants

- Letter formation practice
- Blending practice with easy consonant-vowel-consonant words (e.g., *cat, bed, sit, log, sun*)
- Reading and writing consonant-vowel-consonant words, word family words (e.g., *cat, hat, fat, mat*), and dictated words
- Reading and writing short decodable stories and sentences (e.g., *The dog had a big red hat.*)
- Writing the letters of the alphabet

First Grade

- Phonemic awareness skills (e.g., sound segmentation)
- Short vowels (*a, e, i, o, u*) plus consonants
- Consonant digraphs (*ch, sh, th, wh*)
- Consonant blends (*bl, br, fl, sl, sm, st, tr, pr, str*)
- Silent e (when the e at the end of the word makes the vowel long, as in *same, note, tire, lute*)
- Blending practice with consonant-vowel-consonant words and longer words with initial, medial, and final blends, digraphs, and diphthongs
- Compound words (e.g., *postman, bedroom, cowboy*)
- Vowel digraphs (*ai, ay, ea, ee, oa, ow*)
- Other vowel spelling patterns (*oo, ou, ow, oi, and oy*)
- Word families (e.g., *same, game, tame, name*)
- Endings (*ed, ing,* two sounds for *y* at the end of words)
- Contractions (*I'll, you've, she's, it's, don't*)
- Reading and writing words, decodable stories, and sentences
- Dictation exercises and writing practice to reinforce skill development

Second and Third Grades

- More complex spelling patterns (*ph, ight, ough*)
- More word families
- Soft c (as in *city*) and soft g (as in *gem*)
- Prefixes (*in, un, mis, re, dis*)
- Suffixes (*less, ness, able, ly, ful, est, tion*)
- Silent letters (wr as in *wrap*, mb as in *climb*, gn as in *sign*, kn as in *know*, lk as in *talk*)
- Multisyllabic words
- Root words
- Syllabication strategies (divide between two consonants, *slip/per*, creating a short vowel sound in the first syllable, or divide in front of a single consonant, *pa/per*, creating a long vowel sound in the first syllable, and other strategies)
- Lots of reading practice to make decoding and word identification rapid and automatic
- More writing practice to reinforce skill development

Upper Grades

- Normally phonics skills are not taught in the upper grades. (Most delayed readers, students with learning disabilities, and learners with decoding and word recognition deficits can be taught phonics skills, however, using multisensory, engaging, targeted systematic, explicit phonics instruction and grade-level appropriate decodable texts.)
- Dictation and writing practice are recommended to reinforce skill development.
- High-interest teaching methods and maximum student engagement are recommended to stimulate student motivation.
- Individual tutoring or small-group instruction in phonics may be most effective for learners with reading delays.

Most Children Can Learn to Read

Research reported by the National Reading Panel in 2000 shows that almost all children, even those with learning disabilities and dyslexia, can learn to read, given appropriate phoneme awareness and phonics instruction. In 2004, exciting brain imaging studies using functional magnetic resonance imaging demonstrated that intensive instruction in phoneme awareness and phonics can remap and normalize the neural functioning of dyslexics. Students with normal intelligence who cannot read may simply turn out to be learners who have not received enough focused phoneme awareness and phonics instruction.

Phonics Offers an Array of Benefits

Empirical research demonstrates that systematic, explicit phonics instruction improves the reading of regular education students as well as students with learning disabilities. Phonics improves the word-reading ability of students from both low and high socioeconomic backgrounds. Across all grade levels, systematic phonics instruction improves the ability to spell and, with adequate practice, leads to automatic word recognition and reading fluency. Finally, phonics combined with adequate vocabulary knowledge improves all-important reading comprehension.

But Phonics Isn't Everything

Basically, phonics skills are necessary for learning to read, but they are not the only skills required. Effective reading teachers are mindful of the totality of the reading task and include instruction designed to develop fluency and increase vocabulary and comprehension. Early readers need a great deal of experience reading, especially in connected, leveled, or decodable texts. Reading practice at home and in school (at first aloud and later silently) cements phonics skills and moves the learner toward automatic word recall and reading fluency. Students should also be read *to* both at home and at school, to create a pleasure anchor, to expand background knowledge and vocabulary, and to motivate them to read independently. Written, oral, and computer literacy activities and comprehension skill development are also important ingredients in a total reading curriculum. Phonics alone should not constitute a beginning reading program.

Don't "Drill and Kill"

An essential bridge to word identification, phonics can nonetheless be poorly taught or excessively taught. In some regrettable situations, phonics is not actually taught at all, but daily worksheets are passed out that students are expected to complete independently. Old-fashioned dreary drills and motivation-quashing busywork assignments are clearly not components of effective reading instruction. Active, social, engaging phonics lessons followed with reading in connected text, however, provide vital scaffolding as learners acquire reading strategies.

The Purpose of Phonics Is to Enable Learners to Read Well

The goal is reading. Educators and parents must remember that the purpose of phonics instruction is not to memorize phonics rules or generalizations, but to provide learners with skills they need to read and write easily and well. Effective phonics leads to fluency and reading comprehension, and can engender a lifelong love of reading. It is the means to an end.

—*Lynn Melby Gordon*

See also Whole Language

Further Readings and References

Adams, M. (1990). *Beginning to read: Thinking and learning about print.* Cambridge: MIT Press.

Blevins, W. (1998). *Phonics from A to Z.* New York: Scholastic Professional Books.

Center for the Improvement of Early Reading Achievement. (2001). *Put reading first: The research building blocks for teaching children to read.* Retrieved from http://www .nifl.gov/partnershipforreading/publications/reading_first1 .html

Chall, J., & Popp, H. (1999). *Teaching and assessing phonics: Why, what, when, how.* Cambridge, MA: Educators Publishing Service.

Honig, B. (1997). *Reading the right way: What research and best practices say about eliminating failure among beginning readers.* Retrieved from http://www.aasa.org/publications/ sa/1997_09/honig.htm

International Reading Association's Phonics Special Interest Group, http://www.phonicsbulletin.info

National Institute of Child Health and Human Development. (2000). *Report of the National Reading Panel: Teaching children to read.* Retrieved from http://www.nichd.nih.gov/ publications/nrp/smallbook.htm

Shaywitz, S. (2003). *Overcoming dyslexia: A new and complete science-based program for reading problems at any level.* New York: Alfred A. Knopf

PHONOLOGICAL AWARENESS

Phonological awareness is the sensitivity and ability to manipulate the sound structure of language and the understanding that spoken language is made up of individual and separate sounds. Phonological awareness is now recognized as playing a causal role in learning to read alphabetic script systems and as being the core deficit for most children having difficulty learning to read. Children who enter first grade low in knowledge about the phonological features of words are at a high risk for difficulties in benefiting from early reading instruction. Children delayed in the development of phonological awareness have a very difficult time making sense of phonics instruction because they have trouble noticing the phonemic patterns in written words.

One common misunderstanding is that phonological awareness and phonics are the same thing. Phonological awareness, including phonemic awareness, is not phonics. Phonics is the knowledge that there are predictable relationships between phonemes and the letters that represent those sounds in written language. Phonological awareness is the understanding that the sounds of spoken language are the underlying elements of words. Therefore, phonological awareness is needed to benefit from phonics instruction.

Phonological awareness appears to develop gradually during the preschool and early school years. It is best viewed as a hierarchy of sensitivity or levels of complexity. Higher levels of sensitivity require more explicit awareness and manipulation of smaller-sized language units (e.g., phonemes), whereas more elementary sensitivity requires the manipulation of larger sound units (e.g., syllables). For example, "Say airplane without saying /air/," would be a word-level task. A phoneme-level item would require manipulation or awareness of individual phonemes. For example, "Say hat without saying the /h/ sound."

Children typically achieve syllabic and rhyme sensitivity and sensitivity to onset-rime before they achieve sensitivity to phonemes. The awareness of and ability to manipulate phonemes is often called phonemic awareness or sensitivity. Phonemic awareness appears to be especially important in the development of word decoding skills. Even though phonological awareness is considered to develop in levels, it is now considered to consist of one underlying or unitary construct that is very stable from at least the late preschool period through formal reading instruction.

Tasks used to assess phonological awareness tend to vary substantially, and children can demonstrate phonological awareness in several ways. Broader and more elementary phonological awareness skills can be demonstrated by identifying and making oral rhymes. For example, "Mat wore a (hat)." Other tasks require counting syllables, identifying and isolating onsets or rimes, or identifying and working with the individual phonemes in spoken words. Tasks can also be constructed to require the categorization of words, the blending of word parts, or the segmentation of words. For example, a phoneme blending task would require a child to listen to a sequence of separately spoken phonemes and then combine the phonemes to form a word.

Before children can learn to decode words, they need to become aware of how sounds in words work, that is, that words consist of speech sounds. Effective classroom phonological awareness instruction teaches children to notice, think about, and manipulate sounds in spoken language. Activities that build phonological awareness, especially phonemic awareness, include isolating and identifying the individual sounds in spoken words, blending sounds to make words, and breaking spoken words into their separate sounds. Phonemic awareness instruction is most effective when children are taught to manipulate phonemes by using the letters of the alphabet. Vocabulary development also appears to play a key role in the development of phonological awareness. Other general activities that promote phonological awareness growth are shared reading, letter name and sound play, and rhyming games.

—*Stephen Burgess and Tabitha Smith*

See also Language Development

Further Readings and References

International Reading Association. (1998, July). *Summary of a position statement of the International Reading Association: Phonemic awareness and the teaching of reading.* Retrieved from http://www.reading.org/positions/phonemic.html

Kahill, M. L., Mosenthal, P. B., Pearson, P., & Barr, R. (Eds.). (2000). *Handbook of reading research: Vol. 3.* Mahwah, NJ: Erlbaum.

National Reading Panel. (2000). *Teaching children to read.* Retrieved from http://www.nationalreadingpanel.org/Publications/summary.htm

Torgesen, J. K., & Mathes, P. (2000). *A basic guide to understanding, assessing, and teaching phonological awareness.* Austin, TX: PRO-ED.

PHYSICAL DEVELOPMENT AND GROWTH

Differences in physical growth are apparent from everyday observations of people around us. We differ in terms of height, weight, the relative length of our body proportions, and fitness. We also differ in our abilities to move and perform physical skills and tasks. These differences provide valuable insights into our maturation, overall development, and health. As such, the study of physical growth and development is central to child development, medicine, education, and a host of other disciplines. It is also a subject of personal interest to all people in possession of a body.

STAGES OF PHYSICAL GROWTH

The general pattern of physical growth is similar for all individuals. There can be considerable variations, however, in terms of the rate and timing of growth and the size attained. Chronological age provides an obvious point of reference for observing and recording growth. Its significance should not be overstated, though; biological events and processes follow

Table 1   Stages of Human Growth

Stage	Age / Growth Event
Prenatal Growth	
Ovum Period	First 2 weeks after fertilization Cell division and increasing complexity
Embryo Period	Weeks 2 through 8 Steady growth; differentiation of cells into tissues, organ and systems
Fetus Period	Weeks 9 through 40 Rapid growth in size and mass; changes in body proportions; development of function in tissues, organs and systems
Postnatal Growth	
Infancy	Birth to end of weaning (about 24–36 months)
Early Childhood	Weaning to about seven years of age
Later Childhood	Seven years of age to puberty
Adolescence	Puberty to sexual and physical maturation, at about 20 years of age
Adulthood	20 years of age to end of menopause (for women)
Senescence	Menopause to death

their own schedule. As it is sometimes said, biology does not celebrate birthdays!

Table 1 offers a brief overview of the different stages of human physical growth and the ages and events that often relate to them. Of course, any model of stages of development is necessarily somewhat arbitrary. The one presented here provides one way of understanding the process of physical growth, from conception to death.

The clearest distinction in human growth is between prenatal and postnatal stages. For obvious reasons, studies of prenatal growth are far more difficult to carry out than postnatal studies. However, recent research has offered valuable information and a more complete picture of physical growth throughout the course of life.

Prenatal Growth

There are two common approaches for categorizing growth in the prenatal period, which comprises on average 9 months, or 40 weeks. One way is in terms of the development of the organism as an ovum, an embryo and a fetus. The other approach is the well-known trimester model in which the course of pregnancy is usefully divided into 3-month periods. Discussing prenatal development in terms of trimesters is useful in certain contexts, such as clinical settings with mothers. However, because it only crudely relates to actual biological events, its value is limited. For this reason, the following discussion will consider prenatal growth in terms of biological events, particularly the development of the ovum, the embryo, and the fetus.

The Ovum

Growth begins at the moment of conception with the fertilization of the ovum (the mother's egg) by the father's sperm. The period of the ovum comprises the first 2 weeks after fertilization. It is a process of self-duplication and multiplication from single cells into tens of thousands of new cells. As cell division takes place, the cluster of cells resembles a raspberry and then changes position to form a hollow disk. During the second week after fertilization, the disk implants itself in the wall of the uterus (or womb), and a number of cellular layers become differentiated, including one that develops into the embryo.

The Embryo

Beginning with the formation of the embryo during the second week, this period is characterized by quite rapid growth differentiation of cells. Cells become specialized and organized to form the different tissues, organs, and bodily systems. By the end of this period, at about week 8, the embryo has developed the basic physical and functional features of a human, and changes during subsequent weeks are mainly in the dimension of physical features and refinement of functions. No new anatomical features appear after the embryo period.

The multiplication of cells and the specialization or differentiation of these cells into different organs and tissues makes the early stages of life highly susceptible to growth pathologies due to either genetic abnormalities or harmful environmental conditions, such as mother's poor nutrition or disease.

The Fetus

By week 9, the process of differentiation and specialization into tissues, organs, and bodily systems is largely complete. Growth is rapid during this period, especially from week 20. In fact, 90% of body weight at birth is attained during this second half of pregnancy. As well as marked increases in size and weight, the fetus period is characterized by changes to the body proportions. The embryo has an extremely large head in relation to the rest of the body, but as the fetus develops, the back and limbs grow rapidly in relation to the head, and the fetus takes a form much more recognizably human.

Importantly, from the perspective of the individual's survival after birth, the development of several bodily systems like blood circulation, breathing, and digestion occurs, preparing the fetus for the transition to life outside of the mother's uterus.

Postnatal Growth— The Growth Curve

The introduction of what has become known as the growth curve dates back to 18th-century France. Count Philibert Gueneau de Montbeillard measured the height of his son every 6 months from birth to 18 years of age, and these measurements were reported by his friend and celebrated scientist, George-Louie Leclerc de Buffon. These measurements were significant because they represented a new and valuable approach to measuring physical growth. Before this advance, the most common method for assessing growth was cross-sectional study, in which an individual is measured once. There is an inherent limitation of this approach because it can tell us nothing about individual development from 1 year to the next. It is precisely information about variability and changes in rates of growth that is most useful to both clinicians, wishing to compare an individual's rate to standards, and researchers, studying the relationship between early influences and later physical growth. A difficulty with the original measurements of Montbeillard's son was that they were recorded using antiquated French units. It was not until an American, Richard Scammon, converted these measurements into modern metric units in the early part of the 20th century that the information was made widely available in the form of a chart.

Growth charts are now staple elements of the study of physical growth. Despite the technological advances made in recent years, Montbeillard's measurements were remarkably accurate and reveal distinct phases of growth that continue to be valid today.

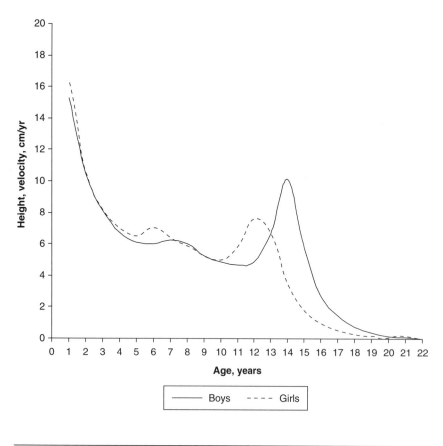

at about 6 to 8 years of age and the second, longer one, beginning at about 10 years for girls and 12 years for boys. Using the evident changes in the rate of growth as a starting point, it is possible to divide postnatal growth into a series of phases, with each phase characterized by distinct growth events and processes.

Phases of Postnatal Growth and Development

Although all human experience has the same basic pattern of growth, there are significant differences in individual rates and timing of growth during the life span. This is not just a point of academic interest. A school teacher of a class of 12-year-old girls or 14-year-old boys may be confronted with students of vastly different degrees of physical maturity, including relatively immature children and mature individuals who are almost adults.

Figure 1   Idealized Mean Velocity Growth Curves for Boys and Girls

Scammon's chart described the height achieved by the boy at all ages between birth and 18. This is called a *distance curve* because it reflects the child's progression toward maturity. Distance curves reveal some important facts about physical growth. There is obviously dramatic growth throughout the first 18 years of life, with a difference in height gains between boys and girls occurring around the early teen years. However, this is nonlinear: the individual does not increase the same amount of height each year, and there are periods of relatively large growth and others of relatively little growth. Although the distance curve can give a hint of these different stages of growth, these stages are far from clear. What is needed to show the differences in rates of growth over time is a *velocity curve*. An idealized velocity curve is shown in Figure 1.

Immediately, it is possible to see that physical growth takes place through quite distinct phases. It is also possible to identify two spurts, the first occurring

Infancy

Infancy begins with birth and ends when the infant changes from lactation to eating solid food. The age of this development varies between different societies, and this variation is exacerbated by the trend in industrialized countries to reduce or eliminate the period of breast-feeding. In more traditional societies, which would seem to offer a more reliable indication, weaning normally ends at about 2 or 3 years.

The first months of postnatal life, called the *neonatal period*, is a time of transition from the womb to the outside environment. The infancy phase is a period of rapid growth in most physical dimensions and bodily systems. Although there is a clear increase in the distance of growth, this period is characterized by a steep decrease in velocity. In many respects, this growth is a continuation of the fetus growth pattern. Alongside increases in height and weight during the first years, changes also occur in body proportions. Particularly

Table 2 Ages at Which Movement Skills Are Achieved

Age Range (months)	Motor Milestone
0.7–4.0	Head held erect
0.7–5.0	Turns from side to back
1.0–5.0	Sits upright with support
4.0–8.0	Unilateral reaching
5.0–9.0	Sits alone unsupported
5.0–12.0	Pulls up to stand position
7.0–12.0	Walks with assistance
9.0–16.0	Stands alone
9.0–17.0	Walks alone

noticeable is the relatively large head during infancy, which represents 25% of the total body length and is almost 70% of its eventual adult size. In the first year, the head accounts for 20% of body length, and by adulthood, it accounts for just 12%, with the legs taking 50% of total stature.

Infancy is associated with the development of the musculoskeletal frame and the nervous system, especially the brain, which grows more rapidly during infancy than any other tissue or organ of the body. This development facilitates a host of cognitive and movement achievements. Most early movement is characterized by reflex actions, which are broadly defined as involuntary actions triggered by a range of external stimuli.

The period from 12 to 24 months is a time for the infant to practice and master many of the actions initiated during the first year and to add new ones. Although the rate of acquisition of skills varies according to each individual, the sequence of skills is quite predictable and seems to transcend social, cultural, and ethnic boundaries. Findings from research during the 1930s and 1940s established the creation of "motor milestones." These are basic to skilled performance as each skill is a landmark in an infant's movement development (see Table 2).

Early Childhood

Following the deceleration of growth during infancy, the years between 3 and 7 witness a period of relatively rapid physical growth. It has often been noted that a characteristic feature of early childhood growth is its predictability, and a common pattern seems to be shared by all healthy children. In fact, this predictability has been used to good effect in clinical and epidemiological settings, to help detect ill health, by assessing deviations from normal growth.

Although children of this age have been weaned, they remain dependent on adult support, mainly because of their still developing cognitive and movement capabilities. Early childhood is a time for developing mastery in basic movement skills and for testing oneself physically in different environments. Movement activities can be viewed from various perspectives, but most are based on the categories of stability (or balance), locomotion (or traveling), and manipulation (or control) because these are found in all ages. One further classification is into fine motor and gross motor activities. Fine motor activities involve movements that require precision and dexterity, usually regulating the use of hands and eyes together. Movement patterns in this category include writing, drawing, cutting, pasting, and the manipulation of small objects and instruments. Gross motor activities involve the whole body or major segments. Often referred to as *fundamental motor skills*, they include such skills as running, jumping, twisting, turning, hopping, throwing, and kicking (see Table 3).

Later Childhood

The transition from early to later childhood is sometimes marked by an increase in growth velocity, called the midgrowth spurt. During the subsequent phase, which occurs between about 7 years of age and the onset of puberty, the rate of growth declines. The rate of growth during later childhood, in terms of height and weight, as well as body tissues and systems, is the slowest since birth. Differences in size between boys and girls are insignificant during both early and later childhood phases. However, an extremely important difference does appear at the end of later childhood, as girls enter puberty some time before boys. Girls' later childhood period ends at about 10 years of age; for boys, it is at about 12 years.

The period between 7 years and puberty is sometimes referred to as the *skill-hungry years*. Occurring between the periods of rapid growth in early childhood

Table 3   Movement Skills in Early Childhood

Age	Fine Skills	Gross Skills
3 years	Picks up blocks	Stands on one foot
	Places shapes in holes	Walks backwards and sideways
	Turns the pages of a book	Jumps down from a step
	Paints at an easel	Kicks a large ball with force
4 years	Holds a pencil in an adult way	Pedals a tricycle
	Copies a square accurately	Hops on the spot and along
	Brings thumbs into opposition	Bounces a large ball
	Colors inside lines	Runs smoothly
5 years	Uses a knife and fork competently	Can touch toes when upright
	Threads a needle and sews	Jumps for height up to 30 cm
	Copies a triangle accurately	Dances rhythmically to music
	Does jigsaws with joining pieces	Walks downstairs with alternating feet
6 years	Ties own shoe laces	Skips with alternate feet
	Writes first and last names	Catches a ball with consistency
	Holds a pencil with finger tips	Kicks a football up to 6 meters
	Builds a straight tower of cubes	Throws a ball using wrists and fingers

and adolescence, it represents a time of relative stability, during which children can extend their physical competence in different contexts. Having already established fundamental movement skills, children now develop their skills in new and challenging situations. They do this by refining, combining, and elaborating on their fundamental movement skills to perform more specialized, often more socially stereotypical actions, such as sports, dance, and games.

Adolescence

Progression to adolescence is marked by a rapid acceleration in the velocity of growth of almost all body parts, although different parts of the body reach their peak rate of growth at different times. The duration of the period of acceleration, called the *adolescent growth spurt*, is usually greater in boys than in girls, although there is a great deal of individual difference. On completion of the adolescent growth spurt, men are, on average, taller and heavier than women. This seems to be common to all societies and ethnicities. The difference in final height and weight between males and females appears to be attributable to two main factors: the delay of the onset of puberty in boys and the greater intensity of the growth spurt in boys. The consequences of these, and other factors, is the adult stature of women averages about 90% of the stature of men.

Adolescence is the time when sexual maturation takes places, with visible signs such as a sudden increase in the density of pubic hair, and, in the case of girls, the development of the breast bud. Other significant events during adolescence include the production of viable sperm in boys and egg cells in girls, although these do not signal full sexual maturity. This is particularly the case in girls, for whom the first menstrual period, or menarche, is often followed by a period of sterility. On average, girls are not fertile until about 14 years of age or later, and a further 4 years are often needed before full sexual maturity is reached. The adolescent stage of growth is also the phase during which secondary sexual characteristics develop, such as changes to the external genitalia and differences in body size and body composition.

Adulthood and Senescence

The transition from adolescence to adulthood is primarily characterized by two events: the end of increases in height and full reproductive maturity. The course of physical growth during adulthood is relatively uneventful. Regular, weight-bearing physical activity will increase muscle mass; regular, low-intensity exercise will generally decrease body fat, whereas overeating will increase the amount of body fat. Generally speaking, however, the adult stage is characterized by its stability.

Western men and women from high socioeconomic groups tend to reach adult height at about 20 years and 18 years, respectively. Other groups tend to achieve adult height a little later, with the cultural differences presumably attributable to degrees of access to quality nutrition and health care. Those suffering from undernutrition may continue to grow for some years later, although they rarely reach the final stature of their healthier, often wealthier peers.

Aging, or senescence, is characterized by a process of decline in an individual's ability to reproduce and adapt to stress. There is a large degree of variability in the onset and nature of senescence. Although some traits, such as loss of skin elasticity, reduced movement capacity, and female menopause, or the end of menstruation at about 45 and 55 years, are common to most societies; others, such as cardiovascular disease, brittle bones, and arthritis, are more likely to be culture-specific consequences of Western lifestyles.

MEASURING GROWTH

The evolution of the study of physical growth has been briefly discussed in the previous section. Essentially, there are two basic kinds of studies: cross-sectional and longitudinal. In cross-sectional studies, individuals are measured once. Typically a large number of individuals are measured at each chronological age, and the average measurements are calculated. Longitudinal studies involve repeated measurements of individuals over a number of years. Compared with cross-sectional studies, longitudinal research is very time consuming and usually necessitates a restricted sample size. This partially accounts for the relative variety of longitudinal studies of growth.

Recent advances have made available a great number of tools for measuring physical growth. Some of these tools involve the use of complex specialist equipment; however, most growth studies continue to use methods that are quite easy to understand and replicate.

The potential measures that could be made of the human body are almost infinite, but certain techniques have been established, and some of these are listed and described in Table 4.

REGULATION OF PHYSICAL GROWTH

The process of physical growth is a complex one, influenced by genetic, hormonal, and environmental factors. Genes offer a potential range for achieving physical size and shape, and the environment partly determines the eventual growth within that range.

Genes do not influence growth directly. They produce proteins that regulate a genetically inherited pattern of growth, mediated by the endocrine and neurological systems. In essence, the endocrine system—the system of glands under neural control responsible for the release of regulatory chemicals—provides the biochemical environment in which genes act. For example, the adolescent growth spurt cannot occur without the release of sufficient quantities of growth and sex-specific hormones into the blood. Harmful environmental insults cause a reduction in the release of growth hormone and other hormones, resulting in reduced growth. To this extent, the endocrine system acts as an intermediary between the action of the genes and the influence of the environment.

Although genes and the endocrine system have significant influence on the regulation of physical growth, environmental factors—those that are nongenetic and external to the organism—can also account for some of the differences between individuals. Unfavorable environmental conditions, such as nutrition, negative psychological and social experiences, and pollutants, can start to affect growth adversely from shortly after the moment of conception, and continue throughout the life span.

The effects of harmful environmental conditions on growth seem to be dependent on the severity and duration of the problem, as well as the age at which it occurs. Young children are particularly vulnerable to such insults. However, there is some evidence to suggest that, when the insult is removed and adequate nutrition is available, retardation of growth is usually followed by a period of catch-up growth, during which the individual rapidly returns to or approaches a normal rate of growth. A useful analogy for this period of catch-up was provided by the British geneticist, C. H. Waddington, who compared physical growth to the movement of a ball down a valley floor. He suggested that an insult may knock the ball away from a central pathway, and the velocity of its movement will then reduce. Once the insult is corrected, though, the ball returns toward the valley floor at an increased speed, upon which normal velocity recommences. If the insult is not corrected, perhaps because of continued poor diet, the individual may resume growth at a relatively slower rate, and skeletal maturation may be delayed, extending the period of growth. Scholars disagree regarding the long-term effects of harmful environmental conditions during infancy and childhood, but there is some evidence

Table 4   Common Measurements of Individual Growth

Stature	Standing	Floor to top of head (no shoes)
	Lying	Feet to top of head while lying on back
	Sitting	Sitting surface/buttocks to top of head
Breadth	Shoulders	Outside of left to outside of right upper arm
	Hips	Outside of left to outside of right hip, at waist
	Knees	Widest aspect
	Elbows	Widest aspect
Circumferences	Upper arm	Midway between shoulder and elbow, with arm hanging loosely to side
	Calf	"Belly" calf, standing
	Head	Forehead level
Skinfold	Triceps muscle	Double-fold of skin at back of upper arm
	Subscapular	Fold beneath shoulder blade
	Suprailiac	Fold above waist

to suggest that severe difficulties can result in negative lasting effects. In most cases, however, it seems to be the case that growth merely slows down in response to harmful conditions, and waits for better times.

Because environmental factors rarely operate in isolation, it can be difficult to quantify the precise relationship between specific influences and physical growth. Nevertheless, there are certain factors that have well-documented effects on physical growth, including nutrition, social and environmental status, psychological stress, and pollutants.

Nutrition

Adequate nutrition is of fundamental importance to physical growth and development. A reduction in the rate of growth is one of the first responses to restricted food intake, and in countries where food is persistently limited, growth delays occur, and children tend to be shorter and lighter than in countries with adequate food supplies. In fact, so strongly associated are growth and nutrition that measurement of physical growth is one of the most widely used indices of nutritional status in children.

Although the effects of poor nutrition can be experienced at all stages of development, including during the prenatal growth, infancy and early childhood represent the periods during which the developing child's system is unusually sensitive to malnutrition. This seems to be, in part, because the first years of life witness the most rapid growth. International studies suggest that about half of all deaths during the first 5 years result from the effects of poor nutrition and the associated inability to fight infectious diseases.

Adolescence is another period when individuals are especially vulnerable to the harmful effects of malnutrition. Nutritional needs are greater during this period than at any other time of life, and although the rate of proportionate growth is somewhat less than during the early years, it persists for much longer. As is well known, adolescence is a time when young people experiment with food choices, and inappropriate choices can have profound and long-lasting effects. Conditions such as anorexia nervosa (a disorder characterized by an abnormal fear of becoming obese) and bulimia nervosa (an eating disorder, in which binge eating is often followed by feelings of guilt and fasting) are especially common among adolescent girls and can seriously threaten both health and physical growth. Aside from retarding an individual's rate of growth, inappropriate diet can also have harmful effects on skeletal development, and insufficient food intake has been associated with the development of osteoporosis, or brittle bones, in women.

Social and Economic Status

Children from poorer families are generally shorter and lighter than their peers in higher-income families. They also consume less food. The timing of growth, rather than growth itself, seems to be most affected by social and economic factors; for example, the onset of puberty occurs earlier in individuals from wealthier groups than those from poorer groups. Studies of preschoolers have reported differences in height, weight, skin-fold thickness, and musculature in favor of children from high social and economic status families. By the time they reach adulthood, much of the difference is reduced or even cancelled. Social and economic factors are most evident among males. In fact, most environmental influences seem to affect males more strongly than females. The reasons for such differences are unclear.

Psychological Stress

There is considerable evidence that extreme stress can slow physical growth and development. The mechanisms involved in such effects are unclear, although stress may negatively affect the secretion of growth hormones. A cluster of factors like maternal care, social isolation, parental substance abuse, and sexual abuse are linked to psychological and emotional ill health. Recent research has also indicated that some children are genetically predisposed to stress and respond to it in an extreme and prolonged manner that results in restricted growth.

Pollutants

Physical growth is sensitive to several pollutants, including lead, air pollution, certain organic compounds, and tobacco smoke. Of course, pollutants are somewhat unavoidable in the modern world, but levels of pollution vary considerably, and so its effects will be different among different groups. To take only one example, smoking by the mother during pregnancy is well known to affect both birth weight and an infant's subsequent growth. It also seems that living in a home with smoking parents is related to reduced height and weight throughout infancy and childhood. The insult to weight seems to be corrected as the individual moves toward adolescence; the deficit in height is probably never made up.

CONCLUSION

Physical growth is essentially a biological process, but it is affected and constrained by the environments in which it takes place. The interaction of biological and environmental factors accounts for the great variation in growth that is evident among both individuals and whole populations. It also influences the development of other physical characteristics, such as movement skills.

Growth is an important, if often overlooked, aspect of human development. Its centrality is most evident during the periods of infancy and childhood, when physical changes make available a wide range of new behaviors and experiences. Physical growth and development affect the way individuals perceive themselves and how others perceive them. Growth also gives visible clues of an individual's stage of overall development and of that individual's state of health and well-being. As such, it warrants attention by all of those interested in human development.

—*Richard Bailey*

Further Readings and References

Bogin, B. (1999). *Patterns of human growth* (2nd ed.). Cambridge, UK: Cambridge University Press.

Brook, C. G. D. (2001). *Clinical paediatric endocrinology* (4th ed.). Oxford, UK: Blackwell Science.

Centers for Disease Control and Prevention. (2000). *Growth charts: United States*. Retrieved from http://www.cdc.gov/growthcharts/

Cogill, B. (2003). *Anthropometric indicators measurement guide* (Rev. ed.). Washington, DC: Food and Nutrition Technical Assistance Project, Academy for Educational Development. Available from http://www.fantaproject.org/publications/anthropom.shtml

Doherty, J., & Bailey, R. P. (2003). *Supporting physical development in the early years*. Buckingham, UK: Open University Press.

Eveleth, P. B., & Tanner, J. M. (1990). *Worldwide variation in human growth* (2nd ed.). Cambridge, UK: Cambridge University Press.

Lohman, T. G., Roche, A. F., & Martorell, R. (1988). *Anthropometric standardization reference manual*. Champaign, IL: Human Kinetics.

Malina, R., & Bouchard, C. (1991). *Growth, maturation and physical activity*. Champaign, IL: Human Kinetics.

Tanner, J. M. (1988). *History of the study of human growth*. New York: Academic Press.

Tanner, J. M. (1989). *Foetus into man* (Revised & enlarged). Cambridge, MA: Harvard University Press.

PIAGET, JEAN (1896–1980)

The Swiss psychologist and renowned scientist in cognitive psychology, Jean Piaget is arguably best known for formulating his influential theory of childhood cognitive development. Piaget was the oldest child of Rebecca Jackson and Arthur Piaget, an academic in the field of medieval literature. Piaget studied the natural sciences at the University of Neuchatel and by the age of 21 had published 25 articles on mollusks. In 1918, he was granted a doctorate degree in biology and began pursuing his interest in incorporating empirical methods into the field of genetic epistemology—the study of the development of knowledge.

Following graduation, Piaget studied psychoanalysis and experimental methodology at the University of Zurich and then at the Sorbonne in Paris. It was in Paris that Piaget collaborated with Alfred Binet and Theodore Simon to construct intelligence tests for children. As such, Piaget observed many of the errors that children made on intelligence tests and began to notice possible sequential steps involved in children's cognitive development.

Piaget viewed cognitive development as a result of the interaction between the individual and the environment. His perspective contrasted with two other dominant views of cognitive development, one positing that cognitive development derived from innate abilities, and the other positing that children's minds were blank slates that passively acquired knowledge from the environment.

Piaget proposed that children progress through four stages of cognitive development that follow an invariant order: (1) the sensorimotor stage (newborn to 2 years), in which infants understand their world through direct actions; (2) the preoperational stage (2–6 years), in which children begin to represent people, objects, and events in an illogical and egocentric manner in their minds; (3) the concrete-operational stage (6–12 years), in which children logically reason about concrete events in the world; and (4) the formal-operational stage (beyond age 12), in which children are capable of abstract and hypothetical thinking. Piaget emphasized that children's minds are not necessarily immature versions of adults' minds; rather, children's cognitive processes qualitatively differ from those of adults.

Overall, Piaget's formulations of cognitive development have yielded major insights into the child's mind. Despite the fact that his theory has been fairly criticized by contemporary researchers, Piaget's ideas have had a lasting effect on the field.

—*Andrew E. Molnar and*
Matthew J. Hertenstein

See also Cognitive Development, Concrete Operational Period, Fluid Intelligence, Theories of Development

Further Readings and References

Flavell, J. H. (1963). *The developmental psychology of Jean Piaget.* Princeton, NJ: Van Nostrand.

Jean Piaget Society, http://www.piaget.org

Piaget, J. (1929). *The child's conception of the world.* New York: Harcourt, Brace.

POLYCHLORINATED BIPHENYLS (PCB)

Polychlorinated biphenyls (PCBs) are a class of organochlorine chemicals that were discovered to be teratogenic in two mass human poisoning incidents due to contaminated cooking oil in Japan in 1968 and in Taiwan in 1978. The acute illness was termed *Yusho* in Japan and *Yu-Cheng* in Taiwan, for "oil disease." The onset of acute symptoms of PCB exposure in adults is delayed after exposure by a month or more. The symptoms of acute PCB exposure include chloracne (a rash with blackheads and acne-like eruptions), fatigue, nausea and vomiting, swollen eyelids, disturbed vision, numbness and pain in the limbs, and altered liver function. Prenatal exposure to PCBs and related chemicals (dibenzofurans and dioxins) in the contaminated cooking oil in Japan and Taiwan caused birth defects including mental retardation, misshapen fingernails, discolored skin, abnormal eye secretions, natal teeth, and dental malformations.

After the discovery of the teratogenic effects of PCBs in these poisoning incidents, prospective longitudinal studies were begun of low-level exposure to PCB residues in food. One longitudinal study found that prenatal exposure to much lower concentrations of PCBs from residues in food (Lake Michigan sport fish) is associated with suboptimal neurological functioning in infancy, lower performance on an infant memory test (the Fagan Test of Infant Intelligence), lower performance on attention and memory tasks in childhood, and lowered intelligence quotient (IQ) and reading test scores in late elementary school. More highly exposed children were slightly smaller, indicating that physical growth is also altered. Research controversies have centered on the replicability of the results, whether PCBs themselves are responsible for the effects as opposed to other contaminants that occur in the presence of PCBs, and what PCB congeners (chemical variants) may actually be responsible for the observed effects.

Other prospective longitudinal studies of PCB and organochlorine chemical exposure in Europe and the United States have largely replicated the results of the study of Lake Michigan fish eaters. In addition, findings indicate that children prenatally exposed to higher levels of PCBs show altered gender-related play, lower immune system functioning, and altered latencies of auditory evoked potentials. Older adults chronically exposed to PCBs in Lake Michigan sport fish show impaired memory performance.

PCBs are lipophilic (have an affinity for fat) and biomagnify up the food chain. PCBs were phased out of use in the United States and most industrialized nations in the late 1970s but remain inside closed systems such as power transformers. However, because of their former widespread use in many industrial and consumer products, PCBs are found in small concentrations in the fat of virtually all animals and are excreted by mammals in breast milk. Global transport by air and biomagnification in the food chain have resulted in high concentrations of PCBs in arctic mammals such as polar bears and walruses. Arctic peoples eating traditional diets of arctic mammals also have high PCB concentrations.

PCBs are endocrine disruptors that can alter thyroid function. Low thyroid hormone was one of the first causes of mental retardation to be discovered. Any substance that alters thyroid functioning in the mother or fetus has potential to affect brain development. PCB body burdens in industrialized countries have dropped since phase out of the chemicals began in the late 1970s. However, the concentrations of chemically related pollutants such as polybrominated diethyl ethers (PBDEs), a substance widely used in flame retardants, are rising rapidly in people and animals. PBDEs are still in use in the United States. PBDEs are also endocrine disruptors and are known to affect thyroid functioning.

—*Colleen F. Moore*

See also Teratogen

Further Readings and References

Agency for Toxic Substances and Disease Registry. (2001). *ToxFAQs for polychlorinated biphenyls (PCBs)*. Retrieved from http://www.atsdr.cdc.gov/tfacts17.html

Jacobson, J. L., & Jacobson, S. L. (2000). Teratogenic insult and neurobehavioral function in infancy and childhood. In C. A. Nelson (Ed.), *The effects of early adversity on neurobehavioral development: The Minnesota symposium on child psychology, Vol. 31*. Mahwah, NJ: Erlbaum.

Masuda, Y. (1985). Health status of Japanese and Taiwanese after exposure to contaminated rice oil. *Environmental Health Perspectives, 60*, 321–325.

Polychlorinated biphenyls, http://www.ec.gc.ca/pcb/eng/index_e.htm

POSITRON EMISSION TOPOGRAPHY (PET)

Positron emission tomography (PET) is a relatively new visual neural-imaging methodology that identifies variations in cerebral blood flow in regions of the brain. This fact makes PET a useful tool for scientists who are interested in identifying specific regions of the brain that are used during the execution of a task.

The logic underlying PET is quite sophisticated. First the patient is injected with a nontoxic, slightly radioactive isotope while engaged in a task. The most common isotope used in cognitive studies is oxygen-15 (^{15}O), an unstable form of oxygen that is usually injected into the bloodstream. As the patient continues to engage in the task, neural activity increases in the regions of their brain that are used to execute the task. These increases in neural activity result in increases in metabolic requirements and, consequently, additional blood flows to these active regions carrying the fuel for neural activity (i.e., glucose) as well as the radioactive isotopes (i.e., oxygen-15). Because the radioactive isotopes are unstable, they rapidly decay by emitting positrons. When these emitted positrons collide with electrons, they annihilate each other, resulting in the formation of gamma rays. More gamma rays are present in brain regions with greater metabolic activity (i.e., blood flow) than in brain regions with less metabolic activity because these regions consume more glucose. The PET scanner, which is essentially a gamma ray detector, locates the origins of gamma rays, and these origins are mapped into an image of the brain by a computer. The computer, which is sensitive to variations in intensities in gamma radiation, color codes the image by using a more intense color for those regions of the brain with more gamma rays (i.e., greater metabolic activity) and a less intense color for those regions of the brain with less gamma rays (i.e., less metabolic activity). In other words, the regions of the brain that are used more heavily during the execution of the task are depicted in the image with an intense color, whereas the regions of the brain that are less active during the execution of the task are depicted with a less intense color.

The main reason scientists use PET is to identify the specific regions of the brain that are used to execute a specific task. However, because the brain executes a number of other activities while the task of experimental interest is being executed, a patient completes two conditions: a control condition and an experimental condition. During the control condition, the patient's cerebral blood flow is scanned as the patient rests or views a blank stimulus screen. This scan is commonly called the *baseline scan*. During the experimental condition, the patient's cerebral blood flow is scanned as the patient executes the task of experimental interest. This scan is called the *load scan*. By subtracting the image of the baseline scan from the image of the load scan, a difference image is created. This difference image reveals those regions of the brain that are unique to the execution of the experimental task of interest.

One of the strengths of PET is its good visual resolution; however, the temporal resolution of PET is quite limited. It takes minutes to record an image using PET, whereas the execution of a task typically occurs within seconds. Consequently, scientists tend to use PET in concert with other neural-imaging methodologies that are known to have much better temporal resolution. Two of these methodologies are event-related potentials and functional magnetic resonance imaging.

—*Brenda A. M. Hannon*

Further Readings and References

Carson, R. E. (1998). *Quantitative functional brain imaging with positron emission tomography.* New York: Academic Press.

Gjedde, A. (2001). *Physiological imaging of the brain with PET.* New York: Academic Press.

POSTPARTUM DEPRESSION

Postpartum depression is depression in mothers that occurs following the birth of their child. Women often feel pressure from others to experience joy and delight after giving birth; however, in reality, normal postpartum adjustment often involves a difficult transition to a new role, decreased freedom, and increased financial constraints. Contrary to media depictions of women with severe postpartum depression who harm their children, most women with postpartum depression experience symptoms of mild to moderate severity that readily respond to treatment. It is well established that depression generally results from a combination of vulnerability factors (e.g., genetics,

pessimistic cognitive style) and stressful life events; examination of depression in the postpartum period provides an opportunity to consider the manner in which vulnerability factors put women at risk for experiencing depression in the context of a discrete, clearly defined stressor.

DIAGNOSIS

Although postpartum depression is readily identified in the research literature and in the media, there is no official diagnosis of postpartum depression per se. Instead, the *Diagnostic and Statistical Manual of Mental Disorders, Fourth Edition (DSM-IV)* indicates that women are assigned a diagnosis of major depressive disorder with postpartum onset if they meet criteria for a major depressive episode within the first 4 weeks following childbirth. A diagnosis of major depressive disorder requires that individuals endorse at least five of the following symptoms: depressed mood, lack of interest or enjoyment in activities, appetite disturbance, sleep disturbance, fatigue, worthlessness or inappropriate guilt, concentration difficulties or indecisiveness, and suicidal ideation. These symptoms must occur more days than not over at least a 2-week period and cause life interference or significant personal distress. Although this is the definition that mental health practitioners use for diagnosing postpartum depression in their clinical practice, some researchers have defined postpartum depression as being either a major or minor depressive episode (i.e., consisting of fewer than five of these symptoms) following childbirth. It also is important for clinicians who diagnose postpartum depression to realize that many features of normal adjustment (e.g., sleep deprivation) overlap with symptoms of depression. Thus, such symptoms should be regarded as indicative of postpartum depression only if they are in excess of what is considered normal adjustment for postpartum women. A useful tool to screen for depression specific to the postpartum period is the Edinburgh Postnatal Depression Rating Scale.

Some researchers have documented that postpartum depression lasts, on average, between 6 and 8 weeks; however, there are many instances in which postpartum depression extends beyond the first year following childbirth. Although the *DSM-IV* postpartum onset specifier indicates that the major depressive episode begins within 4 weeks after childbirth, many women with postpartum depression also report major depression during pregnancy, and there are many instances in which women develop depression several months after childbirth. Recently, researchers have raised the possibility that there might be two types of postpartum depression—discrete episodes that begin following childbirth, and recurrences of non-postpartum depression.

Research conducted in the 1990s indicates that postpartum depression is similar to depression that occurs at other times in women's lives, such that both types of depression are characterized by similar symptom profiles and psychosocial correlates. However, older research suggests that postpartum depression is qualitatively different from non-postpartum depression, in that it is associated with high levels of anxiety, hostility, agitation, and guilt; an external (versus internal) locus of control; and perceived uncontrollability. Older research also has found that women with postpartum depression are less likely to endorse suicidal ideation than women who report depression at other times in their lives.

Postpartum depression is often contrasted with two other instances of postpartum emotional disturbance. The *postpartum blues* is a mild and transient mood disturbance that begins during the first week postpartum and lasts between a few hours and a few days. Between 50% and 80% of postpartum women experience the blues, and it is associated with few negative consequences, although more women who subsequently endorse postpartum depression indicate that they experienced the blues than did women without postpartum depression. Typical blues symptoms include crying, mood lability, irritability, anxiety, and insomnia. In contrast, *postpartum psychosis* characterizes women who exhibit psychotic symptoms following childbirth, such as confused thinking, delusions, hallucinations, and disorganized behavior. The prevalence of postpartum psychosis is between 1 in 500 and 1 in 1,000. The length of postpartum psychosis is variable, and it requires immediate attention and often inpatient hospitalization.

EPIDEMIOLOGY

Meta-analytic studies have estimated the prevalence of major and minor postpartum depression to be about 13%. The time period associated with the definition of postpartum depression has a great impact on observed prevalence rates because the prevalence increases to about 22% when postpartum depression

is defined broadly as depression occurring in the first 6 months after childbirth. Moreover, research has shown that prevalence rates vary substantially depending on whether postpartum depression is diagnosed using structured clinical interviews or high scores on depression self-report inventories, with the use of self-report inventories resulting in prevalence rates as high as 33%. The prevalence of postpartum depression is lower in cultural groups in which there is a high level of support given to new mothers.

RISK FACTORS

The strongest predictors of postpartum depression are a previous history of psychiatric disturbance, psychiatric disturbance during pregnancy, poor marital relationship, lack of social support, and stressful life events, including both major events and ongoing child care stressors. Other documented risk factors for postpartum depression include obstetric complications, worries about infant health, problematic infant behavior (e.g., colic), and emotion-focused (versus task-focused) coping styles. Demographic variables, such as educational level and parity, do not correlate with postpartum depressive symptoms, although some studies have found that women who do not work outside of the home are overrepresented in samples of women with postpartum depression, and recent studies suggest that postpartum depression is more common in very young or very old mothers. Contrary to popular opinion, there is little evidence that abnormal levels of hormones or changes in hormone levels following childbirth are associated systematically with postpartum depression.

IMPACT ON CHILD DEVELOPMENT

Infancy is a critical period of time in which the mother-child relationship provides a scaffold for children to develop emotion regulation and attachments with others. Depressed mothers often have difficulty providing responsive and predictable care to their infants, and depressed mother-child interactions are often characterized by less positive affective expressions than nondepressed mother-child interactions. Research has demonstrated that postpartum depression is associated with dysregulation, which is evidenced by decreased orienting behavior, depressed affect, and irregular sleep patterns. Postpartum depression is also associated with a high rate of preoccupied attachment, behavioral problems, and cognitive delays in young children. Moreover, postpartum depression puts women at risk for experiencing future depressive episodes, and research has demonstrated that maternal depression is associated with child abuse, impairments in cognitive development, behavioral problems, and symptoms of psychopathology in older children. However, research shows that infants have the capacity for resiliency and may only experience adverse effects of postpartum depression if their mother's depression does not abate during the first year. Mothers who maintain high levels of warmth and sensitivity despite experiencing depressive symptoms decrease the likelihood that their children will have emotional and behavioral difficulties.

EFFECTIVENESS OF INTERVENTIONS

There is concern about treating postpartum depression with antidepressant medications during the period in which mothers are breast-feeding because research suggests that metabolites of some medications are available in the breast milk, and the physiological and developmental effects of these substances on infant health generally are unknown. Although antidepressant medications, particularly selective serotonin reuptake inhibitors, are prescribed for moderate to severe postpartum depression, researchers have focused on developing alternative psychosocial interventions to reduce risk for adverse health outcomes in breast-feeding mothers. Small outcome studies have provided preliminary evidence that psychoeducation, supportive group therapy, and cognitive behavioral therapy are effective in treating postpartum depression. A new psychosocial treatment is being developed that involves group therapy for mothers and infants, both separately and together in pairs to facilitate bonding. The largest outcome study to date found that interpersonal psychotherapy (IPT) was more effective than no treatment in reducing depressive symptoms and improving psychosocial functioning in community women with postpartum depression of mild to moderate severity.

SUMMARY

Postpartum depression is a major depressive episode that women experience in the period following childbirth. Infants whose mothers are depressed often exhibit a range of emotional, cognitive, and behavioral difficulties, although the effects of postpartum depression are lessened if the episode is relatively brief. Postpartum depression responds well to treatment, particularly psychosocial treatment with an interpersonal focus. Although women who experience postpartum depression are distressed, only infrequently is postpartum depression associated with catastrophic consequences, such as harm to the infant.

—Amy Wenzel

Further Readings and References

Goodman, S. H., & Gotlib, I. H. (Eds.). (2002). *Children of depressed parents: Mechanisms of risk and implications for treatment.* Washington, DC: American Psychological Association.

Harris, B. (2002). Postpartum depression. *Psychiatric Annals, 32,* 405–415.

Miller, L. J. (Ed.). (1999). *Postpartum mood disorders.* Washington, DC: American Psychiatric Association.

Miller, L. J. (2002). Postpartum depression. *Journal of the American Medical Association, 287,* 762–765.

Murray, L., & Cooper, P. J. (Eds.). (1997). *Postpartum depression and child development.* New York: Guilford.

O'Hara, M. W. (1994). *Postpartum depression: Causes and consequences.* New York: Springer-Verlag.

National Library of Medicine and National Institutes of Health. (2004). *Postpartum depression.* Retrieved from http://www.nlm.nih.gov/medlineplus/postpartumdepression.html

Postpartum Support International, http://www.postpartum.net/

POSTTRAUMATIC STRESS DISORDER (PTSD)

Posttraumatic stress disorder (PTSD) is defined as a set of characteristic symptoms that occur following exposure to an event that seriously threatened the life of the individual or someone very close to that individual. The characteristic symptoms include horror, fear, or helplessness. Re-experiencing the event, avoidance of anything associated with the event, and symptoms of arousal (e.g., distractibility, hypervigilance) that were not present before the traumatic event are also necessary to obtain a diagnosis of PTSD. For a clinical diagnosis, the symptoms of re-experiencing, avoidance, and arousal must have been present for at least 1 month to obtain a diagnosis. The diagnosis is considered acute if the duration of the symptoms lasts fewer than 3 months (this occurs about 50% of the time) and chronic if the symptoms remain for longer than 3 months. The symptoms must also cause significant impairment in at least one major area of functioning (e.g., school, work, home) to qualify for a diagnosis.

PREVALENCE

PTSD symptoms can occur at any age across the life span following a traumatic event. Lifetime prevalence rates for PTSD range from 1% to 14%, whereas at-risk populations, such as war veterans, have prevalence rates ranging from 3% to 58%. Studies have found that as many as 25% of children have experienced at least one potentially traumatic event. Occurrences such as exposure to war, family violence, natural disaster, rape, or serious illness or injury have been associated with PTSD symptoms and diagnoses. A higher incidence of PTSD symptoms has been found for females than males in both pediatric and adult samples.

Prevalence rates vary depending on the types of trauma experienced. Children who have sustained a serious injury have had rates of 16% to 23%, children who have been victims of abuse have had rates of 36% or higher, female rape victims have had rates of 32%, and children who have been witnesses to domestic abuse have had rates of 56%.

ETIOLOGY

There is some evidence that PTSD is heritable among family members. In addition, preexisting or comorbid psychopathology has been related to longer duration and greater severity of PTSD symptoms.

Developmental Considerations

Children and adolescents are more vulnerable to environmental hazards than adults, such that direct trauma to the central nervous system may have long-lasting and possibly permanent effects on their future development. Exposure to such trauma may predispose these individuals to become more vulnerable to future distress, and even normal developmental changes may seem overwhelming for these individuals. In addition, cognitive development also may influence PTSD, in that younger children, who tend to use less effective reasoning strategies, are more likely to assume that they were at fault for a traumatic event and are less likely to use effective coping strategies.

TREATMENT

Cognitive-behavioral therapy (CBT) appears to be the most effective treatment for children and adults with PTSD. For example, one cognitive-based treatment for child- or adolescent-onset PTSD involves the use of a multimodality trauma treatment protocol (MMTT). According to this treatment model, symptoms of PTSD are viewed as an unconditioned response to the trigger symptoms, the conditioned stimuli. The more manual treatment involves the use of storybooks, narratives, cognitive games, and peer modeling for the affected individual to habituate to the anxiety associated with the conditioned stimuli. In addition, trauma-induced schemas are addressed, and strategies are developed for coping with emotions related to the event. Treatment with this intervention has been associated with significant improvement in PTSD symptoms that have been maintained up to 6 months after treatment. In addition, CBT has been demonstrated to be significantly more effective than nondirective supportive therapy in reducing PTSD symptoms in groups of sexually abused preschoolers over the long term. Exposure techniques, such as in vivo or imaginal flooding or gradual exposure, have also been successful in reducing PTSD symptoms. These techniques involve repeated exposure to cues associated with the traumatic event, paired with relaxation exercises, in an attempt to remove the negative emotions from the trauma-associated stimuli. Psychopharmacologic treatment for PTSD, which is often conducted in conjunction with CBT, may involve the use of antidepressants, such as monoamine oxidase inhibitors (MAOIs), tricyclic antidepressants (TCAs), and selective serotonin reuptake inhibitors (SSRIs). MAOIs may reduce symptoms of re-experiencing, avoidance, and arousal. SSRIs typically have few negative side effects and reduce a wide range of symptoms; however, they may take up to 6 weeks to reach therapeutic levels. In addition, medications for sleep may be necessary, especially when nightmares are frequent.

—*Sunnye Mayes and Michael C. Roberts*

Further Readings and References

Aaron, J., Zaglul, H., & Emery, R. E. (1999). Posttraumatic stress in children following acute physical injury. *Journal of Pediatric Psychology, 24,* 335–343.

Ackerman, P. T., Newton, J. E. O., McPherson, W. B., Jones, J. G., & Dykman, R. A. (1998). Prevalence of post traumatic stress disorder and other psychiatric diagnoses in three groups of abused children (sexual, physical, and both). *Child Abuse and Neglect, 22*, 759–774.

Amaya-Jackson, L., Reynolds, V., Murray, M. C., McCarthy, G., Nelson, A., Cherney, M. S., et al. (2003). Cognitive-behavioral treatment for pediatric posttraumatic stress disorder: Protocol and application in school and community settings. *Cognitive and Behavioral Practice, 10*, 204–213.

American Psychiatric Association. (1999). *Let's talk facts about post traumatic stress disorder*. Retrieved from http://www.psych.org/public_info/ptsd.cfm

Department of Veteran Affairs, National Center for PTSD. (n.d.). *Facts about PTSD*. Retrieved from http://www.ncptsd.org/facts/index.html

La Greca, A. M., Silverman, W. K., Vernberg, E. M., & Roberts, M. C. (Eds.). (2002). *Helping children cope with disasters and terrorism*. Washington, DC: American Psychological Association.

Lehmann, P. (1997). The development of posttraumatic stress disorder (PTSD) in a sample of child witnesses to mother assault. *Journal of Family Violence, 12*, 241–257.

March, J. S., Amaya-Jackson, L., Murray, M. C., & Schulte, A. (1998). Cognitive-behavioral psychotherapy for children and adolescents with posttraumatic stress disorder after a single-incident stressor. *Journal of the American Academy of Child and Adolescent Psychiatry, 37*, 585–593.

Resnick, H. S., Kilpatrick, D. G., Dansky, B. S., Saunders, B. E., & Best, C. L. (1993). Prevalence of civilian trauma and posttraumatic stress disorder in a representative national sample of women. *Journal of Consulting Psychology, 61*, 984–991.

Vernberg, E. M., & Varela, R. E. (2001). Posttraumatic stress disorder: A developmental perspective. In M. W. Vasey & M. R. Dadds (Eds.), *The developmental psychopathology of anxiety* (pp. 386–406). New York: Oxford University Press.

POVERTY

Childhood poverty is an issue of concern for policy makers, scientists, and the nation at large. Nearly 2 of every 10 children in the United States live in poverty today, and as many as 1 of every 3 children will spend at least 1 year of their life in poverty. Compared with their nonpoor peers, poor children are at higher risk for developing health, achievement, and social-emotional problems. Understanding this risk requires attention to the demographics of poverty in the United States, the causal mechanisms that result in poverty, and social policies aimed at alleviating negative outcomes for poor children and their families.

INCIDENCE

Poverty is ubiquitous, affecting families across the country of varying structures, ethnicities, and employment statuses. Further, the gap between the wealthiest and poorest in the nation has steadily increased since the 1960s. Using the U.S. Census Bureau's poverty index, for which a family is classified as poor if their annual income is less than their annual financial needs, the nation's poverty rate is currently highest in the South (13.8%) and lowest in the Midwest (10.3%). Although a disproportionate number of the nation's poor live in major metropolitan areas, poverty exists in both suburban and rural areas, with about 9% and 14% of people living in these areas being poor. Risk is greatest among black and Hispanic families and female-headed households. Yet, even as many as 10% of white families and more than 12% of single-parent, male-headed households are poor. In addition, nearly 38% of the poor are employed.

Chronically poor families who are continuously dependent on public assistance are the exception rather than the rule; most families' poverty experiences are relatively short (i.e., 1–3 years). Nonetheless, the risk for being poor remains high for children (younger than 18 years), and they are at greater risk for living in poverty than any other age group.

CAUSES

Causes of poverty generally fall into two categories: (1) macroeconomic forces that affect the distribution of income across the population at large; and (2) family-level processes that affect the economic well-being of individual families. From a macroeconomic perspective, increased numbers of immigrant families with language and educational barriers, increased participation of women and young workers in the labor market, and technological advances that have magnified earning differences between more- and less-educated workers are some factors associated with an increasing income disparity in the United States. Within families, income is often in flux over the life course, especially for lower-income families, who are likely to experience multiple transitions into and out of poverty.

Employment and family composition changes such as divorce and remarriage are two family-level processes that may cause transitions into or out of poverty. For example, decreased earnings (e.g., due to job loss) for fathers and changes in family structure from two- to single-parent households are two of the most frequently occurring precursors to families falling into poverty. On the other hand, increased earnings for both fathers and mothers (in both two-parent and single-parent families) are the most common life events that help lift families out of poverty.

CONTEXT OF POVERTY

Children living in poor families experience a multitude of poor-quality living conditions and negative life events that accompany their financial deprivation. Children living in poverty are, for example, more likely than their nonpoor peers to live in single-parent and less-educated households. Housing quality is also likely to be deficient with regard to size, lighting, exposure to environmental hazards (e.g., lead paint), and general integrity. Further, these children are more apt to live in overcrowded, impoverished neighborhoods with higher rates of joblessness and crime as well as lower-quality schools compared with the neighborhoods in which middle-class children are apt to live.

IMPACT ON CHILD WELL-BEING

One of the most consistent findings in the human development literature concerns the association between childhood poverty and negative developmental outcomes. Recent literature reviews highlight four primary findings with regard to the negative effects of poverty on child development: (1) poverty affects child functioning in most areas of development, although effects are greater for cognitive and language achievement than for physical and mental health; (2) poverty experiences during early childhood have greater effects compared with impoverishment during later life stages; (3) effects become increasingly negative the longer children live in poverty; and (4) effects are transmitted to children through family investments and family stress.

Physical health risks associated with childhood poverty include elevated blood lead levels, chronic illness, and growth retardation. These early problems are, in turn, risk factors for later developmental problems, including increased risk for lowered intelligence, school failure, and obesity. Poverty is also associated with mental health problems in childhood and beyond. Poor children are, for example, more likely than nonpoor children to have both internalizing (e.g., depression) and externalizing (e.g., aggression) behavior problems. Beyond these health problems, poverty poses the greatest risk to children's cognitive and language development and ultimately limits their success in school.

On average, poor children score lower than nonpoor children on cognitive, language, and intelligence tests, even within the first 3 years of life. Compared with their nonpoor peers, poor children are also more likely to be retained in school (i.e., repeat grades), be placed in special education classes, and quit school before graduation. These differences appear to be greatest when children experience economic deprivation early in life, particularly during the preschool years. Further, the longer children remain poor, the greater the achievement gap between these children and their nonpoor peers.

Family income affects achievement and physical health primarily through investments. Having more money is, for example, associated with parents' abilities to buy more learning materials such as books and higher-quality goods such as foods higher in nutritional value that support children's cognitive and language development. On the other hand, family income affects child mental health primarily through social relationships such as the parent-child relationship. More specifically, the stressful context of poverty is associated with parent mental health problems like depression. These mental health problems, in turn, make parenting a more difficult task, with parenting often becoming inconsistent and less warm when families fall into poverty. Such parenting practices then lead to child behavior problems.

SOCIAL POLICY AND INTERVENTION

In 1996, the Personal Responsibility and Work Opportunity Reconciliation Act was signed into law. Replacing the Aid to Families with Dependent Children program, the 1996 welfare reform aimed to reduce poverty in the United States, primarily by giving states increased flexibility to design their own welfare programs, promoting marriage for poor single parents, and requiring welfare recipients to move from public assistance to work. In general, there have been increases in employment rates among poor families and decreases in child poverty rates since the 1996 reform, although it remains controversial to what extent these changes can be attributed to welfare reform, per se, and to what extent these changes also reflect general economic trends. From a child development perspective, the success of welfare reform for improving the well-being of children appears to hinge on whether or not families experienced income gains.

For most children, transitions from welfare to work appear unrelated to developmental outcomes, possibly because many welfare families moved into low-paying jobs and, as such, did not experience financial gains. In fact, experimental evaluations of welfare policies in which families have been randomly assigned to conditions including work requirements without income supplements or work requirements with income supplements have demonstrated that increased employment is likely to improve children's life chances, but only when families increase their economic well-being. These findings have been corroborated in nonexperimental studies demonstrating that income gains can lead to improved achievement and mental health for children living in poverty.

Publicly funded early intervention programs have also been used to mitigate the negative effects of poverty on children's development. Most of these intervention programs, such as the federally funded Head Start and Early Head Start programs, include comprehensive services for children and their families. For example, in addition to high-quality educational services, Head Start programs provide poor preschool-aged children and their families with health, nutrition, and social services. By so doing, early intervention has generally focused on improving children's life chances both directly (e.g., through increased literacy education) and indirectly (e.g., through improved home environment). Indeed, early intervention is associated with cognitive, language, and social-emotional improvements as early as 3 years of age. Further, early intervention participation increases the probability that children born into poverty will graduate from high school and gain employment as young adults, thus decreasing the probability that their children will grow up poor.

—*Eric Dearing and Christine Wade*

See also Malnutrition, Social Security

Further Readings and References

Bane, M. J., & Ellwood, D. T. (1986). Slipping into and out of poverty: The dynamics of spells. *Journal of Human Resources, 21*, 1–23.

Bradley, R. H., & Corwyn, R. F. (2002). Socioeconomic status and child development. *Annual Review of Psychology, 53*(1), 371–399.

Duncan, G. J., & Brooks-Gunn, J. (2000). Family poverty, welfare reform, and child development. *Child Development, 71*, 188–196.

Evans, G. W. (2004). The environment of childhood poverty. *American Psychologist, 59*(2), 77–92.

Future of Children. (1997). Children and poverty: Executive summary. *Future of Children, 7*(2). Available from http://www.futureofchildren.org

Future of Children. (2002). Children and welfare reform: Executive Summary. *Future of Children, 12*(1). Available from http://www.futureofchildren.org

McLoyd, V. C. (1998). Socioeconomic disadvantage and child development. *American Psychologist, 53*, 185–204.

U.S. Census Bureau. (2003, September). *Poverty in the United States: 2002*. Washington, DC: Authors. Retrieved from http://www.census.gov/hhes/www/poverty02.html

PREGNANCY

Pregnancy is a period of intense and rapid development for both the mother and the fetus. Physiologically, anatomically, and psychologically, the rapid transformation of an embryo into an infant and of a woman into a mother is unparalleled. Although not a comprehensive review of pregnancy, this chapter discusses maternal and fetal development in each of the three trimesters, considering the physical and psychological changes that take place.

TRIMESTER 1: WEEKS 1 TO 12

The first sign of pregnancy for most women is a missed menstrual period. Other early signs of pregnancy are tenderness of the breasts—a tingling sensation and special sensitivity of the nipples—and nausea and vomiting (called *morning sickness*, although it may occur at any time of the day). More frequent urination, feelings of fatigue, and a need for more sleep are other early signs of pregnancy. A wide variety of reactions may follow the discovery of a pregnancy. For the woman who has been trying to conceive for several months, the reaction may be joy and eager anticipation. For the teenager who does not feel ready to become a mother, the adult woman who does not want to have children, or the adult woman who feels that she already has enough children, the reaction may be negative—depression, anger, and fear. The presence of a supportive social network is particularly important for such women at this time. The decision to end or continue the pregnancy is typically made within the first trimester.

The relationship between the mother and her partner may begin to change after the discovery of pregnancy. Although a range of patterns and frequencies in sexuality is normal, sexual desire and activity may decrease during pregnancy. Most women attribute this change to fatigue. Expectant fathers are sometimes initially ambivalent about their approaching father role, but trends in North America show fathers becoming more involved in parenting and childbirth preparation. For the couple eagerly awaiting the birth of their new baby, pregnancy can be a time of increased intimacy and relationship satisfaction.

The basic physical change that takes place in the woman's body during the first trimester is a large increase in the levels of hormones, especially estrogen and progesterone, which are produced by the placenta. Many of the other physical signs of the first trimester arise from these endocrine changes. The breasts swell and tingle, resulting from the development of the mammary glands, which are stimulated by the hormones, and the nipples and areolas may darken and broaden. There is often a need to urinate more frequently, which is related to changes in the pituitary hormones' effects on the adrenals, which in turn change the water balance in the body so that more water is retained. The growing uterus also contributes by pressing against the bladder. About 75% of women experience morning sickness, which may be due to high levels of estrogen irritating the stomach. Vaginal discharges may also increase at this time, partly because of the increased hormone levels, which change the vaginal pH, and partly because the vaginal secretions are changing in their chemical composition and quantity. The feelings of fatigue and sleepiness are probably related to the high levels of progesterone, which is known to have a sedative effect.

The development of the fetus during the first trimester is rapid: the small mass of cells implanted in the uterus develops into a fetus with most of the major organ systems present and with recognizable human features. During the third and fourth weeks, the head undergoes a great deal of development as the central nervous system begins to form, and the beginnings of eyes and ears are visible. By the end of the 10th week, the eyes, ears, arms, hands, fingers, legs, feet, and toes are completely formed. By the end of the 7th week,

the liver, lungs, pancreas, kidneys, and intestines have formed and have begun limited functioning. Although the gonads have also formed, the gender of the fetus is not clearly distinguishable until the 12th week. From this point on, development consists mainly of enlargement and differentiation of structures that are already present.

TRIMESTER 2: WEEKS 13 TO 26

During the fourth month, the woman becomes aware of the fetus's movements, known as *quickening*. Many women find this to be an exciting developmental milestone in their pregnancy. In addition, the experience may lessen anxiety about a miscarriage. Around the same time, the physician or midwife can detect the fetal heartbeat. The mother is made even more aware of the pregnancy by her rapidly expanding belly. Some women feel that it is a beautiful and powerful symbol of womanhood; other women may feel awkward and resentful of their bulky shape and may feel insecure about their physical attractiveness.

Most of the physical discomforts of the first trimester, such as morning sickness, disappear in the second trimester. For this reason, the second trimester is usually a period of relative calm and well-being. As a result of the mother's physical changes, constipation (caused by increased progesterone, which inhibits smooth muscle contraction) and nosebleeds (caused by increased blood volume) may occur. For some women, edema may be a problem in the face, hands, wrists, ankles, and feet; it results from increased water retention throughout the body.

By about midpregnancy, the breasts, under hormonal stimulation, have essentially completed their development in preparation for lactation. Beginning about the 19th week, a thin amber or yellow fluid called colostrum may come out of the nipple. Around this same time, the fetus first opens its eyes. By about the 24th week, the fetus is sensitive to light and can hear sounds in utero. Arm and leg movements are vigorous at this time, and the fetus alternates between periods of wakefulness and sleep. These patterns are detected by the mother, whose bond to her developing fetus may strengthen as she becomes more acquainted with its activity.

Throughout pregnancy, it is important that the mother obtain adequate nutrition to support herself and her fetus. Folic acid, calcium, iron, vitamin A, magnesium, and protein are important for maintaining the mother's health and fostering the healthy development of the fetus. Some drugs, such as antibiotics, alcohol, cocaine, marijuana, nicotine, and some prescription drugs, may adversely affect fetal development and lead to birth defects, preterm labor, or even miscarriage.

For about 10% of women, pregnancy may be accompanied by depression. Although women with a history of depression are at increased risk for depression during pregnancy, the depressive episode during pregnancy is the first such episode for about one third of depressed pregnant women. Other risk factors include poor marital quality, inadequate social support, low socioeconomic status, an unwanted pregnancy, and negative life events. Depression during pregnancy increases risk for health problems during pregnancy (e.g., poor fetal weight gain, drug use, and noncompliance with health care) and in the postpartum (e.g., child cognitive, social, emotional, and health problems, as well as postpartum depression). Although the U.S. Food and Drug Administration (FDA) has not approved the use of antidepressant medications during pregnancy, many studies suggest that some antidepressants may safely treat depression during pregnancy.

TRIMESTER 3: WEEKS 27 TO 38

The mother's uterus is very large and hard now, which puts pressure on her other organs and may cause some discomfort. The pressure on the lungs may cause shortness of breath. The stomach is squeezed, often leading to indigestion. The heart is also somewhat strained by the large increase in blood volume. Sleep can also be difficult because of the increased size of the uterus and increasing activity level of the fetus. These physical changes are often accompanied by a further decrease in sexual desire on the part of the mother because the mother's shape may make sexual intercourse uncomfortable at this time.

The weight gain of the second trimester continues in the third trimester, sometimes causing a disturbance in the mother's sense of balance and an increase in lower back pain. Although women typically gain 20 to 30 pounds during pregnancy, excessive weight gain can be a sign of gestational diabetes. Regular aerobic exercise during pregnancy can improve or maintain physical fitness and has not been conclusively shown to be associated with any risks. At the end of the 8th month, the fetus weighs an average of 2,500 grams. The average full-term baby weighs 3,300 grams and is 50 centimeters long.

During the seventh month, the fetus turns in the uterus to assume a head-down position. If this turning does not occur by the time of delivery, there will be a breech presentation. Women can do certain exercises to aid the turning. Physicians and midwives can also perform certain procedures to turn the fetus. Moxibustion (a technique used in Chinese medicine) can be performed by an acupuncturist to aid turning as well. In the last month, the fetus will begin to descend into the pelvis (called *engagement*), sometimes creating slight discomfort in the perineum. During the third trimester, the uterus may also tighten occasionally in painless contractions (called *Braxton-Hicks contractions*). Although not a part of labor, these contractions may help strengthen the uterine muscles in preparation for labor.

CONCLUSION

A mother and her developing fetus experience tremendous and rapid development during pregnancy. As adequate prenatal care and nutrition contribute to the healthy development of the fetus, a supportive social network contributes to the psychological well-being of the mother.

—Nicole M. Else-Quest and Janet Shibley Hyde

See also Gamete, Ultrasound

Further Readings and References

Childbirth.Org. (2001). *Pregnancy.* Retrieved from http://www.childbirth.org/articles/preglinks.html

Enkin, M., Keirse, M. J., Neilson, J., Crowther, C., Duley, L., Hodnett, E., et al. (2000). *A guide to effective care in pregnancy and childbirth* (3rd ed.). New York: Oxford.

Hyde, J. S., & DeLamater, J. D. (2003). *Understanding human sexuality* (8th ed.). New York: McGraw-Hill.

Northrup, C. (1998). *Women's bodies, women's wisdom* (2nd ed.). New York: Bantam.

Simkin, P., Whalley, J., & Keppler, A. (2001). *Pregnancy, childbirth, and the newborn, revised and updated: The complete guide.* Minnetonka, MN: Meadowbrook.

PRENATAL DEVELOPMENT

Prenatal development can be divided into three stages: preimplantation, embryonic, and fetal. The preimplantation period, between fertilization and implantation of the conceptus in the uterine wall, takes an average of 7 days. The embryonic period is considered to be the major period of organogenesis, lasting about 2 months from conception. During the fetal period, lasting until about 38 weeks after conception, growth, functional maturation, and further differentiation of tissues occur.

The prenatal period is highly sensitive to disruption by toxic substances because of the high rate of cell division and the intricate and complex coordination among chemical, cellular, and genetic processes that is necessary for normal development. Toxic insults to the conceptus are thought more likely to be lethal during the preimplantation and embryonic periods than the fetal period. The timing of an exposure or event has a dramatic influence on the developmental effects that will likely result. For example, alterations of hormones such as prostaglandins and the progesterone–estrogen balance can prevent implantation, resulting in embryonic death. During organogenesis, when the molecular, cellular, and morphological structural organization of tissues and organs takes place, the embryo is considered to be most susceptible to structural defects. Animal experiments show that the exact timing of exposure to a teratogen affects the pattern of structural malformations. However, malformations usually occur in more than one organ system because of overlap in the sensitive period of development of different systems. Functional effects and growth retardation, rather than malformations, are considered to be the most likely outcomes of toxic exposures during the fetal period. However, there are exceptions to these generalizations. For example, skeletal abnormalities in mice can be induced during the preimplantation stage.

Susceptibility to teratogens or other causes of untoward birth outcomes also depends on species, genetic characteristics, and the history of the mother herself. Examples of species and genetic influences on the effects of a teratogen are that mice and rats were found to be resistant to the induction of limb defects by thalidomide, whereas rabbits and hamsters showed variable effects, and some species of primates were highly sensitive to the teratogenicity of thalidomide. The life history of the mother can also affect outcome. For example, the sensitivity of the fetus to alcohol appears to increase with the age of the mother, and recent findings suggest second-generation effects of prenatal influences such as nutrition. A female child

born during a famine is more likely to give birth to a low-birth-weight infant, regardless of her own nutritional during pregnancy.

Prenatal exposures can create behavioral and psychological effects by altering aspects of early brain formation such as cell proliferation, dendritic and axonal differentiation, neuronal migration, apoptosis (programmed cell death), synaptogenesis, and myelination. Exactly how alterations in these aspects of brain development create specific behavioral and psychological outcomes is unknown but being studied. Examples of disruptions of intracellular and extracellular processes that can affect brain development include altering ion channels, adhesion molecules on neural cells, hormonal concentrations and balance, neurotransmitter production, and oxidative stress. For example, methylmercury and lead are both thought to alter ion channel functioning and calcium distribution, which in turn may disrupt the neural architecture of the brain. Methylmercury also creates oxidative stress, which, in turn, can cause neural cell death. PCBs (polychlorinated biphenyls) are endocrine disruptors that may alter thyroid functioning of the fetus or mother. Maternal stress alters the levels of hormones such as cortisol, adrenocorticotrophic hormone (ACTH), and corticotrophic-releasing hormone (CRH), all of which can influence the development of the fetal hypothalamic-pituitary-adrenal axis and promote premature birth. In rodents, prenatal stress reduces male sexual behavior and increases emotional behavior in offspring. Insecticides and nicotine alter the concentrations of neurotransmitters that direct embryonic and fetal neural development and affect processes such as apoptosis.

The effects of prenatal toxicants also depend on the dose, the degree to which and form in which a substance is transmitted across the placenta to the fetus, and the developmental status of the fetus's ability to process the toxicant. Higher doses normally increase the likelihood of adverse effects. Transfer across the placenta depends partly on variables such as molecular weight and structure, protein binding, lipid solubility, and ionic charge. Once a potential teratogen enters the fetus, the detoxification of the substance depends on the maturity of the liver, kidneys, and metabolic and enzymatic processes. The toxicity of substances depends not just on initial chemical structure but also on metabolic transformation. For example, ethanol (the alcohol used in beverages) is converted into acetaldehyde, which is itself teratogenic.

The wide variety of potential toxic insults to the conceptus raises the importance of health care and information for pregnant women and women planning pregnancy. In 1985, the U.S. Institute of Medicine concluded that prenatal care is important for the prevention of low birth weight and recommended policies to make prenatal care available to women regardless of eligibility for public aid. Because low birth weight is a risk for a wide range of development problems, including infant mortality, prevention is important. Low birth weight can result from either premature birth or intrauterine growth restriction. In the two decades following the recommendation, the infant mortality rate in the United States fell. Whether this is due to improvements in prenatal care, improved neonatal critical care, or both is unclear. Some segments of the population have not benefited from these policies as much as others. In particular, African Americans with income below the poverty line have higher rates of low-birth-weight infants and higher infant mortality rates than the rest of the American population.

There is also some controversy about whether current prenatal care practices are truly effective in preventing low birth weight. Prenatal care should consist of early and continuing maternal and fetal risk assessment, health promotion, medical and psychosocial interventions, and follow-up. Late initiation of prenatal care (fourth month or later) is associated with higher rates of many types of congenital defects. This finding could be the result of preventative information or treatments during prenatal visits, or it could derive from the fact that late initiation of prenatal care is a signal for poor health behaviors, poor health care utilization, or poor health care availability.

Although one aspect of prenatal care is promoting health behaviors that are important for infant outcome, as many as one third of pregnant women are not advised about eliminating alcohol, tobacco, and illicit drugs during prenatal visits. To develop more effective prenatal care, future research requires better measures of prenatal care content, quality, timing, and prenatal care provider characteristics and training. Examination of the relations between specific components of prenatal care and child and maternal health and behavioral outcomes is also needed.

An emerging area of prenatal care is the prevention of the transmission of human immunodeficiency virus (HIV) to the fetus. HIV can be transmitted from mother to child during pregnancy, during labor and delivery, and after birth. Most mother-to-child transmission occurs during birth and delivery. The likelihood of perinatal transmission of HIV can be greatly reduced by antiretroviral drug therapy for the mother during pregnancy, treatment of the infant shortly after birth, and avoidance of breast-feeding. As a result of more vigorous prenatal HIV testing and counseling in the United States, between 1992 and 1996 the number of newborns diagnosed with HIV fell by more than 40%.

—*Colleen F. Moore and*
Mary L. Schneider

See also Neonate, Preterm Infants

Further Readings and References

Alexander, G. R., & Kotelchuck, M. (2001). Assessing the role and effectiveness of prenatal care: History, challenges, and directions for future research (Practice Articles). *Public Health Reports, 116*(4), 306–311.

Carmichael, S. L., Shaw, G. M., & Nelson, V. (2002). Timing of prenatal care initiation and risk of congenital malformations. *Teratology, 66*, 326–330.

Child Development Institute. (n.d.). *Approximate timetable of prenatal development*. Retrieved from http://www.childdevelopmentinfo.com/development/prenataldevelopment.shtml

Committee on Developmental Toxicology. (2000). *Scientific frontiers in developmental toxicology and risk assessment*. Washington, DC: National Academies Press.

Lummaa, V. (2003). Early developmental conditions and reproductive success in humans: Downstream effects of prenatal famine, birthweight, and timing of birth. *American Journal of Human Biology, 15*, 370–379.

Nelson, C. A. (Ed.). (2000). *The effects of early adversity on neurobehavioral development: The Minnesota symposia on child psychology: Vol. 31*. Mahwah, NJ: Erlbaum.

Slikker, W., Jr., & Chang, L. W. (Eds.). (1998). *Handbook of developmental neurotoxicity*. New York: Academic Press.

PREOPERATIONAL THOUGHT

The young infant develops from an almost entirely reflexive organism to one that can intentionally manipulate symbols that represent objects in the real world. Imagine the tremendous amount of growth that is now possible, given these new tools for exploring and experiencing the environment. The child is no longer bound by perceptual experiences but can go beyond what the environment offers. The child is progressing from a sensorimotor type of intelligence to a symbolic type of intelligence characteristic of the preoperational stage of development. Whereas the first was limited to direct interactions with the environment, the second is characterized by a manipulation of symbols that represent the environment—thus the beginnings of language. The onset and development of language is the most significant event during this stage.

IMPORTANCE OF OPERATIONS IN PIAGET'S THEORY

An operation is an action wherein an object or experience that was transformed can be returned to its original form. An operation is reversible. It is also an action that is performed mentally. The preoperational child is incapable of performing such operations, and this characteristic is a primary distinction between the preoperational child and the child in a more advanced stage of cognitive development.

The processes of addition and subtraction represent a good example of an operation. The fact that 2 plus 4 equals 6 is logically the same operation as 6 minus 4 equals 2 may seem obvious, but it is not obvious to the preoperational child. The preoperational child cannot mentally rearrange a sequence of events into the reverse order from that in which they originally occurred. One of the primary outcomes of Piaget's long and intensive research into this lack of "operationality" is the child's failure to conserve the relationship between different dimensions of an event. If one dimension of an experience changes (such as the shape of one of two pieces of clay), the preoperational child cannot understand how the mass, weight, or another dimension can remain the same. Technically, this is the invariance of one dimension while there is a change in another.

For example, in a conservation of number task, the child is presented with a row of objects (such as a row of pennies). The child is asked to construct a second row of pennies to match the first row exactly. What the child is being asked to do is to establish a type of perceptual equivalence between the two sets of objects. After this task is completed, the experimenter changes the spacing between the pennies in one row so that one row is shorter than the other. When asked which row then has more pennies, the child confuses the dimension of length with that of number and says that the row that is longer has more pennies in it. This is clearly a contradiction of what the child did earlier, when he or she matched each of the pennies in his or her own row with each of those of another row. Yet now the child believes that one row has more pennies than the other. This is a good example of how the child's use of language at this age reflects an immature level of thought.

Conservation of mass tasks are similar in design. For example, a child will be given two balls of clay that are exactly the same shape and size. The experimenter forms one of the balls into another shape (e.g., from a circle to a sausage). Again, the child believes that the mass of the two are now different and that one is "more" than the other. In fact, the child cannot reverse the process that has taken place or mentally make the comparison between the two shapes before and after the manipulation took place.

The preoperational child cannot conserve or understand that just because one dimension of an experience is changed, other qualities of that experience do not have to change as well. The preoperational child has a difficult time simultaneously relating two dimensions of a situation to one another. For example, the preoperational child cannot understand how she can be both a "good girl" and someone's "little sister." In other words, the child does not yet possess the cognitive structures necessary to recognize that a change in one dimension of an experience does not necessarily mean a change in the others. Because of this, the child is still somewhat perceptually bound and cannot manipulate symbolic elements in a reversible sense. In essence, the child believes that what you see is what you get.

EGOCENTRISM IN THE PREOPERATIONAL STAGE

The most important aspect of this phase of intellectual development is the child's increasing use of symbols to represent objects and the development of a complex and sophisticated system of language. It is no surprise that the primary task the child is faced with in the developmental course of egocentricity is the conquest of the symbol. Now that the child has been separated from the world of sensorimotor egocentrism and can distinguish between self and external objects, the next task is differentiating between symbols and their referents. In other words, the child's world is a function of the way in which the child chooses to represent the world. The child cannot assume another perspective than his or her own, and it is doubtful whether the child even knows another perspective exists.

Piaget and his colleagues developed an ingenious task called the *three-mountain task* to examine this lack of perspective by preoperational children. Depending on one's position around the table, one sees a different view of the three mountains. For example, view A reflects a configuration seen from seat A. The child is seated at one of four positions, and a doll is placed at one of the other positions. The child is then asked to choose the picture that the doll sees from a set of pictures representing all possible views. If, for example, the doll was sitting in seat D, the correct response would be view D. Preoperational children almost invariably choose the view that represents their own position rather than that of the doll. This illustrates that the preoperational child cannot assume a perspective other than his or her own. In contrast, the older child almost never fails at this task, and, if incorrect, the error will not be egocentric but nonegocentric, such as choosing view C or view B.

Another dimension of preoperational egocentrism is the way that language is used. Although Piaget believes that language is a necessary prerequisite for the development of adaptive behavior, language alone is not sufficient. Language has some obvious advantages over sensorimotor functioning, such as the more rapid speed with which events can be processed. However, without the structural changes that take place at this time, language cannot be a primary component of logical thought. Language serves the important function of manipulating and rearranging different symbols (and experiences) without the inefficiency of direct physical activity, but language is restricted by the illogical rules the preoperational child applies to it. The preoperational child uses language in an extreme literal sense. For example, he or she may be confused by a statement such as "He has grown a foot," thinking that indeed someone has actually grown another foot.

The preoperational child also illustrates what Piaget calls egocentric speech, in which there is no differentiation between the child and other people. Even though the child is talking with other children, there is a collective monologue wherein no meaningful transmission of information takes place. Language progresses during this period from being basically egocentric, whereby the child's verbalizing has no real communicative purpose (that is, he or she talks at instead of to other people), to sociocentric or socialized speech, where the communication consists of transmitted information.

Egocentric language parallels the way preoperational children follow rules while playing. Even though they often do not follow the rules, they insist that they are correct. Given that the only set of rules they are aware of is their own, it is logical for them to believe these rules are correct. When two preoperational children play a simple game with each other, each of them changes the rules as they go along to fit his or her personal needs. They are playing for themselves and have no knowledge that a set of outside rules might apply to their behavior.

The preoperational stage is a distinct turning point in the course of cognitive development. For the first time, thought becomes a symbolic process for understanding the world. The most obvious example of this is the development of language.

The world of the preoperational child is bounded by direct contact with concrete objects. The child benefits most from experiences with nonabstract elements and events because his or her ability to manipulate events or objects that are not directly tied to perceptual experiences is limited. The child cannot reverse an operation and has difficulty understanding the importance of cause-and-effect relationships in solving certain types of problems.

The preoperational child is in a transitional period. Although his or her perspective on the world expands rapidly, there is still some confusion in the evaluation of cause and effect. The child makes inappropriate generalizations and attributes his or her feelings to inanimate objects, assuming, for example, that clouds cry to make rain.

—*Neil J. Salkind*

See also Concrete Operational Period; Formal Operational Period; Piaget, Jean; Sensory Development

Further Readings and References

Jean Piaget Society, http://www.piaget.org/

Piaget, J., & Inhelder, B. (1956). *The child's conception of space.* London: Routledge & Kegan Paul.

Russell, J. (1999). Cognitive development as an executive process—in part: A homeopathic dose of Piaget. *Developmental Science, 2*(3), 247–295.

PRESCHOOL YEARS

The preschool years, from about 2 to 5 years of age, is a period of remarkable intellectual (cognitive), social, and physical development. It is an age of both amazing abilities and surprising limitations in the ways in which preschool children interact and understand their expanding world. Consider the following scenario from a *false belief* task designed to show what preschool children understand about thinking. Sally, a 3-year-old, is asked what she believes is in a box of crayons. Naturally, she replies "crayons." Next the box is emptied to reveal that there are really candles inside. When the candles are then placed back in the box and she is asked what she first thought was in the box, she answers "candles." She further believes that someone who has never looked inside the box also thinks as she does that there are candles in the box. She does not understand that there can be two different beliefs about the same situation. However, only 18 months later, she will be able to answer such questions. This ability to distinguish conflicting beliefs will affect Sally's participation in social spheres, such as interactions with peers and family members. As this example illustrates, preschool children often misunderstand many aspects of their world, but the development of their understanding quickly blossoms and intersects other facets of their development.

PHYSICAL DEVELOPMENT

The typical 3-year-old weighs about 23 pounds and is a little over 2½ feet tall. By 6 years of age, the child's weight has increased to 50 pounds and height to almost 3½ feet. Of course, as with all aspects of development, there is enormous variability reflecting both biological influences, such as heredity, and environmental influences, such as nutrition and disease. Children's motor skills continue to develop and become more refined and elaborated from infancy. Preschoolers become more coordinated at being able to move around their expanding world. They can run, jump, and climb. Further, they continue to improve in their ability to handle and manipulate objects, such as throwing and catching a baseball or dribbling a basketball.

One of the most significant physical developments is the brain's continued rapid growth that began during the prenatal period. Its continued growth during the preschool years is responsible for many of the cognitive and social changes that take place. In terms of size, by 3 years of age, the brain has reached 80% of its adult weight. Two fundamental processes of brain development that continue during the preschool period are *synaptogenesis* and *myelinization*. Synaptogenesis reflects the formation of synaptic connections between neurons and allows the different areas of the brain to communicate with each other, allowing for more coordinated and sophisticated behavior. The rate of synaptogenesis varies across different brain areas. Synaptogenesis of the prefrontal cortex, responsible for many executive functioning skills, such as planning, peaks at about 4 years of age, whereas synaptogenesis in the visual cortex peaks several years earlier. Interestingly, the elimination of unused neural pathways also occurs across the preschool period. Myelinization refers to the covering of axons with myelin—an insulating sheath that affects the speed of information processing between neurons (brain cells)—and continues to occur during the preschool period. As the brain matures, different areas become *lateralized,* or specialized for different functions. For instance, the left hemisphere becomes increasingly specialized for language. However, during early development, the brain also exhibits *plasticity*— the ability to recover from damage or injury by having other areas take over other functions. As children get older, the degree of plasticity decreases, and thus it becomes more difficult to recover. The brain's development contributes to the many social and cognitive changes described below.

COGNITIVE DEVELOPMENT
Jean Piaget

Perhaps no one has done more to describe the preschool mind than Jean Piaget, a psychologist and biologist who devoted his life to understanding the different stages of cognitive development from infancy to adulthood. Piaget was one of the first to note both the enhanced cognitive abilities of the preschool child compared with the infant and the limitations of the preschool child compared with the elementary school child. According to Piaget, the hallmark of the preschool child is *symbolic* thought. One of the most dramatic indications of symbolic abilities is children's use of words to represent concepts, such as the understanding that the word *dog* represents the entire category of dogs and not simply the one in the back yard. Another symbolic function is *pretend play*, when children begin to use other objects to represent another. Typical examples would be a child using a block to represent a car, or despite the best efforts of parents, using a stick to represent a gun. Children also are capable of *deferred imitation*—witnessing a model perform an action and then imitating it at a later time point.

Piaget was struck by the illogical or limited nature of preschool thought as well. He referred to the preschool period as the *preoperational* or prelogical stage. The best known illustration of this limited thinking is preschoolers' misunderstanding of *conservation*—that the quantity of objects does not change despite changes in appearance. In the conservation of liquid problem, children are shown two glasses of the same size with the same amount of juice in each. As the child watches, the juice from one of the glasses is poured into a taller, thinner glass. The child now thinks the taller beaker has more juice than the original shorter one because they can only focus on the more salient perceptual dimension of height and are unable to understand that the greater height is compensated by a smaller width. Parents often have to struggle with this misunderstanding as they try to hand out equal shares of cookies and juice.

This inability to focus on only one dimension is also reflected in difficulties with *perspective taking*. Preschool children often have difficulty understanding that another person's visual perspective or social perspective is different from their own. In Piaget's classic three-mountain task, children are shown a model of three mountains with different objects on the different sides. As the child is seated on one side of the display, the child is asked what a person on the other side sees. Preschool children respond that the other person sees the same objects that they do. Similarly, they have difficulty understanding that an adult would want a different birthday present than they would—a reflection of *egocentric* or self-focused thought. Often, however, changes in testing demands can improve preschoolers performance on all of these tasks, and some researchers have argued that preschoolers are not as limited in their thinking as Piaget's original work suggested.

Theory of Mind

This pattern of strength and weakness is characteristic of many aspects of preschoolers' cognitive development. Nowhere is this more evident than preschoolers' understanding of the mind or their *theory of mind*. Theory of mind refers to children's understanding of mental states (e.g., emotion, desires, and beliefs) and how these are related to behavior. This ability is a fundamental component of understanding social interactions, such as knowing where someone will look for their keys based on where they think the keys are rather than the actual physical location of the keys. Preschool children understand many different aspects of the mind. Initially, children understand mental states such as *desires* by 2 and 3 years of age. They can predict someone's behavior from knowing their desire, for example, predicting that a child will go to the cookie jar to get a cookie if the child wants one. In addition, 3-year-olds know that different types of perceptual experiences lead to different types of knowledge. They understand that someone who can look inside a box will know what is inside of it, whereas someone who cannot see inside will not. Although they can understand desires, they cannot fully understand beliefs until about 5 years. As the crayon box *false belief* example illustrated, children before age 5 do not understand that people (including themselves) can have different or conflicting beliefs. Once they understand this, however, they learn how to surprise and deceive other people. Similar to this difficulty in understanding beliefs, it is not until about 5 years of age that children understand the *appearance–reality* distinction, recognizing that appearances may mask a different reality. For example, young preschool children are often frightened by people wearing masks or have problems recognizing that someone may appear happy but really be sad. Autistic children have particular difficulty in understanding the mind, which may account for their difficulties in social interactions.

Language

Perhaps there is no area of cognitive development in which children make more progress than language during the preschool years. It is one of children's most remarkable intellectual achievements. During this period, their vocabulary expands rapidly, so that by the time they are 5 years of age, their vocabulary may number 5,000 to 10,000 words. Children's word meaning reflects the concepts that they are acquiring. Preschoolers use a variety of learning strategies to learn word meanings that primarily involve understanding the communicative intentions of others.

Perhaps the most impressive language achievement of the preschool period is the development of a *grammar*—a system of rules for combining words and morphemes (e.g., the past tense marker of *-ed*). The rules of any language are very complex and subtle, and yet children are able to acquire them effortlessly with no direct instruction. Children do make language errors as they acquire their grammar, but these are creative errors reflecting children's ability to extract rules from the language they hear around them. The best illustration of this is the *overregularization* of grammatical morphemes. This occurs when children misapply a rule, for example, adding an *-ed* ending to an irregular verb form, producing words such as *goed* or *wented*. Despite such errors, by the end of the preschool period, children have mastered many of the grammatical rules of language. So impressive is children's skill at learning grammar, that some have proposed that children have innate knowledge of particular linguistic principles common to the world's languages, referred to as *universal grammar*. Others argue that children's language can be explained by more general cognitive and social-cognitive mechanisms that children use in learning about all aspects of their world. This debate regarding whether children have innate, specialized abilities or use more general cognitive learning strategies occurs in other areas of cognitive development as well, such as theory of mind.

Regardless of which position is correct for language, it is clear that preschool children have an advantage over older children and adults in learning a language. It is much easier for preschool children to learn a first or second language than it is for older children or adults. This optimal period for learning language is often referred to as a *critical* or *sensitive period*, which begins to decline at about 6 or 7 years of age. If language learning is not accomplished during this period, it will be much more difficult, if not impossible, to acquire to a native proficiency of language later.

Memory

Thus far, preschool children's understanding of specific cognitive domains or concepts has been explored. There are also changes in more basic cognitive abilities and capacity. One of the most important is in the area of memory development. Information-processing approaches make a distinction between *short-term memory* and *long-term memory*. Short-term memory holds incoming information for a brief period of time before it is transferred to long-term memory, which is long lasting. Children's ability to remember short- and long-term information increases across the preschool years. For example, they can remember longer sequences of random numbers, reflecting an increase in short-term memory.

Two aspects of memory performance that may be particularly limited in the preschool years are *strategies* and *metamemory*. Most preschoolers are not very strategic. For example, if given a set of pictures to remember, most preschoolers will not spontaneously rehearse the picture labels or put them into categories. They can adopt simpler memory strategies to help them remember where a toy is hidden, for example, by staring at its location. The more deliberate or conscious strategies, such as rehearsal, develop later. Similarly, preschool children do not have a very sophisticated metamemory—conscious knowledge of memory and how it operates. Preschoolers may have difficulty knowing what memory tasks are easy or difficult and easily overestimate what they are capable of remembering.

Preschool children can use their knowledge to help them remember. This is most apparent in children's *scripts* for routine events. Scripts are generalized representations of everyday events such as going to a birthday party or going to preschool. Preschoolers can quickly form general memories of these events and recall them in a logically and temporally organized manner.

A significant memory achievement that occurs at about 4 years of age is an *autobiographical memory* system. Although even infants and young preschoolers can remember events, adults typically cannot recall experiences that occurred before age 3 or 4 years. This absence of early memories is referred to as *infantile* or *childhood amnesia*. There have been numerous explanations of the emergence of autobiographical memory at 4 years. One proposal is that children need to have established a *self-concept* to form personally significant memories. Another important contributing factor is *narrative skill*—the ability to tell a story about their past. Interestingly, parent-child interactions appear to be particularly critical to this development. As parents and children jointly discuss past experiences, such as vacations or birthday parties, children learn the narrative structure of how to talk about the past as well as the importance of the past to their own self-concept. Those parents who create elaborative narratives, using rich stories of the past, facilitate children's formation of autobiographical memories more so than parents who are less elaborative.

A related practical memory question is whether preschool children can provide accurate *eyewitness testimony* in court, which may be necessary in cases of abuse when children are the only witnesses. There is some concern that preschool children are too suggestible and can be led to provide false testimony by the asking of leading questions by concerned parents and court authorities. Several high-profile convictions have been overturned because of these concerns. Research does indicate that preschool children are more suggestible than older children, although there is debate about how extensive this is and whether children can provide reliable testimony. Many researchers believe that under appropriate interview conditions, preschool children can give accurate testimony, whereas others urge caution.

Problem Solving

Many of the tasks described so far are actually examples of different types of problems that children learn to solve during the preschool years. As described by David Klahr, *problem solving* involves the development of strategies to overcome an obstacle to achieve a goal. One key to successful problem solving is *planning*. Preschoolers often have difficulty planning out a course of action and often proceed in a trial and error fashion, leading to frequent problem-solving failures. This inability to plan may reflect difficulty in inhibiting actions. Preschoolers tend to plunge ahead without developing a strategic plan. This difficulty in inhibiting an action is reflected in delay of gratification tasks, in which children must decide whether to wait and receive a larger award later or act now and receive a smaller award. Not surprisingly, most preschool children do not wait. The development of planning and inhibition broadly reflect the development of *executive function*—a broad constellation of skills that are thought to reflect the maturation of the brain's frontal lobes.

Finally, other basic processes that influence children's problem solving are *encoding* and *speed of processing*. In solving a problem successfully, it is necessary to encode or attend to the most important aspects of the problem. For instance, to solve Piaget's conservation of liquid problem, children must encode both the height and width of the beaker and not just the height. Preschool children often fail to encode or notice all the important dimensions, although training them to do so can facilitate their success. In addition, the speed with which children can perform basic processes increases dramatically over childhood, including the preschool years, reflecting both brain maturation and experience.

SOCIAL DEVELOPMENT

In addition to the amazing strides children experience cognitively, the preschool years are a time during which children's participation in social interactions also increases. Equipped with their newly improved cognitive abilities born out of social interactions with others, preschoolers become increasingly capable of interacting with other members of their family and forming relationships with members from their peer group. Unlike infancy, preschoolers' social worlds are multilayered and operate beyond that of the parent-child relationship. According to Urie Bronfenbrenner, social participation occurs at multiple levels, represented as concentric circles: microsystem, mesosystem, exosystem, and macrosystem. Thus, children's participation in their social world, such as that with peers and family members, is embedded within larger social contexts, such as their neighborhoods and communities and, ultimately, the attitudes and ideologies of the culture in which they live. The hallmarks of social development during the preschool years include (1) development of the self-concept, (2) role of parents, (3) forming peer relationships, (4) development of play, and (5) effects of day care.

Development of the Self-Concept

Between 18 and 24 months of age, children are able to recognize themselves in the mirror, as evidenced by their reaction to a spot of rouge surreptitiously placed on their nose. However, there is some debate as to whether this form of visual self-recognition truly reveals children's early self-understanding. Others argue that self-awareness continues to develop over the course of the preschool years, emerging as late as 4 years of age, evidenced by their ability to identify themselves on videotape.

This enhanced ability to recognize oneself is accompanied by changes in how children characterize themselves according to other dimensions, the most salient of which is physical characteristics, particularly gender, during the preschool years. Children also describe themselves in relation to what they like and dislike, such as food preferences, as well as items they possess, such as toys and pets. Typical instruments used to assess children's self-description involve interview procedures in which children are asked yes-or-no questions that assess characteristics of their physical, social, and cognitive abilities. However, because children during the preschool years typically possess a heightened (and perhaps overinflated) view of themselves, it is difficult to ascertain the accuracy of their judgments related to their self-perception and self-worth during this time frame.

Perhaps the most central theme that runs through children's self-concept development during the preschool years is the role of gender. Initially, many children exhibit gender-stereotyped behaviors that meet the standard cultural roles prescribed by society. At the same time, children begin to develop *gender constancy*, a term that refers to the fixedness of stereotypically masculine and feminine characteristics, such as males are aggressive and females are emotional. Based on these gender stereotypes, children form schemas for gender-relevant behaviors. Interestingly, preschoolers' gender schemas play a significant role in their ability to recall events. Thus, girls and boys differentially recall gender consistent, as opposed to gender inconsistent, information. This illustrates again how knowledge affects memory. Finally, the role of gender stereotypes is evident in preschoolers' play, such that preschool-age boys' play is characterized as rough and tumble in nature, whereas preschool girls tend to aggregate in group conversations that are often in close proximity to teachers.

Role of Parents

Given their increasing independence cognitively, socially, and personally, it is not surprising that elements of family interactions also change during the preschool years. Individual differences in socialization within the family context, particularly in relation to the manner in which parents regulate their children's positive and negative behaviors, begin to emerge. Specifically, different parental styles emerge, known as authoritative, authoritarian, permissive, and disengaged. *Authoritative* parents are able to strike a balance between disciplining their child and still maintaining a sense of warmth and affection. In contrast, *authoritarian* parents are highly demanding and controlling, absent of warmth and affection. Permissive parents are very warm with their children, but lack effective control over their children's behaviors, whereas those who are *disengaged* are low in warmth and control.

Within the context of predominantly white, middle-class families, Baumrind's classifications of the different parenting styles in relation to positive developmental outcomes, such as success in school and popularity with peers, is linked to the authoritative parenting style, whereas the most negative outcomes are linked to the disengaged parenting style. Children of authoritarian parents tend not to do as well in school and experience behavioral difficulties in adolescence. Differences within other cultural and ethnic groups demonstrate, for example, that children from other countries, such as China, and African American children from the United States experience success in scholastic and social worlds best when exposed to authoritarian styles of parenting.

Parents also serve as social facilitators to enhance the nature of their children's peer interactions. Specifically, parents influence relations within the peer group by structuring opportunities for social interaction, such as play groups, and supporting their children to join clubs and sports teams, such as soccer. Further, parents serve as models of social interaction, from which preschoolers are able to base their manner of interactions with others. Research demonstrates that the extent to which preschoolers are rejected by their peer group is influenced by the communicative style of their parent. This suggests that parents' own abilities to engage in effective communicative interactions directly affect their children's ability to tune into the social, emotional, and linguistic cues of those with whom they interact.

Forming Peer Relationships

During the preschool years, children's concepts of friends shift. At 3 years of age, children typically have one peer of the same sex, which they consider a playmate. These playmates are typically selected based on similarities in play styles and children's ability levels, such as possessing similar linguistic skills. As children move through the preschool years, the quality of their interactions with their peers changes, in part because of children's enhanced cognitive capacity to engage in more quality interactions in play contexts. Besides facilitating play opportunities, peer relationships also serve other functions in preschoolers' lives, such as teaching cooperation and negotiation with others. The mastery of these skills during the preschool years affects children's developing self-concept and their future interactions with others.

Children's *sociometric status* (i.e., social status among peers) begins to increase in meaning by the end of the preschool years. Social status among peers is studied by a peer nomination process in which children indicate, for example, the three children they would most like and least like to play with in their class. By age 5, groups of children are classified as *popular* (those capable of facilitating and maintaining positive interactions in the peer group), *rejected* (those actively rejected by their peers), *neglected* (those not acknowledged by their peers), or *controversial* (those who receive both positive and negative nominations from their peer group).

As children develop cognitively (e.g., theory of mind), they become increasingly capable of interpreting the social behaviors of those around them. Crick and Dodge discuss young children's capabilities to draw on their knowledge database to process the social information of those around them. Those children who are more effective interpreters of those with whom they interact experience more positive than negative social consequences. Further, those children who are considered more socially adept, specifically in the form of popularity, tend to be better consumers of the social information presented to them.

A special form of the peer relationship that buds during the preschool years is the sibling relationship. Because of their increased cognitive and linguistic skills, preschoolers become more capable of participating in quality interactions with their siblings, such as serving as social facilitators and managers of activities such as play and conversation. Preschoolers who are younger siblings or close in age to their older siblings experience a heightened awareness of theory of mind, likely owing to their participation in emotionally charged or deceptively laden interactions with their older siblings.

Development of Play

As previously discussed, preschoolers' solitary play with objects becomes more sophisticated as a result of their increased symbolic understanding. Gradually, children's symbolic representations in play begin to involve other people, particularly peers, as they recruit them to engage in joint symbolic interactions. The development of pretense in play also emerges. Some children begin to engage in fantasy play with imaginary peers, puppets, and stuffed animals by themselves. By the culmination of the preschool years, most children participate in sociodramatic play, the most sophisticated form of play, which involves recruiting other individuals to act out related

roles. For instance, one child plays the role of the teacher while the other enacts the role of a student. The capacity to engage in symbolic and pretend play is beneficial to preschoolers' cognitive advancements. For instance, early instances of pretense, particularly those pretend-play acts constructed in conjunction with parents and peers, is shown to advance the social-cognitive skills of children later on in the preschool years, such as theory of mind.

In addition to its cognitive characterizations, preschoolers' play is often characterized according to the degree to which it involves the social participation of others. Thus, children's participation in play activities can range from merely watching others, to *solitary, independent play*, to *parallel play*, to *cooperative play* in which all members' participation in the activity is fully coordinated. Typically, preschool children between 3 and 5 years of age engage in parallel play, which involves two or more children in close physical approximation to each other engaging in related activities. However, the actions of these children are not coordinated or cooperative in any way.

Effects of Day Care

During the past several decades, numerous studies examining the impact of daycare on preschoolers' social and cognitive abilities have revealed a range of both positive and negative outcomes. Historically, earlier studies examining the influence of day care experiences found that maternal employment was related to less secure parent-child attachment styles. However, these earlier studies were wrought with problems, such as low numbers of participants and inadequate controls, and most important, researchers' ability to replicate the earlier findings varied. To disentangle the exact effects of early day care and maternal employment on children's developmental outcomes, a host of researchers came together, funded by the National Institute of Child Health and Human Development (NICHD), to help resolve the debate over maternal employment and day care.

Since 1991, NICHD researchers from across the United States have established testing sites to assess these issues longitudinally in economically and culturally diverse families. The general patterns of findings reveal that the quality of day care and amount of time spent in day care are most predictive of the types of interactions children share with their caregivers, particularly their mothers. Thus, children who attend low-quality day care centers or spend a lot of time in day care are most likely to develop insecure attachments with their caregivers.

The pattern also holds true for developmental outcomes, such as cognitive and linguistic skills, in that the higher the quality of care, the more likely the child is to experience positive outcomes. In relation to negative outcomes, the effects of early, full-time day care were particularly exacerbated for 3-year-old boys of less sensitive mothers. Specifically, these children scored lower on tests assessing school readiness. In addition, children spending more time in day care have higher rates of behavioral problems during the latter preschool and kindergarten years, regardless of the quality of care these children received. Thus, higher quality of care does not always yield positive benefits.

SUMMARY

During the preschool period, children make enormous strides across cognitive, social, and physical domains. In each of these areas, children show both strengths and limitations. These developments in these domains are interdependent, so that changes in one domain affect changes in the others. For example, the development of better language skills changes the nature of children's social interactions with their parents and peers. All of these developments lay the foundation for the next period of development— middle childhood.

—*M. Jeffrey Farrar and
Joann P. Benigno*

See also Baumrind, Diana; Bronfenbrenner, Urie; Piaget, Jean

Further Readings and References

Borden, M. (1997). *Smart start: The parents' complete guide to preschool education.* New York: Facts on File.

Bowman, B., Donavan, S., & Burns, S. (2000). *Eager to learn: Educating our preschoolers.* Washington, DC: National Research Council.

Bruce, T. (1993). For parents particularly: The role of play in children's lives. *Childhood Education, 69*(4), 237–238.

Developmental psychology links, http://www.socialpsychology .org/develop.htm

Neuman, S., Copple, C., & Bredekamp, S. (1999). *Learning to read and write: Developmentally appropriate practices for young children.* Washington, DC: National Association for the Education of Young Children.

Psi Café. (n.d.). *Developmental psychology.* Available from http://www.psy.pdx.edu/PsiCafe/Areas/Developmental/

U.S. Department of Education, http://www.ed.gov/index.jhtml

PRETERM INFANTS

In comparison with infants born at 40 weeks, the expected length of pregnancy, infants born before they have reached 37 weeks' gestation are considered premature. About one of eight infants, or 12%, is born premature in the United States, resulting in more than 485,000 preterm births. Of these premature infants, about 60,000, or 1.4%, are born at 32 weeks' gestation or earlier. All babies born before their expected due dates are at higher risk for complications that can affect the growing baby and family well into childhood. The earlier the infant is born, the more likely there will be significant medical complications and less optimal developmental outcomes.

The highest rates of premature births are in women younger than 20 and older than 35 years and in African American mothers when compared with mothers of other ethnic backgrounds. Although the cause of prematurity is not known, a variety of contributors to poor pregnancy outcomes have been identified, including poor nutrition during pregnancy, smoking, substance abuse, infections, and multiple-birth pregnancies. The substantial increase in rates of prematurity during the past decade is in part a result of an increase in the number of women who are postponing pregnancy and in part to an increased use of assisted reproductive technologies. These therapies often result in multiple fetuses, which tend to be born prematurely.

Technological and pharmacological advances in reproductive medicine now make it possible for older women to conceive and for couples who were thought to be infertile to become pregnant and have babies. Many assisted pregnancies result in twins, triplets, or higher-order multiples. Any increase in the number of fetuses sharing a uterus also increases the rate of premature birth, which has resulted in an increasing rate of premature, multiple-birth admissions. From 1980 to 1997, pregnancies resulting in multiple births increased by 52% overall, and triplets and higher-order births increased by 404%. Only recently have the rates declined, although twin rates continue to climb. Rates of prematurity and death for twins and higher-order multiples are 4 to 33 times higher than those for single-born babies.

Preterm birth is the number one obstetric challenge and a leading problem for ongoing pediatric care. It is the leading cause of neonatal death in the first month of life in the United States and the second leading cause of death for infants as a whole. Additionally, preterm birth contributes substantially to neonatal and infant illness. Not only does preterm birth have serious health consequences, but it also contributes to significant national health care costs. Intensive care for premature infants is a fairly recent phenomenon.

Technological, pharmacological, and specialty hospital care for infants born early began only in the 1960s. Because infants born prematurely are unable to survive without significant intensive medical support, they are typically cared for in specialty intensive care units, which have been regionalized according to medical acuity. Infants born earliest and with the most severe complications are provided care in intensive care units that have specific expertise and can respond to life-threatening events. Similarly, infants who are born closer to term and do not have life-threatening conditions might be hospitalized in an intensive care unit that has fewer technical and medical intervention requirements.

As a result of increases in medical technology and expertise, smaller and earlier-born infants not only survive, but thrive. High-tech neonatal intensive care units (NICUs) now provide medical, developmental, environmental, and family support for the growing infant. Thanks to these improvements in medical and technological intervention, infants born at 23 to 26 weeks' gestation (typically weighing 500–850 grams) now have a 40% to 60% chance of survival. Babies born at 27 to 28 weeks' gestation (about 750–1000 grams) have about an 85% chance of survival. As the pregnancy goes on, survival rates increase dramatically, so that almost all infants born at 34 weeks' gestation or later survive. However, survival alone does not ensure that the baby will have good health or typical development. Although many infants born prematurely have typical development and do not face long-term medical or developmental complications, about 10% of infants face significant risk for severe neurodevelopmental problems, including major, permanent neurosensory impairments such as blindness and deafness; cognitive and language delays such as mental retardation; motor deficits such as cerebral palsy; and learning disabilities. Children who were born prematurely may experience subtle but substantial neurodevelopmental and socioemotional deficits,

including mild cognitive delays, speech and language disorders, persistent neuromotor problems, and perceptual problems. These difficulties may not be identified until school age, when prematurely born children must use more differentiated language, visual-spatial skills, and social competencies to succeed. In the classroom environment, their developmental and behavioral challenges become increasingly apparent. Typically, they do not subside as prematurely born children grow; rather, these difficulties may persist into adolescence and even young adulthood, although many have adapted well and report a good quality of life. Many of these underlying deficits lead to significant challenges in school for children who began their lives in the NICU.

Prematurity and the NICU experience have long-term effects on parents and siblings, as well as on the growing child. The impact of these early stressful experiences influences family relationships and family functioning and may result in a variety of less than optimal social, economic, and developmental outcomes. Families in crisis because of the premature birth or from ongoing medical, social, or economic distress have a hard time relating to their babies, making relationships between infants and their parents difficult. Effects of early experiences on family functioning and interactions may be reflected long into the child's early years and into adolescence.

Premature infants have difficulty in communicating clearly through their behavior, in comparison with infants born at full term. Consequently, parents have difficulty in understanding and responding appropriately to their newborn's needs and requests. Not surprisingly, relationships between preterm infants and their parents are often difficult. Because infant development occurs in the context of relationships, the preterm infant, whose communication is not well defined, is at significant risk for relationship disruption and subsequent developmental delay. Prematurely born children are at higher risk for abuse and neglect, reflecting early relationship difficulties.

Intervention strategies for modifying the NICU environment and caregiving practices have recently been proposed to address the growing scientific evidence that the environment in which the vulnerable infant grows can have a significant impact on brain development and function. Modifications in sound and light exposure in the NICU that are now implemented address the realization that infant neurological development is exquisitely sensitive to the timing, modulation, and integration of sensory input presented at sensitive periods of development. Similarly, caregiving practices are now modified to reduce painful stimulation, to support the infant's emerging behavioral organization, and to engage the family in care of the infant. Scientists and medical professionals are just beginning to understand how environmental sensory input and caregiving affect the developing premature infant. Available evidence suggests that the best environment for the stable premature infant is his or her parents' faces, voices, and bodies. They are familiar, appropriately complex, multimodal, and specific to the infant's individual expectations and needs, and can readily modify themselves according to the baby's responses. Emphasis is also being focused on prevention and amelioration of painful procedures in the NICU because research suggests that repeated painful interventions in the NICU may have long-term adverse behavioral and physiological effects.

Because prematurely born infants are at higher risk for neurodevelopmental and sensory deficits that may be evident at birth or that may not emerge until the child is older, support for transition from the hospital to the home community is essential. Close follow-up with sequential evaluation of developmental progress is imperative to ensure appropriate development and engagement of the family with the infant, or to provide intervention should the child be found to have developmental delays. Interdisciplinary teams that have experience and specialize in the assessment and treatment of neurodevelopmental sequelae of early birth should be provided to the family in their community. Should the infant have, or develop, significant medical or developmental conditions, they should be referred to appropriate intervention services.

The complexities of premature birth continue to be challenging for health care providers, families, and educational systems. The vulnerability of these babies and their families lasts far beyond the newborn intensive care unit and extends far after discharge. Premature birth can affect the child's cognitive and socioemotional development well into the school years. Therefore, advances in medical care, modifications of early environments and caregiving, and supportive parental relationships must begin early and continue into the child's early years so that they can experience the best developmental outcomes possible.

—*Joy V. Browne*

See also Neonate

Further Readings and References

Anand, K. J., & International Evidence-Based Group for Neonatal Pain. (2001). Consensus statement for the prevention and management of pain in the newborn. *Archives of Pediatrics & Adolescent Medicine, 155*(2), 173–180.

Bennett, F. C. (1999). Developmental outcomes. In G. B. Avery, M. A. Fletcher, & M. G. MacDonald (Eds.), *Neonatology: Pathophysiology and management of the newborn*. Philadelphia: Lippincott, Williams & Wilkins.

Browne, J. V. (2003). New perspectives on premature infants and their parents. *Zero to Three, 24*(2), 4–12.

Hack, M., Flannery, D. J., Schluchter, M., Cartar, L., Borawski, E., & Klein, N. (2002). Outcomes in young adulthood for very-low-birth-weight infants [Comment]. *New England Journal of Medicine, 346*(3), 149–157.

March of Dimes Prematurity Campaign, http://www.modimes.org/prematurity/5126.asp

Martin, J. A., Hamilton, B. E., Ventura, S. J., Menacker, F., & Park, M. M. (2002). Births: Final data for 2000. *National Vital Statistics Reports, 50*(5), 1–101.

MedlinePlus. (2005). *Premature babies*. Retrieved from http://www.nlm.nih.gov/medlineplus/prematurebabies.html

NICU design standards, http://www.nd.edu/~kkolberg/DesignStandards.htm

Talmi, A., & Harmon, R. J. (2003). Relationships between preterm infants and their parents. *Zero to Three, 24*(2), 13–20.

U.S. Department of Health and Human Services. (2002). *Child Health USA 2002*. Retrieved from http://mchb.hrsa.gov/chusa02/index.htm

PREVENTIVE MEDICINE

Preventive medicine is the practice of disease prevention and health promotion. Practitioners of preventive medicine, who may be health care professionals, psychologists, or policy makers, have a knowledge base in clinical medicine, public health, and behavioral medicine. Prevention programs seek to stop the occurrence of a negative outcome before adverse events take place through early identification of problems and early intervention to diminish negative effects. For example, tobacco use has been associated with an increased risk for negative health outcomes, such as heart disease and cancer. Thus, tobacco use reduction programs provide a good example of a current area of focus in preventive medicine and will be used to illustrate the basic concepts of prevention.

Prevention can be implemented at any of three stages of the development of a health problem: primary, secondary, or tertiary. Primary prevention is applied before problems are evident; for example, teaching school-age children not to begin smoking. Secondary prevention interventions might be used when problems are considered likely or when health screenings have shown the problem to be in its early stages so that further development does not occur. For example, secondary prevention programs would be used to help someone who reports being a smoker quit smoking, even though the individual does not have any negative health effects. Tertiary prevention occurs when problems have already developed, and prevention is used to reduce impairment and avoid development of further problems. With tobacco use, tertiary prevention would be used with smokers who require medical attention for a mild respiratory problem that is likely linked to their smoking habit.

Prevention programs may be implemented at a structural level or a behavioral level. Structural prevention involves modifications to the environment, which can range from changing building and city design to passing laws or adding warning labels. In the case of reducing tobacco use, building designs that relegate smokers to small unattractive spaces and laws prohibiting smoking in many public buildings are examples of seeking to decrease smoking rates through structural prevention. Behavioral prevention involves direct modification in human behavior, which would include any of the programs designed to help individuals stop smoking, such as the nicotine patch or smoking cessation classes run through health clinics. In the field of injury and accident prevention, prevention is often discussed as being either passive or active. Passive prevention requires minimal effort by an individual by creating changes to the environment such as governmental standards requiring installation of airbags and building firewalls in apartment complexes. Active prevention requires frequent action by an individual. For example, this may include buckling up during every car trip or installing locks on kitchen cabinets, both of which require correct use every time to gain protective benefit.

Research on the effectiveness of preventive medicine techniques reveals mixed results. Increased knowledge through large-scale community campaigns is sometimes linked to behavioral change. A good example may be the public health campaign for pregnant women to have an adequate intake of folic acid. Also, physician counseling has been shown to increase healthy behaviors, but long-term effects are limited, and overall effects are small. Passive prevention, such as water fluorination and regulation of car seat manufacturing, can be a very effective means of health promotion and injury prevention.

SPECIALIZATIONS

Preventive medicine has been a board certified medical specialty since 1948. Training is primarily through a postmedical school residency program that includes a master's degree in public health and clinical and practicum training in preventive medicine. The core knowledge areas for this training are health services administration, biostatistics, epidemiology, clinical preventive medicine, behavioral aspects of health, and environmental health. This training prepares specialists for jobs in public policy, administration, research, or primary care. A preventive medical specialist in a primary care setting seeks to increase long-term health outcomes through frequent screening for possibly emerging health problems, medical techniques (i.e., medicine and surgery), and behavioral counseling. For example, a patient with high cholesterol (which has been linked to an increased risk for cardiovascular disease) may receive a medication known to reduce cholesterol levels, have blood tests every 6 months to monitor cholesterol levels, and be counseled about dietary and exercise changes to further reduce the possible negative health effects of high cholesterol.

Some medical specialties, such as pediatrics and family medicine, have long adopted prevention and promotion activities with emphasis on immunization, injury prevention, nutrition, and healthy development. Gerontology, the comprehensive study of aging and the problems of the aged, is a related and emerging medical field that has a strong focus on maintaining and improving a high quality of life for older adults. Because quality of life (i.e., minimizing the disabilities and handicaps of old age) is a goal of preventive medicine, gerontology has generally become more effective in integrating preventive medicine with primary medical care. Because a preventive medicine approach encompasses many areas of medicine, gerontology (and preventive medicine in general) recognizes the interaction between mind and body and that easing psychological stress aids physical health. Thus, gerontologists take a holistic approach that is interested in preventing the potentially negative psychosocial effects of aging. For example, a gerontologist may monitor a patient's feelings of loss when no longer able to perform a specific leisure activity (e.g., jogging) and may help the patient identify alternatives (e.g., swimming laps).

HISTORY AND FUTURE

Two historical changes have led to the emergence of the specialty of preventive medicine. First, because cures are available for most infectious diseases, and advances in public health (such as better sanitation systems) have led to longer life spans, medical science has begun to focus on preventable health problems and better management of chronic diseases. Second, the health cost benefits of the prevention and early detection of disease has been recognized. For example, effective management of diabetes not only enhances a person's current quality of life but also helps prevent the development of costly and debilitating conditions such as blindness and kidney failure.

As the field of preventive medicine grows, the list of recommended prevention activities also grows, such that the U.S. Preventive Services Task Force guidelines for an average adult patient suggest a health care provider perform 25 preventive activities and address 15 risk factors. However, many barriers exist for the implementation of many preventive medicine techniques in primary medical settings (i.e., doctor's offices or health clinics). For example, the structure of many health insurance plans will often reimburse doctors for treatment of an already present health condition but not for the prevention of a problem that may occur several years down the road. Consequently, although most health care providers recognize the need for preventive medicine and practice it to a limited degree, they are unable to effectively implement all suggested activities (especially with financial incentives that limit the amount of time spent with each patient).

Overall, preventive medicine is a diverse, dynamic, and growing field. As mentioned previously, decreasing tobacco use and increasing the quality of life for older adults are two current areas of focus for the field. Other areas of interest are the prevention of cardiovascular diseases through changes in diet and exercise, the reduction in the spread of infection diseases such as human immunodeficiency virus (HIV) and hepatitis B through the development and distribution of immunizations, and the public health campaigns to increase screenings for early detection of skin, breast, and colon cancers. The U.S. federal health care initiative

Healthy People 2010 provides an agenda for comprehensive, nationwide health promotion and disease prevention. The health outcome objectives established by *Healthy People 2010* seek to eliminate health disparities, increase quality of life and years of life, and increase awareness and funding for preventive medicine research and interventions.

Important future directions for the field of preventive medicine include continuing to identify what makes people more likely to respond to recommendations to promote healthy behaviors. Current research indicates that perception of disease risk, attitudes about treatment, and motivational readiness are related to the likelihood of behavior change, and future research will likely focus on how best to prepare people (on a community and individual level) for change. Increasing the maintenance of health behavior change through the development of sustainable health interventions and effective follow-up techniques will also continue to be a focus for the field.

Emerging technologies, such as Internet-based information, new genetic research and treatments, new immunizations, and use of computer programs to influence change, will also likely affect the field of preventive medicine. Research to develop these technologies in a way to optimally affect health behaviors will be an important focus for preventive medicine. Finally, preventive medicine will likely continue to be active in creating system-wide health promotion changes through legislation and community public health movements.

—Montserrat C. Mitchell and
Michael C. Roberts

Further Readings and References

American Academy of Family Physicians, http://www.aafp.org

American Academy of Pediatrics, http://www.aap.org

American College of Preventive Medicine, http://www.acpm.org

Gerontological Society of America, http://www.geron.org

Healthy People 2010, http://www.healthypeople.gov

Roberts, M. C., Brown, K. J., Boles, R. E., Mashunkashey, J. O., & Mayes, S. (2003). Prevention of disease and injury in pediatric psychology. In M. C. Roberts (Ed.), *Handbook of pediatric psychology* (pp. 84–98). New York: Guilford.

Siegler, I. C., Bastian, L. A., & Bosworth, H. B. (2001). Health, behavior and age. In A. Baum, T. A. Revenson, & J. E. Singer (Eds.), *Handbook of health psychology* (pp. 469–476). Mahwah, NJ: Erlbaum.

PRIMARY CIRCULAR REACTIONS

Circular reaction is term coined by Jean Piaget (1896–1980), a developmental biologist by training, who devoted his life to studying intellectual abilities from infancy to adolescence. The term describes stages of the infant's cognitive development in the sensorimotor period, the first of the stages identified by Piaget, which lasts from 0 to 24 months of age. During this period, infants discover relationships between actions of their bodies, such as moving the fingers of their hand in order to open their hands or in order to make a fist, and relationships between their bodies and the environment, such as kicking a mobile and making it move, or vocalizing and making the mother appear.

The sensorimotor period is divided into several stages, namely reflexes; primary, secondary, and tertiary circular reactions; and invention of new means through mental combination. The first of these stages is the reflexive stage, from 0 to 2 months, when infants are able to perform simple reflexes such as grasping and sucking, and from these reflexes circular reactions develop. The second stage, according to Piaget's theory, is the stage of primary circular reactions, typically lasting from 1 to 4 months of age. Through exploration of their world, infants at this stage discover associations between events. They orient themselves toward the external world and might show their first social smiles. According to Spitz, the first true emotions occur at this time because reactions at this stage reflect a relation between infants and their observations of familiar objects, such as faces. In cognitive terms, infants learn that specific behaviors lead to specific events. At the stage of primary circular reactions, infants open and close their hands and observe these results. For example, 3-month-olds with the arm extended watch their fingers move; then lowering the arm, they find themselves with their fingers near their mouths and finally manage to insert their fingers into their mouths. Infants have been observed to suck their thumbs even in the womb, but we assume that once they experience this sensation in the sensorimotor period, they gain pleasure from it and hence repeat the event. At the stage of primary circular reactions, infants have a rudimentary ability to anticipate events, but they are not yet able to discern effects they might have on the external world.

The repetition and reorganization of the infant's schema leads to the third stage, that of secondary circular reactions, lasting from 4 to 8 months, in which an infant will, for example, kick a mobile and observe the mobile move, then reproduce the behavior in order to reproduce the event. Through coordination of its activity, the infant learns to produce a result to control physical and social events and thereby learns personal agency. This is in contrast to the stage of primary circular reactions, in which infants learn self-awareness, in the sense of experiencing self (my fingers move) in relation to self (I control the movement of my fingers) but are not yet aware that they are in control of interpersonal events. At the stage of primary circular reactions, infants cry and mother appears, but infants at that stage do not plan to make the mother appear by crying as they can at the stage of secondary circular reactions. From 8 to 12 months, according to Piaget, infants apply what they learned during the stages of primary and secondary circular reactions to new situations. At the time of tertiary circular reactions (12–18 months), infants actively experiment to provoke new effects, such as pouring their cereal from the bowl onto the high chair. Tertiary circular reactions develop at 18 to 24 months into invention of new means through mental combination. At this stage, infants speak their first words and are capable of pretend play.

—*Nadja Reissland*

See also Piaget, Jean

Further Readings and References

Piaget, J. (1952). *The origins of intelligence in children.* New York: Routledge.

Piaget, J. (1954/1999). *The construction of reality in the child.* London: Routledge.

PRIVATE SPEECH

Private speech is the term used by psychologists and scientists to refer to speech that is not addressed to another person and instead is directed at the self. Private speech, or self-talk, refers only to one's overt, audible speech and one's visible, quiet, verbal lip movements, not the unobservable speech that goes on "inside one's head" when one is thinking to oneself in words—typically referred to as *inner speech*. Although children and adults of all ages engage in overt self-talk at times, most of the research focus on private speech has been on children during the preschool years, the period during which private speech is most frequently observed. An example of children's private speech would be a child who, while working alone building a robot out of Legos in his room, says things like "I need two more blues. Where did I see those big blue pieces? Oh. Here they are."

Private speech was first observed scientifically in children in the early 1900s by both Lev Vygotsky (1896–1934), a Russian developmental psychologist, and Jean Piaget (1896–1980), the well-known Swiss scientist and theoretician, who, at the time, referred to such speech as *egocentric speech*, a term no longer used because of its undesired negative connotations. Vygotsky and Piaget differed in their interpretations of children' private speech. For Piaget, private speech was thought of as poor social speech and simply indicative of young children's immature cognitive and language development that made it difficult for them to engage in competent, social, communicative speech with other people. Thus, for Piaget, the developmental movement was one from the internal world of the child to the external social world—children's private speech would eventually disappear with age as their social speech improved.

For Vygotsky, however, private speech was seen as evidence that an important internalization process, from the external social world to the internal cognitive world of the child, was going on. Children first use language for communication with others socially, and then language begins to be used by children not only for communication (social speech) but also as a tool for thought and behavioral regulation (private speech). At first, children's behavior, and much of their cognitive activity as well, is regulated or controlled by others, first physically and later verbally through the language that adults use with children. Then children begin to talk out loud to themselves and use private speech to guide thinking, problem solving, and behavior. Finally, typically in the late preschool and early school years, children's overt private speech is replaced with inner speech, or inner, verbal thought. Today, it is this Vygotskian interpretation of the role of children's private speech that is widely accepted.

Researchers have learned a variety of things about children's use of private speech by observing children's use of self-talk in naturalistic settings and by analyzing videotapes of children of different ages working on problem-solving tasks in structured laboratory settings. First, self-talk is normal, natural, and healthy for children (and adults), and such speech is indeed helpful. Interestingly, young children themselves appear to know this because they report positive effects about their own use of self-talk. Second, people tend to use private speech when they need the extra help to get a task done, either because the task is particularly challenging or because they are cognitively, emotionally, or motivationally spent. Thus, a common pattern is to see increased private speech use in children when the task activity they are engaging in gets more difficult, as if the private speech becomes an extra tool they use to overcome obstacles. Also, children's use of private speech can be influenced by others around them. Children who are exposed to rich language environments at home and at school and are cognitively stimulated and advanced compared with their peers appear to use private speech earlier and internalize their speech earlier (have it replaced with whispers and inner speech) than children from different environments.

The implications for teachers and parents of the research on private speech are relatively clear. Researchers typically recommend that teachers allow, if not encourage, children to use private speech in the classroom, as long as it is not too loud and disruptive to other children, because it is a natural and effective learning tool for youngsters and because quieting down children who find it useful to spontaneously talk out loud to themselves during their work typically hurts their performance. Teachers and parents can also learn a lot about what children are thinking and feeling and about what strategies they are using to solve academic problems by listening carefully to children's private speech. In that sense, children's private speech can be used as an assessment tool by teachers for learning what is going on in the child's head. Also, parents can increase children's use of private speech by working together with their children on appropriately challenging problem-solving tasks, by encouraging the child to speak while the two work together on the task, and by allowing the child the autonomy to do as much of the task as possible by himself or herself.

Children with problems of behavioral self-control, such as those with behavior problems and those diagnosed with attention deficit hyperactivity disorder (ADHD), also use private speech as a tool for self-regulation; however, such children appear to be delayed in their internalization of such speech. That is, they continue to use overt self-talk while other nonproblem children of the same age talk less to themselves or have moved on to quieter, partially internalized forms of speech (whispers or inaudible mutterings) or silent inner speech. There are a variety of intervention programs for such children that attempt to make their private speech more effective in guiding behavior.

Children's private speech appears to internalize (go away and become inner verbal thought) by itself over time as part of a natural process after the child has had sufficient experience successfully talking himself or herself through problems. Thus, although counterintuitive for parents and teachers, who may want children to stop talking to themselves, the way to eventually get them to be quieter and to think to themselves inside their head is actually to foster and encourage children's use of overt self-talk. After sufficient experience doing so, the speech will go underground by itself. Telling children to stop talking does not work and tends to disrupt their performance.

Although this discussion has mostly centered on children's self-talk with behavioral and cognitive self-regulatory functions while youngsters are engaged in various cognitive problem-solving activities, there are other types of private speech that may serve different functions. Some toddlers, for example, talk to themselves at length in their cribs either before going to sleep or after waking. This type of private speech, called *crib speech*, appears to serve several important functions for children as well, such as practice in pronunciation of new words and utterances that the child is currently in the process of mastering and consolidation of memories and processing of emotions from the day's events. Also considered private speech, but of a different type, are all of the utterances young children make (i.e., noises, sound effects, and dialogue) during their solitary fantasy pretend play, with dolls and figurines, for example. These forms of self-talk, however, have not been studied in as much detail.

—*Adam Winsler*

See also Language Development; Scaffolding; Vygotsky, Lev

Further Readings and References

Berk, L. E. (1994). Why children talk to themselves. *Scientific American, 271*(5), 78–83. Retrieved from http://www.abacon.com/berk/ica/research.html

Berk, L. E., & Winsler, A. (1995). *Scaffolding children's learning: Vygotsky and early childhood education*. Washington, DC: National Association for the Education of Young Children.

Diaz, R. M., & Berk, L. E. (Eds.). (1992). *Private speech: From social interaction to self-regulation*. Hillsdale, NJ: Erlbaum.

Landsberger, J. (2004). *Thinking aloud: Private speech*. Retrieved from http://www.studygs.net/thinkingaloud.htm

Nelson, K. (Ed.). (1989). *Narratives from the crib*. Cambridge, MA: Harvard University Press.

Winsler, A., De León, J. R., Wallace, B., Carlton, M. P, & Willson-Quayle, A. (2003). Private speech in preschool children: Developmental stability and change, across-task consistency, and relations with classroom behavior. *Journal of Child Language, 30*, 583–608.

PROBLEM SOLVING

Problem solving occurs when actions are taken to progress from a present situation to a more desired, goal situation, while overcoming any barriers to the goal. The seven stages of problem solving are presented sequentially here; however, the stages compose a flexible problem-solving cycle, and individuals may skip over, repeat, or rearrange stages of the cycle and still problem-solve effectively.

The initial problem-solving stage is problem recognition or identification. This stage includes identifying a goal, goal-path obstacles, and solution errors. Problems can be classified as presented, which are most easily identifiable; as discovered; or as created, which are the most difficult to identify.

The second stage is defining and mentally representing the problem. This stage requires a clear statement of the problem scope and goals. Also, information regarding the current state, goal state, relevant operators, and any restrictions must be cognitively organized for efficient retrieval and application.

The third stage involves forming a strategy for solving the problem. Strategies may entail breaking down the problem into elements (analysis) or rearranging and combining elements (synthesis). It is helpful to brainstorm a variety of possible strategies (divergent thinking) and then to decide on one promising strategy (convergent thinking).

Fourth, the problem solver must gather and reorganize new and old problem-related information. In contrast to the second stage, this fourth stage requires collecting and organizing information in a way that will best support implementation of the specific strategy that was identified in the third stage.

Individuals allocate various resources for problem solving in the fifth stage. Such resources include time, effort, attention, assistance, money, and materials. Mental resources are more effectively spent on initial, global planning rather than on details and strategy implementation.

In the sixth stage, problem solvers monitor their progress toward their goal. Such reflection must occur along the route toward a solution rather than only after the strategy has been entirely implemented so that modifications can be made before resources are spent unnecessarily.

Finally, individuals evaluate the results of their problem solving in terms of their goal state once they are finished. Evaluation immediately following completion, after a delay, or after a great deal of time can confirm or invalidate strategy effectiveness. Additionally, such reflection can provide new insights regarding the situation and all aspects of the problem-solving cycle.

Each problem-solving stage is affected by the definition and structure of a problem. Well-defined problems have easily identifiable solution paths, often involving algorithms or heuristics, but those paths may still be difficult to follow. An ill-defined problem, in contrast, may require insight to identify, define, represent, and formulate a strategy for the problem.

Problem solving can also be affected by development. As proposed by Jean Piaget and later supported empirically, problem solving (strategic behavior and means–end action sequencing) is possible at 8 months of age. With development and knowledge gain, goal-directed behavior on complicated tasks increase, and by 24 to 36 months, children can monitor their performance, make corrections, complete tasks successfully more often, and respond emotionally to success or failure.

Additionally, development affects strategy use, but not in discrete stages as was previously thought. According to the adaptive strategy choice model developed by Robert Siegler, individuals use a variety of strategies on a single problem—sometimes more than one at a time. Strategies are selected depending on the nature of the task, the goals of the individual, and the past effectiveness of a strategy. Additionally, the frequency of use of a single strategy changes over time. Initially, an individual prefers simple strategies, but with practice and maturation, individuals prefer more efficient strategies even if the more efficient strategies require more effort.

—*Anne S. Beauchamp*

See also Cognitive Development, Learning

Further Readings and References

Bjorklund, D. F. (2000). *Children's thinking: Developmental function and individual differences* (3rd ed.). Belmont, CA: Wadsworth.

Davidson, J. E., & Sternberg, R. J. (Eds.). (2003). *The psychology of problem solving.* Cambridge, UK: Cambridge University Press.

Sternberg, R. J. (1999). *Cognitive psychology* (2nd ed.). Fort Worth, TX: Harcourt Brace.

PROSOCIAL BEHAVIOR

Prosocial behaviors are actions children engage in for the good of another person and with no expectation of personal reward. Examples of prosocial behavior include sharing, helping, cooperation, and altruism. The emergence of prosocial behavior depends on cognitive and emotional developments in early childhood, and therefore, truly prosocial behaviors are not observable until the toddler years. Cognitively, children must have an appreciation of others' perspectives or an understanding that other people can think and feel differently than themselves. Emotionally, children must learn to recognize others' emotions and experience complex emotions related to others, including sympathy and empathy. With these cognitive and emotional skills in place, children acquire prosocial behaviors most readily through modeling the behaviors of influential people in their lives, such as siblings, peers, and parents. Over time, prosocial motivations are gradually internalized, so that by the preschool years, children react prosocially in the absence of parents or teachers. Factors influencing the typical development of prosocial behavior and factors that relate to individual differences in the likelihood of displaying prosocial behaviors, including gender, temperament, and developmental disorders, particularly autism, are discussed in more detail below.

COGNITIVE DEVELOPMENT AND PERSPECTIVE TAKING

One precursor to the development of prosocial behavior is perspective taking, the ability to imagine what another person is thinking or feeling. One way that infants learn about another's perspective is through joint attention. Infants initiate joint attention by pointing at an object or looking at their caregiver in order to share an experience, and also respond to their caregiver's initiation of joint attention by looking at and interpreting the caregiver's facial expressions to learn about what he or she is feeling. Infants use these experiences to gain perspective on others' thoughts and feelings. When measured at 12 months of age, an infant's ability to initiate the sharing of experience predicts the development of prosocial behaviors, such as compliance, empathy, and prosocial peer interactions at 30 months of age. Hence, it appears that the groundwork for prosocial behavior begins to be laid in infancy when coordination and sharing of attention with others allows infants to learn about the differences between theirs and others' perspectives. By early childhood, children who are better able to understand others' psychological states are more popular with their peers. Perspective taking plays such a central role in the development of prosocial behavior that attempts to increase perspective taking are often the primary focus in the treatment of antisocial behavior in children and adolescents. Interventions that serve to foster perspective taking through coaching and practice have been shown to increase empathy and prosocial responding in at-risk children.

EMOTIONAL DEVELOPMENT AND EMPATHY AND SYMPATHY

Once children are able to take the perspective of others, they begin to experience complex emotions, including empathy and sympathy. *Sympathy* describes feelings of concern or sorrow for another person. For example, a young child feels sympathy for a friend who is crying because she lost her dog. *Empathy* goes beyond just feeling concern for another to include engaging or feeling with another person and responding in an emotionally similar way. For example, a young child feels empathic when she becomes tearful upon seeing her mother crying over the death of a friend. Often, empathy and sympathy serve as primary motivators for prosocial behavior. That is, when they experience empathy or sympathy, children are motivated to speak or act in a way that will help relieve the other person.

LEARNING THROUGH OBSERVATION

According to social learning theory, prosocial behaviors are most readily learned through exposure to appropriate models. Several studies based in the social learning tradition have demonstrated that young children observe and then imitate the prosocial behaviors of influential people in their environments. For example, children who watched an adult play a bowling game and then choose to donate the winnings to a children's charity fund were much more likely to donate their own winnings when playing the same game than were children who had not previously watched the adult do likewise. That is, children modeled the generosity and sharing behavior of the adult when making decisions about their own behaviors. The extent to which models are effective in eliciting prosocial behaviors depends on characteristics of the children watching as well as the models themselves. Specifically, preschool-age children are particularly influenced by models. In addition, the most influential models are those adults who are (1) warm and responsive in their interactions with children, (2) viewed as competent and powerful, and (3) consistent in what they say a child should do and what they do themselves.

FACTORS INFLUENCING INDIVIDUAL DIFFERENCES IN THE EXPRESSION OF PROSOCIAL BEHAVIOR

Temperament

Temperament describes individual differences in children's emotional reactions and their ability to manage or regulate these reactions (Rothbart & Bates, 1998). For many children, feelings of empathy for others provide the impetus for sharing, helping, or other behaviors that function to aid another person. But for other children, watching others experience some kind of distress makes them feel so empathic that they are overwhelmed by their own emotions to a point that they are unable to help others. Eisenberg and colleagues have suggested that a child's temperament will determine whether the child is able to translate feelings of empathy into prosocial actions. Specifically, sociable, assertive children who are good at regulating their emotions are more likely to respond prosocially to others' needs, whereas children who have difficulty regulating their emotions experience personal distress and therefore are unable to help when exposed to another's negative emotion.

Gender

Across all stages of development, girls are more likely than boys to display prosocial behavior, particularly expressions of kindness and consideration. This may be due in part to girls' greater susceptibility to experiencing feelings of empathy and sympathy, which in turn predicts more prosocial acts. In addition to seeing gender differences in the frequency of prosocial behavior, there are also differences in the types of prosocial behaviors in which girls and boys engage. Specifically, by middle childhood, girls express prosocial behavior through expressions of sympathy, feelings of responsibility for their own actions and the welfare of others, and psychological perspective taking. In contrast, boys display prosocial behaviors through instrumental acts of helping. As is the case with gender differences in many aspects of social behavior, it remains unknown whether these robust differences are a product of biology and inherited differences or a function of gender differences in societal expectations and socialization experiences. It is most likely a combination of both.

Maladaptive Parenting

Given the salience and importance of modeling in the acquisition of prosocial behavior, it is not surprising that unhealthy or maladaptive parenting practices are associated with deficits in children's prosocial responding. For example, preschoolers who have been physically abused are more likely to respond to others' unhappiness with fear, anger, or physical attacks rather than prosocial acts. This is likely because this is how they have observed their own parents respond and because these children have had inadequate opportunities to learn how to regulate their own emotions in adaptive ways.

Developmental Disorders—Autism

Children with autism display clear deficits in prosocial behavior that are evident beginning in infancy when they are largely unaware of other people's points of view. Although typically developing infants between 12 and 18 months look to their caregiver's face in order to share information about how they are feeling about an object or event, children with autism do not. Because of this tendency, autistic children have far fewer experiences from which to learn about the feelings and emotions of others. As such, young children with autism show deficits in behaviors that require an understanding of others,

such as perspective taking, emotion recognition and comprehension, and empathic responding, behaviors that are all necessary for appropriate prosocial behavior. One of the hallmark characteristics of young autistic children is a lack of responsiveness to the needs of those around them. For example, a typically developing toddler, having learned to recognize emotions and having witnessed reactions to such emotions, will offer comfort to his or her caregivers if they are hurt or ill. A child with autism, however, will not show the same awareness of another's feelings and will not offer appropriate comfort. Interestingly, among autistic children, there are gender differences in prosocial behaviors, such that girls with autism are more likely than boys to display prosocial behavior in situations of distress. This suggests that, as with typically developing children, there are a wide range of prosocial abilities within the autistic population.

—*Heather A. Henderson and Caley B. Schwartz*

See also Social Development

Further Readings and References

Bacon, A. L., Fein, D., Morris, R., Waterhouse, L., & Allen, D. (1998). The response of autistic children to the distress of others. *Journal of Autism and Developmental Disabilities, 28,* 129–142

Bandura, A. (1967). The role of modeling processes in personality development. In W. W. Hartup & W. L. Smothergill (Eds.), *The young child: Reviews of research.* Washington, DC: National Association for the Education of Young Children.

Bandura, A. (1977). *Social learning theory.* Englewood Cliffs, NJ: Prentice-Hall.

Baron-Cohen, S. (1995). *Mindblindness: An essay on autism and theory of mind.* Cambridge, MA: MIT Press.

Carlo, G., Knight, G., Eisenberg, N., & Rotenberg, K. (1991). Cognitive processes and prosocial behaviors among children: The role of affective attributions and reasoning. *Developmental Psychology, 27,* 456–461.

Cassidy, K. W., Werner, R. S., Rourke, M., Zubernis, L. S., & Balaraman, G. (2003). The relationship between psychological understanding and positive social behaviors. *Social Development, 12,* 198–221.

Chalmers, J. B., & Townsend, M. A. R. (1990). The effects of training in social perspective taking on socially maladjusted girls. *Child Development, 61,* 178–190.

Corkum, V., & Moore, C. (1995). The development of joint attention. In C. Moore & P. Dunham (Eds.), *Joint attention: Its origins and role in development* (pp. 61–84). Hillsdale, NJ: Erlbaum.

Eagley, A. H., & Crowley, M. (1986). Gender and helping behavior: A meta-analytic review of the social psychological literature. *Psychological Bulletin, 100*, 283–308.

Eisenberg, N. (2003). Prosocial behavior, empathy, and sympathy. In M. H. Bornstein, L. Davidson, C. L. M. Keyes, & K. A. Moore (Eds.), *Well-being: Positive development across the lifecourse* (pp. 253–263). Mahwah, NJ: Erlbaum.

Eisenberg, N., & Fabes, R. A. (1998). Prosocial development. In N. Eisenberg (Ed.), & W. Damon (Series Ed.), *Handbook of child psychology: Vol. 3: Social, emotional, and personality development* (5th ed., pp. 701–778). New York: Wiley.

Eisenberg, N., Fabes, R., Murphy, B., Karbon, M., Smith, M., & Masck, P. (1996). The relations of children's dispositional empathy-related responding to their emotionality, regulation, and social functioning. *Developmental Psychology, 32*, 195–209.

Eisenberg, N., Fabes, R. A., Shepard, S. A., Murphy, B. C., Jones, S., & Guthrie, I. K. (1998). Contemporaneous and longitudinal prediction of children's sympathy from dispositional regulation and emotionality. *Developmental Psychology, 34*, 910–924.

Klimes-Dougan, B., & Kistner, J. (1990). Physically abused preschoolers' responses to peers' distress. *Developmental Psychology, 26*, 599–602.

Kochanska, G., & Murray, K. (2000). Mother-child mutually responsive orientation and conscience development: From toddler to early school age. *Child Development, 71*, 417–431.

Koestner, R., Franz, C., & Weinberger, J. (1990). The family origins of empathic concern: A 26-year longitudinal study. *Journal of Personality and Social Psychology, 58*, 709–717.

Mundy, P., & Gomes, A. (1998). Individual differences in joint attention skill development in the second year. *Infant Behavior and Development, 21*, 469–482.

Mussen, P., & Eisenberg-Berg, N. (1977). *Roots of caring, sharing, and helping.* San Francisco: Freeman.

Pickens, J., Field, T., & Nawrocki, T. (2001). Frontal EEG asymmetry in response to emotional vignettes in preschool age children. *International Journal of Behavioral Development, 25*, 105–112.

Rothbart, M. K., & Bates, J. E. (1998). Temperament. In N. Eisenberg (Ed.) & W. Damon (Series Ed.), *Handbook of child psychology: Vol. 3: Social, emotional, and personality development* (5th ed., pp. 105–176). New York: Wiley.

Rushton, J. P. (1975). Generosity in children: Immediate and long term effects of modeling, preaching, and moral judgment. *Journal of Personality and Social Psychology, 31*, 459–466.

Vaughan, A. (2004). *Contributions of temperament and joint attention to social competence, externalizing, and internalizing behavior in normally developing children.* Unpublished doctoral dissertation, University of Miami, Florida.

Yarrow, M. R., Scott, P. M., & Waxler, C. Z. (1973). Learning concern for others. *Developmental Psychology, 8*, 240–260.

PROSTATE CANCER

Prostate cancer is a malignant tumor that forms in the tissue of the prostate gland, a walnut-shaped gland that produces the semen that transports sperm and is necessary for male reproduction. The prostate gland is located between the bladder and the penis, and the urethra travels through the prostate.

INCIDENCE AND OCCURRENCE

Prostate cancer is the most often diagnosed form of cancer in men in the United States other than skin cancer, with 220,900 new cases of prostate cancer diagnosed in 2003 and 28,900 deaths from this type of cancer occurring annually, only second to lung cancer as a cause for cancer-related deaths in men. Some of the facts about prostate cancer from the Centers on Disease Control and Prevention are as follows:

- About 70% of all diagnosed prostate cancers are found in men aged 65 years or older.
- During the past 20 years, the survival rate for prostate cancer has increased from 67% to 97%.
- The prostate cancer death rate is higher for African American men than for any other racial or ethnic group.
- Compared with other racial and ethnic groups, the Asian/Pacific Islander group has relatively low rates of prostate cancer incidence and mortality.
- Among all racial and ethnic groups, prostate cancer death rates were lower in 1999 than they were in 1990.
- Decreases in prostate cancer death rates during 1990 to 1999 were almost twice as great for whites and Asian/Pacific Islanders as for African Americans, American Indian/Alaska Natives, and Hispanics.

DIAGNOSIS

Prostate cancer can be diagnosed in a variety of ways. First, with a digital rectal examination (DRE), the physician can feel the prostate gland for any abnormalities, including texture and growths. Second, a prostate-specific antigen (PSA) blood test can reveal the presence of a cancer-related antigen in the blood, often an indication of abnormality. This test is recommended for all men older than 50 years, and unusually high or consistent levels of this antigen (above 4) can be a cause for concern, as can a rapid increase in this value from test to test. Although there is good evidence that PSA screening can detect early cancers, it is unclear whether such detection through the PSA test results in better health outcomes. If there is reason to believe that the patient may have prostate cancer, a needle biopsy can be performed, in which very small bits of tissue are taken from both sides of the prostate with a special device that is inserted through the rectum and guided using sonography. Although this is an uncomfortable procedure, it can be done in the doctor's office on an outpatient basis.

TREATMENT

Currently, most men can be cured of prostate cancer if the cancer is detected in its earliest clinical stages. The gold standard for treatment of localized disease (which means the cancer has not spread beyond the prostate gland) is the radical prostatectomy, in which the prostate gland is removed through surgery. This is a major surgical procedure that can involve a somewhat lengthy period of recovery. Possible complications include impotence and incontinence, which vary in their degrees of severity, although various therapies and drugs can successfully treat these side effects in more than 90% of the men who are affected. Other treatments for localized prostate cancer include internal and external radiation and freezing of the cancerous cells, all of which can have side effects as well. Because so many men develop prostate cancer (but do not die from it), some physicians suggest "waiting and watching" and paying close attention to PSA levels and biopsy results until more aggressive treatment is indicated.

If the cancer has spread beyond the prostate, hormonal therapy and alternative treatments ranging from acupuncture to nutritional supplements are available; these are all undergoing clinical trials.

—*Neil J. Salkind*

See also Cancer

Further Readings and References

CDC Cancer Publications Center, http://www.cdc.gov/cancer/publica.htm

Centers for Disease Control and Prevention. (n.d.). *Prostate cancer screening: A decision guide.* Retrieved from http://www.cdc.gov/cancer/prostate/decisionguide/

Prostate Cancer Foundation, http://www.prostatecancerfoundation.org/

Walsh, P. C., & Worthington, J. F. (2001). *Dr. Patrick Walsh's guide to surviving prostate cancer.* New York: Warner Books.

PSYCHOANALYTIC THEORY

Psychoanalytic theorists have emphasized various aspects of development across the human life span since Freud's introduction of the genetic principle—the persistence of the past into the present—over a century ago. Although psychoanalytic developmental theory now encompasses a number of different and sometimes mutually incompatible frameworks, this entry, owing to limitations of space, will briefly review three of the most influential among them. These are Freud's theory of libidinal development, Mahler's separation-individuation theory, and Kohut's "selfobject" theory.

CLASSICAL PSYCHOANALYSIS: LIBIDINAL DRIVE AND THE OEDIPUS COMPLEX

In classical psychoanalysis, the body of thought intimately associated with the theories of Sigmund Freud, human sexuality is understood to have its origins in early childhood. This idea, once considered controversial, asserts that continuity exists between the sexual wishes of childhood and the sexual behavior of adults, and furthermore, that adult sexuality cannot be fully understood without an appreciation of its roots in childhood sexual desires. Sexual desire in childhood, however, is qualitatively distinctive from that in adulthood and is composed of various sensual pleasures experienced in association with sensitive parts of the body, such as the skin, the mouth, the anus, and the genitals. Freud believed that these bodily organs, which he termed the *erogenous zones*, were *cathected* or charged with *libido* or sexual drive energy according to a specific developmental sequence.

The earliest stage of libidinal development, which Freud termed the *oral stage,* begins at birth and continues through the middle of the second year of development. Some psychoanalysts believe that there are two subphases within the oral stage, the first of which involves sucking and the second, oral-sadism (biting and devouring), but there is general recognition of the preeminence of oral needs, perceptions, and an oral mode of expression focused on the mouth, lips, tongue, and oral mucosa during this earliest developmental epoch. The next stage, termed the *anal stage* (about 1–3 years), commences with the neuromuscular maturation of the anal sphincter. Such maturation is regarded as significant inasmuch as it furnishes the infant with appreciably greater voluntary control over the expulsion or retention of fecal products. Freud believed that there was a pleasure associated with the exercise of anal functions, which he termed *anal eroticism*. The anal stage is superseded by the *phallic stage* of development (about 3–5 or 6 years), at which time erotic pleasure becomes firmly linked for the first time to stimulation of the penis or vagina. The phallic stage is followed by a period of libidinal quiescence, referred to as *latency* (about 5–11 years), at which time there is relative inactivity of the libidinal drive, a situation that permits a fuller resolution of oedipal or triangular conflicts. The final stage of the libido is the *genital stage*, which commences with the onset of puberty and extends to young adulthood. Characterized by continuing maturation of the genital-sexual functioning, it is also associated with hormonal and other bodily changes.

Oedipus Complex

The Oedipus complex has a pivotal significance in the classical psychoanalytic literature. It is understood as a configuration of psychological forces characterized by the concentration of sexual wishes directed at one parent, usually of the opposite sex, and the concurrent emergence of hostile feelings toward the remaining parent, the child's rival in love. The Oedipus complex actually consists of both positive oedipal and negative oedipal strivings. The "positive" Oedipus complex is associated with the wish for a sexual union with the parent of the opposite sex and a coterminous wish for the same-sex parent's demise. However, because such wishes give rise both to ambivalence and vulnerability, "negative" oedipal strivings—consisting of the desire for a sexual union with the same-sex parent and feelings of rivalry with the opposite-sex parent—coexist with the positive ones. According to classical theory, the positive Oedipus complex supersedes the negative Oedipus complex, and this is considered a prerequisite for the emergence of a heterosexual orientation and cohesive identity in adulthood.

MAHLER'S SEPARATION-INDIVIDUATION THEORY

Margaret Mahler's theory of the separation-individuation process, later criticisms notwithstanding,

introduced a schema that transformed not only the study of infant and early childhood development, but also that of adolescence; in addition, it has, arguably, left an indelible stamp on contemporary psychoanalytic ideas concerning character pathology. On the basis of pioneering longitudinal investigations of maternal-infant pairs in a nursery setting, Mahler portrayed a process that begins at birth and continues into the child's fourth year. Characterizing infants as essentially nonrelated or objectless at birth (the autistic phase), she described their gradual emergence through a period of maternal-infant symbiosis into four relatively discrete stages of separation and individuation: *differentiation* (5–9 months), *practicing* (9–15 months), *rapprochement* (15–24 months), and the *development of object constancy* (24–36 months and beyond).

During *differentiation*, which supersedes what Mahler had termed the *normal symbiotic phase*, infants attain a heightened level of alertness while awake and begin to explore beyond the confines of the symbiotic orbit with mother, a phenomenon Mahler also referred to as "hatching." *Practicing*, according to Mahler, actually consists of two periods, early practicing and the practicing subphase proper. Early practicing commences with the infant's newly emerging locomotor capacity to move away physically from mother, who is, nevertheless, treated as a sort of "home base" as periodic needs for "emotional refueling" interrupt the infant's exploratory activity. The practicing period proper, the specific developmental location of the infant's psychological "birth" in Mahler's view, is ushered in by the child's capacity for upright locomotion. This monumental achievement, which contributes so meaningfully to the child's sense of psychological separateness, leads to a sustained sense of exhilaration, newfound pleasure in the child's own body, and a radical alteration in the object relationship with the mother, whose importance is at times almost overshadowed by the child's excitement at being able to escape from the earlier maternal-child symbiosis. However, the emerging experience of physical separateness and psychological individuation also reinforces children's awareness of their small stature, physical dependence on caretakers, and sense of vulnerability. Mother's separateness, it seems, also carries with it the inevitability that she may not always be available at times of need, a dawning recognition that leads to the phase of *rapprochement*. As such experiences accrue, they lead to moments of deep anxiety that Mahler has referred to as the *rapprochement crisis*, typically located between 18 and 20 to 24 months. At such times, the child's wishes and desires for separation, autonomy, and omnipotence are moderated by increasing awareness of the need for continued dependence on the mother, a situation that gives rise to a forerunner of the adult experience of ambivalence. In the final phase of separation-individuation, some resolution of the intense conflicts of the rapprochement phase is achieved through the child's consolidation of self-identity and attainment of *libidinal object constancy*. Object constancy, Mahler believed, is possible only when the maternal image becomes intrapsychically available to the child much in the same way the actual mother had been libidinally available—for sustenance, comfort, and love.

KOHUT'S "SELFOBJECT" THEORY

Selfobject theory is derived from a newer psychoanalytic framework, the *psychology of the self*, which is based on the contributions of Heinz Kohut. Unlike either Freud's theory of the libido or Mahler's separation-individuation theory, theories characterized as conflict-based, Kohut's is a *deficit-based* theory focused far more on the availability of certain kinds of psychological supplies thought to be necessary for the evolution of a vital and harmonious self. Kohut and his followers believed that such developmental supplies are made available through three major kinds of relational configurations, termed *selfobject relationships*, so named because they refer to a particular kind of relationship in which the object is actually experienced as an extension of the self, without psychological differentiation. The three selfobject experiences are *mirroring*, *idealizing*, and *partnering*. Each corresponds to a particular domain of self-experience: Mirroring experiences are associated with an intrapsychic structure known as the *archaic-grandiose self*, reflecting the need for approval, interest, and affirmation; idealizing experiences, with the *idealized parent imago*, reflecting the developmental need for closeness and support from an (idealized) other; and partnering experiences, with the *alter ego*, reflecting the need for contact with others who are felt to bear an essential likeness to the self. Collectively, these three domains are called the *tripolar self*.

Kohut, whose theoretical contributions and clinical innovations are far ranging, also placed considerable emphasis on the role of empathy in human development.

He believed that children's capacity to feel themselves into the experience of another, also termed *vicarious introspection*, was only likely to develop in an environment in which the selfobjects are empathically resonant. At the same time, a critical impetus for healthy development of the self involves minor, relatively nontraumatic lapses in parental empathy. Such lapses, when they are *optimally* frustrating, motivate children to "take in" specific functions associated with the selfobjects (ranging from self-calming and self-soothing to pride in one's accomplishments) and shape them to suit their own unique needs. Referred to as "transmuting internalization," this critical intrapsychic developmental process makes possible a gradual, bit-by-bit translocation through which various selfobject functions become enduring parts of the child's own self-structure. The key elements of this sequence are, in order, *optimal frustration, increased tension, selfobject response, reduced tension, memory trace,* and *development of internal regulating structure*. Kohut, like Freud and Mahler, believed that the most critical developmental experiences occur in infancy and early childhood. However, he also maintained that even when healthy consolidation of self structures has culminated in a harmoniously functioning, "cohesive" self, the need for relational or external selfobject "supplies" is never fully extinguished and regularly re-emerges throughout the human life cycle.

—Jerrold R. Brandell

See also Conscience; Ego; Freud, Sigmund; Id; Superego

Further Readings and References

Brandell, J., & Perlman, F. (1997). Psychoanalytic theory. In J. Brandell (Ed.), *Theory and practice in clinical social work* (pp. 38–80). New York: Free Press.

Greenberg, J., & Mitchell, S. (1983). *Object relations in psychoanalytic theory*. Cambridge, MA: Harvard University Press.

Horner, T. (1985). The psychic life of the young infant: Review and critique of the psychoanalytic concepts of symbiosis and infantile omnipotence. *American Journal of Orthopsychiatry, 55,* 324–344.

Kohut, H. (1971). *The analysis of the self.* New York: International Universities Press.

Kohut, H., & Wolf, E. (1978). The disorders of the self and their treatment: An outline. *International Journal of Psychoanalysis, 59,* 413–425.

Leider, R. (1996). The psychology of the self. In E. Nersessian & R. Kopff (Eds.), *Textbook of psychoanalysis* (pp. 127–164). Washington, DC: American Psychiatric Press.

Mahler, M. (1968). *On human symbiosis and the vicissitudes of individuation*. New York: International Universities Press.

Mahler, M., Pine, F., & Bergmann, A. (1975). *The psychological birth of the human infant*. New York: Basic Books.

Meissner, W. (2000). *Freud and psychoanalysis*. Notre Dame, IN: Notre Dame Press.

Moore, B., & Fine, B. (1990). *Psychoanalytic terms and concepts*. New Haven, CT: Yale University Press.

Stern, D. (1985). *The interpersonal world of the infant*. New York: Basic Books.

Theoretical and clinical papers, psychoanalytic links, and other helpful information related to psychoanalytic developmental psychology, http://www.psychematters.com

PSYCHOPATHOLOGY

Psychopathology is often defined as the presence of mental illness or disease, but as a research endeavor, psychopathology can be understood more broadly to refer to the study of abnormal behavior. Defining behavior as abnormal, such that it might be termed a *mental disorder*, is an inherently challenging endeavor. The current edition of the *Diagnostic and Statistical Manual of Mental Disorders, Fourth Edition, Text Revision (DSM-IV-TR)* defines a mental disorder as a psychological dysfunction that produces distress or impairment in functioning in the individual, while acknowledging that the boundaries of a term such as "mental disorder" are unclear. The behaviors constituting a mental disorder are conceptualized as a syndrome or pattern that represents a dysfunction in a behavioral, psychological, or biological aspect of human functioning.

DEFINING ABNORMAL BEHAVIOR

Historically, many approaches have been taken in differentiating abnormal from normal behavior. For example, a statistical definition of abnormal behavior would entail establishing quantifiable cutoffs for the behavior of interest in order to determine that they are statistically deviant from normal, or average. Another approach to defining abnormal behavior might be to label all behavior that deviates from the norms of society as characteristic of mental disorder. A third example may define abnormal behavior as anything that results in distress for an individual. All of these definitions have significant problems when taken in isolation, or when taken as a "gold standard" definition of abnormal behavior. The current definition in the

DSM-IV-TR attempts to address some of these issues by specifying that behavior must be beyond an expected response (such as "normal" distress following the death of a loved one) and must not be behavior that is sanctioned by the individual's culture. Because there is no clear, consistent definition that would apply to the entire range of situations, it is likely that the definition of abnormal behavior will continue to evolve.

APPROACHES TO CLASSIFICATION

Three basic approaches might be used for the classification of psychopathology. A strictly *categorical* approach would divide disorders into mutually exclusive categories. Consistent with a categorical approach, each individual would either fall completely into the category or completely outside of it and would not be allowed to fall into more than one category. A second approach to classification is a *dimensional* approach, which assumes that disorders are better represented by dimensional continua. According to a dimensional approach, individuals can present with varying levels of different types of psychopathology, which may reflect, for example, different severities of the underlying pathology. In addition, unlike a categorical approach, in a dimensional approach individuals can be given a score on all dimensions in the system. Thus, more information is retained about individuals in a dimensional approach versus a strictly categorical approach.

The *DSM-IV-TR* is the primary classification system for mental disorders and uses a *prototypical* approach to classification. The organization of the *DSM* is loosely based on the medical model, with disorders divided into separate categories. Each category consists of lists of symptoms thought to define the disorder. In the prototypical approach, a certain number of symptoms for each disorder must be present for the individual to be deemed close enough to the "prototype" for diagnosis of a given disorder. In addition, within the *DSM* classification scheme, an individual can fall in more than one category. This phenomenon is referred to as *comorbidity*, so that an individual who meets diagnostic criteria for more than one disorder is said to be comorbid for the two disorders. Some major objections that have been raised about the present classification system are the loss of information about individuals by placing them in present versus absent categories, potentially detrimental social effects such as stigmatization based on the labels that are assigned, dehumanizing effects of boxing people in the given categories, and the susceptibility of such labels to political and social influences.

UNDERSTANDING COMORBIDITY

Some researchers employing a dimensional approach to the classification of psychopathology have suggested that many common mental disorders may be conceptualized as undergirded by two dimensions, labeled *internalizing* and *externalizing*. The use of internalizing and externalizing as primary dimensions of psychopathology has been predominant in research and practice with children and adolescents for some time, but recent research shows that these constructs are also applicable to adult psychopathology. Research on comorbidity suggests that certain groups of disorders are more likely to co-occur in the same adults. Specifically, the *internalizing* dimension in adults encompasses mood, anxiety, and somatic disorders, whereas the *externalizing* dimension encompasses substance use disorders and disorders characterized by antisocial behavior. Other major groups of disorders that are included in the *DSM-IV-TR* include schizophrenia and other psychotic disorders, cognitive disorders such as dementia, eating disorders, and dissociative disorders. Seeing how these disorders fit in with, or extend, the internalizing-externalizing model remains an important direction for future research.

APPROACHES TO STUDYING PSYCHOPATHOLOGY

Major theoretical approaches to studying psychopathology are largely defined based on presumed causal factors of psychopathology. One common way of discussing the etiology of psychopathology is the *diathesis-stress* model. The diathesis-stress model states that the development of psychopathology occurs when an individual has a diathesis, such as a biological predisposition, toward a disorder and also encounters stress, or environmental factors that interact with the diathesis to produce the onset of a disorder. Although the diathesis-stress model is typically regarded as a general model that may help us understand the development of many types of psychopathology, most psychopathology researchers align themselves with a more specific school of thought regarding the etiology of psychopathology in order to frame their research.

The predominant schools of thought regarding the origins of mental disorders are the biological approach, the psychosocial approach, and the sociocultural approach. The biological approach to understanding etiology, or causal factors, of psychopathology has been gaining attention, in part because of the many recent scientific advances in fields such as genetics and neuroscience. Support for the biological approach has come from research suggesting that neurotransmitter and hormonal imbalances are linked to certain mental disorders, that many types of psychopathology show substantial genetic influence, and that abnormalities in brain structure and function influence the development of psychopathology. Research methods such as behavioral genetic techniques, which estimate the genetic and environmental influences on a particular trait or disorder, and neuroimaging techniques such as functional magnetic resonance imaging are common research methods used to investigate the etiology of psychopathology from a biological perspective.

The psychosocial approach encompasses a wide variety of viewpoints, including approaches based on psychodynamic and behavioral theories. The psychodynamic approach extends classic psychoanalytic theory, which suggests that early childhood experiences, especially extreme experiences such as deprivation or trauma, play a significant role in shaping later development of psychopathology. This viewpoint emphasizes unconscious processes, such as various methods of coping (often referred to as *defense mechanisms*) with internal conflict and resulting anxiety. From a behavioral perspective, aspects of a person's environment play a central role in learning behaviors, thus in developing, maintaining, and ultimately treating different types of psychopathology. That is, a behavioral approach to understanding psychopathology would seek to identify aspects of the environment that trigger, cause, or exacerbate various psychopathological symptoms. Finally, a sociocultural approach emphasizes aspects of an individual's society and culture that contribute to the development of psychopathology. Epidemiological, or population-based, research has been particularly informative to a sociocultural perspective by providing information on the prevalence and distribution of disorders over time and across various cultures and societies.

—*Jennifer L. Tackett and Robert F. Krueger*

See also Depression

Further Readings and References

Achenbach, T. M., & McConaughy, S. H. (1998). *Empirically based assessment of child and adolescent psychopathology: Practical applications* (2nd ed.). Thousand Oaks, CA: Sage.

American Psychiatric Association. (2000). *Diagnostic and statistical manual of mental disorders* (4th ed., text rev.). Washington, DC: Author.

Krueger, R. F., Chentsova-Dutton, Y. E., Markon, K. E., Goldberg, D., & Ormel, J. (2003). A cross cultural study of the structure of comorbidity among common psychopathological syndromes in the general health care setting. *Journal of Abnormal Psychology, 112,* 437–447.

National Institute of Mental Health, http://www.nimh.nih.gov/

Zuckerman, M. (1999). *Vulnerability to psychopathology: A biosocial model.* Washington, DC: American Psychological Association.

PSYCHOPHARMACOLOGY

Psychopharmacology is an inclusive term referring to the study of the effects of endogenous or exogenous chemicals on the central nervous system and the resulting neuropsychiatric manifestations. Pharmacologic agents of interest include endogenous neurotransmitters such as norepinephrine and serotonin, therapeutic agents such as antipsychotic and antidepressant drugs, and drugs of abuse such as cocaine and opioids. Some agents of interest have not been developed as therapeutic agents but have been useful to identify receptors or elucidate mechanisms of action. The term psychopharmacology is generally applied to both this molecular approach and to clinical manifestations of drugs and of neurotransmitter imbalance.

Psychiatric effects of drugs have been of interest since pharmacology emerged as a science, and the discipline of psychopharmacology can be said to have matured in the mid-20th century with the advent of antipsychotic agents, of which chlorpromazine is the classic example. It was recognized at that time that all these agents had in common the effect of antagonizing the pharmacologic effects of dopamine, and the theory of "dopaminergic excess" began to be evoked as the principal theory of schizophrenia. At that time, differentiation of receptor subtypes was unknown, as were the relationships of receptor types to specific neural pathways in the brain. The identification of receptor types and subtypes with specific neural pathways, and the behavioral aspects of specific pathways, are still imperfectly understood despite intensive work during the past 50 years.

Concurrent with the emergence of antipsychotic agents, the development of tricyclic antidepressant agents proceeded rapidly, with about a dozen drugs available by 1970. The drugs in this category are either secondary or tertiary amines. These early drugs brought about clinical relief of depression through blockade of the reuptake of principally epinephrine (tertiary amines) or norepinephrine (secondary amines, many of which are metabolites of the tertiary amine drugs). Normally, the neurotransmitters are released from the stimulating neuron in a neural pathway, cross the synapse, and occupy and activate receptors on the postsynaptic cell, after which they leave the receptors in a dynamic process of two-way mass transfer (diffusion) and are reabsorbed by the presynaptic cell. The blockade of such reuptake causes a greater quantity of neurotransmitter to remain in the synapse and reoccupy postsynaptic receptors, the gross effect being a general stimulatory effect of the pathway in question; hence, the intuitive utility of these drugs to reverse the low neural activity thought to accompany or cause clinical depression.

Extensive and increasingly specific research has elaborated on these basic models of schizophrenia and depression by discovering a multitude of receptor subtypes specific to individual neural pathways and identification of these pathways' behavioral and cognitive functions. Many endogenous substances whose principal function is other than neurological have also been found to function as neurotransmitters in the brain; examples include corticotropin and angiotensin II. The proliferation of this information has led to the development of "atypical" antipsychotic and antidepressant agents (i.e., those acting primarily on other than dopaminergic or adrenergic systems); at this writing, the exact mechanism of action of many of these drugs is largely unknown.

Since the 1990s, intense attention has also been directed toward pharmacologic mechanisms in other psychiatric disorders. Study of the neural pathways associated with generalized anxiety has yielded progress in the clinical management of generalized anxiety disorders, posttraumatic stress disorder, and the anxiety associated with depression and other syndromes. For example, identification of the "pleasure centers" or "reward centers" of the brain and their association with the neurotransmitter serotonin have been followed by the development of drugs effective in treating tobacco, alcohol, and opioid addiction.

At a systems level, psychopharmacology includes pharmacokinetics (the study of the absorption, distribution, metabolism, and elimination of neurologically active drugs) and pharmacodynamics (the description of the relationship of drug concentrations in the blood and at receptors to pharmacologic effects). Such studies typically occur first in animals, then in small studies of human subjects in Phase I of the U.S. Food and Drug Administration hierarchy of drug development. Additional information is gained through Phase II and III clinical trials with larger numbers of subjects, where aberrant, infrequent, or unexpected clinical effects may be detected; these include drug-food and drug-drug interactions and the effect of disease states on the pharmacokinetics of drugs. The interaction of drugs with other than the target receptors or neural pathways gives rise to side effects and adverse effects of the drugs. The discipline attempts to determine the scientific basis for such effects, some of which bear no apparent relationship to the drug's supposed mechanism of action. Studies of adverse effects of drugs have revealed much about interindividual variations in the response to drugs and have contributed importantly to knowledge of differences in inheritance patterns of drug-metabolizing enzymes, receptor subtypes, and perhaps differences in underlying disease mechanisms.

Finally, at the clinical level, psychopharmacology as a discipline involves the selection of appropriate therapeutic agents for individual patients. Therapeutic and side-effect responses to drugs are affected not only by inherited differences in metabolic pathways, but also by age, gender, nutritional status, and, perhaps most important, concurrent disease states. The selection of an appropriate therapeutic agent must involve consideration of the effects of comorbid conditions on drug-clearing organs, conditions such as acid-base disturbances that alter drug distribution, the presence of other drugs and their effects on organ systems, and individual variability in the manifestations of the underlying disease. An example of the latter is schizophrenic hallucinations; usually, these are auditory and respond to dopaminergic agents, but visual hallucinations that respond better to serotonergic agents also occur. Finally, patient choices regarding dosage schedules, cost, tolerability of adverse effects, and other personal issues are important because these affect the degree of the patient's compliance with dosing instructions.

Recently, the work of basic scientists, physicians, clinical pharmacologists, and clinical pharmacists has expanded to include more extensive studies in elderly patients, women, and children, groups traditionally underrepresented in the drug development process. This is partly because of the late recognition that clinical depression is common in children and adolescents and that age and gender effects on pharmacology and pharmacokinetics exist for many drugs.

As work progresses, the term psychopharmacology will probably be less specific as subdisciplines emerge from this field.

—Roy Parish

Further Readings and References

American Psychological Association Division of Psychopharmacology and Substance Abuse, http://www.apa.org/divisions/div28/
National Institute on Drug Abuse, http://www.nida.nih.gov/
Society for Neuroscience, http://apu.sfn.org/

PSYCHOSOCIAL DEVELOPMENT

Psychosocial development refers to the interaction of both psychological and social forces over the development of individuals across the life span. It is in the domain of socialization influences. The best known single, unifying theory of these concepts was formulated by Erik H. Erikson (1902–1994). Psychosocial development may also include changes in altruistic, prosocial behavior and self-control.

ERIKSON'S THEORY

Unlike Sigmund Freud, Erikson's theory describes development across the life span. His eight stages cover the psychological tasks that all individuals face from infancy through old age. Erikson's theory addresses issues about how personality develops and how people acquire their identity and role as a member of society. Erikson's emphasis on the psychosocial, rather than the Freudian psychosexual, orientation reminds us that the ego aspect of personality is actively involved in developing skills and attitudes to be a productive, responsible citizen.

Erikson's theory, sometimes referred to as "the stages of man," is based on a belief that individuals form self-images (an identity) from both self-perceptions and others' perceptions. His is one of the few

Table 1   Erik Erikson's Theory of Psychosocial Development

Stage or "Crisis"	Approximate Age Range	Important Event	"Desired" Outcome/Trait	"Negative" Outcome
I. Basic trust v. mistrust	Birth–18 months	Feeding, attachment	Hope	Fear, mistrust of others
II. Autonomy v. shame/doubt	18–36 months	Toilet training	Willpower	Self-doubt
III. Initiative v. guilt	3–6 years	Independence	Purpose	Guilt about thought and actions
IV. Industry v. inferiority	6–12 years	School demands	Competence	Lack of competence
V. Identity v. role confusion	12–20 years	Identity and peer relations	Fidelity	Inability to establish a sense of self
VI. Intimacy v. isolation	20–40 years	Love relations	Love	Fear of intimacy
VII. Generativity v. stagnation	40–65 years	Parenting, mentoring	Care	Self-absorption
VIII. Ego integrity v. despair	65–death	Reflection and acceptance	Wisdom	Regret and doubt

psychological theories to account for a person's place in history; everyone must accept responsibility for their individualized outcome that results from person-environment relationships. His theory is presented as a series of stages, each having a dilemma or crisis to be resolved.

People pass through these stages independent of whether they have achieved a resolution. Unresolved conflicts or difficulties are passed on to later stages, which can make their outcome more challenging.

Erikson's theory has been described as a continuum of crises faced over the course of human development. A new crisis or dilemma emerges as people grow and confront new psychological tasks and responsibilities. These tasks are listed in Table 1 as important events. Crises may be seen as opportunities from which to grow and attain positive outcomes, or as misfortunes that can lead to a failed, negative resolution. From each stage, a desired psychological attribute may be acquired. Table 1 summarizes Erikson's theory.

Most data and research interest have been given to stages I, V and VII. In stage I, *basic trust versus mistrust*, infants, in interactions with their caregivers, learn about the world. They must decide whether there is love and security, leading to a basic trust, or whether their needs are not met and the world is unpredictable, leading to fear and mistrust. This stage corresponds to an entire literature on the importance of attachment as a basic task of infancy. Attachment quality becomes a foundation for all future relationships the person will have over his or her life. The work of Mary Ainsworth is important to note here. She first described the various types of attachment outcomes that emerge as a result of the parent-infant interactions over the first years of life. So-called secure or insecure attachments underlie the concept of trust versus mistrust.

In the second stage, *autonomy versus shame and doubt*, Erikson states that children begin to acquire a sense of independent, self-directed behavior, often evidenced by the "terrible 2s" and use of the word, "no." Children who are overdisciplined or otherwise discouraged to be autonomous will develop shame and doubt about their new abilities.

The third stage, *initiative versus guilt*, is characterized by the toddler's need to learn and acquire self-control against the backdrop of developing many new abilities and skills. Initiative refers to the burgeoning autonomy and independence that leads to exploring all parts of their world. Guilt and unworthiness result when the toddler holds himself back because of overcontrol of his impulses and fantasies.

Stage IV is termed *industry versus inferiority*. This stage is marked by school-age children who are gaining abilities in a wide variety of tasks—projects with which they make things, learn to use tools, and gain a variety of skills. Inferiority and inadequacy result if the child does not master age-appropriate abilities and feels inadequate.

In stage V, *identity versus role confusion*, teens face decisions about their future role in life and who they are. This is a crucial stage in determining overall quality of life and may be associated with great turmoil. The need for appropriate role models and influences, as well as experiences, is obvious. James Marcia has written about four possible identity outcomes—achievement, moratorium, foreclosure, and diffusion. Marcia's work has extended, modernized, and elaborated on Erikson's fifth stage.

According to Marcia, a positive outcome, identity achievement, occurs after the teen has had opportunities to explore options and has committed to a set of values or goals. A teen or young adult who is still experimenting without any commitments is said to be in a moratorium or holding pattern. One who commits to a set of values without challenge or exploration has reached foreclosure. Finally, a person who lacks direction because of lack of exploration and commitment is said to be diffused. Failure to resolve these identity questions can result in a rebellious, disorienting outcome related to acting out and experimenting with risky behavior.

In the sixth stage, *intimacy versus isolation*, Erikson states that the healthy individual needs to share himself and commit to another. At one time, this meant marriage, but a contemporary take would refer to any long-term intimate, committed relationship. Intimacy with another completes a person and adds to who they are. Failure to achieve intimacy leads to loneliness.

In stage VII, *generativity versus stagnation*, the middle-age adult attempts to give back to the next generation what they will need to develop successfully. Marriage and parenthood are the important life events to be managed. Generativity refers to nurturant, supportive behaviors such as child rearing, caring for others, and productive, meaningful work such as community service. The generative adult wishes to create something of lasting value. Generativity refers to caring behaviors to guide the next generation—mentoring, teaching, and parenting. If one does not engage in these behaviors, the result can be self-absorption and an emotionally impoverished existence, which Erikson termed *stagnation*. Stagnation is an empty feeling, referred to as an absence of meaningful accomplishment.

The final stage, *ego integrity versus despair*, is the time when an individual looks back on a complete lifetime and prepares for death. A person with ego integrity attains total self-hood, a sense of a life well lived. Despair results if a person obsesses over all their loss of roles as they age.

As can be seen by this review, Erikson's theory captures the process of socialization over the lifetime. His theory remains influential as a source of insightful descriptions of the course of human development. Other important psychosocial variables also affect personal growth and psychological well-being.

OTHER PSYCHOSOCIAL DEVELOPMENTAL VARIABLES

Altruism or *prosocial behavior* is a key process related to psychosocial development. Altruism and prosocial behavior as used here are synonymous; these terms refer to behaviors that benefit another without an expected reward in return. Both are rooted in empathy, the ability to comprehend another person's emotional status and be able to identify and feel the way that another person feels. Behaviorally, empathy refers to a person responding emotionally in support of the other. (Sympathy, a different characteristic, refers to feelings of concern for another's situation.)

In childhood, prosocial behavior is usually associated with sociable, competent children who are also able to regulate their emotions. Parenting and role models play a key role in the development of prosocial behaviors and attitudes. Parents who are warm and responsive and show sympathy lay the groundwork for appropriate responses in their children. These responses persist into the teen years and beyond.

Self-control refers to an individual's capacity to resist an impulse to engage in socially disapproved or unacceptable behavior. It is an essential characteristic for citizenship, morality, and positive social relations. Self-control first emerges in infancy as seen by compliance behaviors. In early childhood, comparable to Erikson's stage II, children learn to obey adult commands and to comply with authority. Appropriate, warm and responsive parenting will create an environment in which the toddler wants to please the adults. In doing so, the child acquires a positive, eager spirit of cooperation within the development of autonomy and self-directed behavior.

Self-control has been found to be stable throughout childhood and adolescence. Authoritative parenting, coupled with appropriate modeling, tends to produce the best outcome—good frustration tolerance, control of emotions, and low impulsivity. In adulthood, these traits are associated with success across every facet of life—in family and peer relationships, at work and in career achievement, and overall life satisfaction.

—*Joseph D. Sclafani*

See also Erikson, Erik

Further Readings and References

Ainsworth, M. D. S., Blehar, M. C., Waters, E., & Wall, S. (1978). *Patterns of attachment.* Hillsdale, NJ: Erlbaum.

Erikson, E. H. (R. Coles, Ed.). (2000). *The Erik Erikson reader.* New York: Norton.

Giesbrecht, N. (1998). Gender patterns of psychosocial development. *Sex Roles: A Journal of Research.* Retrieved from http://www.findarticles.com/cf_dls/m2294/n5-6_v39/212 27883/p1/article.jhtml

Kids Health. (2001). *Teaching your child self-control.* Retrieved from kidshealth.org/parent/emotions/behavior/selfcontrol.html

Marcia, J. E. (1980). Identity in adolescence. In J. Adelson (Ed.), *Handbook of adolescent psychology.* New York: Wiley.

PUBERTY

What signifies the beginning of puberty, a hallmark of the stage of adolescence? For the girl, the first menstruation is often considered the beginning of puberty, but even before it can occur, the sex organs have to develop, and secondary sex characteristics (the nongenital physical features that distinguish men from women) will begin to appear. In the boy, semen, pubic hair, a lower voice, and growth of the penis and testes are often taken as signs of the onset of puberty, but about 1 to 2 years before the outward signs appear, the gonads begin secreting androgen in boys and estrogen in girls. These hormones initiate the striking physical and mental changes of adolescence.

STAGES OF PUBERTY

Puberty can be divided into three stages. In the prepubescent stage, the secondary sex characteristics begin to develop, but the reproductive organs do not yet function. In the pubescent stage, the secondary sex characteristics continue to develop, and the reproductive organs become capable of producing ova and sperm. In the postpubescent stage, the secondary sex characteristics are well developed, and the sex organs are capable of adult functioning. The great majority of American girls have their first menstruation, an event known as menarche, between the ages of 11 and 15. In the United States, the mean age is 12.7 years.

PRIMARY SEX CHARACTERISTICS

The male testes are present at birth, but are only about 10% of their mature size. They grow rapidly during the first 1 or 2 years of puberty, and then grow more slowly, not reaching mature size until the age of 20 or 21. Shortly after the testes begin to develop, the penis starts to grow in length, and the seminal ducts and the prostate gland enlarge. Although the penis is capable of erection by means of contact from birth, only during adolescence does it begin to erect spontaneously or in response to sexually provocative sights, sounds, and thoughts.

The female's uterus, fallopian tubes, and vagina also grow rapidly through puberty. The ovaries grow during puberty, too, and although they begin to function about midway through the period, they do not reach full adult size until the age of 20 or 21. The ovaries produce ova and secrete the hormones needed for pregnancy, menstruation, and the development of the secondary sex characteristics.

Following menarche, menstruation may come at irregular intervals at first. For 6 months to 1 year or more, ovulation may not always occur. Headaches, backaches, and cramps sometimes accompany the early menstrual periods, and the girl may feel tired, depressed, and irritable. As menstruation becomes more regular, these physical and psychological symptoms often diminish or disappear entirely. A good deal of attention has been paid to a reaction called *premenstrual syndrome* (PMS), in which the buildup and concentration of hormones in the woman's body can lead to dramatic changes in personality. There is some evidence that the changes that accompany PMS may be as much a result of changes surrounding the social world of the adolescent female as changes in hormones. For example, peer and other pressures (from parents and from school commitments) may exacerbate, or even be the source of, many of the adolescent mood swings that may be experienced. The biological changes that accompany PMS, along with these other difficulties, make navigating through an ordinarily challenging day even more difficult.

SECONDARY SEX CHARACTERISTICS

The secondary sex characteristics involving breasts, body hair, and voice changes are not directly related to sperm or ovum production. The secondary sex characteristic that first develops in boys is sparse patches of light-colored, straight pubic hair. This hair takes on its characteristically dark, curly appearance after 1 or 2 years. Axillary or underarm and facial hair begins to appear when the pubic hair has almost fully grown. Like pubic hair, this hair at first is light-colored, fine, and sparse. As for facial hair, few boys find that they need to shave before they are 16 or so. Hair also appears on the arms, legs, and shoulders, and later on the chest. Body hair continues to develop for some time, often into adulthood; the amount and density of hair are determined by heredity.

People's skin becomes coarser and thicker during puberty. The sebaceous, or fatty, glands in the skin become active at this time and produce an oily secretion, as individuals suffering from acne know all too well. The sweat *glands* in the armpits begin to function even before the axillary hair appears, and the amount and odor of perspiration increase.

Perhaps the most noticeable change in boys is the deepening of the voice. Usually by the time a boy is 13, his voice has become husky. Only at about age 16 or 17 does it begin to "crack." This may last for 1 or 2 years, until the voice change is complete. The voice change occurs because the male hormones cause the larynx to enlarge and the vocal cords to lengthen. Later in adolescence, the male voice drops an octave or more in pitch, increases in volume, and develops a more even tonal quality.

Girls' secondary sex characteristics generally develop in the same sequence as boys. The first indication of approaching sexual maturity in a girl is change in the shape and size of her hips, which grow wider and rounder. This development is caused in part by enlargement of the pelvic bone and in part by the thickening of the fat that lies under the skin. Both of these changes have their basis in preparation for childbirth. A wider pelvis makes childbirth easier, and additional fat ensures adequate nutrition for the developing baby.

Soon after a girl's hips start to develop, her breasts begin to grow. The first stage of breast development is the bud stage, in which the nipple elevates slightly and the surrounding areola becomes fuller. This occurs at an average age of 10 or 11. Before the menarche, there is an increase in the amount of fat underlying the nipple and the areola, and the breast rises in a conical shape. After menarche, the breasts become larger and rounder with the development of the mammary glands. Girls also experience hair growth in the pubic area, underarms, and legs. The extent of all these changes varies with the individual.

CHANGING GROWTH PATTERNS

Children in widely separated parts of the world seem to be reaching puberty earlier than their parents did, and growing taller and heavier as well. What might be the causes of these trends?

Records show that in America, a young man will, on the average, be 1 inch taller and 10 pounds heavier than his father was. A young woman will probably be almost an inch taller than her mother and 2 pounds heavier and will reach menarche 10 months earlier than her mother did. Today's adolescents are also reaching full adult height earlier than their ancestors. A century ago, boys did not reach full height until age 23 or 24, but now an adolescent boy stops growing by about the age of 18 or 19. At the turn of the century, girls reached full height at the age of 18, whereas the modern girl stops growing at age 16. Evidence of this increase in size can be seen in the clothing and furnishings of past generations. A modern family would find the furniture of a house in colonial Williamsburg far too small. The armor worn by medieval warriors would cramp a modern boy of 12. The first colonists who settled in Jamestown more than 200 years ago were, on the average, less than 5 feet tall.

In addition to growing bigger in height and weight, recent generations also mature earlier than their ancestors did, so that puberty begins at a younger age. This is not a recent phenomenon, nor is it confined to America. Children in China, New Zealand, Italy, and Poland are reaching maturity earlier, and the trend seems to be operating in all populations of these countries. Many studies in recent years have used the menarche as the criterion for tracing this trend.

In Scandinavia, England, and America, the age at menarche has been getting steadily younger at the rate of one-third to one-half year per decade, and the menarche is continuing to arrive earlier. In 1840, Norwegian girls reached menarche at an average age of 17. Since then, the menarche has arrived about 4 months earlier per decade, and today the average Norwegian girl begins to menstruate before her 13th birthday. The female's body is probably programmed in such a way that ova will not be released until the body has enough weight as food to support and nourish an embryo. People nowadays reach that weight (about 106 pounds) earlier in life than they did several decades ago. A set of factors other than nutrition that have been associated with the decreased age at menarche are socioeconomic conditions, number of siblings, race, and especially stress.

With these physical changes has come a correspondingly earlier age of social and intellectual maturity. Sometimes parents do not realize that when they were adolescents, they may have been less mature physically as well as socially than their children are at the same chronological age. Failure to recognize changes in growth patterns (as well as individual variations in development) has led to the *myth of chronological age*. To think about the ages that an adolescent juggles biological, social, emotional, intellectual, and academic concerns makes a mockery of chronological age. To be told that someone is 13 is to be told just about nothing except perhaps grade level in school. In other words, age actually only records the passage of time and tells us nothing about the events that take place within that time period.

Better diet in the 20th century is also a probable cause of earlier maturity. Improvements in agricultural technology have increased crop yields and caloric intake in much of the world. Throughout history, the children of the upper classes have tended to be larger and to reach maturity faster than the children of the lower classes. Upper-class children are growing bigger and maturing sooner these days, too, but children of poorer families have shown a more striking change (perhaps because they have farther to go to reach the norm).

Immunization, a lower incidence of serious childhood diseases, and better general health care (especially during the prenatal period) are all probable factors in promoting growth and maturity among all classes. The recent trend toward smaller families is also associated with the trend in growth patterns. Children in smaller families tend to be larger and better developed than children in large families. The fact that in smaller families there are more food and

medical resources available may contribute to the differences. There is also some speculation that fewer births are easier on the woman and deplete less of what she can biologically give to the child.

Will these trends continue indefinitely? Animal species other than ours seem to have an upper limit on body size, so anthropologists predict that the size of humans, too, will eventually stabilize. Some researchers claim that the trend toward increasingly earlier physical maturity has already ended.

VARYING RATES OF DEVELOPMENT

Within any age group of adolescents, one can observe significant variations in physical maturity and concomitant variations in areas of emotional and intellectual development. One researcher explains that there is no more variable group that we can deal with than adolescents, especially young adolescents. Because of this extreme variability, there can be a 6-year span in biological development between a quickly developing girl and a slowly developing boy, and here I am only talking about biological age.

Early-maturing boys are taller, heavier, and more muscular than their age mates. They tend to excel at sports, achieve popularity, and become leaders in student government and extracurricular activities. Early-maturing boys also tend to be more interested in girls and gain the advantage of acquiring social graces early. In adult life, they are likely to be more successful socially and vocationally and to be more conventional in career and lifestyle choices.

Early-maturing girls are faced with the problem that few other girls and almost no boys are as tall and well developed as they are. Friends may avoid them simply because they are bigger. Early-maturing girls tend to date older boys until their peers catch up with them.

Late-maturing boys are smaller and less well developed than almost everyone in their age group. They may lack interest in dating, and when they do become interested in girls, they often lack social graces or are rebuffed by the prettiest and most popular girls. Late-maturing boys tend to participate in extracurricular activities such as band, the chess club, or the school newspaper, where their lack of physical maturity is not a drawback. In adult life, they tend to be insightful, independent, and less conventionally successful. Little has been written about late-maturing girls, perhaps because they still mature before many of the boys. Late-maturing girls do not face the problems that confront late-maturing boys, but they may be at some social disadvantages if they are less attractive to boys than other girls are.

Although these observations are general, it should be emphasized that rates of growth in various areas of development are not synchronized. For example, a young woman who becomes physically mature more rapidly than her age mates may still be much younger emotionally and socially.

—*Neil J. Salkind*

See also Adolescence

Further Readings and References

Rostosky, S. S. (2005). Adolescent romantic relations and sexual behavior: Theory, research, and practical implications. *Journal of Adolescent Research, 20,* 136–138.

Scharf, M., Shulman, S., & Avigad-Spitz, L. (2005). Sibling relationships in emerging adulthood and in adolescence. *Journal of Adolescent Research. 20,* 64–90.

Sinclair, J., & Milner, D. (2005). On being Jewish: A qualitative study of identity among British Jews in emerging adulthood. *Journal of Adolescent Research, 20,* 91–117.

Society for Research on Adolescence, http://www.s-r-a.org/

PUBLIC POLICY

Social science disciplines concerned with human development have a long, if turbulent, history of interaction with public policy. The origins of current day relations between developmental science and public policy are usually traced back to the reform movements of the late 1800s and early 1900s focused on the urban poor, public health, labor conditions, and juvenile crime. Those seeking social reform explicitly harnessed the evidence provided by those seeking to understand human development for the purpose of improving lives and, thereby, improving society. Their efforts led to the first laws governing child labor, maternal and child health, and compulsory education, as well as to social institutions such as public health and child guidance clinics and the juvenile courts. Since this time, the relationship between the scientific study of human development and public policy has experienced periods of retrenchment initiated by, for example, the emergence of positivist social science during the 1920s, and periods of intensive collaboration

led in by, for example, the "war on poverty" of the 1960s and, more recently, education, juvenile justice, and welfare reform. This tension between social science as an arms-length, objective endeavor and as an explicit tool of social reform remains an abiding dilemma facing the human development and public policy enterprise.

WHAT IS PUBLIC POLICY?

Public policy addresses legal, legislative, and administrative decision making at all levels of government. The range and complexity of the activities this encompasses have confounded efforts to place clear boundaries around the domain of public policy. It can concern a vote in the U.S. Congress or a city council, a court decision, the issuance of regulations guiding implementation of a law, the appointment of an agency director, or an Executive Order. The nature of the human policy issues in question include the familiar domains of health and nutrition, education, labor, social security, and welfare, but also encompass transportation (e.g., seat belt and maximum speed laws), taxation (e.g., child tax credit), agricultural (e.g., use of pesticides), immigration (e.g., family reunification), and defense (e.g., military child care) issues.

Rational models trace the policy process from the transformation of a social problem into a policy issue through to the implementation and evaluation of an enacted policy. In practice, it is difficult to portray the complex dynamics of public policy making. Public policies are not "made" at some discernable place and time, but rather are the product of numerous decisions fashioned incrementally over a prolonged period of time. The process inevitably involves a heterogeneous, largely uncoordinated, and vast number of participants with differing roles, agendas, values, and capacities for influence and thus centers on resolving conflicts of interest. Policies and laws are shaped by a variety of conditions, events, and actors that are intricately, but not logically, interwoven. As a result, rational models must be complemented by portrayals that capture the unpredictability, fragmentation, contentiousness, and multiple influences that bear on the policy process.

SCIENCE-POLICY INTERSECTION

As many have pointed out, this characterization of the policy process contrasts sharply with basic elements of the scientific process. It has been noted, for example, that science seeks truth, legal procedures seek justice, and legislative policy seeks allies. The scientific method attempts to screen out the influence of personal values, whereas the policy process explicitly contends with competing values. Science has led to views of human behavior as multiply determined; policy and legal debates tend to hold individuals responsible for their actions. Rules of evidence also vary dramatically across these differing arenas. Yet, science and policy are both conservative, incremental processes. They attempt to be cumulative insofar as major questions and issues are revisited over time in light of new developments. Policies, like scientific research, are based on hypotheses about human behavior and the actions—interventions, tax incentives, sanctions—that will affect it. Thus, despite a measure of mutual skepticism among those who function in these two realms, there is also substantial common ground.

RATIONALES FOR HUMAN DEVELOPMENT POLICY

Policy involvement in matters of human development derives primarily from two rationales. Police power justifies intervention when public safety is placed at risk. *Parens patriae* (literally, the State as parent) provides the framework for government intervention in the lives of dependent children whose family circumstances place them at risk, as well as for impaired adults. As exemplified by juvenile justice and child welfare (e.g., foster care) policies, these rationales often cast government involvement as a last resort when private (i.e., family) solutions to problems have failed and draw attention away from preventive interventions.

Other rationales, which place a greater emphasis on promoting social goals and avoiding social costs (rather than on preventing harm to individuals), have also been used to argue successfully for policy involvement in human development. A significant legacy of the civil rights movement is a set of policies designed to promote equal opportunity that extend to employment and disability issues. Public education also carries this banner, although the federal role in education remains largely focused on children who are poor or who have disabilities, and thus continues to invoke *parens patraie*. Public health policy emphasizes the avoidance of health and economic costs to the broader society.

Policy for America's aged is somewhat unique in that economic dependency is an inevitable aspect of old age; a condition that occurs through no fault of their own, presumably after a lengthy period of economic contribution. As a result, benefits such as Social Security and Medicare do not carry the ambivalence or stigma that accompany many public benefits for younger populations. Rather, they were established as a right or entitlement, not an act of benevolence; are designed not only to relieve old-age dependency, but to prevent it; and now approach universal coverage.

CONTRIBUTIONS OF RESEARCH

Efforts to identify the salient forces that shape public policy have assigned research a relatively minor, although not inconsequential, role. It competes with (1) contextual factors, including social, economic, demographic, political, and ideological influences, that shape the overall context of policymaking at any given time; (2) constituency pressures exerted by both organized and unorganized individuals and groups; (3) principles and ideas that shape policymakers' visions and policy goals; (4) institutions and institutional actors that establish the infrastructure within which the power to shape policy is defined; and (5) the media and its powerful ability to shape what people think about as well as their opinions about salient issues. All these forces, including research, intersect and interact against the backdrop of existing policy and legal precedent established through prior court decisions, prevailing legal doctrine, and existing legislative frameworks.

The contributions of research, as it enters this mix of influences, have been loosely categorized as (1) knowledge building: contributing to the fundamental understanding of social and behavioral processes, (2) problem-exploring: contributing to the definition of social problems, (3) policy-forming: contributing to the formulation of policies or the resolution of legal questions addressing specific social problems, and (4) program-directing and evaluating: contributing to the design, evaluation, and improvement of established policies and programs.

Across these broad categories of policy-relevant research, efforts to understand how research is used to inform, shape, or support public policy have identified two contrasting models. The first focuses on direct, instrumental applications of research on human development to the resolution of pending legal or policy decision. Submission of amicus briefs and presentation of expert testimony provide clear examples of instrumental applications. The second "enlightenment" model of research utilization emphasizes more subtle, indirect, and circuitous applications by which, for example, generalized evidence from multiple studies (e.g., mental health problems are a deterrent to welfare reform; the reliability of eyewitness testimony is highly situation specific) or concepts derived from research on human development (e.g., successful aging, social capital) shape policymakers' views about issues that warrant their attention and their instincts about how best to address them. Examples of both direct and indirect uses are plentiful, and each can be—and has been—used to promote, delay, or prevent action on a policy issue.

As with virtually all factors that contribute to public policy, research is most likely to play a role when its findings coincide with constituency interests, prevailing values, and other important influences. Case studies of individuals in various policy roles have revealed that the timeliness and relevance of the findings to an active policy debate are prerequisites for use. The perceived quality of the research and its "fit" with the users' prior perceptions and values foster trust in the research and thus enhance its potential for utilization. Its application is then affected by the extent to which the presentation of the research articulates possibilities for action or, at a minimum, studies variables that policymakers can manipulate (e.g., maternal education as distinct from maternal warmth) as well as by its potential to raise new issues for consideration or new perspectives on more long-standing issues.

The circumstances that prevail when research is introduced into the process are also important. Policymakers are more likely to turn to research evidence when confronted with an unfamiliar issue on which they have not formed an opinion (e.g., acquired immunodeficiency syndrome [AIDS] in the 1980s, child witness testimony in the 1980s and 1990s), dealing with a highly contentious policy for which a "sympathetic" empirical finding might tip the balance of opinion or discredit the opponents' arguments (e.g., welfare or health care reform, immigration policy, discrimination law), or seeking to delay action by asserting that research is inconclusive or insufficient to justify policy intervention. These circumstances challenge researchers to maintain credibility in the scientific and policy arenas by advocating the appropriate use of their findings while articulating the limits of their data.

It is now recognized that the relation between science and policy is characterized by interdependence and mutual interests. The exchange brings vital funding for training and research on human development, policies that facilitate empirical inquiry, public relevance, and opportunities for social as well as scientific impact. The ongoing challenge is one of understanding differences between these two enterprises, acknowledging the constraints and opportunities that confront those who operate within them, and constructing an effective working relationship in the service of making a difference in the lives of those we study.

—Deborah A. Phillips, Jennifer Woolard, and Amy Sussman

Further Readings and References

Birkland, T. A. (2001). *An introduction to the policy process: Theories, concepts, and models of public policy making.* Armonk, NY: ME Sharpe.

Bottoms, B. L., Kovera, M. B., & McAuliffe, B. D. (Eds.). (2002). *Children, social science, and the law.* New York: Cambridge University Press.

Erickson, R. J., & Simon, R. J. (1998). *The use of social science data in Supreme Court decisions.* Urbana, IL: University of Chicago Press.

Featherman, D. L., & Vinovskis, M. A. (Eds.). (2001). *Social science and policy-making: A search for relevance in the twentieth century.* Ann Arbor: University of Michigan Press.

Hayes, C. D. (Ed.). (1982). *Making policies for children: A study of the federal process.* Washington, DC: National Academies Press.

Levine, M., & Wallach, L. (2002). *Psychological problems, social issues, and law.* Boston: Allyn & Bacon.

Lorion, R. P., Iscoe, I., DeLeon, P. H., & VandenBos, G. R. (1996). *Psychology and public policy: Balancing public service and professional need.* Washington, DC: American Psychological Association.

Lynn, L. E. (Ed.). (1978). *Knowledge and policy: The uncertain connection: Vol. 5. Study project on social research and development.* Washington, DC: National Academy of Sciences.

Zigler, E. G., & Hall, N. W. (2000). *Child development and social policy: Theory and applications.* Boston: McGraw-Hill.

PUNISHMENT

According to B. F. Skinner's learning theory model, punishment is a procedure involving the arrangement of stimulus conditions, referred to as consequences, for the purpose of reducing or eliminating one or more behaviors being exhibited by some human or nonhuman animal. There are two basic types of punishment: positive and negative. Positive punishment is the application of an unpleasant (undesirable) stimulus contingent on a response for the purpose of decreasing the frequency of that response. Negative punishment is the removal of a pleasant (desirable) stimulus contingent on a response for the purpose of decreasing the frequency of that response. Positive and negative punishing stimuli may be equally effective, depending on the value the organism associates with the stimuli.

Punishing stimuli may be extrinsic (e.g., doing something wrong and being put in "time-out") or intrinsic (e.g., doing something wrong and having internal feelings of remorse) in nature. A punishing stimulus may be defined as natural (e.g., the result of a natural cause-and-effect relationship such as a hand being burned when placed on a hot stove) or contrived (e.g., a child loses his opportunity to play video games because he hit his brother). Natural and contrived punishing stimuli may be equally effective, depending on the value the individual associates with the punishing stimuli.

—*Paul W. Robinson*

See also Reinforcement, Spanking

Further Readings and References

AllPsych Online. (n.d.). *Reinforcement and reinforcement schedules*. Retrieved from http://allpsych.com/psychology 101/reinforcement.html

Learning, http://www.psychology.org/links/Environment_ Behavior_Relationships/Learning/

Reinforcement and punishment, http://www.psychology.uiowa .edu/Faculty/wasserman/Glossary/reinforcement.html

Qualitative Methods

Formal symbolic representation of qualitative entities is doomed to its rightful place of minor significance in a world where flowers and beautiful women abound.

—Albert Einstein

QUALITATIVE METHODS

Qualitative methods include a wide array of scientific methods designed to describe and/or understand patterns related to people's behaviors, thoughts, experiences, or emotions. The goal is often to look for similarities (or differences) within (or across) places (or time).

Qualitative methods are different from experimental methods in that experimental methods artificially control the environment where the research question is studied and then alter one or a few conditions within that controlled environment. The goal of experimental methods is often to predict a small subset of behavior. Another difference is that researchers who ascribe to a *logical positivist* philosophy of science, or believe that there is a truth that can be discovered, often use experimental methods. Researchers who ascribe to a *postpositivist*, *critical*, or *constructivist* philosophy of science, on the other hand, often use qualitative methods. Though these are three different philosophies of science, all theorize multiple truths and hold that there are ways of learning about phenomena of interest other than through artificial manipulation and control. Qualitative methods open up other possibilities for inquiry, allowing different kinds of questions to be addressed.

A similarity between experimental and qualitative methods is that both follow a scientific methodology. With qualitative methods, data are collected through observation, interview procedure, or collecting artifacts. Data are analyzed systematically, and the results are reported. There are several types of qualitative methods, several ways to analyze qualitative data, and several ways to evaluate the methods.

TYPES OF QUALITATIVE METHODS

Some qualitative methods are interviews, observation, action research, and archival research. These methods may have a quantitative (scaled numbers) component to them and thus should not be characterized exclusively as qualitative.

Interviews

Interviews may be done with one person or with a group. *Individual interviews* are used generally when the topic area is private or personal or when the researcher is interested in getting in-depth information. *Focus groups* are often used when the researcher wants to gather a variety of opinions, ideas, or experiences; when group dynamics are of interest; or when the researcher believes the group setting will help participants generate more information.

There are a few options with respect to interview questions. The researcher may choose a *structured format*, where all of the questions are determined beforehand and participants do not help to determine the focus of the interview. With a *semistructured format*, the general areas are determined beforehand but the researcher may ask different questions depending on the direction of the interview. Participants' responses may help determine the direction or focus of the interview. An *unstructured format* means that the researcher has a general idea of areas to be covered, but the questions are not yet determined. With this format, the participants also help determine the focus, scope, and direction of the interview.

Observations

Observations may take the form of "outsider" observations, where the researcher records behavioral observations and does not participate in the events. This method is often referred to as *naturalistic observation*. Examples are a researcher recording college student behavior on the first spring day on the campus quad or studying children's peer interactions behind a one-way mirror at a child care center.

With other observational methods, the researcher participates in at least some aspect of what is studied. This method is typically called *ethnography*. Minimally, the participation takes the form of being in the setting and obviously taking notes. This method is typically considered *conventional ethnography*. For example, Anne Haas Dyson, author and professor of education at University of California, Berkeley, took notes in an elementary classroom and playground for 2 years, recording children's experiences related to literacy, culture, and peer relationships.

Another kind of ethnography is where the researcher participates in setting activities. This method is usually called *participant observation* or *participatory ethnography* (for examples, see books written by William Corsaro, a professor of sociology at Indiana University). An example is a researcher serving as an elementary school teacher while taking notes about those experiences. In either of these cases (i.e., conventional or participatory), the researcher might choose to write from a perspective that highlights what others are doing.

Another option is to write about how the researcher's experiences interact with the events in the setting; this is called *autoethnography*, and requires the researcher to examine his or her own role. For example, one could read books written by Ruth Behar, professor of anthropology at the University of Michigan. To parallel the aforementioned example, an autoethnographic account could be the researcher writing about how his or her own gender, race, and/or social class influenced interactions with students in the elementary school classroom. The goal might be to understand how culture mediates experiences.

Action Research

Action research is a value-based method that is grounded in social justice and designed to facilitate change in the research setting. Action research might or might not be qualitative and might or might not be participatory. In *participatory action research*, the researcher works with participants as collaborators in terms of defining the research question, determining how to study the question, and interpreting the results. An example is school staff and researchers interviewing students about playground behavior and, based on children's input, creating a playground intervention that promotes social justice. Action research, on the other hand, does not include the stakeholders in the design or methodological process of the research, but social justice drives the results and they are given back to the research setting.

Archival Research

Archival research, which encompasses historical research, involves gathering any data that trace the past and seek to understand behavior patterns over time. Archives include written documents such as diaries, clinical notes, and magazines, as well as unwritten physical documents such as examining the wear patterns on playgrounds. An example is looking at school yearbooks to determine if specific groups of students participate in specific types of activities or clubs.

QUALITATIVE DATA ANALYSIS

Just as there are several types of qualitative research, there are also several ways to analyze qualitative research. Some of the more common approaches include content analysis, interpretative phenomenological analysis, narrative analysis, discourse analysis, and grounded theory. The type of analysis done often is informed by the researcher's philosophy of science.

Content Analysis

Content analysis is done typically by identifying recurrent themes in the data (transcripts or field notes) that relate to the research question through a coding process. The research questions or areas are determined before data examination. Some researchers argue that the person who was in the research setting, especially if the research took place over a long period of time, need be the only person involved in analyzing the data because familiarity with the data (including the meaning) will be greater than for an outside person. Some argue that at least two people should code data in order to ensure agreement for conclusions drawn. Still others prefer to use computer software to analyze data. These differences in approach are based in philosophy of science (in terms of how we know things and what kinds of claims can be made).

Interpretive Phenomenological Analysis

Another type of analysis is *interpretive phenomenological*. The goal is usually to describe behavior, places, and the interaction between the two. Here, the researcher starts with everyday experiences and becomes reflective of those experiences. Data are gathered through field notes, transcripts, accounts, archives, etc. In the next step, the researcher attempts to interpret the experience reflected upon. What are the essential aspects of the experience and how are those aspects understood? These meanings and experiences are then linked to broader systems such as culture. In the final step, the researcher describes the findings. With this method, the specific research questions and literature review generally happen after some analysis has been completed so that the data drive the direction of the analysis.

Narrative Analysis

A *narrative analysis* assumes that the data collected are in story format (e.g., a life history, a story about school experience). The story is examined first in its entirety and then divided into smaller substories. Details of the substories are examined, looking for apparent themes or uniqueness among and within substories. Often, links are drawn between the story being told and larger community or dominant narratives. An account is then written, detailing the findings.

Discourse Analysis

A person who is interested in studying conversational patterns or language use might use *discourse analysis*. The first step is to transcribe the text, including all aspects of speech such as words, pauses, stuttering, voice pitch, and emphasis. All parts of speech are viewed as essential to understanding the meaning of the speech act. In the analysis phase, the researcher determines research questions or areas and then identifies instances that are consistent and inconsistent with the researcher's expectations. Patterns or themes are determined, and the analysis is written.

Grounded Theory

With *grounded theory,* the goal is to produce theory from data (rather than test data against a theory). With this analytic approach, data are analyzed and collected simultaneously, so that findings can shape the direction of further data collection. An analysis generally consists of a line-by-line coding of the data, identifying as many themes as possible. The next step is creation of more focused codes based on the line-by-line coding. From there, the researcher creates more general categories. A literature review is then conducted, and the results are written in manuscript form.

EVALUATION OF THE RESEARCH

With respect to judging scientific defensibility, there are several models. With most models, there are three general criteria to be met: believability, applicability, and agreement. *Believability* can be met through long-term engagement in the research setting, using multiple methods, and/or double-checking understanding with participants. *Applicability* is met if other readers have enough detail to understand how results may or may not apply to different settings or conditions. *Agreement* occurs when others agree that the analysis is consistent with the claims made.

SUMMARY

Qualitative methods provide additional ways to examine research questions. Use of qualitative methods allows a researcher to ask questions and provide evidence about research questions that focus on broad, dynamic, multifaceted phenomena.

—Regina Day Langhout

Further Readings and References

Briggs, C. L. (1986). *Learning how to ask: A sociolinguistic appraisal of the role of the interview in social science research*. Cambridge, UK: Cambridge University Press.

Camic, P. M., Rhodes, J. E., & Yardley, L. (Eds.). (2003). *Qualitative research in psychology: Expanding perspectives in methodology and design*. Washington, DC: American Psychological Association.

Denzin, N. K., & Lincoln, Y. S. (Eds.). (2000). *Handbook of qualitative research*. Thousand Oaks, CA: Sage.

Emerson, R. M., Fretz, R. I., & Shaw L. L. (1995). *Writing ethnographic fieldnotes*. Chicago: University of Chicago Press.

Lionnet, F. (1989). *Autobiographical voices: Race, gender, and self portraiture*. Ithaca, NY: Cornell University Press.

Smith, S. E., & Willms, D. G. (Eds.). (1997). *Nurtured by knowledge: Learning to do participatory action-research*. New York: Apex Press.

Tormey, R., Good, A., & MacKeough, C. (1995). *Post-methodology? New directions for research methodologies in the social sciences* [web book]. Retrieved from http://www.iol.ie/~mazzoldi/toolsforchange/postmet/book.html

QUANTITATIVE METHODS

Quantitative methods play a critical role in applying the scientific method to the study of human development. Our observations of behavior must be transformed into data, and our data must be described and used to test hypotheses. Quantitative methods play a role in both of these endeavors, which fall under the general headings of *measurement* and *statistical analysis*.

Formally, *measurement* is defined as the assignment of numbers to represent properties of objects in a lawful way. In recent years, measurement theorists have stressed that measurement is not a simple, mechanical process; rather, measurement involves the application of theory to a behavioral realm. For example, one's theory about intelligence will guide how many numbers are assigned to represent it. A unitary conception of intelligence argues for a single set of numbers being sufficient (e.g., IQ scores), whereas a multidimensional conception argues that several sets of numbers are required to represent intelligence adequately. Good measurement involves, then, not just attention to vital concepts such as reliability and validity but also an understanding of what model underlies the numbers being used to stand in for behavior and how best to test the assumptions of that model. Of course, there are many unique difficulties associated with obtaining good measures of young children that are not encountered when measuring adults.

Even a brief discussion of measurement necessitates mention of Stevens' classic *scale types*, the hierarchy of nominal, ordinal, interval, and ratio scales. Stevens argued, essentially, that if one knew the scale type being used in one's study, then one knew how to interpret the numbers and what statistical analyses were permissible. Stevens' scale type theory was extraordinarily influential in the last half of the 20th century, but many have argued that it is incomplete and does not provide a framework for evaluating the adequacy of our measures. The process of measurement is now more closely aligned with theory testing as, for example, in complicated multitrait, multimethod validity studies.

Statistics can be used to describe data (e.g., providing a scatterplot of intelligence plotted against achievement motivation, or giving a mean and standard deviation for a set of attitude scores) or to test hypotheses about the populations from which samples are drawn (e.g., do children differ in their attachment styles to mothers versus fathers). Some statistical procedures are unique to developmental or "over time" data, and, more generally, the rapid growth of computing power since the 1960s has meant a huge increase in the arsenal of statistical techniques available to researchers, especially those with large numbers of variables and large numbers of participants. Indeed, new professional organizations have sprung up, new journals have been initiated, and new methodological standards have been applied in the submissions of research applications and journal articles. For example, researchers are required to pay more attention to statistical power (the ability to detect real differences in populations) and to effect sizes (the actual magnitude of any statistically significant results). A new technique called *meta-analysis* is designed to evaluate the size of effects across several different studies of the same behaviors.

Sophisticated statistics remains a poor substitute for creative but logical research designs, however. Especially in developmental studies, researchers must work diligently to employ methodologies with appropriate control groups, with representative samples, and with ecological validity (as Bronfenbrenner defined it, namely, the extent to which the study's participants are experiencing the study the way the researcher intended). Quantitative methods are part and parcel of, and can help improve, every stage of the research process—from designing a new measure to testing whether children's standing on the measure changes over time. Indeed, the scientific study of human development rests on the foundation of quantitative methods.

—*James A. Green*

See also Longitudinal Research, Reliability, Validity

Further Readings and References

Appelbaum, M. I., & McCall, R. B. (1983). Design and analysis in developmental psychology. In P. H. Mussen (Ed.), *Handbook of child psychology* (4th ed., Vol. 1, pp. 415–476). New York: Wiley.

Blalock, H. M. (1982). *Conceptualization and measurement in the social sciences.* Beverly Hills, CA: Sage.

Dubois, P. H. (1970). *A history of psychological testing.* Boston: Allyn & Bacon.

Duncan, O. D. (1984). *Notes on social measurement.* New York: Russell Sage Foundation.

Hartmann, D. P. (1988). Measurement and analysis. In M. H. Bornstein & M. E. Lamb (Eds.), *Developmental psychology: An advanced textbook* (2nd ed., pp. 85–147). Hillsdale, NJ: Erlbaum.

Jacoby, W. G. (1991). *Data theory and dimensional analysis.* Newbury Park, CA: Sage.

Messick, S. (1983). Assessment of children. In P. H. Mussen (Ed.), *Handbook of child psychology* (4th ed., Vol. 1, pp. 477–526). New York: Wiley.

QUASI-EXPERIMENTAL DESIGN

In the early 1960s, Donald T. Campbell pioneered the method of quasi-experimentation. A quasi-experiment is a way of methodically gathering data about a topic in its natural environment when that topic cannot be studied in a laboratory. The word "quasi" is derived from the Latin *quam si*, and means "as if," "in some sense or degree," or "resembling in some degree." An experiment is an operation carried out under controlled conditions in order to discover an unknown, to test or establish a hypothesis, or to illustrate a known law. By these definitions, a quasi-experiment approximates the controlled conditions of an experiment to discover an unknown.

An important goal of experimental research is internal validity, or the ability to conclude a causal relationship between the independent and dependent variables. To conclude causality, the only difference between groups should be the independent variable or variables in question. This is achieved by directly manipulating and controlling the levels of the independent variable and by randomly assigning participants to the levels of the independent variable. When the criteria for causality cannot be met, the experiment is considered a quasi-experiment. Thus, causal conclusions cannot strictly be drawn from a quasi-experimental design.

The lack of control in a quasi-experiment can be compensated for in a number of ways. First, large numbers of participants are often recruited in quasi-experimental designs in an attempt to minimize the differences among the groups. In addition, methodological techniques such as matching are used to achieve approximately equivalent groups. Even though these techniques improve the possibility of a causal connection, causality cannot be established through a quasi-experiment.

Regardless of the potential problems, quasi-experiments have a secure place in modern research. Why use a quasi-experimental design? One reason is that it may be impossible to conduct a true experiment. Quasi-experiments are frequently used to study phenomena such as riots or traffic incidents where it is unethical, unlawful, or otherwise unavailable to assign participants into different experimental or control groups. Additionally, a quasi-experiment may be elected because the experimenter wants to maintain external validity or the extent to which the findings can be generalized to other individuals or situations.

Investigating the effect of punishing retailers who sell alcohol to minors is an example of a quasi-experiment. Retailers who have received citations for not checking identification could be compared to retailers who have never been cited. Because participants cannot be randomly assigned to experimental conditions, there are other potential explanations for the results, and causality cannot be inferred. Therefore, this is a quasi-experiment rather than a "true" experiment.

There are different varieties of quasi-experimental designs, including the nonequivalent groups design, interrupted time series design, and proxy pretest design. These differ in the way the procedure is set up and how measurements are taken.

To summarize, a quasi-experimental design is one that approximates a true experiment when a true experiment is not possible or the researcher is concerned with maintaining external validity. The advantages of a quasi-experimental design are the ability to conduct the experiment in a natural setting and a potential increase in external validity. The subsequent disadvantage is that internal validity is compromised and causality cannot be inferred from a quasi-experimental design.

—Danielle Mull and Shannon Whitten

See also Experimental Method

Further Readings and References

Campbell, D. T., & Stanley J. C. (1966). *Experimental and quasi-experimental designs for research.* Chicago: Rand McNally.

O'Connor, T. (2004). *Experimental and quasi-experimental research design.* Retrieved from http://faculty.ncwc.edu/toconnor/308/308lect06.htm

Scribner, R., & Cohen, D. (2001, Fall). The effect of enforcement on merchant compliance with the minimum legal drinking age law. *Journal of Drug Issues, 31*(4), 857–866. Retrieved from http://www.findarticles.com/p/articles/mi_qa3733/is_200110/ai_n8957561/pg_2

Shadish, W. R., Cook, T. D., & Campbell, D. T. (2002). *Experimental and quasi experimental designs for generalized causal inference.* Boston: Houghton-Mifflin.

Trochim, W. M. (2000). *The research methods knowledge base* (2nd ed.). Retrieved from http://trochim.human.cornell.edu/kb/quasiexp.htm

QUINCEAÑERA

La quinceañera is a Latina tradition involving a coming-of-age celebration for young women on their 15th birthdays. The word *quinceañera* comes from the words "quince," which is Spanish for *15*, and "años," which is Spanish for *years*. Although the exact origin of the celebration is unknown, the tradition is thought to have Aztec and Catholic roots. Several centuries ago, girls were separated from other children when they turned 15 in order to prepare for womanhood and learn about their future roles within their families and community.

Today, the event includes a thanksgiving Mass, which represents a young woman's vow to serve her community, church, and family, and the event also includes an extravagant party to celebrate the special occasion. Planning for the quinceañera celebration is elaborate. Much like for a wedding, for her quinceañera the 15-year-old and her family send invitations, buy a formal full-length gown, reserve a reception hall or a party salon, order a cake, and hire photographers and possibly even choreographers. Also, just as a bride and groom pick bridesmaids and groomsmen, the young woman chooses 14 people to be the "chambelanes" (chamberlains) and "damas" (maids of honor) of her court. These 14 court members represent each year of the Quinceañera's life prior to her 15th birthday.

The most important part of a quinceañera is the religious Mass, which occurs at the beginning of the celebration. This ceremony recognizes religious customs and the virtues of family and social responsibility. At this time, the birthday girl thanks God for her blessings and asks for guidance and protection as she begins her new stage of life. She welcomes her role as a woman and defines her goals for the future. Parents and godparents may give a speech at the altar as well.

After Mass, relatives and friends gather for the social part of the evening. Traditionally, the Quinceañera dances her first dance with her father. She changes from flats into high-heeled shoes for this dance to symbolize her entrance into womanhood. She also reserves a dance, typically a choreographed waltz, for one or more of her chambelanes. For the rest of the celebration, family and friends are welcome to dance to the music of the band, which is often a mariachi band. Other highlights of the occasion include the cutting of the cake and a celebratory toast.

On her birthday, the Quinceañera also receives gifts that hold special meaning and indicate her loyalty and commitment to God, family, and community. Traditional quinceañera gifts may include a tiara to symbolize triumph over childhood; a bracelet or ring to denote the unending circle of life; earrings to remind the young woman to always hear and respond to the world around her; a cross to represent the Quinceañera's faith in God, her world, and herself; and a bible to keep close the word of God. The Quinceañera might also receive a personalized pillow to place under her knees as she kneels during the Mass or a Quinceañera doll that serves as a keepsake for the event. To show appreciation toward her guests, the birthday woman of honor, with the help of sisters, cousins, and friends, often gives commemorative favors to those in attendance.

The quinceañera rite of passage began long ago, but the ceremony is still observed in several countries, including the United States. Although some Latina 15-year-olds may prefer to receive a trip or even a car to celebrate, the beginning of a woman's 15th year of life still marks a significant and symbolic life change. Today, the quinceañera remains one of the traditions that affirm the bond of Latinas worldwide.

—*Kristin L. Rasmussen*

See also Adolescence

Further Readings and References

Hoyt-Goldsmith, D., & Migdale, L. (2002). *Celebrating a Quinceañera: A Latina's 15th birthday celebration.* New York: Holiday House.

Quinceanera Boutique. (n.d.). *Traditions.* Retrieved from http://www.quinceanera-boutique.com/quinceaneratradition.htm

Resendes, R. (2005). *The celebration of the Quinceañera.* Retrieved from http://gomexico.about.com/cs/culture/a/quinceanera.htm

R

Reading

Books are the quietest and most constant of friends; they are the most accessible and wisest of counselors, and the most patient of teachers.

—Charles W. Eliot

RAPE

The term *rape* has different meanings for different segments of the population. For example, within the field of psychology, the terms rape and sexual assault are often used interchangeably and encompass a range of nonconsensual acts from touching the breasts, buttocks, or genitals, to forced penetration of the vagina, anus, or mouth, by a penis or an object. In this case, force can involve verbal coercion, threats, physical restraint, or violence. Although laws vary by state, the generally accepted legal definition of rape is an act of sexual intercourse carried out by force or coercion, or when the victim is unable to give consent.

While many people think that stranger rape, the man hiding in the bushes wearing a ski mask, is more common, research indicates that date or acquaintance rape is much more prevalent. Statistics show that about 85% of sexual assaults are committed by someone whom the victim knows, and 57% of assaults are perpetrated by romantic partners. Because of the stigma associated with admitting to having been raped and differing definitions of rape, it is difficult to know what the true incidence and prevalence statistics are for rape. However, across the life span and regardless of age or socioeconomic status, studies consistently demonstrate that prevalence rates for rape are between 15% and 25%. In terms of the age of rape victims, the youngest rape victim ever reported was 2 months old, while the oldest was 97 years old.

Thus far rape has been discussed as it relates to women, yet it is important to realize that men can be victims of rape as well. Typically, men are victimized by other men. Research indicates that while male rape make up about 5% of all reported rapes, 95% of male rape victims do not report the assault. The FBI estimates that 1 in 10 men are the victims of adult sexual assault.

Part of the reason that rape is an underreported crime and one that is viewed with a great deal of skepticism is the presence of rape myths. Rape myths are generally defined as false beliefs about various aspects of rape that inadvertently support the presence of rape within society by denying the prevalence, impact, and severity of the crime. Rape myths essentially call into question the guilt of the perpetrator and the innocence of the victim by focusing attention on irrelevant factors such as the victim's dress or behavior or by implying that certain circumstances justify rape. According to one commonly known rape myth, women often falsely accuse men of rape. In reality, the rate of false reporting of rape is less than 1%, while the false report rate for all other crimes is estimated to be around 3%.

The psychological sequelae of rape are numerous. Research shows that rape produces both initial effects as well as long-term impact on victims. Short-term sequelae of rape include physical and emotional injuries, contracting sexually transmitted diseases, unwanted pregnancy, feelings of guilt, betrayal, responsibility, shame, inadequacy, inability to trust, fear of men, fear of being alone, insomnia, problems concentrating, nightmares, and an increased susceptibility to stress-related illnesses. Long-term effects of rape include depression, drug and alcohol abuse, suicidal ideation, low self-esteem, sexual dysfunction, relationship problems, and posttraumatic stress disorder (PTSD). The most common psychiatric diagnosis given to rape victims postassault is PTSD. The symptoms of PTSD include nightmares, flashbacks, and intrusive images of the assault, feelings of emotional numbness, irritability, anxiety, avoidance of all trauma cues, hypervigilance, difficulty concentrating, and insomnia. Studies indicate that 94% of rape victims meet the criteria for PTSD between 1 and 3 weeks post-assault. While some rape victims can recover either spontaneously or with treatment, others can suffer from symptoms of PTSD for decades after the assault.

—*Judith Conoyer Bronson*

See also Violence

Further Readings and References

Bownes, I. T., O'Gorman, E. C., & Sayers, A. (1991). Psychiatric symptoms, behavioral responses, and posttraumatic stress disorder in rape victims. *Issues in Criminal and Legal Psychology, 1,* 25–33.

Brownmiller, S. (1975). *Against our will: Men, women, and rape.* New York: Simon & Schuster.

Burt, M. R. (1980). Cultural myths and supports for rape. *Journal of Personality and Social Psychology, 38,* 277–322.

Herman, J. (1997). *Trauma and recovery: The aftermath of violence—From domestic violence to political terror.* New York: Basic Books.

Koss, M. P. (2000). *High? Low? Changing?: What's new in rape prevalence.* Retrieved from http://www.nvaw.org/research/newprevalence.shtml

Koss, M. P., Gidycz, C. A., & Wisniewski, N. (1987). The scope of rape: Incidence and prevalence of sexual aggression and victimization in a national sample of higher education students. *Journal of Consulting and Clinical Psychology, 55,* 162–170.

Planned Parenthood Federation of America. (1998). *What is rape? Some legal definitions.* Retrieved from http://www.teenwire.com/index.asp?taStrona=http://www.teenwire.com/warehous/articles/wh_19981201p060.asp

READING

In a split second, a skilled reader identifies words, recovers their meanings, and integrates them with prior words in the passage. The average skilled reader recognizes at least 50,000 words, having read about a hundred million words. Though reading seems automatic, it is a complex cognitive act consisting of several component operations that deal with the sequence of words, phrases, and sentences of a text. These operations act together to achieve the result of reading, which is the comprehension of the text. Reading involves other cognitive processes, including perception, memory, reasoning, and problem solving. Unlike spoken language comprehension, the reading skill requires a long period of instruction and practice. However, the rewards are ample as our society values literacy as a prerequisite for success.

COGNITIVE PROCESSES IN READING

Coherent text is based on the repetition of key concepts in a text. In order to comprehend the text, readers must spot the recurring ideas in the text and integrate them into a mental structure. Because most texts are too long to be processed in one piece, the reader creates a memory representation by processing the text's smaller units, its sentences, and its clauses. A variety of processes at several levels of structure, including letters, words, phrases, and sentences, contribute to comprehension. At the letter level, visual features must be decoded to identify letters. Word-level processes include the encoding of the word into an abstract unit and lexical access by which the word's meaning is retrieved from a mental lexicon. Sentence-level processes include operations that handle both the segments of the sentence and the sentence as a whole. Text-level processes integrate the information from different sentences into the reader's model of the text. To achieve such integration, the reader must maintain the prior information from the current text in memory. All along, inferential processes occur that make use of the reader's general knowledge of the physical and social world.

How does the reader integrate text information with prior knowledge, whether it is from the current text or from other sources? Different models of reading comprehension attempt to find an answer to this question. Memory-based models assume that information in memory is activated automatically during reading. This is a continuous process that requires relatively little mental work. The text concepts currently in focus broadcast a signal to the contents of memory. Concepts in memory are activated by virtue of passive resonance. The degree of activation of a concept in memory depends on its similarity to the specific text concept.

Constructionist models view reading comprehension as an active building of the text representation. The representation captures the causal relations among events in the text. The events include the goals, reactions, and actions of a story's character as advocated by story grammar theory. Situation models focus on what the text is about rather than the repetition of individual concepts. In addition to causal relations, the scenario of a text includes the spatial and temporal context within which the story evolves.

READING RESEARCH

There are four largely independent traditions in reading research. These include research on (1) basic cognitive processes in reading, (2) the precursors of reading, (3) reading instruction, and (4) reading disabilities with special emphasis on dyslexia. Basic researchers and dyslexia researchers increasingly turn to neuroimaging methodologies to complement behavioral assessments of reading.

Basic Research

Basic reading research examines the behavioral and neural manifestations of reading comprehension. The research uses patterns of eye fixations and other behavioral measures, as well as neural images, to track the changing mental load as a person reads a text. Eye fixation studies reveal that reading does not involve the smooth movement of the eyes across the page that one might assume. Rather, the eyes make short and rapid movements, known as the saccades, and then fixate on a text unit, which is typically a word. It is during the fixation that the reader is assumed to extract the meaning of the word. Thus, reading is much like a slide show where words are flashed for about a quarter of a second. The reader controls the exposure duration of each word, albeit unconsciously. The duration of eye fixations reflects the difficulty of a text segment. Unfamiliar words, challenging syntactic structures, and concepts introduced for the first time in a text require longer fixation durations. In addition, both behavioral and brain imaging research have shown that reading involves shifts of activation to currently relevant meanings and active suppression of meanings no longer relevant.

Brain imaging research supports the hypothesis that reading builds on spoken language processing in that reading makes use of the same brain regions implicated in understanding spoken language. In normal readers, these typically are centers in the left hemisphere, the rear-brain parietal region, including Broca's area, and the boundary region between the temporal and occipital lobes. The latter region is presumably implicated in word decoding. Integrating information across clauses and sentences activates centers in the right frontal lobes.

The Precursors of Reading

There is a profound difference between learning to speak and learning to read. Speaking is innate, but reading is not. Children must be instructed to learn to read. Spoken language has existed for at least 50,000 years. The human brain has evolved to produce and comprehend spoken language. Reading is of a more recent vintage, perhaps no older than 5,000 years. Learning to read presumably capitalizes on the brain systems used for spoken language processing.

There is consensus among researchers that phonological awareness is a critical precursor to reading and that it plays a fundamental role in reading acquisition. Phonological awareness refers to our sensitivity to the sounds in words, the phonemes, and our ability to manipulate those phonemes. Phonemes are the smallest sound units in language. Phonological awareness is tested, for example, by asking the person to say *crane* without the *r* or *cat* without the *c*. There are three aspects of phonological awareness: phonological sensitivity, phonological access to the mental lexicon, and phonological memory.

Phonological sensitivity is reflected in the child's ability to identify words that rhyme, to combine phonemes into words, and to delete syllables or phonemes from a word to create another word. Such sensitivity advances the child's understanding of the correspondence between letters and phonemes, which is the basis of alphabetic languages.

Phonological memory involves short-term memory for sound-based information. This is measured by span tests where the child must repeat a sequence of items in the order they were presented. Phonological memory enables a child to maintain a representation of the phonemes corresponding to the letters of a word, as the child processes the text's clauses, sentences, and relations between repeated concepts. Not surprisingly, phonological awareness accounts for much of the difference between poor and good readers. Most children have no trouble manipulating phonemes, but for poorer readers this is a difficult challenge.

Reading Instruction

Throughout the last century, there has been a vocal debate on the best method of reading instruction involving advocates of the whole-word method and the phonics method. Proponents of the whole-word method believe it is best to teach children to read by exposing them to whole words and by reading entire stories. This method works adequately for children who can break the decoding barrier on their own, but not for those who cannot.

The phonics method is more attuned to phonological awareness as a precursor to reading. Recent research evidence from a diverse set of sources has demonstrated that this is more successful for most children than the whole-word method. According to the phonics method, children are instructed to form mental links between letters and sounds, and between sounds and words. Specifically, as noted in the National Reading Panel report (2000) "explicit, systematic instruction in phonemic awareness is more successful in teaching children to read than any other method."

Research on Dyslexia

Whereas the reading level of poor readers is on par with their general intelligence, dyslexic readers read at a level significantly below their level of intelligence. Dyslexia is defined as a learning disability that is neurobiological in origin. Dyslexic individuals have difficulty with fluent word recognition thought to result from a deficit in the phonological component of language. Dyslexic children typically have problems in identifying specific target words visually, even when given unlimited time. As a result, these children encounter problems in understanding passages of text. They tend to read less, thus impeding the growth of their vocabulary and general world knowledge. It is estimated that about 5% of all school-age children, or approximately 2.5 million, are dyslexic.

Brain imaging research reveals a contrast in the brain processes of normal and dyslexic children during reading. In dyslexic readers, including the youngest ones, brain centers other than those in normal readers are activated during reading. Notably, the occipital-temporal word decoding area is not active. Importantly, when performing other cognitive tasks such as problem solving, the brain activation patterns of normals and dyslexics do not differ. When systematic remedial tutoring in phonics and phonological awareness is started early enough with young dyslexic children, their reading skills improve significantly. Indeed, their brains prove to be malleable to such instruction and their brain patterns come to resemble the brain patterns in unimpaired children.

SUMMARY

Much progress has been made in the last decade on basic, instructional, and remedial issues in reading. Nevertheless, as Edmund Huey, the pioneer of reading research, noted nearly a century ago, "to completely understand the mental processes of reading represents the acme of reading research."

—*Karl Haberlandt*

See also School

Further Readings and References

Adams, M. J. (1990). *Beginning to read: Thinking and learning about print.* Cambridge: MIT Press.

Castles, A., & Coltheart, M. (2004). Is there a causal link from phonological awareness to success in learning to read? *Cognition, 91*, 77–111.

Clifton, C., & Duffy, S. (2001). Sentence and text comprehension: Roles of linguistic structure. *Annual Review of Psychology, 52*, 167–196.

Huey, E. B. (1968). *The psychology and pedagogy of reading.* Cambridge: MIT Press. (Original work published 1908)

Lyon, G. R., Shaywitz, S., & Shaywitz, B. (2003). A definition of dyslexia. *Annals of Dyslexia, 53*, 1–14.

National Reading Panel Report. (2000). *Teaching children to read.* Retrieved from http://www.nichd.nih.gov/publications/nrp/smallbook.htm

Reichle, E., Rayner, K., & Pollatsek, A. (2003). The E-Z Reader model of eye-movement control in reading: Comparison to other models. *Behavioral and Brain Sciences, 26*, 445–526.

RECIPROCAL DETERMINISM

Reciprocal determinism refers to mutual back and forth interactions among individuals, objects, or processes. In a recent application, the *principle of Reciprocal Determinism* asserts that there are mutual back-and-forth influences among levels of organization and function in neurobehavioral systems. According to the 19th century neurologist, John Hughlings Jackson, the evolution of the nervous system entails a progressive layering of more newly developed neural systems over lower and more primitive organizations. This progressive layering yields what Jackson termed the re-representation of functions at multiple levels within the neuraxis.

Lower-level systems tend to be relatively simple, limited in scope and function, and inflexible compared to higher systems. The pain withdrawal reflex to a noxious stimulus, for example, is organized at the spinal cord level and comprises a rather simple circuit consisting of a pain afferent (sensory input neuron), a motor efferent (motor neuron to the muscle), and a few interconnecting interneurons within the cord. This provides for a very rapid efficient limb withdrawal response that can occur prior to conscious awareness of the pain. More complex reactions, consisting of escape, defensive reactions, or aggressive reactions, are organized at higher levels of the neuraxis. These higher systems allow for more complex patterns of response to pain. One structure that has received a great deal of attention in this regard is the amygdala, an almond-shaped set of nuclei within the temporal lobe. The amygdala has been shown to be especially important in learned fear responses and in mediating the behavioral effects of emotional reactions.

At the highest level of processing within the cerebral cortex are organized the most general, integrative, and flexible cognitive substrates that support a variety of highly adaptable and flexible *strategies* for avoiding or eliminating aversive conditions. These include efforts such as planning of avoidance strategies, procurement of shelter to escape the cold, and social cooperation to enhance defensiveness (establishment of laws, police forces, armies, etc.). These higher-level systems do not replace lower mechanisms, but provide for the elaboration and further development of adaptive responses. The multiple levels of re-representation can be active concurrently. A pain stimulus may trigger a pain withdrawal reflex as well as a cognitive avoidance strategy. Lower-level systems can bias higher-level processes, and higher-level processes can impact lower-level systems. This is reciprocal determinism.

From the broadest vantage, the principle of reciprocal determinism captures the fact that a given level of organization and function (e.g., the psychological domain) is both impacted by and impacts on other levels of organization and function (e.g., the physiological domain). Interactions are two-way (reciprocal) and mutually influence functions of the other level (i.e., they are determinants). Consequently, a comprehensive understanding of behavior may require attention to both its psychological and biological determinants. This has become evident in the past quarter century of research on addictive behaviors. Drug abuse is fundamentally related to the actions of drugs on brain receptors, so an understanding of addiction will necessarily require attention to the psychopharmacology of drugs. However, drug exposure alone does not necessarily lead to addiction. Psychological states and environmental and sociocultural influences as well as life history can all powerfully influence an individual's reactions to drugs. Moreover, drug taking can alter psychological states and so on go the reciprocal influences underlying drug abuse. Drug abuse is an example of a reciprocally determined phenomenon—the direction of causation between behavioral and physiological processes is not one way.

The principle of reciprocal determinism has a guiding corollary concerning interdisciplinary science and the multiple levels of analysis that can range from the psychological to the organ (brain) level to the cellular to the genetic and ultimately to the molecular level. Because causal influences among processes studied at different levels of organization can be bidirectional, the *Corollary of Interdependence* states that a single level of analysis may not yield a comprehensive understanding of a phenomenon, and that there may be no single, preferred level of analysis that uniformly applies. In this regard, the principle of reciprocal determinism is most consistent with an interdisciplinary, multilevel scientific approach.

—*Gary G. Berntson and John T. Cacioppo*

See also Bandura, Albert

Further Readings and References

Bandura, A. (1978). The self system in reciprocal determinism. *American Psychologist, 33,* 344–358.

Berntson, G. G., & Cacioppo, J. T. (2004) Multilevel analyses and reductionism: Why social psychologists should care about neuroscience and vice versa. In J. T. Cacioppo & G. G. Berntson (Eds.), *Essays in social neuroscience* (pp. 107–120). Boston: MIT Press.

McMaster University. (n.d.). *Psychology 2B3: Theories of personality*. Retrieved from http://www.science.mcmaster .ca/Psychology/psych2b3/lectures/banmisch-1.html

Mischel, W. (2004). Toward an integrative science of the person. *Annual Review of Psychology 55*, 1–22.

REFLEXES

The meaning of the term "reflex" has changed considerably as theories of motor control have evolved. Classically defined as an involuntary and relatively stereotyped response to a particular stimulus, a reflex was considered to be the simplest component of the nervous system able to produce a coherent, elemental reaction. To qualify as a reflex, a response had to be perfectly reproducible, be graded with respect to stimulus intensity, and occur at a specific time after the stimulus. However, over time the term has been applied loosely to a wide range of motor behaviors, ranging from the relatively simple knee jerk in response to a patellar tendon tap to the complex patterns of neuromuscular interactions required to maintain equilibrium. Though reflexes have historically figured prominently in theories of motor control, motor learning, and motor development, contemporary researchers cannot agree on what constitutes a reflex and whether the term even has scientific value, despite the popularity of the term's usage in the scientific literature, clinical settings, and lay conversations.

The Latin translation of the term reflex is "bending back." Descartes referred to reflex systems as neural pathways connecting stimulus with response; however, Georgiy Procháska is credited with first formally defining a reflex as a behavior in response to an excitation, mediated by separate motor and sensory nerves. A number of studies in the 18th, 19th, and 20th centuries showed that a vertebrate spinal cord that was disconnected from the brain was capable of automatically producing movements when externally stimulated. These findings led to the notion that reflexive behaviors were distinct from voluntary behaviors because they were externally triggered, automatically controlled, and highly repeatable. Subsequently, all of these characteristics of reflexes have been called into question. For example, many reflexive behaviors are thought to be internally elicited and even the parameters (e.g., gains) of the simplest reflex circuits can be modified by instructions and other task and contextual factors. Furthermore, these modifications can themselves be learned and unlearned.

Many contemporary researchers now believe that all behavior lies on a continuum from reflexive to voluntary with no specific behaviors being either purely reflexive or purely voluntary. Those who consider the term reflex to be scientifically useful are divided as to whether to differentiate reflexive and voluntary behavior based on the potential for conscious mediation or based on the anatomical/physiological complexity of the circuits (with only the simplest input-output circuits being considered reflexive) involved in behavior. Many researchers would prefer to replace the term reflex with sensorimotor interactions. Others have suggested using terms such as reactions, coordinative structures, and functional synergies, though these terms have typically referred to the more generalized responses to stimuli.

Despite the debate over the usefulness of the term, reflexes have generally been classified according to their function. The most basic reflex circuit is composed of four units: a receptor, an afferent (sensory) neuron projecting to the central nervous system, an efferent (motor) neuron to the muscle, and an effector (e.g., a muscle). Interneurons are not essential but it is rare to find a reflex circuit without one. Reflexes are considered monosynaptic, disynaptic, or polysynaptic depending on whether they have one, two, or more central synapses. The latency of a response is determined by the speed of transmission over the nerve fibers (conduction is faster across larger diameter fibers), the time to cross synapses, the number of synapses, and the time for the muscle to contract. Repeated application of a constant innocuous stimulus leads to an attenuation of a reflex that is referred to as *habituation*. Any detectable change to the stimulus leads to *dishabituation*, where the reflex returns to its baseline state. Repeated application of a noxious stimulus can lead to an enhancement of the reflex referred to as *sensitization*. In some reflexes, it is possible to elicit the response to a novel stimulus if that stimulus is paired in time with the stimulus that typically elicits the response. This type of associative learning creates what are known as *conditioned reflexes*.

The *muscle spindle reflexes* (also referred to as *myotatic* or *stretch reflexes*) are the simplest reactions that have been labeled reflexive. The stretch reflex, which causes a muscle to contract when the muscle or its tendon are tapped or a load is suddenly applied to a limb, is designed to preserve a prespecified muscle length. The receptor is a muscle spindle which lies in parallel with the *extrafusal* muscle fibers. The spindles have their own *intrafusal* muscle fibers that contract when the main muscle fibers contract so that the central region of the spindle stays taut and can respond to any muscle stretch. Afferent fibers project from the spindle to the spinal cord where they synapse with motor neurons that activate fibers of the muscle in which the spindle is located. The stretch reflex has a phasic component that rapidly responds to the rate of muscle stretch and a sustained tonic component that responds to the amplitude of stretch. Stretch reflexes must be overridden to accomplish voluntary movements, and this is achieved by activating the extrafusal and intrafusal muscle fibers at the same time. The spindle reflexes help to regulate muscle stiffness and they are particularly important for damping oscillations at the end of movements and for controlling mechanical interactions among limbs and between the limbs and the environment.

Among the most complex and generalized reactions that have been referred to as reflexive are the postural reflexes. In contrast to the spindle reflexes, which are localized at the level of the spinal cord and respond to mechanical stretch (or electrical stimulation of their afferent fibers, in which case they are called *Hoffman reflexes*), the postural reflexes are organized by the brain stem in response to vestibular, somatosensory, and visual inputs. The *vestibular (labyrinthine) reflexes*, the *neck reflexes*, and the *righting reflexes* are well-known postural reflexes. *Vestibulocollic* and *vestibulospinal reflexes* are labyrinthine reflexes that stabilize head orientation in space. The former activate neck muscles to keep the head upright, whereas the latter act on limb muscles, causing flexion or extension depending on head position. The *cervicocollic* and *cervicospinal reflexes* (often referred to as *tonic neck* reflexes) are neck reflexes that respond to flexion, extension, and rotation of the head about the neck. The former activate neck muscles and the latter activate limb muscles. Cervicocollic and vestibulocollic reflexes generally complement each other, while cervicospinal and vestibulospinal reflexes can work at cross purposes, in which case one is thought to dominate the other. The righting reflexes are those reactions that help reorient the head and/or body to an external frame of reference such as gravity or the surface of support, or that help to reorient body parts (e.g., head and trunk)

relative to each other. They include vestibular and neck righting reflexes, *optical righting reflexes*, and *body righting reflexes*, the latter responding to cutaneous stimuli.

The isolated components of the postural reflexes are difficult to discern in normal motor behavior because the substrates of voluntary movements are typically so highly integrated. However, they often become apparent in stressful activity or during maximal efforts, presumably because they are recruited to reinforce muscle contraction and extend endurance. The postural reflexes are often seen in exaggerated form in brain damaged patients and can be elicited in early infancy. In both cases, lack of inhibition from higher brain centers is thought to account for the ease with which the reflexes can be elicited.

From a developmental perspective, the role of reflexes is hotly debated. Primitive reflexes (labeled primitive because they were first seen in animals more primitive than humans and because they reside at lower levels of the CNS) can be elicited as early as the second or third month after conception, and most of the estimated 27 major infant reflexes are present at or prior to birth but have disappeared by 6 months of age in typically developing children. Infant reflexes are thought to have several functions: they facilitate survival (e.g., the *sucking reflex*), they provide protection (e.g., the *moro reflex* in which all limbs fling outward in response to a sudden displacement of the head and trunk); they stimulate the CNS and muscles and regulate muscle tone, and they permit early exploration of the environment and of the body. In addition, reflexes provide pediatricians with a useful tool for evaluating neurological integrity because the onset and disappearance of most reflexes is fairly well documented. However, there is controversy concerning the link between early reflexes and later voluntary behavior.

Most viewpoints generally agree that early reflexes are integrated into voluntary movements (though we must be mindful of the controversy surrounding the terms "reflex" and "voluntary"). After all, early reflexes appear to be ideally suited to serve as prefabricated building blocks for more complex behaviors. The controversy surrounds the continuity between early and later appearing behaviors. The traditional view is that those reflexes resembling later behaviors must be suppressed by higher brain centers before they can reappear as voluntary behaviors. A related view is that primitive reflexes must disappear and postural and locomotor reflexes must appear before voluntary behavior is possible. A more contemporary view is that early reflexes are rudimentary expressions of later behaviors (i.e., there is continuity across development). Proponents of this viewpoint prefer not to use the term reflex to describe these early patterns because they do not conform to the classic definition of involuntary and relatively stereotyped responses to particular stimuli. Evidence shows that many precocious patterns are not stereotyped in their expression, that they can be modified by task and contextual factors (including reinforcement and infant level of arousal), and that they can be facilitated with training or practice. For example, practice of the *stepping reflex* causes the pattern to persist across the first year of life and is associated with an earlier onset of independent walking. These findings, coupled with newer findings, will continue to contribute to the evolution of our ideas about reflexes in human behavior.

—David I. Anderson, Marianne Barbu Roth,
and Joseph J. Campos

See also Babinski Reflex, Breathing Reflex, Sucking Behaviors

Further Readings and References

Fukuda, T. (1961). Studies on human dynamic postures from the viewpoint of postural reflexes. *Acta Otolaryngologica, 161*[Suppl.], 1–52.

Nichols, T. R., & Houk, J. C. (2004). Reflex control of muscle. In G. Adelman & B. H. Smith (Eds.), *Encyclopedia of neuroscience* (3rd ed.). Amsterdam: Elsevier.

Thelen, E., Fisher, D. M., & Ridley-Johnson, R. (2002). The relationship between physical growth and a newborn reflex. *Infant Behavior and Development, 25*, 72–85.

U.S. National Library of Medicine. (n.d.). *Infantile reflexes.* Retrieved from http://www.nlm.nih.gov/medlineplus/ency/article/003292.htm

Woody, C. D. (2004). Reflex learning. In G. Adelman & B. H. Smith (Eds.), *Encyclopedia of neuroscience* (3rd ed.). Amsterdam: Elsevier.

REGGIO EMILIA CHILDHOOD PROGRAM

In the early 1990s, American early childhood educators began to explore a new philosophy of schooling described by Loris Malaguzzi as a system of relationships. That system is now commonly known as the Reggio Emilia Approach (REA). The system calls for an organization—school/classroom—working closely together to offer the best learning experiences for young children using a variety of media referred to as the "100 Languages of Children." Those languages become the mechanism for children's learning experiences. In addition, the languages foster relationships among children, educators, and families within the greater social context. Teachers, children, and families discuss learning experiences with one another and plan using multiple perspectives.

Curricula are supported by a coordinator referred to as a *pedigogista.* The *pedigogista* is responsible for coordinating the school's curriculum and may work with multiple schools. All Reggio classrooms believe in the richness of fine arts as well. Through the incorporation of an art studio (*atelier*) within the schools, the *atelierista* provides support for the arts. The *atelierista* is usually assigned to only one school and works with multiple classrooms. The *pedigogista*, the *atelierista*, the teachers, and the children all work together on projects.

Although Reggio Emilia is actually a city in Italy, the approach to early childhood education has become world renowned for recognizing the "image of the child." In the Reggio Emilia Approach, children are protagonists of their learning and are competent and capable. Project work, the backbone of the learning experience, encourages children to use their "100 languages" to explore, discover, construct, communicate, and interact in the learning environment. Project work is defined as *progettazione.* American educators have used project work for many years. What distinguishes Reggio Emilia from other approaches is twofold: (a) the notion of emergent curricula that is more complex in planning, and (b) the dynamic process of *documentation* of children's thinking and learning processes. Malaguzzi described children's projects as "long stories."

Documentation serves as a method to demonstrate children's thinking and learning processes. It also is a system of organizing children's work over the life of a project and the development of the child. Within the organization of the project, teachers capture children's actual words through dictation and apply the words directly to the works. Teachers, children, and families "revisit" the work of the children as another system of relating the teaching and learning process among and between all individuals.

This model preschool program supports the notion of quality education for young children. The basic tenets of the approach provide a framework for developmentally appropriate practices and rich meaningful learning experiences for children. When young children are provided learning opportunities through a variety of experiences that include teachers, children, and families, optimal growth and development is enhanced. The Reggio Emilia Approach to early childhood education is a philosophy that outlines such learning opportunities and experiences.

The preschools of Reggio Emilia, Italy, using the approach have deep roots dating back to the mid-1940s. However, many educators did not begin to fully appreciate the philosophy until the mid-1970s. Throughout the 1980s and 1990s, educators from around the world traveled to Italy to study this approach. Today, many writers and researchers continue to study and interpret this ever-evolving approach to early childhood education. As you consider the study of early childhood education and its complexities, the following serves as guiding principles for the Reggio Emilia Approach:

The child as protagonist, collaborator, and communicator.

The teacher as a partner, a guide, as a nurturer, and a researcher.

The parent as a partner too.

The environment becomes a third teacher.

Documentation is a form of communication.

—*Elizabeth M. Elliott*

Further Readings and References

Bruner, J. (1961). *Actual minds, possible worlds.* Cambridge, MA: Harvard University Press.

Dewy, J. (1916). *Democracy and education: An introduction to the philosophy of education.* New York: Macmillan.

Gandini, L. (1996). The Reggio story: History and organization. In J. Hendrick (Ed.), *First steps toward teaching the Reggio way* (pp. 2–13). Columbus, OH: Prentice Hall.

Katz, L. & Chard, S. (1989). *Engaging children's minds: The project approach.* Norwood, NY: Ablex.

Malaguzzi, L. (1993). History, ideas, and basic philosophy. In C. Edwards, L. Gandini, & G. Forman (Eds.), *The hundred languages of children: The Reggio Emilia approach to early childhood education.* Norwood, NY: Ablex.

Reggio Emilia, http://www.reggiochildren.com/

REGGIO-L discussion list, http://ecap.crc.uiuc.edu/listserv/reggio-l.html

REINFORCEMENT

Reinforcement is a process that results in a particular response, or set of responses, occurring more often in similar settings because a particular stimulus was presented or removed following that response. Reinforcement is always defined by its effect. That is, reinforcement always strengthens behavior, or produces an increase in the likelihood of that response in similar future settings.

POSITIVE AND NEGATIVE REINFORCEMENT

Positive reinforcement refers to the addition of a stimulus following a behavior that produces an increase in the future likelihood of that behavior or similar behaviors in similar settings. Negative reinforcement also always produces an increase in the probability of a response, but does so by removing, or subtracting, a stimulus that is aversive following a behavior. Negative reinforcement is often confused with punishment, which actually produces a decrease in responding.

Reinforcement can be intentionally arranged to increase certain behaviors, or it may be produced by naturally occurring environmental relations. When reinforcement is provided to establish a skill, it is called *programmed reinforcement.* Typically, reinforcement is contingent on, or dependent on, the occurrence of a particular response. When a reinforcer is provided at a specified interval regardless of the response that preceded it, it is referred to as *noncontingent reinforcement.*

REINFORCERS

The stimulus that produces the increase in the strength of responding characteristics of reinforcement is called a reinforcer. Reinforcers can include a wide array of stimuli, or of persons, objects, or events in the environment that effect behavior. Responses are present at birth to some stimuli that allow them to function as unconditioned reinforcers, or stimulus conditions that we favor instinctively. For example, infants typically respond to the human voice as an unconditioned reinforcer. However, individuals learn to respond to other stimuli through experiences that occur during their lifetime. The stimuli that we learn to respond to are called *conditioned*, and can also function as reinforcers. Praise or kind words are examples of stimuli that individuals learn to respond to as a conditioned reinforcer. A young child will respond to a soft tone, but with experience they come to discriminate what the words of praise mean. All stimulus effects are individual in that each learner will respond in unique ways, and that the same learner may even respond differently to a given stimulus at different times.

Some reinforcers occur naturally in the environment and some are intentionally arranged, or programmed, to teach a given skill. Stimuli that function as reinforcers can be categorized as tangible, possessions, edible, activity, social, or manipulative. Tangible reinforcers might include items such as a toy, ball, or action figure. A possessional reinforcer could be the learner's favorite stuffed animal or pillow to which they are given limited access contingent on the performance of a particular behavior. Edible or consumable reinforcers include favored foods and drinks. It is important to note that when edible reinforcers are utilized, the learner cannot be satiated on them prior to attempting their use as a reinforcer. However, the learner must not be denied proper and appropriate access to consumable items outside the teaching environment. Thus, the use of edible items as reinforcers requires special considerations. An activity reinforcer might include a video game, time on a playground, or a trip to a favorite restaurant. Social reinforcers include access to or activities with desired people. This may include time alone with the child's mother, a trip to see a playmate, time with grandpa, or undivided teacher attention. Finally, manipulative reinforcers might include sensory toys or stimulation such as playing in a sand tray, building a Lego structure, piecing together a model, or other fine motor activities. It is possible for a single stimulus to be described by a number of labels, such as a programmed unconditioned positive tangible reinforcer or a soft, fuzzy blanket.

Knowing the types of stimuli that the learner responds best to is important to the arrangement of effective consequences for behavior. One might conduct a stimulus preference assessment to determine the relative value of an array of favored items for that individual. Our preferences change, even in the moment, so knowing what a learner prefers during one session might not help us to predict what they will respond strongly to in later sessions. If one has had extensive contact with an item, it might become less desirable for a period of time. This is called *satiation*. Conversely, when an item has been unavailable for a period of time, it may become more interesting due to deprivation. Satiation and deprivation momentarily change the power of stimuli to influence behavior. These two effects are called *establishing* or *motivating operations*.

SCHEDULES OF REINFORCEMENT

In both natural and programmed learning environments, a reinforcer can be provided on a variety of schedules. When establishing new behaviors, continuous reinforcement is the most efficient method. With continuous reinforcement, each behavior is followed by a reinforcer. However, once behavior has been established and shows some consistency, reinforcement can be provided intermittently. Reinforcer delivery on an intermittent schedule can be at fixed or variable increments. Fixed schedules of reinforcement require a predetermined measure of behavior to be observed before reinforcement is provided. In variable schedules of reinforcement, the measure of behavior that is required to produce reinforcement varies about an average.

Behavior can be measured to determine the schedule for reinforcer delivery by examining the frequency of responses, the duration of behavior, or the interval of time between the occurrences of a given behavior. On a *frequency schedule of reinforcement*, the number of occurrences of behavior is counted. Once the count of behavior is provided, either a fixed or variable number of responses will be required to produce reinforcement. In *duration schedules of reinforcement*, the amount of time that a behavior must continuously occur to produce reinforcement is determined. Either a fixed or variable duration of responding may be required. Finally, *interval schedules of reinforcement* require a certain amount of time between occurrences of the same behavior to produce reinforcement. The interval of time between behavior one and behavior two can be fixed or variable. Each of the schedules of reinforcement produces characteristic patterns of responding. Intermittent schedules have the advantage of maintaining behavior over increasingly long periods of time with minimal reinforcer delivery.

—*Deirdre L. Fitzgerald*

Further Readings and References

Cooper, J. O., Heron, T. E., & Heward, W. L. (1987). *Applied behavior analysis*. Englewood Cliffs, NJ: Prentice Hall.

Miltenberger, R. G. (2003). *Behavior modification: Principles & procedures* (3rd ed.). Belmont, CA: Wadsworth.

Reinforcement and punishment, http://www.psychology .uiowa.edu/Faculty/wasserman/Glossary/reinforcement.html

Sulzer-Azaroff, B., & Mayer, G. R. (1991). *Behavior analysis for lasting change*. New York: Holt, Rinehart and Winston.

RELIABILITY

Reliability refers to the consistency or stability of measurements. A test with good reliability means that the respondent will obtain the same score upon repeated testing, as long as no other extraneous factors affect the score. In actuality, a respondent will rarely obtain the exact same score over repeated testing because repeated assessments of any phenomenon will likely be affected by chance errors. Thus, the goal of testing is to minimize chance errors and maximize the reliability of the measurement with the recognition that a perfectly reliable measure is unattainable. Reliability is extremely important because evidence of reliability is necessarily the first step in establishing the scientific acceptance and usefulness of a test. Once reliability is established, the validity of the test can then be evaluated (validity is defined as the extent to which a test accurately measures what it purports to measure). The two most common forms of reliability are *test-retest reliability* and *scale reliability*.

Test-retest reliability is a measure of a test's consistency over a period of time. Test-retest reliability assumes that the construct being measured is relatively stable over time, such as personality. A good test manual should specify the sample, the test-retest interval (typically about 1 week to 1 month), and the reliability coefficient. If the construct is likely to change over time (e.g., perceived stress), then test makers will generally choose a shorter interval (e.g., 1 week). Test-retest reliabilities are reported and interpreted as correlation coefficients and are considered excellent if they are 0.90 or better and good if they are 0.80 or better. If a construct is thought to be relatively stable but the test-retest reliability coefficient for a test of that construct is around 0.50, it likely means that the test is unreliable. Perhaps there are too few questions

on the test or some test questions are poorly worded. Another possibility is that some extraneous variable affected the construct during the interval. One final concern regarding the interpretation of test-retest reliabilities is that they may be spuriously high because of practice effects or memory effects. A respondent may do better on the second testing because the trait being assessed improves with practice. Some people may respond similarly to a second administration of a test because they remember the answers that they gave previously. One possible solution to these problems is the use of *alternate forms* of the same test.

Scale reliability (commonly called *internal consistency*) is a measure of how well the items on a test relate to each other. The standard statistic for scale reliability is Cronbach's (1951) coefficient alpha. One way of understanding Cronbach's alpha is to view it as an average of all of the correlations of each test item with every other test item. The alpha coefficient ranges from 0.00 to 1.00 and is interpreted like a correlation coefficient. Values above 0.80 are considered good and generally reflective of reliable (internally consistent) scales. The alpha coefficient is dependent on three important variables. First, the number of test items impacts alpha: shorter tests will generally yield lower coefficients than longer tests. Second, the alpha coefficient is dependent on a high first factor concentration (i.e., the test is measuring a single concept or trait). A scale that measures two components of a construct will have a lower alpha than a different scale that measures only one core concept. Third, the alpha coefficient is dependent on the number of participants who take the test. A higher number of participants (generally above 200) will yield higher alpha coefficients, whereas a lower number of participants (less than 100) will yield lower alpha coefficients.

—*Daniel L. Segal and*
Frederick L. Coolidge

See also Validity

Further Readings and References

Coolidge, F. L. (2000). *Statistics: A gentle approach*. London: Sage.

Cronbach, L. J. (1951). Coefficient alpha and the internal structure of tests. *Psychometrika, 6*, 297–334.

Nunnally, J. C., & Bernstein, I. H. (1994). *Psychometric theory* (3rd ed.). New York: McGraw-Hill.

Segal, D. L., & Coolidge, F. L. (2003). Structured interviewing and DSM classification. In M. Hersen & S. Turner (Eds.), *Adult psychopathology and diagnosis* (4th ed., pp. 72–103). New York: Wiley.

Segal, D. L., & Coolidge, F. L. (2004). Objective assessment of personality and psychopathology: An overview. In M. Hilsenroth, D. L. Segal (Eds.), & M. Hersen (Ed.-in-Chief), *Comprehensive handbook of psychological assessment, Vol. 2: Personality assessment* (pp. 3–13). New York: Wiley.

Tabachnick, B. G., & Fidell, L. S. (2001). *Using multivariate statistics* (4th ed.). Needham Heights, MA: Allyn & Bacon.

RELIGION

Religion has played a central role in the cultural and community traditions of humankind since the beginning of civilization. Wherever ancient and modern peoples have settled and flourished, there has been a corresponding development of religious traditions that shapes the communities' perceptions of what is sacred and what is profane. Within the family circle, the child soon learns about areas, aspects, or rituals of life that are vital and important (sacred), and those that are merely mundane. That which is sacred transcends the profane. It is soon recognized as holy. Common to the three influential monotheistic traditions of the West, for example, God is described as the omnipotent and omniscient creator of the heavens and the earth who sustains all life and who abundantly provides for his creatures. These ideas and practices associated with the holy and sacred are the accepted doctrines and traditions of the religious community. When carefully woven together, these sacred customs and teachings form the fabric of faith.

While it is possible to describe the role of religion in the early development of the child from a general religious perspective, it is perhaps more appropriate to illustrate the great impact that religious belief can have on child-rearing practices from the perspective of a particular religious tradition, such as Judaism or Christianity. Within the sacred writings of Judaism, the Hebrew Bible (Tanakh), there are several texts that address the importance of passing religious beliefs and practices from one generation to the next. For example, the Deuteronomist records that shortly before his death, Moses, the great liberator and leader of the people of Israel, demanded that the people diligently keep the teachings and commandments given to them by God: "Now this is the commandment—the statues and the ordinances—that the Lord your God charged me to teach you to observe in the land that you are about to cross and occupy, so that you and your children and your children's children may fear the Lord your God all the days of your life, and keep all his decrees and his commandments that I am commanding you, so that your days may be long. Hear therefore, O Israel, and observe them diligently, so that it may go well with you, and so that you may multiply greatly in a land flowing with milk and honey, as the Lord, the God of your ancestors, has promised you." One can clearly see from this religious text the importance of maintaining the sacred traditions and holy doctrines from one generation to the next. Moreover, it is obvious that this religious teaching provides the people with important knowledge concerning their past, promises about their future, and commandments and doctrines about how to live life in the present. In other words, the great philosophical questions about origin (Where did I come from?), reality (Why am I here?), and destiny (Where am I going?) are neatly and definitively answered through religious belief. While most things are known and understood through experience and reason, the most important things concerning life and death can only be known by faith. As principle architect of about half of the New Testament, Saul of Tarsus—better known as the Apostle Paul—admonished the Corinthian Christians to live by the principle of faith, rather than be merely guided by reason alone. Within Judaism, believers would teach their children about God through acts of everyday life, no matter how mundane. Traces of the holy would often be seen in the profane. Moreover, within the sapiential wisdom literature of ancient Israel, there are many texts and traditions that demonstrate how religious beliefs in general inform child-rearing practices in particular. One ancient proverb, for example, matter-of-factly states: "Train children in the right way, and when old, they will not stray."

Through the process of time, children adopt the religious faith and practice of their parents, typically without much modification or change. Within certain Christian scriptures, there are teachings that stress the importance of instructing children and grandchildren about the central truths of the faith. In this way, the continuity of family traditions and religious beliefs will be ensured. In his second letter to his dedicated disciple Timothy, whom he considered to be his son in the faith, the Apostle Paul writes: "I am reminded of your sincere faith, a faith that first dwelt in your grandmother Lois and your mother Eunice and now, I am sure, dwells in you." In yet another important sacred text, Christian children are directly commanded to honor and even obey their parents, while parents, on the other hand, are admonished to nurture and indoctrinate their offspring within the strict traditions and discipline of the faith.

It seems quite clear, therefore, that child-rearing traditions within the sacred texts of both Judaism and Christianity affirm the importance of religious faith and practice within the framework of the family, and that these religious traditions hold the promise of present and future blessings upon those who believe. From a strictly secular perspective, however, the role of religion in the life of a child, and on child-rearing practices, is ambiguous at best and detrimental at worst. Sigmund Freud, in his critical monograph on the subject of religion, for example, considered all formal religion to be simply an illusion of childlike fantasy for people who cannot manage the complex problems and severity of life. This is similar to the projection theory of Feuerbach, where man merely projects human-like attributes or characteristics upon the humanly created concept of God.

Although the phenomenon of religion has been considered to be an illusion or a projection, or even the opium of the people, according to Marx, the presence and influence of religion—in all its varied manifestations—will certainly continue to exist and thrive in the twenty-first century. Modern and even postmodern philosophies and worldviews have been impotent to erase the phenomenon of religion and its universal appeal and influence. It will continue to make its mark on society in general and on the consciousness of the developing child in particular.

—Ramón Anthony Madrigal

See also Buddhism, Catholicism, Islam, Judaism

Further Readings and References

Biblical Studies Info Page, http://www.biblicalstudies.info

Coogan, M. D. (Ed.). (2001). *The New Oxford Annotated Bible* (3rd ed.). Oxford, UK: Oxford University Press.

Eliade, M. (1959). *The sacred and the profane*. New York: Harcourt, Brace & World.

Madrigal, R. (1999). Faith and reason. In F. Jenkins (Ed.), *A place to stand* (pp. 160–180). Temple Terrace: Florida College Press.

Smith, H. (2001). *Why religion matters*. New York: HarperCollins.

RESILIENCY

Resilience refers to the ability to thrive as an individual despite being exposed to serious adverse life circumstances, situations, stressors, and risks. Have you ever noticed how individuals who are exposed to the very same negative life event can react and respond in very different ways? One child in a family who has been exposed to the same marital conflict and bitter divorce walks away from the event apparently unharmed and continues to be happy and do well in school, while the brother or sister, after experiencing the same events, develops serious behavior problems and flunks out of school. In this example, the former child would be said to be more resilient than the latter.

The term *resilience* is used in two different ways. In the first sense, it simply refers to a fundamental characteristic of all children and human beings—that we are, in general, very adaptable, flexible, and quite good at surviving extraordinary negative life events. The human brain, body, and psyche are generally remarkably adept at changing and learning from experiences, and reorganizing themselves to make the best of difficult life circumstances. More commonly, however, the term resilience is used to refer to a psychological quality that varies somewhat from individual to individual. Simply put, some individuals are more resilient than others. Some children are able to recover from trauma and overcome risk factors that for other children seriously impede their development.

Because resilience, by definition, refers collectively to the characteristics of children who do well in the face of adversity, it is important to discuss the types of adversity or negative life experiences that have been studied. Any condition that is known to negatively affect children's development is called a risk factor. Situational risk factors that are known to have significant negative impacts on children's developmental outcomes include poverty, homelessness, child abuse, parental psychopathology (i.e., maternal depression, parental alcoholism, or substance abuse, schizophrenia), teen parenting, unemployment, single-parent homes, exposure to family violence, migrant/refugee status, and war. There are also individual risk factors that describe features of the child that put him or her at increased risk for negative outcomes. These include low birth weight or premature birth or the presence of a serious medical condition or a physical or developmental disability. By definition, resilient children are those children who have been exposed to one or more of these risk factors but are still doing very well and achieving high competence in multiple developmental domains. Unfortunately, the majority of children with prolonged exposure to many of the above risk factors do not thrive or become highly competent individuals. Finally, it is important to note that advantaged children who thrive and do well but have *not* been exposed to any of these serious risk factors are not necessarily resilient; their resiliency can only be assessed after exposure to such risk factors.

The typical research strategy for those interested in resilience is to identify a group of children and families who have clearly been exposed to many of the above risk factors and evaluate how well the children are doing. "Doing well" has sometimes been defined as an absence of psychopathology (behavior problems, delinquency, depression, mental illness) in children, and other times, success is defined as the child having negotiated major developmental tasks of childhood effectively. These tasks vary depending on the age of the child. For infants and toddlers, the developmental tasks include forming a secure attachment relationship with their caregiver, acquiring language, differentiating self from other, and developing sufficient emotional and behavioral self-control. During middle childhood, competence in relevant developmental tasks might include a successful transition to school, the development of peer social skills, establishing friendships, and maintaining satisfactory academic progress in school. In adolescence, additional developmental tasks are introduced such as establishing a cohesive sense of self and identity. It is important to note that while some markers of competence such as acquiring language are more universal, other developmental tasks are greatly influenced by culture. For example, establishing a strong sense of individual identity and autonomy may not be considered an indicator of competence in all cultures.

Regardless of the criteria used to define competence, the next step in a resilience research program is typically to classify the at-risk children into two groups: those who are doing particularly well—the resilient children, and those who do not evidence high competence—the nonresilient children. These two groups of children are then compared using a variety of individual, family, and situational variables to see how resilient children are different from nonresilient children and to see what makes resilient children thrive in the face of adversity. The positive factors that

seem to distinguish resilient children from their similarly at-risk peers are called *protective* or *buffering* factors. Protective factors have been identified as falling into three domains: individual, family, and external supports.

Individual protective factors are intrinsic characteristics of the child. The main individual characteristics that have been found to be associated with competence in the face of life stressors are high IQ or good intellectual functioning, strong language skills, an easygoing disposition or temperament, and strong self-efficacy beliefs or high self-esteem. Children with easy temperaments elicit positive attention and interactions from caregivers and strangers. Good eating and sleeping habits are also a part of an easygoing temperament, which leads to less disruption for parents. High self-esteem and accurate and realistic assessments of one's abilities also appear to be a protective factor for at-risk children. Resilient children often demonstrate a particular talent, a specific activity important to themselves and others that they are particularly good at, such as soccer or playing piano. Success in a particular skill area also facilitates children's subsequent positive interactions with peers and adults.

A close, warm, loving relationship to one's caregiver is the most powerful of the family protective factors that promote resiliency in childhood. Effective parenting characterized by warmth, structure, and high expectations fosters healthy development in unfavorable situations. As resilient children get older, a parent or other caregiver is typically viewed as a source of motivational support. Additionally, resilient children tend to both value and utilize immediate and extended family support more so than their nonresilient peers.

The most important protective factor within the external support category for resilient children is a close connection with at least one nonparent, prosocial, competent adult who acts as a mentor for the child. This is particularly important when little support is available from the child's primary caregivers. A trusted teacher, neighbor, regular caregiver, friend, counselor, community leader, or spiritual advisor has often been found to be a critical source of motivation and support for children able to overcome potentially overwhelming risk factors. As is the case with family support, resilient children appear to be more effective than nonresilient youngsters in securing and relying on external support systems in times of crisis. Finally, close friendships with one or more peers also distinguish resilient children from others who do not weather stressors as well.

One of the advantages of taking a resilience perspective on development is that rather than focusing on the deficits and problems seen in children growing up under adverse circumstance, it places emphasis on children's strengths and the protective factors that help children overcome disadvantageous conditions. In addition, interventions to help at-risk children can be, and have been, based on increasing children's protective factors to help them become more resilient in the face of hardship. As the number of life stressors and risk factors accumulate, children need more and stronger protective factors in order to reach their full potential.

—Sue Hartman and Adam Winsler

Further Readings and References

Gordon Rouse, K. A., Longo, M., & Trickett, M. (n.d.). *Fostering resilience in children* (Bulletin 875-99). Retrieved from http://ohioline.osu.edu/b875/

Grotberg, E. H. (1995). *A guide to promoting resilience in children: Strengthening the human spirit.* The Hague: Netherlands: Bernard van Leer Foundation. Retrieved from http://resilnet.uiuc.edu/library/grotb95b.html

Luthar, S. S., & Zigler, E. (1991). Vulnerability and competence: A review of research on resilience in childhood. *Journal of American Orthopsychiatry, 61,* 6–22.

Masten, A. S., & Coatsworth, J. D. (1998). The development of competence in favorable and unfavorable environments: Lessons from research on successful children. *American Psychologist, 53,* 205–220.

Resiliency in Action, http://www.resiliency.com

Smokowski, P. R., Reynolds, A. J., & Bezruczko, N. (1999). Resilience and protective factors in adolescence: An autobiographical perspective from disadvantaged youth. *Journal of School Psychology, 37*(4), 425–448.

Wang, M. C., & Gordon, E. W. (1994). *Educational resilience in inner-city America: Challenges and prospects.* Hillsdale, NJ: Erlbaum.

Werner, E. E., & Smith, R. S. (1982). *Vulnerable but invincible: A study of resilient children.* New York: McGraw-Hill.

RETENTION

When students fall seriously behind grade-level achievement expectations at school, their parents, teachers, and other school personnel face difficult decisions about how to help them improve. Some parents and educators favor retention—that is, having struggling students repeat a grade—to give them time to mature or build their knowledge and skills in preparation for the next grade. An alternative is to pass the struggling students on to the next grade so that they can remain with their peers. This is called social promotion. In general, research has shown that neither retention nor social promotion alone provide struggling students with the support they need to reach grade-level expectations.

Public opinion favors retention over social promotion, and despite decades of research showing that retention is rarely effective and frequently harmful, it is fairly common. An estimated 7% to 9% of American students are retained each year, and by ninth grade, 30% to 50% of students will have been retained at least once. Retention is higher in first and ninth grade, probably because these are transition years. Retention rates are also higher for boys, minority students, and students from low-income families. Retention rates are likely to remain high in the United States because several states and school districts now require that students pass competency tests before promotion to certain grades. For example, the Chicago Public Schools require students to attain minimum scores on tests in third, sixth, and eighth grades for promotion. Retention is less common in developed nations other than the United States.

Numerous studies have compared retained students with similarly low-achieving students who were socially promoted. Retained students often show some improvement in achievement in the year following retention, but the gains fade over time.

Besides being ineffective, retention has been linked to poor outcomes over the long run. There is a stigma attached to retention, and students find it stressful. (In 2001, sixth graders rated grade retention as more stressful than either the loss of a parent or going blind!) Students who have been retained are older than their classmates and experience puberty ahead them, another possible source of stress. In comparison to other low achievers, students who have been retained are more likely to be assigned to special education, drop out of school, engage in illegal behavior, and have poor employment records.

In evaluating the effects of retention, it is important to consider the characteristics of the children who are retained and the experiences they have during and after retention. Prior to retention, retained students are more likely than low-achieving promoted students to have had behavior problems, including aggression; to have been immature; and to have had poorly educated parents who were uninvolved in their children's education. These characteristics alone would make them more likely to experience long-term problems in school; unfortunately, retained students are frequently assigned to low ability groups. This compounds their problems, because low-ability groups often have many students with behavior problems, teachers with low expectations, and content of little interest.

Retention is more likely to succeed when children have positive attitudes toward school and good social skills, and they experience different teaching methods during their retention year. Educators now realize that regardless of whether struggling students are retained or socially promoted, they need special programs such as tutoring, summer programs, or alternative schools to help them succeed. Early intervention programs for children at risk of failure are also seen as a viable way to reduce the need for either retention or social promotion.

—*Pamela P. Hufnagel*

Further Readings and References

Alexander, K. L., Entwisle, D. R., & Dauber, S. L. (2003). *On the success of failure: A reassessment of the effects of retention in the primary school grades* (2nd ed.). Cambridge, UK: Cambridge University Press.

Jimerson, S. R., & Kaufman, A. M. (2003). Reading, writing, and retention: A primer on grade retention research. *The Reading Teacher, 56,* 622–635.

National Association of School Psychologists. (2003). *Position statement on student grade retention and social promotion.* Retrieved from http://www.nasponline.org/information/pospaper_graderetent.html

North Central Regional Educational Laboratory. (2001). *Critical issue: Beyond social promotion and retention—Five strategies to help students succeed.* Retrieved from http://www.ncrel.org/sdrs/areas/issues/students/atrisk/at800.htm

Shepard, L. A., & Smith, M. L. (Eds.). (1989). *Flunking grades: Research and policies on retention.* London: Falmer.

Trotter, A. (2004, April 14). Studies fault results of retention in Chicago. *Education Week.* Retrieved from http://www.edweek.org/ew/ewstory.cfm?slug=31Chicago.h23&keywords=retention

RETIREMENT

Retirement is often defined as a withdrawal from active working life undertaken by older adults. Unfortunately, such a definition is hardly descriptive of the phenomenon. There are a number of reasons for this. First, the term retirement is used interchangeably to refer to both the act of retiring and the status of being retired. Second, the concept of retirement is a social construction, and as such, it is constantly being redefined by both the larger society in which it takes place and those engaging in it. For instance, social norms play a large role in determining at what point one becomes an "older adult." In addition, the notion that retirement involves withdrawal from active work life may be inaccurate for the many older adults who "retire" yet continue in some form of paid employment in their preretirement positions/occupations, start out on new careers, and so on. The third reason why defining retirement is difficult is because it has been studied by a variety of different disciplines, which have operationalized it in different ways ranging from receiving income from a pension to planned retirement age. Different disciplines have also conceptualized retirement at different levels of aggregation, ranging from macrolevel work force participation rates to macrolevel self-attributions of retirement status.

Although all of these issues make arriving at a clear and unequivocal definition of retirement difficult, we nevertheless define the term retirement here as the process by which older adults come to reduce their reliance on the work role as a source of income, identity, or meaning. Through this definition we recognize retirement as a social, economic, and personal construct. In the section that immediately follows, we describe some of the trends leading toward the phenomenon of retirement. Then, we discuss the retirement process in two parts: In the first part we discuss issues related to the "act," or decision to retire; in the second part we discuss issues related to "status" of being retired.

RETIREMENT TRENDS

Prior to the 1900s, retirement was uncommon, thus retirement is a relatively new phenomenon, having emerged primarily among industrialized nations in just the last century. Most people (predominantly men) who worked outside of the home at that time continued to work as long as physically possible. The reasons for the emergence of retirement can be linked to a number of demographic trends including a decline in the average age at which individuals retire and the decreased workforce participation rates of older adults. At the start of the 1900s, the average age of retirement is estimated to have been about 66 years old. By the end of the century, it had declined to approximately 62 years of age. While at first glance this 4-year decline in the average age of retirement over the course of the last century does not appear very dramatic, it does have an important impact when one considers it at the aggregate level, expressed in terms of the workforce participation rate. For instance, just prior to the start of the 1900s some 75% of men in the United States over the age of 65 participated in the labor force whereas by the year 2000 this number had dropped to only about 18%. We hasten to add, however, that this trend toward lower workforce participation began leveling off after 1985.

These changes in the average age at which an individual retires and the workforce participation rate for older adults become even more significant when one considers the progressive aging and increased longevity of the population. The progressive aging of the population is largely attributable to the aging "baby boom" cohort made up of those born between 1946 and 1964. Currently, the members of this cohort consist of approximately 80 million adults who are quickly reaching the age where retirement is becoming a realistic option. Similar trends are apparent across most industrialized nations. Regarding longevity, within the United States, the average life expectancy at birth has increased from the late 40s in 1900 to the late 70s in 2000. Based on all of these trends, we can surmise that over the next few decades there is going to be a substantial number of people experiencing retirement and that they will be experiencing it for a substantially longer duration than at any time in the past. Thus, it is imperative for us to better understand the factors that contribute to the decision to retire.

The Decision to Retire

Retirement decision making has been the topic of empirical research among those in a number of areas such as economics, sociology, business, industrial/organizational psychology, and gerontology. Perhaps as a result of the variety of perspectives these different areas bring to the study of retirement decision making, there is no universally accepted theory of retirement decision making. Rather, in most cases, each discipline has attempted to explain retirement decision making by applying the theoretical lens from within their own discipline. For example, economists have employed theories about the economic trade-offs between work and leisure that determine whether or not one will work as well as the timing of that work

over the life cycle. In essence, this approach frames the retirement decision as a rational economic choice between when to work and when to spend and, as a result, tends to focus attention on the effects of financial resources on the decision to retire.

Those taking a more sociological perspective have applied theories surrounding the interplay age and the larger social context to examine how social policies, structures, and social norms influence retirement decision making. In the areas of business and industrial/organizational psychology, researchers have applied self-image theory, role attachment theory, and models of organizational withdrawal to retirement decision making. These tend to emphasize the importance of maintaining a positive self-image and membership in valued roles and also direct attention to working conditions and work-related attitudes. Gerontologists have applied theories of adult development and aging to retirement; for example, continuity theory.

Although these various perspectives and approaches to understanding retirement decision making may seem quite different from each other, they share certain commonalities. Perhaps the most important commonality is that each suggests that the decision to retire is a longitudinal process that begins long before the actual decision is made. It is also important to note that each of these different perspectives and approaches has contributed to our understanding of retirement decision making. Taken together, they provide an impressive literature regarding the factors that influence the decision to retire. In the section that immediately follows, we review some of the main findings of this literature.

FACTORS RELATED TO THE DECISION TO RETIRE

Environmental Factors

Perhaps the most important environmental influences on retirement decision making are the availability of public and private pension programs and laws surrounding age discrimination. Chief among the public pension programs is the Old Age, Survivors and Disability Insurance program enacted by the passage of the Social Security Act of 1935, which provides some level of income when one can no longer work. Though the specific ages at which benefits become available is changing, historically this program has provided "full" retirement benefits at age 65 and a reduced level at age 62. Not surprisingly, these are also the ages at which the most significant declines in work force participation rates have occurred, and a long line of research has supported the connection between the two.

Along the same lines as social security, the availability of private pension benefits for those between the ages of 55 and 60 has also been reliably linked to retirement decisions and declines in work force participation rates in that same age range. The 1986 amendment to the Age Discrimination in Employment Act (originally passed in 1967 to protect workers age 40 to 65 from discrimination in employment decisions) eliminated the practice of mandatory retirement for most workers in the United States. While organizations still have a variety of mechanisms by which to encourage retirement (e.g., early retirement incentives), some have linked the lifting of mandatory retirement with the leveling off of the trend toward lower work force participation rates that began to occur after 1986.

In addition to these, three other macrolevel influences are the social norms that have emerged (influenced at least in part by the legal developments above) surrounding retirement, changes in governmental regulations, and general economic conditions. Retirement norms, which set expectations regarding the timing of the decision to retire, do exist. These are established and communicated through the timing of when social security and private pension benefits become available and through interactions with coworkers, friends, and family. Current estimates suggest that many people see ages 62 and 65 as the appropriate and expected retirement age. In addition, changes in governmental regulations, such as the recent removal of earnings limits on social security benefits for those aged 65 to 69, may also impact individuals' decisions about when to retire. Regarding economic conditions, some research suggests that organizational munificence is negatively related to retirement decisions, while a high local unemployment rate may be positively related to retirement decisions.

Working Conditions and Attitudes

It would seem logical that the characteristics of one's job would be related to retirement decision making and the research to date supports this logic. For instance, studies have found that those in physically demanding jobs as well as unrewarding and stressful jobs are more likely to retire earlier. In addition, empirical research supports a reliable relationship between job characteristics such as autonomy, variety, interaction with others, feedback, task identity, and task significance, often combined to form an overall score, and the decision to retire earlier. Some evidence also suggests that positive affective reactions to work (e.g., job satisfaction) are related to the decision to retire later. Similarly, research supports the idea that commitment, including general commitment to work, organizational commitment, and career commitment, are related to the decision to retire later.

Familial Factors

Although not studied as widely as other variables, the decision to retire is often made within the context of the family, and family-related variables do play a role in this part of the retirement process. One general finding is that married couples tend to coordinate their retirement decisions such that they retire at similar times. However, this relationship is by no means universal and may depend on the quality of the marital relationship and family life, the presence of dependents in the home, and the health and gender of the spouse. Because a considerable amount of time spent in the status of retirement may also mean time spent with family, the quality of the marital relationship and family life is important. Those with poorer quality family relationships are less likely to retire than those with higher quality family relationships. With regard to having dependents, including children, grandchildren, and parents in the home, the relationship between this factor and retirement decision making likely depends on gender and the acting out of traditional gender roles. For men, the presence of dependents in the home can be perceived as creating financial demands that must be met through continued work (the "bread winner" role for men). As a result, men are less likely to retire. For women, on the other hand, the presence of dependents in the home can be perceived as creating demands that must be met through care giving. As a result, women are more likely to retire.

Individual Factors

Compared to familial factors, the relationships demographic and other individual factors have with retirement decision making have been studied quite often. Among the demographic factors, age, health, wealth, and education level have probably been studied most often. While it is certainly true that when one considers the entire age range of adults, it is the older adults who retire, there is some evidence that younger workers today intend to retire at earlier ages than older workers. In addition, those with health limitations and those who can financially afford to stop working are more likely to retire than those in good health or who need to maintain their income from paid work. Although the results are somewhat less robust, education level has also been linked to retirement decisions such that those with lower education levels are more likely to retire at earlier ages than those with higher education levels. Beyond these demographic variables, attitudes toward retirement have also been shown to be related to the decision to retire. Not surprisingly, those who view retirement positively tend to express a desire to retire sooner rather than later.

In summary, a number of disciplines have contributed to our understanding of the process of retirement decision making. Still, there are a number of areas that warrant further research attention, one of which involves examining the role of early retirement incentive programs. In addition, recent developments in and increasing access to procedures to model processes over time and at various levels of aggregation (i.e., latent growth curve modeling, random coefficient modeling) could be employed by researchers.

THE STATUS OF RETIREMENT

Theories of Retirement Adjustment

Theory on retirement adjustment has typically taken one of several approaches. The first focuses on examining retirement in terms of role theory. That is, retirement is viewed as a role that individuals engage in and transition to, similar to that of the role of worker, spouse, parent, or other socially created and defined roles. A second theoretical approach to examining retirement adjustment has focused on different retirement styles. For example, some have discussed four different styles or modes of adaptation to retirement, one of which is referred to as *transition to old age,* where the older individual sees retirement as a time to wind down and disengage. The *new beginnings* style entails welcoming retirement with a new

sense of freedom and increased vigor, while older individuals who use a *continuation* style would see little difference from pre- to postretirement. Finally, those retirees having the *imposed transition* style see retirement as a significant role loss. Thus, engaging in different modes or styles of retirement appears to have implications for how retirees transition and adapt to retirement, as well as the significance they place on the role of retiree.

A third theoretical approach to examining retirement adjustment has been to characterize the retirement process as a series of phases or stages that one passes through. One of these models discusses seven phases that individuals *may* go through as they transition into, through, and out of retirement. According to this model, initially individuals are in the *remote* phase where retirement is characterized as a distal event and where individuals typically have only a vague concept of retirement. By the *near* phase, individuals realize that retirement is not that far off and begin serious planning and preparation for retirement. The *honeymoon* phase occurs immediately after the retirement event itself and is typically characterized by a sense of freedom and maybe even euphoria of not having to deal with the daily grind of work. By the *disenchantment* phase, retirees may begin to obtain a sense that retirement may not be exactly what they expected. However, most individuals will go through a fifth *reorientation* phase where they are able to realign their preretirement expectations with the realities experienced once they retired. Most individuals will then settle into the sixth *stability* phase where the role of retiree begins to become more comfortable and routine. In the seventh and final *termination* phase, individuals no longer are engaged in the retiree role, typically due to morbidity or mortality.

While these three broad approaches to understanding and explaining the retirement adjustment process may appear to differ on the surface, they have important common characteristics. For example, all three approaches see retirement as a continuous process of preparation, transition, and then adjustment. Retirement is not viewed as a single decision that older individuals briefly engage in or as an event that occurs ever so briefly. Instead, retirement preparation, transition, and adjustment are viewed as long-term processes that individuals actively engage in. In fact, most people understand that they will eventually retire and begin thinking about it long before the "event" actually takes place.

Retirement Myths

A number of studies have been conducted to examine the process of retirement and how individuals prepare for, transition to, and adjust to this increasingly prominent role in late life. Most empirical studies indicate that several myths regarding retirement and the adjustment to retirement do not appear to hold true. For example, it was long assumed that retirement "caused" illness and poor health. Often is heard the anecdote of so-and-so who retired and got sick and died! Most epidemiological research indicates that those experiencing poor health immediately after retirement were experiencing poor health prior to retirement. Thus, while some health problems are inevitable as we age, it does not appear that retirement itself "causes" these ills.

In addition, the myth that retirement is very stressful and a time of "crisis" has not been supported by research. While some individuals do experience high stress during the transition to retirement, usually coincidental with other stressful life events, a majority of older individuals typically do not experience a true "crisis." Instead, older individuals experience relative continuity in life, where some roles are decreased (worker), while other increase (volunteer, grandparent) to replace the diminished work role. Similarly, another myth is that a majority of older individuals migrate to warm weather climates after retirement. In fact, less than 10% of retirees move out of state after retirement. Family and social contact networks that have evolved over the course of a lifetime are cherished and used to help smooth the transition and adjustment to retirement.

Finally, the myth of the retiring husband suddenly "being under foot" and thus causing marital discord appears to be highly exaggerated. While some adjustment period is warranted in most marriages when one or both spouses retire, most couples report improved, rather than diminished, marital relations after retirement. This of course assumes that the retirement does not coincide with a negative life event such as poor health on the part of the retiree or spouse.

Preretirement Planning

One line of research on retirement adjustment has examined the effects of preretirement planning on the transition to retirement. Not surprisingly, those individuals who engage in more preparation for retirement, whether formal or informal, tend to adjust better to the retirement role than those who fail to prepare. In fact, most retirement planning takes the form of informal discussions with spouse, family, and friends. However, for most individuals, this appears to be adequate to allow for a relatively smooth transition to retirement. In addition, these positive effects of retirement planning appear to hold for both civilian workers and military personnel transitioning to retirement.

Gender Difference in Retirement Adjustment

Another line of retirement adjustment research has examined gender differences in retirement, as well as the extent to which retirement is indeed a "coupled" experience. While early work on retirement focused almost exclusively on men's (predominantly white men's) retirement experiences, more recent work has looked at both men's and women's retirement experiences. The more recent research appears to indicate that men's and women's experiences of retirement can be similar, especially when they have experienced similar work histories. In addition, individuals who are married and in dual career relationships often try to time their retirement to coincide with their spouse's retirement. However, to the extent that men and women have different personal (e.g., health), nonwork (e.g., dependents in the household), and work-related (e.g., work role attachment) dynamics, they will experience retirement in a different way. Given that such gender differences often do exist in these dynamics, some have warned against using the "male model" of retirement to explain women's adjustment to retirement.

Postretirement Employment

The transition to retirement has become a "blurred" process in that most individuals do not simply stop working one day, after 25 or 30 years with the same company. Instead, a majority of individuals transition slowly out of the workforce through phased or partial retirement in the same job or occupation, by engaging in some form of postretirement employment in a different job or occupation, or by moving back and forth between being retired and employed, until eventually exiting the labor force completely. Thus, the effects of postretirement employment (usually referred to as bridge employment) on retirement adjustment have only relatively recently been examined. While bridge employment can have beneficial effects on retirement adjustment, they are by no means universal. In particular, if retirees feel they are forced to return to work for, say, financial reasons, retirement adjustment tends to be negatively impacted. The key to maximizing the beneficial effects of bridge employment on retirement adjustment is the degree of match between the retirees desired level of work involvement in retirement and their actual level of involvement. The better the match, the better adjustment tends to be. This result appears to hold for both paid and volunteer work activities.

In summary, generally older individuals who are healthy, have adequate income, have planned and prepared for retirement, have a strong social network, and who have an adaptive personality style tend to adjust better to retirement than those who do not possess these qualities. While most individuals do tend to eventually adjust well to retirement, continued research is needed to address the reasons why some individuals fail to make this adjustment. Unfortunately, solid research and theory on other behavioral and cognitive strategies for positively adapting to retirement are still lacking. Thus, more research is needed to determine why some fail to adjust well why others adjust well and even thrive in retirement.

—*Gary A. Adams and Kenneth S. Shultz*

See also American Association of Retired Persons (AARP)

Further Readings and References

Adams, G. A., & Beehr, T. A. (2003). *Retirement: Reasons, processes, and results.* New York: Springer.

Administration on Aging, http://www.aoa.dhhs.gov/

Atchley, R. C. (1989). A continuity theory of normal aging. *The Gerontologist, 29,* 183–190.

Blöndal, S., & Scarpetta, S. (1998). *The retirement decision in OECD countries.* OECD Working Paper, No. 202, Paris: OECD.

Costa, D. L. (1998). *The evolution of retirement—An American economic history 1880–1990.* Chicago: University of Chicago Press.

Gruber, J., & Wise, D. A. (1999). *Social security and retirement around the world.* Chicago: University of Chicago Press.

Kim, J. E., & Moen, P. (2001). Moving into retirement: Preparation and transition in late midlife. In M. E. Lachman (Ed.), *Handbook of midlife development* (Chap. 14, pp. 487–527). New York: Wiley.

Schaie, K. W., & Schooler, C. (1998). *Impact of work on older adults.* New York: Springer.

Szinovacz, M. E. (2003). Retirement. *International encyclopedia of marriage and the family.* New York: Macmillan.

Talaga, J. A., & Beehr, T. A. (1989). Retirement: A psychological perspective. In C. L. Cooper & I. T. Robertson (Eds.), *International review of industrial and organizational psychology* (pp. 185–211). New York: Wiley.

RETT SYNDROME

Rett syndrome (RS) is a pervasive neurodevelopmental disorder that almost solely affects females. Of importance for understanding its developmental course, it is not a generative disorder. RS is marked by apparently normal development for 6 to 18 months followed by rapid physical and mental deterioration. Although estimates vary, RS occurs in about 1 in every 10,000 to 15,000 female births worldwide, affecting all racial and ethnic groups.

GENETICS OF RS

The discovery in 1999 that RS is associated with a mutation of the MECP2 gene, located on X-chromosomes, confirmed the disorder's long-inferred genetic basis. The mutated gene on one X-chromosome is sufficient to produce RS. Occurrence of RS appears to owe to random mutation, and is thus genetic but generally not inherited; recurrence rates within the same family are less then 0.4%.

Recent evidence suggests that the mutation most often occurs in the father's sperm. Because the father passes on an X-chromosome to his daughters and a Y-chromosome to his sons, only daughters receive the mutated MECP2 gene. Thus, the theory that RS is lethal prenatally to males is believed to be incorrect. In line with the current theory, RS has been reported in some males with an extra X-chromosome who show characteristics of both Rett and Klinefelter syndromes.

Apparently, the MECP2 gene is normally involved in switching off other genes. The mutated gene allows other genes to inappropriately switch or stay on, disrupting normal development. This previously unknown malfunctioning process has implications for understanding not only RS, but other neurodevelopmental disorders and perhaps even apparently unrelated conditions such as Alzheimer's disease.

DIAGNOSIS AND CHARACTERISTICS

Often misdiagnosed in the past, commonly as autism or cerebral palsy, RS now has agreed upon necessary, supportive, and exclusionary diagnostic criteria. Necessary criteria include apparently normal pre-, peri-, and early postnatal development; deceleration of head growth beginning from 3 to 36 months of age; loss of acquired skills (voluntary hand skills; verbal and nonverbal communication skills) beginning at 3 to 36 months of age; appearance of obvious mental retardation and intense and persistent hand stereotypies (hand wringing/squeezing, washing/patting/rubbing, mouthing/tongue pulling) in early childhood; and gait abnormalities in ambulatory cases.

Supportive criteria include breathing dysfunctions, bloating and marked air swallowing, EEG abnormalities, seizures, spasticity, muscle wasting, peripheral vasomotor disturbances, scoliosis, hypotrophic small and cold feet, and growth retardation. Exclusionary criteria (presence excludes diagnosis of RS) include signs of storage disease, retinopathy or optic atrophy, microcephaly at birth, existence of metabolic or other hereditary degenerative disorder, neurological disorder from severe infection or head trauma, intrauterine growth retardation, and peri- or postnatal brain damage.

DEVELOPMENTAL COURSE

Classic RS generally develops through a four-stage sequence of behavioral and physical changes. However, it has variable expressivity, so individual differences characterize which features are manifested and the age of onset, duration, and transition across stages. (1) *Early-onset stagnation* (onset: 6–18 months; duration: months) is characterized by developmental stagnation, deceleration of head growth, and hyptonia; diminished eye contact, communication, hand-use ability, interest in play and the environment; and development of random movements. (2) *Rapid developmental regression* (onset: 12–36 months; duration: weeks to months) includes the appearance of hand stereotypies; onset of sleep disturbances, breathing irregularities, and seizure-like spells; and deterioration of cognitive functioning, hand use, and expressive language. The child's behavior may resemble, and be diagnosed as, autism. (3) *Pseudostationary* (onset: preschool age; duration: to about 10 years of age) is characterized by a decrease in autistic-like features; fixed gait and stance; increased severity of mental retardation, breathing irregularities, bruxism, body rigidity, and seizures; and development of scoliosis. (4) Late motor deterioration (onset: 10 years of age;

lifelong duration) includes loss or decrease in expressive or receptive language and remaining motor function, including chewing, swallowing, and walking; and increase in rigidity, scoliosis, and muscle wasting. However, many parents report that their adult daughters show improvements: in the form of (a) decreases in sleep problems, irritability, wide mood swings, seizures, panic attacks, and hand stereotypies, and (b) increases in voluntary hand use, such as cup holding, and communication through "eye pointing." Since most diagnosed females with RS are less than 18 years old, information on life expectancy is limited, but many will live well into their 40s.

Treatment

No overall effective treatment for RS is available, although some symptoms can be managed. Treatment is specific to the individual and the severity of symptoms at any particular time. A multidisciplinary approach is necessary, typically beginning with treatment from a neurologist and/or developmental pediatrician. Medication effectively controls, and physical therapy reduces, many symptoms. Lifelong physical, occupational, and speech therapies are often necessary, as are academic, social, vocational, and supportive services. Specific treatments include medication for seizures and agitation, and braces, surgery, and physical therapy for scoliosis. Behavior modification has had limited effectiveness. Alternative communication techniques (e.g., augmentative communication) may be useful. Music therapy is often used to help children with gross motor and manipulative skills, environmental awareness, and receptive and expressive language.

Affected girls will require lifelong care and supervision, placing a heavy burden on caregivers. Families may benefit from regular counseling concerning their daughters' condition and treatment and will often need a variety of supports.

POSSIBLE FUTURE DEVELOPMENTS

The discovery of the genetic basis and recent development of a mouse model have led to several promising avenues of research. These include discovering the mechanisms by which the mutated MECP2 gene manifests itself; determining how to "silence" the effects of the mutation; and developing treatment, such as stem cell transplants, that may halt or reverse the course of the disorder.

—Robert T. Brown and
Kathleen McMillan

Further Readings and References

Brown, R. T., & Hoadley, S. L. (1999). Rett syndrome. In S. Goldstein & C. R. Reynolds (Eds.), *Handbook of neurodevelopmental and genetic disorders in children* (pp. 459–477). New York: Guilford.

Hoadley, S. L., & Brown, R. T. (2003). Rett syndrome. In E. Fletcher-Janzen & C. R. Reynolds (Eds.), *The diagnostic manual of childhood disorders: Clinical and special education applications.* New York: Wiley.

International Rett Syndrome Association, http://www.rettsyndrome.org/index.htm

Kerr, A. (2002). Annotation: Rett syndrome: Recent progress and implications for research and clinical practice. *Journal of Child Psychology and Psychiatry, 43,* 277–287.

WE MOVE. (2004). *Rett syndrome.* Retrieved from http://www.wemove.org/rett/

RH FACTOR

Rhesus monkeys have contributed greatly to our understanding of human physiology but perhaps their most significant role was in the discovery of the Rh factor. So great was their contribution that this protein substance of the red blood cell was named the Rhesus Factor.

It had long been known that some substance present in human blood, when administered to another human, caused "agglutination" or clumping of the recipient's blood. Similar to injection of ABO incompatible blood, the patient would respond by building up antibodies even when the blood groups were the same. In other words, even if two people had type B blood, a transfusion was not always successful.

Having already documented the first three human blood groups—A, B, and O—in 1901, Karl Landsteiner, an Austrian physician, and Alex Wiener, while conducting research 38 years later in New York City, discovered a final clue to the mystery of blood incompatibility. They observed that a protein substance that Landsteiner named the Rhesus factor had the ability to induce intense antibody response when Rhesus monkey blood was transfused into a rabbit. Agglutination or clumping occurred in the majority of specimens. When human blood was mixed with the same rabbit serum, red cells clumped together in a majority of the specimens. Such blood was typed Rh positive. The blood of the remaining specimens lacked the factor and was typed Rh negative.

In normal life circumstances, there are two critical times when bloods of separate individuals mingle—transfusion and pregnancy. In a human without the Rhesus factor, introduction of the factor (the antigen) causes an immunologic response (antibody formation) in the recipient. If an Rh-absent (negative) mother gives birth to an Rh-present (positive) baby, or if Rh-positive blood is transfused into an Rh-negative person, the negative factored person will begin to develop antibodies that attach to the Rh-positive red blood cells, causing them to clump together. The action of these antibodies is *hemolysis* or destruction of the red blood cells. The initial insult (e.g., a first pregnancy) may pass unnoticed; however, introduction of more Rh positive cells (a second pregnancy) may trigger the activation and release of more antibodies, which may cause significant anemia in the mother or destruction of red blood cells or hemolytic disease in the fetus/newborn (erythroblastosis fetalis). Hemolytic disease may be minor and responsive to supportive therapy or treatment, or it may result in significant illness and death.

Every mother is tested at her initial obstetrical visit; her Rh factor is noted as is the presence of any antibodies. If she is Rh negative, a protective dose of "Rh IgG," an immunoglobulin (RhoGAM), is administered by injection at 28 weeks gestation. This suppresses antibody formation for the last trimester of pregnancy. Upon birth, the mother is tested again for antibody formation and, if the baby is Rh positive, another dose of RhoGAM is administered within 72 hours to protect future babies from maternal antibody development that might destroy his or her red blood cells. The immunoglobulin would also be administered in the event of any maternal injury, bleeding in the second or third trimester, or after a miscarriage or induced abortion. Since the introduction of RhoGAM, the risk of Rh incompatibility has been reduced from 10% to 20% to less than 1%.

About 85% of Caucasians and 92 to 96% of African Americans are Rh positive; 99% of Native Americans and those of Chinese and Japanese descent are Rhesus positive, while 30% to 35% of Basque descendants are Rh negative.

—Margaret Plumbo

Further Readings and References

Ballard, C. (2003). *The heart and blood: Injury, illness and health.* Chicago: Heinemann Library.

Cheong, Y., Goodrick, J., & Kyle, P. (2001). Management of anti-Rhesus-D antibodies in pregnancy: A review from 1994 to 1998. *Fetal Diagnosis & Therapy, 16*(5), 294–298.

Cunningham, F. G. (2001). Isoimmunization. In G. Cunningham, N. F. Gant, K. J. Leveno, L. C. Gilstrap, J. C. Hauth, & K. D. Wenstrom (Eds.), *Williams obstetrics* (pp. 1057–1063). New York: McGraw-Hill.

eMedicine. (2004). *Rh incompatibility.* Retrieved from http://www.emedicine.com/emerg/topic507.htm

Gallagher, K. (2004). *Rh immune globulin.* Retrieved from http://my.webmd.com/hw/being_pregnant/hw144853.asp

Hackett, E. (1973). *Blood.* New York: Dutton.

Harmening, D. (1999). *Modern blood banking and transfusion practices.* Philadelphia: F. A. Davis.

Harrod, K. S., Hanson, L., VandeVusse, L., & Heywood, P. (2003). Rh negative status and isoimmunization update: A case-based approach to care. *Journal of Perinatal & Neonatal Nursing, 17*(3), 166–178.

iVillage. (2005). *Incompatibility of blood types and Rh factor.* Retrieved from http://www.ivillage.co.uk/pregnancy andbaby/pregnancy/complicatepreg/qas/0,,15_158142,00 .html

Maisels, M., & Watchko, J. (Eds.). (2000). *Neonatal jaundice.* Amsterdam: Harwood Academic.

March of Dimes. (2001). *Rh disease.* Retrieved from http://www.marchofdimes.com/professionals/681_1220.asp

MoonDragon Birthing Services. (n.d.). *Variations of pregnancy: Maternal blood type—Rh negative.* Retrieved from http://www.moondragon.org/mdbsguidelines/rhneg.html

Neal, J. L. (2001). RhD isoimmunization and current management modalities [Review]. *Journal of Obstetric, Gynecologic, & Neonatal Nursing, 30*(6), 589–606.

Stockman, J. (2001). Overview of the state of the art of Rh disease: History, current clinical management, and recent progress. *Journal of Pediatric Hematology/Oncology, 23*(6), 385–393.

WebMD Health. (n.d.). *Rh sensitization during pregnancy.* Retrieved from http://my.webmd.com/hw/being_pregnant/ hw135945.asp?lastselectedguid={5FE84E90-BC77-4056-A91C-9531713CA348}

Zimmerman, D. R. (1973). *Rh: The intimate history of a disease and its conquest.* New York: Macmillan.

RHEUMATOID ARTHRITIS

Rheumatoid arthritis can occur throughout the life span and takes various forms in childhood and the adult years. We will briefly review these disorders by age group.

CHILDHOOD-ONSET ARTHRITIS

Juvenile rheumatic diseases (JRD) are a heterogeneous group of disabling autoinflammatory diseases. Juvenile rheumatoid arthritis (JRA), systemic lupus erythematosus (SLE), juvenile ankylosing spondylitis (JAS), and juvenile dermatomyositis (JDM) are the primary subtypes of JRD; all are believed to be related to abnormal immunological control. The specific etiology of these diseases is largely unknown, and no cure is presently available. It has been stressed that the occurrences of these diseases are multifactorial, including genetic, immunological, and infectious triggers. Trauma and stress are also possible triggers for JRD. Findings suggest that multiple pathways may result in a diagnosis of JRD, including abnormalities of immunologic regulation, psychological stress, trauma, hormonal abnormalities, and infection.

JRDs have many common features, including an unpredictable disease course with periods of remission and relapse. Children diagnosed with one of these rheumatic diseases commonly experience pain, muscle weakness, fatigue, and functional disabilities. There is also great variation in the rate of onset of the clinical manifestations of these diseases; making a diagnosis can take months or years.

Of all the JRDs, juvenile rheumatoid arthritis (JRA) is the most common. Onset is typically before age 16 and can be as early as 6 months of age. The estimated prevalence rate of children diagnosed with JRA in the United States is approximately between 16 and 150 children per 100,000 individuals, girls being affected twice as often as boys.

The role of psychological variables in JRD has been widely examined. It is believed children and youth with JRD may be more susceptible to psychological complications due to the characteristics of the disease: physical deformity, disability, and chronicity. In addition, the uncertain prognosis, invisibility of the condition, and a remitting disease course serve as additional risk factors for psychological distress. It is not surprising that children with JRD are at increased risk for experiencing a host of psychosocial adjustment difficulties, including depression and dysthymic disorder as well as social difficulties. Increases in both negative daily moods and daily stressful events have been associated with reports of fatigue, stiffness, and decreases in daily activities.

Currently, there is no known cure for the juvenile rheumatic diseases. Treatment aims include controlling inflammation, pain, and range of motion, preventing joint deformities, and maximizing functioning, as well as increasing and amplifying psychosocial adjustment. Additional treatment goals consist of increasing muscle strength and function, managing systemic involvement, and facilitating healthy nutrition and physical development. Children diagnosed with JRD may receive multiple medications and/or utilize resources and treatments from a number of medical specialists (e.g., pediatric rheumatologist, physical therapists, occupational therapist, nurse, nutritionist, psychologist, orthopedic surgeon). Some of the medications commonly utilized to treat JRD include nonsteroidal anti-inflammatory drugs, gold hydroxychloroquine, antimalarial drugs, D-penicillamine, sulfasalazine, methotrexate, intravenous immunoglobulins, monoclonal antibody treatments, and corticosteroids. These medications are primarily designed to control pain, preserve range of motion and function, and manage systemic complications.

ADULT-ONSET ARTHRITIS

Rheumatoid arthritis (RA) in adults is also characterized as an autoimmune disease involving inflammation of the joints, resulting in pain, stiffness, and loss of function. RA typically occurs in symmetrical patterns, and often involves the finger joints closest to the hand, as well as the wrist. RA can also occur in any number of other joints, including the feet, ankles, hips, and neck. Such symptoms may also be accompanied by fatigue, fever, and a general sense of malaise. Not unlike the childhood forms, the causes of RA are thought to be multifactorial, involving a combination of genetic, hormonal, environmental, and stress influences. Once a diagnosis is made, the course of RA may be quite unpredictable, with periods of exacerbations or "flares" followed by periods of remission. Some individuals experience only mild to moderate degrees of disease activity, while others may have severe forms that result in significant joint damage, pain, and disability. It is currently estimated that RA affects approximately 2.1 million Americans. Women are two to three times more likely to be diagnosed with this disease. Onset is most likely to occur in middle-aged to older adults.

Depression and depressive symptomotology are frequently observed phenomena in individuals with RA. Research has also suggested that increased pain and disability are important concomitants of depression. Notably, it has also been demonstrated that individuals with similar levels of pain and disability often experience quite different levels of depression, thereby suggesting the contribution of other intervening psychological variables. Indeed, cognitive appraisal variables, such as attributional style, have been implicated in the development of depressive symptoms.

Just as is the case with childhood forms, RA has no known cure at this time. The primary goals of treatment are to reduce pain and stiffness, to decrease the rate of joint damage, and to enhance the individual's quality of life. A wide variety of treatment approaches have been utilized in the treatment of RA. Lifestyle modifications are typically encouraged and include appropriately designed exercise programs, scheduled rest periods, joint care procedures (e.g., splinting devices), and stress management. Interventions may also include surgeries for joint replacement and tendon reconstruction. A wide variety of medications have also been used to treat the pain and stiffness associated with RA, or to slow its progression. Such medications include the analgesics and nonsteroidal anti-inflammatory drugs (NSAIDs) such as acetaminophen, aspirin, and ibuprofen, corticosteroids such as prednisone, and the disease-modifying anti-rheumatic drugs (DMARDs), including azathioprine, cyclosporine, and methotrexate. A new generation of drugs, known as biologic response modifiers, is also being used now to treat the inflammation and joint damage associated with RA. Examples of such medications include infliximab, adalimumab, and etanercept, all of which work by blocking the action of cytokines.

—Larry L. Mullins, John M. Chaney, and Molly White

Further Readings and References

Cassidy, J. T., & Petty, R. E. (2001). *The textbook of pediatric rheumatology* (4th ed.). Philadelphia: W.B. Saunders.

Chaney, J. M., Mullins, L. L., Wagner, J. L., Hommel, K.A., Page, M. C., & Doppler, M. J. (2004). A longitudinal examination of causal attributions and depression symptomatology in rheumatoid arthritis. *Rehabilitation Psychology, 49,* 126–133.

National Institute of Arthritis and Musculoskeletal and Skin Diseases. (1998). *Handout on health: Rheumatoid arthritis.* Retrieved from http://www.niams.nih.gov/hi/topics/arthritis/rahandout.htm

RIGHT-TO-DIE MOVEMENT

The "right to die" is an umbrella term that denotes not a unified movement but rather a collection of various advocacy groups that have asserted a range of ethical and legal positions about when and how a human life may be deliberately terminated with legal impunity. Among these groups are those who argue for a natural or civil right to self-determination, even over the manner and timing of one's death, a so-called right to "rational suicide" or "self-deliverance" under certain conditions (or, much the same position has been argued on utilitarian grounds, rather than as a matter of individual rights); those who would permit legally assisted euthanasia (or "mercy killing" or "assisted suicide") of terminally ill, brain-dead, or acutely suffering patients, respectively; those who promote a generalized "death with dignity" that clarifies a person's wishes for end-of-life medical treatments through a living will stipulating those terms in advance; and those who participate in hospice outreach care that addresses issues of medical treatment, palliative measures, pain management, and comfort for dying individuals and their families and loved ones. "Passive" euthanasia is often distinguished from "active" euthanasia, which is the difference, for instance, between a physician withholding life-support systems such as feeding tubes versus someone proactively administering lethal drug doses in order to hasten death. Some of the prominent right-to-die groups include the Society for the Right to Die, the Hemlock Society (renamed in 2003 as End-of-Life Choices), Voluntary Euthanasia Society, Dying with Dignity, Death with Dignity, Compassion in Dying Federation, Partnership for Caring, and Dying Well Network. The World Federation of Right to Die Societies, founded in 1980, consists of 38 organizations from 23 countries.

The modern origins of these groups date back to the world's first euthanasia society founded in London in 1935 and the Euthanasia Society of America, founded in New York in 1938 (renamed the Society for the Right to Die in 1974). The following notable historical events led to the formation of the contemporary right-to-die organizations. In 1967, attorney Louis Kutner wrote the first living will. In 1969, Elisabeth Kübler-Ross published *On Death and Dying*, a book that drew wide attention to public issues about dying. In 1976, the New Jersey Supreme Court ruled that the parents of Karen Ann Quinlan, a comatose woman who had suffered brain damage, could disconnect her body from the respirator. In 1984, the Netherlands became the first country to approve voluntary euthanasia. In 1990, the U.S. Supreme Court ruled, in *Cruzan v. Director, Missouri Department of Heath*, that competent adults have a constitutionally protected liberty to refuse medical treatment, though the court insisted on proof of a patient's wishes by "clear and convincing evidence."

In 1991 Derek Humphry, founder of the Hemlock Society, published *Final Exit: The Practicalities of Self-Deliverance and Assisted Suicide*, a book that became a bestseller and helped mobilize a number of state referenda to approve assisted suicide. Only one of those state initiatives passed: In 1994 Oregon voters approved a Death with Dignity referendum which, after legal challenges, took effect in 1997, thus making Oregon the first and only state to legalize physician-assisted suicide. In 1997 the U.S. Supreme Court basically reversed course from the *Cruzan* case, now ruling unanimously in *Washington v. Glucksberg* that states may indeed outlaw doctor-assisted suicide, thus establishing the principle that a general public right to assistance in committing suicide is not a fundamental liberty guaranteed by the Constitution.

In 1999, Dr. Jack Kervorkian was found guilty of second degree murder in Michigan, whereas in the previous 10 years he had assisted in the deaths of 120 people and yet eluded criminal conviction up to that point. In 1998, Michael Schiavo petitioned a Florida court requesting that his wife, Terri, who had been severely brain-damaged in 1990, be removed from life-prolonging medical procedures; the Schiavo case became the latest and one of the nation's most bitterly fought right-to-die cases, winding its way through numerous Florida courts, the Florida legislature, the Florida Governor's office and the Supreme Court of the United States. While most right-to-die controversy has focused on the United States and the Netherlands, numerous right-to-die campaigns involving legal challenges, informational conferences and newsletters, medical and technological research, and other such activities have been initiated in recent years in other countries.

The modern salience of the right-to-die movement is probably symptomatic of a number of large-scale shifts in population demographics, advances in medical technologies, and changes in the economics of health care delivery. The basic sociological fact underwriting much of the movement is that a smaller percentage of the population in industrialized countries now dies a "natural" death, i.e., free of aggressive late-terminal medical intervention. Instead, a host of life-prolonging medical treatments is brought to bear upon the elderly, the infirm, and the dying.

Another facet is that people are living longer. In the United States, for instance, male life expectancy increased from 46.3 years to 74.4 years between 1900 and 2001; female life expectancy during that period rose from 48.3 years to 79.8 years. Yet the site of death has shifted dramatically from residential locations to hospitals and other institutions. In 1936, only 35.1% of all Americans died in hospitals and institutional settings; by 1994, that figure more than doubled, rising to 73.8%. In the majority of cases, physicians and other health care providers have made a concerted effort to keep these increasingly hospitalized patients alive, using the latest medical techniques and technologies available to them. Yet the right-to-die movement does not impact simply the elderly; many of the most dramatic cases have centered on brain-damaged young women, such as Karen Ann Quinlan (1975–1985), Nancy Cruzan (1983–1990), and Terri Schiavo (1990–2005). By 2000, 45 states had authorized both a living will and the appointment of a health care proxy for an "advance directive" in such dire situations; four states permit only a health care agent, and one state permits only a living will. While assisted suicide is legal only in Oregon, right-to-die proponents contend that a de facto practice is widespread throughout the country, enacted, when necessary, by compassionate physicians who quietly withhold medical treatment or else prescribe virtually lethal doses of morphine to hasten death. Whereas American culture once viewed the terms of death primarily as a private family matter, changing demographic, legal, and economic concerns have forced the issue into the public domain, where courts and congresses must now wrestle with and renegotiate the proper boundary lines between privacy rights and public oversight and between state and federal jurisdictions.

Right-to-die advocates frequently contend that the thicket of constitutional, cultural, and technological issues reduces down to a basic ethical insight; to see an anguished family member or loved one suffer at the time of death prompts bystanders and survivors to seek alternative, more humane approaches to the end of a life. Instead of having to shop around for a sympathetic physician—increasingly difficult in an era of bureaucratized health care as well as medical malpractice lawsuits—terminally ill patients and their family members in all states, they contend, should have uniform access to medical assistance (or the refusal of medical intervention) in expediting the inevitable, albeit with proper safeguards in place. Such a position has galvanized a significant backlash as well. A number of groups have organized to contest the ethics of modern euthanasia. Many of these groups espouse a religious perspective, contending that euthanasia is a form of murder and that suicide is never to be condoned. The preservation of life, the unconditional affirmation of the sanctity of life, is of paramount importance, they submit; and a physician's obligation is to prolong life at all costs, regardless of a patient's expressed wishes.

Others argue on more utilitarian grounds against the legalization of assisted euthanasia. They worry that the marginalized of society—the elderly, the disabled, persons of color, the poor, the unloved, the depressed—are more likely to be subject to such termination procedures. They point out that family members may well be factoring in the high cost and financial burden of medical care that may influence their judgment about how long to sanction and to endure life-sustaining procedures. Still others point out that certain comatose patients who were once diagnosed as brain-dead and terminal have, in exceptional cases, recovered; thus, the possibility of misdiagnosis or of miraculous recovery always looms on the horizon. Finally, some physicians point out that the Hippocratic oath states: "To please no one will I prescribe a deadly drug, or give advice which may cause his death." Ending someone's life, for whatever reason, requires that a physician corrupt the traditional practice of medicine, transforming it from an enterprise that helps and saves lives into one that harms and terminates them. Yet, in at least one legal brief, the American Medical Association, while opposing physician-assisted suicide, conceded that physicians face a dilemma in many terminal situations: "For over 2000 years, the predominant responsibility of the physician has not been to preserve life at all costs but to serve the patient's needs while respecting the patient's autonomy and dignity."

—*John Seery*

See also Death, Death with Dignity

Further Readings and References

End of Life Choices, http://www.endoflifechoices.org/ index.jsp

Heifetz, M. D. (1975). *The right to die*. New York: Putnam.

Hendin, H. (1997). *Seduced by death: Doctors, patients, and the Dutch cure.* New York: W. W. Norton.

Humphry, D. (1991). *Final exit: The practicalities of self-deliverance and assisted suicide for the dying.* Secaucus, NJ: Carol Publishing.

Humphry, D., & Clement, M. (1998). *Freedom to die: People, politics, and the right to die movement.* New York: St. Martin's Press.

Kübler-Ross, E. (1969). *On death and dying.* New York: Macmillan.

Moreno, J. D. (Ed.). (1995). *Arguing euthanasia: The controversy over mercy killing, assisted suicide, and the "right to die."* New York: Simon & Schuster.

Public Agenda. (2005). *Right to Die: Overview.* Retrieved from http://www.publicagenda.org/issues/overview.cfm?issue_type=right2die

Singer, P. (1994). *Rethinking life and death: The collapse of our traditional ethics.* New York: St. Martin's Press.

Smith, W. J. (1997). *Forced exit: The slippery slope from assisted suicide to legalized murder.* New York: Random House.

World Federation of Right to Die Societies, http://www.worldrtd.net/

RITALIN

Ritalin (methylphenidate hydrochloride) is a central nervous system (CNS) stimulant medication most commonly prescribed for children and adults diagnosed with attention deficit hyperactivity disorder (ADHD). Ritalin is also occasionally prescribed to treat sleep disorders such as narcolepsy. Ritalin was the first of many stimulant and nonstimulant medications that emerged for treating ADHD and is still the most widely used today, although other prescription drugs are increasing in popularity. Other similar medications used for ADHD include (in order of their appearance on the market) Dexedrine, Adderall, Desoxyn, and Cylert. The alarming 600% increase in the prescription of Ritalin since 1990 has created healthy debates about whether the drug is overprescribed. Each day, nearly 3 million children take Ritalin in the United States.

Although the specific mechanisms through which Ritalin has its effects are not fully known, it appears to temporarily increase the release of dopamine and, to a lesser extent, serotonin (both neurotransmitters) in key parts of the brain involved with behavioral and attention control and regulation, such as the prefrontal cortex. Ritalin is generally fast-acting (behavioral changes are often noticed within 15–30 minutes after ingestion), short-term in nature (effects typically disappear with 4 hours), and quick to leave the body, although slower-acting, sustained-release forms of Ritalin are now available.

Ritalin's popularity is related to the fact that "it works"; however, it is important to understand what "it works" means. Children with ADHD typically have trouble with three aspects of behavioral self-regulation: attention, impulsivity, and hyperactivity. For some children diagnosed with ADHD (about 70%), Ritalin helps them sustain their attention longer on difficult tasks, resist external distractions, sit still longer, follow directions better, and wait their turn better to a degree that is noticeable by parents and teachers. Improvements are also often seen in increased prosocial behavior and reduced oppositional and aggressive behavior. It is important to note that these dramatic effects are short-term (while the medication is active), are not found in all children with ADHD, and can be found for nondiagnosed children as well. Ritalin appears to have minimal long-term effects, however, but this has not been fully established. For these reasons, and the fact that Ritalin does not directly address the other interpersonal, emotional, family, and motivational difficulties often present in those with ADHD, Ritalin should only be used in the context of a comprehensive treatment package that could include other intervention strategies, such as skills training, behavior modification programs, parent training and support programs, educational accommodations, and counseling/therapy as needed. The first three of the other treatment strategies listed above have been shown to be as effective as Ritalin.

Despite its numerous benefits and the critical difference it has made in normalizing the lives of many families with ADHD children, Ritalin does not come without costs/risks. In addition to the extremely rare but occasional idiosyncratic adverse reactions to the medication (tic disorders, convulsions, visual disturbances, panic attacks, irregular heart beat), a sizable minority of users report a variety of side effects from Ritalin, including nervousness, insomnia, headache, nausea/stomach upset, and reduced appetite. Sometimes these problems can be alleviated by modifying the dosage and/or scheduling of the medication. Another common concern is slowed growth rate. In order to avoid this side effect, most recommend implementing "drug holidays"—periods such as weekends, summers, and other breaks from school when Ritalin is not used. Finally, most researchers recommend that Ritalin (and related medications) not be used with children under the age of 6, not only because the side effects tend to be worse with the very young, but also because research on the short- and long-term effects of its use in very young children is lacking.

—*Erin McClaren and Adam Winsler*

See also Attention, Attention Deficit Hyperactivity Disorder (ADHD), Attention Span

Further Readings and References

Breggin, P. R. (2001). *Talking back to Ritalin: What doctors aren't telling you about stimulants and ADHD*. Cambridge, MA: Perseus.

Diller, L. H. (1998). *Running on Ritalin: A physician reflects on children, society, and performance in a pill*. New York: Bantam.

Gainetdov, R. R., Wetsel, W. C., Jones, S. R., Levin, E. D., Jaber, M., & Caron, M. G. (1999, January). Role of serotonin in the paradoxical calming effect of psychostimulants on hyperactivity. *Science*, 397–410.

National Institute of Health. (1998, November 16–18). Diagnosis and treatment of attention deficit hyperactivity disorder. *NIH Consensus Statement, 16*(2), 1–37. Retrieved from http://odp.od.nih.gov/consensus/cons/110/110_state ment.htm

National Institute of Mental Health. (1996). *Attention deficit hyperactivity disorder* [Brochure]. Retrieved from http://www.nimh.nih.gov/publicat/adhd.cfm#adhd10

National Institute of Mental Health. (2000). *NIMH research on treatment for attention deficit hyperactivity disorder (ADHD): The multimodal treatment study—Questions and answers*. Retrieved from http://www.nimh.nih.gov/events/mtaqa.cfm

National Institute on Drug Abuse. (2000). *Methylphenidate (Ritalin)*. Retrieved from http://www.nida.nih.gov/Infofax/ritalin.html

ROGERS, CARL (1902–1987)

Carl Ransom Rogers, an American psychologist born in Oak Park, Illinois, is recognized as one of the most influential individuals in psychology. Rogers's most important achievements include crafting a humanistic approach of psychotherapy known as client-centered therapy and initiating scientific investigation of psychotherapy, prompting some to call him the "father of psychotherapy research."

Rogers's parents devoutly ascribed to the beliefs of fundamentalist Protestantism and accordingly encouraged pragmatic and Christian values. Rogers entered the University of Wisconsin to study agricultural science; however, following an influential trip to China, his interests shifted from practical pursuits to intellectual ones. Rogers received a BA degree in history and entered the Union Theological Seminary in New York City before transferring to Columbia University Teacher's College to study clinical psychology.

While at Columbia, Rogers specialized in the treatment of children. Roger's dissertation, *Measuring Personality Adjustment in Children Nine to Thirteen Years of Age* (1931), offered an objective test of children's attitudes toward their abilities and relationships. In his first book, *The Clinical Treatment of the Problem Child* (1939), Rogers critiqued the major approaches of psychotherapy and presented original thoughts concerning psychotherapist skills that would later become fundamental concepts of client-centered therapy.

Client-centered therapy was inadvertently born in 1940 when Rogers delivered a presentation at the University of Minnesota. Soon after, Rogers wrote *Counseling and Psychotherapy: Newer Concepts in Practice* (1942), which emphasized the use of humanistic principles in psychotherapy. Rogers referred to this new approach as "nondirective." The nature of nondirective psychotherapy greatly contrasted the dominant approaches of behaviorism and Sigmund Freud's psychoanalysis. Like many groundbreaking achievements, nondirective techniques were initially ignored, then met with heated criticism.

In 1945, Rogers left a professorship at The Ohio State University to direct a new counseling center at the University of Chicago. The counseling center was conducive to the cultivation of nondirective techniques, and in 1951 Rogers published *Client-Centered Therapy*. Rogers asserted that client-centered therapy empowers clients to achieve greater self-understanding through the therapist's ability to employ unconditional positive regard, empathy, and genuineness. Much of Rogers' subsequent work sought to refine and promote client-centered therapy, as well as supporting its efficacy by conducting controlled outcome research. Late in his career, Rogers addressed the fields of education and conflict resolution. Rogers published 16 books and more than 200 articles. The American Psychological Association awarded Rogers the first Distinguished Scientific Achievement Award (1956) and the first Distinguished Professional Contribution Award (1972).

—Shawn T. Bubany

Further Readings and References

Carl Rogers, http://oprf.com/Rogers

Rogers, C. (1951). *Client-centered therapy*. New York: Houghton Mifflin.

Rogers, C. (1961). *On becoming a person*. Boston: Houghton Mifflin.

Rogers, C., Kirschenbaum, H., & Henderson, V. (1989). *The Carl Rogers reader*. Boston: Houghton Mifflin.

ROGERS, FRED (1928–2003)

Fred McFeely Rogers was born March 20, 1928, in Latrobe, Pennsylvania, 40 miles east of Pittsburgh. The son of wealthy and devout Presbyterian parents, he earned his bachelor's degree in music from Rollins College (Winter Park, Florida, 1951) and was hired by NBC television in New York to assistant produce *The Voice of Firestone* and, later, floor direct *The Lucky Strike Hit Parade, The Kate Smith Hour,* and the *NBC Opera Theatre.* He married (Sara) Joanne Byrd, Rollins classmate and concert pianist, in 1952, and in November 1953 they returned to Pittsburgh and Western Pennsylvania roots. WQED Pittsburgh, the nation's first community-sponsored educational television station, was preparing to air and had asked Rogers to develop its program schedule. One of his first productions was *The Children's Corner*—hourlong music and puppetry—in which Rogers was off-camera as puppeteer, composer, and organist. It was here that puppets Daniel Striped Tiger, X the Owl, King Friday XIII, Henrietta Pussycat, and Lady Elaine Fairchilde were born and first aired.

Beyond his WQED responsibilities, Rogers attended Pittsburgh Theological Seminary and the University of Pittsburgh's Graduate School of Child Development, receiving his seminary degree and Presbyterian minister ordination in 1963. His ordination charge was to continue utilizing his talents to reach children and their families through the mass media. Later in 1963, CBC Canada asked him to create a children's program called *Mister Rogers*. In this series, Rogers debuted on camera as host and formulated the program elements for *Mister Rogers' Neighborhood*. The *Neighborhood* itself formally aired when Rogers and his family returned to Pittsburgh in 1966. It was distributed first through National Educational Television (NET), later to become the Public Broadcasting Service (PBS). Immediately winning the hearts and minds of children and their parents, the *Neighborhood* ran 33 years, becoming the longest running program for children. En route, Rogers himself received every conceivable honor the nation could accord him, including two Peabody Awards, four Emmys, a "Lifetime Achievement" Award from the National Academy of Television Arts and Sciences, induction into the Television Hall of Fame, a star on the Hollywood Walk of Fame, and the Presidential Medal of Freedom, the nation's highest civilian honor. One of his mother's home-knit red cardigan sweaters hangs in the Smithsonian Institution's Americana Collection in Washington, DC.

As "media parent" to generations of children, Rogers and *Mister Rogers' Neighborhood* identified with children's feelings and experiences; talked with children about difficult topics such as divorce, conflict, adoption, and death; assured children that they were special and that there was no one in the world just like them; and welcomed young viewers to a trolley ride into the "The Neighborhood of Make-Believe." Rogers personified acceptance, love, and caring. A private person who never sought the spotlight, his noblest goal was to be someone who cared deeply about children. When a symposium on creativity and childhood was convened in his honor, bringing together the nation's distinguished academicians and keynoted by Erik Erikson, it seemed crystal clear that Rogers' goal had been realized.

After a December diagnosis and January treatment for stomach cancer, Rogers died at his home in Pittsburgh on February 27, 2003, survived by his wife, (Sara) Joanne, two sons, and two grandsons.

—Edward L. Palmer

Further Readings and References

Collins, M., & Kimmel, M. M. (Eds.). (1996). *Mister Rogers' neighborhood: Children, television, and Fred Rogers*. Pittsburgh, PA: University of Pittsburgh Press.

Family Communications. (n.d.). *Fred Rogers' biography*. Retrieved from http://www.familycommunications.org/mister_rogers_neighborhood/biography.asp

Junod, T. (1998, November). Can you say . . . "hero"? *Esquire*. Retrieved from http://www.keepmedia.com/pubs/Esquire

/1998/11/01/170940?from=search&criteria=Can+you+say
.+.+.hero

Zoba, W. M. (2000, March 6). Won't you be my neighbor? *Christianity Today*. Retrieved from http://www.christianity-today.com/ct/2000/003/1.38.html

RUBELLA (GERMAN MEASLES)

RUBELLA VIRUS AND CONGENITAL RUBELLA SYNDROME

Rubella virus causes a benign disease known as "rubella" or "German measles." The primary symptoms associated with rubella are low-grade fever, enlarged lymph nodes, and rash, and these usually resolve within 3 days of appearance (leading to another name for the infection, "three day measles"). Rubella virus infection is frequently unapparent. The virus is spread by the respiratory route (sneezing and coughing releasing virus present in saliva) and once contracted it establishes a bodywide or systemic infection. An immune response is induced by the infection, which clears the virus and establishes effective lifelong immunity against reinfection. Despite the names attached to rubella virus infection, the virus is distinct and unrelated to measles virus, and as an acute disease, measles is more serious than is rubella.

The serious complication associated with rubella virus infection arises when infection occurs during the first trimester of pregnancy. The systemic nature of the infection allows the virus to reach the placenta where it replicates and crosses the placenta leading to infection of the fetus. The consequences of fetal infection range from fetal death to induction of congenital defects, although fetal infection without consequences does occur. Congenital defects most commonly include deafness, blindness, mental retardation, cardiac malformations, and thrombocytopenia purpura. The latter is a platelet defect that leads to appearance of petechiae or blue spots on the skin, known as "blueberry muffin syndrome," which, when present at birth, is indicative of fetal rubella virus infection. The constellation of defects caused by fetal rubella virus infection is known as "congenital rubella syndrome" or CRS. CRS can be manifested as a single defect or several of these defects, and the most affected CRS patients are severely handicapped and may require institutionalization. The CRS epidemic in 1964 and its aftermath were a major impetus behind proposal and passage of the Children with Disabilities Act by Congress in 1973.

The mechanism by which fetal rubella virus infection leads to CRS is not known. Fetal infection is widespread, affecting all tissues and organs, and CRS patients shed virus for up to a year after birth; however, little frank damage and no immune-mediated tissue destruction is detected. A hallmark of CRS is that small stature and affected organs often have a reduced number of cells. Considering that the critical window for CRS is early in gestation, it is thought that virus infection of progenitor cells may interfere with organ and tissue development. The chances of CRS occurrence following fetal infection are greatest during the first month of gestation, decline during the second and third month, and are nonexistent after the four month.

The link between rubella virus infection during pregnancy and birth defects was first recognized in 1941 by an Australian ophthalmologist, N. M. Gregg, who reportedly heard mothers of newborns in his waiting room commenting on a recent rubella outbreak and an increase in congenital cataracts. Rubella virus was not isolated until 1961. A worldwide pandemic occurred in 1964 leading to over 20,000 CRS cases in the United States. The pandemic spurred the development of live, attenuated vaccines, which were approved and in use in vaccination programs by 1969. Application of the vaccination program has been progressively tightened since introduction of the vaccine, and at present (2005) indigenous rubella has been eliminated from the United States and the small number of cases that occur are imported. Current vaccination requirements in the United States are two doses, one given at 15 to 18 months of age and a second at 4 to 6 years of age. The vaccine is routinely administered as a component of a trivalent vaccine consisting of the live attenuated measles, mumps, and rubella vaccines, known as MMR. Vaccination is enforced as a requirement for primary school and university entry and, in some states, for obtaining a marriage license. In some places, entry into health care (positions in which contact with women in early pregnancy could occur) requires adults to be vaccinated against rubella.

Once fetal infection occurs, there is no intervention available that can alter the course of infection or prevent development of CRS. A woman contracting rubella during the early course of pregnancy is confronted with a definite probability, though not certainty, that her baby will suffer from CRS and the wide range of defects that it presents. Tests to detect the presence of virus or anti-rubella virus fetal antibodies in amniotic or chorionic villous specimens to confirm fetal infection have been developed, but these are not routinely available in the United States because of the infrequency of rubella during pregnancy. Thus, the only options are delivery or termination of the pregnancy. Rubella virus infection during pregnancy is therefore prevented by aggressive national administration of the MMR vaccination program and testing for immunity to rubella virus during prepregnancy counseling. Women found to be nonimmune are vaccinated if not pregnant and vaccinated postpartum if already pregnant. Through implementation of these procedures, the occurrence of CRS is extremely rare in the United States.

—*Teryl Frey*

See also Teratogen

Further Readings and References

The Canadian Deafblind and Rubella Association, http://www .cdbra.ca

Chantler, J. K., & Tingle, A. J. (2001). Rubella. In B. N. Fields, D. M. Knipe, Howley, P. M., et al. (Eds.), *Virology* (4th ed.). Philadelphia: Lippincott-Raven.

The Helen Keller Foundation for Research and Education, http://www.helenkellerfoundation.org

Plotkin, S. A. (1999). Rubella vaccines. In S. A. Plotkin & E. A. Mortimer (Eds.), *Vaccines* (3rd ed., pp. 409–439). Philadelphia: W. B. Saunders.

S

School

I have never let my schooling interfere with my education.

—Mark Twain (1835–1910)

SAMPLING

Research studies typically include a sample group that is presumed to represent a larger population. For example, if the researcher is interested in the understanding of friendship during middle childhood, it is impossible to test all children in that age group. Instead, the researcher tests a sample of children in that age range and, if the sample adequately represents the broader population, then the results of the study may generalize from the sample to the population. Therefore, the sample refers to the specific people or cases that are studied, and the population refers to the entire set of people or cases that the researcher aims to describe.

Researchers should address whether their sample is representative of the larger population and should attend to possible sources of bias in sampling. Randomization in the sampling procedure helps avoid bias in sample selection. Two examples of randomized sampling techniques are simple random sampling and stratified random sampling.

In simple random sampling, each member of the population has an equal chance of being selected for inclusion in the study. Selection is done through a process that is truly random, such as the use of a computerized random number generator. For example, if a company wanted to interview a simple random sample of 10% of its employees, it might assign code numbers to each employee and then use a computer-programmed randomized selection process to choose 10% of the employees by code number.

In this case, the process used would be sampling without replacement, because once that employee's code was chosen, that code would not be put back into the pool of available numbers to select. A different method, sampling with replacement, would be useful in other circumstances and would involve replacing the selected number in the pool, so that it could potentially be selected again.

Stratified random sampling is used when the researcher wants representation from various subgroups, or strata, within a population. For example, in a study of parenting, a researcher might deem it important to include categories defined as parents of one child, parents of two children, and parents of three or more children. Within the available population of parents, the researcher would randomly select a sample of parents in each subgroup.

In studies that are based solely on volunteer participants, the results may generalize to a greater population of those who would volunteer, but may not generalize to the general population. The issue of nonresponse bias is a factor here, because those who choose not to volunteer for the study might differ in critical ways from those who choose to volunteer. Survey research is an example of a type of study where nonresponse bias is a concern.

In many studies in the behavioral sciences, true random sampling is not possible. For example, a researcher interested in studying children's moral development cannot sample randomly from all children of a certain age in some geographic area. Typically, the researcher may be working with certain schools and, within those groups, can test only those children whose parents give informed consent to the experimental procedure. Therefore, even if the researcher takes a random sample of the total group of children whose parents consented within two neighborhood schools, that sample is not necessarily representative of the entire population of children of that age. In addition to potential differences between children whose parents agree to have them participate and children whose parents do not agree, the schools may differ from the broader population of the area in terms of socioeconomic status, race and ethnicity of the students, and other factors. Large-scale, national studies of day care, for example, should address issues of sampling and potential sources of selection bias. In many behavioral science studies, researchers make the best attempt they can to provide a reasonable sample that meets the purposes of their study and minimizes sources of bias.

—*Marie T. Balaban*

Further Readings and References

HyperStat Online Textbook, http://davidmlane.com/hyperstat/index.html

McBurney, D. H. (1994). *Research methods* (3rd ed.). Pacific Grove, CA: Brooks-Cole.

Rosnow, R. L., & Rosenthal, R. (2001). *Beginning behavioral research: A conceptual primer* (4th ed.). Upper Saddle River, NJ: Prentice-Hall.

Trochim, W. M. K. (2002). *Nonprobability sampling*. Retrieved from http://trochim.human.cornell.edu/kb/sampnon.htm

Trochim, W. M. K. (2002). *Probability sampling*. Retrieved from http://trochim.human.cornell.edu/kb/sampprob.htm

Wainer, H. (1989). Eelworms, bullet holes, and Geraldine Ferraro: Some problems with statistical adjustment and some solutions. *Journal of Educational Statistics, 14*, 121–140.

SAT

The College Board Scholastic Aptitude Test (SAT) was first administered in 1926 to more than 8,000 candidates to colleges in the northeastern section of the United States. The first SAT was a multiple-choice examination consisting of nine subtests: definitions, arithmetical problems, classification, artificial language, antonyms, number series, analogies, logical inference, and paragraph reading. In subsequent years the number of subtests was reduced to six. Later the SAT was divided into two separate sections: one section dealing with mathematical ability and the other dealing with verbal ability. With minor modifications, the SAT remains a test of verbal and mathematical abilities much as it had been developed earlier.

The SAT is neither an intelligence test per se nor an educational achievement test, but a mixture of both. The verbal scale of the SAT is basically vocabulary and reading comprehension and, by implication, an index of student facility in linguistic concepts and expression. The mathematical scale is basically a measure of the student's ability to deal with numerical symbols, analyze quantitative relationships, and interpret mathematical problems. In this manner the SAT is a measure of the student's ability to analyze and interpret written materials of the kind encountered in academic coursework. The specific nature of the items, of course, were antonyms, analogies, sentence completions, and paragraph comprehension on the verbal scale and arithmetical computation on the mathematical scale. No total or combined score is reported for the SAT because it is not thought desirable to summate the two scores. Indeed, the verbal scale has the backing of the trivium (rhetoric, grammar, and logic) and the mathematics scale is representative of the quadrivium (astronomy, geometry, music, and arithmetic) in the curriculum of the medieval university. As indicated by the president of Educational Testing Service in his annual report of 1961–1962, the SAT is "quite simply a highly reliable measure of verbal and mathematical ability" and "as such it serves both students and colleges well."

An extensive study of the SAT in 1974 showed that the SAT is indeed useful to both students and colleges. Thirteen years of data from the University System of Georgia norms booklets were analyzed on the premise that the value of the SAT did not lie in its ability to directly and independently predict college performance, but in its incremental effectiveness when used in conjunction with high school records. In other words, the College Board has long advised against the use of the SAT as a single, absolute measure of academic ability and has consistently recommended that the SAT be used in conjunction with other information such as high school records and achievement test scores. The Board has also pointed out that the high school grade point average (HSA) or class rank is the best single predictor of college grades and that the advantage of using the SAT is as a supplement to HSA or other indications of prior educational achievement.

Uses of the SAT have often combined HSAs and SAT scores as multiple predictors of freshman grade point averages. The relative contributions of SAT verbal and SAT mathematic scores vary, of course, from institution to institution. In the University System of Georgia, statistical analysis reveals that the SAT verbal score contributed significantly to the prediction of freshman grades 70% to 80% of the time, while the SAT mathematics score contributed approximately 50% of the time. Both the SAT verbal and the SAT math scores contributed 30% to 40% of the time. Only in approximately 10% of cases did neither the verbal nor the mathematics scores contribute significantly to the prediction of freshman grades.

The analysis of SAT scores over a 13-year period suggested that the public colleges and universities of Georgia could be classified by the mean SAT verbal scores recorded over the years. The university-level institutions consistently had a mean SAT verbal score of 450 or higher, while the 4-year senior colleges had an SAT verbal score between 400 and 450 and the junior or 2-year colleges in the state had a mean verbal score somewhere between 300 and 400. The level of the SAT verbal scores, however, was not related to the extent to which they correlated with college grades. For example, the SAT verbal score of men correlated .36 with grades in junior colleges, .37 with senior college grades, and .35 with university-level grades. Correlations for women were .50, .53, and .45, respectively.

The study consistently showed that a combination of SAT scores and HSA provided the best prediction of college grades. The data also showed that there was some slight loss in predictive efficiency whenever SAT scores were combined prior to their insertion in a regression equation. Multiple correlation coefficients with a differential weighting of SAT-verbal + SAT-math + HSA were .58 for male students and .70 for

female students during the years studied. There were no detectable differences among the three levels of institutions for either men or women.

The predictive efficiency of the SAT was demonstrated by computing an index of forecasting efficiency for the HSA alone and then computing an index of forecasting efficiency for the combination of HSAs and SAT scores. The average gain found in this manner was 6 percentage points for men and 8 percentage points for women. The researcher concluded from the study that the use of the SAT reduced the predictive error an additional 6 points (or 46%) for male students and an additional 8 points (or 43%) for female students.

The study concluded that while the predictive efficiency of the SAT had been amply demonstrated, the use of the SAT should not be based on the increased accuracy of predicted grades alone. There were many indications that numerous benefits had accrued from the use of the SAT over the 13-year period. The norms booklets distributed annually by the University System of Georgia depicted the diversity of institutions within the System and the differential attraction of students with varying levels of high school preparation and measured ability. The normative data gave high school counselors accurate and reliable information about the various institutions of the University System. In turn, the data contained in the norms booklets gave high school seniors appreciable information about the relative difficulty of academic success in the public institutions of Georgia.

The SAT was originally conceived as a measure of academic ability that would be relatively independent of high school preparation, teacher judgments, and HSA. Its primary use over the years has been the prediction of freshman grades and selective admissions to institutions with more applicants than classroom facilities. As the best known and most widely used standardized test of academic ability, the SAT is the frequent target of critics who believe that all standardized tests impede access and equity for students who are socially, economically, or educationally disadvantaged. Ignored in most criticisms is the valuable information that the SAT has provided about the verbal and mathematical abilities of students completing secondary education and entering U.S. colleges and universities.

In many respects the SAT remains a major source of information concerning the abilities and preparation of college students, the general or overall quality of secondary education, and the extension of educational opportunity to minorities in a pluralistic society. Other admission tests, such as the American College Test (ACT), also contribute significant and valuable information, but the SAT is more frequently discussed in matters of national or public policy. Indeed, the SAT is much closer to being, in effect, a national or public examination for students leaving secondary schools and entering institutions of higher education.

The uses and consequences of the SAT and other standardized tests in the United States continue to be involved in more significant issues concerning access, equity, assessment, and accountability in higher education. During the 1980s, criticisms of standardized tests focused more directly on the assessment of educational outcomes. Assessment has been advocated as more appropriate for purposes of accountability and accreditation, and different forms and methods of assessing (as opposed to testing) student performance were part of the public demands placed on schools and colleges. Unfortunately, criticisms of the SAT were often confused. Declining SAT scores were interpreted as evidence of the SAT's irrelevance to educational decisions, and variations in predictive validity coefficients were interpreted as proof of the SAT's technical obsolescence. Changes in the SAT's content were recommended by the SAT's more friendly critics, while complete abolishment was advocated by those who saw no merits in either national testing agencies or their standardized products.

Thus, we witness the continuing national concern over access-and-equity issues in higher education and the public demands for accountability that stem from perceptions of declining quality. The continuing interplay between a periodic quest for "social justice"—as reflected in educational opportunities and outcomes—and the public's interest in assessment as a means of accountability is a fascinating example of differences in national perceptions and expectations. Whatever the American national character, it has often been depicted as "quite willing to enjoy the best of all promising alternatives."

American notions of equity stem from a long-standing concern with proportionate sharing. Regions, states, counties, and cities in the United States have often based their public expectations on concepts of "democratic arithmetic." Reading in the newspaper that a certain percentage of the nation's population resides within their state, citizens and residents may assume that they are entitled to a similar percentage of

the nation's many benefits, advantages, and amenities. Such reasoning was quite pronounced in regional studies of the southern states during the 1930s and in the civil rights movement of the 1960s. Constituting a substantial percentage of the nation's population, minority citizens understandably believe that they are entitled to a more equitable percentage of the rights and privileges in which societal distribution is influenced by public policy.

As other minority groups became aware of their proportionate share of societal benefits and advantages, more frequent references were made to "distributive justice" and institutions of higher education were increasingly perceived as the means by which such "national objectives" were attained. In much the same manner, national security has dictated federal aid to education in the name of national defense.

In the late 1950s and early 1960s, as college enrollments expanded, selective admissions was momentarily regarded as a solution to limited facilities, faculties, and finances. The College Board took the lead in addressing the policy issues involved in limiting enrollments to accommodate institutional resources. Annual symposia, research conferences, professional journals, and the popular press demonstrated a remarkable consensus in their discussions of "an impending tidal wave" of students and the nation's needs for campus facilities and classroom instructors.

The individualistic features of the American national character have also included the expectation that individuals should excel. The discovery and development of talent was a particularly appealing aspect of higher education in its post–World War II years, and as school and college enrollments benefited from a rapidly increasing birthrate, the sifting and sorting of potential talent was a societal responsibility that colleges and universities managed well until overwhelmed in the late 1960s. Jeffersonian notions of a "natural aristocracy of virtue and talent" were quite compatible with the nation's faith in education, and the testing of student aptitudes, abilities, and interests was in keeping with the public interest.

John Gardner's (1961) book on excellence was read as both a national and a personal challenge. Individual differences in athletics, music, art, and drama were widely recognized as natural talents that could be identified early and developed further. Creativity and ingenuity in science and other intellectual disciplines were increasingly recognized as special talents that should be discovered and encouraged. An emerging concept of developed abilities (such as those measured by the SAT) promised to set aside the irreconcilable differences of hereditarian and environmentalistic doctrines, and serious efforts were made to measure educational progress as a rational and developmental sequence in intellectual and/or academic competence. The optimism of that day was short-lived.

In the late 1960s, national thought and discussion were mistakingly preoccupied with idealistic notions of social justice. On college campuses, student protests and faculty dissent produced an educational climate in which neither administrators, faculty, nor students could discuss access, equity, and excellence as complementary concepts without contradiction. In their quest for excellence, colleges and universities were regarded by social critics as serving the screening and credentialing needs of society, business corporations, and government agencies. For some critics, excellence became a code word for elitism and for the exclusion of minorities, women, and other nontraditional students.

In their quest for equality of educational opportunity, schools and colleges witnessed a drastic shift from educational inputs to educational outcomes. The U.S. Congress, unwisely writing into the Civil Rights Act of 1964 a survey of equal educational opportunity, created a demand for instant results that schools and colleges could not supply. In their hurry to meet a congressional mandate, the survey researchers were entrapped by their methodological preferences and concluded, for the most part, that further federal funding was a waste of public resources. Instead of surveying the "availability of equal educational opportunities for individuals by reason of race, color, religion, or national origin," the researchers analyzed the determinants of educational achievement as measured by tests of verbal ability. The major conclusion, as reported in the news media and as heard by too many receptive ears, was that home, family, and community were more important to student learning than school facilities, teachers, classmates, and textbooks. Reanalyses and reinterpretations eventually clarified the confusions of the massive data collected, but not before considerable damage had been done in the world of public opinion and public expectations.

In retrospect, the emergence of equity as a dominant feature in public notions of social (or educational) justice can be viewed as a poorly articulated progression from (a) public expectations of "equal educational opportunities" to (b) strident demands for "equal educational outcomes." From there, public thought and discussion turned to (c) concepts of "equity" in educational opportunities and outcomes and eventually to (d) more realistic concepts of equity as "fairness" in educational access, placement, instruction, evaluation, progression, graduation, and societal benefits or advantages. Concepts of equity as fairness are more in keeping with current concepts of cultural pluralism and give better promise to the future solution of educational problems. Unfortunately, the roadside is still cluttered with the debris of sociological and econometric notions of distributive effects that replaced a constructive "psychology of individual differences" with a militant "sociology of groups." In the process, many schools and colleges found that they could not serve as instruments of worthy public policies without becoming political playgrounds.

In 1994, the Scholastic Aptitude Test was renamed the Scholastic Assessment Test. The change in name was in keeping with a national interest in the assessment of educational outcomes that was clearly evident in the 1980s. Given the nation's previous reliance on testing, measurement, and evaluation—as funded by federal legislation—it is not surprising that the assessment of student outcomes should be widely advocated. National commissions and public leaders were apparently convinced that institutions of higher education could not be accountable without better evidence of congruence between institutional purposes and institutional effectiveness. Despite the inordinate concern with distributive effect in sociological and economic studies of occupational placement, starting salaries, lifetime earnings, socioeconomic status, and professional prestige, many studies were sensitive to the individual abilities of students and graduates as they climbed national career ladders. Some studies were explicit in their recognition that "sophisticated notions" of social origins and socioeconomic status could not account for the distributed benefits of education, occupation, and income without including individual achievement and abilities.

The "assessment movement" of the 1980s was a function of the changing climate of public opinion in which institutions of higher education found themselves. A quarter century of declining test scores, the necessity of teaching basic skills of literacy to thousands of college freshmen, and intense dissatisfaction with the general academic competencies of a large proportion of college students—plus embarrassing criticisms of the literacy of college graduates enrolled in professional or graduate programs—have convinced many public leaders and policy makers that outcomes assessment is necessary to ensure institutional and program effectiveness and accountability to societal benefactors and sponsors.

Current assessment concepts and methods have been influenced by the minimal competency testing movement of the 1970s, the many debates concerning criterion-referenced and norms-referenced testing, and the nation's apparent love-hate relationship with multiple-choice, mechanically scored, computer-processed tests such as the SAT. The U.S. news media, unable to accept the SAT as an empirically developed measure of verbal and mathematical ability and refusing to view standardized testing as a necessary technological innovation in an era of mass education, continued to give headlines to studies that hint at Achilleian heels.

Although interesting methods of assessment are continually sought, genuine, substantive assessment of general (and meaningful) educational outcomes is unlikely until national testing agencies supply "an assessment market" with instruments and methods that will have the practicality, credibility, and fairness of traditional and/or empirically validated tests of the SAT and ACT.

The assessment uses of the SAT are demonstrated best by the useful information it and similar standardized tests provide about student abilities and achievement. No other national organizations serve the public interest in the same way that the College Board, Educational Testing Service, and the American College Testing Program do. Critics of the SAT seldom recognize that the intellectual development of individuals is still an essential purpose and function of higher education. Intellectual competence is still an expected outcome of a college education, and the SAT—with such tests as the Graduate Record Exam (GRE), Law School Admission Test (LSAT), and Medical College Admission Test (MCAT), among others—is still the best measure we have of the intellectual/academic competencies needed in various fields of advanced, specialized, professional study. The verbal and mathematical abilities tapped by the SAT are still the best (general) indication of individual capabilities in the world of education. And intellectual ability is still the best generalized measure of individual achievement. No one doubts individual differences in athletics, literature, music, and art, but too many social critics find it difficult to accept individual (and group) differences in intellectual development.

In addition to information about the abilities and achievements of individuals, the SAT provides relevant information about the distribution of student abilities among institutions and programs of higher education. Within statewide systems of public higher education, the distribution of students among institutions and programs is particularly relevant to many issues in public policy. In the University System of Georgia, the distribution of SAT scores among institutions lends credence to policy decisions that placed public institutions within commuting distance of the great majority (95%) of the state's population. Also implied by such distribution are the beneficial effects of individual choices and institutional decisions in the admission of high school graduates to the state's public colleges and universities.

The assessment uses and implications of the SAT may be summarized in the following manner: As a standardized test of academic ability, the SAT is, in many ways, a measure of basic academic competencies that are used extensively in undergraduate, graduate, and professional education. To no small extent, the test reflects the importance of vocabulary, reading comprehension, and mathematical reasoning in many different phases of conceptual learning. In addition to their usefulness as a general measure of intellectual/academic competence, SAT scores are often useful in advising, counseling, sectioning, and placing students who must choose institutions, programs, services, and activities. Also relevant are the SAT's many uses in institutional research, planning, development, and evaluation that may affect future decisions and choices.

In the long-term advancement of standardized tests and their educational uses, the misuses of the SAT have been dramatically publicized. In 1983, when the National Commission on Excellence in Education issued its report, *A Nation at Risk*, the SAT was used to "rank" the 50 states of the nation. Since that time, the news media have continued to regard the quality of secondary education as a function of SAT scores, as released for publication. To a certain extent, the SAT became the victim of its reputation as a national examination of educational progress. It also became the most visible target in what some regard as "the testing wars" enemy. The SAT, perhaps more than any other nationally administered test, has contributed significantly to the clarification of public policies concerning access and equity. The policy issues concerning standardized tests, group differences, and assessment alternatives to traditional testing concepts involved, in many ways, data and information derived from the SAT or similar tests. For such reasons, the SAT, similar tests, or their modified versions should be used much more extensively in the assessment of educational outcomes—not less!

In the 21st century, the assessment of educational outcomes is, or should be, a search for competence—not excellence. Governing boards and other public officials demand assurances that high school graduates can read and write well enough to become responsible employees, voters, and taxpayers. Social justice, whatever its form, requires that educational opportunities be accessible and that educational outcomes be equitable. The public interest requires better secondary preparation to ensure basic academic competencies that will permit high school graduates to take better advantage of postsecondary opportunities. Thus, it all suggests a remarkable convergence on one form or another of assessment and achievement.

In the assessment of educational outcomes, individual differences will continue to be the major source of variance on the SAT, ACT, and other standardized tests. Neither institutional or program characteristics nor instructional facilities and methods will account for measured or assessed outcomes, or for the intellectual/academic development of individual students. The assessment of educational outcomes thus cannot be statistically significant, educationally meaningful, or publicly creditable without consideration of individual differences in academic or learning ability.

Clearly, the public interest is best served in a society where individual talents, abilities, and achievements are assessed in a fair and creditable manner. Given systematic, objective, valid, reliable, and fair assessments of educational outcomes, individuals and institutions in higher education should be the beneficiaries. Assessed outcomes should serve the public interest in both accountability and accreditation, as well as institutional interests in the improvement of undergraduate education and student development. The assessment of individual competencies should serve social justice by contributing more substantially to self-understanding, academic and career planning, and personal management.

If we seriously ask how effective the SAT has been in facilitating the decisions institutions must make in selectively admitting students—or how helpful SAT scores might be in the choices of students actively recruited—we can turn again to the experiences of the University System of Georgia where SAT scores have been required since 1957 for all students entering its 34 institutions of higher education.

As the nation's fourth-largest statewide system of public higher education, the University System of Georgia has an excellent database from which SAT scores, HSAs, and first-year college grade point averages (GPAs) have been intensively studied. Even more important is the attention that the University System has given to the distribution and organization of its institutions—geographically, regionally, and economically—and to public expectations for diversity, access, and equity. As the largest state (territorially) east of the Mississippi River, Georgia now has a statewide system that has attracted the interest of other states.

In 1986, a more thorough study of the University System of Georgia's cumulative experience with the SAT gave commendable support to its use in admissions, counseling, and overall assessment. This study has involved more than 243,000 students entering units of the University System of Georgia over a 25-year period and consists of at least 883 different regression equations in which HSAs, SAT-verbal, SAT-math, and GPA have been correlated. Because of the large number of subjects involved in the study and because of the large number of equations, there is little observed variance in the mean correlations computed over the 25 years. The analysis shows that almost 41% of the variance in academic achievement by female students in the freshman year can be accounted for by prior preparation in high school and by verbal and mathematical abilities, as measured by the SAT. For male students, the differential weighting of SAT scores and HSAs can account for almost 34% of the variance in freshman grades. Such analysis of SAT scores and HSAs suggests that approximately 60% of the variance in freshman grades for women remain unaccounted for while approximately 64% of the variance in freshman grades for men is similarly unexplained. Thus the conclusion many years ago that we can predict freshman grades as well as we should hope to do so is justified. The unexplained variance of freshman performance—all educators should trust—can be accounted for by such conditions as student effort and quality of instruction.

In brief, the SAT, as a measure of verbal and mathematical abilities and as an indication of the applicant's readiness to meet academic responsibilities, finds many uses in the units of the University System of Georgia. Users of the SAT are familiar with the test and know of its long use within the University System. The most important conclusion to be drawn, however, is that the SAT is valuable in the articulation of students from secondary schools to units of the statewide system of public higher education. Continued use of the SAT in the University System of Georgia has never been justified on the basis of its predictive validity alone, but on the basis of the valuable information the SAT provides about student abilities and achievement.

Currently, the semantic differences between *assessment* and *achievement* are much in evidence. Critics of the SAT Assessment Test advocate the use of SAT Achievement Tests. Their opponents believe this to be unwise—and perhaps a naive effort to develop tests less susceptible to coaching (by entrepreneurial programs that many parents cannot afford for their sons and daughters). From other critics, and in the name of accountability, comes the insistence of the news media in publishing annual rankings of the 50 states—based on state averages of SAT scores and nothing else. Treated as a "national" report card on how well our secondary schools prepare their graduates for higher education, such "reports" mislead their readers into thinking the states with very low college attendance do a better job of preparing students for college than states with higher in-state college attendance.

Whatever the title of the SAT—be it aptitude, ability, assessment, or achievement—the original purpose of the SAT was to assist selective institutions in their decisions to admit individuals, and to help individuals in their choice of colleges and/or universities to attend. Intelligent uses of the SAT have always implied that SAT scores were valuable information to use in conjunction with other valid and reliable information in making a decision to admit (on the institution's part) and in making a choice to attend. High school counselors, if competent, have always used other sources of information in making recommendations to students—and surely, student advisors continue to use other resources in recommending college programs, services, and activities.

—*Cameron Fincher*

See also Standardized Testing

Further Readings and References

ACT Assessment: An ACT program for educational planning, http://www.act.org/aap/

College Board, http://www.collegeboard.com/splash

Fincher, C. (1986). The predictive contribution of the SAT in a statewide system of public higher education. *Measures in the college admissions process: A college board colloquium.* New York: College Entry Examination Board.

Zwick, R. (Ed.). (2004). *Rethinking the SAT: The future of standardized testing in university admissions.* New York: Routledge Farmer.

SCAFFOLDING

Scaffolding occurs during the activities adults and children engage in together every day. *Scaffolding* refers to a particular way in which adults help children learn or assume more responsibility for tasks. Experts in child development view scaffolding as an important process through which children acquire new skills and learn about their world. As the metaphor of scaffolding used in building construction suggests, the idea is that before children are able to stand on their own and complete tasks independently, adults (or more competent peers) provide just the right amount and type of support, assistance, or "scaffolding" children need in order to move to the next level or take on more responsibility for completing a particular task by themselves.

While the term *scaffolding* is not found in the original writings of Lev Vygotsky, the concept is based on his sociocultural theory of learning and development. Vygotsky and his followers believe that child development takes place via the internalization of cultural tools and by the child's increasing appropriation of adult-like roles and participation in cultural activities, not unlike how a student apprentice gradually learns from a master craftsman. Neo-Vygotskian scholars of the 1970s, such as David Wood and Jerome Bruner, began using the term to describe which teaching practices are most effective in promoting the cognitive development of children. Although typically used to refer to a quality of one-on-one adult-child interaction, the concept of scaffolding can also be applied to small-group and classroom teaching/learning processes.

The key features of scaffolding include (a) adult-child joint collaboration on a challenging and culturally meaningful problem-solving activity; (b) the presence of what is called *intersubjectivity*—when both adult and child are trying to accomplish the same thing or share the same goals for the task; (c) the adult contingently adjusting the amount and type of assistance provided to be as minimal as possible, depending on the child's moment-to-moment competence with the task; and (d) an active attempt by the adult to sensitively withdraw his or her assistance as the child's skills increase over time to allow the child as much autonomy as possible. The main goal for the adult who is scaffolding children's problem solving is to keep the level of task difficulty within the child's zone of proximal development—that is, slightly above the level of difficulty at which the child could complete the task independently but still within the range where the child could succeed on the task with some adult assistance. Good scaffolders typically do this by what is called *contingent shifting*—they shift the amount and type of support provided contingent on the child's current success, increasing support when a child is struggling and reducing support when the child does well on the task. Finally, scaffolding is often more successful when it occurs within the context of warm and pleasant interactions and secure relationships between adult and child.

Although the general processes involved in scaffolding appear to be culturally universal, the particular way in which adults scaffold children's learning varies somewhat across cultures. Some cultural groups—for example, when engaging their children in apprenticeship learning situations—use more demonstration and modeling techniques and less overt verbal discussion with children about the activity.

Research shows that scaffolding is not only an effective way for children to learn specific tasks, but it also promotes cognitive, language, motivational, and social-emotional development more generally in important ways. After a good quality scaffolding session, children walk away with not only increased competence on the task they were working on, but also an increased sense of mastery, self-efficacy, task enjoyment, and task persistence, as well as new ideas about how to plan and organize one's problem solving and how to work together with others.

—*Erin Way and Adam Winsler*

See also Vygotsky, Lev

Further Readings and References

Berk, L. E. (2001). *Awakening children's minds: How parents and teachers can make a difference.* London: Oxford University Press.

Berk, L. E., & Spuhl, S. T. (1995). Maternal interaction, private speech, and task performance in preschool children. *Early Childhood Research Quarterly, 10,* 145–169.

Berk, L. E., & Winsler, A. (1995). *Scaffolding children's learning: Vygotsky and early childhood education.* Washington, DC: National Association for the Education of Young Children.

Leong, D., Bodrova, E., Hensen, R., & Henninger, M. (1999). *Scaffolding early literacy through play.* Retrieved from http://www.mcrel.org/PDF/EarlyChildhoodEducation/4006IR_NAEYC_Handout_Play.pdf

Madsen, J., & Gudmundsdottir, S. (2000). *Scaffolding children's learning in the zone of proximal development: A classroom study.* Retrieved from http://www.sv.ntnu.no/ped/sigrun/publikasjoner/ecerjm.html

Pratt, M. W., Kerig, P., Cowan, P. A., & Cowan, C. P. (1988). Mothers and fathers teaching 3-year-olds: Authoritative parents and adult scaffolding of young children's learning. *Developmental Psychology, 24,* 832–839.

Rogoff, B. (1990). *Apprenticeship in thinking: Cognitive development in social context.* New York: Oxford University Press.

Wood, D. J., & Middleton, D. (1975). A study of assisted problem solving. *British Journal of Psychology, 66,* 181–191.

SCHEMA

Starting as early as infancy, children have expectations about their environment, or schemata, which enables them to recognize and understand recurring themes in their daily world. Thus, schemata are mental shortcuts that help people make predictions about the world. These mental shortcuts are derived from experience (often repeated) with specific events. For example, children may develop a schema for attending school, a trip to the zoo, or dining out after one or more experiences with these events. Without schemata, each interaction with an environment (e.g., school) would be like the first time. Developmentally, schemata are believed to be one of the earliest forms of knowledge representations, and are established easily by children. Although repeated exposure to an event strengthens a schema, children can form schemata after a single exposure to an event. Schemata are recognized as important mental processes that develop in early childhood and affect almost every aspect of behavior.

SCHEMATA AND MEMORY

Schemata guide both interactions with new experiences and also later retrieval of information.

Information stored in memory has been conceptualized as being organized around schematic networks. For example, a schematic network concerning a trip to McDonalds would consist of a cluster of items and events relevant to a "normal" trip to McDonalds (e.g., ordering, hamburgers). During acquisition and retrieval of an event, people will encode both schema-typical and schema-atypical details, but they will store the atypical items separately. Over time, memory for the atypical details fade, and the gaps are filled in with schema knowledge. In these cases, schemata can cause memory distortion.

TYPES OF SCHEMATIC KNOWLEDGE

The term *schema* is an umbrella category referring to generic knowledge structures of many types. Scripts are a specific type of schematic knowledge structure that reflects understanding of a temporal, repeated event, such as going to a restaurant or attending school. Stereotypes are another specific type of schema that refers to types and characteristics of people. Children have been found to have scripts and stereotypes at relatively young ages.

AGE DIFFERENCES IN SCHEMA USE

Preschool-aged children may rely more on general schema information when structuring their memory for familiar interactions than older children and adults. As a result, younger children have difficulty recalling information concerning a specific event. As young children develop a schema, until the schematic representation is an established mental framework, it is more difficult for the children to recall unique information about a specific event. As children age, their schemata become more solidified and they become more experienced with differentiating between information that is consistent with the general representation and information that is inconsistent with the general representation. Thus, older children rely less on their schemata to guide their memories than do younger children.

When children rely on their schemata when remembering, they are prone to making memory errors. For example, when children are presented with an event that contains information that is inconsistent with an existing schema, children remember the schema-inconsistent information when asked immediately

following the event. However, as time passes between the event and the recall process, children rely more on their schema representations, causing them to remember the event as being schema consistent. Often this leads to a memory distortion for a specific episode in favor of the schema.

SUMMARY

In summary, schemata are useful because they make interacting with the world more predictable. Schematic knowledge, including scripts and stereotypes, is being acquired from infancy. Schematic information enhances memory when information is consistent with the schema but can cause memory errors when the to-be-remembered information is inconsistent with our expectations.

—*Livia L. Gilstrap and Cindy Laub*

See also Cognitive Development

Further Readings and References

Adams, L. T., & Worden, P. E. (1986). Script development and memory organization in preschool and elementary school children. *Discourse Processes, 9*, 149–166.

Farrar, M. J., & Goodman, G. S. (1992). Developmental changes in event memory. *Child Development, 63*, 173–187.

Fiske, S. T., & Taylor, S. E. (1991). *Social cognition.* New York: McGraw-Hill.

Nelson, K. (1986). *Event knowledge: Structure and function in development.* Hillsdale, NJ: Erlbaum.

Price, D. W., & Goodman, G. S. (1990). Visiting the wizard: Children's memory for a recurring event. *Child Development, 61*, 664–680.

SCHIZOPHRENIA

Schizophrenia is perhaps the most complex, severe, and devastating of all mental illnesses. It can manifest in many different ways and forms. People with schizophrenia can exhibit, for example, a wide combination of psychotic symptoms, behavioral disorganization, and deficits in motivation and affective expression. Schizophrenic individuals may also show a variety of cognitive impairments. All of these symptoms interfere with the person's day-to-day social and occupational functioning. Schizophrenic signs and symptoms typically wax and wane across time and circumstances. Some people with schizophrenia, for example, have periods of time when they think clearly and can function in the community, and other times when their thinking and speech become unclear, and they may lose touch with reality and require psychiatric hospitalization. In other cases, symptoms are refractory and severe enough to result in chronic impairment and major life disruption.

DIAGNOSTIC ORIGINS

In 1883, German psychiatrist Emil Kraepelin developed what is often considered the most comprehensive description of schizophrenia. He used the term *dementia praecox* to describe two important aspects of the disorder: an early onset, typically between 16 and 25 years old (praecox) and a progressive deteriorating course (dementia). Eugen Bleuer, a contemporary of Kraepelin, greatly broadened the definition of dementia praecox and renamed it schizophrenia, from the Greek words *schizein*, which means "to split," and *phrenos*, which means "mind." Bleuer believed that in schizophrenia, one's mental associations, thoughts, and emotions, which are usually integrated with one another, are loosened or split. Today, our conceptualization of the disorder (e.g., in the American Psychiatric Association's *Diagnostic and Statistical Manual of Mental Disorders,* 4th edition, or in the World Health Organization's *International Statistical Classification of Diseases and Related Health Problems,* 10th revision) is research based, more reliable and valid than in the past, and much closer to Kraepelin's description of dementia praecox even though the term *schizophrenia* was retained.

DESCRIPTIVE FEATURES

No single symptom is characteristic of schizophrenia. The diagnosis requires the presence of a number of behavioral and social deficits that significantly impact the functioning of the individual. Characteristic symptoms fall into three broad categories: positive symptoms, disorganized symptoms, and negative signs and symptoms. Positive symptoms reflect an excess of normal functions, such as delusions and hallucinations. *Delusions* are defined as beliefs that are both untrue and uncharacteristic of the individual's culture. They can be categorized as persecutory, somatic, referential, or grandiose. *Hallucinations* are

sensory perceptions in the absence of an external stimulus, and can occur in any sensory modality—auditory, visual, tactile, olfactory, and gustatory. Auditory hallucinations are the most commonly experienced type of hallucination in schizophrenia and are perceived as one or more voices distinct from one's own thought. Disorganized symptoms include speech that is hard to follow and confused motor behavior. Speech may become so disorganized that the individual is almost incoherent and communication is severely impaired. Disorganized or catatonic motor behavior is exhibited in problems with goal-directed behavior, which lead to declining maintenance of activities of daily living as well as inappropriate and/or unpredictable behavior. Catatonic behavior occurs when an individual alternates between motor excitability and a decrease in reactivity to the environment. In extreme cases, the individual may assume an odd, rigid posture or even lose complete awareness of his or her surroundings.

Negative symptoms, in contrast, represent deficits in certain domains of normal functioning. They involve the absence of behaviors rather than the presence of behaviors and include affective flattening, which encompasses a diminished range of facial mobility and vocal expression; alogia, which is decreased fluency and productivity of speech; avolition, which involves the inability to initiate activities; and anhedonia, where the person loses the capacity to experience pleasure. Negative symptoms are more chronic and stable than other symptoms. Additionally it is believed that the severity of negative symptoms, particularly flat affect, is prognostic of a more severe and chronic course of illness.

CURRENT DIAGNOSTIC CRITERIA

Diagnostic and Statistical Manual of Mental Disorders, 4th edition, text revision (*DSM-IV-TR*), criteria for a diagnosis of schizophrenia require that at least two of the characteristic symptoms listed above (i.e., positive, disorganized, and/or negative symptoms) be present for at least 1 month, or if the delusions are bizarre and the auditory hallucinations consist of more than one voice, then only one symptom is required.

In addition to the month of active symptoms, the *DSM-IV* diagnosis of schizophrenia requires significant dysfunction for at least 6 months in major areas of life functioning, such as self-care, work, or interpersonal relations. Depending on the specific symptoms exhibited, schizophrenia can be categorized into several subtypes, such as paranoid, disorganized, catatonic, undifferentiated, and residual.

While cognitive impairment is not part of the formal diagnostic scheme for schizophrenia, many researchers advocate for its inclusion as a diagnostic criterion for the disorder. Cognitive dysfunction in schizophrenia is very common and can take the form of memory impairment, attentional dysfunction, and deficits in abstract reasoning and executive functioning ability. Cognitive deficits may play a major role in the social and occupational deficits exhibited by patients, and recent research suggests that cognitive deficits are a robust predictor of patients' outcome and treatment response.

Because there is such a wide range of manifestations of schizophrenia, differential diagnosis is also of great importance. Many positive and negative symptoms often associated with schizophrenia can occur in other disorders, such as depression, bipolar disorder, and acute substance intoxication. Psychotic symptoms, for example, can be exhibited during depressive episodes as well as manic episodes, and can be exacerbated by or even due to medical illnesses.

PREVALENCE AND DEMOGRAPHIC FACTORS

Schizophrenia affects about 1% of the general population. However, this figure differs depending on where the data were gathered. Schizophrenia is about eight times more common in poor individuals who come from inner-city environments. Some researchers suggest that the many stresses and lack of resources associated with poverty causes increased schizophrenia onset rates (social causation hypothesis). Other theorists speculate that many people with schizophrenia may start out at higher socioeconomic levels but due to schizophrenic illness wind up in the lowest social rungs (social drift hypothesis). It has also been speculated that the schizophrenic individuals found in poor urban areas are what is left after the people with the social and financial resources get out of the decaying neighborhoods (social residual hypothesis). Treatment outcome also varies, and affected individuals living in less stressful rural environments fare better than those people living in urban areas.

There are also gender differences in terms of the onset and prognosis. Women typically have a later onset than men. The age of onset of a first psychotic break in men is generally between the late teens and mid-twenties, while the age of onset for women is typically late twenties to mid-thirties. Onset before adolescence or after age 45 is possible, but relatively rare.

ETIOLOGY

It is indisputable that schizophrenia is, in part, genetically transmitted. First-degree relatives of people with schizophrenia, for example, have a 10 times higher risk for developing the disorder compared with the general population. Twin and adoption studies also support a genetic component to the disorder. Children of mothers with schizophrenia who were adopted away by families with no mental illness also have a 10 times higher risk for developing the disorder than adoptees without a biological parent with schizophrenia. Twin studies reveal that concordance rates are higher for monozygotic twins (about 50% concordance rates) than for dizygotic twins (10%–15% concordance).

The brains of some people with schizophrenia also show deficits in structure and function. Areas of the brain that have reliably shown impairment include the prefrontal cortex and mesolimbic areas. These regions control emotion, cognition, and social reasoning ability. Some studies also find that the ventricles of the brain, which are fluid-filled spaces, are enlarged in people with schizophrenia. This indicates deterioration in surrounding brain tissue.

In terms of neurochemical brain activity, the neurotransmitter dopamine appears to be too high in subcortical regions of the brain and too low in prefrontal brain areas. Further research has indicated that the neurotransmitters serotonin and glutamate may also play roles in the development and manifestation of schizophrenia.

Note that since concordance rates for monozygotic (identical) twins are not 100%, it is clear that nongenetic factors also contribute to the onset of the disorder. Some theorists hypothesize that a prenatal virus (e.g., influenza) affects the genetically susceptible fetus in the second or third trimester of pregnancy. Supporting evidence of immunodysfunction comes from studies that found that the people who were born during major flu epidemics of the 19th and 20th centuries have correspondingly increased rates of schizophrenia. Also some studies (but not all) find that people who eventually are diagnosed with schizophrenia were born closer to the flu season in the winter and early spring months (season of birth effect). Abnormal fetal growth and development, complications during pregnancy, and hypoxic effects during delivery have also been linked to later development of schizophrenia in genetically susceptible individuals.

Researchers have examined psychological mechanisms that may also contribute to schizophrenic psychosis. The psychological factors outlined below are theorized to occur concomitantly with or as a result of biological factors. Research has found, for example, that schizophrenia patients may have increased psychotic behavior because they frequently respond to the most immediate environmental stimuli without regard to the overall context and do not show normal latent inhibition mechanisms. Other studies have found that patients with schizophrenia may be more prone to hallucinate because they readily acquire abnormal sensory conditioned associations and have difficulty in source monitoring. Source monitoring failure has been linked to schizophrenic thought disorder. Schizophrenic patients are also more likely to show attributional biases and reasoning deficits that may contribute to delusional thinking.

ROLE OF THE FAMILY

Although certain aspects of one's family life, such as living in generally stressful circumstances, may contribute to schizophrenia, many theorists see this as a consequence rather than a direct cause of the disorder. Family members who display high expressed emotion (EE) are rated as hostile, overinvolved, and highly critical of their schizophrenic relative. High levels of EE have been found to result in higher relapse rates than in patients returning from the hospital and living with family members who are low on these EE dimensions.

OTHER CONSIDERATIONS

People with schizophrenia are at greatly increased risk for suicide, substance dependence, committing violence against others, being the victim of violence, and being stigmatized by society. The majority of schizophrenic patients also lack awareness of the fact that they have a mental illness (anosognosia). Consequently, patients believe their delusions and hallucinations are real. Although not part of the formal diagnostic criteria, all of these factors may interact to

exacerbate schizophrenic illness. Many schizophrenic patients, for example, are homeless because they have difficulty maintaining employment and are alienated from their families and lack the necessary insight needed to maintain their treatment regimens. Also, the massive closing of psychiatric hospitals and introduction of managed behavioral health care has resulted in significantly fewer mental health services available to patients in need of psychiatric hospitalization or housing. Homelessness may increase the risk for substance misuse, violence, victimization treatment noncompliance, and suicide for the individual with schizophrenia.

It is also important to evaluate symptoms from within the cultural context of the patient when determining a schizophrenia diagnosis. What may be normal behavior in one culture may not be in another. Hallucinations, which are usually seen as abnormal in Western culture, may be normal under some circumstances in other cultural contexts. It may be more acceptable in some Native American, West Indian, and African cultures than in others, for example, to believe family ancestors are speaking to them and exacting a tangible influence on their daily lives. Similarly, some Asian cultures may value more unemotional interactions, which may be misconstrued as flattened affect.

TREATMENT

Schizophrenia is a lifelong disorder. Antipsychotic medication is the most common treatment for symptom alleviation. Perhaps the most widely known neuroleptic medication is chlorpromazine (Thorazine), a phenothiazine that was introduced in the 1950s and was the first drug to effectively reduce positive symptoms in schizophrenic patients. Overall, neuroleptics have been shown to be effective but often produce severe neurological side effects, including extrapryamidal side effects and tardive dyskinesia due to massive dopamine blockade in the subcortex. Newer drugs, known as atypical antipsychotics, such as clozapine (Clozaril), risperidone (Risperdal), and olanzapine (Zyprexa), seem to be at least as effective as phenothiazines without inducing as many side effects. These medications are more selective in their dopamine blockade in the brain and also affect other neurotransmitter systems. Atypical antipsychotics also have been found to be effective in the treatment of patients who did not respond to traditional neuroleptic medications. The advent of atypical antipsychotic medications, particularly clozapine, represent a major step forward in the pharmacological treatment of schizophrenia. They do, however, come with some risks, including a potentially fatal blood illness (if not caught in time) called agranulocytosis (a decrease in the production of white blood cells), occurring in about 1% of clozapine-treated patients. Consequently, clozapine-treated patients require monitoring of the blood every 2 weeks.

However, it is clear that the most effective treatments for schizophrenia combine psychopharmacological with a wide range of psychosocial intervention programs. These behavioral interventions include psychosocial-based learning programs, communication and social skills training, community living training, family intervention, supported employment, assertive community treatment, and cognitive behavioral therapies. Effective management of schizophrenic illness can only come from a combination of psychopharmacotherapy and aggressive application of the evidence-based psychosocial interventions listed above. These treatments may serve to increase functioning, and community involvement, decrease the need for hospitalization, and ultimately significantly improve the quality of life of affected individuals.

—*Mark Serper and Nadine Chang*

Further Readings and References

Abi-Dargham, A. (2004). Do we still believe in the dopamine hypothesis? New data bring new evidence. *International Journal of Neuropsychopharmacology, 7*(Suppl.), 1–5.

Baumeister, A. A., & Francis, J. L. (2002). Historical development of the dopamine hypothesis of schizophrenia. *Journal of the History of Neuroscience, 11*, 265–277.

Bentall, R. (1990). The illusion of reality: A review and integration of psychological research on hallucinations. *Psychological Bulletin, 107*, 82–95.

Boog, G. (2004). Obstetrical complications and subsequent schizophrenia in adolescent and young adult offsprings: Is there a relationship? *European Journal of Obstetric and Gynecological Reproductive Biology, 114*, 130–136.

Cannon, M., Jones, P. B., & Murray, R. M. (2002). Obstetric complications and schizophrenia: Historical and meta-analytic review. *American Journal of Psychiatry, 159*, 1080–1092.

Chadwick, P., & Lowe, C. (1994). A cognitive approach to measuring and modifying delusions. *Behaviour Research and Therapy, 32*, 355–367.

Compton, W. M., & Guze, S. B. (1995). The neo-Kraepelinian revolution in psychiatric diagnosis. *European Archives of Psychiatry and Clinical Neuroscience, 245*, 196–201.

Davies, G., Welham, J., Chant, D., Torrey, E., & McGrath, J. (2003). A systematic review and meta-analysis of Northern Hemisphere season of birth studies in schizophrenia. *Schizophrenia Bulletin, 29*, 587–593.

Eaton, W. W., Thara, R., Federman, E., & Tien A. (1998). Remission and relapse in schizophrenia: The Madras Longitudinal Study. *Journal of Nervous and Mental Disease, 186*, 357–363.

Edgar, E. (2001). *Assertive community treatment promotes recovery: An interview with Joe Phillips.* Retrieved from http://www.nami.org/Template.cfm?Section=ACT-TA_Center&template=/ContentManagement/ContentDisplay.cfm&ContentID=6954

Freeman, H. (1994). Schizophrenia and city residence. *British Journal of Psychiatry, 164*(Suppl. 23), 39–50.

Glazer, W. M., & Dickson, R. A. (1998). Clozapine reduces violence and persistent aggression in schizophrenia. *Journal of Clinical Psychiatry, 59*(Suppl. 3), 8–14.

Goldstein, J. (1997). Sex differences in schizophrenia: Epidemiology, genetics, and the brain. *International Review of Psychiatry, 9*, 399–408.

Gottesman, I. (1991). *Schizophrenia genesis: The origins of madness.* New York: W. H. Freeman.

Harvey, P., & Serper, M. (1990). Linguistic and cognitive failures in schizophrenia: A multivariate analysis. *Journal of Nervous and Mental Disease, 178*, 487–493.

Heinssen, R. K., Liberman, R. P., & Kopelowicz, A. (2000). Psychosocial skills training for schizophrenia: Lessons from the laboratory. *Schizophrenia Bulletin, 26*, 21–46.

Heston, L. (1966). Psychiatric disorders in foster home reared children of schizophrenic mothers. *British Journal of Psychiatry, 112*, 819–825.

Kirch, D. G. (1993). Infection and autoimmunity as etiologic factors in schizophrenia: A review and reappraisal. *Schizophrenia Bulletin, 19*, 355–370.

Kot, T., & Serper, M. (2002). Increased susceptibility to auditory conditioning in hallucinating schizophrenic patients: A preliminary investigation. *Journal of Nervous and Mental Disease, 190*, 282–288.

Leff, J. (1994). Working with the families of schizophrenic patients. *British Journal of Psychiatry, 23*(Suppl.), 71–76.

Limosin, F., Rouillon, F., Payan, C., Cohen, J. M., & Strub, N. (2003). Prenatal exposure to influenza as a risk factor for adult schizophrenia. *Acta Psychiatrica Scandinavica, 107*, 331–335.

Lubow, R., & Gewirtz, J. (1995). Latent inhibition in humans: Data, theory, and implications for schizophrenia. *Psychological Bulletin, 117*, 87–103.

Mednick, S., Machon, R., Huttonen, M., & Bonett, D. (1988). Adult schizophrenia following prenatal exposure to an influenza epidemic. *Archives of General Psychiatry, 45*, 189–192.

Paul, G. L., & Lentz, R. J. (1977/1997). *Psychosocial treatment of chronically ill mental patients: Milieu vs. social learning programs.* Champaign, IL: Research Press.

Salzinger, K. (1980). The immediacy hypothesis in a theory of schizophrenia. In W. D. Spaulding & J. K. Cole (Eds.), *Nebraska symposium on motivation: Theories of schizophrenia and psychosis.* Lincoln: University of Nebraska Press.

Serper, M., & Bergman, A. (2003). *Psychotic violence: Motives, methods, madness.* Madison, CT: International Universities Press/Psychosocial Press.

Serper, M., Bergman, A., Copersino, M., Chou, J., Richarme, D., & Cancro, R. (2000). Learning and memory impairment in cocaine-dependent and comorbid schizophrenia patients. *Psychiatry Research, 93,* 21–32.

Serper, M., & Chou, J. C.-Y. (1997). Novel neuroleptics improve schizophrenic patients attentional functioning. *CNS Spectrums, 46,* 22–26.

Serper, M., Chou, J. C.-Y., Allen, M., Czobor, P., & Cancro, R. (1999). Symptomatic overlap of cocaine intoxication and acute schizophrenia at emergency presentation. *Schizophrenia Bulletin, 25,* 387–394.

Spaulding W. D., Reed, D., Sullivan, M., Richardson, C., & Weiler, M. (1999). Effects of cognitive treatment in psychiatric rehabilitation. *Schizophrenia Bulletin, 25,* 657–676.

Torrey, E. F. (1998). *Out of the shadows: Confronting America's mental illness crisis.* New York: Wiley.

Torrey, E. F., Bowler, A. E., & Clark, K. (1997). Urban birth and residence as risk factors for psychoses: An analysis of 1880 data. *Schizophrenia Research, 25,* 69–76.

Treatment Advocacy Center. (2004). *Hospital closures.* Retrieved from http://www.psychlaws.org/HospitalClosure/Index.htm

van Beilen, M., Kiers, H., Bouma, A., van Zomeren, E., Withaar, F., Arends, J., et al. (2003). Cognitive deficits and social functioning in schizophrenia: A clinical perspective. *The Clinical Neuropsychologist, 17,* 507–514.

van Os, J., Hanssen, M., Bak, M., Bijl, R. V., & Vollebergh, W. (2003). Do urbanicity and familial liability coparticipate in causing psychosis? *American Journal of Psychiatry, 160,* 477–482.

Vaughn, C., & Leff, J. (1976). The measurement of expressed emotion in the families of psychiatric patients. *British Journal of Social and Clinical Psychology, 15,* 157–165.

Volavka, J. (1999). The effects of clozapine on aggression and substance abuse in schizophrenic patients. *Journal of Clinical Psychiatry, 60*(Suppl. 12), 43–46.

Wyatt, R., Alexander, R., Egan, M., & Kirch, D. (1987). Schizophrenia, just the facts: What do we know, how well do we know it? *Schizophrenia Research, 1,* 3–18.

Zartman, K. (2004). *Why we give: A family's struggle with schizophrenia.* Retrieved from http://www.narsad.org/dc/schizophrenia/featured.html

Zorrilla, L., Cannon, T., Kronenberg, S., Mednick, S., Schulsinger F., Parnas, J., et al. (1997). Structural brain abnormalities in schizophrenia: A family study. *Biological Psychiatry, 42,* 1080–1086.

SCHOOL

The term *school* usually refers to formal, institutionalized settings for imparting socially desirable knowledge, skills, and attitudes. In modern societies, children and youth spend many years in such settings, completing tasks assigned primarily by teachers, but interacting primarily with same-age peers. Because schooling is such a major experience, it seems likely both to influence and to be influenced by children's personal development. This article considers both possibilities, starting with how (and whether) children's development affects schooling.

DEVELOPMENTAL EFFECTS ON SCHOOLS

A lot of research and literature takes human development as a given independent variable and argues that school can and should adjust methods to how children grow and change. A specialty that advocates this viewpoint especially strongly is early childhood education (nursery, kindergarten, and the early primary school grades). In early childhood education, "developmentally appropriate practice" includes ample use of "hands-on," sensorimotor experiences, encouragement of elaborated oral language, and leeway for children to choose their own activities. The features are thought to reflect principles of cognitive development as formulated by Piaget and other developmental theorists.

Among older students, pedagogical responses to youthful development are also advocated, although they are not necessarily named as "developmental." The existence of middle schools, for example, and of the former junior high schools, reflects both the research and the popular belief that participating in peer groups is often stressful for adolescents, especially early in this period of life. Middle schools were invented, so to speak, to ease the transition to peers by protecting young adolescents initially from the dominance of older peers, by reducing the initial size of peer cohorts, and by introducing adult-like responsibilities to youngsters more gradually than otherwise possible.

In spite of responses such as these to the development of students, however, the influence of developmental knowledge on schooling has been limited because of both conceptual flaws and practical problems. Conceptually, the assumption that "ages and stages" describe young people is often criticized by developmentalists themselves on the grounds that stages are often imprecise in timing and not easily identified in everyday, nonexperimental conditions. It is hardly fair, therefore, to expect educators to achieve a precision about children's developmental "levels" that developmentalists themselves have not achieved. As a practical matter, furthermore, the very diversity of students makes educational responses to diversity difficult or at times even unrealistic. The vast literature critiquing education, in fact, can be interpreted as testimony to the difficulties of making a mass, compulsory institution truly responsive to the individuality of children and youth.

That said, it is still true that human development influences schooling, but the effects are often not considered "developmental" in the sense of reflecting particular age-related changes in human nature. Research has found, for example, that students' classroom behavior can influence teachers to present a program more (or less) abstractly (or concretely); but such influence can happen at any level of schooling, from kindergarten through high school. Research has also documented (rather obviously) that students' misbehavior can cause teachers to impose stricter controls on behavior and to reduce opportunities for students to self-regulate their behavior. But this effect, too, can happen at any level of schooling, and in this sense is nondevelopmental. The safest generalization is that, overall, human development has contradictory, ambiguous effects on schooling. Whatever tasks are expected on any one occasion can support learning and "growth" in one student but leave another student more confused or even alienated from the demands of "maturity." This fact makes assessment of schooling puzzling and difficult. But given that schooling is institutional and that human development is individual, it seems inevitable.

SCHOOL EFFECTS ON HUMAN DEVELOPMENT

If schooling is taken as the independent variable and human development as the dependent variable, then consistent effects do become visible. Oddly, though, educational research generally shows that the effects have little to do with specific curriculum goals, even though curriculum is the ostensible, explicit purpose of schooling. In the 1960s and 1970s, for example, longitudinal studies of well-designed preschool programs for children from low-income families found few differences in the effects of alternative curricular approaches. Programs that were highly structured and teacher centered had about the same impact as programs that were moderately structured, or even as programs that were open-ended and child centered.

Similar results have been found for curricular initiatives with older students. For example, programs designed to develop middle and high school students' ethical and moral sense ("character education") generally do not have measurable effects on character: They may have impact, but the impact is too complex and contradictory to reveal trends.

But inconsistent curricular impact does not mean that schooling itself has no broad developmental effect on students. The studies of preschool mentioned above, for example, also found that some sort of carefully planned preschool program does benefit children from low-income families; it just does not matter exactly which sort of program is planned. And analysis of character education programs suggests that students' experiences with teachers and schools do influence their ethical sensibilities; but the influence is as much in spite of teachers' efforts as because of them. The conclusion—that effects of schooling are real, but somewhat "accidental"—may not be as ironic as it appears. The breadth, duration, and complexity of most developmental change make school influences both inevitable and reasonable, but also beyond the power of particular teachers or specific curricula to influence broadly.

Effects on Cognition: Literacy

Schooling does seem to affect cognitive development because of its pervasive emphasis on literacy. Virtually all teachers, regardless of grade level or subject area, expect students to acquire and use knowledge of print, and most students do in fact acquire this ability at least to a moderate extent. Because of the nature of text, successful reading eventually fosters forms of metacognition—reflection on or self-awareness of cognition itself. Metacognition appears because reading requires more than "breaking the code." In addition, effective readers must also realize that print (as opposed to oral language) is a second-order symbolic system: It does not represent the world directly but instead represents language that in turn represents the world. The printed set of letters in *caterpillar,* for example, represents the spoken sounds in /caterpillar/, but only the latter directly represents the small worm-like creature that later becomes a butterfly. Young children often do not understand this idea, and therefore think that the printed word *caterpillar* is shorter or smaller than the printed word *train,* because real caterpillars are shorter and smaller than real trains.

Realizing that printed text stands for language rather than for the world leads to important developmental changes in thinking. It makes possible the insight, for example, that what a person says may differ from what the person means. It also creates the belief that words have fixed meanings (enshrined in dictionaries) that are independent of their oral use on any one occasion. These ideas in turn lead to the realization that words can be misused, either accidentally or on purpose; hence, false beliefs (mistaken ideas) become possible, but so does deliberate lying about the truth. In schools, in addition, using words correctly becomes an ongoing issue between teachers and students. Striving for accuracy in language helps to develop achievement motivation for some children. When overdone, though, it can also create pedantic perfectionism or even alienation from schoolwork if children fail chronically to meet teachers' standards of linguistic accuracy.

Effects on Social Relationships: Peers

Schools provide copious contact with same-age peers, and as time goes on, they tend gradually to restrict contact with adults (the teachers) to businesslike, formal relationships. These circumstances make it an increasing challenge for older students to identify with the goals of schooling (preparation for career, self-fulfillment) and hence to develop a confident personal identity. They also make peers increasingly important as alternative sources of meaning. Social psychological studies of life in middle schools and high schools document the salience of peer social systems structured around large "crowds" and smaller "cliques," and organized hierarchically in the minds of the participants. With only a few exceptions, most adolescent crowds and cliques influence individuals to limit or even conceal expressions of academic interest and motivation, whether they feel interest and motivation or not. In some cases peers also increase individuals' vulnerability to high-risk behaviors (e.g., drugs or early sex). Such influences interact, of course, with teenagers' relationships with family members. With an appropriate mixture of support, freedom, and protection at home, potential negative effects of schooling can be moderated substantially. Achieving a healthy, developmentally appropriate mix is often easier said than done. But in principle, at least, parents and family members can frame the long-term purposes of schooling more meaningfully than can peers, and

interpret the short-term expectations of peers in ways that help a child respond to peers more as friends than as a monolithic pressure group.

—*Kelvin L. Seifert*

See also After-School Programs, Charter Schools, Grade Retention, Reading, School Dropouts

Further Readings and References

Adler, P., & Adler, P. (1998). *Peer power: Preadolescent culture and identity.* New Brunswick, NJ: Rutgers University Press.

Amsel, E., & Byrnes, J. (Ed.). (2002). *Language, literacy, and cognitive development.* Mahwah, NJ: Erlbaum.

Association of Childhood Education International, http://www.udel.edu/bateman/acei

Beane, J., & Brodhagen, B. (2001). Teaching in middle schools. In V. Richardson (Ed.), *Handbook of research on teaching* (4th ed., pp. 1157–1174). Washington, DC: American Educational Research Association.

Bredekamp, S., & Copple, C. (Eds.). (1997). *Developmentally appropriate practice in early childhood programs* (Rev. ed.). Washington, DC: National Association for the Education of Young Children.

National Association of School Psychologists, http://www.nasponline.org

Noddings, N. (2002). *Educating moral people: A caring alternative to character education.* New York: Teachers College Press.

Oden, S., Schweinhart, L., Weikart, D., Marcus, S., & Xie, Y. (2000). *Into adulthood: A study of the effects of Head Start.* Ypsilanti, MI: High/Scope Press.

Teachers College Record, http://www.tcrecord.org

SCHOOL DROPOUTS

The importance of earning a high school diploma has increased dramatically over the past 50 years. Dropping out impacts individuals and society on a number of fronts, including employment, finances, and crime. Dropout rates can be measured in two ways. The event dropout rate compares the number of people who are not enrolled in school (and did not graduate but were enrolled during the previous year) to the total enrolled during the previous year. The status dropout rate refers to the percentage of people who are not enrolled in school and have not graduated, regardless of whether they were enrolled during the previous year.

FREQUENCY

Between October 2001 and October 2002, among the civilian noninstitutionalized population, 367,000 students in grades 10 through 12 dropped out of school, translating into an event dropout rate of approximately 1 out of every 30 students in those grades. The 2002 event dropout rate (3.3%) is only slightly below dropout rates between 1967 and 2001, which ranged from 4.0% to 6.7%. Apart from a downward trend during the 1980s, event dropout rates have remained relatively unchanged. Each year since 1990, this consistent school leaving has resulted in more than 3 million people between the ages of 16 and 24 who were not enrolled in school and had not graduated. In 2002, the number reached 3,721,000, a 10.5% status dropout rate in the young population.

DEMOGRAPHICS

Age

Dropping out tends to occur beyond the traditional high school ages. While relatively few students ages 15 to 18 dropped out in 2000 (2.9%, 3.5%, and 6.1%, respectively), 9.6% of 19-year-olds and 16.1% of 20- through 24-year-olds dropped out. In 2002, 55% of people between the ages of 16 and 24 were beyond traditional high school age, but over two-thirds of young status dropouts were between 19 and 24 years old.

Gender

Over the majority of the past three decades, males and females did not experience significantly different event dropout rates. Between October 2001 and October 2002, 3.2% of females and 3.5% of males dropped out of grades 10 through 12. However, 14% of males ages 18 to 24 were not enrolled and had not graduated from high school in 2002, compared with only 10.6% of females in that same group.

Income

Students from low-income families are less likely to stay in school until graduation than students from high-income families. In 2000, only 1.6% of students from families in the top 20% of the income distribution dropped out. That same year, the event dropout rate for students from middle-income families was 5.2% and 10% of students from families with incomes in the lowest 20% dropped out.

Location

Location has been shown to relate to dropout rates. In 2001, high dropout rates were observed most often in large or midsize cities and least often in rural areas. In addition to the size of a city, region impacts dropout rates.

Across the country, regional event dropout rates did not vary widely in 2000, ranging from 3.8% in the West to 6.2% in the South. However, significant regional differences in status dropout rates occurred in 2000, as they have since the mid-1970s. Status dropout rates in the South (12.9%) and West (11.3%) were significantly higher than status dropout rates in the Northeast (8.5%) and Midwest (9.2%). Considering the proportion of young adults living in each region, the Northeast and Midwest experienced disproportionately low dropout rates, the West experienced proportionate dropout rates, and the South experienced disproportionately high dropout rates.

Race/Ethnicity

A great disparity exists among racial/ethnic groups in terms of event and status dropout rates. White non-Hispanics have experienced consistently lower dropout rates than black non-Hispanics since 1967. Additionally, Hispanics have experienced the highest dropout rate each year since the earliest year for which figures are available, 1972. Figures for Asians and Pacific Islanders are available from 1999, showing the lowest dropout rates. In 2002, among the civilian noninstitutionalized population, Asians and Pacific Islanders experienced an event dropout rate of 2.3%, followed by white non-Hispanics (2.4%), black non-Hispanics (4.5%), and those of Hispanic origin (5.3%). That same year, the status dropout rate for Asians and Pacific Islanders was 4.2%, followed by white non-Hispanics (7.5%), black non-Hispanics (13.4%), and Hispanics (30.1%).

Over three decades of records provide evidence that group dropout rates have declined for whites and blacks, while the gap between the groups also decreased. In 1967, the status dropout rate for whites was 5.7 percentage points higher than in 2002 and the status dropout rate for blacks was 20 percentage points higher than in 2002. However, the decline in dropout rates for blacks is partly due to a striking increase in incarceration rates among black high school dropouts since 1980. Incarcerated individuals are removed from the civilian noninstitutionalized population, which is used to determine dropout rates.

While other racial/ethnic groups experienced reduced dropout rates, the event and status dropout rates for Hispanics have remained high. While the highest recorded Hispanic event dropout rate occurred in 1978 (12.3%), similar rates occurred as recently as 1995 (11.6%) and the event dropout rate has yet to fall below 5%. Additionally, Hispanics have repeatedly experienced 40% status dropout rates (40.4% in 1972, 40.3% in 1980, and 39.6% in 1988 and 1991) and the rate has never fallen below 30%.

Hispanics who are born in the United States are less likely to graduate than their peers but are more than twice as likely to graduate as foreign-born Hispanics. Hispanics are the only racial/ethnic group to experience a difference in dropout rates dependent on timing of immigration, which may be due to language difficulties. In 1995, 62.5% of Hispanic dropouts born outside the United States had never enrolled in a U.S. school. Most of this group who had never enrolled reported speaking English "not well" or "not at all" (79.8%).

COSTS

Employment, Income, and Poverty

Since the 1950s, the value of a high school degree has changed from an advantage in the labor market to a minimum requirement for entry-level positions. Employment is a challenge for those who do not graduate. Nearly 30% of people who dropped out between October 2001 and October 2002 were unemployed in June of 2003, while only 16.9% of recent high school graduates who were not enrolled in college were unemployed. Overall, the unemployment rate for dropouts is 60%, while the unemployment rates for high school and college graduates is 40% and 20%, respectively.

A dropout who is able to find work still earns less money than a high school graduate. Just as the need for a high school degree has increased over the past few decades, the hourly wage for high school dropouts has decreased—by 31% (adjusted for inflation) between 1973 and 1997. The result is an average yearly earning for high school dropouts of $9,245 less than for high school graduates and a difference of $369,819 over 40 years. Additionally, compared to

high school graduates who do not go on to college, dropouts are more likely to fall into poverty, to apply for and receive public assistance, and to stay on public assistance longer.

Societal Impact

In addition to effects on the personal level, dropping out impacts the national community. Due to dropouts' reduced income, the country loses lifetime tax revenue estimated between $200 billion and $944 billion for each year's class of dropouts. Additionally, the government spends an estimated $24 billion more due to public welfare and crime for each class.

Increased crime-related expenditure is reflected in the disproportionate amount of dropouts in the nation's jails and prisons. Compared with the percentage of dropouts in the noninstitutionalized adult population (18% in 1997), the institutionalized population is composed of high percentages of dropouts: 31% of probationers (1995), 47% of local jail inmates (1996), 27% of federal prisoners (1997), and 40% of state prisoners (1997) are dropouts.

PROGRAMS TO REDUCE DROPOUT RATES

A number of organizations have identified effective strategies and characteristics of dropout prevention programs. Such characteristics include early identification and programming, personalized attention, innovative structures, experiential learning, safe school climate, high standards, and long-term support. While many programs feature one or more of these characteristics, not all programs have proven effective. Included among the programs that have been proven to reduce dropout rates for participants are Advancement Via Individual Determination; Career Academies—Junior ROTC; Coca-Cola Valued Youth Program; CollegeBound; DeLaSalle Model; Gateway to Higher Education; Graduation, Reality, and Dual-Role Skills; I Have a Dream; Maryland's Tomorrow; Quantum Opportunities Program; SCORE for College; Tech Prep (TX); Turner Technical Arts High School; and Youth River Watch.

SUMMARY

The nation's graduation rate has improved over recent decades. Meanwhile, the importance of a high school degree has grown exponentially. Still, race/ethnicity, income, and region are factors in dropout rates. With prevention programs targeting those most at risk, improvement may continue.

—Anne S. Beauchamp

Further Readings and References

ChildTrends DataBank. (2003). *High school dropout rates.* Retrieved from http://www.childtrendsdatabank.org/indicators/1HighSchoolDropout.cfm

National Center for Education Statistics. (2003). *The condition of education 2003* (NCES No. 2003-067). Washington, DC: U.S. Government Printing Office. Retrieved from http://nces.ed.gov/pubsearch/pubsinfo.asp?pubid=2003067

National Dropout Prevention Center. (2004). *Quick facts: Economic impact.* Retrieved from http://www.dropoutprevention.org/stats/quick_facts/econ_impact.htm

Young, B. A. (2003). *Public high school dropouts and completers from the common core of data: School year 2000–01* (NCES No. 2004-310). Washington, DC: U.S. Department of Education. Retrieved from http://nces.ed.gov/pubsearch/pubsinfo.asp?pubid=2002382

SCHOOL READINESS

"School readiness" has to do with how likely children are to adjust to the school environment and do well in kindergarten and early elementary school. The transition to school is an important period in young children's lives because many important attitudes, beliefs, relationships, and skills are formed during early schooling and these affect children's later academic, social, emotional, and motivational development. Indeed, trying to ensure that every child is ready for, and will thrive in, early school has been an educational and political policy priority for the past 20 years.

Although current researchers and practitioners are beginning to see school readiness as a two-way street—that is, believing that the question "Is the school ready for this child?" is just as important as the question "Is this child ready for school?"—most of the earlier focus has unfortunately been placed on examining only factors within the child that are important for predicting early school success. Even though we know that (1) parenting practices and children's early experiences in the home are critical for school readiness; (2) the type and quality of teacher, the early school setting, and the curriculum

are all important for predicting children's school transition; and (3) the culture of early school settings varies considerably from school to school, the cultural diversity of today's families is great, and the goodness of fit between family culture and the school environment is critical, the focus has largely been on assessing whether the child is ready for what is presumed to be a fixed and universal early school setting.

One typical way of doing this is to look at the child's age and simply set a cutoff age for beginning school. Interestingly, although many parents decide to hold their child back a year and have him or her start school later, thinking that the gift of another year will ensure readiness and success on the part of the child, there is absolutely no support for this practice in the research that has been conducted. Holding kids back a year by itself does not seem to do much good on average and may even have some side effects such as lowering children's motivation and self-esteem and souring attitudes toward school. Because massive variation from child to child in skills and prior experiences still exists even within the span of only 1 year of age, and because birth-date deadlines are not that effective in yielding age-homogeneous groups of kindergarteners anyway, some schools use a wide variety of available standardized (or school-made) readiness assessment checklists, surveys, or tests to determine if children are "ready" for school.

These assessment instruments typically cover children's academic skills (e.g., counting to 10, recognizing letters of the alphabet) and/or developmental milestones (e.g., hopping on one foot, drawing shapes) and are administered before either kindergarten or first-grade placement decisions are made, with the idea being if they pass the test they get to advance to school. The problem is that these school readiness assessments, although fine for their original purpose—to make specific curriculum and intervention decisions on individual children—are not very good for making global program placement, advancement, or retention decisions. Children deemed "unready" by the test who go on to school anyway are often indistinguishable a year later from those classmates deemed "ready" when they took the same test.

The bottom line for school readiness assessment is that there is no easy, magical, or scientific way to definitively determine how well children are going to do as they enter school. It depends on the child's preschool experience; exposure to academic, literacy events, regular routines, and positive social interactions inside and outside of the home; interaction with materials that allow the child to explore and derive a sense of mastery of their environment; and the classroom teacher and environment. If a readiness assessment instrument reveals that there are particular areas of deficiency for a child's learning skills, then what is important is getting the child the specialized therapeutic educational services he or she needs to remediate the problem, not just waiting another year and hoping the problem goes away.

—*Adam Winsler and Martha Carlton*

Further Readings and References

Carlton, M. P., & Winsler, A. (1999). School readiness: The need for a paradigm shift. *School Psychology Review, 28,* 338–352.

National Association for the Education of Young Children. (n.d.). *NAEYC position statement on school readiness.* Retrieved from http://www.naeyc.org/about/positions/psredy98.asp

North Central Regional Educational Laboratory. (n.d.). *Assessment of school readiness.* Retrieved from http://www.ncrel.org/sdrs/areas/issues/students/earlycld/ea5lk11b.htm

Pianta, R. C., & Cox, M. J. (1999). (Eds.). *The transition to kindergarten.* Baltimore: Paul H. Brookes.

Rimm-Kaufman, S. E., & Pianta, R. C. (2000). An ecological perspective on the transition to kindergarten: A theoretical framework to guide empirical research. *Journal of Applied Developmental Psychology, 21,* 491–511.

Saluja, G., Scott-Little, C., & Clifford, R. M. (2000). Readiness for school: A survey of state policies and definitions. *Early Childhood Research and Practice, 2*(2). Retrieved from http://ecrp.uiuc.edu/v2n2/saluja.html

SCHOOL YEARS

The term *school years* refers to the years in which children of many cultures find themselves undergoing formal education. During the approximate ages of 6 to 11, children around the world spend more time away from direct parental supervision and show increasing independence and ability to take on more mature responsibilities. They also become increasingly engaged with their peers. In most industrialized and many nonindustrialized societies, these changes occur at the same time that children are immersed in a school setting. These years are distinctive from other periods of development because children begin, often

in limited ways, to participate directly in the world of adults, and receive deliberate training in the values and important knowledge of this world. However, children in this age group are widely believed not to have the full understanding and expertise held by adults. They also do not typically engage in the romantic or sexual relationships in which adolescents and adults participate.

There are many hallmarks of entry into this period of development, most of which appear across widely differing cultures. Physically, children become larger, stronger, and capable of better balance and coordination, although they have not yet undergone the development of secondary sex characteristics associated with puberty. Cognitively, children in this age group appear better able to think in two ways at the same time. For example, they become more fully capable of considering others' viewpoints, they consider alternative logical possibilities, and they begin to integrate conflicting ideas in areas as diverse as emotional understanding and reasoning about physical concepts. Children in middle childhood are more consistent in their reasoning and more deliberate in planning their activities than when they were younger. Socially, children in the school years become deeply engaged in the world of peers and begin to form a sense of personal identity that includes their role in the larger world as well as in their own families. Children have more independence from their parents, increasingly regulate their own behavior, and are held to higher standards by their parents than in the preschool years. They also begin to participate more fully in cultural institutions such as schools, religious communities, and social organizations.

In the following paragraphs, major changes that occur in the school years are outlined for the broad areas of physical development, cognitive development, emotional development and self-understanding, and social relationships. These areas are thought to overlap and influence one another in many ways. In each of the areas outlined, connections to other aspects of development at this time period are noted. The overall picture of development in the school years is one in which changes in physical and cognitive competence are mirrored in widespread changes in children's self-understanding and social relationships.

PHYSICAL DEVELOPMENT

Many societies recognize that children are starting to leave the preschool years behind when they lose baby teeth. For most children, permanent teeth gradually replace the 20 baby teeth between the ages of 6 and 12. Although the loss of teeth and accompanying "toothless grin" is perhaps the most obvious outward marker of entry into middle childhood, this period is also a time of important skeletal growth. The average child in the United States weighs 45 pounds and is 42 inches tall at age 6. Over the next few years, children grow two to three inches in height and gain about 5 pounds each year. This growth is not as rapid as in early childhood or in adolescence but is still noteworthy. The lower portion of the body grows the most quickly in middle childhood, so that children in the school years often look "leggy" or "lanky" compared with younger children. Children's bones increase in both length and broadness during this time period. Because the ligaments are not yet firmly attached to the bones, children in this age group are quite flexible compared with both younger children and adults. Skeletal growth is associated with new accomplishments in motor development. In particular, children in middle childhood show marked increases in strength, balance, and coordination. They run faster, jump higher and farther, and become accomplished in skills such as kicking balls, swimming, riding bicycles, and climbing trees. At the outset of the school years, girls tend to be slightly smaller and thinner than boys. Girls, however, enter the adolescent growth spurt about 2 years earlier than boys, so that by age 9 girls typically catch up to boys in height and weight, and by age 10 to 11, they often are taller and look more mature than their male age-mates.

In addition to growth in height and weight, children show important brain growth in middle childhood. In particular, the frontal lobes of the cerebral cortex, thought to be responsible for consciousness, planning, and impulse control, increase in weight and undergo myelination. Synaptic pruning is a normal process that leads to the death of unused synaptic connections and increased stability of heavily used connections throughout the brain. This process occurs at different rates in different areas of the brain throughout childhood. Synaptic pruning in the frontal cortex is especially prominent during middle childhood. Other areas undergoing major brain development in middle childhood include the parietal lobes (involved in spatial abilities) and the corpus callosum (allowing enhanced communication between the two hemispheres of the cerebral cortex). These changes are associated with increased lateralization of brain function.

Patterns of electrical activity in the brain, as measured by electroencephalography (EEG), show an increase in alpha waves (characteristic of periods of alert attention in adulthood) and a decrease in theta waves (characteristic of adult sleep) during middle childhood. Before age 5, there is more theta activity than alpha activity. The two types of activity are approximately equal between ages 5 and 7, and then alpha activity is more common than theta activity from age 7 into adulthood. Moreover, different areas of the brain show increased synchronization of electrical activity during middle childhood, suggesting greater coordination of the various brain parts. This increase in EEG coherence is especially marked between the frontal lobes and other areas of the brain.

Other brain changes in this time period are less fully researched, but there is some evidence that synaptic responding to neurotransmitters becomes more selective in middle childhood. It has been suggested that this more specialized chemical responsiveness of synapses may lead to greater efficiency in school-aged thinking. The adrenal glands release more androgens (male sex hormones) in both sexes beginning at around age 7, which may also affect brain organization in middle childhood. Later increases in androgens for males are known to affect brain organization in adolescence, but the effects of androgens on both sexes in middle childhood are less well understood.

COGNITIVE DEVELOPMENT

Most psychologists believe that the many cognitive changes that occur in middle childhood are intimately connected to and enabled by the brain changes described above. Theorists from different perspectives tend to agree that a hallmark of school-aged thinking is the ability to consider several different, even conflicting, aspects of a situation at the same time. Jean Piaget describes this change as an increase in reversibility, that is, an increase in the ability to carry out mental operations flexibly. This change is the main characteristic of entry into the period of concrete operations, a stage in which children show a marked increase in logical reasoning. Entry into this stage is thought to occur around ages 6 to 8 across the world. (Piaget believes, however, that children in the concrete operational stage are only logical when reasoning about tangible objects or events. According to his theory, children do not have the ability to engage in reversible reasoning about abstract or hypothetical problems until they enter the period of formal operations at about age 11 or 12.)

Piaget's best-known method for assessing children's entry into the period of concrete operations is the conservation task. Conservation actually refers to a family of tasks that present children with two equal quantities or qualities, make a change to the outward appearance of one, and require children to recognize that the underlying quantity or quality has not changed despite the change in superficial appearance. For example, the conservation of liquid task is often passed by 7- or 8-year-olds. In this task, the experimenter puts two identical beakers partially filled with liquid (e.g., colored water) on a table in front of the child. The experimenter asks the child if one container has more liquid or if both have the same amount. Both preschoolers and children in middle childhood recognize that the two containers have the same amount of liquid. Next, in full view of the child, the experimenter pours the contents of one beaker into a taller, thinner glass. The other beaker remains unchanged. Now the experimenter repeats the question of whether one container has more liquid or if both have the same amount. Preschoolers answer by referring to only one dimension of the appearance of the liquid in the new container. Typically, they point to the greater height of the liquid and state that there is now more liquid in the new container. School-aged children, however, consider both aspects of the visual appearance of the containers, and state that although the liquid is higher in the new container, it is also narrower. They assert correctly that both containers still have the same amount of liquid.

The increase in reversibility that characterizes concrete operations can be seen in children's "decentrated" responses, in which they can focus on two competing dimensions of the containers at the same time. They recognize that the greater height of the new container is compensated for by its narrower width. The increase in reversibility is also seen in school-aged children's recognition that the experimenter could easily pour the liquid in the new container back into the old container, and it would still be the same amount of liquid as before. Piaget argues that this increase in the ability to consider two conflicting pieces of information together results from maturation of thought structures.

Many recent theorists disagree with Piaget's stage analysis of this shift, arguing that it takes place more gradually than his work suggested. They also report evidence suggesting that the shift reflects changes in a variety of underlying cognitive skills rather than a fundamental reorganization of thought structures. For example, children can sometimes solve conservation tasks correctly as young as 4 years of age when the tasks draw on areas in which they have extensive background knowledge or when the language of the tasks is modified to clarify ambiguities. These findings indicate that even very young children are sometimes capable of more mature thinking. Nonetheless, there is widespread agreement that children do not typically pass Piaget's conservation task until they enter the school years. Despite the fact that younger children may have pockets of capability, and may show advanced logic in certain circumstances, they do not show consistent use of reversible logic until they are in middle childhood.

Another important arena in which Piaget notes an increase in reversible thinking is in taking other people's perspectives. In his three-mountain task, Piaget showed children a three-dimensional model of papier-mâché mountains on a table. He seated each child at one side of the table and asked the child to arrange small cardboard images of the mountains to indicate their appearance to a doll seated on a different side of the table. Piaget found that younger children often arranged the cardboard to show their own view of the mountains rather than the doll's view. Piaget called this inability to take a different visual perspective egocentrism. School-aged children, however, could accurately identify the doll's perspective when it contrasted with their own. Piaget noted that similar difficulties with egocentrism appear in preschoolers' language, in that they often fail to adjust their communication to make it comprehensible to others without the same background information. Concrete operational children, however, typically communicate in ways that account for others' needs and access to relevant information.

More recent research has pursued a similar question in the study of *theory of mind*. This term refers to the fact that we never directly see the contents of other people's minds and, in the absence of direct evidence, must formulate theories about what others think, know, believe, and feel. Most studies agree that children begin to understand other people's minds as distinct from their own sometime around the age of 3, and solidify this understanding at 4 and 5 years of age. Thus, recent research sees a shift in perspective-taking skills as occurring somewhat earlier than Piaget believed. Whether these skills are just beginning, as Piaget argued, or whether they are firmly in place, researchers agree that a major way in which school-aged children differ from younger children is that they are able to consider other people's points of view. This cognitive change reflects the larger tendency to consider conflicting aspects of a situation and has numerous implications for children's functioning in the social world.

Information-processing theorists focus on specific cognitive skills rather than underlying changes in thought structures. They agree that children in the school years show increased logic, consistency, and ability to consider and weigh several pieces of information at once. For example, school-aged children become much more skilled at classifying information, such as categories and subcategories of animals or plants. Children also become more skilled at finding their way through their neighborhoods because they can consider landmarks from several directions and angles at the same time. Information-processing theorists argue that children move from isolated competencies to widespread competencies because of improvements in the ease, speed, and flexibility with which they can deploy specific cognitive skills.

In particular, memory processes improve dramatically in the early school years. The speed with which children can encode new information into memory and retrieve stored information from memory improves, leading to the ability to hold greater numbers of items in working memory—that is, to actively think about more pieces of information at once. Children have a much greater knowledge base with which new information can be interpreted and integrated, leading to improvements in the ability to encode new information. Children also use memory strategies, such as rehearsal and organization of information to be remembered, much more consistently and efficiently in middle childhood. For example, in a classic study conducted by Terrence Keeney, Samuel Cannizzo, and John Flavell, 5- and 10-year-old children were asked to remember sets of seven pictures for periods of 15 seconds. Older children moved their lips while waiting because they repeated, or rehearsed, the lists of items. Younger children rarely showed any evidence of rehearsing the items. Those children who rehearsed remembered more items than those who did not, regardless of the age of the child, and younger children who were taught to use rehearsal did so effectively and

improved their performance. This study indicates that younger children are capable of using strategies to improve their memory, but that they rarely do so. In contrast, school-aged children approach memory tasks differently by choosing to engage in strategies that increase their success. Some psychologists have argued that a major part of development in the school years consists of children's increasing ability to select and use the most efficient strategies to enhance their performance.

Similar findings exist in the area of attention. School-aged children can sustain and direct their attention more skillfully than younger children, so that they deploy attention to various aspects of problems in a systematic fashion rather than having their attention "captured" by random aspects of the task. Children in middle childhood are better at ignoring distractions and choosing what they will pay attention to.

In part due to improvements in memory and attention, children become better able to plan their behaviors or approaches to problems during the school years. They are more likely than younger children to plan their approach to a complex task ahead of time. They can pursue a goal for a longer period of time and meet more subgoals along the way. They can shift means of obtaining the goal along the way, suggesting an ability to consider the goal and the means as separate aspects of a situation.

Overall, a major cognitive development in the school years is metacognition. This is the ability to think about thinking, to reflect on one's approach to a problem at the same time that one is also trying to solve the problem. In many different arenas, children in the school years show increased awareness of their own thought processes and greater skill at finding ways to focus and improve their thinking.

In the area of language, children undergo similar development in the school years. Their vocabulary improves at a tremendous rate; recent estimates indicate that the typical 6-year-old has a vocabulary of 10,000 words, while the typical 10-year-old has a vocabulary of 40,000 words. Children's increased ability to appreciate alternative meanings of words leads to their fondness for jokes involving word play, such as knock-knock jokes. Children also show increasing metalinguistic awareness, that is, the ability not only to use language but also to reflect on it.

In most industrialized and many nonindustrialized societies, children spend many hours of middle childhood in school. Children can benefit more from direct instruction at this age than at earlier ages because of their improved memory, attention, and language skills. In recent years, developmentalists have grown increasingly interested in the question of how schooling itself affects children. Most studies indicate that children acquire large amounts of specific knowledge in school; this knowledge is typically that held important in the larger culture. In most countries, the early school curriculum is focused on mathematics and language arts, and it is in these areas that the most dramatic increases in knowledge and skills occur.

Less clear, however, is the answer to the question of how school affects children's reasoning skills. Some studies have found that children in school, when compared with children from similar backgrounds who do not attend school, show no differences in the ages at which they pass Piagetian tasks. Other studies do show some improvements in reasoning on Piagetian tasks. The current evidence suggests that children in school become more skilled in using memory strategies in particular and metacognitive skills in general, so that overall they approach cognitive tasks more logically and with more planning than children of the same age with little experience in school. Sometimes these skills lead to improved performance on Piagetian tasks. However, the school-related changes seem to affect children's understanding of cognitive testing itself, rather than raw cognitive capacities. Children in school are more used to being asked questions by an adult who already knows the answer, and have better strategies for figuring out how to answer these questions. They are able to reason about problems apart from the real-life context in which the problem might appear. For example, Terezinha Nunes and colleagues studied children with little school experience who were street vendors in Brazil. The study found that the children were very skilled in solving math problems in the context of real transactions in their places of business. However, when given the identical problems in a classroom setting and without a business context, the same children's mathematical reasoning was much less advanced. Schooling appears to enhance children's abilities to marshal their thinking skills to solve abstract problems.

Overall, there are larger effects of school attendance. In most countries, children who attend school later have better access to jobs and higher income than children who do not. In the United States, adult income level is closely associated with years of education. Thus, children who attend school grow up to have more financial resources. They also appear to have better skills in negotiating with health care providers and are more likely to engage in direct teaching with their own children. Thus, some researchers suggest that schooling for children eventually leads them to become parents who are more able or likely to raise their children in ways expected in schooled society.

Children's entry into school is usually the first time that they are expected to sit still for long periods of time and to engage in sustained cognitive activities. Clearly this arrangement suits some children better than others. It is estimated, for example, that 25% of children have great difficulty learning to read when taught by traditional methods. Children are first likely to be diagnosed with disorders related to learning, such as specific learning disabilities and attention deficit disorder, during the school years. Currently, a great deal of educational research is focused on designing alternative classroom styles that allow children to participate more actively in the learning process and provide better learning opportunities for children with different learning skills. There is also a large amount of research on ways to create classrooms that are sensitive to cultural differences in children's learning styles. Many studies have found national differences in school success; for example, Japanese and Chinese children have been found to outperform children from the United States in mathematics. Current research on schooling asks why these differences appear and how education in countries with less academic achievement in some areas can incorporate the best aspects of education in countries where children achieve more.

EMOTIONAL DEVELOPMENT AND SELF-UNDERSTANDING

Many of the social and emotional changes in children's lives during the school years are closely related to the cognitive changes described above. In the area of emotions, children become better able to regulate their emotions (consistent with better regulation of thinking skills) and show less overall emotional negativity than in earlier years. Consistent with their greater logic, children's fears are more likely to be based on realistic (if exaggerated) concerns than on imaginary creatures such as monsters. For example, children in middle childhood report fears for the health of their family members and fears of being victims of violent crimes. When they are harmed, school-aged children are less likely to show anger unless they believe that the person who harmed them intended to do so; this change is related to children's increasing capacity to consider several pieces of information and specifically to recognize other perspectives. School-aged children are also better able to understand and reconcile conflicting emotions in themselves and others, such as excitement about an impending visit to grandparents that occurs in conjunction with sadness about being separated from one's parents.

Given children's increasing abilities to consider several different pieces of information and to reflect on their own thought processes, it is not surprising that children develop a more differentiated and abstract conception of self during the school years. Self-understanding in this age group is likely to involve some analysis of one's traits and some acceptance of these traits as relatively stable aspects of the self. For example, whereas preschoolers may describe themselves in terms of possessions and activities, school-aged children may describe themselves as "smart," "shy," or "good at sports." As in the area of cognitive development, some psychologists believe that younger children are capable of this more refined self-understanding, but that it is not shown consistently and readily until the school years.

Children are much more likely to engage in social comparison in the school years than they did earlier. Many researchers believe that this change is brought about at least in part by the school setting itself, in which children are explicitly and publicly compared to their classmates on a regular basis. It is also likely that children's increasing ability to consider conflicting pieces of information enables them to more accurately compare their own skills to those of others. Whereas most 6-year-olds tend to rank themselves near the top of their class, most 10- and 11-year-olds rank their academic skills relative to the rest of the class very similarly to their teachers' rankings. Children in middle childhood are also increasingly concerned with their peers' opinions of themselves and begin to define themselves in ways that reflect their roles in school and with their peers.

Self-esteem refers to the way in which individuals evaluate and feel about themselves. In middle childhood, self-esteem is based on a wide array of information. Some factors that affect preschoolers' self-esteem, such as beliefs about parental approval, continue to be important in the school years. New

information also comes into play, however. Social comparison processes in areas of performance that children value, such as academic and athletic skill, affect self-esteem in middle childhood. Children's beliefs about their peers' attitudes toward them are also important. Physical attractiveness is also a component of self-esteem in middle childhood, as are children's beliefs about others' opinions of their own background, such as whether they think they live in a neighborhood that other children would dislike. Because children are making more realistic appraisals of themselves in relation to others, self-esteem often shows some decline in the early elementary school years. This decline is thought to be a normal part of development and not especially harmful unless it is extreme.

In cultures around the world, adults believe that success in school is a function not only of cognitive intelligence (defined differently in different countries), but also of less tangible factors such as motivation, effort, and confidence. As children enter the world of school, these factors begin to impact their academic performance and their beliefs about themselves that arise from that performance. Several psychologists (e.g., Carol Dweck, Eric Anderman) suggest that children in North America differ in whether they emphasize learning/mastery goals, or improving their skills, versus performance goals, or obtaining high marks and outward judgments of success. Different cultures, schools, classrooms, and tasks are also thought to give greater emphasis to learning or to performance goals. When children are oriented toward performance goals, they are more likely to respond negatively to failure. They interpret failure as a sign that their ability is low, experience negative emotions about themselves and the task, and often perform at less sophisticated levels or withdraw from the task. In contrast, when children are oriented toward mastering skills and improving their ability, they tend to be less disturbed by academic failure. Rather, they view failure as a temporary reflection of inadequate knowledge or strategies. They improve effort and ultimately their performance. Dweck believes that children who favor performance goals have an underlying view of their intelligence as a stable, unchangeable component of themselves, but that children who favor learning goals tend to think of intelligence as malleable and improvable with effort.

These developments in the area of achievement motivation are well documented among children in the United States by age 10 or 11, and there is evidence that similar patterns occur in younger children as well. The complex interplay of cognitive development with emotional and social development can be seen in this example. Children's ability to compare themselves to others, to think about their own thought processes and others' judgments of themselves, and to think of their own qualities as stable can have negative consequences for some children during the school years. Children are increasingly able to judge themselves and their abilities harshly and then to behave in ways that will prevent future successes.

SOCIAL DEVELOPMENT

During the school years, parents are less often involved in direct supervision of their children. Consistent with children's greater cognitive and physical skills, parents allow children more freedom to spend time out of their sight. Some of this time away from parents is in the care of other adults, such as in school (where, however, only one or two adults are typically responsible for large numbers of children). Children are also increasingly involved in peer clubs (e.g., scouting), athletic teams, and religious organizations that involve both adults and peers from outside the family. Other time is spent with peers away from any adults, often in unsupervised play. Children in many societies bear greater responsibilities for their families, too, whether in doing chores in the home, caring for younger siblings, or contributing economically to their households. In many cases this work takes place without constant monitoring from caregivers.

In the school years, parents are often less overtly affectionate with their children. Parents hold higher standards for their children than in the preschool years, and more frequently criticize children for not meeting those standards. Discipline is less likely to be physical at this age, and more likely to involve loss of privileges. School-aged children in many societies are also more likely than when they were younger to point out inconsistencies in their parents' decisions and to argue with their parents.

Perhaps because of children's greater cognitive understanding as well as the reduced opportunity for direct supervision, parents rely more on coregulation strategies than direct supervision for discipline. That is, they count on children to behave in ways the parents would approve even when the parents are not present, and they often use disciplinary tactics involving guilt and/or reasoning, designed to have continued effects on behavior long after the moment of misbehavior is past. Despite their generally greater distance, however, there is ample evidence that parental involvement in children's lives during the school years is beneficial for children. For example, in the United States, children are more likely to engage in antisocial behavior and to be rejected by their peers when their parents do not know where they are or with whom they are playing.

As parents become less directly involved with their children, children in many cultures are immersed in the world of peers. Whereas preschoolers typically prefer to play in dyads, school-aged children often play in groups. Children still become involved in conflicts with their peers at this age, and still most often resolve conflicts by means of coercion. In general, there is a decline in physical aggression toward peers and an increase in prosocial behavior during the school years. Nonaggressive strategies for conflict resolution become more prevalent.

School-aged children continue to engage in fantasy play, as in the preschool years, but this type of play declines during middle childhood. One activity that increases during the school years across the world is playing games with rules. Although younger children play together, the rules are few and change often. Among school-aged children, however, beliefs about rules are shared by large groups of children and the rules are sustained for long periods of time in the course of game play. It is thought that children's greater perspective-taking skills enable them to set out rules clearly and uphold them for all, and that their more consistent and flexible logic allows them to use the rules for protracted play. Games with rules, not directly supervised by adults, may be occasions for practicing mature relationships and responsibilities.

At this age, children in many cultures segregate themselves by gender, especially when they are not under adult supervision. Although some children in most classrooms report having a handful of cross-gender friendships, most children's best friends and most frequent playmates are of the same gender. It is estimated that children in the school years initiate play with a member of their own gender five times more often than they do with a member of the opposite gender. Gender grouping is common on school playgrounds and in classrooms when children are allowed to choose their own groups, although it is somewhat less apparent when children play with neighbors near their homes. Children who play with members of the opposite gender on a regular basis tend to be less popular with their peers. Eleanor Maccoby, after a review of many studies, suggested that school-aged girls, who tend to have a more cooperative style of interacting with their peers than do boys, find the rough-and-tumble, coercive interactions of boys extremely unpleasant. Boys tend to ignore girls' requests and preferences, and girls may actively seek the company of other girls so that they can experience smoother social interactions. Girls also tend to stay closer to adults than do boys, perhaps as a way of gaining protection from boys' aggressive play. Overall, peer segregation by gender appears to be self-initiated and self-perpetuated.

During the school years, children in industrialized societies differ in the extent to which their peers accept them. Developmental psychologists have identified subgroups of children with different status in their classrooms. "Popular" children are liked by most of their classmates. These children tend to be prosocial, emotionally well regulated, and socially skilled. Although they are rarely aggressive for hostile reasons, they do use aggression occasionally as a means of self-assertion. "Neglected" children make very little impact in their classrooms; rather than being liked or disliked, they are mostly overlooked. These children are not especially sociable or aggressive, but they appear to be of average social competence. "Rejected" children, in contrast, are actively disliked by their classmates. These children fall into several groups. About half of rejected children are aggressive; they tend to be hostile and disruptive in interactions with their peers. A smaller proportion of rejected children are socially withdrawn and timid. These children are not merely shy (as some neglected children may be); rather, they are also immature and show poor emotional regulation. Finally, "controversial" children have a high but mixed profile in their classrooms. They are actively liked by some children and actively disliked by others. They tend to be highly visible and to show both cooperative and hostile behaviors. They are often perceived both as group leaders and as snobs. (Peer acceptance is based on varying criteria across cultures; for example, in China, shyness is associated with peer acceptance during the school years, whereas in North America, shyness is associated with neglected social status.)

Differences in peer status are important in part because of differences in children's feelings about their social experiences. Many rejected children, especially rejected-withdrawn children, report being lonely on a regular basis. Differences in peer status are also important because they are associated with long-term adjustment. Rejected children are at greater risk for a range of later difficulties, including poor academic performance, school dropout, externalizing symptoms such as aggression and substance abuse, and internalizing symptoms such as depression. Peer relations are an important arena for children's development, and disruptions in these relations are considered a risk factor in their own right. It is likely, however, that cause and effect relations are complex in this area, and that children who are rejected by their peers may have other factors in addition to poor peer relations per se that contribute to later adjustment problems.

Bullying and victimization are common problems in the school years that tend to decline in adolescence. Some studies report that most children regularly both bully and are victimized. However, about 20% of children engage in extensive bullying, and about 15% of children are frequent victims. Although girls can bully and be victimized, it is more common for males to be bullies as well as to be victimized. Many victims tend to be passive and visibly upset when bullied, and they have few if any defenders in their peer groups. Other victims also engage in aggressive behaviors, and their occasional violent retaliations may make them targets of more bullying in the future. Many studies now suggest that school-implemented programs are effective in reducing bullying and victimization. These programs are actively encouraged in many schools because of the negative long-term consequences of bullying for the perpetrators and especially the victims.

Friendship is a supportive and mutual one-to-one relationship with another child. It is conceptually distinct from more general peer acceptance. Friendships allow children to develop social skills, experience fun and companionship, and establish models of intimate relationships. Regardless of peer status, children who have at least one reciprocated close friendship have a better chance of long-term adjustment than children without close friends. Even rejected children and victimized children with a best friend show fewer adjustment problems than those with no friends. On the other hand, aggressive and rejected children often have friendships of poorer quality than other children, and it is believed that friendships are more beneficial when they provide greater support and acceptance.

Although younger children have friends, children in the school years are increasingly aware of the qualities of positive friendships. They cite trust, kindness, and emotional support as key components of friendship. During the school years, children gradually engage in more intimate conversation and overt self-disclosure with their friends (as opposed to self-disclosure in the context of make-believe play in the preschool years). They become more selective in their friendships. Whereas preschoolers report having many friends, most children have just a few good friends by age nine. Most children's friends are similar to themselves in social background, personality, peer acceptance, and academic success. Cross-race friendships are common in integrated schools and neighborhoods, but less common in less integrated environments. Friends are typically skilled at resolving conflicts with one another. Children's improved perspective-taking skills are thought to both contribute to and benefit from the deeper friendships that occur as children go through the school years.

One domain closely related to children's experiences with both peers and parents is moral development. Parents' use of coregulation in discipline reflects the belief that children in the school years are beginning to internalize moral values, such that they themselves desire to behave in moral ways even when others are not present to administer consequences. Over the course of the school years, children do in fact show increasing understanding of moral issues and internalization of moral values. They are increasingly likely to consider others' perspectives and intentions when making moral judgments. For example, Piaget believed that children beginning school are governed by a moral framework in which rules are immutable and punishments for rule breaking are amply justified. By age 11 or 12, however, Piaget thought that children have come to value fairness and egalitarianism, and to see rules as flexible products of social agreement. Kohlberg saw morality in the school years as moving from a concern for one's own best interests to a concern for meeting mutual interpersonal needs and expectations. The development of prosocial moral reasoning follows a similar trajectory. When asked to reason about hypothetical dilemmas pitting voluntary helping of another person against personal satisfaction (e.g., helping a boy who has hurt his leg vs. continuing on one's way to a birthday party), school-aged children from widely differing cultures exhibit concern for social approval. Toward the end of this age, children's reasoning reflects greater empathy and concern for the other person. Children in the school years are also better able to distinguish between moral rules (involving fair and just treatment of the self and others) and rules that reflect social conventions (e.g., styles of clothing, table manners). These advances in moral understanding often express themselves in the realm of peer interactions, but it is also the case that extensive peer interactions in the school years contribute to these advances. Overall, in children's moral reasoning, the interplay between their increasingly logical and flexible cognitive skills and their expanding social worlds is clearly illustrated.

SUMMARY

Physically, children in the school years increase in size, strength, and motor coordination. Their brains continue to develop, especially in the frontal cortex responsible for planning. Their cognitive skills reflect underlying brain changes; children's thinking in the school years is more efficient, logical, and consistent than when they were younger. Children are also increasingly able to consider different and conflicting pieces of information and to plan and direct their cognitive activities. Children's emotional development mirrors their increasing ability to consider conflicting information and take others' perspectives. Children come to have more differentiated and realistic views of the self, as a result of both their new cognitive skills and the new social contexts in which they find themselves. These social contexts include more time with peers and less time with parents, although parents remain important in children's lives. The world of peers allows school-aged children to use their perspective-taking skills and logic, and peer interactions in turn contribute to children's abilities to understand other perspectives and to regulate their own behavior. In this phase of development, as in others, the many interconnections between physical, cognitive, emotional, and social development are apparent. In the school years, this interplay prepares children for the more mature responsibilities of adolescence and adulthood.

—*Kathleen M. Cain*

Further Readings and References

About.com. (n.d.). *School age children.* Retrieved from http://pediatrics.about.com/od/schoolagechildren/
Cole, M., Cole, S. R., & Lightfoot, C. (2005). *The development of children* (5th ed.). New York: Worth. (See especially Part IV: Middle Childhood, pp. 449–573)

Dweck, C. S. (1999). *Self-theories: Their role in motivation, personality, and development.* Philadelphia: Psychology Press/Taylor & Francis.

Eisenberg, N., & Fabes, R. (1998). Prosocial development. In W. Damon (Series Ed.) & N. Eisenberg (Vol. Ed.), *Handbook of child psychology: Vol. 3. Social, emotional, and personality development* (5th ed., pp. 701–778). New York: Wiley.

Goswami, U. (2002). *Blackwell handbook of childhood cognitive development.* Malden, MA: Blackwell.

Maccoby, E. E. (2002). Gender and group process: A developmental perspective. *Current Directions in Psychological Science, 11,* 54–58.

Piaget, J., & Inhelder, B. (2000/1969). *The psychology of the child.* New York: Basic Books.

Rogoff, B. (2003). *The cultural nature of human development.* Oxford, UK: Oxford University Press.

Smith, P. K., & Hart, C. H. (2002). *Blackwell handbook of childhood social development.* Malden, MA: Blackwell.

Wigfield, A., & Eccles, J. S. (Eds.). (2002). *Development of achievement motivation.* San Diego, CA: Academic Press.

SCIENTIFIC METHOD

Science plays an important part in our everyday life. If you use automobiles and computers, or if you take prescription medicine, you are benefiting from science. Science has improved our understanding of the world and provided the basis for much of modern technology. Science has also taught us important things about human development, for example, what the normative course of child development is and what child-rearing practices are most likely to be successful.

THE GOALS OF SCIENCE

Science aims to establish general laws or theories concerning natural events and relations among them. The laws and theories in turn allow us to explain and understand phenomena. For example, a general law states that reward (i.e., reinforcement) that reliably follows a behavior will increase the future likelihood of that behavior. Based on that law, we can explain, for example, the occurrence of socially desirable behavior in terms of past reinforcement, and we have gained some understanding of why some children exhibit more socially desirable behavior than others. Further, the law allows us to *predict* how someone may behave in the future based on what behaviors are

currently being reinforced. Finally, the law allows for *control* of behavior by the systematic presentation or removal of rewards following important behaviors.

SCIENCE AND OTHER WAYS OF KNOWING

The scientific approach is a means to gain systematic knowledge. However, there are other ways to gain knowledge. The first one is authority. We say we know something because somebody told us it was true. Everybody gains knowledge from authority, because we cannot test or experience everything for ourselves. If you have ever been influenced by something you read in a newspaper, what you heard the president say, or what you were told by a trusted teacher, you have gained knowledge from authority. Knowledge of this type is often correct and useful, but may also be wrong and even dangerous. History contains many examples of people being misled by authority (e.g., in Nazi Germany).

A second way of knowing is through logic. Logic involves drawing conclusions based on assumptions. For example, somebody may reason the following way:

Assumption 1: All children who have a diagnosis of mental retardation fail in regular classrooms.

Assumption 2: Billy has mental retardation.

Conclusion: Therefore, Billy will fail in a regular classroom.

Logic is useful in reasoning about events in the world, but it only leads to correct conclusions if the assumptions are correct. The correctness of the assumptions needs to be ascertained through means other than logic. In this case, the first assumption (all children with mental retardation fail in regular classrooms) is clearly not true; thus, the reasoning process may lead us to an incorrect conclusion.

A third way of knowing is through common sense, which may be characterized as beliefs shared by a group of people. Common sense is often useful, but shared beliefs are not necessarily correct. For example, it is common sense to immediately talk to a child who has just hit a peer, in order to explain why hitting others is wrong. However, sufficient research has shown that too much attention following undesirable behavior, which may take the form of a dialogue about acceptable behavior, may in fact increase the undesirable behavior. As an aside, it is usually better to proactively teach appropriate ways to interact than telling children what not to do after it has been done. Common sense can thus lead to ineffective practices.

A fourth way of knowing is through scientific methods, which are characterized by six essential features. First, science is empirical, which means that it is based on observation rather than opinion or logic. Second, science is objective, which means that more than one person has to be able to observe and describe the phenomena. The objective nature of science is particularly important, because it allows for replication of studies, which is necessary for results to be widely accepted. Third, science is parsimonious. If two or more explanations are equally correct, the simplest one is chosen. Fourth, science is self-correcting. Because of the emphasis on objective description of procedures and the requirement for replication, results that are anomalous, forged, or otherwise incorrect are likely to be exposed. Fifth, science is progressive, in that a cumulative body of knowledge is built. This requires that scientists be aware of relevant work in their field and design their research to extend prior knowledge. Sixth, scientific knowledge is always tentative. The philosopher Karl Popper pointed out that theories could be experimentally supported, but never proven to be absolutely true, because the possibility of falsification always remains. Thus, scientists try to design experiments whose results may falsify theories or laws. Any scientific theories or laws may be changed or replaced based on new findings. Those decisions are made by scientific communities, which consist of the scientist, the scientists's most immediate colleagues, audiences at conferences, and review boards and readers of scientific journals. Results that are discrepant with previously established findings may result in debates and additional research until the matter is resolved, either by exposing methodological flaws or by proposing a new theory or law that explains the phenomena in a more satisfactory manner.

METHODS OF SCIENCE

Scientific methods relevant to research on human development can be partitioned into three broad categories. First, the anecdotal method involves observing events under naturalistic conditions, and describing what occurred and why it might have occurred. For example, the developmental psychologist Jean Piaget constructed his theory of cognitive development by anecdotal observations of his own children. Anecdotes are lacking in most of the essential characteristics of science, and thus are often considered as starting points of a scientific method. Careful descriptions may generate ideas that can be tested using more stringent methods, as was the case with Piaget's contributions.

Second, descriptive and correlational studies also use observation and description, but the phenomena under study are precisely defined to allow for objective observation and precise description. Researchers have employed precise measures of children's performance on tasks that measure cognitive abilities, and analyzed how the performances change with age. Such studies enable us to describe the normative course of cognitive development, and to describe the correlation between age and cognitive abilities. However, it does not follow that age causes changes in cognitive abilities, because other variables (e.g., biological and environmental factors) that are correlated with age may be more relevant causal factors.

The third category of methods, experiments, is the preferred way to reveal causal relations. Its purpose is to gain control over the subject matter by manipulating potentially influential variables. For instance, researchers have investigated the extent to which attention by parents influences the rate of infant vocalizing and smiling. By showing that infants' vocalizing and smiling increase when and only when parents consistently hold and talk to infants after they smile and vocalize, scientists have convincingly shown the effects of social reinforcement. By conducting sessions under controlled conditions, scientists can minimize the effects of other potentially influential variables (e.g., they can ensure that the infants are similarly well fed and rested prior to each observation), which increases our confidence that the results were indeed due to the variable of interest (i.e., the delivery of parent attention following infant behavior) and not some other factor.

EXPERIMENTAL DESIGNS

In science, relations between phenomena are demonstrated through experimental designs, which come in several varieties. Within-subjects designs use a single individual or group and the influence of a variable is shown by demonstrating that the effects occur when the variable is present, but not when the variable is removed. The believability of the effect is increased with multiple replications both within and across individuals or groups. Between-subjects designs employ two or more groups that are treated differently. For example, one group may receive a certain treatment while the other does not, or groups may receive different levels of treatment. Alternatively, researchers may study naturally existing groups, such as groups of people with different social backgrounds or different habits. For example, a group of children that watches a lot of television may be compared with a group of children that watches little television, with the goal of identifying differences in the respective group's ability to remain academically on task. Statistical tests are typically used to determine whether the differences between groups exceed statistical chance or not. If other potentially influential factors are held constant between groups, statistically significant differences between groups are assumed to be a function of the treatment.

Developmental psychologists, who are interested in how behavior changes over time, employ longitudinal designs, in which a group of people are assessed at different time intervals; cross-sectional designs, in which different age groups are assessed at the same time; or cross-sequential designs, in which two age groups (i.e., cohorts) are compared at different points in time. Through these developmental designs, researchers may gain some understanding of, for example, how people's performance on tests of intelligence or other abilities changes with increased age.

CONCLUSION

Despite past accomplishments of developmental scientists, much remains to be learned about human development. Furthermore, the implementation of already established scientific knowledge (e.g., about best practices in child rearing and education) is still somewhat limited. Those interested in scientific research in human development can thus look forward to many opportunities to enhance understanding and improve people's lives.

—*Einar T. Ingvarsson and
Gregory P. Hanley*

See also Experimental Method, Hypothesis

Further Readings and References

American Association for the Advancement of Science, http://www.aaas.org/

American Psychological Association. (2005). *How to be a wise consumer of psychological research.* Retrieved from http://www.psychologymatters.org//wiseconsumer.html

Braithwaite, R. B. (1959). *Scientific explanation.* London: Cambridge University Press.

Kerlinger, F. N. (1986). *Foundations of behavioral research.* Fort Worth, TX: Harcourt Brace Jovanovich.

Sidman, M. (1960). *Tactics of scientific research.* Boston: Authors Cooperative.

The Skeptic's Dictionary. (2005). *Science.* Retrieved from http://www.skepdic.com/science.html

SEARS, ROBERT (1870–1937)

Robert R. "Bob" Sears was professor and chair of the Psychology Department at Stanford University, as well as dean of Stanford's School of Humanities and Social Sciences. He was born in Palo Alto, California.

Robert Sears's father was a professor in the Stanford School of Education, and Sears met his wife, Pauline Snedden Sears, as an undergraduate at Stanford. Although his interests were initially in literature and drama, he was drawn into the study of psychology while an undergraduate at Stanford. During his graduate work at Yale he was influenced by Clark Hull and he received his PhD in 1932 with a dissertation in physiological psychology.

Sears's first academic appointment was at the University of Illinois, where he taught abnormal and personality psychology. Searching for a method to teach personality to undergraduates, he met with success combining psychodynamic theory with learning theory, informed with examples from literature. Subsequently he conducted empirical studies in which psychodynamic concepts were operationalized and empirically tested, becoming a leading scholar in this area. While at the Institute for Social Relations at Yale, he coauthored *Frustration and Aggression* (1939). He later completed the influential monograph, *A Survey of Objective Studies of Psychoanalytic Concepts* (1943).

Robert Sears entered the field of child psychology in 1942 when he became a professor of child psychology and director of the Iowa Child Welfare Research Station at the University of Iowa. There, with his wife Pauline, he focused on issues of personality and socialization in children. He was interested in parental influences on childhood personality, and was a pioneer in the investigation of child-rearing practices. Balancing good experimental control with ecological validity, he developed rigorous and creative methods for studying children and their parents. These included doll-play procedures to investigate children's fantasies and time sampling of children's behavior in preschool, as well as studies of parent-child interaction in the laboratory using standardized socialization procedures. This groundbreaking work produced numerous publications in professional journals, as well at the coauthored books, *Patterns of Child Rearing* (1957) and *Identification and Child Rearing* (1965). Sears's work at Iowa, and later at Harvard and Stanford, framed the agenda for the study of children's socialization.

During the latter part of his career, Robert Sears returned to the psychobiographical study of Mark Twain, in whom he had a lifelong interest. Sears had taken on the direction of the Terman Study of the Gifted after Lewis Terman's death in 1956. His work with this archive created a rich resource for scholars studying life-span development. His coauthored book, *The Gifted Group in Later Maturity* (1995), extended the study of intellectual giftedness into the aging years.

—*Carole K. Holahan*

Further Readings and References

Holahan, C., Sears, R., & Cronbach, L. (1995). *The gifted group in later maturity*. Stanford, CA: Stanford University Press.

Sears, R. (1941). Non-aggressive reactions to frustration. *Psychological Review, 48,* 343–346.

Sears, R. (1965). *Identification and child rearing*. Stanford, CA: Stanford University Press.

SEATTLE LONGITUDINAL STUDY

With its first data collection occurring in 1956, the Seattle Longitudinal Study (SLS) is one of the longest-running longitudinal studies of cognitive development in adulthood. Study findings have shown that patterns of cognitive change throughout adulthood are ability specific and demonstrate significant interindividual variability. On average, numeric ability and word fluency decline earlier than verbal meaning, spatial orientation, and inductive reasoning abilities. The study also established that cognitive decline related to normal aging generally does not begin until age 60 years or later and that the rate of decline accelerates throughout the period of age 60 years to age 81 years. The cohort differences in cognitive ability have been examined and have been found to be ability specific. An investigation of predictors of cognitive change in adulthood has revealed the important influences of chronic disease (particularly cardiovascular disease), environmental factors such as education level, and the intellectual stimulation of one's environment and personality style. A cognitive intervention component first added to the study in 1984 demonstrated that cognitive decline could be remediated to earlier levels, and these remediated levels could be maintained over time. Examination of neuropsychological data has indicated that individuals at risk for dementia could be identified at points 7 or 14 years prior.

The SLS was begun in 1956 as study founder K. Warner Schaie's doctoral dissertation at the University of Washington. Follow-up testing cycles occurred at 7-year intervals in 1963, 1970, 1977, 1984, 1991, and 1998, with new participants sampled and added to the longitudinal sample that could be resampled at each testing interval. The original sample in 1956 consisted of 500 individuals sampled from the membership of a health maintenance organization (HMO). By 1998, more than 4,800 members of this HMO, representing 13 birth cohorts over the average age range of 25 to 95 years, had been tested at least once as part of the main component of this study, and 38 people had participated in all seven waves. Early work by Schaie contributed to an understanding of the confounded nature of age, period, and cohort effects and to the differential conclusions that can be reached about development from cross-sectional and longitudinal data collections.

The longevity of the SLS has been due in part to the ability of the study to expand in order to take advantage of new methodologies and to answer new and important questions. The basic test battery used in the first four data waves (1956–1977) was augmented in 1984 with multiple indicators of each cognitive ability to examine these abilities at the latent factor level. In 1984, an intervention component was also added to the SLS to investigate whether decline in inductive reasoning and spatial orientation abilities could be remediated. Later waves also examined whether gains due to cognitive training were maintained over time in these older adults. In 1989, a data collection was started for the adult offspring and siblings of SLS participants to examine family similarity in cognitive change. By the 1996 follow-up, over 1,800 family members had been tested at least once. Neuropsychological testing of participants over age 60 was added in 1997, along with the collection of blood data, to examine early detection of dementia. In 2001, grandchildren of SLS participants were tested for the first time, providing three generations of cognitive data for some families. Additional measures have also been added throughout the study history to examine certain areas (e.g., personality, health behaviors, health records, and family environment) in greater detail. With its rich database and history, the SLS continues to be a major source of information about adult cognitive development.

—*Grace I. L. Caskie*

See also Longitudinal Research

Further Readings and References

Schaie, K. W. (2004). *Developmental influences on adult intelligence: The Seattle Longitudinal Study.* New York: Oxford University Press.

Schaie, K. W., Willis, S. L., & Caskie, G. I. L. (2004). The Seattle Longitudinal Study: Relationship between personality and cognition. *Aging, Neuropsychology, and Cognition, 11*, 304–324.

Seattle Longitudinal Study, http://geron.psu.edu/sls

SECOND LANGUAGES

A bright-eyed, anxious, yet excited kindergartner is accompanied by his parents to his first school experience; as his teacher greets his parents, the mother soon realizes that his first language is not that of the school. The teacher assures his parents that he will adjust well and that in a few months he will be speaking the language of the school. A college student interested in becoming a teacher in New York City majors in Spanish and education; a year before her graduation, she applies to and is accepted into a language immersion program where she will live with a Mexican family for 6 months. She is confident that when she returns to New York City, she will be proficient in Spanish. A recent immigrant, excited by all the possibilities of success in America, tries to find employment but realizes he needs to learn English in order to obtain decent employment. He enrolls in an evening class to learn English, believing that within a couple of months he will know enough of this language to obtain employment. However, second language acquisition is a complex and multifaceted process that is affected by factors such as sociocultural beliefs, educational background, proficiency in the first language (language spoken in the home), personality traits, and intellectual abilities.

WHAT IS SECOND LANGUAGE ACQUISITION?

Over the past 20 years, research findings have begun to offer a clearer picture of how children and adults acquire proficiency in a second language and how this process affects learning and achievement in school. Learning a second language is a long process, and not every person learning a second language achieves native-like proficiency. Most second language learners acquire second language skills through social interactions with peers, siblings, parents, coworkers, and teachers. In 1982, Stephen Krashen, in his writings on second language acquisition, identified five stages. These stages include the following.

Preproduction

In this stage the person is developing comprehension skills even though expressive skills in the second language are minimal. Listening is key since the person is now starting to associate sound and meaning. Sometimes individuals spend more time listening than talking, so this period is also known as the silent period; it may last a couple weeks or several months.

Early Production

Adults, parents, and teachers may find that in this stage, the individual comprehension and word usage in the second language is beginning to increase. One or two word utterances or short phrases are common, such as "How are you?" or "Good morning!" The person may mispronounce words, and this is typical of this stage.

Speech Emergence

In this stage, the second language learner is now starting to use longer and more complex sentences or phrases. The person is also starting to create his or her own sentences and can now retell stories in the second language. However, grammatical mistakes that are associated with transferring the rules from the first language to the second language are common.

Intermediate Fluency

Of particular note in this stage is the individual's ability to produce more connected or longer sentences. The second-language learner may comfortably engage in conversations with native speakers of the second language. However, even though understanding and usage of the second language have progressed and the person makes fewer grammatical mistakes, he or she still processes information more slowly in the second language. This means that compared with native speakers of the second language, the individual is slower in fully understanding information received and needed. This happens because the second language learner is probably still translating information from one language to another in order to understand the communication.

Advanced Fluency

This is Krashen's final stage. During this stage, the second language learner demonstrates better receptive (understanding) and expressive (spoken) skills in the second language. Nevertheless, the learner still continues to process information at a slower rate in areas of recalling and acquiring information. The action of processing information in a second language demands time and practice and may persist for years.

For children in school, this means that children who are second language learners may take a little more time understanding classroom demands and instruction even though they may seem to speak the second language well. Moreover, Jim Cummins, who studied second language acquisition issues in Canada, identified different facets of language proficiency. He noted two different aspects of language proficiency: basic interpersonal communication skills (BICS) and cognitive academic language proficiency (CALP). Cummins described BICS as the manifestation of language skills in everyday communicative context. It refers to those language skills that are necessary for day-to-day interaction, and it is a superficial fluency that second language learners acquire through interaction with peers, co-workers, and teachers. It can be referred to as a social language. For example, the individual can speak about the weather, favorite foods, and hobbies; give simple directions; and order items in a store or restaurant. Acquiring BICS may take 2 to 3 years. CALP is the second aspect of language proficiency. It refers to the type of language proficiency that is necessary for learning at the same rate as native speakers. CALP refers to vocabulary, higher-order reasoning, and problem-solving skills in the second language, and it transcends the social language. CALP is associated with literacy in the second language, and its development impacts on achievement. Cummins stated that it takes 5 to 7 years to develop CALP. This means that acquiring proficiency in a second language, which includes literacy skills, requires at least 5 years.

Second language learning involves a developmental progression through various patterns of language usage. This normal process brings about several patterns of language use; these are interlanguage, fossilization, code switching, interference, and language loss.

Interlanguage refers to a separate linguistic system that has a structurally intermediate status between the native and second language. It results from a learner's attempt to produce the second language and it includes a combination of linguistic rules adapted from both languages.

Fossilization is defined as specific second language "errors" or incorrect linguistic forms that remain firmly rooted despite good proficiency in the second language. It is a normal aspect of second language acquisition. It is believed that once a second language learner gains sufficient facility in a language to function in the mainstream culture, the individual stops learning because the level of motivation has decreased.

Code switching is a kind of verbal interaction in bilinguals in which a person switches from the grammatical system of one language to another at the word, phrase, or sentence level. Code switching is a very common occurrence in bilinguals; it is not necessarily a sign of weak proficiency. Moreover, very fluent bilinguals code switch; it can be used as a way of expressing cultural solidarity and to show close ties.

Interference occurs when communicative behaviors from the first language are transferred inappropriately to the second language. Interference from the first language can be found at the level of pronunciation, vocabulary, and meaning.

Language loss refers to the process of losing proficiency in the native language. It is often evident in young second language learners whose first language was neglected to teach the second language. It occurs when a child had inadequate linguistic models, experiences, and instruction in the first or native language.

WHAT FACTORS FACILITATE SECOND LANGUAGE ACQUISITION?

Over the 20 or more years of studying second language acquisition, researchers have found that there are several factors that mediate or influence this process. These factors include proficiency in the first language, educational background, intellectual abilities, personality traits, and sociocultural beliefs.

Proficiency in the First Language

In his work, Cummins found that highly proficient skills in the first language facilitate learning in the second language. A child or adult who has a rich vocabulary and expressive skills in the first language will acquire a second language more quickly because a good language foundation makes it possible to just transfer information from one system to another. On the other hand, if an individual's first language skills are weak, this person will find it more challenging to learn a second language since most of the information is being encoded for the first time.

Educational Background

The ability to read and write in the first language improves a person's ability to develop proficiency in a second language. This occurs because it seems that the common underlying language structures between two languages allow children or adults to transfer information from one language system to another. When children enter a school with very little education in their native language, they often experience great obstacles in learning a second language and in acquiring literacy skills in that second language.

Intellectual Abilities

Intellectual or cognitive abilities play a role in second language acquisition under two conditions: when a person has deficits in cognitive abilities and when children are placed in educational programs in the second language where they do not continue to grow intellectually in their first language. A person who has deficits in intellectual abilities will experience

difficulty learning as a whole; thus, learning a second language can be an arduous process. Carlos Ovando, Virginia Collier, and Mary Carol Combs have done extensive research on second language acquisition, bilingual programs and instruction, and achievement of language minorities. These scholars emphasized that it is critical to facilitate children's cognitive growth in the child's first language at least through the elementary grades because extensive research has demonstrated that children who reach full cognitive development in two languages enjoy intellectual advantages over monolinguals. For children, linguistic, cognitive, and academic developments need to be addressed equally in both first and second languages.

Personality Traits

An individual's self-esteem and his or her motivation to learn a second language contribute to the process of acquiring a second language. Other factors that play a significant role are personality factors such as whether a person is outgoing or extroverted as opposed to someone who is shy or introverted. An outgoing individual will be more comfortable taking risks and expressing himself or herself in the target language. This individual will probably socialize more with native speakers and expose himself or herself to situations that facilitate learning the second language. On the other hand, an introverted person may experience more anxiety and may take fewer risks. A high level of anxiety and discomfort interferes with learning because it not only impairs memory but also decreases the learner's willingness to practice the new language. Therefore, the optimum situation for second language acquisition will be someone who is outgoing, not afraid to take risks, and who is confident and motivated to learn a second language.

Sociocultural Issues

According to Grosjean, language is not only an instrument of communication, it is also a symbol of social or group identity. As such, language is accompanied by attitudes and values held by its members. The willingness to learn a language to identify with a particular social group can be a motivating factor to acquire a second language; conversely, a strong motivation to be accepted by a social group that does not participate in the mainstream culture can become a barrier to gaining second-language proficiency. In other words, if an individual lives in a society that rejects his or her native language or views it in disfavor, this attitude may influence the individual's willingness to learn the second language.

SUMMARY

Second language acquisition is a complex and multilayered process; it takes at least 7 years with appropriate linguistic models to achieve a level of proficiency to support literacy in the second language. Having a strong first language facilitates learning a second language. Moreover, there are other factors that facilitate acquiring a second language, such as being outgoing and motivated, living in a community that encourages learning the second language, demonstrating reading and writing skills in the first language, and being provided with the opportunity to continue growing cognitively in both the first and second language.

—*Tania Thomas-Presswood*

See also Language Development

Further Readings and References

Cook, V. (n.d.). *Second language acquisition topics.* Retrieved from http://homepage.ntlworld.com/vivian.c/SLA/

Cummins, J. (1984). *Bilingualism and special education: Issues in assessment and pedagogy.* San Diego, CA: College Hill Press.

Gopaul-McNicol, S.-A., & Thomas Presswood, T. (1998). *Working with linguistically and culturally different children.* Needham Heights, MA: Allyn & Bacon.

Grosjean, F. (1982). *Life with two languages.* Cambridge, MA: Harvard University Press.

International Commission on Second Language Acquisition, http://www.hw.ac.uk/langwww/icsla/icsla.html

Ovando, C., Collier, V., & Combs, M. C. (2003). *Bilingual and ESL classrooms: Teaching in multicultural contexts* (3rd ed.). New York: McGraw-Hill.

Roseberry-McKibbin, C. (1995). *Multicultural students with special language needs.* Oceanside, CA: Academic Communication Associates.

SECURE ATTACHMENT

Attachment refers to the quality of the relationship between a child and the child's caregiver. The term encompasses a number of different aspects of parent-child interaction, including the degree to which a child seeks comfort from the caregiver, the preference of the primary caregiver to other adults, proximity to the caregiver while exploring his or her environment, and reaction to separation and reunion with the caregiver.

Secure attachment is one classification of attachment. Securely attached infants use their mother or caregiver as a "secure base" from which they explore their environment. For example, the securely attached infant might crawl away from his or her mother to touch an object, but would periodically stop to turn and look at the mother for assurance. Similarly, the securely attached child will actively explore the environment in the presence of the mother and express distress when separated from his or her mother. Upon reunification of the child with caregiver, the child will seek physical comfort to alleviate the distress of the mother leaving.

Infant attachment is frequently assessed via the strange situation paradigm, developed by Mary Ainsworth, a colleague of John Bowlby. The strange situation paradigm is a method of assessing infant attachment that requires observation of a series of "scenes": the infant and mother playing together in a room; a stranger (i.e., a researcher) entering the room; the mother leaving the infant with the stranger for a brief period; and finally, the mother returning.

Ainsworth observed distinct sets of infant behavior, which she believed corresponded with attachment. The most common three sets of behavior (attachment) were referred to as secure, anxious resistant, and anxious avoidant. The secure child typically demonstrated some distress when the mother left, and welcomed the mother back warmly and sought physical contact when she returned. The anxious resistant child also demonstrated distress at the mother's departure, but would resist physical contact upon her return. Finally, the anxious avoidant child demonstrated less distress at the mother's departure, and would ignore the mother when she returned from the brief separation.

Of the three main classifications resulting from the strange situation, the secure child has received the most investigation. Approximately 65% of North American infants fall into the classification of securely attached. About 20% of North American infants have anxious avoidant attachment, and about 10% have anxious resistant attachment. International research suggests that these percentages are variable across cultures.

Attachment theory has never excluded the father as an attachment figure and allows for multiple attachment figures. However, the mother has most frequently stood as the primary attachment figure in research studies. Although Ainsworth's initial classification of secure attachment only included mothers, further research has measured the relationship between fathers and infants in relation to attachment style and yielded similar results.

The long-term benefits of secure attachment have been demonstrated through longitudinal research. In these investigations, infants with secure attachment, in comparison to those with other attachment classifications, were less aggressive with their caregiver, had higher social competence, were more persistent problem solvers, were better able to elicit their caregiver's help when younger, and had higher self-esteem later in childhood. Additionally, studies have found that securely attached infants score higher on developmental and language development tests. However, more research is needed to be certain that these trends are consistent because other studies have offered mixed results. The confounding variable in these studies appears to be the consistency of the caregiver's behavior across development. Changes in the caregiver's behavior can stimulate change in the attachment style of the child. Consequently, the caregiving environment of the child is important, not just in infancy but throughout childhood.

—*Peter K. Stewart and Ric G. Steele*

See also Ainsworth, Mary Salter; Strange Situation

Further Reading and References

Ainsworth, M. D. S. (1979). Infant-mother attachment. *American Psychologist, 34,* 932–937.

Ainsworth, M. D. S. (1983). Infant-mother attachment. In W. Damon (Ed.), *Social and personality development: Essays on the growth of the child.* New York: W. W. Norton.

Ainsworth, M. D. S. (1989). Attachment beyond infancy. *American Psychologist, 44,* 709–716.

SELF-ACTUALIZATION

Self-actualization is the epitome of maturity. It is indicative of sound psychological health and predictive of a creative, meaningful, and happy life. Self-actualized individuals are self-accepting and spontaneous. They are not inhibited by social pressures but confident in themselves, and thus authentic and unpretentious. They accept themselves for what they truly are and are in this sense honest with themselves. This is not to say that they believe themselves to be perfect and unflawed. Rather, they recognize their imperfections and accept them as part of what makes each of us a unique person. You might say that self-actualized persons are high in intrapersonal intelligence.

Not everyone attains self-actualization. Self-actualization apparently occurs only when a variety of basic needs are fulfilled. The needs that must be met before self-actualization is achieved include very fundamental human needs, such as those for food and shelter, and social needs for affiliation. Self-actualization is itself viewed as a need, albeit what Abraham Maslow called a meta-need. If a person's basic needs are met, he or she is in a position to consider meta-needs (for knowledge, justice, spirituality, as well as self-actualization) and may attain the highest level of human development. Self-actualization is a kind of maturity, a result of optimal development.

One of the most important benefits of self-actualization is its support of creative behavior. In fact, the two theorists who did the most to define self-actualization, Carl Rogers and Abraham Maslow, both felt that creativity was inextricable from self-actualization. Indeed, creative persons are spontaneous, uninhibited, open-minded, and flexible. The relationship is apparent from the other perspective: Self-actualized persons are creative. They may not devote themselves to traditional creative fields and produce notable works (books, works of art, inventions), but they are creative in an everyday sense. Like creative persons, self-actualized individuals are open minded, spontaneous, and autonomous.

Much of the thinking about self-actualization was based on clinical studies and qualitative research. It is not easy to examine self-actualization with more rigorous experimental techniques. Then again, according to Carl Rogers and Abraham Maslow, it should not be studied in that fashion. They felt that experimental methods tend to reduce human potentials and behavior in unrealistic ways. They felt that reductionism precluded an accurate understanding of what it is to be human. It should also be noted, however, that some traditional research studies have supported their ideas about self-actualization. There are, for example, several correlational studies showing an association between creative potential and self-actualization.

Self-actualization is viewed as the peak of development because it indicates that human potentials have been fulfilled and that the individual is functioning in an optimal fashion. Importantly, Carl Rogers felt that potentials can be fulfilled in systematic or at least intentional ways. He pointed to both clinical therapy and creative work as efforts to fulfill human potential. The clinical technique that best supports such fulfillment and self-actualization is that which uses unconditional positive regard. As this label implies, the key is to provide the client with assurance that he or she is respected as an individual. This in turn will often lead to the client gaining self-respect and an appreciation for his or her own individuality. This individual is likely to behave in a spontaneous fashion and live in an authentic and creative fashion.

Not surprisingly, Rogers suggests that parents and teachers should also provide unconditional positive regard to their children and students. Recall here the developmental aspect of self-actualization: It is a sign of maturity, the epitome of health and growth, indicative of potentials fulfilled. Without a doubt, self-actualization is an admirable human condition and indeed an important target for those working with children (and anyone else who is interested in development). It is, however, a unique kind of development, and not tied to cognitive or social advancement. Parents and teachers cannot assume that self-actualization will occur, even if they are careful in constructing a developmentally stimulating environment. Certain environments may stimulate intelligence, for example, but do nothing for the individual's self-actualization. Parents and teachers can, however, provide the unconditional positive regard and respect that will allow the individual to accept himself or herself as a unique and self-actualized individual.

KEY TERMS

Basic needs. These must be fulfilled before the individual feels the need for self-actualization. Basic needs include food, shelter, and social contact.

Meta-needs. Self-actualization is a meta-need in that it is only felt when basic needs are fulfilled.

Reductionism. An unfortunate tendency, rejected by theories of self-actualization, to study human behavior and potential by separating and simplifying.

Unconditional positive regard. One prerequisite for the development of self-actualization, given by therapists (to their clients) or perhaps parents (to their children). It is a kind of respect for the individual that does not depend on behavior. It is respect that does not need to be earned.

—*Mark A. Runco*

Further Readings and References

Maslow, A. H. (1971). *The farther reaches of human nature.* New York: Viking Press.

Performance Unlimited. (1998). *Self-actualization.* Retrieved from http://www.performance-unlimited.com/samain.htm

Rogers, C. R. (1961). *On becoming a person.* Boston: Houghton Mifflin.

Runco, M. A. (1999). Self-actualization and creativity. In M. A. Runco & S. Pritzker (Eds.), *Encyclopedia of creativity* (pp. 533–536). San Diego, CA: Academic Press.

Runco, M. A., Ebersole, P., & Mraz, W. (1991). Self-actualization and creativity. *Journal of Social Behavior and Personality, 6,* 161–167.

SELF-CONCEPT

People think about themselves. This observation is hardly surprising, but it reflects something quite unique and extraordinary about human beings. With the exception of chimpanzees and orangutans, humans are the only animals for which self-awareness has been documented scientifically. Humans are unique in other ways, of course, and there is reason to think that these defining features of human nature are linked to, if not made possible by, the capacity to reflect on one's own behavior, psychological processes, and existence. Self-reflection is more than a fleeting mental state (as it likely is for other primates); rather, it promotes an internalized representation or concept of one's competencies, values, personality traits, social worth, and other personal attributes.

People are not born with a self-concept. The capacity for self-reflection, in fact, does not emerge until children are at least 15 months old (usually older). The developmental onset of self-reflection has been documented in studies that assess signs of self-recognition in response to mirrors, videotapes, and photographs. In the mirror studies, for example, the infant's face is marked in some way (e.g., with rouge), he or she is placed in front of a mirror, and an observer notes whether the infant responds to the mark by touching the appropriate region of his or her face rather than the mark's image in the mirror. The emergence of self-recognition coincides with other developmental milestones involving cognitive competence (e.g., grammar in language use) and interpersonal behavior (e.g., embarrassment).

Initially, a child's concept of self is defined in terms of concrete attributes (e.g., physical features, emotional states) and is highly malleable and open to influence. Over time, children develop a sense of their competencies, interests, and general response tendencies. The input for this progressively abstract and internalized self-concept is generally considered to be social in nature, with parents and various significant others (e.g., siblings) playing a particularly influential role. Recent research, however, suggests that children's personality, including their self-concept, is shaped to a large extent by their interactions outside the familial environment (e.g., by peers and schoolmates). The primary mechanism in both cases is commonly assumed to be sensitivity to and acceptance of the feedback provided by others about one's characteristics.

Once a self-concept is formed, it tends to resist substantial change. Self-concept maintenance has been traced to various biases in processing social feedback, most notably self-enhancement (selective attention to positive feedback or positive interpretation of ambiguous feedback) and self-consistency (greater attention to and acceptance of feedback that confirms one's current self-assessment), although these biases (and other self-defense mechanisms) have been investigated primarily in adults. The self-consistency bias is particularly interesting, since it implies that someone with a negative self-concept will actively resist or reinterpret positive feedback from others. Although a negative self-concept can certainly prove problematic, self-concept stability in general is considered essential for effective and autonomous functioning. The failure to maintain a coherent self-concept is associated with identity diffusion, promotes uncertainty and ambivalence in social relations, and undermines commitment to long-term goals and persistence in effortful task performance. A stable self-concept is also fundamental for the self-regulation of thought, mood, and action. Because self-concept is defined to a large degree in terms of values, it provides a frame of reference for evaluating courses of action and thus enables the person to resist impulse, temptation, and peer pressure. A unique set of "self-conscious" emotions is associated with the evaluation of one's behavior against internalized standards and values. By late childhood, children are capable of experiencing such uniquely human affective states as embarrassment, guilt, and shame. The concern with avoiding (or escaping) these states provides a hedonic basis for moral action.

Self-concept, in sum, is a uniquely human characteristic that underlies a host of other psychological processes that distinguish our species. Contemporary research is exploring the evolutionary origins of self-concept. Another recent approach adapts the concepts and methods of dynamical systems theory to investigate the emergence and maintenance of coherence and stability in self-concept.

—*Robin R. Vallacher*

Further Readings and References

Baumeister, R. F., & Twenge, J. M. (2003). The social self. In I. Weiner (Series Ed.), T. Millon, & M. J. Lerner (Vol. Eds.), *Handbook of psychology: Vol. 5. Personality and social psychology* (pp. 327–352). New York: Wiley.

Nowak, A., Vallacher, R. R., Tesser, A., & Borkowski, W. (2000). Society of self: The emergence of collective properties in self-structure. *Psychological Review, 107*, 39–61.

Suls, J., & Greenwald, A. G. (Eds.). (1986). *Psychological perspectives on the self* (Vol. 3). Hillsdale, NJ: Erlbaum.

Tangney, J. P., & Fischer, K. W. (Eds.). (1995). *The self-conscious emotions*. New York: Guilford.

Tesser, A., Felson, R. B., & Suls, J. M. (Eds.). (2000). *Psychological perspectives on self and identity*. Washington, DC: American Psychological Association.

SELF-EFFICACY

Self-efficacy is the belief that one can accomplish certain goals. This belief is important not only to begin planning goals, but it also plays a significant role in attaining those goals.

This belief is a domain-specific belief. Individuals have self-efficacy in a given task in a given situation. Therefore, high or low self-efficacy would not be a trait of an individual, but rather a situational aspect in a person's life. For example, a student may have high self-efficacy while taking a math test, but not while taking a spelling test. However, levels of self-efficacy for individuals are correlated across tasks that are not related.

The construct of self-efficacy falls under social cognitive theory. Within this framework, a person is not passive to the environment, but instead takes what is there and manipulates it to create a self. This active role opposes theories that posit that the environment creates the individual with the individual having no say.

WHERE DOES SELF-EFFICACY COME FROM?

Six sources interact to produce self-efficacy: (a) performance experiences; (b) vicarious experiences; (c) imaginal experiences; (d) verbal persuasion; (e) physiological states; and (f) emotional states. These six sources affect the individual either distally or proximally. Distally means that something happened in the past that has left an impression on the individual that will affect his or her present and future thoughts and actions. Proximally is something that is happening in the present that will affect his or her present and future thoughts and actions.

Performance experiences are the experiences one has had while attempting to attain either a previous or current goal. With a strong background and success in goal achievement in a particular area comes high self-efficacy. Vicarious experiences come from observing someone else attempting to accomplish a task, comparing yourself to that person, and then considering how successful you would be at accomplishing that same task. If you perceive yourself as doing well, you would have high self-efficacy, but if you perceive yourself as performing poorly, you would have low self-efficacy. Imaginal experience is you perceiving your ability to achieve a certain task. Through this creative thought process, your imagined belief dictates your self-efficacy. Verbal persuasion comes from outside sources. This is when another person or group tells you that you have the ability or inability to achieve some tasks. Physiological arousal, whether positive, negative, or neutral, plays a role in self-efficacy. Individuals in a negative state are more likely to have doubting beliefs in themselves; however, when they have neutral or positive physical arousal, they will be more self-confident, thus increasing self-efficacy. Emotional states influence self-efficacy depending on whether one is in a positive or negative mood. In a negative mood, individuals are more likely to doubt themselves, and contrarily, in a positive mood, individuals have more confidence and more self-efficacy.

SELF-EFFICACY AND ITS EFFECTS ON BEHAVIOR

Self-efficacy plays a significant role in shaping behavior and does so through four mechanisms: (a) goal setting; (b) cognition; (c) affect; and (d) selection of environments. Goal setting is a necessary part of human functioning, and if individuals have a high sense of efficacy in a given area, they will be more able and willing to create goals in a certain domain. Contrarily, if they have a low sense of efficacy, they will be more likely to flee from a challenging situation and not create the goals that are necessary to succeed.

Cognition, a necessary mechanism for problem solving, is influenced by self-efficacy. With strong efficacy, individuals believe in their own abilities to succeed in life domains. This allows them to be efficient problem solvers and good decision makers.

Self-efficacy also has a strong connection to affect. With high self-efficacy, individuals in a difficult situation will have positive emotional responses. With low self-efficacy, they experience anxiety and possibly despondency or depression when considering highly desired goals that they believe they will not be able to achieve.

With a high level of self-efficacy, individuals are more likely to select more uncommon environments. They will have the beliefs in themselves that will allow them to try new places and experiences. Individuals with low efficacy would be more likely to stay in the environment that they are comfortable in.

HOW SELF-EFFICACY IS INCREASED IN A GIVEN ENVIRONMENT

Beliefs regarding one's efficacy are continually shown to play a significant role in both motivation and goal attainment. The greatest way to increase an individual's efficacy is through mastery experience. This comes via successfully reaching a difficult goal. Individuals who are able to struggle through a given situation and then achieve what they were pursuing will have more self-efficacy in this area and therefore will be able to face another challenge in this domain. The struggle creates the belief that they will be successful regardless of the challenges. If they were to not be successful in their goal attainment, they would have decreased efficacy, believing that goal attainment is not possible since it did not occur previously.

In the changing state of families, going from nuclear to family members having multiple work duties (e.g., working and taking care of the family), perceived efficacy in these multiple roles has become paramount. Women's beliefs that they can be successful at managing their careers and managing their home lives have more of an effect on both health and emotional strain than family income, occupational workload, or division of child care responsibilities. Also, when parents have a strong sense of efficacy, they are able to increase their children's competencies.

In school, self-efficacy is important in regulating students' abilities to be able to successfully learn and achieve what is desired. Academic development is regulated by three forms of beliefs. The first is students' perception of how well they can achieve understanding of scholastic subjects. The second is the teachers' belief that they can motivate and successful get across the information to the students. The third is the collective belief of the faculty and staff that the program can be successful at having students learn what is being taught.

Career development is another area that is significantly influenced by self-efficacy beliefs. When individuals must decide what careers to look at, their perceived beliefs about what they can accomplish determine what occupations they will perceive as being attainable and what is beyond their ability. Perceptions regarding the ability to navigate learning opportunities influence their belief that they can successfully complete the schooling required for a given field.

In the health arena, efficacy plays an important role in two life aspects. When coping with life stressors, efficacy dictates how successfully an individual will cope with them. Under the biopsychosocial model, where health is affected by both psychosocial and biological factors, life stressors have become ever more a priority when examining individual health. If individuals are able to deal with stressors more successfully, their health will be better than if they were not. The other area of efficacy in health is the perception that individuals can regulate their behavior. Individuals' perceptions of their ability to both control what they eat and control their activity level and types of activity is important to their physical health.

RAISING SELF-ESTEEM

Self-esteem is the discrepancy between where individuals believe they are and where they want to be. Therefore, individuals who have an ideal of where they would like to be and are close to that ideal have high self-esteem. The notion of self-esteem is much broader than that of self-efficacy in that it is not domain specific, but encompasses the whole person.

It has been shown that individuals who are praised, succeed in learning a new ability, or went through psychotherapy have an increased level of self-esteem. Another way to increase self-esteem is for individuals to attain goals. In one study, there were three groups. The first group was told to complete certain tasks. This group attained goals, which resulted in increased levels of self-esteem. In the second and third groups, participants either participated in psychotherapy (group two) or decreased their goals (group three). Participants in both of these groups had lower levels of self-esteem than the group that attained goals.

Other programs have been developed to create increased levels of self-esteem in at-risk youth. Training in some of these programs includes sessions on self-discovery, peer pressure, personal power, drug and alcohol information, and decision making. Participants learn about what positive aspects they see within themselves along with what positive aspects others see in them. Prevention strategies are created so that individuals can learn better ways of coping with pressure to participate in drug use. Also, awards are given to participants to let them know how successful they are within the program. The hope is to increase participants' self-esteem so that they will be able to be successful and be able to resist the pressure of harmful behaviors.

—*Daniel W. Cox*

See also Bandura, Albert; Self-Esteem

Further Readings and References

Bandura, A. (1977). Self-efficacy: Toward a unifying theory of behavioral change. *Psychological Review, 84,* 191–215.

Bandura, A. (Ed.). (1995). *Self-efficacy in changing societies.* New York: Cambridge University Press.

Frank, I. C. (1996). *Building self-esteem in at-risk youth: Peer group programs and individual success stories.* Westport, CT: Praeger.

Information on self-efficacy, http://www.emory.edu/mfp/self-efficacy.html

Kernis, M. H. (Ed.). (1995). *Efficacy, agency, and self-esteem.* New York: Plenum.

Maddux, J. E. (Ed.). (1995). *Self-efficacy, adaptation, and adjustment: Theory, research, and application.* New York: Plenum.

National Association for Self-Esteem, http://www.self-esteem nase.org/

Schwarzer, R. (Eds.). (1992). *Self-efficacy: Thought control of action.* Washington, DC: Hemisphere.

SELF-ESTEEM

In Ernest Becker's *The Birth and Death of Meaning*, he writes "If you . . . want to understand directly what is driving your patient, ask yourself simply how he thinks of himself as a hero, what constitutes the frame of reference for his heroic strivings— or better, for the clinical case, why he does not feel heroic in his life" (p. 77). This quote captures how central our heroic strivings, or in psychology terms, our self-esteem, can be to who we are and what we do. Indeed, self-esteem, our feeling of worth and value as a person, is of considerable psychological importance and, in that light, it is not surprising that it is one of the most widely researched topics in psychology. Having high self-esteem is associated with a wide range of positive outcomes, and although the pursuit of self-esteem may also have its costs, it generally contributes to peoples' psychological and physical health.

The development of self-esteem begins early in childhood and is a lifelong, fundamentally social process that often involves considerable psychological effort and defense to maintain. There are different types and contingencies of self-worth, and the culture in which we exist plays a large role in influencing how we seek to feel good about ourselves.

WHAT IS SELF-ESTEEM?

Self-esteem is often defined as the general attitude or feeling that one has about oneself. William James, the father of a great deal of psychological theorizing, suggested that self-esteem is the result of one's "pretensions," or what one aspires to be, divided by one's successes (or how much one reaches the goals to which one aspires). Similarly, many psychologists define self-esteem as living up to the standards that you, based in large part on cultural values, associate with being a good or significant person.

Self-esteem is often conceptualized as a relatively stable trait, a dispositional characteristic wherein some people may generally—across different time periods—have higher self-esteem whereas others generally have less positive self-regard. Self-esteem is also conceptualized as a state, a situational quality that is temporally raised or lowered by the events that we experience. An employee getting a promotion, or a student getting a good grade on a test, or an athlete playing well may temporally make the person feel better about himself or herself. Of course, this also implies that when an employee is denied the promotion, or a student fails the test, he or she may temporally experience a threat to his or her sense of self-worth. Such experiences can then lead to a variety of psychological defenses that are directed toward bolstering or maintaining an overall sense of self-esteem.

WHY DO WE NEED SELF-ESTEEM?

There are many different reasons why people need self-esteem, but at a very basic level some theorists argue that we need self-esteem because it conveys to us that we are special people and this in turn provides a deep sense of security. People, psychologists point out, have evolved a sufficient level of intelligence that we are aware of our inevitable mortality and all the precariousness of life. This type of awareness can lead to a considerable potential for anxiety. We seek to quell this potential for anxiety by maintaining beliefs that we are valued people that live in a meaningful world. This conveys a sense of order and purpose to our lives. Thus, self-esteem reflects the successful maintenance of these beliefs and therefore serves a fundamental anxiety-buffering function. Some researchers also suggest that we need self-esteem because it conveys to us that we are accepted by others.

HOW DO WE DEVELOP SELF-ESTEEM?

The development of self-esteem begins early in a person's life. At birth, human infants are profoundly immature in terms of their ability to take care of themselves. This state of infantilization means that humans are from birth completely dependent on their caregivers to provide for their basic needs and facilitate their survival. Because of this dependency, the child learns to associate doing what the caregiver wants and pleasing the caregiver with security (and ultimately self-esteem). When Mommy, for example, tells us not to jump on the sofa with our muddy shoes and we refrain from dirtying the decor, we often receive praise and love and this makes us feel secure. When, however, we persist in jumping on the sofa, Mommy may become upset and the ensuing absence of at least overt affection can increase feelings of insecurity. The caregivers thus constitute the basis of the developing child's sense of what it means to be a good person. They communicate to us to what is acceptable and valued behavior and what is unacceptable and bad behavior. As the child develops, the basis for what it takes to be a valued person transfers from the caregivers' standards to those that are drawn from our larger social groups and culture. In this way, the process of developing and maintaining self-esteem begins as, and continues to be, a fundamentally social endeavor.

HOW DO WE MAINTAIN SELF-ESTEEM?

We maintain self-esteem by living up to the standards that we associate with being a valued person. However, we inevitably encounter situations that threaten our sense of value (as when, for example, a student does poorly on an examination), and in such situations people will often employ a variety of psychological defenses to maintain self-esteem. Rather than interpreting such experiences accurately, we often interpret them in ways that reflect a self-serving bias; that is, we interpret experiences in a way that reflects favorably on our own sense of value. Thus, for example, our student who did poorly on the examination may explain this poor performance not by a lack of abilities, but instead attribute it to the teacher designing a poor test, bad luck, or some other external excuse. Indeed, in certain situations, people may go so far as to self-handicap themselves, to sabotage their chances of success so as to create a handy excuse for a failure they might experience (e.g., partying all night right before a test, so that if I subsequently do not do well I can blame it on the after-effects of the partying).

Because self-esteem is a fundamentally social process, a large part of our self-esteem maintenance efforts involve other people. When other people like us, this may often make us feel good about ourselves. And when others dislike us, this can pose a threat to our self-worth. Furthermore, we often try to associate with groups that support our sense of self-worth and reflect positively on us, and avoid associations with groups that do not support our sense of self-worth and

reflect negatively on us. These are just a few of the many ways in which people can try to maintain a positive sense of self-esteem.

ARE THERE DIFFERENT TYPES OF SELF-ESTEEM?

In recent years, research has caught up to classic psychological theory to indicate that there is more to self-esteem than whether it is simply high or low. Rather, it is important to consider the stability of people's self feelings (i.e., how much they fluctuate over time), the contingencies of self-worth or domains from which people derive feelings of self-esteem (e.g., does a person get their self-esteem from being a student or a spouse), as well as the broader distinction of whether people get their self-esteem from doing what they personally value or whether they get it from doing what other people value. In addition, capitalizing on developments in technology, researchers also examine how people may have conscious feelings of self-worth (e.g., feelings about their self they can report) but also unconscious feelings of self-worth (i.e., feelings about the self of which they may not be aware). These distinctions may be important for a number of reasons. For example, research indicates that unstable, externally derived self-esteem can be associated with increased defensiveness as one seeks to sustain personal feelings of value, but stable, internally based self-esteem is not.

WHAT IS THE ROLE OF CULTURE IN SELF-ESTEEM?

Another debate in psychological circles concerns the role that culture plays in feelings of self-worth. Do all people in all cultures need to feel good about themselves or does this reflect the typically Western focus on individualism? One view is that while all people seek to have self-esteem, they can do so in very different ways. For example, whereas a person in an individualistic Western culture may derive self-esteem from accomplishments he or she personally achieves, the self-esteem of people in more collectivistic cultures is tied much more strongly to one's group and one's communal contributions to that group. Or as another example, consider that while in the United States many people may gain self-esteem by accumulating wealth, in other cultures far different behaviors lead to feelings of esteem. Thus, one important anthropological message about self-esteem is to consider that it is culturally relative, in that what confers value in one culture does not necessarily do so in another.

SUMMARY

Self-esteem has been found to be a vital aspect of human social functioning. While much has been learned, there are still many interesting questions about the nature, determinants, and consequences to explore.

—*Jamie Arndt*

Further Reading and References

Becker, E. (1971). *The birth and death of meaning* (2nd ed.). New York: Free Press.

The Ernest Becker Foundation, http://faculty.washington .edu/nelgee/

Goldschmidt, W. *The human career: The self in the symbolic world*. Cambridge, MA: Blackwell.

International Society for Self and Identity, http://www.psych .neu.edu/ISSI/

Kernis, M. H. (Ed.). (1995). *Efficacy, agency, and self-esteem*. New York: Plenum.

Leary, M. R., & Tangney, J. P. (Eds.). (2003). *Handbook of self and identity*. New York: Guilford.

Pyszczynski, T., Greenberg, J., Solomon, S., Arndt, J., & Schimel, J. (2004). Why do people need self-esteem? A theoretical and empirical review. *Psychological Bulletin, 130*, 435–468.

Social Psychology Network, http://www.socialpsychology.org/

Tesser, A., Stapel, D. A., & Wood, J. W. (Eds.). (2002). *Self and motivation: Emerging psychological perspectives*. Washington, DC: American Psychological Association.

SELF-FULFILLING PROPHECY

Whether at home, in school, or at work, what others expect of us, the basis of the self-fulfilling prophecy (SFP), can help determine the outcome of our lives.

HISTORY OF THE SELF-FULFILLING PROPHECY

The term *self-fulfilling prophecy* was coined over a half century ago, but gained more universal attention in the 1960s through the research of Robert Rosenthal. Rosenthal gave his graduate students one of two types of rats, designated "maze-dull" or "maze-bright," to run through a series of maze experiments.

Students with the maze-bright rats were told that their rats would perform normally at first, but, thereafter, their performance would improve markedly. The students with the maze-dull rats were told that their rats were not expected to show much evidence of learning. In reality, the rats had been assigned to student experimenters on a random basis—any differences among the rats existed only in the student experimenters' minds (i.e., their expectations).

By the end of the 5-day study, the maze-bright rats had, in fact, performed significantly better than the maze-dull rats. Perhaps more important than how well the rats actually performed was how the student experimenters rated (described) the rats. Maze-bright rat handlers rated their rats more favorably (e.g., described them as being brighter, more pleasant) than did maze-dull rat handlers.

Rosenthal's follow-up experiment with elementary schoolchildren did much to call attention to the SFP among educators. He and his coauthor, Lenore Jacobson, led the teachers to believe that approximately 20% of their students were expected to "bloom" academically and intellectually during the school year.

Of course, there never actually was any scientific basis for identifying which students were designated to bloom. Instead, the designated student "bloomers" were randomly assigned so that the only differences between the bloomers and the rest of the student body were in the minds of the teachers. At the end of the year, the students designated as "bloomers" did, in fact, show intellectual gains.

Upon completion of the school year, when asked to describe the classroom behavior of their students, the "bloomers," from whom intellectual growth was expected, were described positively by their teachers—being happier, more curious, more appealing, and better adjusted. On the other hand, when the students designated as nonbloomers bloomed, and some did, these same teachers described these students negatively—less likable, less likely to succeed in life, less happy.

The results of this study showed the impact of having a Pygmalion in one's life. Pygmalion was the Greek sculptor who loved his ivory stature so much that Aphrodite, the goddess of love, allowed the statue to come to life. In the modern play, *My Fair Lady*,

Professor Henry Higgins, through his expectations, became a Pygmalion for Eliza Doolittle, transforming her from a flower girl to a princess.

STEPS IN THE SELF-FULFILLING PROPHECY

The SFP is a four-step process. The steps are deceptively simple:

Step 1—Person A forms expectations of person B based on a variety of factors—race, gender, ethnicity, body build, given name, etc.

Step 2—Based on these expectations, person A treats person B differently.

Step 3—Person A's treatment of person B tells person B what behavior and achievement person A expects.

Step 4—If person A's treatment is consistent over time, and if person B does not actively resist, it will tend to shape his or her behavior and achievement.

SUMMARY

The three most important words in parenting, teaching, and managing may well be *expectations, expectations, expectations.* Understanding the SFP is crucial to the acting as a positive Pygmalion in the lives of others.

—*Robert T. Tauber*

Further Readings and References

Brophy, J. E., & Good, T. L. (1970). Teacher's communication of differential expectations for children's classroom performance: Some behavioral data. *Journal of Educational Psychology, 61,* 365–374.

Dusek, J. B. (1975). Do teachers bias children learning? *Review of Educational Research, 45*(4), 661–684.

Eden, D. (1990). *Pygmalion in management: Productivity as a self-fulfilling prophecy.* Lexington, MA: Heath.

Jussim, L. (1989). Teacher expectations: Self-fulfilling prophecies, perceptual biases, and accuracy. *Journal of personality and Social Psychology, 57*(3), 469–480.

Merton, R. K. (1948). The self-fulfilling prophecy. *Antioch Review, 8,* 193–210.

Nanna, M. P., Sheras, P. L, & Cooper, J. (1975). Pygmalion and Galetea: The interactive effect of teacher and student experiences. *Journal of Experimental Social Psychology, 11*(3), 279–287.

Rosenthal, R. (1987). Pygmalion effects: Existence, magnitude, and social importance. *Educational Researcher, 16,* 37–41.

Rosenthal, R., & Jacobson, L. (1969). *Pygmalion in the classroom.* New York: Holt, Rinehart & Winston.

Rosenthal, R., & Lawson, R. (1964). A longitudinal study of the effects of experimenter bias on the operant learning of laboratory rats. *Journal of Psychiatric Research, 2,* 61–72.

Tauber, R. T. (1997). *Self-fulfilling prophecy: A practical guide to its use in education.* Westport, CT: Praeger.

SEMANTIC DEVELOPMENT

A word is a verbal symbol, or a sequence of sounds, that signifies a referent, or object. A referent, however, is not the meaning of the word but simply the object the word symbolizes. The accumulation of words that adult speakers have is referred to as their mental lexicon, or mental dictionary.

SEMANTIC DEVELOPMENT

Children produce their first word at approximately 1 year old and slowly add an average of 8 to 11 words a month to their vocabularies until they hit the 50-word mark. At around this time, approximately 18 months of age, children display a word spurt, or a dramatic increase in the rate at which new words are added to their vocabulary. By their second birthday most children are producing an average of 300 different words. Children's early words are most often words for objects, known as nominals, words for actions or states. A large percentage of these words are nouns because nouns typically have more concrete referents.

Children's early semantic development is characterized by improper or irregular use of words. Children often engage in overextension of a newly learned word and apply the word too broadly to an array of objects or events for which is it not appropriate. For example, a child may call all four-legged animals a *cat.* Children also engage in underextension of a newly learned word and apply the word too narrowly to only one specific object or event. For example, a child may call only his own cat a *cat.*

Children's early word production does not indicate their level of word comprehension; however, children's comprehension skills develop ahead of their production skills. Therefore, children are able to understand much more language than they can produce on their own. According to Nagy and Anderson (1984), in later semantic development, older children expand their vocabulary at an average rate of approximately 3,000 new words a year. They are able to understand more complex concepts; can use puns, metaphors, and irony; and come to understand that words can have multiple meanings.

HOW ARE WORDS LEARNED?

In a typical word-learning situation, a mother and child are in the grocery store and the mother says, "I need lettuce, a tomato, and a radish." The child already has lettuce and tomato in his mental lexicon and as such in this situation would understand that *radish* refers to the unknown object the mother is holding. In an example of fast-mapping, the child would then add the word *radish* to his mental lexicon, after only this one exposure to the word.

In this situation, however, *radish* could mean any number of things about the radish such as its color, shape, or leafy green top. With all the possible meanings for *radish,* how did the child come to decide on *radish* as symbolizing the vegetable the mother was holding? Theories have suggested that children use several hypotheses about what a new word might mean called constraints on word learning (Markman, 1991; 1994). The whole-object assumption states that children assume that a word refers to a whole object, and not parts of the object. So, *radish* would refer to the entire radish and not just its color, shape, or leafy green top. The mutual exclusivity assumption states that children assume objects can have one and only one name. Because the child already knew the names for the lettuce and tomato, these objects could not be the radish. The taxonomic assumption states that children assume new words that extend to other members of the same taxonomic category. So, the child may assume that a turnip is also a radish because it has the same leafy green top. In addition to these proposed early constraints on word learning, once children have acquired enough language, they can use the context in which a word appears and grammar to determine a word's meaning.

—*Susan J. Parault*

Further Reading and Reference

Child Development Institute. (n.d.). *Language and speech development in children.* Retrieved from http://www.child developmentinfo.com/development/language_development .shtml

SENSATION SEEKING

Sensation seeking is a personality trait that is characterized by the tendency to seek varied and novel sensations and experiences. These experiences may include participation in risky physical activities (e.g., mountain climbing or dirt bike racing), an attraction to novel political and philosophical ideologies, or experimentation with both licit and illicit drugs. Individuals vary in their level of sensation seeking, with some people displaying high levels of sensation seeking and others showing low levels of this trait. However, most individuals fall somewhere in between.

Marvin Zuckerman is the psychologist credited with developing the theory of sensation seeking. He suggested that sensation seeking is composed of four general tendencies: thrill and adventure seeking (TAS), experience seeking (ES), disinhibition (DIS), and boredom susceptibility (BS). TAS is characterized by a desire to engage in activities that involve speed or danger. Examples of such activities include bungee jumping, downhill skiing, and mountain climbing. Whereas TAS is expressed through physical pursuits, a second dimension of sensation seeking, ES, reflects the need for novel personal or inner experiences. With this type of sensation seeking there is a preference for new and different experiences that might be achieved through travel to exotic destinations, interaction with people from different cultures, or learning about new philosophies. A third component of sensation seeking, DIS, is characterized by the expression of reduced social restraint. Individuals with this behavioral tendency are less constrained by societal norms and mores so they are more experimental with regard to their behavior. They often report having many sexual partners and may also indicate that they engage in illegal drug use or gambling. However, these individuals also tend to be more creative than those lower in sensation seeking. The final dimension of sensation seeking is labeled BS. BS occurs when an individual reports distaste for anything routine or predictable. Instead, individuals high in BS seek out new people to interact with along with new experiences. Perhaps not surprisingly, people high in this type of sensation seeking often have problems maintaining long-term personal relationships, but they do well in professions involving changing environments (e.g., aviation).

The behavioral tendencies associated with the trait of sensation seeking are thought to reflect underlying neurochemical processes. Specifically, higher levels of sensation seeking are associated with lower levels of monoamine oxidase (MAO). MAO is an enzyme that is involved in the regulation of monoamine neurotransmitters, including serotonin, dopamine, and norepinephrine. Collectively, the monoamine neurotransmitters influence arousal and behavioral approach and avoidance tendencies. Research has shown that MAO levels are at their lowest point during adolescence, while the trait of sensation seeking tends to be at its highest. There is also a reliable sex difference in MAO levels, with males displaying lower levels of the enzyme than do females. Research with infants as young as 3 days old has documented this effect. Males also tend to report higher levels of sensation seeking than do females.

Biometric studies of sensation seeking suggest that there is a strong heritability component of this dimension. Estimates suggest that approximately 55% to 60% of the variance within the trait of sensation seeking is due to genetic factors. For example, research examining correlations of sensation seeking scores of identical twins reared apart, compared with identical twins reared together, showed that the association was essentially the same across both groups ($r = .59$). This finding indicates that genetic factors make a greater contribution to one's level of sensation seeking than does one's family environment. Furthermore, while the remaining 40% variance of the trait of sensation seeking is believed to be environmentally influenced, the influence is believed to reside in environmental factors outside of one's family environment. Specifically, it has been suggested that the culture in which one is raised, along with one's peer influences, contribute to the development of sensation seeking.

—*Rhonda Swickert*

Further Readings and References

Marvin Zuckerman home page, http://www.psych.udel.edu/people/detail.php?firstname=Marvin&lastname=Zuckerman

Zuckerman, M. (1994). *Behavioral expressions and biosocial bases of sensation seeking.* New York: Cambridge University Press.

Zuckerman, M. (2000). Are you a risk-taker? *Psychology Today*, Nov/Dec, 54–87.

Zuckerman, M., & Kuhlman, D. M. (2000). Personality and risk-taking: Common biosocial factors. *Journal of Personality, 68*, 999–1029.

Zuckerman, M., & Kuhlman, D. M. (n.d.). *Sensation seeking scale: Roads and traffic authority.* Retrieved from http://www.rta.nsw.gov.au/licensing/tests/driverqualificationtest/sensationseekingscale/

SENSITIVE PERIOD

The concept of a sensitive period refers to a period of time in development during which certain internal or external events have effects that the same events do not have at earlier or later developmental stages. Certain events may determine long-lasting important characteristics of individuals if they occur within a particular developmental period, even if they have no obvious immediate relevance. Furthermore, these effects might not be susceptible to change in later developmental stages, or, in other words, they may tend to be permanent. An understanding of the time periods during which the individual is particularly sensitive to certain life events is important to understand aspects of typical and atypical behavioral development, and to improve child care and intervention programs.

Some developmental theorists have argued that there are psychological processes that may occur only within precise temporal windows of opportunity, called critical periods. The hypothesis of critical periods was borrowed from embryological studies indicating that, within a critical period, organ tissues tend to differentiate according to adjacent cells. Once the critical period ends, organ tissues lose their plasticity and become unalterably differentiated. However, research has demonstrated that the limits of the time periods affecting psychobiological developmental phenomena are not as rigidly fixed as originally thought. The term *critical period* was therefore replaced by that of *sensitive period*. The term *sensitive period* is similar to that of *critical period*, but it refers to a time window with limits that are graded, rather than abrupt, relatively malleable, and probably depend on the characteristics of particular individuals and their experience.

The notion of sensitive periods is applicable to early childhood experience as well as to prenatal development. It refers to a period of time when a child is especially receptive to certain kinds of environmental events. Furthermore, certain experiences have to occur within the frame of sensitive periods in order for the child's development to proceed normally. If the right experiences do not happen during a prescribed sensitive period, critical aspects of development might be enduringly affected. For example, if early social deprivation occurs at the time of the initial attachment of the child to the mother (or to other caretakers), then attachment is not allowed to form. This might occur in infants who live in institutions, under conditions of abandonment, abuse, or neglect. These infants might show impaired social development as early as 5 months of age. Early social deprivation may also have long-lasting detrimental effects in social and emotional situations, as indicated by heightened aggression, delinquency, and indifference to others, and in cognitive functions, as indicated by impoverished language skills and abstract thinking. However, under appropriate conditions, some of these effects might be found to be at least partially reversed in some adult individuals.

Another clear example of sensitive periods comes from the acquisition of language. Peak proficiency in phonological and syntactic aspects of language can be found among those individuals who were first exposed to the target language during early childhood. As age of exposure increases, average proficiency in language declines, beginning at the ages of 4 to 6 years and continuing until proficiency reaches its plateau for adult learners. Adult learners may also have problems in acquiring the phonetic properties that are relevant for being judged as a native speaker. Furthermore, evidence of a sensitive period in language acquisition comes from second language learners whose age of exposure begins after 7 years. Regions of brain activation do not overlap with those that are active during performance of the native language. Second language learners also display less lateralization and high individual variability.

—*Santiago Pellegrini*

See also Critical Period

Further Readings and References

Bailey, D. B., Bruers, J. T., Symons, F. J., & Lichtman, J. W. (Eds.). (2001). *Critical thinking about critical periods.* Baltimore: Paul H. Brookes.

Glaser, D. (2000). Child abuse and neglect and the brain—A review. *Journal of Child Psychology and Psychiatry and Allied Disciplines, 41,* 97–116.

Jayeon, L. (2003). *A new look at the critical period hypothesis.* Retrieved from http://www.alak.or.kr/2_public/2003_oct/document/200310_feature_article.pdf

Kate, E. (1998). *Critical period in brain development discovered.* Retrieved from http://www.primate.wisc.edu/pin/rh/rhoct19.txt

Papini, M. R. (2002). *Comparative psychology: Evolution and development of behavior.* Upper Saddle River, NJ: Prentice-Hall.

Skuse, D. H., Pickles, A., Wolke, D., & Reilly, S. (1994). Postnatal growth and mental development: Evidence for a "sensitive period." *Journal of Child Psychology and Psychiatry and Allied Disciplines, 35,* 521–545.

Varin, D., Crugnola, C. R., Molina, P., & Ripamonti, C. (1996). Sensitive periods in the development of attachment and the age of entry into day care. *European Journal of Psychology of Education, 11,* 215–229.

SENSORY DEVELOPMENT

The processes by which an organism experiences and interacts with its world begin with sensation. A stimulus event in the world affects the body by producing changes at the sensory receptors. Psychologists often distinguish between the distal world and the proximal information that activates our sensory systems. For example, while watching a purple rubber ball bouncing (distal event), light energy enters the eye (proximal) and stimulates the photoreceptors, providing color, shape, size, movement, and other information, and sound energy enters the ear (proximal) and stimulates the hair cells, providing sounds that correspond to the ball hitting the ground. The traditional five sensory modalities are touch, taste, smell, hearing, and vision. Other sensory processes include awareness of joint and muscle position, balance, and so forth.

BACKGROUND AND KEY CONCEPTS

The study of sensation focuses on the function of the receptors and sensory systems and emphasizes physiology. A related field of study, perception, focuses on how sensory information is used to understand and interpret the world and emphasizes both physiology and psychology. The field of psychophysics relates changes in physical characteristics of a stimulus, such as intensity, to changes in the perceptual experience of a stimulus, such as brightness in vision or loudness in hearing. One key concept is that of the absolute threshold, which refers to the intensity of a stimulus when it becomes detectable to an observer.

Studying the development of human sensory and perceptual abilities is guided by various theoretical approaches. Some of these include the nativist approach, which emphasizes organization and constraints that are present early in life to guide development; the empiricist approach, which emphasizes the acquisition of knowledge through experience; and the ecological approach of Eleanor and James Gibson, which emphasizes the information provided by a person's dynamic interactions in the real world.

In order to study changes over time in sensory abilities, the key concept of a sensitive period must be considered. A sensitive period typically refers to a time during which certain events or inputs are beneficial for optimal development. In studies of binocular vision in cats, the first 6 months is a sensitive period because interruption of input to one eye during that time diminishes binocular abilities. Clinical studies suggest there is a similar sensitive period for human binocular vision during the first few years of life. More generally, animal studies have indicated that enriched early experiences facilitate neural development.

SENSORY DEVELOPMENT OVER THE LIFE SPAN

In considering the development of sensory abilities, many studies focus on the emergence and elaboration of sensory abilities during infancy and on changes in sensory abilities due to aging.

Early Sensory Development

Despite William James's claim that infants might initially find their new sensory worlds confusing, research studies reveal infants' organized sensory and perceptual abilities. Immediately after birth, a newborn is sensitive to touch and temperature, and also highly sensitive to pain, responding with crying and cardiovascular responses. Studies of taste and smell show that babies respond with different facial expressions, suggesting that certain preferences are innate. They tend to prefer sweeter tasting liquids to salty or bitter liquids, and they can discriminate their mother's scent from others'. Regarding hearing, infants respond to sounds even before birth and appear to be especially sensitive to the frequencies of sounds in human speech and to prefer the exaggerated contours of infant-directed speech. Infants are innately ready to respond to sounds of any language, and become more

selectively attuned to their native language later in development. Regarding vision, young infants' visual acuity is about 20/400, which means that an infant can see something at 20 feet that an adult with normal vision could see at 400 feet. Thus, the world probably looks blurry to young infants. They look longer at checkerboards with fewer large squares than with many small squares because of their poor visual acuity. Infants' thresholds for seeing a visual pattern are higher than adults'. Thus, toys for infants are sometimes manufactured with black and white patterns rather than pastel colors because the higher contrast between black and white makes the pattern more visible to the immature visual system. Color vision improves over the first few months of life. By about 6 months, infants' visual acuity improves and approximates adult 20/20 acuity. Sensitivity to binocular depth cues, which require inputs from both eyes, is evident by about 3 months and continues to develop during the first 6 months. Even young infants show preferences for faces and facelike patterns.

Intermodal perception refers to a combination of stimulation from more than one sensory modality. Babies seem to be born with the ability to perceive the world in an intermodal way. For example, infants who sucked on a pacifier with either a smooth or textured surface preferred to look at a corresponding (smooth or textured) visual model of the pacifier. By 4 months, infants can match lip movements with speech sounds and can match other audiovisual events.

Although sensory development emphasizes the afferent processes used to take in information from the environment, these sensory processes can be affected by the infant's developing motor abilities. Reaching, crawling, and other actions allow the infant to see, touch, and organize their his or her experiences in new ways.

Atypical Sensory Development

During childhood, the most common vision problem is myopia, or nearsightedness, which can be corrected with glasses. Regarding more severe visual disorders, legal blindness is defined by acuity less than or equal to 20/200 in a person's better eye. Blindness can occur for various reasons, including damage to the retina of the eye or the optic nerve, or diseases such as glaucoma or cataracts. Congenital blindness refers to blindness that is present at birth. In some cases, newborn blindness results from environmental causes such as rubella or vitamin A deficiency.

Other congenital cases are due to retinopathy of prematurity, retinal diseases, and neural lesions.

Hearing impairments can occur because of congenital problems (abnormal development) and damage to the conduction system of the middle ear. Repeated infections of the middle ear can lead to interference due to accumulation of tissue or to membrane rupture. Hearing impairment and deafness can also occur due to congenital problems and damage to the sensorineural system of the inner ear.

Hearing loss of various severities occurs in about 3 of 1,000 infants at birth, and it is estimated that about half of these cases have genetic causes.

Hearing aids are useful for some children with hearing loss, and a typical communication system for the deaf is American Sign Language. For some people with severe hearing impairment, a cochlear implant can be used to provide auditory input. This electronic device has an external microphone to receive sounds from the environment, an external speech processor that conditions the sounds, and an implanted set of electrodes that transmit electrical impulses to the cochlea to stimulate auditory nerve fibers. In keeping with the idea of a sensitive period for language development, the success of cochlear implants for a person's speech processing and production is often related to the age of the person at the time of the surgery.

Sensory Changes During Adulthood

There are age-related changes in all sensory systems during middle to late adulthood. Touch sensitivity and the ability to sense temperature and vibration tend to decline in older adults. This could be secondary to changes in the skin or circulation.

In vision, the ability to focus on close objects declines from about age 30 on as the lens of the eye changes with age. By about age 40, difficulty with reading small print is common and can often be improved with corrective lenses. Visual acuity and, in particular, night vision can also begin to decline in the middle adulthood years due to physical changes in the eye. The risk for glaucoma, a disease in which increased pressure in the eye affects the optic nerve, increases in middle and late adulthood. Around age 50 to 60, presbyopia ("old eyes") occurs when the lens can no longer adjust well to focus at various distances. In late adulthood, cataracts can develop. These cloudy areas of the lens of the eye can interfere with acuity and, if untreated, can cause blindness. Age-related physical changes in the eye can cause problems in dark adaptation as one moves from a bright to a dark room. Visual acuity tends to decrease with aging, particularly after age 70. Macular degeneration, a leading cause of adult blindness, is due to age-related damage to the retina.

In hearing, sensitivity to sound begins to decrease with aging. About one in six adults in their middle adulthood years in the United States has some hearing loss. The hair cells of the inner ear show age-related changes due to cell death or other factors. Environmental exposure to noise can contribute to hearing loss over time. By about age 50, hearing loss may begin to be evident for high-frequency sounds. By about age 60, the frequencies in the human speech range may be affected and distinguishing a sound, such as speech in a conversation, from background noise may become more difficult. These aging effects on hearing may be more prevalent in men than in women. In late adulthood, hearing shows greater declines, due to hair cell loss as well as to decreased blood supply, membrane stiffening, and neural effects. For some older adults, hearing aids may help to ameliorate some of these declines in hearing.

Changes in the sensory perception of taste and smell occur in late adulthood. This may be due to a decrease in smell receptors, which would affect both smell and taste. There are conflicting descriptions of whether normal aging directly affects these chemical senses, or whether exposure to things such as medicines, pollution, and smoking contribute to the decline. Together, the decline of sensitivity to taste and smell can contribute to a decrease in the enjoyment of food for the elderly.

—*Marie T. Balaban and Casi D. Reisenauer*

See also Piaget, Jean; Smell

Further Readings and References

Belsky, J. K. (1998). *The psychology of aging: Theory, research, and interventions.* Pacific Grove, CA: Wadsworth.

Bower, B. (2001). Faces of perception. *Science News, 160*(1), 10. Retrieved from http://www.sciencenews.org/articles/20010707/bob16.asp

Gilbert, C., & Foster, A. (2001). Childhood blindness in the context of VISION 2020: The right to sight. *Bulletin of the World Health Organization* [online], *79,* 227–232.

Retrieved from http://www.scielosp.org/scielo.php?pid=S0042-96862001000300011&script=sci_arttext&tlng=en

Gopnik, A., Meltsoff, A. N., & Kuhl, P. K. (2000). *The scientist in the crib: What early learning tells us about the mind.* New York: Perennial.

Hain, T. C. (2001). *Congenital deafness.* Retrieved from http://www.american-hearing.org/name/cong_hearing.html

Pick, A. D., & Gibson, E. J. (2000). *An ecological approach to perceptual learning and development.* New York: Oxford.

Soderquist, D. R. (2002). *Sensory processes.* Newbury Park, CA: Sage.

Stern, J.-M. (2004). *The cochlear implant—rejection of culture, or aid to improve hearing?* Retrieved from http://www.deaftoday.com/news/archives/003876.html

SEPARATION ANXIETY

Separation anxiety—the emotional distress displayed by infants and young children due to separation from their attachment figure—is one of the most important and salient developmental events in childhood. Separation anxiety begins to emerge in infants around 8 months of age, peaks for most infants around 13 to 15 months of age, and then begins to wane thereafter. Interestingly, even blind infants show evidence of separation anxiety, indicating that they are capable of perceiving the sudden absence of their mother.

The origins of separation anxiety are thought to derive from the adaptive evolutionary value that such a response confers to the infant by keeping the caregiver in close proximity. Cross-cultural data support the evolutionary origins of separation anxiety, indicating that the onset and developmental progression of separation anxiety are similar in every culture tested to date, including China, Japan, Guatemala, and Israel.

Individual differences in the incidence and severity of separation anxiety exist among infants, with some infants demonstrating high levels of separation anxiety and others displaying little or no evidence of it. Researchers have found in a U.S. sample, for example, that only 42% of 11-month-olds and only 79% of 13-month-olds fretted and cried at the departure of their mothers. Thus, even at the peak of separation anxiety—13 to 15 months of age—one of approximately every five infants exhibits little sign of separation anxiety. Research indicates that differences between infants showing varying degrees of separation anxiety are attributable to infant temperament, the cultures in which infants are raised, and the caregiving practices to which they are exposed.

Developmentalists have uncovered several contextual factors influencing the incidence of separation anxiety among infants. For example, infants tend to display less separation anxiety (a) when they are left in the presence of another familiar caregiver such as a parent, a babysitter, or a grandparent, (b) when they crawl or walk away from the caregiver rather than the caregiver departing them, (c) when they are left with a sibling or stranger compared to being left alone, (d) when they are left with toys, (e) when they are left behind with their pacifiers, and (f) when they can hear and see their caregivers in an adjacent room. These findings make it clear that the presence and intensity of separation anxiety depends on the relations between the infant, the caregiver, and the broader social context.

Given the fact that the children's responses to separation are not due solely to themselves as discussed above, what can caregivers do to reduce the frequency and intensity of separation anxiety? Although verbal gestures such as "bye-bye" are ineffective for 1-year-olds, these types of gestures do appease older children. In addition, caregivers can arrange the child's environment to maximize the likelihood that the child will not be distressed upon separation. For example, caregivers may place toys in the environment, leave the infant with a pacifier, or have a familiar substitute caregiver present during the departure. Finally, the caregiver of a child older than about 2 years should avoid physical contact with the child just before departure and explain what the child could do when the parent is absent (e.g., play with toys or watch a cartoon).

Although separation anxiety diminishes for most children and adolescents, approximately 4% to 5% of infants develop separation anxiety disorder (SAD). This disorder is distinguished by abnormal emotional reactivity to real or imagined separation from attachment figures that disrupts activities of daily living. Epidemiological studies indicate that the majority of children and adolescents with SAD are raised by families with low socioeconomic status and many children with SAD refuse to go to school. Pharmacological, behavioral, and psychotherapeutic treatments for SAD have been shown to be effective.

—*Matthew J. Hertenstein and Margaret A. McCullough*

See also Attachment

Further Readings and References

Bowlby, J. (1980). *Attachment and loss* (Vol. 3). New York: Basic Books.

Children's Hospital Medical Center of Akron. (n.d.). *Separation anxiety.* Retrieved from http://www.akronchildrens.org/tips/pdfs/BP1108.pdf

Durso, B. (2001). *How do I get my child to let me leave him?* Retrieved from http://www.keepkidshealthy.com/development/separation_anxiety.html

Field, T., Gewirtz, J. L., Cohen, D., Garcia, R., Greenberg, R., & Collins, K. (1984). Leave-takings and reunions of infants, toddlers, preschoolers, and their parents. *Child Development, 55,* 628–635.

Weinraub, M., & Lewis, M. (1977). The determinants of children's responses to separation. *Monographs of the Society for Research in Child Development, 42*(Serial No. 172), 1–127.

SEX DIFFERENCES

Are boys and girls really different? Are little boys really, as Mother Goose says, made of snips and snails and puppy dog tails? And are little girls made of sugar and spice and everything nice? If the amount written about the topic is any indication, then this question is of prime interest. A search of the PsycInfo database found 44,621 journal citations in English with the key words *sex difference* from 1840 to April 2004.

Psychologists and others who study this topic divide differences into three types: sex, gender, and sex related. Sex refers to classifications based on genetic makeup, anatomy, and reproductive functions and are biological differences. As we shall see, there are very few "pure" sex differences. The second type, gender, refers to the expectations associated with being female or male in social and cultural settings. These are socially determined. The third type, sex-related differences, implies that the behavior corresponds to sex but it does not say anything about the cause or the etiology of the difference. The majority of the differences between boys and girls and between women and men fall within this definition.

PHYSICAL AND HEALTH DIFFERENCES

Physical Characteristics

Some physical differences clearly are sex differences, whereas others are sex related. Males are heavier and longer at birth and have a greater lung capacity and higher caloric intake. They are more vulnerable to physical handicaps. Females are developmentally older at birth, both in skeletal maturation and central nervous system maturation. They mature faster than males, and they live longer. The life expectancy for a white female born in 2001 is 80.2 years, whereas it is only 75 years for a white male. For a black female born in 2001, life expectancy is 75.5 years and 68.6 for a black male.

Large differences in motor skills do not appear until adolescence, when hormonal differences lead to large height and musculature changes in males. Physical performance of motor skills increases with age; however, there is no difference in the curve of boys and girls until about 5 years of age. Then the curve for girls is lower, but the increases are parallel until adolescence. At adolescence boys show a sharp increase, whereas girls level off or decline.

Puberty begins and ends for girls, on the average, 2 years before boys. There is a great deal of variation within each sex in both the age at which puberty begins and the length of time it takes for changes to be completed. Although primarily a biological function, menarche, or first menstruation, occurs earlier in girls who are well nourished, who live in warmer climates, or who have had sexual intercourse.

In terms of external changes, girls may experience their growth spurt at 9 years whereas boys typically begin their growth spurt after age 11. Most girls are at adult height by 14 to 16 years, but most boys do not stop growing until their late teens.

Men, on the average, are taller and stronger than women. Women, on the other hand, have a higher proportion of body fat than do men.

Brain Size

Even after correcting for body size, men's brains are larger than women's brains. The difference is about 200 cubic centimeters or two and a half golf balls. Most of the difference is in white matter, which is primarily nerve fibers and blood vessels. Women's brains contain a larger proportion of gray matter than do men's brains. Research using magnetic resonance imaging technology indicates that men's corpus callosums, the large band of white matter that connects the two hemispheres, is about 10% larger than women's. Again, the excess is primarily white matter. The difference in volume is spread across all the lobes of the brain such that no one area is larger for one sex. Older women lose less brain volume in old age and do not begin to lose brain volume until an older age than men.

Physical Health

In Western societies, heart disease is the leading cause of death for both women and men. Each year 50,000 more women than men die from cardiovascular disease. However, the onset and progression of cardiovascular diseases occurs earlier in men than in women so that the men who die each year are younger, on average, than are the women. Symptoms of impending heart malfunction are different in men and women. The most common symptom of heart attack for men is chest pain. Although women often experience chest pain, it does not always occur. They may experience indigestion, abdominal or midback pain, nausea, and vomiting in addition to or instead of chest pain. Although 81% of heart transplant patients are men, there are no gender differences in the need for or suitability of heart transplants or in survival rates.

Women who smoke are 70% more likely to develop lung cancer than men who smoke. Most autoimmune diseases affect women more than men, with rheumatoid arthritis, multiple sclerosis, and lupus 75% more likely to occur in women than in men. Although the incidence of type I diabetes does not show sex-related differences, type II diabetes occurs more frequently in women than in men.

There are major sex differences in drug reactions and side effects. Ibuprofen is more effective for pain relief for men than for women, whereas kappa opiate pain medications are more effective for women than for men. Women typically take 7 minutes to wake from anesthesia, whereas men take an average of 11 minutes. Even when they are size matched, women require less alcohol to attain the same blood alcohol levels as men.

Mental Health

Not only do men and women differ in the kinds of physical health problems they experience, but there are differences in the mental health problems they face. Women are more likely to experience anxiety, depression, and neurosis, a relatively benign mental disorder, whereas men are more likely to experience loneliness and psychosis, a severe mental disorder.

In developed countries women are two to three times more likely to have a depressive episode in their lifetime, although recent data from a large national study indicate that the ratio is now 1.74 to 1, suggesting that men's rates are rising. The probability for experiencing an episode in their lifetime is 1 of every 4 women and 1 of every 10 men. Rates in undeveloped countries are equal for women and men and sometimes higher for men than women. This suggests that the underlying causes may be related to psychosocial factors. The preceding data aggregate all forms of depression. However, rates for bipolar disorder, which is a genetically linked disorder, differ from rates for major depression, which stem either from social factors or from an interaction of social and biological factors. The ratio for major depression is somewhere between three to four women for every man. There is no difference in the ratio of women to men for bipolar disorder.

A far too common outcome of depression is suicide. Here the sex-related difference does not reflect that of depression. Suicide is twice as likely among men as among women.

An interesting incidence of sex-related difference occurs in the mental health diagnosis of multiple personality disorder (MPD). North American women are at least three times more likely than men to receive an MPD diagnosis. In Switzerland one study found that 51% of the MPD diagnoses were given to men.

Summary

Sex differences in size and viability appear at birth. Physical differences occurring later in life are more likely a result of an interaction between biological and social factors. There is strong support for the role of social factors in major depressive disorders, although biological factors have an important role in the disorder. As evidenced by the cross-cultural work on MPD and on depressive disorders, psychological diagnoses do seem to be culturally determined.

SOCIAL DIFFERENCES
Traits

Of particular interest is whether women and men differ on personality traits. Men are higher on instrumental traits (e.g., assertiveness, independence, ambition, and the need to dominate), whereas women are higher on expressive traits (e.g., sensitivity to the needs of others, altruism, warmth, and cooperativeness).

Empathy

Although girls and women are believed to be more empathic, research indicates that this depends on how you measure empathy. If you ask people how they feel in certain situations (e.g., "Does seeing someone cry upset you?"), women report more feelings of empathy. However, when physiological reactions are measured or behaviors are observed unobtrusively, no sex-related differences are found.

Helping Behavior

Prosocial behavior, or behavior that is intended to benefit someone else, is a part of the feminine stereotype of nurturance and support. However, research generally finds few differences in helping behavior in young children. When found, the differences typically favor girls who help others more than do boys. Surprisingly the opposite is true for adults. Research indicates that men are more likely to come to the aid of others than are women. This may be a function of how helping behaviors are studied. When individuals are given the opportunity to help a stranger, men are more likely to come to their aid, particularly if the situation is dangerous. When asked about whether they provide psychological assistance and help to friends and family members, women report more helping behaviors. Sex-related differences appear to be greater for kindness/consideration (favoring females) than for instrumental (favoring males) forms of prosocial behavior.

Influence and Persuasion

Women are perceived as more easily influenced and more conforming than men. Social psychologists Alice Eagly and Linda Carli examined the literature and concluded that although there were differences in persuasiveness and conformity, these differences were small. In addition, women were influenced more when the topics were masculine (e.g., sports) and when the researchers were male.

Activity Level

Studies support the stereotype that males are more active than females. However, the difference is small among infants, medium among preschoolers, and large among older children. In addition, the difference is larger in the presence of peers. Boys in groups are much more active than individual boys.

Aggression

Among the most actively debated issues is sex differences in aggressive behavior. The debate focuses on whether differences exist and, if they do, their origin.

Few gender differences in aggression are found in the infancy and toddler years. However, by about age 4 when children begin interacting with others, boys are more physically aggressive than girls. This difference increases over time so that when they begin school there are stable sex differences in the frequency of behavior problems that persist into adulthood. Although there are sex-related differences in frequency of aggressive behaviors, the patterning of these behaviors is similar between the sexes. For both males and females the highest rates of violent crimes occur between the ages of 14 and 24. Men are more likely to commit more serious acts of aggression than are women. The difference seems to be less in quantity of aggression than in type. Relational aggression, where others are harmed through nonphysical hurtful manipulation of peer relationships, occurs more often with girls than with boys.

Psychologists Alice Eagly and Valerie Steffen reviewed studies of adult aggression. They found a small sex-related difference favoring men. The differences were larger in laboratory studies than in field studies that mimic real-life situations. The differences also were larger when physical measures of aggression were used than when psychological measures were used. Men were more aggressive to men than to women. This difference, too, was larger in the laboratory and for physical measures of aggression.

Research on sex-related differences in aggression has focused on differences between the average of the groups. British psychologists John Archer and Karin Westerman asked whether these differences occurred because all boys were more aggressive than all girls or because a few boys were much more aggressive than the average boy or girl. Their study suggests that, at least for 11-year-olds, the differences result from a few individual boys behaving particularly aggressively.

The debate on the origin of aggressive behaviors focuses on biological or social factors. Supporting the biological interpretation is evidence that chimpanzees and boys with higher levels of the masculinizing hormone testosterone tend to be more aggressive.

However, levels of testosterone follow aggressive behavior as well as precede it, clouding this explanation. Evidence reviewed above indicates that levels of aggression do not differ until children begin to interact, suggesting a social explanation. In addition, there is a suggestion that the higher levels of aggression in boys may be due to a few very aggressive boys.

Sexuality

A national probability study asked more than 3,000 adults 18 to 59 years of age about their sexual behaviors. Men reported more frequent masturbation during the past year, and over three times as many men as women reported masturbating in the previous week. More women than men said they had never masturbated to orgasm. Over half of the men reported having more than five sexual partners since age 18, whereas less than a third of the women reported more than five. Other studies report a large sex-related difference favoring men's positive attitudes toward premarital sex, particularly casual sex. Men also are more likely to be accepting of premarital sex and are more likely to have had sex than are women. Although men's attitudes to gay men are more negative than are women's, there is no difference in women's and men's attitudes to lesbians.

Summary

Social differences are primarily sex-related differences. However, it is not clear which differences are primarily socially determined and which are an outcome of social and biological interactions. Differences do occur in traits that are viewed primarily as masculine and feminine, but cross-sex behaviors are common. Evidence on the two closely related areas of empathy and prosocial behavior is not clear, although it appears that situational factors are strong determinants of behaviors in these areas. Again, situational factors appear to be at work in the differences found between women and men in ease of persuasion in that women are more susceptible to persuasion when the topic or the persuader is male.

The last three areas, activity level, aggressive behaviors, and sexuality, are areas where sex differences generally are argued to occur. However, even here the role of biological factors is not unequivocal. Differences in activity level are small early in life but increase in size as children grow older, indicating

some influence of social factors. They also are situationally determined, with boys more active in groups than alone. The potential causal factors for aggressive behaviors were reviewed in the topic area and suggest that the evidence does not support either purely biological or social factors. Research on sexual behavior indicates some consistent differences as well as increasing similarities over time.

COGNITIVE DIFFERENCES

Intelligence

Certainly the question of who is the most intelligent has consumed the attention of scientists and laypersons alike. When asked to estimate their scores on intelligence tests, men estimate their scores as higher than do women. On the other hand, girls have higher grade point averages than do boys.

Evaluating sex-related differences in intelligence using standardized intelligence tests is not possible. The tests are developed so that the test questions either sample from areas where there are no sex-related differences or sample equally from presumed female- and male-advantaged areas. Some have argued that the *g* factor, the general ability that is proposed to underlie all aspects of intelligence, can be measured by scores on a variety of tests designed to measure fluid intelligence. Fluid intelligence is considered to be biologically determined. It is the ability to reason and is unrelated to experience. When both adolescents and college applicants were tested on measures of fluid intelligence, no sex-related differences were found.

Sex-related differences are observed more often in the extremes of ability distributions. Males, on average, score higher on the Scholastic Assessment Test (SAT) and the Graduate Record Examination (GRE) than do females. Although these standardized tests are designed to predict grades in college (SAT) or graduate school (GRE), females, on average, get higher grades than do males. Males who earn an A in mathematics class score higher on the mathematics portion of the SAT than do females earning an A in mathematics.

Spatial Ability

Spatial ability is not a single construct. Three distinct spatial skills are studied, and the size of the difference between men and women depends on the type of spatial skills. Men are better on tests of spatial perception that require one to orient an object in space in relation to his or her body. The difference is of medium size.

Men also are better than women on tests of mental rotation where one must mentally rotate a three-dimensional object depicted in two dimensions in order to match it to a target figure. Women and men are equally accurate at matching the target object, but men perform the task much faster. This difference is large and has been stable in Western societies over a 20-year period. It is found in Asian and African populations as well. However, the male advantage is limited to two-dimensional drawings and disappears with real three-dimensional stimuli. Sex-related differences also are not evident when the participants are not told that it is a spatial task, but are only given directions on what to do.

Women outperform men on tests of embedded figures where one must locate the simple figure inside a complex scene. This is very similar to "can you find the object" games in magazines. The difference between women and men is small, but it is consistent.

Indian psychologist Santha Kumari Kunjayi compared Indian adolescent and middle-aged groups on spatial rotation. Sex-related differences favoring boys were found between adolescent boys and girls. No differences were found between middle-aged women and men, nor were differences found between adolescent boys and middle-aged men. However, middle-aged women outperformed adolescent girls, suggesting that, at least for females, spatial abilities have a learned component.

Although the finding of a sex-related difference favoring males in mental rotation is robust, it is not clear how this applies in the real world. Spatial skills are assumed to account for male's better geographical knowledge and way finding, or the ability to find one's way in a novel environment. In one study, way finding was related to men's scores on a mental rotation task such that those with faster mental rotation scores also completed an orienteering task faster than those with slower mental rotation scores. However, women often performed as well as men on the orienteering task despite having lower mental rotation scores than the men.

Mathematics

Although the common perception is that men are much better in mathematics than are women, a U.S.

Department of Education study found that women and girls make higher grades in college mathematics classes. This occurs both in the general college population and in students who have taken more than 10 college credits in mathematics. Other studies have found small differences in specific math skills, with these differences typically favoring men. The exception is that women outperform men in math calculation. Studies after 1974 find smaller sex-related differences than do studies prior to 1974. Recent reviews have found no sex-related differences in mathematical areas such as fractions, ratio/proportion/percent, algebra, geometry, and measurement.

Girls outperform boys on most tests of arithmetic computation. However, on timed tests, boys score better than girls. There is some evidence indicating that girls learn the correct but slower way to calculate, whereas boys more often resort to estimation, a faster approach. On the mathematics portion of the SAT, girls more often than boys correctly answered problems that involved applying formulas. Problems involving logic or estimation were more often solved correctly by boys.

Using a national probability sample, a Canadian study of secondary schoolchildren found no difference in girls and boys' basic skills and knowledge or in their routine or complex problem-solving abilities in grade 7. Although there is a fan-shaped distribution across students' growth in mathematical skills from grade 7 to grade 11 such that the better students improved at a greater rate than the less skilled students, this did not differ by gender. At grade 11 there was no sex-related difference in these skills.

There is one strong sex-related difference that favors boys. Highly mathematically talented junior high students are predominantly male. The most frequent explanation for this is related to intrasex variability. There is some evidence that the range of mathematic ability varies much more between boys than between girls. If this is the case, then it is proposed that even with the small and decreasing difference in average ability between the sexes, the number of males in the upper end of the distribution, or the most talented, may be as many as 12 to every 1 female.

The relationship of mathematics and spatial skills, particularly mental rotation, has been the subject of much speculation and some research. Many psychometricians, the scientists who study mental processes, have long believed that a single mode of thought underlies both mathematical and spatial reasoning, perhaps causing those who possess this mode to reason differently and more effectively. In a meta-analytic review of the literature, Lynn Friedman, an education psychologist at the University of Minnesota, examined this question. She found that the correlations between mathematical and verbal skills were higher than those between mathematical and spatial skills. Math-space correlations were no higher, and were sometimes lower, than other skills (e.g., social studies and sports information). In addition, math-space correlations were higher in females than in males. Training in spatial skills eliminates sex differences; however, training in spatial skills does not improve mathematical achievement.

Verbal

Differences in verbal ability are observed very early in children. Girls talk about 1 month earlier, develop larger vocabularies, produce longer utterances, and use better grammar than boys. Between the ages of 1 and 5, girls are more proficient in language skills than are boys. By the age of 16 months there is a 13-word difference in vocabulary size favoring girls. This grows to 51 words at 20 months and 115 words at 24 months. This does not appear to be related to a differential rate of mothers speaking to their girls, because they speak as much to their boy babies as to their girl babies.

A small sex-related difference favoring girls and women is found in vocabulary and reading comprehension. Speech production shows a moderately sized sex-related difference that favors girls and women. As with mathematics, the size of the difference is larger in studies conducted prior to 1974 than it is in those conducted after 1974.

An area in which a large sex-related difference exists is writing proficiency. This difference favors girls and women who outperform boys and men at all ages and at all times of assessment. On the other hand, boys outperform girls on verbal analogies.

Memory

On a battery of tests examining different aspects of memory, women were substantially better than men, scoring more than one half of a standard deviation above the men. A similar result occurs on tests of visual memory.

Females score higher on tests of short-term, working, and long-term memory than do males. This difference has been found both in adolescents and in older adults. In addition, females appear to have better memories for spatial locations. Females also have better episodic memory, or memory for events, than do males.

Perceptual Ability

Very early in life some perceptual differences are evident. Girls are able at an earlier age to recognize a new from a previously viewed object and will gaze at a preferred object earlier than will boys. As adults these differences continue. Women see better in the dark than do men, whereas men's vision is better than women's in bright light. There is some evidence that men have mild tunnel vision resulting in greater concentration on depth. Women, on the other hand, have wider peripheral vision. More men than women are color blind.

Infant girls appear to be more sensitive to sound than are infant boys, becoming more irritated and anxious about noise. Girls and women hear better than men, are more sensitive to sound, and are more likely to sing in tune. Auditory acuity varies with the stages of the menstrual cycle.

Women have more touch receptors in their fingertips than do men. As a result they are more sensitive to touch than are men. Even a few hours after birth girls are more sensitive to touch than are boys.

Women have a lower threshold for odor recognition, particularly musk and amyl acetate. They are 1,000 times more sensitive to musk-like odors than are men.

At least early in life, women have a lower threshold for tastes, particularly bitter flavors, than do men. However, one investigator found that the regeneration of taste buds slows down more for women than for men. In older adults, taste thresholds were lower for men for most tastes, particularly sweet tastes.

There is a moderate difference in pain perception with women tending to have lower thresholds than men. Evidence suggests that estrogen, a female sex hormone, and testosterone, a male sex hormone, may be involved. In research with mice, males injected with estrogen appear to have a lower tolerance for pain. The presence of testosterone appears to elevate tolerance for pain in female mice. As usual, however, this is not as straightforward as it appears. When pain perception is examined in more detail, the differences occur only at high levels of neural stimulation.

Culture accounts in part for differences in how men and women receive pain signals. Young boys are taught not to cry, whereas young girls often are held and cuddled when they are in pain. A study of pain tolerance in children 7 to 14 years of age found that younger boys had the lowest levels of tolerance and older boys the highest levels. Tolerance levels were moderate for girls of all ages, suggesting that, at least for boys, tolerance for pain is learned.

Summary

Although humans have worked hard at determining who is most intelligent—men or women—the use of intelligence tests cannot determine this. If intelligence is some underlying factor guiding the ability to reason, then it is fairly clear that no differences occur between the sexes. However, differences occur in some, but not all, of the areas related to intelligence.

Spatial rotation is used as an explanation for men's superior way finding abilities and their mathematics skills. Although there does appear to be some relation of the ability to mentally rotate objects in space to way finding, the evidence is not overwhelming. The male advantage in mathematics is not as well established as that of spatial rotation. With the exception of highly talented mathematics students and scores on timed tests, the male advantage has lessened or disappeared as girls have been encouraged to take more mathematics classes. Finally, math skills are more strongly related to verbal skills than to spatial skills.

Women have a small but consistent advantage in verbal skills, although in most areas, such as vocabulary and speech production, the size of the difference has decreased in recent years. The female advantage in writing, however, is robust. Where differences occur in memory, the advantage is to women. This difference is found across the life span.

It is likely that many of the differences in perceptual abilities are sex differences. Differences in discrimination, preference, and sensitivity to sounds and to touch are evident from birth. Others vary with the menstrual cycle. Other perceptual differences are more likely gender-or sex-related differences. For example, in orthodox Jewish communities, myopia occurs more frequently in boys, but it is most frequent in those boys who spend as much as 16 hours a day reading. Differences that indicate women have lower physiological threshold for pain than do men may be sex differences, although physiological responses can be learned.

CONCLUSIONS

Evidence of sex differences occur across all the areas examined. Certainly differences that occur at or shortly after birth indicate a biological cause. Differences that do not occur until later in life are more likely to be gender differences. Most differences seem to be sex-related.

An issue that has not been addressed is the size of the differences that do occur. Across all the differences reviewed, most are small to medium. The two largest are in spatial rotation scores and in aggressive behaviors. In the other areas, the differences between men and the differences between women are larger than the difference between men and women. Thus, the real behaviors and abilities of real women and men often overlap, with some men and some women being very much alike in a specific area. Although the difference in spatial rotation is large, it is not clear how this impacts daily life. It may make it easier for men to find their way from one point to another, but women can be trained to the average man's level. Men's advantage in mathematics, with a few exceptions, has decreased to the point that spatial rotation, which has remained robust, is now used to explain a small or nonexistent effect.

—Virginia Norris

Further Readings and References

Allen, J. S., Bruss, J., & Damasio, H. (2004). The structure of the human brain. *American Scientist, 92,* 246–253.

Archer, J., & Westman, K. (1981). Sex differences in the aggressive behaviour of schoolchildren. *British Journal of Social Psychology, 20,* 31–36.

Bem, S. L. (2004). Transforming the debate on sexual inequality: From biological difference to institutionalized androcentrism. In J. C. Chrisler, C. Golden, & P. Rozee (Eds), *Lectures on the psychology of women* (3rd ed., pp. 2–15). Rahway, NJ: McGraw-Hill.

Center for the Study of Sex Differences in Health, Aging and Disease. (n.d.). *Why study sex differences?* Retrieved from http://csd.georgetown.edu/why.htm

Cutbertson, F. M. (1997). Depression and gender: An international review. *American Psychologist, 52,* 25–31.

Halpern, D. F., & LaMay, M. L. (2000). The smarter sex: A critical review of sex differences in intelligence. *Educational Psychology Review, 12,* 229–246.

Kimura, D. (2002, May 13). *Sex differences in the brain.* Retrieved from http://www.sciam.com/article.cfm?articleID=00018E9D-879D-1D06-8E49809EC588EEDF

Lips, H. M. (2001). *Sex & gender: An introduction* (4th ed.). Mountain View, CA: Mayfield.

Ma, X. (1999). Gender differences in growth in mathematical skills during secondary grades: A growth model analysis. *Alberta Journal of Educational Research, 45,* 448–466.

McGillicuddy-De Lisi, A., & De Lisi, R. (2002). *Biology, society, and behavior: The development of sex differences in cognition.* Westport, CT: Ablex.

Naglieri, J. A., & Rojahn, J. (2001). Gender differences in planning, attention, simultaneous, and successive (PASS) cognitive processes and achievement. *Journal of Educational Psychology, 93,* 430–437.

Quinsey, V. L., Skilling, T. A., Lalumière, M. L., & Craig, W. M. (2004). *Juvenile delinquency: Understanding the origins of individual differences.* Washington, DC: American Psychological Association.

Society for Women's Health Research. (n.d.). *Sex differences in cardio/cerebrovascular disease.* Retrieved from http://www.womenshealthresearch.org/hs/facts_cardio.htm

Spanos, N. P. (1994). Multiple identity enactments and multiple personality disorder: A sociocognitive perspective. *Psychological Bulletin, 116,* 143–165.

Walsh, M. R. (1997). *Women, men, and gender: Ongoing debates.* New Haven, CT: Yale University Press.

SEX EDUCATION

Sex education, sometimes called sexuality education, is the teaching of information regarding sexual behaviors and their effects. The history of sex education is relatively recent and has been shrouded in much controversy. In the early days of the 20th century, doctors and laypersons could be arrested for disseminating information regarding contraception and family planning. As recently as the 1950s, the topic of sex was not considered appropriate for discussion in polite society and certainly not in public schools. Along with the lifting of other societal taboos, the 1960s brought discussions of sexuality into the public arena and with this, the introduction of sex education into public school classrooms.

CONTROVERSIES

In spite of these public discussions, there remain a variety of controversies. Should we teach sex education in the schools? There are those who believe vehemently that all sex education belongs in the home and those who believe equally strongly that we should rely on schools to provide this information. Between these two extremes are those who believe that parents, at the very least, need to have control over whether or not their children participate in any sex education offered by the public schools. If we are going to teach sex education in schools, what should we be teaching? How effective are the "plumbing" lessons, which teach about body parts and what goes where, with no regard for discussions about the risks and consequences of irresponsible sexual activity? How effective are the comprehensive sexuality education programs versus the abstinence-only programs? In what ways does each of these programs deal effectively with the students who are already engaged in sexual activities?

There are two major divisions in the sex education field that highlight the major controversies.

COMPREHENSIVE SEXUALITY EDUCATION

Comprehensive sexuality education is usually defined as the teaching of information regarding reproductive anatomy and physiology, contraceptive choice, sexual identity, relationships and intimacy issues, and risks and consequences of sexual behavior (e.g., human immunodeficiency virus [HIV] and acquired immunodeficiency syndrome [AIDS], pregnancy, sexually transmitted diseases [STDs]). While comprehensive sexuality programs stress responsible sexual behavior and convey that abstinence is the only guaranteed method for preventing unwanted pregnancies and exposure to STDs, there may also be discussion that includes those teenagers who are already engaging in or will choose to engage in sexual activity. These programs often offer information regarding responsible sexual behavior, safer sex, where contraception can be obtained, and all available alternatives for teenagers who face an unwanted pregnancy.

ABSTINENCE-ONLY SEX EDUCATION

Abstinence-only sex education has as its exclusive purpose teaching the social, psychological, and health gains to be realized by abstaining from sexual activity. It teaches that a mutually faithful monogamous relationship in the context of marriage is the expected standard of sexual activity and sexual activity outside marriage is likely to have harmful side effects. It teaches sexual abstinence outside of marriage is the expected standard for all school-age children and teaches the harmful consequences of having children out of wedlock. It also teaches young people how to reject sexual advances and how alcohol and drug use increase vulnerability to sexual advances. Finally, it teaches the importance of self-sufficiency before engaging in sexual activity. There is no information provided regarding contraception, safer sex, or sexual orientation.

It should be noted that there is broad disagreement among abstinence-only educators and policy makers about what constitutes sexual activity; consequently there is little agreement about what constitutes abstinence. Since 2000, the focus of the federal government has been on promoting abstinence-only education in the public schools.

TEEN PREGNANCY AND SEX EDUCATION

Based on 2000 census data, the pregnancy rate for teenage women 15 to 19 years of age dropped from 106.7 per 1,000 in 1986 to 83.6 per 1,000 in 2000. The pregnancy rate for all teenagers is mathematically the product of two factors: the proportion of young women engaged in intercourse (sexual activity) and the rate at which these young women become pregnant (lack of effective contraceptive use). The most closely studied and analyzed data on this topic were collected between 1988 and 1995, when the teen pregnancy rate dropped from 111.4 per 1,000 in 1988 to 99.6 per 1,000 in 1995. What the calculations using these data indicated was that roughly 25% of the teen pregnancy rate decline was due to delayed onset of sexual intercourse, while 75% of the decline was due to increased use of highly effective contraceptive methods.

CURRENT SEX EDUCATION POLICIES IN THE UNITED STATES

Highlights of the current state of sexuality education in the United States (as of February 2005) are as follows:

- Twenty-two states and the District of Columbia mandate public schools to teach sex education; many place requirements on how abstinence and contraception are treated when taught.
- Twenty-one states require that abstinence be stressed when taught as part of sex education.
- Nine states require simply that abstinence be covered during instruction.

- Fourteen states and the District of Columbia require that sex education programs cover contraception; no state requires that it be stressed.
- Thirty-eight states and the District of Columbia require provision of STD/HIV education; many place requirements on how abstinence and contraception are treated.
- Twenty-five states require abstinence be stressed when taught as part of STD/HIV education.
- Nine states require that it be covered.
- Seventeen states require that STD/HIV programs cover contraception; no state requires that it be stressed.
- Thirty-nine states and the District of Columbia require school districts to permit parental involvement in sexuality and STD/HIV education.
- Three states require parental consent in order for students to participate in sex or STD/HIV education.
- Thirty-six states and the District of Columbia allow parents to remove their children from instruction.

Most states currently offer parents an opt-out alternative to their children participating in sexuality education programs. However, few parents have their children removed from these classes.

Although the controversies remain, sex education in its varied forms is here to stay. While many experts might agree that parents should be the primary educators for their children, not all parents are educated or comfortable enough themselves to deal with these very difficult topics in a productive manner. Many will continue to rely on the public schools to provide, at the very least, some information regarding sexuality, whether it is a comprehensive or abstinence-only sex education program. The program chosen will be determined by federal, state, and district policies and outcomes desired.

—Shelley Dubkin-Lee and
LeoNora M. Cohen

See also Kinsey Institute

Further Readings and References

Alan Guttmacher Institute. (n.d.). *Changing emphases in sexuality education in U.S. public secondary schools, 1988–1999.* Retrieved from http://www.guttmacher.org/pubs/journals/3220400.pdf

Alan Guttmacher Institute. (n.d.). *Sex and STD/HIV education— State policies in brief.* Retrieved from http://www.guttmacher.org/statecenter/spibs/spib_SE.pdf

Bruess, C. E., & Greenburg, J. S. (2004). *Sexuality education: Theory and practice.* Sudbury, MA: Jones & Bartlett.

Irvine, J. M. (2002). *Talk about sex: The battles over sex education in the United States*. San Diego, CA: Greenhaven Press.

Moran, J. P. (2002). *Teaching sex: The shaping of adolescence in the 20th century*. Cambridge, MA: Harvard University Press.

National Campaign to Prevent Teen Pregnancy, http://www .teenpregnancy.org/resources/data/report_summaries/emer ging_answers/default.asp

Roleff, T. L. (1998). *Sex education (opposing viewpoints)*. Berkeley: University of California Press.

Sears, J. T. (1992). *Sexuality and the curriculum: The politics and practices of sexuality education*. New York: Teachers College Press.

Sexuality Information and Education Council of the United States. (n.d.). *State profiles—A portrait of sexuality education and abstinence-only-until-marriage programs in the states*. Retrieved from http://www.siecus.org/policy/states/ index.html

Social Security Online. (n.d.). *Separate program for absti- nence education*. Retrieved from http://www.ssa.gov/OP_ Home/ssact/title05/0510.htm

Taverner, W. J. (2002). *Taking sides: Clashing views on controversial issues in human sexuality*. Dubuque, IA: McGraw-Hill/Dushkin.

SEXUAL ABUSE

Before the mid-1970s, a great deal of the writing about child sexual abuse did not focus on the severity of the problem or the rates of occurrence. However, during the feminist movement of the 1960s and 1970s, more attention was given to the topic, and since that time awareness of child sexual abuse has increased.

WHAT IS CHILD SEXUAL ABUSE?

There is no universally accepted definition for child sexual abuse; definitions vary in legal versus clinical settings. Discrepancies that arise when trying to define child sexual abuse include variations in the age for how old one considers a child to be, as well as what one believes to be inappropriate sexual behavior. In addition, the capacity of a child to give "informed consent" to a sexual activity and a child's vulnerabil- ity to manipulation or coercion are also considered. Regardless of the difficulties in trying to standardize the definition of child sexual abuse, it is often defined based on the types of sexual behavior that occurred, the age and relationship of the offender, and the pat- terns of the abuse. The sexual abuse of children is illegal in all states in the United States. Most child protection agencies handle only cases in which a caregiver of the child is the abuser.

Types of sexually abusive behavior include non- contact sex abuse, fondling, oral sex, and penile pene- tration. Noncontact sexual abuse can include sexually explicit comments to the child, solicitation or sexually inappropriate behavior over the Internet, exposure of intimate body parts, voyeurism (peeping), and obscene phone calls. Fondling is when the child is told to touch the offender's intimate body parts or when the offender touches the child's intimate body parts, either of which can occur above or beneath the clothing. Oral sex con- sists of kissing with or without the use of the tongue, licking, biting, or sucking of the body, breasts, vagina, penis, or the anus. Penile penetration may be per- formed on the child by the offender, and is when the penis is inserted into the vagina or anus.

A sexual act is typically considered abusive when there is an age difference of about five years or more between the offender and victim, when the event occurs for the pleasure of the offender but not for the victim, and usually when the offender has power or influence over the victim. However, abuse can occur between two children of similar ages.

Patterns of sexual abuse usually fall into one of five categories: dyadic sexual abuse, group sexual abuse, sexual exploitation, sex rings, and ritualistic sexual abuse. Dyadic sexual abuse occurs when there is one offender and one victim and may be present within a family or between persons who are not related. Group sexual abuse can occur when the offender begins by having sex with one victim and eventually is abusing several victims at one time or when there is one or more offenders abusing several victims at one time. Sexual exploitation (also referred to as "human traf- ficking") occurs when victims are being used as pros- titutes or to produce pornography (with the Internet and computers playing a growing role). While sexual exploitation is a problem in the United States, it is an extreme problem in Southeast Asia, Latin America, Western Europe, and the Philippines, due to the poor economic conditions in those countries. Adolescents may be lured by promises of jobs as waitresses, dancers, or hotel maids. Some are openly recruited for the sex trade. Sex rings, in which one or more offend- ers typically abuses more than one child, are more commonly created by male pedophiles, or persons who are primarily interested in children to fulfill their sexual needs. Ritualistic abuse can occur when the child is abused physically, psychologically, and sexually in a calculated manner, such as by a cult, in a day care setting, or by a single person.

Indications that a child has been sexually abused can be sexual or nonsexual. Actions that often increase suspicion of child sexual abuse include excessive masturbation by the child, knowledge of sexual activities that are more advanced than appropriate for his or her age, sexual aggression toward other children, sexual advances toward older children or adults, exhibition of inappropriate promiscuous behavior, or presence of sleep, bowel, bladder, eating, emotional, cognitive, and behavior problems. One theory regarding victims of sexual abuse that eventually sexually abuse others is that the victims may feel powerless and out of control, but by creating a situation wherein they are the offender, they feel as if they are gaining an element of control that they did not have during their own abuse.

INCIDENCE/PREVALENCE PATTERNS

The prevalence rates of child sexual abuse are estimated through population surveys conducted over the phone, by personal interviews, and through questionnaires. Prevalence rates can be calculated through information from the victims as well as from volunteers in the field, special populations such as persons in therapy, and samples that are believed to be representative of the population. Different populations, definitions of sexual abuse, and the ways in which the surveys are conducted all may produce varying results in estimates of the prevalence of child sexual abuse. Prevalence rates may not only be more inaccurate than desired because of measurement issues but also because of unreported events, minimizing of the event by adults or professionals due to their own interpretation of sexual abuse, as well as events that are not remembered. Therefore, the reported and actual occurrence rates of sexual abuse may be dramatically different.

In 2002, incidents of child sexual abuse that were reported and confirmed by law enforcement officials or state child protective services were found in 1.2% of children (approximately 88,686 children) in the United States. Furthermore, in 2002, 9.9% of children who had been maltreated, whose cases were investigated and the reports were confirmed, were found to be sexually abused (sexual abuse is less common than child neglect or physical abuse).

However, in contrast to officially reported instances of child sexual abuse, survey or questionnaire studies reveal a higher incidence. Instances of child sexual abuse are typically not reported to legal or child welfare authorities. One study estimated that only one in five instances of child sexual abuse is reported, while another estimate was that only 3% of instances are reported.

Studies of U.S. college students' responses to questionnaires show that about 50% responded that as children they experienced some form of sexual abuse that did not involve contact with their genitals (sexualized kissing, seeing an exhibitionist), and 5% to 10% reported they experienced attempted or completed intercourse. Studies in the United States, Great Britain, Canada, Sweden, and New Zealand provide a wide range of prevalence of child sexual abuse, from 12% to 62% for women, and 3% to 39% for men. The wide range in the prevalence rates is mainly due to the varying definitions employed in the studies and the methods of data collection. Studies in which data are collected in face-to-face interviews by trained interviewers obtain higher reports of abuse than studies using questionnaires or telephone surveys. One study that examined a number of child sexual abuse prevalence studies suggested that the prevalence for the general population (not clinical samples) is between 12% and 17% for women and between 5% and 8% for men. Other researchers conclude that at least 1 in 3 women has experienced sexual abuse during childhood, and at least 1 in 10 men. There is agreement that updated epidemiological studies, employing standard definitions of child sexual abuse and adjustment/outcome measures, are needed.

Research findings suggest that males are more likely to be abused by someone outside of their family than females, possibly because of independence that is given to boys in hopes of creating self-reliance. Research regarding the prevalence rates of men who were sexually abused as children has not been as common as research involving sexually abused females. Underreporting of males who have encountered sexual abuse may be a result of professionals failing to recognize signs of abuse in boys, less supervision of boys than girls, due to the anxiety and stigma that the boy may be "gay" if the abuse were disclosed, or because of cultural training not to express distress to others.

A common problem with the reporting of child sexual abuse is getting the child to disclose that the abuse is occurring. Some children remember the acts and do not want to talk about them and others are not able to remember them. Often, children who are sexually abused experience repression and are unable to remember the experiences clearly or at all due to the traumatic nature of the incident. This may be an adaptive response for the child, and may be used unintentionally so that the child is able to survive without having to reexperience those memories. Unintentional motivations for memory repression may be to avoid becoming overwhelmed, to avoid experiencing the pain of the event, to maintain some type of relationship with the abuser if necessary, and to avoid threats to how the victim views interactions between persons in the outside world. Experiences in which the person's boundaries are betrayed in a relationship and when the person is terrorized (such as experiencing war crimes or sexual abuse) are more likely to be repressed. Events that are frightening, can physically harm the person, but are not viewed as a betrayal by someone else (such as surviving an automobile accident) are considered terrorizing events, but are not as likely to be repressed. Therefore, it is likely that repression serves as a way to protect the person from the pain of the event and the recognition that relationship boundaries are being betrayed with the abuser and those who are aware that the abuse is occurring. Typically, the more dependent the child is on the person abusing him or her, the more intense the act of betrayal will seem.

Oftentimes individuals intentionally and unintentionally focus on other sensory experiences during sexual abuse. By focusing on other sensory experiences, such as the texture of a fabric or a smell, the person is able to avoid dealing with the traumatic event at that time. However, whatever sensation the person focused on during the abuse is often remembered and paired with the emotions that surrounded the event, even if the actual abusive act is not remembered. Therefore, sensations can act as triggers for flashbacks, or the reexperience of the emotions that were associated with the time when the abuse occurred, even if the abuse is not remembered in its entirety or at all.

IMPACT AND EFFECTS

At the time of initial assessment for child abuse, as many as 40% of children do not manifest clinical symptoms. When a broad definition of child sexual abuse is used (that includes a single incident that was not physically invasive) in college student samples, most people surveyed say they have not experienced significant long-term negative consequences. However, there are quite pronounced negative consequences for some. The effects of child sexual abuse are unique and experienced differently for every victim. When sexual abuse causes harm, it can interfere with normal child development and can increase the risk for emotional challenges or maladjustment in adolescence and adulthood. Distressing symptoms and poorer adjustment are more likely following sexual abuse that was more severe in terms of betrayal, coercion, or physical intrusion. Further complicating the assessment of the impact of sexual abuse is the fact that sexual abuse is more likely to occur in families in which there is violence, conflict, or dysfunction. Therefore, it is difficult to sort out the effects of the sexual abuse from the other sources of distress.

Short Term

The physical, emotional, and psychological effects of the abuse can be experienced for a short period of time after the abuse or can be more pervasive and long lasting, often throughout childhood and adulthood. While threats from the offender are a major reason for children to not report abuse, children also may not speak out because they do not feel they will be believed, they fear that they may anger their parents or caregivers, and they fear that the parents may become angry with the offender and perceive them as "creating trouble." Some other reasons for children to withhold disclosure are the fear that people may believe the child was responsible for the abuse, the fear that the parents could be blamed for allowing the abuse to continue, and the child's ambivalent feelings regarding the abuse. It is not uncommon for children to retract true allegations of sexual abuse because of pressure to recant or due to their distress at the response to the allegations.

After-effects of sexual abuse can be intensified when a trusted adult does not believe or support the child. In response, the child may withdraw and internalize, by directing the painful feelings at himself or herself, or may externalize, by directing the feelings toward others or acting out. The child may fear being stigmatized by the disclosure of the abuse, in that he or she may not be "male" or "female" enough, which can often result in behaviors in girls of being more passive or "feminine" and boys being more aggressive or "masculine."

Long Term

Long-term effects that are specifically caused by child sexual abuse are unknown due to the lack of reports, individual differences in response to the abuse, and inadequate research populations, among other factors. Many aspects of personality are formed in childhood, and when traumatic events such as sexual abuse occur in childhood, certain characteristics can be formed and maintained on a long-term basis. As time following the abuse increases, children often associate the feelings and fear that were internalized from the abuse with everyday occurrences and relationships that are not associated with it. Many times children feel that it is necessary to be hypervigilant to protect themselves from future incidents. Another common long-term effect of sexual abuse is for the victim to have a less-defined sense of self and low self-esteem, due in part to feelings of alienation, the confusion of emotions, and contradictions perceived in relationships.

Long-term psychological problems that children often experience as a result of sexual abuse include problems with sleep and relaxation, depression, anxiety, negative beliefs regarding their bodies, flashbacks associated with psychological disorders, and an inability to deal with reality, often referred to as dissociation. Psychological disorders that are often experienced by victims of sexual abuse include depression, eating disorders, anxiety disorders, posttraumatic stress disorder (in which the victim reexperiences the traumatic event and may be hypervigilant and may try to avoid stimuli that trigger flashbacks), borderline personality disorder (in which the victim engages in self-mutilating behavior as a means to deal with psychological pain, dissociation, etc.), and the extremely rare dissociative identity disorder (in which the abuse that the victim encountered was so severe that his or her personality during times of the abuse fragmented as a means to cope, creating different alters or "personalities").

Feelings of anger and guilt toward the abuser, especially when the abuser is someone the child feels they should love or care for, can increase the levels of debilitating emotional turmoil for the victim. Victims of child sexual abuse are also more likely to participate in relationships later in life where they are revictimized emotionally, physically, or sexually. It is common for victims of sexual abuse to encounter some type of sexual dysfunction later in life, even if engaged in a loving relationship.

INTERVENTIONS FOR THE VICTIM/SURVIVOR

Children

A child-centered approach, where the decisions and actions are examined in the child's best interest, is employed by understanding how the abuse affected the child while acknowledging that abuse affects each person differently. In addition to acting in a manner that is congruent with the child's wishes, a child-centered approach also attempts to ensure that the child's best interests have been met.

Individual, group, and family therapy models are used in treatment. When a sexually abused child has posttraumatic stress reactions, abuse-specific cognitive behavior therapy (CBT) has been shown to be helpful, especially with school-aged children. Components of this therapy include psychoeducation (providing information about abuse and offenders, and explaining the principles of CBT), anxiety management (teaching relaxation and coping strategies to reduce fear and anxiety), exposure (talking, drawing, or writing about the abuse to reduce avoidance and to reduce automatic responses that do not promote adjustment), and cognitive therapy (challenging and replacing irrational or unhelpful thoughts about the event or one's self). Parents of the child may also participate in therapy to reduce their distress, learn effective strategies for behavior management, and increase their support of the child. Creating a sense of safety for each family member may also be a focus.

Group therapy has been helpful in reducing the feeling of isolation or "differentness" for some survivors, and may provide normalization and validation of one's experience and reactions. Peers may offer an alternate support system to survivors who lack family support, and may find value and meaning in being of help to others. However, there have been few studies of the efficacy of group therapy with adolescents.

While pharmacological treatment is not recommended as a primary treatment for sexually traumatized children, medications are sometimes used to supplement psychosocial interventions. There have been no placebo-controlled studies of medication with abused children, but there have been some studies suggesting that antidepressants and alpha-adrenergic or beta-blocker drugs may be useful. Since sexual abuse effects may co-occur with other mental health concerns, the other conditions may require treatment as well.

Adults Who Were Abused as Children

When adults who were sexually abused as children enter therapy, often one of the treatment goals may be to improve coping mechanisms that were adopted earlier in their lives. Many times these persons attempt to cope with their abuse through acting out behaviors such as violence, internalizing behaviors such as eating disorders, substance abuse, and the perpetuation of abuse in other relationships. A wide variety of treatments are available for persons who were sexually abused as children, especially through psychotherapy. For many survivors of abuse who engage in individual or group psychotherapy, treatment goals often include an increase of awareness of the abuse and determination to change the thoughts into a more positive experience (labeling oneself as a "survivor" instead of a "victim"), an educational component, an introduction to more positive ways to cope, emphasis on the strengths of the person, and normalization of their responses to the abuse.

The entire therapeutic process is often found to be helpful in better understanding and decreasing the frequency of flashbacks. This is attempted by having the survivor work toward fully confronting the circumstances of the abuse and to reintegrate the triggers into their conscious mind, which in turn would help them to distinguish the past from the present and minimize flashbacks. Other goals of therapy can include, but are not limited to, processing feelings of anger, establishment of age-appropriate sexual knowledge and communication skills, and creating a safe and supportive home environment.

TREATMENT OF PERPETRATORS

Treatment of Children With Sexual Behavior Problems

Girls and boys less than 6 years of age, and even younger, have demonstrated sexually aggressive behaviors against other children. The label of "children with sexual behavior problems" is recommended for such children (instead of "child offenders" or "child perpetrators") because it labels the behavior rather than the child's identity. Since young children do not have cognitive skills comparable with those of adolescents or adults to plan, groom a victim, or rationalize, their aggressive behaviors are more often impulsive. These children are likely to have been exposed to explicit sexual activity (i.e., through experiencing sexual abuse, access to sexually explicit media, poor parental supervision). Helping parents learn effective behavior management techniques is an important part of treatment, as are increasing parental supervision, providing age-appropriate sexuality education, and teaching rules about sexual behavior.

Treatment of Adolescent Perpetrators/Juvenile Sex Offenders

According to the National Incident-Based Reporting System of the FBI, 43% of sexual assaults against children 6 years of age or younger are committed by juvenile offenders. Since the early 1980s, research and treatment for juvenile sex offenders has increased, although very few large-scale studies have been done. About 90% of known adolescent sexual offenders are male. No single personality profile has been identified for adolescent offenders, but many have been observed to have poor social skills, additional behavior problems, learning disabilities, impulsivity, and depression. Their family backgrounds are diverse, with some families having parental alcoholism or other substance abuse, chaotic family patterns, or problems with cohesion or adaptability, while other families are characterized as healthy.

For adult offenders, treatment often focuses on modifying deviant arousal patterns, but this is less useful for adolescent offenders. Cognitive-behavioral and social skills training techniques are often used to build empathy for victims, reduce thinking errors or cognitive distortions (rationalizations that "justify" abuse), improve social skills, and teach techniques for anger management and self-control. Known reoffenses among juvenile sex offenders are low (ranging from 5% to 15% according to treatment studies) in the 5 to 10 years in which follow-up has been done. However, nonsexual reoffending among the youth is frequent.

A promising treatment approach that has been used to address not only the commission of sexual abuse but other delinquent behaviors as well is multisystemic therapy (MST). MST is an intensive home and community-based therapeutic approach that intervenes in the social ecology of a youth and family. Such concerns as parental supervision, school attendance and achievement, and peer networks are addressed. Use of MST has been effective in reducing nonsexual recidivism for treated youth.

Treatment of Adult Perpetrators

On the other hand, recidivism rates for treated adult offenders is higher; a review of 43 treatment studies showed recidivism rates of about 12% for the treated groups and about 17% for comparison groups. Programs that were more likely to reduce recidivism were intensive (lasting at least several months), employed a behavioral or cognitive behavioral approach (in contrast to traditional psychodynamic or nondirective approaches), taught prosocial skills, were firmly but fairly administered, and involved the offender's real-world social network to keep the offender in contact with prosocial people and activities. Cognitive-behavioral techniques include the identification of patterns that lead to offending and learning skills to interrupt those patterns. The skills could include reducing alcohol use; learning problem-solving skills, effective coping, and self-control strategies; and participating in satisfying daily activities. For those with deviant fantasies, cognitive interventions include covert sensitization (imagining negative consequences to sexually offending), masturbatory satiation (masturbating to deviant thoughts until the masturbation becomes boring or uncomfortable), and orgasmic reconditioning (thinking of socially acceptable sexual images just prior to orgasm). Relapse prevention may also be used with other treatment models. It involves identifying triggers to offend and developing a plan to reduce the likelihood. For offenders with brain injury or neurological disease, close supervision and monitoring may also be needed. Treatment is often conducted in a group setting. One of the largest treatment programs operates in Great Britain, but little has been published to date regarding its effectiveness.

Occasionally surgical and pharmacological interventions (use of hormonal medication to reduce arousal) are used with subgroups of adult sexual offenders. Although some people think castration (removal of the testes to reduce testosterone) would be a remedy, in about half of patients it does not prevent erection. For some offenders, "chemical castration" or administration of antiandrogen drugs has reduced the person's sex drive and sexual fantasy. However, side effects and resulting noncompliance with the medication have been problems with this approach. The most recent type of drug used is antidepressants (e.g., sertraline, clomipramine, and fluoxetine). These can be helpful in reducing deviant sex drive and also helping with depressed mood. Drug therapy is typically used in conjunction with cognitive-behavioral interventions, as part of a comprehensive treatment plan.

PREVENTION OF CHILD SEXUAL ABUSE

Decline in Reported Cases of Child Sexual Abuse

During the first decade that reported child abuse case data were reliably collected in the United States (1986–1996), the frequency of child sexual abuse doubled. However, in the past decade, a 40% decrease in substantiated cases has been observed (from 1992 to 2000, substantiated cases decreased from to 140,800 to 89,355). Analysis of these data suggests that a real decline has occurred, and this is not just an artifact of changes in substantiation or data-collection practices. Hypotheses regarding this decline include the impact of aggressive prosecution and incarceration of sex offenders. Between 1991 and 1997 the incarceration in state correctional facilities for sex crimes against children increased nearly 40%. It is also possible that public educational activities of the past two decades, and fears of detection and prosecution, have deterred the potential offenders most able to control their actions, therefore resulting in a decline in the most readily preventable cases. However, there is evidence from one state suggesting the decline may be partly due to a backlash against those reporting sexual abuse.

Prevention Strategies

Despite this decline, sexual abuse remains a significant public health problem. Various prevention approaches have been attempted. David Finkelhor, director of the Crimes Against Children Research Center, identified four preconditions to child sexual abuse:

1. Motivation for sexual abuse (being sexually aroused by children or fantasies involving children)

2. Overcoming internal inhibitors (using alcohol or drugs, acting impulsively)

3. Overcoming external inhibitors (having unsupervised access to children)

4. Overcoming the child's resistance (coercing or manipulating the child into participating)

Treatment of identified sex offenders usually focuses on attempts to reduce the first two factors, reducing deviant arousal and building inhibitions against offending. Law enforcement interventions have typically focused on creating external inhibitors (incarceration, sex offender registration and public notification, and postincarceration civil commitment). All states in the United States now have sex offender registries. There is no evidence to date as to whether registration and notification prevent sexual abuse, but they may result in quicker apprehension of repeat offenders.

Victimization prevention programs often focus on education of children to resist abuse and to disclose victimization. Studies of interventions to promote child resistance reveal that children often have difficulty learning and retaining the concepts in the educational programs (e.g., that an abuser may be someone they know), but the educational programs may increase earlier detection of abuse by encouraging children to report it.

A novel prevention approach has been advanced by Stop It Now!, a nonprofit group that promotes the use of four tools to address the root causes of child sexual abuse. Stop It Now! attempts to develop awareness in potential abusers and urge them to seek help; challenge those who abuse to stop immediately and seek treatment (a helpline and an Internet resource are provided); educate "bystanders" on how to confront abusers; and educate the public and the media to change the social climate to say, "We will no longer tolerate the sexual abuse of our children."

—*Susan McCammon and Sarah Ramby*

Further Readings and References

Baker, C. C. (2002). *Female survivors of sexual abuse: An integrated guide to treatment.* New York: Brunner Routledge.

Conte, J. R. (Ed.). (2002). *Critical issues in child sexual abuse: Historical, legal, and psychological perspectives.* Thousand Oaks, CA: Sage.

Crimes Against Children Research Center, http://www.unh.edu/ccrc/index.html

Durham, A. (2003). *Young men surviving child sexual abuse: Research stories and lessons for therapeutic practice.* Indianapolis, IN: Wiley.

Faller, K. C. (2003). *Understanding and assessing child sexual maltreatment* (2nd ed.). Thousand Oaks, CA: Sage.

Ferrara, F. F. (2002). *Childhood sexual abuse: Developmental effects across the lifespan.* Pacific Grove, CA: Brooks-Cole.

Finkelhor, D., & Jones, L. M. (2004, January). Explanations for the decline in child sexual abuse cases. *Juvenile Justice Bulletin.* Retrieved from http://www.ncjrs.org/pdffiles1/ojjdp/199298.pdf

Haugaard, J. J. (2000). The challenge of defining child sexual abuse. *American Psychologist, 55,* 1036–1039.

Jones, L. M., & Finkelhor, D. (2003). Putting together evidence on declining trends in sexual abuse: A complex puzzle. *Child Abuse and Neglect, 27,* 133–135.

National Center for Missing & Exploited Children, http://www.missingkids.com

National Clearinghouse on Child Abuse and Neglect Information, http://nccanch.acf.hhs.gov

Rind, B., Tromovitch, P., & Bauserman, R. (1998). A meta-analytic examination of assumed properties of child sexual abuse using college samples. *Psychological Bulletin, 124,* 22–53.

Stop It Now! The Campaign to Prevent Child Sexual Abuse, http://www.stopitnow.com

Ward, T., Laws, D. R., & Hudson, S. M. (Eds.). (2003). *Sexual deviance: Issues and controversies.* Thousand Oaks, CA: Sage.

Wolak, J., Mitchell, K., & Finkelhor, D. (2003, November). *Internet sex crimes against minors: The response of law enforcement.* Alexandria, VA: National Center for Missing & Exploited Children.

SEXUAL ACTIVITY

Adolescence is characterized as a period of rapid growth involving dramatic change. This stage of development begins with puberty and involves many physical, cognitive, and emotional changes that mark the shift from childhood to adulthood. Girls reach puberty approximately 12 to 18 months earlier than boys do, with the average age range for beginning puberty being 9.5 to 13.5 years for boys and 8 to 13 years for girls. In addition, these changes lead to an increased interest in sex, including masturbation and sexual experimentation. Adolescent sexual behavior, unfortunately, is also associated with certain risks such as sexually transmissible infections and unplanned pregnancy. The best protection against these problems is knowledge—and making healthy decisions about sex depends on accurate information as well the motivation to make responsible choices.

With the onset of puberty, adolescents begin to experience changes in many realms of life. For one, during this period teenagers demonstrate an increasing ability to use rational and abstract thought. They start to question authority, rules, laws, and customs, and begin to develop their own theories and viewpoints. Not surprisingly, parents often describe their adolescent children as stubborn and rebellious. Furthermore, adolescence is a time when young males and females attempt to establish a sense of who they are, where they fit into their peer group, and what their goals will be. Many adolescents struggle with the answers to the question "Who am I?" This beginning of identity formation, which can persist into adulthood, leads to many questions, including curiosity about dating, sex, and love.

Physically, adolescence brings on dramatic changes involving the body. Development often begins with a growth spurt characterized by significant bone and muscle growth, weight gain, and the maturation of the brain, heart, lungs, and reproductive system. Changes in the reproductive system are the hallmark of adolescent development, known as puberty. For males, puberty brings about a growth in the size of the penis and testes; the production of semen; the appearance of pubic, underarm, and facial hair; and also a deepening of the voice. Many males also experience nocturnal emissions, or wet dreams, when sperm production first begins. For females, puberty is a time during which menarche (the first menstrual period) begins, the vagina elongates, the ovaries and uterus grow, breasts begin to develop, and pubic and underarm hair appear as well. All of these developments begin when a part of the brain, the hypothalamus, signals the release of hormones known as gonadotropins. These hormones then direct the production of testosterone by the testes and estrogen by the ovaries, which in turn direct the body to begin pubertal changes.

These psychological and physical changes signal a growing interest in sexual behavior. Masturbation is the most common form of sexual behavior: 88% of boys and 62% of girls have masturbated by age 16. Frequency of masturbation increases throughout adolescence; among teenagers 16 to 19 years old, more than two thirds of boys and half of girls masturbate weekly. However, many adolescents (females in particular) also feel guilt and shame about masturbating.

Sexual interactions also often begin in adolescence, with most boys and girls progressing through

Table 1   Percentage of Sexually Active High School Students

Category	Ever Had Sexual Intercourse		
	Female	*Male*	*Total*
Race/Ethnicity			
White	43%	41%	42%
Black	61%	74%	67%
Hispanic	46%	57%	52%
Grade			
9th	28%	37%	33%
10th	43%	45%	44%
11th	53%	53%	53%
12th	62%	61%	62%
Total	**45%**	**48%**	**47%**

SOURCE: U.S. Risk Behavior Survey, 2003.

a similar sequence of behaviors. The characteristic progression begins with hugging and kissing ("making out"), followed by fondling ("petting"), rubbing genitals together while clothed, and ultimately sexual intercourse. Some teenagers experiment with oral sex as an alternative to sexual intercourse and to preserve virginity. The age at first intercourse varies, but 46% of high school students report having sex at least once, and one third are currently sexually active. The proportion of sexually active students grows from one-third in the 9th grade to nearly two-thirds by the 12th grade. African American teenagers are more likely to be sexually experienced than their white and Hispanic peers (Table 1). Overall, boys are more sexually active and start earlier than girls. In general, the gender and racial/ethnic differences in sexual behavior dissipate by early adulthood.

Some factors contributing to early intercourse include: early maturation, increased testosterone levels (for males and females), peer norms, peer pressure, academic achievement, athletic involvement, religion, availability of opportunities, and parental influence. Adolescents who perceive that their peers are having sex are more inclined to do so themselves, and direct pressure from peers can increase the likelihood that the adolescent will engage in sexual activity. However, parental communication about sex can offset peer influence—teenagers who report high levels of communication and close relationships with their parents are more likely to delay having sex. For girls, athletic involvement also seems to decrease the likelihood of early intercourse. For both sexes, academic achievement is related to the onset of sexual intercourse. It has been shown that adolescents with low academic achievement and low educational goals are more likely to become sexually active earlier than those with high achievement and goals. Furthermore, adolescents who consider religion an important aspect of their lives are less likely to be sexually active. Finally, opportunity plays a role in early sexual initiation. Research shows that being in a steady relationship predicts early initiation, whereas limited dating is associated with later sexual initiation in girls. Reactions of boys and girls to first intercourse can differ, but both genders report feelings of anxiety and fear about the first time. However, males also report more pleasure and less guilt than females, due in part to the fact that males are significantly more likely to reach orgasm during first intercourse. Both genders report more pleasure and less guilt if they are in a committed rather than a casual relationship, the so-called "love effect."

Unprepared sexual activity leads to some risks—including sexually transmitted infections (STIs) and teenage pregnancy. More than 3 million teenagers in the United States contract one or more STIs each year, and one in four sexually active adolescents will contract an STI. Although rates of gonorrhea in adolescents have dropped over the past 10 years, the rates of chlamydia have risen. However, this may be due in part to improved screening techniques. It is estimated that 26% to 46% of young women are infected with the human papillomavirus (HPV or genital warts), and 15% to 20% of young men and women are infected with genital herpes, another sexually transmitted virus. Adolescent girls are most susceptible to contracting STIs, and if left untreated are at greater risk for developing long-term health problems, which can include infertility. In addition, the rates of infection by the human immunodeficiency virus (HIV) are increasing among adolescents—acquired immunodeficiency syndrome (AIDS) is the seventh-leading cause of death among 15- to 24-year-olds in the United States. One of the main reasons for this increase is that many teenagers do not practice safer sex. Studies show one-third or more of sexually active high school students had not used a condom during their last sexual encounter. Short of abstinence, condoms are the most effective means of protection against STIs, HIV, and another problem of teenage sexuality—unplanned pregnancy.

Each year in the United States there are 870,000 pregnancies in females 15 to 19 years of age, and 80% of these are unintended. Thus, each year more than 7% of adolescents experience an unplanned pregnancy. On a positive note, these figures are at the lowest level in over a decade—adolescent pregnancy rates have dropped 27% since 1990. This decline is attributed to later onset of sexual activity and a greater use of contraception among teenagers. Even so, there are many problems associated with teenage pregnancy. Unintended pregnancies often place the adolescent mother and her child at a disadvantage economically, socially, and financially. Teenage mothers are significantly less likely to complete high school or attend college, more likely to have failed marriages, and are at a greater health risk than other adolescent females. One third of pregnant adolescents do not receive proper prenatal care, and the babies of teenage mothers commonly have low birth weight and other health complications.

In order to allay these complications, interventions have been developed to help educate adolescents about sexuality. School-based programs, such as sexuality education classes, are often used to accomplish this goal and they often do lead to greater and more effective contraceptive use among teenagers. Yet, although the majority of people in the United States favor sexuality education, there is also much controversy around what to teach and how to present this information. Despite fears that sexuality education may actually encourage adolescents to engage in sexual activity, studies dispel this myth.

The majority of programs have one of two goals: comprehensive sexuality education or an exclusive focus on abstinence from sexual activity. Both share the common goal of encouraging adolescents to postpone intercourse until they are prepared for responsible sexual decision making. A successful program would ideally include teaching specific skills for reducing sexual risk behaviors (such as how to obtain and use condoms), techniques for communicating with parents and partners about sex, methods of dealing with peer pressure, and basic information of sexual anatomy and reproduction. Sexuality education programs are even more effective when paired with availability of contraceptives, reproductive and peer counseling, and sexual health services like STI screening. In addition, parents should play a large part in helping adolescents to make healthy decisions—teenagers who are able to discuss their sexuality and related concerns openly with parents have fewer sex partners and are less likely to engage in risky sexual behaviors.

—Jennifer Buckley and
Richard D. McAnulty

Further Readings and References

Alan Guttmacher Institute. (n.d.). *Get "in the know": 20 questions about pregnancy, contraception and abortion.* Retrieved from http://www.guttmacher.org/in-the-know/index.html

Alan Guttmacher Institute. (1994). *Sex and America's teenagers.* New York: Author.

Centers for Disease Control and Prevention. (2004). Youth risk behavior surveillance—United States, 2003. *Morbidity and Mortality Weekly Report, 53*(SS-2).

Crockett, L. J., Raffaelli, M., & Moilanen, K. L. (2003). Adolescent sexuality: Behavior and meaning. In M. D. Berzonsky & G. R. Adams (Eds.), *Blackwell handbook of adolescence.* (pp. 371–392). Malden, MA: Blackwell.

Florsheim, P. (2003). *Adolescent romantic relations and sexual behavior: Theory, research, and practical implications.* Mahwah, NJ: Erlbaum.

Kaiser Family Foundation. (n.d.). *Sex education in the U.S.: Policy and politics.* Retrieved from http://www.kff.org/youthhivstds/3224-02-index.cfm

Kaiser Family Foundation. (2003). *National survey of adolescents and young adults: Sexual health knowledge, attitudes and experiences.* Menlo Park, CA: Author. Retrieved from http://www.kff.org/youthhivstds/3218-index.cfm

SEXUALLY TRANSMITTED DISEASES (STDs)

Sexually transmitted diseases or infections (STDs or STIs) are primarily spread through vaginal, anal, or oral intercourse. Pathogenic organisms, such as bacteria or viruses, are carried by body fluids, such as semen and blood, through vaginal, urethral, cervical, rectal, and oral mucous membranes. A few are transmitted via contact with affected skin or contaminated objects.

It is estimated that hundreds of millions of new STD cases appear worldwide every year. More males are infected with STDs than females, but compared with males, females with STDs tend to be younger. On the whole, 15- to 24-year-olds tend to be at greatest risk. They are most likely to not use condoms, have more than one sexual partner, and have high-risk partners. However, anyone who has sex can contract an STD; the only certain way to avoid an STD is to abstain from sex. Barring abstinence, male and female condoms are about 90% effective in protecting against STDs. Minimizing the number of sexual partners can also reduce the risk for acquiring STDs.

The diagnosis and treatment of STDs requires a physician's special knowledge, skills, and procedures. Using antibiotics, doctors can cure bacterial infections. Parasitic and fungal diseases can be cured with a variety of nonprescription and prescription drugs. There are no drugs, however, that can rid the body of a viral STD, but the symptoms can be eased and controlled with various treatments, including antiviral, antibiotic, and immune system–boosting drugs. Worldwide, STDs cost billions of dollars to treat every year. Although STDs are rarely fatal, some can foster human immunodeficiency virus (HIV) transmission, and if untreated lead to severe discomfort and complications. Additionally, without treatment, infected pregnant women can pass the STD to the fetus in the uterus or to the infant during birth.

STDs can also be emotionally devastating. They strain relationships with family, friends, and significant others, leaving individuals with STDs feeling isolated and rejected. For some, fear of rejection fosters concealment of the disease, but for others, revealing their disease protects them from disappointment with preintimate relationships. Due to increased anxiety and guilt that comes with the fear of transmission, STDs negatively affect sexual relationships, decreasing an individual's ability to have orgasms and to experience the warmth and intimacy associated with sex. Individuals with STDs also experience a drop in self-esteem because they often feel dirty, contaminated, and less sexually attractive. Feelings of depression, self-destructiveness, pessimism, and hostility frequently follow an STD diagnosis. Individuals diagnosed with an STD may exhibit short-term delusional thinking, disorganized speech or behavior, or medical symptoms unrelated to the STD but indicative of trauma-induced stress. Additionally, studies demonstrate that emotional distress and self-revulsion can foster symptom recurrence with some STDs. Counseling and support groups can help STD-diagnosed individuals cope with the stress and stigma of the disease.

BACTERIAL INFECTIONS

Bacteria are single-cell microorganisms existing with or on another organism. Gonorrhea, often called "the clap" or "the drip," is caused by the bacterium *Neisseria gonorrhoeae.* About 2 to 5 days after transmission, males experience burning urination and a yellowish, thick discharge from the penis. If untreated, male gonorrhea can cause fertility and kidney problems. Initially, women may only notice a slight vaginal discharge, but if untreated the bacteria may cause burning urination and irregular menstrual bleeding. It can also result in pelvic inflammatory disease (a major cause of female infertility), ectopic pregnancy, and chronic pelvic pain. During birth, infants can contract gonorrhea of the eyes.

Syphilis is caused by *Treponema pallidum* bacteria. Not only is it spread sexually, but touching the accompanying infectious chancre can also transmit syphilis. In the first stage (2–4 weeks from contamination), a round chancre or sore appears at the infection site; a few weeks later it disappears. Two to four weeks later a skin rash, characterized by raised red bumps that darken and burst, develops. At this stage the infected individual may also have headaches, fever, mouth sores, sore throat, and joint pain. When these symptoms disappear, the disease enters a dormant phase for many years. Within the last stage, a large destructive ulcer can appear anywhere in the body. If untreated, syphilis can attack the central nervous system or cardiovascular system and cause brain damage, paralysis, mental illness, and death. Syphilis can be passed through the placenta, affecting fetal development or causing miscarriage or stillbirth. Infants born with syphilis are at risk for vision, hearing, dental, and bone impairments.

Chlamydia trachomatis bacteria can cause an infection in the male urethra or epididymis and the female urethra, cervix, or endometrium. Most women and men do not experience symptoms, but women may notice frequent painful urination, a vaginal discharge, or lower abdominal pain, and men may experience symptoms similar to but milder than gonorrhea. Chlamydia is also like gonorrhea in that it can cause pelvic inflammatory disease. If chlamydia is transmitted through oral-genital contact, a sore throat is the first symptom. It can also be transmitted to the eye after touching infected genitals and to newborns passing through the birth canal of an infected mother, resulting in eye inflammation and pneumonia.

VIRAL INFECTIONS

Smaller than bacteria, viruses grow and reproduce within living cells. Viral infections include herpes simplex virus type 2 (HSV-2), hepatitis (types A, B, C, and D), human papillomavirus (HPV), and HIV. Although HIV is a sexually transmitted disease, its characteristics and effects are explained in a separate entry of this encyclopedia.

HSV-2, or genital herpes, is most contagious during active outbreaks, and transmission almost always occurs sexually. The primary symptom, itchy red bumps, usually appears on the genitals, thighs, or buttocks 3 to 7 days after exposure. The bumps develop blisters that break and turn into painful ulcers lasting 1 to 2 weeks. They can develop in the vagina or on the cervix accompanied by a vaginal discharge. Fever, burning urination, and aches and pains may also develop. HSV-2 can be spread to the eye after touching the broken blisters. Women with HSV-2 are at greater risk for cervical cancer. HSV-2 can be passed from mother to child during a vaginal birth and cause infant problems and death.

Hepatitis A, B, C, and D can be transmitted via sexual contact or a transfusion with contaminated blood. The virus causes an inflammation of the liver and symptoms that range in severity, including fever, fatigue, abdominal pain, nausea, vomiting, dark urine, light-colored stools, and yellow skin and eyes. Symptoms can be so mild that they go unnoticed and untreated, leading to cirrhosis, cancer of the liver, or death.

Some types of HPV cause genital warts. They are cauliflower-like growths that appear on any part of a woman's vulva, such as the labia, or on the cervix or walls of the vagina. In men they can appear on the penis, foreskin, scrotum, or urethra. Occasionally, they may cause some pain or itching around genital openings. HPV may cause cell changes and therefore has been associated with cervical cancer. The virus is most often transmitted by sexual contact but can be transmitted via contaminated fabrics or objects. In rare cases HPV has been transmitted to infants during birth.

PARASITIC INFECTIONS

There are three parasitic infections or infestations that can be sexually transmitted: trichomoniasis, pediculosis, and scabies. Trichomoniasis, or "trich," is caused by a one-celled animal or protozoan, *Trichomonas vaginalis.* Although some women are asymptomatic, typical symptoms include an itchy burning vulva and a foamy, yellowish and foul-smelling discharge. Men can also be asymptomatic, but they may experience an inflammation of the urethra.

Pediculosis, or "crabs," are pubic lice, *Phthirus publis.* Not only are they transmitted via sexual contact, but also by contact with infested fabrics or objects. Crabs are difficult to see and cause intense itching in hairy pubic areas where the lice burrow into the skin. Scabies, or *Sarcoptes scabiei,* are similar to crabs in that they cause intense itching, but there are visual symptoms such as red lines, welts, and blisters where the mites burrow into the skin. They can also be transmitted via infested fabrics contacting the skin.

CONCLUSION

Approximately 50 STDs have been identified worldwide—only the most common and problematic were reviewed here. Some of those excluded are candidiasis, bacterial vaginosis, HSV-1, chancroid, shigellosis, granuloma inguinale, and lymphogranuloma venereum. The number and variety of STDs may contribute to the difficulty in recognizing specific STD symptoms, making diagnosis more improbable. Considering that some STDs may go undiagnosed and that some are incurable, they are likely to have significant life-long effects throughout our population.

—*Danae E. Roberts*

See also Acquired Immune Deficiency Syndrome (AIDS), Human Immunodeficiency Virus (HIV)

Further Readings and References

AVERT. (2004). *Condoms, history, effectiveness, and testing.* Retrieved from http://www.avert.org/condoms.htm

Centers for Disease Control and Prevention. (2003). *Sexually transmitted disease surveillance, 2002.* Atlanta, GA: U.S. Department of Health and Human Services. Retrieved from http://cdc.gov/std/stats/toc.2002.htm

Communicable Disease Report Weekly. (2003, October 30). Sexually transmitted disease quarterly report: Genital warts and herpes simplex virus infection in the UK. *CDR Weekly, 13*(44). Retrieved from http://www.hpa.org.ul/cdr/PDF files/2003cdr4403.pdf

Edelman, D. (1994). The psychological impact of being diagnosed with genital human papillomavirus. *Dissertation Abstracts International, 55,* 2286 (UMI No. 9434479).

Falvo, D. R. (1994). Risk: Sexually transmitted diseases. *Journal of Applied Rehabilitation Counseling, 25*(1), 43–49.

Fishman, D. M., Lipstitch, M., Hook, E. W., & Goldie, S. J. (2002). Projection of the future dimensions and costs of the genital herpes simplex 2 epidemic in the United States. *Sexually Transmitted Diseases, 29*(10), 608–622.

Frezieres, R. G., Walsh, T. L. W., Nelson, A. L., Clark, V. A., & Coulson, A. H. (1999). Evaluation of the efficacy of a polyurethane condom: Results from a randomized, controlled clinical trial. *Family Planning Perspectives, 31*(2), 81–87.

Lee, J. D., & Craft, E. A. (2002). Protecting one's self from a stigmatized disease . . . once one has it. *Deviant Behavior, 23*(3), 267–299.

Longo, D. J., & Clum, G. A. (1989). Psychosocial factors affecting genital herpes recurrences: Linear vs. mediating models. *Journal of Psychosomatic Research, 33*(2), 161–166.

Moore, S., Rosenthal, D., & Mitchell, A. (1996). *Youth, AIDS and sexually transmitted diseases.* New York: Routledge.

Rathus, S. A., Nevid, J. S., & Fichner-Rathus, L. (2000). *Human sexuality in a world of diversity* (4th ed.). Needham Heights, MA: Allyn & Bacon.

SHORT-TERM MEMORY

The concept of a short-term store has been in existence for many years and is one of the most-researched topics in cognitive science. The importance of short-term memory cannot be overestimated: Nearly every act of cognition—reasoning, planning, problem solving—relies on our ability to store and manipulate information. For instance, imagine you are in the grocery store and need to know whether or not you have enough money for your purchases. If you do not want to take the time to write down all of the prices and add them on paper, you must be able to mentally store all of the prices while you add them together in your head. Although you remember the individual prices long enough to complete the task, you then soon forget them. This type of memory can be distinguished for longer-lasting memories for facts or events.

The study of short-term memory was revolutionized by the experiments of Alan D. Baddeley and colleagues in the 1970s and 1980s. According to their model, short-term or working memory consists of at least two storage buffers: one for visuospatial information and another for verbal information. A unique aspect of their model was its inclusion of a central executive that coordinates the activities of the storage buffers and manipulates information. This newer concept of working memory can be likened to a mental workspace rather than a simple storage device or a conduit into long-term memory. The switch in terminology between short-term memory and working memory reflects this belief in the importance of using this mechanism for performing our mental work.

Much recent short-term memory research has focused on three issues: (1) Are there truly separable stores for different types of information? (2) What is the nature of the central executive? (3) Do individual differences in short-term memory abilities account for different levels of ability to read, plan, and solve problems?

STORAGE

Research suggests at least two distinct storage buffers: one for the verbal information and another for visuospatial information. Much of the evidence for this distinction comes from the logic of double dissociation. According to this logic, two cognitive mechanisms (e.g., verbal and spatial short-term memory) are separate if the task performance is differentially impacted by two different variables. For example, performance on verbal working memory tasks (e.g., remember a set of letters), but not spatial working memory tasks (e.g., remembering a set of locations on a computer screen), is impaired by having to say a syllable or word repeatedly (e.g., "the, the, the") during a memory delay. This is presumably because having to repeat the word or syllable prevents people from silently rehearsing the to-be-remembered letters, a common tactic known as subvocal rehearsal. Conversely, being required to tap a set of computer keys in a spatial pattern interferes with memory for a set of locations in space, but not with memory for a set of letters. Taken together, this set of findings implies that verbal and spatial short-term memory rely on different pools of cognitive resources.

Patricia A. Reuter-Lorenz and Andrea C. Miller used the logic of double dissociation to determine whether verbal and spatial short-term memory rely on different neural mechanisms, by testing patient V. P. on verbal and spatial short-term memory tasks. V. P. had undergone a collosotomy (split-brain) procedure, in which the corpus collosum, the major connecting tract between the two hemispheres, was severed as a treatment for severe epilepsy. Strikingly, Reuter-Lorenz

and Miller found that when the verbal variant of the task was presented to the left hemisphere, performance was markedly superior to when the verbal task was presented to the right hemisphere. The opposite was true when the spatial task was presented to the right hemisphere.

These findings are bolstered by data from neuroimaging and patient studies of the division between verbal and spatial information. For instance, in a positron emission tomography experiment, Edward E. Smith, John Jonides, and Robert A. Koeppe asked participants to perform two variants of an item recognition task. What they found was that the verbal task was mediated largely by left hemisphere neural regions, whereas the spatial task was relatively largely right lateralized.

THE CENTRAL EXECUTIVE

In the original working memory model of Baddeley and Hitch, the central executive was the least developed component, and there has been a great deal of interest in trying to characterize this mechanism. Some have proposed that it coordinates and controls various subparts of the system. Such a conceptualization is consistent with a number of different computational models, such as EPIC by David E. Meyer and David E. Kieras, in that many major architectures contain a mechanism that determines whether goals and subgoals are being met and strategically schedules the initiation of various processes. Others have conceptualized executive function as a collection of processes that serve to manipulate the contents of working memory, including inhibition, attention, and temporal ordering.

INDIVIDUAL DIFFERENCES

One thing that appears to distinguish earlier ideas of short-term memory from working memory is that performance on tasks involving just the short-term storage of information does not predict how well people will perform on higher-order reasoning skills, whereas performance on tasks involving both the simultaneous storage and manipulation of information in memory predicts a host of cognitive skills. For instance, Daneman and Carpenter showed in 1980 that working memory capacity, as defined by the ability to simultaneously store and process information, predicts reading comprehension skill. Working memory capacity also predicts how well people will perform on problem-solving tasks, such as conditional reasoning problems. Thus, it appears that working memory capacity can account for many of the skills that comprise intelligence.

DEVELOPMENT

From a developmental perspective, working memory is critical because it may play a role in learning language, and particularly in vocabulary acquisition. Furthermore, just as working memory capacity can predict performance on higher-order cognitive tasks, working memory ability has been hypothesized to play a role in diverse childhood and adult maladies such as attention deficit hyperactivity disorder, mathematical disabilities, and reading disabilities. Furthermore, children of school age in cultures in which the articulation time to numbers or letters is shorter (e.g., Chinese, as compared to German) show a greater memory capacity earlier in development. This is because verbal memory is language based and limited not just by the number of items, but also by how long it takes to utter them.

Just as important cognitive skills appear to develop with the help of working memory in childhood, working memory declines in older adults appear to be a factor in age-related changes in a range of cognitive tasks. Adults reach their peak working memory capacity in their twenties, conveniently coinciding with the college years for many, then declines steadily over the life span into old age.

SUMMARY AND CONCLUSIONS

As we have seen, short-term, or working, memory is a critical cognitive skill that impacts many acts of cognition. It can be conceptualized as the short-term maintenance and storage of task-relevant information and involves not just passively storing information, but also manipulating information in the service of thought. There are at least two types of working memory, one for verbal information and another for spatial information, as well as a set of processes that either coordinate the buffers or manipulate information—probably both. Working memory is an important concept for developmental psychology because working memory capacity determines reading comprehension and may play a role in language development, particularly in vocabulary acquisition.

—*Christy Marshuetz*

See also Memory Failure

Further Readings and References

Baddeley, A. D. (1986). *Working memory.* Oxford, UK: Clarendon Press.

Baddeley, A. D., Gathercole, S., & Papagno, C. (1998). The phonological loop as a language learning device. *Psychological Review, 105,* 158–173.

Baddeley, A. D., & Hitch, G. J. (1974). Working memory. In G. Bower (Ed.), *Recent advances in learning and motivation* (Vol. III). New York: Academic Press.

Barkley, R. A. (1997). Behavioral inhibition, sustained attention, and executive functions: Constructing a unified theory of ADHD. *Psychological Bulletin, 121,* 65–94.

Daneman, M., & Carpenter, P. A. (1980). Individual differences in working memory and reading. *Journal of Verbal Learning and Verbal Behavior, 19,* 450–466.

Kieras, D. E., & Meyer, D. E. (n.d.). *EPIC: A cognitive architecture for computational modeling of human performance.* Retrieved from http://www.eecs.umich.edu/~kieras/epic.html

Markovitz, H., Doyon, C., & Simoneau, M. (2002). Individual differences in working memory and conditional reasoning with concrete and abstract content. *Thinking & Reasoning, 8,* 97–107.

McLean, J. F., & Hitch, G. J. (1999). Working memory impairments in children with specific arithmetic learning difficulties. *Journal of Experimental Child Psychology, 74,* 240–260.

Orangi, H. (n.d.). *Working memory.* Retrieved from http://coe.sdsu.edu/eet/articles/workingmemory/start.htm

Park, D. C., Polk, T., Mikels, J., Taylor, S. F., & Marshuetz, C. (2001). Cerebral aging: Integration of brain and behavioral models of cognitive function. *Dialogues in Clinical Neuroscience, 3,* 151–165.

Reuter-Lorenz, P. A., & Miller, A. C. (1998). The cognitive neuroscience of human laterality: Lessons from the bisected brain. *Current Directions in Psychological Science, 7,* 15–20.

Smith, E. E., Jonides J., & Koeppe R. A. (1996). Dissociating verbal and spatial working memory using PET. *Cerebral Cortex, 6,* 11–20.

Young, M. L. (2000). *Working memory, language and reading.* Retrieved from http://www.brainconnection.com/topics/?main=fa/memory-language

SHYNESS

Shyness is the term most often used to label feelings of anxiety and inhibition in social situations. Common synonyms include bashfulness, timidity, self-consciousness, reticence, and social anxiety. The experience of shyness typically involves three components. Global feelings of emotional arousal and specific physiological complaints, such as upset stomach, pounding heart, sweating, or blushing define the somatic anxiety component of shyness. Acute public self-consciousness, self-critical thoughts, and worries about being evaluated negatively by others constitute the second, cognitive component of shyness. The third component includes observable behavior such as quietness, cautiousness, awkward body language, avoidance of eye contact, and social withdrawal.

Situations differ in their power to evoke these reactions of social anxiety. Ratings of shyness-eliciting situations reveal that interactions with strangers, encounters requiring assertive behavior, and explicitly evaluative settings such as interviews provoke the strongest feelings of social anxiety. From an evolutionary perspective on emotional development, a moderate amount of wariness regarding strangers and unfamiliar or unpredictable situations has considerable adaptive value. Social anxiety is functional when it motivates preparation and rehearsal for important interpersonal events, and shyness also helps to facilitate cooperative group living by inhibiting individual behavior that is socially unacceptable. Situational shyness as a transitory emotional state appears to be a normal aspect of human development and everyday adult life. For some people, however, shyness is more than a temporary situational response; it occurs with sufficient frequency and intensity to be considered a personality trait. Although some psychologists have argued that the positive connotations of shyness, such as modesty or sensitivity, should be emphasized, it is generally viewed as an undesirable personality characteristic.

In early childhood, shyness is usually manifested as the relative absence or inhibition of normally expected social behaviors. The child appears excessively quiet, with diminished social participation. For shy children, the normal peaks of stranger anxiety (9 months) and separation anxiety (18 months) do not fade away. Shyness is one of the few temperamental traits whose precursors in infancy are often clear. About 15% to 20% of infants typically respond to a new situation or stimulus (e.g., an unfamiliar toy, person, or place) by withdrawing and becoming either emotionally subdued or upset (crying, fussing, and fretting). It has been speculated that this pattern of inhibition to novelty is related to a lower threshold for arousal in sites in the amygdala. Research studies of identical and fraternal twins indicate that the temperamental predisposition for shyness has a substantial genetic component. Infants with this highly reactive temperament in the first year of life are more likely to be wary or fearful of strangers at the end of the second year, and they are also more likely to be described as shy by their kindergarten teachers than are children with an opposite, behaviorally uninhibited temperament.

Temperamental inhibition in infancy does not lead invariably to childhood shyness. Parents who are sensitive to the nature of their inhibited child's temperament, who take an active role in helping the child to develop relationships with playmates, and who facilitate involvement in school activities appear to ameliorate the impact of shyness on the child's subsequent social adjustment. Childhood shyness is a joint product of temperament and socialization experiences within and outside the family. Retrospective reports indicate that 75% of young adults who say they were shy in early childhood continue to identify themselves as shy persons. Equally significant, however, is the fact that about half of shy adults report that they did not become troubled by shyness until they were between the ages of 8 and 14. While about 33% of elementary school–aged children in the United States are shy, the developmental peak for shyness occurs during adolescence, when 60% of the girls and 50% of the boys in seventh and eighth grades identify themselves as shy.

Most of the children who first become shy in later childhood and early adolescence do not have the temperamental predisposition for shyness. Instead, late-developing shyness is usually caused by adjustment problems in adolescent social development. The bodily changes of puberty, the newly acquired cognitive ability to think abstractly about the self and the environment, and the new demands and opportunities resulting from changing social roles combine to make adolescents feel intensely self-conscious and socially awkward. Adolescent self-consciousness gradually declines after age 14, and less than 50% of individuals who first became shy during later childhood and early adolescence still consider themselves to be shy by age 21.

The inability of some adolescents to outgrow late-developing shyness has been linked to several factors. Research on the timing of puberty indicates that early-maturing girls and late-maturing boys suffer more severe social adjustment problems with their peers. Moving to a new neighborhood or school can disrupt the development of social skills, which are most easily practiced in safe and familiar surroundings. Shy adolescents need to experience positive social relationships in order to develop a healthy level of self-esteem. If parents, siblings, teachers, or peers tease and embarrass the shy adolescent, he or she may develop the self-image of being an unworthy and unlikable person. Sex-role socialization puts different pressures on adolescent girls and boys. In the United States, teenage girls experience more symptoms of self-conscious shyness, such as doubts about their attractiveness and worries about what others think of them, whereas teenage boys tend to be more troubled by behavioral symptoms of shyness because the traditional male role requires initiative and assertiveness in social life.

Cultural differences in the prevalence of shyness may reflect the impact of socialization practices. In Israel children tend to be praised for being self-confident and often are included in adult conversations, two factors that may account for the low level of shyness reported by Israelis. In Japan, on the other hand, the incidence of shyness is much higher than in the United States. Japanese culture values harmony and tends to encourage dependency and quiet loyalty to one's superiors. Talkative or assertive individuals risk being considered immature or insincere, and there is a high level of concern about avoiding the shame of failure. All of these values may promote shyness yet also make it a somewhat less socially undesirable personality trait. In contrast, American cultural values that emphasize competition, individual achievement, and material success appear to create an environment in which it is particularly difficult for the shy person to feel secure and worthwhile.

Especially in cultures that value an outgoing, extraverted personality, shyness may be confused with introversion, introspectiveness, or a preference for solitude. Some people prefer to spend time alone rather than with others but also feel comfortable when they are in social settings. Such people are nonanxious introverts, who may be unsociable but are not shy. The opposite of shyness is social self-confidence, not extraversion. The problem for truly shy people is that their anxiety prevents them from participating in social life when they want to or need to. Longitudinal research indicates that when shyness continues into adulthood it can create significant barriers to satisfaction in love, work, recreation, and friendship. As a result, shy adults tend to be lonelier and less happy than those who are not shy. Childhood shyness does not, however, predict psychopathology in adulthood and usually should be considered part of the normal range of individual differences in personality and social behavior.

Nevertheless, extremely shy children may have an increased risk for developing anxiety disorders such as social phobia, and those who appear particularly silent or withdrawn should be screened by a doctor for selective mutism and Asperger's syndrome.

In most cases, the goals of intervention in childhood shyness are essentially proactive and preventative in nature: helping the shy child to achieve better adjustment in his or her current and future social life. It is worth noting that retrospective interviews with painfully shy adults frequently contain complaints that doctors and teachers had ignored their childhood shyness. Advice from psychologists to parents typically emphasizes the need to avoid overprotecting or overindulging shy children. Rather than rushing to soothe away every sign of anxiety, parents should allow the shy child to experience moderate amounts of challenge, frustration, and stress. With emotional support from parents and gradual exposure to new objects, people, and places, the child will have opportunities to learn to cope with his or her own special sensitivity to novelty.

—*Jonathan M. Cheek*

Further Readings and References

Anxiety Disorders Association of America, http://www.adaa.org

Beidel, D. C., & Turner, S. M. (1998). *Shy children, phobic adults: Nature and treatment of social phobia.* Washington, DC: American Psychological Association.

Carducci, B. J. (2003). *The shyness breakthrough: A no-stress plan to help your shy child warm up, open up, and join the fun.* Emmaus, PA: Rodale.

Cheek, J. M., & Krasnoperova, E. N. (1999). Varieties of shyness in adolescence and adulthood. In L. A. Schmidt & J. Schulkin (Eds.), *Extreme fear, shyness, and social phobia: Origins, biological mechanisms, and clinical outcomes* (pp. 224–250). New York: Oxford University Press.

Crozier, W. R. (Ed.). (2001). *Shyness: Development, consolidation, and change.* London: Routledge.

The Shyness Institute, http://www.shyness.com

Zimbardo, P. G., & Radl, S. L. (1999). *The shy child: Overcoming and preventing shyness from infancy to adulthood.* Cambridge, MA: Malor Books.

SIBLINGS

Sibling relationships are those relationships that a person has with a brother or sister. The relationship that develops between siblings is one of the longest-lasting relationships individuals will have throughout their lives. A relationship with a sibling has been established long before one meets a partner or spouse and will last long after one's parents have died. Not only is this one of the longest-lasting relationships, but nearly 80% of children in the United States have at least one sibling. The quality of the relationship between siblings has significant developmental consequences for children and adults. When we speak of quality, we are talking about the type of relationship that exists between siblings with respect to the amount of conflict and rivalry, as well as the amount of affection or closeness in the relationship. Children with warm and friendly sibling relationships are often more caring and share with their brothers and sisters in the early years of childhood and as they reach adolescence can become very effective teachers for their younger siblings. Adult siblings with close ties to their brothers and sisters often use them as confidants and a source of social support. Elderly individuals often report that their relationships with their siblings are some of the last remaining sources of support in their later years.

Conflict and rivalry between siblings is often commonplace, and many parents are concerned about the extent to which their children have disagreements or fight with one another. Although living in a household with squabbling siblings may sometimes be annoying for parents, children and adolescents involved in sibling conflict are learning life-long skills about successful conflict resolution and the fact that others can have perspectives different from their own, skills that will serve them well as they start to establish friendships outside the home. Sibling rivalry and friendly competition between siblings can also foster academic achievement and motivate the children to set higher personal goals and to persevere in meeting those goals.

Even though conflict, warmth, and rivalry can have developmental benefits, this is so only when the conflict or rivalry occurs in the context of a warm and caring relationship between siblings. Sibling relationships characterized by intense rivalries and feelings of hatred toward one another or those involving high levels of aggression and destructive behavior can have devastating consequences for the children involved. Not only do children in such hostile and aggressive relationships risk physical harm at the hands of a more powerful bully, but there are also severe psychological consequences, including lower self-esteem, feelings of loneliness, and in some cases depression. Furthermore, the aggressive exchanges between siblings cannot only escalate conflict and hostile feelings toward one another, but children and adolescents in these destructive relationships often learn that aggression against others is an acceptable means of settling conflict and they can be seen using similar forms of aggression with their peers in school. More aggression and violence occurs between siblings in families than any other family relationship, and as a result, parents may believe that "kids are just being kids" or "all siblings fight" and they will eventually outgrow it. Rather than dismissing physical aggression between siblings as something that all kids do or a stage they are going through, parents would be well advised to intervene early to diminish such dangerous and damaging behavior between their children.

The type of relationship one develops with a sibling starts early in life, often within weeks after the birth of a baby brother or sister. How well children accept a new baby in the house can determine whether or not the siblings eventually develop a close and affectionate relationship as they approach preschool, middle childhood, and adolescence or whether hostility and aggression start to become commonplace as children grow older and enter adulthood. Intense rivalries between adult siblings often have their origins in the early years of childhood. If one's sibling relationship with a sibling in the preschool years was warm and friendly, there's a high likelihood that these children will also have warm and friendly sibling relationships in adolescence.

With the increasing rate of divorce in the United States, stepsiblings and half-siblings have now become commonplace. *Stepsiblings* refers to the typical *Brady Bunch* scenario where children from two different marriages, and therefore two different sets of biological parents, are brought together to live as one family. *Half-siblings* describe the situation where one child is from a previous marriage, but the other child is the product of the current parents' marriage. In other words, the two children share one biological parent, either mother or father, but the second parent is from the previous marriage. When divorced parents remarry, they often worry about how stepchildren will accept the new marriage and how well stepsiblings will get along with one another. Or they worry about how an older sibling will accept the new half-sibling once he or she is born. It is the case that more conflict and rivalry is reported between stepsiblings in remarried families than in nondivorced families, but how parents manage the transition after the divorce and the subsequent remarriage plays a large role in how well children will adjust to their new living arrangement and their new brothers and sisters. Discussions with children and adolescents about what to expect and whether or nor they have fears or concerns about the new family situation should take place. Being realistic with children and talking beforehand about where disagreements might arise can prepare parents and children how to best deal with these potential areas of disagreement before they ever happen.

What parents do with each of their children plays a significant role in how well the siblings will get along with one another. It is the case that some children are more difficult than others and may be more prone to angry outbursts, but parental favoritism, where the parent prefers or loves one child more than the other, is one of the most significant factors in determining the intensity of sibling conflict and rivalry in the family. Children do differ with respect to their ages and their gender, and it is the case that parents may treat older and younger children differently or do different things with their daughters than their sons. Children are individuals, and parents often do things with children based on the child's individual characteristics, thus making it unlikely that parents are treating the children equally. There is a huge difference, though, between disciplining an older child more than a younger child because of age differences and openly expressing more love and affection toward one child to the exclusion of the other child. In the first case, a parent may legitimately expect more mature behavior from an older sibling who should also have a better understanding of right and wrong. In the second instance, the parent, for no apparent reason, shows favoritism toward one child and disfavors the other child. Making clear statements in front of the children that one is a disappointment, can never do anything right, or is clearly not as loveable as the other child not only breeds rivalry and hatred between siblings but also has devastating effects on the disfavored child's psychological well-being and adjustment. Older children and adolescents, however, do understand if a parent treats them differently from a sibling because of age or other personal characteristics and are often not offended by such differences. For instance, a younger sister will understand that her older brother may have the privilege of staying up later than she does without necessarily feeling resentment or hostility toward her parents or her older brother. She, too, will eventually have this privilege as she gets older. But, knowing that her brother always gets more expensive gifts, better opportunities for advancement, or more of dad's time and attention than she ever will may lead that child to wonder whether there may be some failing or deficit on her part that is responsible for such grievous injustice.

Sibling rivalry is a source of concern for many parents, and parents often want to know what they can do to diminish the rivalry and conflict between their children and how they can promote warm and caring sibling relationships. Although there is not much in the way of scientific research looking at sibling relationships, some recommendations as to how to prevent intense sibling rivalry can be made. Besides diminishing parental favoritism, parents must also be willing to discipline both children for misbehavior, but particularly any behaviors that lead to physical harm of one child, destruction of another's property, or verbally abusive and threatening behavior. Sibling conflict can escalate over time, and relations between siblings can deteriorate and become more hostile and aggressive during adolescence without proper intervention by parents to manage such behavior when the children are younger. Parents can also supervise their children's play early on, teaching children not only how to take turns and share, but also how to successfully solve the conflicts that will erupt. Discussing children's feelings at the time of a dispute allows children to see how others are affected by their transgressions, and this discussion can facilitate the development of perspective taking, a moral sense of right and wrong, and a respect and tolerance for others. Demonstrating affection to both children equally while also using age-appropriate discipline to discourage hostile and harmful behaviors between siblings can help ensure that this long-lasting relationship with a brother or sister provides years of emotional and instrumental support throughout their lifetimes.

—*Brenda L. Volling*

Further Readings and References

Aber, L. W., & Yarbroudy, E. (1990). *101 activities for siblings who squabble: Projects and games to entertain and keep the peace.* New York: St. Martins Press.

Brody, G. H. (1996). *Sibling relationships: Their causes and consequences.* Westport, CT: Ablex.

Dunn, J. (2002). *Sibling relationships.* In P. K. Smith & C. H. Hart (Eds.), *Blackwell handbook of childhood social development* (pp. 223–237). Malden, MA: Blackwell.

Faber, A., & Mazlish, E. (1998). *Siblings without rivalry*. New York: Avon Books.

Furman, W., & Lanthier, R. (2002). Parenting siblings. In M. H. Bornstein (Ed.), *Handbook of parenting: Vol. 1: Children and parenting* (2nd ed., pp. 165–188). Mahwah, NJ: Erlbaum.

Goldenthal, P. (1999). *Beyond sibling rivalry: How to help your children become cooperative, caring, and compassionate*. New York: Henry Holt.

Kidshealth. (n.d.). *Sibling rivalry*. Retrieved from http://kidshealth.org/kid/feeling/home_family/sibling_rivalry.html

Stepfamily Association of America, http://www.saafamilies.org/

Volling, B. L. (2003). Sibling relationships. In M. H. Bornstein, L. Davidson, C. L. M. Keyes, K. A. Moore, & the Center for Child Well-being (Eds.), *Well-being: Positive development across the life course* (pp. 205–220). Mahwah, NJ: Erlbaum.

SINGLE-PARENT FAMILY

The U.S. Census Bureau defines single-parent families as those in which the head of household is the only parent present in the home. The parent may be divorced, never married, widowed, or married with an absent spouse. In 2000, single-parent families constituted approximately 27% of all families in the United States. Women are most commonly the head of household in a single-parent family, with 9,969,000 single parent families headed by women, of 12,201,000 single parent families total, in 2002. The number of single-parent family households headed by women increased only slightly between 1998 and 2002, from 9.8 million to about 9.9 million. Single-parent families with men as the head of household increased from 2.1 million in 1998 to approximately 2.3 million in 2002. Overall, the prevalence rate of single-parent families rose from 11.9 million in 1998 to 12.2 million in 2002, as reported by the U.S. Census Bureau.

Because the majority of single-parent households are headed by women, a large amount of research has been conducted on this population. Consequently, relatively few studies have focused on the impact that single-parent families headed by men may have on children.

POVERTY RATES

Roughly 25% of all single-parent family households live below the poverty level. Of the 3.6 million single-parent families living below the poverty level, about 3.2 million of them are headed by women. African American single-parent families headed by women are disproportionately affected by poverty, thus limiting the medical, social, and psychological resources available to children in these families. Some research has found that, controlling for socioeconomic factors, no significant differences exist between single-parent families of color and two-parent families of color with respect to child social skills after accounting for these socioeconomic factors.

EMPLOYMENT EFFECTS

Research focusing on maternal employment in single-parent families has resulted in divergent findings. While numerous studies assert that maternal employment and length of workday, in particular, have adverse effects on children in single-parent families, other studies have found no adverse effects and often positive effects of maternal employment. Recent research focusing on maternal employment status has found it to play a role in children's intellectual functioning and behavior in single-parent families headed by women. Children of mothers who are employed have been found to obtain significantly higher scores on measures of cognitive abilities and achievement. Moreover, these children exhibit fewer externalizing problem behaviors than children of unemployed mothers. However, the beneficial impact of maternal employment may not be due to employment itself, but rather to the financial resources and higher maternal self-esteem associated with being employed. While there remains some controversy as to whether maternal employment actually has a positive impact on children in single-parent families, at the very least, it has not been found to consistently have a negative impact on children.

RISK FACTORS

Certain risk factors have been found to be associated with being raised in a single-parent family versus a two-parent family. Factors such as lower socioeconomic status, greater rates of residential mobility, and lower levels of parental supervision are all linked to a higher risk for delinquency during adolescence. Additionally, research indicates that children from single-parent families are more likely to engage in delinquent activities when they attend school where a greater proportion of students are being raised in single-parent families.

An extensive amount of research has been conducted on parent-child interactions, especially in relation to the mother-child relationship. Due to the high number of maternal-headed single-parent families in the United States, it follows that this type of familial relationship warrants careful examination. Research indicates that, in general, adolescents experience the most severe conflicts with their mothers. Thus, in single-parent families, this discordant relationship may increase a child's risk for engaging in unhealthy behaviors.

PROTECTIVE FACTORS

Recent research has indicated that single-parent families contain many positive elements that had previously been overlooked due to the focus on negative factors associated with them. In fact, many children from single-parent families experience healthy developmental outcomes.

Some factors that serve to protect children growing up in single-parent families from developing delinquent behaviors include positive parental involvement and support; extended family involvement and support; involvement in structured, constructive activities; healthy parental relationships (when parents are divorced or apart); maternal optimism; and healthy psychological well-being of the parent. "Family cohesion" has also been identified by both single-parent families and two-parent families as a strength upon which their family foundations were built, thus recognizing the similarities in perceptions and positive features across these two family structures.

SUMMARY

Single-parent families constitute roughly a quarter of the U.S. family population. While there has been a historical stigma associated with one-parent families— for instance, being characterized by some as a key indication of our society's deterioration—recent research indicates that there are unique strengths associated with this family subtype. Additionally, findings indicate that most children who grow up in this type of family experience healthy, typical development. While research pertaining to delinquent behaviors indicates that children from single-parent families

are at a greater risk for engaging in various types of antisocial behaviors, recent studies have also indicated a number of protective factors associated with positive development and outcomes. Thus, single-parent families are increasingly recognized in research and perceived by the public as a common variation in the array of family structures.

—*Shane R. Jimerson and Sarah M. Woehr*

Further Readings and References

Anderson, A. L. (2002). Individual and contextual influences on delinquency: The role of the single-parent family. *Journal of Criminal Justice, 30*(6), 575–587.

Brody, G. H., McBride Murry, V., Kim, S., & Brown, A. C. (2002). Longitudinal pathways to competence and psychological adjustment among African American children living in rural single-parent households. *Child Development, 73*(5), 1505–1516.

Dworkin, J. B., & Larson, R. (2001). Age trends in the experience of family discord in single-mother families across adolescence. *Journal of Adolescence, 24*, 529–534.

Ford-Gilboe, M. (2000). Dispelling myths and creating opportunity: A comparison of the strengths of single-parent and two-parent families. *Advances in Nursing Science, 23*(1), 41–58.

Kesner, J. E., & McKenry, P. C. (2001). Single parenthood and social competence in children of color. *Families in Society, 82*(2), 136–144.

Larson, R., Dworkin, J., & Gillman, S. (2001). Facilitating adolescents' constructive use of time in one-parent families. *Applied Developmental Science, 5*(3), 143–157.

Parents World, http://www.parentsworld.com/

Single Parent Central, http://www.singleparentcentral.com/

U.S. Census Bureau. (2002). *America's families and living arrangements: March 2002* (Table FG5). Retrieved from http://www.census.gov/population/www/socdemo/hh-fam/cps2002.html

Weinraub, M., Horvath, D. L., & Gringlas, M. B. (2002). Single parenthood. In M. H. Bornstein (Ed.), *Handbook of parenting: Vol. 3: Being and becoming a parent* (2nd ed., pp. 109–140). Mahwah, NJ: Erlbaum.

Youngblut, J. M., Brooten, D., Singer, L. T., Standing, T., Lee, H., & Rodgers, W. L. (2001). Effects of maternal employment and prematurity on child outcomes in single parent families. *Nursing Research, 50*(6), 346–355.

SINGLE PARENTS

The most dramatic change in the structure of the American family over the past 20 years is the increase in single-parent households. While single parenthood due to death of a spouse has remained relatively stable, single parenthood as a choice, single parenthood as a result of teen pregnancy, and single parenthood as a result of divorce have increased dramatically. One in four children is born to a never-married mother. Another 40% of children under the age of 18 will experience parental divorce. More than 27% of all American children currently live in homes headed by single parents. If trends remain consistent from other census data, it will only be a matter of a few years when one third of all children will live with a single parent.

Single parent families are defined as those either headed by a mother or a father, a sole parent, responsible for taking care of herself or himself and a child or children. This includes those created as a result of divorce, abandonment, death, unwed pregnancy, and adoption. In 1970, the total number of single-parent families was slightly fewer than 3.5 million. In 2000, this had quadrupled to 12 million single-parent families. Female-headed single-parent families in 2000 were more than 10 million, while male-headed single-parent families in 2000 were more than 2 million.

There has been much controversy over whether these single-parent families are as healthy as two-parent families for raising children. Past research stated that children from these families were more likely to drop out of school, bear children out of wedlock, and have trouble keeping jobs as young adults. However, we now know, lack of income is the single most important factor in understanding the health of children raised in single-parent households. The latest research finds that, in general, single-parent families are happy, healthy, and well-functioning families, despite the hardships they experience, and that the children of these families learn positive resiliency skills that children of two-parent families do not learn until much later in life.

One of the problems related to understanding single-parent families is that we have stereotyped them into one generic class of people. Yet the single-parent family is dramatically different and faces different developmental challenges based on how that family is formed. Single-parent families fall into three basic structures: single parenthood as a result of death, single parenthood as a result of divorce, and single parenthood as a result of never being married. Whether the single parent is widowed or divorced or never married may be the most important indicator of the quality of life for children in these families. Widowed and divorced single parents have an economic advantage over children living with a never-married single parent. They tend to be older and to have a higher income than never-married single parents. They also tend to have a much stronger support system within their families of origin and within their communities.

Historically, most single-parent families were created by death or desertion of a spouse. The 1950s were the first time that the percentage of single-parent families created by divorce exceeded those created by death. The 1970s ushered in another new trend of unmarried women bearing and raising children by themselves. This trend hit its highest point in 1990, with approximately 20% of white births, 37% of Hispanic births, and 67% of black births to unmarried females. Each particular type of single-parent family provides its own creation of problems and solutions.

The first type, single parenthood as a result of death, involves not only the creation of a new family structure regarding power and boundaries but also coping with issues regarding mourning the loss of a loved one. Even when death is expected, it is always a shock. Single parents must deal not only with their loss of a partner, but must also be able to help their children communicate feelings concerning the loss of a parent. Often these parents have a difficult time attending to the needs of their children because of their own depression and lack of coping skills. It is recommended that these parents find a local community group such as Parents Without Partners to enable them to work through their mourning. Only then will they be able to assist their children through their mourning process. After a time of mourning, the family must move on to the readjustment stage. A big part of this is reassigning tasks and responsibilities, both functional and emotional, to the remaining members of the family and then redefining their identity as a single-parent family.

The second type of single-parent family is the one created as the result of divorce. In 2000, 50% of white, non-Hispanic, single-mother-headed households were the result of divorce. Among black women, 17% were due to a divorce. Divorce is one of the most complicated forms of single-parent families because of the multifaceted relationship that exists between the absent parent and the custodial parent. The loss suffered through a divorce, for both children and parents, is an issue of great significance, regardless of financial or emotional support. It typically takes up to

3 years to adjust to the new single-parent household, during which time there may be frequent moves, which brings additional complications of adjustment for the children. If the children have to change neighborhoods, change schools, and change friends, their lives can be totally disrupted. The fewer changes the new single parent can make during this initial time, the easier it will be for the children. The custodial parent may experience the stressors of rebuilding financial and social networks, with the most stressful time being the first year after the divorce. The parent must also cope with his or her own feelings of anger and resentment toward the parent who has left. Many parents will turn to their children for comfort during this time and will use the children as a sounding board to verbalize their resentment toward the absent parent. This can create a situation in which the children feel caught in the middle, being asked to relay messages between the two parents. This can be devastating for these children. It can affect their school functioning, create conflict with friends, and destroy normal developmental childhood task accomplishments. If the single parent is having difficulty adjusting to his or her divorce, it is recommended that he or she seek a marriage and family therapist for counseling. The American Association for Marriage and Family Therapy has a Web site that can locate therapists throughout the United States and Canada.

Never-married single parents is the third category of single-parent families. This category can be further divided into single parenthood by intent and those by accident such as teen pregnancy. Never-married single-parent families are the fastest growing segment of single parents, especially among black females. In 2000, never-married single mothers accounted for 30% of white, non-Hispanic single-female-headed households, while they accounted for 65% of black single-female-headed households. One reason that has been given for the high percentage of black never-married mothers is the lack of available black males as marriage partners. It is estimated that one in every three black males is involved with the justice system. An unfortunate aspect of this never-married type of single parent is that she usually shoulders the total responsibility financially and emotionally for raising the children. Single never-married mothers in reality are not as TV or the movies would portray them. There is a new organization called Mothers Outside of Marriage (MOMs) that provides education and information for never-married women. There is also a Web site,

UnwedAmerica.com, that provides linkages between unmarried mothers to assist in providing a much needed support system.

Single families, whether by death, by divorce, or by intent, are different, based on whether the single parent is a mother or a father. Single fathers can typically provide greater economic resources for their children, while single mothers often provide greater interpersonal resources such as attention and emotional support. Female-headed single-parent families have historically been the norm, making up approximately 85% of all single-parent families. Therefore, most of the information we know about how these families function is related to mothers raising their children. Thirty-four percent of single mother–headed households live below the poverty level, while only 16% of father-headed households live in poverty. Poverty increases stress in the single-parent family due to the inability to attain simple everyday needs such as food, housing, and child care. Employment of these single mothers is correlated to better health and to more positive self-esteem for the mother. However, because women are paid less than their male counterparts and because the professions available to them are lower-paying professions, these families are still likely to be in poverty.

In comparison with married mothers, single mothers are more socially isolated, receive less emotional and parental support, and have more unstable social networks. Financial strain is one of the strongest predictors of depression in single mothers. Higher levels of depression are predictive of more punitive disciplining of children, less parental nurturance, and increased unhappiness in their parenting role. Violence and abuse are also associated with mother-headed single-parent families who live in poverty. Single mothers in poverty are caught up in a vicious cycle of hopelessness and despair, which is detrimental to both them and their children. Better wages, better access to health insurance, work environments that are flexible, mandatory child support payments such as wage withholdings, and public preschool or day care would assist in breaking this cycle of poverty for mother-headed single-parent families.

Father-headed single-parent families have increased dramatically over the past 10 years. One advantage that single fathers have is that they usually have access to more than twice the financial resources of women. This allows the father to utilize caretakers to relieve him when he chooses to create less role strain and stress over his parenting role. Fathers as single parents express confidence in their role; however, because mothers have been viewed as the gatekeepers for their children, few fathers fight for custody of their children.

Single fathers typically fall into two groups: white, middle-class divorced men or low-income men and men of color who may not have ever married the mother. White middle-class men typically have a strong familial support system and have access to resources to assist them in their role as a single parent. They typically have gone to court to fight for the custody of their children. The only negative that these fathers report is that being the primary caregiver for his children will often force him to take a less dominant role in his movement up the career ladder.

Low-income men and men of color often become single parents by default and are stressed by taking on the full-time, single-parenting role. They report they became parents because of the mother's lack of interest in parenting, the child's removal from the mother's household because of abuse or neglect, or the child actively sought to live with the father. Overall, these fathers report feeling ill prepared to assume sole parental responsibility. These men are more likely than most demographic groups to experience incarceration, crime, unemployment, poor health, and homelessness. These men are likely to rely on relatives and fictive kin for social and economic support. These fathers report a lack of support from public aid and feel they are questioned as to their intentions of being a single parent. However, despite their reluctance to become single fathers, these fathers grow to enjoy the role. Most will then fight to continue their role if the mother comes to reclaim their child.

There are both challenges and strengths that result from single parenting. As stated previously, the single most stressful challenge experienced by single-parent families is poverty. Thirty-four percent of single-mother-headed households and 16% of single-father-headed households live below the poverty level. Higher rates of poverty among women can be attributed to higher earning power of men, lack of child support payments, lack of affordable child care, and poor public assistance programs. Living with a family member can help with some of these problems, such as providing child care and economic support.

One of the biggest internal challenges of the single-parent family lies with defining boundaries and roles.

The democratic nature of the single-parent household can blur needed boundary distinctions between parent and child. Without these appropriate boundaries, chaotic and confusing interactions can occur, which is not to the benefit of the parent or the children. Another challenge that goes along with boundaries is role delineation. Although role flexibility is what often enables these families to survive, it can also create undue stress on particular family members. Sons, particularly for single moms, can be placed in the "man of the house" role, while daughters may be placed in the peer, confidante role. Both of these roles are asking the child to be the emotional support of the parent, which can be detrimental in the long run.

Although children of single parents have increased responsibility in household and family obligations, this can lead to the positive aspects of increased autonomy and self-esteem. According to some current research, children of one-parent households are no more likely to experience emotional and physical problems than children of two-parent households, if financial stressors are reduced.

One strength of single-parent families is that they tend to be more democratic. Because these families usually have an informal way of relating to each other, they tend to take everyone's view into account before making decisions. Another strength is that these children learn at an early age how to be creative because they live with fewer resources. They realize the value of time and money and are therefore more protective of these.

Recent assessment of single-parent homes finds that most provide the structure, values, and nurturance that their children need, despite the hardships they experience and the bad press they receive. Their homes are not "broken," their lives are not miserable, and both parent and children thrive while managing the additional roles required of them. Unfortunately, rather than focusing on these strengths, American society has often chosen to concentrate on the problems. We know that it takes a village to raise a child, and nowhere is this truer than in single-parent families. Communities must praise single parents for their strengths and assist them with their needs. This is our obligation to our children.

—Mary Ann Adams, Jeff Hinton, and Patricia Sims

See also Divorce, Single-Parent Family

Further Readings and References

Amato, P. R. (2000). Diversity within single-parent families. In D. H. Demo, K. R. Allen, & M. A. Fine (Eds.), *Handbook for family diversity* (pp. 149–172). New York: Oxford University Press.

American Association for Marriage and Family Therapy, http://www.aamft.org

Anderson, J. (1990). *The single mother's book: A practical guide to managing your children, career, home, finances, and everything else.* Atlanta: Peachtree.

Cooperative Parenting and Divorce, http://www.cooperative parenting.com

Dickerson, B. (1995). *African American single mothers: Understanding their lives and families.* Sage Series on Race and Ethnic Relations, Vol. 10. Thousand Oaks, CA: Sage.

Dowd, N. E. (1997). *In defense of single-parent families.* New York: University Press.

Ellison, S. (2001). *The courage to be a single mother: Becoming whole again after divorce.* San Francisco: Harper.

Ginsberg, B. G., & Israeloff, R. (2002). *50 wonderful ways to be a single-parent family.* Oakland, CA: New Harbinger.

Mattes, J. (1997). *Single mothers by choice: A guidebook for single women who are considering or have chosen motherhood.* New York: Three Rivers Press.

Mothers Outside of Marriage (MOMs), http://www.singlemothers.org

Parents Without Partners, http://www.parentswithoutpartners.org

Single Parents Association, http://singleparents.org

Sugarman, S. D. (2003). Single parent families. In M. A. Mason, A. Skolnick, & S. D. Sugarman (Eds.), *All our families: New policies for a new century* (pp. 117–143). New York: Oxford University Press.

SKINNER, B. F. (1904–1990)

In establishing a natural science of behavior, developing a philosophy of that science, and advancing their implications for improving the human condition, Burrhus Frederic (B. F.) Skinner became the most eminent psychologist of the 20th century. He was born and raised in Susquehanna, Pennsylvania, as American Progressivism and modernism neared their height. He received an AB in English from Hamilton College in 1926 and a PhD in psychology from Harvard University in 1931. He afterward held positions at Harvard (1931–1936), the University of Minnesota (1936–1945), Indiana University (1945–1947), and Harvard again (1947–1974), retiring as Professor Emeritus in 1974, but continuing to work.

Skinner tried making his mark first as a writer, but writing failed him as a means for understanding human behavior. So, he turned to psychology. With mechanical skills and a belief that understanding was based in empirical research, not contemplation, he invented methods and apparatus (e.g., the "Skinner box") with which he discovered the basic principles of voluntary behavior, notably its selection by consequences (e.g., reinforcement). In synthesizing his methods and results with Pavlov's, he established a science of behavior (*The Behavior of Organisms*, 1938). In adopting and adapting the contributions of Bacon and Mach, he derived a philosophy of the science—radical behaviorism.

While making still further discoveries and advances (e.g., shaping, rule-governed behavior), Skinner extended his science to human behavior. He described an experimental approach to intentional communities (*Walden Two*, 1948); offered behavioral accounts of human action (*Science and Human Behavior*, 1953; *Verbal Behavior*, 1957); applied his science to education and aging (*The Technology of Teaching*, 1968; *Enjoy Old Age*, 1983); naturalized ethical, social, and political philosophy (*Beyond Freedom and Dignity*, 1971); and founded a system of psychology known as behavior analysis. Behavior was its subject matter, not just what it studied; biology was context for environmental contingencies; and mind was public and private behavior in everyday context (*About Behaviorism*, 1974).

The behavior analysis of human development was fully influenced by Skinner's work. Bijou applied the style of Skinner's science to the analysis of child behavior (e.g., discriminative responding); Gewirtz extended its content to social development (e.g., attachment); and Baer provided an age-irrelevant concept of development and behavioral cusps as alternatives to age- and stage-based theories. Skinner's contributions extend across the human life span, with their most significant impact today being in the development and validation of empirically based treatments for atypical development (e.g., autism).

—*Edward K. Morris*

See also Applied Behavior Analysis, Operant Conditioning

Further Readings and References

B. F. Skinner Foundation, http://www.bfskinner.org/

Skinner, B. F. (1938). *The behavior of organisms: An experimental analysis.* New York: Appleton-Century.

Skinner, B. F. (1953). *Science and human behavior*. New York: Macmillan.

Skinner, B. F. (1999). *Cumulative record* (Definitive ed., V. G. Laties & A. C. Catania, Eds.). Cambridge, MA: B. F. Skinner Foundation.

SLEEP

Sleep: We all do it, we all need it. An individual who lives to be 75 will have slept an estimated 22 to 23 years of that time (more than 200,000 hours).

WHAT IS SLEEP?

Sleep is defined in the laboratory by the use of three standard psychophysical measures: electroencephalography (EEG), which records brain wave activity; electrooculography (EOG), which records eye movements; and electromyography (EMG), which measures chin muscle activity, giving an indication of muscle tonus. Information from these instruments indicates sleep and sleep stages. During periods of wakefulness, the EEG pattern shows two basic types of activity. Beta waves occur when the individual is mentally alert and active. This is characterized by low-amplitude, irregular, high-frequency waves (13+ Hz). Alpha waves occur when an individual is resting quietly and is particularly evident when the eyes are closed. Alpha waves are high amplitude, more regular, and lower frequency (8–12 Hz).

There are two types of sleep: non–rapid eye movement (NREM) and rapid eye movement (REM) sleep. Within NREM sleep there are four stages usually recognized in humans.

Stage 1 is the transitional phase between full wakefulness and sleep. EEG activity is theta waves (3–7 Hz). In normal sleepers, stage 1 lasts from 30 seconds to about 7 minutes. During this period, reactivity to outside stimuli is diminished. Mental processes change during stage 1 as thoughts begin to drift, thinking is no longer reality oriented, and short dreams often develop. This is usually accompanied by slow, rolling eye movements. Nevertheless, many people subjectively feel that they are awake during stage 1.

Stage 2 continues to show theta waves and is marked by the appearance of EEG sleep spindles (bursts of 12–14 Hz activity lasting 0.5 second to 2 seconds) and k complexes (well delineated, slow negative EEG deflections that are followed by a positive component). This is the first bona fide sleep stage, and any thoughts during this stage are short, mundane, and fragmented. Slow-rolling eye movements cease when stage 2 begins.

Stage 3 is a transition from lighter sleep to deeper sleep and is distinguished by delta waves (0.5 to 2 Hz), which are high amplitude and very slow, mixed in with theta waves. At least 20% to 50% of an epoch (30-second time frame) must be dominated by delta to be stage 3.

Stage 4 indicates delta waves are present in 50% of the epoch. This is the deepest sleep.

REM sleep EEG patterns resemble those of stage 1 sleep, except that sawtooth waves are often seen. Rapid eye movements and atonia are the physiological characteristic of this sleep stage. Atonia is similar to a paralysis so the sleeper cannot act out dreams. In about 80% of awakenings from REM sleep, people recall dreams, whereas 5% of NREM awakenings result in full-fledged dream reports. In 60% to 80% of NREM awakenings, the sleepers can recall some thought-like fragments.

After going to bed, a sleeper first passes through a stage of relaxed wakefulness, characterized by alpha waves. Later the sleeper passes through stage 1 and into stage 2. Gradually descending deeper into sleep, most young adults enter delta sleep (stages 3 and 4) within 30 to 45 minutes after sleep onset. Depending on the sleeper's age, delta sleep may last from a few minutes up to an hour, then the sleeper "backtracks" to stage 2. About 70 to 90 minutes after sleep onset, the first REM period of the night occurs. It usually lasts about 5 minutes and it is by far the least intense REM period of the night, both in terms of the physiological manifestations of REM sleep and the psychological intensity of dreams. Children frequently do not have this first REM period. Most people cycle through the stages four to six times in a night with approximately a 90-minute cycle (children have a 60-minute cycle). As the night progresses, we spend less and less time in delta sleep. Early in the night, sleep is dominated by delta sleep, whereas early in the morning we tend to alternate between REM and stage 2. As the night progresses, REM periods become more intense, both physiologically and psychologically. The average night for an adult is approximately 5% stage 1, 45% to 50% stage 2, 7% stage 3, 13% stage 4, and 25% to 30% REM.

Our sleep habits change throughout our lifetime. A newborn typically sleeps approximately 16.5 hours per 24-hour period. This is typically polyphasic sleep in that the infant is accumulating the 16.5 hours over several sleep periods throughout the day. By 1 month the infant is averaging 15 hours per 24-hour period and 14 hours by 6 months. By the time children turn 2 they are averaging closer to 10 hours per 24 hours, and by the age of 10 the average is just over 9 hours. During this time period, children become monophasic sleepers, getting their sleep in one consolidated, culturally accepted time frame (nighttime). At 18, the average adult is sleeping approximately 7 to 8 hours and continues this pattern into his or her sixties. By the time an individual turns 70, sleep time averages closer to 6.5 hours, and we see a polyphasic sleep emerging again. One of the major changes seen in the stages of sleep across the life span is the amount of time spent in REM and delta sleep (stages 3 and 4). The average newborn will spend close to 50% of the sleep time in REM, which decreases to 25% to 30% in childhood to about 20% or less after puberty. The amount of delta sleep steadily decreases from childhood to old age.

SLEEP DISORDERS

It is not uncommon for things go wrong with our sleep. Next to the common cold, sleep disorders are the most common health complaint. Sleep disorders are typically divided into four categories: disorders of initiating and maintaining sleep (i.e., insomnia), disorders of excessive somnolence (i.e., narcolepsy), disorders of the sleep-wake schedule (i.e., jet lag), and dysfunctions associated with sleep, sleep stages, or partial arousals (parasomnias—i.e., sleepwalking).

It is common for everyone to experience insomnia at some point in their lives. Insomnia in general means that you feel tired but you have trouble going to sleep or you can go to sleep but cannot sleep through the night. There are many causes of insomnia, with the most likely culprit being stress. There are many over-the-counter sleep aides that typically make the individual feel more relaxed, which makes it easier to fall asleep.

Narcolepsy refers to the disorder in which the individual suddenly falls into several minutes of REM sleep from an active waking state. This is very dramatic because it is accompanied by the atonia found during the REM period. Therefore, the individual literally collapses and remains immobile until a short period after awakening.

Sleep apnea is more common. Individuals suffering from insomnia have difficulty breathing once they have fallen asleep. After falling asleep individuals stop breathing for a short period. The breathing stop triggers these individuals to awaken for a gasp of air, and then they go back to sleep. They usually do not remember the awakenings during the night, but they do report being very tired during the day due to a lack of good, consolidated sleep during the night.

Sleepwalking (somnambulism) and sleep talking (somniloquy) usually occur during stage 4 sleep and not during REM, as most people believe. The normal atonia of REM prevents these events from occurring at that time. These are also more common in children and are typically outgrown.

DREAMING

Dreaming is an intriguing area to all of us. Do all people dream? Do our dreams have meaning? Research suggests that all people dream; if awakened from sleep when the EEG pattern suggests a REM period, the individual will report a dream. Instead of a distinction between dreamers and nondreamers, the distinction seems to be between recallers and nonrecallers (those that remember and those that do not). As for the role of those dreams, there are many theories explaining why we dream, some of which also try to explain the content of our dreams. Many theories look at explaining dreaming as a way for the individual to examine what is happening in their daily lives; the content is affected by the stressors and life events we are trying to deal with each day. Some researchers speculate that dreaming is a by-product of random activity in the brain during the REM stage of sleep and the "storyline" is determined by events or thoughts an individual has had. Others speculate that dreaming is a way of "cleaning house" and ridding the mind of unnecessary clutter. Finally, some suggest it is a time of memory consolidation. Why do we have so many conflicting theories of why we dream? It is a very difficult question to answer and a very difficult phenomenon to study.

SUMMARY

Sleep is an essential aspect of our daily lives, yet still remains somewhat of a mystery.

—Jo Ellen Meerdink

See also Apnea

Further Readings and References

Borbely, A. (1986). *Secrets of sleep*. New York: Basic Books.

Ellman, S. J., & Antrobus, J. (1991). *The mind in sleep*. New York: Wiley.

Empson, J. (2002). *Sleep & dreaming* (3rd ed.). New York: Palgrave.

Foulkes, D. (1982). *Children's dreams: Longitudinal studies*. New York: Wiley.

Hauri, P. (1982). *The sleep disorders*. Kalamazoo, MI: Upjohn.

Hobson, J. A. (1988). *The dreaming brain*. New York: Basic Books.

Moorcroft, W. H. (1993). *Sleep, dreaming, & sleep disorders: An introduction* (2nd ed.). Lanham, MD: University Press of America.

The Sleep Well, http://www.stanford.edu/~dement

Webb, W. B. (1992). *Sleep: The gentle tyrant*. Bolton: Anker.

SMELL

Olfaction, also known as the sense of smell, is important for enjoying food and life, detecting danger (smoke, natural gas leak, rotten food), and communicating social information.

The olfactory receptor genes constitute the largest gene family in vertebrates. Humans have a total of about 350 functional olfactory receptor genes, which are used to detect thousands of different odors. (By contrast, only three photoreceptor genes are involved in making color discriminations.) The study of olfaction is a burgeoning field, albeit still at its early stage. It was not until 1991 that the family of olfactory receptors was first discovered. For this work, Linda Buck and Richard Axel were awarded the Nobel Prize in Medicine in 2004.

The molecular mechanism of olfactory processing is a work in progress. We do know that olfactory receptors bind to odorant molecules and relay the information along the axons of the olfactory neurons to the glomeruli in the olfactory bulb. From there, the information is projected to the areas of the brain involved in processing odor association and discrimination, as well as emotion and memory. These areas include the anterior olfactory nucleus, the amygdalae, the olfactory tubercle, the piriform and periamygdaloid cortical areas, and the rostral entorhinal cortex.

Olfactory learning occurs prenatally. The anatomical and physiological structure of the olfactory system is fully developed in utero, by about 28 gestational weeks. In many altricial animals, olfaction-based mother-infant recognition is essential for the survival of the infant. Olfaction-based mother-infant recognition is also reported in humans. Human newborns as early as 3 days of age orient more toward the smell of their own amniotic fluid over that of an unfamiliar mother. Similarly, newborns orient more toward the breast and underarm smell of their own mother over that of an unfamiliar lactating woman. Olfactory learning continues after birth. A 30-minute exposure to a novel odor (e.g., cherry) minutes after birth can lead to increased orientation toward the exposed odor tested 3 days later.

Hedonic preferences for odors appear to be similar in neonates and adults. Newborns less than 1 day old display facial expressions similar to those of adults to pleasant and unpleasant odors. Similar conclusions apply to children between 1 and 5 years of age, although hedonic differences with regard to specific odors have also been reported.

Olfactory performance can be influenced by a combination of experiential, cognitive, and biological factors. Across odors, absolute olfactory sensitivity threshold is similar in children and young adults. Odor identification, however, is often found to be poorer in children than in adults, possibly due to differences in experience. As early as in one's thirties, olfactory performance can start to decline. The decline becomes pronounced as people reach their sixties and beyond. Olfactory deficit has been reported in almost every major affective disorder and neurodegenerative disease. Research suggests that olfactory deficit used in conjunction with other biological markers may serve as a useful predictor of Alzheimer's disease and other cognitive disabilities. Women in general are better at naming, identifying, and discriminating among smells than men, although their absolute olfactory threshold per se does not appear to differ. Interestingly, women of childbearing age improved significantly in their absolute threshold to certain odors after repeated testing; no such improvement was seen in men of the same age, in postmenopausal women and senior men, or in prepubertal girls and boys.

There is evidence that olfaction plays a role in genetic fitness and interpersonal attractions. Women can sniff out genetic compatibility, and prefer the smell of T-shirts worn by men who are genetically compatible to themselves. Both men and women reported olfactory information as important in mate choice. Chemical signals of sex-specific steroid have been shown to produce gender-specific activations in the brain, as well as impacting on autonomic nervous system responses, and on self-reported mood.

—Denise Chen

See also Sensory Development

Further Readings and References

Dalton, P. (2002). Olfaction. In H. Pashler & S. Yantis (Eds.), *Steven's handbook of experimental psychology. Vol. 1. Sensation and perception* (3rd ed., pp. 691–746). New York: Wiley.

Doty, R. L. (2001). Olfaction. *Annual Review of Psychology, 52,* 423–452.

Schaal, B., Soussignan, R., & Marlier, L. (2003). Olfactory cognition at the start of life: The perinatal shaping of selective odor responsiveness. In C. Rouby, B. Schaal, D. Dubois, R. Gervais, & A. Holley (Eds.), *Olfaction, taste, and cognition* (pp. 421–440). Cambridge, UK: Cambridge University Press.

SMILING

Infant smiles are a prototypical expression of early joy. They are a window on the development of positive emotion. Smiles not only communicate positive engagement and happiness, they also elicit positive engagement and happiness in those around the infant (Figure 1). This interactive process of being positively engaged with another may be part of how joy and social competence develop. Early smiles also help to predict later development.

PREDICTION

Infant smiles—particularly smiles in response to ambiguous stimuli—tell us about how infants will develop. Four-month-olds who smile more in response to a mobile show a more exuberant temperamental style at 4 years when they are more likely to talk and engage with peers. Infant smiling in response to a brief period of parental nonresponsivity—when the parent stops normal play to pose a "still-face"—may index a certain emotional resilience. In comparison with infants who did not smile, 6-month-old infants who smile during the still-face are more likely to be securely attached at 12 months. Their parents also perceive them as having fewer externalizing behaviors

such as being loud and rough than infants who did not smile during the parental still-face. Infants who smile when the going gets rough appear to develop socially appropriate relationships. But exactly what is a smile?

WHAT IS SMILING AND HOW DOES IT DEVELOP?

The zygomatic major muscle pulls the corners of the lips upward and sideways to form a smile. Newborn infants typically smile during states of active sleep, although infrequent smiles occur in non-sleep states as well. These early smiles sometimes have a relatively mature form, but occur against a backdrop of frequent lip and mouth movements. Through 1 month of age, smiles often occur during states of drowsiness when they are elicited by high-pitched tones. Blind infants also develop smiling during this period. After 1 month, smiles among sighted infants are increasingly elicited by visual stimuli such as gazing at a face or an image of a face. These smiles are thought to occur when the infant experiences a sudden relaxation in cognitive tension related to recognizing the visual stimulus.

It might seem advantageous for newborn infants to gaze at their parents and smile at them shortly after birth. But this activity—known as social smiling—does not develop until the second month of life. Social smiling signals the infant's active, positive participation in the relationship. Social smiling at 2 to 6 months of age is often studied during face-to-face play with a parent (Figure 1). The development of infant smiling in interaction involves both changes in the timing of smiles and in the form of the smiles themselves.

The Timing of Smiles

In early interaction, infants tend to smile (often repeatedly) while gazing continuously at their parent. The infant's positive affect, represented by the smile, appears to be dependent on continual visual contact with the parent. At 3 to 6 months of age, infant smiling becomes less dependent on the parent. Infants are more likely to initiate smiles while the parent is neither smiling nor vocalizing. Infants continue to smile during a gaze at the parent but become more likely to gaze away from the parent during the course of the smile. This suggests that infants are increasingly

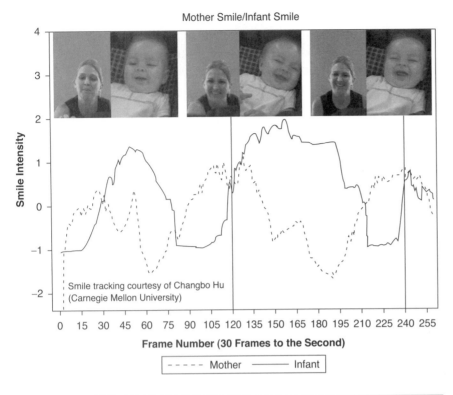

Mother Smile/Infant Smile

Smile tracking courtesy of Changbo Hu
(Carnegie Mellon University)

Frame Number (30 Frames to the Second)

- - - - - Mother ———— Infant

Figure 1   Social Smiling During Face-to-Face Play

controlling their own positive emotion by exercising control over both the onsets and offsets of their own smiles.

During face-to-face interactions, infant smiles are often the high point of play and may be avidly sought after by the infant's parents, relatives, and friends. Parents tend to respond to the infant's smile with a smile of their own. A parent smile makes the infant smile more likely, but certainly does not guarantee that the infant will smile. Paradoxically, infants will be more likely to smile if they are allowed time to not smile. When playing with infants, it is important to be alert to the infant's timing. Infants need time to disengage, turn away, and then look back at the person they are playing with.

The Form of Smiles and the Intensity of Positive Emotion

Infant smiles appear to be part of a process of feeling and expressing positive emotion. Infant smiles tend to occur in response to situations expected to elicit positive emotion such as peek-a-boo games. Smiles are recognized as expressions of positive emotion (even

among infants with serious facial deformities). Some smiles, however, are more joyful and positive than others. Infant smiles that involve the raising of the cheeks around the eyes—the Duchenne smile, a smile of joy in adults—involve patterns of left frontal brain activity thought to be associated with joyful engagement. Infant smiles involving mouth opening also seem to involve particularly strong joy and arousal.

Smiles that involve both mouth opening and cheek raising involve the strongest smiling actions. These smiles are perceived by adults (including the parents of young infants) as more emotionally positive than other smiles. They also are more likely than other smiles to occur when the infant is gazing at its smiling parent. This likelihood grows as infants approach 6 months of age. So the form of infant smiles as well as their timing changes with development. Just as infants exercise more control over when they smile at 3 to 6 months of age, they also become more capable of using very intense smiles to participate in highly arousing social situations.

Vocalizations and laughter are another index of emotional intensity. When a vocalization occurs with a smile, it tends to begin during the smile and end before the smile finishes. Laughter is a smile-linked vocalization that becomes more common at 4 to 12 months of age, when it may signify the most intense positive emotion. Smiles and laughter accompany both physically stimulating games such as tickling (which is similar to the play-aggression games of nonhuman primates) and visual or psychologically stimulating games such as peek-a-boo. Infants in the first year of life take an increasingly active role in games like these and, more generally, in all types of interaction. This increasingly evident agency might be seen as the infant's smiles and laughs as the infant, rather than the mother, uncovers the mother's hands from the mother's face in a game of peek-a-boo.

Through 6 months of age, infant smiles reflect here-and-now emotional interchange with a partner.

By 12 to 15 months, infants are intentionally communicating to the partner about objects. How does this development occur? Anticipatory smiling—in which infants smile at an object and then gaze at an adult while continuing to smile—may be the first step. Anticipatory smiling rises sharply at 8 to 10 months of age. Anticipatory smiles seem to communicate that the infant wants to share with the adult a funny experience the infant had with a toy. These may be among the first types of communicative reference in which the infant seems to be referring to an object or experience by expressing something like, "That was a funny toy, wasn't it?"

Theorists like Alan Sroufe see smiling as a response to tension reduction, a type of arousal regulation linked to a decrease in heart rate. This helps explain similarities in a young infant's smiling response to a relatively unfamiliar face and an older infant's smiling response to a mother walking like a penguin. Both involve tension in trying to understand an event, and then sudden relaxation as the event is interpreted as having safe, familiar, and interesting elements. This interpretation is similar to the idea that joy and smiles arise when a desired goal is attained faster than anticipated. One difficulty with these ideas is that arousal is hard to measure (heart rate is sensitive to many factors) and that young infants often do not have clear goals. It is possible, however, that even in the pell-mell of play, infants are responding to interesting and arousing events that the infant has a role in creating. The infant may smile and laugh as part of the realization that these events, though arousing, are safe and part of larger patterns that the infant is in the process of interactively creating with a partner.

Both smiles and the joyful processes to which they are linked rise and fall in time. It is thought that at a moment-to-moment level, infant and parent are continuously communicating, sharing, and creating emotional information. Specifically, infant expressions of joys are mirrored and intensified by the parent, and the infant responds to this intensification with either intensified engagement or disengagement. New developments in computer vision are allowing researchers such as Jeffrey Cohn to explore these real-time interactive dynamics (Figure 1). Computer vision and other automated tools for measuring smiles will allow researchers to understand how infants and parents create joyful moments together. They will also shed light on differences between infants and parents in how they respond to one another emotionally through smiles.

—*Daniel Messinger*

See also Infancy, Social Development

Further Readings and References

Automated Face Analysis Project, http://www-2.cs.cmu.edu/~face/index2.htm

Fogel, A., Nelson-Goens, G. C., Hsu, H., & Shapiro, A. F. (2000). Do different infant smiles reflect different emotions? *Social Development, 9*(4), 497–522.

Fox, N., & Davidson, R. J. (1988). Patterns of brain electrical activity during facial signs of emotion in 10 month old infants. *Developmental Psychology, 24*(2), 230–236.

Messinger, D. S. (2002). Positive and negative: Infant facial expressions and emotions. *Current Directions in Psychological Science, 11*(1), 1–6.

Oster, H. (2003). Emotion in the infant's face: Insights from the study of infants with facial anomalies. *Annals of the New York Academy of Sciences, 1000*, 197–204.

Sroufe, L. A. (1995). *Emotional development: The organization of emotional life in the early years.* New York: Cambridge University Press.

Venezia, M., Messinger, D. S., Thorp, D., & Mundy, P. (2004). Timing changes: The development of anticipatory smiling. *Infancy, 6*(3), 397-406.

SOCIAL ANXIETY DISORDER

Until recently, Social Anxiety Disorder (SAD) was referred to as social phobia. The label of phobia, and the inclusion of SAD among the subtypes of specific phobia, created the false impression that pathology based on social apprehension was less severe than other anxiety disorders. Mounting evidence shows that SAD is a serious and debilitating disorder that frequently leads to social, occupational, and education disability, as well as serious correlates such as secondary mood disorders and substance abuse.

The *Diagnostic and Statistical Manual of Mental Disorders* defines SAD along several dimensions:

- Persistent fear of one or more social situations. The fear is of potential embarrassment and/or rejection.
- Exposure to the feared situation virtually always leads to anxiety (which may be described as a panic attack).
- The individual recognizes the excessive and unreasonable nature of the fear.

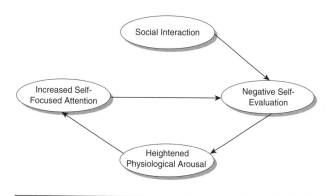

Figure 1   Automatic Negative Self-Evaluations in Social Anxiety Disorder

- Social situations are avoided.
- Significant impairment of functioning due to avoidance of social situations.
- Symptoms are not due to the effects of a substance or medical condition.

While the vast majority of people may report occasions of anxiety in social situations or the common fear of public speaking, the occurrence of SAD is far less frequent. It is the intensity of the anxiety experienced, the wider range of feared social situations, and the profound negative impact on functioning that sets SAD apart from milder instances of social apprehension.

SAD may be of two forms: specific and generalized. Some individuals experience social anxiety for a small and discrete set of social situations. However, the more severe and more common variant of SAD is the generalized type. In this case, anxiety is triggered in virtually all social interactions (e.g., meeting an individual one-on-one as well as meeting a small group of people all at once). Epidemiological data suggest that the prevalence of SAD (referred to as social phobia in the most recent surveys) is approximately 2.4% in the general population, although there are wide variations depending on culture (i.e., as low as 0.5% in South Korea, and as high as 3.0% in New Zealand).

SYMPTOMS OF SOCIAL ANXIETY DISORDER

Physiological Reactivity

It has been noted that during exposure to social situations, individuals with SAD may experience situational panic attacks wherein the physical symptoms closely resemble panic. Specifically, the SAD sufferer may experience trembling, sweating, dizziness, tachycardia, depersonalization, numbness in the extremities, and other signs of sympathetic arousal. Reacting with panic-like symptoms when exposed to social situations is frequently accompanied by increases in warmth around the cheeks, resulting in blushing.

Behavioral Features

One of the principal observable aspects of SAD involves avoidance of social interactions. This specific symptom is the key disabling feature of SAD, leading to significant personal distress among SAD sufferers. Self-report assessments, such as the Social Interaction Anxiety Scale, generally focus on the anxiety associated with social interaction. This scale, used in conjunction with the Social Phobia Scale, provides a detailed self-report evaluation of the severity of social anxiety.

Cognitive Aspects

Most models of the etiology of SAD have a prominent cognitive component that is primarily concerned with self-focused attention and self-evaluative statements that occur either during or immediately following social situations. Specifically, individuals with SAD evaluate social situations as more threatening, and others are highly likely to evaluate the SAD sufferer negatively. Numerous investigations have demonstrated experimentally that individuals with SAD consistently evaluate their performances negatively as well as make attributions that others perceive their performance negatively. The process of negative self-evaluation immediately following social interactions is sometimes referred to as the negative postmortem. These spontaneously occurring negative self-evaluations set up a pernicious feedback loop, depicted in Figure 1.

Additional Common Complicating Factors in Social Anxiety Disorder

Given the degree of anxiety experienced by individuals suffering from SAD and the ubiquity of social interactions, the SAD sufferer cannot completely avoid severe anxiety-provoking situations. This problem frequently leads to significant difficulties aside from the primary presenting problem. For example, there is a higher probability of alcohol abuse among individuals with SAD. In addition, individuals with SAD have higher levels of depression, as well as higher levels of suicidal ideation and attempts. Finally, those with SAD are significantly more likely to drop out of school compared with other anxiety disorder groups.

Treatment Approach and Outcome

The primary psychosocial intervention for SAD is cognitive-behavioral therapy (CBT). There have been numerous trials examining CBT for SAD (or social phobia), with generally favorable results. There are two major components to this treatment package. The first involves behavioral mastery of specific situations that formerly triggered anxious responding. This frequently involves imaginal and in vivo exposure designed to develop better methods of coping with anxiety-provoking situations, as well as provide an opportunity for the clinician to assess specific cognitive distortions that contribute to the maintenance of social anxiety. The second component overlaps with the behavioral procedures and involves cognitive restructuring. This additional element is essential to train the SAD sufferer in methods for challenging the accuracy of his or her negative self-evaluations and to break the negative cycle depicted in Figure 1 that frequently leads to a real breakdown in social performance. While treatment may be conducted individually, interventions are often enhanced in social anxiety groups, where fellow group members assist by proving an opportunity for exposure and offering feedback in the service of support and mastery.

—*Dean McKay and Kevin McKiernan*

Further Readings and References

American Psychiatric Association. (2000). *Diagnostic and statistical manual of mental disorders* (4th ed., text revision). Washington, DC: Author.

Amerigen, M. V., Mancini, C., & Farvolden, P. (2003). The impact of anxiety disorders on educational achievement. *Journal of Anxiety Disorders, 17,* 561–571.

The Anxiety Network. (n.d.). *Social anxiety disorder.* Retrieved from http://www.anxietynetwork.com/sphome .html

Beidel, D. C., & Turner, S. M. (1998). *Shy children, phobic adults: Nature and treatment of social phobia.* Washington, DC: American Psychological Association Press.

Boegels, S. M., Rijsemus, W., & de Jong, P. J. (2002). Self-focused attention and social anxiety: The effects of experimentally heightened self-awareness on fear, blushing, cognitions, and social skills. *Cognitive Therapy and Research, 26,* 461–472.

Carrigan, M. H., & Randall, C. L. (2003). Self-medication in social phobia: A review of the alcohol literature. *Addictive Behaviors, 28,* 269–284.

Heimberg, R. G., & Becker, R. E. (2002). *Cognitive-behavioral group therapy for social phobia: Basic mechanisms and clinical strategies.* New York: Guilford.

Heimberg, R. G., Liebowitz, M. R., Hope, D. A., & Schneier, F. R. (1994). *Social phobia: Diagnosis, assessment, and treatment.* New York: Guilford.

Mattick, R. P., & Clark, J. C. (1998). Development and validation of measures of social phobia scrutiny fear and social interaction anxiety. *Behaviour Research and Therapy, 36,* 455–470.

Social Phobia/Social Anxiety Disorder Association, http:// www.socialphobia.org/

Wells, A., & Clark, D. M. (1997). Social phobia: A cognitive approach. In G. C. L. Davey (Ed.), *Phobias: A handbook of theory, research and treatment* (pp. 3–26). Chichester, UK: Wiley.

SOCIAL CLASS

Everyone belongs to a certain social class. Whether one is abundant with material wealth or whether one is deprived and poor, people most usually classify oneself, others, or a group as having a certain socio-economic status. Being part of a social class is commonly accompanied by sentiments and feelings that range from pride, security, arrogance, and contentment to inferiority, self-pity, sadness, and anger.

Social class has existed as long as material belongings and physical possession have taken importance in people's existence. In psychology, therapists and policy makers would often need to consider and be respectful of clients' and communities' potentials and limitations that are borne out of people's social class. Along with gender, age, race, culture, sexual orientation, religion, and ability, social class is an essential source of diversity that needs to be considered in practice and in research. In the field of developmental psychology and specifically in the world of children, the family's and society's social class naturally dictate the amount of resources available to children's growth. Social class thereby has a global, direct, and subtle influence on children's capacities, futures, potentials, and, at unfortunate times, their limitations.

WHAT IS SOCIAL CLASS?

Social class is a mobile construct. Because it is most usually defined by material possession, investments, or economic acquisitions, social class is temporary and may change drastically depending on the increase or loss of this material wealth in a natural or man-made disaster, by winning the lottery, or during war and other political unrest. Moreover, it can also change gradually through time, in the event of attaining further education, in relation to a country's increased gross domestic product (GDP), or in increased inflation or habits such as addiction to gambling. The sources of one's social class include (1) structural, (2) familial, (3) interpersonal, (4) intrapersonal, and (5) circumstantial influences. Defining one's social position may be highly dictated by the structure of the society one is born into—the opportunities for employment or lack thereof; the affordability of food, clothing, housing, health care, and education; and economic well-being of one's country, in terms of inflation, inequalities, development, and technological infrastructure. Additionally, one's social class may also be highly influenced by the family one is born into—parents' wealth, presence of impending inheritance, a cycle of deprivation, intergenerational businesses and professions, or support for education. Social class is affected by interpersonal factors—other people's choices, actions, generosity or greed, the way people react to any person's gender, age, ability, race, culture, religion, sexual orientation, power, and lifestyle. One's social class may also be largely dependent on forces that are personal—personality characteristics such as resilience, perseverance, determination, and laziness, as well as the actions and decisions people make, the values and priorities people choose, and the attitudes and beliefs people have. Finally, circumstantial factors affect social class—the unexpected occurrences of error, luck, and timing.

Social class, because of its temporal and elusive nature, is often loosely defined by people in empirical research on the basis of different correlates and on the basis of standards that are often relative. Many elements influence the definition and position of any one person's social class, at any given time. Needless to say, the perspective, biases, prejudices, and stereotypes of the person needing or having to consider another's social class in research, practice, or training impacts the definition of this social class. For instance, this is exemplified by children's definition of social class, when they refer to their schoolmate as rich like them because they also have each a cellular phone in their family, or a child who says that they are poorer than their neighbor because their toys are often older and less numerous compared with their neighbor's.

CORRELATES OF SOCIAL CLASS

The correlates or indicators of social class include housing, safety, food, clothing, education, health care, transportation/mobility, and leisure. The privilege, deprivations, or amount of security experienced in one's social class is closely related to the circumstances of one's housing (i.e. where one lives, with whom one lives, the experience of privacy or density, the safety, danger, or predictability of having a roof over one's head). Whether an individual or a family lives in an apartment, a single family home, or in the streets depends on what they can afford. One's social class also affects the adequacy of food and clothing, and determines the extent to which children are hungry, undernourished, and go by without their needs met. The affordability of education, the kind of education, and the expense of education are largely influenced by the family's social class. Whether a child goes to elementary school, finishes high school, or pursues college or even graduate school certainly says something about one's cultural expectations in that social class. The experience or lack thereof of adequate and reliable health care is certainly dictated by one's social class. The experience of mobility and level of control over one's transportation highly correlates with one's social class. For instance, especially living in a place where public transportation is not accessible or efficient, not being able to afford a car, car insurance, and maintenance expenses explicitates one's social class. Although not as clear a correlate as the others, the exposure to a variety of places, people, experiences, avocations, and vacations largely depends on one's social class.

HOW IS SOCIAL CLASS ASSESSED?

In psychology, social class is often overlooked as a variable in research because of the complexity of its definition, the inherent biases and controversies in its perception, and its temporary and ever-changing nature brought by different standards and different perspectives (i.e., social class being relative to the one defining it). Moreover, the salience of the assessment and measurement of social class is necessitated by its function. For instance, social class positions and inequalities were highlighted in research studies conducted in the 1960s in the aftermath of World War II or the Great Depression. In the current time, social class discussions and assessments come to the fore along with multicultural psychology and with the waves of immigration that highly correlate minority status with specific social classes.

In the objective sense, especially in research, social class has been assessed using one or a combination of the following: educational attainment, income, power, or prestige. In demographic information sheets and when used as a variable of study, preconceived levels, figures, or rankings have already been defined and participants are asked to identify these descriptors in order to eventually categorize their social class.

The subjective sense is the one that laypeople (i.e., nonpsychologists) rely on in assessing social class. Although qualitative researchers are starting to use the subjective measure in their studies, scientists generally tend to adhere to the objective measures. The subjective measure is one's own attribution of belonging to a level of social class that an individual identifies with. This is usually the position that the person expresses, for a number of reasons, to be the social class the person genuinely feels he or she belongs to. Using the subjective measure, for instance, a person is asked what his or her social class is, and is then asked to define or relate why that identification was made. This recognizes the categories or levels of social class the person uses and the reasons for such classification. In other instances, the individual is given a measure of 1 to 10, with 1 being poor and 10 being wealthy, and then is asked for his or her social class given the scale. The subjective measure of social class then gives the person the flexibility to use the standards, the classifications, and the labels he or she believes in, and at the same time acknowledges and respects the sense of belonging and definition of social class the person finds truthful and useful.

WHY IS SOCIAL CLASS IMPORTANT IN STUDYING CHILDREN?

Children are in positions where they are mostly helpless recipients of resources accorded to them for their growth. When studying children it is necessary to know the socioeconomic status they and their families are in, in order to assess the distribution of these resources (food, clothing, shelter, education, health care, safety), to identify their specific needs to ensure their healthy development and well-being, to inform policy makers to further advocate for the needs of our children, and to achieve higher ideals of economic equality and social justice.

The identification of social class is important in the early intervention for children. For example, the identification of poor neighborhoods and financially deprived communities facilitates the identification of social class and thereby the interventions for high-risk children, high-risk pregnancies, juvenile delinquents, emotional and behavioral problems of children, children with a tendency toward violence, and mental health risks of children. Identification of social class for children is relevant for the early detection of their needs for help, and the assurance of interventions.

Social class and the importance of social class in our studies dealing with children are certainly a point of education and intervention for the values we want to teach children. Although social class is often overlooked as a variable of study, it is often used in judging people's social positions and undeniably fuels people's self-esteem, biases, prejudices, and stereotypes. With children, then, using social class as a variable of study can potentially educate them in acceptance, respect, and sensitivity for other children and adults who are of social classes different from theirs. These studies can inculcate social justice and values of concern and generosity toward others, and can process issues of hatred, indifference, self-pity, or anger toward others who are of a different social class. And most importantly, these studies can help children develop through adulthood acknowledging the privilege, potential, deprivations, narrowness of experiences, and limitations brought on by their social class.

Children in Developed Countries

Social class is important in identifying the children in developed countries who need early intervention: children born to poor families, those who have minority status, those whose resources are distributed among many children, those who are lacking in emotional and material resources in parenting, those who are in single-parent households, those who are raised in unsafe circumstances, and those whose opportunities for the future are limited by social class.

Children in So-Called Third World Countries

In the global world and in the international community, there are many children in underdeveloped or Third World countries where the effect of social class is not just essential to look into, but is almost a moral obligation. For children in these countries, resources are scarce, and they do live in circumstances that are unique to underdeveloped countries: children raising themselves; children raised by a stranger or by extended families; children whose parent or parents are overseas workers; children in societies where health care is scarce, where there is no health insurance and social security, and where they can be easily refused for health care when they do not have resources; children who have never visited a doctor or a dentist; children who cannot afford to go to school because they are expected to work; child laborers (e.g., children having to work as cigarette and newspaper vendors, prostitutes, farmers, and construction workers); children who live in the streets; children who grow up deprived of any technology or books in their homes or even in their schools; children who are victims of war, political warfare, terrorism, and graft and corruption in their governments; and children who have difficulty discerning right from wrong because of the prevalence of violence, bribery, and deceit.

SUMMARY

Social class is a rather influential aspect of one's position in society that dictates one's past, present, and future privileges, opportunities, deprivations, and experiences. Especially for children who are mostly reliant on the resources their family's social class can offer them, a lot of their development, expectations, and attitudes in life, and the values they imbibe, are largely in the power of their social class.

—*Teresa G. Tuason*

See also Socioeconomic Status

Further Readings and References

AcademicDB. (n.d.). *Sociology/poverty*. Retrieved from http://www.academicdb.com/Sociology/Poverty/

Argyle, M. (1994). *The psychology of social class*. London: Routledge.

Fouad, N., & Brown, M. T. (2001). Role of race and social class in development: Implications for counseling psychology. In S. D. Brown & R. W. Lent (Eds.), *Handbook of counseling psychology* (pp. 379–408). New York: Wiley.

Frable, D. E. S. (1997). Gender, racial, ethnic, sexual, and class identities. *Annual Review of Psychology, 48*, 139–162.

Liu, W. M., Ali, S. R., Soleck, G., Hopps, J., Dunston, K., Pickett, T., Jr. (2004). Using social class in counseling psychology research. *Journal of Counseling Psychology, 51*, 3–18.

Lott, B. (2002). Cognitive and behavioral distancing from the poor. *American Psychologist, 57*, 100–110.

Marmot, M. (1999). *The social determinants of health inequalities*. Retrieved from http://www.worldbank.org/poverty/health/library/nov99seminar.pdf

Pope-Davis, D. B., & Coleman, H. L. K. (Eds.). (2001). *The intersection of race, class, and gender in multicultural counseling*. Thousand Oaks, CA: Sage.

Tudor, J. F. (1971). The development of class awareness in children. *Social Forces, 49*, 470–476.

U.S. Census Bureau. (2000). *Poverty in the United States 2002*. Retrieved from http://www.census.gov/hhes/www/poverty02.html

SOCIAL COGNITION

How is it that two individuals can interact with the same person yet come away with vastly different impressions of the person? Can we feel good about ourselves, yet still have concerns about our basic worth? Why do our moods have such a profound effect on our judgments and decision making? Why do we sometimes experience negative thoughts about members of certain ethnic groups? Can we control these thoughts if we want to?

Questions such as these are the focus of social cognition researchers. Specifically, social cognition is a sub-area of psychology that focuses on the mental processes that come into play when individuals interact with one another. In this sub-area, mental processes are defined very broadly. They include thoughts, feelings, and motivations, and researchers have studied the role these processes play in a wide range of behaviors such as self-perception, the perception of others, judgments of life satisfaction, and stereotyping.

As the context of investigating these topics, social cognitive researchers have raised a number of more fundamental questions about human nature. To what extent do individuals guide their thoughts, feelings, and behaviors consciously as opposed to automatically? To the extent we act in unintentional, automatic ways, why is this so and can we do anything about it? Do our thoughts, feelings, and behavior accurately reflect our situation or are they systematically biased by self-serving, defensive motivations? Are our conceptions of ourselves stable or are they constructed in different ways in different situations?

An interesting and representative social cognition study was conducted by Baldwin and colleagues. They began with the assumption that individuals come to think about themselves more or less as they believe significant others in their life (e.g., parents, friends, teachers) think about them. If so, then it should be possible to influence the way individuals feel about themselves by changing which individuals they bring to mind. To test this possibility, Baldwin and colleagues asked Roman Catholic females who did or did not describe themselves as strict practitioners to read a description of a sexually permissive dream. Although not explicit, the description did allude to activities that were of questionable moral value for a strict, practicing Catholic. Thus, strict Catholics might not feel especially good about themselves after reading the description. This should be especially true, though, if these strict Catholics had their religious standards brought to mind (e.g., What would the Pope think about me reading that description?).

To make it likely some women in the study had these standards on their mind, Baldwin and colleagues had the women respond as quickly as they could to flashes on a computer screen. The women did this after they had read the description of the dream and before they rated themselves. The flashes were actually photographs presented too briefly for the women to detect consciously. For some participants, the photograph was of an individual unknown to them. For others, it was the Pope. If the subliminal presentations of the Pope's photograph activated the internal representation of the Pope (i.e., religious standards), then women who described themselves as practicing Catholics and who had been exposed to the Pope's picture would report the lowest feelings about themselves after reading about the sexually permissive dream. This is precisely what Baldwin and colleagues found.

This study showed that a person's momentary sense of self can be shaped by the activation of an internal representation of the presumed evaluation of a significant other. It showed more generally that individuals play an active role in determining their own thoughts, feelings, and behavior—even when they are not aware of it. This active role is what social cognition researchers investigate.

—*Leonard L. Martin*

Further Readings and References

Baldwin, M. W., Carrell, S. E., & Lopez, D. F. (1990). Priming relationship schemas: My advisor and the Pope are watching me from the back of my mind. *Journal of Experimental Social Psychology, 25*, 435–454.

Brewer, M. B., & Hewstone, M. (2004). *Social cognition.* Malden, MA: Blackwell.

Devine, P. G., Hamilton, D. L., & Ostrom, T. M. (1994). *Social cognition: Impact on social psychology.* San Diego, CA: Academic Press.

Higgins. E. T., & Kruglanski, A. W. (1996). *Social psychology: Handbook of basic principles.* New York: Guilford.

Huitt, W. (2002). Social cognition. In *Educational psychology interactive.* Valdosta, GA: Valdosta State University. Retrieved from http://chiron.valdosta.edu/whuitt/col/soccog/soccog.html

Martin, L. L., & Clark, L. F. (1990). Social cognition: Exploring the mental processes involved in human social interaction. In M. W. Eysenck (Ed.), *Cognitive psychology: An international review* (pp. 265–310). Chichester, UK: Wiley.

Moskowitz, G. B. (2005). *Social cognition: Understanding self and others.* New York: Guilford.

SOCIAL DEVELOPMENT

Social development is the change over time in an individual's understanding of, attitudes concerning, and behavior toward others; for example, a developmental change in how people behave with members of the other gender or their understanding of what friendship entails. These changes are perceived to occur due to socialization processes as well as physical and cognitive maturation. Socialization, however, is not a unidirectional influence, where society simply affects the individual. Instead, relationships are perceived as bidirectional. That is, the parent affects the child's development, as well as the child impacting the parent's. Initial relationships may be the most important as they serve as models of what infants and children should expect in their future relationships. Over the course of the life span, relationships with parents, siblings, peers, and romantic partners play integral roles for social development.

Because these relationships do not exist in a vacuum, they are affected by the social and cultural contexts in which they exist. Cultural, ethnic, and religious differences affect the manner in which people interact with each other and subsequently children's development within those contexts. Individuals' gender and social economic standing (SES) also affect how they think, feel about, and behave toward others, as well as how other people respond to them.

INITIAL RELATIONSHIPS

John Bowlby, a prominent ethologist, proposed that infants develop attachments to their primary caregivers. He argued that attachments are reciprocal relationships; the infants become attached to their caregivers and the caregivers become attached to the infants. Attachments are theorized to serve an evolutionary purpose because they increase the likelihood that the caregivers will protect and care for the infant. Attachments between infants and caregivers develop gradually over time as the infants and caregivers improve their ability to read and respond to each other's signals. Typically, infants form clear-cut attachments to familiar caregivers by 7 months of age.

Attachments provide children with emotional support. The child is able to use the familiar caregiver as a secure base from which to explore his or her surroundings. Because infants look to their familiar caregivers for support, they are more willing to explore their environment when their caregivers are present than when they are absent. Caregivers also serve as sources of comfort when the infants become distressed.

Bowlby proposed that infants grow to understand what their caregivers are like and how they typically respond when the infants are stressed. These initial working models, or expectations concerning social relationships, are theorized to guide their expectations about future relationships during childhood, adolescence, and adulthood. If infants had warm relationships with their caregivers and their needs were met, they may expect positive relations with others. However, if these relationships were negative, they may expect to be hurt by others and become more defensive in future relationships.

Mary Ainsworth, a contemporary of Bowlby's, developed the "strange situation" to examine the quality of children's attachments to their caregivers. In this test, 1-year-old infants encounter a number of stressful situations, from interacting with strangers to

having their caregivers leave. The children are classified into different attachment styles based on how they cope with these situations.

Children with secure attachments are distressed at separation, but are easily comforted when their caregiver returns, and are more willing to explore when the caregiver is present. Three categories of insecure attachments have been observed. Children with an avoidant attachment style tend to be unresponsive to their caregivers when they are present and display little distress at separation. These children are slow to respond or avoid the caregivers when they return. Children who display resistant attachment styles seek closeness to their caregivers and often fail to explore their environment. They are very distressed at separation and frequently display angry, resistant behavior at reunion. Finally, abused infants usually display a disorganized/disoriented attachment style. These infants often are afraid of their caregivers and display a combination of avoidant and resistant behaviors.

An important determinant of attachment style is the quality of care the infants receive. Mothers of securely attached children tend to be warm, sensitive to their children's signals, and encourage their children to explore the world. Mothers of insecurely attached children provide less sensitive parenting. Mothers of resistant children often provide inconsistent feedback; sometimes they are enthusiastic and other times they ignore the children. These babies become anxious and resentful as they realize they cannot count on their mothers for support and comfort. Two patterns of parenting styles are related with avoidant babies. Mothers of avoidant infants often overstimulate their children or are unresponsive to the babies' signals and express negative attitudes toward them. In both cases, infants learn that they can reduce negative stimulation by avoiding the parent. Whereas infant characteristics, such as being premature or having a difficult temperament, may make an insecure attachment more likely, caregiver qualities seem to be more important for attachment than the infant's qualities.

Because of cross-cultural differences in child rearing, the percentage of children who fall into the secure and insecure attachment styles varies across cultures. For example, German culture promotes independence in their children and discourages clingy behavior. Not surprisingly, German infants tend to display more avoidant attachment than do babies raised in the United States. In Japanese culture, parents rarely leave their infants in the care of strangers. Therefore,

Japanese children tend to display greater separation anxiety and more resistant attachment than do children raised in the United States.

There is significant evidence to support Bowlby's claim that early attachments influence subsequent social relationships. During the preschool years, children who were classified as securely attached tend to be more sociable with their peers and have more friends and more positive interactions with peers than do insecurely attached children. In middle childhood, children who had secure attachments have better relationships with peers and closer friendships than insecurely attached children. Furthermore, there are intergenerational effects of attachment. Adults' attachments to their parents are correlated with how their children are attached to them. This likely occurs because the parents' attachment style affects how they behave with their children. Typically the best outcomes occur when the children are securely attached to both parents and the worst outcomes are when both attachments are insecure. For the quality of the attachment to be maintained, it is necessary that sensitive caregiving continue throughout childhood.

PARENTING STYLES

In addition to warm, responsive parenting, Erik Erikson and others have claimed that a second dimension of parenting, the amount of demands and controls the parents place on their children, also plays an integral role in children's and adolescents' social development. Parents can be categorized as being either high or low on each of these dimensions (Table 1).

In the 1960s and 1970s, Diana Baumrind conducted extensive research on how parents interact with their children. She observed three patterns of parenting styles. Authoritative parents display high levels of warmth and affection and place demands on their children. These parents tend to be responsive to their children's thoughts and feelings, and encourage age-appropriate independence while placing controls on their actions. Whereas authoritarian parents also place high levels of control on their children, they display low levels of warmth. These parents tend to impose many rules and expect compliance from their children. They often rely on punitive or coercive measures to obtain obedience. Permissive parents place few demands on their children but are warm and caring toward their children. Parents often take this approach

Table 1 Classifications of Parenting Styles

	Responsive	*Unresponsive*
Demanding	Authoritative	Authoritarian
Undemanding	Permissive	Uninvolved

if they lack the confidence to control their children or feel it is best if the children make their own decisions. Developmental psychologists Eleanor Maccoby and John Martin added the fourth category, uninvolved parenting. These parents display little warmth and place few demands or expectations on their children.

Children raised by authoritative parents have the best social and academic outcomes. They have high self-esteem, are successful in school, and are well liked by their peers. Children raised in authoritarian households tend to have average social and cognitive competencies and during adolescence tend to be more conforming to their peers. Children raised by permissive parents tend to have low cognitive and social competencies. They often are immature and lack self-control and are more likely to get involved with delinquent behavior than children whose parents set controls for them. The worst outcomes are associated with uninvolved parenting. These children tend to perform poorly in school, display aggressive behavior during childhood, and are at risk for delinquent behavior as adolescents.

Because these findings are correlational, the outcomes are not necessarily due to the parenting style. It is possible that easy-going, intelligent children elicit more authoritative parenting than do difficult children. As stated earlier, whereas parents influence their children, the children also impact the parents.

Working-class parents are more likely to take an authoritarian approach to parenting, and tend to display less warmth than do middle-class parents. In addition, they are less likely to reason with, negotiate with, or foster curiosity and independence in their children. These differences can be explained by the power differences in blue- and white-collar occupations. Working-class parents tend to have little power in the outside world and have to defer to their bosses. This leads to a perception of the world as hierarchical. These parents therefore stress obedience to their children, because it is a skill that will help them survive in a blue-collar world. Middle- and upper-class parents also attempt to teach their children skills that will help them negotiate their futures. These parents focus on instilling initiative, curiosity, and creativity because these skills are relevant in a white-collar environment.

SIBLINGS

The longest-lasting relationships most people have are with their siblings. Older siblings typically assume dominant roles, such as determining which activities to engage in, or how they should be played. They tend to initiate both more prosocial and combative behavior than younger siblings. Younger siblings are more likely to imitate their older brothers and sisters. As siblings age, the importance of birth order lessens and the relationship becomes more egalitarian by early adolescence.

A number of factors affect sibling relationships, including the genders of the siblings, the age gap between them, and their relationship with their parents. Although same-sex siblings tend to be closer than brother and sister pairs, the most conflict is seen in brother-brother relationships. By middle childhood, girls tend to report more warmth and intimacy in their sibling relationships than do boys. This trend continues into adulthood, where sister relationships tend to be the strongest and most intimate. Siblings whose ages are close together tend to display more warmth and closeness but also more conflict during childhood. This occurs because there are more direct comparisons and more frequent conflict over resources or perceived unequal treatment when the age gap is small.

The treatment children receive from their parents also influences their relationship. When parents favor one child, not only does sibling antagonism increase, but the least-favored child is also at risk for adjustment difficulties. The greatest problems occur when the children believe their parents care more about one child than another.

Sibling rivalry begins with the arrival of the new baby. This typically leads to a decline in positive interactions between mothers and the older children, such as joint play, cuddling, and talking. However, negative interactions, such as restrictive and punitive behavior, increase in frequency. This can lead to jealousy if the older children associate these changes with the baby.

Sibling rivalry tends to increase when the younger child reaches 1½ to 2 years of age. The younger siblings can now try to hold their own by hitting back or getting the parents' attention. Sibling rivalry continues increasing into middle childhood and is usually more intense when the children are the same gender or are close in age. Sibling rivalry declines during adolescence as the siblings develop their own social worlds and the frequency of their interactions with each other decreases.

There are a number of positive aspects to sibling relationships. First, they can provide social support. Older children can provide emotional support when their younger siblings are dealing with uncertain situations. Sisters play an important social support role, because relationships with sisters are more intimate. Second, older children can serve as models or tutors to their siblings. They can help their younger siblings master cognitive, physical, or social tasks through direct instruction or modeling behavior. Both older and younger siblings benefit from the tutoring. Children who tutor their siblings tend to do better on academic aptitude tests then same-age children who do not have these experiences. Third, interactions with older siblings aid in younger children's social cognitive development. This helps younger children develop social skills and enhance their emotional understanding and perspective-taking abilities.

PEER RELATIONSHIPS

Parents both directly and indirectly influence their children's peer relationships. Parents choose which neighborhoods they live in, which schools and religious services they attend, and whether or not they participate in after-school programs. These decisions affect who their children's potential peers are. Furthermore, they act as gatekeepers or booking agents in scheduling play dates for young children. Parents also serve as positive or negative role models of how to act toward others, and they can actively coach how to deal with peers. Finally, the parenting style they employ is related to peer sociability. Children raised by authoritative parents tend to have better social skills than those raised by authoritarian or uninvolved parents.

This is important because children's social skills strongly affect their popularity. Popular children tend to be calm, outgoing, and friendly. They act prosocially and are rarely disruptive or aggressive. In addition, they tend to have better perspective-taking skills than their peers. Two patterns of social interaction styles have negative consequences for popularity. Hostile, impulsive children tend to be poor perspective takers and often interpret other children as having a hostile intent. Because of this perspective, they are more likely than others to respond to other children's behavior with aggression. Children with this interaction style are at risk for becoming delinquent adolescents.

A subset of withdrawn children are passive and socially awkward. These children are aware that others dislike them and expect their peers to treat them poorly. They are very sensitive to negative feedback because this information supports their belief that they are disliked. Because of this, they tend to have a submissive interaction style and withdraw from social interactions. Subsequently, they often feel lonely and are at risk for depression and low self-esteem. However, not all children who have low rates of interactions with others are socially inept. Some of these children are socially well adjusted but just have a preference for interacting with only a few friends.

Physical appearance also impacts popularity, because attractive children tend to be more popular than their unattractive peers. The timing of the onset of puberty is influential as well. Boys who mature early tend to be more popular than later maturing boys. As early maturers are bigger and stronger than their peers, they excel in sports, which boosts their social status. In contrast, early maturing girls tend to be slightly less popular than later developing girls. Because these girls are the first in their cohort to reach puberty, they are likely to be teased, especially by the boys.

Gender differences in peer relationships begin much earlier than the onset of puberty. During early childhood, children begin to show preferences for playing with their own gender. Girls prefer to play with other girls by age 2, and boys start to prefer playing with other boys the following year. Young children not only prefer same-sex playmates, they also actively avoid the other gender. Because children segregate along gender lines, boys and girls live in different social worlds. Among other distinctions, boys and girls differ in their style of play, toy choices, what they do with their friends, and how they deal with conflict.

Boys are more active and aggressive, and are more likely to engage in rough-and-tumble play than girls. Furthermore, boys tend to play in larger groups and play more competitive games than do girls. Boys' groups tend to develop dominance hierarchies with power plays to determine where each child stands in the group. Because boys are concerned with their status within the group, their communication often focuses on dominance. When conflict arises, such as a fight over toys, they are likely to use verbal or physical aggression to resolve it.

In contrast to boys, girls are more vocal and nurturing. They are more likely to play with only one or two best friends. These friendships tend to be emotionally close and intimate. Typically, girls claim to have closer friendships than boys do from middle childhood on. When conflict does occur, girls are likely to compromise and try to work things out. When girls act aggressively, it is more likely to be an attempt to hurt someone's social relationships than to cause physical harm.

Children base their friendships on shared activities—the people they do things with. By adolescence, friendships become more focused on trust and intimacy, especially for girls. Adolescent girls turn to their friends for emotional support and understanding. Although adolescent boys disclose more to their friends than they did as children, they primarily continue to base their friendships on shared recreational activities.

In addition to the changes in the intimacy of friendships, a number of other changes occur in the transition to adolescence. Both the size of peer groups and their gender makeup change from childhood to adolescence. Cliques, which are small groups of approximately five or six friends who spend most of their time together, develop during preadolescence. Clique members usually are similar in terms of their gender, age, grade, and ethnic background. Larger reputation-based groups, called crowds, emerge in adolescence. Crowds are mixed gender groups that can contain multiple cliques. Crowd members tend to share similar norms, values, and interests. A crowd, such as jocks or brains, not only provides a group identity to adolescents but also a status level within the peer context.

Australian ethnographer Dexter Dunphy proposed a model of how peer group structures change during adolescence. Initially, boys and girls are relatively isolated from each another because they mainly associate with members of their same-sex cliques. In Dunphy's second stage, crowds begin to form as boys' and girls' cliques begin to interact at an intergroup level. Dating ensues between the higher status boys and girls in the third stage. These individuals serve as models for romantic relationships as well as mentors for the other members of their cliques. Crowds become fully developed in the fourth stage, as the youth begin to interact with members of the other sex at an interpersonal level. Finally, in the last stage, crowds begin to disintegrate, leaving loosely associated groups of couples.

There is considerable support to the premise that these changes in peer group structure influence dating and romantic relationships. Youth who had close other-sex friends during early adolescence are more likely to be integrated in mixed-sex social networks in mid-adolescence. This, in turn, is related to an enhanced likelihood of being in a romantic relationship. Furthermore, interactions with other-sex peers are associated with social and romantic competence.

Dates in early adolescence tend to be superficial and often occur in group settings. Whereas early dating relationships provide an opportunity to engage in leisure activities and explore sexual feelings, attachment and caregiving are not central to these relationships. According to B. Bradford Brown, a psychology professor at the University of Wisconsin, youth focus less on the qualities of their romantic relationships and more on characteristics of themselves during this phase of adolescent dating. This initial foray into dating provides adolescents with an opportunity to gain confidence in their ability to relate to the other gender and to view themselves as capable dating partners.

In the next developmental phase, youths focus on how their romantic relationships will be perceived by their peers. For status reasons, simply having a romantic partner may be more important than the relationship itself. Whereas a relationship can enhance an adolescent's status, it is important that the relationship be with the "right" type of partner. Dating the wrong person or performing non–socially accepted dating behaviors could damage a youth's social status.

Youth subsequently orient away from how their relationships are viewed by others toward a focus on the relationship itself. This occurs when they become more confident in their ability to interact in romantic relationships as well as more accepting of their reputation and social status among their peers. At this point, true attachments to romantic partners can be formed. Because these relationships are more emotionally intense and intimate, they tend to be more satisfying then those in the previous phases. In late adolescence or early adulthood, a third shift is proposed toward a focus on whether to form a long-term commitment to the romantic partner.

Adolescents with withdrawn or aggressive interaction styles may face problems developing healthy romantic relationships. Withdrawn adolescents may have difficulty entering into same-sex cliques and subsequently into mixed-sex peer groups. Thus, these youth are likely to lack the learning environment provided by informally dating within the peer group. This becomes problematic when they begin to date because they lack a support network to explore ideas related to romantic relationships and they may have problems developing the right level of intimacy with romantic partners.

Aggressive youth face a different set of problems. Although these teenagers have a peer group, it consists of other delinquent youth. Therefore, their romantic partners often display antisocial behaviors as well. Because these adolescents have developed aggressive interaction styles, their romantic relationships are at risk for psychological and physical aggression. In addition, they tend to engage in earlier sexual activity than their peers.

Maturing early also places adolescents at risk because they tend to begin romantic relationships earlier than on-time or late-maturing adolescents. Early-maturing girls tend to date older boys who frequently have a delinquent orientation. This places these girls at risk for both deviance and early sexual activity. Unfortunately, not only do early-maturing girls typically engage in sexual activity prior to their peers, but they also are at a higher risk for acquiring sexually transmitted diseases and becoming pregnant.

ADULT RELATIONSHIPS

In Brown's fourth phase of romantic relationships, people search for partners to whom they can commit long term. Finding a marriage partner seems to be beneficial, because people who are married tend to be happier, healthier, and wealthier than unmarried people. One explanation for this effect is that people with these qualities are more likely to get married. However, there seem to be actual benefits to marriage because people who have lost their marriage, such as widowed and divorced individuals, tend to do worse than single individuals. This finding implies that the benefits of marriage are not solely due to a self-selection effect.

In terms of emotions and psychological well-being, men seem to benefit from marriage more than women do. More men report being happily married than do women, and being married is related to gains in men's physical and emotional health. For women, relationship quality is more important than just whether or not they are married. Marriage seems to be beneficial for women if the relationship is going well; however, if the relationship is going poorly, women tend to suffer more than do men. One possible reason for this gender difference is that men are more likely than women to only have their spouse as a significant outlet for emotional intimacy and social support.

Gender differences also are observed in other family relationships. Because women seem to be better at kin-keeping skills, such as calling, sending birthday cards, and visiting, family relationships involving women tend to be closer than those involving men. Because they tend to have poorer kin-keeping skills, men are at greater risk for losing intimacy with their children after a divorce. This gender difference also is observed when examining adults' relationships with their parents. Daughters are more likely than sons to provide direct social support and care to elderly parents. When sons are the primary caregivers, they tend to be managers of care rather than direct providers.

People's longest-lasting relationships are with their siblings. Sibling relationships tend be more important early and late in life. During early and middle adulthood, sibling relationships become more secondary because adults tend to focus on their families and careers. Siblings become a more important source of support in late adulthood. Strong relationships with sisters during late adulthood seem to be protective against depression, but close relationships with brothers do not. The positive impact of relationships with sisters is probably due to the high levels of intimacy in these relationships.

People's relationships with their peers also change throughout adulthood. The number of friends people have tends to decline after young adulthood as their family and career concerns take precedence. However, the number of close, intimate friendships tends to remain stable throughout adulthood. As in earlier stages of life, women's friendships tend to be more intimate friendships than men's. Whereas women often discuss personal issues with their friends, men are more likely to engage in leisure activities.

COMMUNITY EFFECTS

About 20% of U.S. infants and children live in families below the poverty threshold. Children and adolescents growing up in poor neighborhoods are more likely to deal with crowded housing, poor-quality schools, inadequate nutrition and health care, and the presence of violence and drugs in their community than those from middle- or upper-class neighborhoods. Thus, it is not surprising that living in a low-SES neighborhood is related to negative outcomes on a wide range of variables. Children in these neighborhoods are at greater risk than those in middle- or high-SES neighborhoods for poor physical health; lower intellectual attainment and poor school performance;

social, emotional, and behavioral problems; and engaging in crime, delinquency, and high-risk sexual behavior. Typically, the worst outcomes are for children and adolescents living in extreme or enduring poverty.

Three theories have been proposed to explain the effects of poverty on child and adolescent outcomes. The first model is that the quality, quantity, and diversity of community resources, such as schools, social services, recreational and social programs, and employment, mediate well-being. The second model is that parent attributes and characteristics of the home environment mediate the relationship between the parents' and children's well-being. Because these parents are often under economic hardship and stress, their ability to provide quality parenting to their children is negatively influenced. A number of studies have found that parental stress is related to low warmth and harsh parenting. High parental warmth and monitoring of the children seem to be protective factors against the negative effects of low-SES environments. The third model is that formal and informal community institutions act to monitor the residents' behavior in line with social norms. However, in poor neighborhoods, especially where there are high rates of single parents, there tends to be less social organization and subsequently higher rates of crime and vandalism. This is compounded because when there are low levels of neighborhood monitoring, peer groups tend to have negative effects on adolescent outcomes.

—*Joshua Susskind*

See also Antisocial Behavior, Prosocial Behavior

Further Readings and References

Adams, G. R., & Berzonsky, M. D. (Eds.). (2003). *Blackwell handbook of adolescence.* Oxford, UK: Blackwell.

Adolescence Directory On-Line, http://education.indiana.edu/cas/adol/adol.html

Bornstein, M. H., Davidson, L., Keyes, C. L. M., & Moore, K. A. (Eds.). (2003). *Well-being: Positive development across the life course.* Mahwah, NJ: Erlbaum.

Brody, G. H. (1998). Sibling relationship quality: Its causes and consequences. *Annual Review of Psychology, 49,* 1–24.

Darling, N. (1999, March). *Parenting styles and its correlates.* Champaign: ERIC Clearinghouse on Elementary and Early Childhood Education, University of Illinois at Urbana-Champaign. Retrieved from http://www.kidneeds.com/diagnostic_categories/articles/parentcorre01.htm

Durkin, K. (1995). *Developmental social psychology: From infancy to old age.* Oxford, UK: Blackwell.

Furman, W., Brown, B. B., & Feiring, C. (1999). *The development of romantic relationships in adolescence.* Cambridge, UK: Cambridge University Press.

Gifford-Smith, M. E., & Brownell, C. A. (2003). Childhood peer relationships: Social acceptance, friendships, and peer networks. *Journal of School Psychology, 41,* 235–284.

Lerner, R. M., & Steinberg, L. (Eds.). (2004). *Handbook of adolescent psychology* (2nd ed.). Hoboken, NJ: Wiley.

Luthar, S. S. (Ed.). (2003). *Resilience and vulnerability: Adaptation in the context of childhood adversities.* Cambridge, UK: Cambridge University Press.

Smith, P. K., & Hart, C. H. (Eds.). (2002). *Blackwell handbook of childhood social development.* Oxford, UK: Blackwell.

University of Minnesota, Center for Early Education and Development. (n.d.). *Attachment and bonding.* Retrieved from http://education.umn.edu/ceed/publications/early report/winter91.htm

Walsh, F. (Ed.). (2003). *Normal family processes: Growing diversity and complexity* (3rd ed.). New York: Guilford.

Zimmer-Gembeck, M. J. (2002). The development of romantic relationships and adaptations in the system of peer relationships. *Journal of Adolescent Health, 31*(Suppl. 6), 216–225.

SOCIAL SECURITY

In the United States, the term *Social Security* typically refers to the federal Old-Age, Survivors, and Disability Insurance (OASDI) program. This program provides three separate types of benefits. First, it provides cash benefits to retired workers and their spouses and dependent children. Second, it provides cash benefits to the surviving spouses and dependent children of deceased workers. Finally, it provides cash benefits to disabled workers and their spouses and dependent children and pays for rehabilitation services for disabled workers.

One of the country's largest and most successful social welfare programs, Social Security covers about 96% of the workforce. In July 2004, the program paid over 47 million beneficiaries a total of $40 billion in monthly benefits. This included almost 30 million retired workers receiving an average monthly benefit of $926, almost 5 million widows and widowers receiving survivor benefits averaging $878 per month, and more than 6 million disabled workers receiving an average monthly benefit of $866. (The other beneficiaries included spouses and children of retired and disabled workers.)

Social Security constitutes the largest single source of income for most elderly Americans. Indeed, it accounts for more than half of all income for two out of three elderly beneficiaries. When Social Security was originally enacted in 1935, 50% of the elderly lived in poverty, and the poorhouse was a reality for many older Americans near the end of their lives. Today, in contrast, only about 12% of the elderly are subject to poverty, thanks in large part to Social Security.

Social Security is a contributory system; that is, it is funded by contributions or payroll taxes imposed on employers and employees. The Federal Insurance Contributions Act (FICA) requires that employers and employees each contribute 6.2% of wages, up to a maximum taxable wage base (equal to $87,900 in 2004) that is indexed for inflation, to fund old age, survivor, and disability benefits. The contributions are mandatory; employers and employees cannot opt out of the system.

The compulsory character of the Social Security program serves a number of purposes. First, it permits the program to redistribute protection from the higher paid to the lower paid. Second, it prevents the problem of adverse selection that would occur if individuals could decide whether, and to what extent, they wanted to participate in Social Security. Finally, the system's mandatory nature reduces the need for public assistance by requiring the improvident to pay their share of their future retirement needs.

Social Security benefits are typically paid in the form of a life annuity; that is, beneficiaries receive a monthly benefit for life. Unlike most private pensions, Social Security benefits are adjusted each year for inflation. The amount of benefits is calculated through the use of a complex benefit formula. The old age benefit formula bases benefits on workers' average earnings over a 35-year period. The disability benefit formula is similar but may base benefits on fewer than 35 years of earnings.

The benefit formula is progressive in that it replaces a higher percentage of income for lower-wage workers than for higher-wage workers. Thus, in absolute dollar terms, higher-wage earners receive more benefits (larger benefit checks) than do lower-wage workers, but the benefits of higher-wage workers replace a smaller percentage of their average earnings than do the benefits of lower-wage workers. In 2004, the Social Security Administration estimated that Social Security benefits would replace about 57% of the average earnings of low-wage workers, 43% of the average earnings of average-wage workers, and 35% of the wages of high-wage earners.

Under current law, a worker is entitled to receive "full benefits" at "normal retirement age." From the inception of Social Security until 2000, the normal retirement age was 65 years, but for workers born in 1938 and after, the normal retirement age is gradually increasing to 67 by 2022. A worker may elect to receive actuarially reduced benefits as early as age 62; benefits for these workers are reduced because workers who retire earlier are likely to receive benefits over a longer period of time. Similarly, workers may delay the receipt of benefits beyond normal retirement age and receive increased benefits to reflect the shorter period of time they are likely to receive benefits.

Upon reaching the normal retirement age, the spouse of a retired or disabled worker is entitled to receive a spouse benefit equal to 50% of the worker's benefit. The spouse may elect to receive an actuarially reduced benefit as early as age 62. The surviving spouse of an insured worker is entitled to receive a surviving spouse benefit equal to 100% of the deceased worker's benefit if the surviving spouse is age 65 or older. Surviving spouses as young as age 60 may elect to receive an actuarially reduced benefit. Dependent children may also receive benefits of 50% of the worker's benefit in the case of a retired or disabled worker or 75% of the worker's benefit in the case of a deceased worker. Family benefits, however, are limited to a maximum of 150% to about 188% of the worker's benefit, depending on the size of the benefit.

Social Security began as a relatively small and discrete program. As originally enacted in 1935, it covered about 55% of the civilian workforce, provided for limited monthly benefits solely for workers, and benefits were set to begin on January 1, 1942. In 1939, however, before the first benefits were paid, the system was completely revamped. Under the revised program, benefits were extended to wives, widows, and children, benefit amounts in the early years were substantially increased, and the payment of benefits was advanced to 1940. In 1950, coverage was extended to most self-employed individuals, and in 1956 disability insurance began. Over the years, Congress has tinkered with the benefit formula and made other adjustments, but the program has retained its basic form since 1956.

When originally enacted, Social Security provided for the creation of a substantial reserve to fund future Social Security benefits. The creation of such a reserve, however, was widely criticized, and Congress amended the program in 1939 to increase benefits to the first generation of retirees and shift the program towards a "pay-as-you-go" system where current contributions are used to fund current benefits. In 1977, and again in 1983, Congress amended Social Security to move away from a pure pay-as-you go system toward a system with temporary partial-reserve financing where reserves are built up for a few decades and then used to pay for future benefits. Thus, under the system today, most current contributions are used to finance current benefits, although some current contributions are set aside in a trust fund to fund future benefits. The trust fund reserves are currently invested in interest-bearing U.S. Treasury bonds and totaled $1.5 trillion at the end of 2003.

As a result of Social Security's pay-as-you-go financing and changing demographics, Social Security faces serious long-term financing difficulties. Specifically, in 2004, Social Security's Board of Trustees predicted that contributions to the system will exceed benefits paid by the system until 2018. Beginning in 2018, Social Security will need to draw down the assets held in the trust fund in order to pay full benefits, and the trust fund itself will be exhausted by 2042. At that point in time, under present tax rates, contributions will only cover 73% of scheduled benefits in 2042 and 68% of scheduled benefits in 2078.

There are two principal demographic changes behind Social Security's long-term financing difficulties. First, life expectancy is increasing. When the first Social Security benefits were paid in 1940, a 65-year-old man had a life expectancy of 12 years and a 65-year-old woman had a life expectancy of 13 years. Today, in contrast, the average 65-year-old man has a life expectancy of 16 years while the average 65-year-old woman has a life expectancy of 19 years, and life expectancy is expected to continue to increase. Second, 79 million "baby boomers" will begin retiring in 2008, and the baby boom generation is followed by much smaller generations. As a result of these changes, there will be fewer and fewer workers supporting more and more retirees. Currently, there are about 3.3 workers paying into Social Security for every beneficiary. By 2040, the ratio of workers to beneficiaries is expected to drop to 2 to 1.

The American Social Security program is not alone in facing long-term financing difficulties. Retirement systems throughout the Western world are facing similar demographic shifts, and thus similar financing difficulties. In recent years, many European countries, including France, Italy, Sweden, Switzerland, and

Germany, have amended their retirement systems to address these funding difficulties.

Experts throughout the United States generally agree that the American Social Security system should also be amended to address its long-term financing difficulties. Experts, however, disagree about how the system should be reformed. Some experts contend that the system should be "partially privatized" so that some, but not all, benefits are provided through prefunded individual accounts. Other experts contend that the current structure is fundamentally sound and only modest changes, such as a modest increase in the normal retirement age or a modest increase in the payroll tax, are necessary to address the system's long-term deficit.

—*Kathryn L. Moore*

See also Poverty

Further Readings and References

Aaron, H., and Reischauer, R. (1998). *Countdown to reform: The great Social Security debate.* New York: Century Foundation Press.

Sacks, A. (2004). *2004 Social Security explained.* Chicago: CCH.

Social Security Online, http://www.ssa.gov

SOCIETY FOR RESEARCH IN CHILD DEVELOPMENT

The Society for Research in Child Development (SRCD) is an organization of more than 5,000 members from various academic disciplines concerned with the study of child development. Disciplines include, but are not limited to, anthropology, home economics, linguistics, neuroscience, nursing, nutrition, pediatrics, psychiatry, psychology, public health, and sociology. In addition to being multidisciplinary, the society's membership is also international.

The child development movement in the United States started in the early 1920s, but its roots are much earlier. In contrast to many sciences, it arose from external pressures broadly based on desires for better health, rearing, education, legal, and occupational treatment of children. Movements related to child health, child study, and mental hygiene were prominent by the late 19th and early 20th centuries. From these activities came the conception of the child as a responsibility of the society at large.

The scientific status of the field of child development received formal recognition in 1923 through the appointment of the Committee on Child Development, appointed by the National Research Council, a division of the National Academies of Science. The purpose of the committee was to integrate research activities and to stimulate research in child development. In 1927 the first volume of *Child Development Abstracts and Bibliography* was published, SRCD's first publication, which continued until 2000.

In 1933 the Committee on Child Development disbanded and the newly organized Society for Research in Child Development emerged. The mission of SRCD is to promote multidisciplinary research on infant, child, and adolescent development in diverse contexts and its life-long implications; to foster the exchange of information among scientists and other professionals worldwide; and to encourage applications of research-based knowledge.

The society currently publishes three journals:

Child Development—published bimonthly; contains original articles on development research and theory.

Monographs of the Society for Research in Child Development—published four times each year; consists primarily of comprehensive reports of large-scale research projects or integrated programs of research.

Social Policy Report—published quarterly; each issue focuses on a single topic affecting children, youth, or families and includes analyses of legislation and syntheses of research on issues of social policy and children.

The society hosts a biennial meeting with attendance of more than 5,000. These internationally attended meetings include individual research reports, symposia, invited lectures, and discussion sessions, among other timely and historical programs.

Sixteen percent of SRCD's members are from nations outside the United States, representing over 50 countries throughout the world. Special efforts are made by the society to increase communication and interaction among researchers in human development throughout the world. The society also has a commitment to research and training in diversity. Increasing and disseminating research on children from many racial and ethnic minorities is a specific goal.

The society maintains the Office of Policy and Communications (OPC) in Washington, DC. The director supervises the SRCD Fellows Program in Child Development. The goals of this program are to contribute to the effective use of scientific knowledge, to educate the scientific community about public policy, and to establish effective liaisons among scientists, federal, and congressional offices. Fellows spend a year in federal agencies or in congressional offices working to facilitate the translation of findings of research to societal issues regarding children and families. The OPC also has programs to communicate research to the media and to the public.

The society welcomes persons interested in child development. Membership is open to any individual actively engaged in research in human development or any of the related basic sciences, and/or engaged in teaching relevant to human development, or otherwise furthering the purposes of the society. SRCD is located at 3131 S. State St. Suite 301, Ann Arbor, MI, 48108.

—*John W. Hagen and*
Nicholas G. Velissaris

Further Reading and Reference

Society for Research in Child Development, http://www .srcd.org

SOCIOBIOLOGY

The study of ethology stresses how behavior is seen within a gene-environment interaction with an emphasis on the influence of ecological factors on genetically based behaviors. Although one's genetic endowment takes precedence, environmental factors and selective pressure to change are critical components as well.

A more recent extension of some of these ethological principles helps form a relatively new discipline called sociobiology or psychobiology. A major difference between ethology and sociobiology is that sociobiologists view all aspects of development as being controlled and caused by specific genes and very little importance is given to factors that originate outside the organism.

Not a great deal of research has been done applying sociobiological principles to human behavior. It is primarily for this reason that the limitations of such a new approach have to be considered, but at the same time appreciate its suggestions for different and perhaps better ways of understanding development.

THE THEORETICAL OUTLOOK

One of the ongoing arguments as far as human development is whether humans are distinct and separate from their primate ancestors (such as great apes), or are simply a continuation or an extension of them, only at a more "advanced" level.

Most ethologists would agree that human's ancestors contribute a great deal to their current repertoire of biological and psychological potentialities. Sociobiologists would agree with this as well, but would take this argument one step further and discuss biological and psychological determinism.

They contend that the continuity between an individual's current evolutionary status and that of the immediate and past genetic ancestry is almost unbroken. What this means is that, first, the actions of genetic endowment as the cause of behavior are paramount. Second, it means that humans are not as morally and spiritually unique as some people would like to think. In fact, most sociobiologists believe that even our most prized attribute—that of altruism or sacrifice—has a genetic basis.

Sociobiology has been popularly defined by Edmund Wilson (a very important influence) as the systematic study of the biological basis of all social behavior, with social behavior defined as the interaction between organisms. The ardent sociobiologist has no qualms about considering even the most complex of human behaviors, such as the selection of a spouse or the rearing of children, as having a biological basis in nature. These complex behaviors are the outcome of millions of years of evolutionary "progress," do not result from learning, and are highly similar to the same category of behaviors in other animals in form and function.

The task of the sociobiologist is to study the social acts of animals and demonstrate how the animal's actions assist the developing organism in adapting to its environment. More specifically, the "prime directive" of the organism becomes the development of such patterns that contribute to the successful reproduction of the species, often at any and all costs to the parent generation.

For example, it is not uncommon in the animal world for parents to sacrifice their food, shelter, and at times their very lives for their young. All of these sacrifices represent an effort to increase the chances of the young to prosper and reproduce. In terms of human behaviors, we can look to the Eskimos for such an example of the ultimate sacrifice within this sociobiological model.

In the Eskimo culture, grandparents retain a position of honor and respect. This deference comes from the real and legendary sacrifices they have made for their young when it was time to find a new home, yet the amount of supplies were not sufficient to carry all the family members through to the journey's end. Instead of eating their share of food at the expense of the other (younger) people in the tribe or family (and the breeders of the next generation), they would forgo their share, stay behind, and quietly die.

A sociobiological interpretation of this would be that the grandparents, who have lived a full and rewarding life, made the only choice they could. This was a sacrifice, on an individual level, for the good of the entire tribe, to ensure that the species (and the gene pool) continued to survive. Furthermore, the motivation for such sacrifice comes not from the recognition these people will receive as honored and revered members of the society, but theoretically from one's genetic inheritance.

The major problem with this argument, however, is that it is certainly impossible to adequately test, let alone prove. The notion that people sacrifice certain things, and even their lives under specific conditions, can either be the result of some genetic predisposition or in fact a learned or culturally acquired phenomenon. The only way to settle the question would be to manipulate one's genetic potential and observe the outcomes in future generations. We might be able to do this with fruit flies in the laboratory, but certainly not humans. We have neither the technical capability to accomplish this, nor the ethical and social mechanisms to deal with such experimentation.

THE CAUSES OF BEHAVIOR

Sociobiologists believe that there are two general categories of causes that we can look to for an understanding of what precipitates animal (including of course human) behavior. These are called first level and second level causes.

Second level causes, which are further removed from the actual behavior (or less directly influential), consist of phylogenetic inertia and ecological pressure. These in turn influence what are called first level causes, identified as demographic variables, the rate of gene flow, and the coefficient of relationship. All of these result in what we generally know as social behaviors, leading up to the reproduction of the species and the sharing of the most adaptive genes.

Both of these categories of causes are somewhat "removed" as direct influences on behavior. First level causes are, however, more immediate and more traceable as influences. That is, they are more closely related, and perhaps more clearly a cause of the specific behavior or pattern of behavior under consideration.

SECOND LEVEL CAUSES OF BEHAVIOR

The first second level cause is phylogenetic inertia, which emphasizes the strong nature orientation of sociobiology. In the sociobiological sense, phylogenetic inertia can be defined as the tendency to remain genetically unchanged or the tendency to continue as formulated. It is the ease with which an organism's genetic endowment and tendencies might be alterable. In some cases this inertia may be high, and change is difficult to accomplish, while in others the opposite may be the case. What are some factors that might be involved?

Four factors determine the degree of phylogenetic inertia that is associated with any pattern of behavior. The first of these is the degree of genetic variability that exists in the species. The higher the degree of variability (and the accompanying increased opportunity for new combinations of genes to take place), the lower the inertia or the resistance to change on the part of the organism. This also means that there is an increased likelihood of generating new and more adaptive behaviors, a very important function for all animals to be able to perform. On the other hand, if there is very little variability available, then the level of inertia will probably be quite high. In sum, an opportunity to increase the gene pool decreases phylogenetic inertia since more new material is being introduced, and the likelihood of a change increases.

Antisocial factors are the second determinant, or anything that encourages the species (as represented by the individual) to isolate itself. In doing so, the likelihood of increased genetic variability goes down (because of fewer potential partners to chose from), phylogenetic inertia increases, and there are reduced chances for adaptive changes. This is clearly an argument against inbreeding of species. Not only does it exaggerate the recessive and often nonadaptive traits and characteristics, but also minimizes the chances for genetic variability. A sociobiologist would argue that the social taboos we have against incest have their origin at this level of isolation from other sources of potential variation.

The third factor is the complexity of the behavior. The more elaborate the behavior is, the more component parts there are likely to be to the behavior. The more component parts, the higher the inertia needs to be to keep these parts together and functioning, hence the more difficult the behavior may be to change. This can be seen while examining such a complex human behavior as parenting, which consists of a great number of highly interrelated and complex behaviors. The very reason why it may be so difficult to change one's parenting practices (as any parent will tell you) is because the phylogenetic inertia associated with these complex practices is so high.

Finally, the last factor is the effect of the change in behavior on other traits and characteristics. If a behavior is complex (and, as we have just argued, the phylogenetic inertia is high), it takes a major effort to alter the behavior. When one part of a complex system is altered, it probably results in the alteration of other parts as well. In others, the degree to which a change in one part of the system affects a change in another part of the system helps to determine the degree of phylogenetic inertia.

The next of these two kinds of second level causes is called ecological pressure, most simply defined as aspects of environment that encourage the organism to change. For the sociobiologist, ecological pressure represents the nurture side of the nature-nurture debate.

As one might expect, certain ecological or environmental events have no impact on the social evolution of animals, while others are very important. For example, one of the most significant forms of ecological pressure is the presence of predators. This is because predators are probably the primary threat to the animal's existence, and therefore to the passing on of that animal's most adaptive genes.

Given this pressure, what has evolved among all animals are very sophisticated and well-designed means for defending oneself against predators. For example, a primary predator of the brown sparrow is the hawk, which will attack these small birds in flight. When a hawk is flying below the sparrows, and they are not threatened, the sparrows usually fly in a loose grouping. When the hawk is above the sparrows, however, and in position to strike, the sparrows bind together in a closely knit flying group. The hawk is much less likely to try and penetrate the group and risk injuring a vulnerable part of its body. Consequently,

the likelihood of survival for the sparrows increases, and the opportunity for them to pass on their genetic endowment to a subsequent generation is increased as well.

Another major source of ecological pressure is the availability of food. Most directly, when food is not available, it is impossible for a species to survive. In such a situation, animals are forced to move on to a new location where nourishment might be more available. For example, many African animals are nomadic in that they move seasonally from location to location following the growth of certain types of plants to feed on. Even today, in some less technologically advanced cultures, tribes follow herds of animals for food and other necessities, such as hides for clothing. It is only relatively recently that humans have learned how to make food grow in spite of hostile environmental conditions.

Probably the most applicable example of a change due to ecological pressure in the human species is when we made the transition from being a tree-based animal to one that was land based. We began to walk on all fours at first, then later used our hind legs to eventually assume an upright posture. Some sociobiologists believe there was pressure for us to leave our loftier heights to have better access to food. One of the consequences of a more upright posture is a larger and stronger pelvis to help support the viscera and upper body.

A larger pelvis also allows for another change in human evolution, the easier delivery of the newborn with less potential for damage from coming through a too-small birth canal. As our heads became larger, more adaptive changes occurred in the structure of the female's body to compensate.

Finally, as E. O. Wilson concludes, "manipulation of the physical environment is the ultimate adoption," since it is not until animals manipulate their environment that they seek to control it. And, as Wilson notes, once animals control their environment, the indefinite survival of the species can almost be assured. Humans have made tremendous gains in controlling their environment in a very "short" period of time on the evolutionary clock. Once we discovered the use of tools such as bones to beat animal skins, we in a sense were on our way.

The control we have of our environment has increased dramatically through the design and use of tools, including everything from the wheel and plow to the space shuttle. The past half century of human progress has seen incredible increases in human ingenuity and tool usage, but less than comparable progress in adapting to the social impact of these advances. The implications of manipulating genes, maintaining life when there is no mental activity, and going beyond our own solar system (as radio waves are about to do) leave an opening in our evolutionary progress. This opening suggests that the ecological pressures associated with these "advances" are so great that the adaptation process is slow and almost, at times, unnoticeable.

—Neil J. Salkind

Further Readings and References

Greene, S. (1994). Biological determinism: Persisting problems for the psychology of women. *Feminism and Psychology, 14,* 431–435.

International Society of Developmental Psychobiology, http://www.oswego.edu/isdp/

Singh, D. (1995). Female judgment of male attractiveness and desirability for relationships: Role of waist to hip ratio and financial status. *Journal of Personality and Social Psychology, 69,* 1089–1101.

SOCIOECONOMIC STATUS

Socioeconomic status (SES) is a construct of great importance to the study of human development. Much controversy exists among researchers in the field about the definition and measurement of socioeconomic status. Bornstein and Bradley in 2003 pointed out that there is little debate, however, that SES bears meaningful relation to developmental outcomes and that those of higher SES have greater access than those of lower SES to many resources useful for supporting positive development. Although our understanding of the nature and course of SES-developmental relations is in its infancy, the robust relations that SES shares with cognitive, health, and socioemotional indicators supports its study as a variable of primary interest and as a control in developmental research.

Socioeconomic status can be defined in basic terms as one's position in a stratified society, where people are rank ordered according to the amount of a socially valued commodity they possess (Wohlfarth, 1997). Such a commodity can be skills, education, income, social connections, or another valued good. The functional necessity of stratification is assumed; that within a society there are certain positions to be filled and that these positions have different values for the survival of the society. Furthermore, the proposed basis for stratification lies in individual characteristics, implying some degree of personal responsibility for one's position. Within this frame, your place in society or socioeconomic status is important because it reflects implicitly your prestige.

This definition demarcates the boundaries between SES and social class. Whereas SES is situated within a model that presumes a functional necessity of stratification, prestige as the basis for one's position, and quantitative gradations in status, social class theories suppose oppression as the genesis of stratification, control as the basis for one's position, and conflictual relations between qualitatively distinct levels in the social hierarchy (Wohlfarth, 1997). The distinction between SES and social class highlights issues unique to the study of SES, such as the inextricability of socioeconomic status from socioeconomic inequality and the potential for individually powered status mobility.

Socioeconomic status can be conceptualized as a function of capital. Traditional models represent SES through combinations of three specific forms of capital: income, education, and occupation. The Hollingshead four-factor index of social status (Hollingshead, 1975), for instance, is based on the education and occupation of each employed householder in the home, where *householder* is defined as a person who has or shares financial responsibility for maintaining the home and supporting the family members living there (Hauser, 1994). Such representations are well tested and tend to bear meaningful relations to developmental outcomes. They fall short, however, of fully capturing the complexity of certain persons' roles in relation to the family's status, such as a retired grandparent who has substantial wealth tied up in investments, a mother with a doctoral degree who is staying home to raise her children while her husband works, or a teenage father who does not reside in the family household but takes care of his children each day.

Current models often take a broader focus and represent socioeconomic status using Coleman's 1988 concept of financial capital, human capital, and social capital. These categories allow for the inclusion of a wider array of status indicators than traditional representations and may better capture the complexities of socioeconomic position. Financial capital includes income and occupation as well as indices of wealth such as accounts and assets. Human capital incorporates formal education and other training and skills. Furthermore, social capital taps the resources achieved through social connections. Such an interpretation of SES is better able than traditional models to account for potential access as well as realized access to resources. A drawback is that the terms of financial, human, and social capital are vague and encompass a wide variety of constructs, leading to challenges in interpreting and comparing demonstrated relations to developmental outcomes.

The case of financial capital exemplifies important measurement challenges facing researchers who study SES. Although material resources are seemingly the easiest of the three forms of capital to quantify, conceptual and practical issues obstruct a uniform measure of financial assets. Critical distinctions exist between concepts such as labor market earnings, hourly wage rate, monthly rent, and wealth—including liquid and other forms of income. Questions about single versus multiple indicators introduce a tug-of-war between specificity and power. Additionally, the study of financial resource is entangled in issues of privacy and shame such that practical concerns about obtaining honest and accurate responses often drive the selection of indicators.

Beyond the question of which indicators to choose lies the puzzle of whose capital to measure. Particularly for children, there is a question of whose assets best reflect their own access to resources. Moreover, the traditional view of SES as an individual characteristic has been usurped by the notion that multiple levels of SES bear relevance for developmental outcomes. Family per capita income, calculated by dividing the sum of income from all sources coming into the household over a certain period of time by the number of people living in the home, presently holds favor over individual income. Also, researchers now concern themselves with the measurement of neighborhood and school level capital.

Institutional resources, norms/collective efficacy, and relationships, according to Leventhal and Brooks-Gunn, are three forms of capital used to characterize neighborhood SES. Institutional resources capture material benefits of neighborhood residence, such as schools, health care services, employment opportunities, and child care. Norms/collective efficacy includes shared values, group behavior, and regulatory mechanisms that serve to monitor community

activity. And relationships, much like social capital, comprise the support networks, home environments, and the relationships of community members. Neighborhood SES accounts for variance in developmental outcomes beyond that explained by individual or household SES (Leventhal & Brooks-Gunn, 2003). Yet the challenges involved in measuring a community's SES are equal to if not greater than those of selecting indicators for a single person or home.

Neighborhood of residence, family structure, and employment are increasingly fluid constructs. Poor families, especially, face uncertainty and change in their access to financial and other forms of capital. The dynamic nature of socioeconomic conditions means that snapshots of family functioning at a single point in time may misrepresent the effects of SES on human development. Researchers now prefer to pull for annual income rather than tapping hourly wages or monthly earnings, and most consider multiyear measures superior still. Questions about "usual" income, on the other hand, are vulnerable to inaccuracy and might best be avoided.

The persistence of one's socioeconomic position warrants attention, particularly given evidence suggesting that cumulative effects of income volatility over time may have greater influence on the adjustment of economically disadvantaged children than average income levels (McLoyd & Smith, 2002). Furthermore, developmental outcomes may depend on the life course timing of socioeconomic conditions. Whereas early childhood supports the strongest relations between family income and cognitive ability (Duncan & Brooks-Gunn, 1997), the teenage years play host to an increased relation between neighborhood SES and behavioral outcomes (Leventhal & Brooks-Gunn, 2000). Moreover, the effects of gradations in socioeconomic conditions are nonlinear (Duncan and Magnuson, 2003), and changes in SES over time may matter more for those who have less. These issues justify a growing focus among developmentalists on longitudinal studies of SES.

Despite unresolved problems of representation and measurement, the correlations between SES and important developmental outcomes are strong. SES positively predicts child birth weight, school achievement, behavior, socioemotional development, and pubertal timing (Entwisle & Astone, 1994) as well as adult physical and mental health and life expectancy (Blacksher, 2002). Concomitantly, the advantage of analyzing SES holistically rather than as separate indices is questionable. Income, education, and occupation, for example, all relate to physical health, yet, according to Liberatos, Link, and Kelsey (1988), are not themselves highly intercorrelated. Indeed, each indicator is often associated with health outcomes independent of the other two. Currently the favored method among researchers is to measure multiple components of SES but enter them separately in analyses (Ensminger & Fothergill, 2003).

The trend away from aggregation and simplification and toward greater specificity and sophistication characterizes the current state of research on SES and human development. SES earns the reputation of a catch-all variable because indices of income, education, and occupation typically stand as markers for all of the cognitive and socioemotional traits that contribute to a certain level of SES (Jeynes, 2002). With few experimental studies manipulating socioeconomic conditions, the causal effects of SES indicators are often difficult to determine.

Studying moderators and mediators of SES in its relation to developmental outcomes may map pathways through which socioeconomic conditions influence human development, yet this endeavor is in its early stages. Many hold parenting practices as key mediators of SES-developmental relations, but the study of this linkage currently falls short of establishing a causal pathway between parenting and child outcomes (Duncan & Magnuson, 2003). An alternative though not contradictory conception is that parenting practices may moderate the effects of SES. Similarly, although economic models hold that families with greater financial capital are better able to purchase or produce inputs important to child development, specific routes of influence remain elusive due to selection effects and third variable problems.

Selection effects refer to the phenomenon whereby individuals with characteristics in common select similar environments—in this case, socioeconomic conditions. The idea is that such shared characteristics represent a third variable that may explain environmental relations to development. Genes stand as the ultimate third variable, and deterministic accounts posit that all socialization can be reduced to the actions of genes on behaviors (Rowe, 1994). Yet quasi-experimental manipulations of income show benefits of financial gain for child development (Costello, Compton, Keeler, & Angold, 2003) and recent adoption studies provide compelling evidence for a causal role of socioeconomic status by revealing

greater IQ gains for children adopted into families with higher SES (Duyme, Dumaret, & Tomkiewicz, 1999).

The causal contributions of SES to developmental outcomes seem likely, if not well charted. Rather than presupposing that socioeconomic indicators operate unidirectionally and in isolation, researchers today tend to view SES within a dynamic system of influence. The notion of parallel causation suggests that several different factors may be sufficient but not simultaneously necessary to produce a particular outcome. Convergent causation refers to the idea that a particular process may be necessary but not sufficient to produce a given outcome. Additionally, the principle of reciprocal causation states that a developmental outcome may depend on the bidirectional influences of multiple factors interacting across time (Bornstein & Bradley, 2003). Each of these ideas deserves consideration in the study of SES-developmental relations.

Growing evidence supports the notion that various components of SES influence one another (Jeynes, 2002). Occupation, for instance, influences one's relationships and therefore one's social capital, while relationships, in turn, may create employment opportunities (Bradley & Corwyn, 2002). Furthermore, ecological and living systems theories propose dynamic and bidirectional relations between contextual factors and individual characteristics. Research showing that job conditions shape workers' values, personalities, and even cognitive skills (Parcel & Menaghan, 1994) exemplifies such interplay. The complexities of dynamic influence speak at once to the fluidity of status, as well as to the pervasiveness of inequality and challenge of individual escape. Indeed, this latter idea resonates with theories of social class and calls into question the validity of core assumptions of the SES model.

The relationship between SES and age, gender, and race/ethnicity (among other person variables) remains a frontier for research. To avoid oversimplification, developmentalists typically leave categories for age, gender, and race/ethnicity out of indices of SES, choosing instead to analyze these variables separately (see Oakes & Rossi, 2003). Yet such person variables may be part and parcel of socioeconomic position in ways that are not easily captured by indices of financial, human, and social capital.

One issue is the influence of age, gender, and race/ethnicity on socioeconomic attainment. Much concern surrounds gender and racial and ethnic gaps in socioeconomic indicators such as educational achievement (for children) and wages (for adults). Current interest centers on separating effects of oppression and institutional barriers from those of gender or cultural orientations toward status indicators. A somewhat separate issue is that our current models fall short of accounting for status inconsistencies associated with age, gender, and race/ethnicity such as the greater respect afforded a white mill worker than a black teacher (Stuckey, 1990).

Also, growing evidence supports person variables such as age, gender, and race/ethnicity as moderators of SES-developmental relations. Although socioeconomic conditions predict mental health problems, for instance, after controlling for SES, African Americans, Native Americans, and Hispanics are less likely to report or to be reported as having such problems (Saaman, 2000). Findings such as this call into question the cultural sensitivity of our models of SES. Indeed, certain SES constructs such as marital status may have little bearing (Ackerman, Schoff D'Eramo, Umylny, Schultz, & Izard, 2001) for cultural groups such as African Americans where unmarried cohabitation arrangements are the norm (McLoyd, 1998) and our models may lack indices to capture the capital available through certain cultural connections and perspectives.

The potential insensitivity of our models to age, gender, and racial/ethnic differences in the meaning and relevance of status indicators is at once perplexing and not surprising. Although the study of SES and human development aims to understand complexities of status, we are at the same time products of our socioeconomic system, and the difficulty of gaining objective perspective on that system cannot be overestimated. This is perhaps the best explanation that can be offered for why our study of SES has been limited until recently to a deficit model where heterogeneous socioeconomic groups provide data on middle-SES constructs. Indeed, when the assumed functionality of stratification underlies our concept of SES, it is hard to escape a circular justification of socioeconomic position.

Within this traditional frame, it should come as little surprise that low-SES individuals appear deficient. Undeniably, social address powerfully predicts problematic developmental outcomes. Yet a deficit model falls short of illuminating how low SES translates to maladjustment, why low-SES individuals show different types of problematic outcomes, or what allows some low-SES children to dodge the risks and maintain functional behavior and health. Indeed, recent studies

suggest that contextual elements that correlate with financial capital across socioeconomic strata vary independently within lower-SES brackets and may exert independent influence on child development (Ackerman, Brown, & Izard, 2003, 2004; Duncan & Brooks-Gunn, 1997, 2000). Only by abandoning a deficit model and creating an alternative frame can we tackle the theoretical and empirical issues that are critical to a complex understanding of socioeconomic risk.

Growing awareness of the issues, tightening designs and measurements, and increasingly powerful statistical techniques all drive advances in the study of SES. Yet, as our models gain sophistication, the importance of socioeconomic conditions persists. The strong relations that SES shares with cognitive, health, and socioemotional outcomes supports its use as a primary variable of interest and as a control in developmental research. So long as we live in a stratified society, the study of socioeconomic status is likely to remain critical to an understanding of human development.

—*Eleanor D. Brown*

Further Readings and References

Ackerman, B. P., Brown, E., & Izard, C. E. (2003). Continuity and change in levels of externalizing behavior in school of children from economically disadvantaged families. *Child Development, 74*, 694–704.

Ackerman, B. P., Brown, E., & Izard, C. E. (2004). The relations between persistent poverty and contextual risk and children's behavior in elementary school. *Developmental Psychology, 40*, 367–377.

Ackerman, B. P., Schoff D'Eramo, K., Umylny, L., Schultz, D., & Izard, C. (2001). Family structure and the externalizing behavior of children from economically disadvantaged families. *Journal of Family Psychology, 15*, 288–300.

Blacksher, E. (2002). On being poor and feeling poor: Low socioeconomic status and the moral. *Theoretical Medicine and Bioethics, 23*, 455–470.

Bornstein M. H., & Bradley, R. H. (2003). Introduction. In M. H. Bornstein & R. H. Bradley (Eds.), *Socioeconomic status, parenting, & child development* (pp. 1–12). Mahwah, NJ: Erlbaum.

Bradley, R. H., & Corwyn, R. F. (2002). Socioeconomic status and child development. *Annual Review of Psychology, 53*, 371–399.

Coleman, J. S. (1988). Social capital in the creation of human capital. *American Journal of Sociology, 94*(Suppl.), 95–120.

Costello, E. J., Compton, S. N., Keeler, G., & Angold, A. (2003). Relationships between poverty and psychopathology: A natural experiment. *Journal of the American Medical Association, 290*, 2023–2029.

Duncan, G. J., & Brooks-Gunn, J. (1997). Income effects across the life span: Integration and interpretation. In G. J. Duncan & J. Brooks-Gunn (Eds.), *Consequences of growing up poor* (pp. 596–610). New York: Russell Sage Foundation.

Duncan, G. J., & Brooks-Gunn, J. (2000). Family poverty, welfare reform, and child development. *Child Development, 71,* 188–196.

Duncan, G. J., & Magnuson, K. A. (2003). Off with Hollingshead: Socioeconomic resources, parenting and child development. In M. H. Bornstein & R. H. Bradley (Eds.), *Socioeconomic status, parenting, & child development* (pp. 83–106). Mahwah, NJ: Erlbaum.

Duyme, M., Dumaret, A. C., & Tomkiewicz, S. (1999). How can we boost IQs of "dull children"?: A late adoption study. *Proceedings of the National Academy of Sciences, 96,* 8790–8794.

Ensminger, M. E., & Fothergill, K. (2003). A decade of measuring SES: What it tells us and where to go from here. In M. H. Bornstein & R. H. Bradley (Eds.), *Socioeconomic status, parenting, & child development* (pp. 13–28). Mahwah, NJ: Erlbaum.

Entwisle, D. R., & Astone, N. M. (1994). Some practical guidelines for measuring youth's race/ethnicity and socioeconomic status. *Child Development, 65,* 1521–1540.

Hauser, R. M. (1994). Measuring socioeconomic status in studies of child development. *Child Development, 65,* 1541–1545.

Hollingshead, A. B. (1975). *The four-factor index of social status.* Unpublished manuscript, Yale University, New Haven, CT.

Jeynes, W. H. (2002). The challenge of controlling for SES in social science and education research. *Educational Psychology Review, 14,* 205–221.

Leventhal, T., & Brooks-Gunn, J. (2000). The neighborhoods they live in: The effects of neighborhood residence upon child and adolescent outcomes. *Psychological Bulletin, 126,* 309–337.

Leventhal, T., & Brooks-Gunn, J. (2003). Moving on up: Neighborhood effects on children and families. In M. H. Bornstein & R. H. Bradley (Eds.), *Socioeconomic status, parenting, & child development* (pp. 203–230). Mahwah, NJ: Erlbaum.

Liberatos, P., Link, B. G., & Kelsey, J. L. (1988). The measurement of social class in epidemiology. *Epidemiologic Reviews, 10,* 87–121.

McLoyd, V. C. (1998). Socioeconomic disadvantage and child development. *American Psychologist, 53,* 185–204.

McLoyd, V. C., & Smith, J. (2002). Physical discipline and behavior problems in African American, European American and Hispanic children: Emotional support as a moderator. *Journal of Marriage and the Family, 64,* 40–53.

Oakes, J. M., & Rossi, P. H. (2003). The measurement of SES in health research: Current practice and steps toward a new approach. *Social Science and Medicine, 56,* 769–784.

Parcel, T. L., & Menaghan, E. G. (1994). *Parents' jobs and children's lives.* New York: deGruyter.

Rowe, D. C. (1994). *The limits of family influence: Genes, experience and behavior.* New York: Guilford.

Saaman, R. A. (2000). The influences of race, ethnicity and poverty on the mental health of children. *Journal of Health Care for the Poor and Underserved, 11,* 100–110.

Stuckey, J. E. (1999). *The violence of literacy.* Portsmouth, NH: Boynton/Cook.

Wohlfarth, T. (1997). Socioeconomic inequality and psychopathology: Are socioeconomic status and social class interchangeable? *Social Science and Medicine, 45,* 399–410.

SPANKING

Definitions of spanking or corporal punishment vary widely depending on the source. Much of this variation can be attributed to differences in individual agendas. For example, Murray Straus, on record as being opposed to striking children in any form, classed it as "minor violence," clearly a pejorative term. He then goes on to define corporal punishment as "a legally permissible violent act, carried out as part of the parenting role." James Dobson, on the other hand, writes that a lovingly administered spanking is an essential part of teaching children healthy boundaries.

Public perceptions vary just as widely. Although a large majority of American parents use spanking as part of their repertoire of disciplinary techniques, and 80% to 90% of adolescents report having been spanked as a child, only about half report having been "physically disciplined." Furthermore, only a small percentage of these adolescents reported feeling abused by their parents. Clearly there is a dichotomy between what parents and adolescents report and what some experts are saying about physical punishment.

Spanking is an issue that raises strong emotions. Not that long ago, spanking—striking a child on the buttocks with the flat of the hand or an implement such as a belt—was considered a necessary part of responsible parenting. As rates of violence and abuse in American society continue to grow, developmental researchers have come to the conclusion, not always supported by research, that hitting children under the guise of punishment is contributing to this rise in violence. These researchers have called for restrictions on parents that range from "rules" about how to spank a child to laws like those in Sweden and other countries that outlaw spanking completely. Yet, an issue this complex cannot be resolved that simply.

Anecdotally, many American adults will tell you that they can "just tell" which children have been spanked at home and which have not, with the implication being that those who are not spanked are "spoiled brats." Researchers tell us that those children who are spanked tend to be more aggressive and have poorer mental health. The truth very probably lies somewhere in the middle. Elizabeth Gershoff's 2002 meta-analysis (a statistical procedure in which the results of 88 different studies were combined) concluded that physical punishment is detrimental, but Diana Baumrind noted in her commentary on Gershoff that much of the research on spanking fails to adequately discriminate between spanking administered in the context of a healthy parent-child relationship and spanking in an abusive relationship. Baumrind and other authors, including Nancy Darling and Laurence Steinberg, and Joan Grusec and Jacqueline Goodnow, note that the context of a spanking, the child's interpretations of the reasons for it, and the attitudes formed by the spanking are perhaps more important that the spanking itself. Parents who use a variety of disciplinary methods, who are not prone to screaming or yelling, and who talk to their children and lay out clear expectations are very likely to see different outcomes from a spanking than parents who use harsh spanking as a first resort. Yet if researchers merely ask, "Do you spank your child?" these distinctions are soon lost.

Other research has examined the effectiveness of spanking as a disciplinary method. Generally, children who are spanked show more immediate compliance to adult demands, but studies also show that they are less likely to internalize morals. This is most likely linked to a lack of explanations for why specific behaviors are wrong and what the appropriate correct behavior would have been. Otherwise, spanking has few demonstrated positive effects and has not been shown to be preferable to other forms of discipline that may be more effective at maintaining the parent-child relationship, protecting the child's self-esteem, and allowing the child to understand the reasons for parental directives.

Clearly, a need exists for better-controlled studies on spanking within the context of healthy parent-child relationships, on long-term outcomes of children who are spanked, and on the effectiveness of spanking as a disciplinary technique.

—*Susan L. O'Donnell and Gregory Lonigan*

See also Punishment

Further Readings and References

Baumrind, D., Larzelere, R. E., & Cowan, P. A. (2002). Ordinary physical punishment: Is it harmful? Comment on Gershoff (2002). *Psychological Bulletin, 128*(4), 580–589.

Darling, N., & Steinberg, L (1993). Parenting style as context: An integrative model. *Psychological Bulletin, 113*(3), 487–496.

Gershoff, E. T. (2002). Corporal punishment by parents and associated child behaviors and experiences: A meta-analytic and theoretical review. *Psychological Bulletin, 128*(4), 539–579.

Gershoff, E. T. (2002). Corporal punishment, physical abuse, and the burden of proof: Reply to Baumrind, Larzelere, and Cowan (2002), Holden (2002), and Parke (2002). *Psychological Bulletin, 128*(4), 602–611.

Grusec, J. E., & Goodnow, J. J. (1994). Impact of parental discipline methods on the child's internalization of values: A reconceptualization of current points of view. *Developmental Psychology, 30*(1), 4–19.

Robinson, B. A. (n.d.). *Corporal punishment of children. Spanking: All points of view.* Retrieved from http://www .religioustolerance.org/spanking.htm

Whipple, E. E., & Richey, C. A. (1997). Crossing the line from physical disciple to child abuse: How much is too much? *Child Abuse & Neglect, 21*(5), 431–444.

SPECIAL NEEDS CHILDREN

Special needs children, or students with exceptionalities, describes all students who require special education and related services in order to develop their full potential. This definition further suggests that students receiving special education represent a subset of the general population of students and that they exhibit interindividual variation (i.e., developmental differences from one child to the next). Students with exceptionalities are a heterogeneous, or diverse, group and they require special education because they are markedly different from the general population of students in one or more areas because of their disability or limitation, or, in the case of gifted children, because of their special gifts and talents. The federally funded categories of disabilities include specific learning disabilities, speech or language impairments, mental retardation, serious emotional disturbance, hearing, orthopedic, or visual impairments, multiple disabilities, deaf-blindness, autism and traumatic brain injury, developmental delay, and preschool disabled. Furthermore, disabilities may vary greatly in cause, degree of severity, and effect on educational progress, and the effects, in turn, may vary depending on the individual's age, gender, and life circumstances.

On the national level, nearly 15% of all preschool and school-aged children qualify as having a disability. In the 1999 to 2000 school year, almost 5.75 million students, between 5 and 21 years of age, received some kind of special education, and this number has been steadily growing. With regard to gender, more than two-thirds of all students receiving special education are male, with boys outnumbering girls in two categories: learning disabilities and emotional disturbance. The two most prevalent categories of disabilities are specific learning disabilities (50.5%) and speech and language impairments (19.1%), followed by mental retardation (10.8%) and emotional disturbance (8.2%). The fastest growing category is that of learning disabilities. The number of children with attention deficit disorder and attention deficit/hyperactivity disorder (ADHD) has also increased dramatically since 1992, which may be largely attributed to a federal memorandum stipulating that these children were eligible for services under other-health impaired category.

In addition to federally funded categories, another category of exceptionality, gifted and talented, is also used to describe children with special needs who require special education services. Prevalence rates of children identified as gifted and talented vary greatly by state as a function of a particular definition, ranging from a conservative 2% of all students when high IQ and achievement test scores cut-offs are used, to a more liberal 10% to 15% when a flexible, multiple-criteria approach is used. Additionally, researchers have devoted increasing attention to describing characteristics and needs of twice-exceptional students, or students who have both gifts and disabilities and/or learning disabilities, including hearing-disabled gifted students, high potential students with cerebral palsy, and academically gifted students with ADHD and/or learning disabilities, the latter being the most prevalent and widely studied category of twice-exceptional learners. As is the case with students with learning disabilities as well as gifted students, prevalence rates of gifted learning-disabled students is a function of a particular definition, with rather conservative estimates ranging from 2% to 5% of the total population of children with disabilities. Currently, there is a heated debate among the proponents of gifted education concerning how to best identify and serve gifted and talented children.

Generally, students may receive special education/gifted and talented services if they meet a certain set of cut-off criteria. However, if the student with exceptionalities fails to meet these criteria, this student is often left to struggle in school without much support and, thus, potential may be lost. Teachers need training in how to address the needs of children with exceptionalities. Because manifestations of exceptionalities may change as the child matures, educators and service providers are encouraged to take a developmental perspective of students with special needs. In sum, it is generally agreed that in identifying and serving the needs of children with special needs, the emphasis should be on recognizing abilities rather than focusing on disabilities.

—*Lilia M. Ruban and*
F. Richard Olenchak

See also Americans with Disabilities Act, Inclusion/Mainstreaming, Individualized Education Programs (IEP), Individuals with Disabilities Education Act (IDEA), School

Further Readings and References

Baum, S. M., Owen, S. V. (2004). *To be gifted and learning disabled: Strategies for helping bright students with LD, ADHD, and more.* Mansfield, CT: Creative Learning Press.

Bradley, R., Danielson, L., & Hallahan, D. P. (Eds.). (2002). *Identification of learning disabilities: Research to practice.* Mahwah, NJ: Erlbaum.

Council for Exceptional Children, http://www.cec.sped.org

Davis, G. A., & Rimm, S. B. (2004). *Education of the gifted and talented students* (5th ed.). Boston: Pearson.

Hallahan, D. P., & Kauffman, J. M. (2003). *Exceptional learners: Introduction to special education* (9th ed.). Boston: Allyn & Bacon.

Meece, J. L. (2002). *Child and adolescent development for educators* (2nd ed.). Boston: McGraw-Hill.

National Research Center on the Gifted and Talented, http://www.gifted.uconn.edu

STAGES OF DEVELOPMENT

The concept of developmental stages has been applied widely in the literature on human development. Many theorists believe that individuals progress through various stages as they develop into fully functioning human beings. The types, length, and characteristics of stages vary depending on the theory one reads. This entry will briefly define the concept of developmental stages and discuss the characteristics of three widely cited theorists in this area: Sigmund Freud, Jean Piaget, and Erik Erikson.

DEFINITION OF A DEVELOPMENTAL STAGE

Many theories of human development are based on the idea that individuals progress to adulthood through a series of identifiable stages. In general, the term *stage* refers to the period of time in one's development in which biological, psychological, and social forces interact to promote the growth of the individual. Individual stages can be conceptualized as dynamic rather than static and are related to other stages in a sequential manner. Theoretically, a series of stages comprises a pathway that individuals need to progress through in order for development to be actualized. In addition, each stage progressively builds on the stage(s) immediately preceding it, and some contend that earlier stages may be revisited later in life.

CHARACTERISTICS OF STAGES

The characteristics of specific stages (e.g., type, length) vary according to the specific theory of human development. Some theorists have proposed a sequence of stages that primarily focus on the child and adolescent, while others consider development across the life span. One of the earliest and most influential theories of development was described by Sigmund Freud. He believed that individuals are influenced by unconscious forces inside the person (i.e., id, ego, superego) and are largely motivated by sexual (i.e., libido) and aggressive drives. His theory of development is based on a psychosexual perspective and largely focuses on the first 12 years of an individual's life. In fact, Freud believed that an individual's personality was largely determined by the developmental process that takes place early in one's life. In addition, the specific stages he described (Table 1) are named from the areas of the body the libido is most centered on during that point of development.

Jean Piaget is another influential theorist who focused on the cognitive development of the individual. He believed that a significant amount of cognitive development (thinking processes) takes place during the first 12 years of life. Specifically, he suggested that a child's development of cognitive skills (Table 1) progresses over time beginning with the sensorimotor stage (ages 0–2) and ending with the ability to engage in abstract reasoning during the formal operational stage (ages 12 and older). The name of each stage reflects the type of cognitive development taking place for the child at that particular time in his or her life.

In contrast to Freud and Piaget, Erik Erikson's psychosocial theory considers human development across

Table 1   Comparison of Freud, Piaget, and Erikson's Developmental Stages

Developmental Stage	Freud	Piaget	Erikson
1	Oral (0–1)	Sensorimotor (0–2)	Basic trust vs. basic mistrust (0–2)
2	Anal (1–3)	Preoperational (2–7)	Autonomy vs. shame and doubt (2–3)
3	Phallic (3–5)	Concrete operational (7–12)	Initiative vs. guilt (3–5)
4	Latency (5–12)	Formal operational (12 and older)	Industry vs. inferiority (5–12)
5	Genital (12 & above)	—	Identity vs. role confusion (12–18)
6	—	—	Intimacy vs. isolation (18–30)
7	—	—	Generativity vs. stagnation (30–65)
8	—	—	Ego integrity vs. despair (65 and above)

NOTE: Numbers in parentheses are approximate ages for the stage.

the life span. Erikson believed that development is an interactional process between the biology of the individual and the environment. He described a series of eight psychosocial stages through which an individual progresses from birth to geriatrics (Table 1). At each of Erikson's stages, individuals are faced with a specific challenge or struggle termed a crisis. The successful resolution of a crisis allows the individual to acquire the necessary skills for that particular stage and to continue progressing to the following stage. In addition, Erikson asserted that individuals are faced with challenges throughout the life span continuing into older age (e.g., integrity vs. despair).

SUMMARY

The concept of stages has long been used, by various theorists, to explain the process of human development. Freud, Piaget, and Erikson are three of the major theorists who have each described a series of stages that individuals progress through on their way to becoming fully functioning individuals. More specifically, Freud and Piaget focused their developmental theories on the first 12 years of life while Erikson extended his theory to include the entire life span. Each of these theorists provides a divergent yet unique way to understand human development from a psychosexual, cognitive, and psychosocial perspective.

—*Jason J. Burrow-Sanchez*
and Robert March

See also Adolescence, Development, Early Childhood, Embryo, Emerging Adulthood, Fetus, Infancy, Middle Adulthood, Nature–Nurture, Older Adulthood, Oldest Old Age, Preschool Years

Further Readings and References

Berryman, J. C., Smythe, P. K., Taylor, A., Lamont, A., & Joiner, R. (2002). *Developmental psychology and you* (2nd ed.). Malden, MA: Blackwell.

Erikson, E. (1963). *Childhood and society* (2nd ed.). New York: W. W. Norton.

Erikson, E. (1980). *Identity and the life cycle.* New York: W. W. Norton.

Freud, S. (1949). *An outline of psychoanalysis.* New York: W. W. Norton.

Hall, C. S. (1954). *A primer of Freudian psychology.* Cleveland, OH: World.

National Network for Child Care, http://www.nncc.org/

Piaget, J. (1976). Piaget's theory. In P. B. Neubauer (Ed.), *The process of child development* (pp. 164–212). New York: New American Library.

Piaget, J., & Inhelder, B. (1969). *The psychology of the child.* New York: Basic Books.

Sugarman, L. (2001). *Life-span development.* New York: Taylor & Francis.

STAGES OF DYING

WHEN DOES DYING BEGIN AND END?

Before one can consider whether there are stages of dying, one needs to determine when dying begins and ends. Theoretically, dying begins when bodily functions start an irreversible decline toward total cessation of all bodily functions and final death. A more practical working definition might be that dying begins when medical experts have obtained and analyzed sufficient information to judge with a high degree of probability that a patient is terminal. In this case, the judgment of physicians or medical experts determines when dying begins. Determining the beginning of dying is important because it may influence the kind of treatment or care proposed, and patients' readiness to accept it.

From the viewpoint of patients, dying may begin when physicians communicate their judgment to patients (or when patients accept it, which may not occur immediately).

The end of dying is also difficult to determine. Theoretically, dying ends when there is total cessation of all bodily functions and the body begins the first stages in decaying. On a practical level, this is not an easy point to determine. Death is not an event such that one is alive one second and dead the next. Under natural conditions, "deathing" is a process where one becomes dead in a series of steps. Bodily functions end at different rates of speed depending on how long a particular part of the body can function without oxygen. Thus, a pronouncement of death and final death (total cessation of all bodily functions) are not the same.

However, practical considerations in modern society (e.g., decisions on inheritance, organ transplants, solving homicides) call for a pronouncement of death at the earliest possible moment in the deathing process when one can assume that the subsequent steps will inevitably follow. The pronouncement of death is relative to the scientific and cultural criteria used at a given period in time, which will continue to evolve in the future.

It is also important to consider the duration of the interval between the beginning and end of dying. For some, the duration of dying may be a few years, and for others it may be only a few hours. When people are dying, they are still alive, and one must consider their needs and concerns as both living and dying individuals. When individuals are dying gradually, they are "living while dying" and still must face many of the problems of everyday life. If they have only hours to live, then they are "dying while living," where the focus is more on just surviving from moment to moment.

Should Individuals Be Told They Are Dying?

Many people feel that patients should definitely be told that they are dying. Under the Federal Patient Self Determination Act of 1991, hospitals must inform patients of their condition because patients have the right to make decisions about their subsequent medical treatment. However, the custom of some subgroups in our multicultural society (e.g., Asians and Hispanics) is that the physician should tell the family but not the patient. Beyond this, some people feel that if patients are told they are dying, they may be unable to face the news, lose all hope, or develop anxiety and depression that will only accelerate the decline.

Types of Awareness Contexts

In a classic study, Glaser and Strauss identified four types of awareness contexts in the communication system between the dying patient and medical staff in institutions. The first is called closed awareness, where the staff knows but avoids letting patients know that they are going to die. The second type is called suspected awareness, where patients suspect that they are going to die and attempt to seek confirmation of their doubts (e.g., by learning about their condition, monitoring changes in treatment and any failure to respond to treatment, observing the behavior of others, and observing others with similar conditions). The third type is called mutual pretense, where both patients and staff know the patient is dying but both pretend not to know. The fourth type is open awareness, where both patients and staff know, and there is open discussion about dying.

PHYSICAL HEALTH CHANGES IN THE DYING PROCESS

Throughout the dying process, there are changes in health status, energy level, fatigue, frailty, mobility, weaknesses, and pain, and emergence of more specific symptoms. The latter may be due partially to the disease itself, the side effects of the treatment, and deficiencies of eating, sleeping, and activity. In active dying during the last few days of life, most patients have a reduced level of consciousness, loss of appetite, decreased thirst, disorientation (with or without visual and auditory hallucinations), restlessness, irregular breathing patterns, excessive pulmonary secretions, decreased urine production and incontinence, and progressively cool, purple extremities. Most people do not have a clear grasp of the physical decline that may occur while they are dying.

Trajectories

Based on a diagnosis and prognosis of a particular condition, a trajectory is an expectation of the duration and course of the dying process, that is, whether dying will proceed slowly or rapidly, vacillate, maintain a certain plateau, and so on. Having some idea of the trajectory can help the medical staff plan terminal care and help patients plan their lives.

PSYCHO-EMOTIONAL-SOCIAL ASPECTS OF DYING: STAGE THEORIES

Stage theories of dying are concerned with the psycho-emotional-social aspects of dying, beginning with the patient's first knowledge that he or she is dying. Unfortunately, no theory is sufficiently complete or adequate in describing and explaining all that is involved in dying. Nevertheless, these theories do provide some insights into the dying process.

Kübler-Ross's Stages of Dying

Based on interviews with dying cancer patients, Kübler-Ross identified five different emotional stages or reactions to the dying process. First, individuals go into denial when becoming aware of dying; denial helps keep anxiety under control and buys time while they try to verify the diagnosis or search for answers. Once the diagnosis is accepted, the second stage of anger begins, manifested in aggressive and demanding behavior as patients ask, "Why me?" Once the anger subsides, patients enter the bargaining stage, trying to make a deal with God or fate to exchange something to postpone the inevitable. Eventually, as patients become sicker, depression sets in—a sadness that life is coming to an end. Patients may cope by beginning to separate themselves from others. Finally, the acceptance of death occurs, which is simply peace and hope for what is to come.

Various criticisms of this stage theory exist. Individuals may not exhibit all stages or follow any fixed sequence of stages; they may experience certain stages simultaneously, shift back and forth, and so on. Most important, many other aspects of the dying process are not captured in the five stages of emotional responses. The lasting importance of Kübler-Ross's contribution is to show that a variety of feelings are going on during the dying process, and patients do want to talk about them.

Pattison's Phases of Dying

Pattison viewed the dying process in terms of three phases rather than stages. (These phases are broader than stages and are related to the amount of anxiety that exists.) The first phase, an acute crisis period when anxiety increases to a peak point, is initiated when patients become aware of impending death. Dying individuals need to reevaluate their self-identity, reformulate meaningful goals, and make approaching death more acceptable. As they adjust to being gravely ill, the anxiety gradually diminishes, and patients enter a chronic living-dying phase, where they must face not only the problems of dying but also the problems of living (such as maintaining a job, family relationships, and so on). Many specific fears emerge (e.g., fears of bodily deterioration, loss of control, pain and suffering, loneliness, financial insecurity, and so on). Finally, patients enter the terminal phase and begin to withdraw from people, objects, and events. Hope fades and patients accept the reality of imminent death.

Individuality in Dying

Although stage theories of dying provide insights into the dying process, they assume that individuals go through a common process of dying, that is, that there is only one path rather than multiple paths to dying. The predominant view today is that there is no common or universal set of stages that people go through in dying. Individual differences are important, and the dying process depends on many factors, such as the nature of the disease and treatment (and possible side effects), the environment of the hospital or institution, the patient's personality, the quality of interpersonal relationships, ethnicity, and gender differences.

Some research exists describing the help that patients themselves want while going through the dying process, including reduction or elimination of pain and symptoms, control of treatment and care, maintaining a relationship with loved ones without becoming a burden, maintaining their energy level and cognitive capacities as much as possible, and maintaining degrees of hope. All these factors and many others need to be integrated with existing knowledge about the dying process to gain a fuller picture of how patients' psycho-emotional-social states may vary at different "stages" of the dying process.

—*Victor G. Cicirelli*

See also Death, Death with Dignity, Dying

Further Readings and References

Cicirelli, V. G. (2002). *Older adults' views on death.* New York: Springer. (Chapter 5: Views and expectations about the dying process)

Corr, C. A. (1991–1992). A task-based approach to coping with dying. *Omega, 24,* 81–94.

Glaser, B. G., & Strauss, A. L. (1965). *Awareness of dying.* Chicago: Aldine.

Jennings, B., Gemmill, C., Bohman, B., & Lamb, K. (n.d.). *PHI350: The stages in the dying process.* Retrieved from http://www.uky.edu/Classes/PHI/350/kr.htm

Kastenbaum, R., & Thuell, S. (1995). Cookies baking, coffee brewing: Toward a contextual theory of dying. *Omega, 31,* 175–187.

Kübler-Ross, E. (1969). *On death and dying.* New York: Macmillan.

Pattison, E. M. (1977). *The experience of dying.* Englewood Cliffs, NJ: Prentice Hall.

STAGES OF MORAL DEVELOPMENT

Josie's mother asked her to run into the convenience store to pay for their gasoline. She handed her 10-year-old daughter a $20 bill. When Josie reached the checkout counter, the cashier said, "That will be $14.85, please." Josie handed the clerk the $20.00. After the clerk gave Josie her change, she began looking around the store at all the candy and soda pop. Suddenly, Josie looked down into her hands to see how much money was left over and realized that the clerk had given her too much change; he gave her a ten dollar bill instead of a $5 bill! She could buy

$5.00 worth of candy and her mother would never know. What should Josie do—return the change or buy some extra treats?

All individuals will encounter moral dilemmas such as the one described above. How does each of us handle these situations and why do we differ in our responses? According to *Webster's Dictionary*, morality refers to "the quality of being in accord with standards of good or right conduct." Individual variability in perceptions of what is "good" or "right" behavior exists. In addition, behavioral responses to moral dilemmas differ among people.

The study of moral development has been ongoing for a number of years and has become more popular within the past decade. With increases in societal problems such as violence in our schools and heavy drug use among children and youth, the topic of moral development is currently being treated as a critical one in the field of psychology (Damon, 1999). Most of the psychological research in this area has focused around the work of Lawrence Kohlberg, a primary theorist in moral development.

KOHLBERG'S THEORY

Using Piaget's (1932) theory of moral judgment for children, Lawrence Kohlberg (1958) developed a comprehensive stage theory of moral development. This theory is cognitive in nature, focusing on the thinking process that occurs when one decides whether a behavior is right or wrong. Thus, Kohlberg's theoretical emphasis is on how one decides to respond to a moral dilemma, not what one decides or what one actually does. For instance, a young child and an adult may both decide to return extra change to a cashier, but the reasons they give for that decision may be entirely different.

Kohlberg's theoretical framework consists of six stages arranged sequentially in successive tiers of complexity. He organized his six stages into three general levels of moral development.

Level 1: Preconventional Level

At the preconventional level, morality is externally controlled. Rules imposed by authority figures are conformed to in order to avoid punishment or receive rewards. This perspective involves the idea, What is right is what one can get away with or what is personally satisfying.

Stage 1: Punishment/ Obedience Orientation

Behavior is determined by consequences. The individual will obey in order to avoid punishment. For instance, Josie (the character in the introductory hypothetical story) may choose to return the extra change out of fear that her mother may punish her if she keeps it. On the other hand, Josie may choose to keep the extra money because she is confident that she will not get caught and there will be no punishment.

Stage 2: Instrumental Purpose Orientation

Behavior is determined again by consequences. The individual focuses on receiving rewards or satisfying personal needs. For example, Josie may choose not to return the extra money because she can buy candy and soda pop for herself. Or Josie may choose to return the money because she thinks the cashier will give her a monetary reward for being honest.

Level 2: Conventional Level

At the conventional level, conformity to social rules remains important to the individual. However, the emphasis shifts from self-interest to relationships with other people and social systems. The individual strives to support rules that are set forth by others such as parents, peers, and the government in order to win their approval or to maintain social order.

Stage 3: Good Boy/ Nice Girl Orientation

Behavior is determined by social approval. The individual wants to maintain or win the affection and approval of others by being a "good person." Josie may return the extra money because her mother will be so proud of her. Conversely, Josie may choose not to return the extra change because her friends will think she's "cool" because she got away with it.

Stage 4: Law and Order Orientation

Social rules and laws determine behavior. The individual now takes into consideration a larger perspective, that of societal laws. Moral decision making becomes more than consideration of close ties to others. The individual believes that rules and laws maintain social order that is worth preserving. For example, Josie may choose to return the extra change to the cashier because she knows that keeping the money would be breaking the law.

Level 3: Postconventional or Principled Level

At the postconventional level, the individual moves beyond the perspective of his or her own society. Morality is defined in terms of abstract principles and values that apply to all situations and societies. The individual attempts to take the perspective of all individuals.

Stage 5: Social Contract Orientation

Individual rights determine behavior. The individual views laws and rules as flexible tools for improving human purposes. That is, given the right situation, there are exceptions to rules. When laws are not consistent with individual rights and the interests of the majority, it does not bring about good for people and alternatives should be considered. For instance, Josie may return the extra change because she knows it would not be fair to the cashier because his cash drawer will come up short at the end of the day.

Stage 6: Universal Ethical Principle Orientation

According to Kohlberg, this is the highest stage of functioning. However, he claimed that some individuals will never reach this level. At this stage, the appropriate action is determined by one's self-chosen ethical principles of conscience. These principles are abstract and universal in application. This type of reasoning involves taking the perspective of every person or group that could potentially be affected by the decision. In regards to Josie, her decision not to keep the extra change would be based on taking into consideration how her dishonesty would affect the cashier, the store owner, other customers, her mother, and possibly other family members.

BASIC TENETS OF KOHLBERG'S THEORY

The numerous studies investigating moral reasoning based on Kohlberg's theory have confirmed basic tenets regarding the topic area. Cross-sectional data have

shown that older individuals tend to use higher stages of moral reasoning when compared with younger individuals (Kohlberg, 1969), while longitudinal studies report "upward" progression, in accordance with Kohlberg's theoretical order of stages (Kohlberg, 1978). In addition, comprehension studies have revealed that comprehension of the stages is cumulative (e.g., if a person understands stage 3, he or she understands the lower stages but not necessarily the higher stages), and comprehension of higher stages is increasingly difficult (Rest, 1973). Moreover, age trends in moral development have received cross-cultural support (Snarey, Reimer, & Kohlberg, 1984). Lastly, data support the claim that every individual progresses through the same sequence of development; however, the rates of development will vary.

MEASUREMENT OF MORAL DEVELOPMENT

Since the development of Kohlberg's theory, a number of measurement tools that purport to measure moral reasoning have been constructed. The Moral Judgment Interview (Kohlberg, 1969) is a rather lengthy structured interview requiring trained interviewers and scorers. Other instruments include the Defining Issues Test (Rest, 1979) and the Measure of Conscience (Hoffman, 1970). These measures, ranging from projective tests to structured, objective assessments, all consist of a set of hypothetical stories involving moral dilemmas.

CONCLUSION

Moral development plays an important role in our social interactions. Understanding how and why individuals make decisions regarding moral dilemmas can be very useful in many settings. Kohlberg's theory of moral development provides a framework in which to investigate and begin to comprehend how moral reasoning develops within individuals.

—*Cheryl E. Sanders*

See also Kohlberg, Lawrence; Moral Development

Further Readings and References

Barger, R. N. (2000). *A summary of Lawrence Kohlberg's stages of moral development.* Notre Dame, IN: University of Notre Dame. Retrieved from http://www.nd.edu/~rbarger/kohlberg.html

Craig, J. (1999). *Kohlberg's research and theories: 6 stages of moral development.* Chicago: University of Chicago. Available from http://www.ccp.uchicago.edu/

Damon, W. (1999). The moral development of children. *Scientific American, 281*(2), 72–78.

Hoffman, M. (1970). Conscience, personality, and socialization techniques. *Human Development, 13*, 90–126.

Kohlberg, L. (1958). *The development of modes of moral thinking and choice in the years 10–16.* Doctoral dissertation, University of Chicago, Chicago.

Kohlberg, L. (1969). Stage and sequence: The cognitive-developmental approach to socialization. In D. Goslin (Ed.), *Handbook of socialization theory and research.* Chicago: Rand McNally.

Kohlberg, L. (1978). The cognitive developmental approach to moral education. In P. Scharf (Ed.), *Readings in moral education.* Washington, DC: Winston Press.

Mulder, B. (1999). *Kohlberg's theory of moral development.* Notre Dame, IN: University of Notre Dame. Retrieved from http://www.psy.pdx.edu/PsiCafe/Areas/ Developmental/ MoralDev/

Piaget, J. (1932). *The moral judgment of the child.* New York: Free Press.

Rest, J. R. (1973). The hierarchical nature of moral judgment. *Journal of Personality, 41*, 86–109.

Rest, J. R. (1979). *Development in judging moral issues.* Minneapolis: University of Minnesota Press.

Snarey, J., Reimer, J., & Kohlberg, L. (1984). The socio-moral development of Kibbutz adolescents: A longitudinal, cross-cultural study. *Developmental Psychology, 21*, 3–17.

STANDARDIZED TESTING

The term *standardized testing* is often used as synonymous with the kind of multiple-choice, large-scale group testing that takes place in schools and that is aimed at assessing academic achievement. This meaning of the term originated in educational settings as a way of distinguishing printed, commercially available instruments—such as the Stanford Achievement Test or the Iowa Test of Basic Skills (ITBS)—from non-standardized, teacher-made classroom tests. However, while it is true that such testing is standardized, many other types of cognitive ability tests, as well as personality assessment instruments, can also qualify as standardized.

When educational or psychological tests or assessment instruments are described as "standardized," that description refers to two distinct, yet interrelated, aspects of the instruments. The first aspect of standardization consists of uniformity in the administration and scoring procedures of a test. In this sense, a test is standardized if it is administered and scored according to preestablished, carefully delineated guidelines that are to be followed whenever the instrument is used—regardless of the setting in which it is used or the particular individual or group with whom it is used—in an effort to maintain fairness and objectivity. Details such as the directions to be given to examinees, the time limits for a test, the materials to be used, and the way test takers' questions should be addressed must be specified by the test author in the documentation that accompanies a test. The emphasis on strict control of the procedures under which the behavior samples that make up educational and psychological tests are gathered and recorded is a legacy dating back to the earliest period of experimental psychology as it developed in 19th-century Germany. At that time, experimenters became keenly aware that such things as the directions given to research participants and the conditions of the environment in which experiments took place could affect results. Thus, standardization of procedures has been a hallmark of psychological testing from its inception and constitutes an important part of the process of test development.

The second aspect of standardization in test development refers to the process wherein data based on the performance of samples of individuals are collected—under standardized conditions—and tabulated, for the purpose of setting a standard by which the performance of subsequent test takers can be evaluated. These data, in the form of score distributions, means, and standard deviations, are the norms of a test and they constitute the primary basis for norm-referenced test score interpretation; the groups from whom they are obtained are called the normative or standardization samples. In order to provide a meaningful standard of comparison, standardization samples should be representative of the kinds of test takers for whom a test is intended. Norm-referenced test score interpretation typically involves transforming the raw scores obtained by examinees into standard scores that reflect the percentile rank position of the examinee's score within the distribution of scores of an appropriate standardization group. Thus, for example, a standard score equivalent to the 75th percentile indicates that the examinee's level of performance on the test equaled or exceeded the performance of 75% of the individuals in the standardization sample against which the person's score is being compared.

One of the problems inherent in norm-referenced test interpretation is that the normative frame of reference by its very nature is a relative viewpoint from which to evaluate performance and is wholly dependent on the characteristics of the standardization sample. Criterion-referenced or performance-based testing, also known as mastery testing, provides an alternative framework for test score interpretation that is becoming increasingly popular in educational settings. This framework uses preestablished standards of performance at various levels of mastery against which the performance of examinees can be evaluated in order to determine their location within the standards-based continuum of ability, knowledge, or skills that the test encompasses. In recent years, publishers of the major standardized tests used in educational settings, such as the SAT and the ITBS, have begun to incorporate both norm-referenced and criterion-referenced procedures, as well as open-ended items, into their test development in order to provide more flexibility in the way scores are used and a greater range in the behaviors they sample.

—*Susana Urbina*

See also SAT

Further Readings and References

American Educational Research Association, American Psychological Association, & National Council on Measurement in Education. (1999). *Standards for educational and psychological testing.* Washington, DC: Authors.

Lichtenberg, J. W., & Goodyear, R. K. (Eds.). (1999). *Scientist-practitioner perspectives on test interpretation.* Boston: Allyn & Bacon.

Lyman, H. B. (1999). *Test scores and what they mean* (6th ed.). Boston: Allyn & Bacon.

STATISTICAL SIGNIFICANCE

In research studies, a difference on a measure compared between groups or treatment conditions could occur by chance, or it could occur because of actual group or treatment differences. In order to quantify these possibilities, researchers use tests for statistical significance. These tests are called *inferential statistics* because they allow the researcher to draw conclusions about whether results are likely or unlikely to be due to chance. For example, suppose a researcher discovers that children who study while hearing classical music outperform children who study while hearing white noise. The researcher must test whether the difference between groups is statistically significant.

There are many different types of statistical analyses and their appropriateness must be determined based on the type of data collected and the data analysis questions that are asked. In general, an inferential statistical test results in a test statistic, and the magnitude

Table 1 True State of the World

Researcher's Conclusion	Treatments Do Not Have Different Effects	Treatments Have Different Effects
No differences between treatments	Correctly conclude that null hypothesis cannot be rejected	Type II error: fail to reject the null hypothesis when it is false
Significant difference between treatments	Type I error: reject the null hypothesis when it is true	Correctly conclude that null hypothesis is rejected

of that test statistic is associated with a probability of that result occurring by chance. The probability (*p*) of the result happening by chance ranges from 0.0 to 1.0. As a rule of thumb, many researchers use a criterion level of $p < .05$ in order to evaluate significance of the result. This means that if the statistical test shows that the probability of a difference between treatments happening by chance is, for example, $p < .023$, then the researcher would conclude that there is a significant difference between treatments (because *p* is less than .05), but if the statistical test shows a probability of, for example, $p > .27$, then the researcher would conclude that there is not a significant difference between treatments (because *p* is not less than .05). This arbitrary cut-off of .05 means that there is a 5% (or 1 in 20) chance that the difference between treatment groups measured in this study occurred by chance.

In a simple experiment, the logic of significance testing begins with the comparison of two possible states that are opposite to each other and describe all the possible outcomes. One is called the *null hypothesis*, and it typically refers to the absence of an effect. The other is the *alternate hypothesis*, and it typically describes an effect. For example, researchers might propose to test a new method of teaching children geometry. The treatment conditions would be the standard teaching method and the new teaching method. The null hypothesis might be that there is no effect of teaching method on students' later test performance. The alternate hypothesis might be that there is an effect of teaching method on students' later test performance. The results from the study are evaluated in terms of whether the null hypothesis can be rejected. This approach comes from the attempt to discover evidence to disconfirm theories in science. If the test scores between the two groups are analyzed using inferential statistical tests, and the difference between the groups is significant, the researcher concludes that the null hypothesis is rejected and there is a difference between the two teaching methods.

Two correct conclusions and two possible error patterns result from significance testing using the null and alternate hypotheses, as shown in Table 1.

Although statistical significance testing is widely used, some researchers have suggested that there is an overreliance on this technique. The importance of considering other aspects of statistical analyses, such as effect sizes, has been proposed. Effect size helps to indicate what portion of the variation in the results stems from the treatment. If an effect is statistically significant at the $p < .05$ level, but the effect size is very small, than the importance of the treatment effect may be questioned.

—*Marie T. Balaban*

See also Meta-Analysis

Further Readings and References

Berger, J. O., & Berry, D. A. (1988). Statistical analysis and the illusion of objectivity. *American Scientist, 76*, 159–165.

Harris, R. J. (1997). Significance tests have their place. *Psychological Science, 8*, 8–11.

Krueger, J. (2001). Null hypothesis significance testing: On the survival of a flawed method. *American Psychologist, 56*, 16–26.

The Psi Cafe. (n.d.). *Research in Psychology: Diagnosis and interpretation of stats*. Retrieved from http://www .psy.pdx.edu/PsiCafe/Research/Stats-Diag&Interp.htm

Rice Virtual Lab in Statistics. (n.d.). *HyperStat online textbook*. Retrieved from http://davidmlane.com/hyperstat/index.html

Rosnow, R. L., & Rosenthal, R. (2001). *Beginning behavioral research: A conceptual primer* (4th ed.). Upper Saddle River, NJ: Prentice-Hall.

Wilkinson, L., & the Task Force on Statistical Inference. (1999). Statistical methods in psychology journals: Guidelines and explanations. *American Psychologist, 54*, 594–604.

STEPFAMILIES

Although sources vary slightly in their definition of stepfamilies, in general, *stepfamilies* refers to a married couple in which there is at least one stepchild in the family unit. Stepfamilies can either be simple or complex. Simple stepfamilies are stepfamilies in which only one partner in the marriage brings a child (or children) to the family. Complex stepfamilies are stepfamilies in which both partners bring a child (or children) to the family. Approximately 86% of stepfamilies are composed of biological mothers and stepfathers versus biological fathers and stepmothers. Moreover, research has found that African Americans under the age of 18 are more likely to be members of a stepfamily than their Hispanic or white peers. In fact, African Americans constitute 32.3% of all stepfamilies, while Hispanics and whites comprise 16.1% and 14.6%, respectively.

According to the 2000 U.S. Census Bureau, 120 million Americans, or approximately 54% of Americans older than age 15, were married; 41 million or approximately 18% were widowed, separated, or divorced. In 1999, *Data Digest* reported that the divorce rate in the United States was 50.6%, meaning that half of all couples that married would eventually divorce. Additionally, Norton and Miller estimate that approximately 70% of divorced individuals will eventually remarry, resulting in an estimated 35% of children born in the 1980s experiencing the divorce and remarriage of their custodial parent during their childhood or adolescent years. Subsequently, there are an increasing number of stepfamilies because a large percentage of these divorced individuals that remarry have children. In fact, it is estimated that by the year 2010, stepfamilies will be the most prevalent type of family in the United States, accounting for more than 50% of all families.

Despite the rapid growth of stepfamilies across all ethnic groups in the United States, most research concerning family units has been conducted on intact families (families consisting of both married biological parents residing in the same household) and inappropriately generalized to stepfamilies. Using this type of methodology may result in erroneous conclusions about stepfamilies because the dynamics and interactions among members in stepfamilies can be quite different from those of intact, biological families. However, research specific to stepfamilies has recently begun to emerge. A large focus of research has been on the well-being of children and adolescents from stepfamily environments in a variety of areas, including academic performance, psychological well-being, social well-being, emotional well-being, and physical well-being. There is some evidence that children raised in stepfamilies are at an increased risk for developing a host of problems compared with their peers raised in intact families. For example, Hanson, McLanahan, and Thomson found that children in stepfamilies performed poorer in school, had higher rates of externalizing and/or internalizing negative behaviors, showed less initiative in school, and experienced a lower quality of life when compared with children from intact, biological families. The effect sizes revealed that the differences found in externalizing negative behavior were moderate differences ($\eta^2 = .09$), while the differences in quality of life were quite large ($\eta^2 = .22$). Similarly, Dunn, Deater-Deckard, Pickering, O'Conner, and Golding studied 4-year-old children growing up in stepfamilies and found that these children (and their older siblings) had more emotional problems, more peer problems, and higher levels of hyperactivity than their peers from intact, biological families. However, unlike Hanson and colleagues, Dunn and colleagues noted that the differences found between the groups for "total difficulties" was small (based on an effect size of .23).

A limitation of the aforementioned studies is that there is no indication of comparability between individuals from the intact families and the stepfamilies on variables such as age, ethnicity, gender, and income, meaning the differences found could simply be a function of those variables. Love and Murdock compared the psychological well-being of two samples of undergraduate college students from intact families and stepfamilies. To address the limitations of previous studies, Love and Murdock ensured equality between groups by matching both samples on several demographic variables such as age, gender, class rank, ethnicity, income, parental income, and parental level of education. They found that members of the stepfamily group reported significantly less psychological well-being than their peers from intact, biological families. Additionally, the study found that individuals' family environment (intact family vs. stepfamily) was a significant indicator of the level of psychological health that the individuals experience, but only explained a small portion of the variance associated with psychological well-being (5.9%). Finally, a meta-analysis by Amato and Keith reported that children from stepfamilies had poorer outcomes in numerous areas such as academic skills, psychological well-being, and social well-being compared with their peers from intact, biological families.

Numerous studies have sought to explain why individuals in stepfamilies have poorer levels of adjustment than individuals from intact, biological families, but definitive answers have yet to be reached. For instance, Hanson and colleagues theorized that the increased levels of household conflict associated with stepfamily environments would account for the differences found in levels of well-being between individuals from stepfamilies and individuals from intact biological families, but their theory was not supported. Love and

Murdock found that children in stepfamilies had not bonded as well to their biological parents as children from intact families. As such, Love and Murdock theorized that the less secure parent-child bonds would account for the discrepancy. However, because the researchers did not gather information about the parent-child bonds after the divorce, but prior to the remarriage, it is difficult to determine if the lack of bonding is a result of the remarriage or other factors. Love and Murdock's theory was partially supported, for they found that individuals' level of bonding with their parents partially explained some the discrepancy in adjustment outcomes, but parent-child bonds could not explain the phenomenon in its entirety. These findings suggest that there are other undetermined factors that account for the differences in adjustment for youth from stepfamilies versus those from intact, biological families.

Research is continually being conducted to delineate factors that account for the discrepancy, but the current research has some limitation that must be addressed to provide an accurate account of the experiences of individuals from stepfamilies. Several studies have directly compared individuals from intact families and stepfamilies. However, they have not excluded an important comparison group, individuals from divorced families who are not members of a stepfamily. By comparing all three groups, researchers would be able to determine if outcomes for individuals from stepfamilies are a function of the stepfamily environment, or are more related to a product of divorce.

Despite studies that have found less favorable outcomes for children and adolescents from stepfamilies, all stepfamily members do not necessarily experience negative outcomes. Many stepfamilies function as well as, if not better than, intact, biological families. Several factors have been identified that can facilitate the successful formation and existence of a stepfamily unit, including minimizing the amount of conflict between the stepparent and the noncustodial parent, and/or conflict within the stepfamily environment. Custodial parents should encourage the noncustodial parent to stay active in the child's life. A detrimental sense of abandonment may occur when children's noncustodial parents cease to be involved in their child's life, which may interfere with "healthy" life functioning. Custodial parents should strive to improve their levels of "closeness" with their children in the stepfamily. Love and Murdock found that parental bonds between children and their custodial biological parents partially explained the low levels of adjustment for individuals in stepfamilies. Therefore, working to improve parent-child relations may improve individuals' transition into the stepfamily environment and facilitate their positive adjustment in various aspects of life. Open communication should be encouraged between all members of the stepfamily, and each member should work to develop a sense of cohesion between family members. Because issues such as discipline and money may create conflicts in stepfamily environment, the custodial parent and stepparent should clearly define roles that each parent will play in the children's lives before they become problematic. These tips are just some factors that may be useful to members of stepfamilies or for individuals who work with stepfamilies in a professional manner.

—*Keisha M. Love and*
Tamera B. Murdock

See also Divorce

Further Readings and References

Amato, P., & Keith B. (1991). Parental divorce and the well-being of children. *Psychological Bulletin, 110,* 26–46.

Arnaut, G., Fromme, D., Stoll, B., & Felker, J. (2000). A quantitative analysis of stepfamilies: The biological parent. *Journal of Divorce and Remarriage, 33*(3–4), 111–128.

Data Digest, http://www.data-digest.com

Dunn, J., Deater-Deckard, K., Pickering, K., O'Conner, T., Golding, J., & ALSPAC Study Team. (1998). Children's adjustment and prosocial behavior in step-single-parent, and non-stepfamily settings: Findings from a community study. *Journal of Child Psychology and Psychiatry, 39,* 1083–1095.

Hanson, T., McLanahan, S., & Thompson, E. (1996). Double-jeopardy: Parental conflict and stepfamily outcomes for children. *Journal of Marriage and the Family, 58,* 141–154.

Kreider, R., & Simmons, T. (2003). *Marital status: 2000.* Census 2000 Brief, C2KBR-30. Washington, DC: U.S. Census Bureau. Retrieved from http://www.census.gov/prod/2003pubs/c2kbr-30.pdf

Love, K., & Murdock, T. (2004). Attachment to parents and psychological well-being: An examination of young adult college students in intact families and stepfamilies. *Journal of Family Psychology*, 18(4), 600–608.

Norton, A., & Miller, L. (1992). *Marriage, divorce, and remarriage in the 1990's.* Current Population Reports (Series P23-180). Washington, DC: Government Printing Office. Retrieved from http://www.census.gov/population/socdemo/marr-div/p23-180/p23-180.pdf

Stepfamily Association of America, http://www.saafamilies.org

STORM AND STRESS

G. Stanley Hall, a monumental figure in the field of child and adolescent development, described adolescence as suggestive of some ancient period of "storm and stress." Hall's recapitulation theory of human development predicted storm and stress to be the norm of adolescence, rather than an exception, because each individual has to go through the major evolutionary stages, with the period of adolescence recapitulating the time from savagery to civilization. Adolescents have to experience pubertal changes and juggle myriad tasks to overcome chaos and become stable, responsible adults. This process of breaking the old moorings to attain higher levels will inevitably incur storm and stress. However, the sky will clear up after the storm is over—for most adolescents, the outcome is optimistic.

The school of psychoanalysis also upholds this storm and stress view of adolescence. According to Freud's psychosexual developmental theory, the onset of puberty marks the beginning of the genital stage, directing the psychic energy to genitally centered sexuality. The battle between the sexual pleasure-seeking id and the morally inhibiting superego puts the ego under tremendous tensions and pressures. Adolescents' need to end their infantile sexual lives associated with their parents, and their urge to find new love objects for true affection and for relief of sexual tension, pushes them to resolve the renewed Oedipus complex. Conquering these conflicts in the process of rebirth is the source of stress and turmoil. As Anna Freud put it, the upheaval in adolescence is a reflection of internal conflict and psychic disequilibrium.

The figurative term *storm and stress* has been easily accepted by the general public and frequently reinforced in literature and media. Although popular, this view has been criticized for its biological determinism that leaves no room for cultural variations. Margaret Mead's claim that coming of age was relatively easy for Samoan girls challenged for the first time the assumption of universal storm and stress in adolescence, alerting the researchers to the impact of culture and the possibility of different developmental paths in adolescence. Mead also contended that that storm and stress in adolescence cannot be considered a biological inevitability. Instead, the adolescent's affliction results from growing up in the American society, where there are conflicting standards and pressure on the adolescent to make his or her own choices on matters of importance. Although Mead's conclusions have been questioned and her methods criticized, contemporary researchers recognize the importance of sociocultural influences.

While the classical notion of storm and stress persists as a myth, the empirical data have suggested that adolescence is a relatively peaceful period for the majority of adolescents. To balance the negative implications associated with storm and stress such as adolescents' mood swings and rebellious behaviors, positive interpretations of these expressions have been provided. For example, adolescents' questioning the authority of adults, demanding autonomous decision making, and exploring various possibilities might very well be the results of their cognitive achievements. Jeffrey Arnett has modified the traditional storm and stress view of adolescence to incorporate both individual differences and cultural variations. Not all adolescents experience storm and stress, but storm and stress is more likely during adolescence than at other ages. Modernization and globalization tend to increase the likelihood of storm and stress. Coleman's focal theory of adolescence disagrees with the assumption in the storm and stress view that all issues come at once for an adolescent's attention and resolution so that high levels of stress are inevitable. It proposes that different themes come into the focuses of individuals at different times as they develop during adolescence.

In summary, the traditional storm and stress view of adolescence is characteristic of only a small group of adolescents, and it attributes the inevitable storm and stress to the biological mechanism only. Current researchers are developing more balanced, interdisciplinary theories that typically view adolescence as a period during which the adolescent tries to understand his or her biological, cognitive, social, and emotional changes as a function of a developing person adapting to a changing world, and to reorganize these experiences into a coherent, healthy identity.

—*Ling-Yi Zhou*

Further Readings and References

Arnett, J. J. (1999). Adolescent storm and stress, reconsidered. *American Psychologist, 54*(5), 317–326.

Coleman, J. C. (1978). Current contradictions in adolescent theory. *Journal of Youth & Adolescence, 7*(1), 1–11.

Cote, J. E. (1994). *Adolescent storm and stress: An evaluation of the Mead-Freeman controversy*. Hillsdale, NJ: Erlbaum.

Freeman, D. (1983). *Margaret Mead and Samoa: The making and unmaking of an anthropological myth*. Cambridge, MA: Harvard University Press.

Freud, A. (1956). Adolescence. *Psychoanalytic Study of the Child, 13*, 255–278.

Hall, G. S. (1904). *Adolescence: Its psychology and its relations to physiology, anthropology, sociology, sex, crime, religion and education*. New York: D. Appleton and Company.

Mead, M. (1928). *Coming of age in Samoa*. New York: Morrow.

Oldham, D. G. (1978). Adolescent turmoil: A myth revisited. *Adolescent Psychiatry, 6*, 267–279.

Petersen, A. C. (1993). Presidential address: Creating adolescents: The role of context and process in developmental trajectories. *Journal of Research on Adolescence, 3*(1), 1–18.

Susman, E. J., Dorn, L. D., & Schiefelbein, V. (2003). Puberty, sexuality, and health. *Handbook of Psychology: Developmental Psychology, 6*, 295–324.

STRANGE SITUATION

Professor Mary Ainsworth and her student Barbara Wittig at Johns Hopkins University devised the strange situation procedure in the 1960s to demonstrate concepts central to John Bowlby's ethological theory of attachment. Although originally designed to elicit behaviors presumed to be universal among infants under stress, the strange situation instead was found to elicit systematic differences in the behavioral strategies used by infants. Ainsworth's theoretical conceptualization of these patterns, in conjunction with later contributions by her former student Mary Main at the University of California, Berkeley, expanded Bowlby's theory of attachment dramatically.

Bowlby proposed that all ground-dwelling primates possess a biologically based attachment behavioral system that operates to alert an individual to potential dangers, threats, and stresses. Threat is often signaled by the presence of natural clues to danger such as separation from the attachment figure and unfamiliarity of surroundings. The function of the attachment system is to motivate an individual to seek protection from another specific individual when faced with threat and, consequently, increase the individual's chance of survival. In the absence of threat, the activation of the attachment system diminishes, allowing behavioral systems such as exploration to operate. Individuals form enduring emotional bonds (attachments) to other members of their species who provide these "haven of safety" functions; infants form their first attachments to their significant caregivers. The strange situation procedure activates the attachment system in a laboratory setting via the controlled presence of natural clues to danger.

STRANGE SITUATION PROTOCOL

Outlined in *Patterns of Attachment*, a 1978 book authored by Mary Ainsworth and her colleagues, the strange situation is conducted in an unfamiliar toy-filled room by an unfamiliar experimenter (the "stranger") and involves a series of eight episodes. The first episode lasts 1 minute, whereas the remaining seven episodes last 3 minutes each. In the first episode, the stranger introduces the infant and parent to the room then quietly exits. In the second episode, the infant explores the toys on the floor, while the parent sits in a chair and thumbs through a magazine. In the third episode, the stranger enters the room, casually speaks to the mother, then plays with the infant. In the fourth episode (first separation), the parent exits the room, leaving the infant with the stranger. In the fifth episode (first reunion), the parent returns and the stranger exits quietly. In the sixth episode (second separation), the parent again exits, leaving the infant completely alone. In the seventh episode, the stranger enters the room and interacts with the infant. In the eighth and final episode (second reunion), the parent returns and the stranger again exits quietly. The protocol specifies a variety of standardized instructions to be followed by the parent and stranger during these eight episodes; for example, the parent is instructed to leave her purse next to the chair during the separations and to pick up the infant during the second reunion.

The strange situation is currently conducted with only one modification from the original protocol, based on a theoretically grounded concern. The separations are designed to generate just enough stress to activate an infant's attachment behavioral system, yet not generate so much stress that the child cannot employ a coping strategy. As a result, the separations (episodes 4 and 6) are typically curtailed after the infant has demonstrated distress for under 30 seconds. Curtailing the separations in this way helps ensure that an infant's behavior on reunion is a reflection of the quality of the infant-parent relationship rather than simply a reflection of extreme levels of distress that become increasingly difficult to quell.

Other modifications to the strange situation threaten its validity. It is critical that the procedure not be conducted in the child's home or day care classroom and that the "stranger" role not be filled by an adult whom the infant has met previously. Familiarity with the room or stranger tampers with the appropriate presentation of the natural clues to danger that ground the procedure. In addition, it is critical that the strange situation not be shortened to include only one separation. The procedure relies on the gradual build-up of stress, with the first separation leaving the child with the stranger and the second separation leaving the child alone. Many infants appear calm during the first separation but become quite distressed upon the second separation; this change in behavior influences classification. Furthermore, it is critical that the strange situation is used only with infants between the ages of 12 and 18 months. Younger children may not yet have become selectively attached to a specific caregiver or may not be capable of crawling to seek proximity to the caregiver, whereas older children are simply not stressed enough by the procedure to adequately trigger the attachment behavioral system.

INDIVIDUAL DIFFERENCES IN INFANT STRANGE SITUATION BEHAVIOR

The strange situation is videotaped and coded based on the infant's overt behaviors. Based on her original sample, Ainsworth identified three general classifications of behavioral patterns, which since have been documented in hundreds of samples worldwide. In the mid-1980s, Mary Main and her student Judith Solomon added a fourth classification that accounted for a diverse group of previously unclassifiable infants. All four of the strange situation classifications reflect the quality of an infant's relationship with a specific caregiver, and thus may be different with respect to each parent. In addition, these classifications refer to the quality, not strength, of attachment. Being attached to someone—even someone who does not provide optimal care—is critical to the survival of all infants. Except under anomalous circumstances, all infants become attached, even when caregivers are maltreating. Furthermore, quality of attachment is not reflected in the amount a child cries when the attachment system is activated. Although an infant's temperament relates to the amount of distress experienced during separation in the strange situation, it is not associated with the infant's classification. An infant's behavior during the separation is useful for placing the reunion behavior in context, but it is primarily the behavior toward the parent on reunion that provides insight into the quality of the attachment relationship.

Infants are classified as secure in the strange situation when they demonstrate the behavioral pattern considered optimally adaptive by Bowlby's theory: balancing their behaviors and attention between attachment (in the presence of threat) and exploration (in the absence of threat). Many of these infants show a prototypical pattern of being distressed on separation, then promptly calming and returning to play upon reunion with the parent. However, some securely classified infants are highly distressed during separation and are slow to calm upon reunion, whereas others are not overtly distressed and do not seek direct comfort from the parent. However, all infants classified as secure show signs of missing the parent when separated and being pleased at the parent's return. In middle-class samples, approximately 60% of infants typically are classified as secure.

Infants are classified as resistant-ambivalent when they demonstrate behaviors and attention that is inflexibly oriented toward the parent, thus inhibiting exploration even after the threat has passed. These infants are highly distressed upon separation, yet inconsolable upon reunion. For example, many infants classified as ambivalent-resistant cling to the parent upon reunion while simultaneously squirming and pushing away. Infants are classified as avoidant when they show the opposite pattern: behaviors and attention inflexibly oriented away from the parent. These infants do not show overt signs of missing the parent on separation, then actively avoid the parent on reunion. For example, many infants classified as avoidant casually turn their backs toward the parent upon reunion while focusing intently on a toy. Even though avoidant infants appear calm, data on heart rate, stress hormones, and quality of play all reveal that these infants are as stressed as other infants.

Rather than showing a specific and coherent pattern, infants classified as disorganized/disoriented show any of an array of brief yet odd behaviors. For example, these infants may display anomalous postures, stilling, freezing, hand-to-mouth gestures, stereotypes such as constant rocking, and contradictory behavior patterns such as approaching the parent with head averted or starting to approach the parent then suddenly turning away before achieving proximity. These behaviors typically appear within the context of an otherwise organized attentional strategy (secure, resistant-ambivalent, avoidant), which collapses briefly. As a result, the disorganized classification is always assigned in conjunction with the best alternative organized strategy—the strategy thought to collapse.

CORRELATES OF STRANGE SITUATION CLASSIFICATIONS

Strange situation classifications are thought to reflect an infant's expectations of a particular parent's availability in times of stress, based on the history of their interactions. Indeed, the procedure has been validated largely by its moderate to strong associations to parental behavior in the home. An infant's security in the strange situation is predicted by the parent's sensitivity of care during the first year. Specifically, parents of secure babies identify and correctly interpret their infants' social signals such as crying, then respond to those signals promptly and appropriately. In contrast, avoidant and ambivalent-resistant patterns are associated with a variety of forms of insensitive caregiving. Parents of avoidant infants are especially likely to reject infant bids for attachment and to show discomfort with physical contact, whereas parents of ambivalent-resistant infants are especially likely to be inconsistent and unpredictable.

Whereas these organized patterns are associated with parental sensitivity or insensitivity, disorganized infant behavior is associated with parental behavior that is either maltreating or subtly frightening (e.g., quasi-dissociative). As Bowlby originally proposed, when frightened, a baby is motivated to flee from the source of alarm and toward the attachment figure. However, as Mary Main and Erik Hesse later pointed out, when the attachment figure actually is the source of alarm, the baby is placed in a behavioral paradox. The behavioral collapse observed in these human infants mirrors collapses shown by other primates experiencing the activation of conflicting behavior systems.

The strange situation has been validated across gender, temperament, and culture. In addition, the procedure has served as a source of validation for a range of additional attachment assessments in childhood and adulthood, including the widely used Adult Attachment Interview, devised by Main and colleagues. Furthermore, security in the strange situation predicts a variety of behaviors, mental representations, and mental health variables throughout childhood and, when environmental and relationship conditions remain stable, into adulthood as well. Overall, the strange situation is one of the most theoretically grounded and widely used instruments in the study of human development.

—*Kirsten Blount-Matthews and Matthew J. Hertenstein*

See also Ainsworth, Mary Salter; Stranger Anxiety

Further Readings and References

Ainsworth, M. D. S., Blehar, M. C., Waters, E., & Wall, S. (1978). *Patterns of attachment.* Hillsdale, NJ: Erlbaum.

Attachment Theory and Research at Stony Brook, http://www.johnbowlby.com

Lyons-Ruth, K., & Jacobvitz, D. (1999). Attachment disorganization: Unresolved loss, relationship violence, and lapses in behavioral and attentional strategies. In J. Cassidy & P. Shaver (Eds.), *Handbook of attachment*. New York: Guilford.

Main, M., & Solomon, J. (1990). Procedures for identifying infants as disorganized/disoriented during the Ainsworth strange situation. In M. T. Greenberg, D. Cicchetti, & E. M. Cummings (Eds.), *Attachment in the preschool years* (pp. 121–160). Chicago: University of Chicago Press.

Solomon, J., & George, C. (1999). The measurement of attachment security in infancy and childhood. In J. Cassidy & P. Shaver (Eds.), *Handbook of attachment: Theory, research, and clinical applications* (pp. 287–318). New York: Guilford.

van IJzendoorn, M. H. (1995). Adult attachment representations, parental responsiveness, and infant attachment: A meta-analysis on the predictive validity of the Adult Attachment Interview. *Psychological Bulletin, 117*, 387–403.

van IJzendoorn, M. H., & Kroonenberg, P. M. (1988). Cross-cultural patterns of attachment: A meta-analysis of the strange situation. *Child Development, 58*, 147–156.

Waters, E., Hamilton, C. E., & Weinfield, N. S. (2000). The stability of attachment security from infancy to adulthood: General introduction. *Child Development, 71*, 684–689.

Weinfield, N. S., Sroufe, L. A., Egeland, B., & Carlson, E. A. (1999). The nature of individual differences in infant-caregiver attachment. In J. Cassidy & P. Shaver (Eds.), *Handbook of attachment: Theory, research, and clinical applications* (pp. 68–98). New York: Guilford.

STRANGER ANXIETY

Stranger anxiety—the emotional distress displayed by infants and young children due to the approach of an unfamiliar person—is a significant and adaptive developmental achievement in the child's life. The presence of stranger anxiety is rare in the first 6 months of life, common by about 8 months, and peaks around the child's first birthday. On average, girls display it slightly earlier than boys. Research indicates that stranger anxiety is universal cross-culturally among most infants and is signaled by a host of infant behaviors, including crying, gaze aversion, crawling or walking away from the stranger, hiding their faces, and self-soothing (e.g., sucking their thumb). The presence of such behaviors in response to strangers indicates that infants are capable of distinguishing between familiar and unfamiliar adults, a critical cognitive task.

Considerable individual variation exists among infants, with some infants exhibiting more stranger anxiety than others. Two factors have been linked to individual differences in stranger anxiety: temperament and attachment. Researchers have found that infants who are temperamentally "fussy" are more likely to respond more negatively to the approach of a stranger than temperamentally "easy-going" infants. In addition, researchers have found that infants who have been indexed as securely attached to their caregiver are more sociable and less wary of strangers than infants identified as insecurely attached. Infants who are securely attached tend to have caregivers who are sensitive and responsive to their infants' emotional signals, while infants who are insecurely attached tend to have caregivers who are either inconsistently sensitive and responsive to their infants' emotional signals or ignore their infants' signals altogether.

The incidence and severity of stranger anxiety are influenced by a multitude of contextual factors. Infants tend to display greater stranger anxiety (a) when the caregiver is not present, (b) when the stranger is either tall, unattractive, male, approaches quickly, or touches the infant, (c) when the infant is physically restrained (e.g., in a high chair), and (d) when the infant is in a familiar setting such as the home. The latter finding is explained by considering that infants seem to expect novel stimuli such as strangers in unfamiliar settings. When a stranger enters a familiar setting, it violates the infant's expectations. Taken as a whole, the above findings suggest that not only is stranger anxiety a function of the infant, but of how the infant perceives his or her relationship with the outside world.

Caregivers often wonder how the incidence and severity of stranger anxiety can be reduced. Infants tend to display fewer negative emotional displays if the stranger slowly approaches them and does not tower over them; if the stranger approaches them in the context of playing with them (e.g., peek-a-boo); if the stranger behaves contingently with infants' behaviors (e.g., smiling when the infant smiles); if infants are allowed time to familiarize themselves with a novel environment; if infants are allowed to crawl or walk away from the stranger rather than being restrained in a high-chair or similar apparatus; and if the caregiver is present.

In sum, stranger anxiety is an adaptive response that is a normal and healthy behavioral reaction. The incidence of stranger anxiety is influenced by several factors, including the context in which infants find themselves as well as how strangers approach them. These factors and others can be modified to modulate infant wariness toward strangers.

*—Matthew J. Hertenstein
and Rachel Holmes*

See also Strange Situation

Further Readings and References

Bronson, G. (1972). Infants' reactions to unfamiliar persons and novel objects. *Monographs of the Society of Research in Child Development, 37*(3, Serial No. 148).

Brooks, J., & Lewis, M. (1976). Infants' response to strangers: Midget, adult, and child. *Child Development, 47,* 323–332.

Center for Effective Parenting. (n.d.). *Stranger anxiety.* Retrieved from http://www.parenting-ed.org/handouts/Specific%20Concerns%20and%20Problems/stranger%20anxiety.doc

Johnson, C. J. (n.d.). *Stranger anxiety: When your baby is afraid of newcomers.* Retrieved from http://www.babiestoday.com/resources/articles/stranger.htm

Sroufe, L.A. (1977). Wariness of strangers and the study of infant development. *Child Development, 48,* 731–746.

STRESS

Many children experience stressful events in their lives. Stress can influence the development of psychological and medical problems, but can also have positive effects if successfully resolved. Research on stress poses many challenges, including how best to measure it and test it as a risk factor for later problems.

WHAT IS STRESS?

Stress has been conceptualized in a number of ways. Specifically, it can be conceptualized as an accumulation of major life events, or an accumulation of small, minor events (hassles). Stress can be conceptualized as a single event, such as a serious accident, or as a chronic situation, such as a physical disability or poverty. For some stressful experiences, it is unclear which conceptualization makes the most sense. Is parental divorce an event or a chronic situation?

One feature of childhood stress that distinguishes it from adult stress is that of controllability. Most stressful experiences during childhood occur independently of the child; they occur because something happens to the parents, or the parents do something or do not do something to the child. Adults have more control over their environment and are therefore more responsible, at least in part, for their life circumstances.

HOW IS STRESS MEASURED?

Stressor Checklists

The most widely used method for assessing stressors affecting children and adolescents is the self-report (or parent-report) checklist. Checklists are easy to administer, thus allowing investigators to collect data on large samples and to evaluate the relationships between stress and psychological and health outcomes. In the literature, there are at least 11 general stressor checklists for adolescents, and at least five for children. Adolescent checklists are usually designed to be self-report measures, whereas many child checklists are designed for parents to complete.

Although stressful event checklists are widely used and efficient, they have a number of limitations. For example, it is unclear if they actually assess "objectively stressful" events. The specific items on stressor checklists have typically been chosen by researchers based on their own personal opinion, general consensus about the nature of stressful experiences of children, or information generated in small focus groups.

Checklists usually do not assess the timing of events, and therefore are limited in their ability to determine whether stressors cause, or contribute to, the emergence of psychological and medical symptoms. In addition, most stressor checklists fail to distinguish between stressors that are independent of the child's behavior and those that are not. Independent events are less confounded with psychopathology, and therefore represent a cleaner picture of environmental input. In any case, a very significant problem with the research literature is that different researchers use different checklists, making it very difficult to summarize findings in the field.

Stressor Interviews

Stressor interviews were developed in part to address the problems of stressor checklists. Stressor interviews provide relatively objective ratings of the degree of threat and loss that is associated with stressful events. Older children and adolescents can be interviewed directly, whereas parents are interviewed for younger children. Interviews are used to generate a list of the various types of stressful events that have been encountered and the context of these events. Questions for each experienced event include a description of what happened, when it happened, who was involved, and the objective consequences of the event. External raters use a detailed scoring manual to evaluate the level of threat and loss associated with each event and situation, or the severity of impact of each event. These ratings are then summed, or a consensus is reached, to form an objective evaluation of the stressors that each child or adolescent has encountered.

Compared with checklists, interviews are more useful for research on particularly severe events, because they provide more detailed information. Interviews might also be better suited to study effects on mental health and medical outcomes, because they can date the occurrence of life events and ascertain the temporal order of stressful events and specific symptoms.

The biggest problem with interviews concerns their length and expense. A checklist can be administered and scored in a few minutes and can be group-administered to a large sample of individuals. An interview takes much longer, requires training for its administration and scoring, and can only be given to one person at a time.

EFFECTS OF STRESS ON PSYCHOLOGICAL AND MEDICAL OUTCOMES

More than 1,500 studies have examined the relationship between child and adolescent life stress and psychological outcomes. Common outcome measures assess depression, anxiety, substance abuse, eating disorders, and conduct problems. Stress is such an important component of theory and research on psychopathology that the most influential model is called the diathesis-stress model. In this model, individuals with the diathesis (vulnerability factor), which can be genetic or psychological, are at risk for a disorder if they are also exposed to sufficient life stress.

Cross-Sectional and Prospective Research Designs

However, the strength and regularity of the child stress–mental health relationship is unclear. One major reason for this uncertainty involves research methodology. The most typical methodology is a cross-sectional design in which life stress and outcome measures are administered at one point in time. However, this type of design is inadequate to measure the causal effects of life stress. It is possible that psychological status caused life stress rather than vice versa, or that a third variable (e.g., personality) influenced both life stress and psychological status. A prospective design is a more appropriate design, although it is

harder to implement. In this design, life stress and psychological status are measured at one point in time, and then psychological status is measured again at a later time. Statistical analyses then test whether life stress can predict change in status from time 1 to time 2.

Daily Assessment Research Design

A recent methodological development in stress research is the use of a daily assessment design. In this type of study, stress and mood (or behavioral or health) variables are measured daily, or several times each day, over several days or weeks. Using a type of statistical procedure called multilevel modeling, researchers can examine the daily relationship between stress and outcomes such as mood and health, and also evaluate whether certain types of individuals (who vary on age, gender, or psychiatric status) show stronger or weaker daily stress-outcome relationships. For youth, these types of studies are being conducted to evaluate the daily relationships between stress and drinking, smoking, and binge eating.

There is also a large body of literature on the relationship between child and adolescent life stress and medical symptoms and outcomes. The same issues apply. A prospective design is superior to a cross-sectional design when testing the etiological (causal) role of life events. Daily studies are being conducted to test the daily relationships between stress and medical symptoms (e.g., pain) and health behaviors (e.g., medical compliance).

Positive Effects of Stress

Recently, stress theorists and researchers have begun to examine the positive consequences of life stress. For example, with adults, stress researchers have studied how cancer patients and victims of natural disasters have grown from these experiences and have gained wisdom and perspective as a result of these traumas. Obviously, growth takes time, and can only occur once coping efforts have been successful. But the same process might occur for children and adolescents. In other words, some children might benefit from some traumatic experiences, in the long run anyway. Future research is needed to determine which children might grow from which types of stress, experienced at which developmental period.

Moderators and Mediators

The terms *moderators* and *mediators* are very important when discussing the relationship between child/adolescent stress and psychological and medical outcomes. A moderator is a variable that influences the strength of the stress-outcome relationship. Some stressors might be strongly predictive of symptoms if experienced at a younger age compared with an older age, or if combined with an unsupportive family environment compared with a supportive family environment.

A mediator variable is a variable that "explains" the stress-outcome relationship. In short, it is the mechanism that underlies the causal relationship between stressful life events and symptoms. For example, a stress-depression relationship might be mediated by parental conflict. Family stressful events cause parental conflict, which then upsets a child. With respect to medical outcomes, life stress can affect the stress response of the hypothalamic-pituitary-adrenal axis, and immune functioning, which then causes health problems.

Current research is examining variables that moderate and mediate the psychological and medical effects of child stress. Although inconclusive to date, this research should contribute to our understanding of child development and to the development of preventive and treatment interventions for children and adolescents who experience high levels of stress.

SUMMARY

Stress is all too common in the lives of children and adolescents. There are various ways to define and measure stress, and various methodological approaches to study its effects on psychological and medical outcomes. Stress can cause a variety of mental health and medical problems. Fortunately, many children do not suffer as a result of stress, and some might benefit from the experience.

*—Angela Farrehi, Kimberly Dasch,
and Lawrence H. Cohen*

Further Readings and References

ChildTrauma Academy, http://www.childtrauma.org/ctamaterials/ptsd_interdisc.asp

Grant, K., Compas, B., Stuhlmacher, A., Thurm, A., McMahon, S., & Halpert, J. (2003). Stressors and child and adolescent psychopathology: Moving from markers to mechanisms of risk. *Psychological Bulletin, 129,* 447–466.

Grant, K., Compas, B., Thurm, A., McMahon, S., & Gipson, P. (2004). Stressors and child and adolescent psychopathology: Measurement issues and prospective effects. *Journal of Clinical Child and Adolescent Psychology, 33*(4), 412–425.

Johnson, S., Hayes, A., Field, T., Schneiderman, N., & McCabe, P. (Eds.). (2000). *Stress, coping, and depression.* Mahwah, NJ: Erlbaum.

The Nemours Foundation. (n.d.). *Childhood stress.* Retrieved from http://kidshealth.org/parent/emotions/feelings/stress.html

Snyder, C. R. (Ed.). (1999). *Coping: The psychology of what works.* New York: Oxford University Press.

Tedeschi, R., & Calhoun, L. (1995). *Trauma and transformation.* Thousand Oaks, CA: Sage.

Zautra, A. (2003). *Emotions, stress, and health.* New York: Oxford University Press.

STROKE

Stroke symptoms were first described in the 4th century BC and, like many medical writings from the Classical Age of Greece, these descriptions are credited to Hippocrates. The disorder was termed "apoplexy," a Late Middle English word derived from the Greek *apoplexia* [æpYpleksi] meaning "being struck down" and *plexe* implying "a stroke" or "to beat." The word may refer to the most frequent symptom of stroke, hemiplegia, a sudden paralysis of one side of the body, often with loss of consciousness in a seemingly healthy person. In antiquity, sudden afflictions including apoplexy and epilepsy were attributed to possession or an attack by the gods, a belief not shared by Hippocrates. No questions into the cause of stroke were raised until the Renaissance and a "scientific revolution." During this period, the approach to understanding nature by thoughtful contemplation and reliance on writings by classical Greek scholars was replaced by using direct observation to test hypotheses. In the mid-1600s Jacob Wepfer conducted autopsies of patients who died after apoplexy and observed a blockade or bleeding of blood vessels in their brains and began the continuing experimental study of the cause of stroke. The venerable word *apoplexy* endured until the 1920s, when replaced by the term *stroke* during classification of its types. Recently, *brain attack* was introduced and is used interchangeably with *stroke* to convey an urgent need to seek medical attention.

There are two types of stroke: ischemic and hemorrhagic. Ischemic stroke is the most common type, accounting for approximately 88% of all brain attacks. They occur when blood clots stop blood flow in small branches of arteries supplying a focal brain region (Figure 1). Blood clots are classified as thrombotic or embolic, depending on where they form, an important consideration for patient management. A thrombus or thrombotic clot develops in brain arteries damaged by fatty buildups, or atherosclerosis, which stops blood flow supplying a focal brain region. An embolus or embolic clot forms outside of the brain and is carried in the bloodstream until it lodges in an artery leading to or within the brain, blocking blood flow. Embolic clots can result from "atrial fibrillation," an irregular heartbeat slowing blood flow, which allows formation of clots in pooled blood, causing 8% to 15% of all strokes.

As seen in Figure 1, the area of neuronal death in the left hemisphere is dark black and surrounded by regions of "temporarily stunned cells" or "dysfunctional neurons." Dysfunctional brain regions can now be detected using functional brain imaging methods, and appear in areas adjacent to the region of cell death and in structures remote from the injury as depicted in the cerebellum of the right hemisphere. Measuring both dysfunctional regions and the extent of dead cells gives a better account of stroke symptoms and are a target for experimental therapy. Gray areas labeled "speech," "motor functions," and so forth indicate symptoms likely to result when stroke involves that region. Since the extent of neuronal death is unchanged, amplification of any weak capacity of remaining cells related to symptoms is one hypothesis for the lessening of symptoms observed in most patients over the first 3 months after stroke. Symptoms of focal ischemia are often confused with the function of the damaged area but show the functional capacity of remaining viable brain areas.

Hemorrhagic strokes occur when a blood vessel wall ruptures, resulting in bleeding inside the cranium.

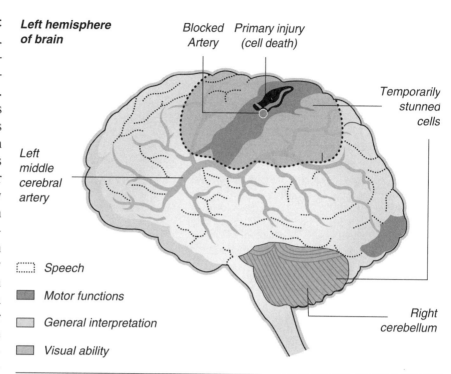

Figure 1   Illustration of the left hemisphere depicting some consequences of an ischemic stroke after a clot blocking blood flow in a branch of a major cerebral artery

There are two types of hemorrhages: subarachnoid and intracerebral. A subarachnoid hemorrhage occurs upon rupture of a blood vessel on the brain surface, and blood flows into the space between skull and brain. An intracerebral hemorrhage occurs when a blood vessel within the brain ruptures, flooding cells with blood components. Hemorrhagic strokes often result from head trauma and also can result from a ruptured aneurysm, blood-filled pouches formed at weak areas of vessel walls. These appear like defects in balloons after repeated inflation, and if untreated, a small aneurysm may continue expanding, further weakening the vessel wall. Hemorrhagic strokes also can result from an arteriovenous malformation, a cluster of enlarged blood vessels that form during fetal development. Their weakened vessel walls can rupture from forces exerted by normal blood flow. Depending on the amount of blood from a ruptured artery that increases pressure on the brain, pushing the brain against the skull, such strokes are often lethal because they suppress vital functions. By 1 month after a hemorrhagic stroke, approximately 38% of patients die, compared with 8% to 12% of ischemic stroke patients.

COMMON STROKE SYMPTOMS

- Numbness or weakness of the face, arms, or legs on one side of the body
- Inability to speak, read, or understand speech
- Confusion or loss of judgment
- Loss of memory
- Persistent headache with no known cause
- Marked change of personality, often depression
- Difficulty swallowing
- Disturbances of vision in one or both eyes
- Dizziness, loss of coordination and balance

Risk factors are characteristics or behaviors that increase the likelihood of stroke and include individual traits such as age and gender, lifestyle (such as smoking), and the presence of high blood pressure (HBP). Some risk factors, such as race, age, or family history of stroke, are unchangeable. Compared with white men of comparable age, African American men have twice the risk for stroke, are stricken at a younger age, and are more likely to die from stroke. However, this may be partly due to a higher incidence of other risk factors in black men compared with white men, such as HBP, obesity, and diabetes. Many risk factors can be controlled by changes in lifestyle or medication to reduce the likelihood of stroke. The most important risk factor for stroke is HBP, which affects 20% of Americans, but because it has no obvious signs, approximately 30% of those with HBP do not know they have it. Often HBP can be lowered by minor changes in lifestyle, such as consuming a healthier diet and increasing exercise. If necessary, drugs to control blood pressure are available by prescription. The more risk factors an individual has, the higher his or her chances of having a stroke. After age 55, the chance of having a stroke more than doubles for each decade of life, but numerical age is not the same as biological age. Few Americans discuss stroke with their physicians, even those who know someone who has had a brain attack. The importance of discussing stroke with a physician cannot be overemphasized because methods to prevent stroke by controlling risk factors are well established.

A type of risk factor, often not considered important enough to seek medical advice, are very short periods of stroke symptoms lasting only a few minutes. Short-lasting epochs of stroke symptoms, lasting less than 24 hours, are called transient ischemic attacks (TIAs) and are a warning that an ischemic stroke may be imminent. Most TIAs last less than 5 minutes, averaging less than a minute and often ignored. However, within 2 days after a TIA, 5% of patients suffer an ischemic stroke, and within 90 days, 10% have a stroke. A TIA is occasionally called a "mini-stroke," but it is a major risk factor, so one should call 911 promptly.

SOME CONTROLLABLE STROKE RISK FACTORS

- People with HBP have a four to six times higher risk for stroke, but blood pressure can be lowered and reduces the likelihood of a brain attack.

- The risk for stroke in heavy smokers (40-plus cigarettes per day) is twice that of light smokers (10-plus cigarettes per day). After stopping smoking, the risk for brain attack significantly decreases within 2 years, and by 5 years the risk is no higher than for nonsmokers.

- After age 55, periodic measures of cholesterol levels should be requested, especially if there are other risk factors. While high cholesterol levels may be metabolic, in many cases diet changes can reduce cholesterol intake and lessen the chance for stroke.

- Being overweight increases the risk for brain attack, and routine vigorous exercise, combined with a healthy diet, lowers the risk.

- Heavy alcohol consumption increases the risk for all types of strokes. Reports that moderate alcohol consumption reduces the risk for stroke are unclear. Some reports of reduced ischemic stroke in moderate drinkers also report increased hemorrhagic stroke in moderate drinkers.

- Some prescription drugs, including Vioxx and the over-the-counter pain reliever Aleve (naproxen), increase the likelihood of stroke.

- If at risk, inexpensive medications such as aspirin can prevent stroke.

The impact of a brain attack is personally and economically devastating. In the United States and other developed countries, stroke is the leading cause of severe disability and is the third leading cause of mortality after heart disease and cancer. In the United States a stroke occurs every 45 seconds, affecting more than 750,000 Americans every year, and of these, 20% (160,000) die within a year after a stroke. For those older than 65, the mortality rate is higher. Stroke is often considered a problem of the elderly, but it occurs throughout our life span. Although rare in children, during the first 30 days after birth the likelihood increases, and 5 deaths in every 100,000 live births are caused by stroke.

Most patients survive a stroke but have some permanent disability that interferes with their ability to conduct daily activities. For patients over age 65, by 6 months after a stroke, more than 30% cannot walk without assistance and 19% have aphasia, the loss of some component of language, ability to speak, comprehend, read, or write. Within a year after stroke, 26% of stroke patients over age 65 are institutionalized in a nursing home. In the United States, the direct medical costs and loss of income average more than $50 billion every year, and the personal costs are incalculable. The estimated loss of quality-adjusted life-years caused by stroke is greater than for any other disease, resulting in an enormous economic burden on families and society. Without improved prevention or development of an effective therapy, the problem of stroke will increase due to the aging of the population.

There is no approved medical therapy for most stroke patients, and treatment primarily consists of supportive care. Only 3% to 5% of ischemic stroke patients can be administered tissue plasminogen activator (tPA), a "clot buster" that restores blood flow to prevent brain cell death and dysfunction. The 3-hour time limit is essential because tPA administration later than 3 hours after onset of symptoms fails to improve outcome and greatly increases the risk for severe hemorrhagic stroke. Additionally, tPA treatment is not recommended unless the facility is appropriately staffed and equipped. An appropriate center for tPA treatment of ischemic stroke requires diagnosis by a physician with expertise in diagnosing stroke that can be confirmed by neuroimaging. Because of the risk for tPA-induced hemorrhagic stroke, the facility must be able to handle bleeding complications and provide adequate emergent ancillary care. Not all hospitals have proper facilities, so for those at risk, an appropriate center should be located. Of those treated with tPA, 35% to 50% recover without significant disabilities, and others do not respond. For a small percentage of patients at high risk for stroke, surgical treatment is appropriate. If a patient had a TIA and has a fatty buildup in a neck artery that has reduced blood flow

to the brain by 70%, a carotid endarterectomy may be warranted. To improve blood flow, the plaque is stripped away from the inner lining of the occluded artery, which reduces the risk for stroke.

Until recently, stroke was considered a human tragedy, not a treatable medical problem. Because symptoms were attributed to irreversible cell death from loss of blood supply, a curative "therapy" was thought impossible, especially for patients with a completed stroke who were transferred to "rehab." The quite limited goal of rehabilitation medicine was described in 1976 by the World Health Assembly to "help victims accept what is inevitable, to correct what is correctable and (learning to) adapt to new circumstances." It was clearly distinguished from the curative goals of scientifically based medicine. However, over the past two decades, experimental and clinical evidence has changed this dismal outlook to cautious optimism for development of a stroke therapy. In the 1980s, laboratory studies on brain injury suggested two qualitatively different strategies for developing a stroke therapy to lessen residual symptoms or promote functional recovery. The first was the observation of delayed neuronal death following cerebral ischemia or trauma. That many brain cells survive for several days rather than the few minutes for complete cell death broke a widely held assumption. This prompted extensive study of neuroprotective drugs that reduced delayed death in diverse laboratory models of stroke and trauma, and it was hypothesized that neuroprotective agents would also lessen symptoms in patients with brain injury. This received no support by any of the over 65 clinical trials administering neuroprotective drugs to stroke patients, but several clinical trials reported significant worsening of patient outcome. The second strategy for a stroke therapy was the observation that drugs increasing levels of noradrenaline enhanced hemiplegia recovery after ischemia or destruction of cerebral cortex. Further studies indicated that an enduring enhancement of recovery of hemiplegia required administration of drugs increasing noradrenaline levels, combined with active physical therapy and attempts to walk. While this approach has received much less attention than neuronal rescue, it has been extended to stroke patients. An increasing number of clinical trials of stroke patients report noradrenergic-enhanced physical therapy improves recovery of hemiplegia and aphasia. Importantly, this experimental treatment enhanced recovery even when treatment was begun weeks to months after stroke onset, and the improved outcome endures for 8 to 10 months after stopping treatment. The association of increased noradrenaline levels with enhanced recovery is complimented by reduced noradrenaline levels slowing hemiplegia recovery in both laboratory studies and clinical trials using stroke patients. Drugs reducing noradrenaline levels are prescribed for HBP in stroke patients, and the clinical and laboratory data indicate that those drugs are contraindicated during recovery after brain injury. This enhanced recovery is proposed to involve dysfunctional neurons as described in Figure 1, one of many effects on brain function included in the concept of "neuroplasticity." These data initiated the study of "rehabilitation pharmacology," since drugs produce unique effects in brain-injured patients that alter the recovery process. The goal of rehabilitation is changing from adapting to a disability to improving outcome and developing a scientific base for "curative" goals during the rehabilitation phase for the treatment of stroke.

—*Dennis M. Feeney*

Further Readings and References

American Heart Association. (n.d.). *Stroke*. Retrieved from http://www.americanheart.org/presenter.jhtml?identifier=4755

Bogousslavsky, J. (Ed.). (2002). *Long term effects of stroke*. New York: Marcel Dekker.

The Cleveland Clinic. (2004). *Stroke*. Retrieved from http://www.clevelandclinic.org/health/health-info/docs/2100/2179.asp?index=9074

Ginsberg, M., & Bogousslavsky, J. (Eds.). (1998). *Cerebrovascular disease: Pathophysiology, diagnosis and management. Vols. I. & II*. Cambridge, MA: Blackwell.

Goldstein, L. B. (Ed.). (1998). *Advances in the pharmacology of recovery after stroke. Restorative neurology*. Armonk, NY: Futura.

HealthCentersOnline. (n.d.). *Stroke center*. Retrieved from http://www.heartcenteronline.com/The_Stroke_Center.html?WT.srch=1

NINDS stroke information page, http://www.ninds.nih.gov/disorders/stroke/stroke_pr.htm

STRUCTURAL AND FUNCTIONAL BRAIN IMAGING

Understanding the structure and function of the human brain is an essential key to understanding the development of personality and consciousness, and assists in the diagnosis and treatment of neurological and psychiatric illnesses. However, the direct study of the healthy human brain was not possible until recently. Being encased by the skull, the brain was not directly accessible for study except by invasive means. For many years, such information could only be obtained from humans using autopsy tissue or from neurological patients with severe head trauma. These data often lacked a clear relationship between brain structure and function. Information was also obtained from test animals, but the usefulness of this was limited by differences between humans and animals. Even given such limitations, many important findings have been made using these methods. However, in order to understand the workings of the normal healthy human brain, and to diagnose and treat neurological and psychiatric patients with a minimum of harm, information had to be obtained from healthy humans noninvasively and while still alive and able to function. Techniques now exist to examine the human brain without damage to the brain itself. There are two basic types of brain imaging: anatomical imaging that provides information about the inner structure of the brain and functional imaging that provides information about the activity of the brain.

ANATOMICAL BRAIN IMAGING

Anatomical imaging began with the discovery of X-rays by Wilhelm Roentgen in 1895, for which he was awarded the first Nobel Prize in physics in 1901. X-rays are a highly energetic form of light wave that can pass through soft tissue (such as skin, brain tissue, and muscle) but are stopped by hard tissue such as bone. By 1896 Thomas Edison had developed the first fluoroscope, which was used to produce and image X-rays, and many hospitals were using them routinely by the turn of the century. More recently, computer-assisted tomography (CAT) has been developed to produce three-dimensional images using X-rays. By injecting a radiopaque dye into the bloodstream that stops X-rays, it is possible to obtain images of veins and arteries in the brain. This can be used to detect malformations in blood vessels as well as tumors and strokes. However, this method is still limited by its inability to image the brain in detail, and to distinguish between gray and white matter.

Structural imaging of the brain began in earnest with the development of magnetic resonance imaging

(MRI). The first MRI was created by Paul Lauterbur in 1972. By 1980, MRI had become a viable technique for medical imaging. MRI is used to produce images of atomic nuclei through the use of radio waves and magnetic fields. A typical MRI has a magnetic field of 1.5 Tesla, which is about 30,000 times stronger than Earth's magnetic field. This has the effect of making the nuclei precess (or rotate about their spin axis) at a frequency proportional to the strength of the field that they experience. The hydrogen nucleus, which is composed of a single proton, is the most commonly imaged since hydrogen is the most common atom in the body. A 1.5-Tesla field makes the hydrogen atoms precess at approximately 63.9 megahertz, which is a slightly lower frequency than a typical FM radio signal. Radio waves of this frequency are transmitted into the brain and are absorbed by the protons, and after a short time these protons are induced to send radio waves back in return. Depending on how the scan is obtained, MRI can be used to produce a map of the density and environment of water in each part of the brain. Since gray matter and white matter differ in the amount of water, complex fats, and proteins they contain, they appear as different intensities in the final MRI. This method provides beautifully detailed images of the human brain where even subtle damage can be observed. MRI has proven invaluable for the diagnosis of many neurological disorders. Paul Lauterbur and Peter Mansfield shared the 2003 Nobel Prize in medicine for their development of methods for performing MRI.

Because MRI can be repeated often in the same individual, and is safe to use in children, it has been used to show patterns of normal and abnormal development from birth through old age. MRI can be used to obtain a variety of measurements from the human brain. Diffusion tensor imaging (DTI) recently was developed to map the course of axonal fibers that connect neurons in the brain. This may eventually be used to examine how the brain is "wired" together, and thus tell us something about how brain regions communicate and transfer information. While imaging the anatomy of the brain is valuable in many ways, equally important is gaining an understanding of how the brain functions.

FUNCTIONAL BRAIN IMAGING

The earliest method for imaging brain function was electroencephalography (EEG), discovered by Hans Berger in 1925. Neurons produce small electrical and magnetic fields as they function. Their activity leads to changes in the EEG that can be recorded using sensitive electrodes and amplifiers. The earliest studies revealed that the brain produces electrical activity of different frequencies during different stages of consciousness. Rapid activity is seen during alert wakefulness, slowing during rest, and becoming slower still with sleep, coma, and finally stopping in death. EEG has been used by clinicians to detect brain damage, such as spikes in the EEG associated with epilepsy, and slowing of EEG frequency associated with brain damage.

Evidence of thought processes can also be observed in the EEG, such as activity evoked by the perception of sound or light. However, most such responses are too small to be seen in the large ongoing background EEG. Event-related potentials (ERPs) are obtained by averaging multiple EEG responses to the same stimulus repeated many times. This reduces the size of the random background EEG so that the average event-related response can be seen. ERPs have been used by clinicians to check for deafness or visual acuity problems in patients who cannot respond, such as babies, and have been used as a method of communication for patients who are completely unable to move any part of their body after severe brain damage, called "locked-in syndrome." ERPs provide the only way that these patients can communicate with the outside world. ERPs have been used to examine healthy human brain functions, including sensory perception, attention, language, motor control, and memory, among many others. One disadvantage to EEG and ERPs is that it is difficult to identify the exact brain regions where the activity was generated. This results in part from the high electrical resistance of the skull, which reduces the passage of electrical fields, and problems with identifying the exact size and position of electrical sources in the brain from surface recordings.

While the skull is resistive to electrical fields, it allows magnetic fields to pass almost unimpeded. Magnetoencephalography (MEG) is similar to EEG but records magnetic impulses. Because these fields are so small, a device is used with very sensitive coils that are cooled to the temperature of liquid nitrogen. This makes the coils able to detect small magnetic fields. While MEG is more expensive than EEG, its ability to detect the location of epileptic foci and other types of brain damage has made it a valuable technique for diagnosis and treatment of these disorders.

Functional imaging methods that use radioisotopes are single positron emission computed tomography (SPECT) and positron emission tomography (PET). These methods can be used to examine blood flow, metabolism, neurotransmitter release, and receptor density as well as other aspects of brain chemistry and function. PET and SPECT employ radioactive nuclei joined to chemicals similar to those found normally in the body. Once injected, these chemicals are used by the body, and PET and SPECT are used to find where they are present in the body and at what concentration. This information is used to infer something about how these chemicals are used and what the body is doing.

More recent methods for examining brain activity use MRI to detect changes in blood oxygenation, volume, and/or flow, called functional magnetic resonance imaging (fMRI). The most commonly used methods for fMRI depend on a peculiar magnetic property of blood. As the brain works, it uses oxygen that is supplied by hemoglobin, which contains iron attached to a protein. As the brain works harder, it sends a signal to the blood vessels to increase the amount of blood being delivered to that region. This changes the amount of hemoglobin present, and the level of oxygen in the hemoglobin. When hemoglobin has oxygen, it has little interaction with magnetic fields. However, when it loses oxygen, it develops a stronger magnetic field than the one it is exposed to, called paramagnetism. MRIs can be obtained in a way that makes them susceptible to these small changes in magnetic fields. Because the body supplies more oxygenated blood than is used by the brain, an increase in brain metabolism results in an increase in oxygenated blood, and this leads to an increase in MRI signal. By comparing changes in MRI signal intensity with changes in an experimental task, this allows one to find brain regions involved in the task. This method has been used to identify brain regions involved in such disparate activities as navigating through space, recognizing faces and other objects, selective attention, vigilance and attentional control, and many others. It has also proven useful for documenting changes in brain function associated with psychiatric disorders such as obsessive compulsive disorder, antisocial disorder, schizophrenia, and drug abuse, among others.

Magnetic resonance spectroscopy (MRS) is another MRI-based method that can be used to detect and measure changes in brain function. MRS measures certain metabolites, including neurotransmitters such as GABA, glutamine, and glutamate, among others. In normal aging, there is a reduction in N-acetyl aspertate (NAA) levels with increasing age, which is related to the health and activity level of neurons. Some brain disorders, such as schizophrenia, show a faster reduction in NAA with age, suggesting more rapid brain degeneration than normal.

SUMMARY

Using anatomical imaging techniques such as X-ray, CAT and MRI, and functional imaging techniques such as EEG, MEG, PET, SPECT, and fMRI has led us to a better understanding of the structure and function of the human brain, and the development of new methods for the diagnosis and treatment of neurological and psychiatric illnesses. Further research will lead to improvements upon what we have already discovered, and will provide us with a deeper understanding of the structure and function of the human brain.

—Vincent P. Clark

See also Brain Development

Further Readings and References

Cabeza, R., & Nyberg, L. (2000). Imaging cognition II: An empirical review of 275 PET and fMRI studies. *Journal of Cognitive Neuroscience, 12*(1), 1–47.

Clark, V. P., Courchesne, E., & Grafe, M. (1992). *In vivo* myeloarchitectonic analysis of human striate and extrastriate cortex using magnetic resonance imaging. *Cerebral Cortex, 2,* 417–424.

Clark, V. P., Fan, S., & Hillyard, S. A. (1995). Identification of early visual evoked potential generators by retinotopic and topographic analyses. *Human Brain Mapping, 2,* 170–187.

Clark, V. P., Keil, K., Maisog, J. M., Courtney, S. M., Ungerleider, L. G., & Haxby, J. V. (1996). Functional magnetic resonance imaging of human visual cortex during face matching: A comparison with positron emission tomography. *NeuroImage, 4*(1), 1–15.

Culham, J. (n.d.). *fMRI for dummies.* Retrieved from http://defiant.ssc.uwo.ca/Jody_web/fmri4dummies.htm

Drevets, W. C. (1998). Functional neuroimaging studies of depression: The anatomy of melancholia. *Annual Review of Medicine, 49,* 341.

Hämäläinen, M., Hari, R., Ilmoniemi, R. J., Knuutila, J., & Lounasmaa, O. V. (1993). Magnetoencephalography— theory, instrumentation, and applications to noninvasive studies of the working human brain. *Reviews of Modern Physics, 65*(2), 413–497.

Huettel, S. A., Song, A. W., & McCarthy, G. (2004). *Functional magnetic resonance imaging.* Sunderland, MA: Sinauer.

Jezzard, P., Matthews, P. M., & Smith, S. M. (Eds.). (2001). *Functional MRI: An introduction to methods.* Oxford, UK: Oxford University Press.

Mathias, R. (1996, November/December). The basics of brain imaging. *NIDA Notes, 11*(5). Retrieved from http://www.nida.nih.gov/NIDA_Notes/NNVol11N5/Basics.html

Posner, M. I., & Dehaene, S. (1994). Attentional networks. *Trends in Neurosciences, 17*(2), 75–79.

Smith, E. E., & Jonides, J. (1999). Neuroscience—Storage and executive processes in the frontal lobes. *Science, 283*(5408), 1657–1661.

Society for Neuroscience Brain Briefings, http://web.sfn.org/content/Publications/BrainBriefings/brain_imaging.html

Strauss, L. G., & Conti, P. S. (1991). The applications of pet in clinical oncology. *Journal of Nuclear Medicine, 32*(4), 623–648.

Ungerleider, L. G. (1995). Functional brain imaging studies of cortical mechanisms for memory. *Science, 270*(5237), 769–775.

STUTTERING

Stuttering is a communication disorder in which the flow of speech is broken by repetitions (t-t-t-t-today), prolongations (rrrrrrestaurant), blocks (silent or audible pauses in speech), or circumlocutions (word substitutions to avoiding stuttering on certain words). Everyone is disfluent at times and may have repetitions and prolongations at times. However, normal disfluencies tend to be a repetition of whole words or the interjection of syllables like *uh* and *er*, while stuttering tends to be repetitions or prolongations of sounds and syllables, not whole words. People who stutter often experience a feeling of loss of control regarding their speech, and for some people who stutter, talking is accompanied by excessive tension in the facial muscles and/or body.

The onset of stuttering typically occurs between the ages of 2 and 7, although onset can be later. It is estimated that approximately 5% of children stutter at some point in their development; however, approximately 75% spontaneously recover and regain normal speech fluency. Males stutter more frequently than females. The male-to-female ratio is approximately 4 or 5 to 1; however, at onset the ratio is closer to 2 to 1, indicating that girls are more likely to recover than boys.

Numerous theories about the cause of stuttering have been proposed. Early theories about stuttering typically focused on a single cause. More recent thinking focuses on a combination of factors coming together to cause stuttering, and it is probable that the cause of stuttering is not the same for all individuals. Although the definitive cause or causes of stuttering have not been pinpointed through research, it is likely that genetics and physiology play a key role in the onset of stuttering. Approximately 60% of people who stutter have a family member who stutters. Recent neurophysiological research also indicates that people who stutter process speech in different areas of the brain than those who do not stutter. Although environmental factors do not cause stuttering, the pressure to speak quickly and precisely may play a role in determining whether stuttering will manifest in a particular child. Children and adults who stutter are no more likely to have psychological problems that those who do not stutter, and there is no evidence to suggest that emotional trauma causes stuttering.

The goals of speech therapy treatment for stuttering are to increase fluency and to communicate effectively and freely. There are no scientific data that indicate the general superiority of any specific treatment approach. Typical treatment strategies include gentle onset of sounds, starting air flow just prior to initiating speech, maintaining continuous airflow while talking, articulating lightly, and reducing the rate of speech. For very young children, speech therapy is often "indirect," encouraging parents and caregivers to use a slower rate of speech with longer pauses to reduce speaking pressure the child may feel and to model desired speech. More direct therapy for preschoolers has been gaining popularity recently, in which the child is instructed to identify stuttered speech and then retry the stuttered sentence "without the bumps."

Since many children who stutter by the time they reach school age will continue to do so to some extent for the rest of their lives, stuttering for older children, teenagers, and adults also focuses on dealing effectively with stuttering so that it does not become a burden or hinder effective communication. For older children, teenagers, and adults, therapy often includes strategies for reducing physical tension during moments of stuttering and reducing the overall severity of stuttering. Therapy for teenagers and adults may involve desensitization exercises or activities to help increase acceptance of their stuttering. Paradoxically, greater acceptance of stuttering using leads to increased ability to utilize speech therapy techniques, increased fluency, and less negative impact from stuttering on daily communication.

—John C. Wade

See also Language Development

Further Readings and References

Bloodstein, O. (1995). *A handbook on stuttering* (5th ed.). San Diego, CA: Singular.

Curlee, R., & Siegel, G. (1997). *Nature and treatment of stuttering: New directions* (2nd ed). Needham Heights, MA: Allyn & Bacon.

Kehoe, D. T. (1997). *Stuttering: Science, therapy & practice: The most complete book about stuttering*. Boulder, CO: Casa Futura Technologies.

National Stuttering Association, http://www.nsastutter.org

Peters, T., & Barry, G. (1998). *Stuttering: An integrated approach to its nature and treatment* (2nd ed.). Baltimore: Williams & Wilkins.

Starkweather, C. W. (1987). *Fluency and stuttering*. Englewood Cliffs, NJ: Prentice-Hall.

St. Louis, K. (2001). *Living with stuttering*. Morgantown, WV: Populore.

Stuttering Foundation of America, http://www.stutteringhelp.org

The Stuttering Home Page, Minnesota State University, Mankato, http://www.stutteringhomepage.com

SUCKING BEHAVIORS

The act of sucking is a complex task for the neonate demanding coordination of sucking, swallowing, and breathing. Thus, a full-term infant is more likely than a preterm infant to handle the complex demands of feeding with ease. Understanding the organization of nutritive sucking in the newborn may assist in early identification of infants at risk not only for feeding dysfunction, but also for neurobehavioral delays. The significance of this cannot be underestimated because it helps us identify infants at risk for later feeding and/or developmental problems.

An infant with an intact central nervous system is able to react to the feeding stimulus with increasing efficiency. In contrast, an infant who has experienced a neurologic insult may not develop a mature pattern of sucking through the early weeks of life. The rhythmic activity of sucking is seen in most full-term newborns during the first hour of life, with increasing sophistication of organization during the first days of life. Initially newborn sucking is entirely reflexive,

relying on rooting, latching, and sucking activities. The establishment of rhythmicity of sucking patterns is dependent on the nuclei ambiguous, solitarius, and hypoglossus in the lower portion of the medulla and the nucleus trigeminalis. Thus, with medullary neuronal injury after hypoxic-ischemic insults there is a disturbance of the sucking organization. Maturation of sucking behaviors appears with infant volition through both sensory input and feeding experience and is a complex enough activity to help us understand much about the central nervous system of these infants almost instantaneously.

A variety of methods have been used to quantify nutritive sucking, including ultrasonography with recording electrocardiography and respiratory patterns; documentation of the infant's oral responses necessary for effective feeding; the implementation of the revised Neonatal Oral Motor Assessment Scale (NOMAS); and use of a suckometer with videotaping and visual observation of the infant's performance. The most frequently used method has been the pressure transducer embedded in the nipple with the ultimate goal of quantitative analysis of the sucking process because it appears to be the most objective measurement form. Typical sucking parameters that have been quantified include the number of sucks, number of bursts, number of sucks per burst, time between sucks, time between bursts, consumption (pressure × length of suck), and mean maximum pressure. The complexity of measures allows us to see not only how infants suck at a particular age but also how their sucking organization improves over time.

In the preterm infant, nutritive sucking organization improves with increasing maturity, with increasing gestational age or increasing postconceptional age (PCA). For example, as an infant matures from 32 to 36 weeks PCA, a typical sucking record would show an increase in the number of sucks, number of sucks per burst, decrease in time between bursts, and increasing sucking rate. Using a cross-sectional age approach, the same pattern is true when examining sucking patterns of infants with varying gestational ages (GA), so that an infant born at 33 weeks GA would have a less mature sucking pattern than the infant born at 35 weeks GA during the first week of feeding. By term, infants with gestational ages between 32 and 35 weeks have nutritive patterns similar to those of full-term infants. In contrast, to term sucking patterns of infants born at 24 to 29 weeks GA appear less mature than either preterm infants with longer GAs or full-term infants.

At present, assessment of sucking rhythms has been confined to research protocols, but has the potential to become part of routine neonatal clinical practice. It offers clinician and researchers the opportunity to evaluate an infant's neurologic status during the earlier stages of the neonatal period resulting in more appropriate intervention for the infant at risk for developmental delays.

—*Barbara Medoff-Cooper*

See also Reflexes

Further Readings and References

Bosma, J. (1985). Postnatal ontogeny of performances of the pharynx, larynx and mouth. *American Review of Respiratory Disease, 131*(5, Suppl.), 10–15.

Bu'Lock, F., Woolridge, M. W., & Baum, J. D. (1990). Development of co-ordination of sucking, swallowing and breathing: Ultrasound study of term and preterm infants. *Developmental Medicine & Child Neurology, 32*(8), 669–678.

Medoff-Cooper, B., Bilker, W., & Kaplan, J. (2001). Sucking behavior as a function of gestational age: A cross-sectional study. *Infant Behavior and Development, 24*, 83–94.

Medoff-Cooper, B., McGrath, J., & Bilker, W. (2000). Nutritive sucking and neurobehavioral development in VLBW infants from 34 weeks PCA to term. *MCN: American Journal of Maternal Child Nursing*, April/May, 64–70.

Medoff-Cooper, B., McGrath, J., & Shults, J. (2002). Feeding patterns of full term and preterm infants at forty weeks postconceptional age. *Journal of Developmental and Behavioral Pediatrics, 23*(1), 231–236.

Wolff, P. (1968). The serial organization of sucking in the young infant. *Pediatrics, 42*(6), 943–956.

SUDDEN INFANT DEATH SYNDROME (SIDS)

Sudden infant death syndrome (SIDS) is the term used when the death of a healthy infant (a) occurs suddenly and unexpectedly and (b) medical and forensic investigation findings are inconclusive. Because an infant's death is diagnosed as SIDS when no other cause of death can be determined, the factors surrounding the cause of SIDS have generated a recent increase in the research and educational efforts to better understand SIDS. Although there has been a recent spike in SIDS interest, cases of infant deaths for no apparent reason—other than assumed smothering, because the infant was found in the parent's bed—have been long documented. The criteria for the diagnosis of SIDS have changed over the history of the research.

In the 1940s, for example, the leading cause of SIDS was thought to be infectious disease. In the 1960s and 1970s, SIDS conferences brought together researchers from multiple backgrounds yielding research goals and a consensus on the broad epidemiological components of SIDS. Researchers concluded that the diagnosis of SIDS is warranted only when a healthy infant unexpectedly dies and autopsy reveals no clear cause of death. In the 1980s, the definition of SIDS was again modified to include a thorough investigation of the death scene before the diagnosis could be issued.

A leading hypothesis in the medical literature suggests that infants who die from SIDS have abnormalities in the area of the brainstem responsible for regulating breathing. Other hypotheses are derived from the idea that a parent or caregiver is responsible for the suffocation of the infant. If the definition of SIDS includes intentionality, then it may be presumed that there are cases diagnosed as SIDS, when in fact the infant was murdered. Beginning in the 1980s, research indicated that (a) 2% to 10% of cases diagnosed as SIDS were in fact filicides and (b) more than 50% of SIDS cases were in fact cases of physical abuse, neglect, and accident.

Due to the ambiguities of the nature of SIDS, uncovering the characteristics surrounding SIDS may appear a daunting task for researchers. With the developing research that suggests that many SIDS cases are murders, it is imperative that forensic scientists and those in the social and behavioral sciences focus greater effort on identifying the predictors of SIDS.

—*Viviana A. Weekes-Shackelford
and Todd K. Shackelford*

See also Death, Infant Mortality

Further Readings and References

Bass, M., Kravath, R. E., & Glass, L. (1986). Death scene investigation in sudden infant death. *New England Journal of Medicine, 315*, 100–105.

Iyasu, S., Randell, L. L., Welty, T. K., Hsai, J., Kinney, H. C., Mandell, F., et al. (2002). Risk factors for sudden infant death syndrome among Northern Plains Indians. *Journal of the American Medical Association, 288*, 2717–2723.

Lipsitt, L. P. (2003). Crib death: A biobehavioral phenomenon? *Current Directions in Psychological Science, 12*, 164–170.

National SIDS/Infant Death Resource Center, http://www.sid scenter.org/

SUICIDE

Human beings are remarkable for their resilience, ability to cope with adversity, and fierce will to survive; they are also unique in the animal kingdom in their propensity for self-destruction. Attempts to come to terms with this puzzle are present throughout literature, from Hamlet's soliloquy ("To be or not to be . . .") to Camus' observation that suicide constitutes "the only really serious philosophical problem."

Suicide, the intentional act of ending one's own life, accounts for more than 1 million deaths per year worldwide. As a violent cause of death exceeding war and homicide combined, it constitutes a major public health problem, yet is regarded as one of the top preventable causes of death. Suicide is observed in all societies, across geographic and historical locales, although its meaning and frequency differ considerably from one place to another.

HISTORY

Suicide has been documented throughout recorded history. As early as the third millennium BC, Egyptian history reveals accounts of completed suicides, suicide notes, and even suicide threats to obtain sympathetic treatment. Historian Flavius Josephus wrote extensively about suicide, documenting individual and mass suicides between 1500 BC and 73 AD. Among these was the famous incident at Masada, wherein 960 soldiers killed themselves rather than face defeat and possible capture by the Romans.

Attitudes about suicide have varied through the ages, from neutral tolerance or implicit approval to total condemnation. Ancient Egyptians, because they saw death only as passage to another state of being, viewed suicide rather neutrally, whereas the Romans considered suicide an appropriate and honorable means of avoiding defeat or humiliation. At the opposite end of the spectrum were the ancient Judaic prohibitions against suicide. Elements of this prohibition survive to this day in contemporary Judaism, Christianity, and Islam, although views have softened somewhat in modern times. For example, the Catholic Church now teaches that, rather than being condemned to eternal damnation, people who kill themselves are likely suffering from an illness and are therefore unable to make a truly free choice.

SUICIDE SCIENCE

Modern theorists generally consider suicide as part of a collection of suicidal behaviors, including suicidal ideation (contemplating suicide without taking action), suicide attempts (engaging in self-harming behaviors that do not result in death), and suicide (intentional, self-inflicted death, sometimes referred to as suicide completion). The term *suicide attempt* is problematic because intentional self-harm is not always intended to end life but may serve a communication function such as a "cry for help." For this reason, such behavior is sometimes referred to as deliberate self-harm or parasuicide.

In the United States, suicide consistently ranks among the top 10 causes of death, taking nearly 30,000 lives per year. The suicide rate in the United States has seen a slight, steady decline in recent years, from about 12 per 100,000 population per year through the 1980s and early 1990s to 10.8 per 100,000 per year in 2001. Suicide rates are strongly and consistently associated with an assortment of population characteristics, including sex, race, age, and geographic location. Although females make suicide attempts two to three times as often as males, fully 80% of deaths by suicide are males. Whites commit suicide more often than any other racial group, accounting for more than 90% of all suicides in the United States. African Americans commit suicide at only half the rate of whites.

The age group at greatest risk for suicide is the elderly, with suicide risk rising sharply after age 65 (this mainly reflects high rates of suicide among elderly males). The suicide rate for adolescents has risen sharply in recent decades, to the point that teenagers now commit suicide at a rate comparable with that of the general population. Suicide rates vary sharply from state to state and region to region, with the highest rates generally appearing in the Rocky Mountain states and the lowest rates in the Northeast.

Suicide is also a leading cause of death internationally, with gradually rising rates in recent years. Male suicide rates are much higher than female rates in almost every country, although China is a notable exception. The World Health Organizations' 2003 statistics showed that countries with the highest suicide rates include Lithuania, Russia, Belarus, Latvia, Ukraine, Slovenia, and Hungary. Countries with the lowest suicide rates include Antigua and Barbuda, the Dominican Republic, Honduras, Jordan, Saint Kitts and Nevis, and Saint Vincent and the Grenadines. However, it is difficult to compare suicide rates among countries; data are often not up to date, and data-gathering procedures are sometimes unreliable and vary from one country to another.

CAUSES OF SUICIDE

Why would anyone intentionally end his or her own life? There is no single, proven cause for suicide; to the contrary, suicide is now recognized as a complex phenomenon resulting from multiple influences. These include biological, environmental, and psychological factors.

Biological factors are reflected in family studies suggesting genetic influences, although it is unclear whether suicidal tendencies themselves are inherited or whether people merely inherit a genetic predisposition to mental disorders that are associated with suicide risk. Neurobiological studies have consistently demonstrated involvement of dysregulated serotonin systems in the brain, which are thought to raise the likelihood of impulsive and aggressive behaviors.

Environmental factors play key roles as well, as indicated by studies showing heightened risk in individuals lacking in social support or with childhood histories of neglect or abuse. Physical illness also seems to play a role, since one third of adult suicide victims are physically ill at the time of their deaths. However, studies also have shown that suicidal ideation among terminally ill patients is not typical and is usually more a result of clinical depression than the terminal condition.

Psychological factors also play important roles. Perhaps the best understood influence is mental illness. "Psychological autopsy" studies consistently have shown that more than 90% of people who die by suicide have histories of some psychological disorder, most notably clinical depression, bipolar illness (manic-depression), schizophrenia, or alcoholism. In addition, studies of thinking patterns of suicidal individuals have consistently shown the importance of hopelessness, deficient problem solving, sense of being a burden to others, perceived lack of belongingness, perfectionism, memory deficits, and other cognitive vulnerabilities.

SUICIDE PREVENTION

Preventing suicide requires recognition of risk factors and warning signs. Factors known to be associated with increased risk for suicide include history of a previous suicide attempt, family history of suicide, diagnosed psychiatric disorder, depressed mood (especially if combined with anxiety or agitation), hopelessness, multiple recent losses, social isolation, abuse or neglect in childhood, impulsivity, aggressiveness, and chronic anger.

Recognizing warning signs that a person is contemplating suicide can be crucial in obtaining help for that individual. Suicidal communications should be taken seriously: studies have shown that more than two-thirds of people who committed suicide gave some indication of their intentions prior to the act. Other warning signs include preparations for death (making out a will, suddenly taking out life insurance, giving away prized possessions, "mending fences" with loved ones), expressions of hopelessness, uncharacteristic risk-taking behaviors or other dramatic changes in behavior, preoccupation with death, and references to suicide in drawings, writings, or songs.

Although the vast majority of suicidal individuals suffer from treatable disorders, more than half never receive appropriate diagnosis and treatment. However, there is little doubt that suicidal individuals can be helped. Both psychotherapy and psychotropic medications (such as antidepressants) are effective for most conditions that predispose to suicide, and often are used in combination. A collaborative therapeutic relationship with a competent professional is a key ingredient in the effective treatment of suicidal individuals.

Public health approaches to suicide prevention have increased dramatically in recent years. The U.S. Surgeon General issued the Call to Action to Prevent Suicide in 1999, identifying suicide as a major public health problem and urging public health officials at all levels to help reduce the suicide rate in the United States. This was followed by the National Strategy for Suicide Prevention in 2001, in which steps to reduce suicide are outlined, including broadening the public's awareness of suicide and its risk factors, enhancing services and programs throughout the country, and advancing the science of suicide prevention.

—Thomas E. Ellis and
Pamela R. Tenney

See also Assisted Suicide, Cluster Suicide, Parasuicide

Further Readings and References

American Association of Suicidology, http://www.suicidology .org

American Foundation for Suicide Prevention, http://www.afsp .org

Colt, G. H. (1991). *The enigma of suicide.* New York: Simon & Schuster.

Ellis, T. E., & Newman, C. F. (1996). *Choosing to live: How to defeat suicide through cognitive therapy.* Oakland, CA: New Harbinger.

Hawton, K., & van Heeringen, K. (2000). *International handbook of suicide and attempted suicide.* Chichester, UK: Wiley.

Jamison, K. R. (1999). *Night falls fast: Understanding suicide.* New York: Knopf.

Maris, R. W., Berman, A. L., & Silverman, M. M. (2000). *Comprehensive textbook of suicidology.* New York: Guilford.

Samaritans, http://www.samaritans.org

Suicide Awareness Voices of Education, http://www.save.org

Suicide Prevention Action Network, http://www.spanusa.org

SUPEREGO

Sigmund Freud coined the term *superego* in 1923 in his work *The Ego and the Id.* In that work, Freud developed what has been called his structural model of the mind. In that model, the mind is divided into three psychic agencies: the ego, the id, and the superego. The superego refers to the part of the mind responsible for conscience. Self-criticism, shame, and guilt emanate from the superego, as does self-acceptance. The superego evaluates the self in terms of moral standards and approves or disapproves of the self accordingly.

Freud viewed the superego from a developmental perspective. The superego is based on identifications with parental approval and disapproval. Yet the child perceives parental approval and disapproval through the distorting prism of his or her own wishes, conflicts, anxieties, and defenses. Freud believed that the superego arises as a resolution of the Oedipus complex.

The child wishes to have an incestuous relationship with the desired parent and wishes to murder the rival parent. These forbidden wishes give rise to feelings of guilt and fears of retribution, such as castration for the little boy. The fear of punishment for these forbidden incestuous and parricidal wishes becomes the basis of the superego. The child identifies with the rival parent and decides to marry someone like the desired parent when the child grows up.

The superego is perceived as omnipotent and omniscient just as the young child views the parents as all-powerful and all-knowing. The child is motivated to listen to the superego not simply out of fear of punishment but also out of a wish to grow up and enjoy adult prerogatives, privileges, and powers, especially those related to adult sexuality. Freud believed that precursors to the superego could be seen in the child's acceptance of parental discipline during the anal phase of psychosexual development when the child is being toilet trained.

Melanie Klein added to Freud's superego theory by suggesting an earlier origin of the superego in the infant's initial relationship with a nurturing mother during the oral phase of development. Klein suggested that the infant deals with frustration of dependency needs by projecting that infantile rage onto the mother, who is then perceived as a bad, angry mother. Fear of a "bad" mother who is hostile to the child's needs becomes the basis of a particularly harsh and punitive superego. Klein suggested that the child feels a primitive form of guilt when the child worries that his or her aggression has damaged the mother. The urge to make reparations, to assume responsibility for fixing the damage wrought by one's own aggression, becomes the inspiration for mature superego functioning.

In psychoanalytic theory, the superego is multifaceted. It has permissive and prohibitive, harshly punitive and lovingly accepting, rational and irrational aspects. The superego is only partially conscious, since the harsher aspects are often repudiated out of fear of punishment. Certain forms of psychopathology have been thought to derive from an unduly harsh superego. Depression derives from a cruel superego that generates irrational self-blame. Obsessional self-doubt and worry derive from a perfectionistic superego that is excessively fault-finding.

—Lawrence Josephs

See also Ego; Ego Development; Freud, Sigmund; Psychoanalytic Theory

Further Readings and References

Freud, S. (1923). *The ego and the id. Standard edition of the complete psychological works of Sigmund Freud* (Vol. 19, pp. 1–66). London: Hogarth Press.

Klein, M. (1975). *Love, guilt, and reparation and other works, 1921–1945*. New York: Delta.

SURROGATE MOTHERS

The term *surrogate mother* is occasionally used to mean the foster caregiver of orphaned children, often an older sibling or a maternal relative. Most commonly, however, surrogate motherhood refers to participation in the conception and gestation of a child by a woman who will not be a primary caregiver after the child is born. A woman may act as a surrogate mother when she becomes pregnant by artificial insemination, gives birth, and surrenders the child to another woman who will care for the child and act as the child's social and emotional mother. She may also be termed a surrogate mother when another woman's fertilized ovum is implanted and develops to term in her uterus, and the newborn infant is given to another woman (sometimes the source of the ovum, sometimes not) who will act socially and emotionally in the role traditionally called "mother," whom we may call the caregiving parent. In either case, the woman who carries the child may be called a *gestational surrogate*, and this term may be preferable to *surrogate mother* because it does not imply a social role as "mother" does.

HISTORICAL BACKGROUND

Some forms of artificial insemination have been possible as long as fertilization has been understood, but gestational surrogacy as a practice first came to public notice with the much-publicized case of Mary Beth Whitehead and Baby M in 1986. Mrs. Whitehead had entered into a contract with a childless couple, agreeing to be inseminated with the husband's sperm, to bear and surrender the resulting child, but after the birth she was reluctant and gave up the little girl only after months of negotiation. By 1994, complex forms of assisted reproductive technology (ART) had developed, creating a variety of beginnings for gestational surrogacy, as well as attempts to solve some of the legal problems inherent in the practice.

INCIDENCE AND TECHNOLOGY

At least a thousand births a year in the United States result from gestational surrogacy. Depending on the reasons for the couple's childlessness, the technology involved ranges from fertilization in vivo with sperm from a donor or from the intended caregiving father, to hormonal stimulation of ovulation to obtain an ovum from a donor or from the intended caregiving mother, followed by in vitro fertilization with sperm from a donor or the intended caregiving father, and transfer of the fertilized ovum to the uterus of the gestational surrogate.

OUTCOMES AND RISKS

Risks to Infant

Risks are increased with all forms of gestational surrogacy that involve ART procedures rather than simple artificial insemination. For all ART procedures, whether or nor gestational surrogacy is involved, the proportion of resulting live-born infants is about 25%. The increased likelihood of multiple births with ART is associated with complications of pregnancy, premature births, low birth weights, and long-term disabilities resulting from these conditions.

Risks to Donors, Surrogates, and Families

Ovum donors in ART procedures experience some medical risk factors connected with stimulation of ovulation by medications, as well as the surgical procedure that retrieves the ovum. In some procedures, the gestational surrogate also undergoes increased risk because of medical and surgical treatment. The gestational surrogate has a slight increase of risk factors as a result of childbirth, as compared with her risk if she did not bear a child.

Families with a history of childlessness and the experience of ART, with or without gestational surrogacy, have emotional concerns that are different from those of "natural" family formation, and may benefit from counseling for parents and for children as the children grow up.

LEGAL AND ETHICAL ISSUES

Early gestational surrogacy arrangements were often made as personal contracts, with the potential for ethical and legal flaws. Today's practice of arrangement of surrogacy through a clinic has lessened the possibility that one party or another will be exploited.

One of the first major ethical concerns about gestational surrogacy was the idea that the childless persons were buying a baby by contract, as some of the first surrogacy agreements implied. Direct purchase of a child, or of an embryo or ovum, is not legal in the United States. However, practical considerations for the gestational surrogate include the possible loss of income during the pregnancy, interruptions to employment or schooling, and medical fees not generally covered by health insurance. Reimbursement of the gestational surrogate for these expenses is appropriate, as is some reimbursement to ovum donors for their time and inconvenience.

Suitable informed consent documentation should be carried out with both gestational surrogates and ovum donors, as it would be for medical procedures done for other purposes. The New York State Task Force on Life and the Law has also recommended that clinics waive charges when carrying out experimental treatments with no clear evidence basis.

A potential problem for gestational surrogate arrangements arises if either the surrogate or the intended caregiving parent changes her mind about the agreement. Court decisions have tended to favor the gestational surrogate as the "real mother" if she wants to keep the child. In one case, neither the surrogate nor the intended caregiving parent wanted to care for a handicapped child born of a surrogacy arrangement.

After the child's birth, the caregiving parents are faced with ethical decisions about disclosing the family's unusual history, either to the child or to others. Lack of knowledge on the part of the child may be a cause of a later unintentional consanguineous marriage, however.

Ethical and legal views of gestational surrogacy are shifting. In 2004, Italy prohibited all ART procedures, including procedures related to gestational surrogacy. Laws and court decisions in the United States are also changing as new problems arise, such as the question of disposal of unneeded embryos after a pregnancy has been achieved.

RELIGIOUS AND CULTURAL CONCERNS

Gestational surrogacy has been regarded with suspicion by some major religious groups. The Roman Catholic Church takes the approach, consistent with its views on abortion, that conception and birth need to occur in the context of marriage and as a result of natural events; this excludes gestational surrogacy as well as all forms of ART. Muslims consider these forms of reproduction wrong, especially in light of their long tradition of foster parenting without formal adoption or family membership. In Judaism, the tradition of passing Jewish identity from mother to child raises questions if either the surrogate or the caregiving mother was not Jewish.

Culture-based attitudes are also important here. In Japan, surrogate motherhood is not approved, and in one recent case children born of a surrogate in the United States as a result of insemination from a Japanese father were not considered to be Japanese by a Japanese court.

The difficulty and expense of gestational surrogacy make cultural attitudes irrelevant outside a few industrialized societies.

MOTIVATIONAL AND ATTITUDINAL FACTORS

One reason for couples' seeking to arrange gestational surrogacy is the very real emotional distress associated with infertility, a problem experienced by 7% to 8% of American couples. Both men and women react with grief and distress to the realization of difficulties with reproductive success, and marriages may be negatively affected, no matter which partner is "at fault." Gestational surrogacy may be a way of ensuring a sense of reproductive success to the husband, when a physical condition of the wife prevents their shared parenthood. Gestational surrogacy may actually be more accessible to some couples in the United States than adoption of a healthy infant.

Couples dealing with infertility may wish for gestational surrogacy using their own sperm and ova, if possible, to ensure that the child will resemble at least one of the caregiving parents as much as possible. This resemblance may be related to important aspects of the marital relationship, or may be desired as a way to obscure the couple's reproductive problems, potentially made public by a child who was very different in appearance.

Male same-sex couples who wish to be parents may find that gestational surrogacy, arranged through a clinic, is more appealing than either adoption, with its scrutiny of lifestyle, or informal arrangements with women.

Finally, we may note that some potential parents share a folk belief that a genetic connection is a factor in a good parent-child relationship, with attachment deriving partly from the genetic relationship; for these people, surrogacy would be more desirable than adoption of an unrelated child.

THE FUTURE OF SURROGATE MOTHERHOOD

The future of gestational surrogacy may be assured by a continuing increase in fertility problems, possibly related to a tendency to delay childbearing until later in life. Risks to the child's health, in the case of ART procedures, may be lessened as guidelines for limiting the number of embryos are developed. Better understanding of and help for families' psychological concerns may also be achieved as the history of gestational surrogacy continues.

—*Jean Mercer*

Further Readings and References

Japanese Justice Ministry denies citizenship to twins whose parents used U.S. surrogate (2003, October 27). *Kaiser Daily Reproductive Health Report*. Available from http://www.kaisernetwork.org?dailyreports/

New York State Task Force on Life and the Law. (n.d.). *Executive summary of assisted reproductive technologies: Analysis and recommendations for public policy*. Retrieved from http:// www.health.state.ny.us/nysdoh/taskfce/execsum.htm

Perrin, E., & the Committee on Psychosocial Aspects of Child and Family Health. (2002). Technical report: Coparent or second-parent adoption by same-sex parents. *Pediatrics, 109*(2), 341–344.

President's Council on Bioethics. (n.d.). *U.S. public policy and the biotechnologies that touch the beginnings of human life: A detailed overview*. Retrieved from http://bioethicsprint.bioethics.gov/background/biotechnology.html

Shapiro, V. B., Shapiro, J. R., & Paret, I. H. (2001). *Complex adoption and assisted reproductive technology*. New York: Guilford.

Society for Assisted Reproductive Technology and the American Society for Reproductive Medicine. (n.d.). *Assisted reproductive technology in the United States: 1999 results generated by the American Society for Reproductive Medicine/Society for Assisted Reproductive Technology Registry*. Retrieved from http://www.asrm.org/Professionals/Fertility&Sterility/1999sartresults.pdf

Turone, F. (2004). Italy to pass new law on assisted reproduction. *British Medical Journal, 328*, 9.

Whitehead, M. B. (1989). *A mother's story*. New York: St. Martin's.

SYMBOLIC PLAY

Symbolic play is play that involves mentally transforming people, objects, or events, or acting as if something were true. Consider a child who pretends to "feed the baby" by putting a block to the lips of a doll; the doll is treated as though it were alive and the block as though it were a bottle of milk. Such activities foreshadow the ability to engage in hypothetical reasoning and immerse oneself in fictional worlds.

Symbolic play usually appears in the second year as single, self-directed actions with realistic objects (e.g., the child holds an empty cup to the lips, as though drinking). With development, the scenario may incorporate more actions (in the earlier example of giving the "baby" the "bottle," the child may add "burping" the "baby"), may include actors other than the self (e.g., the "baby"), and may involve less realistic objects (e.g., the block as "bottle"). Both role assignments and object use follow predictable developmental pathways, increasing in complexity and abstractness.

Children's understanding of pretense as creating an imaginary reality also undergoes developmental change. Even 2-year-olds understand that, once an imaginary situation has been created, subsequent actions must be consistent with that alternate universe. For example, if an empty cup is said to contain "coffee" which is "poured" on the floor, the child will use a sponge to "clean up." Preschoolers communicate the boundaries of the pretend universe, stepping "out of character" to negotiate the next phase of the play, or to converse briefly with an outsider. However, children under age 4 may not recognize that pretense is a mental, rather than physical, activity. If they are introduced to a character described as knowing nothing about kangaroos, and yet is hopping up and down like a kangaroo, very young children will typically say that the character is pretending to be a kangaroo (i.e., they apparently do not understand that knowledge, not action, is critical to pretense).

Symbolic play development is closely linked with other important cognitive and social achievements. As predicted by Jean Piaget's theory of cognitive development, the appearance of symbolic play actions and sequences parallel first words and first sentences. Children who are adept at role play or at social pretend play tend to have an advanced "theory of mind" (understanding of mental states), possibly because they practice "putting themselves into another person's shoes." Theorist Lev Vygotsky argued that conforming to the rules and/or social roles of the pretend universe supports children's ability to distinguish between thought and actions, facilitating the development of abstract thinking and self-control.

Pretending is often a social activity, and although it is apparently universal, it is shaped by cultural beliefs and practices. In middle-class European American homes, parents often support children's early symbolic play development by structuring play scenarios. For example, the parent of a 15-month-old might suggest, "Let's cook dinner," stir some blocks in a pan, and offer the child a "taste." In some other cultures, adults do not engage in pretend activities, and a sibling or other child may provide the social structure for emerging play abilities.

Clinicians use symbolic play as a marker of developmental progress and as a window into children's emotional states. Symbolic play may be absent or delayed in developmental disabilities (e.g., children with autism rarely engage in symbolic play and show

limited theory of mind development as well). Children's play may help them work through emotionally significant issues such as connection or separation from others, a sense of their own power versus weakness, and physical health versus harm. Thus, symbolic play has both cognitive and emotional significance in children's development.

—*Cecilia M. Shore*

Further Readings and References

Göncü, A., Patt, M. B., & Kouba, E. (2002). Understanding young children's pretend play in context. In P. K. Smith & C. H. Hart (Eds.), *Blackwell handbook of childhood social development* (pp. 418–427). Malden, MA: Blackwell.

Lillard, A. (2002). Pretend play and cognitive development. In U. Goswami (Ed.), *Blackwell handbook of childhood cognitive development* (pp. 188–205). Malden, MA: Blackwell.

Saracho, O. N., & Spodek, B. (1988). *Multiple perspectives on play in early childhood education*. Albany: State University of New York Press.

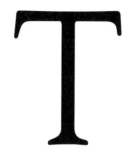

Testosterone

He's a guy. They don't talk, they fight. It's all that crazy testosterone.

—Samantha, *Sex and the City*

T CELLS

T cells or T lymphocytes are a subset of white blood cells that play a major role in eliminating pathogens and cancer cells that escape the body's first line of defenses. On the basis of their function in the immune response, T cells are divided into two categories: T helper (TH) lymphocytes and cytotoxic T lymphocytes (CTLs). TH cells orchestrate the activity of other cells of the immune system by releasing messenger molecules known as cytokines and are subdivided into T helper type 1 (TH1) and T helper type 2 (TH2) cells on the basis of the cytokines they produce. TH1 cytokines preferentially direct immune responses against pathogens that invade cells and against tumors, whereas TH2 cytokines preferentially direct immune responses against extracellular pathogens. CTLs eliminate target cells, such as tumor cells or cells infected by viruses, by producing molecules that form pores on their surface. CTLs then use the pores on the target to insert additional molecules that specifically induce cell death.

All mature T cells express a specialized molecule on their cell surface. This molecule, or T cell receptor (TCR), is used to recognize a small portion (antigen) of the pathogen. Each T cell (and each of its daughter cells) expresses a unique TCR that recognizes only one or a few closely related antigens. T cell progenitors are produced in the bone marrow and then migrate to the thymus to mature, hence the etiology of the name T cells. Once T cells mature, they leave the thymus and circulate in the blood and lymphatic system. The antigen recognition process requires the encounter of the TH cells with other specialized cells of the immune system. These cells are called antigen-presenting cells because their function is to display the antigen to the TCR expressed on the cell surface of the TH cell. If the TH cell recognizes the antigen, it becomes activated, proliferates, and differentiates, thus producing a set of molecules necessary to induce other cells of the immune system to eliminate the pathogen. CTLs encounter target cells at the site of infection. After performing their specific function, most of the responding T cells die. However, some T cells become memory T cells and persist for a long time. In subsequent exposures to the same pathogen, memory T cells are responsible for faster immune responses that may prevent disease development.

When functional T cell numbers are below normal, immunodeficiencies result. Immunodeficient individuals are highly susceptible to infections and tumors. Two heritable immune deficiencies are DiGeorge syndrome and severe combined immune deficiency (SCID).

In DiGeorge syndrome the thymus fails to develop and consequently few T cells mature. Individuals with SCID fail to produce functional T cells and B cells because of mutations that disrupt the mechanism for gene rearrangement responsible for TCR expression. B cells also require this mechanism to produce antibodies. Human immunodeficiency virus (HIV) causes acquired immunodeficiency syndrome (AIDS). HIV indirectly and directly kills TH cells and leads to a progressive decline in TH cell numbers. Healthy individuals usually have 500 to 1500 TH cells per cubic millimeter of blood. AIDS develops generally once this level declines below 200. Inappropriate T cell responses can lead to autoimmune diseases. During maturation in the thymus, T cells that strongly recognize the body's own molecules die by a process called negative selection. Some autoimmune diseases involve self-reactive T cells that escape this selection process. In type I diabetes, T helper cells recognize and direct the destruction of pancreas cells that produce insulin. These types of disorders demonstrate the crucial role that T cells play in the immune response and emphasize the importance of maintaining balanced T cell functions.

—*Roberta Attanasio and
Kenneth A. Rogers*

See also Human Immunodeficiency Virus (HIV)

Further Readings and References

Fabbri, M., Smart, C., & Pardi, R. (2003). T lymphocytes. *The International Journal of Biochemistry & Cell Biology, 35*, 1004–1008.

Kimball, J. (2004). *B cells and T cells*. Retrieved from http://users.rcn.com/jkimball.ma.ultranet/BiologyPages/B/B_and_Tcells.html

Mosmann, T., & Sad, S. (1996). The expanding universe of T-cell subsets: Th1, Th2 and more. *Immunology Today, 17*, 139–146.

Roep, B. O. (2003). The role of T-cells in the pathogenesis of Type 1 diabetes: from cause to cure. *Diabetologia, 46*, 305–321.

Schindler, L. W. (n.d.). *Understanding the immune system*. Retrieved from http://rex.nci.nih.gov/behindthenews/uis/uisframe.htm

Simonte, S. J., & Cunningham-Rundles, C. (2003). Update on primary immunodeficiency: Defects of lymphocytes. *Clinical Immunology, 109*, 109–118.

TABULA RASA

English philosopher John Locke proposed that the mind of the newborn infant is a tabula rasa, or blank slate, on which experience writes. Locke was an empiricist. Development, in the empiricist view, is the product of an active environment operating on a passive mind.

One alternative to empiricism is nativism. Nativists propose that the human genetic heritage includes knowledge accumulated over the course of evolution. Thus the mind of the newborn, far from being a blank slate, represents the knowledge of generations. Development, in the nativist view, is a maturational process directed by the genes. It is genes, not environments, that account for developmental change.

An alternative to both empiricism and nativism is constructivism. Constructivists propose that the mind is an active agent in its own development, and not just an outcome of environmental and/or hereditary forces. Development, in the constructivist view, is a creative process directed by an active mind.

There is evidence for all three of these views. Research on learning, socialization, and enculturation shows the powerful influence of environmental and cultural forces in directing the course of development, as expected by empiricists. Research on infant cognition has shown remarkable competencies at unexpectedly early ages, supporting the nativist view. And research on children of all ages shows that ongoing processes of interpretation, reflection, coordination, and reconstruction are indispensable to developmental change, as argued by constructivists.

The existence of evidence for all three of these views rules out strong versions of any of them. If environments, genes, and minds are all important sources of developmental change, then none of these alone is the basis for development. Virtually all developmental psychologists see development as an ongoing interaction of environmental, hereditary, and constructive forces. Theorists differ, however, in which factors they highlight and in how they conceptualize those ongoing interactions.

The intellectual descendants of Locke are learning theorists who stress the role of the environment. Over the past several decades, however, learning has increasingly been viewed as an active process of construction made possible by the genetic heritage of the human species. Thus, differences among contemporary theorists are mostly a matter of differing emphases rather than stark disputes over what single factor causes development.

For parents, teachers, and others who work with children, there is no doubt that environments can and should be organized to promote learning and development. Empiricism reminds us that, no matter what else is going on, children are learning from their environments, and such learning contributes to their development. Thus, empiricism supports the assumption that socialization and education are worth the effort.

Blank slate empiricism goes too far, however, in its presumption of environmental determinism. We cannot determine the course of development for our children or students. Development is a self-regulated process guided, in part, by genes and mental actions. Parents and teachers who understand this process may be able to encourage it, contribute to it, and even influence its course. If we think we can direct and control a child's development, however, we may intervene in ways that do more harm than good.

The infant is surely not a tabula rasa, and its development is not simply caused by its environment. Psychologists continue to debate, however, how much knowledge we should attribute to the infant at birth, and how minds, genes, and environments interactively generate developmental change.

—*David Moshman*

See also Locke, John

Further Readings and References

Gopnik, A., Meltzoff, A. N., & Kuhl, P. K. (2001). *The scientist in the crib: What early learning tells us about the mind.* New York: Perennial.

Moshman, D. (2005). *Adolescent psychological development: Rationality, morality and identity* (2nd ed.). Mahwah, NJ: Erlbaum.

TASTE

Taste is often described as a primitive sense. In order to successfully feed; identify kin, mates, and individuals; and avoid noxious and hazardous compounds, all creatures have a need to detect the chemicals in their environment. The senses of taste, smell, and chemesthesis (chemically activated pain, touch, and temperature) work in unison to allow them to do so. The sense of taste detects relatively small, water-soluble chemicals, and when ingesting foods it is often combined with the sense of smell, which detects comparatively large, air-soluble compounds. Taste begins functioning in humans before birth and,

despite large individual differences, it remains relatively stable throughout the life span.

WHAT IS TASTE?

In everyday usage, the term "taste" is used to refer to all the sensations experienced when eating a food or drinking a beverage. However, once a substance is placed in the mouth, the individual experiences a multitude of sensations, including taste, smell, touch, temperature, sound, and sometimes even pain and irritation; this collection of sensations is more accurately referred to as "flavor." More precisely, taste is restricted to the sensations that arise from the stimulation of taste receptor cells found throughout the mouth, especially on the tongue. These taste receptors are stimulated by water-soluble compounds that are relatively small. The spectrum of taste sensations is far more limited than those of smell; just how limited is still a matter of debate.

Taste receptor cells are sensory receptor cells that transduce, or convert, a taste compound into a neural signal that is transmitted to the brain. These receptors are organized into taste buds, which are made up of taste receptor cells and supporting cells. Taste buds, in turn, are contained within papillae, of which there are four types. In the oral cavity, all but one type (filiform) contain taste buds. Fungiform papillae are scattered over the front two thirds of the tongue and can be seen as red bumps that stand out in contrast to the pinkness of the rest of the tongue. Circumvallate papillae are located toward the very back of the tongue in an inverted "V". Foliate papillae are very far back on the sides of the tongue and look like a series of folds or lines. The filiform papillae, which do not contain taste buds, cover the remaining surface of the top of the tongue. Taste buds are also found on the back of the throat (epiglottis) and the soft palate (the rear portion of the roof of the mouth).

Are There Four Basic Tastes?

For over a century, the predominant view has been that taste sensations are limited to four basic tastes: sweet, sour, salty, and bitter. However, this hypothesis has never been proven and there are now many prominent researchers who believe in the existence of a fifth basic taste, called "umami." This taste is associated with the taste of MSG (monosodium glutamate, the primary ingredient in Accent seasoning) and is often described as a "brothy" or "savory" taste. There are still others who believe that the entire concept of basic tastes is flawed and feel that the evidence supporting this idea is based more upon language limitations than on perceptual or physiological ones. In fact, to date, no precise definition of a "basic taste" or "taste primary" (other than a list of four or five distinct sensations) has been accepted, nor have four or five physiological mechanisms or structures of taste been discovered. Regardless, it is clear that there are far fewer categories of taste sensation than smell sensation.

The Taste Map

The biggest and most pervasive myth regarding taste is that sweet, sour, salty, and bitter are perceived only on certain distinct regions of the tongue. In actuality, all taste compounds can be tasted in every region of the tongue, as long as taste receptor cells are stimulated. There are regional differences in sensitivity to different compounds, but the taste map grossly oversimplifies this reality and ignores taste receptors that are located on the palate and the back of the throat.

If tasting is believing, it is simple enough to prove to yourself that you can taste sweet, sour, salty, bitter, and umami at the tip of your tongue. Simply collect a few items that are characterized by these flavors (e.g., sugar, salt, lemon juice, coffee, and Accent) and dab each on the tip of your tongue in succession. You can readily perceive each of these distinct tastes, and there is no need to wait for the coffee to touch the back of your tongue, lemon juice the sides, etc. You can further examine falsity of this myth by dabbing a cotton swab containing each of the compounds on other regions of your tongue as well.

TASTE THROUGHOUT THE LIFE SPAN

Humans begin perceiving taste in the womb and continue to taste chemicals throughout their entire life span. Taste is thought to help guide in food selection, acceptance, and rejection. Sweetness is typically an indication of a high-calorie food source and typically elicits a positive hedonic response. In contrast, bitterness (possibly an indicator of alkaloid poisons) and sourness (possibly an indicator of food spoilage or lack of ripeness) are more likely to elicit a negative response, although this is dependent upon intensity levels, context, and familiarity. Umami tends to elicit positive responses, while responses to saltiness show the greatest amount of inconsistency, varying from positive to neutral to negative.

Taste Before Birth

By late gestation, the number and distribution of papillae are similar to those found throughout childhood and adulthood. By the sixth month of gestation, the taste system is functioning and the fetus can be observed to respond to the presence of taste compounds.

Taste in a Newborn

Newborns can perceive sweet, sour, salty, bitter, and umami compounds. Under all testing conditions, they respond positively to sweetness, while their responses to other tastes are more dependent upon the testing conditions. In general, responses to umami compounds are positive, responses to sour and bitter compounds are negative, and responses to saltiness show individual reactions that range from positive to negative.

Taste in Children

Children perceive taste much in the same way that young adults do. They differ from newborns in that experience and context have a larger impact on preferred levels of taste compounds. For example, as compared to their intake of water, toddlers will increase the amount of sucrose solution they consume with increasing concentration, but unlike younger children they will reduce their consumption of salt solutions with increasing concentration. However, toddlers prefer salted to unsalted soup and cereals, suggesting that the context in which the compounds are tasted, in solution versus in a food, impacts preference.

Ratings of taste intensity in older children is very similar to that of adults, although there do seem to be differences in preferences. Children have a tendency to prefer higher concentrations of salt and sucrose, presumably due to differences in nutritional needs. Cultural and gender differences are evident at this stage, with research indicating that both can influence preferences.

Changes With Advancing Age

From the ages of 20 to around 70, there are small but reliable decreases in taste sensitivity, while after 80 there are larger decreases. Taste thresholds rise slightly with age (indicating less sensitivity to low concentrations), taste identification decreases slightly and taste intensity ratings decline for some, but not all, taste compounds. For which gender and at what age sensitivity lessens are questions that are complex and not fully resolved. Also unresolved are for which compounds these sensitivity reductions occur, at what rate, and at what magnitude. It is clear that there are some small reductions in sensitivity with age, but that these age-related decreases for taste are typically later in time and lesser in degree than those that occur for other senses, such as vision and hearing.

—Jeannine Frances Delwiche

See also Sensory Development

Further Readings and References

Broomfield, J. (2000). *Aging changes in the senses.* Retrieved from http://health.discovery.com/diseasesandcond/encyclopedia/508.html

Cowart, B. J. (1981). Development of taste perception in humans: Sensitivity and preference throughout the life span. *Psychological Bulletin, 90,* 43–73.

Cowart, B. J. (1989). Relationships between taste and smell across the adult life span. *Annals of the New York Academy of Sciences, 561,* 39–55.

Delwiche, J. F. (1996). Are there "basic" tastes? *Trends in Food Science and Technology, 7,* 411–415.

Granchrow, J. R., & Mennella, J. A. (2003). The ontogeny of human flavor perception. In R. L. Doty (Ed.), *Handbook of olfaction and gustation* (2nd ed., pp. 823–846). New York: Marcel Dekker.

Monell Chemical Senses Center, http://www.monell.org

OSU SSG Explains, http://ssg.fst.ohio-state.edu/Extension/explains.asp

Schiffman, S. S. (1997). Taste and smell losses in normal aging and disease. *Journal of the American Medical Association, 278,* 1357–1362.

Smith, D. V., & Margolskee, R. F. (2001, March). Making sense of taste. *Scientific American,* 32–39.

TAY-SACHS DISEASE

Tay-Sachs disease was named after two physicians, British ophthalmologist Warren Tay and American neurologist Bernard Sachs. Both described the disease independently in 1881 and 1887, respectively. Tay-Sachs disease is an inborn error associated with the abnormal breakdown of a particular sugar-containing lipid called GM2 ganglioside. The important hallmarks of Tay-Sachs disease are a massive storage of GM2 ganglioside in the brain and also in the macular region of the eye, on which an ophthalmologist can detect the characteristic "cherry red spot." Clinical onset of this disease is usually at 5 to 6 months of age, and the symptoms include retardation in development, loss of motor function and intellectual capacity, and blindness. The disease progresses rapidly and is usually fatal by the age of 3 to 4 years old. However, some with milder cases have lived into teens and adulthood. The disease incidence in Ashkenazi Jewish population is about 1 in 4,000 births, while the incidence in non-Jews is one hundred times lower. The disease is inherited from parents in an autosomal recessive manner. This means that each parent, though not affected by the disease, carries a defective gene in an autosome (the chromosomes other than the sex chromosome), and the affected child has inherited a pair of chromosomes both containing the defective gene.

The normal breakdown of GM2 ganglioside requires a specific enzyme, β-hexosaminidase A (Hex A), and a helper protein called GM2 activator. Thus, Tay-Sachs disease can be caused by the deficiency or defect of either Hex A or GM2 activator. Human tissues contain two forms of β-hexosaminidases, Hex A and Hex B. Hex A contains two different protein chains, alpha- and beta-chains, and Hex B contains two beta-chains. Therefore, Tay-Sachs disease can result from the mutations in any one of the three genes, which are responsible for making the alpha-chain, the beta-chain, and the GM2 activator. Based on the mutations in these three genes, Tay-Sachs disease can be classified into three types: type B (also called classical Tay-Sachs disease), mutations in the gene for making the alpha-chain; type O (also called Sandhoff disease), mutations in the gene for making the beta-chain; and type AB, mutations in the gene for making the GM2 activator. Among these three, Sandhoff disease is the most severe type.

There is no treatment for Tay-Sachs disease at present. Since this disease primarily affects the brain, the effective introduction of therapeutic agents to the brain and to the proper location of the brain cells has been a continuous challenge. Various therapeutic options have been considered, such as (1) enzyme replacement therapy to provide a purified normal enzyme or an activator protein; (2) bone marrow transplantation to provide cells that can produce the functionally active enzyme or activator protein; (3) reduction of GM2 ganglioside formation to minimize its accumulation; and (4) gene therapy to correct the defective gene. However, these methods of treatment are currently only in experimental stages. Simple and rapid analytical methods are available for detecting the Hex A activity, as well as the gene mutations for carrier screening and prenatal diagnosis. The establishment of effective screening procedures represents one of the most important contributions to Tay-Sachs disease. These analyses, together with genetic counseling, have greatly reduced the incidence of Tay-Sachs disease in the Ashkenazi Jewish population, and the disease is now considered a rare disorder. To date, the clinical management of this disease is limited to a patient's supportive care and prevention or treatment of the secondary illness, if occurring. The National Organization for Rare Disorders (NORD), a voluntary health organization, has been established to help people with rare diseases and to provide assistance to the organizations that serve them. The activity of NORD is centered on the identification, treatment, and cure of rare disorders through programs of education, advocacy, research, and service.

—*Su-Chen Li and Yu-Teh Li*

Further Readings and References

Desnick, R. J., & Kaback, M. M. (Eds.). (2001). *Tay-Sachs disease*. San Diego, CA: Academic Press.

Gravel, R. A., Kaback, M. M., Proia, R. L., Sandhoff, K., Suzuki, K., & Suzuki, K. (2001). The GM2 gangliosidoses. In C. R. Scriver, A. L. Beaudet, D. Valle, W. S. Sly, B. Childs, K. W. Kinzler, et al. (Eds.), *The metabolic and molecular basis of inherited diseases* (pp. 3827–3876). New York: McGraw-Hill.

National Organization for Rare Disorders (NORD), http://www.rarediseases.org

National Tay-Sachs and Allied Diseases Association, http://www.ntsad.org

Tay-Sachs Disease Hub, http://www.genomelink.org/taysachs

TEENAGE PREGNANCY

When a fetus is conceived in a woman or female adolescent under the age of 20, it is considered a teenage or adolescent pregnancy. In the early 21st century, 30% to 60% of all female adolescents became pregnant and as many as 78% of those pregnancies were unplanned. In many countries this represented 30 years of decreasing rates; however, in some countries teenage pregnancy rates continued to climb.

PROBLEMS IN TEENAGE PREGNANCY

Although normal human development includes puberty and increased sexual interest, a resulting teenage pregnancy has many developmental risks for both mother and child during pregnancy, at birth, and throughout life. First, adolescent pregnancy tends to postpone or stop a female adolescent's formal education. With little education, teenage mothers are likely to have little earning potential and economic security. Research from the United States also suggests that adolescent fathers lose as much as 15% of their educational achievement and earning potential. Additionally, fathers of children born to adolescent mothers rarely provide enough income to fully support their children, so many teenage mothers and their children live in poverty and use social welfare programs to survive.

A teenage pregnancy also limits a female adolescent's social and personal growth. Adolescent mothers tend to have more pregnancies and spend more of their young adulthood as single parents than women who postpone childbearing until adulthood. Considering that their sexual partners tend not to marry them and that many cultures prohibit childbearing outside of marriage, teenage mothers also experience a great deal of social stigma. In addition, teenage mothers have fewer chances of future marriage, and if they do marry their chances of being abused, abandoned, or divorced increase.

In view of the educational, economic, social, and personal challenges facing pregnant teenagers, some turn to abortion. In many countries, adolescents have difficulty finding and paying for safe abortions. Furthermore, teenagers often delay obtaining an abortion until later gestation, which can lead to life-threatening medical complications. Although emotional problems from abortion are rare, they are more likely to occur when the adolescent delays obtaining the abortion, is undecided about the abortion, has no support for the abortion, or has psychological problems outside of the abortion.

Pregnancy is a leading cause of death for teenage females because their bodies are not completely ready for childbearing. Approximately 70,000 pregnant adolescents die each year in developing countries. In developed countries, pregnant adolescents (17 and younger) are 2 to 4 times more likely to die during childbirth than women in their 20s. Pregnant teens are also at greater risk for complications including toxemia, hypertension, anemia, placenta previa, and premature delivery. Poverty contributes to these complications because poor teens are often malnourished. Moreover, malnourished or growing female adolescents are likely to have undersized pelvises causing prolonged or obstructed labor. Compared to pregnant adults, pregnant adolescents are more likely to smoke, less likely to gain adequate weight, and less likely to receive timely and adequate prenatal care (resulting in unidentified and untreated pregnancy complications).

These potential conditions also put the infant in danger. Infants of adolescent pregnancies are more likely to die (more than 1 million each year in developing countries), to be born prematurely, and to be a low birth weight (less than 5.5 pounds). They are more likely to have organs that are not fully developed, leading to brain, vision, intestinal, urinary tract, or lung problems (such as respiratory distress syndrome). These infants can also have malformed limbs, especially if the mother smoked early in her pregnancy. Teenage pregnancy infants are also at risk for acquiring, dying from, and being impaired by sexually transmitted diseases (STDs) if their mother has an untreated STD. Adolescent mothers are at high risk for untreated STDs because young people have the highest rates of STD acquisition and STDs in females are often undetected.

Children born to adolescents are also likely to experience many problems as they grow up. First of all, teenage parents have few parenting skills and few resources for dealing with parenting stress. Therefore, these children tend to have less developmentally stimulating environments and experience more mistreatment of all kinds, such as abuse and neglect. Consequently, they are likely to experience less educational, economic, and social success than other children. In the United States, for example, they tend to abuse drugs, drop out of school, initiate sex early, engage in criminal activity, have emotional and behavioral problems, and experience teen pregnancy themselves. Moreover, these outcomes can be aggravated if the child is deprived of a close connection to the father.

Teenage pregnancy also has serious consequences for society. In the United States, millions of tax dollars are spent each year for health care, foster care, criminal justice, and public assistance due to teenage pregnancy. Furthermore, the loss in academic achievement due to teenage pregnancy leads to lost productivity and a loss in human potential for society.

FACTORS ASSOCIATED WITH TEENAGE PREGNANCY

Although pregnancy occurs from sexual intercourse between a male and a female, there are many other overlapping and interrelated factors that may foster the incidence of adolescent sexual intercourse and pregnancy. Worldwide improvements in health and nutrition contribute to lowering the average age of menarche and to increasing teenage fertility, so more female adolescents are capable of becoming pregnant. Additionally, early menarche is associated with increased risk for teenage pregnancy.

Access to and knowledge of contraceptives are also factors in teenage pregnancy. If an adolescent is sexually active over a 12-month period without using contraception, she has a 90% chance of becoming pregnant. Consequently, wherever birth control licensing, advertising, selling, and services are restricted, adolescent contraceptive use is constrained and teenage pregnancy rates are higher. These barriers to youth reproductive control are created by laws, policies, and media censorship that are frequently fostered by social taboos, gender bias, and opposition from religious leaders.

Poverty exemplifies another set of teenage pregnancy factors. When communities are compared worldwide, adolescent childbearing tends to be more common in those communities with high rates of poverty, mobility, unemployment, crime, and teen suicide. In addition, early childbearing is rarely thought to be a source of concern in poor communities; it is often considered a normal part of life, even a measure of success or adulthood. Considering that education may be unavailable or seem unattainable in these communities, childbearing may seem to be a more reachable goal. It is therefore understandable that adolescents who give birth are three times as likely to have low levels of educational achievement.

Teenage pregnancy is also linked to several family factors. For example, being raised in a single parent family, in a large family, away from parents, or with a mother or sister who was a teenage parent tends to increase an adolescent's risk for pregnancy. Additionally, parents of pregnant teenagers often have low levels of education and income. Moreover, pregnant teenagers tend to experience poor parental communication and insecure parental attachment, as well as maltreatment and abuse.

Many behavioral factors are also associated with teenage pregnancy such as early dating, many sexual partners, same-sex behavior, cigarette or marijuana smoking, alcohol or drug use, and delinquent activity. Pregnant teenagers are less involved in friendships and school, family, and community activities than those who are not pregnant. The friends of pregnant adolescents tend to be teenage parents themselves. Moreover, an adolescent female who becomes pregnant is likely to have a sexual partner who is married, is 3 or more years older, or is abusive.

Emotional, perceptual, and cognitive factors are also related to teen pregnancy. Adolescents with low self-esteem, low educational expectations, little faith in their future, and depression are at high risk for pregnancy. Furthermore, pregnant teenagers and their partners tend to perceive little or no opportunity for success, ease in childbearing and parenting, low educational expectations from parents, or pregnancy as a symbol of manhood. These factors may also contribute to a perception of pregnancy as a positive step for some teenagers. Sexually active adolescents, not reliably using contraceptives, tend to lack the ability for thought reversal and consideration of alternatives. Furthermore, they tend to believe that pregnancy is not a likely consequence of their sexual behavior. Pregnant teenagers tend to exhibit an external locus of control (i.e., believe their lives are controlled by forces outside their own behavior). Emotional problems, cognitive immaturity, and perceptual disempowerment may intermingle in adolescent sexual decision making and place them at risk for pregnancy.

PREVENTING TEENAGE PREGNANCY

Considering the risks and costs in an adolescent pregnancy, programs to prevent teenage pregnancies have developed worldwide. These programs focus on sexual or nonsexual factors related to teen pregnancy. Programs based on nonsexual factors do not deal directly with teen sexual behavior. They try to improve the cognitive development of children via early childhood programs or strengthen youth academic and vocational skills or youth ties to the community, school, or family. These programs have some success in reducing sexual activity and teenage pregnancies.

Programs based on sexual factors evolve from several perspectives: abstinence until marriage or adulthood, sexual functioning and contraceptive education, reproductive health services (i.e., information, professional health care counseling, and contraceptives), peer counseling and discussion groups, and parent communication on sex. To date no abstinence-only program has shown a significant positive change in teenage sexual behavior. However, sex education programs that discuss contraception tend to reduce the number of sexual partners for adolescents. Moreover,

providing adolescents with contraceptive information or with access to contraceptives does not bring about an earlier onset to sexual intercourse nor does it foster an increase in the amount of sexual intercourse or number of sexual partners. The most effective programs focus on sexual behavior, contraceptive use, abstinence as the safest protection, and contraception as the second safest protection from pregnancy.

—*Danae E. Roberts*

See also Adolescence, Puberty

Further Readings and References

Cocoran, J., Franklin, C., & Bennet, P. (2003). Ecological factors associated with adolescent pregnancy and parenting. *Social Work Research, 24*(1), 29–39.

National Campaign to Prevent Teen Pregnancy. (2002). *Not just another single issue: Teen pregnancy prevention's link to other critical social issues*. Washington, DC: Author.

National Center for Health Statistics. (2003). Crude birth rates, fertility rates, and birth rates by age of mother, according to race and Hispanic origin: United States, selected years 1950–2001. Hyattsville, MD: U.S. Department of Health and Human Services, Centers for Disease Control. Retrieved from http://www.cdc.gov/nchs/data/hus/tables/2003/03hus003.pdf

Rosen, J. (2000). *Advocating for adolescent reproductive health: Addressing cultural sensitivities*. Research Triangle Park, NC: Family Health International. Available from http://www.fhi.org

Young, T. M., Martin, S. S., Young, M. E., & Ting, L. (2001, Summer). Internal poverty and teen pregnancy. *Adolescence, 36*(142), 289–304.

TELEVISION

The effects of television viewing on child development have been contested since the medium's inception in the early 20th century. Some have argued that television clearly has negative effects on youth, while others believe these effects are, at best, ambiguous. While it is uncertain which perspective is right or wrong, it is quite certain that this debate has galvanized social scientists, parents, and politicians, exemplified by the weight this issue carries each election year.

EARLY FINDINGS

As commercial television flourished in the United States in the 1940s, interest began to foment with regard to television's effects on the first generation of individuals raised alongside the new medium. In 1949, the Columbia Broadcasting System, also known as CBS, sponsored a study conducted by Rutgers University that found television increased family unity, did not promote viewer passivity, and did not replace other valued diversions, such as outdoor activities and social interactions. This landmark report was one of the first and most widely disseminated of its kind, and several more would follow in the forthcoming decade. Soon, however, questions were raised about whether television viewing decreased dialogue between children and parents, and whether children could be expected to maintain academic progress as their average total viewing time increased to then-shockingly high numbers of more than 20 hours a week. Eventually, broadcasters capitalized upon these youthful watchers by developing targeted programs such as puppet shows and Saturday morning cartoons. Although these were highly popular, many children were also watching wrestling shows, TV westerns, and mystery-crime dramas, all of which incorporated a significant amount of violence into their storylines. This, in turn, raised even more concerns about the impact of television on American youth.

RESEARCH ON THE EFFECTS OF TELEVISION VIOLENCE ON CHILDREN

In a significant number of studies, Albert Bandura found that children learn from and imitate the behavior of individuals they observe, specifically when the individual is rewarded for aggressive acts. This research finding corroborated the admonitions of those who suggested that children who constantly witnessed their favorite TV "heroes" being praised for beating up or killing the "bad guy" would, in turn, incorporate aggressive acts into their own repertoire of behaviors for use in situations characterized by conflict. Throughout the following decades, psychologists, sociologists, criminologists, and other social scientists have argued a number of different perspectives with respect to whether television violence facilitates or triggers violent behaviors in children. Some believe that watching violence on television likely causes a significant number of children to behave violently. Others have agreed that this may be true, but only with children already susceptible to exhibiting violence. As a result, some have argued for tighter controls, either voluntary or legislative, concerning

what should and should not be allowed on the airwaves. Alternately, some have blamed parents instead of the broadcasting industry, and contended that mothers and fathers are ultimately to blame for their children's television viewing habits. A general point of agreement (or compromise) among the research community is that television can have effects on the behaviors of children, but that it must be considered as one of many determinants that may or may not cause a child to act in a particular manner.

OTHER POTENTIAL EFFECTS OF TELEVISION VIEWING ON CHILDREN

The debate of whether violence on television begets violence in children may be the most salient issue, but some social scientists argue that television programming has negative effects on children beyond promoting aggressive behavior. For example, television shows appear to perpetuate gender and racial stereotypes, and in general offer young viewers a largely unrealistic perspective of how the world and its people behave and exist. In addition, parents have complained about the content of certain shows, contending that even the most "child-friendly" programming may present values that contradict those they wish to pass on to their offspring. The most common examples involve how sex, alcohol or tobacco use, or illicit drug use can be found in most television broadcasts. Similarly, commercials promoting alcohol, tobacco, or other products inappropriate for children have been singled out.

Health care professionals have also raised concerns about how much time children spend watching television, rather than what they are watching during that time. For example, they believe that children who spend more time watching television are going to spend less time engaging in physical activity. This trend, along with the ubiquity of fast food advertisements during such programs, may be largely responsible for America's current obesity epidemic. Additionally, psychologists argue that the large amount of time spent watching TV threatens the cohesiveness of the family. These negative effects may also include inhibiting the social development of children by diminishing the number of conversations between them and their family members.

Despite all of the negative influences attributed to television, some commentators note that the medium can have a positive effect on youth. For instance, television programs are quite commonly used in school classrooms, and teachers may use educational videos or segments recorded from network broadcasts to accentuate their lessons and enhance interest in students not amenable to learning from the traditional lecture format. Also, television programming has provided individuals exposure to a wider array of cultures and societies. Additionally, more young people are aware of political and social issues of the day because of television viewing, which in turn may increase their influence on their respective nation's government. In contrast, critics have deemed in-classroom channels like "Channel One" as simply guises by which advertisers can reach younger buyers.

POLICY ISSUES

Over time, politicians have realized that the promotional value of television is a significant element in elections. Not only do candidates rely on television to reach potential voters, but also to raise television's proposed effects on youth as a campaign issue. For example, in 1992, U.S. Vice President Dan Quayle criticized the television show *Murphy Brown* for its positive depiction of a single mother, and in 2001, former U.S. vice presidential candidate and Connecticut Senator Joe Lieberman criticized the MTV cable network for airing a show titled *Jackass* that highlighted gratuitous, masochistic violence among youth. Consequently, the realm of public policy has been affected, as legislators have advocated for stricter regulation of what is shown on TV. In the U.S. in 1996, Congress mandated that V-chips, devices that parents can use to block out programming inappropriate for children, be installed in every television set produced after 1999. In 1997, the entertainment industry, pressured by Congress to enact a ratings system to work in conjunction with the V-chip technology, developed the "TV Parental Guidelines," a ratings system based somewhat on the Motion Picture Association of America's long-standing system of rating movies, where television shows are marked as "G," "PG," "R," and so on. Despite these efforts, the content of television appears to have become increasingly more violent and sexually charged. Studies indicate that most parents do not utilize the V-chip in their homes, which may render the effects of such legislation negligible.

Although the television broadcasting community has been largely compliant in providing ratings and guidelines for their shows, they generally challenge governmental attempts to restrict their product. In essence, they argue that television is part of the free enterprise system, and any attempt to control the content of it violates constitutional principles. Critics of this position argue that most countries have laws that ensure that television programming is regulated in order to make certain that what is aired does not contradict laws guarding against public indecency and obscenity. Further, the European Union has integrated the minimum television programming standards of its 15 member nations to reflect the supposed values of its constituency. These include the restriction or prohibition of discrimination based on race, sex, or nationality and the limitation of shows highlighting behavior detrimental to one's health or safety. Another example includes Australia, where there has been an added emphasis in recent years to curb the amount of violence seen on television. Regardless, television broadcasters continue to resist such measures, contending that the content of their programming is a reflection of the world around us, not the cause of it.

CONCLUSION

The effect of television viewing on children's behavior is a highly contested topic that arouses a range of reactions from researchers, parents, and politicians alike. In essence, it is hard to argue that today's youth are not affected by what is broadcast on TV. However, it is equally difficult to pinpoint particular shows or genres of programming as causing specific behaviors in children without considering the innumerable amount of alternate influences that may have an effect on the actions of young individuals.

—John L. Powell III and
Michael C. Roberts

Further Readings and References

American Psychological Association, http://www.apa.org/pubinfo/violence.html

Basta, S. S. (2000). *Culture, conflict, and children: Transmission of violence to children.* Lanham, MD: University Press of America.

Comstock, G., & Paik, H. (1991). *Television and the American child.* San Diego, CA: Academic Press.

Luke, C. (1990). *Constructing the child viewer: A history of the American discourse on television and children, 1950–1980.* New York: Praeger.

National Institute on Media and the Family, http://www.mediafamily.org/index.shtml

Roberts, D. F., Foehr, U. G., Rideout, V. J., & Brodie, M. (2004). *Kids and media in America: Patterns of use at the millennium.* New York: Cambridge University Press.

TEMPERAMENT

Temperament is the emotional and regulatory core of personality, incorporating traitlike individual differences in emotional, attentional, and motor reactivity and self-regulation. It is present early in life and has a biological basis, and develops through a person's interaction with the environment. For example, shy children avoid social interactions with unfamiliar others. An initial temperamental predisposition of shyness can lead to differential approach and avoidance of strangers throughout childhood. In addition, people engage in "niche picking" or selecting environments that match their temperament type. Outgoing surgent individuals are more likely to participate in team sports and other community activities. Temperamental characteristics also *evoke* different responses from others in the environment. Individuals prone to irritability are sometimes approached more cautiously by others. Temperament includes both reactivity and self-regulation. As self-regulation develops across childhood, it influences emotional, attentional, and motor expression. Attention systems shift from a more reactive system to a more executive system early in childhood, and individuals have more conscious control over their emotions and activity.

TEMPERAMENT AND PERSONALITY DISTINCTIONS

Along with experience, temperament influences the development of personality. Personality is a broader concept, including habits, skills, goals, values, needs, the content of individual thought, and the perception of the self in relation to others. By studying individuals across development, there is some evidence that child fearfulness and irritability correspond to the adult personality dimension of neuroticism, whereas child positive approach and activity level correspond to extraversion. Similarly, childhood persistence may be related to adult constraint.

DIMENSIONS OF TEMPERAMENT

The most well-known and widely used theory of temperament was developed by Alexander Thomas and Stella Chess. They defined temperament as the stylistic component of behavior. Based on parental descriptions of infant behavior, they identified nine dimensions of temperament for further investigation.

These nine dimensions are approach/withdrawal, quality of mood, distractibility, persistence, threshold, adaptability, rhythmicity, intensity of reaction, and activity level. From these dimensions they formed three temperamental types: *Easy* children are high in rhythmicity (high regularity in sleep, eating, defecating), high in adaptability (accept change readily), and are not overly active, intense, or moody. The second type is called *slow-to-warm-up*; these children have slower adaptability and higher negative responsivity. Over time, these children do adapt positively to novelty. Lastly, *difficult* children are characterized by irregularity in bodily functions (low rhythmicity), low adaptability, and high negative moodiness.

Children classified under this system as difficult are more likely to experience later behavior problems than easy or slow-to-warm-up children, although the prediction depends on the *goodness of fit* with their environments. Goodness of fit characterizes the match between the child's temperament and the demands of the situation or expectations of others. A good fit predicts healthy development, whereas a poor fit generates stress and leads to problem behaviors and disorders.

More recent empirical examination of the dimensions in this framework has revealed the nine dimensions to be highly intercorrelated and conceptually overlapping. In fact, several studies have revealed that the item pool can be reduced to a smaller number of dimensions, which are outlined in Table 1.

MEASURING TEMPERAMENT

Temperament is most commonly assessed through parental report, examiner report, or behavioral observation techniques. There are structured (e.g., the Laboratory Temperament Assessment Battery) and unstructured (e.g., observation on the playground) behavioral observation paradigms. Behavior is typically videotaped and scored later for facial, vocal, and/or motoric indicators of temperament. Emotionality and activity are characterized by individual differences in the latency to, peak intensity of, and duration of response, and the extent to which self-regulation modulates the reactivity.

Each method comes with advantages and disadvantages. Parental report, for example, is inexpensive and taps the extensive knowledge of parents who have seen the child in a variety of contexts over a long period of time. However, parents only observe their

Table 1 Dimensions of Temperament

Dimension	Descriptor	Example item
Fearful Distress	Distress and withdrawal in new situations	"Is afraid of loud noises"
Irritability	Fussiness, anger, frustration	"Gets mad when even mildly criticized"
Positive Emotion/ Approach	Smiling and laugher, cooperative	"Smiles and laughs during play"
Persistence	Duration of orienting toward objects of interest	"When drawing or coloring a book, shows strong concentration"
Activity Level	Amount a child moves	"Tends to run, rather than walk, from room to room"

child's behavior in their own presence, and children may act quite differently when not in the presence of their parents. Parents also may bias their responses because they are worried about making an impression on the researcher. Structured observational assessment, on the other hand, allows the researcher to have precise control over the situation, but is more expensive and constrained in what kinds of behaviors may be elicited and measured.

Temperament is hierarchically organized and thus can be assessed on various levels, including the biological. In addition to considering observed behavioral responses to the environment, individual differences in cardiac reactivity, stress hormone responsivity, and activation patterns in the prefrontal cortex of the brain are considered indicators of temperament. Thus, temperament researchers come from a variety of perspectives, from emphasizing the importance of mothers' perceptions of their child's temperament to considering mutual hemispheric regulation of approach versus withdrawal tendencies.

Temperament is an important concept for human development because of its biological basis, relative continuity across development, relations to important influences such as attachment and parenting, and its predictive power for child and adult adjustment.

GENETIC AND ENVIRONMENTAL INFLUENCES ON TEMPERAMENT

Behavioral genetics studies have underscored the important role genetics play in temperament. Heritability is the extent to which genetic variation is important for variation in a population, and twin study approaches have yielded substantial heritability estimates for infant and childhood temperament. Specifically, genetic effects account for approximately half of the variation in Fearful Distress, Irritability, and Activity Level, and both genetic effects and the shared environment account for variation in Positive Emotion/Approach and Persistence in infants. Aspects of the environment that create differences among people are important for all dimensions. Although genetic influences play a role in temperamental differences among people, these influences do not act in isolation.

RELATIONS WITH ATTACHMENT STYLE, PARENTING, AND FUTURE ADJUSTMENT

Attachment research has established the importance of caregiver sensitivity for infant and child development. Secure attachment indicates that the child can depend on the caregiver and feels safe, leading to increased self-value. The relationship with parents can influence how secure children feel and how they feel about themselves and others, so securely attached children show more positive emotion and less anxiety and have better future relationships with other people. Some studies have found that child temperament predicts behavior during the Strange Situation attachment assessment (a series of parental separations and reunions), but does not predict the attachment classifications of secure or insecure. Mother report of temperamental negative reactivity is modestly associated with attachment security assessing attachment using Q-sort methods (raters sort descriptive statements into categories indicating how typical the descriptions are of the child's behavior). Thus, temperament and attachment are conceptually distinct, yet related to the extent that they both tap children's reactions and coping with stress.

Temperament plays an important role in children's *adjustment*. Fear-prone children are more likely to have anxiety and depression problems at older ages. In one study conducted by Avshalom Caspi and Terrie Moffitt and their colleagues, children who were distress prone, impulsive, and unregulated as 3-year-olds tended to have more problems such as not getting along with others and getting into trouble with the law as adolescents and adults. They also had few people to provide them with social support as adults. Overall, children high on Fearful Distress are at risk for future mood and anxiety disorders, whereas individuals high on Irritability are at risk for future conduct problems. Those high on Activity Level and low on Persistence are at risk for future attention and hyperactive problems.

SUMMARY

Temperament is at the core of personality, and has a strong influence on responding to the surrounding environment. Although it is biologically based and genes account for a significant amount of the variation in temperament among people, the childrearing environment has a strong impact on temperament. The goodness of fit between a child's temperament and their environment influences future positive or negative adjustment.

—*Kathryn S. Lemery*

Further Readings and References

Behavioral-Developmental Initiatives, http://www.temperament.com/

Caspi, A., Henry, B., McGee, R. O., Moffitt, T. E., & Silva, P. A. (1995). Temperamental origins of child and adolescent behavior problems: From age three to age fifteen. *Child Development, 66,* 55–68.

Goldsmith, H. H., Lemery, K. S., Buss, K. A., & Campos, J. (1999). Genetic analyses of focal aspects of infant temperament. *Developmental Psychology, 35,* 972–985.

Goldsmith, H. H., Lemery, K. S., & Essex, M. J. (2004). Temperament as a liability factor for behavioral disorders of childhood. In L. DiLalla (Ed.), *Behavioral genetic principles—development, personality, and psychopathology* (pp. 19–39). Washington, DC: American Psychological Association.

Mary Rothbart's Temperament Laboratory at the University of Oregon, http://darkwing.uoregon.edu/~maryroth/

Rothbart, M. K., & Bates, J. E. (1998). Temperament. In W. Damon (Ed.-in-Chief) & N. Eisenberg (Vol. Ed.), *Handbook of child psychology: Vol. 3, Social, emotional, and personality development* (5th ed., pp. 105–176). New York: Wiley.

Thomas, A., & Chess, S. (1977). *Temperament and development.* Oxford, UK: Brunner/Mazel.

TERATOGEN

A teratogen is an environmental agent that can adversely affect the unborn child, thus producing a birth defect. Most children are exposed to at least one teratogen while in utero. However, even if there is an exposure, it does not always affect the developing child, and even if there is an effect, it may not present at birth. The impact is dependent on an interaction of multiple factors. Although this is a topic with some uncertainties, there is considerable scientific proof that associates the exposure of teratogens to certain birth defects.

Teratogens include infectious agents, chemicals, and physical or mechanical instruments. Infectious teratogens consist of viruses (e.g., rubella), bacteria (e.g., syphilis), and parasites (e.g., toxoplasmosis). For instance, rubella (German measles) can result in blindness, deafness, brain damage, or heart abnormalities. Chemical exposures can occur through lifestyle choices (e.g., alcohol, smoking, drugs) or exposure to environmental hazards (e.g., environmental chemicals). For example, heavy consumption of alcohol during pregnancy can be harmful to the developing child. In extreme cases, children may be born with fetal alcohol syndrome (FAS). Children with FAS display growth retardation, facial deformities, and in some cases mental retardation. Smoking during pregnancy has been associated with increased rates of spontaneous abortion, lower birth weights, and delayed growth. Prescription, over-the-counter, and illegal drugs can also function as teratogens. For instance, mothers who use cocaine during their pregnancy are more likely to have children with lower birth weights. Physical or mechanical agents include radiation (e.g., X-rays). Exposure to radiation from X-rays may alter the genetic makeup of the unborn child.

The teratogenicity, or nature and extent of harm to the fetus, is influenced by fetal genetic vulnerability, type and amount of teratogen, and timing of the exposure during pregnancy. Fetal genetic vulnerability refers to the genetic differences in both the mother and unborn child that can influence the type and severity of effect. This includes differences in placental transport, absorption, metabolism, and distribution of the agent. For instance, an exposure to a teratogen may not result in harm if the mother's metabolism can quickly remove the substance. Teratogenicity is also influenced by the type and amount of exposure.

For instance, a teratogen may be harmless until it reaches a certain level. Once it exceeds that level (dose threshold), it is more likely to result in harm. Also, certain teratogens may have adverse effects only during critical periods of prenatal development. Prenatal development occurs in three phases: germinal, embryonic, and fetal. Each period is characterized by differing developmental changes. The germinal period is characterized by systematic cell division. Differentiation and development of the major organs and body systems occur during the embryonic period whereas organs become more differentiated and operational during the fetal period. As a result of the changes occurring during prenatal development, a certain teratogen may have a minimal impact at one point in time, and a detrimental effect at a different time in development. In general, teratogens have minimal impact during the germinal stage because the developing child is not yet connected to the mother's body. However, just 2 to 3 weeks after conception, the sensitivity to teratogens begins. Major structural harm is more likely to occur during the embryonic period whereas physiological harm and minor structural harm is likely to occur during the fetal period. There are some teratogens (e.g., alcohol) that may adversely affect the developing child at any time during prenatal development.

There are possible exceptions to these principles in which teratogenic exposures may not result in negative effects. There are also agents and conditions with possible, but unproven effects on fetuses. Therefore, it is important to check with a knowledgeable source for possible consequences.

—Deena R. Palenchar

Further Readings and References

Brendt, R. L., & Beckman, D. A. (1990). Teratology. In R. D. Eden, F. H. Boehm, M. Haire, & H. S. Jonas (Eds.), *Assessment and care of the fetus: Physiological, clinical, and medicolegal principles* (pp. 223–244). Norwalk, CT: Appleton & Lange.

Kolberg, K. J. S. (1999). Environmental influences on prenatal development and health. In T. L. Whitman, T. V. Merluzzi, & R. D. White (Eds.), *Life-span perspectives on health and illness* (pp. 87–103). Mahwah, NJ: Erlbaum.

O'Rahilly, R., & Muller, F. (1992). *Human embryology and teratology.* New York: Wiley-Liss.

Schettler, T., Solomon, G., Valenti, M., & Huddle, A. (1999). *Generations at risk: Reproductive health and the environment.* Cambridge: MIT Press.

TESTOSTERONE

Testosterone (T) is produced in the adrenal cortex and ovary of females, but it is made in far greater amounts by the male testis. Castration of humans and animals has long been practiced to prevent fertility and the development of secondary sexual characteristics, cause docility, reduce sex drive, and, in butchered animals, to produce fatter, more tender meat. Castrating a male chick, for example, makes its adult flesh more edible, and the capon fails to develop the rooster's red comb and wattles, does not crow or court hens, and does not fight other cocks. In Asia, eunuchs were presumed to be safe harem guards because of their lack of both interest and ability to copulate. Male sopranos and contraltos, emasculated to maintain their prepubescent voice range, were prominent in the opera and church music of 17th- and 18th-century Europe.

T affects human males importantly but differently at three stages of life: perinatally (in utero and shortly after birth), during puberty, and in adulthood. The fetus begins with undifferentiated sexual parts. A gene on the male chromosome causes the asexual gonads to develop as testes; lacking this gene they become ovaries. The testes then produce T during gestation and for a month or two after birth, causing the external genitalia to form into penis and scrotum rather than clitoris and labia. Internal ducts take the male form, and the central nervous system is masculinized. For the rest of childhood, T stays at low level in both sexes.

Male T rises sharply during puberty, physically converting boys into men. Some T is required for a full repertoire of male sexual behaviors, including libidinous feelings and ejaculation. However, there is no consistent evidence that men with high T are unusually sexy. T is no different in homosexual men than in heterosexuals.

T does not importantly change the male body during adulthood, but the circulating hormone seems to affect sexual and dominance behavior, if not to the degree that is often presumed. The popular belief that men with especially high T are prone to violence or "roid rages" is a myth. A stronger case can be made that elevated T influences men to act in a self-assured, dominant way.

As American men enter middle age, they tend to put on weight, which may be one reason that T declines with age. (T does not lessen in men who maintain constant body fat.) There are similar age trends for male libido, aggressiveness, and antisocial deviance, all being highest among teenagers and men in their early 20s, then diminishing. However, the causal connection from hormone to behavior has not been demonstrated. Among older men, T level does not correlate with sexuality or frequency of coitus, and older men can perform sex adequately when their hormone levels are barely measurable.

T not only affects behavior but also responds to it. The act of competing for dominant status, as in an athletic contest, affects male T in two ways. First, T rises in the face of a challenge, as if it were an anticipatory response to impending competition. Second, after the competition, T rises in winners and declines in losers. There has been insufficient study to know if similar effects occur in women.

—*Allan Mazur*

See also Adolescence, Puberty

Further Readings and References

Dabbs, J. 2000. *Heroes, rogues, and lovers*. New York: McGraw-Hill.

Kemper, T. 1990. *Social structure and testosterone*. New Brunswick, NJ: Rutgers University Press.

Mazur, A., & Booth, A. (1998). Testosterone and dominance in men. *Behavioral and Brain Sciences, 21*, 353–363.

Mazur, A., Mueller, U., Krause, W., & Booth, A. (2002). Causes of sexual decline in aging married men: Germany and America. *International Journal of Impotence Research, 14*, 101–106.

THALASSEMIA

The name *thalassemia* corresponds to a specific group of genetic blood disorders. Thalassemia is closely related to the process through which blood is made; hence, before discussing this disorder, it would be helpful to understand a little about how blood is made in our body.

Hemoglobin is an essential component of the "blood making" process as it carries oxygen to the red blood cells. It consists of two different proteins, an alpha and a beta protein. If the body does not produce enough of either of these two proteins, the red blood cells do not form correctly and cannot carry sufficient oxygen throughout the body. This chronic condition results in anemia that begins in early childhood and continues throughout the individual's lifetime.

Thalassemia is not a single disorder but rather a group of related disorders that affect the human body in similar ways. The different forms of thalassemia are outlined below. Individuals who do not produce enough alpha globin protein chains have alpha thalassemia. This disorder is most commonly found in Africa, the Middle East, India, Southeast Asia, southern China, and occasionally the Mediterranean region. As mentioned above, thalassemia is a genetic blood disorder meaning that the transmission of the disorder occurs through genes (from one generation to the next). Alpha globin protein is made by four genes. Depending on how many abnormal genes are inherited, there are four types of alpha thalassemia that range from mild to severe in terms of their effect on the body. An individual that is a *silent carrier* experiences no health problems because the lack of alpha protein is so small that the hemoglobin functions normally. The individual who is diagnosed with *alpha thalassemia trait* has a greater lack of alpha protein that the silent carrier. Patients with this condition have smaller red blood cells and a mild anemia, although many patients do not experience symptoms. The most severe form of alpha thalassemia is *alpha thalassemia major* where there are no alpha genes in the individual's DNA. This lack in alpha protein causes the formation of an abnormal hemoglobin named hemoglobin Barts. Most individuals with this condition die before or shortly after birth. Individuals whose hemoglobin does not produce enough beta protein have beta thalassemia. This form of the disorder is commonly found in people of Mediterranean heritage, and is also found in the Arabian Peninsula, Iran, Africa, Southeast Asia, and southern China. Much like in alpha thalassemia discussed above, there are three types of beta thalassemia that also range from mild to severe in their effect on the human body.

Those diagnosed with *thalassemia trait* have deficiencies in beta protein that are not great enough to cause problems in the normal functioning of the hemoglobin. A person with this condition simply carries the genetic trait for thalassemia and will usually experience no health problems other than a possible mild anemia. In *thalassemia intermedia* the lack of beta protein in the hemoglobin is significant enough to create significant health problems, including moderately severe anemia, bone deformities, and enlargement of the spleen. Patients diagnosed with this condition require blood transfusions to improve the quality of their lives, but do not need blood transfusions to survive. In *thalassemia* major or *Cooley's anemia,* there is a complete lack of beta protein in the hemoglobin that causes life-threatening anemia. The anemia requires regular blood transfusions and other medical interventions. These extensive and ongoing blood transfusions, which last throughout the life span, usually lead to iron overload, which must be treated with *chelation therapy* (removal of iron from the system) to prevent early death from organ failure. In addition to alpha and beta thalassemia, there are a few other forms of thalassemia that occur less frequently, such as *E beta thalassemia* and *sickle beta thalassemia.*

The main treatment approach for all forms of thalassemia is red blood cell transfusions. These transfusions are necessary and they provide the patient with a temporary healthy supply of red blood cells that are composed of normal hemoglobin and hence are capable of transporting necessary amounts of oxygen to all of the patient's organs. Currently, most patients diagnosed with a major form of thalassemia receive blood transfusions every 2 to 3 weeks to improve their quality of life. However, the resulting iron overload that becomes toxic to tissues and organs, especially the liver and heart, must be treated with chelation. Unfortunately, this treatment can be very difficult, painful, and uncomfortable, and many patients choose to not comply.

Thalassemia can be a devastating genetic blood disorder. In its most severe form, this disease can be fatal. Individuals with severe forms of thalassemia must undergo blood transfusions and chelation therapy to enhance their quality of life and survive.

—*Natalie N. Politikos*

Further Readings and References

Cooley's Anemia Foundation, http://www.thalassemia.org

Mahajan, B. S., Mahjan, B. S., & Rajadhyaksha, M. S. (1999). *New biology and inherited diseases.* Oxford, UK: Oxford University Press.

Nathan, D. G. (1995). *Genes, blood and courage: A boy called Immortal Sword.* Cambridge, MA: Harvard University Press.

Weatherall, D. J., & Clegg, J. B. (2001). *The thalassaemia syndromes* (4th ed.). Oxford, UK: Blackwell.

THALIDOMIDE

Thalidomide, a drug prescribed for morning sickness in the 1950s, made headlines when it was linked with stunting the growth of fetal limbs. Fifty years later, it was back in the headlines, this time for stunting the growth of tumors. Will thalidomide's tragic past allow the drug to have a future for the treatment of hitherto incurable cancers?

THE PAST

Thalidomide was first synthesized in 1953 by the Swiss company Ciba, who discontinued its development because of apparent lack of pharmacological effects. The white crystalline powder was resynthesized a year later by the German company Chemie Grunenthal when searching for drugs that might be useful for treating epilepsy. Thalidomide was ineffective in that regard, but it was noted that the drug was very effective in causing rapid deep sleep, and the company marketed thalidomide in 1956 as a sedative. It soon became the most widely used sleeping pill in Germany because of its lack of hangover and other side effects. Compared with other sedatives, thalidomide was considered nontoxic and so safe that it was prescribed for morning sickness during pregnancy, a use that led to the tragedy of nearly 12,000 "thalidomide babies" being born with deformed limbs, facial defects, and malformed gastrointestinal tracts. Approximately 40% of the thalidomide babies died within their first year. Strong advocacy groups, including Thalidomide Victims Association of Canada (TVAC), are helping those who have reached adulthood to cope with their severe physical defects.

ANTI-INFLAMMATORY EFFECTS

Although withdrawn 4 years after it entered the market, thalidomide did not completely disappear, due to the serendipitous findings of an Israeli physician, Dr. Jacob Sheskin. He prescribed the drug as a sedative to alleviate painful symptoms associated with erythema nodosum leprosum (ENL), a complication of leprosy, but found that the lesions surprisingly cleared. Its miraculous effects on ENL led to thalidomide being tested in other inflammatory disorders where it has shown usefulness for alleviating symptoms associated with arthritis, inflammatory bowel disease, Crohn's disease, multiple sclerosis, Lupus, and many other auto-immune diseases.

ANTI-CANCER EFFECTS

Following demonstration of its teratogenicity, it was reasoned that if it could cause severe defects to a fetus, thalidomide might also be deleterious to tumors. Early trials of thalidomide as an anti-cancer agent in the late 1950s did not produce any notable activity, and consideration of thalidomide for the treatment of cancer remained dormant for 40 years. The resurgence of thalidomide for cancer therapy followed from the demonstration in 1994 by Harvard University scientists, led by Dr. Judah Folkman, that the drug could inhibit angiogenesis—the formation of new blood vessels. Since all tumors have a dependency on the production of new blood vessels to grow, drugs that inhibit angiogenesis can potentially be effective for treating cancer. A new era for thalidomide began when it was shown to be extremely successful against an incurable hematological malignancy, multiple myeloma. It is promising also in the treatment of cancers of the prostate, kidney, and some forms of brain tumors, and cancer patients welcome its return to clinical use.

THE FUTURE

The beneficial effects, both in the treatment of cancer and for inflammatory diseases, are extremely compelling for thalidomide's comeback into clinical practice. However, its tragic past still haunts us, and TVAC has asserted that "we will never accept a world with thalidomide in it." To reach a middle ground, pharmaceutical companies have focused on developing related, new compounds that possess some of thalidomide's therapeutic effects but without its teratogenicity. Revlimid, from Celgene Corporation in the United States, is the first of its kind to reach clinical trials for cancer. Perhaps these new generation drugs can push thalidomide into retirement.

—*Lai-Ming Ching*

Further Readings and References

D'Amato, R. J., Loughnan, M. S., Flynn, E., & Folkman, J. (1994). Thalidomide is an inhibitor of angiogenesis. *Proceedings of the National Academy of Sciences of the USA, 91*, 4082–4085.

Lenz, W. (1992). A personal perspective on the thalidomide tragedy. *Teratology, 46*, 417–418.

Thalidomide Victims Association of Canada, http://www.thalidomide.ca

THEORIES OF AGING

For more than 40 years, researchers in gerontology have commented on the need for theories of aging. K. Warner Schaie suggested that theories were needed to integrate the large amount of research data that was accumulating across disciplines. Timothy Salthouse has commented that the field of cognitive aging has virtually no theories that can account for a wide range of phenomena. More recently, Vern Bengtson and colleagues have stated that many gerontology researchers have not focused on theory building, and therefore, the development of theories of aging has not progressed as rapidly as the accumulation of data. Despite this lag in theory building, some theories of aging have emerged that have influenced the conduction of many research studies in aging. The focus of the present chapter is to give an overview of these existing theories in the domains of psychology, sociology, and biology.

According to Bengtson, *theory* can be defined as "the construction of explicit explanations in accounting for empirical findings." In their view, theories of aging can help us understand and explain the normal aging process. More specifically, theories have several functions: (1) integration of knowledge, (2) explanation of knowledge, (3) predictions about what is not yet known or observed, and (4) interventions to improve human conditions. Theories allow integration of knowledge by providing a coherent framework for organizing a large amount of data obtained in empirical studies into a "brief statement that describes linkages among the crucial observations, variables, or theoretical constructs."

One of the most dominant agendas relevant to interventions is the goal of "successful aging," a theme that has guided much research in hopes of identifying the potential of aging and ways to improve the aging process. Indicators of successful aging have been defined in terms of length of life, biological health, mental health, cognitive efficacy, social competence and productivity, personal control, and life satisfaction. To understand how to age successfully and to develop theories accordingly, Paul and Margaret Baltes offered seven propositions about the nature of human aging:

1. *There are major differences between normal, optimal, and sick (pathological) aging.* This proposition suggests that declines produced by dementia and other age-related illnesses are not typical of the normal aging process.

2. *There is much heterogeneity (variability) in aging.* This proposition proposes that the aging process is not uniform; individuals age differently from each other.

3. *There is much latent reserve.* Reserve refers to the idea that we have a *reserve capacity*, or pool of resources that can be activated through learning, exercise, or practice. Older adults do not necessarily use their reserve capacities all the time, but when encouraged to do so, they can benefit to the same degree as young adults on a variety of tasks. For example, older adults benefit from practice with a task.

4. *There is an aging loss near limits of reserve.* Research has shown that performance in older adults declines when the limits of their reserve are reached. For example, older adults are unable to perform at the level of younger adults in tasks involving speed, even under the most optimal conditions.

5. *Knowledge-based pragmatics and technology can offset age-related decline in cognitive mechanics.* Even when the limits of reserve are reached, older adults can *compensate* for age-related declines by using their preexisting knowledge. For example, Salthouse showed that older typists were able to compensate for their slowing in tapping speed by reading farther ahead in the text to be typed, resulting in equivalent or sometimes better typing performance than younger typists.

6. *With aging, the balance between gains and losses becomes less positive.* A gain can be defined as an expected change with age that is desirable, such as becoming more intelligent, whereas a loss is an expected change that is undesirable, such as becoming less healthy. As we age, the ratio of gains to losses is thought to decrease.

7. *The self remains resilient in old age.* Older adults do not hold more negative views about themselves. In fact, older adults do not differ from young adults in reports of life satisfaction, personal control, or self-efficacy.

Several strategies and multidisciplinary theories for successful aging have been developed across fields of study in response to these propositions. One such theory, for example, emphasizes that increasing mental and physical functioning and decreasing the risk of disease and disability by eating healthy and exercising can reduce the occurrence of pathological conditions that disrupt the normal aging process. Additionally, it promotes active engagement with life.

Another theory, selective optimization with compensation, promotes successful aging through planning. Adults should: (1) select activities and abilities that are most important to their sense of well-being and concentrate their efforts on maintaining those abilities, (2) find strategies that will help them optimize performance on the chosen abilities, and (3) find ways to compensate for declines in other abilities.

Another successful aging theory maintains that aging is characterized by loss and decline in many areas. Successful aging is measured by how well older adults adapt to the unavoidable challenges they face as a result of age-related decline. The theory also establishes four tasks that older adults can perform to help them age successfully: (1) find a replacement for the ability that has been lost, (2) attempt to retrain faculties that are declining with age, (3) learn to make do with less, or (4) retain the remaining functioning.

In many respects, aging seems to be an individual process, demonstrating considerable variability between individuals. For example, two 82-year-olds may be very different in terms of health, their ability to live independently, and their cognitive abilities. Keeping the aforementioned multidisciplinary propositions and theories in mind, we turn to theories that can explain more discipline-specific aspects of the aging process: how and why we age the way we do.

PSYCHOLOGICAL THEORIES

Much research has gone into the problems associated with old age, including dementias such as Alzheimer's disease and Parkinson's disease. Large bodies of literature in psychology, medicine, sociology, and other fields focus on aspects of aging for specific groups of individuals (e.g., clinical patients) whose aging experience can be quite different from the norm. Until fairly recently, few researchers concentrated on studying normal, healthy older adults to get a sense of which aspects of our mental states change over time, which remain stable, and how those changes or stabilities manifest themselves in older adults' daily lives.

Cognitive Aging

Cognitive theories of aging attempt to explain the nature of age-related differences in cognition, the factors responsible for these differences, and the mechanisms underlying why age-related differences occur. Although cognitive theories have developed primarily in the past 20 years, several dominant frameworks have emerged: (1) reduced processing resources, (2) general slowing, (3) inhibition deficits, and (4) transmission deficits.

One theory of cognitive aging proposes reduced processing resources in old age, where a processing resource is defined as some internal input necessary for processing that is available in limited quantities at any given point during processing. A variety of resources required for cognitive processing have been named, including working memory, attention, speed of processing, and inhibition, where the latter two have evolved into their own theories. In a reduced processing resources framework, people have a limited pool of processing resources from which they can draw when performing cognitive tasks, and the amount of available resources decreases as we get older. Therefore, age-related declines in cognitive performance are expected whenever a cognitive task requires more of these resources, e.g., more complex tasks. Consistent with this view, older adults exhibit greater decrements in performance on a variety of complex tasks, such as comprehension of syntactically complex sentences, mental arithmetic, and verbal reasoning.

A second class of theories, theories of general slowing, suggests that a major factor contributing to age-related differences in cognitive functioning is a reduction in older adults' processing speed, or the speed of executing cognitive operations. This age-related slowing occurs in the central nervous system and therefore affects all tasks regardless of complexity. Some researchers have proposed that the rate of slowing in older adults is predictable. For example, some researchers have suggested that young and older adults' processing speeds are linearly related. Others have argued that cognitive processes slow down at a constant rate; more specifically, older adults' processing speed is one and a half times slower than young adults. Although most researchers accept the idea that speed of processing slows with age, there is considerable debate over whether this slowing is the cause of all age differences.

A third cognitive theory of aging proposes that older adults have a deficit in their inhibitory processes: Aging impairs the ability to inhibit or suppress irrelevant information that becomes activated in the course of cognitive processing. Inhibitory processes serve two functions: to prevent irrelevant information from entering working memory (where people hold and manipulate information that is currently being focused on) and to delete information that is no longer relevant to the task at hand. When inhibitory processes are impaired, people will get more interference from irrelevant information because of their inability to suppress it. Inefficient inhibitory mechanisms have been used to explain why older adults are more likely to entertain thoughts that are irrelevant to cognitive processing, such as personally relevant thoughts or daydreams, or why they produce speech that is off-topic when describing events related to their lives.

The fourth cognitive theory of aging uses a connectionist framework where words are represented as nodes that are connected on many levels, including phonology (or sounds), orthography (or spelling), and semantics (or meanings). The Transmission Deficit hypothesis proposes older adults' connections weaken over time by virtue of aging. As a result, any task involving weak connections will be susceptible to age declines. Therefore, older adults are particularly susceptible to cognitive declines when new connection formation is required (as it is for new learning) or when preexisting connections have weakened, as will happen over time when words are not used frequently or recently. Research on older adults' memory, both for tasks involving new learning and for retrieval of infrequently used, existing knowledge, has shown declines, consistent with this theory.

Developmental Theories

Most theories of human development take one of two views of development: the life stage perspective or the life-span perspective.

Life stage perspectives view development as a series of stages through which all people pass in their lives. Progression through the stages occurs in a fixed order, and movement from one stage to another depends on performance in the earlier stage. Generally, later stages are seen as more advanced than earlier stages.

Erik Erikson's theory of psychosocial development, in which development takes place over eight stages, is the most widely known stage theory dealing with older adulthood. Each stage is characterized by two conflicting ways of dealing with life events typically encountered at that stage, called a psychosocial crisis. For example, the period of late adulthood, roughly after age 65, is marked by the struggle between integrity, or looking back on one's life positively, and despair, or feeling negatively about the life one has led. The adaptive resolution to the crisis is the acceptance that death is relatively near and the ability to review one's life with satisfaction. Successful resolution of this crisis brings with it the development of wisdom. However, this development is a lifelong process, as each psychosocial crisis is never fully resolved.

Daniel Levinson describes life as a series of four 25-year eras, or major life stages. As in Erikson's theory, each era is marked by a general developmental goal, such as becoming independent. However, Levinson's stages are further divided into developmental periods, which are alternately stable and transitional as life goals and circumstances change.

While Erikson's and Levinson's theories characterize the life trajectory as that of a series of stages (e.g., birth, middle age, death) that all humans go through, other theories are more consistent with the life-span developmental perspective. The life-span perspective emphasizes development as the result of a lifelong interaction between a person and his or her environment. In this view, development is composed of growth and decline throughout life, in every area of functioning, caused by many different factors. The rate of growth and decline is quite changeable, and individuals can experience several periods of gains and losses in a single domain, such as cognitive functioning, over a lifetime. Development is affected by the individual's historical, cultural, and social environments as well as by the physical environment, and as such is best understood by drawing on several different fields of knowledge.

The stress process framework proposes a mechanism by which people deal with the life changes associated with old age. It is based on the interaction of stressors, such as undesirable events and/or chronic problems; the moderators, or resources, marshaled to deal with the problems; and the outcomes or net effectiveness of the moderators in dealing with the stressor.

Examples of stressors include the loss or change of a societal role, such as retiring from employment or becoming a widow. Stresses often proliferate, and a primary stressor such as losing a spouse can prompt the occurrence of a secondary stressor, such as financial difficulty. Chronic strains such as illness also function as stressors. Moderators can take the form of internal resources that are rooted in one's personality, such as a preferred coping style or feelings of self-efficacy. Other people, in the form of social support

networks, also serve to moderate the effects of stress on older adults. Successful moderators can also bolster people's ability to deal with future stressors, while moderators that are ineffective in dealing with problems can be adapted or discarded.

Similarly, continuity theory posits that people do not deal with stressors in order to resolve a specific developmental challenge, as Erikson argues. Instead, they develop, maintain, and change coping strategies over a lifetime, monitoring their effectiveness and changing strategies to fit each individual situation. Both the stress process framework and continuity theory emphasize the role that individual characteristics play in dealing with stressors, as well as the reciprocal effects stressors and moderators have on each other.

SOCIOLOGICAL THEORIES

In contrast to developmental theories, which focus on age-related change within individuals, sociological theories attempt to explain the relationship of older adults as a group to the rest of society. Most sociological theories tend to emphasize the life course perspective, examining how social norms, including cultural, historical, and familial contexts, influence older adults' social roles and role transitions. The timing of a particular event (e.g., childbearing) in an individual's life and the historical context in which the event occurred are particularly important to the life course perspective.

A social role comprises not only one's personal self-concept but also the ideas held by the rest of society about how a person of a certain status should act. A problem facing most older adults is that of changing roles: from employed to retired, from spouse to widow, from being generally healthy to facing more frequent health problems. According to some researchers, societies have cultural age deadlines or general ages at which people are expected to have completed life milestones, such as marrying, having children, and retiring. Problems arise when these life milestones are completed "off time," or in a drastically different manner from the rest of society.

The role-theory framework focused on the negative changes that came with losing social roles after retirement age and gaining social roles that were less desirable, such as widowed or dependent on others. Studies carried out under this framework found that older adults who were unemployed, widowed, over 70 years old, or who simply viewed themselves as being elderly or old, were less accepting of old age than their working, married, under 70 years old counterparts who viewed themselves as middle aged. Additionally, when studying personality traits and adjustment to social roles, older adults whose personality incorporated both masculine and feminine traits were more accepting of their age than adults whose traits were strongly masculine or strongly feminine.

Activity theory takes the view that older adults' social needs do not diminish with age, even as the actual amount of social interaction declines. Adults who continue previous as well as new social interactions as they transition into old age will have higher life satisfaction than will adults who are more segregated from the rest of society. Although some studies have supported activity theory, other studies have found that older adults voluntarily decrease the amount of their social involvement for a variety of reasons. Additionally, activity theory does not make predictions about the activity level for adults whose environment changes.

In contrast, disengagement theory posits that older adults naturally withdraw from society as they age, becoming more self-involved and less involved with others. Concurrently, society withdraws from the individual, who is seen to have less to offer with increasing age. Later researchers have argued for differential disengagement, whereby older adults become less involved with some activities, but remain active in other ways. While disengagement theory and activity theory are responsible for generating a considerable amount of research on adjustment in late life, some researchers feel the theories fail to incorporate individual differences and preferences sufficiently to adequately explain social interactions in old age.

Continuity theory is a relatively recent sociological theory. As discussed in the previous section, it posits that older adults seek to maintain a stable environment. This environment can be maintained either externally, by remaining in the same physical and social contexts as in previous years, or internally, by maintaining beliefs, attitudes, and personality traits as in younger years. A mismatch between the desired and actual levels of continuity can be problematic; too little continuity (i.e., too many new experiences) can induce anxiety, while too much continuity can induce boredom with current circumstances.

Another recent theory is the socioenvironmental theory, which emphasizes the effects of one's surroundings on one's social interactions. Older adults are more likely to interact in situations where there are many older adults close by, as opposed to when there are fewer older adults or they are far away. This theory accounts for the popularity of large retirement communities and apartment buildings with large numbers of older adults and has been supported by research findings on friendship patterns in older adults.

Social exchange theory is based on the idea that social interactions are conducted with the understanding that both partners will benefit equally from the contact. Interactions may also be conducted without expecting reciprocity, simply to help another person. In this framework, interactions with older adults would tend to fall under the second category, as society views older adults as having very little to give and much to receive, in terms of assistance, time, and money. Studies conducted with older adults on the amount of aid given to and received from others have found mixed results.

BIOLOGICAL THEORIES

One of the early theories about biological aging was the "wear and tear" theory, or the idea that the body was analogous to a machine. Aging occurred simply because the machine was gradually wearing out. More recently, biological theories of aging have more precisely focused on specific factors that contribute to age-related declines, and these theories can be categorized into two groups: theories that argue that the aging process is largely genetically preprogrammed (although it is an oversimplification, one may think of these as "nature" theories), and theories that hold that the aging process is due to events that occur as a part of everyday life (these can be described as "nurture" theories). One current view, however, takes the approach that aging is due to an interaction of genetic and environmental factors.

While recent physiological aging theories have postulated that our aging process was encoded in our DNA and thus predetermined even before we were born, it is currently thought by some researchers that only 10 to 30% of longevity differences are inherited. Nevertheless, many researchers concentrate their efforts on people who have remained healthy into very old age, studying them and their relatives in an effort to determine what genetic characteristics these older adults share that may contribute to their longevity.

Other researchers believe that aging is due to problems at the cellular level. The *error catastrophe* hypothesis claims that errors or mutations sometimes occur during the process of transcribing DNA into RNA and RNA into proteins. As the cell divides and multiplies, these errors are passed on, and eventually impair the cell's functioning or lead to cellular death.

Free radical theories are the aging theories with which the general public is most familiar. Free radicals are byproducts of cell metabolism, and they damage other parts of the cell, thus reducing cellular functioning. Free radicals are unpaired electrons, commonly produced during radiation (e.g., sun exposure) or oxygenation. Much research has gone into the use of topical or ingested antioxidants to pair with the free radical's electron, thus rendering them harmless.

Physiological changes in the body's regulatory and immune systems also contribute to physical aging. The immune system becomes less effective with age, as do the body's other systems and organs. However, declines in immune system functioning lead to a decreased ability to detect and fight diseases, making older adults more vulnerable to illnesses such as influenza. Studies have shown that long-lived individuals have well-preserved immune systems.

In addition, the endocrine system has been shown to become less efficient with age at preserving the body's natural balance in areas such as blood sugar levels or hormones. When environmental changes such as lower blood sugar levels occur, the damage is exacerbated by the body's inability to repair the damage and restore balance as quickly as it did when it was younger.

CONCLUSIONS

This chapter has covered only a handful of the theories of aging that have arisen in the past 40 years. While these are the dominant theories, many other theories exist that are in varying stages of development. In addition, theories are constantly being tested and modified in conjunction as new data from aging research emerge. It is only in the last half-century that researchers have begun to focus their attention on older adults as a population worthy of special consideration. While earlier theories of aging were few in number, narrowly focused, and generally negative, recent theories have emerged that establish aging as a multidimensional process. These theories view aging as characterized by positive as well as negative qualities and are more interactive in nature. They emphasize the interaction of biological, physical, and social

factors in each individual's age trajectory, and attempt to explain how older adults can minimize the negative and maximize the positive aspects of aging, in order to more fully enjoy the increased life span that comes with living in the 21st century.

—*Jennifer H. Stanley and Lise Abrams*

See also Older Adulthood

Further Readings and References

The American Geriatrics Society, http://www.americangeri atrics.org

The American Society on Aging, http://www.asaging.org

Baltes, P. B., & Baltes, M. M. (1990). Psychological perspectives on successful aging: The model of selective optimization with compensation. In P. B. Baltes & M. M. Baltes (Eds.), *Successful aging: Perspectives from the behavioral sciences* (pp. 1–34). New York: Cambridge University Press.

Bengtson, V. L., Rice, C. J., & Johnson, M. L. (1999). Are theories of aging important? Models and explanations in gerontology at the turn of the century. In V. L. Bengtson & K. W. Schaie (Eds.), *Handbook of theories of aging* (pp. 3–20). New York: Springer.

The Gerontological Society of America, http://www.geron.org

Lockshin, R. A., & Zakeri, Z. F. (1990). MINIREVIEW: Programmed cell death: New thoughts and relevance to aging. *Journal of Gerontology: Biological Science, 45,* B135–B140.

Salthouse, T. A. (1991). *Theoretical perspectives on cognitive aging.* Hillside, NJ: Erlbaum.

THEORIES OF DEVELOPMENT

Any one theory of development is an effort to explain complexities of change that occur over the life span, from conception through death. Each tends to represent a different worldview and is based on different fundamental assumptions about the developmental process and can usually be placed into one of the following four categories: biological models, psychoanalytic models, behavioral models, and cognitive developmental models.

THE MATURATIONAL AND BIOLOGICAL MODELS

Arnold Gesell, the foremost maturationalist in developmental psychology, represents a unique approach to the study of human development. As a physician, Gesell believed that the sequence of development is determined by the biological and evolutionary history of the species. In other words, development of the organism is essentially under the control of biological systems and the process of maturation. Although the environment is of some importance, it acts only in a supportive role and does not provide any impetus for change.

While working with G. Stanley Hall within the tradition of the Darwinian influence that was very popular during the 1920s, Gesell applied the tenets of recapitulation theory to the study of individual development (or ontogenesis). Recapitulation theory states that the development of the species is reflected in the development of the individual. In other words, the child progresses through a series of stages that recount the developmental sequence that characterized the species.

Gesell believed that the most important influences on the growth and development of the human organism were biological directives. He summarized this theory in five distinct principles of development, which he later applied to behavior. All of these principles assume that the formation of structures is necessary before any event outside the organism can have an influence on development. Interestingly, the notion that "function follows structure" was pursued not only by Gesell, but later on, designers, architects, and engineers also found a great deal of truth in these words as well.

Gesell also believed that behavior at different stages of development has different degrees of balance or stability. For example, at 2 years of age, the child's behavior might be characterized by a groping for some type of stability (the so-called terrible twos). Shortly thereafter, however, the child's behavior becomes smooth and consolidated. Gesell believed that development is cyclical in nature, swinging from one extreme to another, and that by means of these swings, the child develops and uses new structures.

Because he placed such a strong emphasis on the importance of biological processes, the majority of Gesell's work and that of his colleagues (most notably Frances Ilg and Louise B. Ames) focused on biological systems as a beginning point to understanding development. Through Gesell's use of cinematic (moving picture) records, stop-action analysis provided the foundation for his extensive descriptions of "normal" development. This technique allowed Gesell to examine the frame-by-frame progression of certain motor tasks from their earliest reflex stage at birth through a system of fully developed and integrated behaviors. For example, his detailed analysis of walking provided the first graphic record of the sequence this complex behavior follows.

Gesell also made significant contributions with the development of the co-twin method for comparing the relative effects of heredity (nature) and environment (nurture) on development. One identical twin would receive specific training in some skill (such as stair climbing), and the other twin would receive no training in the skill. The rationale for this strategy was that because the children had an identical genetic makeup (they were identical twins), any difference in stair-climbing ability must be the result of training. This is the basic paradigm that Gesell used to question some very interesting and controversial statements about the nature of intelligence.

Unquestionably, Gesell's greatest contribution has been to the understanding of the development of the "normal" child. His detailed cinematic records, their analyses, and their translation into books for the popular press have influenced child-rearing patterns in this country as much as that of the famous Dr. Spock (who incorporates many of Gesell's principles into his philosophy).

Gesell's ideas and theoretical approach never entered the mainstream of current thought about developmental psychology. Perhaps this is because much of his work was seen as too biological in nature and not sufficiently theoretical. Both from a historical and applied perspective, however, his contribution was and still is an outstanding one.

Over the last few years, there has been a heightened interest in other maturational approaches, most notably ethology and sociobiology. These views, even more than Gesell's, emphasize the importance of biological and evolutionary principles as determinants of behavior. For example, the primary assumption of sociobiology is that social behavior is somewhat patterned and controlled by an evolutionary-founded need to maintain one's genetic legacy—in effect, to spread ones genetic characteristics onto subsequent generations. Similarly, ethologists talk about innate mechanisms that regulate human behavior and prompt human beings to behave in certain fashions. For example, the disproportionately large eyes that characterize young infants (as is present in many other type of animal young) serve to engage humans in caretaking behavior.

THE PSYCHOANALYTIC MODEL

The psychoanalytic model, developed initially by Sigmund Freud, presents a view of development that is revolutionary in both its content and its implications for the nature of development. The basic assumption of this model is that development consists of dynamic, structural, and sequential components, each influenced by a continuously renewed need for the gratification of basic instincts. How psychic energy (or the energy of life, as it is sometimes called) is channeled through these different components constitutes the basis of the developmental process and individual differences.

The dynamic or economic component of Freud's tripartite system characterizes the human mind (or psyche) as a fluid, energized system that can transfer energy from one part to the other where and when needed. The structural or topographical component of the theory describes the three separate, yet interdependent, psychological structures called the id, ego, and superego and the way in which they regulate behavior. Finally, the sequential or stage component emphasizes a progression from one stage of development to the next, focusing on different zones of bodily sensitivity (such as the mouth) and accompanying psychological and social conflicts.

It is difficult to identify the philosophical roots of psychoanalytic theory, because most psychoanalytic theorists would consider their roots to be in embryology, the biological study of the embryo from conception until the organism can survive on its own. This identification with a biological model has a great deal to do with Freud's training as a physician, his work in neuroanatomy, and his belief that biological needs play a paramount role in development. Some people believe that the philosophical tradition of preformationism (which in its extreme holds that all attitudes and characteristics are formed at birth and only expand in size) is basic to the psychoanalytic model, but this may be untrue. The preformationists stress the lack of malleability of the developing individual, while the psychoanalytic model describes a flexible character for the individual and the potential for change.

Freudian theory places an important emphasis on the resolution of conflicts that have their origin at an unconscious level. It states that the origin of these conflicts is biological and passed on from generation to generation. Development (and the development of individual differences) is an ongoing process of resolving these conflicts.

If the roots of behavior are located in the unconscious, how can they be accessible to study? Through a series of historical accidents, Freud was introduced to hypnotism as a method of treatment. This technique, in turn, gave birth to his now famous method called free association, in which individuals are encouraged to freely associate anything that comes to mind in response to certain words or phrases. Freud believed that such an exposition of underlying needs and fears was the key to understanding a typical behavior. This method is a highly subjective way to collect information, and a large part of the criticism leveled against Freud and many of his followers was directed at this practice.

The theory itself, however, is based on abstract and subjective judgments, and the fact that the behaviors under study are not easily amenable to scientific verification has caused controversy for years. However, the richness and diversity that Freud brought to a previously stagnant conception of development started a tradition that is healthy and strong even today. Perhaps Freud's most significant accomplishment was the first documentation and systematic organization of a theory of development.

The major impact of the psychoanalytic model and the work of such theorists as Freud and Erik Erikson has undoubtedly been in the study of personality and the treatment of emotional and social disorders. Erikson, unlike Freud, focused mainly on the social rather than the sexual dimension of behavior (hence the psychosocial nature of this approach). The impact and significance of both men's contributions cannot be overstated.

THE BEHAVIORAL MODEL

The behavioral model characterizes a movement that is peculiar to American psychology and distinct from any other theoretical model. The behavioral perspective views development as a function of learning and one that proceeds according to certain laws or principles of learning. Most important, it places the major impetus for growth and development outside of the individual and in the environment, rather than within the organism itself.

The importance placed on the environment varies with specific theories within this general model, but, in all cases, the organism is seen as reactive instead of active.

Within almost every behavioral theory, the assumption is incorporated that behavior is a function of its consequences. If the consequences of a behavior (such as studying) are good (such as high grades), studying is likely to continue in the future. If they are not good (losing privileges), the behavior (staying out past curfew) will change (perhaps to an earlier hour) or to not going out at all on weekday nights.

The behavioral model makes the laws of learning and the influence of the environment paramount in the developmental process. Through processes such as classical conditioning and imitation, individuals learn what behaviors are most appropriate and lead to adaptive outcomes. Given that this model views development as a learned phenomenon, behaviors can be broken down into their basic elements. This leads people to view the behavioral model perhaps as being "reductionistic."

The behavioral perspective views the newborn child as naive and unlearned. John Locke's notion of tabula rasa best exemplifies the philosophical roots of the behavioral tradition. Literally, tabula rasa means "blank slate." The newborn child is like a blank page waiting to be written on, with only the most fundamental biological reflexes (such as sucking) operative at birth. The organism is malleable, and behavior develops and changes as a result of events or experiences. This is a more open view than the maturationist and psychoanalytic perspectives, because it sees human potential as unlimited by internal factors. Sometimes, however, biological endowment (an internal factor) can limit developmental outcomes, as in the case of genetic diseases or familial retardation. But even in the case of the severely retarded child, a restructuring of the environment can greatly affect basic competencies and caretaking functions such as eating and toilet training.

Given that the emphasis within the behavioral perspective is placed on events that originate in the environment and their effects on the organism, it is no surprise that the variable of primary interest to the behaviorist is the frequency or number of times a behavior occurs. For example, if one is interested in studying an aspect of sibling interaction, behaviors are explicitly defined (or operationalized) and must be objective enough to be reliably measured. Constructs as "nice feelings" would not meet such criteria, but "number of times brother touches friend" would.

Using frequency of behavior, the traditional way of studying development is to examine what effect certain environmental events have on behavior. This is most often done by identifying and observing those events in the environment that control behavior and then, if necessary, manipulating these events to see if the behavior under observation changes. In other words, if a child's speech is delayed, the psychologist might want to observe the events that surround the child's verbalizations when left to run their course. Some intervention wherein the parents are encouraged to respond more directly might be suggested, and then additional observation might be done to see if there is any change. This type of design is frequently used in the area of behavior analysis. It illustrates the way in which the effects of certain contingencies can be isolated and identified.

Most interesting, however (given the behaviorists' deemphasis of biological age or stages of development), is the viewpoint that the sequence of experience is the critical factor in development. In other words, when discussing developmental status, experience—and not age—is the important factor. Although age and experience are somewhat related, age should not be thought of as a determinant (or cause) of behavior but only a correlate (a simultaneous outcome).

A more recently popular approach (within the last 50 years or so) to understanding development is through social learning theory and the work of such people as Robert Sears and Albert Bandura. A social learning theory approach is very much based on the same assumptions of the more traditional behavioral approach. A major difference, however, is that the social learning theory model incorporates ideas such as vicarious (or indirect) reinforcement. Here the individual does not need to directly experience something to actually learn it. This approach still reflects the importance of the environment, while at the same time suggests that individual differences contribute something as well.

The most significant impact this model has had is on the systematic analysis of behavior, on the treatment and management of deviant behaviors, and in educational applications such as programmed instruction.

THE COGNITIVE-DEVELOPMENTAL MODEL

The cognitive-developmental model of human development stresses the individual's active rather than reactive role in the developmental process. The basic assumptions of the model are that:

1. Development occurs in a series of qualitatively distinct stages.
2. These stages always follow the same sequence, but do not necessarily occur at the same times for all individuals.
3. These stages are hierarchically organized such that a later stage subsumes the characteristics of an earlier one.

Another characteristic of the cognitive-developmental model that sets it apart from other theoretical models is the presence of psychological structures and the way in which changes in these underlying structures are reflected in overt changes in behavior. The form these changes take depends on the individual's developmental level. Many people categorize the cognitive-developmental perspective as an "interactionist" model because it encourages one to view development as an interaction between the organism and the environment.

The philosophical roots of this perspective are found in the predeterminist approach, which views development as a "process of qualitative differentiation or evolution of form." Jean-Jacques Rousseau, the noted 18th-century French philosopher, wrote that development consists of a sequence of orderly stages that are internally regulated, and that the individual is transformed from one into the other. Although Rousseau believed that the child is innately good (and most of the early predeterminists believed that the environment plays a very limited role), modern cognitive-developmental theorists would not tacitly accept such a broad assumption.

Although the environment is decisive in determining the content of these stages, the important biological or organismic contribution is the development of structures within which this content can operate. For example, all human beings are born with some innate capacity to develop language and to imitate behavior. Human beings are not, however, born with a capacity to speak a specific language, or even to imitate particular behavior. Children born in the United States with French-speaking parents would certainly not be expected to speak French (or any other language) without exposure to that language. Within the organismic model the capacity for development emerges as part of the developmental process. Although the environment is an important and influential factor, the biological contribution is far more important because it is the impetus for further growth and development. The sequence and process of development are predetermined, but the actual content of behavior within these stages is not.

Of primary interest to the cognitive-developmental psychologist is the sequence of stages and the process of transition from one stage to the next. It is for this reason that the set of stage-related behaviors and their correlates across such dimensions as cognitive or social development have been the focus of study. For example, a psychologist might be interested in examining how children of different ages (and presumably different developmental stages) solve a similar type of problem. After observing many children of different ages, the psychologist can then postulate the existence of different types of underlying structures responsible for the strategies children use.

A great deal of Jean Piaget's work has been directed at a better understanding of the thinking process that children at different developmental levels use to solve problems. In fact, much of the Piagetian tradition emphasizes that these different ways of solving problems reflect, in general, different ways of seeing the world.

Considering the cognitive-developmental psychologist's interest in the concept and use of stages, it is not surprising that the primary method used to study behavior is through the presentation of problems that emphasize differences in structural organization. The infant might depend on purely sensory information (such as touch or smell) to distinguish between different classes of objects, yet the older child might place a group of objects in categories based on more abstract criteria, such as "these are all toys, and these are food." The "how" of development is seen to be reflected in the strategies that children use at qualitatively different developmental levels to solve certain types of problems. More important, however, psychologists focus their attention on *why* these differences are present. Such studies have resulted in a model that hypothesizes that different underlying structures are operative at different stages.

Undoubtedly, the cognitive-developmental theorist has had the greatest impact in the different areas of education. Since much of the research conducted over the past 50 years by these theorists has focused on the general area of "thinking," this may be no surprise. Basically, the educational philosophy and practices that have resulted from this theoretical perspective have emphasized the unique contribution that children make to their own learning through discovery and experience. The child is allowed to explore within an environment that is challenging enough to facilitate development within the child's current stage of development, and one that is not boring.

—*Neil J. Salkind*

See also Cognitive Development, Maturation, Physical Development and Growth

Further Readings and References

Freud, S. (1933). *New introductory lectures on psychoanalysis*. New York: W. W. Norton.

Piaget, J. (1952). *The origins of intelligence in children*. New York: International Universities Press.

Skinner, B. F. (1948, 1976). *Walden two*. New York: Macmillan.

Wright, R. (1995). *The moral animal*. New York: Vintage.

THEORY OF MIND

Like all social animals, human children develop in a complicated social world, filled with numerous events involving the actions of other social agents. The ability to reason about the behaviors of these social agents is one of the most essential tasks in all of human cognition. For this reason, the question of how children come to reason about their social world has been a hot topic in the field of developmental psychology for some time. Much of this developmental work surrounds the question of how and when children develop a *theory of mind*. A theory of mind (ToM) can be defined as the capacity to represent the mental states—the beliefs, thoughts, perceptions, desires, and intentions—of oneself and others. The term "theory of mind" was originally coined by Premack and Woodruff, who examined whether a chimpanzee was able to reason about the intentions of others. Their original study of ToM in chimpanzees sparked a flurry of interest in the development of these capacities in humans.

Beginning in the 1980s, developmental psychologists devoted considerable empirical effort to the question of how and when children develop an understanding of one aspect of the mind of others: the ability to represent *beliefs*. This work led to the now classic test of belief understanding known as the "false belief task." In this type of task, children are asked to predict what another individual believes about an event in situations where that individual's belief differs from their own. In one version, children are asked what they think is inside a box of Smarties candy. Most participants answer that they think Smarties candy is inside the Smarties box. The experimenter then reveals that the participant is wrong; something unexpected (e.g., pencils) is actually inside the box. The experimenter then asks children what another person who has not looked inside the box will think is inside. Children 4 years of age and older correctly respond that another person will have a false belief about the contents of the box; a person who has not yet looked in the box will mistakenly think that there are Smarties inside. Children younger than 4 years of age, however, answer that another person will think that pencils are inside the box; they incorrectly reason that other people will have the same belief about the contents of the box as they do.

These data and others suggest that children undergo a developmental shift in their ability to represent the false beliefs of others sometime between 3 and 4 years of age. The exact nature of this developmental change, however, is still the subject of much debate in the field of cognitive development. Some researchers have argued that children learn to represent the beliefs of others through the development of simulation mechanisms, techniques for imagining the mental states of others (see Harris, 1991, for a version of this so-called simulation theory). Others have advanced the view that children's developing knowledge of beliefs emerges through a process of conceptual change, much like process of theory change in science. Still others champion the view that children's developmental shift in representing beliefs results from the emergence of innate structures for reasoning about the minds of other.

More recent work on the development of ToM abilities has focused on the question of when children come to understand mental states other than beliefs. This newer work suggests that children successfully represent mental states such as *desires* and *intentions* long before they pass false belief tests; even infants seem to think of the actions of others in terms of goals and intentions. Before the first year of life, infants expect human hands and other agents to move in goal-directed ways. Similarly, 18-month-olds correctly reason about the intention behind an unsuccessful action; when shown an action that an adult attempts but fails, such as trying to hang a loop on a metal prong, infants typically imitate the intended action, even though they have never directly witnessed this action. Infants also use their expectation that humans act in goal-directed ways when acquiring other knowledge, such as the meaning of words. Similarly, infants recognize that adults have *perceptions*, and pay specific attention to where other individuals are looking when reasoning about action. For example, 14-month-olds expect human adults to act on objects at which they are looking. Infants of this age also use information about where human experimenters are looking when inferring the referent of a new word and the meaning of a negative emotional expression.

Although most work in theory of mind has focused on human children, comparative psychologists have also investigated whether nonhuman animals—particularly primates—share out mind-reading capacities. Much of the classic work on this subject has suggested that non-human primates know little about the mental states of others. Chimpanzees, for example, typically fail to take into account what human experimenters see and know when choosing whom to ask for food. More recent evidence using different paradigms has indicated that chimpanzees may know about what other individuals see and know in the context of competition. As is the case with work on the development of ToM, these new primate studies continue to be the subject of much controversy and debate in the field.

—*Laurie R. Santos*

See also Cognitive Development

Further Readings and References

Baldwin, D. A., & Moses, L. M. (1994). Early understanding of referential intent and attentional focus: Evidence from language and emotion. In C. Lewis & P. Mitchell (Eds.), *Children's early understanding of mind: Origins and development*. Hillsdale, NJ: Erlbaum.

Bloom, P. (2004). *Descartes' baby: How the science of child development explains what makes us human*. New York: Basic Books.

de Villiers, J. G., & Pyers, J. E. (2003). Complements to cognition: A longitudinal study of the relationship between complex syntax and false-belief-understanding. *Cognitive Development, 17*, 1037–1060.

Leslie, A. M. (1994). ToMM, ToBy, and agency: Core architecture and domain specificity. In L. Hirschfeld & S. Gelman (Eds.), *Mapping the mind: Domain specificity in cognition and culture* (pp. 119–148). New York: Cambridge University Press.

Meltzoff, A. M. (1995). Understanding the intentions of others: re-enactments of intended acts by 18-month-old children. *Developmental Psychology, 31*, 838–850.

Premack, D., & Woodruff, G. (1978). Does the chimpanzee have a theory of mind? *Behavioral and Brain Sciences, 4*, 515–526.

Wellman, H. M., Cross, D., & Watson, J. (2001). Meta-analysis of theory-of-mind development: The truth about false belief. *Child Development, 72*(3), 655–684.

TODDLERHOOD

Toddlerhood typically begins around the first birthday and extends to the end of the third year. During this time, the crawling, babbling infant who was dependent on others to meet basic needs emerges into a walking, talking, and increasingly autonomous preschooler. The developmental accomplishments of the toddler period are often considered to be among the most profound that occur during the life course. The physical, cognitive-linguistic, and social-emotional abilities that first appear during this phase of development provide a foundation for later learning and relating to others.

PHYSICAL DEVELOPMENT

The word *toddler* is derived from "toddle," which means "to walk with short unsteady steps." To be sure, walking is a major accomplishment of this period. The child's first steps, which typically emerge around the first birthday (with the normal range of development between 9 and 17 months), mark the beginning of toddlerhood. At first, the child toddles with legs wide apart, toes pointed outward, and arms raised for balance. Toddlers quickly become adept at this new skill and will engage in more mature walking patterns within 6 months of their first steps. Once walking forward (and backward, at a slightly later age) is mastered, toddlers develop other large motor skills including running, jumping, and climbing. Ask any caregiver of a toddler and you will hear that toddlers are busy people!

Perhaps less striking, although equally important, toddlers also develop greater fine motor coordination, especially with respect to hand and finger skills. Younger toddlers, for instance, become adept at using their thumbs and forefingers to manipulate small objects, hold a spoon, scribble, or stack blocks. Older toddlers will further hone these hand and finger skills, and by the end of toddlerhood, children are able to draw, turn pages of a book, dress and undress themselves, and use a cup single-handedly.

A great challenge to caregivers of toddlers is providing opportunities to practice and polish emerging motor skills, while keeping the toddler safe. Caregivers may facilitate physical development by providing large, soft materials (e.g., pillows, mats, foam blocks) and toddler-sized climbing and sliding equipment that permit toddlers to play safely. Additionally, the availability of blocks, stacking toys, crayons, paints, and puzzles will help to stimulate and foster fine motor skills. Of course, boys and girls alike should have opportunities to engage in a variety of large-motor and fine-motor activities—from playing run-and-chase games or wrestling on the floor to sitting quietly while coloring or turning pages of books.

COGNITIVE-LINGUISTIC DEVELOPMENT

The large motor skills achieved by toddlers in the second year (especially walking upright) allow the child to view the world from a whole new perspective, and the increasing fine motor skills enable the toddler to manipulate and explore objects in ways that were not possible during infancy. Jean Piaget (1896–1980), a Swiss philosopher and psychologist, proposed that children actively construct knowledge about the world. Infants, for instance, learn about objects through the coordination of their senses and motor abilities (e.g., seeing a toy and reaching for it). Piaget labeled this phase the sensorimotor stage of cognitive development. Between 18 and 24 months, toddlers gain the capacity for symbolic thought, which marks the beginning of Piaget's preoperational stage of cognitive development. This newfound ability for symbolic mental representation is reflected in toddlers' ability to imitate actions that they've observed in the past, engage in pretend play, think about what they will do before doing it, and use language.

Indeed, toddlers' rapid gains in receptive and expressive language abilities mark one of the most dramatic changes of this period. Receptive language (i.e., the child's understanding of what others say) emerges before expressive language, and by 24 months most toddlers can understand names of familiar people and objects, point to named objects or pictures, and follow simple commands. These skills further develop between 24 and 36 months, with the ability to follow two-step commands and understand full sentences. Clearly, toddlers also make impressive gains in expressive language (i.e., the ability to put thoughts into words). Between 12 and 15 months of age, toddlers typically say their first words, and by 24 months most toddlers will have a 50-word vocabulary and use two-word sentences and questions (e.g., "more juice," "what that?"). Such utterances are called telegraphic speech because they resemble the abbreviated messages found in telegrams. By the end of the toddler period, children will use complete sentences and basic rules of grammar (e.g., adding "-ed" to the end of verbs to indicate past tense) and will have a 200-plus-word vocabulary.

Caregivers can promote toddlers' cognitive and language development in numerous ways, including naming objects, talking about events that happen throughout the day, reading picture books, and singing. Through these experiences, toddlers not only build strong vocabularies but learn correct grammar and social conventions of language, such as turn-taking in conversations. Having a variety of play materials available that encourage hands-on sensory exploration (e.g., Play-Doh, sand or water tables, paints) and pretend play props that encourage imaginative play (e.g., dress up clothes, cars and trains, dolls) will also help toddlers make full use of their new cognitive abilities and interests.

SOCIAL-EMOTIONAL DEVELOPMENT

Toward the end of the second year, as the capacity for forming mental representations emerges, toddlers develop a sense of an independent self. Signs of this budding sense of self can be found in the toddler's self-references ("Me do it!"), the ability to recognize his/her own image in the mirror, and the increasing likelihood to meet parental requests with an emphatic "NO!" Erik Erickson (1902–1994), a developmental psychologist who proposed a life span theory of psychosocial development, considered achieving a sense of autonomy to be a key task of the toddler period. Toddlers who have the opportunity to engage in self-help skills (e.g., feeding and dressing themselves) and make simple decisions tend to develop an autonomous sense of self. When caregivers do not permit toddlers to make simple choices or do things for themselves, or consistently reject bids for autonomy, the toddler's sense of personal agency may become riddled by feelings of shame and doubt. Importantly, the toddler may swing sharply between striving for autonomy and clinging to caregivers, especially when tired, ill, or afraid. This mixed desire for independence, on one hand, and the security of the caregiver's lap, on the other, is a central tension of toddlerhood. In this sense, the toddler period has been referred to as the "first adolescence."

In conjunction with an emerging sense of self, toddlers demonstrate a growing awareness of and interest in others, especially other children. Toddlers in the second year of life will typically play side by side with little or no interaction. Throughout the third year, though, toddlers will show increasing ability to interact with peers and these interactions often stem from toddlers' propensity to imitate others. Two-year-olds are also able to distinguish among playmates and may develop playmate preferences. Thus, peer interactions in the toddler years pave the way for the advent of friendships in the preschool years.

Finally, as the toddler develops a sense of self as separate from others, new emotions emerge that were not present during infancy. For instance, toddlers are openly affectionate and show signs of empathy and concern toward others' injuries or distress. Toddlers also show positive self-evaluations (a precursor to pride) when accomplishing a goal and shame when behaving in a socially unacceptable or prohibited manner. These emotions are often labeled "social" or "self-conscious" emotions because they reflect feelings about the self in relation to others. As a result of increasing awareness of the social rules for appropriate behavior and the emotions that may accompany such awareness, toddlers may begin to develop a sense of a "moral self."

Given the toddler's frequent demands to "have it all" and the "clash of wills" that may result when the goals of the parent oppose those of the toddler, it is no wonder that the toddler years are challenging for parents and children alike. Older toddlers, in particular, are famous for their increased negativity, thus the label the "terrible twos." Yet, such negativism reflects the child's increasing wish for autonomy and is a normal part of toddler development, especially in Western cultures. Caregivers can promote a positive sense of self by respecting the toddler's need for autonomy. At the same time, when the toddler seeks the caregiver's comfort or protection, it is important to provide reassurance that support is available. By the end of this period, children who have learned that caregivers are available and responsive when needed will be more secure and independent than children who have been "pushed" toward independence. In light of the increasing physical and cognitive capacities of the growing toddler, caregivers tend to first establish rules for behavior during this period. Caregivers should strive to consistently hold to a clear set of rules that serve the safety and well-being of toddlers and others around them. Providing simple reasons for rules may also foster toddlers' understanding of others' feelings and perspectives. Remarkable physical, social-emotional, and cognitive-linguistic growth mark the toddler years, and it is likely that children will benefit when caregivers are responsive to the toddlers' need to "do it myself," provide safe and simple choices, and keep an open mind and sense of humor during these busy times!

—*Nancy L. McElwain*

Further Readings and References

Edwards, C. P. (1995). Parenting toddlers. In M. H. Bornstein (Ed.), *Handbook of parenting, Vol. 1: Children and parenting* (pp. 41–63). Mahwah, NJ: Erlbaum.

Gonzalez-Mena, J., & Eyer, D. W. (2001). *Infants, toddlers, and caregivers* (5th ed.). Mountainview, CA: Mayfield.

National Network for Child Care: Toddler Development, http://www.nncc.org/Child.Dev/todd.dev.html

Parent-to-Parent, http://p2p.uiuc.edu

Shatz, M. (1994). *A toddler's life: Becoming a person.* New York: Oxford University Press.

Shelov, S. P. (Ed.-in-Chief). (1998). *Caring for your baby and young child: Birth to Age 5.* New York: Bantam.

Zero to Three, http://www.zerotothree.org/

TOILET TRAINING

Toilet training is an important developmental milestone in every child's life. Although toilet training is universal, variation exists in everything from the timing to the method of the training. Cultural and societal norms have a significant influence on the practice of toilet training. In the United States, the suggested age of initiating toilet training has ranged from 1 month to 24 months of age. In other industrialized societies, recommendations for the timing of training vary widely, as well. Children have been thought to be "ready" at approximately 5 months in London, 8 months in Paris, and just over 1 year in Stockholm.

The variation in beliefs about readiness may be related to the methods used and attitudes toward toilet training. In some cultures, the responsibility for toilet training falls primarily on the child's caregiver. For example, in the Digo tribe in East Africa, caregivers are trained to recognize and tend to a child's need to urinate or defecate. Children are expected to attain complete dryness by 1 year of age. In contrast, in the United States and other Western societies, the responsibility is placed largely on the child to be independent and therefore dryness is achieved at a much later age.

Despite all the disparity in beliefs and practices related to the timing of toilet training, research indicates that most children are successfully trained by 24 to 36 months of age, with nearly all children being trained by the age of 4. One factor contributing to successful training is the child's level of physical and intellectual maturity. Physical readiness includes a fairly regular pattern of wetting during the day that occurs less frequently (e.g., 4 times per day). Also it is helpful if the child has developed the level of physical dexterity needed to raise and lower his or her pants quickly. Thirdly, the child needs to both understand and be able to convey concepts such as *wet*, *dry*, and *potty*. Finally, for toilet training to be successful and efficient, a child must be able to comply with simple requests given by the parent. All of these "prerequisites" signal that a child is likely to be effectively trained. Given the readiness criteria, it is not surprising that the later training is initiated, the faster dryness is accomplished. For example, children who begin toilet training at 26 months or later tend to be successfully trained twice as fast as those whose training begins before 24 months.

As the differences are great regarding the age of initiating toilet training, opinions about the method of toilet training are equally wide-ranging. Over the years, the prevalent thinking regarding toilet training in the United States has varied between gentle child-centered approaches and intense prescribed methods designed for rapid training in as little as 4 hours. Many diverse techniques and strategies are included in training methods such as the use of scheduled toilet sits, charts, rewards, books, and dolls to assist the child's learning. Despite their differences, varying methods appear to have similar rates of success, given that approximately 90% of children are successfully trained by age 4.

Although toilet training is typically achieved by the age of 4, it is not uncommon for accidents to occasionally occur in children of 3 to 6 years of age. Typical accidents occur when children are intently involved in play activities. Professional guidance is rarely needed in these cases. However, up to 25% of boys and 15% of girls have persistent problems with wetting the bed or their pants. Additionally, from 1.5 to 5% of children have difficulty with soiling or defecating in their pants. These persistent concerns can be effectively treated, but may warrant professional assistance from a physician and/or psychologist.

—*Eve A. Herrera*

See also Parent-Child Relationships, Parenting

Further Readings and References

Berk, L. B., & Friman, P. C. (1990). Epidemiologic aspects of toilet training. *Clinical Pediatrics, 29,* 278–282.

Christophersen, E. R., Walter, M., & Reichman, E. (1997). Toilet training. In *Little people: Guidelines for common sense child rearing* (4th ed., pp. 107–113). Shawnee Mission: Overland Press.

Foxx, R. M., & Azrin, N. H. (1973). Dry pants: A rapid method of toilet training children. *Behaviour Research and Therapy, 11,* 435–442.

iVillage, Inc. (2001, June 20). *Potty training: 10 Steps to toilet teaching your toddler.* Retrieved from http://www.parentsoup.com/toddlers/potty/articles/0,,262585_260941, 00.html

Safer Child, Inc. (2003). *Toilet training.* Retrieved from http://www.saferchild.com/potty.htm

Schaefer, C. E., & DiGeronimo, T. F. (1997). *Toilet training without tears* (Rev. ed.). New York: Signet.

Schroeder, C. S., & Gordon, B. N. (2002). Toileting: Training, enuresis, and encopresis. In *Assessment & treatment of childhood problems* (2nd ed., pp. 115–158). New York: Guilford.

TOUCH

Touch typically refers to sensations that occur when skin receptors are triggered by external stimuli. Touch has been described as one of the most fundamental means of contact with the world and the simplest and most straightforward of all sensory systems. It is the first sense to develop in utero and by 14 weeks after gestation, the surface of the fetus is almost entirely sensitive to tactile stimulation. By adulthood, the skin constitutes the largest organ of the body, covering 1.8 square meters of the average person.

The importance of touch has been implicated in several domains of life across the life span, particularly in early life. Touch helps us learn about the world around us and plays an integral role in biological, cognitive, and social development. Below, each of these domains is described along with the physiological underpinnings and physical dimensions of touch that help make it such a rich and important modality in life.

THE PHYSIOLOGICAL UNDERPINNINGS AND PHYSICAL DIMENSIONS OF TOUCH

As mentioned, the skin is the largest organ of the human body and weighs between six and ten pounds. The skin is a multilayered structure containing several receptors, each of which sends unique signals to the brain via neurons via the spinal cord. Information from the spinal cord enters the thalamus—the "relay station" of the brain—and input from there is sent to a strip of the brain called the somatosensory cortex located on the parietal cortex. The more area on the somatosensory cortex that is dedicated to a given area of skin on the body, the more sensitive that area of skin is to tactile stimulation. Thus, areas of the body such as the fingers and lips—two of the most sensitive areas of the body to tactile stimulation—are well represented on the somatosenory cortex compared to less sensitive areas of the skin such as the back.

When considering the impact of touch, one must consider not only the physiological underpinnings of the modality but the physical dimensions of tactile stimulation on the skin. The dimensions of touch can be divided by the *qualities* of touch (the actual tactile stimulus that is administered) and the *parameters* of touch (where and how much touch is administered). The following constitute the qualities and parameters of touch:

Qualities

- Action: the specific movements on the skin (e.g., stroking, squeezing)
- Intensity: the degree of pressure on the skin
- Velocity: the rate at which something is impressed upon or across the skin
- Abruptness: the acceleration or deceleration that the skin is touched
- Temperature: the temperature of the tactile stimulus on the skin

Parameters

- Location: where the tactile stimulus is on the skin
- Frequency: the number of times that the skin is touched
- Duration: the elapsed time that the skin is touched
- Extent of surface area touched: the amount of surface area that is covered

Together, these dimensions of touch comprise the richness of the tactile modality.

LEARNING ABOUT THE WORLD VIA TOUCH

Throughout life we actively explore the world with our hands to learn about objects in the world—a process known as haptic perception. Haptic perception, in conjunction with vision, is particularly important for infants to learn about the world. Research indicates that by 3 months of age infants can distinguish objects by size and shape (e.g., a cube from a hollow square), by 6 months of age they can distinguish objects by hardness and texture, by 9 months of age they can distinguish objects by weight, and by 15 months of age they can distinguish between shapes that are similar in features but differ in spatial arrangement.

EFFECTS OF TOUCH ON BIOLOGY

Touch plays an instrumental role in brain development and growth, especially in early life. Without adequate tactile stimulation early in life, the brain does not grow to a normal size and the synapses between neurons do not develop properly. In addition, adequate tactile stimulation early in life can buffer the effects of tactile deprivation later in life. Thus, exposure to adequate amounts of touch early in life seems to form a foundation for later nervous system development.

The importance of touch does not wane later in life. Research indicates that when nonhuman animals are provided extra tactile stimulation later in life, their brains increase in size and the synapses between neurons increase. Moreover, tactile stimulation can help stimulate neuronal growth due to brain lesions and infarcts in the brain later in life.

In addition to studying the effects of touch on the brain, researchers have investigated the effects of touch on premature infants' growth. In one study a group of premature infants received a 10-day protocol of massage therapy comprised of tactile/kinesthetic stimulation while a control group did not receive the massage therapy protocol. Compared to the control group, the treatment group gained 47% more weight, was more active and alert, and spent 6 fewer days in the hospital. If all of the premature infants in the country received massage therapy, an estimated total of $4.7 million would be saved in medical costs annually.

Massage therapy improves a host of other biological and health related phenomena. Children and adults receiving massage therapy experience less anxiety, lower levels of stress hormones (cortisol, norepinephrine, and epinephrine), enhanced immune system functioning, and heightened alertness as indexed by EEG. Massage therapy can also play a role in the treatment of several medical conditions including juvenile rheumatoid arthritis, fibromyalgia, chronic lower back pain, migraine headaches, depression, autism, attention deficit hyperactivity disorder, post-traumatic stress disorder, and some eating disorders.

EFFECTS OF TOUCH ON COGNITION

Touch has a significant impact on cognitive development. A wide body of literature suggests that cognitive development is intimately tied to brain development in the childhood years and, as mentioned, touch plays a pivotal role in neuronal development in the early years of life. Parental aversions to touch as well as harsh touch have been implicated as factors in the development of language and learning disorders. In addition, research suggests that parents who use touch to stimulate the central nervous system regularly and appropriately have children that are more likely to develop an accurate and sophisticated body image. These parents provide a variety of forms of tactile stimulation to a number of areas on the body.

EFFECTS OF TOUCH ON EMOTION AND SOCIAL INTERACTION

Touch plays an integral role in the caregiver-child relationship from the beginning of life. In one U.S. sample, infants were touched for 33% to 61% of the time during brief interactions with their mothers. The frequency of contact is much higher in some cultures such as the !Kung and the Efe tribe of Zaire where mothers spend approximately 75% of the time in contact with their infants.

In infancy, caregivers' touch is thought to serve a variety of communicative functions while they are in contact with their infants. Two of the most important are the communication of emotions, as well as the communication of security. A number of studies indicates that touch is capable of communicating and eliciting positive and negative emotions. One powerful demonstration of the power of touch to elicit positive emotions has been shown when researchers use the "still-face paradigm" to study infant emotionality. The still-face paradigm is comprised of a period of interaction when the caregiver assumes a still-face, thereby not responding to the infant's actions. During this period, infants typically react negatively because this is an unusual event in most infants' lives. Several studies indicate that if caregivers touch their infants during the still-face period, their infants' emotional displays are significantly less negative and more positive compared to infants who are not touched during the still-face period.

The quality of caregiver-infant touch is a central feature of the responsive and available caregiving environment that is necessary to foster an infant's sense of security. Several studies suggest that touch between the caregiver and infant is the "ultimate signal" of security of the infant. In one experimental study, researchers compared how infants were attached to their caregivers when they carried their infants ventrally in soft infant carriers versus those who were carried in harder infant seats. The researchers found that infants carried in the soft infant carriers were significantly more likely to be securely attached to their caregivers than infants who were carried in the infant seats. This study and others strongly suggest that touch plays a key role in the communication of security to children.

Touch continues to play an integral role in social communication in adulthood. For example, touch communicates power and emotions to others, as well as aids in persuading others to comply with our requests. In addition, touch increases verbal interaction among people, gains attention from others, and communicates our attraction toward others.

In sum, touch not only helps us learn about the world in which we live but plays an integral role in several other domains of life including biological, cognitive, and social development. Although touch may be one of the most powerful and most important sensory modalities across the life span, the study of touch has remained minimal. Future work on touch will continue to unravel the mysteries of touch.

—*Matthew J. Hertenstein*

See also Sensory Development

Further Readings and References

Anisfeld, E., Casper, V., Nozyce, M., & Cunningham, N. (1990). Does infant carrying promote attachment? An experimental study of the effects of increased physical contact on the development of attachment. *Child Development, 61*, 1617–1627.

Field, T. (2001). *Touch.* Cambridge: MIT Press.

Hertenstein, M. J. (2002). Touch: Its communicative functions in infancy. *Human Development, 45*, 70–94.

Montagu, A. (1986). *Touching: The human significance of the skin* (3rd ed.). New York: Harper & Row.

Stack, D. M., & Muir, D. W. (1992). Adult tactile stimulation during face-to-face interactions modulates five-month-olds' affect and attention. *Child Development, 63*, 1509–1525.

Tronick, E. Z. (1995). Touch in mother-infant interaction. In T. M. Field (Ed.), *Touch in early development* (pp. 53–65). Mahwah, NJ: Erlbaum.

Touch Research Institute, http://www.miami.edu/touch-research/

TOURETTE'S SYNDROME

Tourette's syndrome (TS) is a neurobehavioral disorder named after the French neurologist Georges Gilles de la Tourette who in 1885 described nine patients with TS symptoms including verbal and motor childhood-onset tics and other behavioral problems including poor impulse control and obsessive-compulsive behaviors. The disease, once believed to be extremely rare, is now considered to be quite common, affecting approximately 2% percent of the population. The disease afflicts males 5 times more often than females. The onset of TS, as characterized by the emergence of motor and vocal tics, typically emerges between the ages of 3 and 8 with a reduction in these symptoms occurring by age 20.

SYMPTOMS

The hallmarks of TS are the motor and verbal tics. These tics vary in complexity, duration (ranging from 1 year to lifelong), intensity (from mild to severe), and frequency (from rare to constant). Tics are brief movements or sounds that appear unpredictably. They emerge individually or in choreographed clusters and can be expressed either intermittently or continuously for hours. These tics fall into one of several categories: (1) motor tics which can include intense eye blinking, throat clearing, and neck and arm twitching; (2) phonic tics such as repeated utterance of a particular word, shouting (obscenities), or grunting; (3) aggressive phenomenon such as self-injury, hitting, kicking, or biting self or others; and (4) compulsive behaviors that may include hand-washing, door locking, checking and organizing objects, and touching or tapping others and objects.

The motor and phonic symptoms typically wax and wane. This waxing and waning is most likely influenced by ongoing brain developmental changes and environmental influences such as stress. Additionally, medications for TS can also cause changes in the brain that result in corresponding behavioral changes. The repertoire and severity of symptoms of TS patients, therefore, require constant monitoring by the patient and family, as well as by the physician who will adjust the dose and type of medication accordingly. Studies have reported that the highest incidence and severity of tics occur with anticipation or resolution of emotional changes. Consistent with this, stress, anxiety, and fatigue exacerbate tics, and ironically, the very urge and attempt to control the tic can itself lead to additional stress and anxiety. Altogether, the disease and its consequences can often lead to problems in school performance and self-esteem, and also in a variety of social and behavioral problems at school, at home, and in society in general.

GENETICS

Tourette's syndrome has a significant genetic component. Several genes have been identified through family studies, segregation analyses, candidate gene studies, and linkage studies. TS inheritance may involve several mechanisms including autosomal dominant, bilinear, or polygenic mechanisms. Candidate genes for TS pose a genetic susceptibility with such factors as pre- or postnatal stress, and other environmental factors such as viral infections or stress, increasing their likelihood of expression. It is critical therefore to continue studies designed to identify specific gene-environmental interactions. The candidate genes identified thus far appear to be involved in the regulation of brain development and neurochemical signaling. For example, several dopamine (DA) receptor (D1, D2, D4, D5) and noradrenergic receptor (ADRA2a, ADRA2c and DBH) genes and a few serotonin genes have been identified. In conclusion, many candidate genes that pose a susceptibility to developing TS have been identified. The heterogeneity of identified TS genes together with their varying etiologies and environmental interactions make it impossible to provide a single or simple explanation for the etiology of TS. Research progress in this area will lead to a better understanding and predictability of the etiology of TS and improved treatments for these patients.

NEUROBIOLOGY

Numerous neuroanatomical and brain imaging (fMRI, PET, SPECT) studies have identified the prefrontal cortex (PFC)–basal ganglia (BG) circuit as the major system involved in Tourette's syndrome. This circuit is involved primarily in regulating a variety of motor, limbic, and cognitive functions. The dorsal striatum (consisting of the caudate and putamen) of the BG is implicated primarily in motor control and habit formation, whereas the ventral striatum is implicated in compulsivity and addiction. The prefrontal cortex is involved in such higher-order executive decisions as impulse control. Other related areas such as the brain stem, which has been implicated in eye blink reflex, have also been implicated as well as other areas that interact with the PFC-BG circuit including motor, cingulate, temporal, and parietal cortical areas, Broca's area, thalamus, and cerebellum.

The overriding problem in TS appears to be the overactivity of motor and motivational/reinforcement systems with an inability of the prefrontal cortex to override or inhibit those related behaviors. TS patients, like patients with prefrontal damage, reveal poor performance on impulsivity control tasks. A functional neuroimaging study revealed an increase in neural activity in the prefrontal and caudate nucleus and a decrease in the motor-related putamen and globus pallidus in a tick suppression task. Performance on tasks requiring other higher-order functions such as learning and memory, however, remained normal in TS patients.

Examination of the specific neuroanatomical abnormality of the prefrontal-BG circuit has revealed a decrease in the volume of these brain areas in TS patients. It remains unclear, however, as to whether these brain differences are necessarily due to damage or due to compensatory mechanisms. The compensatory nature of the brain further suggests that these individuals may develop alternative cognitive and behavioral strengths that are not dependent on the damaged brain areas. Special efforts should be made by the family, educators, and physicians to help the patient identify such strengths and talents.

Detailed synaptic and receptor microcircuitry abnormalities within the PFC-BG circuits, however, have not been fully explored. The identification of specific cellular and biochemical circuits will help to improve site-specific targeted treatments for this disorder. For example, striatal cholinergic neurons of the striatum are known to signal reward and in turn influence motor signaling as well as incoming prefrontal cortical signals. Dr. Alcantara's work has implicated these neurons and their corresponding dopamine D2 receptors to play a key role in the development of drug abuse and possibly in the treatments designed to treat addiction. Further investigations should examine whether these cholinergic neurons are also critical for motor and impulse control in TS patients.

TS patients express comorbidity with two other PFC-BG related disorders: obsessive-compulsive disorder (OCD) and attention-deficit-hyperactivity disorder (ADHD; which involves increased inattention, hyperactivity, and impulsivity). TS patients also have a high incidence of depression, anxiety, and aggression. Additionally, family members of TS patients show a higher than normal incidence for OCD, ADHD, drug or alcohol dependency, depression, anxiety, eating disorders, and panic disorders, all of which share a common neuroanatomical and biochemical basis with TS.

NEUROTRANSMITTER SYSTEMS

Two neurotransmitter systems most likely affected by TS are the dopaminergic and norepinephrine systems. The dopamine system, central to the PFC-BG circuit, is suggested to be hypofunctional, further implicating the supersensitivity of dopamine D2 receptors and therefore requiring drugs that block these receptors. The norepinephrine (NE) system originating in the brain stem influences motivation, attention, and arousal in the PFC-BG circuit and is also suggested to be hypofunctional, requiring the use of adrenergic (NE) receptor agonists.

TREATMENTS

Pharmacological Treatments

Two classes of antipsychotic drugs that target the DA and NE systems are most widely used. These include the neuroleptics, including fluphenazine, haloperidol, pimozide, sulpiride, and tiapride, which are effective in reducing the symptoms of TS (side effects include sedation or dysphoria). Additionally the alpha2 adrenergic agonists such as clonidine, desipramine, guanfacine, and risperidone often show benefit (side effects include sedation and irritability).

Behavioral Treatments

Behavioral treatment or combined behavioral treatment with drugs is the most effective in treating the symptoms of TS. Cognitive behavior therapy (CBT) is the main behavioral treatment of choice. CBT includes habit reversal, which is the most promising treatment consisting of awareness training, self-monitoring, relaxation training, competing response training, and contingency management. Also hypnotherapy, biofeedback, conductual therapies, acupuncture, electroconvulsive therapy, meditation, and surgery have been employed. Surgery, however, is the most invasive and can lead to subsequent brain circuit deterioration. Both drug and behavioral treatments can target and modify the affected brain areas and related receptor and synaptic microcircuits. These treatments thereby show much promise for the successful long-term treatment of TS. Continued research in the areas of TS and improved animal models should continue to shed light on our understanding of the etiology of TS and the development of improved site-specific targeted behavioral and pharmacological treatments for Tourette's syndrome.

—Adriana A. Alcantara

Further Readings and References

Berlanga, M. L., Olsen, C. M., Chen, V., Ikegami, A., Herring, B. E., Duvauchelle, C. L., et al. (2003). Cholinergic interneurons of the nucleus accumbens and dorsal striatum are activated by the self-administration of cocaine. *Neuroscience, 120,* 1149–1156.

Gerard, E., & Peterson, B. S. (2003). Developmental processes and brain imaging studies in Tourette syndrome. *Journal of Psychosomatic Research, 55*(1), 13–22.

Leckman, J. F. (2002). Tourette's syndrome. *The Lancet, 360*(9345), 1577–1586.

Pauls, D. L. (2003). An update on the genetics of Gilles de la Tourette syndrome. *Journal of Psychosomatic Research, 55*(1), 7–12.

Tourette Syndrome Association, http://www.tsa-usa.org/

TOXOPLASMOSIS

Toxoplasmosis (toxo) is a common parasitic infection that, often completely asymptomatic when acquired by adults, may have serious adverse consequences when transmitted by a pregnant woman to her embryo/fetus. The responsible parasite, *toxoplasma gondii* occurs worldwide, but infections are more common in warmer climates. Infection generally occurs through eating undercooked meat or unwashed fruit/vegetables or contact with infected cat feces or soil.

ADULT INFECTION

Testing reveals evidence of toxo in many adults. In a minority of normal adults with primary adult infections, symptoms do occur and may include fever, general malaise, and enlargement of lymph nodes. Subsequently, the parasite forms cysts throughout the body which may remain latent for years. Reactivation of the cysts in the eyes of a small percent of affected individuals may cause recurrent vision problems. In adults with severely impaired immune systems, primary toxo infection may have serious consequences, including death. Primary infection generally leads to development of antibodies that protect against reinfection.

PRENATAL/CONGENITAL INFECTION

Major concern with toxo is its potential congenital effects. Toxo is one of several infections that may have serious adverse effects on offspring if primary infection of a pregnant woman is transmitted pre- or perinatally to her embryo/fetus. Such infections are variously called prenatal/perinatal, congenital, or maternal infections. Since newborns affected by these infections share characteristics, identification of the particular agent is often only through laboratory analysis.

Overall probability across pregnancy of congenital infection of the embryo/fetus is about 30%. However, probability of infection is inversely related to duration of gestation: Risk is very low early in pregnancy and only about 6% at 13 weeks, but thereafter rises virtually exponentially to about 80% just before birth.

Congenital toxo can lead to intrauterine growth retardation (IUGR) and, rarely, stillbirth. Many children with congenital toxo are asymptomatic. In those who do show symptoms, the most common is retinochoroiditis. Hydrocephalus, intracranial calcification, mental retardation, and other neurological deficits may also occur. Hearing impairment may develop in childhood. Incidence and severity of adverse effects are inversely related to time in gestation at which infection occurs: Adverse impact is greatest with infection early in pregnancy and diminishes thereafter. Ocular lesions can occur and reoccur at any age, but again, risk appears to diminish with gestation age at time of primary maternal infection. When a toxo infection is identified, which may not be until 12 months of age, antiparasitic agents may be administered.

IDENTIFICATION AND PREVENTION

Since primary *T. gondii* infection leads to subsequent production of antibodies that protect the embryo/fetus from infection, concern is with women who have no antibodies at the beginning of pregnancy. Serological testing can identify women who do not have *T. gondii* antibodies at the outset of pregnancy and retesting can identify development of antibodies, indicating a primary infection. Ultrasound detection of signs such as enlarged cerebral ventricles and intracranial calcification are suggestive of prenatal toxo. Diagnosis can be confirmed through detection of the parasite in amniotic fluid. In cases of maternal or embryonic infection, pregnant women may be treated with antiparasitic agents in an attempt to prevent adverse effects. However, although such identification programs and treatments are common in Europe, their use involves risks to the embryo/fetus, and their effectiveness is controversial. In cases of confirmed diagnosis, the pregnancy may be terminated. See Gilbert (2000) for a detailed discussion.

The best prevention of congenital toxo is for pregnant women to avoid primary infection. Given that the most severe adverse consequences occur with early prenatal infection, much damage to the embryo may occur if a woman suffers primary *T. gondii* infection before learning she is pregnant. The best prevention is for women who may become pregnant to avoid primary infection by not eating undercooked meat, washing hands and work surfaces after preparing raw meat, washing fruits and vegetables, and avoiding contact with used cat litter or soil that may contain animal feces.

—Robert T. Brown

Further Readings and References

Gilbert, R. (2000). Toxoplasmosis. In M.-L. Newell & J. McIntyre (Eds.), *Congenital and perinatal infections: Prevention, diagnosis and treatment* (pp. 305–315). Cambridge, UK: Cambridge University Press. (ebook)

Hill, J. B., & Hafner, W. H. J. (2003). Growth before birth. In M. L. Batshaw (Ed.), *Children with disabilities* (5th ed., pp. 43–53). Baltimore, MD: Brookes.

Ramsey, P. S., & Goldenberg, R. L. (2000). Maternal infections and their consequences. In M.-L. Newell, & J. McIntyre (Eds.), *Congenital and perinatal infections: Prevention, diagnosis and treatment* (pp. 32–63). Cambridge, UK: Cambridge University Press.

TWIN STUDIES

Twin studies represent one of the oldest scientific methods of evaluating the influence of heredity on human development and behavior. During the course of the 20th century, twin studies became more versatile and have encompassed a wider range of behavioral constructs. As the field advanced, debates about whether nurture or nature is more influential have been replaced with the notion of nature *via* nurture. This ideological shift has been driven by an increasing number of twin studies demonstrating that certain environments in combination with genetic influences produce a particular developmental outcome. What follows is a brief overview of the twin study method and applications of the method that have led to discoveries in human development.

BEHAVIORAL GENETICS AND THE TWIN STUDY METHOD

Behavioral genetics is the study of the influence of genes and environment on variation in human behavior. In traditional non-twin family study designs, genetic and environmental influences are confounded with each other, making it difficult to determine the relative degree to which familial resemblance reflects contributions from genes and environment. The basic twin study method treats twinning as a natural experiment that makes use of monozygotic (MZ) twins, who share 100% of their genetic material, and dizygotic (DZ) twins, who on average share only 50% of their genetic material (like ordinary siblings). The environment is assumed to affect members of both types of twin pairs equally, so observed differences in similarity between MZ and DZ pairs are interpreted as reflecting genetic effects. Genetic influences are inferred by the degree to which MZ twins are more similar than their DZ counterparts. Possible limitations to the twin design include the representativeness of twins to the general population and difficulties recruiting the large-scale samples of twins necessary to estimate adequately genetic effects. Nevertheless, twin studies, when combined with traditional family and adoption designs (where parents and their children are not genetically related) have provided many insights into genetic influences on human behavior.

Three types of influences on behavior can be estimated from the basic twin method: genetic factors, shared environmental factors, and nonshared environmental factors. An estimate of genetic influence gleaned from the twin method is referred to as *heritability* or the proportion of variation in a given behavior that is due to genetic factors. Heritability estimates range from 0.0 to 1.0, with a value of 1.0 indicating that 100% of the variability in the trait can be accounted for by genetic factors. *Shared environmental factors* refer to environmental experiences that members of a twin pair share in common, and act to make individuals similar to each other. Examples of shared environment include growing up in the same neighborhood and being reared by the same parents. Shared environmental effects are inferred when the similarity of DZ twins approaches that of MZ twins. *Nonshared environmental factors* refer to those unique factors that members of a twin pair do not share, and thus act to make individuals different from each other. An example of nonshared environmental influence is distinct peer group influence for each member of the pair. Such nonshared environmental effects are inferred from the degree to which MZ twins are dissimilar for a trait of interest. At this most basic level, behavioral geneticists estimate degree of genetic, shared and nonshared environmental influences, but such an analysis cannot identify specific environments or genes influencing behavior.

A variation of the basic twin design is the *twins reared-apart method.* This method identifies rare sets of MZ twins separated early in development and reared in different families. Any similarity in behavioral traits observed in such twins can be attributed to genetic effects because they did not share common rearing environments. Thomas Bouchard, a leading scientist in the twins reared-apart method, collected extensive behavioral data on a relatively large sample of such twins. His data showed striking behavioral similarities between reared-apart identical twins, many of whom met for the first time in his laboratory. Similarities were found for diverse attributes, including personality, vocational choices, attitudes, and religious beliefs, providing compelling evidence for the influence of genes on the development of numerous facets of behavior and psychological functioning.

The twin design can also be used to evaluate the effects of specific environments on a behavior. In the *discordant twin method,* researchers focus on MZ twins who are discordant (or lack similarity) on a given behavior or trait. Sets of twins who are discordant for the behavior are then examined on the basis of measured environmental variables. For example, studies of twins discordant for schizophrenia have shown that the structure of the affected twin's brain differs from that of the healthy co-twin, indicating that some environmental factor has led to the development of anomalous brain anatomy in the MZ twin with schizophrenia.

Key environmental variables have also been integrated into the basic twin method to elucidate the effects of particular environments on behavior. For example, a researcher seeking to test whether the environmental effects on the initiation of substance use are attributable to peer influence may examine the association between these two factors within MZ and DZ twin pairs to determine if peer influence accounts for a substantial proportion of the individual differences in substance use initiation attributable to environmental influence. In this type of twin investigation, specific environmental effects are evaluated in the presence of genetic influences.

Longitudinal Twin Studies

Twin studies using a *longitudinal design,* or repeated measurements on individuals at several intervals over time, provide a unique opportunity to examine the complex nature of genes and environments over the life span. Wattington put forth the concept of *canalization,* or the idea that as individuals mature, their range of possible developmental outcomes narrows. Similarly, evidence from longitudinal twin studies have generally suggested that genetic influence on behavior increases as individuals grow older. Large-scale twin studies spanning infancy, adolescence, adulthood, and late adulthood have been undertaken in several countries. Results of these studies have offered insights into the nature of environmental influence on alcohol and drug use behaviors ranging from initiation of alcohol use to severe forms of alcoholism. Studies of Danish twins during the course of very late adulthood have offered insights into the effects of genes on normal aging.

Gene-Environment Correlation and Interaction

Sandra Scarr, a developmental behavior geneticist, has emphasized how heredity and environment work synergistically rather than independently. Genes and environments are *correlated* when individuals with certain inherited propensities develop associations with environments partial to their genetic inclinations. For example, a child with genes favoring the development of musical talent may seek out friends who enjoy music and join a band. Rather than environmental exposure simply encouraging the development of musical talent, genetic proclivities encourage the selection of musically relevant environments. A *gene-environment interaction* results when an inherited tendency is more likely to be expressed in one environment than another. For instance, heritability estimates of alcohol use may differ in urban and rural environments. In urban settings, where there is less community monitoring and accountability and more avenues to access alcohol, more opportunities exist for increased expression of genetic dispositions to drink alcohol.

THE APPLICATION OF TWIN STUDIES TO UNDERSTAND DEVELOPMENTAL PHENOMENA

The study of human development has benefited from the use of twin studies, and psychologists have used the method to evaluate several psychological domains. In his 1929 pioneering study, Gesell used twins to demonstrate the influence of genes on learning. A pair of infant twins was compared on stair-climbing behavior. One twin was trained in the behavior and one twin was not. The untrained twin soon independently learned the behavior, thus demonstrating that without explicit training (or environmental intervention), a natural developmental phenomena can take place.

Twin studies have also offered insights into the development of temperament and emotion regulation. Goldsmith and colleagues examined infant twins on measures of temperament, behavioral inhibition, and responses to strangers. His studies demonstrated that a significant proportion of variation in early temperament can be attributed to genetic factors. Thus, genes may influence an infant's shyness or soothability. These scientific developments provided convincing evidence that infants were not born *tabula rasa* (or "blank slates"); rather, some significant amount of emotion and behavior can be accounted for by genes.

One of the most significant advances in understanding the causes of schizophrenia originated from the findings of twin studies. In the early 20th century, a predominant etiological theory of schizophrenia placed the blame for the development of this psychosis on poor parenting. Twin studies by Irving Gottesman demonstrated that, contrary to the importance assigned to family environment, schizophrenia is strongly influenced by heredity. The information gleaned from such twin research has led to shifts in how schizophrenia is treated and studied, including providing the rationale behind the push to identify candidate genes influencing schizophrenia's development.

The Future of Twin Studies

Twin research remains a viable natural experiment that helps to elucidate the effects of genes and environments. The application of state-of-the art scientific methods to the area of twin studies (including brain neuroimaging techniques and molecular genetics) will offer exciting new opportunities to understand how genes and environments combine to influence behavioral attributes.

SUMMARY

Twin studies provide a useful natural experiment to evaluate the degree to which genetic and environmental influences determine variability in a given trait. Life-span studies of twins have offered specific insights into normal and abnormal developmental processes, ranging from the development of stair-climbing to the emergence of alcohol misuse and schizophrenia. Results of twin studies are used to guide research into the development of a broad array of psychological attributes.

—*Serena King and William G. Iacono*

See also Multiple Births, Twins

Further Readings and References

International Society for Twin Studies, http://www.ists .qimr.edu.au

McGue, M. (1994). Behavioral genetic models of alcoholism. In K. Leonard (Ed.), *Psychological theories of drinking and alcoholism* (pp. 372–421). New York: Guilford.

Plomin, R., DeFries, J. C., McClearn, G. E., & McGuffin, P. (2001). *Behavioral genetics* (4th ed.). New York: Worth.

Scarr, S., & McCartney, K. (1983). How people make their own environments: A theory of genotype environment effects. *Child Development, 54*(2), 424–435.

TWINS

Twins are a biological fact. As such, they occur in at least two different ways. One pattern involves one egg, fertilized by one sperm, which splits sometime during the first fourteen days after fertilization, thus producing *monozygotic* (uniovular) or "identical" twins. These twins have the same genetic make-up as each other and are always the same sex, being both boys or both girls.

The other twin pattern involves two eggs, each egg fertilized by a separate sperm. Eventually they produce *dizygotic* (binovular) or "fraternal" or "nonidentical" twins. Nonidentical twins may either be of the same sex, that is, two boys or two girls, or unlike sex pairs, that is, a boy and a girl. Genetically, either type of nonidentical twin, same sex or unlike sex pairs, are genetically as similar as any other two siblings. This genetic relationship can range from 25% to 75% of genetic similarity.

There are also some rarer types of twins. These categories include: mirror-image twins, who are identical twins; polar body twins, called half-identical twins; or conjoined (Siamese) twins, who are identical twins.

With the increasing use of ultrasound scans, twins have been detected early in a pregnancy but have "vanished" according to subsequent ultrasounds. This phenomenon has been termed the vanishing twin syndrome.

The incidence of identical twins has remained more or less constant; this constancy applies to most cultures over any given time period. Roughly about one third of all twins are identical and two thirds of all twins are fraternal.

In both the United States and the United Kingdom, the probability of having twins as of 1999/2000 is roughly 1 in 35 pregnancies. The chances of having twins in these two countries has risen recently mainly due to older mothers having babies and the increasing use of fertility treatments.

Rates of fraternal twins vary in different countries, with African countries producing the highest rates and Asian countries the lowest rates of twinning.

MYTHS ABOUT TWINS

Myths about twins picture twins as being both positive and negative, harmonious and rivalrous, happy and unhappy, divine and human. Throughout the world's cultures, myths identify twins as gods who are deified men or women (such as in North and South American cultures). Other twin myths are foundation myths such as in the Biblical story of Jacob and Esau, indicating that two nations are to be born, or the most famous myth about the founding of Rome by twins Romulus and Remus.

Still other myths treat the issue of double paternity; that is, one twin is depicted as the child of a human father while the other twin has a different and divine father. One version of the *Dioscuri*, Castor and Pollux, otherwise known to us as the Heavenly Twins constellation, Gemini, falls into this group. Some myths attempt to provide answers to the culturally unanswerable. Some North American indigenous peoples, such as the Mohave, believe twins function as rainmakers; others believe that human twins are sent from heaven to bring both rain and fertility.

Thus the very many mythologies and cultures of the world contain quite a considerable number and diversity of myths about twins.

EXPLAINING TWIN BIRTH

The birth of twins occurs in all cultures of the world. In most, the appearance of twins itself is a matter of surprise, even shock, both for the parents and the community at large.

In more traditional, nonindustrial societies, the birth of twins often disrupted the structure of the family and the position of individuals within the family. Twins caused a disturbance to the normal order of things. Sometimes this even involved a potential threat to the social order, so that in some extreme cases one or both twins were faced with infanticide; occasionally, the mother also faced death or, at the very least, ostracism. In these societies, concern about the question of who actually fathered the twins and the ensuing anxiety about the real (or even the imagined) disruptions to the established social system were expressed.

In more industrialized societies, due to the intervention of hospital equipment such as scanners and the increasing use of fertility drugs, which are one of the main reasons for the recent increase in twins and higher multiples, dealing with twinship begins at a much earlier stage, although some parallels with nonindustrial societies can be made.

Attitudes toward twins in different societies are mixed: Whether positive, negative or even ambivalent, these attitudes have been and are currently complex and intense. These qualities of complexity and intensity may include feelings of disturbance, anxiety, and unease about identity, especially individual identity.

TWINS IN THE MEDIA

Twins have provided an endless source of fascination for writers over the centuries. Initially, the overwhelming focus of attention was on the comic potential of mistaken identity, especially for monozygotic or "identical" twins. Subsequently, however, writers began to explore stereotypical—opposite—characteristics of twins, such as moral opposites of good versus evil, or opposites of identity, like versus unlike, twins as same versus twins as fundamentally different. Fiction writers also used the double (or the *doppelganger*) in their writing.

Alongside questions of identity, twins have been used by writers to illustrate a range of human behavior associated with twinship. One ever-present theme of this type would be the closeness of twins, such as is found in Bruce Chatwin's famous novel *On the Black Hill*. Another example of the very strong bond thought to exist between twins is found in Thornton Wilder's *The Bridge of San Luis Rey*. In children's literature, we find *Sweet Valley Twins*, where identical twin girls look so much alike it is virtually impossible to tell them apart, but yet they are described as having very different personalities.

In films, twins have been used in general to illustrate and explore themes of personal, psychological, and social identity. Several look at mistaken identity and its consequences, such as in *The Parent Trap*; others explore the indelible effects of twinship, such as Jodie Foster's twin portrayal in *Nell*. But the very refreshing and recent expression of the dichotomy of twins is Ivan Reitman's *Twins* where Danny DeVito and Arnold Schwarznegger play twin brothers, causing the audience to think that they can't be twins because they do not look anything alike, let alone look identical!

Twins in the press fare somewhat differently. Articles often appear about famous twins and famous parents of twins, such as agony aunts Ann Landers and Abigail van Buren or parents of twins Mia Farrow or James Stewart. Other articles focus on the unusual nature of being a twin, exploring the possible psychic affinity between twins, especially looking at those twins who were separated for one reason or another early in their lives. The actual birth of twins and the subsequent parenting of twins forms another category, followed by articles explaining or exploring what it is actually like to be a twin. Finally there are articles revolving around science and nature, often using twins to measure intelligence.

UNIQUE RELATIONSHIPS AND CHARACTERISTICS

The bottom line for analyzing the unique relationship between twins must be the fact that unlike singletons, twins are two babies who are born more or less at the same time. This biological fact has consequences for the twins from the first prenatal stages of their lives, through the birth itself, and quite obviously for their subsequent development as children, as young people, and eventually as adults.

Scientists studying twins are currently debating about the role that genetics plays in relation to environment, also known as the nature versus nurture debate. Twins have been used to prove the greater influence of either nature or nurture on behavior, although more and more studies accept the interplay between the two (influences). This is vital for actually understanding the determinants of behavior of different sets of twins.

Knowing whether a twin is identical or fraternal is also vitally important for those scientists hoping to explain behavior and development by twin type. The most popular current method of *zygosity* determination (determining whether twins are fraternal or identical) is by DNA testing; a swab of cheek cells from each twin will determine whether they are identical or not.

Much twin research has focused on the different types of twins, hoping to establish relationships concerning the role that genetics plays. Other social scientists are concentrating on the role that environment plays, but they are now not assuming that twins necessarily share the same environment, any more that any other sibling in a family shares the same environment. In other words, each twin has another person (his or her twin) directly or immediately in their environment, virtually from the moment of conception. And this other person, the twin, modifies and determines the environment in which they both live. They are defined and often treated as twins, although like other siblings they also face varying environments due to gender differences, positions in the family, relation to parents, and so on. Nonetheless, they share the "twin factor."

SUMMARY

Twins are different, distinct, special, and fascinating. They have been studied, analyzed, and written about for a long time in all cultures, yet there is still a great deal to learn both about twins and from twins.

—*Elizabeth A. Stewart*

See also Fraternal Twins, Identical Twins

Further Readings and References

Bryan, E. (1995). *Twins, triplets and more: Their nature, development and care.* London: The Multiple Births Foundation.

Farmer, P. (1996). *Two or the book of twins and doubles.* London: Virago Press.

Freidrich, E., & Rowland, C. (1990). *The parenting guide to raising twins.* New York: St. Martin's Press.

Multiple Births Association, http://www.mbf.org

National Organisation of Mothers of Twins Clubs, http://www.nomotc.org

Sandbank, A. C. (1999). *Twin and triplet psychology.* London: Routledge.

Siegel, N. (2000). *Entwined lives: Twins and what they tell us about human behavior.* New York: Plume.

Stewart, E. A. (2003). *Exploring twins: Towards a social analysis of twinship.* New York: St. Martin's Press.

Twins and Multiple Births Association, http://www.tamba.org

U

Utopianism

Without the Utopias of other times, men would still live in caves, miserable and naked. It was Utopians who traced the lines of the first city.... Out of generous dreams come beneficial realities. Utopia is the principle of all progress, and the essay into a better future.

—Anatole France

ULTRASOUND

The use of ultrasound in medical diagnosis had its beginnings as *sonar* (sound and navigation ranging) used in the First World War by submarines for underwater navigation. Ultrasound generation and detection was based on the use of a piezoelectric crystal such as quartz or PZT (lead zirconate titanate) whose inherent composition allowed it to convert electric to mechanical energy, as well as the reverse. An electrical impulse was used to excite the crystal, which generated a wave of high-frequency sound (above 1 million cycles per second, or 1 megahertz) that traveled through any solid or fluid medium but not through air. When this pulse wave encountered a material of differing density, some of the energy would pass into it and some would be reflected back to the emitting crystal. If the crystal was kept inactive, it would detect the returning pulse wave and would convert this mechanical vibration into an electrical impulse that would be displayed on a monitor or oscilloscope.

In the early 1940s, the piezoelectric effect was used to detect flaws in metal. Using one of these early systems, Karl Theodore Dussik, a neurologist at the University of Vienna, detected some brain tumors. In Denver, Joseph Holmes, a kidney specialist and acting director of Medical Research, had his engineers build the first two-dimensional ultrasound scanner in 1951. The patient was placed in a water bath while the ultrasound probe moved around the abdomen. This unit was called the Somascope and was featured in the Medicine section of *Life* magazine in 1954.

Ian Donald, a professor of Obstetrics and Gynecology in Glasgow, saw the potential of this technique and first reported on its use in women to detect masses and to differentiate solid from fluid-filled or cystic masses. With the help of some engineers, he built an ultrasound scanner that did not require placing the patient in a water bath, thereby making the technique much more accessible. The case that changed his life was that of a woman who had been diagnosed with a large abdominal mass thought to be an inoperable tumor. Using ultrasound, he saw that the mass was a simple fluid-filled ovarian cyst, promptly removed it, and "saved" her life. Ian Donald was a remarkable individual with whom I had the privilege of studying in the early 1970s. He was not only a leading obstetrician and researcher but also an accomplished painter, pianist, scientific writer, and sailor, all the while suffering heart failure from a leaking mitral valve.

Ultrasound has been used during pregnancy routinely since the late 1970s. It can visualize the pregnancy

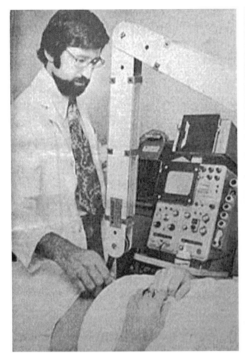

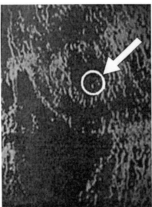

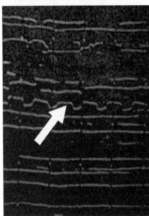

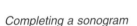

Completing a sonogram

from 5 to 40 weeks of gestation; determine the correct fetal age by measuring the fetus' length, head, abdomen, and legs; and monitor fetal growth. The fetus can be examined using ultrasound, and most abnormalities in all of its vital organs can be detected. It can detect multiple pregnancies and ectopic pregnancies. The position of the placenta is also routinely examined by ultrasound during pregnancy.

Ultrasound is used in more than 75% of pregnant women to accurately establish the age of the fetus and to detect abnormalities in the fetus, amniotic fluid, and placenta. Ultrasound scanners are found in most hospitals around the world and in many obstetricians' offices.

An ultrasound scanner today is basically a computer, and as computers get smaller and faster, so too does the scanner. It is now capable of producing stunning three-dimensional images. Finally, even though the technology is sophisticated, it requires a trained operator, technologist, and physician to accurately interpret the information collected.

—*Edward A. Lyons*

Further Readings and References

Rumack, C. M., Wilson, S., & Charboneau, W. (2004). *Diagnostic ultrasound.* New York: Elsevier Mosby.

Woo, J. S. K. (n.d.). A short history of the development of ultrasound in obstetrics and gynecology. Retrieved from http://www.ob-ultrasound .net/history1.html

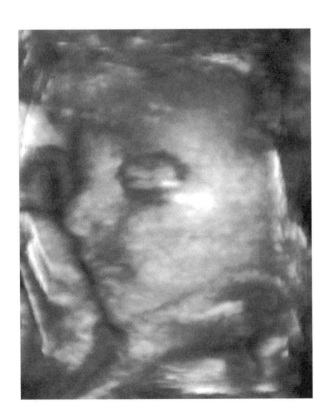

UNIVERSAL GRAMMAR

The definition of universal grammar has evolved considerably since first it was postulated and, moreover, since the 1940s, when it became a specific object of modern linguistic research. It is associated with work in generative grammar and it is based on the idea that certain aspects of syntactic structure are universal. Universal grammar consists of a set of atomic grammatical categories and relations that are the building blocks of the particular grammars of all human languages, over which syntactic structures and constraints on those structures are defined. A universal grammar would suggest that all languages possess the same set of categories and relations and that in order to communicate through language, speakers make infinite use of finite means, an idea that Wilhelm von Humboldt suggested in the 1830s. From this perspective, a grammar must contain a finite system of rules that generates infinitely many deep and surface structures, appropriately related. It must also contain rules that relate these abstract structures to certain representations of sound and meaning—representations that, presumably, are constituted of elements that belong to universal phonetics and universal semantics, respectively.

This concept of grammatical structure is an elaboration of Humboldt's ideas but harkens back to earlier efforts. In *Cartesian Linguistics*, Noam Chomsky traces precursory work related to UG in the writings of Panini, Plato, and both rationalist and romantic philosophers, such as René Descartes (1647), Claude Faure Vaugelas (1647), Cesar Chesneau DuMarsais (1729), Denis Diderot (1751), James Beattie (1788), and Wilhelm von Humboldt (1836). Chomsky focuses in particular on early efforts by the 17th-century Port Royal grammarians, whose rationalist approach to language and language universals was based on the idea that humans in the "civilized world" share a common thought structure. Moreover, he traces the conception of linguistic structure that marked the origins of modern syntactic theory to Lancelot and Arnaud's 1660 Port Royal work, *Grammaire generale et raisonnee*, which postulated a link between the natural order of thought and the ordering of words. Much of what came to be known as modern linguistics in the 20th century belied philosophy in favor of behaviorist currents and various structuralist approaches that on the one hand narrowed this domain of inquiry, while on the other hand providing an expanded database that came to be critical for those willing to use it in a return to traditional concerns. The rejection of historical approaches occurred in part because of the newfound optimism, inspired by contemporary scientific methods and by the "new methods" in linguistics, about the possibilities for making real advances in our understanding of how language functions. In the background of this optimism lie the great discoveries in mathematics and physics, the promise of a new computer and telecommunications industry, the political requirements for enhanced language research, and the concomitant funding offered for such endeavors by the American government, particularly after 1939.

Consistent with earlier work on universals, Universal Grammar came to refer to aspects of the grammatical structure that form the makeup of grammars of all "natural languages." According to Chomsky's early work, there are two keys to the understanding of human language, universal grammar and deep structure, the former described as a sort of metatheory, the latter a technical term pertaining to the particular grammar and designating a precise stage in the derivation of a sentence. To advance our understanding of both, his early goals were threefold: first, to determine what is the nature of the intuitive, unconscious knowledge that permits the speaker to use his or her language; second, to construct an explanatory theory; and third, to consider the general principles of language as the properties of a biologically given system that underlies the acquisition of language.

Chomsky enters the scene in the 1940s, at the height of the optimism, and in a project that both furthered and challenged this work, he wrote an undergraduate thesis called "Morphophonomenics of Modern Hebrew," later expanded to a master's thesis with the same title in 1951. That work was a "generative grammar" in the contemporary sense because it contained a rudimentary generative syntax. Chomsky claims it as the first example thereof, but also recalls classical precedents, including Panini's grammar of Sanskrit and, at the level of morphology and phonology, Leonard Bloomfield's *Menomini Morphophonemics*, published only a few years earlier. The goal of this work was an attempt to demonstrate that the generative grammar presented was the simplest possible grammar in a well-defined technical sense: namely, given a certain framework for the formulation of rules and a precise definition of "simplicity," the grammar was "locally optimal" in the sense that any interchange of order of rules would lead to a less simple grammar. This work was undertaken for Zellig Harris, who at that time was involved in a related, but differently focused, problem of transformations in a structuralist paradigm. Chomsky's early sense was that the discovery procedures and the methods employed by structural linguists such as Zellig Harris were in principle correct, and that only some refinements were necessary to make them work, in the sense of being able to produce a correct grammar with infinite descriptive scope from a finite corpus of the language.

What irked Chomsky early on, however, was Harris's deferring to behaviorist and empiricist models, which he resisted, on the basis of his "Cartesian" belief that one should assume that the general form of the resulting system of knowledge should be given in advance. For Chomsky, the system required to produce human language could not be constructed gradually, step by step, by induction, segmentation and classification, generalization and abstraction, and so on. This was different for Zellig Harris, for whom the goal was to use certain "transformations" to "normalize" the discourse, to transform complex sentences into uniform simple structures to which the methods of structural linguistics might apply: segmentation of sequences, substitution of elements, classification, and so on, all of which suggested that transformations were simply systematic relations between sentences and surface structures. If Harris's assumptions were right, then obviously machines could play a role in such a project, and indeed he believed, along with many others, that computers were going to permit the automation of discovery procedures in linguistics. The idea would be to present a corpus of material to the computer so that it would work out the grammar of the text, on the assumption that the taxonomic procedures of analysis that had been developed were in essence sufficient and adequate to determine grammatical structure. It was quite generally supposed within such circles that B. F. Skinner's theory of behavior approached adequacy, and that the notions developed within the theory of communication furnished a general framework for the study of language within this structuralist paradigm. Chomsky rejected the empiricism of this model, so that even in his earliest work, a transformation is not a relation between two sets of sentences, or between two surface structures; it is a rule within a system of rules that assigns structural descriptions to an infinite class of sentences. In the derivation of a particular sentence, a transformational rule applies to an abstract representation of this sentence and transforms it into another abstract representation. The initial representation is the so-called *deep structure*, which is transformed step by step into terminal (or surface) structure through transformational rules. These surface structures take on a particular phonological form and emerge as the sentences one actually hears.

With Chomsky, therefore, a shift in scientific paradigms in the work of linguistics occurs that works on universal grammar away from the ambitions of mathematics, structuralism, empiricism, and behaviorism and toward biology and a branch of cognitive psychology wherein the basic problem is posed by the human capacity to acquire a natural language, something that he insisted we should see as remarkable, with regard both to what the child experiences and to what he or she acquires. What the child acquires is an indefinitely extensive creative capacity to produce and to understand an open-ended set of sentences that he or she has never heard before. To explain the gross disproportion between what is acquired (in the form of competence) and what is experienced (in the form of speech), Chomsky posited a strongly constrained, internal, innate mechanism that, when triggered by the experience of speech, builds a cognitive structure, a grammar of the language, within limits set by very specialized schemas. Because any child can learn naturally any human language, these schemas had to be universal; thus, when Chomsky referred to the properties of the innate mechanism, he indicated that each of us possesses, indeed knows, the principles of a universal grammar. What exactly is involved in the innate component, what principles the language-acquisition device is armed with, are the technical matters that make reading Chomsky's work so complex; however, in terms of overall objectives, the more general question is to describe their presence, which he did through the terminology of unconscious, innate *knowledge* that, once again, is his way of connecting his theories with those rationalist thinkers of the 17th century.

Therefore, from the early 1960s, the universal grammar objective was to abstract general principles from the complex rule systems devised for particular languages, leaving rules that are simple, constrained in their operations by underlying principles. By the mid-1970s, many particular aspects of the theory had changed, notably on the matter of the relations between syntax and semantics, leading Chomsky to abandon the "standard" theory of *Aspects of the Theory of Syntax* (1965), by which semantic interpretation was applied to deep structure, and instead to apply semantic interpretation to surface structure. He also abandoned his use of the term *deep structure* for those initial abstract base sentences to which the transformations are applied because not only these base sentences, but also processes applied at the level of surface structure, were deemed "deep" in the sense that they express important and hidden human powers. This is the shift that is familiar to those who have read more recent work by Chomsky because it insists on the power of linguistic theory to reveal the depth of the human mind. It implies an uncovering of lower, but continuously related, levels of human thought, further questioning the shallower and more mechanical view of the empiricist outlook, which incidentally can be easily associated with a denial that there is a human nature, an idea that perhaps had currency for its ability to be employed for manipulative and authoritarian conceptions of purposes, one of the few links between language and politics in Chomsky's work.

As far as methodology was concerned, in Chomsky's early universal grammar work, much effort was exerted to extract and describe a great number of rules, and no distinction between rules and conditions of rules was made at this stage; by the 1970s, Chomsky was trying to do the opposite, to limit the expressive power of the rules. Thus, there is considerable evolution in the theory of universal grammar, even while there is consistency, as he himself notes in the Minimalist Program. Chomsky maintains some underlying factual assumptions that date back to his work in the 1950s, notably that there is a component of the human mind or brain dedicated to language and the language faculty, which interacts with other systems. He also maintains that performance systems are in part language specific (and hence are components of the language faculty) and that the cognitive system interacts with the performance systems by means of levels of linguistics representation. Thus, for the model, the cognitive system is deemed to interact with the articulatory-perceptual system and with the conceptual-intentional system through two interface levels—phonetic form at the articulatory-perceptual interface and logical form at the conceptual-intentional system—which links his work to earlier ideas about the relation of sound to meaning. What is new, and what has led to recent works such as Baker's *The Atoms of Language,* is the emphasis on principles and parameters, which holds that languages have no rules in anything like the familiar sense and no theoretically significant grammatical constructions except as taxonomic artifacts. There are universal principles and a finite array of options for how they apply (parameters), but no language-particular rules and no grammatical constructions of the traditional sort within or across languages. The resulting project aims to show that the apparent richness and diversity of linguistic phenomena is illusory and epiphenomenal, the result of interaction of fixed principles under slightly varying conditions. As Chomsky put it, these are the "new horizons in the study of languages and the mind"—new in emphasis, ancient in ambition.

—Robert F. Barsky

See also Chomsky, Noam; Language Development

Further Readings and References

Baker, M. C. (2002). *The atoms of language.* New York: Basic Books.

Barsky, R. F. (1997). *Noam Chomsky: A life of dissent.* Cambridge: MIT Press.

Chomsky, N. (1957). *Syntactic structures.* The Hague, Netherlands: Mouton.

Chomsky, N. (1959). Review of Skinner, *Verbal behaviour. Language, 35,* 26–58.

Chomsky, N. (1964). *Current issues in linguistic theory.* The Hague, Netherlands: Mouton.

Chomsky, N. (1964). *Language and information: Selected essays on the theory and application.* Reading, MA: Addison-Wesley; Jerusalem: The Jerusalem Academic Press.

Chomsky, N. (1965). *Aspects of the theory of syntax.* Cambridge: MIT Press.

Chomsky, N. (1966). *Cartesian linguistics: A chapter in the history of rationalist thought.* New York: Harper and Row.

Chomsky, N. (1968). *Language and mind.* New York: Pantheon.

Chomsky, N. (1971). *Problems of knowledge and freedom: The Russell lectures.* New York: Pantheon.

Chomsky, N. (1971). Review of Skinner, *Beyond freedom and dignity. New York Review of Books,* December 30.

Chomsky, N. (1972). *Studies on semantics in generative grammar.* The Hague, Netherlands: Mouton.

Chomsky, N. (1975). *Logical structure of linguistic theory.* New York: Plenum.

Chomsky, N. (1980). *Rules and representations.* New York: Columbia University Press.

Chomsky, N. (1981). *Lectures on government and binding: The Písa lectures.* Dordrecht, Netherlands: Foris. (Corrected edition, 1982)

Chomsky, N. (1982). *The generative enterprise.* Dordrecht, Netherlands: Foris.

Chomsky, N. (1984). *Modular approaches to the study of the mind.* Distinguished Graduate Research Lecture Series I, 1980. Berkeley: California State University Press.

Chomsky, N. (1986). *Barriers.* Cambridge: MIT Press.

Chomsky, N. (1986). *Knowledge of language: Its nature, origin and use.* New York: Praeger.

Chomsky, N. (1987). *Generative grammar: Its basis, development and prospects.* Kyoto, Japan: Kyoto University of Foreign Studies.

Chomsky, N. (1995). *The minimalist program.* Cambridge: MIT Press.

Noam Chomsky: A Life of Dissent, http://cognet.mit.edu/library/books/chomsky/chomsky/

U.S. BUREAU OF THE CENSUS

The U.S. Census Bureau, also known as the U.S. Bureau of the Census, has existed as a separate agency since 1903. The primary task emanates from the constitutional mandate for the taking of a census every 10 years for purposes of apportioning political representation among the states according to the distribution of the population. Just as dramatic changes occurred over time in implementing this count, as technologies evolved from hand calculations and early tabulating machines to efficient, high-capacity computers and the population grew and diversified, according to the Census Bureau, the mission has become "to be the preeminent collector and provider of timely, relevant and quality data about the people and economy of the United States. We will succeed by valuing our employees, innovating in our work, and responding to our customers." The crucial topics are people, housing, business, and governments, and the major resource is the decennial census of population and housing, although this leading statistical agency is increasingly central for other sources (surveys, administrative statistics, and other information).

The U.S. Census has been taken 22 times. Early census information appears not only in yellowed volumes but also online for 1790 to 1870, as does 1990 and 2000 census information. These statistics are the population's historical record and appear in compilations (e.g., Statistical Abstracts) and comprehensive reviews, other publications, and the integrated public-use microdata sets from the University of Minnesota. As a federal agency pioneering electronic dissemination of reports in the past decade, the Census Bureau releases data promptly, and this empowers data users with easy access and capabilities. The decennial censuses account for core activities to gather data on the demographic, social, and economic characteristics of the U.S. population that are reported in government publications, scholarly articles, and census monographs supported by the Russell Sage Foundation, which help explain changes during the decade. The Census Bureau staff implements other federal surveys that examine labor force trends, health status, and program participation, and one of these, the Current Population Survey, provides the basis for annual poverty and income measures.

The first census in the new millennium has been noted as the best census ever, and the 2000 census may also have been the last census that involved collection of detailed characteristics. The usual positive correlation of economic development with statistical infrastructure simply may not be applicable for the United States confronted with considerable capabilities for gathering statistics on a complex population given the escalating costs of that effort. The 2010 census is to be the reengineered census, with the American Community Survey regarded as the way to collect detailed characteristics nationally on a continuous basis.

Censuses have historically compensated for serious gaps in statistical systems, and regular counts are especially valuable, with 10s of millions of migrants in a world on the move. From about 2 million in 1950, the U.S. Hispanic population has grown quickly to 35 million in 2000, particularly affecting states and metropolitan areas of high immigration of the West and South. Demographers are intrigued not only by the classical questions of changing composition and changing propensity but also by quantifying population change. After the 2000 U.S. Census count of 281.4 million was higher than expected, several studies concluded recent unauthorized immigration in the 1990s was higher than officially allowed. Thus, census demographers have been able to benchmark the population estimates with more "correct" components of population change.

The overall population growth as a consequence of fertility and immigration of Asians, Latinos, and others means the United States is the only developed nation projected in the top 20 countries by 2050. Amnesty programs for unauthorized residents and agricultural workers in the late 1990s transformed the U.S. Mexican population as to lawful presence, unauthorized migration continued despite intensified enforcement at the southern border, and authorized immigration continued, especially of family members, enhancing integration within American places and institutions. Scholars are building a collection of new immigrant and new ethnicity studies on the basis of statistical portraits from census and surveys in conjunction with rich, qualitative studies.

—*Karen A. Woodrow-Lafield*

Further Readings and References

Bean, F. D., Corona R., Tuiran R., Woodrow-Lafield K. A., & Van Hook J. (2001). Circular, invisible, and ambiguous migrants: Components of difference in estimates of the number of unauthorized Mexican migrants in the United States. *Demography, 38*(3), 411–422.

Department of Economic and Social Affairs Population Division, http://www.unpopulation.org

Hobbs, F., & Stoops N. (2002). *Demographic trends in the 20th century*. Census 2000 Special Reports. Series CENSR-4. Washington, DC: U.S. Government Printing Office.

U.S. Census Bureau, http://www.census.gov

Woodrow-Lafield, K. A. (1995). *Potential sponsorship by IRCA-legalized immigrants.* Washington, DC: U.S. Commission on Immigration Reform.

Woodrow-Lafield, K. A. (2001). Implications of immigration for apportionment. *Population Research and Policy Review, 20*(4), 267–289.

UTOPIANISM

Utopian dreaming is not unique to one historical period but represents a theme that runs throughout human history. Although Thomas More coined the term *utopia* in 1516, utopian thought is evident in ancient texts and stories, including Greek and Roman mythology, Plato's *Republic*, the Hebrew account of the Garden of Eden, and Christian conceptions of "a transcendent heaven of splendor" (Pitzer, 1997, p. 4). Utopian scholars are loath to say that utopianism is part of "human nature," but it is probably accurate to say that all people dream of a better life, if not for themselves, at least for those who are wanting. As Sargent (1994) puts it, "At its root, then, utopianism is the result of the human propensity to dream while both asleep and awake" (p. 4).

Utopianism is evident not simply in literature but also in experimentation. Today, numerous utopian communities can be found around the world, some of them relatively well known and established. Although these communities share the goal of working toward a better world, their differences in religion, politics, economics, governmental structure, and lifestyle often outweigh their similarities. Examples of contemporary utopian communities, as described in 2000 in the Fellowship for Intentional Community's *Communities Directory*, include the following:

- Auroville, a community of more than 1,000 people in India, whose purpose is "to realize human unity"

- The Federation of Damanhur, founded in 1977 in Italy, with a current population of more than 400 people. "Since the very first day of its foundation, Damanhur has been engaged in creating a sustainable way of life."

- Findhorn Community, founded in 1962 in Scotland, which works toward "a joyful, loving and sustainable future on Earth"

- The Kibbutz movement in Israel, which traces its beginnings to 1910 and currently includes about 123,000 people in more than 250 kibbutzim. One group, Kibbutz Lotan, works to create a community based on Reform Zionist Jewish values "including equality, economic cooperation, living in harmony with the environment, mutual respect and the betterment of ourselves, our people and the world."

- The Farm community in the United States, formed in 1971, which is "a place where we can relate to each other and the natural environment in a sustainable way, draw upon the collective strength of the community, and contribute to the positive transformation of the world."

- The Twelve Tribes Network, founded in 1972, which is an international network of communities with a focus to serve God and "to love each other as our Master Yashua loved us, to love our Creator with all our heart, soul, mind and strength and to love our neighbors who live around us as we love ourselves."

- The Emissaries of Divine Light, founded in the 1940s, which is "a worldwide spiritual organization dedicated to the spiritual regeneration of humankind."

- Comunidad Los Horcones, in Mexico, which is a community inspired by B. F. Skinner's novel, *Walden Two*, and whose "basic objectives are to design a society where people cooperate for a common good, share property and reinforce egalitarian, pro-ecological and pacifist behaviors."

As Levitas wrote in 1990, "utopia expresses and explores what is desired; under certain conditions it also contains the hope that these desires may be met in reality, rather than merely in fantasy. The essential element in utopia is not hope but desire—the desire for a better way of being."

—*Deborah E. Altus*

Further Readings and References

Fellowship for Intentional Community. (2000). *Communities directory.* Rutledge, MO: Author.

Levitas, R. (1990). *The concept of utopia.* Syracuse, NY: Syracuse University.

Pitzer, D. (1997). *America's communal utopias.* Chapel Hill: University of North Carolina.

Sargent, L. T. (1994). The three faces of utopianism revisited. *Utopian Studies, 5*, 1–37.

Volunteering

Be of service. Whether you make yourself available to a friend or co-worker, or you make time every month to do volunteer work, there is nothing that harvests more of a feeling of empowerment than being of service to someone in need.

—Gillian Anderson

VACCINATION

Vaccination is a process that artificially confers immunity to an individual against a specific type of disease caused by infectious microorganisms (viruses, bacteria, fungi, or parasites). Vaccines work by using the body's ability to remember previous infections. When an individual becomes infected by an infectious organism for the first time, the immune system recognizes and then destroys it by mounting an immune response specific for that organism. Upon an individual's second exposure to the same microorganism, the immune system recognizes and eliminates it by mounting immune responses that occur more rapidly and are greater in magnitude than those induced on the first encounter. Thus, the infection will not develop to a severe level or to the disease stage. This ability to remember infections, called *immune memory*, allows people to become immune to a disease after they have caught it once. A vaccine simulates that first infection by exposing an individual to a particular microorganism or portions of that microorganism without causing infection and illness. There are several disease-causing microbes for which vaccines

exist. Thus, these diseases can be prevented. Some of the most common vaccine-preventable diseases are diphtheria, tetanus, pertussis, some forms of bacterial meningitis, pneumococcal pneumonia, measles, mumps, rubella, chickenpox, influenza, hepatitis A, hepatitis B, poliomyelitis, and rabies. However, there are still many diseases for which effective vaccines are not available. Some of these diseases are the acquired immunodeficiency syndrome (AIDS), malaria, and schistosomiasis.

Vaccines are made from either all or portions of the microorganism against which the vaccine protects. These portions of the microorganisms are called *antigens* and, in most cases, are proteins, glycoproteins, or polysaccharides. There are three traditional types of vaccines. *Inactivated vaccines* are made from organisms that have been killed in such a way that they still retain most of their original structure. Examples are the inactivated polio vaccine and the influenza vaccine. *Live-attenuated vaccines* are made of live organisms that have been weakened so that they replicate poorly in the human host and therefore do not cause disease. Examples are measles, rubella, and chickenpox vaccines. *Subunit vaccines* are made from only some portions of the organism. These often

1295

contain toxins that have been altered so that they are no longer dangerous, and are called *toxoids*, as, for example, the tetanus and the diphtheria vaccines. Other subunit vaccines contain recombinant protein antigens, as, for example, the hepatitis B vaccine. A particular class of subunit vaccines is represented by conjugate vaccines, which consist of bacterial polysaccharides linked to protein carriers. An example is the *Haemophilus influenzae* type B vaccine.

Several types of vaccines are still in the experimental stages and will be part of a new generation of vaccines in the future. These include *DNA vaccines*, which use the gene encoding a particular protein from an organism, and *recombinant vector vaccines*, which use an attenuated virus or bacterium to introduce a gene from another microorganism into the host, thus eliciting an immune response against the antigen encoded by that gene. A third type of experimental vaccine is one that does not target microorganisms, but rather is designed to aid in the elimination of cancer cells. This type of vaccine, termed *dendritic cell vaccine*, relies on the host's own dendritic cells, a category of white blood cells responsible for the activation of T lymphocytes, to recognize cancer cells and therefore contribute to the mechanisms necessary for their elimination.

Vaccine efficacy is usually improved through the use of adjuvants. These include natural or synthetic compounds used in vaccine formulations that aid in enhancing the immune response to vaccines. Although there are hundreds of compounds being evaluated as vaccine adjuvants, the alum (aluminum hydroxide) adjuvant, first described in 1926, remains the only one used in human vaccines licensed in the United States. Vaccine efficacy is also improved by giving recurrent doses of a vaccine. This practice, called *boosting*, is done to allow the immune system to remember previous vaccinations by exposing it to the vaccine more than once, and therefore to produce stronger memory immune responses that are effective for an extended period of time.

The U.S. Food and Drug Administration (FDA) requires extensive research and testing to ensure vaccine safety and efficacy. Before a vaccine can be licensed for general use, preclinical studies must take place, usually in the form of laboratory and animal testing. Researchers test candidate vaccines using cell cultures and animals such as mice, rabbits, guinea pigs, or monkeys. If the vaccine is successful in these preclinical studies, it can go on to be tested in humans. Human studies involve a series of clinical trials consisting of four phases. Phase I studies enroll up to 20 people and primarily test for safety. Phase II studies involve 50 to several hundred people. These studies continue to test for safety and try to determine the best dosage and gather preliminary data on a vaccine's effectiveness. Phase III studies involve thousands of people and are designed for thorough testing of vaccine efficacy. Finally, phase IV studies are conducted to test for rare or delayed adverse reactions that might not have been detected in the smaller studies leading to licensure.

An important goal in vaccine efficacy is to protect an entire community against disease. Individuals who are vaccinated have antibodies and immune cells against a disease-causing organism, so they are much less likely to become infected and transmit that organism to others. This allows individuals who have not been vaccinated or whose vaccines are not fully effective to be protected. This concept is known as *herd immunity*. As the percentage of vaccinated individuals increases, the rate of herd immunity increases.

Since the conception of vaccines, their use has been strongly debated. Several literature reports claim that vaccines have failed and have sometimes caused adverse reactions. In 1998, the American Medical Association reported that measles, a typical childhood disease, is becoming more prevalent among adults as the immune response to the vaccine eventually wears off. The inefficacy of the whole-cell pertussis vaccine was demonstrated when the Centers for Disease Control and Prevention (CDC) released reports that, in 1993, pertussis was at the highest levels since 1976. The failure of manufacturers to sometimes do sufficient research before releasing a product became evident when in 1999 the FDA cancelled use of the rotavirus vaccine almost 1 year from the day it was released. This vaccine protected children against the leading cause of childhood diarrhea but resulted in a dangerous bowel obstruction in infants. Incidents such as seizures, brain damage, ataxia, aseptic meningitis, paralysis, learning difficulties, and deaths have been documented within days or weeks following certain vaccinations. In 1986, the federal government established the National Vaccine Injury Compensation Program (NVICP) to compensate those who suffer from adverse effects of vaccines. Since that time, more than $1 billion has been paid in injury awards to these individuals.

Another concern regarding vaccines relates to the chemicals that are used in the manufacturing process. Chemicals such as formalin and thimerosal are often used as preservatives and bactericidals in vaccines, whereas aluminum salts are commonly used as adjuvants. There is concern about the exposure to these chemicals, which may be toxic. Although studies indicate that the levels of chemicals used as preservatives in manufacturing vaccines are within a safe range, the CDC, FDA, Academy of Pediatrics, and Public Health Service have recognized this as a legitimate concern. As a result, the FDA has encouraged pharmaceutical companies to manufacture single-dose vials of the vaccines without thimerosal, formalin, or other chemicals.

Despite reports of adverse reactions linked to vaccines and the chemicals used in the manufacturing process, statistics show that the numbers of such reports are extremely low compared to the number of children vaccinated each year. Very few reports have shown definitive evidence linking vaccines to all adverse effects. Illness occurring after a vaccination is regarded as an adverse effect of that vaccine, although the exact cause may be unknown. Further studies are needed to document evidence of vaccines causing adverse reactions.

In the early 20th century, infectious diseases were widely prevalent and had an enormous toll on the population because few effective treatment and preventive measures existed. Since then, substantial achievements have been made in the control of many vaccine-preventable diseases in many countries. Smallpox, which once caused rampant epidemics, was officially eradicated in 1980 as a result of the World Health Organization (WHO) mass vaccination campaign. Poliomyelitis and measles are other infectious diseases targeted for eradication. The rate of occurrence of vaccine-preventable diseases has dramatically decreased in the past decades. The use of vaccines is one of the few approaches that can prevent a disease from occurring, rather than attempting to cure it after it has developed. In general, the risks for adverse effects to vaccines are considered insignificant compared with the benefits of vaccination. According to the CDC, vaccination rates are at an all-time high, and occurrences of childhood diseases are at an all-time low. Thus, although few concerns exist, it is clear that vaccine benefits outweigh the risks.

—*Roberta Attanasio and Feda Masseoud*

Further Readings and References

Centers for Disease Control and Prevention, http://www.cdc .gov

Levine, M. M., Kaper, J. B., Rappuoli, R., Liu, M. A., & Good, M. F. (Eds.). (2004). *New generation vaccines*. New York: Marcel Dekker.

Muraskin, W. A. (Ed.). (1998). *The politics of international health: The children's vaccine initiative and the struggle to develop vaccines for the third world*. Albany: State University of New York Press.

Offit, P. A., & Bell, M. L. (Eds.). (1999). *Vaccines: What every parent should know*. New York: IDG Books.

Paoletti, L. C., & McInnes, P. M. (Eds.). (1999). *Vaccines, from concept to clinic: A guide to the development and clinical testing of vaccines for human use*. Boca Raton, FL: CRC Press.

Stratton, K. R., Durch, J. S., & Lawrence R. S. (Eds.). (2000). *Vaccines for the 21st century: A tool for decisionmaking*. Washington, DC: National Academy Press.

Understanding Vaccines (NIAID & NIH), http://www.niaid .nih.gov/publications/vaccine/pdf/undvacc.pdf

World Health Organization, http://www.who.org

VALIDITY

Validity refers to the extent to which a test measures the construct it purports to measure. Essentially, validity has to do with the meaningfulness and usefulness of the specific inferences made from test scores. For example, regarding a measure of assertiveness, the question of its validity would be whether it actually measures assertive behaviors. A truism is that a test can be reliable (i.e., stable and consistent) but not valid, but a test cannot be valid without first being reliable. The different types of validity include *face, content, criterion*, and *construct validity*.

Face validity is the simplest type of validity and refers to how well items on a test reveal the purpose or meaning of the test. For example, the test item "I feel sad all the time" has obvious face validity as an item measuring depression. The downside of test items with clear face validity is that they may be easily manipulated by respondents, either to minimize or exaggerate problems. Some psychometricians appreciate tests that lack face validity but still possess general validity. Test items that still measure what they purport to measure but lack face validity are harder for respondents to manipulate.

Content validity of a test refers to the adequacy of sampling of content across the construct being measured. Given the published literature on a particular construct, are all aspects of that concept represented by items on the test? Consider a psychological theory of depression that holds that depression is caused by negative thoughts about oneself, the world, and the future. A test of depression according to this model should include items that measure these three aspects. A strategy testmakers follow to achieve content validity is to summarize what experts claim to be the nature of a particular construct and then create test items to reflect the consensus. Items measuring a construct should appear in equal proportion to what the literature search reveals or what the experts claim about that particular construct.

Criterion validity (also called *predictive* or *concurrent validity*) refers to the comparison of scores on a test with some other external measure of performance that is theoretically related to the first measure. The relationship can be assessed by a simple correlation coefficient. Some psychometricians further divide criterion validity into predictive or concurrent validity. With predictive validity, the new test is given to a group of participants who are followed over time to see how well the original assessment predicts some important variable at a later point in time. In concurrent validity, a new test is given to a group of participants who complete other theoretically related measures concurrently (at the same time). How can a testmaker demonstrate concurrent validity if he or she is the first to create such a test? Unfortunately, this is not easy. The testmaker must use forms of validity other than concurrent validity if there are no other known measures of that construct. This problem is particularly troublesome for diagnostic measures in psychology. Because there are no definitive biological markers used for the diagnosis of any mental disorder, there are no objective gold standards for diagnostic accuracy. This fact makes it difficult to assess the criterion-related validity of any diagnostic test in psychology.

Construct validity refers to the extent to which a test captures a specific theoretical construct or trait. This requires a test to be anchored in a theory that delineates clearly the meaning of the construct, its uniqueness, and its relationship to other variables measuring similar domains. Psychometricians typically assess construct validity by giving other measures of a trait along with the new proposed measure of a trait and then testing prior hypothesized relationships among the measures. Such hypothesized relationships typically include a mixture of meaningful positive relationships and meaningful negative relationships.

—Daniel L. Segal and
Frederick L. Coolidge

See also Reliability

Further Readings and References

Coolidge, F. L. (2000). *Statistics: A gentle approach.* London: Sage.

Nunnally, J. C., & Bernstein, I. H. (1994). *Psychometric theory* (3rd ed.). New York: McGraw-Hill.

Segal, D. L., & Coolidge, F. L. (2003). Structured interviewing and DSM classification. In M. Hersen & S. Turner (Eds.), *Adult psychopathology and diagnosis* (4th ed., pp. 72–103). New York: Wiley.

Segal, D. L., & Coolidge, F. L. (2004). Objective assessment of personality and psychopathology: An overview. In M. Hilsenroth, D. L. Segal (Eds.), & M. Herson (Ed.-in-Chief), *Comprehensive handbook of psychological assessment, Vol. 2. Personality assessment* (pp. 3–13). New York: Wiley.

Tabachnick, B. G., & Fidell, L. S. (2001). *Using multivariate statistics* (4th ed.). Needham Heights, MA: Allyn & Bacon.

VERY LOW BIRTH WEIGHT (VLBW)

The birth of a newborn infant is a joyous event, but for many families, the reality of an extremely premature baby can be sudden and unexpected. Recent changes in prenatal care practices have enabled the survival of many infants that would have otherwise died after birth. Very low birth weight (VLBW) is part of a larger category of low birth weight. In 1950, the World Health Organization adopted the figure of less than 2,500 grams (5 lb., 8 oz.) as a universal cutoff to determine low-birth-weight status. Within this definition, very-low-birth-weight cutoffs were determined at weights less than 1,500 grams (3 lb., 4 oz.), and extremely low-birth-weight was defined as less than 750 grams (less than 2 lb.). VLBW infants are all born preterm (less than 37 weeks' gestational age) and are likely to experience varying degrees of intrauterine growth failure. Today, VLBW children constitute 1.5% of all births in the United States and less than 15% of low-birth-weight births. Racial differences are apparent within this range: 1.2% of white infants and 3.1% of black infants are born at VLBW.

SURVIVAL AND TREATMENT

VLBW is a natural result of preterm delivery, describing babies born chronologically too soon, and is defined as a live-born infant born before the end of the 37th week of gestation (compared with full-term gestation of 40–42 weeks). Gestational age is a predictor of survival, and even a few days may make the difference between survival and death. For example, very few 22-week-old babies have survived. About 50% of 23-week-old babies and 75% of 24-week-old babies given intensive care survive. At 25 weeks' gestation and beyond, although much risk still remains, the chances that a baby will survive and be healthy in the long run are better.

Table 1 shows outcomes based on information obtained from babies less than 29 weeks' gestation born in 1996 in 50 neonatal intensive care units. This table contains information on the survival rate, short-term complications, and treatments, highlighting the importance of gestational age to health outcomes.

An individual baby's chances of surviving depend on four factors: (1) the time into that week (a baby barely 23 weeks' gestation is less likely to do well than a baby almost 24 weeks); (2) the baby's gender (girls tend to do better than boys); (3) multiple pregnancy (singletons tend to do better than individual babies from multiple pregnancies); and (4) whether there was time before birth to give steroid shots to the mother, which helps the baby's chance of surviving and avoiding severe brain bleeding. Depending on these factors, estimates for an individual baby's chances for survival can be anywhere from 25% to 75%.

For babies as small as 500 and 600 grams born at about 24 weeks' gestation, newborn intensive care can currently improve survival. Typically, intensive care may be reconsidered after the first 3 days, when breathing and blood pressure problems are usually resolving and the first brain ultrasound has been reviewed. Most extremely premature babies who survive have at least some degree of handicap. The problems related to the brain are by far the most important because brain injuries often affect uniquely human traits and characteristics, and because brain injuries cannot heal themselves. There is much medical uncertainty of decisions about instituting intensive care in very preterm infants, thus causing difficult ethical decisions for anxious parents.

COMPLICATIONS AND RISKS

Health outcomes are often more favorable when a baby has minimal difficulty with immature lungs, blood pressure, infections, and other problems that can result from an extremely premature birth. Unfortunately, an additional complication is the problem of severe bleeding into the brain, which happens to some extremely premature babies. Small amounts of bleeding in the brain can have little or no effect on a baby, whereas severe bleeding in the brain often cause significant permanent handicaps. When severe bleeding occurs, it almost always happens in the first 3 days after birth. If no severe bleeding is seen, a major hurdle has been successfully cleared. If severe bleeding is seen, the possibility of surgeries for hydrocephalus (excessive fluid accumulation within the brain) and cerebral palsy increases. There is also a greater likelihood that the child will develop serious disorders, including developmental delays, seizures, and learning disabilities.

Several additional health complications are possible, such as retinopathy of prematurity (ROP), an abnormal growth of blood vessels in the retina. ROP occurs because the vascular system in the baby's eye hasn't fully developed. Many cases of ROP disappear on their own, but sometimes the condition leads to scarring. Some premature infants are also at risk for a potentially severe intestinal problem known as necrotizing enterocolitis (NEC). In the most serious cases, this condition can be life threatening. Premature babies are also at increased risk for sudden infant death syndrome (SIDS), a condition in which babies die in their sleep, which claims the lives of about 2,500 infants each year.

Not all preemies have medical or developmental problems. By 28 to 30 weeks' gestation, the risk for these complications is much lower. For babies born between 32 and 35 weeks, most medical problems are short term. Finally, infections in VLBW infants are also common and can cause a baby to become much sicker or die. Unfortunately, the ventilators that help babies breathe and keep them alive also damage the lungs. This can lead to problems with pneumonia through the early childhood years, requiring more time in the hospital.

DEVELOPMENTAL IMPLICATIONS

Of the possible handicaps, perhaps the most important is cerebral palsy, found to be 25 times more

Table 1　Outcomes From Babies Less Than 29 Weeks' Gestation Born in 1996

	Gestation in Weeks			
Estimates for survivors	23	24	25–26	27–28
Total no. of babies admitted to NICU in 1996 (% of babies who survive)	209 (18)	291 (52)	455 (81)	761 (91)
% with breathing problems needing asst ventilation	100	98	98	90
Average no. of days in hospital before going home	130	97	91	69
Significant abnormal brain scans %	23	20	19	10

common in children who had been VLBW infants. VLBW children experience combinations of various neurosensory, developmental, and health problems, which can worsen clinical and educational outcomes. For example, VLBW infants perform more poorly on extensive batteries of neuropsychological tests than do infants born either at higher weights or at term. As they age, there is an increased risk for behavioral problems, especially among boys, including conduct disorder, hyperactivity, and attentional weaknesses. Patterns of shyness, unassertiveness, and withdrawn behavior have also been documented.

School Age

Generally, predictions of future outcomes for VLBW infants depend on waiting until these children are at least 8 years old. Some cognitive skills may be more compromised than others in low-birth-weight children, and this may eventually be reflected in school performance and academic achievement. Levels of achievement in reading, spelling, and math are lower for VLBW children than for children born at full term. These problems are reflected in much higher proportions of low-birth-weight children than normal-birth-weight children who are enrolled in special education programs or repeat grades. About 50% of all low-birth-weight children are enrolled in special education programs.

Within the VLBW group, different classifications of handicap are evident and show different outcomes

for the conditions stated previously. VLBW children who are classified in the *moderate* handicap group have borderline intelligence that falls between low-normal and mildly mentally retarded and also often have mild cerebral palsy. With the cerebral palsy, children have permanent difficulties with muscle control, need physical therapy, and usually begin to walk much later than most children. Vision may be impaired even when using glasses. Most children in this group need special education in school. Many children in this group are not able to live independently as adults.

Children in the *severe* handicap group are mentally retarded or have severe cerebral palsy, usually to a degree that keeps them from ever walking without assistance. Children in this group also tend to have the most serious problems with their vision. Although blindness is quite rare, vision is often impaired enough to be a significant problem, even with the best possible glasses. Virtually all children in this group need special education in school, and most are not able to live independently as adults.

Family Considerations

Family issues can become part of the larger picture from the start, particularly when the birth is well-ahead of expectations. Poor parental understanding in the hospital can result from many interactions: poor communication techniques and lack of time in consultations, contradictory messages, parent denial, inexperience in terminology, unwillingness to ask questions, and the lack of opportunity to review the information given. Family-centered neonatal care has been created to empower parents with support, respect, and encouragement, thus enhancing parental strength and competence.

There is always grief when a baby is born extremely prematurely because, no matter how well things go thereafter, the dream of a full-term pregnancy and a healthy baby has been lost. When children grow up to have serious handicaps, it is hard to predict how the family will be affected. A seriously handicapped child can be a cherished member of one family, whereas another family may be torn apart by the experience. Other children in the family may feel neglected because of the greater attention a seriously handicapped child requires, but they may also learn important lessons in compassion. Having a child with many medical problems can also be a heavy strain on family finances. Even when the infant eventually develops normally, families can be affected greatly by the experience of having an extremely premature baby. Some marriages fall apart under the stress, and varying degrees of depression may occur. Parenting an extremely premature baby can be a difficult, frustrating experience, but with the proper medical and parental education and social supports in place, parents can help their children to flourish.

–AnnJanette Alejano-Steele

See also High-Risk Infants, Low Birth Weight (LBW)

Further Readings and References

March of Dimes, http://www.modimes.org

Parents of Premature Babies Inc., http://www.Preemie-L.org

Rossetti, L. (1989). *High-risk infants: Identification, assessment and intervention*. Boston: College Hill Press.

Widerstrom, A. H., Mowder, B. A., & Sandall, S. R. (1991). *At-risk and handicapped newborns and infants. Development, assessment and intervention*. Englewood Cliffs, NJ: Prentice Hall.

VERY OLD AGE

Because of the growing population of older adults in technologically advanced countries, researchers in a number of disciplines are becoming increasingly more interested in examining differences between older adults and *very* old adults as well as the transition to very late adulthood. Very old adults (also referred to as *the oldest old*) are typically defined in the literature as those adults who are 85 years old or older; however, some researchers set the criterion at 75 years old. In general, this population has a higher percentage of women compared with other age groups and is characterized by a high degree of comorbidity (i.e., multiple illnesses or conditions), a lower level of education in relation to other age groups, and high rates of institutionalization. The focus of this entry will be on the physical, psychological, emotional, and social characteristics of this group as well as changes that occur in these domains when older adults

transition into being part of the oldest old population. It is important to note that this population is characterized by a high degree of heterogeneity, making generalizations very difficult.

PHYSICAL CHARACTERISTICS

As people age, the functioning of bodily systems tends to decline. In addition, the likelihood of adults older than 65 years having one chronic illness is extremely high (80%), with 50% having two or more conditions. These percentages are even higher in adults older than 85 years. The most prevalent of these diseases are cardiovascular disorders, arthritis, and diabetes, with many attributable to health risk behaviors (e.g., smoking, poor diet). In addition, the percentage of very old adults living with Alzheimer's disease increases from 3% in those who are 65 to 74 years old, to 18.7% of those 75 to 84 years old, to 47% of those living past 85 years old. Alzheimer's disease is also the most common reason for institutionalization. Another factor related to institutionalization is functional ability, or the ability to perform activities of daily living (ADLs). Functional ability is generally at a lower level in the oldest old compared with the young old. Research suggests that about one fifth of young-old adults require assistance with at least one ADL, whereas about one third of the very old require assistance with at least one ADL.

Sensory functioning also tends to be at a lower level in the oldest old compared with young-old adults. Longitudinal studies have also found that most (70%) older adults tested for visual and hearing acuity at age 70 had no visual or hearing impairment, and there was no coexistence of visual and hearing impairment. When tested again at age 81, about 10% demonstrated normal visual or hearing, and about 5% demonstrated a coexistence of hearing and visual impairment. At age 88, none of the men and fewer than 10% of the women had normal hearing and vision, and 8% to 13% demonstrated coexistence. In addition, mild impairment was evident in only 0.5% of the sample when tested at age 70, but increased to 23% and 9% for visual and hearing acuity, respectively, at age 88.

PSYCHOLOGICAL CHANGES

The psychological functioning of the oldest old has also received increased attention recently. The most commonly studied aspects of psychological functioning are cognitive abilities. Research suggests that cognitive decline in the oldest old differs from that in young-old adults in that it is more broad, more marked, less amenable to interventions, and more constrained by biological factors compared with cultural factors. For example, longitudinal research has found that the loss trajectory becomes markedly more negative after the age of 80 in terms of perceptual speed, memory, and fluency. Knowledge (e.g., vocabulary), on the other hand, tends to remain stable until about 90 years of age. Much of the variance in cognitive loss can be accounted for by sensory decline. This has been suggested by some researchers to represent an age-related slowing of the central nervous system (also referred to as the *common cause hypothesis*). Factors such as education, socioeconomic status, ethnicity, sex, and the presence of certain chronic conditions (e.g., diabetes, cardiovascular disease, Alzheimer's disease) also contribute to the heterogeneity of cognitive abilities in late adulthood. However, in general, old-old adults are more likely to be assessed as having lower psychological functioning than young-old adults.

Another research question is whether personality and self-identity remain stable into and throughout this stage. For example, it has been found that very old adults have a relatively stable sense of self, despite believing that some of their characteristics have changed. This suggests that there is a continuity of self into very late adulthood. Research has also found that self-esteem begins to decline in late adulthood. However, rather than being negative, this may represent an increased comfortableness and acceptance with one's self and personal faults. Finally, cross-sectional research examining stability of personality traits as measured by the revised NEO Personality Index (NEO-PI-R), found that the oldest old scored lower on extraversion and on the facet traits of impulsiveness, warmth, and positive emotions in relation to the young-old group, but were similar in terms of neuroticism, openness to experience, conscientiousness, and agreeableness, thus suggesting an overall stability of personality.

SOCIAL RELATIONSHIPS

It is widely recognized that as people enter later adulthood, their social networks tend to decrease in size. Activity theory suggests that this decrease is a result of factors such as decreased mobility, death of people in the social network, and other obstacles to social contact. In contrast, disengagement theory suggests that there is a mutual disengagement between society and old adults in preparation for impending death. However, recent research suggests that older adults are proactive in selecting their social partners in later life. Laura Carstensen's socioemotional selectivity theory posits that as people age, the importance of emotional support and regulation increases, while the salience of acquiring information decreases. Thus, older adults actively select relationships on which to focus their potentially decreasing resources in order to maximize the likelihood of positive experiences. Often this results in a decrease in the number of less close social contacts and stability in the relatively small, but very close and meaningful, social partners.

Another factor affecting social relationships in this age group is the high likelihood of being widowed. Because men have a shorter life expectancy, women are much more likely to be widowed and men are more likely to be married, thus providing men with a more salient source of social support.

EMOTIONAL CHANGES

Research has found conflicting results concerning changes in the experience and expression of emotion in very late adulthood. Some researchers suggest that because of increasing disability and role loss, the amount of negative affect experienced increases, whereas the amount of positive affect decreases. It has also been suggested that the experience of both negative and positive affect decreases because of less exposure to affect-inducing events or because of increased emotional regulation, and that positive affect increases and negative affect decreases as a result of older adults actively selecting situations that optimize the likelihood of experiencing positive affect. In a meta-analysis of the literature, it was found that negative affect does tend to increase and positive affect tends to decrease in the oldest old, and that the frequency and intensity of experiencing high-arousal emotions also decreases.

Research on depression in older adults generally suggests that age is not predictive of clinical depression, but depressive *symptoms* do tend to increase when transitioning into later life. Many researchers suggest that this increase is due to increased scores on negative symptoms and not decreased scores on items assessing well-being. Also of interest is that the relationship of functional ability, cognitive impairment, and depression is often mediated by psychological resources (e.g., mastery). This suggests that it may not merely be the presence of disabilities that lead to depression, but the ways in which they are interpreted.

CONCLUSION

Because the population of people older than 85 years is the fastest growing population in terms of age groups, research examining this age period is becoming more important. Although researchers have identified trends, the heterogeneity of this age group cannot be underemphasized, thus increasing the need for longitudinal studies examining intraindividual change. Caution should also be taken when interpreting the results from studies examining the oldest old because participants typically represent a very positive selection of the population and of their cohort. Finally, because of the relationships between the aspects of aging discussed (e.g., sensory ability and cognition, social relationships and emotion), there is a need for multidisciplinary research to further explicate when and how these interactions occur.

—*Brian J. Ayotte*

Further Readings and References

Alford, D. M. (n.d.). *Nursing care of the oldest old.* Retrieved from http://www.nurseducation.org/oldestold.htm

Baltes, P. B., & Mayer, K. U. (Eds.). (1999). *The Berlin Aging Study: Aging from 70 to 100.* Cambridge, UK: Cambridge University Press.

Berlin Aging Study. (2002). *Berlin aging study.* Retrieved from http://www.base-berlin.mpg.de/Introduction.html

Birren, J. E., & Schaie, K. W. (Eds.). (1996). *Handbook of the psychology of aging* (5th ed.). San Diego, CA: Academic Press.

Carstensen, L. L. (1992). Social and emotional patterns in adulthood: Support for socioemotional selectivity theory. *Psychology and Aging, 7,* 331–338.

Dulay, M. F., & Murphy, C. (2002). Olfactory acuity and cognitive function converge in older adulthood: Support for the common cause hypothesis. *Psychology and Aging, 17*(3), 392–404.

Grundy, E., & Bowling, A. (1999). Enhancing the quality of extended life years: Identification of the oldest old with a very good and very poor quality of life. *Aging and Mental Health, 3*(3), 199–212.

Lindenberger, U., Scherer, H., & Baltes, P. B. (2001). The strong connection between sensory and cognitive performance in old age: Not due to sensory acuity reductions operating during cognitive assessment. *Psychology and Aging, 16*(2), 196–205.

Roepke, S., McAdams, L. A., Lindamer, L. A., Patterson, T. L., & Jeste, D. V. (2001). Personality profiles among normal aged individuals as measured by the NEO-PI-R. *Aging and Mental Health, 5*(2), 159–164.

Singer, T., Lindenberger, U., & Baltes, P. B. (2003). Plasticity of memory for new learning in very old age: A story of major loss? *Psychology and Aging, 18*(2), 306–317.

Singer, T., Verhaeghan, P., Ghisletta, P., Lindenberger, U., & Baltes, P. B. (2003). The fate of cognition in very old age: Six-year longitudinal findings in the Berlin Aging Study (BASE). *Psychology and Aging, 18*(2), 318–331.

Smith, J., & Baltes, P. B. (1997). Profiles of psychological functioning in the old and oldest old. *Psychology and Aging, 12*(3), 458–472.

Smith, J., Borchelt, M., Maier, H., & Jopp, D. (2002). Health and well-being in the young old and oldest old. *Journal of Social Issues, 58*(4), 715–732.

U.S. Census Bureau. (1996). *65+ in the United States.* Current Population Reports, Special Studies, P23-190. Washington, DC: U.S. Government Printing Office. Retrieved from http://www.census.gov/prod/1/pop/p23-190/p23-190.pdf

VIDEO GAMES

ORIGIN AND GROWTH OF THE VIDEO GAME INDUSTRY

The first interactive computer game, *Spacewar*, was written in 1961 by an MIT student named Steve Russell on a Digital Equipment PDP-1 computer. The first consumer video game, *Pong*, was released a decade later in 1972. Throughout the 1970s and into the 1980s, most video games were played in arcades (in this chapter, we define video games to include arcade games, computer games, and home console games such as PlayStation). Several recurring themes began to emerge at this time: multiple companies vied for market dominance, displacing older systems with each new technological advance; the popularity and cultural impact consistently grew over time; and concerns arose regarding the effects games might have. Concerns about video game violence first became highly salient in 1976 with the game *Death Race*, in which the goal was to drive a car over stick figures called "gremlins."

Currently, video game images are created out of many polygons; therefore, the number of polygons processed per second (pg/s) is a common measure of graphics quality. The Sony PlayStation, released in 1995, processed 350,000 pg/s. Sega's Dreamcast, released in 1999, leaped ahead to more than 3 million. A year later, Sony's PlayStation 2 jumped to 66 million pg/s. One year after that, Microsoft's Xbox boasted 125 million pg/s. The stated goal for Sony's PlayStation 3 is 1 billion. At the same time, this increased speed and graphic capacity allowed for games to become more realistic, including far more realistic and graphic violence. Returning to an old theme, the top-selling video games from 2001 to 2003 were the *Grand Theft Auto* series, which included running down pedestrians with cars, and killing police, prostitutes, and others with a variety of weapons. The video game industry is now bigger than Hollywood, raking in more than $10 billion annually in the United States in 2002 and 2003. As games have taken up more of children's time and become more realistic and engaging, researchers have begun to study children's uses of video games and the varied effects they may have.

CHILDREN'S USE OF VIDEO GAMES AND SEX-CORRELATED DIFFERENCES

The amount of time children spend playing video games has increased over the past three decades. Considering both home and arcade playing in the mid-1980s, children averaged about 4 hours per week. By the early 1990s, home playing had increased and arcade playing had decreased, and sex-correlated differences had begun to emerge. Girls played an average of about 2 hours per week, with boys playing an average of 4 hours per week. In the mid-1990s, home play had increased for fourth-grade girls to 4.5 hours per week and 7.1 hours per week for boys. In 1999, school-age children (boys and girls combined) averaged 7 hours per week. Most recently in elementary and middle-school populations, girls are playing about 5.5 hours per week and boys average 13 hours per week. Perhaps surprisingly, the average amount of television watched has not dropped as video game playing time has increased.

It is still unclear at what age video game playing begins, but it is likely to be younger with each passing year. In a nationally representative survey, parents reported that children aged 2 to 7 play an average of 43 minutes per day. In studies of preschool children, even preschoolers aged 2 to 5 play an average of 28 minutes per day. It is also unclear when play peaks, if it does, and when it declines, if it does. Regardless of when children start playing, and whether there is a normative

peak time, it is clear that gamers do not stop playing once they turn 18. The average age of a video game player has risen steadily, and is currently 29. It is important not to let this average mask the fact that video games have become ubiquitous in youth culture, with 92% of 2- to 17-year-olds playing.

Three sex-correlated differences have been found consistently across studies. First, males are more likely to play video games than females. Second, males are more likely to spend more time playing video games. Third, males prefer more violence in their video games. Most researchers define violence in games as when the player can intentionally harm other characters in the game. Content analyses show that most games contain some violent content, and about half of those include violence that would result in serious injuries or death. When asked, a majority of fourth- to eighth-grade children prefer violent games.

VIDEO GAME EFFECTS

Video games are natural teachers. Children find them highly motivating; by virtue of their interactive nature, children are actively engaged with them; they provide repeated practice; and they include rewards for skillful play. These facts make it likely that video games could have large effects, some of which are intended by game designers, and some of which may not be intended. We review several of these intended and unintended effects below, grouped into what could be considered "positive" and "negative" effects.

Positive Effects

The educational value of educational software and video games (known as *discrete educational software*) has been so widely accepted that such software is second only to word processing software in its availability and use in school classrooms. Although the quality of research in this domain varies widely, meta-analyses of recent high-quality studies of the efficacy of discrete educational software show an effect size of 0.38. That is, the average correlation between student use of educational software and student achievement is 0.38. The average correlation is 0.35 for educational games teaching reading skills and 0.45 for games teaching math skills. The efficacy for teaching prereading skills may be even greater than for teaching reading skills. The average correlation between educational software/games and reading skills is

0.44 for prekindergarten and kindergarten children.

Video games with other specific types of content have also shown positive effects. Video games have been used to teach children healthy skills for the self-care of asthma and diabetes and have been successful in imparting the attitudes, skills, and behaviors that they were designed to teach. In a study of college students, playing a golf video game improved students' actual control of force when putting, even though the video game gave no proprioceptive feedback on actual putting movement or force.

Some researchers have argued that video games are the "training wheels" for computer literacy. Computer literacy includes skills beyond traditional literacy skills, specifically iconic skills (image representation and manipulation). Research suggests that people can learn iconic, spatial, and visual attention skills from video games. For example, a study with college students to determine relative ability to keep track of several different things on a computer screen at the same time (a skill similar to those needed by flight controllers) concluded that expert video game players were better at maintaining divided visual attention than novices. In a second study, 5 hours of playing a video game led to increased response speed in the visual attention task, regardless of previous video game experience. Other studies have documented relations between video game play and visual selective attention, spatial visualization, mental rotation, and reaction times. Video games can also provide opportunities for practice in following directions and in the use of fine motor skills. There have even been studies with adults showing that experience with video games is related to better surgical skills.

Negative Effects of Violent Video Games

Of several negative effects that have been studied, the one that has received the most attention is aggressive behavior. Dozens of studies have been conducted on the relation between playing violent video games

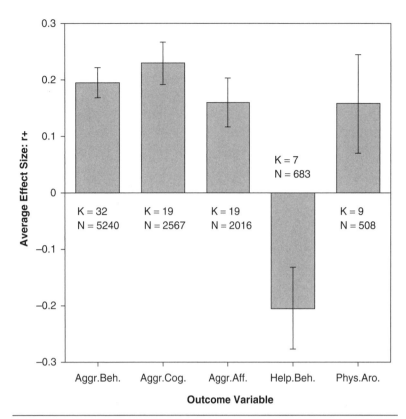

Figure 1   Effects of Violent Video Games on Aggressive Behavior, Aggressive Cognition, Aggressive Affect, Helping Behavior, and Physiological Arousal, All Samples

SOURCE: Anderson, C. A. (2004). An update on the effects of violent video games. *Journal of Adolescence, 27*, 133–122. Copyright by Craig A. Anderson and Academic Press. Reprinted by permission.

NOTES: K = number of independent samples. N = total number of participants. Vertical capped bars are the upper and lower 95% confidence intervals.

and aggression-related variables. When analyzed using modern meta-analytic techniques, these studies show remarkably consistent results that are in line with theoretical predictions and with the much larger research literature on violent television and film effects. As can be seen in Figure 1, there are five major effects of playing violent video games.

1. *Violent video games increase physiological arousal.* Experimental studies show short-term increases in physiological arousal, such as heart rate and blood pressure.

2. *Violent video games increase aggressive cognitions.* Experimental and correlational studies show short-term and long-term increases in aggressive cognitions. Measures have included reaction times to

aggression-related and unrelated words, aggressive content of story completions, hostile attributions to ambiguous provocations, and aggressive completions of word fragments, among others.

3. *Violent video games increase aggressive feelings.* Experimental and correlational studies show short-term and long-term increases in aggressive affect, sometimes labeled *anger* or *state hostility*.

4. *Violent video games increase aggressive behaviors.* Experimental and correlational studies show short-term and long-term increases in aggressive affect. Aggressive behaviors have been measured in several ways, ranging from highly ecologically valid approaches such as physical fights at school to highly controlled (and internally valid) laboratory approaches such as attempts to deliver highly noxious noise blasts to a game opponent. These effects have been found in children and adults, and in males and females, in nonaggressive and highly aggressive individuals. In a recent longitudinal study of third to fifth graders, violent video game play was related to increases in verbally and physically aggressive behaviors even after controlling for sex, hostile attribution bias, amount of screen time, parental involvement, and prior aggression levels.

5. *Violent video games decrease prosocial behaviors.* Experimental and correlational studies show short-term and long-term decreases in positive or prosocial behaviors.

As may be seen from this meta-analysis, violent video games appear to be every bit as good at teaching aggressive skills as educational video games are at teaching reading skills.

Incidental Negative Effects

Several studies have documented relations between video game play and a wide array of other negative effects, most notably academic performance. This appears to be related to the amount of play more than the content of the games, in that students who spend a lot of time playing video games tend to get poorer grades.

There are also a number of concerns about the potential effects of heavy video game play on children's physical health, including obesity, video-induced seizures, and postural, muscular, and skeletal disorders such as tendinitis, nerve compression, and carpal tunnel syndrome. The causes for these types of disorders vary from posture at the computer to the repetitive nature of movements used with input devices (e.g., keyboards,

mice, and joysticks). Most of the information on these types of disorders has been collected on adults. However, some have been documented in pediatric populations. In March 2000, Nintendo of America, a major video game manufacturer, acknowledged the problem by agreeing to provide protective gloves to about 1.2 million children because of numerous reports of hand injuries caused by the control stick of a particular game. Excessive video game playing has also led to documented cases of a form of tendinitis dubbed "Nintendinitis," caused by repeatedly pressing buttons with the thumb during game play.

Finally, some studies are beginning to document the existence of what appears to be video game "addiction." Studies suggest that perhaps as many as 15% to 20% of video game players could be considered "addicted" by criteria similar to the *Diagnostic and Statistical Manual of Mental Disorders,* Fourth Edition *(DSM-IV)* criteria for gambling addiction. Although the correlates of video game addiction are only recently being investigated, it appears that this may be a growing problem.

SUMMARY

Children are becoming more engaged with video games as the technology advances and brings more realistic and exciting games into millions of homes. Partly because so many children play games for increasing amounts of time, researchers have begun to ask what the consequences of play may be. In short, video games appear to be excellent teachers. Many of the things they teach are intended (e.g., reading or math skills), but many are not (e.g., aggressive attitudes and behaviors, visual attention skills). Furthermore, the amount of time spent with video games may also have a negative impact on school performance and physical health for many children.

The question of whether video games are "good" or "bad" for children is oversimplified. Playing a first-person shooter game for hours every day could have a negative effect on school performance, a negative effect on aggressive behaviors, and a positive effect on visual attention skills. We prefer to recognize that video games can have powerful effects on children, for good or ill.

—*Douglas A. Gentile and Craig A. Anderson*

Further Readings and References

Anderson, C. A., & Bushman, B. J. (2001). Effects of violent video games on aggressive behavior, aggressive cognition, aggressive affect, physiological arousal, and prosocial behavior: A meta-analytic review of the scientific literature. *Psychological Science, 12,* 353–359.

Anderson, C. A., Gentile, D. A., & Buckley, K. E. (under review). Violent video game effects on children and adolescents: Further developments and tests of the general aggression model.

Children Now. (2001). *Fair play? Violence, gender and race in video games.* Los Angeles: Author.

Gentile, D. A., & Anderson, C. A. (2003). Violent video games: The newest media violence hazard. In D. A. Gentile (Ed.), *Media violence and children* (pp. 131–152). Westport, CT: Praeger.

Green, C. S., & Bavelier, D. (2003, May 29). Action video game modifies visual selective attention. *Nature, 423,* 534–537.

Lieberman, D. A. (1997). Interactive video games for health promotion: Effects on knowledge, self-efficacy, social support, and health. In R. L. Street, W. R. Gold, & T. Manning (Eds.), *Health promotion and interactive technology: Theoretical applications and future directions* (pp. 103–120). Mahwah, NJ: Erlbaum.

Murphy, R., Penuel, W., Means, B., Korbak, C., & Whaley, A. (2001). *E-DESK: A review of recent evidence on the effectiveness of discrete educational software.* Menlo Park, CA: SRI International. Retrieved from http://ctl.sri.com/publications/downloads/Task3_FinalReport3.pdf

Roberts, D. F., Foehr, U. G., Rideout, V. J., & Brodie, M. (1999). *Kids & media @ the new millennium.* Menlo Park, CA: Kaiser Family Foundation. Retrieved from http://www.kff.org/entmedia/1535-index.cfm

VIOLENCE

Violence is an act of physical force or threat of force that causes damage or is intended to produce harm. The damage inflicted by violence may be physical, psychological, or both. Violence may be distinguished from aggression, a more general type of hostile behavior that may be physical, verbal, or passive in nature.

TYPES OF VIOLENCE

Violence can be categorized in a number of ways. Violent crimes are typically divided into four main categories, based on the nature of the behavior: homicide (intentionally ending the life of another person), assault (attacking another person with the intent to cause harm), robbery (forcibly taking something from another person), and rape (forcing someone to engage in sexual activity). Other forms of violence overlap with these categories, such as child sexual abuse (engaging in sexual acts with a child) and domestic violence (violent behavior between relatives, usually spouses).

Violence can also be categorized according to the motivation for it. Reactive, or emotional, violence typically involves the expression of "hot-blooded" anger—a hostile desire to hurt someone—that arises in response to perceived provocation. Proactive, or instrumental, violence is more "cold blooded" and calculated, done in anticipation of a reward. Psychologist Kenneth Dodge found that these two types of violence involve distinct physiological states: a person engaging in reactive violence experiences increased autonomic nervous system arousal (i.e., increased heart rate and breathing, sweating), whereas a person committing an act of proactive aggression experiences low autonomic arousal.

Another method of categorizing violent behavior involves distinguishing between predatory and affective violence. Predatory violence involves planned acts of hostile force. Affective violence is more impulsive and unplanned. Other types of violence have been suggested, including irritable (motivated by frustration), territorial (motivated by intrusion into one's perceived territory or space), fear-induced (motivated by fear), and maternal (motivated by a threat to one's child) violence.

FREQUENCY OF VIOLENT BEHAVIORS

Since the time of early civilizations, violence has occurred throughout the world, in forms ranging from war between countries to individuals behaving violently toward other individuals. In recent decades, rates of violent crimes committed by individuals have been documented by the United Nations. Although every country experiences violence, rates of violence (calculated as the number of crimes per 100,000 people) vary considerably across countries. For example, in 2000, the reported homicide rate was relatively low in countries such as Greece (0.76), Japan (0.50), Pakistan (0.05), and Switzerland (0.96). Much higher homicide rates were reported that year in Colombia (62.74), Jamaica (33.69), Russia (19.80), and South Africa (51.39). In 2000, the homicide rate in the United States was 5.5 per 100,000 people. In the United States, 1,426,325 violent crimes were reported to the police in 2002; the violent crime rate that year was 494.6 per 100,000. Assaults accounted for the largest proportion (62.7%) of reported violent crimes in the United States, followed by robbery (29.5%), rape (6.7%), and homicide (1.1%). These rates do not account for all violence that occurs in the United

States, however. The Department of Justice's National Criminal Victimization Survey indicates that a large number of violent crimes are not reported to the police. Assault seems to be the most frequently under-reported act of violence, with 79% of assaults not reported to police in 2002. Sixty-two percent of rapes were unreported that year, whereas only 8% of robberies were not reported to police.

The frequency of violent behavior changes across the life span. Very young children (i.e., younger than 8 years) are least likely to engage in serious violence. Older children show some violence, but less than adolescents. Older adolescents and young adults (i.e., 16 to 25 years of age) are more violent than any other age group. Beyond the 20s, the frequency of violence decreases steadily with age. To see changes in violence over the life span, consider homicide as an example. A few very young (i.e., under 8 years) murderers exist, with rates increasing slightly with age until a noticeable increase occurs in the 13- to 16-year-old age group. The homicide rate peaks in the 20- to 24-year-old age group, and then declines steadily with age.

Gender differences exist in the rates of violent crime in the United States. Males are much more likely than females to behave violently. The victims of violent crimes such as homicide and assault are also more likely to be males. Rape victims are most likely to be females, though, as are the victims of domestic violence.

CAUSES OF VIOLENCE

With so much violence occurring all over the globe, it is natural to wonder what causes people to behave violently. Researchers have been attempting to answer this question by examining a variety of possible causal factors. The one point that all researchers seem to agree on is that violence is multicausal, meaning that no single factor is responsible for violent behavior. Instead, violence results from a combination of variables within a person, factors in the social or cultural environment, and immediate situational forces. Researchers have examined multiple factors within a person that may contribute to violence, including genetic predisposition, neurochemical abnormalities (e.g., high testosterone levels), personality characteristics (e.g., lack of empathy for others), information-processing deficits (e.g., tendency to view others' actions as hostile), and experiencing abuse or neglect as a child.

EFFECTS OF VIOLENCE

Regardless of its cause, violence has a negative impact on those who witness or experience it. Violence can cause physical damage as well as psychological harm. Several psychological disorders, including posttraumatic stress disorder, dissociative identity disorder, and borderline personality disorder, are associated with experiencing or witnessing violence. Other psychological symptoms, such as depression, anxiety, and mood swings, are common in victims of violence.

Children seem to be particularly susceptible to the negative effects of violence. Children who experience or witness violence may develop a variety of problems, including anxiety, depression, insecurity, anger, poor anger management, poor social skills, pathological lying, manipulative behavior, impulsiveness, and lack of empathy. As these examples show, some children may respond to violence in "internalizing" ways, such as feelings of insecurity, anxiety, and depression, whereas others may react in "externalizing" ways, such as feeling angry and behaving in an antisocial manner. Although some of the effects of violence may manifest during childhood, others may not appear until adulthood. For example, abused girls are more likely than nonabused girls to have substance abuse problems as adults.

Exposure to violence can also increase violent behavior in children. Psychologist Albert Bandura showed that children often imitate violent behaviors, especially if those acts are committed by trusted adults (e.g., parents). Children also imitate violence shown on television and in other forms of media. Children exposed to greater amounts of media violence are more likely than other kids to become violent adults. This is particularly true if the child identifies with the violent characters and if the child believes that media violence represents reality.

PREVENTION OF VIOLENCE

Once a person engages in violent behavior, the likelihood of future violence is quite high. Of those individuals convicted of a violent crime, a large proportion of them reoffend if released from prison. Research also suggests that many arrestees commit several violent crimes before being arrested for the first time; for example, the average rapist rapes seven women before being caught. As a result of these high rates of reoccurrence of violence, mental health professionals have recognized the need to develop effective violence prevention programs.

Because the tendency to behave violently develops during childhood, most prevention programs target young people. Many of these programs are school based, although some involve the family or the community. The most successful violence prevention programs are those that target all children, not just those who are considered to be at risk for violence. In addition, the most success has been found in school-based programs with committed and involved teachers and programs that include parent training.

An example of an effective school-based violence prevention program is the Resolving Conflict Creatively Program, developed in the New York City public schools. This program includes the training of teachers and students in conflict resolution, problem-solving lessons for students aimed at promoting nonaggressive choices, and peer mediation to facilitate conflict resolution. Effective community-based programs include those that provide children with positive after-school activities and nonviolent role models. Family-based prevention is most successful if the parents are taught to be firm, clear, and understanding and to use nonviolent methods of discipline.

A variety of programs have been developed to reduce or prevent violence in individuals who have already shown a tendency toward violence. For example, a number of prison-based programs attempt to reduce the likelihood of reoffending among violent and nonviolent criminals. These programs often involve a variety of components. Violent offenders may receive training to improve parenting and other relationship skills. A mental health component may be included, such as substance abuse treatment. Job training is another common component of prison-based prevention programs. Occasionally, drugs such as antidepressants, beta-blockers, and benzodiazepines may be used in addition to other methods. Overall, the most successful programs for preventing future violence are those that teach behavioral changes.

SUMMARY

Violence is a relatively common type of human behavior that occurs throughout the world. People of all ages may be violent, although older adolescents and young adults are most likely to engage in violent behavior. Violence has a number of negative effects on those who witness or experience it; children are especially susceptible to its harm. Fortunately, various programs have been successful at preventing and reducing violence.

—*Kristine M. Jacquin*

See also Firearms, Injuries, Rape

Further Readings and References

Bureau of Justice Statistics. (2004). *National Criminal Victimization Survey, 2002.* Retrieved from http://www.ojp.usdoj.gov/bjs/cvictgen.htm

DeJong, W. (1994). *Building the peace: The Resolving Conflict Creatively Program.* Washington, DC: U.S. Department of Justice, National Institute of Justice.

Elliott, D. S., Hamburg, B. A., & Williams, K. R. (Eds.). (1998). *Violence in American schools: A new perspective.* New York: Cambridge University Press.

Federal Bureau of Investigations. (2004). *Uniform crime reports: Crime in the United States 2002.* Retrieved from http://www.fbi.gov/ucr/02cius.htm

Kurst-Swanger, K., & Petcosky, J. L. (2003). *Violence in the home: Multidisciplinary perspectives.* London: Oxford University Press.

North Central Regional Educational Laboratory. (2004). *Resolving Conflict Creatively Program.* Retrieved from http://www.ncrel.org/sdrs/areas/issues/envrnmnt/drugfree/sa2lk16.htm

Rapp-Paglicci, L. A., Roberts, A. R., & Wodarski, J. S. (Eds.). (2002). *Handbook of violence.* New York: Wiley.

Ross, D. M. (2003). *Childhood bullying, teasing, and violence: What school personnel, other professionals, and parents can do* (2nd ed.). Alexandria, VA: American Counseling Association.

Silberman, M. (Ed.). (2003). *Violence and society: A reader.* Upper Saddle River, NJ: Prentice Hall.

VISUAL CLIFF

The visual cliff, designed by Richard D. Walk and Eleanor J. Gibson, is an apparatus used for testing depth perception of human infants and animals. Visual cliffs are constructed by placing patterned surfaces (e.g., checkerboard) on each side of a central platform. Both surfaces are covered by a sheet of glass. One surface is directly beneath the sheet of glass, however, whereas the other surface is dropped several feet below the glass. This creates shallow and deep "visual cliffs" on the opposing sides. Organisms are placed on the platform of the apparatus and allowed to locomote or are coaxed toward the deep cliff.

Early research using the visual cliff found that a variety of species, including rats, cats, goats, and human infants, avoided the deep cliff as soon as they could locomote independently. This avoidance was interpreted as evidence that the organism could perceive the depth or height of the cliffs. The findings that avoidance occurred early in development for most species, when the animals had little motor or perceptual experience, was also interpreted as supporting that this avoidance or wariness was innate or independent of experience.

Subsequent research has offered alternative interpretations for the avoidance response of human infants. Nancy Rader and John E. Richards presented a maturational interpretation of the avoidance response, arguing that the initial avoidance seen in early infancy is not based on fear, but on a response-specific visual-motor program. Their research provided evidence that avoidance behavior is predicted by crawling onset age. Additionally, infants avoided the deep side of the cliff when crawling but not when placed in a walker, suggesting that avoidance does not reflect a generalized fear response to heights.

An experiential interpretation of infant avoidance reactions, presented by Joseph J. Campos, Bennett I. Berthenthal, and colleagues, argued that infants' avoidance does reflect their wariness of heights and that this wariness is related to self-produced locomotion. This research revealed that wariness and avoidance of depth are related to amount of independent locomotion and that wariness is accelerated in infants who are not yet crawling but who have experienced "artificial" locomotion through use of walkers. This research measured infants' behavioral avoidance responses and their heart rate responsiveness when placed over the deep and shallow cliffs. Accelerative heart rate responsiveness, which indicates fear or wariness, was related to locomotor experience. Decelerative heart rate responses, indicating attentional responses but not fear, were recorded in prelocomotor infants. These decelerative responses indicated that precrawling infants could detect differences in depth, but were not yet responding to depth with wariness. According to Campos and colleagues, several processes may underlie the development of wariness. As infants begin coordinating crawling with goal-directed behaviors, the infants may fall, resulting in negative affect becoming associated with these situations. Infants also experience negative emotional reactions of their parents in situations in which they are likely to fall.

These experiences contribute to their wariness of situations involving depth or height. Additionally, as infants acquire crawling experience, they coordinate normally co-occurring visual and vestibular inputs. Wariness is experienced when visual and vestibular cues do not match, such as being lowered over the edge of a surface (e.g., the deep cliff). This experiential interpretation of human infants' depth perception and avoidance reactions is consistent with accumulating data from studies of nonhuman species (e.g., cats, rats, chicks) that depth perception and avoidance of depths is dependent on specific types of visual and locomotor experiences.

—*Melanie J. Spence*

Further Readings and References

Bertenthal, B. I., & Campos, J. J. (1984). A reexamination of fear and its determinants on the visual cliff. *Psychophysiology, 21*, 413–417.

Campos, J., Bertenthal, B., & Kermoian, R. (1992). Early experience and emotional development: The emergence of wariness of heights. *Psychological Science, 3*, 61–64.

Campos, J. J., Langer, A., & Krowitz, A. (1970). Cardiac responses on the visual cliff in prelocomotor human infants. *Science, 170*, 196–197.

Gibson, E. J., & Walk, R. D. (1960). The "visual cliff." *Scientific American, 202*, 64–71. Retrieved from http://www.wadsworth.com/psychology_d/templates/student_resources/0155060678_rathus/ps/ps05.html

Richards, J. E., & Rader, N. (1983), Affective, behavioral, and avoidance responses on the visual cliff: Effects of crawling onset age, crawling experience, and testing age. *Psychophysiology, 20*, 633–642.

VITAMIN DEFICIENCY

Vitamins are organic *substances* needed for their catalytic activities and cannot be synthesized by humans. They are essential to body metabolism and bioactivities.

FAT-SOLUBLE VITAMINS

Vitamin A

There are three forms of vitamin A: retinols, which are found in animal sources of food; beta-carotene, which is the plant source of retinol from which mammals make two thirds of their vitamin A; and carotenoids. Vitamin A is the third most common nutritional deficiency worldwide and is also seen in patients with disorders associated with fat malabsorption.

Vitamin A deficiency can affect the eyes, causing night blindness, complete blindness, and xerophthalmia; less common are Bitot's spots, corneal perforation, keratomalacia, and punctate keratopathy. For the skin, hyperkeratosis, phrynoderma, and destruction of hair follicles can result from vitamin A deficiency. Immunity-related effects include impairment of the humoral and cell-mediated immune system through effects on the phagocytes and T cells.

Vitamin D

Vitamin D is found in fortified milk, fatty fish, cod-liver oil, and eggs. When there's deficiency in vitamin D, reduced intestinal absorption of calcium and phosphorus and demineralization of bones leads to osteoporosis in adults and rickets in children. Hypocalcemia causes a secondary hyperparathyroidism that leads to bone resorption and osteomalacia.

Vitamin E

Vitamin E is an antioxidant that protects cell membranes from destruction. Vitamin E deficiency occurs in patients with disorders associated with fat malabsorption. Neuromuscular disorders associated with vitamin E deficiency include skeletal myopathy, spinocerebellar ataxia, and pigmented retinopathy. Some studies suggest an association between development of Alzheimer's disease and vitamin E deficiency. In premature infants, hemolytic anemia is encountered in the presence of vitamin E deficiency. Congenital hemolytic disorders may be associated with low vitamin E plasma levels.

Vitamin K

The name *vitamin K* comes from the German/Danish word koagulationsvitamin (clotting vitamin). Dietary vitamin K1 (phylloquinones) is found in green vegetables such as spinach and broccoli. Gut microflora synthesize vitamin K2 (menaquinone). Vitamin K deficiency leads to impaired coagulation manifested by easy bruisability, mucosal bleeding, and melena. Hemorrhagic disease of the newborn is due to an immature liver, low vitamin K content of breast milk, a sterile gut, and poor placental transfer of vitamin K.

WATER-SOLUBLE VITAMINS

Vitamin B$_1$ (Thiamine)

Thiamine serves as a catalyst in the conversion of pyruvate to acetyl coenzyme A. Deficiency of thiamine is associated with beriberi. Infantile beriberi is clinically apparent between the ages of 2 and 3 months, manifested as fulminant cardiac syndrome with cardiomegaly, tachycardia, a loud piercing cry, cyanosis, dyspnea, and vomiting. For adults, dry beriberi is a symmetrical sensory and motor peripheral neuropathy. Wet beriberi includes a neuropathy and cardiac involvement with cardiomegaly, cardiomyopathy, and congestive heart failure.

Wernicke-Korsakoff syndrome is largely described in chronic alcoholics. Wernicke's disease is a triad of nystagmus, ophthalmoplegia, ataxia, and confusion. Korsakoff's psychosis is impaired short-term memory and confabulation with otherwise grossly normal cognition.

Leigh's syndrome is a subacute necrotizing encephalomyopathy, leading to symmetrical foci of spongy necrosis and demyelinating changes in the thalami, brain stem, pons, and even peripheral nerves. It is manifested with ataxia, dysarthria, movement disorders, areflexia, muscle atrophy, and weakness.

Vitamin B$_2$ (Riboflavin)

Riboflavin is an essential component of coenzymes involved in multiple cellular metabolic pathways. Riboflavin deficiency is often accompanied by other water-soluble vitamin deficiencies in patients with anorexia nervosa, malabsorptive syndromes, rare inborn errors of metabolism, and long-term use of barbiturates. It is characterized by sore throat, cheilitis, stomatitis, glossitis, normocytic-normochromic anemia, and seborrheic dermatitis.

Vitamin B$_3$ (Niacin)

Nicotinic acid and nicotinamide are the two common forms of the vitamin most often referred to as niacin. Niacin occurs in alcoholics and in poorer countries where diet intake is inadequate. It is associated with carcinoid syndrome, prolonged use of isoniazid, and Hartnup's disease. It manifests as a symmetric hyperpigmented rash on exposed areas of skin, a red tongue, diarrhea and vomiting, insomnia, disorientation, delusions, dementia, and encephalopathy.

Vitamin B₅ (Pantothenic Acid)

Vitamin B₅ is an essential cofactor in many acetylation reactions. It is found mainly in egg yolk, liver, broccoli, and milk. Deficiency of vitamin B₅ is mainly seen in severely malnourished individuals. It is manifested by paresthesias and dysesthesias, referred to as *burning feet syndrome.*

Vitamin B₆ (Pyridoxine)

Meats, whole grains, vegetables, and nuts are the best sources of vitamin B₆. Deficiency is usually manifested as nonspecific stomatitis, glossitis, cheilosis, irritability, confusion, and depression. It can lead to elevations in plasma homocysteine concentrations, a risk factor for the development of atherosclerosis and venous thromboembolism.

Vitamin B₁₂ (Cobalamin) and Folic Acid

Cobalamin and folate deficiency share many similarities. Animal products provide the only dietary source of cobalamin for humans. Folate comes from animal products and leafy vegetables. Cobalamin deficiency is usually a result of inadequate absorption associated with pernicious anemia or gastric disease and also occurs in elderly people.

Hematologic

Megaloblastic anemia presents with symptoms of anemia, atrophic glossitis, and mental sluggishness.

Neurologic

Subacute combined degeneration of the dorsal and lateral spinal columns is characteristic. Neuropathy, paresthesias and ataxia, and loss of vibration and position sense can progress to severe weakness, spasticity, clonus, or paraplegia.

Folate deficiency is due to poor diet, alcoholism, elderly age, and drug-induced (e.g., trimethoprim, methotrexate, and phenytoin) interference with folate metabolism. There is an increased requirement in pregnancy and lactations and in patients with hemolytic anemias and exfoliative skin disease. The hematologic manifestations are similar to those of cobalamin deficiency, without neurologic abnormalities.

Hyperhomocysteinemia

Deficiencies in these vitamins can lead to elevations in plasma homocysteine levels, which is a risk factor for the development of atherosclerosis and venous thromboembolism.

Biotin

Biotin is found in yeast and liver. Biotin functions as a cofactor to the carboxylase enzyme. In the setting of biotin deficiency, pyruvate levels rise and are converted to lactic acid. Nonspecific symptoms may include changes in mental status, myalgia, anorexia, and nausea. Chronic deficiency can lead to maculosquamous dermatitis of the extremities, seborrheic dermatitis, and alopecia.

Multiple carboxylase deficiency is manifested by a slow but progressive loss of biotin in the urine, leading to the typical organic aciduria of multiple carboxylase deficiency. The neonatal type is seen in the first week of life, and the late onset type is generally seen before 1 year of age.

Vitamin C

Vitamin C functions as a cofactor, enzyme complement, cosubstrate, or a strong antioxidant in a variety of metabolic processes. Vitamin C deficiency is related to scurvy. Scurvy is a clinical syndrome, largely due to impaired collagen synthesis. It occurs mostly in severely malnourished individuals, drug and alcohol abusers, or with inadequate oral intake. Symptoms include ecchymoses, bleeding gums, petechiae, hyperkeratosis, and impaired wound healing.

—*Carroll B. Leevy and Hany A. Elbeshbeshy*

Further Readings and References

Baumgartner, E. R., & Suormala, T. (1997). Multiple carboxylase deficiency: Inherited and acquired disorders of biotin metabolism. *International Journal for Vitamin and Nutrition Research, 67,* 377.

Cantorna, M. T., Nashold, F. E., & Hayes, C. E. (1995). Vitamin A deficiency results in a priming environment conducive for Th1 cell development. *European Journal of Immunology, 25,* 1673.

Cervantes-Laurean, N., McElvaney, G., & Moss, J. (2000). Niacin. In M. Shils (Ed.), *Modern nutrition in health and medicine* (p. 401). Philadelphia: Lippincott Williams & Wilkins.

Green, R., & Kinsella, L. J. (1995). Editorial: Current concepts in the diagnosis of cobalamin deficiency. *Neurology, 45,* 1435.

Grundman, M. (2000). Vitamin E and Alzheimer disease: The basis for additional clinical trials. *American Journal of Clinical Nutrition, 71,* 630S.

Jacob, R. (2000). Vitamin C. In M. Shils, J. Olson, M. Shike, & A. C. Ross (Eds.), *Modern nutrition in health and disease* (p. 467). Philadelphia: Lippincott Williams & Wilkins.

Leevy, C. M., & Baker, H. (1968). Vitamins and alcoholism. *American Journal of Clinical Nutrition, 21,* 1325.

Pincus, J. H. (1972). Subacute necrotizing encephalomyelopathy (Leigh's disease): A consideration of clinical features and etiology. *Developmental Medicine and Child Neurology, 14,* 87.

Rimm, E. B., Willett, W. C., Hu, F. B., Sampson, L., Colditz, G. A., Manson, J. E., et al. (1998). Folate and vitamin B6 from diet and supplements in relation to risk of coronary heart disease among women. *Journal of the American Medical Association, 279,* 359.

Sumner, A. E., Chin, M. M., Abrahm, J. L., Berry, G. T., Gracely, E. J., Allen, R. H., et al. (1996). Elevated methylmalonic acid and total homocysteine levels show high prevalence of vitamin B12 deficiency after gastric surgery. *Annals of Internal Medicine, 124,* 469-476.

Vermeer, C., & Schurgers, L. J. (2000). A comprehensive review of vitamin K and vitamin K antagonists. *Hematology/Oncology Clinics of North America, 14,* 339.

VOLUNTEERING

Volunteering is a term used to describe a broad range of helping behaviors intended to benefit a variety of recipients, including large organizations, smaller groups of disadvantaged individuals, and even family members, neighbors, and friends. There are many ways to help others, such as by donating money or time (instrumental help) or by being willing to listen if another person needs to talk (emotional support). Emerging life-span perspectives on volunteerism and service emphasize the importance of providing help to others for feeling useful, especially in older age.

Recent evidence within behavioral medicine, epidemiology, and health psychology suggests that volunteerism and helping others may be an important part of why social relationships are beneficial to the health of older adults. Volunteerism has been shown to improve physical and mental health, and the act of helping others has been shown to reduce distress and improve satisfaction within interpersonal relationships. Among elderly populations, providing support to others improves physical functioning and promotes

longevity. For example, a prospective study of bereavement and mortality demonstrated that older adults who provided tangible forms of assistance (e.g., help with child care, transportation, errands) to friends, relatives, and neighbors were between 40% and 60% less likely to die during a 5-year period, compared with individuals who did not provide this type of assistance to others. Furthermore, providing emotional support to a spouse (e.g., making a spouse feel loved and cared for) was also protective, leading to a 30% lower chance of mortality risk during the same period. Individuals who reported receiving support from others (e.g., feeling loved and cared for by a spouse or other family members) did not have a similar decrease in their mortality risk.

Added to the direct health benefits shown to be associated with volunteering and helping others, indirect evidence links perceptions that may be associated with volunteering, such as a sense of meaning, purpose, belonging, mattering, self-efficacy, and self-esteem, to happiness and reduced depression. These benefits of volunteering and related feelings may reflect the fact that there are adaptive, evolutionary benefits of helping others. For example, kin selection and reciprocal altruism theory suggest that helping others is necessary to ensure inclusive fitness—our own reproductive success plus the reproductive success of individuals who share our genes. Helping others would have maximized inclusive fitness either by enhancing the welfare of relatives who would survive and pass on common genes or by enhancing the welfare of reciprocal altruists who would survive and direct future acts of altruism toward the helper or toward individuals who share the helper's genes.

Both kin selection and reciprocal altruism theory specify the circumstances that altruism could have evolved; however, they do not address the motivational mechanisms that would have impelled individuals to give away their own valuable resources to help others. Selective investment theory was advanced to address the motivational basis for allocating valuable resources to others on a long-term basis, and even in the absence of reciprocity. According to selective investment theory, giving, and not receiving, is the evolutionary function of interpersonal relationships that are characterized by a social bond. Other evolutionary theories of relationship processes have made similar arguments, suggesting that emotional commitments between individuals may have evolved, in part, to promote altruism.

These evolutionary theories of altruism and close relationships have important implications for volunteering. Most notably, they suggest that individuals will be more motivated to volunteer, and may provide the most help to another person, when there exists the potential to develop a personal relationship with the recipient. The possibility that interpersonal relationship processes play an important role in stimulating and maintaining volunteerism is a new area of research that awaits further study.

—Stephanie L. Brown

Further Readings and References

Brown, S. L., Nesse, R., Vinokur, A. D., & Smith, D. M. (2003). Providing support may be more beneficial than receiving it: Results from a prospective study of mortality. *Psychological Science, 14,* 320–327.

Institute for Volunteering Research, http://www.ivr.org.uk/

Omoto, A. M., Synder, M., & Martino, S. C. (2000). Volunteerism and the life course: Investigating age-related agendas for action. *Basic & Applied Social Psychology: Special Issue: The Social Psychology of Aging, 22,* 181–197.

VYGOTSKY, LEV (1896–1934)

Born in 1896 in Orsha, Byelorussia, Lev Semenovich Vygotsky is best known for his sociocultural approach to human development, a very influential set of ideas about how the child's social world and culture affect development. His ideas about how children develop within sociocultural context, now required reading for contemporary scholars of psychology and education, were themselves a reflection of the cultural-historical context of his time—namely Marxist socialism of early 20th-century revolutionary Russia.

Vygotsky's early life experiences were constrained by the limited opportunities afforded to Jewish families at that time. He grew up in the city of Gomel and went to a combination of public and private schools for his education. Vygotsky studied law at Moscow University and also enrolled in the "unofficial" Shaniavsky People's University. After graduation, Vygotsky returned to Gomel, where he taught at Gomel's Teacher's College. Following his marriage to Roza Smekhova and the birth of his daughter Gita,

Vygotsky moved to Moscow, where he began his career as a researcher and psychologist and where he started his fruitful collaboration with students A. R. Luria and A. N. Leont'ev.

Vygotsky maintains that what is unique about human development is that it occurs through the internalization of language and cultural tools and symbols. All higher-order cognitive abilities first appear socially in interactions between people and then become part of children's individual mental lives. Language is seen as the primary cultural tool that children internalize as private speech (self-talk) to guide their own thinking and behavior. Because different cultures have different languages, customs, and primary activities, children's cognitive and behavioral development can be very different across cultures.

Vygotsky's contributions to educational and psychological practice include the notions that (a) instruction should take place in the zone of proximal development (ZPD), a hypothetical region defined by the distance between what a child can accomplish alone and what the child can do with the help of someone else; (b) child assessment should be dynamic (done over time, examining cognitive changes due to teaching) rather than static (standardized individual tests); and (c) that children with special needs should be exposed to as normal social interactions and environments as possible.

The fundamentals of Vygotsky's theory appear in *Thought and Language* and in *Mind in Society*. Vygotsky frantically wrote as much as possible before his untimely death from tuberculosis in 1934. His 180 works had not begun to be translated into English until the 1960s, and his complete works in English were not available until 1999.

—Erin McClare and Adam Winsler

See also Scaffolding, Zone of Proximal Development (ZPD)

Further Readings and References

Berk, L. E., & Winsler, A. (1995). *Scaffolding children's learning: Vygotsky and early childhood education.* Washington, DC: National Association for the Education of Young Children.

Kozulin, A. (1990). *Vygotsky's psychology: A biography of ideas.* Cambridge, MA: Harvard University Press.

Moll, L. C. (Ed.). (1990), *Vygotsky and education: Instructional implications and applications of sociohistorical psychology.* New York: Cambridge University Press.

van der Veer, R., & Valsiner, J. (1991). *Understanding Vygotsky: A quest for synthesis*. Cambridge, MA: Blackwell.

Vygotsky, L. S. (1962). *Thought and language* (E. Hanfmann & G. Vakar, Eds. & Trans.). Cambridge: MIT Press. (Original work published 1934)

Vygotsky, L. S. (1978). *Mind in society: The development of higher mental processes* (M. Cole, V. John-Steiner, S. Scribner, & E. Souberman, Eds. & Trans.). Cambridge, MA: Harvard University Press. (Original work published 1930–1935)

Vygotsky, L. S., & Luria, A. R. (1993). *Studies on the history of behavior: Ape, primitive, and child* (V. I. Golod & J. E. Knox, Eds. & Trans.). Hillsdale, NJ: Erlbaum. (Original work published 1930)

Wertsch, J. V. (1985). *Vygotsky and the social formation of mind*. Cambridge, MA: Harvard University Press.

Work

Far and away the best prize that life offers is the chance to work hard at work worth doing.

—Theodore Roosevelt

WATSON, JOHN B. (1876–1958)

John Broadus Watson was born a poor rural boy from Traveler's Rest, South Carolina, raised by his mother in urban Greenville, at a time when American Progressivism was making a university education and graduate specialization a means for individual, social, and cultural advancement. He received a master's degree in philosophy from Furman University (1899) and achieved the University of Chicago's first PhD in psychology (1903). He was then an instructor at Chicago (1903–1908) and a professor at Johns Hopkins University (1908–1920), but a scandal forced him to leave academe. Undeterred, he became the first "pop" psychologist and a successful advertising executive in New York City (1921–1945).

Watson began as an animal and comparative psychologist, where some of his research was the earliest and best work in ethology. For this, experimental psychology had to be the study and science of behavior, not the then-standard introspection of conscious contents ("Psychology as the Behaviorist Views It," 1913). The former became Watson's classic behaviorism, which was taken seriously because of the high regard in which his research was held. Indeed, his

stature was such that he became the editor and founder of prestigious journals (e.g., *Psychological Review, Journal of Experimental Psychology*) and president of the American Psychological Association.

As a systematist, Watson held that psychology's goal was to formulate the laws and principles of human behavior through systematic observation and experimentation (*Psychology from the Standpoint of a Behaviorist*, 1919, 1929). For this, he advanced prediction and control as a means for understanding behavior, promoting behaviorism, and advancing cultural change. He adopted the conditioned reflex as a basic principle of behavior. He analyzed thinking, feeling, and imagining as implicit responses, not as independent mental processes. And, he viewed anatomy and physiology, not instincts, as the biological basis of human behavior (*Behaviorism*, 1924, 1930).

In extending his science to human development, Watson focused on infancy and early childhood. He made groundbreaking observations of normative emotional development. He pioneered in studying conditioned emotional reactions and their elimination. Watson published articles in the popular press on childrearing (e.g., *Cosmopolitan*), culminating in *Psychological Care of Infant and Child* (1928). Here, he was an early opponent of corporal punishment and an advocate for sex education, but advised unwisely about emotional attachment. His advice, though, was not based on classic behaviorism, but was more personal. Empirically validated child-rearing advice would await the emergence of human development as a science.

—*Edward K. Morris*

Further Readings and References

Buckley, K. W. (1989). *Mechanical man: John Broadus Watson and the beginnings of behaviorism.* New York: Guilford.

John B. Watson, http://www.psy.pdx.edu/PsiCafe/KeyTheorists/Watson.htm#About

Watson, J. B. (1913). Psychology as the behaviorist views it. *Psychological Review, 20*, 158–177.

Watson, J. B. (1930). *Behaviorism* (Rev. ed.). Chicago: University of Chicago Press.

WECHSLER ADULT INTELLIGENCE SCALE (WAIS)

The Wechsler Adult Intelligence Scale (WAIS) measures intellectual ability in 16- to 89-year-olds. The first version of the WAIS was released in 1955. The WAIS-III, released in 1997, is the most recent version. The WAIS is currently the most widely used, individually administered adult intelligence test in the world.

The WAIS is one of three Wechsler intelligence scales. The others are the Wechsler Preschool and Primary Scale of Intelligence, for 2.6- to 7.3-year-olds, and the Wechsler Intelligence Scale for Children, for 6- to 16-year-olds.

The WAIS is divided into two major subscales: Verbal and Performance. The Verbal scale measures verbal knowledge, verbal reasoning, and attention to verbal materials. It includes seven subtests: Arithmetic, which measures the ability to perform arithmetic operations; Comprehension, which measures the understanding of practical and social issues; Digit Span, which measures memory for digits; Information, which measures knowledge of factual information; Letter-Number Sequencing, which measures sequential memory for digits and letters; Similarities, which measure the ability to infer relationships between concepts; and Vocabulary, which measures the ability to define words.

The Performance scale measures fluid reasoning, spatial processing, attention to detail, and visual-motor coordination. It includes seven subtests: Block Design, which measures the ability to build a model with blocks; Digit Symbol-Coding, which measures the ability to learn a code of digits and symbols; Matrix Reasoning, which measures the ability to infer a rule in a sequence of geometric shapes; Object Assembly, which measures the ability to assemble a puzzle; Picture Arrangement, which measures the ability to sequence pictures to tell a story; Picture Completion, which measures the ability to identify a missing element in a picture; and Symbol Search, which measures the ability to identify a target symbol within a group.

The WAIS provides normative, age-corrected intelligence quotient (IQ) scores for the Verbal and Performance scales. It also provides a full-scale intelligence quotient (FSIQ) score, which measures general mental ability. By convention, the average FSIQ within an age group is set at 100 and the standard deviation is set at 15.

In addition to the IQ scores, the WAIS provides four index scores of specific cognitive processes. The Verbal Comprehension index measures verbal knowledge and reasoning. The Perceptual Organization Index measures fluid reasoning, attention to detail, and visual-motor coordination. The Working Memory Index measures the ability to hold and manipulate information in memory. The Processing Speed Index measures the ability to process information quickly.

The psychometric properties of the WAIS are excellent. The test–retest stability of WAIS FSIQ (retest interval: 2–12 weeks) is extremely high for 16- to 89-year-olds ($r = 0.95$, corrected for the variability of the standardization sample). The internal consistency reliability of test items used to compute WAIS FSIQ is also extremely high for 16- to 89-year-olds ($r \geq .97$).

Intercorrelations among the WAIS subtests are almost always positive. This indicates that all the WAIS subtests measure the same latent construct, which has been labeled *g*. The *g* loading of a WAIS subtest (i.e., the correlation between the subtest and *g*) can be determined using factor analysis. Factor analysis shows that some WAIS subtests have relatively high *g* loadings (Vocabulary and Block Design), whereas others have relatively low *g* loadings (Digit Span and Digit Symbol-Coding).

The pattern of WAIS subtest and index scores is related to a number of psychological disorders, including mental retardation, attention deficit hyperactivity disorder, reading and math learning disabilities, Parkinson's disease, traumatic brain injury, and schizophrenia. The WAIS scores are also related to cognitive tests of academic achievement (Wechsler Individual Achievement Test), attention and concentration (Trail-Making Test), memory (California Verbal Learning Test), fine motor dexterity (Grooved Pegboard), and executive functioning (Wisconsin Card Sorting Test).

—Thomas R. Coyle

See also Intelligence, Multiple Intelligences

Further Reading and Reference

The Psychological Corporation. (2002). *WAIS-III—WMS-III technical manual.* San Antonio, TX: Author.

WECHSLER INTELLIGENCE SCALE FOR CHILDREN (WISC)

The Wechsler Intelligence Scale for Children (WISC) was developed in 1949 by David Wechsler to be an individually administered assessment of the cognitive abilities of children aged 5 through 15. The WISC was initially a downward extension of Wechsler's adult intelligence test, the Wechsler-Bellevue Intelligence Scale (WBIS, 1939). The WBIS provided a measure of verbal, performance, and overall intelligence by using 12 subtests. Wechsler retained 11 of these subtests for the WISC and added an additional subtest (mazes) as a means of assessing a child's planning and perceptual abilities. The other 11 subtests are Information, Arithmetic, Similarities, Vocabulary, Digit Span, Comprehension, Picture Completion, Picture Arrangement, Block Design, Object Assembly, and Coding.

Since its initial publication, there have been three revisions of the test in order to meet changing testing needs and to reflect current research. In 1974, the WISC-R was published with some updated test items while retaining the original 12 subtests. The age range was increased to cover ages 6 through 16. The WISC-III, released in 1991, retained the original 12 subtests with a few updated test items and also added a new subtest, Symbol Search, as a means of assessing perceptual discrimination, processing speed, and freedom from distraction. Some additional changes to the test makeup were performed with the newest revision, the WISC-IV, released in 2003. The addition of three new subtests, Matrix Reasoning, Cancellation, and Picture Concepts, and the elimination of the Mazes subtest brought the total number of subtests to 15. Yet, throughout the changes and editions of the test, the basic goals have remained the same: to be able to assess the child's general intellectual ability (full-scale intelligence quotient [FSIQ]) as well as other more specific cognitive domains (Index Scores).

In previous editions of the test, the individual's performance was divided into verbal and performance (nonverbal) measures of intelligence. This separation did not reflect a belief in different forms of intelligence, but rather reflected different means of measuring the one underlying general level of intelligence (Spearman's *g*). However, the WISC-IV focuses on measuring more specific cognitive domains represented by the four indices—Verbal Comprehension, Working Memory, Perceptual Reasoning, and Processing Speed—in addition to the overall FSIQ score. Each index is composed of subtests that collectively measure a specific cognitive domain. The Verbal Comprehension Index is composed of Similarities, Vocabulary, and Comprehension. The Perceptual Reasoning Index is composed of Block Design, Picture Concepts, and Matrix Reasoning. The Working Memory Index includes Digit Span and Letter-Number Sequencing, whereas the Perceptual Speed Index has Coding and Symbol Search.

Upon completion of the WISC-IV, an FSIQ score can be derived. Historically, an IQ score was the ratio (or quotient) of an individual's mental age (MA) to her or his chronological age (CA), as shown below.

$$IQ = \frac{\text{MA}}{\text{CA}} \times 100$$

Today, instead of using the quotient method, standard scores are derived by comparing an individual's score with a set of normative scores within the individual's age range. Thus, the FSIQ represents the child's ability in relation to her or his peers. The average FSIQ score is 100, with 68% of scores falling between 85 and 115; 95% of scores range from 70 to 130. Standard scores are often represented as percentile rankings. Someone with a standard score of 100 would have a percentile ranking of 50%, meaning that the child scored greater than or equal to 50% of her or his peers.

The WISC-IV is used in clinical, counseling, and school settings to assess the cognitive abilities and deficits of children. Many institutions use this instrument to assess for admittance into "gifted" programs and to assist in the diagnosis of learning disabilities or mental retardation.

—Peter K. Stewart and Ric G. Steele

See also Intelligence, Multiple Intelligences

Further Readings and References

Sattler, J. M. (2001). *Assessment of children: Cognitive applications.* La Mesa, CA: Jerome M. Sattler.

Wechsler, D. (2003). *WISC-IV technical and interpretive manual.* San Antonio, TX: The Psychological Corporation.

WEIGHT

Weight refers to the amount or quantity of heaviness or body mass, that is, the force that gravity exerts on an individual or thing. A person's body weight includes the heaviness of the skeleton, muscles, bodily fluids (e.g., blood, water), internal organs, and adipose (i.e., fat) tissue that surrounds and protects the bone and organs. Adipose tissue (also known as *body fat*) also stores energy for later use. Without fat cells, people could not afford to skip a meal; thus, famine or illnesses that interfere with appetite would lead to certain death.

Height and weight are correlated. As human bodies grow and develop, they generally increase in both stature and mass. Failure to thrive, malnutrition, and metabolic disorders are among the reasons infants might not gain weight, and all are obvious reasons for concern. The rate at which infants gain weight varies. It depends not only on the infants' general health and the amount of food they are offered but also on genetic differences in metabolic rate and the initial size and number of their fat cells. As children grow, their activity levels also affect their body weight, as some use more of their energy stores than others.

There are certain times in human development when people are more or less prone to add fat cells or for existing cells to increase in size. For example, boys' percentage of body fat tends to increase during prepubertal phases of development and to decrease during the adolescent growth spurt (i.e., they become leaner following puberty). In contrast, girls' percentage of body fat is relatively stable in childhood, but increases during the adolescent growth spurt. Between ages 10 and 15, on average, the percentage of body fat in boys decreases from 17.8% to 11.2%, and the percentage in girls increases from 16.6% to 23.5%. Girls' pubertal increase in body fat is a necessary prerequisite for menarche, the initiation of the menstrual cycle. Other reproductive milestones (e.g., pregnancy, menopause) also result in weight gain for women. Epidemiologic studies indicate that between the ages of 20 and 50, men's percentage of body fat doubles and women's percentage increases by about 50%. Furthermore, metabolic rate slows as people age. Therefore, if older people do not cut their caloric intake below levels that were typical for them at midlife, they are likely to gain weight. Chronic illness or disability may result in decreased activity level, which also increases the likelihood of weight gain.

There is considerable evidence to support what scientists call the *set-point hypothesis*, that is, the idea that all animals (including humans) are designed to maintain their weight within a certain genetically programmed range, the middle of which is known as the set-point. The system works much like the thermostat connected to a furnace. If people increase their activity levels, the brain increases their appetites and slows down their metabolism so that their body weight will remain about the same. Similarly, if people increase their eating or decrease their activity levels, the brain increases the metabolic rate and decreases appetite in an attempt to maintain the "preferred" weight range. The set-point moves during growth and development to accommodate the changes described earlier. It may also move or become inefficient if the system is dysregulated by, for example, binge-purge behavior, yo-yo dieting, medication side effects, or metabolic disorders.

CONSEQUENCES OF SIGNIFICANT WEIGHT LOSS OR GAIN

Failure to thrive and undiagnosed metabolic disorders (e.g., diabetes mellitus) can result in death. Severe protein malnutrition (rarely seen in developed countries) results in kwashiorkor, a disorder in which a child's stomach, face, and legs swell with water even though their arms are as thin as sticks and their skeletal growth has ceased. More common results of malnutrition are vitamin and mineral deficiencies (e.g., beriberi, pellagra, anemia), cognitive deficiencies (e.g., memory difficulty, slowness of thought, depression), weak bones, and digestive problems (e.g., constipation, heartburn). Malnutrition during adolescence and adulthood can result in the cessation of menstrual cycles (i.e., amenorrhea), and malnutrition during pregnancy can result in miscarriage, low birth weight, or premature birth.

Anorexia nervosa is an eating disorder that is characterized by excessive dieting, distorted body image, an intense fear of gaining weight, and, in women and girls, amenorrhea. Although it is classified as a psychiatric disorder, anorexia nervosa is a form of self-starvation, which results in malnutrition and other physical signs and symptoms, such as brittle bones, bone marrow failure, reduced thyroid function, dry and yellowed skin, slowed breathing and cardiac rhythm, intolerance of cold temperatures, swollen joints, reduced muscle mass, brittle hair and nails, anemia, feeling faint, dehydration, and kidney abnormalities. As many as 5% to 10% of anorexics die from either starvation or suicide. The disorder can occur in either sex, but it is more common in girls and women.

Excessive weight gain can also have serious consequences for individuals. Excessive weight, especially in the form of adipose tissue that collects around the waist, is a risk factor for a number of chronic illnesses, including diabetes, hypertension, heart disease, arthritis, gallbladder disease, and some forms of cancer. Extra weight means extra stress on the joints and cardiovascular system, which can result in decreased stamina and flexibility and make it difficult to maintain physical fitness. Furthermore, heavy people who live in societies that value thinness (and believe that only thin people can be attractive) are often subject to discrimination (e.g., in hiring, promotion, college admissions) and social prejudice (e.g., teasing, bullying).

Lifestyle changes during the decades of the 20th century in industrialized societies have made it increasingly likely that people will gain excess weight. As economies have shifted from agricultural and heavy manufacturing to light manufacturing and service industries, people have used less energy to perform their jobs. The ubiquity of automobiles has resulted in less time spent walking or bicycling, and entertainment and leisure activities have also changed in a more sedentary direction. People are now more likely to watch sports than to participate in them, and television, computers, and electronic games have become

the favorite pastimes of many children and adolescents. In addition, high-calorie foods (e.g., those high in fat and sugar) are increasingly available and heavily advertised. Sociocultural pressures to eat more and exercise less can lead to dysregulation of the set-point system because the body can only do so much to compensate for the energy imbalance that people create. Furthermore, fad diets and diet products can also dysregulate the set-point system. If people suddenly and significantly restrict their caloric consumption, the brain reacts the same way it does when a natural famine occurs. The metabolic rate will slow as much as possible, which makes it much harder to lose weight while on the diet and much easier to gain it back once the diet is over.

HOW MUCH WEIGHT IS TOO MUCH? HOW LITTLE IS TOO LITTLE?

Individuals' "ideal" weight may be determined genetically, the set-point described previously. However, the set-point is theoretical and cannot be measured. Physicians who worked for the Metropolitan Life Insurance Company reviewed thousands of files of their customers in an attempt to determine the average weights of the healthiest and unhealthiest. Their research led to the construction of tables of ideal weight ranges based on small, medium, and large body frames, and these tables were used as guidelines for many years. Unfortunately, the data in the tables came primarily from white, midlife, middle-class men, the people who were most likely to buy life insurance. There is no way to be sure that the weight ranges are actually ideal for any given person, and the determination of body frame size is, in many cases, arbitrary.

The calculation of body mass index (BMI) avoids the frame size controversy by dividing weight (in kilograms) by the square of height (in meters). However, the cutoff points that divide healthy from unhealthy BMIs remain arbitrary, may not be culturally appropriate, and do not allow us to distinguish between the weight of constituent parts of the body. Percentage and location of body fat seem to be more important to health than is body weight. Methods of calculating the percentage of body fat (bioelectrical impedance analysis, hydrostatic weighing, caliper tests) have been developed; however, their accuracy is debatable, and the amount of fat that is considered ideal remains an arbitrary cultural construction. Perhaps the only way ever to know how much weight is too much and how little is too little is when symptoms of malnutrition or chronic illness appear. No one wants to test that hypothesis; thus, the best advice we can follow is to take steps to prevent weight-related illnesses.

FOCUS ON HEALTH, NOT WEIGHT

Once people lose or gain a great deal of body weight, the set-point makes it difficult to return to a healthy weight range. Therefore, people should eat a variety of healthy foods and avoid eating large amounts of high-calorie snacks and desserts. Foods high in fat and sugar content should be considered "treats" and eaten occasionally, as opposed to daily. The amount of dietary fat people need varies with developmental stage; infants and young children need greater amounts than midlife and older people do, and consumption should change with age. Don't forget the other side of the energy equation: Most people in industrialized societies should increase their activity levels. At every developmental stage, people need to get regular exercise by engaging in sports or walking or jogging regularly. Work activities (e.g., vacuuming) and hobbies (e.g., gardening) help us to maintain physical fitness and keep our energy intake and expenditure in balance, as do small lifestyle changes, such as parking farther away from our destination and taking stairs instead of elevators.

People have much less control over their body weight and shape than most Americans believe, but there are steps we can take to increase our chances of being healthy and physically fit. A focus on health rather than weight is very important. Our body is our friend, not our enemy, and we should treat it with respect rather than with loathing. Respect includes proper feeding and exercising, so that we work with our body, not against it.

—*Joan C. Chrisler*

Further Readings and References

Bray, G. A., Bouchard, C., & James, W. P. T. (Eds.). (1998). *Handbook of obesity*. New York: Marcel Dekker.

Hsu, L. K. G. (1990). *Eating disorders*. New York: Guilford.

National Association to Advance Fat Acceptance, http://www.naafa.org

National Association of Anorexia Nervosa and Associated Disorders, http://www.anad.org

National Institute of Diabetes and Digestive and Kidney Diseases, http://www.niddk.nih.gov/health/nutrit/nutrit.htm

Willett, W. C. (1994). Diet and health: What should we eat? *Science, 264*, 532–537.

WELL-BABY CHECKUP

Physicians typically use well-baby checkups to monitor a child's growth and development, conduct necessary medical tests and interventions, and provide parents with anticipatory guidance. Thus, well-baby checkups are an invaluable means of promoting the health and development of infants and young children, although the events of each appointment may vary according to the child's age and issues unique to the child or family. Typically, physicians check a child's growth by measuring head circumference, height, and weight and then calculating a body mass index (BMI). Thus, health care providers are able to track a child's growth over time and ensure that growth is following a healthy trajectory.

Physicians also use regular baby checkups to observe and ask parents questions about their child's development. All aspects of development can be evaluated, including gross motor, fine motor, speech, and social-emotional development, as well as hearing and sight. For newborns, physicians likely would inquire about an infant's ability to move all four extremities, sucking reflex and visual tracking, and response to the parent's face and voice. For older infants, physicians' questions likely would include whether the infant is able to sit and crawl, whether the baby is grasping and mouthing objects, and whether the baby is babbling, smiling, and laughing.

Conducting recommended medical tests and interventions allows the physician to check for signs of illness. Each infant's temperature, heart rate, and respiratory rate are measured, and a thorough physical examination is conducted, including the infant's skin, eyes, ears, mouth, abdomen, and joints. A hearing screening is often conducted at some point. Tests are run for metabolic and blood disorders. If risk factors are present, children may also be tested for lead exposure. In the well-child appointment, mandatory immunizations are conducted according to a schedule set by the Centers for Disease Control and Prevention. Mandatory immunizations for infants include hepatitis B, diphtheria, tetanus, and pertussis (DTaP); *Haemophilus influenzae* type B (HiB); measles, mumps, and rubella (MMR); varicella; pneumococcal vaccine (PCV); and inactivated polio virus (IPV). If certain risk factors are present, physicians may recommend additional vaccines.

Well-baby checkups also provide parents with anticipatory guidance regarding issues such as injury and illness prevention, developmental expectations, and family and community issues. For newborns, anticipatory guidance topics may include putting infants to sleep on their backs to prevent sudden infant death syndrome, securing infants properly into car seats, and feeding infants. For older infants, physicians are likely to address issues such as home safety, setting rules and limits, and how to handle sibling interactions, as applicable. Discussion of these and other topics provides parents with important information and opens the door for parents to ask further questions about their child's health, development, and behavior. Physicians may also consider referring a family to community resources, if needed.

Well-baby checkups promote the prevention, early detection, and treatment of medical and developmental problems and help ensure a child's healthy growth. Checkups also allow parents the opportunity to ask questions about their child's health and development. Children should receive well-baby checkups at the times designated by the National Center for Education in Maternal and Child Health: at birth, within the first week of life, and at 1 month, 2 months, 4 months, 6 months, and 9 months of age. For young children, checkups should occur at 1 year, 15 months, 18 months, 2 years, 3 years, and 4 years of age.

SUMMARY

Regular well-baby checkups serve several important functions, including monitoring children's growth and development, conducting necessary medical tests and interventions, and providing parents with anticipatory guidance.

—Christy Kleinsorge and
Michael C. Roberts

Further Readings and References

American Academy of Pediatrics, Committee on Psychosocial Aspects of Child and Family Health. (2002). *Guidelines for health supervision III*. Elk Grove Village, IL: Author.

Centers for Disease Control and Prevention. (2004). *Recommended childhood and adolescent immunization schedule: United States, January–June 2004*. Retrieved from http://www.cdc.gov/nip/recs/child-schedule.htm#Printable

Green, M., Palfrey, J. S., Clark, E. M., & Anastasi, J. M. (Eds.). (2002). *Bright futures: Guidelines for health supervision of infants, children, and adolescents* (2nd ed., revised). Arlington, VA: National Center for Education in Maternal and Child Health.

U.S. National Library of Medicine and National Institutes of Health. (2003). *Medical encyclopedia: Well-child visits*. Retrieved from http://www.nlm.hih.gov/medlineplus/ency/article/001928.htm

WHOLE LANGUAGE

Whole language, now largely discredited, was a popular educational philosophy and style of reading instruction that emerged in the late 1970s and flourished until the mid-1990s. Influential whole language theorists likened reading development to the natural and effortless emergence of oral language in young children, and a process that students would spontaneously acquire if they were immersed in a nurturing, literature-rich environment. Advocates such as Marie Clay, Kenneth Goodman, and Reggie Routman helped transform the teaching of reading by rhapsodically describing whole language classrooms as student centered (not teacher centered), meaning centered (not skill centered), and focused on literature (not on discreet letters and sounds or on phonics-based basal readers).

During the era of its popularity, whole language teachers rejected traditional instruction that used phonics, spelling lessons, and reading skill workbooks. Teachers came to embrace the idea that literacy concepts were to be discovered, not taught, and that learning to read should be natural, playful, easy, and meaningful. Professors in teachers' colleges, classroom teachers, and publishers quickly jumped on the whole language bandwagon.

CLASSROOM PRACTICES

A variety of teaching practices were associated with the whole language movement. Whole language teachers were encouraged to read literature aloud to students, give "picture walks" (talk about story illustrations) before guided reading, affix labels to objects in the classroom, and read big books while sweeping their hands under the lines of text. Beginning readers were encouraged to memorize short stories, rhymes, and predictable books. Daily activities focused on literature appreciation, enjoyable projects, discussions, and writing activities.

Whole language classrooms were typically organized into learning centers or cooperative pods, rather than in rows facing the teacher. Words were often posted on "word walls" around the room. Many schools mandated schoolwide DEAR (drop everything and read) or SSR (sustained silent reading) time to provide for independent student reading. Because whole language advocates railed against standardized testing and instead promoted the use of "authentic assessments," teachers were urged to evaluate students based on portfolio evidence, conferences, and student reflections.

FALLING OUT OF FAVOR

Although much was written about the ecstasy of the whole language classroom (and some reports did show increased student motivation with certain practices), several comprehensive meta-analytic reports of empirical reading research have compellingly debunked whole language ideology, pointing instead to the crucial importance of systematic, explicit instruction in phonemic awareness and phonics for beginning readers. Research shows that most students learn to read when they are carefully taught to read and not merely exposed to good literature and fun literacy experiences.

WHOLE LANGUAGE LEAVES A LEGACY

Although many analysts blame whole language practices for years of plummeting reading achievement scores, the movement can actually be credited with bringing several benefits to the field. Whole language brought a renewed understanding of the importance of good literature in schools, a fresh emphasis on the importance of daily writing practice, the necessity for allowing "invented spelling" or "temporary spelling" while beginning writers practice sound and symbol generalizations, the idea that spelling is developmental, the essential importance of the teacher–learner relationship, and the necessity of reading instruction being exciting and pleasurable for students.

Although the U.S. government has now strongly endorsed phonemic awareness and phonics as essential components of beginning reading instruction, whole language practices persist in many classrooms. Certainly some teachers who identify themselves as whole language teachers artfully combine literature-based learning with more recently mandated research-based phonics instruction. But phonics experts (sometimes teasingly called *phonicators)* and whole language enthusiasts (sometimes termed *holy*

languagers or *holey languagers*) continue their pedagogical debates in the persistent so-called reading wars. The whole language movement inspired controversy that lingers today.

—*Lynn Melby Gordon*

See also Language Development

Further Readings and References

Adams, M. (1990). *Beginning to read: Thinking and learning about print*. Cambridge: MIT Press.

Goodman, K. S., & Goodman, Y. M. (1979). Learning to read is natural. In L. B. Resnick & P. A. Weaver (Eds.), *Theory and practice of early reading: Vol. 1* (pp. 137–154). Hillsdale, NJ: Erlbaum.

Goodman, K. S. (1986). *What's whole in whole language?* Portsmouth, NH: Heinemann Educational Books.

Moats, L. C. (2000). *Whole language lives on: The illusion of "balanced reading" instruction*. Washington, DC: Fordham Foundation. Retrieved from http://www.edexcellence.net /doc/moats.pdf

National Institute of Child Health and Human Development. (2000). *Report of the National Reading Panel. Teaching children to read: An evidence-based assessment of the scientific research literature on reading and its implications for reading instruction*. Retrieved from http://www .nichd.nih.gov/publications/nrp/smallbook.htm

Watson, D. (1989). Defining and describing whole language. *Elementary School Journal, 90,* 130–141.

Weaver, C. (1990). *Understanding whole language: From principle to practice*. Portsmouth, NH: Heinemann Educational Books.

WIDOWHOOD AND WIDOWERHOOD

The loss of a spouse is typically characterized as one of life's most stressful events, and older adults often state that the loss of a spouse is the defining event of their later years. A wide range of reactions is possible when a person enters into widowhood or widowerhood. Although research has suggested that widowed individuals experience a variety of challenges, it is important to remember that each person's reaction is highly influenced by his or her specific situation. Factors such as length of marriage, age of widow or widower, social and family support, financial resources, type of loss, and many other features make each situation unique.

According to the 2003 U.S. Census, about 2.5% of men (widowers) and 9.7% of women (widows) older than 15 years were classified as widowed. This translates into almost 14 million Americans who have lost a spouse and have not remarried. Research on widowhood and widowerhood has typically focused on the challenges faced by older widows. This is likely because about 62% of all widowed individuals are women older than 65. Conversely, there has been comparatively little research done on widowers, younger widows, and individuals who have lost a same-sex partner.

Both widows and widowers face significant challenges as they adjust to the loss of their partner. Studies have shown that widowed individuals face notably higher rates of health problems. Older widows and widowers also experience higher rates of disability and mortality than married controls. Not surprisingly, both widows and widowers have significantly higher rates of depression than their married counterparts. Often these elevated rates of depression can continue for many years.

It is difficult to determine whether men or women are affected more negatively by the loss of their spouse. Widowers tend to seek out and receive less social support. They are also less inclined to openly express their emotions regarding their loss. Conversely, widows tend to seek out social support and tend to openly convey their grief. Many researchers have argued that marriage tends to be more beneficial for men, and so the loss of their spouse has a greater negative impact. Additionally, many men expect to precede their spouse in death and therefore are surprised when the opposite occurs. Some men have difficulty dealing with the daily aspects of living alone, including eating healthy meals and maintaining a clean living environment. On the other hand, widows often have difficulty sustaining the same standard of living and managing their financial affairs.

An area of specific concern for widowers, especially older widowers, is the markedly increased rates of suicide. Older widowers have a suicide rate about 12 times as high as the rate for older widows. Widowers also demonstrate an increased rate of alcohol abuse compared with other men of the same age.

Some widowed individuals, especially younger widows and widowers, remarry at some point in their life. Research has shown that men are more likely than women to remarry, and younger widows are more likely than older widows to remarry. A significant factor in remarriage is the availability of suitable partners, which explains the relatively low rate of remarriage by older widows. However, it is interesting to note that older widowers do not have a higher rate of remarriage than younger widowers. This suggests that some widowed individuals, especially older individuals, simply choose not to remarry.

—*Jason M. Troyer*

See also Death

Further Readings and References

AARP—Grief and Loss, http://www.aarp.org/life/griefand loss/
GROWW—Grief and Recovery Online (founded by) Widows & Widowers, http://www.groww.com
Lee, G., Willetts, M. C., & Seccombe, K. (1998). Widowhood and depression: Gender differences. *Research on Aging, 20,* 611–630.
Stroebe, M. S., Hansson, R. O., Stroebe, W., & Schut, H. (Eds.). (2001). *Handbook of bereavement research: Consequences, coping, and care.* Washington, DC: American Psychological Association.
U.S. Census Bureau. (2003). *American community survey profile* [2003, Table PCT013]. Retrieved from http://www.census.gov/acs/www/index.html
Widow Net—Resources for Widows and Widowers, http://www.widownet.org

WISDOM

What comes to mind when thinking of wise people? Individuals might think of religious leaders, gurus, priests, medicine men, shamans, and sometimes politicians or therapists. These don't necessarily need to be famous people. On a personal level, someone might think of one's grandfather or grandmother and remember a situation in which their advice shed new light in a situation and was therefore eye opening.

What all these people have in common is a certain age. Rarely is wisdom attributed to a young woman or man. It is attributed to people in *late adulthood* who have had many experiences in life. This is the case in most cultures around the world. On the one hand, wisdom can be a goal of development, that is, something people strive for; on the other hand, wisdom can be the prerequisite for successful coping with life tasks during a certain life period. In any case, wisdom is something positive and admirable.

To get a better grasp of the concept, wisdom has often been discussed in the context of *intelligence*. Cattell distinguished between fluid and crystallized intelligence. Fluid intelligence is related to deductive reasoning, abstract thinking, heuristics for coping with new situations, and the speed of processing information. Fluid intelligence has its peak in young adulthood and declines with age. Crystallized intelligence refers to the whole body of experiences, skills, algorithms, and factual knowledge. Crystallized intelligence almost always increases with age. The increase in crystallized intelligence can make up for the loss in fluid intelligence. Crystallized intelligence can be seen as the basis of wisdom. However, there are some differences between crystallized intelligence and wisdom. First, crystallized intelligence is assessed in intelligence tests on information, vocabulary, facts, and school learning. Wisdom can hardly be measured because it is related to concrete knowledge about life experiences, including life's uncertainties and paradoxes. Second, contrary to intelligence, wisdom is less related to the current sociopolitical conditions. Wisdom encompasses a broader timeframe, learning from history, knowing the past to inform the future and to reflect on the present. Third, wisdom is more then just a body of theoretical knowledge. It has cognitive, motivational, affective, and interpersonal qualities.

For example, professors are often seen as very knowledgeable and bright, but not always necessarily as wise. The *cognitive* component of wisdom refers to experiential and practical knowledge of life. Wise advice is given with a profound understanding of the person and the situation. Wisdom is often connected with thinking outside the box and interpreting the situation from a different angle. It can be seen as the ability to deal successfully with the uncertainties, complexities, and problems of life. As the philosopher Karl Popper stated, "Living is problem solving. Problems and life entered the world together and with them problem solving." Wisdom often refers to creative strategies of problem solving. Strategies are abstract prescriptions on how to interpret and solve life problems, for example, being patient and sacrificing the immediate for the long-term good.

A wise person is not *motivated* by power, glory, or fame. Wise advice is given without considering one's own personal interest and benefits. The person in need or the society in need benefits from the wise advice. The motivation is to care and to be responsible for others. This is the interpersonal component of wisdom. *Emotionally*, a wise person is often described as courageous, fearless, and calm, with a healthy distance from the situation.

The description of the different components of wisdom sheds new light on the question of whether wisdom has a strong *genetic* component or can be *learned*. Often, the genetic side of wisdom has been emphasized. However, wisdom could be partly acquired by being available for reflection and reflexivity in one's life experiences, learning values of responsibility for oneself and the community, learning that giving is sometimes more than receiving, deciding and acting on choices that benefit more people in the long term rather than focusing on the immediate and sole gratification of a few people, and understanding the essentials of life, including the paradoxes and realities, in more detail.

Wisdom of individuals can become part of the wisdom of a collective, for example, a cultural group's *sayings* or *proverbs*. Von Senger, for example, analyzed such proverbs in the Chinese language. Especially relevant today, yet conceived more than 2,300 years ago, Sun Tsu analyzed the art of war in China, according to successful and unsuccessful strategies, for example, "Know your enemy, know yourself, and your victory will not be threatened. Know the terrain, know the weather, and your victory will be complete." Or "No country has ever benefited from a protracted war." Or "The supreme art of war is to subdue the enemy without fighting." However, such sayings or proverbs do not always give clear prescriptions for acting because they are often contradictory, for example, "Don't put off until tomorrow what you can do today" but "Sleep on it," meaning either act right away or wait before you act. Wisdom refers to the ability to consider the demands of the situation. In some situations, it might be appropriate to wait. Time might lead to a clearer mental representation of the problem situation and thus be helpful for coming up with a solution. In other situations, it might be appropriate to act right away. The situation might change, the chance of the moment might be lost, or waiting might aggravate the problem. A wise person, then, is one who considers the value of timing and context of the situation, and adheres to the greater good of people.

To summarize, wisdom refers to the understanding of people in concrete life situations. Wisdom is based on a huge body of life experience and knowledge of problem-solving strategies and on an emotional distance and fearlessness when giving advice without having one's own intentions in mind.

—C. Dominik Güss

Further Readings and References

Cattell, R. B. (1987). *Intelligence: Its structure, growth, and action*. New York: Elsevier.

Clayton, V. (1982). Wisdom and intelligence: The nature and function of knowledge in the later years. *International Journal of Aging and Human Development, 15*(4), 315–321.

Griffith, S. B. (1963). *Sun Tzu: The art of war*. Oxford, UK: Oxford University Press.

Güss, D. (2002). Planning in Brazil, India, and Germany: A cross-cultural study, a cultural study, and a model. In W. J. Lonner, D. L. Dinnel, S. A. Hayes, & D. N. Sattler (Eds.), *Online readings in psychology and culture*. Bellingham: Western Washington University, Department of Psychology, Center for Cross-Cultural Research. Available from http://www.wwu.edu/~culture

Kunzmann, U., & Baltes, P. B. (2003). Wisdom-related knowledge: Affective, motivational, and interpersonal correlates. *Personality and Social Psychology Bulletin, 29*(9), 1104–1119.

Marchand, H. (n.d.). *An overview of the psychology of wisdom*. Retrieved from http://www.prometheus.org.uk/Publishing/Journal/Papers/MarchandOnWisdom/Main.htm

von Senger, H. (Ed.). (1999). *Die List* [The cunning]. Frankfurt am Main, Germany: Suhrkamp.

WORK

Work is commonly defined as an activity that involves effort and sometimes reward. The result of work could be the achievement of a goal, the meeting of a demand, the completion of a task, or the generation of income. This variety of results of work reflects the different meanings that have been and continue to be attached to the activity of work. These differing results of work are associated with a range of psychological and development factors. Work can be considered from a historical perspective but also in terms of its developmental and psychological consequences. The sorts of activities that many in the Western world call work are very different from those pursued by our ancestors. However, some of our current approaches and attitudes toward work may be more than 2 million years old.

Evidence of work as a fundamental activity of human development is often inferred from discoveries of fossilized tools. Using this approach, work has been documented occurring at least 2 million years ago in the Olduvai Gorge in Tanzania. The extinct species of the genus *Homo habilis* apparently used stone chopping tools to butcher dead animals. About 700,000 years ago, hand axes were in use, and thereafter, there is evidence of specialized industries being established based on crafting stone or flint into a variety of different tools.

Debate continues about the degree of organization that existed in production of these crude tools and about the degree of organization in the trade and deployment of such tools. The traditional view is that work was no more than an attempt to meet direct survival demands. Indeed, many accounts of early humans portray them as working as scavengers and behaving like savages. However, there are intriguing examples from relatively modern times that may point to a more sophisticated role of work in the earliest human groups. Aboriginal tribes in the Northern Territory of Australia did not develop tools beyond stone axes at the time of their first contact with white settlers in the 19th century. However, they had developed advanced trade and distribution networks for their tools.

It appears that even primitive forms of work were focused on more than just survival demands. Trade and distribution of tools require planning, logistics, and demarcation of roles. Passing on skills to the next generation requires training and development. Furthermore, it appears that survival demands were not as unrelenting and fraught as some have supposed. Studies of modern hunter-gatherer societies reveal that they often have time for activities other than those associated with the immediate survival of the group, such as hunting, gathering, and fighting rival groups. These other activities included social interactions within and beyond the group, ceremonies, rituals, and religious and aesthetic pursuits. All these activities tended to blend into a kind of "group or tribal life" and were not divided up as in modern developed societies. For example, such tribe people painted the animals they hunted, married and procreated for the survival of the group, and engaged in religious activities often to enlist the favor of the Spirit or Spirits for ongoing personal health and community well-being.

WORK AND SLAVERY

As agrarian societies developed, work and all other aspects of farming life were determined by the seasons. Life and work were cyclical—sow, tend, harvest, store. Amid the vicissitudes of climate (good and bad seasons, floods and droughts), there was a rhythm to existence. Agrarian societies initiated the establishment of private ownership of land. Agriculture also was more specialized and required markets for commodities. With a scarcity of labor and advances in technology, slavery was supplied through either conquest or purchase, and a life of work developed in various parts of the world.

Slavery underpinned some of the greatest civilizations in history. Although slaves predominantly engaged in manual labor, particularly agricultural work, some slaves worked as tradespeople, teachers, domestics, and doctors. Slavery is one of the most powerful examples of the stratification of society through the division of labor. Slaves were often seen by the ruling class as an unruly rabble that was temperamentally work-shy and untrustworthy. This "rabble mentality" was echoed in management theories of the early 20th century and is still evident in some current confrontational management practices. The dependency on slave labor has been associated with the decline of the Roman Empire because of the loss of a work ethic among the citizens.

Slavery reminds us of the central role of freedom and discretion in work. Slaves did not have freedom of expression, congregation, worship, representation, decision making, fear, or want. The distinction between slavery and freedom is not as clear-cut as it might seem. An interesting question is whether the slave of Roman times would identify with a modern executive living in a company-paid house, driving a company car, working 85 hours a week, espousing the company values and vision statement, and being at the beck and call of his or her employer by mobile telephone and email.

WORK AND RELIGION

In less developed societies, religion served to foster the success of survival activities such as cultivation, gathering, hunting, and harvesting. However, in European civilization for about 1,000 years, the organizational prowess of the Christian Church resulted in large landholdings and massive building projects, which in turn afforded a range of work opportunities. These created significant wealth for the Church and with it material and mercantile temptations.

Protestantism provided a potent doctrine that combined religious devotion with the extolling of hard

work. The Protestant Work Ethic emphasized thrift, industry, wealth, and discipline as fundamental virtues. Whereas in the past, Roman Catholic orthodoxy had interpreted the Bible as presenting work was a curse, Protestants reinterpreted work as a blessing. For example, in the book of Genesis in the Old Testament, God is presented as a worker who creates the world in 6 days and ceases from his labors to rest on the 7th day. Moreover, Adam in his unfallen state is commanded to work, tending and ruling creation as God's steward. It is a naïve misreading of the text (still prevalent in textbooks today) to interpret work as a curse after the Fall. Work was originally viewed as good and as part of what humans were made for; however, like every good thing, after the introduction of sin, its blessing became its curse. That is, work in Biblical terms is not a curse in itself; instead, work has become cursed in that we encounter frustration, toil, and obstruction. Protestantism, especially Puritanism and Quakerism, was exported to and flourished in America. The emphasis on hard work and community led to an unprecedented organization of labor into jobs and work shifts. In addition to manufacturing endeavors such as Cadburys in England and Hershey in America, Quakers opened banks and established lines of credit outside of the normal confines of the city.

SPECIALIZATION OF WORK

As settled societies developed towns and new technologies, further specialization of work functions occurred. In particular, a stratum of society sat between the slaves, peasants, laborers, and serfs and the ruling classes of soldiers, lords, knights, and kings. These were the craftsmen who organized themselves along functional lines into part trade unions and part trade associations. In medieval Britain, they were called guilds, but similar organizations developed around the world. Hierarchies existed within these *guilds*, with long apprenticeships to reach the level of a journeyman. The highest level, Master, was achieved after many years of work and the production of a "masterpiece" accepted by the guild.

Guilds provided a powerful mechanism for the control of skilled labor. Guilds in some towns had significant political power as a result of their control of skilled labor. As guilds became more sophisticated, the emphasis moved toward trading the skills and away from the development of the skills. Masters of guilds restricted the number entering and progressing through the guilds to maintain control over the supply of skilled labor. As a result of this, many workers were employed as "wagemen," as opposed to apprentices or journeymen. This created a new class of employer-employee relationship.

The industrialization of Western societies in the late 18th and early 19th centuries dramatically severed the necessary nexus of work and the natural world. Increasingly, work became linked to technology, usually centralized in factories and mills, necessitating massive and unparalleled urbanization around the new sources of employment. Economic power determined the nature and conditions of the work available and, as a consequence, the life circumstances of millions of employees. As a result, employees eventually organized into unions to bargain over the pay and conditions of work. In the process, the field of industrial relations emerged and has remained one of the central characteristics of contemporary working life in developed economies. The change from an agrarian to an industrial era was difficult for many workers. Many resented the loss of autonomy of having a farm of their own, being forced to move to the city often to live in squalor, being underpaid and forced to work in dangerous conditions, having no control over the work process, and being consigned to repetitive and seemingly useless sets of duties. Work became associated with mass production and mass production with worker alienation, which sometimes found expression in industrial sabotage. As industrialism developed, work became increasingly fragmented, simplified, and repetitive.

WORK AND TECHNOLOGY

Technology has profoundly influenced work practices throughout history. Two inventions in the past century that have generated dramatic change are the internal combustion engine and the microcomputer. The internal combustion engine greatly enhanced the mechanization of work. For the first time, workers were not necessarily undertaking the primary work tasks, but were instead tending, operating, or maintaining machines that did. This created an explosion in productivity as production was no longer directly related to worker effort or skill. The Ford Motor Company is often credited with the introduction of the production line method of working; however, Ford management had observed a Chicago meat-packing

business where carcasses were hung from moving hooks and were butchered as they moved along. Until 1909, cars were assembled in teams, with all the workers being involved in the process of construction from start to finish. When production lines were introduced, productivity jumped, and the cost of a Model T Ford halved in 3 years. Workers were reduced to doing one or two activities on a product as it moved along a conveyor belt. These same activities were repeated thousands of time per day, and yet at the end of the day, there was still an apparently endless stream of further products to be processed the same way. People often reported being treated either as part of one of the machines or like a monkey. Such work robbed the workers in many cases of a sense of achievement, a sense of ownership, a sense of skill and personal development, and a sense of meaning through work.

As the quality of working life declined in industrial societies, the value of nonwork time increased. The demarcation of work to a specific location and a number of hours per week delimited work and how it was understood by many in industrialized societies. The problem that increased production created for Ford was that supply outstripped demand because the working hours at the time were so long, individuals did not have time to devote to other activities for which a motor vehicle might be required. Henry Ford's solution was to cut the hours of work so that workers would be able to use the cars that he was producing. The widespread availability of motor vehicles to large portions of society further fueled the pace of change. Workers were able to live further from their place of work, creating suburbs and commuters. Furthermore, there was a large increase in tourism because ordinary people were now able to access distant parts of the country rapidly. This stimulated a nascent tourism and service industry that was already benefiting from enhanced rail infrastructure. The relationship between work and nonwork and leisure has become a major field of theory and research.

Communications technology also had a dramatic effect on work in the late 19th and 20th centuries. The telegraph and then the telephone made the world a smaller place and enabled information to be exchanged at a hitherto unheard-of pace. By the mid-20th century, the computer was developed, and it began to be used by governments and large organizations in the 1950s and 1960s. However, the development of the microprocessor chip led to the first personal computers being widely available for business and home use. The IBM Personal Computer was launched with Microsoft software in 1981. The Apple Corporation had already released the Apple II computer. The impact of the introduction of the personal computer was almost instant. These machines were capable of doing many of the routine clerical tasks in offices faster and more accurately than human clerks. In the same way that machinery had led rapidly to redundancies in manufacturing jobs, computers cut a swathe through clerical jobs. Computers were also employed to control machines, creating robots for a range of tasks, including motor vehicle manufacture.

The combination of communication technology and computer technology has led to further rapid changes in how we work. Telecommuting is now a fact of life for many workers. Employees do not need to be physically present in the workplace; indeed, the notion of the workplace is changing. The mobile phone, laptop computer, and Internet have brought the workplace back into the home for the first time in hundreds of years for some sections of the workforce. This has further complicated the separation of work and nonwork.

With rapid growth in the use of technology, efficiency of production and process has very often come at the expense of employment opportunities and at the cost of nonwork time.

Technological advancement has significantly lengthened the hours of work for some well-educated people in the workforce while at the same time presented long-term unemployment for less-skilled workers. Furthermore, the employer-employee relationship is no longer as intimate as it once was because of globalization. Employees can no longer rely on the quality of their work or their personal qualities to ensure continuing employment but rather are subject to the fluctuations of the international money markets. The complexity and rapidly changing nature of work have spawned at least two specializations within the field of psychology—industrial and organizational psychology and vocational psychology. Central to these endeavors has been the notion of work adjustment and well-being of the worker and organization.

Improvements in manufacturing efficiency continued apace throughout the 20th century, which also saw the development of jet propulsion and affordable air travel and transport as well as large and reliable motorized shipping. This has greatly increased world trade opportunities and development of global organizations.

FORMAL AND INFORMAL WORK

About one third of our time available for living is taken up with work and 20% with leisure. Despite the central role work plays in most of our lives, its purpose, meaning, and psychological influence remain vexed questions. For instance, there is a plethora of research from social and organizational psychology that suggests that work is injurious. A recent study found that most people replied that they "wished they were doing something else" when asked while they were at work. In another study, 19% of women and 14% of men reported having unpleasant emotional strain for more than half of the previous working day. This suggests that many people do not enjoy the experience of work and may experience significant deleterious effects from work. However, other studies point to the benefits of work and our reluctance to forego work. A survey of more than 500 lottery winners concluded that people with psychologically and financially rewarding jobs continued working regardless of the amount they won, whereas those who worked in low-paying semi-skilled and unskilled jobs were far more likely to quit the labor force. In another study, 80% of Americans said they would not retire from working even if they had enough money to live off comfortably. Hence, we end up with the paradox that work is a source of frustration, yet one we are reluctant to forego. However, what constitutes work and leisure is increasingly difficult to define. For instance, whereas working as a mechanic would be seen as work to most people, is working at home tuning your car's engine work or leisure? The difference perhaps is between formal and informal work.

Formal work tends to be associated with income and most commonly with monetary reward defined by some legal arrangement such as employee-employer, self-employed, business partners, subcontractor, agent, or representative. Generally in such arrangements there is a financial exchange between the worker and some other party, such as an employer or a customer or client. These forms of work have been studied extensively from many different perspectives, including industrial relations, sociology, psychology, philosophy, economics, and business studies.

Informal work constitutes activities that fall outside the definition of formal work but still possesses at least one of the characteristics set out in the definition of work. Domestic chores around the house and garden would fall into this informal category, along with charity and voluntary work. In many societies, this work has been traditionally performed by women.

WORK AND DEMOGRAPHY

In 1997, married women in Australia spent an average of 1 hour, 47 minutes per day more on domestic work than men. Women spent an average of 3 hours, 46 minutes on household work, compared with 2 hours, 30 minutes for men. There was evidence of clear demarcation in the type of household work done by men and women. Women did more food preparation and clean-up than men, 30 minutes more laundry work, and 30 minutes more general housework. Men did 25 minutes more grounds and animal care and 25 minutes more home maintenance. Large discrepancies between the amount of informal work done by men and women have been linked to divorce rates. The requirement to do domestic informal work is common for most people, with the exception of the very wealthy who have continued to employ domestic staff, thereby formalizing this type of work.

In 1870, 52% of employed women were engaged in paid domestic work. At the end of the 19th century, the figure was 1.5 million. By 1920, 28% of employed women were paid domestic workers; the proportion decreased further to 18% in 1940, which was the last time the job was at the top of the list of women's occupations. By 1970, the percentage had declined to 5.1%, and then to 2.5% in 1980. The decline in domestic jobs for women was in part due to the widespread availability of clerical roles. At the same time, some of this work was outsourced to restaurants and child care centers.

In American Colonial homes that produced goods, neighborhood girls helped the housewife with cooking, clothes making, baking bread, and producing dairy products in return for room and board and an apprenticeship in these skills. This position changed from a "helper" to a formalized "live-in servant" who was expected to do the household chores employing all of the new facilities, such as gas and electricity, and their attendant appliances. Typically, these were rural workers attracted to the higher wages available in the city.

Domestic work remained a low-status job and became identified with women of color as white women moved into clerical occupations. Between 1920 and 1940, the proportion of African American women in domestic work rose from 46% to 60%. The most common form of domestic work by the 1980s was day cleaning, performed by a range of people of color. Teenage babysitters constituted the largest group of white Americans who were listed as domestic service workers.

Domestic work, whether formal or informal, was excluded from most legal protections and social security entitlements, and even denied protection in the form of a union until the 1970s, when the industry was in sharp decline. However, both formal and informal domestic work is becoming increasingly recognized as a valid form of work that may be associated with psychological outcomes. With women's dramatically increased participation in the workforce in the late 20th century, there has been a resurgence in the formalization of domestic work to assist busy dual income couples. There has been an increase in employment of cleaners, child care assistants, cooks, and butlers. This has been extended to dog walkers and "Saturday Dads" who take children to weekend sporting events. These changes in working patterns have caused a blurring between work and leisure. For instance, time spent with and caring for children is classified by some as work, whereas others classify this as leisure.

WORK AND UNEMPLOYMENT

One way to look at the importance and role of work in human life and development is to examine what happens when people are deprived of the opportunity to work. In her classic research investigations into the effects of unemployment, Marie Jahoda delineated most of the major psychosocial benefits of work in addition to pay and conditions. She found that work performs five psychosocial functions for the individual and that those without work face the challenge of meeting these needs in some other way. First, work enables and often demands social contact. Such contact fosters the development of social skills, the establishing of social networks, and opportunities for mutual support. Second, work demands activity and almost always demands at least a minimal level of physical activity. There are many studies illustrating the physical and psychological benefits of regular activity in sustaining fitness, energy levels, mental alertness, and work conditioning. Third, work in most societies gives people a social role and social identity. Knowing someone's occupation, especially when meeting him or her for the first time, usually gives us a great of information about him or her—education, intelligence, personality, success, income, social status, and how much he or she is or is not like us. Work is a major way in which people define themselves and others within the community. Fourth, work gives structure to people's time. Work usually demands that activities be undertaken at specific hours of employment. This benefit provides a pattern to people's lives, allowing them to make arrangements about nonwork tasks. Fifth, work links people with goals larger than themselves and their own immediate concerns. By having to direct attention away from self to another task external to our individual focus, work usually is an opportunity for external orientation to others and the work in general.

Other researchers have considered the less positive effects of work. In particular, the concept of occupational stress has been extensively researched and is probably the most commonly researched area of work now. Although definitions of stress appear in 16th-century dictionaries, it is generally agreed the term became popular after the Second World War. The term *stress* has passed into the modern idiom despite significant confusion over its meaning. Stress is classically defined as a nonspecific response of the body to any demand made on it. In this scheme, there are three stages of the stress reaction: alarm, resistance, and exhaustion. Other definitions focus on a range of negative affective and physiological responses. Some researchers, most notably Robert Karasek and Roy Payne, have considered the relationship between the characteristics of a person's job and his or her stress response. Both researchers have argued that perceived job demands and perceived control over meeting those demands will predict stress. Jobs that are high in demands and low in control are predicted to be the most stressful. The relationship among job demands, control, and stress has been well documented in the literature for more than 20 years. In addition, other factors, such as the degree of social support enjoyed in the workplace, have been shown to predict stress levels.

Work has been a central activity of all human societies and has provided significant material, societal, and psychological benefits. However, at the same time, it is clear that work in and of itself can be not only unsatisfying but also positively deleterious for psychological and physical well-being. Perhaps

John Paul Getty, the industrialist, best summed up the nature of jobs when he said, "if you haven't got a problem, you haven't got a job." Work is about solving problems, and employment is about delegating this task to others.

SOME CONCLUDING COMMENTS

Work is now recognized as broader than merely having a job. Much essential work is carried on outside of the labor market. There is increasing recognition of the value of such activity for communities and nations as a whole. Moreover, as noted several times, the distinction between work and nonwork is often difficult to delineate—so much so that modern formulations of "career" typically encompass not only worker as employee but also all the multiple roles that individuals take up, shed, and resume at various times in their ongoing development. Writers about the future of work expect that work will continue to change with new occupations developing while old ones perish; that there will be an increasing emphasis in work on academic, creative, and intellectual skills, in comparison with manual and mechanical skills; that work training will become a lifelong learning process and will be conducted increasingly through distance education and the Internet; and that work will be conducted in increasingly globalized and multicultural contexts.

The paradox of work remains with us. Most of us get a sense of contribution and well-being from work as well as an income to help us live. We are confronted by frustration, toil, and boredom while working. We expose ourselves to significant risk: physical injury, stress, bullying, harassment, mockery, and reputation harm through work. Yet work also provides opportunities to turn preoccupations into occupations for growth, enlightenment, contribution, service, and achievement.

—*Jim E. H. Bright and Robert G. L. Pryor*

Further Readings and References

Donkin, R. (2001). *Blood, sweat and tears: The evolution of work.* New York: Texere.

Dudden, F. E. (1983). *Serving women: Household service in nineteenth-century America.* Middletown, CT: Wesleyan University Press.

Hill, R. (1996). *History of work ethic.* Retrieved from http://www.coe.uga.edu/~rhill/workethic/hist.htm

Kaplan, H. R. (1987). Lottery winners: The myth and reality. *Journal of Gambling Behavior, 3*(3), 168–178.

Karasek, R. A., & Theorell, T. (1990). *Healthy work: Stress, productivity and the reconstruction of working life*. New York: Basic Books.

Kasser, T. (2002). *The high price of materialism*. Cambridge: Bradford Books/MIT Press.

Savickas, M. L. (1997). The spirit in career counseling: Fostering self-completion through work. In D. P. Bloch & L. J. Richmond (Eds.), *Connections between spirit and work in career development: New approaches and practical perspectives* (pp. 3–25). Palo Alto, CA: Davies-Black.

The World of Work. (n.d.). *History of work in Minnesota*. Retrieved from http://www.rb-29.net/graa/wowork/index.html

WORLD HEALTH ORGANIZATION

The World Health Organization (WHO) was established in 1948 as a specialized agency for the United Nations devoted to issues of health. It is governed by the 192 Member States of the United Nations, with headquarters in Geneva, Switzerland. A nation can be a member of WHO without being a member of the United Nations. There are six regional offices throughout the world:

Regional Office for Africa in Brazzaville, Republic of Congo

Regional Office for Europe in Copenhagen, Denmark

Regional Office for South East Asia in New Delhi, India

Regional Office for the Americas/Pan American Health Organization in Washington, DC

Regional Office for the Eastern Mediterranean in Cairo, Egypt

Regional Office for the Western Pacific in Manila, Philippines

The main functions of the WHO are as follows:

1. To give worldwide guidance in areas related to health

2. To set global standards for health

3. To cooperate with governments in strengthening national health programs

4. To develop and transfer appropriate technology, information, and standards

The services include a day-to-day information database on the incidence of internationally significant diseases; publishing a list of diseases, injuries, and deaths; monitoring adverse reactions to drugs; and establishing world standards for antibiotics and vaccines. There is a strong training component and resources to strengthen the delivery of health services.

Efforts to control and eradicate infectious diseases have been a main focus for the WHO. One of the major accomplishments of the WHO was the elimination of smallpox. Smallpox was endemic in 31 countries and claimed almost 2 million lives a year. In 1967, a systematic effort to vaccinate selected populations in endemic countries was initiated. By 1972, the disease was present in only 8 countries. The last case of smallpox was discovered in Somalia in 1977. Today, the WHO is focusing on the eradication of polio, neonatal tetanus, leprosy, and iron-deficiency disease.

In 1977, the World Health Assembly, which consists of the member nations, set the goal of "health for all by the year 2000." This slogan does not mean that there will be an end to all disease or disability, but rather that basic health care will be available to everyone. The focus is on health care in community settings, such as homes, schools, and the workplace.

In 1978, representatives from 134 countries met with WHO delegates in Almatay, Kazakhstan, and agreed to implement the "health for all" motto through primary health care. Primary health care emphasizes the responsibility of the community to use health strategies that are appropriate and affordable. Such services would include health education, adequate food supply, safe water, basic sanitation, maternal and child care, family planning, immunizations, prevention and control of local endemic diseases, appropriate treatment of common diseases and injuries, and provision of essential drugs.

Recognizing the threats to the public health posed by accidental or intentional release of harmful agents, the WHO in 2001 made specific recommendations regarding global health security. The WHO issued a resolution that every country should be able to detect, verify, and respond appropriately to epidemic-prone threats when they arise, resulting in the development of the Department of Communicable Disease Surveillance and Response (CSR). This unit aims to attain global health security through the containment of known risks, such as emerging infections; response to unexpected events, such as global outbreaks; and improved preparedness by strengthening national capacity. The aspect of improved preparedness is addressed through an integrated approach providing expert assistance in epidemiology and enhancement of laboratory skills.

—Linda Spencer

Further Readings and References

Publications from WHO include the *Bulletin of the World Health Organization, Pan American Journal of Public Health, Weekly Epidemiological Record, World Health Report,* and *WHO Drug Information.*

World Health Organization (WHO), http://www.who.int/aboutwho

World Health Organization InterNetwork Access to Research Initiative, http://www.healthinternetwork.org

WRIGHT, JOHN C. (1933–2001)

John Cook Wright was born in Los Angeles and grew up in Washington, DC, and Tucson, Arizona. He graduated from Phillips Exeter Academy in 1950, received a bachelor's degree from Harvard University in 1954, and after a 2-year stint in the army, earned his doctoral degree in psychology from Stanford University in 1960. His dissertation was a study of noncontingent reinforcement, supervised by Alex Bavelis, and he also worked with Robert R. Sears on a classic study of child rearing and child development.

Wright spent his long career as a college professor, researcher, social activist, and advocate for the welfare of children. He taught at the University of Minnesota (1960–1968), the University of Kansas (1968–1996), and the University of Texas at Austin (1996–2001). With his wife, Dr. Aletha Huston, he founded and directed the Center for Research on the Influences of Television on Children (CRITC).

Employing innovative experimental methods, Wright applied developmental theories of perceptual attention to describe the mental processes of the young television viewer. His research showed that children are active during viewing; they work deliberately to decode, interpret, and understand the content presented. The formal features of television (production techniques such as cuts, fades, pacing, and animation) are critical tools that children use to judge what content is interesting, comprehensible, and meets their viewing goals. Wright developed his traveling-lens model as a framework to explain that children dedicate the most time and attention to television segments that are both comprehensible and stimulating. As children mature, content that was previously incomprehensible becomes more desirable and engaging.

With a team of colleagues, Wright performed the premier longitudinal studies measuring the effects of early educational television viewing. This line of research revealed that viewing *Sesame Street* at ages 2 and 3 years is related to higher language abilities and better school preparation at age 5. These positive effects do not dissipate after kindergarten—especially for boys, preschool educational viewing predicts higher grades in high school. Wright claimed that early viewing of educational television helps set boys on a positive educational trajectory that begins at school entry and translates into higher levels of success in high school. Informed by the results of these studies, he argued that television as a medium is neither good nor bad—the content viewed determines the effects on the viewer. Contrary to Marshall McLuhan's famous dictum, "The medium is the message," Wright staunchly proclaimed, "The message is the message."

—David S. Bickham

See also Television

Further Reading and Reference

Hymowitz, K. S. (1995, Autumn). *On Sesame Street, it's all show.* Retrieved from http://www.city-journal.org/html/5_4_on_sesame_street.html

Y

Young Adulthood

Youth cannot know how age thinks and feels. But old men are guilty if they forget what it was to be young.

—J. K. Rowling

YOUNG ADULTHOOD

What does it mean to become an adult? Most people rate the top criteria for marking the entry to adulthood as accepting responsibility for one's self, making independent decisions apart from parents, establishing egalitarian relationships with parents, and achieving financial independence. Although self-sufficiency has been attained in young adulthood, the period of the twenties and early thirties, young adults continue to grow and change in multiple arenas: biological, cognitive, psychosocial, and social.

BIOLOGICAL CHANGES DURING YOUNG ADULTHOOD

Typically, full height is attained in middle to late adolescence. Yet growth is not complete; the size and shape of the body continue to change in young adulthood. Both accumulation of fat and growth of muscle continue such that women reach their full breast and hip size and men their full shoulder and arm size in their early twenties. Throughout the twenties, physical strength and athletic skill increase, peaking at about age 30 and declining thereafter. All the body systems

(e.g., the digestive, respiratory, circulatory, immune, and reproductive) reach peak levels of functioning in early adulthood. When physical growth stops, senescence, or age-related gradual physical decline, begins.

Generally, the first noticeable age-related changes occur in the skin. The connective tissue of the body, collagen, begins to decrease at about age 20, by about 1% each year. The skin thins and loses elasticity, making wrinkles visible, especially around the eyes. These age-related changes in the skin occur all over the body but are most noticeable on the face. At about 30, reductions in the number of pigment-producing cells in the head lead to the emergence of gray hair. At this age, hereditary baldness in men becomes apparent; hair also begins to thin because of hormonal changes and reductions in the blood supply to the skin.

There is a great deal of variability in the process and timing of aging. Connections between age and physical change in adulthood are loose and not as predictable as developments during earlier periods in life. Change varies widely across parts of the body, with some parts affected more than others. For example, a given individual's liver may age more quickly than his or her lungs, particularly if he or she consumes heavy amounts of alcohol. In addition, there are tremendous individual differences in the aging process. Some individuals age more quickly than others, because of genetic and lifestyle differences.

COGNITIVE CHANGES DURING YOUNG ADULTHOOD

Most of us recognize the changes in cognition that children and adolescents undergo, but cognition continues to develop in young adulthood.

Postformal Reasoning: From Dualism to Relativism

During young adulthood, many people progress beyond Jean Piaget's formal operational stage of reasoning to postformal reasoning, entailing a shift from dualistic thinking to relativistic thinking. Dualistic thinking entails a belief in absolutes regarding information, authority, and values. Individuals who think in dualistic terms believe that there are concrete right and wrong answers to every question. Adolescents, for example, tend to think in dualistic terms, always looking for the one "right" answer. With time, experience, and exposure to diversity, young adults transition to relativistic thinking in which they realize that there are many perspectives on any given topic. Instead of one absolute truth, relativistic thinkers consider multiple truths, relative to given contexts and perspectives.

The postformal reasoner understands that an individual's perspective is one of many views and that there are few absolute answers; knowledge is not fixed, but changes. Therefore, postformal thinking is flexible, permitting us to attend to both the problem and its context, which is needed to adapt our cognitive problem-solving skills to real-world situations. Postformal reasoning combines objectivity, or abstract logic, and subjectivity, or situation- and individual-based feelings and experiences. In young adulthood, we are confronted with problems in work, marriage, and family life that do not have single correct solutions. Yet how we handle these problems influences our future and life course. Mature thinking entails integrating logical and objective processing with sensitivity to context and personal perspective.

Dialectical Thought

At its best, the cognitive flexibility of formal operational reasoning reaches the level of dialectical thought, an advanced level of reasoning. Dialectical reasoners understand that every idea also suggests the opposite idea. Dialectical reasoners are capable of considering both poles simultaneously, integrating and synthesizing them, and adapting to the resulting continual changes. Dialectical thinking entails integrating and synthesizing our experiences and ideas with the contradictions and inconsistencies we encounter, resulting in a constantly changing perspective of oneself and the world. It is understood that few questions have single unchangeable answers; however, unlike relativistic reasoners, dialectical reasoners recognize that although there are many perspectives or viewpoints on a given situation, some hold more merit or can be better justified than others and permit a more solid foundation for decision making.

Although we first become capable of postformal operational thinking in young adulthood, and many young adults transition to relativistic thinking, only some young adults develop the capacity for dialectical reasoning. Many people do not become dialectical thinkers until middle adulthood, if at all.

Effect of College on Cognition

How does college influence thinking? With college education, people tend to become more tolerant of differing political, social, and religious views and more flexible in their attitudes and consideration of differing perspectives. Research suggests a progression by which the more exposure students have to college, the greater the level of cognitive development, from dualism, to relativism, and, in some individuals, dialecticism.

First-year college students, for example, tend to believe in absolute truth (dualistic thinking); they are often disappointed when professors answer their questions with lengthy generalities (i.e., "it depends on a variety of factors"). Then students enter a phase of extreme relativism in which they question the notion of a universal truth and become lost in a sea of perspectives, recognizing that there are multiple perspectives and each can hold merit, varying by context (relativistic thinking). Finally, students come to realize that although there are multiple perspectives, each can be weighed, and they differ in terms of overall merit. They become committed to particular values, can recognize multiple perspectives, and remain open-minded. True dialectical thought in which contradictions are synthesized into a complex and dynamic perspective occurs for some, but not most, college students.

The intellectual challenge, social interactions, and exposure to a variety of perspectives through class discussions, peers, books, and professors that is typical of a college education stimulate students to consider new questions and thoughts and thus progress cognitively. Generally, the more years of college education and life experience one has, the more likely one is to demonstrate advanced levels of reasoning. However, young adults who are not enrolled in college may advance cognitively if they are confronted with similar opportunities to be intellectually challenged, engage in social interaction and issue-focused discussions, and be confronted with multiple perspectives.

Expertise and Cognition

During the college years, we not only develop our thinking skills but also gain expertise in a given field. We choose a college major, or a field in which to specialize. As we take courses in that field, we develop a knowledge base that influences how we process information. This is also true regarding life experience, regardless of education. As we gain more experiences within a given context, we develop expertise, enabling us to think in more complex and efficient ways. Compared with novices, experts remember and reason more quickly and effectively. We develop more abstract ways of thinking about the material within our area of expertise, which helps us better organize and reason with it.

Moral and Self-Concept Development

Changes in cognitive development and in social experience also bring changes in moral development. We encounter moral dilemmas throughout our daily life. As we advance cognitively, we think in new ways about our lives. Events in our lives, such as committing to a relationship, job promotions, psychotherapy, and serious illness, can lead to a disequilibrium, a mismatch between our perspective and experience, and stimulate reflection. Reflecting on these experiences leads to deeper convictions about our values, self, and place in the world.

Vocation

Vocational exploration and choice begins in childhood, when we fantasize and imagine what different careers are like. In adolescence, we explore and evaluate potential careers in light of our skills and abilities, and choose educational experiences that prepare us for possible careers. In young adulthood, we narrow our options based on our experiences, interests, personalities, and opportunities. Our families and social contexts influence our vocational decisions in the sense that we tend to choose vocations similar to those to which we have been exposed. People who grow up in higher socioeconomic status homes and communities are more likely to select high status vocations such as lawyer, doctor, and scientist, whereas those who grow up in low-income homes and communities are more likely to consider less prestigious occupations. Those individuals who enter college often sample majors, to further exploration and determine where their interests lie. Then they choose a major and explore careers within that field. Some people may not choose an occupation until well after college. Occupational choice does not end with college graduation or entry into the first job. Unlike prior generations when adults could expect to put in a lifetime of work at the same company, retiring with a gold watch and a pension, most young adults can expect to be employed in a range of positions, even changing occupations several times through life. The consideration of various careers and vocational growth and change continues throughout young adulthood.

Young adults who do not attend college have more limited vocational choices. Twenty-five percent of young people with a high school diploma have no plans to go to college. North American young adults who do not attend college often find it hard to find a job other than the one held as a student. Of American recent high school graduates who do not continue their education, about 20% are unemployed. North American young adults who are not college bound have few alternatives to turn to for vocational counseling, training, and job placement. Many flounder after high school graduation because most North American employers perceive high school graduates as poorly prepared for occupations. When high school graduates find work, they often are limited to low-paid and unskilled jobs.

PSYCHOSOCIAL TASKS OF YOUNG ADULTHOOD

Young adults are faced with several psychosocial tasks: solidifying autonomy, further shaping and committing to an identity, and developing a capacity for intimacy.

Autonomy

Autonomy refers to self-governance, the ability to make decisions independently of others. Although the development of autonomy is a lifelong process beginning in toddlerhood and becoming more obvious in adolescence, many people do not establish a full sense of autonomy until young adulthood, when education is complete, work life has begun, and the individual is living on his or her own, apart from parents and formal institutions. A sense of autonomy permits young adults to maintain close bonds with family members, seek family members' advice in problem solving, and ultimately make and carry out their own decisions based on considering their values and opinions. The task for young adults is to gain experience and feel more comfortable in exerting their autonomy.

Identity

Like autonomy, identity development begins in adolescence when individuals experiment with possibilities and explore alternatives in order to ultimately make enduring decisions in the areas of career, love, and worldview. Identity refers to a sense of self. In young adulthood, the individual has committed to an identity and the commitment strengthens. The identity also undergoes change and refinement as the young adult takes on new roles, such as worker, spouse, and parent.

Intimacy

According to life-span development theorist Erik Erikson, the primary psychosocial task of young adulthood is developing a capacity for intimacy. The development of intimacy refers to the ability to establish close, committed relationships with others that will last a lifetime and that will support the individual's maturing identity throughout life. Managing this task entails balancing the opposing needs for independence, or autonomy, and connections, or intimacy. We learn to experience intimacy by making and maintaining important attachments with others. Intimacy entails giving of oneself, openness, and vulnerability—sharing without asking what will be received in return.

SOCIAL CHANGES OF YOUNG ADULTHOOD

Young adulthood is a time of great social change—we progress to full independence and take on adult roles. As we take on adult roles, the impulsivity characteristic of adolescence and emerging adulthood wanes. For example, after the early twenties, particularly college graduation, substance use, such as alcohol and marijuana consumption, declines.

Friendship

Friendship is important at all ages in life because it is a source of emotional support, positive feelings, and self-esteem. Young adulthood is a time in which we sort through and solidify existing friendships and make new ones. The overall absence of marital and family obligations permits young adults time to form extensive and varied social networks, forming friendships at college or at work; among political, cultural, athletic, or religious groups; and even on the commute to work or on vacation. Young adults have many social opportunities from which they select people who provide information, advice, companionship, and empathy.

Friends are usually similar in age, sex, and socioeconomic status. They also share common interests, experiences, and needs. Friends share their thoughts and feelings with one another, revealing themselves and making themselves vulnerable. In adult friendships, trust and loyalty are important. Friends often come and go throughout life, but some adult friendships continue for many years. Women are more likely to experience lifelong friendships and tend to see their friends more often than do men.

Women friends get together to talk. Male friends get together to do things such as play sports. Men are more likely to report barriers to intimacy such as feeling in competition with other male friends. Because they are free of marital and family obligations, open to new people, and exposed to many people, young adults in their early to middle twenties experience low levels of loneliness comparable to other ages in life. Young adults who live alone tend to form an extensive circle of friends and spend nearly as much time with friends as they do alone.

As young adults enter the thirties, family obligations and changing lifestyles cause some friendships to intensify and others wane. A lack of time, caused by juggling work, home life, and child care, makes maintaining friendships more challenging. Because we tend to form friendships with people who are similar to us, a change in marital status or parenting status can change the dynamics of friendship. Some friends, therefore, drift apart, and new friendships are made based on similarities such as children, occupation, and neighborhood. Despite the changes, most people report a few lifelong friends.

Sexuality

In young adulthood, sexual activity increases in prevalence, with fewer people remaining virgins and more people regularly engaging in intercourse. Sexual activity increases through the twenties as people marry or cohabit. At around age 30, sexual activity begins to decline, despite few changes in hormonal levels. The decline in sexual activity is associated with the multiple roles and demands of adult life, work, family, and child care.

Males and females display a similar pattern of sexual activation, arousal, release through orgasm, refraction, and recovery. For males, sexual arousal and excitement can occur very quickly in response to many stimuli, in addition to or in lieu of an arousing partner. Over the course of young adulthood and particularly toward the end of young adulthood, males may notice a gradual increase in refractory period and slower arousal, requiring additional stimulation and additional time between arousal and full erection, erection and ejaculation, and orgasm and recovery.

Generally speaking, in females, sexual arousal, excitement, and orgasm take longer than in males. As females progress through young adulthood, arousal and orgasm become more likely. In adolescence, girls are often advised to protect their virginity and may be conditioned to resist their own desire, and instead emphasize their control over sexual experiences. In young adulthood, many women explore their sexuality through multiple partners and different sexual experiences, becoming more comfortable with and appreciating their sexuality, and experiencing orgasm on a regular basis.

Like friends, we tend to choose partners to date, cohabitate, or marry based on similarity. Our partners tend to be similar in age (within 5 years), education, ethnicity, and often religion. We tend to meet our partners for long-lasting relationships through introductions by family or friends, at work, school, or through activities based on common interests.

Cohabitation

Cohabitation refers to the lifestyle of unmarried couples who live together, sharing intimacy, a sexual relationship, and a residence. Cohabitation is more common today than ever before, especially among young adults. For example, more than one half of all women aged 25 to 40 in the United States have lived with a man outside of marriage. Many couples view cohabitation as an opportunity to test the relationship and get used to living together. Others view it as an alternative to marriage, a long-term arrangement with the rewards of companionship while maintaining independence. Homosexual adults often find no alternative to cohabitation because few states recognize homosexual relationships in formal partnerships. Increasingly, cohabitation includes children.

Marriage

Young adults are waiting longer than ever before to marry. The overall rate of first marriages in young adulthood is the lowest it has been in 50 years. Sixty percent of young adults aged 20 to 30 in the United States are not yet married, and 3% are already divorced. More young adults choose to remain single, cohabitate, and, after divorce, do not remarry.

The transition to marriage itself is a challenge. The transition to marriage entails a great deal of work in defining the relationship and each person's roles within the relationship. For example, negotiating the marital relationship requires deciding who does what in completing the myriad details of daily life. Who will cook? What will be eaten? When is leisure time and what is on the agenda? How will the household and financial tasks be decided? These decisions may be particularly challenging for today's young adults and therefore make the transition to marriage more difficult because of changes in gender roles and the tendency of young adults to live farther away from family members (and thus have fewer sources of support and guidance) than prior generations. Cohabitation before marriage may make marriage less of a turning point; however, many young adults report transitional stress despite prior cohabitation.

Generally, spouses with similar backgrounds in terms of socioeconomic status, education, religion, and age tend to report higher levels of marital satisfaction. Overall stability in other areas of life, such as stable financial and employment status, are also associated with higher levels of marital satisfaction. Although similarity in interests and in background is ideal, most successful married couples share some critical values and interests and learn to compromise, adjust, and agree to disagree about others.

The maturity of the partners also contributes to the overall success of a marriage. Generally, the younger the bride and groom, the less successful the marriage. A full sense of identity is needed before one can establish intimacy. Because many young adults in their early twenties are still determining and solidifying their identity, shared intimacy, compromise, and growth as a couple are difficult. Before a full sense of identity is achieved, passion may be valued over the true predictors of marital success: openness, trust, loyalty, intimacy, and commitment. Young adults who married early may find that their values and roles diverge with those of their spouses as they mature. Those who wait until their late twenties and thirties to marry are less likely to divorce.

Divorce and Remarriage

About one half of all marriages in the United States end in divorce. Most divorces occur within 5 to 10 years of marriage. Divorce itself is a stressful experience for men and women, who both show signs of depression and anxiety, which typically declines within 2 years. Men show a more positive and quick adjustment when they remarry shortly afterward. Most women prefer their new single lives over unhappy marriages, despite increases in loneliness and reduced income. However, some women, particularly those who were in traditional marriages and who highly identified with their roles as wives, find divorce particularly challenging and are likely to remain anxious and depressed over time, experience drops in self-esteem, and tend to form other unsuccessful romantic relationships. Overall, the economic and psychological health of divorced women are enhanced by career advancement through education and job training and social support from family and friends.

After divorcing, two thirds of men and more than one half of women remarry. Typically, remarriage occurs within 4 years of divorce. Men remarry more quickly than do women. Remarriages face many of the same challenges of first marriages, with higher rates of divorce in the first few years. The practical reasons that often influence second marriages, such as financial security, social acceptance, relief from loneliness, and help in raising children, may not provide a basis for a solid marriage. Also, after a failed marriage, people may be more likely to view divorce as an acceptable solution when marital difficulties resurface. Finally, stepfamilies are stressful; children from prior marriages place stress on new marriages. Although the first few years of second marriages are at higher risk for divorce than first marriages (about 7% higher), afterward the divorce rates are about the same.

Parenthood

Recent generations of young adults have come to recognize parenthood as a choice. Some adults choose to remain childless and, because of changing cultural values, are less likely to experience social criticism and rejection than those of prior generations.

The physiological ability to produce children, reproductive capacity, is highest in the early twenties and declines with age. Females' ovulation is most consistent in young adulthood and becomes more erratic in the mid- to late thirties. Males, on the other hand, experience little to no change in sperm production throughout young adulthood. Despite their reproductive capacity, young adults are having children later in life than ever before. Most births occur to women older than 25. The number of women who give birth in their thirties is higher than ever. Families also are having fewer children, with the average number per couple at 1.8.

Young adults note many advantages of parenthood, particularly opportunities for love and change: the giving and receiving of warmth and affection, experiencing the stimulation and fun that children add to life, and the growth and learning opportunities that add meaning to life. They tend to report the sense of accomplishment and creativity from helping children grow and from someone to carry on after one's death as other advantages of parenthood. Parenthood is also an additional marker of adulthood; some young adults view parenthood as an opportunity to learn to be less selfish and to learn to sacrifice as well as to become accepted as a responsible and mature member of the community.

However, young adults also recognize that parenthood entails disadvantages, such as a loss of freedom, financial strain, and worries over children's health and well-being. Parenthood is associated with a decline in marital satisfaction; couples have less time to spend together and experience more stress and sleep loss. Parenthood is associated with a shift toward more traditional roles in the relationship such that the mother usually takes a larger role in child care. Women who have been very active in their careers before parenthood may find this transition particularly challenging and may experience a greater decline in marital satisfaction and mental health than men.

Couples who postpone parenthood until their late twenties and thirties tend to experience a less stressful and easier transition. Couples who have achieved some of their occupational goals and have acquired life experience and maturity navigate new parenthood more successfully and with less of a decline in marital satisfaction. Men in their late twenties and thirties tend to participate more actively in child care, and women this age are more likely to encourage their husbands to share in the housework and child care. Despite this, in most families, women manage most of the parenting, caregiving, and household responsibilities, which can lead to fatigue and stress and sometimes be a detriment to their careers.

SUMMARY

The twenties and early thirties, young adulthood, is a time of biological, cognitive, psychosocial, and social change. Our body reaches the peak of maturation and begins senescence. Our mind undergoes further development, permitting us to think in new ways. Young adults become more comfortable asserting their autonomy, further refine their identities, and develop a capacity for intimacy. Young adulthood is also a time in which we begin to make decisions about relationships. More young adults choose to remain single, cohabitate, and, after divorce, do not remarry.

Those who marry do so at later ages than ever before, and about one half divorce. Likewise, young adults are waiting longer to become parents. In all, it appears that the social changes of young adulthood, the transition to marriage and parenthood, are delayed among today's young adults, as compared with prior generations. The nature of young adulthood itself is undergoing change as we proceed into the new millennium.

—*Tara L. Kuther*

Further Readings and References

Arnstein, R. L (1989). Overview of normal transition to young adulthood. In S. C. Feinstein & A. H. Esman (Eds.), *Adolescent psychiatry: Developmental and clinical studies, Vol. 16.* (pp. 127–141). Chicago: University of Chicago.

Crispi, E. L., & Fisher, C. B. (1994). Development in adulthood. In J. L. Ronch & W. Van Ornum (Eds.), *Counseling sourcebook: A practical reference on contemporary issues* (pp. 343–357). New York: Crossroad.

Gilligan, C. (1993). *In a different voice.* Cambridge, MA: Harvard University Press.

The Network on Transitions to Adulthood, http://www.pop.upenn.edu/transad/

Sassler, S. (2004). The process of entering into cohabiting unions. *Journal of Marriage & the Family, 66,* 491–504.

Society for Research on Adolescence. (n.d.). *Emerging adulthood SIG.* Available from http://www.s-r-a.org/easigrelated websites.html

Z

Zone of Proximal Development

What the child can do in cooperation today he can do alone tomorrow. Therefore the only good kind of instruction is that which marches ahead of development and leads it; it must be aimed not so much at the ripe as at the ripening functions.

—Lev Vygotsky

ZONE OF PROXIMAL DEVELOPMENT (ZPD)

The zone of proximal development (ZPD), as a concept, was introduced by the Russian psychologist Lev Semenovich Vygotsky (1896–1934) in the early 1930s. The ZPD is situated within the context of children's education and cognitive development. It refers to an imaginary zone that represents the gap between what an individual can do independently with no assistance and what he or she can do with careful assistance by an adult or more competent member of his or her culture. Consistent with the Marxist principles of socialism and dialectical materialism of the time, Vygotsky's ZPD emphasizes the importance of social interaction and children's participation in sociocultural activities for learning and development.

The idea is that individuals learn best when working together with others during joint collaboration, and it is through such collaborative endeavors with more skilled persons that children learn and internalize new concepts, psychological tools, and skills. The main goal of education from this perspective is to keep children in their own ZPDs as often as possible by giving them interesting and culturally meaningful learning and problem-solving tasks that are slightly more difficult than what they do alone, such that they will need to work together either with another, more competent peer or with a teacher or adult to finish the task. The idea is that after completing the task jointly, the child will likely be able to complete the same task individually next time, and through that process, the child's ZPD for that particular task will have been raised. This process is then repeated at the higher level of task difficulty that the child's new ZPD requires.

Vygotsky originally proposed the idea of the ZPD in the context of assessing the skills and abilities of children with special needs in the form of serious physical, developmental, or learning disabilities. During the late 1920s, the Soviet Union encountered record numbers of mentally retarded and physical disabled children. Although standard methods of intellectual assessment, such as Binet's intelligence quotient (IQ) test, were becoming popular, Vygotsky's views differed. He argued that such measures limited the assessment of children's intellectual ability because they only assessed a child's individual "static" functioning and therefore missed the really interesting story—what children are capable of learning in the future with help. He argued that children's intellectual assessment should be based on what they are demonstrating with the help of another person, not just what they can already do well by themselves. The ZPD became the central theoretical grounding for a very important and fairly recent movement, called "dynamic assessment," that has endeavored to develop assessment instruments that assess children's learning potential and ongoing learning processes, rather than just their static IQ.

Vygotsky would often give an example similar to the following for why the ZPD is important and why we need to take a dynamic approach to intellectual assessment. Suppose there were two boys who came to the clinic for intellectual assessment due to parents' and teachers' concerns over their learning and academic progress. Each child was given a standard IQ test, and both children performed identically on the static test, yielding an IQ score of 73. According to the standard procedure, these two children would be seen as having the same intellectual potential, and the same educational recommendations would be made for both children. However, let's imagine that both children were then given a dynamic assessment procedure in which a challenging cognitive problem-solving task was first given to the children for them to complete individually and the experimenter noted how well the child could perform the task. Each boy then participated in a 20-minute interactive joint (adult and child) teaching session in which the adult carefully assisted the child on the task and taught the child how it works while they completed the task together. Afterward, the child was given the same task again and asked to complete it on his own, and the experimenter noted how well he did now. One of the boys, it turns out, was able to learn the task easily and made huge gains in what he could do with the task by himself before and after the teaching session. The other child, however, made little gains and never really understood what to do with the task. He continued to struggle even though he had participated in the same sensitive teaching session with the adult as the other child, and his postteaching individual performance score was basically the same as it was before the joint session. According to the static IQ score, these two children are the same intellectually. However, it becomes clear from the dynamic teaching session that these two children are very different in their learning potential and capacity to benefit from instruction. The former child has a much wider ZPD than the latter, at least for this particular task, and the educational placement and curricular recommendations for the two boys are likely to be very different as well.

An important implication of Vygotsky's ZPD for teachers and parents is that it is the learning that takes place during social interaction between adults and children, and between children and other children, that spurs cognitive growth and development for the child. This places much responsibility on the part of teachers and parents as agents of development for children. The goal is to assess each child's ZPD for a given activity (know what the child's skill and motivation level are for a given task) and then pitch sensitive instruction to children at their upper limit of the zone. It is here where children learn with the support and guidance of capable instructors. As the child learns more and more and as his or her skill level increases, the teacher gradually reduces the assistance and gives the opportunity for the child to execute the task alone (a process called "scaffolding"). Eventually, the child masters the required skills needed to accomplish the task. Thus, it is through the teacher's guidance that the child is able to complete the task that he or she would otherwise not be able to complete. Once the task is accomplished, the result is the development of a new, higher ZPD.

A second important implication of Vygotsky's ZPD is the idea that we must assess children's cognitive potential dynamically, over time, and involving others providing assistance in the ZPD, as described earlier. Such assessment procedures provide information about what type of instruction works for the child and allow teachers to tailor their instruction to the student's actual needs rather than on the student's assumed needs based on his or her age or grade level, as is the case with standardized assessment procedures. Finally, the ZPD also suggests that children learn best in small groups, especially if the task is at the right level of difficulty.

Vygotsky's notion of the ZPD, originally developed in the 1930s in the Soviet Union, has much to offer contemporary educational and psychological practice. Indeed, the ZPD is probably the most widely known concept of all of Vygotsky's sociocultural theories, and it continues to inspire researchers and practitioners.

—Luis Espinoza and Adam Winsler

See also Scaffolding; Vygotsky, Lev

Further Readings and References

Berk, L. E., & Winsler, A. (1995). *Scaffolding children's learning: Vygotsky and early childhood education.* Washington, DC: National Association for the Education of Young Children.

Lidz, C. S., & Elliott, J. G. (Eds.). (2000). *Dynamic assessment: Prevailing models and applications.* Amsterdam: JAI/Elsevier Science.

Morris, C. (2002). *Lev Semyonovich Vygotsky's zone of proximal development.* Retrieved from http://www.igs.net/~cmorris/zpd.html

Newman, D., Griffin, P., & Cole, M. (1989). *The construction zone: Working for cognitive change in school.* New York: Cambridge University Press.

Tharp, R. G., & Gallimore, R. (1988). *Rousing minds to life: Teaching, learning, and schooling in social context.* New York: Cambridge University Press.

Vygotsky, L. S. (1978). *Mind in society: The development of higher psychological processes.* Cambridge, MA: Harvard University Press.

Wells, G. (1999). The zone of proximal development and its implications for learning and teaching. *Dialogic inquiry: Towards a sociocultural practice and theory of education.* New York: Cambridge University Press. Retrieved from http://tortoise.oise.utoronto.ca/~gwells/resources/ZPD.html

ZYGOTE

At conception, a sperm from the father penetrates an egg from the mother, resulting in a zygote. A human zygote contains 46 chromosomes in two sets. One set is donated from the sperm (father), and the other set is donated by the egg (mother). The zygote will develop into a male if the sperm that fertilized the egg carries a Y chromosome, and the zygote will develop into a female if the sperm carries an X chromosome. The zygote also contains the appropriate factors necessary to direct the proper formation of the early embryo.

Monozygotic twins (identical) derive from the same zygote and share all of the same genetic material. Dizygotic (fraternal) twins derive from different zygotes and share only 25% of their genetic material, the same amount that any two siblings share.

Zygotes that receive an abnormal number of chromosomes from the gametes that joined together may be unviable or may produce an individual with a genetic syndrome such as Down's syndrome (an extra chromosome number 21), Turner's syndrome (only one X chromosome), or Klinefelter's syndrome (more than two sex chromosomes).

—Therese Poole

Further Readings and References

Farlex, Inc. (n.d.). *Zygote.* Retrieved from http://encyclopedia.thefreedictionary.com/zygote

Pierce, B. (2002). *Genetics: A conceptual approach.* San Francisco: WH Freeman.

Appendix 1

Tables and Figures on Selected Aspects of Human Development

Americans 65 Years and Older As a Percentage of Total U.S. Population, 1950–2050

Year	Total	65 years and over	75 years and over
1950	150,216,110	12,256,850	3,852,395
1960	179,325,657	16,207,237	5,359,338
1970	203,211,926	20,065,502	7,630,046
1980	226,545,805	25,549,427	9,968,822
1990	248,709,873	31,078,895	13,033,400
2000	281,421,906	34,991,753	16,600,767
2010	308,935,581	40,243,713	18,974,204
2020	335,804,546	54,631,891	22,852,732
2030	363,584,435	71,453,471	33,505,538
2040	391,945,658	80,049,634	44,579,726
2050	419,853,587	86,705,637	48,763,200

SOURCE: U.S. Census (2000).

Annual Number of Births, 1946 to 2001 (in thousands)

Year	Number of births	Year	Number of births
1946	3,426	1974	3,160
1947	3,834	1975	3,144
1948	3,655	1976	3,168
1949	3,667	1977	3,327
1950	3,645	1978	3,333
1951	3,845	1979	3,494
1952	3,933	1980	3,612
1953	3,989	1981	3,629
1954	4,102	1982	3,681
1955	4,128	1983	3,639
1956	4,244	1984	3,669
1957	4,332	1985	3,761
1958	4,279	1986	3,757
1959	4,313	1987	3,809
1960	4,307	1988	3,910
1961	4,317	1989	4,041
1962	4,213	1990	4,158
1963	4,142	1991	4,111
1964	4,070	1992	4,065
1965	3,801	1993	4,000
1966	3,642	1994	3,953
1967	3,555	1995	3,900
1968	3,535	1996	3,891
1969	3,626	1997	3,881
1970	3,739	1998	3,942
1971	3,556	1999	3,959
1972	3,258	2000	4,063
1973	3,137	2001	4,028

SOURCE: U.S. Department of Health and Human Services, National Center for Health Statistics (NCHS), Annual Summary of Births, Marriages, Divorces, and Deaths: United States, various years, *National Vital Statistics Report* (2003).

Average Reading, Mathematics, and Science Literacy Scores[1] of 15-Year-Olds, by Sex, 2000

Country	Reading literacy			Mathematics literacy			Science literacy		
	Total	Male	Female	Total	Male	Female	Total	Male	Female
Australia	528	513	546	533	539	527	528	526	529
Austria	507	495	520	515	530	503	519	526	514
Belgium	507	492	525	520	524	518	496	496	498
Canada	534	519	551	533	539	529	529	529	531
Czech Republic	492	473	510	498	504	492	511	512	511
Denmark	497	485	510	514	522	507	481	488	476
Finland	546	520	571	536	537	536	538	534	541
France	505	490	519	517	525	511	500	504	498
Germany	484	468	502	490	498	483	487	489	487
Greece	474	456	493	447	451	444	461	457	464
Hungary	480	465	496	488	492	485	496	496	497
Iceland	507	488	528	514	513	518	496	495	499
Ireland	527	513	542	503	510	497	513	511	517
Italy	487	469	507	457	462	454	478	474	483
Japan	522	507	537	557	561	553	550	547	554
Korea, Republic of	525	519	533	547	559	532	552	561	541
Luxembourg	441	429	456	446	454	439	443	441	448
Mexico	422	411	432	387	393	382	422	423	419
Netherlands	—	517	547	—	569	558	—	529	529
New Zealand	529	507	553	537	536	539	528	523	535
Norway	505	486	529	499	506	495	500	499	505
Poland	479	461	498	470	472	468	483	486	480
Portugal	470	458	482	454	464	446	459	456	462
Spain	493	481	505	476	487	469	491	492	491
Sweden	516	499	536	510	514	507	512	512	513
Switzerland	494	480	510	529	537	523	496	500	493
United Kingdom	523	512	537	529	534	526	532	535	531
United States	504	490	518	493	497	490	499	497	502

SOURCE: World Health Organization.

1. Average score equals 500.

Basic Indicators of World Health Organization Members, 2001

Member State	Total population (in thousands)	Annual growth rate (%)	Percentage of population aged 60+ years		Total fertility rate	
	2001	1991–2001	1991	2001	1991	2001
Afghanistan	22,473	4.5	4.7	4.7	7.1	6.8
Albania	3,144	−0.5	7.9	9.2	2.9	2.4
Algeria	30,841	1.9	5.7	6.0	4.3	2.9
Andorra	90	5.0	19.4	21.1	1.5	1.3
Angola	13,527	3.2	4.7	4.5	7.2	7.2
Antigua and Barbuda	65	0.3	9.1	10.0	1.9	1.6
Argentina	37,487	1.3	13.0	13.4	2.9	2.5
Armenia	3,787	0.5	10.4	13.2	2.2	1.2
Australia	19,338	1.2	15.6	16.5	1.9	1.8
Austria	8,074	0.4	20.0	21.1	1.5	1.3
Azerbaijan	8,095	1.1	8.2	10.5	2.7	1.6
Bahamas	307	1.7	6.7	8.1	2.6	2.3
Bahrain	651	2.6	3.7	4.8	3.6	2.4
Bangladesh	140,368	2.2	4.7	5.0	4.5	3.6
Barbados	268	0.4	15.1	13.2	1.6	1.5
Belarus	10,146	−0.1	16.8	18.8	1.8	1.2
Belgium	10,263	0.3	20.7	22.2	1.6	1.5
Belize	230	2.0	6.0	5.9	4.3	3.0
Benin	6,445	3.0	4.7	4.2	6.6	5.8
Bhutan	2,141	2.2	6.0	6.5	5.8	5.2
Bolivia	8,516	2.4	5.9	6.2	4.9	4.1
Bosnia and Herzegovina	4,066	−0.2	10.7	15.1	1.6	1.3
Botswana	1,553	2.0	3.6	4.6	5.0	4.1
Brazil[a]	172,558	1.4	6.8	8.0	2.6	2.2
Brunei Darussalam	334	2.4	4.0	5.2	3.2	2.6
Bulgaria	7,866	−1.0	19.5	21.7	1.6	1.1
Burkina Faso	11,855	2.5	5.2	4.8	7.2	6.8
Burundi	6,501	1.2	4.7	4.3	6.8	6.8
Cambodia	13,440	3.0	4.4	4.4	5.5	4.9
Cameroon	15,202	2.4	5.6	5.6	5.8	4.8
Canada	31,014	1.0	15.7	16.9	1.7	1.6
Cape Verde	436	2.3	6.8	6.3	4.1	3.3
Central African Republic	3,781	2.3	6.2	6.1	5.6	5.0
Chad	8,134	3.1	5.2	4.9	6.7	6.7
Chile	15,401	1.5	9.1	10.4	2.6	2.4
China	1,292,378	0.9	8.6	10.0	2.1	1.8
Colombia	42,802	1.8	6.3	7.0	3.1	2.7
Comoros	726	3.0	4.0	4.2	6.0	5.1
Congo	3,109	3.1	5.3	5.0	6.3	6.3
Cook Islands	20	0.7	5.8	6.9	4.1	3.3
Costa Rica	4,112	2.7	6.4	7.6	3.1	2.7
Côte d'Ivoire	16,348	2.3	4.3	5.0	6.1	4.8
Croatia	4,654	0.3	17.3	20.5	1.6	1.7
Cuba[a]	11,236	0.5	11.8	14.0	1.7	1.6
Cyprus	790	1.3	14.8	15.9	2.4	1.9
Czech Republic	10,260	0.0	17.8	18.6	1.7	1.2

a. Figures not endorsed by member state as official statistics.

(Continued)

(Continued)

Member State	Total population (in thousands)	Annual growth rate (%)	Percentage of population aged 60+ years		Total fertility rate	
	2001	*1991–2001*	*1991*	*2001*	*1991*	*2001*
Democratic People's Republic of Korea	22,427	1.0	7.8	10.4	2.4	2.1
Democratic Republic of the Congo	52,521	3.2	4.6	4.5	6.7	6.7
Denmark	5,332	0.3	20.3	20.2	1.7	1.7
Djibouti	643	2.2	4.1	5.7	6.3	5.9
Dominica	71	−0.1	9.1	10.0	2.1	1.8
Dominican Republic	8,506	1.7	5.5	6.7	3.3	2.8
Ecuador	12,879	2.1	6.2	7.0	3.7	2.9
Egypt	69,079	1.9	6.1	6.3	4.0	3.0
El Salvador	6,399	2.1	6.6	7.2	3.6	3.0
Equatorial Guinea	469	2.7	6.3	5.9	5.9	5.9
Eritrea	3,815	2.0	4.4	4.7	6.2	5.4
Estonia	1,376	−1.3	17.5	20.3	1.8	1.2
Ethiopia	64,458	2.8	4.5	4.7	6.9	6.8
Fiji	822	1.2	4.9	5.8	3.4	3.0
Finland	5,177	0.3	18.6	20.2	1.8	1.6
France	59,452	0.4	19.3	20.5	1.7	1.8
Gabon	1,261	2.7	9.1	8.6	5.1	5.4
Gambia	1,337	3.3	4.8	5.2	5.8	4.9
Georgia	5,238	−0.4	15.3	18.9	2.0	1.4
Germany	82,006	0.3	20.5	23.7	1.4	1.3
Ghana	19,733	2.4	4.6	5.1	5.5	4.3
Greece	10,623	0.4	20.4	23.7	1.4	1.3
Grenada	94	0.3	9.1	10.0	4.1	3.5
Guatemala	11,686	2.7	5.1	5.3	5.5	4.6
Guinea	8,273	2.7	4.4	4.5	6.5	6.0
Guinea-Bissau	1,226	2.4	5.9	5.6	6.0	6.0
Guyana	762	0.4	6.7	6.9	2.6	2.4
Haiti	8,269	1.6	5.7	5.6	5.1	4.1
Honduras	6,574	2.7	4.5	5.1	5.1	3.9
Hungary	9,916	−0.4	19.1	19.9	1.8	1.3
Iceland	281	0.9	14.6	15.1	2.2	1.9
India	1,025,095	1.8	6.9	7.7	3.8	3.1
Indonesia	214,839	1.5	6.3	7.8	3.2	2.4
Iran, Islamic Republic of	71,368	1.8	4.7	5.3	4.8	2.9
Iraq	23,583	2.9	4.5	4.6	5.8	4.9
Ireland	3,840	0.9	15.2	15.3	2.1	2.0
Israel	6,171	2.9	12.5	13.1	3.0	2.8
Italy	57,502	0.1	21.5	24.3	1.3	1.2
Jamaica	2,598	0.9	10.0	9.6	2.8	2.4
Japan[a]	127,334	0.3	18.0	23.8	1.5	1.4
Jordan	5,050	3.9	4.6	4.6	5.7	4.4
Kazakhstan	16,094	−0.4	9.7	11.2	2.6	2.0
Kenya	31,292	2.5	4.1	4.2	5.8	4.3
Kiribati	84	1.4	6.0	6.9	4.4	4.6
Kuwait	1,970	−0.6	2.1	4.8	3.4	2.7
Kyrgyzstan	4,986	1.2	8.3	8.9	3.6	2.5

a. Figures not endorsed by member state as official statistics.

Member State	Total population (in thousands)	Annual growth rate (%)	Percentage of population aged 60+ years		Total fertility rate	
	2001	1991–2001	1991	2001	1991	2001
Lao People's Democratic Republic	5,402	2.5	6.0	5.6	6.0	5.0
Latvia	2,405	−1.0	17.9	21.1	1.8	1.1
Lebanon	3,555	2.5	8.2	8.5	3.1	2.2
Lesotho	2,057	1.8	6.0	6.6	5.1	4.5
Liberia	3,107	4.0	5.2	4.4	6.8	6.8
Libyan Arab Jamahiriya	5,407	2.1	4.3	5.6	4.6	3.5
Lithuania	3,688	−0.1	16.4	18.8	1.9	1.3
Luxembourg	441	1.4	19.0	19.4	1.6	1.7
Madagascar	16,436	2.9	4.8	4.7	6.2	5.8
Malawi	11,571	1.8	4.3	4.7	7.3	6.5
Malaysia	22,632	2.2	5.8	6.7	3.7	3.0
Maldives	299	3.0	5.3	5.2	6.3	5.5
Mali	11,676	2.6	5.3	5.8	7.0	7.0
Malta	391	0.8	14.8	17.2	2.0	1.8
Marshall Islands	52	1.4	6.0	6.9	5.5	5.7
Mauritania	2,746	3.0	4.9	4.7	6.1	6.0
Mauritius	1,170	0.9	8.3	9.1	2.3	1.9
Mexico	100,367	1.7	5.9	7.1	3.3	2.6
Micronesia, Federated States of	126	2.6	6.0	6.9	4.8	5.1
Monaco	34	−2.9	18.4	20.5	1.8	1.8
Mongolia	2,558	1.2	5.9	5.6	3.8	2.4
Morocco	30,430	1.9	6.0	6.4	4.1	3.1
Mozambique	18,644	2.9	5.1	5.1	6.4	6.0
Myanmar[a]	48,363	1.6	6.7	6.8	3.9	3.0
Namibia	1,787	2.3	5.5	5.6	5.9	5.0
Nauru	13	2.6	6.0	6.9	4.4	4.5
Nepal	23,592	2.4	5.8	5.9	5.1	4.6
Netherlands[a]	15,929	0.6	17.4	18.4	1.6	1.5
New Zealand	3,807	1.1	15.3	15.7	2.1	2.0
Nicaragua	5,207	2.9	4.4	4.6	4.9	4.0
Niger	11,226	3.5	3.5	3.3	8.0	8.0
Nigeria	116,928	2.8	4.7	4.8	6.5	5.6
Niue	2	−1.4	5.8	6.9	3.2	2.6
Norway	4,487	0.5	20.8	19.6	1.9	1.7
Oman	2,621	3.5	3.8	4.3	6.9	5.6
Pakistan	144,971	2.6	5.6	5.8	5.9	5.2
Palau	20	2.3	6.0	6.9	2.6	2.8
Panama	2,898	1.7	7.3	8.2	3.0	2.5
Papua New Guinea	4,919	2.5	4.2	4.2	5.1	4.4
Paraguay	5,635	2.6	5.3	5.4	4.7	3.9
Peru	26,092	1.7	6.2	7.3	3.6	2.7
Philippines	77,130	2.1	4.9	5.6	4.3	3.4
Poland	38,576	0.1	15.1	16.6	2.0	1.3
Portugal	10,032	0.1	19.3	21.0	1.5	1.5

(Continued)

(Continued)

Member State	Total population (in thousands)	Annual growth rate (%)	Percentage of population aged 60+ years		Total fertility rate	
	2001	1991–2001	1991	2001	1991	2001
Qatar	574	2.1	2.1	3.3	4.3	3.4
Republic of Korea	47,068	0.8	7.9	11.3	1.7	1.5
Republic of Moldova	4,284	−0.2	12.9	13.6	2.3	1.5
Romania	22,387	−0.3	16.0	18.9	1.7	1.3
Russian Federation	144,663	−0.3	16.2	18.5	1.7	1.2
Rwanda	7,948	2.1	4.1	4.2	6.8	5.9
Saint Kitts and Nevis	38	−0.8	9.1	10.0	2.8	2.4
Saint Lucia	149	1.2	8.6	7.6	3.2	2.6
Saint Vincent and the Grenadines	114	0.7	9.1	10.0	2.2	1.9
Samoa	158	−0.1	6.1	6.7	4.7	4.3
San Marino	27	1.4	21.5	24.3	1.5	1.3
Sao Tome and Principe	140	1.8	6.8	6.3	6.2	6.0
Saudi Arabia	21,027	2.9	4.1	4.9	6.8	5.7
Senegal	9,661	2.5	4.6	4.2	6.2	5.2
Seychelles	81	1.4	8.3	9.1	2.1	1.8
Sierra Leone	4,587	1.1	5.0	4.7	6.5	6.5
Singapore	4,107	2.9	8.6	10.8	1.7	1.5
Slovakia	5,402	0.2	14.9	15.5	2.0	1.3
Slovenia	1,984	0.3	17.3	19.5	1.5	1.2
Solomon Islands	462	3.5	4.4	4.1	5.9	5.4
Somalia	9,156	2.4	4.2	3.9	7.3	7.3
South Africa	43,791	1.7	5.1	5.8	3.4	2.9
Spain	39,920	0.1	19.6	22.0	1.3	1.1
Sri Lanka	19,103	1.0	8.1	9.5	2.5	2.1
Sudan	31,809	2.3	5.0	5.5	5.4	4.6
Suriname	418	0.4	6.8	8.1	2.6	2.1
Swaziland	937	1.8	4.9	5.4	5.5	4.5
Sweden	8,832	0.2	22.6	22.7	2.0	1.4
Switzerland	7,169	0.4	19.2	21.7	1.5	1.4
Syrian Arab Republic[a]	16,609	2.7	4.5	4.7	5.3	3.8
Tajikistan	6,135	1.3	6.3	6.8	4.7	3.1
Thailand	63,583	1.4	6.4	8.3	2.2	2.0
The former Yugoslav Republic of Macedonia	2,043	0.6	11.8	14.6	1.9	1.6
Togo	4,656	2.8	4.8	4.9	6.3	5.5
Tonga	99	0.3	5.8	6.9	4.7	3.8
Trinidad and Tobago	1,299	0.6	8.8	9.7	2.3	1.6
Tunisia	9,561	1.4	7.0	8.4	3.4	2.2
Turkey	67,632	1.7	7.3	8.5	3.3	2.4
Turkmenistan	4,834	2.5	6.2	6.4	4.2	3.3
Tuvalu	10	1.4	5.8	6.9	3.6	2.9
Uganda	24,022	3.0	4.1	3.8	7.1	7.1
Ukraine	49,111	−0.6	18.6	20.7	1.7	1.1
United Arab Emirates	2,653	2.4	2.7	5.5	4.0	3.0
United Kingdom[a]	59,541	0.3	20.8	20.7	1.8	1.6
United Republic of Tanzania	35,964	2.9	3.8	4.0	6.0	5.2

a. Figures not endorsed by member state as official statistics.

Member State	Total population (in thousands)	Annual growth rate (%)	Percentage of population aged 60+ years		Total fertility rate	
	2001	1991–2001	1991	2001	1991	2001
United States of America[a]	285,925	1.1	16.6	16.2	2.0	2.0
Uruguay	3,360	0.7	16.5	17.2	2.5	2.3
Uzbekistan	25,256	1.9	6.5	7.1	3.8	2.5
Vanuatu	201	2.8	5.2	4.8	4.9	4.4
Venezuela, Bolivarian Republic of	24,631	2.1	5.8	6.7	3.4	2.8
Viet Nam	79,174	1.6	7.3	7.5	3.5	2.3
Yemen	19,113	4.6	4.1	3.6	7.6	7.6
Yugoslavia	10,537	0.3	15.6	18.4	2.0	1.6
Zambia	10,648	2.5	4.4	4.5	6.3	5.8
Zimbabwe	12,851	2.0	4.6	4.7	5.7	4.7

SOURCE: World Health Organization, *The World Health Report 2002.*

Child Care Arrangements of Preschool Children, by Age, Race/Ethnicity, and Type of Child Care Arrangement, 1999

Characteristics	Percent in nonparental arrangements			Percent with parental care only
	Relative care	Nonrelative care	Center-based program	
Total	22.8	16.1	59.7	23.1
Age				
3 years old	24.4	16.2	45.7	30.8
4 years old	22	15.9	69.6	17.7
5 years old	20.2	16.1	76.5	13.5
Race/ethnicity				
White, non-Hispanic	18.8	19.4	60	23.2
Black, non-Hispanic	33.4	7.4	73.2	13.7
Hispanic	26.5	12.7	44.2	33.4
Other	30.2	10.4	66.1	16.6

SOURCE: Department of Education.

Death Rates for Leading Causes of Death for All Ages: United States, 1950–2002

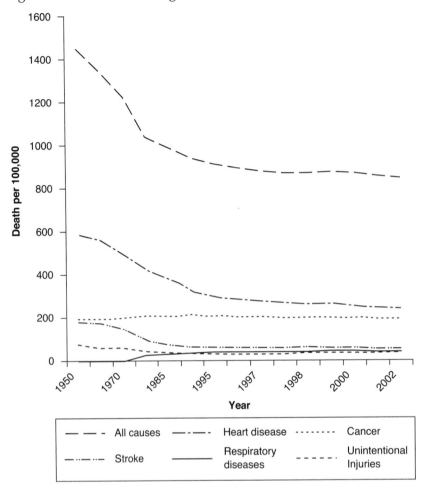

SOURCE: U.S. Department of Education.

Enrollment in Grades K–8 and 9–12 of Elementary and Secondary Schools (in thousands)

Year	Total			Public			Private		
	K–12[1]	K–8[1]	9–12	K–12[1]	K–8[1]	9–12	K–12[1]	K–8[1]	9–12
1988	45,430	32,537	12,893	40,188	28,501	11,687	5,242	4,036	1,206
1989	45,741	33,187	12,554	40,543	29,152	11,390	5,198	4,035	1,163
1990	46,451	33,962	12,488	41,217	29,878	11,338	5,234	4,084	1,150
1991	47,322	34,619	12,703	42,047	30,506	11,541	5,275	4,113	1,162
1992	48,145	35,264	12,882	42,823	31,088	11,735	5,322	4,175	1,147
1993	48,812	35,719	13,093	43,465	31,504	11,961	5,348	4,215	1,132
1994	49,610	36,233	13,376	44,111	31,898	12,213	5,498	4,335	1,163
1995	50,503	36,806	13,697	44,840	32,341	12,500	5,662	4,465	1,197
1996	51,375	37,316	14,060	45,611	32,764	12,847	5,764	4,551	1,213
1997	51,968	37,696	14,272	46,127	33,073	13,054	5,841	4,623	1,218
1998	52,475	38,048	14,427	46,539	33,346	13,193	5,937	4,702	1,235
1999	52,876	38,253	14,623	46,857	33,488	13,369	6,018	4,765	1,254
2000	53,385	38,584	14,801	47,223	33,709	13,514	6,162	4,875	1,287
2001	53,890	38,832	15,058	47,688	33,952	13,736	6,202	4,880	1,322
				Projected					
2002	54,158	38,827	15,331	47,918	33,942	13,976	6,241	4,885	1,356
2003	54,296	38,719	15,577	48,040	33,843	14,198	6,256	4,876	1,379
2004	54,455	38,541	15,914	48,175	33,669	14,506	6,279	4,871	1,408
2005	54,615	38,412	16,203	48,304	33,534	14,770	6,311	4,878	1,433
2006	54,907	38,522	16,385	48,524	33,589	14,936	6,383	4,933	1,449
2007	55,049	38,605	16,445	48,640	33,654	14,986	6,409	4,950	1,458
2008	55,124	38,766	16,358	48,690	33,791	14,899	6,434	4,975	1,459
2009	55,223	38,995	16,228	48,761	33,994	14,767	6,461	5,001	1,461
2010	55,386	39,283	16,103	48,890	34,243	14,648	6,495	5,040	1,455
2011	55,618	39,688	15,930	49,084	34,597	14,487	6,534	5,091	1,443
2012	55,946	40,154	15,792	49,367	35,006	14,361	6,579	5,148	1,430
2013	56,364	40,638	15,726	49,737	35,430	14,307	6,627	5,208	1,419

SOURCE: U.S. Department of Education.
1. Includes most nursery school enrollment.

General Statistics of Public Libraries, by Population, 2000

Number of public library service outlets	17,182	5,749	4,205	1,790	2,140	1,108	2,190
Central libraries	8,915	5,423	2,582	499	281	73	57
Branch libraries	7,383	255	1,326	1,113	1,693	964	2,032
Bookmobiles	884	71	297	178	166	71	101
Collections, in thousands							
Books and serial volumes	760,513	99,639	185,480	91,633	112,461	75,126	196,173
Audio and video materials and films	54,021	5,456	13,020	6,662	8,241	5,184	15,458
Serial subscriptions	1,944	276	487	209	254	193	523
Paid staff, in full-time equivalents							
Librarians	43,118	6,016	11,317	5,156	6,018	4,195	10,416
Librarians with ALA-MLS	29,519	1,221	6,904	3,761	4,858	3,441	9,334
Other staff	86,984	5,479	20,404	11,770	15,787	9,492	24,053
Income, in thousands							
Total operating income	$7,702,768	$499,840	$1,744,932	$967,817	$1,246,162	$858,994	$2,385,022
Source of operating income (percent)							
Federal	0.7	1.5	0.6	0.6	0.7	0.6	0.9
State	12.8	7.8	12.3	15.2	11.6	13.0	13.3
Local	77.1	69.3	77.4	76.0	80.2	79.0	75.9
Other and private	9.4	21.4	9.8	8.2	7.5	7.4	10.0

SOURCE: U.S. Department of Education.

Health Insurance Coverage by Age Group in United States

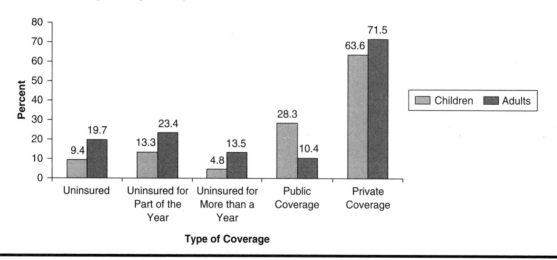

SOURCE: Centers for Disease Control.

High School Graduates 1987–1988 to 2012–2013 (in thousands)

Year ending	Total	Public	Private
1988	2,773	2,500	273
1989	2,744	2,459	285
1990	2,589	2,320	269
1991	2,493	2,235	258
1992	2,478	2,226	252
1993	2,481	2,233	247
1994	2,464	2,221	243
1995	2,519	2,274	246
1996	2,518	2,273	245
1997	2,612	2,358	254
1998	2,704	2,439	265
1999	2,759	2,486	273
2000	2,833	2,554	279
2001	2,852	2,569	283
Projected			
2002	2,917	2,630	287
2003	2,986	2,685	301
2004	3,002	2,698	305
2005	3,037	2,728	308
2006	3,101	2,785	316
2007	3,172	2,850	322
2008	3,262	2,931	331
2009	3,274	2,942	332
2010	3,262	2,930	331
2011	3,237	2,906	331
2012	3,202	2,870	331
2013	3,176	2,843	333

SOURCE: National Center for Educational Statistics.

Life Expectancy in All Member States of World Health Organization in 2001

Country	Total	Males at birth	Males at age 60	Females at birth	Females at age 60
Japan	73.6	71.4	17.1	75.8	20.7
Switzerland	72.8	71.1	16.9	74.4	19.4
San Marino	72.2	70.4	16.3	74.0	19.1
Sweden	71.8	70.5	16.5	73.2	18.5
Australia	71.6	70.1	16.4	73.2	18.8
Monaco	71.3	69.0	16.3	73.5	19.4
France	71.3	69.0	16.1	73.5	19.1
Iceland	71.2	70.5	16.8	71.9	17.6
Italy	71.0	69.2	15.5	72.9	18.2
Austria	71.0	68.9	15.7	73.0	18.5
Andorra	70.9	68.8	15.8	73.0	18.5
Spain	70.9	68.7	15.2	73.0	18.2
Norway	70.8	69.3	15.6	72.2	17.9
Luxembourg	70.6	68.6	15.1	72.7	18.3
Greece	70.4	69.0	15.7	71.9	17.1
New Zealand	70.3	69.1	15.9	71.5	17.7
Germany	70.2	68.3	15.0	72.2	17.7
Finland	70.1	67.7	15.2	72.5	18.1
Denmark	70.1	69.3	15.5	70.8	16.7
Netherlands	69.9	68.7	15.0	71.1	17.3
Canada	69.9	68.2	15.3	71.6	17.9
Belgium	69.7	67.7	14.8	71.8	17.8
United Kingdom	69.6	68.4	15.0	70.9	16.9
Israel	69.4	68.0	15.8	70.8	16.9
Malta	69.2	67.6	14.3	70.9	16.5
Ireland	69.0	67.6	13.9	70.4	16.1
Singapore	68.7	67.9	14.5	69.5	15.8
Slovenia	67.7	65.1	13.3	70.3	16.6
United States of America	67.6	66.4	14.9	68.8	16.6
Republic of Korea	67.4	64.5	12.9	70.3	16.6
Portugal	66.8	64.3	13.4	69.4	16.2
Czech Republic	66.6	63.8	12.8	69.5	16.0
Cuba	66.6	64.7	14.4	68.5	16.6
Cyprus	66.2	65.3	13.2	67.2	14.5
Chile	66.1	64.4	13.3	67.8	15.5
Kuwait	64.9	64.1	12.2	65.8	13.0
Costa Rica	64.8	62.6	12.9	67.0	15.3
Uruguay	64.7	61.2	12.3	68.3	16.8
Poland	64.3	62.1	11.9	66.6	14.6
Barbados	64.3	61.0	12.3	67.6	16.4
Slovakia	64.1	61.6	11.5	66.6	14.6
Panama	64.1	61.2	13.6	66.9	16.4
Mexico	63.8	62.6	14.5	65.0	14.9
Croatia	63.3	59.7	10.1	66.9	14.4
China	63.2	62.0	12.7	64.3	14.2
Argentina	63.1	60.6	11.9	65.7	15.1
Bulgaria	63.0	60.8	11.5	65.2	13.9
Jamaica	62.8	61.1	11.8	64.5	13.9

Country	Total	Males at birth	Males at age 60	Females at birth	Females at age 60
United Arab Emirates	62.5	61.7	10.6	63.3	12.3
Bosnia and Herzegovina	62.5	60.0	11.3	64.9	14.3
The former Yugoslav Republic of Macedonia	62.2	60.4	11.4	63.9	13.0
Yugoslavia	62.1	60.7	11.0	63.6	12.8
Dominica	62.1	59.4	13.0	64.8	15.0
Brunei Darussalam	62.0	60.4	10.5	63.7	12.8
Estonia	62.0	58.0	11.1	66.1	15.0
Bahrain	61.8	62.3	10.5	61.3	9.4
Hungary	61.8	58.0	10.4	65.5	14.4
Tunisia	61.3	58.9	10.8	63.7	13.4
Qatar	61.2	59.2	9.4	63.1	12.7
Lithuania	61.1	56.9	11.0	65.4	14.8
Venezuela, Bolivarian Republic of	61.1	57.1	11.6	65.0	15.0
Romania	60.9	58.6	11.1	63.3	13.5
Saint Kitts and Nevis	60.8	58.8	11.1	62.8	13.5
Saint Lucia	60.6	58.9	11.0	62.4	13.5
Cook Islands	60.5	58.3	10.2	62.6	12.7
Trinidad and Tobago	60.4	58.9	11.5	62.0	12.8
Oman	60.4	59.0	10.4	61.7	12.3
Malaysia	60.4	57.6	9.2	63.2	12.0
Latvia	60.0	55.2	10.0	64.9	14.4
Saudi Arabia	60.0	57.4	10.0	62.5	13.0
Saint Vincent and the Grenadines	59.8	57.5	11.3	62.2	14.0
Georgia	59.8	57.5	10.3	62.2	12.1
Turkey	59.8	58.5	11.2	61.1	12.4
Antigua and Barbuda	59.7	56.9	10.3	62.6	13.4
Libyan Arab Jamahiriya	59.6	56.8	9.8	62.4	12.9
Ecuador	59.5	56.6	11.6	62.4	14.2
Lebanon	59.4	56.5	10.0	62.2	12.9
Syrian Arab Republic	59.2	58.0	10.0	60.5	11.5
Seychelles	59.1	55.4	8.6	62.9	13.1
Niue	59.1	56.4	10.0	61.9	13.0
Belize	58.9	56.3	10.4	61.5	12.9
Sri Lanka	58.9	55.2	8.8	62.6	12.7
Fiji	58.8	56.8	10.0	60.8	12.3
Tonga	58.8	57.1	10.0	60.4	11.9
Colombia	58.7	55.3	10.7	62.1	12.9
Albania	58.7	55.9	8.8	61.5	12.7
Paraguay	58.7	55.4	9.6	61.9	12.9
Viet Nam	58.6	55.9	9.9	61.4	12.5
Bahamas	58.6	54.7	11.1	62.5	14.7
Thailand	58.6	56.4	12.0	60.8	12.6
Jordan	58.5	57.2	9.9	59.9	11.5
Belarus	58.4	53.9	9.5	62.8	13.0
Armenia	58.3	55.4	9.2	61.1	12.2
Algeria	57.8	55.8	10.3	59.9	12.2
Nicaragua	57.8	54.4	10.7	61.3	13.7

(Continued)

(Continued)

Country	Total	Males at birth	Males at age 60	Females at birth	Females at age 60
Samoa	57.7	56.0	9.3	59.5	11.6
Palau	57.7	55.5	9.2	59.9	11.7
Grenada	57.5	56.0	10.1	59.0	12.1
Republic of Moldova	57.5	54.2	9.3	60.8	11.7
Suriname	57.5	54.2	9.4	60.7	12.6
El Salvador	57.4	53.7	11.2	61.2	13.5
Peru	57.4	54.7	10.7	60.1	13.2
Ukraine	57.4	52.9	8.8	61.8	12.2
Mauritius	57.1	56.4	9.4	57.7	11.2
Iran, Islamic Republic of	56.7	55.5	9.8	57.9	11.4
Indonesia	56.7	56.1	10.6	57.2	11.1
Russian Federation	56.7	51.5	8.5	61.9	12.7
Egypt	56.7	56.4	9.4	57.0	9.2
Brazil	56.7	52.2	9.4	61.1	13.0
Cape Verde	56.5	52.2	9.2	60.8	12.3
Dominican Republic	56.4	53.0	9.7	59.8	13.1
Honduras	55.9	52.1	9.3	59.6	12.6
Micronesia, Federated States of	55.8	54.0	9.3	57.5	11.2
Democratic People's Republic of Korea	55.8	53.5	10.7	58.1	13.2
Philippines	55.5	51.1	8.0	59.8	11.9
Morocco	55.4	54.9	9.2	55.9	10.0
Vanuatu	54.9	53.4	8.9	56.3	10.8
Solomon Islands	54.8	52.6	8.7	56.9	11.0
Guatemala	54.3	51.4	10.4	57.2	11.6
Guyana	54.1	51.6	9.4	56.7	12.1
Mongolia	53.9	49.9	9.7	58.0	12.7
Tuvalu	53.9	52.0	8.8	55.7	11.0
Uzbekistan	53.5	50.9	8.2	56.1	10.8
Kiribati	53.2	51.1	8.7	55.4	10.8
Azerbaijan	52.8	50.3	8.5	55.4	11.0
Nauru	52.7	48.8	6.8	56.6	10.4
Marshall Islands	52.6	50.4	7.9	54.7	10.3
Kazakhstan	52.4	49.0	8.7	55.8	10.8
Bangladesh	52.1	51.7	9.4	52.6	10.9
Maldives	51.9	49.6	5.7	54.3	7.5
Kyrgyzstan	51.5	47.7	6.9	55.4	10.4
Bhutan	51.4	50.0	9.2	52.9	11.1
India	51.4	51.5	9.7	51.3	10.2
Sao Tome and Principe	51.4	48.1	8.2	54.7	10.8
Pakistan	50.9	50.4	9.3	51.5	10.8
Bolivia	50.8	48.0	8.4	53.6	11.0
Iraq	50.5	47.7	8.1	53.3	11.0
Turkmenistan	50.3	46.7	6.8	53.8	9.7
Tajikistan	50.1	47.0	8.4	53.2	11.8
Comoros	49.9	47.0	7.6	52.8	10.2
Gabon	49.9	48.2	9.1	51.5	11.0
Papua New Guinea	49.8	47.9	8.2	51.8	10.4
Myanmar	48.9	46.5	9.0	51.4	11.0

Country	Total	Males at birth	Males at age 60	Females at birth	Females at age 60
Nepal	48.9	48.7	8.9	49.1	10.5
Yemen	48.4	45.5	7.0	51.2	10.4
Gambia	48.0	45.1	7.8	51.0	10.3
Ghana	47.8	45.8	8.4	49.7	10.6
Cambodia	46.4	43.0	7.6	49.9	10.5
Sudan	45.5	42.9	7.4	48.1	9.9
Senegal	45.4	43.1	7.4	47.7	9.8
Madagascar	44.5	42.2	7.4	46.7	9.8
Lao People's Democratic Republic	44.2	42.4	7.5	46.0	9.8
Eritrea	44.1	42.3	8.0	45.9	10.3
Equatorial Guinea	43.8	41.7	7.7	45.9	10.0
Congo	43.0	40.9	7.7	45.2	10.6
Haiti	42.9	38.5	8.4	47.3	11.2
Togo	42.7	40.6	7.6	44.9	10.2
Guinea	42.4	40.0	7.3	44.7	9.6
Benin	42.1	40.1	7.1	44.1	9.5
Nigeria	41.9	40.0	7.0	43.8	9.5
Mauritania	41.6	39.6	6.9	43.6	9.4
South Africa	41.3	40.0	8.9	42.7	11.4
Kenya	40.8	39.5	8.1	42.1	10.7
Namibia	40.4	39.8	8.7	41.1	10.9
Cameroon	40.4	38.8	7.3	42.0	9.9
Djibouti	40.1	37.9	6.9	42.3	9.6
Ethiopia	38.8	36.9	7.0	40.7	9.4
Chad	38.7	35.9	6.3	41.5	9.3
Guinea-Bissau	38.3	36.1	6.9	40.6	9.4
Uganda	38.0	36.2	6.9	39.8	9.4
Côte d'Ivoire	37.8	36.3	7.3	39.3	9.7
United Republic of Tanzania	37.8	36.3	6.8	39.3	9.5
Liberia	37.5	35.3	6.6	39.6	9.1
Mozambique	36.0	34.4	6.9	37.7	9.5
Mali	35.7	33.7	6.5	37.7	9.2
Burkina Faso	35.1	33.9	7.0	36.3	9.4
Somalia	35.0	32.5	6.3	37.4	8.8
Democratic Republic of the Congo	34.8	32.3	6.3	37.3	9.2
Central African Republic	34.0	32.3	6.0	35.6	9.2
Swaziland	33.9	33.8	9.0	34.1	11.0
Rwanda	33.8	31.7	6.7	36.0	9.6
Burundi	33.7	31.7	6.8	35.7	9.6
Afghanistan	33.4	31.1	4.9	35.7	8.7
Lesotho	33.4	33.2	8.4	33.6	10.6
Niger	33.2	31.7	6.1	34.7	8.6
Botswana	32.9	33.0	9.1	32.7	12.2
Zimbabwe	31.3	31.6	8.6	31.0	10.7
Zambia	30.9	30.5	7.5	31.4	10.0
Malawi	29.8	29.0	7.2	30.7	9.5
Angola	28.7	25.7	5.8	31.7	9.2
Sierra Leone	26.5	24.0	5.5	29.0	8.5

SOURCE: World Health Organization.

Mortality Causes Under 5 Years Old in 2002

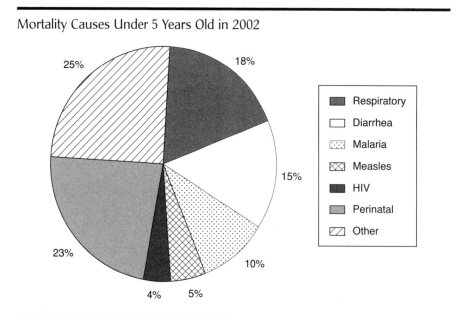

SOURCE: World Health Organization.

Number of People Age 60 and Older

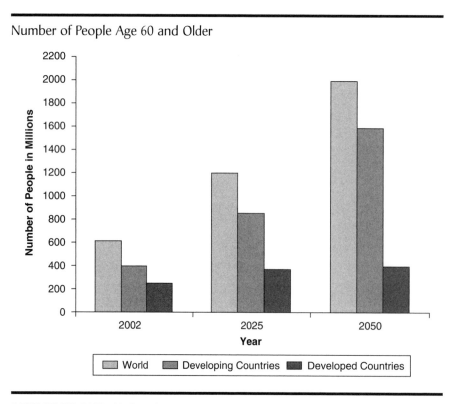

SOURCE: World Health Organization.

Number of School Associated Violent Deaths, 1992–2000

	Ages 5–19		Ages 5–19	
Year	*Homicides at school*	*Homicides away from school*	*Suicides at school*	*Suicides away from school*
1992–1993	34	3,583	6	2,199
1993–1994	29	3,806	7	2,263
1994–1995	28	3,546	7	2,220
1995–1996	32	3,303	6	2,113
1996–1997	28	2,950	1	2,108
1997–1998	34	2,728	6	2,055
1998–1999	33	2,366	4	1,855
1999–2000	16	2,124	6	1,922
Total	234	24,406	43	16,735

SOURCE: National Center for Education Statistics.

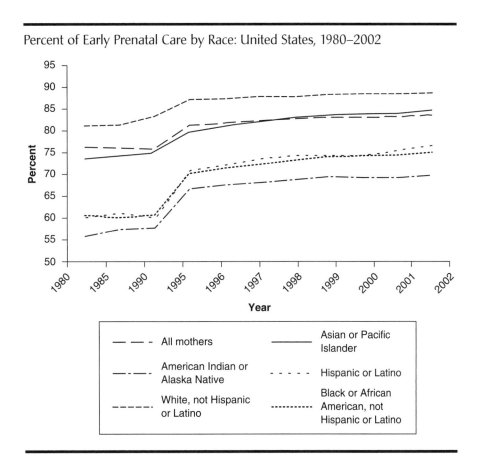

Percent of Early Prenatal Care by Race: United States, 1980–2002

Legend:
- – – – All mothers
- –·–· American Indian or Alaska Native
- – – – White, not Hispanic or Latino
- ——— Asian or Pacific Islander
- - - - - Hispanic or Latino
- ··········· Black or African American, not Hispanic or Latino

SOURCE: National Center for Education Statistics.

Percent of Families With Income Below the Poverty Level

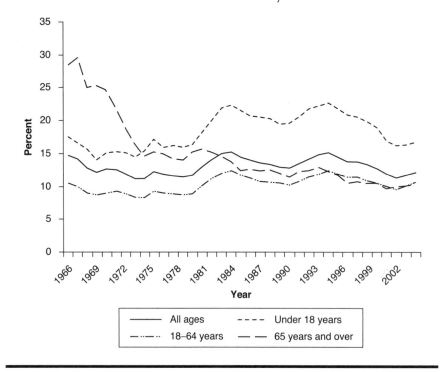

SOURCE: U.S. Census Bureau.

Percent Overweight and Obesity by Age: United States, 1960–2002

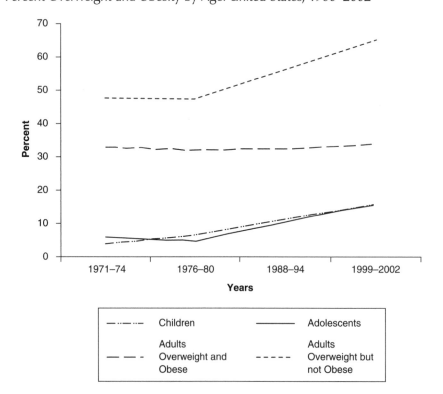

SOURCE: Centers for Disease Control.

Percentage of Children Ages 3–5 Not Yet Enrolled in Kindergarten Who Participated in Home Literacy Activities With a Family Member Three or More Times per Week

Child and family characteristics	Read to		Told a story		Taught letters, words, or numbers		Taught songs or music	
	1993	2001	1993	2001	1993	2001	1993	2001
Total	78.3	84.1	43	54.3	57.7	74.2	41	54.1
Age								
3 Years	79.4	83.6	46.4	54.5	57.2	71.2	45	59.9
4 Years	77.8	85.2	41.2	54.6	58.1	77.1	38.9	51.7
5 Years	75.9	81.5	35.8	52	57.9	74.6	33.1	40.6
Race/Ethnicity								
Asian/Pacific Islander	68.8	87.4	52.1	58.1	61.8	77.9	35.9	50.4
Black	65.9	76.7	39	51.2	62.7	77.5	48.9	53.9
White	84.8	89.4	44.3	57.9	57.2	74.8	40.2	53.4
Other[1]	75.9	86.5	48.1	61.8	56	78.4	31.3	57.9
Hispanic	58.2	70.7	37.7	42.3	53.9	68.2	38.7	56.6
Poverty Status								
Below poverty threshold (poor)	67.5	73.7	39.1	50.7	59.6	72.4	45.2	57
At or above poverty threshold (nonpoor)	82.1	87.1	44.3	55.3	57	74.7	39.5	53.3

SOURCE: U.S. Department of Education, NCES, School Readiness and Early Childhood Education Program Participation Surveys of the National Household Education Surveys Program.
1. Other includes American Indian and Alaska Native.

Selected Chronic Health Conditions Causing Limitation of Activity Among Working-Age Adults by Age: United States, 2000–2002

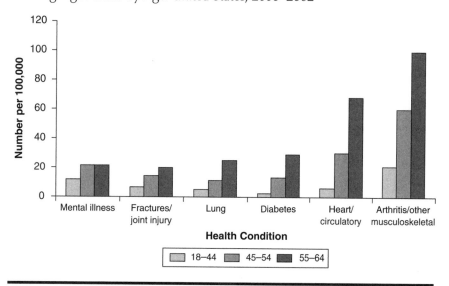

SOURCE: U.S. Department of Education.

Use of Illicit Drugs in the Past Month by Age, 2003

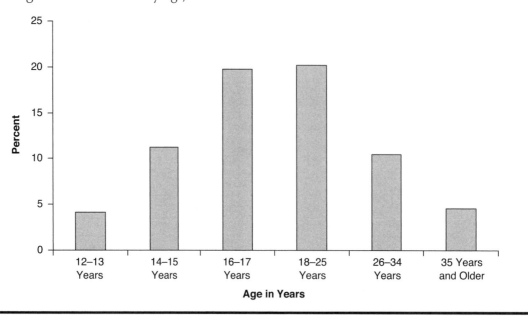

SOURCE: U.S. Department of Education.

Years of Life Lost in Thousands by Risk Factor and Sex, 2000 (Global)

	Males	*Females*
Childhood and maternal undernutrition		
Underweight	64,119	62,766
Iron deficiency	11,891	13,967
Vitamin A deficiency	11,276	14,727
Zinc deficiency	13,459	13,167
Other diet-related risks and physical inactivity		
Blood pressure	30,206	25,342
Cholesterol	19,373	15,600
Overweight	11,276	11,868
Low fruit and vegetable intake	13,463	10,014
Physical inactivity	8,562	7,278
Sexual and reproductive health risks		
Unsafe sex	36,918	40,052
Lack of contraception	—	4,206
Addictive substances		
Tobacco	37,913	7,708
Alcohol	28,035	4,662
Illicit drugs	3,841	978
Environmental risks		
Unsafe water, sanitation, and hygiene	24,917	24,315
Urban air pollution	3,533	2,871
Indoor smoke from solid fuels	17,341	17,805
Lead exposure	1,888	914
Climate change	2,415	2,530
Occupational risks		
Risk factors for injury	6,674	433
Carcinogens	1,105	271
Airborne particulates	1,344	143
Ergonomic stressors	4	1
Noise	0	0
Other selected risks to health		
Unsafe health care injections	5,504	3,675
Childhood sexual abuse	784	908

SOURCE: World Health Organization.

Appendix 2

Master Bibliography

Aaron, H., & Reischauer, R. (1998). *Countdown to reform: The great Social Security debate.* New York: Century.

Aaron, J., Zaglul, H., & Emery, R. E. (1999). Posttraumatic stress in children following acute physical injury. *Journal of Pediatric Psychology, 24,* 335–343.

AARP The Magazine, http://www.aarpmagazine.org

AARP—Grief and Loss, http://www.aarp.org/life/griefandloss

Abe, J. A., & Izard, C. E. (1999). The developmental functions of emotions: An analysis in terms of differential emotions theory. *Cognition and Emotion, 13,* 523–549.

Abe, J. A., & Izard, C. E. (1999). A longitudinal study of emotion, expression and personality relations in early development. *Journal of Personality and Social Psychology, 77*(3), 566–577.

Aber, L. W., & Yarbroudy, E. (1990). *101 activities for siblings who squabble: Projects and games to entertain and keep the peace.* New York: St. Martins Press.

Abi-Dargham, A. (2004). Do we still believe in the dopamine hypothesis? New data bring new evidence. *International Journal of Neuropsychopharmacology, 7*(Suppl.), 1–5.

Abidin, R. R., Golladay, W. M., & Howerton, A. L. (1971). Elementary school retention: An unjustifiable, discriminatory, and noxious policy. *Journal of School Psychology, 9,* 410–414.

Abitbol, M. M. (1988). Effect of posture and locomotion on energy expenditure. *American Journal of Physical Anthropology, 77,* 191–199.

About ageism. (n.d.). Retrieved from http://www.21stcenturyschools.com/Ageism.htm

About.com. (n.d.). *School age children.* Retrieved from http://pediatrics.about.com/od/schoolagechildren

About, Inc. (n.d.). *Allergies.* Retrieved from http://allergies.about.com/

About, Inc. (n.d.). *Science: Correlational vs. experimental.* Retrieved from http://psychology.about.com/library/weekly/aa070102b.htm

Abramowitz, J. S. (1998). Does cognitive-behavioral therapy cure obsessive-compulsive disorder? A meta-analytic evaluation of clinical significance. *Behavior Therapy, 29,* 339–355.

Abramowitz, J. S., Franklin, M. E., Schwartz, S. A., & Furr, J. M. (2003). Symptom presentation and outcome of cognitive-behavioral therapy for obsessive-compulsive disorder. *Journal of Consulting and Clinical Psychology, 71,* 1049–1057.

AcademicDB. (n.d.). *Sociology/poverty.* Retrieved from http://www.academicdb.com/Sociology/Poverty

Academy for Eating Disorders, http://www.aedweb.org/index.cfm

Academy for Eating Disorders. (n.d.). *About eating disorders.* Retrieved from http://www.aedweb.org/eating_disorders/index.cfm

Achbar, M. (1994). *Manufacturing consent: Noam Chomsky and the media.* Montréal, Canada: Black Rose Books.

Achenbach, T. M. (1974). *Developmental psychopathology* (Vol. 1). New York: Wiley.

Achenbach, T. M. (1978). *Research in developmental psychology: Concepts, strategies, methods.* New York: The Free Press.

Achenbach, T. M., & McConaughy, S. H. (1998). *Empirically based assessment of child and adolescent psychopathology: Practical applications* (2nd ed.). Thousand Oaks, CA: Sage.

Ackerman, B. P., Brown, E., & Izard, C. E. (2003). Continuity and change in levels of externalizing behavior in school of children from economically disadvantaged families. *Child Development, 74,* 694–704.

Ackerman, B. P., Brown, E., & Izard, C. E. (2004). The relations between persistent poverty and contextual risk and children's behavior in elementary school. *Developmental Psychology, 40,* 367–377.

Ackerman, B. P., Schoff D'Eramo, K., Umylny, L., Schultz, D., & Izard, C. (2001). Family structure and the externalizing behavior of children from economically disadvantaged families. *Journal of Family Psychology, 15,* 288–300.

Ackerman, P. L. (2003). Cognitive ability and non-ability trait determinants of expertise. *Educational Researcher, 32*(8), 15–20. Available from http://www.aera.net/

Ackerman, P. T., Newton, J. E. O., McPherson, W. B., Jones, J. G., & Dykman, R. A. (1998). Prevalence of post traumatic stress disorder and other psychiatric diagnoses in three groups of abused children (sexual, physical, and both). *Child Abuse and Neglect, 22,* 759–774.

The ACNM Certification Council, http://www.accmidwife.org

ACT Assessment: An ACT program for educational planning, http://www.act.org/aap/

Adams, G. A., & Beehr, T. A. (2003). *Retirement: Reasons, processes, and results.* New York: Springer.

Adams, G. R., & Berzonsky, M. D. (Eds.). (2003). *Blackwell handbook of adolescence.* Oxford, UK: Blackwell.

Adams, L. T., & Worden, P. E. (1986). Script development and memory organization in preschool and elementary school children. *Discourse Processes, 9,* 149–166.

Adams, M. (1990). *Beginning to read: Thinking and learning about print.* Cambridge: MIT Press.

Adams, R. D., Victor, M., & Ropper, A. H. (1997). *Principles of neurology* (6th ed.). New York: McGraw-Hill.

Adamson, G. D., & Baker, V. L. (2003). Subfertility: Causes, treatment and outcome. *Best Practice & Research Clinical Obstetrics & Gynaecology, 17,* 169–185.

Adler, A. (1925). *The practice and theory of individual psychology* (P. Radlin, Trans.). London: Routledge Kegan Paul.

Adler, A. (1928). Characteristics of the first, second, and third child. *Children: The Magazine for Parents, 5,* 14.

Adler Graduate School, http://www.alfredadler.edu

Adler, I., & Kandel, D. B. (1981). Cross-cultural perspectives on developmental stages in adolescent drug-use. *Journal of Studies on Alcohol, 42,* 701–715.

Adler, P., & Adler, P. (1998). *Peer power: Preadolescent culture and identity.* New Brunswick, NJ: Rutgers University Press.

Administration on Aging, http://www.aoa.dhhs.gov/

Administration of Children and Families: Head Start Bureau, http://www.acf.hhs.gov/programs/hsb/

Administration on Children, Youth and Families (ACYF). (2000). *FACES findings: New research on Head Start program quality and outcomes.* Washington, DC: Author.

Administration on Developmental Disabilities. (n.d.). *Making a difference in the lives of people with developmental disabilities. ADD Fact Sheet.* Retrieved from http://www.acf.hhs.gov/

Adolescence Directory On-Line, http://education.indiana.edu/cas/adol/adol.html

Adolph, K. (1977). Learning in the development of infant locomotion. *Monographs for the Society for Research in Child Development, 62*(3, Serial No. 251).

Adolph, K. E., Vereijken, B., & Denny, M. A. (1998). Learning to crawl. *Child Development, 69,* 1299–1312.

Adrados, J. L. (1995). The influence of family, school, and peers on adolescent drug misuse. *International Journal of the Addictions, 30,* 1407–1423.

Advanced Bionics Corporation, http://www.advancedbionics.com

African American time line 1852–1925, http://www.africanamericans.com/Timeline.htm

African Americans by the numbers, http://www.africanamericans.com/AADemographics.htm

Agency for Toxic Substances and Disease Registry. (2001). *ToxFAQs for polychlorinated biphenyls (PCBs).* Retrieved from http://www.atsdr.cdc.gov/tfacts17.html

Aging Parents and Elder Care, http://www.aging-parents-and-elder-care.com

Agnew, C. R. (1999). Power over interdependent behavior within the dyad: Who decides what a couple does? In L. J. Severy & W. B. Miller (Eds.), *Advances in population: Psychosocial perspectives: Vol. 3.* London: Jessica Kingsley.

Agran, P., Anderson, C., Winn, D., Trent, R., & Walton-Haynes, T. (2003). Rates of pediatric injuries by 3-month intervals for children 0 to 3 years of age. *Pediatrics, 111,* 683–692.

A. H. Maslow Publications, http://www.maslow.com/

Ahrons, C., & Rodgers, R. (1989). *Divorced families: Meeting the challenge of divorce and remarriage.* New York: W. W. Norton.

AIDS Information. (2003). *HIV treatment guidelines.* Retrieved from http://www.aidsinfo.nih.gov/drugs

Ainsworth, M. D. S. (1967). *Infancy in Uganda: Infant care and the growth of love.* Baltimore: Johns Hopkins University Press.

Ainsworth, M. D. S. (1979). Infant-mother attachment. *American Psychologist, 34,* 932–937.

Ainsworth, M. D. S. (1983). Infant-mother attachment. In W. Damon (Ed.), *Social and personality development: Essays on the growth of the child.* New York: W. W. Norton.

Ainsworth, M. D. S. (1989). Attachment beyond infancy. *American Psychologist, 44,* 709–716.

Ainsworth, M. D. S., & Wittig, B. A. (1969). Attachment and the exploratory behaviour of one-year-olds in a strange situation. In B. M. Foss (Ed.), *Determinants of infant behaviour* (Vol. 4, pp. 113–136). London: Methuen.

Ainsworth, M. D. S., Blehar, M. C., Waters, E., & Wall, S. (1978). *Patterns of attachment: A psychological study of the strange situation.* Hillsdale, NJ: Erlbaum.

Ainsworth, M. S. (1979). Infant-mother attachment. *American Psychologist, 34,* 932–937.

Aish International, http://www.aish.edu

Ajzen, I. (1985). From intentions to actions: A theory of planned behavior. In J. Kuhl & J. Beckmann (Eds.), *Action-control: From cognition to behavior* (pp. 11–39). Heidelberg, Germany: Springer-Verlag.

Ajzen, I. (2002). Perceived behavioral control, self-efficacy, locus of control, and the theory of planned behavior. *Journal of Applied Social Psychology, 32*(4), 665–683.

Alan Guttmacher Institute. (1994). *Sex and America's teenagers.* New York: Author.

Alan Guttmacher Institute. (2004). *Contraception in the United States: Current use and continuing challenges.* Retrieved from http//www.guttmacher.org/pubs/contraception-us.html

Alan Guttmacher Institute. (2004). *Facts in brief: Induced abortion.* Retrieved from http://www.agi.usa.org/pubs/fb_induced_abortion.html

Alan Guttmacher Institute. (n.d.). *Changing emphases in sexuality education in U.S. public secondary schools, 1988–1999.* Retrieved from http://www.guttmacher.org/pubs/journals/3220400.pdf

Alan Guttmacher Institute. (n.d.). *Get "in the know": 20 questions about pregnancy, contraception and abortion.* Retrieved from http://www.guttmacher.org/in-the-know/index.html

Alan Guttmacher Institute. (n.d.). *Sex and STD/HIV education—State policies in brief.* Retrieved from http://www.guttmacher.org/statecenter/spibs/spib_SE.pdf

Alberto, P. A., & Troutman, A. C. (2003). *Applied behavior analysis for teachers* (6th ed.). Upper Saddle River, NJ: Merrill.

Alcoholics Anonymous, http://www.alcoholics-anonymous.org/

Alcoholics Anonymous World Services. (1939). *Alcoholics Anonymous: The story of how many thousands of men and women have recovered.* New York: Works.

Alexander, G. R., & Kotelchuck, M. (2001). Assessing the role and effectiveness of prenatal care: History, challenges, and directions for future research (Practice Articles). *Public Health Reports, 116*(4), 306–311.

Alexander, K. L., & Entwisle, D. R. (1988). Achievement in the first 2 years of school: Patterns and processes. *Monographs of the Society for Research in Child Development, 53,* Serial No. 218.

Alexander, K. L., Entwisle, D. R., & Dauber, S. L. (2003). *On the success of failure: A reassessment of the effects of retention in the primary school grades* (2nd ed.). Cambridge, UK: Cambridge University Press.

Alford, D. M. (n.d.). *Nursing care of the oldest old.* Retrieved from http://www.nurseducation.org/oldestold.htm

Alfred Adler Institutes. (n.d.). *Classical Adlerian psychology.* Retrieved from http://ourworld.compuserve.com/homepages/hstein/hompage.htm

Alfred Binet. (n.d.). Retrieved from http://elvers.stjoe.udayton.edu/history/people/Binet.html

All About Vision, http://www.allaboutvision.com/conditions/myopia.htm

Allen, J. S., Bruss, J., & Damasio, H. (2004). The structure of the human brain. *American Scientist, 92,* 246–253.

AllPsych Online. (n.d.). *Reinforcement and reinforcement schedules.* Retrieved from http://allpsych.com/psychology101/reinforcement.html

Allyn & Bacon. (n.d.). *Exploring child development.* Retrieved from http://www.abacon.com/fabes/pages/timeline.html

Almeling, R., Tews, L., & Dudley, S. (1998). Abortion training in U.S. obstetrics and gynecology residency programs. *Family Planning Perspectives, 32*(2000), 268–320.

Al-Qur'an. (Ahmed Ali, Trans.). (1988). Princeton, NJ: Princeton University Press.

Alred, G., Garve, B., & Smith, R. (2000). *The mentoring pocketbook.* Herndon, VA: Stylus.

Altbach, P. G., Berdahl, R. O., & Gumport, P. J. (Eds.). (1999). *American higher education in the twenty-first century: Social, political, and economic challenges.* Baltimore: Johns Hopkins University Press.

Altepeter, T. S., & Korger, J. N. (1999). Disruptive behavior: Oppositional defiant disorder and conduct disorder. In S. D. Netherton, D. Holmes, & C. E. Walker (Eds.), *Child and adolescent psychological disorders.* New York: Oxford University Press.

Alternatives to Marriage Project. (n.d.). *Statistics.* Retrieved from http://www.unmarried.org/statistics.html

Alzheimer's Association, http://www.alz.org

Alzheimer's Disease Education and Referral Center of the National Institute on Aging, http://www.alzheimers.org

Amato, P. R. (2000). Diversity within single-parent families. In D. H. Demo, K. R. Allen, & M. A. Fine (Eds.), *Handbook for family diversity* (pp. 149–172). New York: Oxford University Press.

Amato, P., & Keith B. (1991). Parental divorce and the well-being of children. *Psychological Bulletin, 110,* 26–46.

Amaya-Jackson, L., Reynolds, V., Murray, M. C., McCarthy, G., Nelson, A., Cherney, M. S., et al. (2003). Cognitive-behavioral treatment for pediatric posttraumatic stress disorder: Protocol and application in school and community settings. *Cognitive and Behavioral Practice, 10,* 204–213.

American Academy of Child and Adolescent Psychiatry, http://www.aacap.org/

American Academy of Child and Adolescent Psychiatry. (n.d.). *Facts for families and other resources.* Retrieved from http://www.aacap.org/info_families/index.htm

American Academy of Family Physicians, http://www.aafp.org

American Academy of Neurology, http://www.neurology.org/

American Academy of Neurology. (1995). Practice parameters for determining brain death in adults (summary statement). The Quality Standards Subcommittee of the American Academy of Neurology. *Neurology, 45*(5), 1012–1014.

American Academy of Pediatrics Committee on Genetics. (2001). Maternal phenylketonuria. *Pediatrics, 107,* 427–428.

American Academy of Pediatrics Committee on Nutrition. (1998). Supplemental foods for infants. In R. Kleinman (Ed.), *Pediatric nutrition handbook* (4th ed., pp. 43–54). Elk Grove Village, IL: Author.

American Academy of Pediatrics Committee on Psychosocial Aspects of Child and Family Health. (1998). Guidance for effective discipline. *Pediatrics, 101*(4), 723–728. Retrieved from http://aappolicy.aappublications.org/cgi/content/full/pediatrics;101/4/723

American Academy of Pediatrics Committee on Psychosocial Aspects of Child and Family Health. (2002). *Guidelines for health supervision III.* Elk Grove Village, IL: Author.

American Academy of Pediatrics, http://www.aap.org

American Academy of Pediatrics. (1987). Report of special Task Force. Guidelines for the determination of brain death in children. American Academy of Pediatrics Task Force on Brain Death in Children. *Pediatrics, 80*(2), 298–300.

American Academy of Pediatrics. (2004). *We believe in the inherent worth of all children.* Chicago: Author.

American Academy of Pediatrics. (2005). *Dedicated to the health of all children: 75 years of caring 1930–2005.* Chicago: Author.

American Association for the Advancement of Science, http://www.aaas.org/

American Association of Chronic Fatigue Syndrome, http://www.aacfs.org/

American Association for Marriage and Family Therapy, http:// www.aamft.org

American Association of Pediatrics, http://www.aap.org

American Association of Retired Persons (AARP), http://www.aarp.org

American Association of Suicidology, http://www.suicidology.org

American Association of University Women. (1998). *How schools shortchange girls.* Washington, DC: National Education Association.

American Association on Mental Retardation. (2002). *Mental retardation: Definition, classifications, and systems of support* (10th ed.). Washington, DC: Author.

American Association on Mental Retardation. (2004). *Definition of mental retardation.* Retrieved from http://aamr.org/Policies/faq_mental_retardation.shtml

American Board of Internal Medicine. (1996). *Caring for the dying: Identification of and promotion of physician competency. Educational research documents.* Philadelphia: Author.

American Cancer Society, http://www.cancer.org

American College of Nurse-Midwives, http://www.midwife.org

American College of Nurse-Midwives. (n.d.). *Home birth.* Retrieved from http://www.acnm.org/prof/factsheet.cfm

American College of Obstetricians and Gynecologists, http://www.acog.org

American College of Preventive Medicine, http://www.acpm.org

American College of Sports Medicine, http://www.acsm.org/

American Council on Alcoholism (ACA), http://www.aca-usa.org/

American Creativity Association, http://www.amcreativityassoc.org/

American Diabetes Association, http://www.diabetes.org

American Educational Research Association, American Psychological Association, & National Council on Measurement in Education. (1999). *Standards for educational and psychological testing.* Washington, DC: Authors.

American Epilepsy Society, http://www.aesnet.org

American Federation for Aging Research. (2002). *Theory of aging information center.* Retrieved from http://www.infoaging.org/b-the-home.html

American Federation of Teachers, http://www.aft.org/topics/charters/index.htm

American Foundation for Suicide Prevention, http://www.afsp.org

The American Geriatrics Society, http://www.americangeriatrics.org

American Heart Association, http://www.americanheart.org

American Heart Association. (2003). *Heart disease and stroke statistics—2004 update.* Dallas, TX: Author.

American Heart Association. (n.d.). *Atherosclerosis.* Retrieved from http://www.americanheart.org/presenter.jhtml?identifier=4440

American Heart Association. (n.d.). *Congestive heart failure.* Retrieved from http://www.americanheart.org/presenter.jhtml?identifier=4585

American Heart Association. (n.d.). *Stroke.* Retrieved from http://www.americanheart.org/presenter.jhtml?identifier=4755

American Heart Association Task Force on Risk Reduction. (1998). Primary prevention of coronary heart disease: Guidance from Framingham. *Circulation, 97,* 1876–1887.

American Hospice Foundation, http://www.americanhospice.org

American Journal of Distance Education, http://www.ajde.com/

American Medical Association. (2004). *Family medical guide* (4th ed.). Hoboken, NJ: Wiley.

American Professional Society on the Abuse of Children, http://www.apsac.org/

American Psychiatric Association. (1994). *Diagnostic and statistical manual of mental disorders* (4th ed.). Washington, DC: Author.

American Psychiatric Association. (1999). *Let's talk facts about post traumatic stress disorder.* Retrieved from http://www.psych.org/public_info/ptsd.cfm

American Psychiatric Association. (2000). *Diagnostic and statistical manual of mental disorders* (4th ed., text rev.). Washington, DC: Author.

American Psychiatric Association. (2000). Eating disorders. *Diagnostic and statistical manual of mental disorders* (4th ed., text rev., pp. 583–595). Washington, DC: Author.

American Psychological Association, http://www.apa.org

American Psychological Association. (1994). *Guidelines for child custody evaluations in divorce proceedings.* Retrieved from http://www.apa.org/practice/childcustody.html

American Psychological Association. (1998). *Hate crimes today: An age-old foe in modern dress.* Retrieved from http://www.apa.org/pubinfo/hate

American Psychological Association. (1998). *Violence and the family: Report of the APA Presidential Task Force on Violence and the Family—Executive Summary.* Washington, DC: Public Interest Directorate of the American Psychological Association.

American Psychological Association. (2000). *Diagnostic and statistical manual of mental disorders* (4th ed., text revision). Washington, DC: Author.

American Psychological Association. (2002). *Elder abuse and neglect: In search of solutions.* Retrieved from http://www.apa.org/pi/aging/eldabuse.html

American Psychological Association. (2002). *Ethical principles of psychologists and code of conduct.* Retrieved from http://www.apa.org/ethics/code2002.html

American Psychological Association. (2002). *The publication manual of the American Psychological Association* (5th ed.). Washington, DC: Author.

American Psychological Association. (2004). Congratulations to this year's award winners. *Monitor on Psychology, 35*(5), 72–79.

American Psychological Association. (2005). *How to be a wise consumer of psychological research.* Retrieved from http://www.psychologymatters.org//wiseconsumer.html

American Psychological Association. (2005). *Violence on television—What do children learn? What can parents do?* Retrieved from http://www.apa.org/pubinfo/violence.html

American Psychological Association. (n.d.). *Answers to your questions about sexual orientation and homosexuality.* Retrieved from http://www.apa.org/pubinfo/answers.html

American Psychological Association. (n.d.). *Topics: Women & men.* Available from http://www.apa.org/topics/topicwomen men.html

American Psychological Association—Division 20. Adult Development and Aging, http://apadiv20.phhp.ufl.edu/

American Psychological Association—Division 28, Psychopharmacology and Substance Abuse, http://www.apa.org/divisions/div28/

American Psychological Association—Division 40, Clinical Neuropsychology, http://www.div40.org/

American Psychological Society, http://www.psychological science.org

American Society on Aging, http://www.asaging.edu

American Society for Reproductive Medicine, http://www.asrm.org/

American Society of Reproductive Medicine. (n.d.). *Menopause and osteoporosis.* Retrieved from http://www.asrm.org/Patients/topics/menopause.html

American Youth Policy Forum. (n.d.). *Abecedarian program.* Retrieved from http://www.aypf.org/rmaa/pdfs/Abecedarian.pdf

Americans for Divorce Reform, http://www.divorcereform.org

Americans with Disabilities Act of 1990, Pub. L. No. 101–336. (1990). Retrieved from http://www.usdoj.gov/crt/ada/statute.html

Amerigen, M. V., Mancini, C., & Farvolden, P. (2003). The impact of anxiety disorders on educational achievement. *Journal of Anxiety Disorders, 17,* 561–571.

Ames, L., & Ilg, F. (1979). *Your six-year-old: Loving and defiant.* New York, NY: Dell.

Ames, L. A. (1967). *Is your child in the wrong grade?* New York: Harper & Row.

Ames, L. B. (1989). *Arnold Gesell: Themes of his work.* New York: Human Sciences Press.

Ames, L. B., & Ilg, F. L. (1964). Gesell behavior tests as predictive of later grade placement. *Perceptual and Motor Skills, 19,* 719–722.

Ames, L., Ilg, F., & Haber, C. (1982). *Your one-year-old: The fun-loving, fussy 12- to 24-month-old.* New York: Dell.

Amory, J. K., Anawalt, B. D., Paulsen, C. A., & Bremner, W. J. (2000). Klinefelter's syndrome. *Lancet, 356,* 333–335.

Amsel, E., & Byrnes, J. (Eds.). (2002). *Language, literacy, and cognitive development.* Mahwah, NJ: Erlbaum.

Anand, K. J., & International Evidence-Based Group for Neonatal Pain. (2001). Consensus statement for the prevention and management of pain in the newborn. *Archives of Pediatrics & Adolescent Medicine, 155*(2), 173–180.

Anastasi, A. (1988). *Psychological testing* (6th ed.). New York: Macmillan.

Anastasi, A., & Urbina, S. (1997). *Psychological testing* (7th ed.). Upper Saddle River, NJ: Prentice-Hall.

Anders, T. F., & Taylor, T. R. (1994). Babies and their sleep environment. *Children's Environments, 11,* 123–134.

Anderson, A. L. (2002). Individual and contextual influences on delinquency: The role of the single-parent family. *Journal of Criminal Justice, 30*(6), 575–587.

Anderson, B. (1995). *Imagined communities.* London: Verso.

Anderson, C. A., & Bushman, B. J. (2001). Effects of violent video games on aggressive behavior, aggressive cognition, aggressive affect, physiological arousal, and prosocial behavior: A meta-analytic review of the scientific literature. *Psychological Science, 12,* 353–359.

Anderson, C. A., & Bushman, B. J. (2002). Human aggression. *Annual Review of Psychology, 53,* 27–51.

Anderson, C. A., Gentile, D. A., & Buckley, K. E. (under review). Violent video game effects on children and adolescents: Further developments and tests of the general aggression model.

Anderson, J. (1990). *The single mother's book: A practical guide to managing your children, career, home, finances, and everything else.* Atlanta, GA: Peachtree.

Anderson, R., & Murphy, P. (1995). Outcomes of 11,788 planned home births attended by certified nurse-midwives. *Journal of Nurse-Midwifery, 6,* 584–492.

Anderson, R. N., & Smith, B. L. (2003). *Deaths: Leading causes for 2001.* Retrieved from http://www.cdc.govnchs/data/nvsr/nvsr52/nvsr52_09.pdf

Anderson, V. L. (1993). Gender differences in altruism among holocaust rescuers. *Journal of Social Behavior and Personality, 8,* 43–58.

Anderson, V., Northam, E., Hendy, J., & Wrennal, J. (2001). *Developmental neuropsychology: A clinical approach.* London: Psychology Press.

Anderssen, N., Amlie, C., & Ytteroy, E. A. (2002). Outcomes for children with lesbian or gay parents: A review of studies from 1978–2000. *Scandinavian Journal of Psychology, 43,* 335–351.

Andrews, J., Leigh, I. W., & Weiner, M. (2004). *Deaf people: Evolving perspectives from psychology, education, and sociology.* Boston: Allyn & Bacon.

Anisfeld, E., Casper, V., Nozyce, M., & Cunningham, N. (1990). Does infant carrying promote attachment? An experimental study of the effects of increased physical contact on the development of attachment. *Child Development, 61,* 1617–1627.

Anorexia and Related Eating Disorders, Inc. (2002). *ANRED: Information and resources.* Retrieved from http://www.anred.com

Ansbacher, H. L., & Ansbacher, R. R. (Eds.). (1956). *The individual psychology of Alfred Adler: A systematic presentation in selections from his writings.* New York: Harper Torchbooks.

Ansel, D. A. (1999). *Infant colic.* Retrieved from http://www.chmed.com/mod.php?mod=userpage&page_id=101&menu=1522

Anthony, S. (1972). *The discovery of death in childhood and after.* New York: Basic Books.

Anti-Defamation League. (n.d.). *Education.* Retrieved from http://www.adl.org/education

Antony, M. M., & Barlow, D. H. (2002). Specific phobias. In D. H. Barlow (Ed.), *Anxiety and its disorders* (2nd ed., pp. 380–417). New York: Guilford.

Anxiety Disorders Association of America, http://www.adaa.org

The Anxiety Network. (n.d.). *Social anxiety disorder.* Retrieved from http://www.anxietynetwork.com/sphome.html

Anxiety Network International, generalized anxiety home page, http://www.anxietynetwork.com/gahome.html

Anxiety Network International, panic home page, http://www.anxietynetwork.com/pdhome.html

Anxiety and Panic, http://www.anxietypanic.com/

APA Online. (2002). *Ethical principles of psychologists and code of conduct.* Retrieved from http://www.apa.org/ethics/code2002.html

Apgar, V., & Beck, J. (1972). *Is my baby all right?* New York: Trident.

Apgar, V., & James, L. (1962). Further observations on the newborn scoring system. *American Journal of Diseases of Children, 104,* 419–428.

Appelbaum, M. I., & McCall, R. B. (1983). Design and analysis in developmental psychology. In P. H. Mussen (Ed.), *Handbook of child psychology* (4th ed., Vol. 1, pp. 415–476). New York: Wiley.

Apple, D. (1956). The social structure of grandparenthood. *American Anthropologist, 58,* 656–663.

Applied Ethology, http://www.usask.ca/wcvm/herdmed/appliedethology/

Applied Knowledge Research Institute. (n.d.). *Human memory models.* Retrieved from http://www.akri.org/cognition/hummod.htm

The Arc. (2004). *Information about mental retardation and related topics.* Retrieved from http://www.thearc.org/infomr.html

Archambault, F. A., Jr., Westberg, K. L., Brown, S. W., Hallmark, B. W., Emmons, C. L., & Zhang, W. (1993). *Regular classroom practices with gifted students: Results of a national survey of classroom teachers* (Research Monograph No. 93102). Storrs: The National Research Center on the Gifted and Talented, University of Connecticut.

Archer, J., & Westman, K. (1981). Sex differences in the aggressive behaviour of schoolchildren. *British Journal of Social Psychology, 20,* 31–36.

Arden, H., & Wall, S. (1990). *Wisdomkeepers: Meetings with Native American spiritual elders.* Hillsboro, OR: Beyond Words.

Arendt, H. (1973). *The origins of totalitarianism.* New York: Harcourt.

Argyle, M. (1994). *The psychology of social class.* London: Routledge.

Arlin, P. K. (1975). Cognitive development in adulthood: A fifth stage. *Developmental Psychology, 11,* 602–606.

Armstrong-Dailey, A., & Zarbcok, S. (Eds.). (2001). *Hospice care for children.* New York: Oxford University Press.

Arnaut, G., Fromme, D., Stoll, B., & Felker, J. (2000). A quantitative analysis of stepfamilies: The biological parent. *Journal of Divorce and Remarriage, 33*(3–4), 111–128.

Arnett, J. J. (1998). Learning to stand alone: The contemporary transition to adulthood in cultural and historical context. *Human Development, 41*(5/6), 295–316.

Arnett, J. J. (1999). Adolescent storm and stress, reconsidered. *American Psychologist, 54*(5), 317–326.

Arnett, J. J. (2000). Emerging adulthood: A theory of development from the late teens through the twenties. *American Psychologist, 55*(5), 469–480.

Arnett, J. J. (2004). *Emerging adulthood: The winding road from the late teens through the twenties.* New York: Oxford University Press.

Arnett, J. J., & Tabor, S. (1994). Adolescence terminable and interminable: When does adolescence end? *Journal of Youth and Adolescence, 23*(5), 517–538.

Arnstein, R. L (1989). Overview of normal transition to young adulthood. In S. C. Feinstein & A. H. Esman (Eds.), *Adolescent psychiatry: Developmental and clinical studies, Vol. 16.* (pp. 127–141). Chicago: University of Chicago.

Arntz, A. (2002). Cognitive therapy versus interoceptive exposure as treatment of panic disorder without agoraphobia. *Behaviour Research and Therapy, 40,* 325–341.

Arp, D., Arp, C., Stanley, S., Markman, H., & Blumberg, S. (2000). *Fighting for your empty nest marriage: Reinventing your relationship when the kids leave home.* San Francisco: Jossey-Bass.

Aschoff, J. (1960). Exogenous and endogenous components in circadian rhythms. *Cold Spring Harbor Symposia on Quantitative Biology, 25,* 11–28.

Aschoff, J., Fatranská, M., Giedke, H., Doerr, P., Stamm, D., & Wisser, H. (1971). Human circadian rhythms in continuous darkness: Entrainment by social cues. *Science, 171,* 213–215.

AskDrSears.com, http://www.askdrsears.com

Asperger, H. (1991). "Autistic psychopathy" in childhood. In U. Frith (Ed. & Trans.), *Autism and Asperger syndrome* (pp. 37–92). Cambridge, UK: Cambridge University Press. (Original work published 1944)

Assaiante, C., & Amblard, B. (1995). An ontogenetic model for the sensorimotor organization of balance control in humans. *Human Movement Science, 14,* 13–43.

Assisted Living Federation of America, http://www.alfa.org

Association of Behavior Analysis, http://www.abainternational.org

Association for Bilingual Education (NABE), http://www.nabe.org/

Association of Childhood Education International, http://www.udel.edu/bateman/acei

Association for Conflict Resolution, http://www.acrnet.org

Association of Family and Conciliation Courts, http://www.afccnet.org

Association of Family and Conciliation Courts. (n.d.). *Resource center*. Available from http://www.afccnet.org/resources/index.asp

Association for Gerontology in Higher Education, http://aghe.org

Association of MultiEthnic Americans, http://www.ameasite.org

Association of SIDS and Infant Mortality Programs, http://www.asip1.org/

Association for the Study of Higher Education, http://www.ashe.ws

Atchley, R. C. (1989). A continuity theory of normal aging. *The Gerontologist, 29,* 183–190.

Atiya, A. S. (1962). *Crusade, commerce and culture.* Bloomington: Indiana University Press.

Atlanta Alliance on Developmental Disabilities. (n.d.). *What are developmental disabilities?* Retrieved from http://www.aadd.org/html

Attachment Theory and Research at Stony Brook, http://www.johnbowlby.com

Ault, A. (1996). Ambiguous identity in an unambiguous sex/gender structure: The case of the bisexual woman. *The Sociological Quarterly, 37,* 449–463.

Austin, B. S. (n.d.). *The Holocaust/Shoah page.* Retrieved from http://www.mtsu.edu/%7Ebaustin/holo.html

Autism Research Institute, http://www.autism.com

Autismsociety.org, http://www.autismsociety.org/

Autism Society of America, http://autism-society.org

Automated Face Analysis Project, http://www-2.cs.cmu.edu/~face/index2.htm

AVERT. (2004). *AIDS orphans in Africa.* Retrieved from http://www.avert.org/aidsorphans.htm

AVERT. (2004). *Condoms, history, effectiveness, and testing.* Retrieved from http://www.avert.org/condoms.htm

Avetisov, E. S., Tarutta, E. P., Iomdina, E. N., Vinetskaya, M. I., & Andreyeva, L. D. (1997). Nonsurgical and surgical methods of sclera reinforcement in progressive myopia. *Acta Ophthalmologica Scandinavica, 75,* 618–623.

Aylsworth, A. S. (2005). Clinical genetics and phenotype definition. In J. L. Hains & M. A. Pericak-Vance (Eds.), *Genetic analysis of complex disease* (2nd ed.). New York: Wiley-Liss.

Azar, S. T. (2002). Parenting and child maltreatment. In M. H. Bornstein (Ed.), *Handbook of parenting* (Vol. 4, 2nd ed., pp. 361–388). Mahwah, NJ: Erlbaum.

Azrin, N. H., Donohue, B., Teichner, G., Crum, T., Howell, J., & DeCato, L. (2002). A controlled evaluation and description of individual cognitive problem-solving and family behavioral therapies in conduct-disordered and substance dependent youth. *Journal of Child and Adolescent Substance Abuse, 11*(1), 1–43.

BabyCenter LLC, http://www.babycenter.com/

Bachman, R., & Saltzman, L. E. (1996). *Violence against women: Estimates from the redesigned survey* (Bureau of Justice Statistics special report, NCJ No. 154348). Rockville, MD: U.S. Department of Justice.

Bachu, A. (1999, May). *Is childlessness among American women on the rise?* (Population Division Working Paper No. 37). Washington, DC: U.S. Census Bureau, Population Division, Fertility and Family Statistics Branch. Retrieved from http://www.census.gov/population/www/documentation/twps0037/twps0037.html

Bacon, A. L., Fein, D., Morris, R., Waterhouse, L., & Allen, D. (1998). The response of autistic children to the distress of others. *Journal of Autism and Developmental Disabilities, 28,* 129–142.

Baddeley, A. (1999). *Essentials of human memory.* Hove, UK: Psychology Press.

Baddeley, A. D. (1986). *Working memory.* Oxford, UK: Clarendon Press.

Baddeley, A. D., Gathercole, S., & Papagno, C. (1998). The phonological loop as a language learning device. *Psychological Review, 105,* 158–173.

Baddeley, A. D., & Hitch, G. J. (1974). Working memory. In G. Bower (Ed.), *Recent advances in learning and motivation* (Vol. III). New York: Academic Press.

Baddeley, A. D., Kopelman, M. D., & Wilson, D. A. (Eds.). (2002). *The handbook of memory disorders* (2nd ed.). West Sussex, UK: Wiley.

Bailey, D. B., Bruer, J. T., Symons, F. J., & Lichtman, J. W. (Eds.). (2001). *Critical thinking about critical periods.* Baltimore: Paul H. Brookes.

Bailey, D. B., McWilliam, R. A., Darkes, L. A., Hebbler, K., Simeonsson, R. J., Spiker, D., et al. (1998). Family outcomes in early intervention: A framework for program evaluation and efficacy research. *Exceptional Children, 64,* 313–328.

Baillargeon, R., & DeVos, J. (1991). Object permanence in young infants: Further evidence. *Child Development, 62,* 1227–1246.

Bainbridge, D. (2000). *Making babies: The science of pregnancy.* Cambridge, MA: Harvard University Press.

Baker, C. C. (2002). *Female survivors of sexual abuse: An integrated guide to treatment.* New York: Brunner Routledge.

Baker, C., & Cokely, D. (1980). *American Sign Language: A teacher's resource text on grammar and culture.* Silver Spring, MD: TJ Publishers.

Baker, M. C. (2002). *The atoms of language.* New York: Basic Books.

Bakhurst, D., & Shanker, S. (Eds.). (2001). *Jerome Bruner: Language, culture, self.* Thousand Oaks, CA: Sage.

Baldwin, D. A., & Moses, L. M. (1994). Early understanding of referential intent and attentional focus: Evidence from language and emotion. In C. Lewis & P. Mitchell (Eds.), *Children's early understanding of mind: Origins and development.* Hillsdale, NJ: Erlbaum.

Baldwin, J. M. (1973). *Social and ethical interpretations in mental development.* New York: Arno Press.

Baldwin, M. W., Carrell, S. E., & Lopez, D. F. (1990). Priming relationship schemas: My advisor and the Pope are watching me from the back of my mind. *Journal of Experimental Social Psychology, 25,* 435–454.

Baldwin Grossman, J., Price, M. L., Fellerath, V., Jucovy, L. Z., Kotloff, L. J., Raley, R., & Walker, K. E. (2002). *Multiple choices after school: Findings from the Extended-Service Schools Initiative.* Philadelphia: Public/Private Ventures. Retrieved from http://www.mdrc.org/publications/48/full.pdf

Bale, J. R., Stoll, B. J., & Lucas, A. O. (Eds.). (2003). *Reducing birth defects: Meeting the challenge in the developing world.* Washington, DC: National Academies Press. Retrieved from http://books.nap.edu/openbook/0309086086/html/index.html

Balkenius, C. (2000). *Cognitive aspects of conditioning and habituation.* Retrieved from http://lucs.lu.se/People/Christian.Balkenius/Conditioning.Habituation/

Ball, R. M. (1995). What Medicare's architects had in mind. *Health Affairs, 14,* 62–72.

Ballard, C. (2003). *The heart and blood: Injury, illness and health.* Chicago: Heinemann Library.

Baltes, P. B. (1968). Longitudinal and cross-sectional sequences in the study of age and generation effects. *Human Development, 11,* 145–171.

Baltes, P. B., & Baltes, M. M. (1990). Psychological perspectives on successful aging: The model of selective optimization with compensation. In P. B. Baltes & M. M. Baltes (Eds.), *Successful aging: Perspectives from the behavioral sciences* (pp. 1–34). New York: Cambridge University Press.

Baltes, P. B., & Baltes, M. M. (1993). *Successful aging: Perspectives from the behavioral sciences.* Cambridge, UK: Cambridge University Press.

Baltes, P. B., & Mayer, K. U. (Eds.). (1999). *The Berlin Aging Study: Aging from 70 to 100.* Cambridge, UK: Cambridge University Press.

Baltes, P. B., & Smith, J. (2002). New frontiers in the future of aging: From successful aging of the young old to the dilemmas of the fourth age. Keynote address given at the Valencia Forum, Valencia, Spain. Retrieved from http://www.valenciaforum.com/Keynotes/pb.html

Baltimore Longitudinal Study of Aging, http://www.grc.nia.nih.gov/branches/blsa/blsa.htm

Bandura, A. (1967). The role of modeling processes in personality development. In W. W. Hartup & W. L. Smothergill (Eds.), *The young child: Reviews of research.* Washington, DC: National Association for the Education of Young Children.

Bandura, A. (1969). *Principles of behavior modification.* New York: Holt, Rinehart & Winston.

Bandura, A. (1973). *Aggression: A social learning theory analysis.* Englewood Cliffs, NJ: Prentice-Hall.

Bandura, A. (1977). Self-efficacy: Toward a unifying theory of behavioral change. *Psychological Review, 84,* 191–215.

Bandura, A. (1977). *Social learning theory.* Englewood Cliffs, NJ: Prentice-Hall.

Bandura, A. (1978). The self system in reciprocal determinism. *American Psychologist, 33,* 344–358.

Bandura, A. (1986). *Social foundations of thought and action: A social cognitive theory.* Englewood Cliffs, NJ: Prentice-Hall.

Bandura, A. (Ed.). (1995). *Self-efficacy in changing societies.* New York: Cambridge University Press.

Bandura, A., & Walters, R. (1963). *Social learning and personality development.* New York: Holt, Rinehart & Winston.

Bane, M. J., & Ellwood, D. T. (1986). Slipping into and out of poverty: The dynamics of spells. *Journal of Human Resources, 21,* 1–23.

Banks, J. B. (2002). Childhood discipline: Challenges for clinicians and parents. *American Academy of Physicians.* Retrieved from http://www.aafp.org/afp/20021015/1447.html

Barbus, A. (1975). The dying person's bill of rights. *American Journal of Nursing, 1,* 99.

Bardy, B. G., Oullier, O., Bootsma, R. J., & Stoffregen, T. A. (2002). Dynamics of human postural transitions. *Journal of Experimental Psychology: Human Perception and Performance, 28,* 499–514.

Barger, R. N. (2000). *A summary of Lawrence Kohlberg's stages of moral development.* Notre Dame, IN: University of Notre Dame. Retrieved from http://www.nd.edu/~rbarger/kohlberg.html

Barker, R. G. (1968). *Ecological psychology: Concepts and methods for studying the environment of human behavior.* Stanford, CA: Stanford University Press.

Barker, R. G., & Gump, P. (1964). *Big school, small school: High school size and student behavior.* Stanford, CA: Stanford University Press.

Barker, R. G., & Schoggen, P. (1973). *Qualities of community life.* San Francisco: Jossey-Bass.

Barker, R. G., & Wright, H. F. (1955). *Midwest and its children.* New York: Harper & Row.

Barkley, R. (2000). *Taking charge of ADHD* (2nd ed.). New York: Guilford.

Barkley, R. A. (1997). Behavioral inhibition, sustained attention, and executive functions: Constructing a unified theory of ADHD. *Psychological Bulletin, 121,* 65–94.

Barkley, R. A. (1998). *Attention deficit hyperactivity disorder: A handbook for diagnosis and treatment* (2nd ed.). New York: Guilford.

Barkley, R. A. (2002). Psychosocial treatments for attention-deficit/hyperactivity disorder in children. *Journal of Clinical Psychiatry, 63,* 36–43.

Barlow, D. H. (2002). *Anxiety and its disorders: The nature and treatment of anxiety and panic* (2nd ed.). New York: Guilford.

Barnett, O. W., Miller-Perrin, C. L., & Perrin, R. D. (2004). *Family violence across the lifespan* (2nd ed.). Thousand Oaks, CA: Sage.

Barnett, W. S. (1992). Benefits of compensatory preschool education. *Journal of Human Resources, 27*(2), 279–312.

Bar-On, R., & Parker, J. D. (Eds.). (2000). *The handbook of emotional intelligence: Theory, assessment, and application at home, school, and in the workplace.* San Francisco: Jossey-Bass.

Baron-Cohen, S. (1995). *Mindblindness: An essay on autism and theory of mind.* Cambridge: MIT Press.

Barr, D. A. (2002). *Introduction to US health policy: The organization, financing, and delivery of health care in America.* New York: Benjamin Cummings.

Barr, R., Dowden, A., & Hayne, H. (1996). Developmental changes in deferred imitation by 6- to 24-month-old infants. *Infant Behavior and Development, 19,* 159–171.

Barr, R., & Hayne, H. (2000). Age-related changes in imitation: Implications for memory development. In C. Rovee-Collier, L. P. Lipsitt, & H. Hayne (Eds.), *Progress in infancy research* (Vol. 1, pp. 21–67). Mahwah, NJ: Erlbaum.

Barr, R., & Hayne, H. (2003). It's not what you know, it's who you know: Older siblings facilitate imitation during infancy. *International Journal of Early Years Education, 11,* 7–21.

Barsky, R. F. (1997). *Noam Chomsky: A life of dissent.* Cambridge: MIT Press.

Barth, R., Courtney, M., Berrick, J., & Albert, V. (1994). *From child abuse to permanency planning.* New York: Aldine De Gruyter.

Bartholomew, K. (1990). Avoidance of intimacy: An attachment perspective. *Journal of Social and Personal Relationships, 7,* 140–178.

Bartlett, S. J., Wadden, T. A., & Vogt, R. A. (1996). Psychosocial consequences of weight cycling. *Journal of Consulting and Clinical Psychology, 64,* 587–592.

Bass, G. J. (2000). *Stay the hand of vengeance.* Princeton, NJ: Princeton University Press.

Bass, M., Kravath, R. E., & Glass, L. (1986). Death scene investigation in sudden infant death. *New England Journal of Medicine, 315,* 100–105.

Basseches, M. (1980). Dialectical schemata: A framework for the empirical study of the development of dialectical thinking. *Human Development, 23,* 400–421.

Basta, S. S. (2000). *Culture, conflict, and children: Transmission of violence to children.* Lanham, MD: University Press of America.

Batchelor, J. A. (1999). *Failure to thrive in young children: Research and practice evaluated.* London: The Children's Society.

Bateson, P. (2001). Fetal experience and good adult design. *International Journal of Epidemiology, 30,* 928–934.

Bateson, P. P. G. (1978). How do sensitive periods arise and what are they for? *Animal Behaviour, 27,* 470–486.

Bateson, P., Barker, D., Clutton-Brock, T., Deb, D., D'Udine, D., Foley, R. A., et al. (2004). Developmental plasticity and human health. *Nature, 430,* 419–421.

Bateson, P., & Martin, P. (1999). *Design for a life: How behaviour develops.* London: Jonathan Cape.

Batshaw, M. (1991). *Your child has a disability: A complete sourcebook of daily and medical care.* New York: Little, Brown.

Batshaw, M. L. (1997). PKU and other inborn errors of metabolism. In M. L. Batshaw (Ed.), *Children with disabilities* (4th ed., pp. 389–404). Baltimore: Paul H. Brookes.

Batshaw, M. L. (2002). *Children with disabilities* (5th ed.). Baltimore: Paul H. Brookes.

Batshaw, M. L., & Perret, M. A. (1992). *Children with disabilities: A medical primer.* Baltimore: Paul H. Brookes.

Batshaw, M. L., & Tuchman, M. (2003). PKU and other inborn errors of metabolism. In M. L. Batshaw (Ed.), *Children with disabilities* (5th ed., pp. 333–345). Baltimore: Paul H. Brookes.

Batson, C. D., Sager, K., Garst, E., Kang, M., Rubchinsky, K., & Dawson, K. (1997). Is empathy-induced helping due to self-other merging? *Journal of Personality and Social Psychology, 73,* 495–509.

Bauer, P. J. (1992). Holding it all together: How enabling relations facilitate young children's event recall. *Cognitive Development, 7,* 1–28.

Bauer, P. J., Wenner, J. A., Dropik, P. L., & Wewerka, S. S. (2000). Parameters of remembering and forgetting in the transition from infancy to early childhood. *Monographs of the Society for Research in Child Development, 65*(4, Serial No. 263).

Bauer, Y. (1982). *History of the Holocaust.* New York: Franklin Watts.

Baum, A., & Fleming, I. (1993). Implications of psychological research on stress and technological accidents. *American Psychologist, 48*(6), 665–672.

Baum, D. (1996). *Smoke and mirrors: The war on drugs and the politics of failure.* Boston: Little, Brown.

Baum, S. M., & Owen, S. V. (2004). *To be gifted and learning disabled: Strategies for helping bright students with LD, ADHD, and more.* Mansfield, CT: Creative Learning Press.

Baumeister, A. A., & Francis, J. L. (2002). Historical development of the dopamine hypothesis of schizophrenia. *Journal of the History of Neuroscience, 11,* 265–277.

Baumeister, R. F., & Twenge, J. M. (2003). The social self. In I. Weiner (Series Ed.), T. Millon, & M. J. Lerner (Vol. Eds.), *Handbook of psychology: Vol. 5. Personality and social psychology* (pp. 327–352). New York: Wiley.

Baumgartner, E. R., & Suormala, T. (1997). Multiple carboxylase deficiency: Inherited and acquired disorders of biotin metabolism. *International Journal for Vitamin and Nutrition Research, 67,* 377.

Baumrind, D. (1967). Child care practices anteceding three patterns of preschool behavior. *Genetic Psychology Monographs, 75,* 43–88.

Baumrind, D. (1971). Current patterns of parental authority. *Developmental Psychology Monograph, 4*(1, Part 2), 1–101.

Baumrind, D. (1989). Rearing competent children. In W. Damon (Ed.), *Child development today and tomorrow.* San Francisco: Jossey-Bass.

Baumrind, D. (1991). The influence of parenting style on adolescent competence and substance use. *Journal of Early Adolescence, 11,* 5695.

Baumrind, D. (1996). The discipline controversy revisited. *Family Relations, 45,* 405–411.

Baumrind, D. (1997). Necessary distinctions. *Psychological Inquiry, 8*(3), 176–229.

Baumrind, D., Larzelere, R. E., & Cowan, P. A. (2002). Ordinary physical punishment: Is it harmful? Comment on Gershoff (2002). *Psychological Bulletin, 128*(4), 580–589.

Bauserman, R. (2002). Child adjustment in joint-custody versus sole-custody arrangements: A meta-analytic review. *Journal of Family Psychology, 16*(1), 91–102.

Bayley, N. (1926). Performance tests for three-, four-, and five-year-old children. *Journal of Genetic Psychology, 33,* 435–454.

Bayley, N. (1956). Implicit and explicit values in science as related to human growth and development. *Merrill-Palmer Quarterly, 2,* 121–126.

Bayley, N. (1993). *Bayley scales of infant development.* New York: Psychological Corporation.

Bayley, N., & Schaefer, E. S. (1964). Correlations of maternal and child behaviors with the development of mental abilities: Data from the Berkeley Growth Study. *Monographs of the Society for Research in Child Development, 29*(6, Serial No. 97), 1–80.

BBC. (n.d.). *Gene stories: Nature/nurture.* Retrieved from http://www.bbc.co.uk/health/genes/lifestyle/nature_nurture.shtml

Beal, A. C., Co, J. P., Dougherty, D., Jorsling, T., Kam, J., Perrin, J., et al. (2004). Quality measures for children's health care. *Pediatrics, 113*(1, Pt. 2), 199–209.

Beal, M. F. (2000). Energetics in the pathogenesis of neurodegenerative diseases. *Trends in Neurosciences, 23*(7), 298–304.

Bean, F. D., Corona, R., Tuiran, R., Woodrow-Lafield, K. A., & Van Hook, J. (2001). Circular, invisible, and ambiguous migrants: Components of difference in estimates of the number of unauthorized Mexican migrants in the United States. *Demography, 38*(3), 411–422.

Beane, J., & Brodhagen, B. (2001). Teaching in middle schools. In V. Richardson (Ed.), *Handbook of research on teaching* (4th ed., pp. 1157–1174). Washington, DC: American Educational Research Association.

Bearison, D. J., & Mulhern, R. K. (1994). *Pediatric psychooncology: Psychological perspectives on children with cancer.* Oxford, UK: Oxford University Press.

Beasley, R., Crane, J., Lai, C. K. W., & Pearce, N. (2000). Prevalence and etiology of asthma. *Journal of Allergy and Clinical Immunology, 105,* S466–S472.

Beatty, B. (1997). *Preschool education in America.* New Haven, CT: Yale University Press.

Beaudet, A. L., Scriver, C. R., Sly, W. S., & Valle, D. (2001). Genetics, biochemistry, and molecular bases of variant human phenotypes. In C. R. Scriver, A. L. Beaudet, W. S. Sly, & D. Valle (Eds.), *Metabolic and molecular bases of inherited disease.* New York: McGraw-Hill.

Beaujot, R. (1991). *Population change in Canada: The challenge of policy adoption.* Toronto, Ontario: Oxford University Press.

Beaujot, R., & McQuillan, K. (1982). *Growth and dualism: The demographic development of Canadian society.* Toronto, Ontario: Gage.

Beausang, C. C., & Razor, A. G. (2000). Young Western women's experiences of menarche and menstruation. *Health Care for Women International, 21,* 517–528.

Beck, A. M., & Katcher, A. H. (1996). *Between pets and people: The importance of animal companionship.* West Lafayette, IN: Purdue University Press.

Becker, E. (1971). *The birth and death of meaning* (2nd ed.). New York: Free Press.

Becker, J. B., Breedlove, S. M., Crews, D., & McCarthy, M. (2002). *Behavioral endocrinology.* Cambridge: MIT Press.

Bedny, G. Z., & Karwowski, W. (2004). Activity theory as a basis for the study of work. *Ergonomics, 47,* 134–153.

Beek, P. J., & Van Santvoord, A. M. (1996). Dexterity in cascade juggling. In M. Latash & M. T. Turvey (Eds.), *Dexterity and its development* (pp. 377–391). Mahwah, NJ: Erlbaum.

Behavior Analyst, http://www.abainternational.org/tbajournal/index.htm

Behavioral-Developmental Initiatives, http://www.temperament.com/

Beidel, D. C., & Turner, S. M. (1998). *Shy children, phobic adults: Nature and treatment of social phobia.* Washington, DC: American Psychological Association Press.

Beijing Times. (2003, December 10). Retrieved from http://english.peopledaily.com.cn/200312/10/eng20031210_130093.shtml

Beilin, H. (1992). Piaget's enduring contribution to developmental psychology. *Developmental Psychology, 28,* 191–204.

Beins, B. C. (2004). *Research methods: A tool for life.* Boston: Pearson.

Beirne-Smith, M., Ittenbach, R. F., & Patton, J. R. (2002). *Mental retardation* (6th ed.). Upper Saddle River, NJ: Prentice-Hall.

Bekker, M. H. J. (1996). Agoraphobia and gender: A review. *Clinical Psychology Review, 16,* 129–142.

Belsky, J. (1999). Modern evolutionary theory and patterns of attachment. In J. Cassidy & P. Shaver (Eds.), *Handbook of attachment.* New York: Guilford.

Belsky, J. K. (1998). *The psychology of aging: Theory, research, and interventions.* Pacific Grove, CA: Wadsworth.

Bem, S. L. (1974). The measurement of psychological androgyny. *Journal of Consulting and Clinical Psychology, 42,* 155–162.

Bem, S. L. (1993). *The lenses of gender: Transforming the debate on sexual inequality.* New Haven, CT: Yale University Press.

Bem, S. L. (2004). Transforming the debate on sexual inequality: From biological difference to institutionalized androcentrism. In J. C. Chrisler, C. Golden, & P. Rozee (Eds.), *Lectures on the psychology of women* (3rd ed., pp. 2–15). Rahway, NJ: McGraw-Hill.

Benaisch, A. A., & Leevers, H. J. (2003). Processing of rapidly presented auditory cues in infancy: Implications for later language development. In H. Hayne & J. Fagen (Eds.), *Progress in infancy research* (Vol. 3, pp. 245–288). Mahwah, NJ: LEA.

Bendersky, M., Gambini, G., Lastella, A., Bennet, D. S., & Lewis, M. (2003). Inhibitory motor control at five years as a function of prenatal cocaine exposure. *Journal of Developmental Behavioral Pediatrics, 24,* 345–351.

Bendheim Thoman Center for Research on Child Wellbeing (CRCW), Woodrow Wilson School of International and Public Affairs, http://crcw.princeton.edu/

Bengtson, V. L., Rice, C. J., & Johnson, M. L. (1999). Are theories of aging important? Models and explanations in gerontology at the turn of the century. In V. L. Bengtson & K. W. Schaie (Eds.), *Handbook of theories of aging* (pp. 3–20). New York: Springer.

Bengston, V. L., & Schrader, S. (1982). Parent-child relations: The measurement of intergenerational interaction and affect in old age. In D. Mangen & W. Peterson (Eds.), *Research instrument in social gerontology.* Minneapolis: University of Minnesota Press.

Benjamin, L. T. (1997). The origin of psychological species: History of the beginnings of American Psychological Association divisions. *American Psychologist, 52,* 725–732.

Bennett, F. C. (1999). Developmental outcomes. In G. B. Avery, M. A. Fletcher, & M. G. MacDonald (Eds.), *Neonatology: Pathophysiology and management of the newborn.* Philadelphia: Lippincott Williams & Wilkins.

Bennett, L., Jr. (1975). *The shaping of black America: The struggles and triumphs of African-Americans, 1619–1900s.* Chicago: Johnson.

Bennett, L., Jr. (1988). *Before the Mayflower: A history of black America* (6th ed.). Chicago: Johnson.

Bennett, R. (2005). *Ageism.* Retrieved from http://timegoesby.net/ageism

Benson, C. (2003). The unthinkable boundaries of self: The role of negative emotional boundaries in the formation, maintenance and transformation of identity. In R. Harre & F. Moghaddam (Eds.), *The self and others.* Westport, CT: Praeger.

Benson, P. L., Sharma, A. R., & Roehlkepartain, E. C. (1994). *Growing up adopted.* Minneapolis, MN: Search Institute.

Bentall, R. (1990). The illusion of reality: A review and integration of psychological research on hallucinations. *Psychological Bulletin, 107,* 82–95.

Ben-Zeev, S. (1977). The influence of bilingualism on cognitive strategy and cognitive development. *Child Development, 48,* 1009–1018.

Berenbaum, M. (1990). *A mosaic of victims: Non-Jews persecuted and murdered by the Nazis.* New York: New York University Press.

Bergen, D. (2002). Finding the humor in children's play. In J. L. Roopnarine (Ed.), *Conceptual, social-cognitive, and contextual issues in the fields of play* (pp. 209–220). Westport, CT: Ablex.

Berger, J. O., & Berry, D. A. (1988). Statistical analysis and the illusion of objectivity. *American Scientist, 76,* 159–165.

Berk, L. B., & Friman, P. C. (1990). Epidemiologic aspects of toilet training. *Clinical Pediatrics, 29,* 278–282.

Berk, L. E. (1991). *Child development* (2nd ed.). Needham Heights, MA: Allyn & Bacon.

Berk, L. E. (1994). Why children talk to themselves. *Scientific American, 271*(5), 78–83. Retrieved from http://www.abacon.com/berk/ica/research.html

Berk, L. E. (2001). *Awakening children's minds: How parents and teachers can make a difference.* London: Oxford University Press.

Berk, L. E., & Spuhl, S. T. (1995). Maternal interaction, private speech, and task performance in preschool children. *Early Childhood Research Quarterly, 10,* 145–169.

Berk, L. E., & Winsler, A. (1995). *Scaffolding children's learning: Vygotsky and early childhood education.* Washington, DC: National Association for the Education of Young Children.

Berk, R. A. (Ed.). (1984). *A guide to criterion-referenced test construction.* Baltimore: John Hopkins University Press.

Berkeley Mortality Database, http://www.cdc.gov/nchs/fastats/lifexpec.htm

Berko-Gleason, J. (1997). *The development of language* (4th ed.). Boston: Allyn & Bacon.

Berkowitz, M. W., & Grych, J. H. (1998). Fostering goodness: Teaching parents to facilitate children's moral development. *Journal of Moral Education, 27*(3), 371–391. Retrieved from http://parenthood.library.wisc.edu/Berkowitz/Berkowitz.html

Berlanga, M. L., Olsen, C. M., Chen, V., Ikegami, A., Herring, B. E., Duvauchelle, C. L., et al. (2003). Cholinergic interneurons of the nucleus accumbens and dorsal striatum are activated by the self-administration of cocaine. *Neuroscience, 120,* 1149–1156.

Berlin Aging Study. (2002). *Berlin aging study.* Retrieved from http://www.base-berlin.mpg.de/Introduction.html

Bernal, M. E., Knight, G. P., Ocampo, K. A., Garza, C. A., & Cota, M. K. (1993). *Ethnic identity: Formation and transmission among Hispanics and other minorities.* Albany: State University of New York Press.

Bernstein, N. (1996). On dexterity and its development. In M. L. Latash & M. T. Turvey (Eds.), *Dexterity and its development* (pp. 3–244). Mahwah, NJ: Erlbaum.

Berntson, G. G., & Cacioppo, J. T. (2004). Multilevel analyses and reductionism: Why social psychologists should care about neuroscience and vice versa. In J. T. Cacioppo & G. G. Berntson (Eds.), *Essays in social neuroscience* (pp. 107–120). Boston: MIT Press.

Berrueta-Clement, J. R., Schweinhart, L. J., Barnett, W. S., Epstein, A. S., & Weikart, D. P. (1984). *Changed lives: The effects of the Perry Preschool Project on youths through age 19.* Ypsilanti, MI: High/Scope Educational Research Foundation.

Berry, J. W., Dasen, P. R., & Saraswathi, T. S. (1997). *Handbook of cross-cultural psychology: Vol. 2. Basic processes and human development* (2nd ed.). Boston: Allyn & Bacon.

Berryman, J. C., Smythe, P. K., Taylor, A., Lamont, A., & Joiner, R. (2002). *Developmental psychology and you* (2nd ed.). Malden, MA: Blackwell.

Bertenthal, B. I., & Campos, J. J. (1984). A reexamination of fear and its determinants on the visual cliff. *Psychophysiology, 21,* 413–417.

Bertenthal, B. I., & Clifton, R. K. (1998). Perception and action. In W. Damon (Series Ed.), D. Kuhn & R. Siegler (Vol. Eds.), *Handbook of child psychology: Vol. 2. Cognition, perception, & language* (pp. 51–102). New York: Wiley.

Bertrand, R., & Lachman, M. E. (2002). Personality development in adulthood and old age. In R. M. Lerner, M. A. Easterbrooks, & J. Mistry (Eds.), *Comprehensive handbook of psychology: Vol. 6. Developmental psychology.* New York: Wiley.

Bethel, E. R. (1995). *AIDS: Readings on a global crisis.* Boston: Allyn & Bacon.

B. F. Skinner Foundation, http://www.bfskinner.org/

Bhugra, D., & DeSilva, P. (1997). Dimensions of bisexuality: An exploratory study using focus groups of male and female bisexuals. *Sexual and Marital Therapy, 13,* 145–157.

Bialystok, E. (1991). *Language processing in bilingual children.* Cambridge, UK: Cambridge University Press.

Bialystok, E., & Hakuta, K. (1994). *In other words: The science and psychology of second language acquisition.* New York: Basic Books.

Biblical Studies Info Page, http://www.biblicalstudies.info

Bicego, G, Rutstein, S., & Johnson, K. (2003). Dimensions of the orphan crisis in sub-Saharan Africa. *Social Science and Medicine, 56*(6), 1235–1247.

Bielby, W., & Bielby, D. (1992). I will follow him: Family ties, gender role beliefs, and reluctance to relocate for a better job. *American Journal of Sociology, 97,* 1241–1267.

Bigler, E. D. (1988). *Diagnostic clinical neuropsychology* (Revised ed.). Austin: University of Texas Press.

Bigner, J. J. (2002). *Parent-child relations: An introduction to parenting.* Upper Saddle River, NJ: Merrill/Prentice-Hall.

Bijleveld, C., Kamp, L., Mooijaart, A., Kloot, W., Leeden, R., & Burg, E. (2004). *Longitudinal data analysis: Designs, models, and methods.* Thousand Oaks, CA: Sage.

Bijou, S. W. (1996). *New directions in behavior development.* Reno, NV: Context Press.

Binet, A., & Henri, V. (1896). La psychologie individuelle [Individual psychology]. *Annee Psychologique, 2,* 411–465.

Biringen, Z. (2000). Emotional availability: Conceptualization and research findings. *American Journal of Orthopsychiatry, 70,* 104–114.

Birkland, T. A. (2001). *An introduction to the policy process: Theories, concepts, and models of public policy making.* Armonk, NY: ME Sharpe.

Birren, J. E., & Schaie, K. W. (2001). *Handbook of the psychology of aging* (5th ed.). San Diego, CA: Academic Press.

Birth Defects Research for Children, Inc., http://www.birth defects.org

The Bisexual Network of British Columbia. (n.d.). *A bisexuality primer: "Bisexuality 101."* Retrieved from http://binetbc.bi .org/primer.html

Bjorklund, D. F. (1989). *Children's thinking: Developmental function and individual differences.* Pacific Grove, CA: Brooks/Cole.

Bjorklund, D. F. (2000). *Children's thinking: Developmental function and individual differences* (3rd ed.). Belmont, CA: Wadsworth.

Bjorklund, D. F., & Bering, J. M. (2003). A note on the development of deferred imitation in enculturated juvenile chimpanzees (*Pan troglodytes*). *Developmental Review, 23,* 389–412.

Black, C. (2001). *It will never happen to me: Growing up with addiction as youngsters, adolescents, adults.* Minneapolis, MN: Hazelden.

Black, D. W. (1996). Epidemiology and genetics of OCD: A review and discussion of future directions for research. *CNS Spectrums, 1,* 10–16.

Black, M. (1999). *Essentials of Bayley Scales of Infant Development. II. Assessment.* New York: Wiley.

Black, M. M. (1995). Failure to thrive: Strategies for evaluation and intervention. *School Psychology Review, 24*(2), 171–185.

Blacksher, E. (2002). On being poor and feeling poor: Low socioeconomic status and the moral. *Theoretical Medicine and Bioethics, 23,* 455–470.

Blackwood, E. (2000). Culture and women's sexualities. *Journal of Social Issues, 56,* 223–238.

Blake, J. (1980). *Family size and achievement.* Berkeley: University of California Press. Available from http://ark .cdlib.org/ark:/13030/ft6489p0rr/

Blalock, H. M. (1982). *Conceptualization and measurement in the social sciences.* Beverly Hills, CA: Sage.

Blanchfield, B., Dunbar, J., Feldman, J., & Gardner, E. (1999). *The severely to profoundly hearing impaired population in the United States: Prevalence and demographics.* Bethesda, MD: Project HOPE Center for Health Affairs. Available from http://www.projhope.org

Bland, J. (1998). *About gender: Differences.* Retrieved from http://www.gender.org.uk/about/00_diffs.htm

Blanton, P. W., & Vandergriff-Avery, M. (2001). Marital therapy and marital power: Constructing narratives of sharing relational and positional power. *Contemporary Family Therapy, 23,* 295–308.

Blaze-Temple, D., & Lo, S. K. (1992). Stages of drug use: A community survey of Perth teenagers. *British Journal of Addictions, 87,* 215–225.

Blazer, D. (2000). Psychiatry and the oldest old. *American Journal of Psychiatry, 157*(12), 1915–1924.

Blevins, W. (1998). *Phonics from A to Z.* New York: Scholastic Professional Books.

Blieszner, R., & Adams, R. G. (1992). *Adult friendship.* Newbury Park, CA: Sage.

Blincoe, L., Seay, A., Zaloshnja, E., Miller, T., Romano, E., Luchter, S., et al. (2002). *The economic impact of motor vehicle crashes, 2000.* Washington, DC: National Highway Traffic Safety Administration, U.S. Department of Transportation. Retrieved from http://www.nhtsa.dot.gov/people/economic/econimpact2000/index.htm

Bliss, T. V., & Lomo, T. (1973). Long-lasting potentiation of synaptic transmission in the dentate area of the anaesthetized rabbit following stimulation of the perforant path. *Journal of Physiology, 232*(2), 331–356.

Block, J. (1995). A contrarian view of the five-factor approach to personality description. *Psychological Bulletin, 117,* 187–215.

Blöndal, S., & Scarpetta, S. (1998). *The retirement decision in OECD countries.* OECD Working Paper, No. 202, Paris: OECD.

Bloodstein, O. (1995) *A handbook on stuttering* (5th ed.). San Diego, CA: Singular.

Bloom, P. (2004). *Descartes' baby: How the science of child development explains what makes us human.* New York: Basic Books.

Blos, P. (1962). *On adolescence.* Glencoe, NY: Free Press.

Blum, D. (2002). *Love at Goon Park: Harry Harlow and the science of affection.* Cambridge, MA: Perseus.

Blumstein, P., & Schwartz, P. (1983). *American couples: Money, work, sex.* New York: Morrow.

BMJ (British Medical Journal). (n.d.). *Meta-analysis.* Retrieved from http://bmj.bmjjournals.com/collections/ma.htm

Bock, V. (n.d.). *The secret weapon: An IQ-to-grade conversion chart.* Retrieved from http://www.gtworld.org/iqgrade.html

Bodner, M., Muftuler, L. T., Nalcioglu, O., & Shaw, G. L. (2001). fMRI study relevant to the Mozart effect: Brain areas involved in spatial-temporal reasoning. *Neurological Research, 23,* 683–690.

Bodyteen.com, http://www231.pair.com/grpulse/bt/sefeme.html

Boegels, S. M., Rijsemus, W., & de Jong, P. J. (2002). Self-focused attention and social anxiety: The effects of experimentally heightened self-awareness on fear, blushing, cognitions, and social skills. *Cognitive Therapy and Research, 26,* 461–472.

Bogin, B. (1999). *Patterns of human growth* (2nd ed.). Cambridge, UK: Cambridge University Press.

Bogousslavsky, J. (Ed.). (2002). *Long term effects of stroke.* New York: Marcel Dekker.

Bond, L. A. (1996). *Norm and criterion-referenced testing.* Washington, DC: ERIC Clearinghouse on Assessment and Evaluation. (ERIC Document Reproduction Service No. ED410316). Retrieved from http://www.ericdigests.org/1998-1/norm.htm

Boog, G. (2004). Obstetrical complications and subsequent schizophrenia in adolescent and young adult offsprings: Is there a relationship? *European Journal of Obstetric and Gynecological Reproductive Biology, 114,* 130–136.

Boone, T., & Spann, S. (2004). Overactive bladder: Antimuscarinic therapy in primary care. *Patient Care for the Nurse Practitioner,* May (Special edition).

Booth, A., Crouter, A. C., & Clements, M. (Eds.). (2001). *Couples in conflict.* Mahwah, NJ: Erlbaum.

Borbely, A. (1986). *Secrets of sleep.* New York: Basic Books.

Borden, L. M., Donnermeyer, J. F., & Scheer, S. D. (2001). The influence of extra-curricular activities and peer influence on substance use. *Adolescent and Family Health, 2,* 12–19.

Borden, M. (1997). *Smart start: The parents' complete guide to preschool education.* New York: Facts on File.

Borkowski, J. G., Ramey, S. L., & Bristol-Power, M. (Eds.). (2002). *Parenting and the child's world: Influences on academic, intellectual, and social-emotional development.* Mahwah, NJ: Erlbaum.

Bornstein, M. H. (1989). Sensitive periods in development: Structural characteristics and causal interpretations. *Psychological Bulletin, 105,* 179–197.

Bornstein, M. H. (Ed.). (2002). *Handbook of parenting.* Mahwah, NJ: Erlbaum.

Bornstein M. H., & Bradley, R. H. (2003). Introduction. In M. H. Bornstein & R. H. Bradley (Eds.), *Socioeconomic status, parenting, and child development* (pp. 1–12). Mahwah, NJ: Erlbaum.

Bornstein, M. H., & Bradley, R. H. (Eds.). (2003). *Socioeconomic status, parenting, and child development.* Mahwah, NJ: Erlbaum.

Bornstein, M. H., Davidson, L., Keyes, C. L. M., & Moore, K. A. (Eds.). (2003). *Well-being: Positive development across the life course.* Mahwah, NJ: Erlbaum.

Boskind-White, M., & White, W. C. (2000). *Bulimia/anorexia: The binge/purge cycle and self-starvation.* New York: W. W. Norton.

Bosma, J. (1985). Postnatal ontogeny of performances of the pharynx, larynx and mouth. *American Review of Respiratory Disease, 131*(5, Suppl.), 10–15.

Boston Women's Health Book Collective. (1992). *The new our bodies, ourselves.* New York: Simon & Schuster.

Boston Women's Health Book Collective. (1998). *Our bodies, ourselves for the new century: A book by and for women.* New York: Simon & Schuster.

Boswell, J. (1994). *Same-sex unions in pre-modern Europe.* New York: Villard.

Bottoms, B. L., Kovera, M. B., & McAuliffe, B. D. (Eds.). (2002). *Children, social science, and the law.* New York: Cambridge University Press.

Bouchard, C., Shephard, R. J., & Stephens, T. (Eds.). (1994). *Physical activity, fitness, and health: International proceedings and consensus statement.* Champaign, IL: Human Kinetics.

Bouchery, E., & Harwood, H. (2001). *The economic costs of drug abuse in the United States 1992–1998* (Publication

No. NCJ-190636). Washington, DC: Executive Office of the President, Office of National Drug Control Policy. Available from http://www.whitehousedrugpolicy.gov

Bould, S., Sanborn, B., & Reif, L. (1989). *Eighty-five plus: The oldest old.* Belmont, CA: Wadsworth.

Boushey, H., Gundersen, B., Chauna Brocht, C., & Bernstein, J. (2001). *Hardships in America: The real story of working families.* Washington, DC: Economic Policy Institute.

Boushey, H., & Wright, J. (2004). *Working moms and child care.* Washington, DC: Center for Economic Policy Research.

Bower, B. (2001). Faces of perception. *Science News, 160*(1), 10. Retrieved from http://www.sciencenews.org/articles/20010707/bob16.asp

Bowlby, J. (1969). *Attachment and loss: Vol. 1. Attachment.* New York: Basic Books.

Bowlby, J. (1979). *The making and breaking of affectional bonds.* London: Tavistock Publishers.

Bowlby, J. (1980). *Attachment and loss* (Vol. 3). New York: Basic Books.

Bowlby, J. (1988). *A secure base.* New York: Basic Books.

Bowman, B., Donavan, S., & Burns, S. (2000). *Eager to learn: Educating our preschoolers.* Washington, DC: National Research Council.

Bownes, I. T., O'Gorman, E. C., & Sayers, A. (1991). Psychiatric symptoms, behavioral responses, and posttraumatic stress disorder in rape victims. *Issues in Criminal and Legal Psychology, 1,* 25–33.

Brabant, S. (2004). Death in two settings: The acute care facility and hospice. In C. D. Bryant (Ed.), *Handbook of death and dying: Vol. 1. The presence of death* (pp. 475–484). Thousand Oaks, CA: Sage.

Bradley, R. A. (1996). *Husband coached childbirth.* New York: Bantam.

Bradley, R. H., & Corwyn, R. F. (2002). Socioeconomic status and child development. *Annual Review of Psychology, 53,* 371–399.

Bradley, R., Danielson, L., & Hallahan, D. P. (Eds.). (2002). *Identification of learning disabilities: Research to practice.* Mahwah, NJ: Erlbaum.

Braine, M. D. S. (1978). On the relation between the natural logic of reasoning and standard logic. *Psychological Review, 85,* 1–21.

Braithwaite, R. B. (1959). *Scientific explanation.* London: Cambridge University Press.

Brandell, J., & Perlman, F. (1997). Psychoanalytic theory. In J. Brandell (Ed.), *Theory and practice in clinical social work* (pp. 38–80). New York: Free Press.

Bransford, J. (1979). *Human cognition: Learning, understanding and remembering.* Belmont, CA: Wadsworth.

Braun, K. L., Pietsch, J. H., & Blanchette, P. L. (Eds.). (2000). *Cultural issues in end-of-life decision making.* Thousand Oaks, CA: Sage.

Braunschweig, C. L., Gomez, S., Sheean, P., Tomey, K. M., Rimmer, J., & Heller, T. (2004). High prevalence of obesity and low prevalence of cardiovascular and type 2 diabetes risk factors in urban community dwelling adults with

Down syndrome. *American Journal on Mental Retardation, 109,* 186–193.

Braver, S. L., & O'Connell, D. (1998). *Divorced dads: Shattering the myths.* New York: Tarcher/Putnam.

Braverman, R. (1986). Locke, Defoe, and the politics of childhood. *English Language Notes, 24,* 36–48.

Bray, G. A., Bouchard, C., & James, W. P. T. (Eds.). (1998). *Handbook of obesity.* New York: Marcel Dekker.

The Brazelton Institute, http://www.brazelton-institute.com

Brazelton, T. B. (1973). *Neonatal Behavioral Assessment Scale.* Clinics on Developmental Medicine, No. 50. Philadelphia: William Heinema Medical Books.

Brazelton, T. B. (1985). Early parent infant reciprocity. *Progress in Reproductive Biology and Medicine, 2,* 1–13.

Brazelton, T. B. (1992). *Touchpoints: Your child's emotional and behavioral development.* Cambridge, MA: Perseus.

Brazelton, T. B., & Nugent, J. K. (1995). *The Neonatal Behavioral Assessment Scale.* London: McKeith Press.

Brazelton, T. B., & Sparrow, J. D. (2001). *Touchpoints three to six.* Cambridge, MA: Perseus. Available from http://www.brazelton-institute.com

Bredekamp, S., & Copple, C. (Eds.). (1997). *Developmentally appropriate practice in early childhood programs* (Rev. ed.). Washington, DC: National Association for the Education of Young Children.

Breger, L. (2000). *Freud: Darkness in the midst of vision.* New York: Wiley.

Breggin, P. R. (2001). *Talking back to Ritalin: What doctors aren't telling you about stimulants and ADHD.* Cambridge, MA: Perseus.

Brendt, R. L., & Beckman, D. A. (1990). Teratology. In R. D. Eden, F. H. Boehm, M. Haire, & H. S. Jonas (Eds.), *Assessment and care of the fetus: Physiological, clinical, and medicolegal principles* (pp. 223–244). Norwalk, CT: Appleton & Lange.

Breniere, Y., Bril, B., & Fontaine, R. (1989). Analysis of the transition from upright stance to steady state locomotion in children with under 200 days of autonomous walking. *Journal of Motor Behavior, 21,* 20–37.

Brent, D., May, D. C., & Kundert, D. K. (1996). The incidence of delayed school entry: A twelve-year review. *Early Intervention and Care, 7*(2), 121–135.

Brent, R. L. (1996). Developmental effects following radiation exposure: Counseling the pregnant and nonpregnant patient about these risks. In W. R. Hendee & F. M. Edwards (Eds.), *Health effects of exposure to low-level ionizing radiation.* Philadelphia: Institute of Physics.

Bretherton, I. (2003). Mary Ainsworth: Insightful observer and courageous theoretician. In G. A. Kimble & M. Wertheimer (Eds.), *Portraits of pioneers in psychology* (Vol. 5). Washington, DC: American Psychological Association.

Brewer, M. B., & Hewstone, M. (2004). *Social cognition.* Malden, MA: Blackwell.

Brian, J. A., Landry, R., Szatmari, P., Niccols, A., & Byson, S. (2003). Habituation in high-risk infants: Reliability and patterns of responding. *Infant and Child Development, 12,* 387–394.

Briggs, C. L. (1986). *Learning how to ask: A sociolinguistic appraisal of the role of the interview in social science research.* Cambridge, UK: Cambridge University Press.

British United Provident Association (BUPA). (2003, October). *Colic.* Retrieved from http://hcd2.bupa.co.uk/fact_sheets/html/infant_colic.html

Broderick, P. B. (n.d.). *Chomsky for philosophers.* Retrieved from http://www.personal.kent.edu/~pbohanbr/Webpage/New/newintro.html

Brody, B. (1998). *The ethics of biomedical research: An international perspective.* New York: Oxford University Press.

Brody, G. H. (1996). *Sibling relationships: Their causes and consequences.* Westport, CT: Ablex.

Brody, G. H. (1998). Sibling relationship quality: Its causes and consequences. *Annual Review of Psychology, 49,* 1–24.

Brody, G. H., McBride Murry, V., Kim, S., & Brown, A. C. (2002). Longitudinal pathways to competence and psychological adjustment among African American children living in rural single-parent households. *Child Development, 73*(5), 1505–1516.

Brody, L. R. (1985). Gender differences in emotional development: A review of theories and research. *Journal of Personality, 53,* 102–149.

Brodzinsky, D., & Pinderhughes, E. (2002). Parenting and child development in adoptive families. In M. Bornstein (Ed.), *Handbook of parenting* (Vol. 1, pp. 279–311). Hilldale, NJ: Erlbaum.

Bronfenbrenner, U. (1970). *Two worlds of childhood: U.S. and U.S.S.R.* New York: Russell Sage Foundation.

Bronfenbrenner, U. (1977). Toward an experimental psychology of human development. *American Psychologist, 32,* 513–531.

Bronfenbrenner, U. (1979). *The ecology of human development: Experiments by nature and design.* Cambridge, MA: Harvard University Press.

Bronfenbrenner, U. (n.d.). Personal Web site. Retrieved from http://www.people.cornell.edu/pages/ub11/

Bronfenbrenner, U., & Ceci, S. J. (1994). Nature-nurture reconceptualized: A bio-ecological model. *Psychological Review, 101,* 568–586.

Bronfenbrenner, U., & Morris, P. A. (1998). The ecology of developmental processes. In W. Damon & R. Lerner (Eds.), *Handbook of child psychology* (5th ed.). New York: Wiley.

Bronson, G. (1972). Infants' reactions to unfamiliar persons and novel objects. *Monographs of the Society of Research in Child Development, 37*(3, Serial No. 148).

Brook, C. G. D. (2001). *Clinical paediatric endocrinology* (4th ed.). Oxford, UK: Blackwell Science.

Brooks, J., & Lewis, M. (1976). Infants' response to strangers: Midget, adult, and child. *Child Development, 47,* 323–332.

Brooks-Gunn, J., Berlin, L. J., & Fuligni, A. S. (2000). Early childhood intervention programs: What about the family? In J. P. Shonkoff & S. J. Meisels (Eds.), *Handbook of early childhood intervention* (2nd ed., pp. 549–587). New York: Cambridge University Press.

Brooks-Gunn, J., Duncan, G., & Aber, J. (1997). *Neighborhood poverty: Vol. 1. Context and consequences for children. Vol. 2. Policy implications in studying neighborhoods.* New York: Russell Sage Foundation.

Broomfield, J. (2000). *Aging changes in the senses.* Retrieved from http://health.discovery.com/diseasesandcond/encyclopedia/508.html

Brophy, D. R. (2000–2001). Comparing the attributes, activities, and performance of divergent, convergent, and combination thinkers. *Creativity Research Journal, 13,* 439–455.

Brophy, J. E., & Good, T. L. (1970). Teacher's communication of differential expectations for children's classroom performance: Some behavioral data. *Journal of Educational Psychology, 61,* 365–374.

Brott, A. (n.d.). *Imaginary friends: Should you be concerned?* Retrieved from http://www.familyresource.com/parenting/6/551/

Brown, B. B. (1999). "You're going out with who?" Peer group influences on adolescent romantic relationships. In W. Furman, B. B. Brown, & C. Feiring (Eds.), *The development of romantic relationships in adolescence* (pp. 291–329). Cambridge, UK: Cambridge University Press.

Brown, B. B., & Klute, C. (2003). Friendships, cliques, and crowds. In G. R. Adams & M. D. Berzonsky (Eds.), *Blackwell handbook of adolescence* (pp. 330–348). Malden, MA: Blackwell.

Brown, D., & Brooks, L. (1996). *Career choice and development: Applying contemporary theories to practice* (3rd ed.). San Francisco: Jossey-Bass.

Brown, G., Malmkjær, K., & Williams, J. (Eds.). (1996). *Performance and competence in second language acquisition.* Cambridge, UK: Cambridge University Press.

Brown, R. (1973). *A first language: The early stages.* Cambridge, MA: Harvard University Press.

Brown, R. T., & Hoadley, S. L. (1999). Rett syndrome. In S. Goldstein & C. R. Reynolds (Eds.), *Handbook of neurodevelopmental and genetic disorders in children* (pp. 459–477). New York: Guilford.

Brown, R. W. (1958). *Words and things.* Glencoe, IL: Free Press.

Brown, R. W. (1973). *A first language: The early stages.* Cambridge, MA: Harvard University Press.

Brown, S. D., & Lent, R. W. (Eds.). (2004). *Career development and counseling: Putting theory and research to work.* New York: Wiley.

Brown, S. L., & Booth, A. (1996). Cohabitation versus marriage: A comparison of relationship quality. *Journal of Marriage and the Family, 58,* 668–679.

Brown, S. L., Nesse, R., Vinokur, A. D., & Smith, D. M. (2003). Providing support may be more beneficial than receiving it: Results from a prospective study of mortality. *Psychological Science, 14,* 320–327.

Browne, J. V. (2003). New perspectives on premature infants and their parents. *Zero to Three, 24*(2), 4–12.

Brownell, K. D., & Fairburn, C. G. (Eds.). (2002). *Eating disorders and obesity: A comprehensive handbook* (2nd ed.). New York: Guilford.

Brownmiller, S. (1975). *Against our will: Men, women, and rape.* New York: Simon & Schuster.

Bruce, T. (1993). For parents particularly: The role of play in children's lives. *Childhood Education, 69*(4), 237–238.

Bruce, V. G. (1960) Environmental entrainment of circadian rhythms. *Cold Spring Harbor Symposia on Quantitative Biology, 25,* 29–48.

Bruer, J. T. (1999). *The myth of the first three years.* New York: Free Press.

Bruess, C. E., & Greenburg, J. S. (2004). *Sexuality education: Theory and practice.* Sudbury, MA: Jones & Bartlett.

Bruner, J. (1961). *Actual minds, possible worlds.* Cambridge, MA: Harvard University Press.

Bruner, J. (1990). *Acts of meaning.* Cambridge, MA: Harvard University Press.

Bryan, E. (1995). *Twins, triplets and more: Their nature, development and care.* London: Multiple Birth Foundation.

Bryan, J. (2003). *Fighting for respect: African-American soldiers in WWI military history.* Retrieved from http://www.militaryhistoryonline.com/wwi/articles/fightingforrespect.aspx

Bryce, J., el Arifeen, S., Pariyo, G., Lanata, C., Gwatkin, D., Habicht, J. P., et al. (2003). Reducing child mortality: Can public health deliver? *Lancet, 12,* 362(9378), 159–164.

Buckley, K. W. (1989). *Mechanical man: John Broadus Watson and the beginnings of behaviorism.* New York: Guilford.

Buddha 101: The history, philosophy, and practice of Buddhism, http://www.buddha101.com

BuddhaNet, http://www.buddhanet.net

Bukowski, W. M., Newcomb, A. F., & Hartup, W. W. (Eds.). (1996). *The company they keep: Friendship in childhood and adolescence.* Cambridge, UK: Cambridge University Press.

Bullough, V. L., & Brundage, J. A. (Eds.). (1996). *Handbook of medieval sexuality.* London: Garland.

Bu'Lock, F., Woolridge, M. W., & Baum, J. D. (1990). Development of co-ordination of sucking, swallowing and breathing: Ultrasound study of term and preterm infants. *Developmental Medicine & Child Neurology, 32*(8), 669–678.

Burchinal, M. R., Campbell, F. A., Bryant, D. M., Wasik, B. H., & Ramey, C. T. (1997). Early intervention and mediating processes in cognitive performance of children of low-income African American families. *Child Development, 68,* 935–954.

Bureau of Justice Statistics. (2004). *National Criminal Victimization Survey, 2002.* Retrieved from http://www.ojp.usdoj.gov/bjs/cvictgen.htm

Burnside, L. H. (1927). Coordination in the locomotion of human infants. *Genetic Psychology Monographs, 2,* 284–372.

Burt, M. R. (1980). Cultural myths and supports for rape. *Journal of Personality and Social Psychology, 38,* 277–322.

Bush, A., & Beail, N. (2004). Risk factors for dementia in people with Down syndrome: Issues in assessment and diagnosis. *American Journal on Mental Retardation, 109,* 83–97.

Buss, D. M. (1989). Sex differences in human mate preferences: Evolutionary hypotheses tested in 37 cultures. *Behavioral and Brain Sciences, 12,* 1–49.

Buss, D. M. (1999). *Evolutionary psychology: The new science of the mind.* Needham Heights, MA: Allyn & Bacon.

Busse, E. W. (1969). Themes of aging. In E. W. Busse & E. Pfeiffer (Eds.), *Behavior and adaptation in late life.* Boston: Little, Brown.

Bussey, K., & Bandura, A. (1999). Social cognitive theory of gender development and differentiation. *Psychological Review, 106,* 676–713.

Butler, R. N. (1969). Age-ism: Another form of bigotry. *Gerontologist, 9,* 243–246.

Butterworth, G., & Bryant, P. (Eds.). (1990). *Causes of development: Interdisciplinary perspectives.* Hillsdale, NJ: Erlbaum.

Buysse, V., & Bailey, D. B. (1993). Behavioral and developmental outcomes in young children with disabilities in integrated and segregated settings: A review of comparative studies. *Journal of Special Education, 26,* 434–461.

Byock, I. (1997). *Dying well: The prospect for growth at the end of life.* New York: Riverhead Books.

Byrd, R. S., Weitzman, M., & Auinger, P. (1997). Increased behavior problems associated with delayed school entry and delayed school progress. *Pediatrics, 100*(4), 1–8.

Cabeza, R., & Nyberg, L. (2000). Imaging cognition II: An empirical review of 275 PET and fMRI studies. *Journal of Cognitive Neuroscience, 12*(1), 1–47.

Cacioppo, J. T., Hawkley, L. C., & Bernston, G. G. (2003). The anatomy of loneliness. *Current Directions in Psychological Science, 12*(3), 71–74.

Cacioppo, J. T., Hawkley, L. C., Crawford, L. E., Ernst, J. M., Burleson, M. H., Kowalewski, R. B., et al. (2002). Loneliness and health: Potential mechanisms. *Psychosomatic Medicine, 64,* 407–417.

Calabresi, P., Pisani, A., & Bernardi, G. (1996). The corticostriatal projection: From synaptic plasticity to dysfunctions of the basal ganglia. *Trends in Neurosciences, 19*(1), 19–24.

Calder, B. J., & Malthouse, E. C. (2003). The behavioral score approach to dependent variables. *Journal of Consumer Psychology, 13,* 387–394.

California Birth Defects Monitoring Program, http://www.cbdmp.org

Callahan, C. (2000). Intelligence and giftedness. In R. J. Sternberg (Ed.), *Handbook of intelligence* (pp. 159–175). New York: Cambridge University Press.

Cambridge Center for Behavioral Studies, http://www.behavior.org

Camic, P. M., Rhodes, J. E., & Yardley, L. (Eds.). (2003). *Qualitative research in psychology: Expanding perspectives in methodology and design.* Washington, DC: American Psychological Association.

Campbell, D. T., & Stanley J. C. (1966). *Experimental and quasi-experimental designs for research.* Chicago: Rand McNally.

Campbell, F. A., Pungello, E. P., Miller-Johnson, S., Burchinal, M., & Ramey, C. T. (2001). The development of cognitive and academic abilities: Growth curves from an early childhood educational experiment. *Developmental Psychology, 37,* 231–242.

Campbell, F. A., & Ramey, C. T. (1994). Effects of early intervention on intellectual and academic achievement: A follow-up study of children from low-income families. *Child Development, 65,* 684–698.

Campbell, F. A., & Ramey, C. T. (1995). Cognitive and school outcomes for high-risk African-American students at middle adolescence: Positive effects of early intervention. *American Educational Research Journal, 32,* 743–772.

Campbell, F. A., Ramey, C. T., Pungello, E. P., Sparling, J., & Miller-Johnson, S. (2002). Early childhood education: Young adult outcomes from the Abecedarian Project. *Applied Developmental Science, 6*(1), 42–57.

Campbell, J. (1999). *Student discipline and classroom management: Preventing and managing discipline problems in the classroom.* Springfield, IL: Charles C Thomas.

Campbell, L., White, J., & Stewart, A. (1991). The relationship of psychological birth order to actual birth order. *Individual Psychology, 47,* 380–391.

Campos, J., Bertenthal, B., & Kermoian, R. (1992). Early experience and emotional development: The emergence of wariness of heights. *Psychological Science, 3,* 61–64.

Campos, J. J., Anderson, D. I., Barbu-Roth, M., Hubbard, E. M., Hertenstein, M. J., & Witherington, D. (2000). Travel broadens the mind. *Infancy, 1,* 149–219.

Campos, J. J., Langer, A., & Krowitz, A. (1970). Cardiac responses on the visual cliff in prelocomotor human infants. *Science, 170,* 196–197.

The Canadian Deafblind and Rubella Association, http://www.cdbra.ca

Canclini, M., Saviolo-Negrin, N., Zanon, E., Bertoletti, R., Girolami, A., & Pagnan, A. (2003). Psychological aspects and coping in haemophilic patients: A case-control study. *Haemophilia, 9,* 619–624.

Candlelighters Childhood Cancer Foundation, http://www.candlelighters.org

Cannon, M., Jones, P. B., & Murray, R. M. (2002). Obstetric complications and schizophrenia: Historical and meta-analytic review. *American Journal of Psychiatry, 159,* 1080–1092.

Cantorna, M. T., Nashold, F. E., & Hayes, C. E. (1995). Vitamin A deficiency results in a priming environment conducive for Th1 cell development. *European Journal of Immunology, 25,* 1673.

Caplan, P. (1987). *The cultural construction of sexuality.* London: Tavistock.

Carducci, B. J. (2003). *The shyness breakthrough: A no-stress plan to help your shy child warm up, open up, and join the fun.* Emmaus, PA: Rodale.

Carey, J. R. (2003). *Longevity: The biology and demography of life span.* Princeton, NJ: Princeton University Press.

Carl Rogers, http://oprf.com/Rogers

Carlo, G., Knight, G., Eisenberg, N., & Rotenberg, K. (1991). Cognitive processes and prosocial behaviors among children: The role of affective attributions and reasoning. *Developmental Psychology, 27,* 456–461.

Carlson, N. R. (2001). *Physiology of behavior* (7th ed.). Boston: Allyn & Bacon.

Carlton, M. P., & Winsler, A. (1999). School readiness: The need for a paradigm shift. *School Psychology Review, 28,* 338–352.

Carmichael, S. L., Shaw, G. M., & Nelson, V. (2002). Timing of prenatal care initiation and risk of congenital malformations. *Teratology, 66,* 326–330.

Carolina Abecedarian Project, http://www.fpg.unc.edu/~abc/

Carrigan, M. H., & Randall, C. L. (2003). Self-medication in social phobia: A review of the alcohol literature. *Addictive Behaviors, 28,* 269–284.

Carroll, J. B. (1976). Psychometric tests as cognitive tasks: A new "structure of intellect." In L. Resnick (Ed.), *The nature of intelligence* (pp. 27–56). Hillsdale, NJ: Erlbaum.

Carroll, J. B. (1993). *Human cognitive abilities: A survey of factor-analytic studies.* New York: Cambridge University Press.

Carroll, J. B. (1997). The three-stratum theory of cognitive abilities. In D. P. Flanagan, J. L. Genshaft, & P. L. Harrison (Eds.), *Contemporary intellectual assessment: Theories, tests, and issues* (pp. 122–130). New York: Guilford.

Carson, R. E. (1998). *Quantitative functional brain imaging with positron emission tomography.* New York: Academic Press.

Carstensen, L. L. (1992). Social and emotional patterns in adulthood: Support for socioemotional selectivity theory. *Psychology and Aging, 7,* 331–338.

Carter, J. (1998). *The virtues of aging.* New York: Ballantine.

Caruso, D. (n.d.). *Emotional intelligence.* Available from http://www.emotionaliq.com

Carver, P. R., Yunger, J. L., & Perry, D. G. (2003). Gender identity and adjustment in middle childhood. *Sex Roles, 49,* 95–109.

Casarett, D. J., Hirschman, K. B., & Henry, M. R. (2001). Does hospice have a role in nursing home care at the end of life? *Journal of the American Geriatrics Society, 49,* 1493–1498.

Casey, B. J., Tottenham, N., & Fossella, J. (2002). Clinical, imaging, lesion, and genetic approaches toward a model of cognitive control. *Developmental Psychobiology, 40,* 237–254.

Casey, B. M., McIntire, D. D., & Leveno, K. J. (2001). The continuing value of the Apgar score for the assessment of newborn infants. *New England Journal of Medicine, 344,* 467–471.

Caspi, A., Henry, B., McGee, R. O., Moffitt, T. E., & Silva, P. A. (1995). Temperamental origins of child and adolescent behavior problems: From age three to age fifteen. *Child Development, 66,* 55–68.

Caspi, A., Sugden, K., Moffitt, T. E., Taylor, A., Craig, I. W., Harrington, H., et al. (2003). Influence of life stress on depression: Moderation by a polymorphism in the 5-HTT gene. *Science, 301,* 386–389.

Cassar, E., Ward, T., & Thakker, J. (2003). A descriptive model of the homicide process. *Behaviour Change, 20,* 76–93.

Cassidy, J. T., & Petty, R. E. (2001). *The textbook of pediatric rheumatology* (4th ed.). Philadelphia: W. B. Saunders.

Cassidy, K. W., Werner, R. S., Rourke, M., Zubernis, L. S., & Balaraman, G. (2003). The relationship between psychological understanding and positive social behaviors. *Social Development, 12,* 198–221.

Castells, M. (1997). Immigrant workers and class struggles in advanced capitalism: The Western European experience. In R. Cohen & Z. Layton-Henry (Eds.), *The politics of migration* (pp. 33–61). Northampton, MA: Elgar.

Castles, A., & Coltheart, M. (2004). Is there a causal link from phonological awareness to success in learning to read? *Cognition, 91,* 77–111.

Catalyst. (1998). *Advancing women in business—the Catalyst guide: Best practices from the corporate leaders.* San Francisco, CA: Jossey-Bass.

Catalyst. (2000). *2000 Catalyst census of women corporate officers and top earners.* Available from http://www.catalystwomen.org/

Catalyst. (2003). *2003 Catalyst census of women board directors.* Available from http://www.catalystwomen.org/

Catania, A. C. (1998). *Learning* (4th ed.). Upper Saddle River, NJ: Prentice-Hall.

Catholic answers. (n.d.). Available from http://www.catholic.com/

Catholic encyclopedia. (n.d.). Retrieved from http://www.newadvent.org/cathen/

Cattaneo, E., Rigamonti, D., Goffredo, D., Zuccato, C., Squitieri, F., & Sipione, S. (2001). Loss of normal huntingtin function: New developments in Huntington's disease research. *Trends in Neurosciences, 24*(3), 182–188.

Cattell, R. B. (1943). The measurement of adult intelligence. *Psychological Bulletin, 40,* 153–193.

Cattell, R. B. (1957). *Personality and motivation structure and measurement.* New York: World Book.

Cattell, R. B. (1963). Theory of fluid and crystallized intelligence: A critical experiment. *Journal of Educational Psychology, 54,* 1–22.

Cattell, R. B. (1971). *Abilities: Their structure, growth and action.* Boston: Houghton Mifflin.

Cattell, R. B. (1987). *Intelligence: Its structure, growth, and action.* New York: Elsevier.

Cavanaugh, C. (2002). Distance education quality: Success factors for resources, practices and results. In R. Discenza, C. Howard, & K. Schenk (Eds.), *The design and management of effective distance learning programs.* Hershey, PA: Idea Group Press.

Cavanaugh, M. P. (1996). History of teaching English as a second language. *English Journal, 85,* 40–44.

CDC Cancer Publications Center, http://www.cdc.gov/cancer/publica.htm

Ceci, S. J., & Bruck, M. (1995). *Jeopardy in the courtroom: A scientific analysis of children's testimony.* Washington, DC: American Psychological Association.

Ceci, S. J., Gilstrap, L. L., & Fitneva, S. (2002). Children's testimony. In M. Rutter (Ed.), *Child and adolescent psychiatry: Modern approaches* (pp. 117–127). London: Blackwell Scientific.

Ceci, S. J., & Hembrooke, H. (Eds.). (1998). *Expert witnesses in child abuse cases: What can and should be said in court.* Washington, DC: American Psychological Association.

Census Bureau facts pertaining to African Americans, http://www.africanamericans.com/CensusBureauFacts.htm

Center for Adult English Language Acquisition, http://www.cal.org/caela

Center of Child Abuse and Neglect (CCAN), http://w3.ouhsc.edu/ccan/

Center for Communication and Social Policy, University of California-Santa Barbara National Television Violence Study. (n.d.). *Project overview.* Retrieved from http://www.ccsp.ucsb.edu/ntvs.htm

Center for Cross-Cultural Research, Western Washington University. (n.d.). *Online readings in psychology and culture.* Retrieved from http://www.ac.wwu.edu/~culture/readings.htm

The Center for Effective Discipline, http://stophitting.org

Center for Effective Parenting. (n.d.). *Stranger anxiety.* Retrieved from http://www.parenting-ed.org/handouts/ Specific%20Concerns%20and%20Problems/stranger%20anxiety.doc

Center for Evolutionary Psychology, http://www.psych.ucsb.edu/research/cep/

Center for the Future of Children. (1995). *The future of children: Low birth weight* (Vol. 5, pp. 176–196). Princeton, NJ: Brookings Institute.

Center for the Improvement of Early Reading Achievement. (2001). *Put reading first: The research building blocks for teaching children to read.* Retrieved from http://www.nifl.gov/partnershipforreading/publications/reading_first1.html

Center for International Development and Conflict Management, http://www.cidcm.umd.edu

Center for Reproductive Law and Policy. (1997). *Women of the world: Laws and policies affecting their reproductive lives: Latin America and the Caribbean.* Available from http://www.crlp.org

Center for the Study of Multiple Birth, http://www.MultipleBirth.com

Center for the Study of Sex Differences in Health, Aging and Disease. (n.d.). *Why study sex differences?* Retrieved from http://csd.georgetown.edu/why.htm

Center for Substance Abuse Treatment (CSAT). (1997). *Proceedings of the National Consensus Meeting on the use, abuse, and sequelae of abuse of methamphetamine with implications for prevention, treatment, and research.* DHHS Pub. No. (SMA) 96–8013. Rockville, MD: Department of Health and Human Services.

Centers for Disease Control and Prevention (CDC), http://www.cdc.gov

Centers for Disease Control and Prevention. (1998). Recommendations to prevent and control iron deficiency in the United States. *Morbidity and Mortality Weekly Report, 47,* 1–36. Retrieved from http://www.cdc.gov/mmwr/preview/mmwrhtml/00051880.htm

Centers for Disease Control and Prevention. (2000). *Growth charts: United States.* Retrieved from http://www.cdc.gov/growthcharts/

Centers for Disease Control and Prevention. (2000). *Safe motherhood: Preventing pregnancy-related illness and death.* Washington, DC: U.S. Department of Health and Human Services.

Centers for Disease Control and Prevention. (2001). HIV and AIDS: United States, 1981–2000. *MMWR, 50*(21), 430–434.

Centers for Disease Control and Prevention. (2001). School health guidelines to prevent unintentional injuries and violence. *Morbidity and Mortality Weekly Report, 50,* RR22. Retrieved from http://www.cdc.gov/mmwr/preview/mmwrhtml/rr5022a1.htm

Centers for Disease Control and Prevention. (2002). Annual smoking-attributable mortality, years of potential life lost, and economic costs—United States, 1995–1999. *Morbidity and Mortality Weekly Report, 51*(14), 300–303. Retrieved from http://www.cdc.gov/tobacco/research_data/economics/mmwr5114.highlights.htm

Centers for Disease Control and Prevention. (2002). Involvement of young drivers in fatal alcohol-related motor-vehicle crashes—United States, 1982–2001. *Morbidity and Mortality Weekly Report, 51,* 1089–1091.

Centers for Disease Control and Prevention. (2002). Surveillance for asthma—United States, 1980–1999. *Surveillance Summaries, 51,* 1–13.

Centers for Disease Control and Prevention. (2003). *2001 Assisted Reproductive Technology success rates.* Atlanta, GA: U.S. Department of Health and Human Services. Retrieved from http://www.cdc.gov/reproductivehealth/ART01/index.htm

Centers for Disease Control and Prevention. (2003). *HIV/AIDS surveillance report: U.S. HIV and AIDS cases reported through December 2002.* Retrieved from http://www.cdc.gov/hiv/stats/hasr1402

Centers for Disease Control and Prevention. (2003). Self-reported asthma prevalence and control among adults—United States, 2001. *Morbidity and Mortality Weekly Report, 52,* 381–384.

Centers for Disease Control and Prevention. (2003). *Sexually transmitted disease surveillance, 2002.* Atlanta, GA: U.S. Department of Health and Human Services. Retrieved from http://cdc.gov/std/stats/toc.2002.htm

Centers for Disease Control and Prevention. (2004). *Recommended childhood and adolescent immunization schedule: United States, January–June 2004.* Retrieved from http://www.cdc.gov/nip/recs/child-schedule.htm#Printable

Centers for Disease Control and Prevention. (2004). Youth risk behavior surveillance—United States, 2003. *Morbidity and Mortality Weekly Report, 53*(SS-2).

Centers for Disease Control and Prevention. (n.d.). *CDC recommends* [database]. Available from http://www.phppo.cdc.gov/CDCRecommends/AdvSearchV.asp

Centers for Disease Control and Prevention. (n.d.). Firearms. Retrieved from http://www.cdc.gov/search.do?action=search&queryText=firearms

Centers for Disease Control and Prevention. (n.d.). *Prostate cancer screening: A decision guide.* Retrieved from http://www.cdc.gov/cancer/prostate/decisionguide/

Centers for Disease Control and Prevention, National Center on Birth Defects and Developmental Disabilities, http://www.cdc.gov/ncbddd

Centers for Disease Control and Prevention, National Center for Chronic Disease Prevention and Health Promotion. (n.d.). *Chronic disease prevention.* Retrieved from http://www.cdc.gov/nccdphp/

Centers for Disease Control and Prevention, National Center for Infectious Diseases Centers, http://www.cdc.gov/ncidod/index.htm

Centers for Disease Control and Prevention, National Center for Infectious Diseases. (n.d.). *Chronic fatigue syndrome.* Retrieved from http://www.cdc.gov/ncidod/diseases/cfs/

Centre for Menstrual Cycle and Ovulation Research, http://www.cemcor.ubc.ca/

Cepeda, N. J., Kramer, A. F., & Gonzalez de Sather, J. C. (2001). Changes in executive control across the life span: Examination of task-switching performance. *Developmental Psychology, 37*(5), 715–730.

Cervantes-Laurean, N., McElvaney, G., & Moss, J. (2000). Niacin. In M. Shils (Ed.), *Modern nutrition in health and medicine* (p. 401). Philadelphia: Lippincott Williams & Wilkins.

Chadwick, P., & Lowe, C. (1994). A cognitive approach to measuring and modifying delusions. *Behaviour Research and Therapy, 32,* 355–367.

Chall, J. (1983). *Learning to read: The great debate.* New York: McGraw-Hill.

Chall, J., & Popp, H. (1999). *Teaching and assessing phonics: Why, what, when, how.* Cambridge, MA: Educators Publishing Service.

Challem, J. (1999). *ABC's of hormones.* New York: McGraw-Hill.

Chalmers, J. B., & Townsend, M. A. R. (1990). The effects of training in social perspective taking on socially maladjusted girls. *Child Development, 61,* 178–190.

Chamberlain, G., Wraight, A., & Crowley, P. (1999). Birth at home: A report of the national survey of home births in the UK by the National Birthday Trust. *Practising Midwife, 2,* 35–39.

Chan, J., Edman, J. C., & Koltai, P. J. (2004). Obstructive sleep apnea in children. *American Family Physician, 69,* 1147–1154, 1159–1160.

Chaney, J. M., Mullins, L. L., Wagner, J. L., Hommel, K. A., Page, M. C., & Doppler, M. J. (2004). A longitudinal examination of causal attributions and depression symptomatology in rheumatoid arthritis. *Rehabilitation Psychology, 49,* 126–133.

Chantler, J. K., & Tingle, A. J. (2001). Rubella. In B. N. Fields, D. M. Knipe, Howley, P. M., et al. (Eds.), *Virology* (4th ed.). Philadelphia: Lippincott-Raven.

Chapman, S. A. (2005). Theorizing about aging well: Constructing a narrative. *Canadian Journal of Aging, 24*(1), 12–17.

The Character Education Partnership, http://www.character.org/

Cheatum, B. A., & Hammond, A. A. (2000). *Physical activities for improving children's learning and behavior: A guide to sensory motor development.* Champaign, IL: Human Kinetics.

Cheek, J. M., & Krasnoperova, E. N. (1999). Varieties of shyness in adolescence and adulthood. In L. A. Schmidt & J. Schulkin (Eds.), *Extreme fear, shyness, and social phobia: Origins, biological mechanisms, and clinical outcomes* (pp. 224–250). New York: Oxford University Press.

Cheng, M., & Hannah, M. E. (1993). Breech delivery at term: A critical review of the literature. *Obstetrics and Gynecology, 82,* 605–618.

Cheong, Y., Goodrick, J., & Kyle, P. (2001). Management of anti-Rhesus-D antibodies in pregnancy: A review from 1994 to 1998. *Fetal Diagnosis & Therapy, 16*(5), 294–298.

Cheron, G., Bouillot, E., Dan, B., Bengoetxea, A., Draye, J., & Lacquaniti, F. (2001). Development of a kinematic coordination pattern in toddler locomotion: Planar covariation. *Experimental Brain Research, 137,* 455–466.

Chesney-Lind, M., & Hagedorn, J. (Eds.). (1999). *Female gangs in America: Essays on girls, gangs, and gender.* Chicago: Lakeview Press.

Chess, S., & Thomas, A. (1996). Temperament: Theory and practice. *Basic principles into practice series: Vol. 12.* Philadelphia: Bruner/Mazel.

Chess, S., & Thomas, A. (2002). Temperament. In M. Lewis (Ed.), *Child and adolescent psychiatry: A comprehensive textbook.* (3rd ed., pp. 170–180). Philadelphia: Lippincott Williams & Wilkins.

Chesselet, M. F., & Delfs, J. M. (1996). Basal ganglia and movement disorders: An update. *Trends in Neurosciences, 19*(10), 417–422.

Child Abuse Prevention Network, http://child-abuse.com/

Child and Adolescent Health and Development. (n.d.). *Neonatal health.* Retrieved from http://www.who.int/child adolescent-health/overview/hni/neonatal.htm

Child Development Institute. (2004). *Temperament and your child's personality.* Retrieved from http://www.childdevelopmentinfo.com/development/temperament_and_your_child.htm

Child Development Institute. (n.d.). *Approximate timetable of prenatal development.* Retrieved from http://www.childdevelopmentinfo.com/development/prenataldevelopment.shtml

Child Development Institute. (n.d.). *Language and speech development in children.* Retrieved from http://www.childdevelopmentinfo.com/development/language_development.shtml

Child Trends, http://www.childtrends.org/

Child Welfare League of America, http://www.cwla.org/

Childbirth.Org. (2001). *Pregnancy.* Retrieved from http://www.childbirth.org/articles/preglinks.html

The Childfree-by-Choice Pages, http://www.childfree.net/

Childhelp USA. (n.d.). *Treatment and prevention of child abuse.* Retrieved from http://www.childhelpusa.org/hotline.htm

Children and Adults with Attention Deficit Hyperactivity Disorder, http://www.chadd.org

Children Now. (2001). *Fair play? Violence, gender and race in video games.* Los Angeles: Author.

Children's grief and loss issues and how we can help them. (n.d.). Available from http://www.childrensgrief.net

Children's Hospital Medical Center of Akron. (n.d.). *Separation anxiety.* Retrieved from http://www.akronchildrens.org/tips/pdfs/BP1108.pdf

Children's Medical Center of the University of Virginia. (n.d.). *Asthma tutorial.* Retrieved from http://www.people.virginia.edu/~smb4v/tutorials/asthma/asthma1.html

ChildTrauma Academy, http://www.childtrauma.org/ctamaterials/ptsd_interdisc.asp

ChildTrends DataBank. (2003). *High school dropout rates.* Retrieved from http://www.childtrendsdatabank.org/indicators/1HighSchoolDropout.cfm

Chobanian, A. V., Bakris, G. L., & Black, H. R. (2003). The seventh report of the Joint National Committee on the Prevention, Detection, Evaluation, and Treatment of High Blood Pressure: The JNC 7 Report. *JAMA, 289,* 2560–2571.

Chochinov, H. M. (2002). Dignity-conserving care—A new model for palliative care. *Journal of the American Medical Association, 287,* 2253–2260.

Choi, N., & Fuqua, D. R. (2003). The structure of the Bem Sex Role Inventory: A summary report of 23 validation studies. *Educational and Psychological Measurement, 63,* 872–877.

Chomsky, N. (1957). *Syntactic structures.* The Hague, Netherlands: Mouton.

Chomsky, N. (1959). A review of B. F. Skinner's *Verbal Behavior. Language, 35,* 26–58.

Chomsky, N. (1964). *Current issues in linguistic theory.* The Hague, Netherlands: Mouton.

Chomsky, N. (1964). *Language and information: Selected essays on the theory and application.* Reading, MA: Addison-Wesley; Jerusalem: The Jerusalem Academic Press.

Chomsky, N. (1965). *Aspects of the theory of syntax.* Cambridge: MIT Press.

Chomsky, N. (1966). *Cartesian linguistics: A chapter in the history of rationalist thought.* New York: Harper & Row.

Chomsky, N. (1968). *Language and mind.* New York: Pantheon.

Chomsky, N. (1969). *American power and the new Mandarins.* New York: Pantheon.

Chomsky, N. (1970). *At war with Asia.* New York: Pantheon.

Chomsky, N. (1971, December 30). The case against B. F. Skinner. [Review of the book *Beyond freedom and dignity*]. *New York Review of Books, 17*(11), 322.

Chomsky, N. (1971). *Problems of knowledge and freedom: The Russell Lectures.* New York: Pantheon.

Chomsky, N. (1972). *Language and mind.* New York: Pantheon.

Chomsky, N. (1972). *Studies on semantics in generative grammar.* The Hague, Netherlands: Mouton.

Chomsky, N. (1973). *For reasons of state.* New York: Pantheon.

Chomsky, N. (1975). *Logical structure of linguistic theory.* New York: Plenum.

Chomsky, N. (1980). *Rules and representations.* New York: Columbia University Press.

Chomsky, N. (1980). *The debate between Chomsky and Piaget.* Cambridge, MA: Harvard University Press.

Chomsky, N. (1981). *Lectures on government and binding: The Písa lectures.* Dordrecht, Netherlands: Foris. (Corrected edition, 1982)

Chomsky, N. (1982). *The generative enterprise.* Dordrecht, Netherlands: Foris.

Chomsky, N. (1983). *The fateful triangle: The United States, Israel and the Palestinians.* Boston: South End Press.

Chomsky, N. (1984). *Modular approaches to the study of the mind.* Distinguished Graduate Research Lecture Series I, 1980. Berkeley: California State University Press.

Chomsky, N. (1986). *Barriers.* Cambridge: MIT Press.

Chomsky, N. (1986). *Knowledge of language: Its nature, origin, and use.* New York: Praeger.

Chomsky, N. (1987). *Generative grammar: Its basis, development and prospects.* Kyoto, Japan: Kyoto University of Foreign Studies.

Chomsky, N. (1993). *Year 501: The conquest continues.* Boston: South End Press.

Chomsky, N. (1995). *The minimalist program.* Cambridge: MIT Press.

Chrisler, J. C. (2004). *From menarche to menopause: The female body in feminist therapy.* Binghamton, NY: Haworth Press.

Christ, S. E., White, D. A., Mandernach, T. B., & Keys, B. A. (2001). Inhibitory control across the life-span. *Developmental Neuropsychology, 20*(3), 653–669.

Christakis, N. A., & Iwashyna, T. J. (2003). The health impact of health care on families: A matched cohort study of hospice use by decedents and mortality outcomes in surviving, widowed spouses. *Social Science and Medicine, 57,* 465–475.

Christensen, K. (Ed.). (2000). *Deaf plus: A multicultural perspective.* San Diego, CA: DawnSignPress.

Christian, B. (2003). Growing up with chronic illness: Psychosocial adjustment of children and adolescents with cystic fibrosis. *Annual Review of Nursing Research, 21,* 151–172.

Christopher, F. S., & Sprecher, S. (2000). Sexuality in marriage, dating, and other relationships: A decade review. *Journal of Family and Marriage, 62,* 999–1017.

Christophersen, E. R., & Mortweet, S. L. (2003). *Parenting that works: Building skills that last a lifetime.* Washington, DC: American Psychological Association.

Christophersen, E. R., Walter, M., & Reichman, E. (1997). Toilet training. In *Little people: Guidelines for common sense child rearing* (4th ed., pp. 107–113). Shawnee Mission: Overland Press.

Chronic Fatigue Syndrome Project, http://condor.depaul.edu/~ljason/cfs/

Chronicle of Higher Education, http:///www.chronicle.com

Chudler, E. H. (2004). *Brain facts and figures.* Retrieved from http://faculty.washington.edu/chudler/facts.html

Churchill, J. D., Galvez, R., Colcombe, S., Swain, R. A., Kramer, A. F., & Greenough, W. T. (2002). Exercise, experience and the aging brain. *Neurobiology of Aging, 23,* 941–955.

Cialdini, R., Brown, S., Lewis, B., Luce, C., & Neuberg, S. (1997). Reinterpreting the empathy-altruism relationship: When one into one equals oneness. *Journal of Personality and Social Psychology, 73,* 481–494.

Ciardiello, A. (2003). *Question types: Level 2—Convergent thinking.* Retrieved from http://www.sasaustin.org/library/ConvergentThinkingQuestions.htm

Cicirelli, V. G. (2002). *Older adults' views on death.* New York: Springer. (Chapter 5: Views and expectations about the dying process)

Cincinnati Children's Hospital Medical Center. (n.d.). *Conditions and diagnoses: Obstructive sleep apnea.* Retrieved from http://www.cincinnatichildrens.org/health/info/chest/diagnose/obstruct_sleep_apnea.htm

Circumcision Information and Resource Pages, http://www.cirp.org/

Clapp, J. D., & McDonnell, A. L. (2000). The relationship of alcohol promotion and peer drinking norms to alcohol problems reported by college students. *Journal of College Student Development, 41*(1), 19–26.

Clapp, J. F. (2002). *Exercising through your pregnancy.* Omaha, NE: Addicus Books.

Clark University. (2003). *The Sigmund Freud and Carl Jung lectures at Clark University.* Retrieved from http://www.clarku.edu/offices/library/archives/Freud&Jung.htm

Clark, D. A. (2004). *Cognitive-behavioral therapy for OCD.* New York: Guilford.

Clark, D. M. (1986). A cognitive approach to panic. *Behaviour Research and Therapy, 24,* 461–470.

Clark, G. M., Tong, Y. C., & Patrick, J. F. (Eds.). (1990). *Cochlear prostheses.* Edinburgh, UK: Churchill Livingstone.

Clark, J. E., & Phillips, S. J. (1987). The step cycle organization of infant walkers. *Journal of Motor Behavior, 19,* 421–433.

Clark, J. E., Phillips, S. J., & Petersen, R. (1989). Developmental stability in jumping. *Developmental Psychology, 25,* 929–935.

Clark, J. E., Truly, T. L., & Phillips, S. J. (1990). A dynamical systems approach to understanding the development of lower limb coordination in locomotion. In H. Bloch & B. Bertenthal (Eds.), *Sensory-motor organizations and development in infancy and early childhood* (pp. 363–378). Amsterdam: Kluwer.

Clark, R. F. (2002). *The war on poverty: History, selected programs and ongoing impact.* Lanham: University Press of America.

Clark, V. P., Courchesne, E., & Grafe, M. (1992). *In vivo* myeloarchitectonic analysis of human striate and extrastriate cortex using magnetic resonance imaging. *Cerebral Cortex, 2,* 417–424.

Clark, V. P., Fan, S., & Hillyard, S. A. (1995). Identification of early visual evoked potential generators by retinotopic and topographic analyses. *Human Brain Mapping, 2,* 170–187.

Clark, V. P., & Hillyard, S. A. (1996). Spatial selective attention affects early extrastriate but not striate components of the visual evoked potential. *Journal of Cognitive Neuroscience, 8*(5), 387–402.

Clark, V. P., Keil, K., Maisog, J. M., Courtney, S. M., Ungerleider, L. G., & Haxby, J. V. (1996). Functional magnetic resonance imaging of human visual cortex during face matching: A comparison with positron emission tomography. *NeuroImage, 4*(1), 1–15.

Clark, V. P., Lai, S., & Deckel, A. W. (2002). Altered functional MRI responses in Huntington's disease. *Neuroreport, 13*(5), 703–706.

Clausen, J. M., Landsverk, J., Ganger, W., Chadwick, D., & Litrownik, A. (1998). Mental health problems of children in foster care. *Journal of Child & Family Studies, 7,* 283–296.

Clayton, V. (1982). Wisdom and intelligence: The nature and function of knowledge in the later years. *International Journal of Aging and Human Development, 15*(4), 315–321.

Clearinghouse on Abuse and Neglect of the Elderly (CANE), http://db.rdms.udel.edu:8080/CANE

Clendinen, D., & Nagourney, A. (1999). *Out for good: The struggle to build a gay rights movement in America.* New York: Simon & Schuster.

The Cleveland Clinic. (2004). *Stroke.* Retrieved from http://www.clevelandclinic.org/health/health-info/docs/2100/2179.asp?index=9074

Cleveland Clinic, Neuroscience Center, http://www.clevelandclinic.org

Cleverly, J., & Phillips, D. C. (1986). *Visions of childhood: Influential models from Locke to Spock.* New York: Teachers College Press.

Clifford, E. (1999). Neural plasticity: Merzenich, Taub, and Greenough [Review]. *The Harvard Brain, 6*(1), 16–20. Retrieved from http://hcs.harvard.edu/~husn/BRAIN/v016/p16–20-Neuronalplasticity.pdf

Clifton, C., & Duffy, S. (2001). Sentence and text comprehension: Roles of linguistic structure. *Annual Review of Psychology, 52,* 167–196.

Clinton, W. J. (2000, November 20). Statement on signing the Older Americans Act Amendments of 2000. *Weekly Compilation of Presidential Documents, 36*(46), 2864–2866.

Clipper, S. E. (1998). *Huntington's disease: Hope through research.* Bethesda, MD: Office of Scientific and Health Reports, National Institute of Neurological Disorders and Stroke, National Institutes of Health.

Coakley, J. (2004). *Sport in society: Issues and controversies.* New York: McGraw-Hill.

Cochlear, Inc., http://www.cochlear.com

Cockerham, W. C. (1997). *This aging society.* Upper Saddle River, NJ: Prentice-Hall.

Cocoran, J., Franklin, C., & Bennet, P. (2003). Ecological factors associated with adolescent pregnancy and parenting. *Social Work Research, 24*(1), 29–39.

Coen, E. (1999). *The art of genes.* Oxford, UK: Oxford University Press.

Cogill, B. (2003). *Anthropometric indicators measurement guide* (Rev. ed.). Washington, DC: Food and Nutrition Technical Assistance Project, Academy for Educational Development. Available from http://www.fantaproject.org/publications/anthropom.shtml

Cognitive styles. (n.d.). Retrieved from http://www.cognitivestyles.com

Cognitive styles and the Myers-Briggs type inventory (MBTI). (n.d.). Available from http://www.personalitytype.com/

Cohen, J. D., & Servanschreiber, D. (1992). Context, cortex, and dopamine: A connectionist approach to behavior and biology in schizophrenia. *Psychological Review, 99*(1), 45–77.

Cohen, L. B. (2001). *Uses and misuses of habituation: A theoretical and methodological analysis.* Retrieved from http://homepage.psy.utexas.edu/homepage/Group/CohenLab/pubs/Uses_and_Misuses_of_Habit.pdf

Cohen, L. G., & Spenciner, L. J. (2003). *Assessment of children and youth with special needs.* Boston: Allyn & Bacon.

Cohen, L. M., & Kim, Y. (1999). Piaget's equilibration theory and the young gifted child: A balancing act. *Roeper Review, 21*(3), 201–206.

Cohen, S., Krantz, D. S., Evans, G. W., & Stokols, D. (1981). Cardiovascular and behavioral effects of community noise. *American Scientist, 69,* 528–535.

Coie, J. D., Dodge, K. A., & Coppotelli, H. (1982). Dimensions and types of social status: A cross-age perspective. *Developmental Psychology, 18,* 557–570.

Colby, A., & Kohlberg, L. (1987). *The measurement of moral judgment.* Cambridge, UK: Cambridge University Press.

Colby, C. L., & Goldberg, M. E. (1999). Space and attention in parietal cortex. *Annual Review of Neuroscience, 22,* 319–349.

Cole, M. (1996). *Cultural psychology: A once and future discipline.* Cambridge, MA: Harvard University Press.

Cole, M., & Cole, S. (1996). *The development of children.* New York: W. H. Freeman.

Cole, M., & Engeström, Y. (1993). A cultural historical approach to distributed cognition. In G. Salomon (Ed.), *Distributed cognitions: Psychological and educational considerations* (pp. 1–46). Cambridge, UK: Cambridge University Press.

Cole, M., & Scribner, S. (1974). *Culture and thought: A psychological introduction.* New York: Wiley.

Cole, M., Cole, S. R., & Lightfoot, C. (2005). *The development of children* (5th ed.). New York: Worth. (See especially Part IV: Middle Childhood, pp. 449–573)

Cole, T. J., Bellizzi, M. C., Flegal, K. M., & Dietz, W. H. (2000). Establishing a standard definition for child overweight and obesity worldwide: International survey. *British Medical Journal, 320*(7244), 1240–1243.

Coleman, J. C. (1978). Current contradictions in adolescent theory. *Journal of Youth & Adolescence, 7*(1), 1–11.

Coleman, J. S. (1988). Social capital in the creation of human capital. *American Journal of Sociology, 94*(Suppl.), 95–120.

Coleman, L. (1987). *Suicide clusters.* Boston: Faber & Faber.

College Board, http://www.collegeboard.com/splash

College of Midwives of British Columbia. (n.d.). *Bylaws, standards, and guidelines/Standards of practice/Indications for planned place of birth.* Available from http://www.cmbc.bc.ca

Collins, G., & Clinton, T. (1992). *Baby Boomer blues.* New York: Word Publishing.

Collins, M., & Kimmel, M. M. (Eds.). (1996). *Mister Rogers' neighborhood: Children, television, and Fred Rogers.* Pittsburgh, PA: University of Pittsburgh Press.

Collins, M., Laverty, A., Roberts, S., Kyle, R., Smith, S., & Eaton Evans, J. (2004). Eating behavior and food choices in children with Down's syndrome, autistic spectrum disorder or cri du chat syndrome and comparison groups of siblings: Diet and preventive dentistry. *Journal of Learning Disabilities, 8,* 331–350.

Collins, R. (2004). *Interaction ritual chains.* Princeton, NJ: Princeton University Press.

Collins, V. L., Dickson, S. V., Simmons, D. C., & Kameenui, E. J. (n.d.). *Metacognition and its relation to reading comprehension: A synthesis of the research* (Technical Report No. 23). Eugene: National Center to Improve the Tools of Educators, University of Oregon. Retrieved from http://idea.uoregon.edu/~ncite/documents/techrep/tech23.html

Collins, W. A., Maccoby, E. E., Steinberg, L., Hetherington, E. M., & Bornstein, M. H. (2000). Contemporary research on parenting: The case for nature and nurture. *American Psychologist, 55,* 218–232.

Colt, G. H. (1991). *The enigma of suicide.* New York: Simon & Schuster.

The Columbia Electronic Encyclopedia. (2003). *Imprinting, psychology and psychiatry.* Retrieved from http://reference.allrefer.com/encyclopedia/I/imprinti.html

Commission on Classification and Terminology of the International League Against Epilepsy. (1981). Proposal for the revised clinical and electroencephalographic classification of epileptic seizures. *Epilepsia, 22,* 489–501.

Commission on Classification and Terminology of the International League Against Epilepsy. (1989). Proposal for revised classification of epilepsies and epileptic syndromes. *Epilepsia, 30*(4), 389–399.

Committee for Children. (n.d.). *Resources and information.* Retrieved from http://www.cfchildren.org/bully.html

Committee on Developmental Toxicology. (2000). *Scientific frontiers in developmental toxicology and risk assessment.* Washington, DC: National Academies Press.

Committee on Environmental Health. (1997). Noise: A hazard for the fetus and newborn. *Pediatrics, 100*(4), 724–727.

Communicable Disease Report Weekly. (2003, October 30). Sexually transmitted disease quarterly report: Genital warts and herpes simplex virus infection in the UK. *CDR Weekly, 13*(44). Retrieved from http://www.hpa.org.ul/cdr/PDF files/2003cdr4403.pdf

Compas, B. E., & Luecken, L. J. (2002). Psychological adjustment to breast cancer: Cognitive and interpersonal processes. *Current Directions in Psychological Science, 11,* 111–114.

Compton, W. M., & Guze, S. B. (1995). The neo-Kraepelinian revolution in psychiatric diagnosis. *European Archives of Psychiatry and Clinical Neuroscience, 245,* 196–201.

Comstock, G., & Paik, H. (1991). *Television and the American child.* San Diego, CA: Academic Press.

Comtois, K. (2002). A review of interventions to reduce the prevalence of parasuicide. *Psychiatric Services, 53*(9), 1138–1144.

Conflict Research Consortium, http://www.conflict.colorado.edu

Connell, R. W. (1995). *Masculinities.* Berkeley: University of California Press.

Connelly, E. R. (2000). *Child abuse and neglect: Examining the psychological consequences.* Philadelphia: Chelsea House.

Connolly, M. (2005). *Protection and support for orphans and families affected by HIV/AIDS.* New York: UNICEF.

Conrad, C. F., & Trani, E. P. (1990). Challenges met, challenges facing the modern university and its faculty. In C. Wingfield (Ed.), *Faculty responsibility in contemporary society* (pp. 1–25). Washington, DC: American Association of State Colleges and Universities.

Consortium for Research on Emotional Intelligence in Organizations, http://www.EQconsortium.org

The Construction of Reality in the Child. (n.d.). Retrieved from http://www.marxists.org/reference/subject/philosophy/works/fr/piaget2.htm

Consumer Consortium on Assisted Living, http://www.ccal.org

Conte, J. R. (Ed.). (2002). *Critical issues in child sexual abuse: Historical, legal, and psychological perspectives.* Thousand Oaks, CA: Sage.

Contento, I., Balch, G. I., Bronner, Y. L., Lytle, L. A., Maloney, S. K., Olson, C. M., et al. (1995). The effectiveness of nutrition education and implications for nutrition education policy, programs and research: A review of the research. *Journal of Nutrition Education, 27,* 277–418.

Convergent thinking. (2001). *Gale encyclopedia of psychology* (2nd ed.). Detroit, MI: Gale Group. Retrieved from http://www.findarticles.com/cf_dls/g2699/0004/2699000427/p1/article.jhtml

Conway, F., & Stricker, G. (2003). An integrative assessment model as a means of intervention with the grandparent caregiver. In B. Hayslip, Jr., & J. H. Patrick (Eds.), *Working with custodial grandparents* (pp. 45–57). New York: Springer-Verlag.

Conway, M. A. (Ed.). (1997). *Recovered memories and false memories.* London: Oxford University Press.

Conway, S. (1998). Transition from pediatric to adult-orientated care for adolescents with cystic fibrosis. *Disability and Rehabilitation, 20,* 209–216.

Coogan, M. D. (Ed.). (2001). *The New Oxford Annotated Bible* (3rd ed.). Oxford, UK: Oxford University Press.

Coogler, O. J. (1978). *Structured mediation in divorce settlement: A handbook for marital mediators.* Lexington, MA: Lexington Books.

Cook, S. D. (Ed.). (2001). *Neurological disease and therapy series: Vol. 53. The handbook of multiple sclerosis* (3rd ed.). New York: Marcel Dekker.

Cook, V. (n.d.). *Second language acquisition topics.* Retrieved from http://homepage.ntlworld.com/vivian.c/SLA/

Cooley's Anemia Foundation, http://www.thalassemia.org

Coolidge, F. L. (2000). *Statistics: A gentle approach.* London: Sage.

Cooper, J. O., Heron, T. E., & Heward, W. L. (1987). *Applied behavior analysis.* Englewood Cliffs, NJ: Prentice-Hall.

Cooperative Learning Center at the University of Minnesota, http://www.co-operation.org/

Cooperative Parenting and Divorce, http://www.cooperativeparenting.com

Corkin, S. (1984). Lasting consequences of bilateral medial temporal lobectomy: Clinical course and experimental findings in H. M. *Seminars in Neurology, 4,* 249–259.

Corkum, V., & Moore, C. (1995). The development of joint attention. In C. Moore & P. Dunham (Eds.), *Joint attention: Its origins and role in development* (pp. 61–84). Hillsdale, NJ: Erlbaum.

Corpun. (2004). *World corporal punishment research.* Retrieved from http://www.corpun.com/

Corr, C. A. (1991–1992). A task-based approach to coping with dying. *Omega, 24,* 81–94.

Corr, C. A., Nabe, C. M., & Corr, D. M. (2003). *Death and dying: Life and living* (4th ed.). Pacific Grove, CA: Brooks/Cole.

Costa, D. L. (1998). *The evolution of retirement—An American economic history 1880–1990.* Chicago: University of Chicago Press.

Costa, P. T., & McCrae, R. R. (1988). Personality in adulthood: A six year longitudinal study of self-reports and spouse ratings on the NEO Personality Inventory. *Journal of Personality and Social Psychology, 54,* 853–863.

Costello, E. J., & Angold, A. (2000). Developmental psychopathology and public health: Past, present and future. *Development and Psychopathology, 12,* 599–618.

Costello, E. J., Compton, S. N., Keeler, G., & Angold, A. (2003). Relationships between poverty and psychopathology: A natural experiment. *Journal of the American Medical Association, 290,* 2023–2029.

Cote, J. E. (1994). *Adolescent storm and stress: An evaluation of the Mead-Freeman controversy.* Hillsdale, NJ: Erlbaum.

Cotton, K. (n.d.). *Developing empathy in children and youth.* Retrieved from http://www.nwrel.org/scpd/sirs/7/cu13.html

Council for Exceptional Children, http://www.cec.sped.org

Council for Exceptional Children. (1997). *Discover IDEA: CD 2000.* Arlington, VA: Author.

Council for Exceptional Children. (n.d.). *The new IDEA: CEC's summary of significant issues.* Retrieved from http://www.cec.sped.org/pp/IDEA_120204.pdf

Courtois, C. (1988). *Healing the incest wound.* New York: W. W. Norton.

Cowart, B. J. (1981). Development of taste perception in humans: Sensitivity and preference throughout the life span. *Psychological Bulletin, 90,* 43–73.

Cowart, B. J. (1989). Relationships between taste and smell across the adult life span. *Annals of the New York Academy of Sciences, 561,* 39–55.

Cox, M. J., Burchinal, M., Taylor, L. C., Frosch, C., Goldman, B., & Kanoy, K. (2004). The transition to parenting: Continuity and change in early parenting behavior and attitudes. In R. D. Conger, F. O. Lorenz, & K. A. S. Wickrama (Eds.), *Continuity and change in family relations: Theory, methods, and empirical findings* (pp. 201–239). Mahwah, NJ: Erlbaum.

Cox, M. J., & Harter, K. S. (2003). Parent-child relationships. In M. H. Bornstein, L. Davidson, C. L. M., Keyes, & K. A. Moore (Eds.), *Well being: Positive development across the life course.* Mahwah, NJ: Erlbaum.

Coyle, S., Moore, A. H., Rubin, D. C., Hall, W. G., & Goldberg-Arnold, J. S. (2000). Olfactory conditioning facilitates diet transition in human infants. *Developmental Psychobiology, 37,* 144–152.

Cozby, P. C. (2001). *Methods in behavioral research* (7th ed.). Palo Alto, CA: Mayfield.

Craig, G. C., & Baucum, D. (2002). *Human development.* Upper Saddle River, NJ: Prentice-Hall.

Craig, J. (1999). *Kohlberg's research and theories: 6 stages of moral development.* Chicago: University of Chicago. Available from http://www.ccp.uchicago.edu/

Craik, R. (1989). Changes in locomotion in the aging adult. In M. Woollacott & A. Shumway-Cook (Eds.), *The development of posture and gait across the lifespan* (pp. 176–201). Columbia: University of South Carolina Press.

Crain, W. C. (1999). *Theories of development.* Upper Saddle River, NJ: Prentice-Hall.

Cramer, C., Flynn, B., & LaFave, A. (1997). *Erik Erikson's 8 Stages of Psychosocial Development.* Retrieved from http://facultyweb.cortland.edu/~ANDERSMD/ERIK/welcome.html

Craske, M. G. (1999). *Anxiety disorders: Psychological approaches to theory and treatment.* Boulder, CO: Westview.

Craske, M. G. (2003). *Origins of phobias and anxiety disorders: Why more women than men?* Amsterdam: Elsevier.

Craske, M. G., Rachman, S., & Tallman, K. (1986). Mobility, cognitions and panic. *Journal of Psychopathology and Behavioral Assessment, 8,* 199–210.

Cratty, B. J. (1986). *Perceptual and motor development in infants and children.* Englewood Cliffs, NJ: Prentice-Hall.

Crawford, J. (1999). *Bilingual education: History, politics, theory and practice.* Los Angeles: Bilingual Educational Services.

Crawford, L. I., & Domjan, M. (1993). Sexual approach conditioning: Omission contingency tests. *Animal Learning and Behavior, 21,* 42–50.

Crawley, J. B. (1998–1999). Is the honeymoon over for common-law marriage: A consideration of the continued viability of the common-law marriage doctrine. *Cumberland Law Review, 29,* 399, 401.

Creasey, R., Resnick, R., & Iams, J. (2004). *Maternal-fetal medicine.* Philadelphia: WB Saunders.

Crews, F. (Ed.). (1998). *Unauthorized Freud: Doubters confront a legend.* New York: Penguin.

Crick, N. R., & Grotpeter, J. K. (1995). Relational aggression, gender, and social-psychological adjustment. *Child Development, 66,* 710–722.

Crimes Against Children Research Center, http://www.unh.edu/ccrc/index.html

Crisp, A. H. (1980). *Anorexia nervosa: Let me be.* London: Academic Press.

Crispi, E. L., & Fisher, C. B. (1994). Development in adulthood. In J. L. Ronch & W. Van Ornum (Eds.), *Counseling sourcebook: A practical reference on contemporary issues* (pp. 343–357). New York: Crossroad.

Crockett, L. J., Raffaelli, M., & Moilanen, K. L. (2003). Adolescent sexuality: Behavior and meaning. In M. D. Berzonsky & G. R. Adams (Eds.), *Blackwell handbook of adolescence.* (pp. 371–392). Malden, MA: Blackwell.

Cronbach, L. J, & Snow, R. E. (1977). *Aptitudes and instructional methods: A handbook for research on interactions.* New York: Irvington.

Cronbach, L. J. (1951). Coefficient alpha and the internal structure of tests. *Psychometrika, 6,* 297–334.

Cronbach, L. J. (1971). Test validation. In R. L. Thorndike (Ed.), *Educational measurement* (2nd ed., pp. 443–506). Washington, DC: American Council on Education.

Cronbach, L. J. (2002). *Remaking the concept of aptitude: Extending the legacy of Richard E. Snow.* Mahwah, NJ: Erlbaum.

Cropley, A. J. (1999). Creativity and cognition: Producing effective novelty. *Roeper Review, 21,* 253–260.

Cross, W. E. (1971). Negro-to-Black conversion experience. *Black World, 20,* 13–27.

Crown, W. H. (Ed.). (1996). *Handbook on employment and the elderly.* Westport, CT: Greenwood Press.

Crozier, W. R. (Ed.). (2001). *Shyness: Development, consolidation, and change.* London: Routledge.

Culham, J. (n.d.). *fMRI for dummies.* Retrieved from http://defiant.ssc.uwo.ca/Jody_web/fmri4dummies.htm

Culligan, P. J., & Heit, M. (2000). Urinary incontinence in women: Evaluation and management. *American Family Physician, 62,* 2433–2444, 2447, 2452.

Cummings, E. M., & Davies, P. (1994). *Children and marital conflict: The impact of family dispute and resolution.* New York: Guilford.

Cummings, E. M., Davies, P. T., & Campbell, S. B. (2000). New directions in the study of parenting and child development. In *Developmental psychopathology and family process: Theory, research, and clinical implications* (pp. 200–250). New York: Guilford.

Cummings, S. M. (2002). Predictors of psychological well-being among assisted living residents. *Health and Social Work, 27*(4), 293–302.

Cummings, S. R., & Melton, L. J. (2002). Epidemiology and outcomes of osteoporotic fractures. *Lancet, 359,* 1761–1767.

Cummins, J. (1984). *Bilingualism and special education: Issues in assessment and pedagogy.* San Diego, CA: College Hill Press.

Cunningham, F. G. (2001). Isoimmunization. In G. Cunningham, N. F. Gant, K. J. Leveno, L. C. Gilstrap, J. C. Hauth, & K. D. Wenstrom (Eds.), *Williams obstetrics* (pp. 1057–1063). New York: McGraw-Hill.

Curlee, R., & Siegel, G. (1997). *Nature and treatment of stuttering: New directions* (2nd ed). Needham Heights, MA: Allyn & Bacon.

Currie, J. (2000, May). *What we know about early childhood interventions* (2000 Joint Center for Poverty Research, Policy Brief, Vol. 2, No. 10). Retrieved from http://www.jcpr.org/policybriefs/v012_num10.html

Curry, T. E., Jr., & Osteen, K. G. (2003). The matrix metalloproteinase system: Changes, regulation, and impact throughout the ovarian and uterine reproductive cycle. *Endocrinology Review, 24*(4), 428–465.

Curtin, B. J. (1985). *The myopias: Basic science and clinical management.* Philadelphia: Harper & Row.

Curtis, P. A., Dale, G. J., & Kendall, J. C. (1999). *The foster care crisis: Translating research into policy and practice.* Lincoln: University of Nebraska Press.

Cutbertson, F. M. (1997). Depression and gender: An international review. *American Psychologist, 52,* 25–31.

Cutler, B. L., & Penrod, S. D. (1995). *Mistaken identification: The eyewitness, psychology, and the law.* Cambridge, UK: Cambridge University Press.

Cystic Fibrosis Foundation. (n.d.). *About cystic fibrosis: What is CF?* Retrieved from http://www.cff.org/about_cf/what_is_cf.cfm

Czeisler, C. A., & Wright, K. P., Jr. (1999). Influence of light on circadian rhythmicity in humans. In F. W. Turek & P. C. Zee (Eds.), *Regulation of sleep and circadian rhythms* (pp. 149–180). New York: Marcel Dekker.

Dabbs, J. (2000). *Heroes, rogues, and lovers.* New York: McGraw-Hill.

Dagenbach, D., & Carr, T. H. (1994). *Inhibitory processes in attention, memory, and language.* San Diego, CA: Academic Press.

Dalai Lama, http://www.dalailama.com

Dalton, P. (2002). Olfaction. In H. Pashler & S. Yantis (Eds.), *Steven's handbook of experimental psychology. Vol. 1. Sensation and perception* (3rd ed., pp. 691–746). New York: Wiley.

D'Amato, R. J., Loughnan, M. S., Flynn, E., & Folkman, J. (1994). Thalidomide is an inhibitor of angiogenesis.

Proceedings of the National Academy of Sciences of the USA, 91, 4082–4085.

Damon, W. (1999). The moral development of children. *Scientific American, 281*(2), 72–78.

Daneman, M., & Carpenter, P. A. (1980). Individual differences in working memory and reading. *Journal of Verbal Learning and Verbal Behavior, 19,* 450–466.

Danielson, H., & Bushaw, K. (n.d.). *Talking to children about death.* Retrieved from http://www.ext.nodak.edu/extpubs/yf/famsci/fs441w.htm

Darling, N. (1999). *Parenting style and its correlates.* Retrieved from http://www.athealth.com/Practitioner/ceduc/parentingstyles.html

Darling, N. (1999, March). *Parenting styles and its correlates.* Champaign: ERIC Clearinghouse on Elementary and Early Childhood Education, University of Illinois at Urbana-Champaign. Retrieved from http://www.kidneeds.com/diagnostic_categories/articles/parentcorre01.htm

Darling, N., & Steinberg, L. (1993). Parenting style as context: An integrative model. *Psychological Bulletin, 113*(3), 487–496.

Das, J. P., Naglieri, J. A., & Kirby, J. R. (1994). *Assessment of cognitive processes: The PASS theory of intelligence.* Needham Heights: MA: Allyn & Bacon.

Data Digest, http://www.data-digest.com

D'Auria, J., Christian, B., & Richardson, L. (1997). Through the looking glass: Children's perceptions of growing up with cystic fibrosis. *Canadian Journal of Nursing Research, 29,* 99–112.

Dave's ESL Cafe, http://www.eslcafe.com

Davey, A., Janke, M., & Savla, J. (2004). Antecedents of intergenerational support: Families in context and families as context. In M. Silverstein, R. Giarrusso, & V. L. Bengston (Eds.), *Annual Review of Gerontology and Geriatrics* (Vol. 24). New York: Springer-Verlag.

Davey, G. C. L. (1994). Pathological worrying as exacerbated problem-solving. In G. Davey & F. Tallis (Eds.), *Worrying: Perspectives on theory, assessment, and treatment* (pp. 35–59). Chichester, UK: Wiley.

David and Lucile Packard Foundation. (1994, Spring). Children and divorce. *The Future of Children, 4*(1).

David and Lucile Packard Foundation. (1999). When school is out. *The future of children* (Vol. 9). Los Altos, CA: Author. Retrieved from http://www.futureofchildren.org/usr_doc/v019n02.pdf

Davidson, J. E., & Sternberg, R. J. (Eds.). (2003). *The psychology of problem solving.* Cambridge, UK: Cambridge University Press.

Davidson, R., & Hugdahl, K. (Eds.). (1998). *Brain asymmetry.* Cambridge: MIT Press.

Davies, G., Welham, J., Chant, D., Torrey, E., & McGrath, J. (2003). A systematic review and meta-analysis of Northern Hemisphere season of birth studies in schizophrenia. *Schizophrenia Bulletin, 29,* 587–593.

Davis, C. (Ed.). (2002). *Programs and plans of the National Center for Education Statistics* (2002 ed.). Washington, DC: U.S. Department of Education, National Center for Education Statistics.

Davis, G. A., & Rimm, S. B. (2004). *Education of the gifted and talented students* (5th ed.). Boston: Pearson.

Davis, R. C., & Taylor, B. G. (1999). Does batterer treatment reduce violence? A synthesis of the literature. In L. Feder (Ed.), *Women and domestic violence: An interdisciplinary approach* (pp. 69–93). New York: Haworth Press.

Dawis, R. V. (1992). The individual differences tradition in counseling psychology. *Journal of Counseling, 39,* 7–19.

Dawkins, R. (1986). *The blind watchmaker.* New York: W. W. Norton.

Deater-Deckard, K. D., Dodge, K. A., Bates, J. E., & Pettit, G. S. (1996). Physical discipline among African American and European American mothers: Links to children's externalizing behaviors. *Developmental Psychology, 32,* 1065–1072.

Death with Dignity National Center, http://www.deathwithdignity.org/

DeBord, K. (2000). *Childhood anger and aggression.* Retrieved from http://www.ces.ncsu.edu/depts/fcs/smp9/anger.html

DeCasper, A. J., & Fifer, W. P. (1980). Of human bonding: Newborns prefer their mothers' voices. *Science, 208,* 1174–1176.

DeCasper, A. J., & Spence, M. J. (1986). Prenatal maternal speech influences newborns' perceptions of speech sounds. *Infant Behavior and Development, 9,* 133–150.

Deci, E., Koestner, R., & Ryan, R. (1999). A meta-analytic review of experiments examining the effects of extrinsic rewards on intrinsic motivation. *Psychological Bulletin, 125,* 627–668.

Deci, E., & Ryan, R. (1985). *Intrinsic motivation and self-determination in human behavior.* New York: Plenum.

Deci, E., & Ryan, R. (2004). *Self-determination theory: An approach to human motivation and personality.* Retrieved from http://www.psych.rochester.edu/SDT/

Deductive and inductive arguments. (n.d.). Retrieved from http://webpages.shepherd.edu/maustin/rhetoric/deductiv.htm

De Houwer, J., Thomas, S., & Baeyens, F. (2001). Association learning of likes and dislikes: A review of 25 years of research on human evaluative conditioning. *Psychological Bulletin, 127,* 853–869.

DeJong, G. (1979). Independent living: From social movement to analytic paradigm. *Archives of Physical Medicine and Rehabilitation, 60,* 435–466.

DeJong, W. (1994). *Building the peace: The Resolving Conflict Creatively Program.* Washington, DC: U.S. Department of Justice, National Institute of Justice.

Delcomyn, F. (1996). *Foundations of neurobiology.* New York: W. H. Freeman.

Delcourt, M. A. B., Loyd, B. H., Cornell, D. G., & Goldberg, M. D. (1994). *Evaluation of the effects of programming arrangements on student learning outcomes* (Research Monograph 94108). Storrs: The National Research Center on the Gifted and Talented, University of Connecticut.

DeLeo, D., Scocco, P., Marietta, P., Schmidtke, A., Bille-Brahe, U., Kerkhof, A. J. F. M., et al. (1999). Physical illness and parasuicide: Evidence from the European parasuicide study interview schedule (EPSIS/WHO-EURO). *International Journal of Psychiatry in Medicine, 29*(2), 149–163.

Dellinger, A. M., Bolen, J., & Sacks, J. J. (1999). A comparison of driver- and passenger-based estimates of alcohol-impaired driving. *American Journal of Preventive Medicine, 16*(4), 283–288.

Delmas, P. D. (2002). Treatment of postmenopausal osteoporosis. *Lancet, 359,* 2018–2026.

Delta Society, http://deltasociety.org/

Delwiche, J. F. (1996). Are there "basic" tastes? *Trends in Food Science and Technology, 7,* 411–415.

Dementia.com, http://www.dementia.com/

Dempster, R. N. (1992). The rise and fall of the inhibitory mechanism: Toward a unified theory of cognitive development and aging. *Developmental Review, 12,* 45–75.

Denenberg, V. H. (Ed.). (1978). *The development of behavior.* Stamford, CT: Sinauer.

Denham, S. A. (1998). *Emotional development in young children.* New York: Guilford.

Denzin, N. K., & Lincoln, Y. S. (Eds.). (2000). *Handbook of qualitative research.* Thousand Oaks, CA: Sage.

Department of Economic and Social Affairs Population Division, http://www.unpopulation.org

Department of Health. (1993). *Changing childbirth: Parts I and II.* London: HMSO Publications.

Department of Health and Human Services, Administration on Aging. (2004). *Older Americans Act.* Available from http://www.aoa.dhhs.gov/about/over/over_mission.asp

Department of Health and Human Services. National Heart, Lung, and Blood Institute, http://www.nhlbi.nih.gov/

Department of Veteran Affairs, National Center for PTSD. (n.d.). *Facts about PTSD.* Retrieved from http://www.ncptsd.org/facts/index.html

The descent of man, and selection in relation to sex. (n.d.). Retrieved from http://www.zoo.uib.no/classics/descent.html

Desnick, R. J., & Kaback, M. M. (Eds.). (2001). *Tay-Sachs disease.* San Diego, CA: Academic Press.

DeSpelder, L. A., & Strickland, A. L. (2002). *The last dance: Encountering death and dying* (6th ed.). Boston: McGraw-Hill.

Detrick, S. (1999). *A commentary on the United Nations Convention on the Rights of the Child.* The Hague, Netherlands: Kluwer Law International.

Deutsch, M. (1973). *The resolution of conflict: Constructive and destructive processes.* New Haven, CT: Yale University Press.

Developmental psychology links, http://www.socialpsychology.org/develop.htm

de Villiers, J. G., & Pyers, J. E. (2003). Complements to cognition: A longitudinal study of the relationship between complex syntax and false-belief-understanding. *Cognitive Development, 17,* 1037–1060.

Devine, P. G., Hamilton, D. L., & Ostrom, T. M. (1994). *Social cognition: Impact on social psychology.* San Diego, CA: Academic Press.

Dewsbury, D. (Ed.). (2000). *Unification through division: Histories of the divisions of the American Psychological Association* (Vols. 1–5). Washington, DC: American Psychological Association.

Dewy, J. (1916). *Democracy and education: An introduction to the philosophy of education.* New York: Macmillan.

Dexter, P. (2003). *Countering the counterfeit: A case for traditional marriage.* Available from http://www.pointofview.net

DharmaNet International, http://www.dharmanet.org

Diamond, J. (1993). *The third chimpanzee.* New York: HarperCollins.

Diamond, M. C., Krech, D., & Rosenzweig, R. (1964). The effects of an enriched environment on the histology of the rat cerebral cortex. *Journal of Comparative Neurology, 123,* 111–120.

Diana Baumrind, http://ihd.berkeley.edu/baumrind.htm

Diaz, R. M., & Berk, L. E. (Eds.). (1992). *Private speech: From social interaction to self-regulation.* Hillsdale, NJ: Erlbaum.

Diaz-Rico, L. T., & Weed, K. Z. (2002). *The crosscultural, language and academic development handbook: A complete K-12 reference guide.* Boston: Allyn & Bacon.

Dickerson, B. (1995). *African American single mothers: Understanding their lives and families.* Sage Series on Race and Ethnic Relations, Vol. 10. Thousand Oaks, CA: Sage.

DiClemente, R. J., & Peterson, J. L. (Eds.). (1994). *Preventing AIDS: Theories and methods of behavioral interventions.* New York: Plenum.

DiFranza, J. R., Aligne, C. A., & Weitzman, M. (2004). Prenatal and postnatal environmental tobacco smoke exposure and children's health. *Pediatrics, 113*(4, Suppl), 1007–1115.

Digman, J. M. (1990). Personality structure: Emergence of the five-factor model. *Annual Review of Psychology, 41,* 417–440.

Diller, L. H. (1998). *Running on Ritalin: A physician reflects on children, society, and performance in a pill.* New York: Bantam.

Dinwiddie, S. (n.d.). *Effective parenting styles: Why yesterday's models won't work today.* Retrieved from http://www.kidsource.com/better.world.press/parenting.html

DiPietro, J. A., Bornstein, M. H., & Costigan, K. A. (2002). What does fetal movement predict about behavior during the first two years of life? *Developmental Psychobiology, 40,* 358–371.

Distance-Educator.com, http://www.distance-educator.com/

Ditto, P. H. (2005). Self-determination, substituted judgment and the psychology of end-of-life medical decision making. In J. Werth & D. Blevins (Eds.), *Attending to psychosocial issues at the end of life: A comprehensive guidebook.* Washington, DC: American Psychological Association Press.

Division for Early Childhood. (1999, October). *Concept paper on the identification of and intervention with challenging behavior*. Missoula, MT: Author. Retrieved from http://www.dec-sped.org/pdf/positionpapers/Concept%20Challenging%20Behavior.pdf

Divorce Headquarters, http://www.divorcehq.com

Dixon, J. W. (2001). *Battered woman syndrome*. Retrieved from http://www.psychologyandlaw.com/battered.htm

Dixon, R. A., Lerner, R. M., & Hultsch, D. F. (1991). The concept of development in the study of individual and social change. In P. van Geert & L. P. Mos (Eds.), *Annals of theoretical psychology* (Vol. 7, pp. 279–323). New York: Plenum.

Dodge, K. A., & Coie, J. D. (1987). Social information-processing factors in reactive and proactive aggression in children's peer groups. *Journal of Personality and Social Psychology, 53*, 389–409.

Dodge, K. A., & Pettit, G. S. (2003). A biopsychosocial model of the development of chronic conduct problems in adolescence. *Developmental Psychology, 39*, 349–371.

Doggrell, S. A. (2003). Recurrent hope for the treatment of preterm delivery. *Expert Opinions in Pharmacotherapy, 4*(12), 2363–2366.

Doh, H. S., & Falbo, T. (1999). Social competence, maternal attentiveness, and overprotectiveness: Only children. *International Journal of Behavioral Development, 23*(1), 149–162.

Doherty, J., & Bailey, R. P. (2003). *Supporting physical development in the early years*. Buckingham, UK: Open University Press.

Dohrman, K. R. (2003). *Outcomes for students in a Montessori Program*. Rochester, NY: Association Montessori Internationale/USA.

Doka, K. J. (1996). *Living with grief after sudden loss*. Washington, DC: Hospice Foundation of America. Hospice Net. (n.d.). *Talking to children about death*. Available from http://www.hospicenet.org

Donaldson, M. (1987). The origins of inference. In J. S. Bruner & H. Haste (Eds.), *Making sense: The child's construction of the world* (pp. 97–107). New York: Methuen.

Donkin, R. (2001). *Blood, sweat and tears: The evolution of work*. New York: Texere.

Dorne, C. K. (2002). *An introduction to child maltreatment in the United States: History, public policy and research* (3rd ed.). New York: Criminal Justice Press.

Doty, R. L. (2001). Olfaction. *Annual Review of Psychology, 52*, 423–452.

Dovidio, J. F., & Esses, V. M. (2001). Immigrants and immigration: Advancing the psychological perspective. *Journal of Social Issues, 57*, 375–387.

Dowd, N. E. (1997). *In defense of single-parent families*. New York: University Press.

Down syndrome prevalence at birth: United States, 1983–1990. (1994). *Morbidity and Mortality Weekly Report, 43*, 617–622.

Drecktrah, M. E., & Marchel, M. A. (2004, March 26). *Functional assessment: Analyzing child behavior*. Retrieved from http://www.earlychildhood.com/Articles/index.cfm?FuseAction=Article&A=255

Drevets, W. C. (1998). Functional neuroimaging studies of depression: The anatomy of melancholia. *Annual Review of Medicine, 49*, 341.

Drotar, D. (1991). The family context of non-organic failure to thrive. *American Journal of Orthopsychiatry, 6*(1), 23–34.

Drug Policy Alliance. (n.d.). *Methadone maintenance treatment research brief*. Retrieved from http://www.lindesmith.org/library/research/methadone.cfm

Dubbert, P. M. (2002). Physical activity and exercise: Recent advances and current challenges. *Journal of Consulting and Clinical Psychology, 70*(3), 526–536.

Dubois, P. H. (1970). *A history of psychological testing*. Boston: Allyn & Bacon.

Dudden, F. E. (1983). *Serving women: Household service in nineteenth-century America*. Middletown, CT: Wesleyan University Press.

Dulay, M. F., & Murphy, C. (2002). Olfactory acuity and cognitive function converge in older adulthood: Support for the common cause hypothesis. *Psychology and Aging, 17*(3), 392–404.

Duncan, G. J., & Brooks-Gunn, J. (1997). Income effects across the life span: Integration and interpretation. In G. J. Duncan & J. Brooks-Gunn (Eds.), *Consequences of growing up poor* (pp. 596–610). New York: Russell Sage Foundation.

Duncan, G. J., & Brooks-Gunn, J. (2000). Family poverty, welfare reform, and child development. *Child Development, 71*, 188–196.

Duncan, G. J., & Magnuson, K. A. (2003). Off with Hollingshead: Socioeconomic resources, parenting and child development. In M. H. Bornstein & R. H. Bradley (Eds.), *Socioeconomic status, parenting, and child development* (pp. 83–106). Mahwah, NJ: Erlbaum.

Duncan, J., Burgess, P., & Emslie, H. (1995). Fluid intelligence after frontal lobe lesions. *Neuropsychologia, 33*, 261–268.

Duncan, O. D. (1984). *Notes on social measurement*. New York: Russell Sage Foundation.

Dunkle, R., Roberts, B., & Haug, M. (2001). *The oldest old in everyday life: Self perception, coping with change and stress*. New York: Springer-Verlag.

Dunlap, G., Newton, J. S., Fox, L., Benito, N., & Vaughn, B. (2001). Family involvement in functional assessment and positive behavior support. *Focus on Autism and Other Developmental Disabilities, 16*, 215–221.

Dunn, D. S. (1999). *The practical researcher*. Boston: McGraw-Hill.

Dunn, J. (1988). *The beginnings of social understanding*. Cambridge, MA: Harvard University Press.

Dunn, J. (2002). *Sibling relationships*. In P. K. Smith & C. H. Hart (Eds.), *Blackwell handbook of childhood social development* (pp. 223–237). Malden, MA: Blackwell.

Dunn, J., Deater-Deckard, K., Pickering, K., O'Conner, T., Golding, J., & ALSPAC Study Team. (1998). Children's adjustment and prosocial behavior in step-single-parent, and non-stepfamily settings: Findings from a community study. *Journal of Child Psychology and Psychiatry, 39,* 1083–1095.

DuPaul, G. J., & Hoff, K. E. (1998). Attention/concentration problems. In S. Watson & F. M. Greham (Eds.), *Handbook of child behavior therapy* (pp. 99–126). New York: Plenum.

Dupont, J.-M., & Edwards, P. (n.d.). *Transition to adulthood.* Retrieved from http://www.growinghealthykids.com/english/transitions/adulthood/home/index.html

Dupont, R. L. (1984). *Getting tough on gateway drugs: A guide for the family.* Washington, DC: American Psychiatric Press.

Durham, A. (2003). *Young men surviving child sexual abuse: Research stories and lessons for therapeutic practice.* Indianapolis, IN: Wiley.

Durkin, D. (1989). *Teaching them to read.* (5th ed.). Boston: Allyn & Bacon.

Durkin, K. (1995). *Developmental social psychology: From infancy to old age.* Oxford, UK: Blackwell.

Durso, B. (2001). *How do I get my child to let me leave him?* Retrieved from http://www.keepkidshealthy.com/development/separation_anxiety.html

Dusek, J. B. (1975). Do teachers bias children learning? *Review of Educational Research, 45*(4), 661–684.

Dutton, M. A. (1996, September). *Critique of the "battered woman syndrome" model.* Retrieved from http://www.vaw.umn.edu/documents/vawnet/bws/bws.html

Duyme, M., Dumaret, A. C., & Tomkiewicz, S. (1999). How can we boost IQs of "dull children"?: A late adoption study. *Proceedings of the National Academy of Sciences, 96,* 8790–8794.

Dweck, C. S. (1999). *Self-theories: Their role in motivation, personality, and development.* Philadelphia: Psychology Press/Taylor & Francis.

Dweck, C. S., & Leggett, E. L. (1988). A social-cognitive approach to motivation and personality. *Psychological Review, 95*(2), 256–273.

Dworkin, G. (1998). *Euthanasia and physician-assisted suicide.* Cambridge, UK: Cambridge University Press.

Dworkin, J. B., & Larson, R. (2001). Age trends in the experience of family discord in single-mother families across adolescence. *Journal of Adolescence, 24,* 529–534.

Dyer, C. B., Pavlik, V. N., Murphy, K. P., & Hyman, D. J. (2000). The high prevalence of depression and dementia in elder abuse or neglect. *Journal of the American Geriatrics Society, 48*(2), 205–208.

DyingWell.org. (n.d.). *Defining wellness through the end of life: Resources for people facing life-limiting illness, their families, and their professional caregivers.* Available from http://www.dyingwell.com

Dykens, E. M., Hodapp, R. M., & Finucane, B. M. (2000). *Genetics and mental retardation syndromes. A new look at behaviour and interventions.* Baltimore: Paul H. Brookes.

Eagly, A. (1995). The science and politics of comparing women and men. *American Psychologist, 50,* 145–158.

Eagly, A. H., & Chaiken, S. (1998). Attitude structure and function. In D. Gilbert & S. Fiske (Eds.), *Handbook of social psychology* (Vol. 1, 4th ed., pp. 269–322). New York: McGraw-Hill.

Eagly, A. H., & Crowley, M. (1986). Gender and helping behavior: A meta-analytic review of the social psychological literature. *Psychological Bulletin, 100,* 283–308.

Eaker, E. D., Sullivan, L. M., Kelly-Hayes, M., D'Agostino, R. B., & Benjamin, E. J. (2004). Anger and hostility predict the development of atrial fibrillation in men in the Framingham Offspring Study. *Circulation, 109,* 1267–1271.

Earleywine, M. (2002). *Understanding marijuana: A new look at the scientific evidence.* New York: Oxford University Press.

Early Childhood and Parenting Collaborative, http://ecap.crc.uiuc.edu/info/

Eating Disorders Association. (2004). *Welcome to the EDA home page.* Retrieved from http://www.edauk.com/

Eaton, W. W., Dryman, A., & Weissman, M. M. (1991). Panic and phobia. In L. N. Robins & D. A. Regier (Eds.), *Psychiatric disorders in America: The epidemiological catchment area study.* New York: Free Press.

Eaton, W. W., Thara, R., Federman, E., & Tien A. (1998). Remission and relapse in schizophrenia: The Madras Longitudinal Study. *Journal of Nervous and Mental Disease, 186,* 357–363.

Ebel, R. L. (1979). *Essentials of educational measurement* (3rd ed.). Englewood Cliffs, NJ: Prentice-Hall.

Eccles, J. S. (1994). Understanding women's educational and occupational choices: Applying the Eccles et al. model of achievement-related choices. *Psychology of Women Quarterly, 18,* 585–609.

Eccles, J. S., & Gootman, J. A. (Eds.). (2002). *Community programs to promote youth development.* Committee on Community-Level Programs for Youth. Board on Children, Youth, and Families, Commission on Behavioral and Social Sciences and Education, National Research Council and Institute of Medicine. Washington, DC: National Academies Press.

Eccles, J. S., & Templeton, J. (2002). Extracurricular and other after-school activities for youth. *Review of Research in Education, 26,* 113–180.

EchoHawk, M. (1997). Suicide: The scourge of Native American people. *Suicide and Life-Threatening Behavior, 27,* 6–67.

Edelman, D. (1994). The psychological impact of being diagnosed with genital human papillomavirus. *Dissertation Abstracts International, 55,* 2286 (UMI No. 9434479).

Eden, D. (1990). *Pygmalion in management: Productivity as a self-fulfilling prophecy.* Lexington, MA: Heath.

Edgar, E. (2001). *Assertive community treatment promotes recovery: An interview with Joe Phillips.* Retrieved from http://www.nami.org/Template.cfm?Section=ACT-TA_Center&template=/ContentManagement/ContentDisplay.cfm&ContentID=6954

Edwards, C. P. (1995). Parenting toddlers. In M. H. Bornstein (Ed.), *Handbook of parenting, Vol. 1: Children and parenting* (pp. 41–63). Mahwah, NJ: Erlbaum.

Edwards, R. (n.d.). *Parenting styles.* Retrieved from http://www.unt.edu/cpe/module1/blk2styl.htm

Egan, S. K., & Perry, D. G. (2001). Gender identity: A multidimensional analysis with implications for psychosocial adjustment. *Developmental Psychology, 37,* 451–463.

Ego Development Research & Applications Network, http://owl.webster.edu/egodev.htm

Eichenbaum, H. E., & Cohen, N. J. (2001). *From conditioning to conscious recollection: Memory systems of the brain.* Upper Saddle River, NJ: Oxford University Press.

Eisen, G. (1988). *Children and play in the Holocaust: Games among the shadows.* Amherst: University of Massachusetts Press.

Eisenbarth, G. S., Polonsky, K. S., & Buse, J. B. (2003). Type 1 diabetes mellitus. In P. R. Larsen, H. M. Krononberg, S. Melmed, & K. S. Polonsky (Eds.), *Williams textbook of endocrinology* (10th ed., pp. 1500–1504). Philadelphia: Saunders.

Eisenberg, N. (1992). *The caring child.* Cambridge, MA: Harvard University Press.

Eisenberg, N. (2003). Prosocial behavior, empathy, and sympathy. In M. H. Bornstein, L. Davidson, C. L. M. Keyes, & K. A. Moore (Eds.), *Well-being: Positive development across the lifecourse* (pp. 253–263). Mahwah, NJ: Erlbaum.

Eisenberg, N., & Fabes, R. (1998). Prosocial development. In W. Damon (Series Ed.) & N. Eisenberg (Vol. Ed.), *Handbook of child psychology: Vol. 3. Social, emotional, and personality development* (5th ed., pp. 701–778). New York: Wiley.

Eisenberg, N., Fabes, R., Murphy, B., Karbon, M., Smith, M., & Masck, P. (1996). The relations of children's dispositional empathy-related responding to their emotionality, regulation, and social functioning. *Developmental Psychology, 32,* 195–209.

Eisenberg, N., Fabes, R. A., Shepard, S. A., Murphy, B. C., Jones, S., & Guthrie, I. K. (1998). Contemporaneous and longitudinal prediction of children's sympathy from dispositional regulation and emotionality. *Developmental Psychology, 34,* 910–924.

Eisenberg, N., & Strayer, J. (1987). *Empathy and its development.* New York: Cambridge University Press.

Eisenberger, R., Pierce, D., & Cameron, J. (1999). Effects of reward on intrinsic motivation—Negative, neutral, and positive. *Psychological Bulletin, 125,* 677–691.

Eisenson, J. (1997). *Is my child's speech normal?* (2nd ed.). Austin, TX: Pro-Ed.

Eisenstein, E. M., Eisenstein, D., & Smith, J. C. (2001). The evolutionary significance of habituation and sensitization across phylogeny: A behavioral homeostasis model. *Integrative Physiological & Behavioral Science, 36*(4), 251–265.

Eiser, J. R. (1994). *Attitudes, chaos and the connectionist mind.* Cambridge, MA: Blackwell.

Eisinger, J. (1982). Lead and wine: Eberhard Gockel and the Colica Pictonum. *Medical History, 26,* 279–302.

Elam-Evans, L. D., Strauss, L. T., Herndon, J., Parker, W. Y., Bowens, S. V., Zane, S., & Berg, C. J. (2003). Abortion surveillance—United States, 2000. *MMWR Surveillance Summaries, 52*(SS12), 1–32.

Elderhostel, http://www.elderhostel.org

Eliade, M. (1959). *The sacred and the profane.* New York: Harcourt, Brace & World.

Elizabeth F. Loftus, http://faculty.washington.edu/eloftus/

Elkind, D. (1967). Egocentrism in adolescence. *Child Development, 38,* 1025–1034.

Elliott, B. (2003). *Containing the uncontainable: Alcohol misuse and the Personal Choice Community Programme.* London: Whurr.

Elliott, D. S., Hamburg, B. A., & Williams, K. R. (Eds.). (1998). *Violence in American schools: A new perspective.* New York: Cambridge University Press.

Elliott, M. R., Fisher, K., & Ames, E. W. (1988). The effects of rocking on the state and respiration of normal and excessive cryers. *Canadian Journal of Psychology, 42*(2), 163–172.

Elliott, M. R., Pedersen, E. L., & Mogan, J. (1997). Early infant crying: Child and family follow-up at three years. *Canadian Journal of Nursing Research, 29*(2), 47–67.

Elliott, M. R., Reilly, S. M., Drummond, J., & Letourneau, N. (2002). The effect of different soothing interventions on infant crying and on parent-infant interaction. *Infant Mental Health Journal, 23*(3), 310–328.

Ellis, B. J., & Symons, D. (1990). Sex differences in sexual fantasy: An evolutionary psychological approach. *Journal of Sex Research, 27,* 490–521.

Ellis, T. E., & Newman, C. F. (1996). *Choosing to live: How to defeat suicide through cognitive therapy.* Oakland, CA: New Harbinger.

Ellison, S. (2001). *The courage to be a single mother: Becoming whole again after divorce.* San Francisco: Harper.

Ellman, S. J., & Antrobus, J. (1991). *The mind in sleep.* New York: Wiley.

Ellsworth, J., & Ames, L. J. (Eds.). (1998). *Critical perspectives on project Head Start: Revisioning the hope and challenge.* Albany: State University of New York Press.

Elrod, L. D., & Buchele, J. P. (2001). *Kansas family law* (Kansas Law and Practice) § 3.3. St. Paul, MN: Thomson West.

eMedicine. (2004). *Rh incompatibility.* Retrieved from http://www.emedicine.com/emerg/topic507.htm

Emerson, R. M., Fretz, R. I., & Shaw L. L. (1995). *Writing ethnographic fieldnotes.* Chicago: University of Chicago Press.

Emmelkamp, P. M. J., Krijn, M., Hulsbosch, A. M., de Vries, S., Schuemie, M. J., & van der Mast, C. A. P. G. (2002). Virtual reality treatment versus exposure in vivo: A comparative evaluation in acrophobia. *Behaviour Research and Therapy, 40,* 509–516.

Employer-Based Insurance, http://my.webmd.com

Empson, J. (2002). *Sleep & dreaming* (3rd ed.). New York: Palgrave.

Encyclopedia Britannica Online. (n.d.). *Dieting.* Retrieved from http://www.britannica.com/ebc/article-9030400

Encyclopedia Britannica Online. (n.d.). *Ego.* Retrieved from http://www.britannica.com/ebc/article-9363461

End of Life Choices, http://www.endoflifechoices.org/index.jsp

Enders, A. (n.d.). *Where are the U.S. centers for independent living?* Retrieved from http://rtc.ruralinstitute.umt.edu/CIL/

Engel, J., & Pedley, T. A. (1998). *Epilepsy. A comprehensive textbook.* Philadelphia: Lippincott-Raven.

Engeström, Y., Miettinen, R., & Punamäki, R.-L. (Eds.). (1999). *Perspectives on activity theory.* Cambridge, UK: Cambridge University Press.

Enkin, M., Keirse, M. J., Neilson, J., Crowther, C., Duley, L., Hodnett, E., et al. (2000). *A guide to effective care in pregnancy and childbirth* (3rd ed.). New York: Oxford University Press.

Enright, J. T. (1965). Synchronization and ranges of entrainment. In J. Aschoff (Ed.), *Circadian clocks* (pp. 112–124). Amsterdam: North-Holland.

Ensminger, M. E., & Fothergill, K. (2003). A decade of measuring SES: What it tells us and where to go from here. In M. H. Bornstein & R. H. Bradley (Eds.), *Socioeconomic status, parenting, & child development* (pp. 13–28). Mahwah, NJ: Erlbaum.

Entwisle, D. R., & Astone, N. M. (1994). Some practical guidelines for measuring youth's race/ethnicity and socioeconomic status. *Child Development, 65,* 1521–1540.

Epilepsy Foundation of America, http://www.epilepsyfoundation.org/

Epley, N., Morewedge, C., & Keysar, B. (2004). Perspective taking in children and adults: Equivalent egocentrism but differential correction. *Journal of Experimental Social Psychology, 40,* 760–768.

Epstein, L. H., Myers, M. D., Raynor, H. A., & Saelens, B. E. (1998). Treatment of pediatric obesity. *Pediatrics, 101,* 554–570.

Ercal, N., Gurer-Orhan, H., & Aykin-Burns, N. (2001). Toxic metals and oxidative stress: Part I. Mechanisms involved in metal-induced oxidative damage. *Current Topics in Medicinal Chemistry, 1,* 529–539.

Erickson, G. F. (2003). *Morphology and physiology of the ovary.* Retrieved from http://www.endotext.org/female/female1/female1.htm

Erickson, M. F., & Egeland, B. (2002). Child neglect. In J. B. Myers, L. Berliner, J. Briere, C. T. Hendrix, C. Jenny, & T. A. Reid (Eds.), *The APSAC handbook of child maltreatment.* Thousand Oaks, CA: Sage.

Erickson, R. (1993). Reconceptualizing family work: The effects of emotion work on perceptions of marital quality. *Journal of Marriage and the Family, 55,* 888–900.

Erickson, R. J., & Simon, R. J. (1998). *The use of social science data in Supreme Court decisions.* Urbana, IL: University of Chicago Press.

Erik Erikson's Developmental Theory, http://www.azaz.essortment.com/psychosocialdev_rijk.htm

Erikson, E. (1950). *Childhood and society.* New York: W. W. Norton.

Erikson, E. (1963). *Childhood and society* (2nd ed.). New York: W. W. Norton.

Erikson, E. (1968). *Identity: Youth and crisis.* New York: W. W. Norton.

Erikson, E. (1980). *Identity and the life cycle.* New York: W. W. Norton.

Erikson, E. H. (1959). Identity and the life-cycle. *Psychological Issues, 1,* 18–164.

Erikson, E. H. (1982). *The life cycle completed: Review.* New York: W. W. Norton.

Erikson, E. H. (R. Coles, Ed.). (2000). *The Erik Erikson reader.* New York: W. W. Norton.

Eriksson, P., & Talts, U. (2000). Neonatal exposure to neurotoxic pesticides increases adult susceptibility: A review of current findings. *Neurotoxicology, 21*(1–2), 37–48.

The Ernest Becker Foundation, http://faculty.washington.edu/nelgee/

Eron, L. D., Gentry, J. H., & Schlegel, P. (Eds.). (1994). *Reason to hope: A psychological perspective on violence and youth.* Washington, DC: American Psychological Association.

Espenshade, T. H., & Hempstead, K. (1995). Contemporary American attitudes toward U.S. immigration. *International Migration Review, 30,* 535–570.

Espey, L. L. (1994). Ovulation. In E. Knobil & J. D. Neill (Eds.), *Encyclopedia of reproduction, Vol. 1* (pp. 725–780). San Diego, CA: Academic Press.

Esposito, J. L. (2002). *What everyone needs to know about Islam.* Oxford, UK: Oxford University Press.

Esses, V. M., Dovidio, J. F., Jackson, L. M., & Armstrong, T. L. (2001). The immigration dilemma: The role of perceived group competition, ethnic prejudice, and national identity. *Journal of Social Issues, 57,* 389–412.

Eternal Word Television Network, http://www.ewtn.com/

Ettenberg, A. (2004). Opponent process properties of self-administered cocaine. *Neuroscience and Biobehavioral Reviews, 27,* 721–728.

European Association on Early Intervention (Eurlyaid), http://www.eurlyaid.net/index.php

Evan B. Donaldson Adoption Institute, http://www.adoptioninstitute.org

Evans, G. W. (2004). The environment of childhood poverty. *American Psychologist, 59*(2), 77–92.

Evans, G. W., Hygge, S., & Bullinger, M. (1998). Chronic noise exposure and physiological stress: A prospective study of children living under environmental stress. *Psychological Science, 9,* 75–77.

Evans, R. B., Sexton, V. S., & Cadwallader, T. C. (1992). *The American Psychological Association: A historical perspective.* Washington, DC: American Psychological Association.

Eveleth, P. B., & Tanner, J. M. (1990). *Worldwide variation in human growth* (2nd ed.). Cambridge, UK: Cambridge University Press.

Evengard, B., Schacterle, R. S., & Komaroff, A. L. (1999). Chronic fatigue syndrome: New insights and old ignorance. *Journal of Internal Medicine, 246*(5), 455–469.

Everitt, B. S. (2001). *Statistics for psychologists.* Mahwah, NJ: Erlbaum.

Everything ESL, http://www.everythingesl.net

Experiments. (n.d.). Retrieved from http://sun.science.wayne.edu/~wpoff/cor/bas/experim.html

Eyberg, S. M., & Robinson, E. A. (1982). Parent-child interaction training: Effects on family functioning. *Journal of Clinical Child Psychology, 11,* 130–137.

Fabbri, M., Smart, C., & Pardi, R. (2003). T lymphocytes. *The International Journal of Biochemistry & Cell Biology, 35,* 1004–1008.

Fabricius, W. V., & Hall, J. A. (2000). Young adults' perspectives on divorce living arrangements. *Family and Conciliation Courts Review, 38*(4), 446–461.

Fagen, J. W., & Ohr, P. S. (2001). Learning and memory in infancy: Habituation, instrumental conditioning, and expectancy formation. In L. T. Singer & P. S. Zeskind (Eds.), *Biobehavioral assessment of the infant* (pp. 233–273). New York: Guilford.

Fairburn, C. G. (1995). *Overcoming binge eating.* New York: Guilford.

Fairburn, C. G., & Brownell, K. D. (2002). *Eating disorders and obesity: A comprehensive handbook* (2nd ed.). New York: Guilford.

Fairburn, C. G., & Wilson, G. T. (1993). *Binge eating: Nature, assessment, and treatment.* New York: Guilford.

Fairen, A., Morante-Oria, J., & Frassoni, C. (2002). The surface of developing cerebral cortex: Still special cells one century later. *Progress in Brain Research, 136,* 281–191.

Faller, K. C. (2003). *Understanding and assessing child sexual maltreatment* (2nd ed.). Thousand Oaks, CA: Sage.

False Memory Syndrome Foundation, http://www.fmsfonline.org/

Falvo, D. R. (1994). Risk: Sexually transmitted diseases. *Journal of Applied Rehabilitation Counseling, 25*(1), 43–49.

Families for Early Autism Treatment, http://feat.org

Family Communications. (n.d.). *Fred Rogers' biography.* Retrieved from http://www.familycommunications.org/mister_rogers_neighborhood/biography.asp

Family Village: A Global Community of Disability Related Resources, http://familyvillage.wisc.edu

Family Voices, Inc., http://www.familyvoices.org

Fancher, R. E. (1985). *The intelligence men: Makers of the IQ controversy.* New York: W. W. Norton.

Fantl, J. A., Newman, D. K., Colling, J., DeLancey, J. O. L., Keeys, C., Loughery, R., et al. (1996). *Urinary incontinence in adults: Acute and chronic management.* Clinical Practice Guideline, No. 2, 1996 Update (AHCPR Publication No. 96–0682). Rockville, MD: U.S. Department of Health and Human Services, Public Health Service, Agency for Health Care Policy and Research.

Fantuzzo, J. W., Polite, K., & Grayson, N. (1990). An evaluation of reciprocal peer tutoring across elementary school settings. *Journal of School Psychology, 28,* 309–333.

Faria, M.A., Jr. (2002). Statistical malpractice: Firearm availability and violence. I. Politics or science? *Medical Sentinel, 7*(4), 132–133.

Farlex, Inc. (n.d.). *Allele.* Retrieved from http://encyclopedia.thefreedictionary.com/allele

Farlex, Inc. (n.d.). *Chromosome.* Retrieved from http://encyclopedia.thefreedictionary.com/chromosome

Farlex, Inc. (n.d.). *Gamete.* Retrieved from http://encyclopedia.thefreedictionary.com/gamete

Farlex, Inc. (n.d.). *Inductive reasoning.* Retrieved from http://encyclopedia.thefreedictionary.com/Inductive+reasoning

Farlex, Inc. (n.d.). *Zygote.* Retrieved from http://encyclopedia.thefreedictionary.com/zygote

Farmer, P. (1996). *Two or the book of twins and doubles.* London: Virago Press.

Farooque, R., & Ernst, F. (2003). Filicide: A review of eight years of clinical experience. *Journal of the National Medical Association, 95,* 90–94. Retrieved from http://www.nmanet.org/Filicide.pdf

Farrar, M. J., & Goodman, G. S. (1992). Developmental changes in event memory. *Child Development, 63,* 173–187.

Farrington, D. P. (1992). Explaining the beginning, progress, and ending of antisocial behavior from birth to adulthood. In J. McCord (Ed.), *Advances in criminological theory* (pp. 253–286). New Brunswick, NH: Transaction.

Favazza, P. C., Phillipsen, L., & Kumar, P. (2000). Measuring and promoting acceptance of young children with disabilities. *Exceptional Children, 66*(4), 491–508.

Featherman, D. L., & Vinovskis, M. A. (Eds.). (2001). *Social science and policy-making: A search for relevance in the twentieth century.* Ann Arbor: University of Michigan Press.

Federal Bureau of Investigation. (2003). *Hate crime statistics.* Retrieved from http://www.fbi.gov/ucr/hatecrime2002.pdf

Federal Bureau of Investigations. (2004). *Uniform crime reports: Crime in the United States 2002.* Retrieved from http://www.fbi.gov/ucr/02cius.htm

Federal Interagency on Aging Related Statistics, http://agingstats.gov

Federal Interagency Forum on Aging-Related Statistics. (2000). *Older Americans 2000: Key indicators of well-being.* Washington, DC: U.S. Government Printing Office.

Federal Interagency Forum on Child and Family Statistics, http://www.childstats.gov/

Federal Interagency Forum on Child and Family Statistics. (n.d.). *America's children: Key national indicators of well-being.* Available from http://childstats.gov

Feldkamper, M., & Schaeffel, F. (2003). Interactions of genes and environment in myopia. *Developments in Ophthalmology, 37,* 34–49.

Feldman, R. S., Meyer, J. S., & Quenzer. L. F. (1997). *Principles of neuropsychopharmacology* (pp. 568–590). Sunderland, MA: Sinauer.

Fellowship for Intentional Community. (2000). *Communities directory.* Rutledge, MO: Author.

Ferber, R. (1986). *Solve your child's sleep problems.* New York: Simon & Schuster.

Ferguson, C. A. (1964). Baby talk in six languages. *American Anthropologist, 66,* 103–114.

Ferguson, J. M. (1999). High school students' attitudes toward inclusion of handicapped students in the regular education classroom. *The Educational Forum, 63*(2), 173–179.

Fergusson, D. M., Beautrais, A. L., & Horwood, L. J. (2003). Vulnerability and resiliency to suicidal behaviors in young people. *Psychological Medicine, 33,* 61–73.

Fernald, A., Taeschner, T., Dunn, J., Papousek, M., Boysson-Bardies, B., & Fukui, I. (1989). A cross-language study of prosodic modifications in mothers' and fathers' speech to preverbal infants. *Journal of Child Language, 16,* 477–501.

Fernie, D. (1988). *The nature of children's play.* Urbana, IL: ERIC Clearinghouse on Elementary and Early Childhood Education. (ERIC Document Reproduction Service No. ED307967). Retrieved from http://www.kidsource.com/kidsource/content2/nature.of.childs.play.html

Ferrara, F. F. (2002). *Childhood sexual abuse: Developmental effects across the lifespan.* Pacific Grove, CA: Brooks-Cole.

Feschbach, S. (1970). Aggression. In P. H. Mussen (Ed.), *Carmichael's manual of child psychology* (pp. 159–259). New York: Wiley.

Feshbach, N. D. (1982). Sex differences in empathy and social behavior in children. In N. Eisenberg (Ed.), *The development of prosocial behavior.* New York: Academic Press.

Festinger, L. (1957). *A theory of cognitive dissonance.* New York: Row, Peterson.

Field, M. J., & Cassel, C. K. (1997). *Approaching death: Improving care at the end of life.* Washington, DC: National Academy Press.

Field, T. (2001). *Touch.* Cambridge: MIT Press.

Field, T., Gewirtz, J. L., Cohen, D., Garcia, R., Greenberg, R., & Collins, K. (1984). Leave-takings and reunions of infants, toddlers, preschoolers, and their parents. *Child Development, 55,* 628–635.

Fincham, F. D., & Bradbury, T. N. (Eds.). (1990). *The psychology of marriage: Basic issues and applications.* New York: Guilford.

Fincher, C. (1986). The predictive contribution of the SAT in a statewide system of public higher education. *Measures in the college admissions process: A college board colloquium.* New York: College Entry Examination Board.

FindLaw, http://public.findlaw.com/divorce

Fine, M. A., Coleman, M., & Ganong, L. H. (1999). A social constructionist multi-method approach to understanding the stepparent role. In E. M. Hetherington (Ed.), *Coping with divorce, single parenting, and remarriage: A risk and resiliency perspective* (pp. 273–294). Mahwah, NJ: Erlbaum.

Finer, L. B., & Henshaw, S. K. (2003). Abortion incidence and services in the United States in 2000. *Perspectives on Sexual and Reproductive Health, 35*(2003), 6–24.

Finkelhor, D. (1984). *Child sexual abuse: New theory and research.* New York: The Free Press.

Finkelhor, D. (1994). Current information on the scope and nature of child sexual abuse. *Future of Children, 4,* 31–53.

Finkelhor, D., & Dziuba-Leatherman, J. (1994). Victimization of children. *American Psychologist, 49,* 173–183.

Finkelhor, D., & Dziuba-Leatherman, J. (1995). Victimization prevention programs: A national survey of adult men and women: Prevalence, characteristics, and risk factors. *Child Abuse & Neglect, 19,* 120–139.

Finkelhor, D., & Jones, L. M. (2004, January). Explanations for the decline in child sexual abuse cases. *Juvenile Justice Bulletin.* Retrieved from http://www.ncjrs.org/pdffiles1/ojjdp/199298.pdf

Finley, G. E. (2002). The best interest of the child and the eye of the beholder [Review of C. Panter-Brick & M. T. Smith (Eds.), *Abandoned children*]. *Contemporary Psychology, APA Review of Books, 47*(5), 629–631.

Firestein, B. A. (1996). *Bisexuality: The psychology and politics of an invisible minority.* Thousand Oaks, CA: Sage.

Fisch, B. J. J. (2000). *Fisch and Spehlmann's EEG primer* (3rd ed.). New York: Elsevier.

Fishbein, M., & Ajzen, I. (1975). *Belief, attitude, intention, and behavior: An introduction to theory and research.* Reading, MA: Addison-Wesley.

Fishman, D. M., Lipstitch, M., Hook, E. W., & Goldie, S. J. (2002). Projection of the future dimensions and costs of the genital herpes simplex 2 epidemic in the United States. *Sexually Transmitted Diseases, 29*(10), 608–622.

Fiske, S. T., & Taylor, S. E. (1991). *Social cognition.* New York: McGraw-Hill.

Fitzpatrick, P., Schmidt, R. C., & Lockman, J. J. (1996). Dynamical patterns in the development of clapping. *Child Development, 67,* 2691–2708.

Flanagan, D. P., McGrew, K. S., & Ortiz, S. O. (2000). *The Wechsler intelligence scales and Gf-Gc theory: A contemporary approach to interpretation.* Boston: Allyn & Bacon.

Flavell, J. H. (1963). *The developmental psychology of Jean Piaget.* Princeton, NJ: Van Nostrand.

Flavell, J. H. (1985). *Cognitive development.* Englewood Cliffs, NJ: Prentice-Hall.

Flavell, J. H. (1996). Piaget's legacy. *Psychological Science, 7,* 200–203.

Flavell, J. H. (1999). Cognitive development: Children's knowledge about the mind. *Annual Review of Psychology, 50,* 145–156.

Flavell, J. H., Green F. L., & Flavell, E. R. (1995). Young children's knowledge about thinking. *Monographs of the Society for Research in Child Development,* Serial No. 243, *60*(1).

Flavell, J. H., Miller, P. H., & Miller, S. A. (1993). *Cognitive development.* Englewood Cliffs, NJ: Prentice-Hall.

Flavell, J. H., Miller, P. H., & Miller, S. A. (2002). *Cognitive development* (4th ed.). Upper Saddle River, NJ: Prentice-Hall.

Fleshman, M. (2001, October). AIDS orphans: Facing Africa's silent crisis. *Africa Recovery, 15*(3).

Florida Department of Corrections. (1999). *Selected community corrections residential programs.* Retrieved from http://www.dc.state.fl.us/pub/rop/rop99-06/programtypes .html

Florsheim, P. (2003). *Adolescent romantic relations and sexual behavior: Theory, research, and practical implications.* Mahwah, NJ: Erlbaum.

Fogel, A., Nelson-Goens, G. C., Hsu, H., & Shapiro, A. F. (2000). Do different infant smiles reflect different emotions? *Social Development, 9*(4), 497–522.

Folberg, J., Milne, A., & Salem, P. (Eds.). (2004). *Divorce and family mediation: Models, techniques, and applications.* New York: Guilford.

Folbre, N., & Nelson, J. A. (2000). For love or money—Or both? *Journal of Economic Perspectives, 14*(4), 1230–1240.

Food Research and Action Center. (2004). *State of the states.* Retrieved from http://www.frac.org/htm

Foos, P. W., & Clark, M. C. (2003). *Human aging.* Boston: Pearson Education.

Foote, R. C., Schuhmann, E. M., Jones, M. L., & Eyberg, S. M. (1998). Parent-child interaction therapy: A guide for clinicians. *Clinical Child Psychology and Psychiatry, 3,* 361–373.

Ford-Gilboe, M. (2000). Dispelling myths and creating opportunity: A comparison of the strengths of single-parent and two-parent families. *Advances in Nursing Science, 23*(1), 41–58.

Forehand, R., & Kotchick, B. A. (1996). Cultural diversity: A wake-up call for parent training. *Behavior Therapy, 27,* 187–206.

Forehand, R. L., & Long, N. (2002). *Parenting the strong-willed child: The clinically proven five-week program for parents of two- to six-year-olds* (2nd ed.). New York: McGraw-Hill.

4Girls Health. (n.d.). *Getting your period.* Retrieved from http://www.4girls.gov/body/period.htm

Forman, G. E., & Kuschner, D. S. (1983). *Piaget for teaching children.* Washington, DC: NAEYC.

Forssberg, H., Stokes, V., & Hirschfeld, H. (1992). Basic mechanisms of human locomotor development. In M. Gunnar & C. Nelson (Eds.), *Developmental behavioral neuroscience* (Minnesota Symposia on Child Psychology, Vol. 24, pp. 37–73). Hillsdale, NJ: Erlbaum.

Foss, P. W., & Clark, M. C. (2004). *Human aging.* Boston: Allyn & Bacon.

Foss, R. D., Feaganes, J., & Rodgman, E. (2001). Initial effects of graduated driver licensing on 16-year-old driver crashes in North Carolina. *JAMA, 286,* 1588–1592.

Foster, A. M., van Dis, J., & Steinauer, J. (2003). Educational and legislative initiatives affecting residency training in abortion. *JAMA, 290,* 1777–1778.

Fouad, N., & Brown, M. T. (2001). Role of race and social class in development: Implications for counseling psychology. In S. D. Brown & R. W. Lent (Eds.), *Handbook of counseling psychology* (pp. 379–408). New York: Wiley.

Foucault, M. (1976; reprinted 1980). *The history of sexuality, volume 1: An introduction.* New York: Vantage.

Foulkes, D. (1982). *Children's dreams: Longitudinal studies.* New York: Wiley.

Foundation for Grandparenting, http://www.grandparenting .org/

Foundation Press. Sacks, A. (2004). *2004 Social Security explained.* Chicago: CCH.

Fournier, G., & Jeanrie, C. (2003). Locus of control: Back to basics. In S. J. Lopez & C. R. Snyder (Eds.), *Positive psychological assessment: A handbook of models and measures* (pp. 139–154). Washington, DC: American Psychological Association.

Fowers, B. (2000). *Beyond the myth of marital happiness.* San Francisco: Jossey-Bass.

Fox, L., Dunlap, G., & Cushing, L. (2002). Early intervention, positive behavior support, and transition to school. *Journal of Emotional and Behavioral Disorders, 10*(3), 149–157. Available from http://www.questia.com/PM.qst?a=o&d= 5000816369

Fox, M. K., Pac, S., Devaney, B., & Jankowski, L. (2004). Feeding infants and toddlers study: What foods are infants and toddlers eating? *Journal of the American Dietetic Association, 104*(Suppl. 1), 22–30.

Fox, N., & Davidson, R. J. (1988). Patterns of brain electrical activity during facial signs of emotion in 10 month old infants. *Developmental Psychology, 24*(2), 230–236.

Foxx, R. M., & Azrin, N. H. (1973). Dry pants: A rapid method of toilet training children. *Behaviour Research and Therapy, 11,* 435–442.

Frable, D. E. S. (1997). Gender, racial, ethnic, sexual, and class identities. *Annual Review of Psychology, 48,* 139–162.

Frank, I. C. (1996). *Building self-esteem in at-risk youth: Peer group programs and individual success stories.* Westport, CT: Praeger.

Frank, R. H. (1988). *Passions within reason: The strategic role of the emotions.* New York: W. W. Norton.

Frasure-Smith, N., & Lesperance, F. (1999). Psychosocial risks and cardiovascular diseases. *Canadian Journal of Cardiology, 15,* 93G–97G.

Frazer, J. G. (1922). *The golden bough.* New York: Macmillan.

Freedman, M. (2002). *Prime time: How Baby Boomers will revolutionize retirement and transform America.* Washington, DC: PublicAffairs.

Freeman, D. (1983). *Margaret Mead and Samoa: The making and unmaking of an anthropological myth.* Cambridge, MA: Harvard University Press.

Freeman, D. E., & Freeman, Y. S. (2001). *Between worlds: Access to second language acquisition.* Portsmouth, NH: Heinemann.

Freeman, H. (1994). Schizophrenia and city residence. *British Journal of Psychiatry, 164*(Suppl. 23), 39–50.

Freidrich, E., & Rowland, C. (1990). *The parenting guide to raising twins.* New York: St. Martin's Press.

French, L. A. (2004). Alcohol and other drug addictions among Native Americans: The movement toward tribal-centric treatment programs. *Alcoholism Treatment Quarterly, 22,* 81–91.

Freud, A. (1956). Adolescence. *Psychoanalytic Study of the Child, 13,* 255–278.

Freud, S. (1923). *The ego and the id. Standard edition of the complete psychological works of Sigmund Freud* (Vol. 19, pp. 1–66). London: Hogarth Press.

Freud, S. (1933). *New introductory lectures on psychoanalysis.* New York: W. W. Norton.

Freud, S. (1946). *Totem and taboo.* New York: Vintage.

Freud, S. (1949). *An outline of psychoanalysis.* New York: W. W. Norton.

Freud, S. (1961). *Civilization and its discontents.* New York: W. W. Norton. (Original work published 1930)

Freud, S. (1962). *Three essays on the theory of sexuality* (Standard Edition, 7). London: Hogart. (Original work published 1905)

Freud, S. (1965). *The problem of anxiety.* New York: W. W. Norton. (Original work published 1936)

Freyd, J. (1998). *Betrayal trauma.* Boston: Harvard University Press.

Frezieres, R. G., Walsh, T. L. W., Nelson, A. L., Clark, V. A., & Coulson, A. H. (1999). Evaluation of the efficacy of a polyurethane condom: Results from a randomized, controlled clinical trial. *Family Planning Perspectives, 31*(2), 81–87.

Frick, P. J. (2001). Effective interventions for children and adolescents with conduct disorder. *The Canadian Journal of Psychiatry, 46,* 26–37.

Frick, P. J. (2004). Integrating research on temperament and childhood psychopathology: Its pitfalls and promise. *Journal of Clinical Child and Adolescent Psychology, 33,* 2–7.

Frick, P. J., & Morris, A. S. (2004). Temperament and developmental pathways to conduct problems. *Journal of Clinical Child and Adolescent Psychology, 33,* 54–68.

Frick, W. B. (2000). Remembering Maslow: Reflections on a 1968 interview. *Journal of Humanistic Psychology, 40,* 128–147.

Friedan, B. (1994). *The fountain of age.* New York: Simon & Schuster.

Friedberg, F., & Jason, L. A. (1998). *Understanding chronic fatigue syndrome: An empirical guide to assessment and treatment.* Washington, DC: American Psychological Association.

Friedman, E. A. (1978). Evolution of graphic analysis of labor. *American Journal of Obstetrics and Gynecology, 132,* 824–827.

Friedman, M. A., Schwartz, M. B., & Brownell, K. D. (1998). Differential relation of psychological functioning with history and experience of weight cycling. *Journal of Consulting and Clinical Psychology, 66,* 646–650.

Friedmann, E., Katcher, A. H., Lynch, J. J., & Thomas, S. A. (1980). Animal companions and one-year survival of patients after discharge from a coronary care unit. *Public Health Reports, 95,* 307–312.

Friedrich, D. (2003). Personal and societal intervention strategies for successful ageing. *Ageing International, 28,* 3–36.

Frisco, M. L., & Williams, K. (2003). Perceived housework equity, marital happiness, and divorce in dual earner households. *Journal of Family Issues, 24,* 51–73.

Frith, C. D., & Frith, U. (1999). Cognitive psychology: Interacting minds—a biological basis. *Science, 286*(5445), 1692–1695.

Frith, U. (1989). *Autism: Explaining the enigma.* Oxford, UK: Blackwell.

Frondizi, R. (1971). *The nature of self: A functional interpretation.* Carbondale: Southern Illinois University Press.

Fuentes R., Gómez-Sanz, J. J., & Pavón, J. (2004). Activity theory for the analysis and design of multi-agent systems. *Lecture Notes in Computer Science, 2935,* 110–122.

Fukuda, K., Straus, S. E., Hickie, I., Sharpe, M. C., Dobbins, J. G., Komaroff, A., et al. (1994). The chronic fatigue syndrome: A comprehensive approach to its definition and study. *Annals of Internal Medicine, 12,* 953–959.

Fukuda, T. (1961). Studies on human dynamic postures from the viewpoint of postural reflexes. *Acta Otolaryngologica, 161*[Suppl.], 1–52.

Fulmer, T., Firpo, A., Guadagno, L., Easter, T. M., Kahan, F., & Paris, B. (2003). Themes from a grounded theory analysis of elder neglect assessment by experts. *Gerontologist, 43,* 745.

Fulmer, T., Paveza, G., Abraham, I., & Fairchild, S. (2000). Elder neglect assessment in the emergency department. *Journal of Emergency Nursing, 26*(5), 436–443.

Funderstanding. (n.d.). *Observational learning.* Retrieved from http://www.funderstanding.com/observational_learning.cfm

Furman, W., Brown, B. B., & Feiring, C. (1999). *The development of romantic relationships in adolescence.* Cambridge, UK: Cambridge University Press.

Furstenberg, F., Jr., Cook, T., Eccles, J., Elder, G., Jr., & Sameroff, A. (1999). *Managing to make it: Urban families and adolescent success.* Chicago: University of Chicago Press.

Furth, H. G. (1981). *Piaget and knowledge* (2nd ed.). Chicago: University of Chicago Press.

The Future of Children, http://www.futureofchildren.org (see, especially, volume 5, issue 3, "Long-term outcomes of early childhood programs")

Future of Children. (1997). Children and poverty: Executive summary. *Future of Children, 7*(2). Available from http://www.futureofchildren.org

Future of Children. (2002). Children and welfare reform: Executive Summary. *Future of Children, 12*(1). Available from http://www.futureofchildren.org

Gabell, A., & Nayak, U. (1984). The effect of age on variability in gait. *Journal of Gerontology, 39,* 662–666.

Gage, N. L., & Berliner, D. C. (1979). *Educational psychology* (2nd ed, pp. 306–307, 333–348, 467). Chicago: Rand McNally College Publishing.

Gagne, E., Yekovich, C., & Yekovich, F. (1993). *The cognitive psychology of school learning.* New York: HarperCollins.

Gainetdov, R. R., Wetsel, W. C., Jones, S. R., Levin, E. D., Jaber, M., & Caron, M. G. (1999, January). Role of serotonin in the paradoxical calming effect of psychostimulants on hyperactivity. *Science,* 397–410.

Galanter, M. (Ed.). (2002). *Alcohol and violence: Epidemiology, neurobiology, psychology, family issues.* New York: Kluwer Academic.

Galanti, G. (1997). *Caring for patients from different cultures: Case studies from American hospitals* (2nd ed.). Philadelphia: University of Pennsylvania Press.

Gallagher, K. (2004). *Rh immune globulin.* Retrieved from http://my.webmd.com/hw/being_pregnant/hw144853.asp

Gallahue, D. L., & Ozmun, J. C. (1995). *Understanding motor development: Infants, children, adolescents, adults.* Madison, WI: Brown & Benchmark.

Gallup Organization. (1995). *Disciplining children in America: A Gallup poll report.* Princeton, NJ: Author.

Galton, F. (1883). *Inquiries into human faculty and its development.* London: Macmillan.

Gandini, L. (1996). The Reggio story: History and organization. In J. Hendrick (Ed.), *First steps toward teaching the Reggio way* (pp. 2–13). Columbus, OH: Prentice-Hall.

Gangstead, S. W., & Thornhill, R. (1997). The evolutionary psychology of extra-pair sex: The role of fluctuating asymmetry. *Evolution and Human Behavior, 18,* 69–88.

Gangstead, S. W., Thornhill, R., & Garver, C. E. (2001). Changes in women's sexual interests and their partners' mate-retention tactics across the menstrual cycle: Evidence for shifting conflicts of interest. *Proceedings of the Royal Society of London, B, 269,* 975–982.

Garber, M. (1995). *Vice versa: Bisexuality and the eroticism of everyday life.* New York: Simon & Schuster.

Gardner, H. (1983). *Frames of mind: The theory of multiple intelligences.* New York: Basic Books.

Gardner, H. (1993). *Multiple intelligences: The theory in practice.* New York: Basic Books.

Gardner, H. (1999). *Intelligence reframed: Multiple intelligences for the 21st century.* New York: Basic Books.

Gardner, R. (1981). *The boys and girls book about divorce.* New York: Bantam.

Gardner, R. A. (1989). *Family evaluation in child custody mediation, arbitration, and litigation.* Cresskill, NJ: Creative Therapeutics.

Garner, D. M., & Barry, D. (2001). Treatment of eating disorders in adolescents. In C. E. Walker & M. C. Roberts (Eds.), *Handbook of clinical child psychology* (pp. 692–713). New York: Wiley.

Garner, D. M., & Garfinkel, P. E. (Eds.). (1997). *Handbook of treatment for eating disorders* (2nd ed.). New York: Guilford.

Garrity, C., & Baris, M. (1994). *Caught in the middle: Protecting the children of high-conflict divorce.* New York: Lexington Books.

Gaskin, I. M. (1990). *Spiritual midwifery* (3rd ed.). Summertown, TN: Book Publishing Co.

Gass, G. H., & Kaplan, H. M. (1996). *Handbook of endocrinology.* Boca Raton, FL: CRC Press.

Gates, H. L., Jr. (1994). *Colored people: A memoir.* New York: Random House.

Gathercole, S. (1998). The development of memory. *Journal of Child Psychology and Psychiatry, 39,* 3–27.

Gathorne-Hardy, J. (1998). *Sex the measure of all things: A life of Alfred C. Kinsey.* Bloomington: Indiana University Press.

Gavrilov, L. A., & Gavrilova, N. S. (2002). Evolutionary theories of aging and longevity. *Scientific World Journal, 2,* 339–356. Retrieved from http://longevityscience.org/Evolution.htm

Gay, P. (1988). *Freud: A life for our time.* New York: W. W. Norton.

Gaynor, J. L. R., & Runco, M. A. (1992). Family size, birth order, age-interval, and the creativity of children. *Journal of Creative Behavior, 26,* 108–118.

Gazmararian, J. A., Petersen, R., Spitz, A. M., Goodwin, M. M., Saltzman, L. E., & Marks, J. S. (2000). Violence and reproductive health: Current knowledge and future research directions. *Maternal and Child Health Journal, 4*(2), 79–84.

Gedo, J. E. (2001). The enduring scientific contributions of Sigmund Freud. In J. A. Winer & J. W. Anderson (Eds.), *The annual of psychoanalysis volume XXIX: Sigmund Freud and his impact on the modern world* (pp. 105–115). Hillsdale, NJ: Analytic Press.

Geen, R. G., & Donnerstein, E. (Eds.). (1998). *Human aggression: Theories, research and implications for social policy.* San Diego, CA: Academic Press.

Geffner, R., Jaffe, P. G., & Suderman, M. (2000). *Children exposed to domestic violence: Current research, interventions, prevention, & policy development.* New York: Haworth Press.

Geiger, R. L. (Ed.). (2000). *The American college in the nineteenth century.* Nashville, TN: Vanderbilt University Press.

Gelman, S. A. (1988). The development of induction within natural kind and artifact categories. *Cognitive Psychology, 20,* 65–95.

Gelman, S. A., & Markman, E. M. (1986). Categories and induction in young children. *Cognition, 23,* 183–209.

Gemelli, R. (1996). *Normal child and adolescent development.* Washington, DC: American Psychiatric Press.

General Accountability Office, http://www.gao.gov/

Generations Together, http://www.gt.pitt.edu/

Generations United, http://www.gu.org

Genishi, C., Ryan, S., Ochsner, M., & Yarnall, M. (2001). Teaching in early childhood education: Understanding practices through research and theory. In V. Richardson (Ed.), *Handbook of research on teaching* (4th ed., pp. 1175–1210). Washington, DC: American Educational Research Association.

Gentile, D. A. (Ed.). (2003). *Media violence and children: A complete guide for parents and professionals.* Westport, CT: Praeger.

Gentile, D. A., & Anderson, C. A. (2003). Violent video games: The newest media violence hazard. In D. A. Gentile (Ed.), *Media violence and children* (pp. 131–152). Westport, CT: Praeger.

Gerontological Society of America, http://www.geron.org

Gershoff, E. T. (2002). Corporal punishment by parents and associated child behaviors and experiences: A meta-analytic and theoretical review. *Psychological Bulletin, 128*(4), 539–579.

Gershoff, E. T. (2002). Corporal punishment, physical abuse, and the burden of proof: Reply to Baumrind, Larzelere, and Cowan (2002), Holden (2002), and Parke (2002). *Psychological Bulletin, 128*(4), 602–611.

Gesell Institute of Human Development, http://www.gesell institute.org

Gesell, A. (1935). Cinemanalysis: A method of behavior study. *Journal of Genetic Psychology, 47,* 3–26.

Gesell, A. (1954). The ontogenesis of infant behavior. In L. Carmichael (Ed.), *Manual of child psychology.* New York: Wiley.

Gesell, A. (1966). *The first five years of life: A guide to the study of the preschool child.* London: Methuen. (Original work published 1930)

Gesell, A., & Ames, L. B. (1940). The ontogenetic organization of prone behavior in human infancy. *Journal of Genetic Psychology, 56,* 247–263.

Gesell, A., & Ilg, F. L. (1937). *Feeding behavior of infants: A pediatric approach to the mental hygiene of early life.* Philadelphia: JB Lippincott.

Gesell, A., Ilg, F. L., & Ames, L. B. (1940). *The first five years of life.* New York: Harper.

Gesell, A., Ilg, F. L., & Ames, L. B. (1946). *The child from five to ten.* New York: Harper & Row.

Getchell, N., & Roberton, M. A. (1989). Whole body stiffness as a function of developmental level in children's hopping. *Developmental Psychology, 25,* 920–928.

Gibb, G. S., & Dyches, T. T. (2000). *Guide to writing individualized education programs: What's best for students with disabilities?* Boston: Allyn & Bacon.

Gibbons, R. D., Clark, D. C., & Fawcett, J. A. (1990). A statistical method for evaluating suicide clusters and implementing cluster surveillance. *American Journal of Epidemiology, 132,* 183–191.

Gibson, E. J. (2000). Commentary on perceptual and conceptual processes in infancy. *Journal of Cognition and Development, 1,* 43–48.

Gibson, E. J., & Walk, R. D. (1960). The "visual cliff." *Scientific American, 202,* 64–71. Retrieved from http://www.wadsworth.com/psychology_d/templates/student_resources/0155060678_rathus/ps/ps05.html

Gibson, J. J. (1979). *The ecological approach to visual perception.* Boston: Houghton Mifflin.

Giesbrecht, N. (1998). Gender patterns of psychosocial development. *Sex Roles: A Journal of Research.* Retrieved from http://www.findarticles.com/cf_dls/m2294/n5–6_v39/212 27883/p1/article.jhtml

Gifford-Smith, M. E., & Brownell, C. A. (2003). Childhood peer relationships: Social acceptance, friendships, and peer networks. *Journal of School Psychology, 41,* 235–284.

Gilbert, C., & Foster, A. (2001). Childhood blindness in the context of VISION 2020: The right to sight. *Bulletin of the World Health Organization* [online], *79,* 227–232. Retrieved from http://www.scielosp.org/scielo.php?pid=S0042-96862001000300011&script=sci_arttext&tlng=en

Gilbert, R. (2000). Toxoplasmosis. In M.-L. Newell & J. McIntyre (Eds.), *Congenital and perinatal infections: Prevention, diagnosis and treatment* (pp. 305–315). Cambridge, UK: Cambridge University Press. (ebook)

Gilbert, W. M., & Danielsen, B. (2003). Pregnancy outcomes associated with intrauterine growth restriction. *American Journal of Obstetrics and Gynecology, 188,* 1596–1601.

Gill, D. (1980). *Quest: The life of Elisabeth Kübler-Ross.* New York: Harper & Row.

Gillberg, C. (2002). *A guide to Asperger syndrome.* Cambridge, UK: Cambridge University Press.

Gilligan, C. (1982). *In a different voice: Psychological theory and women's development.* Cambridge, MA: Harvard University Press.

Gilligan, C. (1993). *In a different voice: Psychological theory and women's development* (2nd ed., with new preface by the author). Cambridge, MA: Harvard University Press.

Gilligan, C. (2002). *The birth of pleasure.* New York: Alfred A. Knopf.

Gilligan, C., & Attanucci, J. (1988). Two moral orientations: Gender differences and similarities. *Merrill-Palmer Quarterly, 34,* 223–237.

Gilligan, C., & Brown, L. (1992). *Meeting at the crossroads: Women's psychology and girls' development.* Cambridge, MA: Harvard University Press.

Gillooly, J. (1998). *Before she gets her period: Talking with your daughter about menstruation.* Glendale, CA: Perspective.

Gilmartin, B. (2004). Myopia: Precedents for research in the twenty-first century. *Clinical and Experimental Ophthalmology, 32,* 305–324.

Gilmartin, B., & Rosenfield, M. (Eds.). (1998). *Myopia and near work.* Oxford, UK: Butterworth-Heinemann.

Ginsberg, B. G., & Israeloff, R. (2002). *50 wonderful ways to be a single-parent family.* Oakland, CA: New Harbinger.

Ginsberg, M., & Bogousslavsky, J. (Eds.). (1998). *Cerebrovascular disease: Pathophysiology, diagnosis and management. Vols. I. & II.* Cambridge, MA: Blackwell.

Ginsburg, H. P., & Opper, S. (1988). *Piaget's theory of intellectual development: An introduction* (3rd ed.). Englewood Cliffs, NJ: Prentice-Hall.

Gjedde, A. (2001). *Physiological imaging of the brain with PET.* New York: Academic Press.

Glaser, B. G., & Strauss, A. L. (1965). *Awareness of dying.* Chicago: Aldine.

Glaser, B. G., & Strauss, A. L. (1968). *Time for dying.* Chicago: Aldine.

Glaser, D. (2000). Child abuse and neglect and the brain—A review. *Journal of Child Psychology and Psychiatry and Allied Disciplines, 41,* 97–116.

Glass Ceiling Act of 1991, Pub. L. No. 102–166, Sec. 201–210, 105 Stat. 1081 (1991).

Glass, G. V., McGraw, B., & Smith, M. L. (1981). *Meta-analysis in social research.* Beverly Hills, CA: Sage.

Glazer, W. M., & Dickson, R. A. (1998). Clozapine reduces violence and persistent aggression in schizophrenia. *Journal of Clinical Psychiatry, 59*(Suppl. 3), 8–14.

Gleason, T. (2002). Social provisions of real and imaginary relationships in early childhood. *Developmental Psychology, 38,* 979–992.

Gleason, T., Sebanc, A., & Hartup, W. (2000). Imaginary companions of preschool children. *Developmental Psychology, 36,* 419–428.

Glenn, N. D. (1977). *Cohort analysis.* Beverly Hills, CA: Sage.

Global Early Intervention Network (GEIN), http://www .atsweb.neu.edu/cp/ei/

Glover, I., & Branine M. (2001). *Ageism in work and employment.* Burlington, VT: Ashgate.

Glover, J. A., Ronning, R. R., & Reynolds, C. R. (1989). *Handbook of creativity: Perspectives on individual differences.* New York: Plenum.

Gluck, J. P., DiPasquale, T., & Orlans, F. B. (2002). *Applied ethics in animal research: Philosophy, regulation, and laboratory applications.* West Lafayette, IN: Purdue University Press.

Gluck Lab Online, http://www.gluck.edu/memory/

Godfrey, J. J. (1987). *A philosophy of human hope.* Dordrecht, Netherlands: Martinus Nijhoff.

Goel, V., & Dolan, R. J. (2001). Functional neuroanatomy of three-term relational reasoning. *Neuropsychologia, 39,* 901–909.

Goer, H. (1995). *Obstetric myths versus research realities: A guide to the medical literature.* Westport, CT: Bergin & Garvey.

Golan, M., & Crow, S. (2004). Parents are key players in the prevention and treatment of weight-related problems. *Nutrition Reviews, 62,* 39–50.

Goldberg, E. (2001). *The executive brain.* New York: Oxford University Press.

Goldberg, I. (n.d.). *Dr. Ivan's depression central.* Retrieved from http://www.psycom.net/depression.central.html

Goldberg, L. R. (2004). *International personality item pool: A scientific collaboratory for the development of advanced measures of personality traits and other individual differences.* Retrieved from http://ipip.ori.org/ipip/

Goldfield, E. C. (1995). *Emergent forms: Origins and early development of human action and perception.* New York: Oxford University Press.

Goldfield, E. C., Kay, B., & Warren, W. H., Jr. (1993). Infant bouncing: The assembly and tuning of action systems. *Child Development, 64,* 1128–1142.

Goldman, A. (1996). Home care of the dying child. *Journal of Palliative Care, 12,* 16–19.

Goldsby, R. A., Kindt, T. J., Osborne, B. A., & Kuby, J. (2003). *Immunology* (5th ed.). San Francisco: W. H. Freeman.

Goldschmidt, E. (2003). The mystery of myopia. *Acta Ophthalmologica Scandinavica, 81,* 431–436.

Goldschmidt, W. (1990). *The human career: The self in the symbolic world.* Cambridge, MA: Blackwell.

Goldsmith, H. H., Lemery, K. S., Buss, K. A., & Campos, J. (1999). Genetic analyses of focal aspects of infant temperament. *Developmental Psychology, 35,* 972–985.

Goldsmith, H. H., Lemery, K. S., & Essex, M. J. (2004). Temperament as a liability factor for behavioral disorders of childhood. In L. DiLalla (Ed.), *Behavioral genetic principles—development, personality, and psychopathology* (pp. 19–39). Washington, DC: American Psychological Association.

Goldstein, A. (2001). *Addiction: From biology to drug policy* (2nd ed.). New York: Oxford University Press.

Goldstein, A. P., & Michaels, G. Y. (1985). *Empathy: Development, training, and consequences.* Hillsdale, NJ: Erlbaum.

Goldstein, G. W. (1990). Lead poisoning and brain cell function. *Environmental Health Perspectives, 89,* 91–94.

Goldstein, J. (1997). Sex differences in schizophrenia: Epidemiology, genetics, and the brain. *International Review of Psychiatry, 9,* 399–408.

Goldstein, J. (2002). *One Dharma: The emerging Western Buddhism.* San Francisco: HarperSanFrancisco.

Goldstein, L. B. (Ed.). (1998). *Advances in the pharmacology of recovery after stroke. Restorative neurology.* Armonk, NY: Futura.

Goldstein, L., & McNeil, C. (2004). *Clinical neuropsychology: A practical guide to assessment and management for clinicians.* London: Wiley.

Goleman, D. (1995). *Emotional intelligence: Why it can matter more than IQ.* New York: Bantam.

Golub, S. (1992). *Periods: From menarche to menopause.* Newbury Park, CA: Sage.

Gomez, J. E. (2000). Growth and maturation. In A. J. Sullivan & S. J. Anderson (Eds.), *Care of the young athlete* (pp. 25–32). Park Ridge, IL: American Academy of Orthopaedic Surgeons, and Elk Grove Village, IL: American Academy of Pediatrics.

Göncü, A., Patt, M. B., & Kouba, E. (2002). Understanding young children's pretend play in context. In P. K. Smith & C. H. Hart (Eds.), *Blackwell handbook of childhood social development* (pp. 418–427). Malden, MA: Blackwell.

Gondolf, E. W., & Fisher, E. R. (1988). *Battered women as survivors: An alternative of learned helplessness.* Lexington, MA: Lexington Books.

Gone, J. P. (2004). Mental health services for Native Americans in the 21st century United States. *Professional Psychology: Research and Practice, 35,* 10–18.

Gonsiorek, J. C., & Rudolph, J. R. (1991). Homosexual identity: Coming out and other developmental events. In J. C. Gonsiorek & J. D. Weinrich (Eds.), *Homosexuality: Research implications for public policy.* Newbury Park, CA: Sage.

Gonzalez-Mena, J., & Eyer, D. W. (2001). *Infants, toddlers, and caregivers* (5th ed.). Mountainview, CA: Mayfield.

Goodchild, L. F. (1996). G. Stanley Hall and the study of higher education. *Review of Higher Education, 20,* 69–99.

Goodchild, L. F., & Wechsler, H. S. (Eds.). (1997). *The history of higher education* (2nd ed.). ASHE Reader Series. Boston: Pearson Custom Publishing.

Goodenough, F. L. (1931). *Anger in young children.* Minneapolis: University of Minnesota Press.

Goodman, K. S. (1986). *What's whole in whole language?* Portsmouth, NH: Heinemann Educational Books.

Goodman, K. S., & Goodman, Y. M. (1979). Learning to read is natural. In L. B. Resnick & P. A. Weaver (Eds.), *Theory and practice of early reading: Vol. 1* (pp. 137–154). Hillsdale, NJ: Erlbaum.

Goodman, S. H., & Gotlib, I. H. (Eds.). (2002). *Children of depressed parents: Mechanisms of risk and implications for treatment.* Washington, DC: American Psychological Association.

Goodwin, C. J. (2003). *Research in psychology: Methods and design* (3rd ed.). Hoboken, NJ: Wiley.

Goossens, L., Beyers, W., Emmen, M., & van Aken, M. A. G. (2002). The imaginary audience and personal fable: Factor analyses and concurrent validity of the "New Look" measures. *Journal of Research on Adolescence, 12,* 193–215.

Gopaul-McNicol, S.-A., & Thomas Presswood, T. (1998). *Working with linguistically and culturally different children.* Needham Heights, MA: Allyn & Bacon.

Gopnik, A., Meltsoff, A. N., & Kuhl, P. K. (2000). *The scientist in the crib: What early learning tells us about the mind.* New York: Perennial.

Gopnik, M., & Crago, M. (1991). Familial aggression of a developmental language disorder. *Cognition, 39,* 139–141.

Gordon Rouse, K. A., Longo, M., & Trickett, M. (n.d.). *Fostering resilience in children* (Bulletin 875–99). Retrieved from http://ohioline.osu.edu/b875/

Gore, S. A., Brown, D. M., & West, D. S. (2003). The role of postpartum weight retention in obesity among women: A review of the evidence. *Annals of Behavioral Medicine, 26,* 149–159.

Goswami, U. (2001). Analogical reasoning in children. In D. Gentner, K. J. Holyoak, & B. N. Kokinov (Eds.), *The analogical mind: Perspectives from cognitive science* (pp. 437–470). Cambridge: MIT Press.

Goswami, U. (2002). *Blackwell handbook of childhood cognitive development.* Malden, MA: Blackwell.

Goswami, U. (2002). Inductive and deductive reasoning. In U. Goswami (Ed.), *Blackwell handbook of child cognitive development* (pp. 282–302). Malden, MA: Blackwell.

Gotlib, I. H., & Hammen, C. L. (2002). *Handbook of depression.* New York: Guilford.

Gottesman, I. (1991). *Schizophrenia genesis: The origins of madness.* New York: W. H. Freeman.

Gottfredson, L. S., & Deary, I. J. (2004). Intelligence predicts health and longevity, but why? *Current Directions in Psychological Science, 13*(1), 1–4.

Gottlieb, D. J., Vezina, R. M., Chase, C., Lesko, S. M., Heeren, T. C., Weese-Mayer, D. E., et al. (2003). Symptoms of sleep-disordered breathing in 5-year-old children are associated with sleepiness and problem behaviors. *Pediatrics, 112,* 870–877.

Gottlieb, G. (1971). *Development of species identification in birds.* Chicago: University of Chicago Press.

Gottlieb, G. (1997). *Synthesizing nature-nurture: Prenatal roots of instinctive behavior.* Mahwah, NJ: Erlbaum.

Gottman Institute, http://www.gottman.com

Gottman, J. M. (1979). *Marital interaction: Experimental investigations.* New York: Academic Press.

Gottman, J. M. (1994). *What predicts divorce? The relationship between marital processes and marital outcomes.* Mahwah, NJ: Erlbaum.

Gottman, J. M. (2002). *The relationship cure: A 5 step guide to strengthening your marriage, family, and friendships.* New York: Crown.

Gottman, J., & DeClaire, J. (1997). *The heart of parenting: How to raise an emotionally intelligent child.* New York: Simon & Schuster.

Gottman, J., Murray, J., Swanson, C., Tyson, R., & Swanson, K. (2002). *The mathematics of marriage: Dynamic nonlinear models.* Cambridge: MIT Press.

Goubet, N., & Clifton, R. K. (1998). Object and event representation in 6½-month-old infants. *Developmental Psychology, 34,* 63–76.

Gould, M. S., Wallenstein, S., & Kleinman, M. (1990). Time-space clustering of teenage suicide. *American Journal of Epidemiology, 131,* 71–78.

Graf, P., & Ohta, N. (2002). *Lifespan development of human memory.* Cambridge: MIT Press.

Graham, S. (1991). A review of attribution theory in achievement contexts. *Educational Psychology Review, 3*(1), 5–39.

Graham, S., & Juvonen, J. (1998). Self-blame and peer harassment in middle school: An attributional analysis. *Developmental Psychology, 34,* 587–599.

Granchrow, J. R., & Mennella, J. A. (2003). The ontogeny of human flavor perception. In R. L. Doty (Ed.), *Handbook of olfaction and gustation* (2nd ed., pp. 823–846). New York: Marcel Dekker.

Grandjean, P., Murata, K., Budtz-Jorgensen, E., & Weihe, P. (2004). Cardiac autonomic activity in methylmercury neurotoxicity: 14-year follow-up of a Faroese birth cohort. *Journal of Pediatrics, 144*(2), 169–176.

Grant, K., Compas, B., Stuhlmacher, A., Thurm, A., McMahon, S., & Halpert, J. (2003). Stressors and child and adolescent psychopathology: Moving from markers to mechanisms of risk. *Psychological Bulletin, 129,* 447–466.

Grant, K., Compas, B., Thurm, A., McMahon, S., & Gipson, P. (2004). Stressors and child and adolescent psychopathology: Measurement issues and prospective effects. *Journal of Clinical Child and Adolescent Psychology, 33*(4), 412–425.

Grapes, B. J. (Ed.). (2001). *Child abuse: Contemporary issues.* San Diego, CA: Greenhaven.

Gratz, K. L. (2003). Risk factors for and functions of deliberate self-harm: An empirical and conceptual review. *Clinical Psychology: Science & Practice, 10*(2), 192–205.

Gravel, R. A., Kaback, M. M., Proia, R. L., Sandhoff, K., Suzuki, K., & Suzuki, K. (2001). The GM2 gangliosidoses. In C. R. Scriver, A. L. Beaudet, D. Valle, W. S. Sly, B. Childs, K. W. Kinzler, et al. (Eds.), *The metabolic and molecular basis of inherited diseases* (pp. 3827–3876). New York: McGraw-Hill.

Gray, J. R., Chabris, C. F., & Braver, T. S. (2003). Neural mechanisms of general fluid intelligence. *Nature Neuroscience, 6,* 316–322.

Gray, J. R., & Thompson, P. M. (2004). Neurobiology of intelligence: Science and ethics. *Nature Reviews Neuroscience, 5,* 471–482.

Gray Panthers. (n.d.). *Gray Panthers' history.* Retrieved from http://www.graypanthers.org/graypanthers/history.htm

Gray Panthers. (n.d.). *Gray Panthers' selected achievements.* Retrieved from http://www.graypanthers.org/graypanthers/achieve.htm

Graybiel, A. M., Aosaki, T., Flaherty, A. W., & Kimura, M. (1994). The basal ganglia and adaptive motor control. *Science, 265*(5180), 1826–1831.

Green, C. D. (n.d.). *Classics in the history of psychology.* Retrieved from http://psychclassics.yorku.ca/Bandura/bobo.htm

Green, C. S., & Bavelier, D. (2003, May 29). Action video game modifies visual selective attention. *Nature, 423,* 534–537.

Green, M., Palfrey, J. S., Clark, E. M., & Anastasi, J. M. (Eds.). (2002). *Bright futures: Guidelines for health supervision of infants, children, and adolescents* (2nd ed., revised). Arlington, VA: National Center for Education in Maternal and Child Health.

Green, R., & Kinsella, L. J. (1995). Editorial: Current concepts in the diagnosis of cobalamin deficiency. *Neurology, 45,* 1435.

Greenberg, J., & Mitchell, S. (1983). *Object relations in psychoanalytic theory.* Cambridge, MA: Harvard University Press.

Greenbert, G., & Haraway, M. M. (2002). *Principles of comparative psychology.* Boston: Allyn & Bacon.

Greene, S. (1994). Biological determinism: Persisting problems for the psychology of women. *Feminism and Psychology, 14,* 431–435.

Greenfield, D. N. (1999). *Virtual addiction.* Oakland, CA: New Harbinger.

Greenfield, P. M., & Cocking, R. R. (1994). *Cross cultural roots of minority child development.* Hillsdale, NJ: Erlbaum.

Greenfield, P., et al. (1990). Jerome Bruner—Construction of a scientist. *Human Development, 33,* 325–355.

Greenough, W. T., Black, J. E., & Wallace, C. S. (1987). Experience and brain development. *Child Development, 58,* 539–559.

Greenspan, F. S., & Gardner, D. G. (2003). *Basic and clinical endocrinology.* Norwalk, CT: Appleton & Lange.

Greer, D. S., & Mor, V. (1986). An overview of national hospice study findings. *Journal of Chronic Disease, 39,* 5–7. Growth of Hospice, http://www.amda.com/caring/may2004/hospice.htm

Gregory, R. F. (2001). *Age discrimination in the American workplace: Old at a young age.* New Brunswick, NJ: Rutgers University Press.

Greil, A. L. (1997). Infertility and psychological distress: A critical review of the literature. *Social Science and Medicine, 45,* 1679–1704.

Greisberg, S., & McKay, D. (2003). Neuropsychology of obsessive-compulsive disorder: A review and treatment implications. *Clinical Psychology Review, 23,* 95–117.

Greydanus, D. E., Pratt, H. D, & Patel, D. R. (2004). The first three years of life and the early adolescent: Influences of biology and behavior-implications for child rearing. *International Pediatrics, 19*(2), 70–78.

Greydanus, D. E., Pratt, H. D., Spates, C. R., Blake-Dreher, A. E., Greydanus-Gerhart, M. A., & Patel, D. R. (2003). Corporal punishment in schools: Position paper of the Society for Adolescent Medicine. *Journal of Adolescent Health, 32*(5), 385–393.

Grezlik, A. G. (1999). *G. Stanley Hall.* Retrieved from http://fates.cns.muskingum.edu/~psych/psycweb/history/hall.htm

GriefNet, http://griefnet.org

Griffith, S. B. (1963). *Sun Tzu: The art of war.* Oxford, UK: Oxford University Press.

Grisso, T. (1998). *Forensic evaluation of juveniles.* Sarasota, FL: Professional Resource Press.

Griswald, R. (1993). *Fatherhood in America: A history.* New York: Basic Books.

Grosjean, F. (1982). *Life with two languages.* Cambridge, MA: Harvard University Press.

Grossman, A. W., Churchill, J. D., McKinney, B. C., Kodish, I. M., Otte, S. L., & Greenough, W. T. (2003). Experience effects on brain development: Possible contributions to psychopathology. *Journal of Child Psychology and Psychiatry, 44*(1), 33–63.

Grossman, H. J. (Ed.). (1983). *Classification in mental retardation.* Washington, DC: American Association on Mental Deficiency.

Grotberg, E. H. (1995). *A guide to promoting resilience in children: Strengthening the human spirit.* The Hague: Netherlands: Bernard van Leer Foundation. Retrieved from http://resilnet.uiuc.edu/library/grotb95b.html

Grotevant, H. D. (1997). Coming to terms with adoption: The construction of identity from adolescence into adulthood. *Adoption Quarterly, 1*(1), 3–27.

Grotevant, H. D., & Kohler, J. (1999). Adoptive families. In M. E. Lamb (Ed.), *Parenting and child development in "nontraditional" families* (pp. 161–190). Mahwah, NJ: Erlbaum.

Grotevant, H. D., & McRoy, R. G. (1998). *Openness in adoption: Exploring family connections.* Thousand Oaks, CA: Sage.

Growth House, http://www.growthhouse.org

GROWW—Grief and Recovery Online (founded by) Widows & Widowers, http://www.groww.com

Gruber, J., & Wise, D. A. (1999). *Social security and retirement around the world.* Chicago: University of Chicago Press.

Grunbaum, J. A., Kann, L., Kinchen, S. A., Williams, B., Ross, J. G., Lowry, R., et al. (2002). Youth risk behavior surveillance—United States, 2001. *Morbidity and Mortality Weekly Report, 51*(SS04), 1–64. Retrieved from http://www.cdc.gov/mmwr/preview/mmwrhtml/ss5104a1.htm

Grundman, M. (2000). Vitamin E and Alzheimer disease: The basis for additional clinical trials. *American Journal of Clinical Nutrition, 71*, 630S.

Grundy, E., & Bowling, A. (1999). Enhancing the quality of extended life years: Identification of the oldest old with a very good and very poor quality of life. *Aging and Mental Health, 3*(3), 199–212.

Grusec, J. E., & Goodnow, J. J. (1994). Impact of parental discipline methods on the child's internalization of values: A reconceptualization of current points of view. *Developmental Psychology, 30*(1), 4–19.

Grusec, J. E., & Kuczynski, L. (1997). *Parenting and children's internalization of values: A handbook of contemporary theory.* New York: Wiley.

Guanipa-Ho, C., & Guanipa, J. A. (n.d.). *Ethnic identity and adolescence.* Retrieved from http://edweb.sdsu.edu/people/CGuanipa/ethnic.htm

Guardian Newspaper, http://www.guardian.co.uk/gayrights

Guilford, J. P. (1950). Creativity. *American Psychologist, 5*, 444–454.

Guilford, J. P. (1967). *The nature of human intelligence.* New York: McGraw-Hill.

Guilford, J. P. (1973). *Creativity tests for children.* Orange, CA: Sheridan Psychological Services.

Guillot, M. (2003). Life tables. In P. Demeny & G. McNicoll (Eds.), *Encyclopedia of population* (Vol. 1, pp. 594–602). New York: The Gale Group.

Guns and Gunpowder, http://www.pbs.org/wgbh/nova/lost empires/china/age.html

Guralnick, M. J. (2000). Early childhood intervention: Evolution of a system. In M. L. Wehmeyer & J. R. Patton (Eds.), *Mental retardation in the 21st century* (pp. 37–58). Austin, TX: Pro-Ed.

Gurer, H., & Ercal, N. (2000). Can antioxidants be beneficial in the treatment of lead poisoning. *Free Radical Biology & Medicine, 29*, 927–945.

Güss, D. (2002). Planning in Brazil, India, and Germany: A cross-cultural study, a cultural study, and a model. In W. J. Lonner, D. L. Dinnel, S. A. Hayes, & D. N. Sattler (Eds.), *Online readings in psychology and culture.* Bellingham: Western Washington University, Department of Psychology, Center for Cross-Cultural Research. Available from http://www.wwu.edu/~culture

Gutman, A. (1993). *EEO law and personnel practices.* Newbury Park, CA: Sage.

Gutman, A. (2000). *EEO law and personnel practices* (2nd ed.). London: Sage.

Gutmann, D. (1998). The paternal imperative. *American Scholar, 67,* 118–126.

Hack, M., Flannery, D. J., Schluchter, M., Cartar, L., Borawski, E., & Klein, N. (2002). Outcomes in young adulthood for very-low-birth-weight infants [Comment]. *New England Journal of Medicine, 346*(3), 149–157.

Hack, M., Klein, N. K., & Taylor, H. G. (1995). Long-term developmental outcomes of low birth weight infants. *The Future of Children, 5*(1), 176–196.

Hackett, E. (1973). *Blood.* New York: Dutton.

Hackett, G., & Betz, N. E. (1981). A self-efficacy approach to career development of women. *Journal of Vocational Behavior, 18,* 326–339.

Hadaway, N. L., Vardell, S. M., & Young, T. A. (2002). *Young literature-based instruction with English language learners K-12.* Boston: Allyn & Bacon.

Hagedorn, J. M. (1998). *People and folks: Gangs, crime, and the underclass in a rustbelt city* (2nd ed.). Chicago: Lakeview Press.

Hagerman, R. J., & Hagerman, P. J. (2002). *Fragile X syndrome: Diagnosis, treatment, and research* (3rd ed.). Baltimore: Johns Hopkins University Press.

Hahn, S., & Suprenant, L. J. (1998). *Catholic for a reason: Scripture and the mystery of the family of God.* Steubenville, OH: Emmaus Road.

Haidt, J., McCauley, C., & Rozin, P. (1994). Individual differences in sensitivity to disgust: A scale sampling seven domains of disgust elicitors. *Personality and Individual Differences, 16,* 701–713.

Hain, T. C. (2001). *Congenital deafness.* Retrieved from http://www.american-hearing.org/name/cong_hearing.html

Haith, M. M. (1980). *Rules that babies look by.* Hillsdale, NJ: Erlbaum.

Hakuta, K. (1986). *The mirror of language: The debate on bilingualism.* New York: Basic Books.

Halfon, N., Mendonca, A., & Berkowitz, G. (1995). Health status of children in foster care: The experience of the center for the vulnerable child. *Archives of Pediatric Adolescent Medicine, 149,* 386–392.

Hall, C. S. (1954). *A primer of Freudian psychology.* Cleveland, OH: World.

Hall, G. S. (1904). *Adolescence: Its psychology and its relations to physiology, anthropology, sociology, sex, crime, religion and education* (Vols. 1 & 2). New York: Appleton.

Hall, G. S. (1906). *Youth: Its education, regiment, and hygiene.* New York: Appleton.

Hall, G. S. (1911). *Educational problems* (Vols. 1 & 2). New York: Appleton.

Hall, G. S. (1917). *Jesus, the Christ, in the light of psychology* (Vols. 1 & 2). Garden City, NY: Doubleday.

Hall, G. S. (1920). *Morale: The supreme standard of life and conduct.* New York: Appleton.

Hall, G. S. (1923). *The life and confessions of a psychologist.* New York: Appleton.

Hall, G. S. (1923). *Senescence: The last half of life.* New York: Appleton.

Hall, M., Fingerhut, L., & Heinen, M. (2004, November). *National trend data on hospitalization of the elderly for injuries, 1979–2001.* Presented at the annual meeting of the American Public Health Association, Washington, DC.

Hallahan, D. P., & Kauffman, J. M. (2000). *Exceptional learners: Introduction to special education* (8th ed.). Boston: Allyn & Bacon.

Hallahan, D. P., & Kauffman, J. M. (2003). *Exceptional learners: Introduction to special education* (9th ed.). Boston: Allyn & Bacon.

Halpern, D. F., & LaMay, M. L. (2000). The smarter sex: A critical review of sex differences in intelligence. *Educational Psychology Review, 12,* 229–246.

Halverson, C. F., Jr., Kohnstamm, G. A., & Martin, R. P. (Eds.). (1994). *The developing structure of temperament and personality from infancy to adulthood.* Mahwah, NJ: Erlbaum.

Halverson, L. E., Roberton, M. A., Langendorfer, S., & Williams, K. (1979). Longitudinal changes in children's overarm throw ball velocities. *Research Quarterly, 50,* 256–264.

Hamaguchi, P. (1995). *Childhood speech, language, & listening problems: What every parent should know.* New York: Wiley.

Hämäläinen, M., Hari, R., Ilmoniemi, R. J., Knuutila, J., & Lounasmaa, O. V. (1993). Magnetoencephalography—theory, instrumentation, and applications to noninvasive studies of the working human brain. *Reviews of Modern Physics, 65*(2), 413–497.

Hamilton, W. (1964). The evolution of altruistic behavior. *American Naturalist, 97,* 354–356.

Hammen, C. (2003). Mood disorders. In G. Stricker, T. A. Widiger, & I. B. Weiner (Eds.), *Handbook of psychology: Clinical psychology* (Vol. 8, pp. 93–118). New York: Wiley.

Hanks, H., & Hobbs, C. (1993). Failure to thrive: A model for treatment. *Baillière's Clinical Paediatrics, 1*(1), 101–119.

Hanna, G. L. (2000). Clinical and family-genetic studies of childhood obsessive-compulsive disorder. In W. K. Goodman, M. V. Rudorfer, & J. D. Maser (Eds.), *Obsessive-compulsive disorder: Contemporary issues in treatment* (pp. 87–103). Mahwah, NJ: Erlbaum.

Hannah, M. E., Hannah, W. J., Hewson, S. A., Hodnett E. D., Saigal S., & Willan, A. R. (2000). Planned caesarean section versus planned vaginal birth for breech presentation at term: A randomized multicenter trial. Term Breech Trial Collaborative Group. *Lancet, 356,* 1375–1383.

Hansen, D. E., & Vandenberg, B. (1997). Neuropsychological features and differential diagnosis of sleep apnea syndrome in children. *Journal of Clinical Child Psychology, 26,* 304–310.

Hansen, D. J., Christopher, J. S., & Nangle, D. W. (1992). Adolescent heterosexual interactions and dating. In V. D. Van Hasselt & M. Hersen (Eds.), *Handbook of social development: A lifespan perspective* (pp. 371–394). New York: Plenum.

Hanson, T., McLanahan, S., & Thompson, E. (1996). Double-jeopardy: Parental conflict and stepfamily outcomes for children. *Journal of Marriage and the Family, 58,* 141–154.

Harada, M. (1995). Minamata disease: Methylmercury poisoning in Japan caused by environmental pollution. *Critical Reviews in Toxicology, 25,* 1–24.

Hardill, I. (2002). *Gender, migration and the dual career household.* New York: Routledge.

Hareven, T. K. (2001). Historical perspectives on aging and family relations. In R. Binstock & L. K. George (Eds.), *Handbook of aging and social sciences* (5th ed., pp. 141–159). San Diego, CA: Academic Press.

Harkness, S., & Super, C. (1996). *Parents' cultural belief systems.* New York: Guilford.

Harkness, S., & Super, C. M. (2002). Culture and parenting. In M. H. Bornstein (Ed.), *Handbook of parenting: Vol. 2. Biology and ecology of parenting* (2nd ed.). Mahwah, NJ: Erlbaum.

Harlow, H. (1958). The nature of love. *American Psychologist, 13,* 673–685. Available from http://psychclassics.yorku.ca/Harlow/love.htm

Harmening, D. (1999). *Modern blood banking and transfusion practices.* Philadelphia: F. A. Davis.

Harmon-Jones, E., & Mills, J. (1999). *Cognitive dissonance: Progress on a pivotal theory in social psychology.* Washington, DC: American Psychological Association.

Harris, B. (2002). Postpartum depression. *Psychiatric Annals, 32,* 405–415.

Harris, D. B. (Ed.). (1957). *The concept of development: An issue in the study of human behavior* (pp. 125–148). Minneapolis: University of Minnesota Press.

Harris, J. R. (1995). Where is the child's environment? A group socialization theory of development. *Psychological Bulletin, 102,* 458–489.

Harris, P. L. (2000). *The work of the imagination.* Oxford, UK: Blackwell.

Harris, R. J. (1997). Significance tests have their place. *Psychological Science, 8,* 8–11.

Harrod, K. S., Hanson, L., VandeVusse, L., & Heywood, P. (2003). Rh negative status and isoimmunization update: A case-based approach to care. *Journal of Perinatal & Neonatal Nursing, 17*(3), 166–178.

Hart, B., & Risley, T. (2002). *Meaningful differences in the everyday experience of young American children.* Baltimore: Paul H. Brookes.

Hart, L. A. (2004). Social support and psychological adjustment among women who have experienced miscarriage. *Dissertation Abstracts International: Section B: The Sciences and Engineering, 65,* 1029.

Harter, S. (1999). *The construction of the self: A developmental perspective.* New York: Guilford.

Hartmann, D. P. (1988). Measurement and analysis. In M. H. Bornstein & M. E. Lamb (Eds.), *Developmental psychology: An advanced textbook* (2nd ed., pp. 85–147). Hillsdale, NJ: Erlbaum.

Hartup, W. W. (1997). Friendships and adaptation in the life course. *Psychological Bulletin, 121,* 355–370.

Hartup, W. W., & Laursen, B. (1991). Relationships as developmental contexts. In R. Cohen & A. W. Siegel (Eds.), *Context and development* (pp. 253–279). Hillsdale, NJ: Erlbaum.

Harvard Graduate School of Education. (2000, October 1). Reconstructing Larry: Assessing the legacy of Lawrence Kohlberg. *HGSE News/Ed.* Retrieved from http://www.gse.harvard.edu/news/features/larry10012000_page2.html

Harvard University Description of Intergenerational Longitudinal Studies, http://www.radcliffe.edu/documents/murray/0627StudyDescription.pdf

Harvey, J. A. (2004). Cocaine effects on the developing brain: Current status. *Neuroscience and Biobehavioral Review, 27,* 751–764.

Harvey, J. A., & Kosofsky, J. A. (Eds.). (1998). Cocaine: Effects of the developing brain. *Annals of the New York Academy of Sciences, 846.*

Harvey, P., & Serper, M. (1990). Linguistic and cognitive failures in schizophrenia: A multivariate analysis. *Journal of Nervous and Mental Disease, 178,* 487–493.

Harvey, S. M., Beckman, L. J., & Satre, S. J. (2001). Choice of and satisfaction with methods of medical and surgical abortion among U.S. clinic patients. *Family Planning Perspectives, 33,* 212–216.

Harwood, H. (2000). *Updating estimates of the economic cost of alcoholism: Estimates, updating methods, and data.* Bethesda, MD: National Institute on Alcohol Abuse and Alcoholism. Retrieved from http://www.niaaa.nih.gov/publications/economic_2000

Hashway, R. M. (1998). *Developmental cognitive styles: A primer to the literature including an introduction to the theory of developmentalism.* New York: Austin & Winfield.

Haslam, N., Williams, B. J., Kyrios, M., & McKay, D. (in press). Subtyping obsessive-compulsive disorder: A taxometric analysis. *Behavior Therapy.*

Hatcher, R. A., Trussell, J., Stewart, F., Cates, W., Stewart, G. K., Guest, F., et al. (2004). *Contraceptive technology* (18th ed.). New York: Ardent Media.

Haugaard, J. J. (2000). The challenge of defining child sexual abuse. *American Psychologist, 55,* 1036–1039.

Haugaard, J., & Hazan, C. (2002). Foster parenting. In M. H. Bornstein (Ed.), *Handbook of parenting. Vol. 1. Children and parenting* (2nd ed., pp. 313–327). Mahwah, NJ: Erlbaum.

Haupt, S. (Producer). (2002). *Facing death* [Videorecording]. Brooklyn, NY: First Run/Icarus Films.

Hauri, P. (1982). *The sleep disorders.* Kalamazoo, MI: Upjohn.

Hauser, R. M. (1994). Measuring socioeconomic status in studies of child development. *Child Development, 65,* 1541–1545.

Hauser, S. T. (1991). *Adolescents and their families: Patterns of ego development.* New York: Free Press.

Hawes, C., Rose, M., & Phillips, C. D. (1999). *A national survey of assisted living for frail elderly.* Washington, DC: U.S. Department of Health and Human Services and General Accounting Office.

Hawker, D. S. J., & Boulton, M. J. (2000). Twenty years' research on peer victimization and psychosocial maladjustment: A meta-analytic review of cross-sectional studies. *Journal of Child Psychology and Psychiatry, 41,* 441–455.

Hawton, K., & van Heeringen, K. (2000). *International handbook of suicide and attempted suicide.* Chichester, UK: Wiley.

Hayes, C. D. (Ed.). (1982). *Making policies for children: A study of the federal process.* Washington, DC: National Academies Press.

Haynes, S. G., Feinleib, M., & Kannel, W. B. (1980). The relationship of psychosocial factors to coronary heart disease in the Framingham Study. III. Eight-year incidence of coronary heart disease. *American Journal of Epidemiology, 111,* 37–58.

Haynes, S. G., Feinleib, M., Levine, S., Scotch, N., & Kannel, W. B. (1978). The relationship of psychosocial factors to coronary heart disease in the Framingham Study. II. Prevalence of coronary heart disease. *American Journal of Epidemiology, 107,* 384–402.

Hayslip, B., & Patrick, J. H. (2002). *Working with custodial grandparents.* New York: Springer.

Hayslip, B., Ragow-O'Brien, D., & Guarnaccia, C. A. (1998–1999). The relationship of cause of death to attitudes toward funerals and bereavement adjustment. *Omega, 38,* 297–312.

Haywood, K. M. (2001). *Life span motor development.* Champaign, IL: Human Kinetics.

Haywood, K., & Getchell, N. (2001). *Life span motor development* (3rd ed.). Champaign, IL: Human Kinetics.

Healey, K., Smith, C., & O'Sullivan, C. (1998). *Batterer intervention: Program approaches and criminal justice strategies.* Washington, DC: Offices of Justice Programs, National Institute of Justice.

HealthCentersOnline. (n.d.). *Stroke center.* Retrieved from http://www.heartcenteronline.com/The_Stroke_Center.html?WT.srch=1

Health Council of the Netherlands: Committee on the Health Impact of Large Airports. (1999). *Public health impact of large airports.* The Hague: Health Council of the Netherlands.

Healthy People 2010, http://www.healthypeople.gov

Heather, N., & Stockwell, T. (Eds.). (2004). *The essential handbook of treatment and prevention of alcohol problems.* Chichester, UK/Hoboken, NJ: Wiley.

Heatherton, T. F., Herman, C. P., Polivy, J., King, G. A., & McGree, S. T. (1988). The (mis)measurement of restraint: An analysis of conceptual and psychometric issues. *Journal of Abnormal Psychology, 97,* 19–28.

Hebb, D. O. (1949). *Organization of behavior.* New York: Wiley.

Hebert, L. E., Scherr, P. A., Bienias, J. L., Bennett, D. A., & Evans, D. A. (2003). Alzheimer disease in the U.S. population: Prevalence estimates using the 2000 census. *Archives of Neurology, 60,* 1119–1122.

The Hebrew University of Jerusalem, http://ca.huji.ac.il

Heffner, G. J. (2000). *Echolalia and autism.* Retrieved from http://groups.msn.com/TheAutismHomePage/echolaliafacts.msnw

Heffner, G. J. (2000). *Treating echolalia.* Retrieved from http://groups.msn.com/TheAutismHomePage/treatingecholalia.msnw

Heggenhougen, K., Sabin, L., & Lawrence, K. (Eds.). (2004). *Comparative studies of orphans and non-orphans in Uganda* (p. 103). Monograph, Center for International Health and Development, Boston University School of Public Health.

Heidemann S., & Hewitt, D. (1992). *Pathways to play: Developing play skills in young children.* St. Paul, MN: Redleaf Press.

Heifetz, M. D. (1975). *The right to die.* New York: Putnam.

Heimberg, R. G., & Becker, R. E. (2002). *Cognitive-behavioral group therapy for social phobia: Basic mechanisms and clinical strategies.* New York: Guilford.

Heimberg, R. G., Liebowitz, M. R., Hope, D. A., & Schneier, F. R. (1994). *Social phobia: Diagnosis, assessment, and treatment.* New York: Guilford.

Heimberg, R. G., Turk, C. L., & Mennin, D. S. (2004). *Generalized anxiety disorder: Advances in research and practice.* New York: Guilford.

Heinrich, R. K., Corbine, J. L., & Thomas, K. R. (1990). Counseling Native Americans. *Journal of Counseling & Development, 17,* 4–13.

Heinssen, R. K., Liberman, R. P., & Kopelowicz, A. (2000). Psychosocial skills training for schizophrenia: Lessons from the laboratory. *Schizophrenia Bulletin, 26,* 21–46.

Heit, E. (2000). Properties of inductive reasoning. *Psychonomic Bulletin and Review, 7,* 569–592.

The Helen Keller Foundation for Research and Education, http://www.helenkellerfoundation.org

Helgeson, V. S. (1994). Relation of agency and communion to well-being: Evidence and potential explanations. *Psychological Bulletin, 116,* 412–428.

Helgeson, V. S., Snyder, P., & Seltman, H. (2004). Psychological and physical adjustment to breast cancer over 4 years: Identifying distinct trajectories of change. *Health Psychology, 23*(1), 3–15.

Helmreich, W. B. (1996). *Against all odds: Holocaust survivors and the successful lives they made in America.* New Brunswick, NJ: Transaction Publishers.

Helms, J. E. (1990). *Black and White racial identity: Theory, research, and practice.* New York: Greenwood.

Hemenway, D., & Miller, M. (2000). Firearm availability and homicide rates across 26 high-income countries. *Journal of Trauma-Injury Infection & Critical Care, 49*(6), 985–988.

Hendin, H. (1997). *Seduced by death: Doctors, patients, and the Dutch cure.* New York: W. W. Norton.

Henning, M. B., & Mitchell, L. C. (2002). Preparing for inclusion. *Child Study Journal, 32*(1), 19–30.

Henry, S., & Peterson, G. W. (1995). Adolescent social competence, parental qualities, and parental satisfaction. *American Journal of Orthopsychiatry, 65,* 249–262.

Hepburn, L., & Hemenway, D. (2004). Firearm availability and homicide: A review of the literature. *Aggression and Violent Behavior, 9,* 417–440.

Hepburn, T., & Page, A. C. (1999). Effects of images about fear and disgust upon responses to blood-injury phobic stimuli. *Behavior Therapy, 30,* 63–77.

Herman, J. (1997). *Trauma and recovery: The aftermath of violence—From domestic violence to political terror.* New York: Basic Books.

Herschkowitz, N., & Herschkowitz, E. C. (2002). *A good start in life: Understanding your child's brain and behavior.* Washington, DC: Joseph Henry Press.

Hertenstein, M. J. (2002). Touch: Its communicative functions in infancy. *Human Development, 45,* 70–94.

Hesse, E. (1999). The Adult Attachment Interview: Historical and current perspectives. In J. Cassidy & P. Shaver (Eds.), *Handbook of attachment.* New York: Guilford.

Heston, L. (1966). Psychiatric disorders in foster home reared children of schizophrenic mothers. *British Journal of Psychiatry, 112,* 819–825.

Hetherington, E. M., & Stanley-Hagan, M. (2000). Diversity among stepfamilies. In D. H. Demo, K. R. Allen, & M. Fine (Eds.), *Handbook of family diversity* (pp. 173–196). New York: Oxford University Press.

Hetzen, L., & Smith, A. (2001, October). *The 65 years and over population: 2000* (Census 2000 Brief, U.S. Census Bureau). Washington, DC: U.S. Government Printing Office.

Hewitt, J. A. (2003). *Heterosexuality.* Retrieved from http://www.sexandphilosophy.co.uk/heterosexuality.htm

Higgins, S. T., & Katz, J. L. (1998). *Cocaine abuse: Behavior, pharmacology, and clinical applications.* San Diego, CA: Academic Press.

Higgins, E. T., & Kruglanski, A. W. (1996). *Social psychology: Handbook of basic principles.* New York: Guilford.

Higginson, I. J., Finlay-Illora, G., Goodwin, D., Hood, K., Edwards, A. G., Cook, A., et al. (2003). Is there evidence that palliative care teams alter end-of-life experiences of patients and their caregivers? *Journal of Pain and Symptom Management, 25,* 150–168.

High, E. C. (2003). Sweat lodge. *Appalachia Journal, 30,* 355.

High/Scope Educational Research Foundation, http://www.highscope.org

Hilberg, R. (2003). *The destruction of the European Jews.* New Haven, CT: Yale University Press.

Hill, J. B., & Hafner, W. H. J. (2003). Growth before birth. In M. L. Batshaw (Ed.), *Children with disabilities* (5th ed., pp. 43–53). Baltimore: Paul H. Brookes.

Hill, P., Lake, R., & Celio, M. (2002). *Charter schools and accountability in public education.* Washington, DC: Brookings Institute.

Hill, R. (1996). *History of work ethic.* Retrieved from http://www.coe.uga.edu/~rhill/workethic/hist.htm

Hillyard, D., & Dombrink, J. (2001). *Dying right: The death with dignity movement.* New York: Routledge.

Hillyard, S. A., Hink, R. F., Schwent, V. L., & Picton, T. W. (1973). Electrical signs of selective attention in human brain. *Science, 182*(4108), 171–180.

Himelstein, B. P., Hilden, J. M., Boldt, A. M., & Weissman, D. (2004). Medical progress: Pediatric palliative care. *New England Journal of Medicine, 350,* 1752–1762.

Hinde, R. (1970). *Animal behaviour: A synthesis of ethology and comparative psychology.* New York: McGraw-Hill.

Hinde, R. A. (1997). *Relationships: A dialectical perspective.* Hove, UK: Psychology Press.

Hines, D. A., & Malley-Morrison, K. (2005). *Family violence in the United States: Defining, understanding, and combating abuse.* Thousand Oaks, CA: Sage.

Hingson, R., Heeren, T., Levenson, S., Jamanka, A., & Voas, R. (2002). Age of drinking onset, driving after drinking, and involvement in alcohol related motor-vehicle crashes. *Accident Analysis & Prevention, 34*(1), 85–92.

Hinton, R. (2002). Osteoarthritis: Diagnosis and therapeutic considerations. *American Family Physician, 65*, 841–848.

Hiroto, D. S., & Seligman, M. E. P. (1975). Generality of learning helplessness in man. *Journal of Personality and Social Psychology, 31*, 311–327.

Hirsh, D. (2003). *Law against genocide: Cosmopolitan trials.* London: GlassHouse.

Hispanic Federation. (1999). *Hispanic New Yorkers on Nueva York: Seventh annual survey of Hispanic New Yorkers* (Report 3: Profile of the Puerto Rican Community). Retrieved from http://www.hispanicfederation.org/sv993.htm

History of influences in the development of intelligence theory and testing (interactive map), http://www.indiana.edu/~intell/map.shtml

Hitti, P. K. (1968). *History of the Arabs from the earliest times to the present.* New York: St. Martin's Press.

Hoadley, S. L., & Brown, R. T. (2003). Rett syndrome. In E. Fletcher-Janzen & C. R. Reynolds (Eds.), *The diagnostic manual of childhood disorders: Clinical and special education applications.* New York: Wiley.

Hoagies' Gifted Education, http://www.hoagiesgifted.com

Hobbs, F., & Stoops N. (2002). *Demographic trends in the 20th century.* Census 2000 Special Reports. Series CENSR-4. Washington, DC: U.S. Government Printing Office.

Hobbs, N., Perrin, J., & Ireys, H. (1985). *Chronically ill children and their families.* San Francisco: Jossey-Bass.

Hoben, T., & Gilmore, R. O. (2004). Habituation assessment in infancy. *Psychological Methods, 9*(1), 70–92.

Hobson, J. A. (1988). *The dreaming brain.* New York: Basic Books.

Hoff, E. (2001). *Language development.* Belmont, CA: Wadsworth/Thomson Learning.

Hoffman, C., & Kamps, B. (Eds.). (2003). *HIV medicine.* Flying Publisher. Available from http://www.HIVMedicine.com

Hoffman, E. (1994). *The drive for self: Alfred Adler and the founding of individual psychology.* Reading, MA: Addison-Wesley.

Hoffman, E. (Ed.). (1996). *Future visions: The unpublished papers of Abraham Maslow* (pp. 128–147). Thousand Oaks, CA: Sage.

Hoffman, L. (1989). Effects of maternal employment in the two-parent family. *American Psychologist, 44*, 283–293.

Hoffman, M. (1970). Conscience, personality, and socialization techniques. *Human Development, 13*, 90–126.

Hoffman, M. L. (1988). Moral development. In M. H. Bornstein & M. E. Lamb (Eds.), *Developmental psychology: An advanced textbook* (2nd ed., pp. 497–548). Hillsdale, NJ: Erlbaum.

Hoffman, M. L. (2000). *Empathy and moral development: Implications for caring and justice.* New York: Cambridge University Press.

Hofmann, A. D. (1997). Adolescent growth and development. In A. D. Hofmann & D. E. Greydanus (Eds.), *Adolescent medicine* (3rd ed., pp. 11–22). Stamford, CT: Appleton & Lange.

Hogan, J. D., & Sexton, V. S. (1991). Women and the American Psychological Association. *Psychology of Women Quarterly, 15*, 623–634.

Hogan, R., Johnson, J., & Briggs, S. (Eds.). (1997). *Handbook of personality psychology.* San Diego, CA: Academic Press.

Holahan, C., Sears, R., & Cronbach, L. (1995). *The gifted group in later maturity.* Stanford, CA: Stanford University Press.

Holden, C. (2001). "Behavioral" addictions: Do they exist? *Science, 294*, 980–982.

Holden, G., Geffner, R., & Jouriles, E. (Eds.). (1998). *Children exposed to marital violence: Theory, research, and applied issues.* Washington, DC: American Psychological Association.

Holland, J. L. (1985). *Making vocational choices: A theory of vocational personalities and work environments* (2nd ed.). Odessa, FL: Psychological Assessment Resources.

Holland, J. L. (1997). *Making vocational choices: A theory of vocational personalities and work environments* (3rd ed.). Odessa, FL: Psychological Assessment Resources.

Hollingshead, A. B. (1975). *The four-factor index of social status.* Unpublished manuscript, Yale University, New Haven, CT.

Holmberg, B. (1989). *Theory and practice of distance education.* London: Routledge.

Holmes, C. T. (1989). Grade-level retention effects: A meta-analysis of research studies. In L. A. Shepard & M. L. Smith (Eds.), *Flunking grades: Research and policies on retention* (pp. 16–33). London: Falmer.

Holmes, C. T., & Matthews, K. M. (1984). The effects of nonpromotion on elementary and junior high school pupils: A metaanalysis. *Reviews of Educational Research, 54*, 225–236.

Holmes, D. L. (1998). *Autism through the lifespan: The Eden model.* Bethesda, MD: Woodbine House.

Holstein, C. S. (1976). Irreversible, stepwise sequence in the development of moral judgment: A longitudinal study of males and females. *Child Development, 47*, 51–61.

Holt, B. J. (1994, September/October). Targeting in federal grant programs: The case of the Older Americans Act. *Public Administration Review, 54*(5), 444–450.

Holzinger, K. J. (1936). Recent research on unitary mental traits. *Character & Personality, 4*, 335–343.

Holzkamp, K. (1991). Societal and individual life processes. In C. W. Tolman & W. Maiers (Eds.), *Critical psychology: Contributions to an historical science of the subject* (pp. 50–64). Cambridge, UK: Cambridge University Press.

Home Office, Great Britain, www.homeoffice.gov.uk

Honig, B. (1997). *Reading the right way: What research and best practices say about eliminating failure among beginning readers.* Retrieved from http://www.aasa.org/publications/sa/1997_09/honig.htm

Hood, K. K., & Eyberg, S. M. (2003). Outcomes of parent-child interaction therapy: Mothers' reports of maintenance three to six years after treatment. *Journal of Clinical Child and Adolescent Psychology, 32,* 419–429.

The Hormone Foundation, http://www.hormone.org

Horn, J. L. (1986). Intellectual ability concepts. In R. J. Sternberg (Ed.), *Advances in the psychology of human intelligence* (pp. 35–77). Hillsdale, NJ: Erlbaum.

Horn, J. L. (1988). Thinking about human abilities. In J. R. Nesselroade & R. B. Cattell (Eds.), *Handbook of multivariate psychology* (2nd ed., pp. 645–685). New York: Academic Press.

Horn, J. L. (1991). Measurement of intellectual capabilities: A review of theory. In K. S. McGrew, J. K. Werder, & R. W. Woodcock (Eds.), *Woodcock-Johnson technical manual* (pp. 197–232). Chicago: Riverside.

Horn, J. L. (1994). Theory of fluid and crystallized intelligence. In R. J. Sternberg (Ed.), *Encyclopedia of human intelligence* (pp. 443–451). New York: Macmillan.

Horn, J. L., & Cattell, R. B. (1966). Refinement and test of the theory of fluid and crystallized general intelligences. *Journal of Educational Psychology, 57,* 253–270.

Horn, J. L., & Cattell, R. B. (1967). Age differences in fluid and crystallized intelligence. *Acta Psychologica, 26,* 107–129.

Horn, J. L., & Masunaga, H. (2000). New directions for research into aging and intelligence: The development of expertise. In T. J. Perfect & E. A. Maylor (Eds.), *Models of cognitive aging* (pp. 125–159). Oxford, UK: Oxford University Press.

Horn, J. L., & Noll, J. (1997). Human cognitive capabilities: Gf-Gc theory. In D. P. Flanagan, J. L. Genshaft, & P. L. Harrison (Eds.), *Contemporary intellectual assessment: Theories, tests, and issues* (pp. 53–91). New York: Guilford.

Horn, T. (Ed.). (2002). *Advances in sport psychology* (2nd ed.). Champaign, IL: Human Kinetics.

Horner, T. (1985). The psychic life of the young infant: Review and critique of the psychoanalytic concepts of symbiosis and infantile omnipotence. *American Journal of Orthopsychiatry, 55,* 324–344.

Hospice Association of America, http://www.hospice-america.org

Hospice Foundation of America, http://www.hospicefoundation.org

Hospice Web, http://www.hospiceweb.com

House Select Committee on Aging, U.S. Congress. (1991). *Elder abuse: What can be done?* Washington, DC: U.S. Government Printing Office.

House, J. S., Landis, K. R., & Umberson, D. (1988). Social relationships and health. *Science, 241,* 540–545.

Howard Gardner, http://www.howardgardner.com

Howell, J. C. (1999). *Youth gang programs and strategies.* Washington, DC: U.S. Department of Justice, Office of Justice Programs, Office of Juvenile Justice and Delinquency Prevention.

Howes, C. (1996). The earliest friendships. In W. M. Bukowski, A. F. Newcomb, & W. W. Hartup (Eds.), *The company they keep: Friendship in childhood and adolescence* (pp. 66–86). Cambridge, UK: Cambridge University Press.

Howlin, P., & Udwin, O. (Eds.). (2002). *Outcomes in neurodevelopmental and genetic disorders.* New York: Cambridge University Press.

Hoyert, D. L., Kochanek, K. D., & Murphy, S. L. (1999). *National Vital Statistics Report, 47.*

Hoyt-Goldsmith, D., & Migdale, L. (2002). *Celebrating a Quinceañera: A Latina's 15th birthday celebration.* New York: Holiday House.

Hsu, L. K. G. (1990). *Eating disorders.* New York: Guilford.

Hudson, L. M., & Gray, W. M. (1986). Formal operations, the imaginary audience and the personal fable. *Adolescence, 21*(84), 751–765.

Huettel, S. A., Song, A. W., & McCarthy, G. (2004). *Functional magnetic resonance imaging.* Sunderland, MA: Sinauer.

Huey, E. B. (1968). *The psychology and pedagogy of reading.* Cambridge: MIT Press. (Original work published 1908)

Huff, C. R. (1996). *Gangs in America* (2nd ed.). Thousand Oaks, CA: Sage.

Hughes, B. A., & James, G. (1980). *American Academy of Pediatrics: The first 50 years.* Chicago: American Academy of Pediatrics.

Hughes, J. R., Daaboul, Y., Fino, J. J., & Shaw, G. L. (1998). The "Mozart effect" in epileptiform activity. *Clinical Electroencephalography, 29,* 101–119.

Hughes, S. M., & Gallup, G. G. (2003). Sex differences in morphological predictors of sexual behavior: Shoulder to hip and waist to hip ratios. *Evolution and Human Behavior, 24,* 173–178.

Huitt, W. (1997). Cognitive development: Applications. *Educational psychology interactive.* Valdosta, GA: Valdosta State University. Retrieved from http://chiron.valdosta.edu/whuitt/col/cogsys/piagtuse.html

Huitt, W. (2002). Social cognition. In *Educational psychology interactive.* Valdosta, GA: Valdosta State University. Retrieved from http://chiron.valdosta.edu/whuitt/col/soccog/soccog.html

Huitt, W. (2003). *The information processing approach.* Retrieved from http://chiron.valdosta.edu/whuitt/col/cogsys/infoproc.html

Huitt, W., & Hummel, J. (2003). Piaget's theory of cognitive development. *Educational psychology interactive.* Valdosta, GA: Valdosta State University. Retrieved from http://chiron.valdosta.edu/whuitt/col/cogsys/piaget.html

Huitt, W., & Hummel, J. (2004). *Cognitive development.* Retrieved from http://chiron.valdosta.edu/whuitt/col/cogsys/piaget.html

Hukanovic, R. (1997). *The tenth circle of Hell.* London: Little, Brown.

Hull, C. (1943). *Principles of behavior.* New York: Appleton-Century-Crofts.

Hull, C. L. (1928). *Aptitude testing.* Yonkers-on-Hudson, NY: World Book.

The human genome. (2001, February 16). Retrieved from http://www.sciencemag.org/content/v01291/issue5507/index.html

The human genome. (n.d.). Retrieved from http://www.nature.com/genomics/human/papers/articles.html

Human Rights Watch. (2003). *Non-discrimination in civil marriage: Perspective from international human rights law and practice.* Available from http://www.hrw.org/lgbt/

Human Rights Watch. (2005). *Orphans and abandoned children.* Retrieved from http://www.hrw.org/children/abandoned.htm

Humphrey, J. H. (1992). *Motor learning in childhood education.* Springfield, IL: Thomas.

Humphry, D. (1991). *Final exit: The practicalities of self-deliverance and assisted suicide for the dying.* Secaucus, NJ: Carol Publishing.

Humphry, D., & Clement, M. (1998). *Freedom to die: People, politics, and the right to die movement.* New York: St. Martin's Press.

Humphry, D., & Wickett, A. (1986). *The right to die.* Eugene, OR: The Hemlock Society.

Hunt, E. (1971). What kind of computer is man? *Cognitive Psychology, 2,* 57–98.

Hunter, R. H. F. (2003). *Physiology of the graafian follicle and ovulation.* Cambridge, UK: Cambridge University Press.

Huntington's Disease Association, http://www.hda.org.uk/

Huntington's Disease Society of America, http://www.hdsa.org/

Hurley, V. M., Mitchell, H. L., & Walsh, N. (2003). In osteoarthritis, the psychosocial benefits of exercise are as important as physiological improvements. *Exercise Sport Science Review, 31,* 138–143.

Hussey-Gardner, B. (n.d.). *Parenting to make a difference: Social skills.* Retrieved from http://www.parentingme.com/social.htm

Huttenlocher, P. R. (2002). *Neural plasticity.* Cambridge, MA: Harvard University Press.

Hyde, J. S., & DeLamater, J. D. (2003). *Understanding human sexuality* (8th ed.). New York: McGraw-Hill.

Hyman, I. A., McDowell, E., & Rains, B. (1977). Corporal punishment and alternatives in the schools: An overview of theoretical and practical issues. *National Institute of Education: Proceedings: Conference on Corporal Punishment Schools: A National Debate, February 18–20, 1977.* Washington, DC: U.S. Government Printing Office.

Hymes, D. (1974). *Foundations in sociolinguistics.* Philadelphia: University of Pennsylvania Press.

Hymowitz, K. S. (1995, Autumn). *On Sesame Street, it's all show.* Retrieved from http://www.city journal.org/html/5_4_on_sesame_street.html

HyperStat Online Textbook, http://davidmlane.com/hyperstat/index.html

Ickes, W. (Ed.). (1997). *Empathic accuracy.* New York: Guilford.

IDEA Practices, http://www.ideapractices.org

Iglehart, J. K. (2004). The new Medicare prescription-drug benefit: A pure power play. *New England Journal of Medicine, 350,* 826–833.

In re Estate of Antonopoulos, 268 Kan. 178, 189, 993 P.2d 637 (1999).

Indian Health Service. (2001). *Domestic violence and child abuse prevention initiative.* Available from http://www.ihs.gov/

Individuals with Disabilities Education Act (IDEA) Amendments of 1997, PL 105–17, 20 U.S.C. §§ *et seq.*

Information on self-efficacy, http://www.emory.edu/mfp/self-efficacy.html

Innocence Lost. A PBS/Frontline production on several famous daycare child abuse cases. Retrieved from http://www.pbs.org/wgbh/pages/frontline/shows/innocence/

Innocence Project. *DNA based reversals of guilty convictions.* Available from http://www.innocenceproject.org/

The Institute for Applied Psychometrics, http://www.iapsych.com

Institute for Community Inclusion, http://www.communityinclusion.org/

Institute of Human Development at University of California, Berkeley, http://ihd.berkeley.edu/hm2.htm

Institute for Learning Technologies. (n.d.). *Rousseau's Emile, ou l'education.* Retrieved from http://projects.ilt.columbia.edu/pedagogies/rousseau/contents2.html

Institute of Medicine. (1997). *Approaching death: Improving care at the end of life* (M. J. Field & C. K. Cassell, Eds.). Washington, DC: National Academy Press.

Institute of Medicine, Committee on Palliative and End-of-Life Care for Children and Their Families (M. J. Field & R. E. Behrman, Eds.). (2002). *When children die: Improving palliative and end-of-life care for children and their families.* Washington, DC: National Academies Press.

Institute of Medicine of the National Academies. (2003). *When children die: Improving palliative and end-of-life care for children and their families.* Washington, DC: National Academies Press.

Institute for Personal Growth. (n.d.). *Bisexuality in women: Myths, realities, and implications for therapy.* Retrieved from http://www.ipgcounseling.com/bisexuality_in_women.html

Institute for Personality and Social Research at the University of California at Berkeley, http://ls.berkeley.edu/dept/ipsr/IPSRArchiveWeb/ArchivesStart.htm

Institute for the Study of Aging and the International Longevity Center–USA, http://www.aging-institute.org

Institute for the Study of Youth Sports, Michigan State, http://ed-web3.educ.msu.edu/ysi

Institute for Volunteering Research, http://www.ivr.org.uk/

International Association for Conflict Management, http://www.iacm-conflict.org

International Association for Cross-Cultural Psychology, http://www.iaccp.org/

International Birth Defects Information System, http://www.ibis-birthdefects.org

International Commission on Second Language Acquisition, http://www.hw.ac.uk/langwww/icsla/icsla.html

The InterNational Council on Infertility Information Dissemination, Inc., http://www.inciid.org/

International Criminal Tribunal for the Former Yugoslavia, http://www.un.org/icty/

International Dyslexia Association, http://www.interdys.org

International Gay and Lesbian Association, http://www.ilga.com

International Human Genome Sequencing Consortium. (2004, October 21). Finishing the euchromatic sequence of the human genome. *Nature, 431,* 931–945. Retrieved from http://www.nature.com/cgi-taf/DynaPage.taf?file=/nature/journal/v431/n7011/full/nature03001_fs.html

International Journal on E-Learning, http://www.aace.org/pubs/ijel/default.htm

International League Against Epilepsy (ILAE), http://www.ilae-epilepsy.org

International Personality Item Pool. (2001). *A scientific collaboratory for the development of advanced measures of personality traits and other individual differences.* Available from http://ipip.ori.org/

International Reading Association. (1998, July). *Summary of a position statement of the International Reading Association: Phonemic awareness and the teaching of reading.* Retrieved from http://www.reading.org/positions/phonemic.html

International Reading Association's Phonics Special Interest Group, http://www.phonicsbulletin.info

International Rett Syndrome Association, http://rettsyndrome.org

International Society of Developmental Psychobiology, http://www.oswego.edu/isdp/

International Society on Infant Studies, http://www.isisweb.org

International Society for Self and Identity, http://www.psych.neu.edu/ISSI/

International Society for Twin Studies, http://www.ists.qimr.edu.au

Iowa State University, University Extension. (1999). *Living with your teenager: Understanding emotional changes.* Retrieved from http://www.extension.iastate.edu/Publications/PM944A.pdf

Irvine, J. M. (2002). *Talk about sex: The battles over sex education in the United States.* San Diego, CA: Greenhaven Press.

Isabella, R. A. (1995). The origins of infant-mother attachment: Maternal behavior and infant development. *Annals of Child Development, 10,* 57–81.

Isabella, R. A., Belsky, J., & von Eye, A. (1989). Origins of infant-mother attachment: An examination of interactional synchrony during the infant's first year. *Developmental Psychology, 19,* 418–426.

Issacharoff, S., & Harris, E. W. (1997). Is age discrimination really age discriminations? The ADEA's unnatural solution. *New York University Law Review, 72,* 780–840.

Isser, N. K., & Schwartz, L. L. (2000). *Endangered children: Neonaticide, infanticide, and filicide.* Boca Raton, FL: CRC Press.

iVillage, Inc. (2001, June 20). *Potty training: 10 steps to toilet teaching your toddler.* Retrieved from http://www.parentsoup.com/toddlers/potty/articles/0,,262585_260941,00.html

iVillage. (2005). *Incompatibility of blood types and Rh factor.* Retrieved from http://www.ivillage.co.uk/pregnancyand-baby/pregnancy/complicatepreg/qas/0,,15_158142,00.html

Iwaniec, D. (1995). *The emotionally abused and neglected child: Identification, assessment and intervention.* Chichester, UK: Wiley.

Iwaniec, D. (2004). *Children who fail to thrive: A practice guide.* Chichester, UK: Wiley.

Iyasu, S., Randell, L. L., Welty, T. K., Hsai, J., Kinney, H. C., Mandell, F., et al. (2002). Risk factors for sudden infant death syndrome among Northern Plains Indians. *Journal of the American Medical Association, 288,* 2717–2723.

Jackson, D. J., Lang, J. M., Swartz, W. H., Ganiats, T. G., Fulleron, J., Eckers, F., et al. (2003). Outcomes, safety, and resource utilization in a collaborative care birth center program compared with traditional physician-based prenatal care. *American Journal of Public Health, 93*(6), 999–1006.

Jacob, R. (2000). Vitamin C. In M. Shils, J. Olson, M. Shike, & A. C. Ross (Eds.), *Modern nutrition in health and disease* (p. 467). Philadelphia: Lippincott Williams & Wilkins.

Jacobowitz, R. S. (Ed.). (1999). *The estrogen answer book: 150 Most-asked questions about hormone replacement therapy.* Boston: Little, Brown.

Jacobs, L. (1987). *The book of Jewish belief.* Mahwah, NJ: Behrman House.

Jacobs, L. (1987). *The book of Jewish practice.* Mahwah, NJ: Behrman House.

Jacobs, P. A., & Strong, J. A. (1959). A case of human intersexuality having a possible XXY sex-determining mechanism. *Nature, 183,* 302–303.

Jacobsen, P. B., & Breitbart, W. (2002). Managing pain in chronic illness. In Chesney, M. A., & Antoni, M. H. (Eds.), *Innovative approaches to health psychology: Prevention and treatment lessons from AIDS* (pp. 219–234). Washington, DC: American Psychological Association.

Jacobson, J. L., & Jacobson, S. L. (2000). Teratogenic insult and neurobehavioral function in infancy and childhood. In C. A. Nelson (Ed.), *The effects of early adversity on neurobehavioral development: The Minnesota symposium on child psychology, Vol. 31.* Mahwah, NJ: Erlbaum.

Jacoby, W. G. (1991). *Data theory and dimensional analysis.* Newbury Park, CA: Sage.

James, L. E., & MacKay, D. G. (2001). H. M., word knowledge, and aging: Support for a new theory of long-term retrograde amnesia. *Psychological Science, 12*(6), 485–492.

Jamison, K. R. (1995). *An unquiet mind.* New York: Knopf.

Jamison, K. R. (1999). *Night falls fast: Understanding suicide.* New York: Knopf.

Jamison, S. (1997). *Assisted suicide: A decision-making guide for health professionals.* San Francisco: Jossey-Bass.

Janeway, C., Travers, P., Walport, M., & Shlomchik, M. J. (2005). *Immunobiology: The immune system in health and disease* (6th ed.), Oxford, UK: Garland Science.

Janos, P. M., Fung, H. C., & Robinson, N. M. (1985). Self-concept, self-esteem, and peer relations among gifted children who feel different. *Gifted Child Quarterly, 29*(2), 78–82.

Janssen, P. A., Holt, V. L., Sugg, N. K., Emanuel, I., Critchlow, C. M., & Henderson, A. D. (2003). Intimate partner violence and adverse pregnancy outcomes: A population-based study. *American Journal of Obstetrics and Gynecology, 188*(5), 1341–1347.

Janssen, P. A., Lee, S. K., Ryan, E. M., Etches, D. J., Farquharson, D. F., Peacock, D., et al. (2002). Outcomes of planned home births versus planned hospital births after regulation of midwifery in British Columbia. *Canadian Medical Association Journal, 166*, 315–323.

Japanese Justice Ministry denies citizenship to twins whose parents used U.S. surrogate (2003, October 27). *Kaiser Daily Reproductive Health Report.* Available from http://www.kaisernetwork.org?dailyreports/

Jarrett, R. (1997). African American family and parenting strategies in impoverished neighborhoods. *Qualitative Sociology, 20*(2), 275–287.

Jarvinen, D. W., & Nicholls, J. G. (1996). Adolescents' social goals, beliefs about the causes of social success, and satisfaction in peer relations. *Developmental Psychology, 32*(3), 435–441.

Jason, L. A., Fennell, P., & Taylor, R. R. (Eds.). (2003). *Handbook of chronic fatigue syndrome.* New York: Wiley.

Jason, L. A., Richman, J. A., Friedberg, F., Wagner, L., Taylor, R., & Jordan, K. M. (1997). Politics, science, and the emergence of a new disease: The case of chronic fatigue syndrome. *American Psychologist, 52*, 973–983.

Jayeon, L. (2003). *A new look at the critical period hypothesis.* Retrieved from http://www.alak.or.kr/2_public/2003_oct/document/200310_feature_article.pdf

Jean Piaget Society, http://www.piaget.org

Jean Piaget Society. (n.d.). *Internet resources.* Retrieved from http://www.piaget.org/links.html

Jelalian, E., & Saelens, B. E. (1999). Empirically supported treatments in pediatric psychology: Pediatric obesity. *Journal of Pediatric Psychology, 24*, 223–248.

Jenike, M. A. (1998). Drug treatment of obsessive-compulsive disorders. In M. A. Jenike, L. Baer, & W. E. Minichiello (Eds.), *Obsessive-compulsive disorders: Practical management* (3rd ed., pp. 469–532). St. Louis, MO: Mosby.

Jennings, B., Gemmill, C., Bohman, B., & Lamb, K. (n.d.). *PHI350: The stages in the dying process.* Retrieved from http://www.uky.edu/Classes/PHI/350/kr.htm

Jensen, A. R. (1998). *The g factor.* Westport, CT: Praeger.

The Jewish Theological Seminary, http://www.jtsa.edu/about/cj

Jeynes, W. H. (2002). The challenge of controlling for SES in social science and education research. *Educational Psychology Review, 14*, 205–221.

Jezzard, P., Matthews, P. M., & Smith, S. M. (Eds.). (2001). *Functional MRI: An introduction to methods.* Oxford, UK: Oxford University Press.

Jimerson, S. R. (1999). On the failure of failure: Examining the association between early grade retention and education and employment outcomes during late adolescence. *Journal of School Psychology, 37*, 243–272.

Jimerson, S. R. (2001). Meta-analysis of grade retention research: Implications for practice in the 21st century. *School Psychology Review, 30*, 420–437.

Jimerson, S. R. (n.d.). *Beyond grade retention and social promotion.* Retrieved from http://www.education.ucsb.edu/jimerson/retention

Jimerson, S. R., Anderson, G. E., & Whipple, A. D. (2002). Winning the battle and losing the war: Examining the relation between grade retention and dropping out of high school. *Psychology in the Schools, 39*(4), 441–457.

Jimerson, S. R., Carlson, E., Rotert, M., Egeland, B., & Sroufe, L. A. (1997). A prospective, longitudinal study of the correlates and consequences of early grade retention. *Journal of School Psychology, 35*, 3–25.

Jimerson, S. R., Ferguson, P., Whipple, A. D., Anderson, G. E., & Dalton, M. J. (2002). Exploring the association between grade retention and dropout: A longitudinal study examining socio-emotional, behavioral, and achievement characteristics of retained students. *California School Psychologist, 7*, 51–62.

Jimerson, S. R., & Kaufman, A. M. (2003). Reading, writing, and retention: A primer on grade retention research. *The Reading Teacher, 56*(8), 622–635.

Joe, S., & Marcus, S. C. (2003). Datapoints: Trends by race and gender in suicide attempts among U.S. adolescents, 1991–2001. *Psychiatric Services, 54*(4), 454.

Johanson, C. E., & Schuster, C. R. (1995). Cocaine. In F. J. Bloom & D. J. Kupfer (Eds.), *Psychopharmacology: The fourth generation of progress* (pp. 1685–1690). New York: Raven Press.

John B. Watson, http://www.psy.pdx.edu/PsiCafe/KeyTheorists/Watson.htm#About

John C. Liebeskind History of Pain Collection. (1998). *Relief of pain and suffering.* Retrieved from http://www.library.ucla.edu/libraries/biomed/his/painexhibit/index.html

Johnson, C. J. (n.d.). *Stranger anxiety: When your baby is afraid of newcomers.* Retrieved from http://www.babiestoday.com/resources/articles/stranger.htm

Johnson, C. L., & Barer, B. M. (1997). *Life beyond 85: The aura of survivorship.* New York: Springer.

Johnson, D. J. (2002). *The psychology of wisdom: Evaluation and analysis of theory.* Unpublished dissertation, Fielding Graduate University, Santa Barbara, CA.

Johnson, D., & Fein, E. (1991). The concept of attachment: Applications to adoption. *Children and Youth Services Review, 13*, 397–412.

Johnson, D. W., & Johnson, R. T. (1996). Conflict resolution and peer mediation programs in elementary and secondary schools: A review of the research. *Review of Educational Research, 66*, 459–506.

Johnson, J. K., Cotman, C., Tasaki, C. S., & Shaw, G. L. (1998). Enhancement in spatial-temporal reasoning after a Mozart listening condition in Alzheimer's disease. *Neurological Research, 20,* 61–72.

Johnson, K. O. (1995). *Why do Catholics do that? A guide to the teachings and practices of the Catholic Church.* New York: Random House.

Johnson, M. H., Munakata, Y., & Gilmore, R. O. (Eds.). (2002). *Brain development and cognition: A reader* (2nd ed.). Oxford, UK: Blackwell.

Johnson, M. K., Hashtroudi, S., & Lindsay, D. S. (1993). Source monitoring. *Psychological Bulletin, 114,* 3–28.

Johnson, S., Hayes, A., Field, T., Schneiderman, N., & McCabe, P. (Eds.). (2000). *Stress, coping, and depression.* Mahwah, NJ: Erlbaum.

Johnson, W. B. (2002). The intentional mentor: Strategies and guidelines for the practice of mentoring. *Professional Psychology: Research and Practice, 33,* 88–96.

Johnson-Laird, P. (1983). *Mental models.* Cambridge, MA: Harvard University Press.

Johnston, L. D., O'Malley, P. M., & Bachman, J. G. (2002). *National survey results on drug use from the Monitoring the Future Study, 1975–2001: Volume I, secondary school students* (NIH Publication No. 02–5106). Bethesda, MD: National Institute on Drug Abuse.

Johnston, L. D., O'Malley, P. M., & Bachman, J. G. (2003). *Monitoring the Future national survey results on drug use 1975–2002: Vol. 1. Secondary school students* (NIH Publication No. 03-5375). Bethesda, MD: National Institute on Drug Abuse. See also http://www.monitoringthefuture.org

Joiner, T. E., Jr. (1999). The clustering and contagion of suicide. *Current Direction in Psychological Science, 8*(3), 89–92.

Joint custody from the child's point of view, http://www.gocrc.com

Joint custody from the father's point of view, http://www.deltabravo.net

Joint custody from the mother's point of view, http://www.now.org

Joint United Nations Programme on HIV/AIDS. (2004). *UNAIDS.* Retrieved from http://www.unaids.org

Jonas, H. (1970). Philosophical reflections on experimenting with human subjects. In P. Freund (Ed.), *Experimentation with human subjects* (pp. 1–31). New York: Braziller.

Jones, A. (2002). The National Nursing Home Survey: 1999 summary. National Center for Health Statistics. *Vital Health Statistics, 13,* 152.

Jones, E. (1953/1957). *Sigmund Freud: Life and work* (3 vols.). London: Hogarth Press.

Jones, G., Steketee, R. W., Black, R. E., Bhutta, Z. A., Morris, S. S., & the Bellagio Child Survival Study Group. (2003). How many child deaths can we prevent this year? *Lancet, 362*(9377), 65–71.

Jones, J. S. (2003). *Overcoming impotence: A leading urologist tells you everything you need to know.* Amherst, NY: Prometheus Books.

Jones, L. M., & Finkelhor, D. (2003). Putting together evidence on declining trends in sexual abuse: A complex puzzle. *Child Abuse and Neglect, 27,* 133–135.

Jones, M. L. (1996). *Phonics in ESL literacy instruction: Functional or not?* Santa Barbara, CA: Santa Barbara City College. Retrieved from http://www.literacyonline.org/products/ili/pdf/ilprocmj.pdf

Jones, R. K., & Henshaw, S. K. (2002). Mifepristone for early medical abortion: Experiences in France, Great Britain and Sweden. *Perspectives on Sexual and Reproductive Health, 34,* 154–161.

Jones, W. H., & Carver, M. (1991). The experience of loneliness: Adjustment and coping implications. In R. Snyder & D. Forsyth (Eds.), *Handbook of social and clinical psychology* (pp. 395–415). New York: Plenum.

Jorde, L. B. (Ed.). (2005). *Encyclopedia of genetics, genomics, proteomics, and bioinformatics: Vol. 1. Genetics.* New York: Wiley.

Journal of Applied Behavior Analysis, http://seab.envmed.rochester.edu

Judaism 101. (n.d.). *Bar Mitzvah, Bat Mitzvah and Confirmation.* Available at http://Jewfaq.org/barmitz.htm

Junco, F. (1993). Acquisition of a filial preference in an altricial bird without food reinforcement. *Animal Behaviour, 46*(6), 1237–1239.

Junco, F. (1993). Filial imprinting in blackbird nestlings, *Turdus merula,* after only one feeding session. *Animal Behaviour, 45*(3), 619–622.

Junod, T. (1998, November). Can you say . . . "hero"? *Esquire.* Retrieved from http://www.keepmedia.com/pubs/Esquire/1998/11/01/170940?from=search&criteria=Can+you+say.+.+.hero

Jusczyk, P. (1997). *The discovery of spoken language.* Cambridge: MIT Press.

Jussim, L. (1989). Teacher expectations: Self-fulfilling prophecies, perceptual biases, and accuracy. *Journal of Personality and Social Psychology, 57*(3), 469–480.

Juvenile Justice Information Center, http://www.juvenilejusticeinfocenter.com

Juvonen, J., & Graham, S. (Eds.). (2001). *Peer harassment in school: The plight of the vulnerable and victimized.* New York: Guilford.

Kagan, J. (1994). *Galen's prophecy.* New York: Basic Books.

Kahill, M. L., Mosenthal, P. B., Pearson, P., & Barr, R. (Eds.). (2000). *Handbook of reading research: Vol. 3.* Mahwah, NJ: Erlbaum.

Kahn, R. L. (2003). Successful aging: Intended and unintended consequences of a concept. In L. W. Poon, S. H. Gueldner, & B. M. Sprouse (Eds.), *Successful aging and adaptation with chronic diseases.* New York: Springer.

Kahneman, D., & Treisman, A. (1992). The reviewing of object files: Object-specific integration of information. *Cognitive Psychology, 24*(2), 175–219.

Kaiser, A. P., & Hester, P. P. (1997). Prevention of conduct disorder through early intervention: A social-communicative perspective. *Behavioral Disorders, 22,* 117–130.

Kaiser Family Foundation. (2003). *National survey of adolescents and young adults: Sexual health knowledge, attitudes and experiences.* Menlo Park, CA: Author. Retrieved from http://www.kff.org/youthhivstds/3218-index.cfm

Kaiser Family Foundation. (n.d.). *Medicare.* Retrieved from http://www.kff.org/medicare/index.cfm

Kaiser Family Foundation. (n.d.). *Sex education in the U.S.: Policy and politics.* Retrieved from http://www.kff.org/youthhivstds/3224-02-index.cfm

Kalat, J. W. (1998). *Biological psychology* (6th ed.). Pacific Grove, CA: Brooks/Cole.

Kaldor, M. (1999). *New and old wars: Organized violence in a global era.* London: Polity.

Kalish, R. A. (Ed.). (1985). *The final analysis.* Farmingdale, NY: Baywood.

Kalman, M. B. (2000). Adolescent menstrual lay literature. *Journal of Multicultural Nursing and Health, 6*(1), 35–41.

Kamerman, S. B. (Ed.). (2001). *Early childhood education and care: International perspectives.* New York: Institute for Child and Family Policy, Columbia University.

Kamo, Y. (2000). Racial and ethnic differences in extended family households. *Sociological Perspectives, 4,* 211–229.

Kamo, Y., & Zhou, M. (1994). Living arrangements of elderly Chinese and Japanese in the United States. *Journal of Marriage and the Family, 56,* 544–558.

Kamphaus, R. W. (1993). *Clinical assessment of children's intelligence.* Boston: Allyn & Bacon.

Kamphaus, R. W. (1998). Intelligence test interpretation: Acting in the absence of evidence. In A. Prifitera & D. Saklofshe (Eds.), *WISC-III clinical use and interpretation: Scientist-practitioner perspectives* (pp. 39–57). New York: Academic Press.

Kamphaus, R. W., Petoskey, M. D., & Morgan, A. W. (1997). A history of test intelligence interpretation. In D. P. Flanagan, J. L. Genshaft, & P. L. Harrison (Eds.), *Contemporary intellectual assessment: Theories, tests, and issues* (pp. 32–51). New York: Guilford.

Kamps, D. M., Tankersley, M., & Ellis, C. (2000). Social skills interventions for young at-risk students: A 2-year follow-up study. *Behavioral Disorders, 25,* 310–324.

Kandel, D. B. (1975). Stages in adolescent involvement in drug use. *Science, 190,* 912–914.

Kandel, D. B. (2002). Examining the gateway hypothesis: Stages and pathways of drug involvement. In D. B. Kandel (Ed.), *Stages and pathways of drug involvement: Examining the gateway hypothesis* (pp. 3–15). New York: Cambridge University Press.

Kandel, E. R. (2002). *Habituation involves a depression of synaptic transmission.* Retrieved from http://www.geocities.com/celllearning/habituation.htm

Kandel, E. R., Schwartz, J. H., & Jessell, T. M. (2000). Cellular mechanisms of learning and the biological basis of individuality. In E. R. Kandel, J. H. Schwartz, & T. M. Jessell (Eds.), *Principles of neural science* (4th ed., pp. 1247–1279). New York: McGraw-Hill.

Kane, M. J., & Engle, R. W. (2002). The role of prefrontal cortex in working-memory capacity, executive attention, and general fluid intelligence: An individual-differences perspective. *Psychonomic Bulletin and Review, 9,* 637–671.

Kane, R. J., & Yacoubian, G. S., Jr. (1999). Patterns of drug escalation among Philadelphia arrestees: An assessment of the gateway theory. *Journal of Drug Issues, 29,* 107–120.

Kanis, J. A. (2002). Diagnosis of osteoporosis and assessment of fracture risk. *Lancet, 359,* 1929–1936.

Kannel, W. B., & Eaker, E. D. (1986). Psychosocial and other features of coronary heart disease: Insights from the Framingham Study. *American Heart Journal, 112*(5), 1066–1073.

Kanner, L. (1943). Autistic disturbances of affective content. *Nervous Child, 2,* 217–250.

Kantor, G., & Straus, M. A. (1990). The "drunken bum" theory of wife beating. In M. A. Straus & R. J. Gelles (Eds.), *Physical violence in American families* (pp. 203–224). New Brunswick, NJ: Transaction.

Kaplan, H. R. (1987). Lottery winners: The myth and reality. *Journal of Gambling Behavior, 3*(3), 168–178.

Kaplan, J. R., Adams, M. R., Clarkson, T. B., Manuck, S. B., & Shively, C. A. (1991). Social behavior and gender in biomedical investigations using monkeys: Studies in atherogenesis. *Laboratory Animal Science, 41,* 334–343.

Kaplan, N. M. (Ed.). (2002). *Clinical hypertension* (8th ed.). New York: Lippincott Williams & Wilkins.

Kaptelinin, V., & Nardie, B. (1997). *Activity theory: Basic concepts and applications.* Retrieved from http://www.acm.org/sigchi/chi97/proceedings/tutorial/bn.htm

Karasek, R. A., & Theorell, T. (1990). *Healthy work: Stress, productivity and the reconstruction of working life.* New York: Basic Books.

Karen, R. (1994). *Becoming attached: Unfolding the mystery of the infant-mother bond and its impact on later life.* New York: Warner Books.

Karnes, M., Shewedel, A., & Williams, M. (1983). A comparison of five approaches for educating young children from low-income homes. In Center for Longitudinal Studies (Ed.), *As the twig is bent: Lasting effects of preschool programs* (pp. 133–171). Hillsdale, NJ: Erlbaum.

Karoly, L. A., Greenwood, P. W., Everingham, S. S., Hoube, J., Kilburn, M. R., Rydell, C. P., et al. (1998). *Investing in our children: What we know and don't know about the costs and benefits of early-childhood interventions.* Santa Monica, CA: Rand.

Kasser, T. (2002). *The high price of materialism.* Cambridge: Bradford Books/MIT Press.

Kassinove, H., & Tafrate, R. C. (2002). *Anger management: The complete treatment guidebook for practitioners.* Atascadero, CA: Impact.

Kastenbaum, R. J. (1992). *The psychology of death* (2nd ed.). New York: Springer.

Kastenbaum, R., & Thuell, S. (1995). Cookies baking, coffee brewing: Toward a contextual theory of dying. *Omega, 31,* 175–187.

Kastner, S., & Ungerleider, L. G. (2000). Mechanisms of visual attention in the human cortex. *Annual Review of Neuroscience, 23,* 315–341.

Kate, E. (1998). *Critical period in brain development discovered.* Retrieved from http://www.primate.wisc.edu/pin/rh/rhoct19.txt

Katz, J. (1988). *Seductions of crime: Moral and sensual attractions in doing evil.* New York: Basic Books.

Katz, J. N. (1995). *The invention of heterosexuality.* New York: Dutton.

Katz, L. & Chard, S. (1989). *Engaging children's minds: The project approach.* Norwood, NY: Ablex.

Kauffman, S. (1993). *The origins of order.* New York: Oxford University Press.

Kaufman, A. S. (1979). *Intelligent testing with the WISC-R.* New York: Wiley.

Kaufman, A. S. (2000). Intelligence tests and school psychology: Predicting the future by studying the past. *Psychology in the Schools, 37,* 7–16.

Kaufman, A. S., & Kaufman, N. L. (1983). *Kaufman Assessment Battery for Children.* Circle Pines, MN: American Guidance Service.

Kazdin, A. (1987). Treatment of antisocial behavior in children: Current status and future directions. *Psychological Bulletin, 102,* 187–203.

Kazdin, A. E. (2001). *Behavior modification in applied settings* (6th ed.). Belmont, CA: Wadsworth.

Kazdin, A. E. (2003). Problem-solving skills training and parent management training for conduct disorder. In A. E. Kazdin & J. R. Weisz (Eds.), *Evidence-based psychotherapies for children and adolescents* (pp. 241–262). New York: Guilford.

Kazdin, A. E., & Weiss, J. R. (2003). *Evidence-based psychotherapies for children and adolescents.* New York: Guilford.

Kearsley, G. (1994). *Information processing theory: G. Miller.* Retrieved from http://www.gwu.edu/~tip/miller.html

Kearsley, G. (2000). *Online education.* Belmont, CA: Wadsworth.

Keating, K. (1992). *What Catholics really believe—setting the record straight: 52 answers to common misconceptions about the Catholic faith.* San Francisco: Ignatius Press.

Keegan, D. (1986). *The foundations of distance education.* London: Croom Helm.

Keep Kids Healthy. (2002). *Failure to thrive.* Retrieved from http://www.keepkidshealthy.com/welcome/conditions/failure_to_thrive.html

Kegan, R. (1982). *The evolving self: Problem and process in human development.* Cambridge, MA: Harvard University Press.

Kehoe, D. T. (1997). *Stuttering: Science, therapy & practice: The most complete book about stuttering.* Boulder, CO: Casa Futura Technologies.

Keidel, G. S. (2002). Burnout and compassion fatigue among hospice caregivers. *American Journal of Hospice and Palliative Care, 19,* 200–205.

Keisjers, G. P. J., Hoogduin, C. A. L., & Schaap, C. P. D. R. (1994). Prognostic factors in the behavioral treatment of panic disorder with and without agoraphobia. *Behavior Therapy, 25,* 689–708.

Keith, L. G., Oleszczuk, J. J., & Keith, D. M. (2000). Multiple gestation: Reflections on epidemiology, causes and consequences. *International Journal of Fertility, 45*(3), 206–214.

Keith, L. G., Papiernik, E., Keith, D. M., & Luke, B. (Eds.). (1995). *Multiple pregnancy—Epidemiology, gestation, and perinatal outcome* (pp. 163–190). New York: Parthenon.

Kellermann, A., Somes, G., Rivara, F., Lee, R. K., & Banton, J. (1998). Injuries and deaths due to firearms in the home. *Journal of Trauma-Injury Infection & Critical Care, 45*(2), 263–267.

Kelley, R. I. (1996). Metabolic diseases. In A. J. Capute & P. J. Accardo (Eds.), *Developmental disabilities in infancy and childhood* (2nd ed., pp. 113–136). Baltimore: Paul H. Brookes.

Kelly, K., & Colangelo, N. (1984). Academic and social self-concepts of gifted, general, and special students. *Exceptional Children, 50*(6), 551–554.

Kelso, J. A. S., & DeGuzman, G. C. (1992). The intermittent dynamics of coordination. In G. E. Stelmach & J. Requin (Eds.), *Tutorials in motor behavior II* (pp. 549–561). Amsterdam: Elsevier.

Kempe, C. H., Silverman, F., Steele, B., Droegmueller, W., & Silver, H. (1962). The battered child syndrome. *Journal of the American Medical Association, 181,* 17–24.

Kemper, T. (1990). *Social structure and testosterone.* New Brunswick, NJ: Rutgers University Press.

Kenrick, D. (1991). Proximate altruism and ultimate selfishness. *Psychological Inquiry, 2,* 135–137.

Kenrick, D. T., & Keefe, R. C. (1992). Age preferences in mates reflect sex differences in reproductive strategies. *Behavioral and Brain Sciences, 15,* 75–133.

Kenrick, D., Neuberg, S., & Cialdini, R. (1999). *Social psychology: Unraveling the mystery.* Boston: Allyn & Bacon.

Kerlinger, F. N. (1986). *Foundations of behavioral research.* Fort Worth, TX: Harcourt Brace Jovanovich.

Kernis, M. H. (Ed.). (1995). *Efficacy, agency, and self-esteem.* New York: Plenum.

Kerr, A. (2002). Annotation: Rett syndrome: Recent progress and implications for research and clinical practice. *Journal of Child Psychology and Psychiatry, 43,* 277–287.

Kersting, A., Dorsch, M., Kreulich, C., & Baez, E. (2004). Psychological stress response after miscarriage and induced abortion. *Psychosomatic Medicine, 66,* 795–796.

Kesner, J. E., & McKenry, P. C. (2001). Single parenthood and social competence in children of color. *Families in Society, 82*(2), 136–144.

Kessel, F. S. (Ed.). (1988). *The development of language and language researchers: Essays in honor of Roger Brown.* Hillsdale, NJ: Erlbaum.

Kessler, R. C., McGonagle, K. A., Zhao, S., Nelson, C. B., Hughes, M., Eshleman, S., et al. (1994). Lifetime and 12-month prevalence of DSM-III-R psychiatric disorders in the United States: Results from the National Comorbidity Survey. *Archives of General Psychiatry, 51*(1), 8–19.

Kevin Leman, http://www.drleman.com

Kibbutz, http://www.jewishvirtuallibrary.org/jsource/Society_&_Culture/kibbutz.html

Kibbutzim, http://www.kibbutz.org.il/eng/welcome.htm

Kidd, A. H., & Kidd, R. M. (1985). Children's attitudes toward their pets. *Psychological Reports, 57,* 15–31.

KidsHealth, http://www.kidshealth.org/

KidsHealth. (2001). *Teaching your child self-control.* Retrieved from http://www.kidshealth.org/parent/emotions/behavior/self_control.html

KidsHealth. (2004). *Bullying and your child.* Retrieved from http://www.kidshealth.org/parent/emotions/feelings/bullies.html

Kieras, D. E., & Meyer, D. E. (n.d.). *EPIC: A cognitive architecture for computational modeling of human performance.* Retrieved from http://www.eecs.umich.edu/~kieras/epic.html

Kiernan, K. (2003). *Cohabitation and divorce across nations and generations.* London: Centre for Analysis of Social Exclusion. Retrieved from http://sticerd.lse.ac.uk/dps/case/cp/CASEpaper65.pdf

Kim, J. E., & Moen, P. (2001). Moving into retirement: Preparation and transition in late midlife. In M. E. Lachman (Ed.), *Handbook of midlife development* (Chap. 14, pp. 487–527). New York: Wiley.

Kimball, J. (2004). *B cells and T cells.* Retrieved from http://users.rcn.com/jkimball.ma.ultranet/BiologyPages/B/B_and_Tcells.html

Kimball, J. R. (2005). *Hormones of the reproductive system.* Retrieved from http://users.rcn.com/jkimball.ma.ultranet/BiologyPages/S/SexHormones.html

Kimel et al. v. Florida Board of Regents (1999). No. 98–791, slip op. (S. Ct. January 11, 1999).

Kimura, D. (2002, May 13). *Sex differences in the brain.* Retrieved from http://www.sciam.com/article.cfm?articleID=00018E9D-879D-1D06-8E49809EC588EEDF

King, P. M., & Kitchener, K. S. (1998). The reflective judgment model: Twenty years of research on epistemic cognition. In B. K. Hofer & Paul R. Pintrich (Eds.), *Personal epistemology: The psychology of beliefs about knowledge and knowing* (pp. 37–61). Mahwah, NJ: Erlbaum.

Kinoy, B. P. (Ed.). (2001). *Eating disorders: New directions in treatment and recovery.* New York: Columbia University Press.

Kinsella, K., & Velkoff, V. A. (2001). *An aging world.* U.S. Census Bureau, Series P95/01-1. Washington, DC: U.S. Government Printing Office.

Kinsey, A. C., Pomeroy, W. B., & Martin, C. E. (1998). *Sexual behavior in the human male.* Philadelphia: W. B. Saunders; Bloomington: Indiana University Press. (Original work published 1948)

Kinsey, A. C., Pomeroy, W. B., Martin, C. E., & Gebhard, P. H. (1953). *Sexual behavior in the human female.* Philadelphia: WB Saunders.

Kinsey, A. C., Pomeroy, W. B., Martin, C. E., & Gebhard, P. H. (1998). *Sexual behavior in the human female.* Philadelphia: W. B. Saunders; Bloomington: Indiana University Press. (Original work published 1953)

The Kinsey Institute, http://www.kinseyinstitute.org

Kinzl, J., Mangweth, B., Traweger, C., & Biebl, W. (1996). Sexual dysfunction in males: Significance of adverse childhood experiences. *Child Abuse & Neglect, 10,* 759–766.

Kirch, D. G. (1993). Infection and autoimmunity as etiologic factors in schizophrenia: A review and reappraisal. *Schizophrenia Bulletin, 19,* 355–370.

Kirk, R. E. (1995). *Experimental design: Procedures for behavioral sciences* (3rd ed.). Pacific Grove, CA: Brooks/Cole.

Kitzman, K. M., Cohen, R., & Lockwood, R. L. (2002). Are only children missing out? Comparison of the peer-related social competence of only children and siblings. *Journal of Social and Personal Relationships, 19*(3), 299–316.

Klaus, M. (1998). Mother and infant: Early emotional ties. *Pediatrics, 102,* 1244–1246.

Klein, A. J. (Ed.). (2003). *Humor in children's lives: A guidebook for practitioners.* Westport, CT: Praeger.

Klein, A. P., Duggal, P., Lee, K. E., Klein, R., Bailey-Wilson, J. E., & Klein, B. E. (2005). Support for polygenic influences on ocular refractive error. *Investigative Ophthalmology and Visual Science, 46,* 442–446.

Klein, F. (1993). *The bisexual option* (2nd ed.). New York: Harrington Park.

Klein, F., Sepekoff, B., & Wolf, T. J. (1985). Sexual orientation: A multivariate dynamic process. *Journal of Homosexuality, 11,* 35–49.

Klein, M. (1975). *Love, guilt, and reparation and other works, 1921–1945.* New York: Delta.

Kliewer, W. (1997). Children's coping with chronic illness. In S. A. Wolchik & I. N. Sandler (Eds.), *Handbook of children's coping: Linking theory and intervention. Issues in clinical child psychology* (pp. 275–300). New York: Plenum.

Klimes-Dougan, B., & Kistner, J. (1990). Physically abused preschoolers' responses to peers' distress. *Developmental Psychology, 26,* 599–602.

Klinefelter, H. F., Jr., Reifenstein, E. C., Jr., & Albright, F. (1942). Syndrome characterized by gynecomastia, aspermatogenesis without aleydigism and increased excretion of follicle-stimulating hormone. *Journal of Clinical Endocrinology, 2,* 615–627.

Knight, R. T. (1997). Distributed cortical network for visual attention. *Journal of Cognitive Neuroscience, 9*(1), 75–91.

KnowKidding, http://www.uab.edu/knowkidding

Knox, G. W. (2000). *An introduction to gangs* (5th ed.). Peotone, IL: New Chicago School Press.

Knox, S. S. (2001). Psychosocial stress and the physiology of atherosclerosis. *Advances in Psychosomatic Medicine, 22,* 139–151.

Kochanek, K. D., & Smith, B. L. (2004). Deaths: Preliminary data for 2002. *National Vital Statistics Reports, 52,* 13, 1–48.

Kochanska, G., & Murray, K. (2000). Mother-child mutually responsive orientation and conscience development: From toddler to early school age. *Child Development, 71,* 417–431.

Koestner, R., Franz, C., & Weinberger, J. (1990). The family origins of empathic concern: A 26-year longitudinal study. *Journal of Personality and Social Psychology, 58,* 709–717.

Kogan, N., & Mills, M. (1992). Gender influences on age cognitions and preferences: Sociocultural or sociobiological? *Psychology and Aging, 7,* 98–106.

Kohlberg, L. (1958). *The development of modes of moral thinking and choice in the years 10–16.* Doctoral dissertation, University of Chicago, Chicago.

Kohlberg, L. (1969). Stage and sequence: The cognitive-development approach to socialization. In D. A. Goslin (Ed.), *Handbook of socialization theory and research* (pp. 347–480). Chicago: Rand McNally.

Kohlberg, L. (1975). The cognitive-developmental approach to moral education. *Phi Delta Kappan, 56,* 670–677.

Kohlberg, L. (1978). The cognitive developmental approach to moral education. In P. Scharf (Ed.), *Readings in moral education.* Washington, DC: Winston Press.

Kohlberg, L. (1981). *Essays on moral development: The philosophy of moral development: Vol. 1.* New York: Harper & Row.

Kohlberg, L. (1981). *The philosophy of moral development: Moral stages and the idea of justice.* San Francisco: Harper & Row.

Kohlberg, L. (1984). *Essays on moral development: The psychology of moral development: Vol. 2.* San Francisco: Harper & Row.

Kohlberg, L. (1984). *The psychology of moral development: Moral stages and the idea of justice.* San Francisco: Harper & Row.

Kohlberg, L., Levine, C., & Hewer, A. (1983). Moral stages: A current formulation and a response to critics. In J. A. Meacham (Ed.), *Contributions to human development* (Vol. 10). Basel: Karger.

Kohlberg's ideas of moral development. (n.d.). Retrieved from http://facultyweb.cortland.edu/andersmd/kohl/kidmoral.html

Kohn, A. (1990). *The brighter side of human nature: Altruism and empathy in everyday life.* New York: Basic Books.

Kohut, H. (1971). *The analysis of the self.* New York: International Universities Press.

Kohut, H., & Wolf, E. (1978). The disorders of the self and their treatment: An outline. *International Journal of Psychoanalysis, 59,* 413–425.

Kokuritsu Shakai Hosho Jinko Mondai Kenkyujyo [National Institute of Population and Social Security Research]. (2003). *Jinko Tokei Shiryo-shu.* Tokyo: Author.

Kolb, B., & Whishaw, I. Q. (2003). *Fundamentals of human neuropsychology* (5th ed.). New York: Worth Publishers.

Kolberg, K. J. S. (1999). Environmental influences on prenatal development and health. In T. L. Whitman, T. V. Merluzzi, & R. D. White (Eds.), *Life-span perspectives on health and illness* (pp. 87–103). Mahwah, NJ: Erlbaum.

Konrad Lorenz, http://www.nobel.se/medicine/laureates/1973/lorenz-autobio.html

Koob, G. F., Ahmed, S. H., Boutrel, B., Chen, S. A., Kenny, P. J., Markou, A., et al. (2004). Neurobiological mechanisms in the transition from drug use to drug dependence. *Neuroscience and Biobehavioral Review, 27,* 739–750.

Koss, M. P. (2000). *High? Low? Changing?: What's new in rape prevalence.* Retrieved from http://www.nvaw.org/research/newprevalence.shtml

Koss, M. P., Gidycz, C. A., & Wisniewski, N. (1987). The scope of rape: Incidence and prevalence of sexual aggression and victimization in a national sample of higher education students. *Journal of Consulting and Clinical Psychology, 55,* 162–170.

Kot, T., & Serper, M. (2002). Increased susceptibility to auditory conditioning in hallucinating schizophrenic patients: A preliminary investigation. *Journal of Nervous and Mental Disease, 190,* 282–288.

Kovalenko, P. A., Hoven, C. W., Wu, P., Wicks, J., Mandell, D. J., & Tiet, Q. (2001). Association between allergy and anxiety disorders in youth. *Australian and New Zealand Journal of Psychiatry, 35,* 815–821.

Kozak, M. J., & Foa, E. B. (1994). Obsessions, overvalued ideas, and delusions in obsessive-compulsive disorder. *Behaviour Research and Therapy, 32,* 343–353.

Kozulin, A. (1990). *Vygotsky's psychology: A biography of ideas.* Cambridge, MA: Harvard University Press.

Kraemer, H. C., Berkowitz, R. I., & Hammer, L. D. (1990). Methodological difficulties in studies in obesity: Measurement issues. *Annals of Behavioral Medicine, 12,* 112–118.

Kramer, A. F., & Willis, S. L. (2002). Enhancing the cognitive vitality of older adults. *Current Directions in Psychological Science, 11*(5), 173–177.

Kreider, R., & Simmons, T. (2003). *Marital status: 2000.* Census 2000 Brief, C2KBR-30. Washington, DC: U.S. Census Bureau. Retrieved from http://www.census.gov/prod/2003pubs/c2kbr-30.pdf

Kreipe, R. E. (1994). Normal somatic adolescent growth and development. In E. R. McAnarney, R. E. Kreipe, D. P. Orr, & G. D. Comerci (Eds.), *Textbook of adolescent medicine* (pp. 44–67). Philadelphia: WB Saunders.

Krueger, J. (2001). Null hypothesis significance testing: On the survival of a flawed method. *American Psychologist, 56,* 16–26.

Krueger, R. F., Chentsova-Dutton, Y. E., Markon, K. E., Goldberg, D., & Ormel, J. (2003). A cross cultural study of the structure of comorbidity among common psychopathological syndromes in the general health care setting. *Journal of Abnormal Psychology, 112,* 437–447.

Kruger, D. J. (2003). Evolution and altruism: Combining psychological mediators with naturally selected tendencies. *Evolution and Human Behavior, 24,* 118–125.

Kruger, D. J. (n.d.). *Evolution and altruism.* Retrieved from http://www-personal.umich.edu/~kruger

Kübler-Ross, E. (1969). *On death and dying.* New York: Macmillan.

Kübler-Ross, E. (1997). *The wheel of life: A memoir of living and dying.* New York: Scribner.

Kuhn, D. (1999). Metacognitive development. In C. Tamis LeMonda (Ed.), *Child psychology: A handbook of contemporary issues.* New York: Garland.

Kuhn, D., & Bennett, D. A. (2003). *Alzheimer's early stages: First steps for family, friends, and caregivers* (2nd ed.). Alameda, CA: Hunter House Publishers.

Kuhn, M. (1991). *No stone unturned: The life and times of Maggie Kuhn.* New York: Ballantine.

Kung, E. M., & Farrell, A. D. (2000). The role of parents in early adolescent substance abuse: An examination of mediating and moderating effects. *Journal of Child and Family Studies, 9,* 509–528.

Kunzmann, U., & Baltes, P. B. (2003). Wisdom-related knowledge: Affective, motivational, and interpersonal correlates. *Personality and Social Psychology Bulletin, 29*(9), 1104–1119.

Kurnit, D. M., Layton, W. M., & Matthysse, S. (1987). Genetics, chance, and morphogenesis. *American Journal of Human Genetics, 41,* 979–995.

Kurst-Swanger, K., & Petcosky, J. L. (2003). *Violence in the home: Multidisciplinary perspectives.* London: Oxford University Press.

La Greca, A. M., Silverman, W. K., Vernberg, E. M., & Roberts, M. C. (Eds.). (2002). *Helping children cope with disasters and terrorism.* Washington, DC: American Psychological Association.

Lack, L. C., & Bootzin, R. R. (2003). Circadian rhythm factors in insomnia and their treatment. In M. Perlis & K. Lichstein (Eds.), *Treatment of sleep disorders: Principles and practice of behavioral sleep medicine.* Hoboken, NJ: Wiley.

LaFreniere, P. J. (2000). *Emotional development: A biosocial perspective.* Belmont, CA: Wadsworth.

Lakoff, G. (1987). *Women, fire, and dangerous things: What categories reveal about the mind.* Chicago: University of Chicago Press.

Lamaze Institute for Normal Birth, http://normalbirth.lamaze .org/institute/CarePractices Midwife Archives. (n.d.). *Midwives support unmedicated birth because it's better for the baby.* Retrieved from http://www.gentlebirth.org/archives/nodrugs.html

Lamb, M. E. (2002). Placing children's interests first: Developmentally appropriate parenting plans. *Virginia Journal of Social Policy and Law, 10,* 98–119.

The Lampinen Lab, http://comp.uark.edu/~lampinen/lab.html

Landsberger, J. (2004). *Thinking aloud: Private speech.* Retrieved from http://www.studygs.net/thinkingaloud.htm

Landy, U., Steinauer, J. E., & Ryan, K. J. (2001). How available is abortion training? *Family Planning Perspectives, 33,* 88–89.

Lane, H., Hoffmeister, R., & Bahan, B. (1996). *A journey into the deaf-world.* San Diego, CA: DawnSignPress.

Lane, K., Gresham, F., MacMillan, D., & Bocian, K. (2001). Early detection of students with antisocial behavior and hyperactivity problems. *Education and Treatment of Children, 24,* 294–308.

Langer, O., Berkus, M. D., Huff, R. W., & Samueloff, A. (1991). Shoulder dystocia: Should the fetus weighing greater than or equal to 4000 grams be delivered by cesarean section? *American Journal of Obstetrics and Gynecology, 165,* 831–837.

Lapp, D. C. (1995). *Don't forget! Easy exercises for a better memory.* New York: Perseus.

Lapsley, D. (1996). *Moral psychology.* Boulder, CO: Westview Press.

Lapsley, D. K. (1993). Toward an integrated theory of adolescent ego development: The "new look" at adolescent egocentrism. *American Journal of Orthopsychiatry, 63,* 562–571.

Larson, R. W. (2000). Toward a psychology of positive youth development. *American Psychologist, 55,* 170–183.

Larson, R., Dworkin, J., & Gillman, S. (2001). Facilitating adolescents' constructive use of time in one-parent families. *Applied Developmental Science, 5*(3), 143–157.

Last Acts, http://www.lastacts.org/

Latane, B., & Darley, J. (1970). *The unresponsive bystander: Why doesn't he help?* New York: Appleton-Century-Crofts.

Lattimore, P. J., & Halford, J. C. (2003). Adolescence and the diet-dieting disparity: Healthy food choice or risky health behavior? *British Journal of Health Psychology, 8,* 451–464.

Lauer, J., & Lauer, R. (1999). *How to survive and thrive in an empty nest.* Oakland, CA: New Harbinger.

Laughlin, E. H. (2002). *Coming to terms with cancer: A glossary of cancer-related terms.* Atlanta, GA: American Cancer Society.

Laumann, E. O., Gagnon, J. H., Michael, R. T., & Michaels, S. (1994). *The social organization of sexuality: Sexual practices in the United States.* Chicago: University of Chicago Press.

Laursen, B., & Collins, W. A. (1994). Interpersonal conflict during adolescence. *Psychological Bulletin, 115,* 197–209.

Lavie, N. (1995). Perceptual load as a necessary condition for selective attention. *Journal of Experimental Psychology—Human Perception and Performance, 21*(3), 451–468.

Lawton, M. P., & Brody, E. M. (1969). Assessment of older people: Self-maintaining and instrumental activities of daily living. *Gerontologist, 9,* 179–186.

Lazar, I., Darlington, R., Murray, H., Royce, J., & Snipper, A. (1982). Lasting effects of early education: A report from the consortium for longitudinal studies. *Monographs of the Society for Research in Child Development, 47* (Serial No. 195).

LD Online, http://www.ldonline.org

Leal, C. (2001) *Portraits of Huntington's.* Belleville, Ontario: Essence.

Leaper, C. (2002). Parenting girls and boys. In M. H. Bornstein (Ed.), *Handbook of parenting: Vol. 1. Children and parenting* (2nd ed., pp. 127–152). Mahwah, NJ: Erlbaum.

Learning, http://www.psychology.org/links/Environment_Behavior_Relationships/Learning/

Learning Disabilities Online, http://www.ldonline.org/ld_indepth

Learning Theories, http://www.emtech.net/learning_theories.htm

Leary, M. R., & Tangney, J. P. (Eds.). (2003). *Handbook of self and identity.* New York: Guilford.

Ledger, L. D. (1997). *Intelligence testing.* Retrieved from http://www.liberalartsandcrafts.net/contentcatalog/learning/IQtests.shtml

Lee, G., Willetts, M. C., & Seccombe, K. (1998). Widowhood and depression: Gender differences. *Research on Aging, 20,* 611–630.

Lee, J. D., & Craft, E. A. (2002). Protecting one's self from a stigmatized disease . . . once one has it. *Deviant Behavior, 23*(3), 267–299.

Lee, R. (2003). The transracial adoption paradox: History, research, and counseling; Implications for cultural socialization. *Counseling Psychologist, 31,* 711–744.

Leevy, C. M., & Baker, H. (1968). Vitamins and alcoholism. *American Journal of Clinical Nutrition, 21,* 1325.

Lefcourt, H. M. (1991). Locus of control. In J. P. Robinson, P. R. Shaver, & L. S. Wrightsman (Eds.), *Measures of personality and social psychological attitudes* (pp. 413–499). San Diego, CA: Academic Press Unlimited.

Lefcourt, H. M. (2001). *Humor: The psychology of living buoyantly.* New York: Kluwer Academic/Plenum.

Leff, J. (1994). Working with the families of schizophrenic patients. *British Journal of Psychiatry, 23*(Suppl.), 71–76.

Lehmann, P. (1997). The development of posttraumatic stress disorder (PTSD) in a sample of child witnesses to mother assault. *Journal of Family Violence, 12,* 241–257.

Lehr, F., & Osborn, J. (Eds.). (1994). *Reading, language, and literacy: Instruction for the twenty-first century.* Hillsdale, NJ: Erlbaum.

Leider, R. (1996). The psychology of the self. In E. Nersessian & R. Kopff (Eds.), *Textbook of psychoanalysis* (pp. 127–164). Washington, DC: American Psychiatric Press.

Leland, L., Kirsch, J., & Stone, S. M. (2004). *The effects of pets on elderly citizens' blood pressure and heart rate.* Kansas City, MO: Great Plains Research Conference.

Leming, M. R. (2004). The history of the hospice approach. In C. D. Bryant (Ed.), *Handbook of death and dying: Vol. 1. The presence of death* (pp. 485–494). Thousand Oaks, CA: Sage.

Lemkin, R. (1944). *Axis rule in occupied Europe: Laws of occupation, analysis of government, proposals for redress.* Washington, DC: Carnegie Endowment for International Peace, Division of International Law.

Leng, X., & Shaw, G. L. (1991). Toward a neural theory of higher brain function using music as a window. *Concepts in Neuroscience, 2,* 229–258.

Lenneberg, E. H. (1967). *Biological foundations of language.* New York: Wiley.

Lenney, E. (1991). Sex roles: The measurement of masculinity, femininity, and androgyny. In J. P. Robinson, P. R. Shaver, & L. S. Wrightsman (Eds.), *Measures of social psychological attitudes* (Vol. 1, pp. 573–660). San Diego, CA: Academic Press.

Lenz, W. (1992). A personal perspective on the thalidomide tragedy. *Teratology, 46,* 417–418.

Leong, D., Bodrova, E., Hensen, R., & Henninger, M. (1999). *Scaffolding early literacy through play.* Retrieved from http://www.mcrel.org/PDF/EarlyChildhoodEducation/4006IR_NAEYC_Handout_Play.pdf

Leong, F. T. L. (1985). *Career development and vocational behavior of racial and ethnic minorities.* Mahwah, NJ: Erlbaum.

Leont'ev, A. N. (1978). *Activity, consciousness and personality.* Englewood Cliffs, NJ: Prentice-Hall.

Lepper, M. R., Greene, D., & Nisbett, R. E. (1973). Undermining children's intrinsic interest with extrinsic rewards: A test of the overjustification hypothesis. *Journal of Personality and Social Psychology, 28,* 129–137.

Lerman, D., & Iwata, B. A. (1995). Prevalence of the extinction burst and its attenuation during treatment. *Journal of Applied Behavior Analysis, 28,* 93–94.

Lerner, R. M. (2002). *Concepts and theories of human development* (3rd ed.). Mahwah, NJ: Erlbaum.

Lerner, R. M., & Steinberg, L. (Eds.). (2004). *Handbook of adolescent psychology* (2nd ed.). Hoboken, NJ: Wiley.

Leslie, A. M. (1994). ToMM, ToBy, and agency: Core architecture and domain specificity. In L. Hirschfeld & S. Gelman (Eds.), *Mapping the mind: Domain specificity in cognition and culture* (pp. 119–148). New York: Cambridge University Press.

Lester, D. (1997). *Suicide in American Indians.* New York: Nova Science.

Letherby, G. (1999). Nonmotherhood: Ambivalent autobiographies. *Feminist Studies, 25*(3), 719–729.

Leu, D. J., Jr., & Kinzer, C. K. (1999). *Effective literacy instruction* (4th ed.). Upper Saddle River, NJ: Prentice-Hall.

Levenson, R. W. (2000). Expressive, physiological, and subjective changes in emotion across adulthood. In S. H. Qualls & N. Abeles (Eds.), *Psychology and the aging revolution: How we adapt to longer life* (pp. 123–140). Washington, DC: American Psychological Association.

Leventhal, T., & Brooks-Gunn, J. (2000). The neighborhoods they live in: The effects of neighborhood residence on child and adolescent outcomes. *Psychological Bulletin, 126*(2), 309–337.

Leventhal, T., & Brooks-Gunn, J. (2003). Moving on up: Neighborhood effects on children and families. In M. H. Bornstein & R. H. Bradley (Eds.), *Socioeconomic status, parenting, & child development* (pp. 203–230). Mahwah, NJ: Erlbaum.

Levin, J. (2002). *The violence of hate.* Boston: Allyn & Bacon.

Levine, M. D. (2000). Neurodevelopmental dysfunction in the school age child. In R. E. Behrman, R. M. Kliegman, & H. B. Jenson (Eds.), *Nelson textbook of pediatrics* (16th ed., pp. 94–100). Philadelphia: WB Saunders.

Levine, M. M., Kaper, J. B., Rappuoli, R., Liu, M. A., & Good, M. F. (Eds.). (2004). *New generation vaccines.* New York: Marcel Dekker.

Levine, M., & Wallach, L. (2002). *Psychological problems, social issues, and law.* Boston: Allyn & Bacon.

LeVine, R. A. (1974). Parental goals: A cross-cultural view. *Teachers College Record, 76,* 226–239.

Levinson, B. M. (1969). *Pet-oriented child psychotherapy.* Springfield, IL: Charles C Thomas.

Levinson, J. (1978). *The seasons of a man's life.* New York: Knopf.

Levitas, R. (1990). *The concept of utopia.* Syracuse, NY: Syracuse University.

Levitt, M. J. (2003). *Methods of studying aging.* Retrieved from http://www.fiu.edu/~levittmj/agmethod.html

Levy, C. (1988). *A people's history of independent living.* Lawrence: Research and Training Center on Independent Living at the University of Kansas.

Lewin, K. (1951). *Field theory in social science: Selected theoretical papers.* New York: Harper.

Lewis, B. (1995). *The Middle East: A brief history of the last 2,000 years.* New York: York: Touchstone.

Lewis, B. (2003). *The assassins: A radical sect in Islam.* New York: Basic Books.

Lewis, C., & Lamb, M. E. (2003). Fathers' influence on children's development: The evidence from two parent families. *European Journal of Psychology of Religion, 18,* 211–228.

Lewis, M. (1992). *Shame: The exposed self.* New York: Free Press.

Ley, R. (1985). Blood, breath, and fears: A hyperventilation theory of panic attacks and agoraphobia. *Clinical Psychology Review, 5,* 271–285.

Leyser, Y., & Tappendorf, K. (2001). Are attitudes and practices regarding mainstreaming changing? A case of teachers in two rural school districts. *Education, 121*(4), 751–761.

Lezak, M. D. (1995). *Neuropsychological assessment* (3rd ed.). New York: Oxford University Press.

Li, L., van den Bogert, E., Caldwell, G. E., van Emmerik, R., & Hamill, J. (1999). Coordination patterns of walking and running at similar speed and stride frequency. *Human Movement Science, 18,* 67–85.

Liberatos, P., Link, B. G., & Kelsey, J. L. (1988). The measurement of social class in epidemiology. *Epidemiologic Reviews, 10,* 87–121.

Libreria Editrice Vaticana. (1994). *Catechism of the Catholic Church.* New York: William H. Sadlier.

Lichtenberg, J. W., & Goodyear, R. K. (Eds.). (1999). *Scientist-practitioner perspectives on test interpretation.* Boston: Allyn & Bacon.

Lickliter, R. (2000). Atypical perinatal sensory stimulation and early perceptual development. Insights from developmental psychobiology. *Journal of Perinatology, 20,* 45–54.

Lidz, C. S., & Elliott, J. G. (Eds.). (2000). *Dynamic assessment: Prevailing models and applications.* Amsterdam: JAI/Elsevier Science.

Lieberman, D. A. (1997). Interactive video games for health promotion: Effects on knowledge, self-efficacy, social sup-port, and health. In R. L. Street, W. R. Gold, & T. Manning (Eds.), *Health promotion and interactive technology: Theoretical applications and future directions* (pp. 103–120). Mahwah, NJ: Erlbaum.

Lieberman, T. (2000). *Consumer Reports complete guide to health services for seniors.* New York: Three Rivers Press.

Lieblich, A. (1986). Successful career women at midlife: Crises and transitions. *International Journal of Aging and Human Development, 23,* 301–312.

Lillard, A. (2002). Pretend play and cognitive development. In U. Goswami (Ed.), *Blackwell handbook of childhood cognitive development* (pp. 188–205). Malden, MA: Blackwell.

Lillard, A. (2005). *Montessori: The science behind the genius.* New York: Oxford University Press.

Limosin, F., Rouillon, F., Payan, C., Cohen, J. M., & Strub, N. (2003). Prenatal exposure to influenza as a risk factor for adult schizophrenia. *Acta Psychiatrica Scandinavica, 107,* 331–335.

Lindenberger, U., Scherer, H., & Baltes, P. B. (2001). The strong connection between sensory and cognitive performance in old age: Not due to sensory acuity reductions operating during cognitive assessment. *Psychology and Aging, 16*(2), 196–205.

Lindsay, D. S., & Read, J. D. (1994). Psychotherapy and memories of childhood sexual abuse: A cognitive perspective. *Applied Cognitive Psychology, 8,* 281–338.

Lindsay, R. C. L., Brigham, J. C., Brimacombe, C. A. E., & Wells, G. (2002). Eyewitness research. In J. Ogloff (Ed.), *Taking psychology and law into the 21st century.* New York: Kluwer Academic/Plenum.

Linehan, M. (1986). Suicidal people: One population or two? *Annals of the New York Academy of Sciences, 487,* 16–33.

Linn, R. L. (Ed). (1989). *Educational measurement* (3rd ed.). New York: American Council on Education–Macmillan.

Linscheid, T. R., Budd, K., & Rasnake, L. K. (2004). Pediatric feeding problems. In M. Roberts (Ed.), *Handbook of pediatric psychology* (pp. 481–498). New York: Guilford.

Linscheid, T. R., & Butz, C. (2003). Anorexia nervosa and bulimia nervosa. In M. C. Roberts (Ed.), *Handbook of pediatric psychology* (pp. 636–651). New York: Guilford.

Lionnet, F. (1989). *Autobiographical voices: Race, gender, and self portraiture.* Ithaca, NY: Cornell University Press.

Lips, H. M. (2001). *Sex & gender: An introduction* (4th ed.). Mountain View, CA: Mayfield.

Lipsitt, L. P. (2003). Crib death: A biobehavioral phenomenon? *Current Directions in Psychological Science, 12,* 164–170.

Literacy and Deaf Students, Gallaudet Research Institute, Gallaudet University, http://gri.gallaudet.edu/Literacy/

Literacy.org, http://www.literacyonline.org (jointly sponsored by the International Literacy Institute [ILI] and the National Center on Adult Literacy [NCAL] at the University of Pennsylvania Graduate School of Education)

Litin, S. C. (Ed.). (2002). *Mayo Clinic family health book* (3rd ed.). New York: HarperCollins.

Liu, W. M., Ali, S. R., Soleck, G., Hopps, J., Dunston, K., Pickett, T., Jr. (2004). Using social class in counseling psychology research. *Journal of Counseling Psychology, 51,* 3–18.

Lobo, R. A., Kelsey, J., & Marcus, R. (Eds.). (2000). *Menopause: Biology and pathobiology* (pp. 215–227). San Diego, CA: Academic Press.

Locke, L. M., & Prinz, R. J. (2002). Measurement of parental discipline and nurturance. *Clinical Psychology Review, 22,* 895–929.

Lockman, J. J., & Thelen, E. (1993). Developmental biodynamics: Brain, body, behavior connections. *Child Development, 64,* 953–959.

Lockshin, R. A., & Zakeri, Z. F. (1990). MINIREVIEW: Programmed cell death: New thoughts and relevance to aging. *Journal of Gerontology: Biological Science, 45,* B135–B140.

Loeber, R., & Farrington, D. P. (2000). Young children who commit crime: Epidemiology, developmental origins, risk factors, early interventions, and policy implications. *Development and Psychopathology, 12,* 737–762.

Loeber, R., Farrington, D. P., Stouthamer-Loeber, M., & Van Kammen, W. B. (1998). *Antisocial behavior and mental health problems: Explanatory factors in childhood and adolescence.* Mahwah, NJ: Erlbaum.

Loeber, R., & Stouthamer-Loeber, M. (1998). Development of juvenile aggression and violence: Some common misconceptions and controversies. *American Psychologist, 53,* 242–259.

Loevinger, J. (1976). *Ego development: Conceptions and theories.* San Francisco: Jossey-Bass.

Loftus, E. F. (1996). *Eyewitness testimony.* Cambridge, MA: Harvard University Press.

Lohman, T. G., Roche, A. F., & Martorell, R. (1988). *Anthropometric standardization reference manual.* Champaign, IL: Human Kinetics.

Longo, D. J., & Clum, G. A. (1989). Psychosocial factors affecting genital herpes recurrences: Linear vs. mediating models. *Journal of Psychosomatic Research, 33*(2), 161–166.

Lopes, M. (1993). *Young children benefit from conversations about feelings.* Retrieved from http://www.nncc.org/Guidance/yng.benefit.feel.html

Lorenz, K. (1937). Imprinting. *Auk, 54,* 245–273.

Lorenz, K. Z. (1937). The companion in the bird's world. *Auk, 54,* 245–273.

Lorion, R. P., Iscoe, I., DeLeon, P. H., & VandenBos, G. R. (1996). *Psychology and public policy: Balancing public service and professional need.* Washington, DC: American Psychological Association.

Lott, B. (2002). Cognitive and behavioral distancing from the poor. *American Psychologist, 57,* 100–110.

Lott, B., & Eagly, A. H. (1997). Research priorities: Should we continue to study gender differences? In M. R. Walsh (Ed.), *Women, men, & gender: Ongoing debates* (pp. 15–31). New Haven, CT: Yale University Press.

Lou, Y., Abrami, P. C., & d'Apollonia, S. (2001). Small group and individual learning with technology: A meta-analysis. *Review of Educational Research, 71*(3), 449–521.

Loulan, J. (1990). *The lesbian erotic dance: Butch, femme, androgyny and other rhythms.* San Francisco: Spinsters.

Love, K., & Murdock, T. (2004). Attachment to parents and psychological well-being: An examination of young adult college students in intact families and stepfamilies. *Journal of Family Psychology, 18*(4), 600–608.

Love, S. (2000). *Dr. Susan Love's breast book* (3rd ed.). New York: HarperCollins.

Loving, J., Ransom, A., & White, L. (Ed.). (2001). *Building universal preschool in partnership with the private early education and care system: Essential elements for partnerships between public and private early care and education systems.* Conyers, GA: National Child Care Association.

Lowe, M. R. (1993). The effects of dieting on eating behavior. *Psychological Bulletin, 114,* 100–121.

Lubinski, D. (2000). Scientific and social significance of assessing individual differences: "Sinking shafts at a few critical points." *Annual Review of Psychology, 51,* 405–444.

Lubow, R., & Gewirtz, J. (1995). Latent inhibition in humans: Data, theory, and implications for schizophrenia. *Psychological Bulletin, 117,* 87–103.

Lucile Packard Children's Hospital. (n.d.). *Respiratory disorders: Apnea of prematurity.* Retrieved from http://www.lpch.org/DiseaseHealthInfo/HealthLibrary/respire/apneapre.html

Luck, S. J., Chelazzi, L., Hillyard, S. A., & Desimone, R. (1997). Neural mechanisms of spatial selective attention in areas V1, V2, and V4 of macaque visual cortex. *Journal of Neurophysiology, 77*(1), 24–42.

Luepnitz, D. (1988). *The family revisited.* New York: Basic Books.

Luescher, K., & Pillemer, K. (1998). Intergenerational ambivalence: A new approach to the study of parent-child relations in later life. *Journal of Marriage and the Family, 60,* 413–425.

Luiselli, J. K., Matson, J. L., & Singh, N. N. (Eds.). (1992). *Self-injurious behavior.* New York: Springer-Verlag.

Luke, C. (1990). *Constructing the child viewer: A history of the American discourse on television and children, 1950–1980.* New York: Praeger.

Lummaa, V. (2003). Early developmental conditions and reproductive success in humans: Downstream effects of prenatal famine, birthweight, and timing of birth. *American Journal of Human Biology, 15,* 370–379.

Luria, A. R. (1976). *Cognitive development: Its cultural and social foundation* (L. Solotaroff, Trans.). Cambridge, MA: Harvard University Press.

Luszcz, M. A., & Nettelbeck, T. (Eds.). (1989). *Psychological development: Perspectives across the life-span.* Amsterdam: Elsevier Science.

Luthar, S. S. (Ed.). (2003). *Resilience and vulnerability: Adaptation in the context of childhood adversities.* Cambridge, UK: Cambridge University Press.

Luthar, S. S., & Zigler, E. (1991). Vulnerability and competence: A review of research on resilience in childhood. *Journal of American Orthopsychiatry, 61,* 6–22.

Lye, J. (1996). *Psychoanalysis and literature*. Retrieved from http://www.brocku.ca/english/courses/4F70/psychlit.html

Lyman, H. B. (1998). *Test scores and what they mean* (6th ed.). Boston: Allyn & Bacon.

Lynam, D. R. (1996). Early identification of chronic offenders: Who is a fledgling psychopath? *Psychological Bulletin, 120,* 209–234.

Lynn, J., Schuster, J. L., & Kabcenell, A. (2000). *Improving care for the end of life: A sourcebook for health care managers and clinicians.* Oxford, UK: Oxford University Press.

Lynn, L. E. (Ed.). (1978). *Knowledge and policy: The uncertain connection: Vol. 5. Study project on social research and development.* Washington, DC: National Academy of Sciences.

Lyon, G. R. (1995). Toward a definition of dyslexia. *Annals of Dyslexia, 45,* 3–27.

Lyon, G. R., Shaywitz, S., & Shaywitz, B. (2003). A definition of dyslexia. *Annals of Dyslexia, 53,* 1–14.

Lyons, N. P. (1983). Two perspectives: On self, relationship, and morality. *Harvard Educational Review, 53,* 125–145.

Lyons-Ruth, K., & Jacobvitz, D. (1999). Attachment disorganization: Unresolved loss, relationship violence, and lapses in behavioral and attentional strategies. In J. Cassidy & P. Shaver (Eds.), *Handbook of attachment.* New York: Guilford.

Ma, X. (1999). Gender differences in growth in mathematical skills during secondary grades: A growth model analysis. *Alberta Journal of Educational Research, 45,* 448–466.

MAAP Services, Inc. (n.d.). *The source: Autism, Asperger's Syndrome, pervasive developmental disorders.* Available from http://maapservices.org

Maccoby, E. E. (1998). *The two sexes: Growing up apart, coming together.* Cambridge, MA: Belknap Press of Harvard University Press.

Maccoby, E. E. (2002). Gender and group process: A developmental perspective. *Current Directions in Psychological Science, 11,* 54–58.

Maccoby, E. E., & Martin, J. A. (1983). Socialization in the context of the family: Parent child interaction. In E. M. Hetherington (Ed.), *Handbook of psychology: Vol. 4. Socialization, personality, and social development* (pp. 1–101). New York: Wiley.

Mace, N. L., & Rabins, P. V. (1999). *The 36-hour day.* Baltimore: Johns Hopkins University Press.

MacFadven, L., Hastings, G., & Mackintosh, A. M. (2001). Cross sectional study of young people's awareness of and involvement with tobacco marketing. *British Medical Journal, 322,* 513–517.

Machens, K., & Schmidt-Gollwitzer, K. (2003). Issues to debate on the Women's Health Initiative (WHI) study. Hormone replacement therapy: An epidemiological dilemma? *Human Reproduction, 18*(10), 1992–1999.

MacKinnon, L. T. (1992). *Exercise and immunity.* Champaign, IL: Human Kinetics.

Macleod, C. M. (1991). Half a century of research on the Stroop effect: An integrative review. *Psychological Bulletin, 109*(2), 163–203.

Maddux, J. E. (Ed.). (1995). *Self-efficacy, adaptation, and adjustment: Theory, research, and application.* New York: Plenum.

Madhavan, S. (2004). Fosterage patterns in the age of AIDS: Continuity and change. *Social Science and Medicine, 58*(7), 1443–1454.

Madrigal, R. (1999). Faith and reason. In F. Jenkins (Ed.), *A place to stand* (pp. 160–180). Temple Terrace: Florida College Press.

Madsen, J., & Gudmundsdottir, S. (2000). *Scaffolding children's learning in the zone of proximal development: A classroom study.* Retrieved from http://www.sv.ntnu.no/ped/sigrun/publikasjoner/ecerjm.html

Magai, C., & McFadden, S. H. (Eds.). (1996). *Handbook of emotion, adult development and aging.* San Diego, CA: Academic Press.

Magee, S. K., & Ellis, J. (2000). Extinction effects during the assessment of multiple problem behaviors. *Journal of Applied Behavior Analysis, 33,* 313–316.

Mahaffey, K. R. (1990). Environmental lead toxicity: Nutrition as a component of intervention. *Environmental Health Perspectives, 89,* 75–78.

Mahajan, B. S., Mahjan, B. S., & Rajadhyaksha, M. S. (1999). *New biology and inherited diseases.* Oxford, UK: Oxford University Press.

Mahler, M. (1968). *On human symbiosis and the vicissitudes of individuation.* New York: International Universities Press.

Mahler, M., Pine, F., & Bergmann, A. (1975). *The psychological birth of the human infant.* New York: Basic Books.

Mahoney, J. L., Larson, R. W., & Eccles, J. S. (2005). *Organized activities as contexts of development: Extracurricular activities, after-school and community programs.* Mahwah, NJ: Erlbaum.

Maier, S. F., Seligman, M. E. P., & Solomon, R. L. (1969). Pavlovian fear conditioning and learned helplessness: Effects on escape and avoidance behavior of (a) the CS-US contingency, and (b) the independence of the US and voluntary responding. In B. A. Campbell & R. M. Church (Eds.), *Punishment.* New York: Appleton-Century-Crofts.

Mail, P. D. (Ed.). (2002). *Alcohol use among American Indians and Alaska Natives: Multiple perspectives on a complex problem.* Bethesda, MD: U.S. Dept. of Health and Human Services, Public Health Service, National Institutes of Health, National Institute on Alcohol Abuse and Alcoholism.

Main, M., Kaplan, N., & Cassidy, J. (1985). Security in infancy, childhood, and adulthood: A move to the level of representation. In I. Bretherton & E. Waters (Eds.), Growing points of attachment theory and research. *Monographs of the Society for Research in Child Development, 50,* 66–104.

Main, M., & Solomon, J. (1990). Procedures for identifying infants as disorganized/disoriented during the Ainsworth strange situation. In M. T. Greenberg, D. Cicchetti, & E. M. Cummings (Eds.), *Attachment in the preschool years* (pp. 121–160). Chicago: University of Chicago Press.

Maisels, M., & Watchko, J. (Eds). (2000). *Neonatal jaundice.* Amsterdam: Harwood Academic.

Makame, V., & Grantham-McGregor, S. (2002). Psychological well-being of orphans in Dar El Salaam, Tanzania. *Acta Paediatrica, 91*(4), 459.

Malaguzzi, L. (1993). History, ideas, and basic philosophy. In C. Edwards, L. Gandini, & G. Forman (Eds.), *The hundred languages of children: The Reggio Emilia approach to early childhood education.* Norwood, NY: Ablex.

Malina, R., & Bouchard, C. (1991). *Growth, maturation and physical activity.* Champaign, IL: Human Kinetics.

Maltby, N., Kirsch, I., Mayers, M., & Allen, G. J. (2002). Virtual reality exposure therapy for the treatment of fear of flying: A controlled investigation. *Journal of Consulting and Clinical Psychology, 70,* 1112–1118.

Manchester, J. (2003). Beyond accommodation: Reconstructing the insanity defense to provide an adequate remedy for postpartum psychotic women. *Journal of Criminal Law and Criminology, 93,* 713–752.

Mangun, G. R., & Hillyard, S. A. (1991). Modulations of sensory-evoked brain potentials indicate changes in perceptual processing during visual spatial priming. *Journal of Experimental Psychology—Human Perception and Performance, 17*(4), 1057–1074.

Manlove, J., Ryan, S., & Franzetta, K. (2003). Patterns of contraceptive use within teenagers' first sexual relationships. *Perspectives on Sexual and Reproductive Health, 35,* 246–255.

March of Dimes. (2001). *Rh disease.* Retrieved from http://www.marchofdimes.com/professionals/681_1220.asp

March of Dimes. (2004). *Diabetes in pregnancy.* Retrieved from http://www.modimes.org/printableArticles/168-1197.asp?printable=true

March of Dimes. (n.d.). *Pregnancy and newborn health education center.* Retrieved from http://www.marchofdimes.com/pnhec/pnhec.asp

March of Dimes Birth Defects Foundation, http://www.modimes.org

March of Dimes Prematurity Campaign, http://www.modimes.org/prematurity/5126.asp

March, J. S., Amaya-Jackson, L., Murray, M. C., & Schulte, A. (1998). Cognitive-behavioral psychotherapy for children and adolescents with posttraumatic stress disorder after a single-incident stressor. *Journal of the American Academy of Child and Adolescent Psychiatry, 37,* 585–593.

Marchand, H. (2002). *Some reflections on post-formal thought.* Retrieved from http://www.prometheus.org.uk/Publishing/Journal/Papers/MarchandOnPostFormalThought/Main.htm

Marchand, H. (n.d.). *An overview of the psychology of wisdom.* Retrieved from http://www.prometheus.org.uk/Publishing/Journal/Papers/MarchandOnWisdom/Main.htm

Marcia, J. E. (1980). Identity in adolescence. In J. Adelson (Ed.), *Handbook of adolescent psychology.* New York: Wiley.

Marcus, C. L., Greene, M. G., & Carroll, J. L. (1998), Blood pressure in children with obstructive sleep apnea. *Journal of Respiratory Critical Care Medicine, 157,* 109–1103.

Marini, Z., & Case, R. (1994). The development of abstract reasoning about the physical and social world. *Child Development, 65,* 147–159.

Maris, R. W., Berman, A. L., & Silverman, M. M. (2000). *Comprehensive textbook of suicidology.* New York: Guilford.

Mark, E. J., & Barkley, R. A. (2003). *Child psychopathology* (2nd ed.). New York: Guilford.

Marker, R. L. (n.d.). *Assisted suicide: The continuing debate.* Retrieved from http://www.internationaltaskforce.org/cd.htm

Markman, H. J., Stanley, S. M., & Blumberg, S. L. (2001). *Fighting for your marriage: Positive steps for preventing divorce and preserving a lasting love.* New York: Jossey-Bass.

Markovitz, H., Doyon, C., & Simoneau, M. (2002). Individual differences in working memory and conditional reasoning with concrete and abstract content. *Thinking & Reasoning, 8,* 97–107.

Markowitz, M. (2000). Lead poisoning: A disease for the next millennium. *Current Problems in Pediatrics, 3,* 62–70.

Markstrom, C. A. (2005). *Puberty and ritual expressions: Empowerment of Native North American girls.* Morgantown: West Virginia University Press.

Markstrom, C. A., & Iborra, A. (2003). Adolescent identity formation and rites of passage: The Navajo Kinaaldá ceremony for girls. *Journal of Research on Adolescence, 13,* 399–425.

Markstrom, C. A., Stamm, B. H., Stamm, H. E., Berthold, S. M., & Wolf, R. P. (2003). *Ethnicity and rural status in behavioral health care.* In B. H. Stamm (Ed.), *Rural behavioral health care* (pp. 231–243). Washington, DC: American Psychological Association.

Marmor, T. (2000). *The politics of Medicare.* New York: Aldine de Gruyter.

Marmot, M. (1999). *The social determinants of health inequalities.* Retrieved from http://www.worldbank.org/poverty/health/library/nov99seminar.pdf

Marschark, M., Lang, H., & Albertini, J. (2002). *Educating deaf students: From research to practice.* New York: Oxford University Press.

Marschark, M., & Spencer, P. (Eds.). (2003). *Oxford handbook of deaf studies, language, and education.* New York: Oxford University Press.

Martin, C. L., & Ruble, D. (2004). Children's search for gender cues. *Current Directions in Psychological Science, 13,* 67–70.

Martin, J. A., Hamilton, B. E., Ventura, S. J., Menacker, F., & Park, M. M. (2002). Births: Final data for 2000. *National Vital Statistics Reports, 50*(5), 1–101.

Martin, J. A., MacDorman, M. F., & Mathews, T. J. (1997). Triplet births: Trends and outcomes, 1971–94. *Vital and Health Statistics, 21*(55).

Martin, J. A., & Park, M. M. (1999). Trends in twin and triplet births: 1980–97. *National Vital Statistic Reports, 47*(24).

Martin, J. N., Bradford, L. J., Drzewiecka, J. A., & Chitgopekar, A. S. (2003). Intercultural dating patterns among young white U.S. Americans: Have they changed in the past 20 years? *The Howard Journal of Communications, 14*, 53–73.

Martin, L. L., & Clark, L. F. (1990). Social cognition: Exploring the mental processes involved in human social interaction. In M. W. Eysenck (Ed.), *Cognitive psychology: An international review* (pp. 265–310). Chichester, UK: Wiley.

Martin, R., Hohlfeld, R., & McFarland, H. F. (1996). Multiple sclerosis. In T. Brandt, L. R. Caplan, J. Dichgans, H. C. Diener, & C. Kennard (Eds.), *Neurological disorders: Course and treatment* (pp. 483–506). New York: Academic Press.

Martinez, F. D. (2002). Development of wheezing disorders and asthma in preschool children. *Pediatrics, 109*, 362–367.

Martínez, R. S. (2003). Impact of a graduate class on attitudes toward inclusion, perceived teaching efficacy and knowledge about adapting instruction for children with disabilities in inclusive settings. *Teacher Development, 7*(3), 395–416.

Marvin Zuckerman home page, http://www.psych.udel.edu/people/detail.php?firstname=Marvin&lastname=Zuckerman

Mary Rothbart's Temperament Laboratory at the University of Oregon, http://darkwing.uoregon.edu/~maryroth

Masami, T., & Overton, W. F. (2002). Wisdom: A culturally inclusive developmental perspective. *International Journal of Behavioral Development, 3*(26), 269–277.

Maser, J. D., & Cloninger, C. R. (Eds.). (1990). *Comorbidity of mood and anxiety disorders.* Washington, DC: American Psychiatric Press.

Mash, E. J., & Wolfe, D. A. (1999). *Abnormal child psychology.* Belmont, CA: Wadsworth.

Masliah, E., Mallory, M., Hansen, L., DeTeresa, R., & Terry, R. D. (1993). Quantitative synaptic alterations in the human neocortex during normal aging. *Neurology, 43*(1), 192–197.

Maslow, A. H. (1954). *Motivation and personality.* New York: Harper.

Maslow, A. H. (1962). *Toward a psychology of being.* New York: Van Nostrand.

Maslow, A. H. (1969). A theory of metamotivation: The biological rooting of the value-life. *Humanitas, 4*, 301–343.

Maslow, A. H. (1969). Toward a humanistic biology. *American Psychologist, 24*, 724–735.

Maslow, A. H. (1971). *The farther reaches of human nature.* New York: Viking Press.

Masten, A. S., & Coatsworth, J. D. (1998). The development of competence in favorable and unfavorable environments: Lessons from research on successful children. *American Psychologist, 53*, 205–220.

Masuda, Y. (1985). Health status of Japanese and Taiwanese after exposure to contaminated rice oil. *Environmental Health Perspectives, 60*, 321–325.

Maternity Center Association, http://www.maternitywise.org

Mathias, R. (1996, November/December). The basics of brain imaging. *NIDA Notes, 11*(5). Retrieved from http://www.nida.nih.gov/NIDA_Notes/NNV0111N5/Basics.html

Mattes, J. (1997). *Single mothers by choice: A guidebook for single women who are considering or have chosen motherhood.* New York: Three Rivers Press.

Matthews, D. O. (Ed.). (2001). *Eating disorders sourcebook: Basic consumer health information about eating disorders, including information about anorexia nervosa.* Detroit, MI: Omnigraphics.

Mattick, R. P., & Clark, J. C. (1998). Development and validation of measures of social phobia scrutiny fear and social interaction anxiety. *Behaviour Research and Therapy, 36*, 455–470.

Mattson, M. P. (2000). Apoptosis in neurodegenerative disorders. *Nature Reviews Molecular Cell Biology, 1*(2), 120–129.

Maume, D. J., Jr. (2004). Is the glass ceiling a unique form of inequality? Evidence from a random-effects model of managerial attainment. *Work and Occupations, 31*, 250–274.

Mavin Foundation, http://www.mavin.net

May, E. T. (1995). *Barren in the promised land: Childless Americans and the pursuit of happiness.* Cambridge, MA: Harvard University Press.

Mayo Clinic, http://www.mayoclinic.org

Mayo Clinic. (2003). *Cardiovascular disease: A blueprint for understanding the leading killer.* Retrieved from http://www.mayoclinic.com/invoke.cfm?objectid=E5B48F78–76024182–9B484B9817E940C6

Mayo Clinic. (2003). *Ultrasound in pregnancy: What can it tell you?* Retrieved from http://www.mayoclinic.com/invoke.cfm?id=PR00054

Mayo Clinic. (n.d.). *Popular diets: The good, the fad and the iffy.* Retrieved from http://mayoclinic.com/invoke.cfm?id=HQ00654

Mayo Foundation for Medical Education and Research. (2004, May 18). *Creutzfeldt-Jakob disease.* Retrieved from http://www.mayoclinic.com/invoke.cfm?id=DS00531

Mayo Foundation for Medical Education and Research. (2004). *Phenylketonuria.* Retrieved from http://www.mayoclinic.com/invoke.cfm?id=DS00514

Mays, V. M., Albee, G. W., & Schneider, S. F. (Eds.). (1989). *Primary prevention of AIDS.* Newbury Park, CA: Sage.

Mazur, A., & Booth, A. (1998). Testosterone and dominance in men. *Behavioral and Brain Sciences, 21*, 353–363.

Mazur, A., Mueller, U., Krause, W., & Booth, A. (2002). Causes of sexual decline in aging married men: Germany and America. *International Journal of Impotence Research, 14*, 101–106.

Mazur, J. E. (1998). *Learning and behavior* (4th ed.). Upper Saddle River, NJ: Prentice-Hall.

Mazure, C. M., Keita, G. P., & Blehar, M. C. (2002). *Summit on women and depression: Proceedings and recommendations.* Washington, DC: American Psychological Association. Retrieved from http://www.apa.org/pi/wpo/women&depression.pdf

McArdle, J. J., Ferrer-Caja, E., Hamagami, F., & Woodcock, R. W. (2002). Comparative longitudinal structural analyses of the growth and decline of multiple intellectual abilities over the life span. *Developmental Psychology, 38,* 115–142. Available from http://www.apa.org

McBrien, N. A., & Gentle, A. (2003). Role of the sclera in the development and pathological complications of myopia. *Progress in Retinal and Eye Research, 22,* 307–338.

McBurney, D. H. (1994). *Research methods* (3rd ed.). Pacific Grove, CA: Brooks/Cole.

McCallum, P. (2002, January). Cultural memory and the Royal Shakespeare Company Productions: "This England." *Early Modern Literary Studies, 7.3,* 15.1–15.8.

McCarton, C. M., Brooks-Gunn, J., Wallace, I. F., & Bauer, C. R. (1997). Results at age 8 years of early intervention for low-birth-weight premature infants: The infant health and development program. *Journal of the American Medical Association, 277,* 126–132.

McCarty, M. E., & Ashmead, D. H. (1999). Visual control of reaching and grasping in infants. *Developmental Psychology, 35,* 620–631.

McCrae, R. R., & Costa, P. T. (1997). Personality structure as a human universal. *American Psychologist, 52,* 509–516.

McCrae, R. R., & John, O. P. (1992). An introduction to the five-factor model and its applications. *Journal of Personality, 60,* 175–215.

McDermott, D., & Snyder, C. R. (1999). *Making hope happen.* Oakland/San Francisco: New Harbinger Press.

McDonough, L., Mandler, J. M., McKee, R. D., & Squire, L. R. (1995). The deferred imitation task as a nonverbal measure of declarative memory. *Proceedings of the National Academy of Sciences, 92,* 7580–7584.

McGillicuddy-De Lisi, A., & De Lisi, R. (2002). *Biology, society, and behavior: The development of sex differences in cognition.* Westport, CT: Ablex.

McGinnis, S. L. (2003). Cohabitation, dating, and perceived costs of marriage: A model of marriage entry. *Journal of Marriage and Family, 65,* 105–116.

McGrath, P. J., Finley, G. A., & Ritchie, J. (1994). *Pain, pain, go away: Helping children with pain.* Retrieved from http://is.dal.ca/~pedpain/ppga/ppga.html

McGue, M. (1994). Behavioral genetic models of alcoholism. In K. Leonard (Ed.), *Psychological theories of drinking and alcoholism* (pp. 372–421). New York: Guilford.

McIntire, D. (2000). How well does A.A. work? An analysis of published A.A. surveys (1968–1996) and related analyses/comments. *Alcoholism Treatment Quarterly, 18,* 1–18.

McKay, D., Abramowitz, J. S., Calamari, J., Kyrios, M., Sookman, D., Taylor, S., et al. (2004). A critical evaluation of obsessive-compulsive disorder subtypes: Symptoms versus mechanisms. *Clinical Psychology Review, 24,* 283–313.

McKay, D., & Tsao, S. (in press). A treatment most foul: Handling disgust in cognitive-behavior therapy. *Journal of Cognitive Psychotherapy.*

McKay, M., Blades, P., Rogers, J., & Gosse, R. (1984). *The divorce book.* Oakland, CA: New Harbinger.

McKenna, J. J. (2000). Cultural influences on infant and childhood sleep biology, and the science that studies it: Toward a more inclusive program. *Zero to Three, 20,* 9–18.

McKim, W. A. (2003). *Drugs and behavior: An introduction to behavioral pharmacology* (5th ed.). Upper Saddle River, NJ: Prentice-Hall.

McKinnon, J. (2003). *The Black population in the United States: March 2002* (Current Population Reports, Series P20-541). Washington, DC: U.S. Census Bureau. Retrieved from http://www.census.gov/prod/2003pubs/p20-541.pdf

McKusick-Nathans Institute for Genetic Medicine, Johns Hopkins University, & National Center for Biotechnology Information, National Library of Medicine. (2000). *Online mendelian inheritance in man (OMIM).* Retrieved from http://www.ncbi.nlm.nih.gov/omim/

McLanahan, S., & Sandefur, G. (1994). *Growing up with a single parent: What hurts, what helps?* Cambridge, MA: Harvard University Press.

McLean, J. F., & Hitch, G. J. (1999). Working memory impairments in children with specific arithmetic learning difficulties. *Journal of Experimental Child Psychology, 74,* 240–260.

McLoyd, V. C. (1998). Socioeconomic disadvantage and child development. *American Psychologist, 53,* 185–204.

McLoyd, V. C., & Smith, J. (2002). Physical discipline and behavior problems in African American, European American and Hispanic children: Emotional support as a moderator. *Journal of Marriage and the Family, 64,* 40–53.

McMahon, R. J., & Forehand, R. (1984). Parent training for the noncompliant child: Treatment outcome, generalization and adjunctive therapy procedures. In R. F. Dangel & R. A. Polster (Eds.), *Behavioral parent training: Issues in research and practice.* New York: Guilford.

McMahon, R. J., & Forehand, R. L. (2003). *Helping the noncompliant child: Family based treatment for oppositional behavior* (2nd ed.). New York: Guilford.

McMahon, R. J., & Wells, K. C. (1998). Conduct problems. In E. R. Mash & R. A. Barkley (Eds.), *Treatment of childhood disorders* (2nd ed., pp. 111–207). New York: Guilford.

McMaster University. (n.d.). *Psychology 2B3: Theories of personality.* Retrieved from http://www.science.mcmaster.ca/Psychology/psych2b3/lectures/banmisch-1.html

McMillan, N., & Swales, D. M. (2004). *Quality indicators for child care programmes: East and central Africa.* London: Save the Children.

McNally, R. J. (1994). Atypical phobias. In G. C. L. Davey (Ed.), *Phobias: A handbook of theory, research, and treatment* (pp. 183–199). Chichester, UK: Wiley.

McNally, R. J. (1994). *Panic disorder: A critical analysis.* New York: Guilford.

McNally, R. J., & Eke, M. (1996). Anxiety sensitivity, suffocation fear, and breath-holding duration as predictors of response to carbon dioxide challenge. *Journal of Abnormal Psychology, 105,* 146–149.

McPherson, M., Arango, P., Fox, H., Lauver, C., McManus, M., Newacheck, P. W., et al. (1998). A new definition of children with special health care needs [Commentary]. *Pediatrics, 102,* 137–140.

McShane, J. (1991). *Cognitive development: An information-processing approach.* Cambridge, MA: Blackwell.

McSweeney, F. K., & Murphy, E. S. (2000). Criticisms of the satiety hypothesis as an explanation for within-session decreases in responding. *Journal of the Experimental Analysis of Behavior, 74,* 347–361.

McSweeney, F. K., & Swindell, S. (2002). Common processes may contribute to extinction and habituation. *Journal of General Psychology, 129*(4), 1–37.

Mead, G. H. (1962). *Mind, self, and society: From the standpoint of a social behaviorist.* Chicago: University of Chicago Press.

Mead, M. (1928). *Coming of age in Samoa.* New York: Morrow.

Mead, M. (1970). *Culture and commitment: A study of the generation gap.* Garden City, NY: Doubleday.

MED-EL, http://www.medel.com

Medicaid, http://www.cms.hhs.gov/publications/overview medicare-medicaid/default4.asp

Medicare Information Resource, http://www.cms.hhs.gov/medicare/

Medin, D. L., & Atran, S. (Eds.). (1999). *Folkbiology.* Cambridge: MIT Press.

Medin, T., Ross, B. H., & Markman, A. B. (2002). *Cognitive psychology* (3rd ed.). New York: Wiley.

MedlinePlus. (2003). *Immune response.* Retrieved from http://www.nlm.nih.gov/medlineplus/ency/article/000821.htm

MedlinePlus. (2003). *Lungs and breathing topics.* Retrieved from http://www.nlm.nih.gov/medlineplus/lungsandbreathing.html

MedlinePlus. (2004). *Methylmercury poisoning.* Retrieved from http://www.nlm.nih.gov/medlineplus/ency/article/001651.htm

MedlinePlus. (2005). *Disasters and emergency preparedness.* Retrieved from http://www.nlm.nih.gov/medlineplus/disastersandemergencypreparedness.html

MedlinePlus. (2005). *Fine motor control.* Retrieved from http://www.nlm.nih.gov/medlineplus/ency/article/002364.htm

MedlinePlus (2005). *Malnutrition.* Retrieved from http://www.nlm.nih.gov/medlineplus/ency/article/000404.htm

MedlinePlus. (2005). *Parenting.* Retrieved from http://www.nlm.nih.gov/medlineplus/parenting.html

MedlinePlus. (2005). *Phobias.* Retrieved from http://www.nlm.nih.gov/medlineplus/phobias.html

MedlinePlus. (2005). *Premature babies.* Retrieved from http://www.nlm.nih.gov/medlineplus/prematurebabies.html

Mednick, S., Machon, R., Huttonen, M., & Bonett, D. (1988). Adult schizophrenia following prenatal exposure to an influenza epidemic. *Archives of General Psychiatry, 45,* 189–192.

Medoff-Cooper, B., Bilker, W., & Kaplan, J. (2001). Sucking behavior as a function of gestational age: A cross-sectional study. *Infant Behavior and Development, 24,* 83–94.

Medoff-Cooper, B., McGrath, J., & Bilker, W. (2000). Nutritive sucking and neurobehavioral development in VLBW infants from 34 weeks PCA to term. *MCN: American Journal of Maternal Child Nursing,* April/May, 64–70.

Medoff-Cooper, B., McGrath, J., & Shults, J. (2002). Feeding patterns of full term and preterm infants at forty weeks post-conceptional age. *Journal of Developmental and Behavioral Pediatrics, 23*(1), 231–236.

Meece, J. L. (2002). *Child and adolescent development for educators* (2nd ed.). Boston: McGraw-Hill.

Meissner, W. (2000). *Freud and psychoanalysis.* Notre Dame, IN: Notre Dame Press.

Melson, G. F., & Fogle, A. (1989). Children's ideas about animal young and their care: A reassessment of gender differences in the development of nurturance. *Anthrozoos, 2,* 265–273.

Meltzoff, A. M. (1995). Understanding the intentions of others: Re-enactments of intended acts by 18-month-old children. *Developmental Psychology, 31,* 838–850.

Meltzoff, A. N. (1985). Immediate and deferred imitation in fourteen- and twenty-four-month-old infants. *Child Development, 56,* 62–72.

Meltzoff, A. N. (1990). Towards a developmental cognitive science: The implications of cross-modal matching and imitation for the development of representation and memory in infancy. In A. Diamond (Ed.), *The Development and Neural Bases of Higher Cognitive Functions (Annals of the New York Academy of Sciences,* Vol. 608), 1–37.

Meltzoff, A. N. (2002). Imitation as a mechanism of social cognition: Origins of empathy, theory of mind, and the representation of action. In U. Goswami (Ed.), *Blackwell handbook of childhood cognitive development* (pp. 6–25). Malden, MA: Blackwell.

Meltzoff, A. N., & Gopnik, A. (1993). The role of imitation in the understanding of a theory of mind. In S. Baron-Cohen, H. Tager-Flusberg, & D. J. Cohen (Eds.), *Understanding other minds: Perspectives from autism* (pp. 335–366). Oxford, UK: Oxford University Press.

Meltzoff, A. N., & Moore, M. K. (1977). Imitation of facial and manual gestures by human neonates. *Science, 198,* 75–78.

Meltzoff, A. N., & Moore, M. K. (1994). Imitation, memory, and the representation of persons. *Infant Behavior and Development, 17,* 83–89.

Memory Disorders Project at Rutgers University. (n.d.). *Age-associated memory impairment (AAMI).* Retrieved from http://www.memorylossonline.com/glossary/aami.html

Menard, S. (2002). *Longitudinal research.* Thousand Oaks, CA: Sage.

Mendez, M. F., & Cummings, J. L. (2003). *Dementia: A clinical approach* (3rd ed.). Philadelphia: Butterworth-Heinemann.

Menopause Online. (n.d.). *Common discomforts.* Retrieved from http://www.menopause-online.com/discomfort.htm

Mentor Peer Resources, http://www.peer.ca/mentor.html

Merck & Co., Inc. (n.d.). *Malnutrition.* Retrieved from http://www.merck.com/mrkshared/mmanual/section1/chapter2/2a.jsp

Merenstein, G., Kaplan, D., & Rosenburg, A. (1997). *Handbook of pediatrics* (18th ed.). Stamford, CT: Appleton & Lange.

Merkur, D. (2002). The Ojibwa vision quest. *Journal of Applied Psychoanalytic Studies, 4,* 149–170.

Merriam-Webster's collegiate dictionary (11th ed.). (2003). Springfield, MA: Merriam-Webster.

Merrill, K. W. (2003). *Behavioral, social, and emotional assessment of children and adolescents.* Mahwah, NJ: Erlbaum.

Merton, R. K. (1948). The self-fulfilling prophecy. *Antioch Review, 8,* 193–210.

Mesibov, G. B., Shea, V., & Adams, L.W. (2001). *Understanding Asperger syndrome and high functioning autism.* New York: Kluwer Academic/Plenum.

Messerly, J. G. (1996). *Piaget's conception of evolution.* Lanham: Rowman & Littlefield.

Messiah, A., & Pelletier, A. (1996). Partner-specific sexual practices among heterosexual men and women with multiple partners: Results from the French national survey, ACSF. *Archives of Sexual Behavior, 25,* 233–247.

Messick, S. (1983). Assessment of children. In P. H. Mussen (Ed.), *Handbook of child psychology* (4th ed., Vol. 1, pp. 477–526). New York: Wiley.

Messinger, D. S. (2002). Positive and negative: Infant facial expressions and emotions. *Current Directions in Psychological Science, 11*(1), 1–6.

Mesulam, M. M. (1998). From sensation to cognition. *Brain, 121,* 1013–1052.

Metcalfe, J., & Shimamura, A. P. (Eds.). (1994). *Metacognition: Knowing about knowing.* Cambridge: MIT Press.

Meyer, C., & Oberman, M. (2001). *Mothers who kill their children: Understanding the acts of moms from Susan Smith to the "Prom Mom."* New York: New York University Press.

Michel, K., Ballinari, P., Bille-Brahe, U., Bjerke, T., Crepet, P., De Leo, D., et al. (2000). Methods used for parasuicide: Results of the WHO/EURO Multicentre Study on Parasuicide. *Social Psychiatry & Psychiatric Epidemiology, 35*(4), 156–163.

Michigan State University College of Nursing, http://nursing.msu.edu/habi/

Middlemiss, W. (2004). Defining problematic infant sleep: Shifting the focus from deviance to difference. *Zero to Three, 24,* 46–51.

Middlemiss, W. (2004). Infant sleep: A review of normative and problematic sleep and interventions. *Early Child Development and Care, 174,* 99–122.

Middleton, D. B., Zimmerman, R. K., & Mitchell, K. B. (2003). Vaccine schedules and procedures 2003. *The Journal of Family Practice, 52*(1 suppl), S36–S46.

Mid-Hudson Regional Information Center. (n.d.). *Career development.* Retrieved from http://www.mhric.org/edlinks/careers.html

Midkif, D., Shaver, C. M., Murry, V., Flowers, B., Chastain, S., & Kingore, B. (2002, November 2). *The challenge of change: Identifying underrepresented populations.* Presentation at the 49th Annual Convention of the National Association for Gifted Children (NAGC), Denver, CO.

Midwives Alliance of North America, http://www.mana.org

Milbrodt, T. (2002). Breaking the cycle of alcohol problems among Native Americans: Culturally-sensitive treatment in the Lakota community. *Alcoholism Treatment Quarterly, 20,* 19–43.

Miller, B. M. (2003). *Critical hours: After-school programs and educational success.* Quincy, MA: Nellie Mae Educational Foundation. Retrieved from http://www.nmefdn.org/uimages/documents/Critical_Hours.pdf

Miller, G. A., Galanter, E., & Pribram, K. H. (1960). *Plans and the structure of behavior.* New York: Holt, Rinehart & Winston.

Miller, J. (1991). Quantifying productive language disorders. In J. F. Miller (Ed.), *Research on child language disorders: A decade of progress* (pp. 211–220). Austin, TX: Pro-Ed.

Miller, J. (2001). *One of the guys: Girls, gangs, and gender.* New York: Oxford University Press.

Miller, J. B. (2000). Urinary incontinence: A classification system and treatment protocols for the primary care provider. *Journal of the American Academy of Nurse Practitioners, 12*(9), 374–379.

Miller, J. F., & Chapman, R. S. (1981). The relation between age and mean length of utterance in morphemes. *Journal of Speech and Hearing Research, 24,* 154–161.

Miller, J., Maxson, C. L., & Klein, M. W. (2001). *The modern gang reader* (2nd ed.). Los Angeles: Roxbury.

Miller, L. B., & Bizzell, R. P. (1983). The Louisville experiment: A comparison of four programs. In Center for Longitudinal Studies (Ed.), *As the twig is bent: Lasting effects of preschool programs* (pp. 171–199). Hillsdale, NJ: Erlbaum.

Miller, L. B., & Bizzell, R. P. (1984). Long-term effects of four preschool programs: Ninth- and tenth-grade results. *Child Development, 55*(4), 1570–1587.

Miller, L. B., & Dyer, J. L. (1975). Four preschool programs: Their dimensions and effects. *Monographs of the Society for Research in Child Development, 40,* 94–130.

Miller, L. J. (Ed.). (1999). *Postpartum mood disorders.* Washington, DC: American Psychiatric Association.

Miller, L. J. (2002). Postpartum depression. *Journal of the American Medical Association, 287,* 762–765.

Miller, M., Azrael, D., & Hemenway, D. (2002). Firearm availability and unintentional firearm deaths, suicide, and homicide among 5–14 year olds. *Journal of Trauma-Injury Infection & Critical Care, 52*(2), 267–275.

Miller, S. A. (1998). *Developmental research methods* (2nd ed.). Upper Saddle River, NJ: Prentice-Hall.

Miller, T. R., Cohen, M. A., & Wiersema, B. (1996). *Victims costs and consequences: A new look* (NCJ No. 155282, p. 11). Washington, DC: U.S. Department of Justice.

Miller, W. B. (1986). Proception: An important fertility behaviour. *Demography, 23,* 579–594.

Milling, L. S. (2001). Depression in preadolescents. In C. E. Walker & M. C. Roberts (Eds.), *Handbook of clinical child psychology* (3rd ed., pp. 373–413). New York: Wiley.

Mills, E. S. (1993). *The story of Elderhostel.* Hanover, NH: University Press of New England.

Miltenberger, R. G. (2003). *Behavior modification: Principles & procedures* (3rd ed.). Belmont, CA: Wadsworth.

Minow, M. (1998). *Between vengeance and forgiveness: Facing history after genocide and mass violence.* Boston: Beacon Press.

Mirowsky, J., & Ross, C. E. (1999). Well-being across the life course. In A. V. Horowitz & T. L. Scheid (Eds.), *A hand-book for the study of mental health: Social contexts, theories, and systems* (pp. 328–347). New York: Cambridge University Press.

Mischel, W. (2004). Toward an integrative science of the person. *Annual Review of Psychology 55,* 1–22.

The MIT Press. (n.d.). *Noam Chomsky: A life of dissent* [online version]. Available from http://cognet.mit.edu/library/books/chomsky/chomsky/

Moats, L. C. (2000). *Whole language lives on: The illusion of "balanced reading" instruction.* Washington, DC: Fordham Foundation. Retrieved from http://www.edexcellence.net/doc/moats.pdf

Moerk, E. L. (2000). *The guided acquisition of first language skills.* Westport, CT: Ablex.

Moffitt, T. E. (2003). Life-course persistent and adolescence-limited antisocial behavior: A 10-year research review and research agenda. In B. B. Lahey, T. E. Moffitt, & A. Caspi (Eds.), *Causes of conduct disorder and juvenile delinquency* (pp. 49–75). New York: Guilford.

Moll, L. C. (Ed.). (1990). *Vygotsky and education: Instructional implications and applications of sociohistorical psychology.* New York: Cambridge University Press.

Monell Chemical Senses Center, http://www.monell.org

Money, J., & Ehrhardt, A. (1972). *Man and woman, boy and girl.* Baltimore: Johns Hopkins University Press.

Monsour, M. (2002). *Women and men as friends: Relationships across the lifespan in the 21st century.* Mahwah, NJ: Erlbaum.

Montagu, A. (1986). *Touching: The human significance of the skin* (3rd ed.). New York: Harper & Row.

Montepare, J. M., & Zebrowitz, L. A. (2002). A social-developmental view of ageism. In T. D. Nelson (Ed.), *Ageism: Stereotyping and prejudice against older persons* (pp. 77–128). Cambridge: MIT Press.

Monthly Vital Statistics Report, http://www.cdc.gov/nchs/products/pubs/pubd/mvsr/mvsr.htm

Moon, M. (2001). Medicare. *New England Journal of Medicine, 344,* 928–931.

MoonDragon Birthing Services. (n.d.). *Variations of pregnancy: Maternal blood type—Rh negative.* Retrieved from http://www.moondragon.org/mdbsguidelines/rhneg.html

Moorcroft, W. H. (1993). *Sleep, dreaming, & sleep disorders: An introduction* (2nd ed.). Lanham, MD: University Press of America.

Moore, B., & Fine, B. (1990). *Psychoanalytic terms and concepts.* New Haven, CT: Yale University Press.

Moore, C. (2003). *The mediation process* (2nd ed.). San Francisco: Jossey-Bass.

Moore, C. F. (2003). *Silent scourge: Children, pollution, and why scientists disagree.* New York: Oxford University Press.

Moore, K. L., & Persaud, T. V. N. (2003). *Before we are born: Essentials of embryology and birth defects.* Philadelphia: Saunders.

Moore, K. L., & Persaud, T. V. N. (2003). *The developing human: Clinically oriented embryology* (7th ed.). Philadelphia: Saunders.

Moore, M., & Kearsley, G. (1996). *Distance education: A systems view.* Belmont, CA: Wadsworth.

Moore, S., Rosenthal, D., & Mitchell, A. (1996). *Youth, AIDS and sexually transmitted diseases.* New York: Routledge.

Moore-Ede, M., Sulzman, F. M., & Fuller, C. A. (1982). *The clocks that time us.* Cambridge, MA: Harvard University Press.

Moores, D. F. (2001). *Educating the deaf: Psychology, principles, and practices.* Boston: Houghton Mifflin.

Mor, V., & Masterson-Allen, S. (1990). A comparison of hospice vs conventional care of the terminally ill cancer patient. *Oncology, 4,* 85–91.

Morales, P. C. (1999). Lesch-Nyhan syndrome. In S. Goldstein & C. R. Reynolds (Eds.), *Handbook of neurodevelopmental and genetic disorders of children* (pp. 478–498). New York: Guilford.

Moran, J. P. (2002). *Teaching sex: The shaping of adolescence in the 20th century.* Cambridge, MA: Harvard University Press.

Moran, R. F. (2001). *Interracial intimacy.* Chicago: University of Chicago Press.

Moreno, J. (1995). *Arguing euthanasia: The controversy over mercy killing, assisted suicide, and the "right to die."* New York: Touchstone.

Moreno, J. D. (Ed.). (1995). *Arguing euthanasia: The controversy over mercy killing, assisted suicide, and the "right to die."* New York: Simon & Schuster.

Morgan, I., & Rose, K. (2005). How genetic is school myopia? *Progress in Retinal and Eye Research, 24,* 1–38.

Morgan, J. L., & Demuth, K. D. (Eds.). (1996). *Signal to syntax: Bootstrapping from speech to grammar in early language acquisition.* Mahwah, NJ: Erlbaum.

Morgan, J. R., Riley, D., & Chesher, G. B. (1993). Cannabis: Legal reform, medicinal use and harm reduction. In N. Heather, A. Wodak, E. Nadelmann, & P. O'Hare (Eds.), *Psychoactive drugs and harm reduction* (pp. 211–219). London: Whurr.

Morris, B. (2004). *The birth of the Palestinian refugee problem, 1947–1949.* Cambridge, UK: Cambridge University Press.

Morris, C. (2002). *Lev Semyonovich Vygotsky's zone of proximal development.* Retrieved from http://www.igs.net/~cmorris/zpd.html

Morris, D. B. (2001, November). Ethnicity and pain. *Pain Clinical Updates, IX*(4).

Morris, S. S., Black, R. E., & Tomaskovic, L. (2003). Predicting the distribution of under-five deaths by cause in countries without adequate vital registration systems. *International Journal of Epidemiology, 32*(6), 1041–1051.

Morris, T. L., & March, J. S. (Eds.). (2004). *Anxiety disorders in children and adolescents* (2nd ed.). New York: Guilford.

Morrison, A. M., White, R.P., Van Velsor, E., & the Center for Creative Leadership. (1992). *Breaking the glass ceiling: Can women reach the top of America's largest corporations?* (Updated ed.). Reading, MA: Addison-Wesley.

Morrison, V., & Plant, M. (1991). Licit and illicit drug initiations and alcohol-related problems amongst illicit drug users in Edinburgh. *Drug and Alcohol Dependence, 2,* 19–27.

Morrow, A., & Brown, R. T. (2003). Phenylketonuria, maternal. In E. Fletcher-Janzen & C. R. Reynolds (Eds.), *The diagnostic manual of childhood disorders: Clinical and special education applications* (pp. 502–503). New York: Wiley.

Moshman, D. (1998). Cognitive development beyond childhood. In D. Kuhn & R. S. Siegler (Eds.), *Handbook of child psychology: Vol. 2. Cognition, perception, and language* (5th ed.). New York: Wiley.

Moshman, D. (2005). *Adolescent psychological development: Rationality, morality and identity* (2nd ed.). Mahwah, NJ: Erlbaum.

Moskowitz, G. B. (2005). *Social cognition: Understanding self and others.* New York: Guilford.

Mosmann, T., & Sad, S. (1996). The expanding universe of T-cell subsets: Th1, Th2 and more. *Immunology Today, 17,* 139–146.

Moss, D. (Ed.). (1999). *Humanistic and transpersonal psychology: A historical and biographical sourcebook.* Westport, CT: Greenwood.

Moster, D., Lie, R. T., Irgens, L. M., Bjerkedal, T., & Markestad, T. (2001). The association of Apgar score with subsequent death and cerebral palsy: A population-based study in term infants. *Journal of Pediatrics, 138,* 798–803.

Mother-Baby Behavioral Sleep Laboratory, http://www.nd.edu/~jmckenn1/lab/

Mother & Child Glossary. (n.d.). *Innate neonate capacities.* Retrieved from http://www.hon.ch/Dossier/MotherChild/postnatal/reflexes.html

Mothers Against Drunk Driving (MADD), http://www.madd.org/home

Mothers Outside of Marriage (MOMs), http://www.single-mothers.org

Mounts, N. S., & Steinberg, L. (1995). An ecological analysis of peer influence on adolescent grade point average and drug use. *Developmental Psychology, 31,* 915–922.

MSN Encarta. (2004). *African Americans.* Retrieved from http://encarta.msn.com/encyclopedia_761587467_2/African_Americans.html#endads

Mu Soeng. (2000). *The diamond sutra: Transforming the way we perceive the world.* Somerville, MA: Wisdom.

Mulder, B. (1999). *Kohlberg's theory of moral development.* Notre Dame, IN: University of Notre Dame. Retrieved from http://www.psy.pdx.edu/PsiCafe/Areas/Developmental/MoralDev/

Müller, U., Gibbs, P., & Ariely, S. (2003). Adults who were adopted contacting their birthmothers: What are the outcomes, and what factors influence these outcomes? *Adoption Quarterly, 7*(1), 7–26.

Müller, U., & Perry, B. (2001). Adopted persons' search for and contact with their birth parents. I. Who searches and why? *Adoption Quarterly, 4*(3), 5–38.

Multi-Health Systems. (n.d.). *Emotional intelligence.* Retrieved from http://www.emotionalintelligencemhs.com

Multimedia Neuroscience Education Project. (1998). *Synaptic transmission: A four step process.* Retrieved from http://www.williams.edu:803/imput/

Multiple Births Association, http://www.mbf.org

Mundy, P., & Gomes, A. (1998). Individual differences in joint attention skill development in the second year. *Infant Behavior and Development, 21,* 469–482.

Muraskin, W. A. (Ed.). (1998). *The politics of international health: The children's vaccine initiative and the struggle to develop vaccines for the third world.* Albany: State University of New York Press.

Murdoch, W. J., & McDonnel, A. C. (2002). Roles of the ovarian surface epithelium in ovulation and carcinogenesis. *Reproduction, 123*(6), 743–750.

Murphy, R., Penuel, W., Means, B., Korbak, C., & Whaley, A. (2001). *E-DESK: A review of recent evidence on the effectiveness of discrete educational software.* Menlo Park, CA: SRI International. Retrieved from http://ctl.sri.com/publications/downloads/Task3_FinalReport3.pdf

Murray Research Center, http://www.radcliffe.edu/murray/index.php

Murray, L., & Cooper, P. J. (Eds.). (1997). *Postpartum depression and child development.* New York: Guilford.

Murstein, B. I. (1986). *Paths to marriage.* Beverly Hills, CA: Sage.

Mussen, P., & Eisenberg-Berg, N. (1977). *Roots of caring, sharing, and helping.* San Francisco: Freeman.

Muth, A. S. (Ed.). (2002). *Allergies sourcebook* (2nd ed.). Detroit, MI: Omnigraphics.

The Myelin Project, http://www.myelin.org

Myths About Only Children, http://utopia.utexas.edu/articles/opa/only_children.html

Nachtigall, R. D. (1993). Secrecy: An unresolved issue in the practice of donor insemination. *American Journal of Obstetrics and Gynecology, 168,* 1846.

Nachtigall, R. D., Becker, G., Szkupinski-Quiroga, S. S., & Tschann, J. M. (1997). The disclosure decision: Concerns and issues of parents of children conceived through donor insemination. *American Journal of Obstetrics and Gynecology, 178,* 1165–1170.

Nachtigall, R. D., Tschann, J. M., Pitcher, L., Szkupinski-Quiroga, S. S., & Becker, G. (1997). Stigma, disclosure, and family functioning among parents of children conceived through donor insemination. *Fertility and Sterility, 68,* 83–89.

Nadeau, K. (1994). *Survival guide for college students with ADD or LD*. New York: Magination Press.

Naglieri, J. A., & Rojahn, J. (2001). Gender differences in planning, attention, simultaneous, and successive (PASS) cognitive processes and achievement. *Journal of Educational Psychology, 93*, 430–437.

Nagy, M. (1948). The child's theories concerning death. *Journal of Genetic Psychology, 73*, 3–27.

Naimi, T. S., Brewer, R. D., Mokdad, A., Denny, C., Serdula, M. K., & Marks, J. S. (2003). Binge drinking among U.S. adults. *Journal of the American Medical Association, 289*(1), 70–75.

Nakamura, S., Wind, M., & Danello, M. A. (1999). Review of hazards associated with children placed in adults beds. *Archives of Pediatric and Adolescent Medicine, 153*, 1019–1023.

Nanna, M. P., Sheras, P. L., & Cooper, J. (1975). Pygmalion and Galetea: The interactive effect of teacher and student experiences. *Journal of Experimental Social Psychology, 11*(3), 279–287.

Nansel, T. R., Overpeck, M., Pilla, R. S., Ruan, W. J., Simons-Morton, B., & Scheidt, P. (2001). Bullying behaviors among US youth: Prevalence and association with psychosocial adjustment. *Journal of the American Medical Association, 285*, 2094–2100.

NARAL Pro-Choice America. (2002, March 26). *Talking about freedom of choice: 10 Important facts about abortion.* Retrieved from http://www.naral.org/facts/loader.cfm?url=/commonspot/security/getfile.cfm&PageID=1548

Nardi, B. (Ed.). (1996). *Context and consciousness: Activity theory and human-computer interaction.* Cambridge: MIT Press.

Narvaez, D., Bock, T., & Endicott, L. (2003). Who should I become? Citizenship, goodness, human flourishing, and ethical expertise. In W. Veugelers & F. K. Oser (Eds.), *Teaching in moral and democratic education* (pp. 43–63). Bern, Switzerland: Peter Lang.

Nathan, D. G. (1995). *Genes, blood and courage: A boy called Immortal Sword.* Cambridge, MA: Harvard University Press.

Nathanielsz, P. (2001). *The prenatal prescription.* New York: HarperCollins.

National Academy on an Aging Society, http://agingsociety.org

National Academy of Sciences. (1993). *Pesticides in the diets of infants and children.* Washington, DC: National Academies Press.

National Adoption Information Clearinghouse, http://naic.acf.hhs.gov

National Alliance for Autism Research, http://www.naar.org

National Alliance for the Mentally Ill. (n.d.). *Asperger syndrome.* Retrieved from http://www.nami.org/Content/ContentGroups/Helpline1/Asperger_Syndrome.htm

National Archive of Computerized Data on Aging, http://www.icpsr.umich.edu/NACDA

National Assessment of Educational Progress. (2004, February). *The nation's report card.* Retrieved from http://nces.ed.gov/nationsreportcard

National Assessment Governing Board, http://www.nagb.org

National Association to Advance Fat Acceptance, http://www.naafa.org

National Association of Anorexia Nervosa and Associated Disorders, http://www.anad.org

National Association of Anorexia Nervosa and Associated Disorders. *Eating disorder info and resources.* Retrieved from http://www.anad.org/site/anadweb/section.php?id=2118

The National Association of Childbearing Centers, http://www.birthcenters.org

National Association for the Education of Young Children, http://www.naeyc.org

National Association for the Education of Young Children. (n.d.). *NAEYC position statement on school readiness.* Retrieved from http://www.naeyc.org/about/positions/psredy98.asp

National Association for the Education of Young Children. (n.d.). *Where we stand on school readiness.* Retrieved from http://www.naeyc.org/about/positions/pdf/readiness.pdf

National Association for Family Child Care, http://www.nafcc.org/

National Association for Gifted Children (NAGC), http://www.nagc.org

National Association of School Psychologists, http://www.nasponline.org

National Association of School Psychologists. (2003). *Position statement on student grade retention and social promotion.* Retrieved from http://www.nasponline.org/information/pospaper_graderetent.html

National Asthma Education and Prevention Program. (2002). Expert Panel Report: Guidelines for the diagnosis and management of asthma. Update on Selected Topics—2002. *Journal of Allergy Clinical Immunology, 110*, S141–S219.

National Campaign to Prevent Teen Pregnancy, http://www.teenpregnancy.org/resources/data/report_summaries/emerging_answers/default.asp

National Campaign to Prevent Teen Pregnancy. (2002). *Not just another single issue: Teen pregnancy prevention's link to other critical social issues.* Washington, DC: Author.

National Cancer Institute, http://www.cancer.gov

National Cancer Institute. (2004). *Annual report to the nation finds cancer incidence and death rates on the decline: Survival rates show significant improvement.* Retrieved from http://www.nci.nih.gov/newscenter/pressreleases/ReportNation2004release

National Cancer Institute. (n.d.). *Understanding the immune system.* Retrieved from http://press2.nci.nih.gov/sciencebehind/immune/immune00.htm

National Career Development Association. (1992). NCDA reports: Career counseling competencies. *The Career Development Quarterly, 40*, 379–386.

National Center on Addiction and Substance Abuse at Columbia University, http://www.casacolumbia.org/

National Center for Assisted Living, http://www.ncal.org

National Center for Biotechnology Information. (2003). Phenylketonuria. *Genes and disease* (section 234). Bethesda, MD: National Library of Medicine. Retrieved from http://www.ncbi.nlm.nih.gov/books/bv.fcgi?call= bv.View..ShowSection&rid=gnd.section.234

National Center for Complementary and Alternative Medicine. (2004, December). *Acupuncture.* Retrieved from http:// nccam.nih.gov/health/acupuncture/

National Center for Education in Maternal and Child Health, Georgetown University. Maternal and Child Health Library. (2004). *Knowledge path: Children and adolescents with special health care needs.* Retrieved from http://www .mchlibrary.info/knowledgePaths/kp_CSHCN.html

National Center for Education Statistics, http://nces.ed.gov

National Center for Education Statistics. (2003). *The condition of education 2003* (NCES No. 2003-067). Washington, DC: U.S. Government Printing Office. Retrieved from http://nces .ed.gov/pubsearch/pubsinfo.asp?pubid=2003067

National Center on Elder Abuse, http://www.elderabusecenter .org

National Center on Elder Abuse. (1998). *The National Elder Abuse Incidence Study.* Retrieved from http://www.aoa .dhhs.gov/abuse/report/Cexecsum.htm

National Center for Fathering, http://www.fathers.com/

National Center for Health Statistics, http://www.cdc.gov/nchs

National Center for Health Statistics. (1995). *Contraceptive use in the United States: 1982–1990.* Advance Data 1995. Washington, DC: U.S. Government Printing Office.

National Center for Health Statistics. (1997). Births, marriages and deaths for 1996. Monthly vital statistics report (Vol. 45, No. 12). Hyattsville, MD: Author.

National Center for Health Statistics. (2003). *Crude birth rates, fertility rates, and birth rates by age of mother, according to race and Hispanic origin: United States, selected years 1950–2001.* Hyattsville, MD: U.S. Department of Health and Human Services, Centers for Disease Control. Retrieved from http://www.cdc.gov/nchs/data/hus/tables/ 2003/03hus003.pdf

National Center for Health Statistics. (2004, March). *Fast stats A to Z. Table 27: Life expectancy at birth, at 65 years of age, and at 75 years of age, according to race and sex: United States, selected years 1900–2001.* Retrieved from http:// www.cdc.gov/nchs/data/hus/tables/2003/03hus027.pdf

National Center for Health Statistics. (2004). *National trends in injury hospitalization, 1979–2001.* Washington, DC: Centers for Disease Control.

National Center for Infectious Diseases. (n.d.). *Creutzfeldt-Jakob disease.* Retrieved from http://www.cdc.gov/ncidod/ diseases/cjd

National Center for Learning Disabilities, http://www.ld.org

National Center for Missing & Exploited Children, http:// www.missingkids.com

National Child Care Association, http://www.nccanet.org/

National Clearinghouse on Child Abuse and Neglect Information, http://nccanch.acf.hhs.gov

National Clearinghouse for Drug and Alcohol Abuse Information, http://www.health.org

National Coalition Against Domestic Violence, http://www .ncadv.org/

National Commission on Marihuana and Drug Abuse. (1972). *Marihuana: A signal of misunderstanding.* Retrieved from http://www.druglibrary.org/schaffer/Library/studies/nc/nc menu.htm

National Committee for the Prevention of Elder Abuse, http:// www.preventelderabuse.org

National Comorbidity Survey. (n.d.). Retrieved from http:// www.hcp.med.harvard.edu/ncs

National Council on Disability. (2000). *Promises to keep: A decade of federal enforcement of the Americans with Disabilities Act.* Washington, DC: Author. Available from http://www.ncd.gov

National Council on Disability. (2001). *National disability policy: A progress report, November 1999–November 2000.* Washington, DC: Author. Available from http://www .ncd.gov

National Dissemination Center for Children with Disabilities. (2004). *Mental retardation.* Retrieved from http://www .nichcy .org/pubs/factshe/fs8txt.htm

National Dissemination Center for Children with Disabilities (NICHCY). (n.d.). *Connections to the disability community— Information about specific disabilities.* Retrieved from http://www.nichcy.org/disbinf.html

National Down Syndrome Congress, http://www.ndsccenter .org

National Down Syndrome Society, http://www.ndss.org

National Dropout Prevention Center. (2004). *Quick facts: Economic impact.* Retrieved from http://www.dropoutprevention .org/stats/quick_facts/econ_impact.htm

National Eating Disorder Information Centre. (n.d.). *Information and resources on eating disorders and weight preoccupation.* Retrieved from http://www.nedic.ca/default .html

National Eating Disorders Association, http://www .nationaleatingdisorders.org

National Fatherhood Initiative, http://www.fatherhood.org

National Fragile X Foundation, http://www.fragilex.org/

National Gang Crime Research Center, http://www.ngcrc.com

National Head Start Association, http://www.nhsa.org

National Heart, Lung and Blood Institute. (1997). *Expert Panel Report 2: Guidelines for the diagnosis and management of asthma.* NIH Publication 97–4051. Bethesda, MD: National Institutes of Health.

National Heart, Lung and Blood Institute. (n.d.). *Your guide to lowering high blood pressure.* Retrieved from http://www .nhlbi.nih.gov/hbp

National Hemophilia Foundation. (n.d.). *Information center: Types of bleeding disorders.* Retrieved from http://www .hemophilia.org/bdi/bdi_types1.htm

National Highway Traffic Safety Administration, U.S. Department of Transportation. (2003). *Traffic safety facts 2002: Alcohol.* Washington, DC: Author. Retrieved from http:// www-nrd.nhtsa.dot.gov/pdf/nrd-30/NCSA/TSF2002/2002alcfacts .pdf

National Hospice Foundation. (n.d.). *About NHF.* Available from http://www.nationalhospicefoundation.org

National Hospice Organization. (1997). *Hospice fact sheet.* Arlington, VA: Author.

National Hospice and Palliative Care Organization, http://www.nhpco.org

National Human Genome Research Institute, http://www.genome.gov/

National Immunization Program. (2001). *Parents guide to childhood immunization.* Atlanta, GA: Centers for Disease Control and Prevention. Retrieved from http://www.cdc.gov/nip/publications/Parents-Guide/default.htm#pguide

National Immunization Program. (2004). *Epidemiology and prevention of vaccine-preventable diseases* (8th ed.). Atlanta, GA: Centers for Disease Control and Prevention. Retrieved from http://www.cdc.gov/nip/publications/pink/def_pink_full.htm

National Information Center for Children and Youth with Disabilities, http://www.nichcy.org

National Institute on Aging, http://www.nia.nih.gov/

National Institute on Alcohol Abuse and Alcoholism. (2001). *Alcoholism: Getting the facts.* Retrieved from http://www.niaaa.nih.gov/publications/booklet.htm

National Institute on Alcohol Abuse and Alcoholism. (2003). *Databases.* Bethesda, MD. Retrieved from http://www.niaaa.nih.gov/databases/qf.htm

National Institute on Alcohol Abuse and Alcoholism. (n.d.). *College drinking: Changing the culture.* Available from http://www.collegedrinkingprevention.gov

National Institute of Arthritis and Musculoskeletal and Skin Diseases. (1998). *Handout on health: Rheumatoid arthritis.* Retrieved from http://www.niams.nih.gov/hi/topics/arthritis/rahandout.htm

National Institute of Arthritis and Musculoskeletal and Skin Disorders. (2003, March). *NIAMS pain research: An overview.* Retrieved from http://www.niams.nih.gov/hi/topics/pain/pain.htm

National Institute of Child Health and Human Development, http://www.nichd.nih.gov

National Institute of Child Health and Human Development. (1991). *Education of students with phenylketonuria (PKU). Information for teachers, administrators and other school personnel* (Report No. NIH-92–3318). Bethesda, MD: Author. (ERIC Document Reproduction Service No. ED402717)

National Institute of Child Health and Human Development. (1997). The effects of infant care on infant-mother attachment security: Results of the NICHD study of early child care. *Child Development, 68,* 860–879.

National Institute of Child Health and Human Development. (2000). *Report of the National Reading Panel. Teaching children to read: An evidence-based assessment of the scientific research literature on reading and its implications for reading instruction.* Retrieved from http://www.nichd.nih.gov/publications/nrp/smallbook.htm

National Institute of Child Health and Human Development. (2001). *From cells to selves: Biobehavioral development.* Washington, DC: Author.

National Institute of Child Health and Human Development. (n.d.). *Families and Fragile X syndrome.* Retrieved from http://www.nichd.nih.gov/publications/pubs/fragileX/index.htm

National Institute on Deafness and Other Communication Disorders. (2000, April). *Speech and language: Developmental milestones.* Retrieved from http://www.nidcd.nih.gov/health/voice/speechandlanguage.asp

National Institute of Diabetes and Digestive and Kidney Diseases, http://www.niddk.nih.gov/health/nutrit/nutrit.htm

National Institute on Drug Abuse, http://www.nida.nih.gov/

National Institute on Drug Abuse. (1995). *Infofacts. Costs to society.* Retrieved from http://www.nida.nih.gov/Infofax/costs.html

National Institute on Drug Abuse. (2000). *Methylphenidate (Ritalin).* Retrieved from http://www.nida.nih.gov/Infofax/ritalin.html

National Institute for Early Education Research, http://nieer.org

National Institute for Early Education Research. (n.d.). *A benefit-cost analysis of the Abecedarian Early Childhood Intervention.* Retrieved from http://nieer.org/docs/index.php?DocID=57

National Institute of Health. (1998, November 16–18). Diagnosis and treatment of attention deficit hyperactivity disorder. *NIH Consensus Statement, 16*(2), 1–37. Retrieved from http://odp.od.nih.gov/consensus/cons/110/110_statement.htm

National Institute on Media and the Family, http://www.mediafamily.org/index.shtml

National Institute of Mental Health, http://www.nimh.nih.gov/

National Institute of Mental Health. (1994/1996). *Attention deficit hyperactivity disorder: A decade of the brain* (pp. 1–25). Bethesda, MD: U.S. Government Printing Office (NIH Publication No. 96–3576). Retrieved from http://www.nimh.gov/publication/adhd.cfm

National Institute of Mental Health. (1995). Perception, attention, learning, and memory. *Basic behavioral science research for mental health: A national investment.* A report for the National Advisory Mental Health Council (NIH Publication No. 96–3682). Retrieved from http://www.nimh.nih.gov/publicat/baschap3.cfm

National Institute of Mental Health. (1996). *Attention deficit hyperactivity disorder* [Brochure]. Retrieved from http://www.nimh.nih.gov/publicat/adhd.cfm#adhd10

National Institute of Mental Health. (1999). *Schizophrenia.* Retrieved from http://www.nimh.nih.gov/publicat/schizoph.cfm

National Institute of Mental Health. (2000). *NIMH research on treatment for attention deficit hyperactivity disorder (ADHD): The multimodal treatment study—Questions and answers.* Retrieved from http://www.nimh.nih.gov/events/mtaqa.cfm

National Institute of Mental Health. (2003). *Attention deficit hyperactivity disorder.* Retrieved from http://www.nimh.nih.gov/Publicat/ADHD.cfm

National Institute of Mental Health. (2003). Do you suffer from a mental disorder? Or do you know someone who does? Find out more here. *For the public at National Institute for Mental Health, 2003.* Retrieved from http://www.nimh.nih.gov/publicat/index.cfm

National Institute of Mental Health. (2004). *Depression.* Retrieved from http://www.nimh.nih.gov/publicat/depression.cfm

National Institute of Mental Health Panic Disorder, http://www.anxietynetwork.com/pdhome.html

National Institute of Mental Health Therapy Advisor, http://www.therapyadvisor.com

National Institute of Neurological Disorders and Stroke, http://www.ninds.nih.gov/

National Institute of Neurological Disorders and Stroke. (n.d.). *Creutzfeldt-Jakob.* Retrieved from http://www.ninds.nih.gov/health_and_medical/disorders/cjd.htm

National Institute of Neurological Disorders and Stroke. (n.d.). *Huntington's disease information page.* Retrieved from http://www.ninds.nih.gov/health_and_medical/disorders/huntington.htm

National Institutes of Health (NIH), http://www.nih.gov/PHTindex.htm

National Institutes of Health. (1998). *Research report series: Methamphetamine abuse and addiction.* DHHS Pub. No. 98–4210. Rockville, MD: U.S. Department of Health and Human Services.

National Institutes of Health Clinical Center. (2002). *Facts about dietary supplements.* Retrieved from http://www.cc.nih.gov/ccc/supplements/

National Institutes of Health—National Heart, Lung and Blood Institute, http://www.nhlbi.nih.gov

National Institutes of Health—National Heart, Blood, and Lung Institute. (2002). *Framingham Heart Study.* Retrieved from http://www.nhlbi.nih.gov/about/framingham/index.html

National Institutes of Health—National Human Genome Research Institute. (2001). *Developing a haplotype map of the human genome for finding genes related to health and disease.* Retrieved from http://www.genome.gov/10001665

National Institutes of Health, Office of Human Subjects Research. (1979). *Regulations and ethical guidelines: The Belmont Report.* Retrieved from http://ohsr.od.nih.gov/guidelines/belmont.html#gob2

National Kidney and Urologic Diseases Information Clearinghouse, http://kidney.niddk.nih.gov

National Latino Fatherhood and Family Initiative, http://www.nlffi.org

National Library of Medicine and National Institutes of Health. (2004). *Postpartum depression.* Retrieved from http://www.nlm.nih.gov/medlineplus/postpartumdepression.html

National Mental Health Association, http://www.nmha.org/infoctr/factsheets/31.cfm

National Mentoring Partnership, http://www.mentoring.org

National Multiple Sclerosis Society, http://www.nmss.org

National Network for Child Care, http://www.nncc.org

National Network for Child Care: Toddler Development, http://www.nncc.org/Child.Dev/todd.dev.html

National Organization on Disability, http://www.nod.org

National Organization on Disability/Harris. (2000). *Survey of Americans with disability.* Washington, DC: Author. Available from http://www.nod.org

National Organization of Mothers of Twins Clubs, http://www.nomotc.org

National Organization for Rare Disorders (NORD), http://www.rarediseases.org

National Organization for Victim Assistance, http://www.trynova.org/

National Osteoporosis Foundation, http://www.nof.org/

National Reading Panel. (2000). *Teaching children to read: An evidenced-based assessment of the scientific research literature on reading and its implication for reading instruction.* Washington, DC: National Institute of Child Health and Human Development. Retrieved from http://www.nichd.nih.gov/publications/nrp/smallbook.htm

National Reporting System Information and Resources, http://www.headstartinfo.org/nrs_i&r.htm

National Research Center on the Gifted and Talented (NRC/GT), http://www.gifted.uconn.edu

National Research Council. (1999). *Hormonally active agents in the environment.* Washington, DC: National Academies Press.

National Research Council. (2003). *Elder mistreatment: Abuse, neglect, and exploitation in an aging America.* Washington, DC: The National Academies Press.

The National Resource Center on Supportive Housing and Home Modification, http://www.homemods.org/

National Resource Council. (2001). *Educating children with autism.* Washington, DC: National Academy Press.

National Rifle Association. (2004). *Firearms fact sheet.* Retrieved from http://www.nraila.org/Issues/FactSheets/Read.aspx?ID=83

National Rifle Association Glossary, http://www.nraila.org/Issues/FireArmsGlossary/

National SIDS/Infant Death Resource Center, http://www.sidscenter.org/

National Stuttering Association, http://www.nsastutter.org

National Tay-Sachs and Allied Diseases Association, http://www.ntsad.org

National Vital Statistics Reports, http://www.cdc.gov/nchs/products/pubs/pubd/nvsr/nvsr.htm

National Vital Statistics System, http://www.cdc.gov/nchs/ nvss.htm

National Women's Health Information Center, http://www.4woman.gov

National Women's Health Information Center. (2004). *Anemia.* Retrieved from http://www.4woman.gov/faq/anemia.htm

National Women's Health Network, http://www.nwhn.org

National Women's Health Report. Retrieved from http://www.healthywomen.org/healthreport/apri12004/pg4.html

National Youth Gang Center, http://www.iir.com/nygc

National Youth Violence Prevention Resource Center. (n.d.). *Bullying facts and statistics.* Retrieved from http://www.safeyouth.org/scripts/faq/bullying.asp

Natural Child Project, http://www.naturalchild.com/

Neal, J. L. (2001). RhD isoimmunization and current management modalities [Review]. *Journal of Obstetric, Gynecologic, & Neonatal Nursing, 30*(6), 589–606.

Needleman, H. L. (1994). Preventing childhood poisoning. *Preventive Medicine, 23,* 634–637.

Needleman, H. L., Schell, A., Bellinger, D., Levinton, A., & Allred, E. N. (1990). Long term effects of childhood exposure to lead at low dose: An eleven year follow-up report. *New England Journal of Medicine, 322,* 82–88.

Neeleman, J., Wilson-Jones, C., & Wessely, S. (2001). Ethnic density and deliberate self harm; A small area study in southeast London. *Journal of Epidemiology & Community Health, 55*(2), 85–90.

Neihart, M. (1999). The impact of giftedness on psychological well-being. *Roeper Review, 22*(1), 10–17.

Neimeyer, R. A., Stewart, A. E., & Anderson, J. (2004). AIDS-related death anxiety: A research review and clinical recommendations. In H. E. Gendelman, S. Swindells, I. Grant, S. Lipton, & I. Everall (Eds.), *The neurology of AIDS* (2nd ed., pp. 787–799). New York: Chapman & Hall.

Neisser, U. (1967). *Cognitive psychology.* New York: Appleton-Century-Crofts.

Nelson, C. A. (Ed.). (2000). *The effects of early adversity on neurobehavioral development: The Minnesota symposia on child psychology: Vol. 31.* Mahwah, NJ: Erlbaum.

Nelson, J. (1987). *Positive discipline.* New York: Ballantine.

Nelson, K. (1986). *Event knowledge: Structure and function in development.* Hillsdale, NJ: Erlbaum.

Nelson, K. (Ed.). (1989). *Narratives from the crib.* Cambridge, MA: Harvard University Press.

Nelson, R. J. (2000). *An introduction to behavioral endocrinology* (2nd ed.). Sunderland, MA: Sinauer Associates.

Nelson, T. D. (Ed.). (2002). *Ageism: Stereotyping and prejudice against older persons.* Cambridge: MIT Press.

Nelson, T. O. (Ed.). (1992). *Metacognition: Core readings.* Boston: Allyn & Bacon.

The Nemours Foundation. (n.d.). *Childhood stress.* Retrieved from http://kidshealth.org/parent/emotions/feelings/stress .html

The Nemours Foundation. (n.d.). *Dealing with peer pressure.* Retrieved from http://kidshealth.org/kid/feeling/friend/peer_pressure.html

The Nemours Foundation. (n.d.). *What is ADHD?* Retrieved from http://www.kidshealth.org/parent/medical/learning/adhd.html

Nesse, R. M. (2001). *Evolution and the capacity for commitment.* New York: Russell Sage.

Netting, F., Wilson, C., & New J. (1987). The human-animal bond: Implications for practice. *Social Work, 32,* 60–64.

The Network on Transitions to Adulthood, http://www.pop .upenn .edu/transad

Neugarten, D. A. (Ed.). (1996). *The meanings of age: Selected papers of Bernice L. Neugarten.* Chicago: University of Chicago Press.

Neuman, M. G. (1998). *Helping your kids cope with divorce the sandcastles way.* New York: Random House.

Neuman, S., Copple, C., & Bredekamp, S. (1999). *Learning to read and write: Developmentally appropriate practices for young children.* Washington, DC: National Association for the Education of Young Children.

Neumark-Sztainer, D., Hannan, P., Story, M., Croll, J., & Perry, C. (2003). Family meal patterns: Associations with socio-demographic characteristics and improved dietary intake among adolescents. *Journal of the American Dietetics Association, 103,* 317–322.

Neurosciences on the Internet, http://www.neuroguide.com/

New York State Department of Health. (1999). *Clinical practice guideline: Autism/pervasive developmental disorders* (No. 4215). Albany, NY: Health Education Services.

New York State Task Force on Life and the Law. (n.d.). *Executive summary of assisted reproductive technologies: Analysis and recommendations for public policy.* Retrieved from http://www.health.state.ny.us/nysdoh/taskfce/execsum .htm

Newacheck, P. W., & Halfon, N. (1998). Prevalence and impact of disabling chronic conditions in childhood. *American Journal of Public Health, 88,* 610–617.

Newberger, E. (1999). *Computer use in the United States.* Washington, DC: U.S. Census Bureau. Retrieved from http://www.census.gov/prod/99pubs/p20–522.pdf

Newell, A. (1973). Production systems of control processes. In W. G. Chase (Ed.), *Visual information processing* (pp. 463–526). New York: Academic.

Newell, A., & Simon, H. A. (1972). *Human problem solving.* Englewood Cliffs, NJ: Prentice-Hall.

Newman, D. K. (2002). *Managing and treating urinary incontinence.* Baltimore: Health Professions Press.

Newman, D., Griffin, P., & Cole, M. (1989). *The construction zone: Working for cognitive change in school.* New York: Cambridge University Press.

Ney, T. (Ed.). (1995). *True and false allegations of child sexual abuse: Assessment and case management.* New York: Brunner/Mazel.

NICHD. (2004). Study of Early Child Care (SECC) and Youth Development. Retrieved from http://www.nichd.nih.gov/od/secc/index.htm

NICHD Early Child Care Research Network. (2001). Does quality of time spent in children care predict socioemotional adjustment during the transition to kindergarten? *Child Development, 74,* 976–1005.

NICHD Early Child Care Research Network. (2001). Nonmaternal care and family factors in early development: An overview of the NICHD Study of Early Child Care. *Journal of Applied Developmental Psychology, 22,* 457–492.

NICHD Early Child Care Research Network. (2002). Early child care and children's development prior to school entry: Results from the NICHD Study of Early Child Care. *American Educational Research Journal, 39,* 133–164.

NICHD Early Child Care Research Network. (2003). Social functioning in first grade: Associations with earlier home and child care predictors and with current classroom experiences. *Child Development, 74*(6), 1639–1662.

NICHD Early Child Care Research Network. (in press). Multiple pathways to early academic achievement. *Harvard Educational Review.*

NICHD and Research Triangle Institute. (2004). The NICHD Study of Early Child Care and Youth Development. Retrieved from http://secc.rti.org/home.cfm

Nichols, T. R., & Houk, J. C. (2004). Reflex control of muscle. In G. Adelman & B. H. Smith (Eds.), *Encyclopedia of neuroscience* (3rd ed.). Amsterdam: Elsevier.

Nicolai, T., Pereszlenyiova-Bliznakova, L., Illi, S., Reinhardt, D., & von Mutius, E. (2003). Longitudinal follow-up of the changing gender ratio in asthma from childhood to adulthood: Role of delayed manifestation in girls. *Pediatric Allergy and Immunology, 14,* 280–283.

NICU design standards, http://www.nd.edu/~kkolberg/DesignStandards.htm

Niles, S. G., Harris-Bowlsby, J. (2004). *Career development in the 21st century* (2nd ed.). Englewood Cliffs, NJ: Prentice-Hall.

NINDS stroke information page, http://www.ninds.nih.gov/disorders/stroke/stroke_pr.htm

Noack, P., & Buhl, H. M. (2004). Child-parent relationships. In F. R. Lang & K. L. Fingerman (Eds.), *Growing together: Personal relationships across the lifespan* (pp. 45–75). New York: Cambridge University Press.

Noam Chomsky home page, http://web.mit.edu/linguistics/www/chomsky.home.html

Noam Chomsky: A Life of Dissent, http://cognet.mit.edu/library/books/chomsky/chomsky/

Noble, L. (2003). Developments in neonatal technology continue to improve infant outcomes. *Pediatric Annals, 32*(9), 595–603.

Noddings, N. (2002). *Educating moral people: A caring alternative to character education.* New York: Teachers College Press.

Noel, A. M., & Newman, J. (2003). Why delay kindergarten entry? A qualitative study of mothers' decisions. *Early Education & Development, 14*(4), 479–497.

Nolan, C. V., & Shaikh, Z. A. (1992). Lead nephrotoxicity and associated disorders: Biochemical mechanisms. *Toxicology, 73,* 127–146.

Nord, D. (1997). *Multiple AIDS-related loss.* Philadelphia: Taylor & Francis.

Norman, S. (2001). *Parenting an only child.* New York: Broadway.

North American Menopause Society, http://www.menopause.org

North American Menopause Society. (2003). *The menopause guidebook: Helping women make informed healthcare decisions through perimenopause and beyond.* Cleveland, OH: Author.

North American Registry of Midwives, http://www.narm.org

North Central Regional Educational Laboratory. (2001). *Critical issue: Beyond social promotion and retention—Five strategies to help students succeed.* Retrieved from http://www.ncrel.org/sdrs/areas/issues/students/atrisk/at800.htm

North Central Regional Educational Laboratory. (2004). *Resolving Conflict Creatively Program.* Retrieved from http://www.ncrel.org/sdrs/areas/issues/envrnmnt/drugfree/sa21k16.htm

North Central Regional Educational Laboratory. (n.d.). *Assessment of school readiness.* Retrieved from http://www.ncrel.org/sdrs/areas/issues/students/earlycld/ea51k11b.htm

Northrup, C. (1998). *Women's bodies, women's wisdom* (2nd ed.). New York: Bantam.

Norton, A., & Miller, L. (1992). *Marriage, divorce, and remarriage in the 1990's.* Current Population Reports (Series P23-180). Washington, DC: U.S. Government Printing Office. Retrieved from http://www.census.gov/population/socdemo/marr-div/p23-180/p23-180.pdf

Notarius, C. I., & Markman, H. J. (1994). *We can work it out: How to solve conflicts, save your marriage, and strengthen your love for each other.* New York: Perigee.

Novak, G. (1996). *Developmental psychology: Dynamic systems and behavior analysis.* Reno, NV: Context Press.

Nowak, A., Vallacher, R. R., Tesser, A., & Borkowski, W. (2000). Society of self: The emergence of collective properties in self-structure. *Psychological Review, 107,* 39–61.

Nowicki, E., & Sandieson, R. (2002). A meta-analysis of school-age children's attitudes towards persons with physical or intellectual disabilities. *International Journal of Disability, Development and Education, 49*(3), 243–265.

Nucci, L. P. (1981). Conceptions of personal issues: A domain distinct from moral or societal concepts. *Child Development, 52,* 114–121.

Nucci, L. P. (2002). The development of moral reasoning. In U. Goswami (Ed.), *Blackwell handbook of childhood cognitive development* (pp. 303–325). Malden, MA: Blackwell.

Nuland, S. B. (1994). *How we die: Reflections on life's final chapter.* New York: Alfred A. Knopf.

Nunnally, J. C., & Bernstein, I. H. (1994). *Psychometric theory* (3rd ed.). New York: McGraw-Hill.

Nyambedha, E., Wandibba, S., & Aagaard-Hansen, J. (2003). Changing patterns of orphans care due to HIV epidemic in western Kenya, *Social Science and Medicine, 57*(2), 301–311.

Nyanatiloka. (1970). *Buddhist dictionary: Manual of Buddhist terms and doctrines.* Taiwan: The Buddha Educational Foundation.

Nyberg, D., McGahan, J., Pretorius, D., & Pilu, G. (2002). *Diagnostic imaging of fetal anomalies.* Philadelphia: Lippincott Williams & Wilkins.

Nyhan, W. L. (1973). The Lesch-Nyhan syndrome. *Annual Review of Medicine, 24,* 41–60.

Oakes, J. M., & Rossi, P. H. (2003). The measurement of SES in health research: Current practice and steps toward a new approach. *Social Science and Medicine, 56,* 769–784.

Oberlander, J. (2003). *The political life of Medicare.* Chicago: University of Chicago Press.

OBGYN.net, http://www.obgyn.net

O'Brien, L. M., Holbrook, C. R., Mervis, C. B., Klaus, C. J., Bruner, J. L., Raffield, T. J., et al. (2003). Sleep and neurobehavioral characteristics of 5- to 7-year-old children with parentally reported symptoms of attention-deficit/hyperactivity disorder. *Pediatrics, 111,* 554–563.

Observational Learning, http://sun.science.wayne.edu/~wpoff/cor/mem/cognobsr.html

Obsessive-Compulsive Foundation, http://www.ocfoundation.org

O'Connor, T. (2004). *Experimental and quasi-experimental research design.* Retrieved from http://faculty.ncwc.edu/toconnor/308/3081ect06.htm

Oden, S., Schweinhart, L., Weikart, D., Marcus, S., & Xie, Y. (2000). *Into adulthood: A study of the effects of Head Start.* Ypsilanti, MI: High/Scope Press.

Oehlert, G. W. (2000). *A first course in design and analysis of experiments.* New York: Freeman.

Office of Juvenile Justice and Delinquency Prevention, http://ojjdp.ncjrs.org

Office of Juvenile Justice and Delinquency Prevention. (1995). *OJJDP fact sheet* (No. 21). Rockville, MD: Juvenile Justice Clearing House.

Office of National Drug Control Policy. (2004, March). *The president's national drug control strategy.* Retrieved from http://www.whitehousedrugpolicy.gov/publications/policy/ndcs04/healing_amer.html

Offit, P. A., & Bell, M. L. (Eds.). (1999). *Vaccines: What every parent should know.* New York: IDG Books.

Offord Centre for Child Studies, McMaster University, Toronto, http://www.fhs.mcmaster.ca/cscr/autism/Early%20Intervention.html

Ogle, K., Mavis, B., & Wang, T. (2003). Hospice and primary care physicians: Attitudes, knowledge, and behaviors. *American Journal of Hospice and Palliative Care, 20,* 41–49.

Oh, H., Yamazaki, Y., & Kawata, C. (1998). Prevalence and a drug use development model for the study of adolescent drug use in Japan. *Japanese Journal of Public Health, 45,* 870–882.

O'Hara, M. W. (1994). *Postpartum depression: Causes and consequences.* New York: Springer-Verlag.

Older Americans Resources and Services, Duke University. (1975, revised 1988). *The OARS Multidimensional Functional Assessment Questionnaire.* Durham, NC: Duke University Press.

Oldham, D. G. (1978). Adolescent turmoil: A myth revisited. *Adolescent Psychiatry, 6,* 267–279.

Oliver, T. R., Lee, P. R., & Lipton, H. L. (2004). A political history of Medicare and prescription drug coverage. *The Milbank Quarterly, 82,* 283–354.

Olson, L., & Houlihan, D. (2000). A review of behavioral treatments used for Lesch-Nyhan syndrome. *Behavior Modification, 24,* 202–222.

Olweus, D. (1978). *Aggression in the schools: Bullies and whipping boys.* Washington, DC: Hemisphere.

Olweus, D. (1979). Stability of aggression reaction patterns in males: A review. *Psychological Bulletin, 86,* 852–875.

Olweus, D. (1993). *Bullying at school: What we know and what we can do.* Oxford, UK: Blackwell.

Omdahl, B. L. (1995). *Cognitive appraisal, emotion, and empathy.* Mahwah, NJ: Erlbaum.

Omoto, A. M., Synder, M., & Martino, S. C. (2000). Volunteerism and the life course: Investigating age-related agendas for action. *Basic & Applied Social Psychology: Special Issue: The Social Psychology of Aging, 22,* 181–197.

On the origin of the species by means of natural selection. (n.d.). Retrieved from http://www.zoo.uib.no/classics/origin.html

Online Asperger Syndrome Information and Support, http://udel.edu/bkirby/asperger

The Online Library of Liberty. (n.d.). Rousseau's *Discourse on the arts and sciences.* Available from http://oll.libertyfund.org/Home3/index.php

Online Psychological Services, http://www.psychologynet.org/dsm.html

Open Learning Technology Corporation Limited. (1996). *Information-processing theory.* Retrieved from http://www.educationau.edu.au/archives/cp/04h.htm

Optimal Breathing, http://www.breathing.com

O'Rahilly, R., & Muller, F. (1992). *Human embryology and teratology.* New York: Wiley-Liss.

Orangi, H. (n.d.). *Working memory.* Retrieved from http://coe.sdsu.edu/eet/articles/workingmemory/start.htm

Oregon Social Learning Center, http://www.oslc.org

Orem, R. A. (2001). Journal writing in adult ESL: Improving practice through reflective writing. *New Directions for Adult and Continuing Education, 90,* 69–77.

Ornstein, A. C. (1993). Norm-referenced and criterion-referenced tests: An overview. *NASSP Bulletin, 77*(555), 28–39.

Orphan Train Heritage Society of America, http://www.orphantrainriders.com/res.matII.html

Ortner, S., & Whitehead, H. (1981). *Sexual meanings: The cultural construction of gender and sexuality* (pp. 1–27). Cambridge, UK: Cambridge University Press.

Osborne, G. L. (in press). Using the self-report free recall technique to explore everyday memory failures in the aging adult. *Cognitive Technology, 10.*

Osher, D., Kendziora, K. T., VanDenBerg, J., & Dennis, K. (1999). Growing resilience: Creating opportunities for resilience to thrive. *Reaching Today's Youth, 3*(4), 38–45.

Öst, L. G., & Hellstrom, K. (1994). In G. C. L. Davey (Ed.), *Phobias: A handbook of theory, research, and treatment* (pp. 63–80). Chichester, UK: Wiley.

Öst, L. G., Hellstrom, K., & Kaver, A. (1992). One versus five sessions of exposure in the treatment of injection phobia. *Behavior Therapy, 23,* 263–282.

Öst, L. G., Sterner, U., & Lindahl, I. L. (1984). Physiological responses in blood phobics. *Behaviour Research and Therapy, 22,* 109–117.

Oster, H. (2003). Emotion in the infant's face: Insights from the study of infants with facial anomalies. *Annals of the New York Academy of Sciences, 1000,* 197–204.

OSU SSG Explains, http://ssg.fst.ohio-state.edu/Extension/explains.asp

Oswalt, W. H. (2005). *This land was theirs: A study of Native North Americans* (8th ed.). New York: Oxford University Press.

Ovando, C., Collier, V., & Combs, M. C. (2003). *Bilingual and ESL classrooms: Teaching in multicultural contexts* (3rd ed.). New York: McGraw-Hill.

Owens, R. E. (1996). *Language development* (4th ed.). Boston: Allyn & Bacon.

Owram, D. (1997). *Born at the right time: A history of the Baby Boomer generation.* Toronto: University of Toronto Press.

Oxford Reference Online. (n.d.). *Ego.* Available from http://www.oxfordreference.com

Ozkaya, N., & Nordin, M. (1999). *Fundamentals of biomechanics.* New York: Springer-Verlag.

Ozonoff, S., Dawson, G., & McPartland, J. (2002). *A parent's guide to Asperger syndrome and high-functioning autism: How to meet the challenges and help your child thrive.* New York: Guilford.

Pajares, F. (2004). *Albert Bandura: Biographical sketch.* Retrieved from http://www.emory.edu/EDUCATION/mfp/bandurabio.html

Palermo, G. P., Schlegel, P. N., Sills, E. S., Veeck, L. L., Zaninovic, N., Menendez, S., et al. (1998). Births after intracytoplasmic injection of sperm obtained by testicular extraction from men with non-mosaic Klinefelter syndrome. *New England Journal of Medicine, 338,* 588–590.

Paley, V. G. (2004). *A child's work: The importance of fantasy play.* Chicago: University of Chicago Press.

Palkovitz, R. (2002). *Involved fathering and men's adult development: Provisional balances.* Mahwah, NJ: Erlbaum.

Palmer, M. H. (2004). Urinary stress incontinence: Prevalence, etiology and risk factors in women at 3 life stages. *American Journal for Nurse Practitioners,* May(suppl.), 5–14.

Palmore, E. B. (1999). *Ageism: Negative and positive.* New York: Springer.

Paoletti, L. C., & McInnes, P. M. (Eds.). (1999). *Vaccines, from concept to clinic: A guide to the development and clinical testing of vaccines for human use.* Boca Raton, FL: CRC Press.

Papathanasopoulos, M. A., Hunt. G. M., & Tiemessen, C. T. (2003). Evolution and diversity of HIV-1 in Africa: A review. *Virus Genes, 26,* 151–163.

Papini, M. R. (2002). *Comparative psychology: Evolution and development of behavior.* Upper Saddle River, NJ: Prentice-Hall.

Papini, M. R., & Bitterman, M. E. (1990). The role of contingency in classical conditioning. *Psychological Review, 97,* 396–403.

Papini, M. R., & Bitterman, M. E. (1993). The two-test strategy in the study of inhibitory conditioning. *Journal of Experimental Psychology: Animal Behavior Processes, 19,* 342–352.

Parasuraman, R. (Ed.). (1998). *The attentive brain.* Cambridge: MIT Press.

Parcel, T. L., & Menaghan, E. G. (1994). *Parents' jobs and children's lives.* New York: deGruyter.

Parent Soup, http://parentsoup.com

Parent-to-Parent, http://p2p.uiuc.edu

Parenthood, http://parenthoodweb.com

Parenting the Only Child, http://forums.adoption.com/f704.html

Parenting.Org, http://www.parenting.org

Parents and Teachers Against Violence in Education (PTAVE). (n.d.). *Project NoSpank.* Retrieved from http://www.nospank.net/toc.htm#cpchart

Parents Anonymous Inc., http://www.parentsanonymous.org

Parents Anonymous. (2002). *Program bulletin: The model for parent education.* Claremont, CA: Author. Retrieved from http://www.parentsanonymous.org/paTEST/publications1/ProgBulletin.pdf

Parents for Inclusion, http://www.parentsforinclusion.org/

Parents of Premature Babies, Inc., http://www.Preemie-L.org

Parents Without Partners, http://www.parentswithoutpartners.org

Parents World, http://www.parentsworld.com/

Park, D. C., Polk, T., Mikels, J., Taylor, S. F., & Marshuetz, C. (2001). Cerebral aging: Integration of brain and behavioral models of cognitive function. *Dialogues in Clinical Neuroscience, 3,* 151–165.

Park, D. C., & Schwarz, N. (1999). *Cognitive aging: A primer.* Philadelphia: Psychology Press.

Parke, R. D., & Slaby, R. G. (1983). The development of aggression. In P. Mussen (Series Ed.) & E. M. Hetherington (Vol. Ed.), *Handbook of child psychology: Vol. 4. Socialization, personality, and social development* (4th ed., pp. 547–641). New York: Wiley.

Parker, J. N. (2002). *The 2002 official patient's sourcebook on impotence.* San Diego, CA: Icon Health.

Parkin, A. J. (1997). *Memory and amnesia: An introduction* (2nd ed.). Oxford, UK: Blackwell.

Parry, J. K., & Ryan, A. S. (1995). *A cross-cultural look at death, dying, and religion.* Chicago: Nelson-Hall.

Parsons, T., & Bales, R. F. (1955). *Family, socialization and interaction process.* New York: The Free Press.

Parten, M. (1932). Social participation among preschool children. *Journal of Abnormal and Social Psychology, 27,* 243–269.

Partners Against Hate. (2003). *Addressing youthful hate crime is imperative.* Available from http://www.partnersagainsthate.org/

Partnership for Caring, http://www.partnershipforcaring.org

The Partnership for Reading. (2000). *Put reading first: Helping your child learn to read.* Retrieved from http://www.nifl.gov/partnershipforreading/publications/Parent_br.pdf

Partnership for Reading (Producer). (2003, Spring). *A child becomes a reader: Birth through preschool* (2nd ed.). Portsmouth, NH: RMC Corporation. Retrieved from http://www.nifl.gov/partnershipforreading/publications/pdf/low_res_child_reader_B-K.pdf

Partnership for Reading (Producer). (2003, Spring). *A child becomes a reader: Kindergarten through grade 3* (2nd ed.). Portsmouth, NH: RMC Corporation. Retrieved from http://www.nifl.gov/partnershipforreading/publications/pdf/low_res_child_reader_K-3.pdf

Partnership for Reading (Producer). (2003). *Research based principles for adult basic education reading instruction.* Portsmouth, NH: RMC Corporation. Retrieved from http://www.nifl.gov/partnershipforreading/publications/adult_ed_02.pdf

Partnership for Reading. (n.d.). *Put reading first: The research building blocks for teaching children to read, kindergarten through grade 3.* Retrieved from http://www.nifl.gov/partnershipforreading/publications/reading_first1.html

Paternity Angel, http://www.paternityangel.com

Patrick Bateson's home page, http://www.cus.cam.ac.uk/~ppgb

Patten, M. L. (2004). *Understanding research methods* (4th ed.). Glendale, CA: Pyrczak.

Patterson, G. R. (1982). *Coercive family process.* Eugene, OR: Castalia Press.

Patterson, G. R., DeBaryshe, B. D., & Ramsey, E. (1989). A developmental perspective on antisocial behavior. *American Psychologist, 44,* 329–335.

Patterson, G., & Forgatch, M. (1987). *Parents and adolescents: Living together.* Eugene, OR: Castalia Press.

Patterson, G. R., Forgatch, M. S., Yoerger, K. L., & Stoolmiller, M. (1998). Variables that initiate and maintain and early-onset trajectory for juvenile offending. *Development and Psychopathology, 10,* 531–547.

Patterson, L. B., & Dorfman, L. T. (2002). Family support for hospice caregivers. *American Journal of Hospice and Palliative Care, 19,* 315–323.

Pattison, E. M. (1977). *The experience of dying.* Englewood Cliffs, NJ: Prentice-Hall.

Paul, G. L., & Lentz, R. J. (1977/1997). *Psychosocial treatment of chronically ill mental patients: Milieu vs. social learning programs.* Champaign, IL: Research Press.

Paux, M. (1984). *Childless by choice: Choosing childlessness.* New York: Doubleday.

Pavlov, I. P. (1927). *Conditioned reflexes* (G. V. Anrep, Trans.). London: Oxford University Press.

PBS. (n.d.). *Social and emotional development.* Retrieved from http://www.pbs.org/wholechild/abc/social.html

Pearlin, L. I., Pioloi, M. F., & McLaughlin, A. E. (2001). Caregiving by adult children. In R. Binstock & L. K. George (Eds.), *Handbook of aging and social sciences* (5th ed., pp. 238–254). San Diego, CA: Academic Press.

Pearson, D., Rouse, H., Doswell, S., Ainsworth, C., Dawson, O., Simms, K., et al. (2001). Prevalence of imaginary companions in a normal child population. *Child: Care, Health and Development, 27*(1), 13.

Pedhazur, E. J., & Schmelkin, L. P. (1991). *Measurement, design, and analysis: An integrated approach.* Hillsdale, NJ: Erlbaum.

Peeke, P. (2004, April). Looking for relief? Change your lifestyle. *National Women's Health Report.*

Peele, S., & Brodsky, A. (1997). Gateway to nowhere: How alcohol came to be scapegoated for drug abuse. *Addiction Research, 5,* 419–425.

Peer Pressure, http://library.thinkquest.org/3354/Resource_Center/Virtual_Library/Peer_Pressure/peer.htm

Peled, E., Jaffe, P. G., & Edleson, J. L. (1995). *Ending the cycle of violence: Community responses to children of battered women.* Thousand Oaks, CA: Sage.

Pelham, B. W., & Goldberg, R. (2002). *Conducting research in psychology: Measuring the weight of smoke.* Stamford, CT: Wadsworth/Thompson.

Pellegrino, J. W., & Glaser, R. (1979). Cognitive correlates and components in the analysis of individual differences. *Intelligence, 3,* 187–218.

Peplau, L. A., & Garnets, L. D. (2000). A new paradigm for understanding women's sexuality and sexual orientation. *Journal of Social Issues, 56,* 329–350.

Peplau, L. A., & Perlman, D. (Eds.). (1982). *Loneliness: A sourcebook of current theory, research, and therapy.* New York: Wiley-Interscience.

Percy, S. L. (2001). Challenges and dilemmas in implementing the Americans with Disabilities Act: Lessons from the first decade. *Policy Studies Journal, 29,* 633–640.

Peregoy, S. F., & Boyle, O. F. (2001). *Reading, writing, & learning in ESL: A resource book for K-12 teachers.* Reading, MA: Addison Wesley Longman.

Perez, R. M., DeBord, K. A., & Bieschke, K. J. (2000). *Handbook of counseling and psychotherapy with lesbian, gay, and bisexual clients.* Washington, DC: American Psychological Association.

Performance Unlimited. (1998). *Self-actualization.* Retrieved from http://www.performance-unlimited.com/samain.htm

Perkins, H. W., DeJong, W., & Linkenbach, J. (2001). Estimated blood alcohol levels reached by "binge" and "nonbinge" drinkers: A survey of young adults in Montana. *Psychology of Addictive Behaviors, 15*(4), 317–320.

Perlman, D. (1988). Loneliness: A life-span developmental perspective. In P. Milardo (Ed.), *Families and social networks* (pp. 190–220). Newbury Park, CA: Sage.

Perrin, E., & the Committee on Psychosocial Aspects of Child and Family Health. (2002). Technical report: Coparent or second-parent adoption by same-sex parents. *Pediatrics, 109*(2), 341–344.

Perrin, E., Newacheck, P., Pless, I. B., Drotar, D., Gortmaker, S. L., Leventhal, J., et al. (1993). Issues involved in the definition and classification of chronic health conditions. *Pediatrics, 91,* 787–793.

Perry, E. L., Kulik, C. T., & Bourhis, A. C. (1996). Moderating effects of personal and contextual factors in age discrimination. *Journal of Applied Psychology, 81,* 628–647.

Pet-Me Pets Therapeutic Animals, http://www.petmepets.org

Peters, A. (2002). Structural changes that occur during normal aging of primate cerebral hemispheres. *Neuroscience and Biobehavioral Reviews, 26*(7), 733–741.

Peters, T., & Barry, G. (1998). *Stuttering: An integrated approach to its nature and treatment* (2nd ed.). Baltimore: Williams & Wilkins.

Petersen, A. C. (1993). Presidential address: Creating adolescents: The role of context and process in developmental trajectories. *Journal of Research on Adolescence, 3*(1), 1–18.

Peterson, C., Maier, S. F., & Seligman, M. E. P. (1993). *Learned helplessness: A theory for the age of personal control.* New York: Oxford University Press.

Peterson, R. A., & Reiss, S. (1992). *Anxiety Sensitivity Index revised manual.* Worthington, OH: International Diagnostic Systems Publishing.

Petty, R. E., & Wegener, D. T. (1998). Attitude change: Multiple roles for persuasion variables. In D. Gilbert & S. Fiske (Eds.), *Handbook of social psychology* (Vol. 1, 4th ed., pp. 323–390). New York: McGraw-Hill.

Pew Health Professions Commission. (1995). *State Health Personnel Handbook.* San Francisco: UCSF Center for the Health Professions.

Pfau-Effinger, B. (1998). Gender cultures and the gender arrangement—A theoretical framework for cross-national gender research. *Innovation, 11*(2), 147–166.

Pfurtscheller, G., & Lopes da Silva, F. H. (Eds.). (1975–1976). *Handbook of electroencephalography and clinical neurophysiology, Volume 6, Event-related Desynchronization.* Amsterdam: Elsevier.

The Philosophy of John Locke, http://radicalacademy.com/phillocke.htm

Phinney, J. S. (1991). Ethnic identity and self-esteem: A review and integration. *Hispanic Journal of Behavioral Sciences, 13,* 193–208.

Phobia List, http://www.phobialist.com/

Physicians for Reproductive Choice and Health (PRCH) and The Alan Guttmacher Institute (AGI). (2003, January). *An overview of abortion in the United States.* Retrieved from http://www.agi-usa.org/presentations/abort_slides.pdf

Piaget, J. (1929). *The child's conception of the world.* New York: Harcourt Brace.

Piaget, J. (1930). *The child's conception of physical causality.* New York: Harcourt Brace.

Piaget, J. (1932/1965). *The moral judgment of the child.* New York: Free Press.

Piaget, J. (1952). *The child's concept of number.* New York: W. W. Norton.

Piaget, J. (1952). *The origins of intelligence in children.* New York: International Universities Press.

Piaget, J. (1954/1999). *The construction of reality in the child.* London: Routledge.

Piaget, J. (1955). *The construction of reality in the child.* Retrieved from http://www.marxists.org/reference/subject/philosophy/works/fr/piaget2.htm

Piaget, J. (1962). *Play, dreams and imitation in childhood* (C. Gattegno & F. M. Hodgson, Trans.). New York: W. W. Norton.

Piaget, J. (1966). *Psychology of intelligence.* Totowa, NJ: Littlefield, Adams.

Piaget, J. (1970). Piaget's theory. In P. H. Mussen (Ed.), *Carmichael's manual of child psychology: Vol. 1.* New York: Wiley.

Piaget, J. (1972). Intellectual evaluation from adolescence to adulthood. *Human Development 15*(1), 1–12.

Piaget, J. (1976). Piaget's theory. In P. B. Neubauer (Ed.), *The process of child development* (pp. 164–212). New York: New American Library.

Piaget, J. (1977). *Problems of equilibration.* In M. H. Appel & L. S. Goldberg (Eds.), *Topics in cognitive development* (Vol. 1, pp. 3–14). New York: Plenum.

Piaget, J. (1977). *The development of thought: Equilibration of cognitive structures.* New York: The Viking Press. (Originally published in French, 1975)

Piaget, J. (1980). *Adaptation and intelligence: Organic selection and phenocopy.* Chicago: University of Chicago Press. (Originally published in French, 1974)

Piaget, J. (1985). *The equilibration of cognitive structures.* Chicago: University of Chicago Press. (Original work published 1975)

Piaget, J., & Inhelder, B. (1956/1967). *The child's conception of space.* London: Routledge & Kegan Paul.

Piaget, J., & Inhelder, B. (1969/2000). *The psychology of the child.* New York: Basic Books.

Piaget, J., & Inhelder, B. (1974). *The child's construction of quantities.* London: Routledge & Kegan Paul.

Piaget, J., & Szeminska, A. (1952). *The child's conception of number.* New York: Humanities Press.

Piaget's theory of cognitive development. (n.d.). Retrieved from http://chiron.valdosta.edu/whuitt/col/cogsys/piaget.html

Pianta, R. C., & Cox, M. J. (1999). (Eds.). *The transition to kindergarten.* Baltimore: Paul H. Brookes.

Pianta, R. C., Tietbohl, P. J., & Bennett, E. M. (1997). Differences in social adjustment and classroom behavior between children retained in kindergarten and groups of age and grade matched peers. *Early Education and Development, 8,* 137–152.

Pick, A. D., & Gibson, E. J. (2000). *An ecological approach to perceptual learning and development.* New York: Oxford University Press.

Pick, H. L., Jr. (1989). Motor development: The control of action. *Developmental Psychology, 25,* 867–870.

Pick, H. L., Jr. (2003). Development and learning: A historical perspective on the acquisition of motor control. *Infant Behavior and Development, 26,* 441–448.

Pickens, J., Field, T., & Nawrocki, T. (2001). Frontal EEG asymmetry in response to emotional vignettes in preschool age children. *International Journal of Behavioral Development, 25,* 105–112.

Picton, T. W. (1992). The p300 wave of the human event-related potential. *Journal of Clinical Neurophysiology, 9*(4), 456–479.

Pierce, B. (2002). *Genetics: A conceptual approach.* San Francisco: WH Freeman.

Pincus, J. H. (1972). Subacute necrotizing encephalomyelopathy (Leigh's disease): A consideration of clinical features and etiology. *Developmental Medicine and Child Neurology, 14,* 87.

Pinker, S. (1994). *The language instinct.* New York: W. Morrow.

Pinker, S. (1997). *How the mind works.* New York: W. W. Norton.

Pistillo, F. (1989). Preprimary care and education in Italy. In P. P. Olmsted & D. P. Weikart (Eds.), *How nations serve young children: Profiles of child care and education in 14 countries*. Ypsilanti, MI: HighScope Press.

Pitzer, D. (1997). *America's communal utopias*. Chapel Hill: University of North Carolina.

Planned Parenthood Federation of America. (1998). *What is rape? Some legal definitions*. Retrieved from http://www.teenwire.com/index.asp?taStrona=http://www.teenwire.com/warehous/articles/wh_19981201p060.asp

Pleis, J., & Coles, R. (2002). Summary health statistics for U.S. adults: National Health Interview Survey, 1998. National Center for Health Statistics. *Vital Health Statistics, 10*(209).

Plomin, R., DeFries, J. C., McClearn, G. E., & McGuffin, P. (2001). *Behavioral genetics* (4th ed.). New York: Worth.

Plotkin, S. A. (1999). Rubella vaccines. In S. A. Plotkin & E. A. Mortimer (Eds.), *Vaccines* (3rd ed., pp. 409–439). Philadelphia: W. B. Saunders.

Plous, S. (1993). *The psychology of judgment and decision making*. New York: McGraw-Hill.

Plucker, J. A. (Ed.). (2003). *Human intelligence: Historical influences, current controversies, teaching resources*. Retrieved from http://www.indiana.edu/~intell/binet.shtml

Poliakov, L. (2003). *History of anti-Semitism* (Vols. 1–4). Philadelphia: University of Pennsylvania Press.

Polivy, J., & Herman, C. (1985). Dieting and binging: A causal analysis. *American Psychologist, 40,* 193–201.

Polivy, J., & Herman, C. P. (2002). Causes of eating disorders. *Annual Review of Psychology, 53,* 187–214.

Polland, W. (2004). Myopic artists. *Acta Ophthalmologica Scandinavica, 82,* 325–326.

Polychlorinated biphenyls, http://www.ec.gc.ca/pcb/eng/index_e.htm

Ponton, L. E. (1997). *The romance of risk: Why teenagers do the things they do*. New York: Basic Books.

Poon, L. W., Gueldner, S. H., & Sprouse, B. M. (Eds.). (2003). *Successful aging and adaptation with chronic diseases*. New York: Springer.

Pope-Davis, D. B., & Coleman, H. L. K. (Eds.). (2001). *The intersection of race, class, and gender in multicultural counseling*. Thousand Oaks, CA: Sage.

Popham, J. W. (1978). *Criterion referenced measurement*. Englewood Cliffs, NJ: Prentice-Hall.

Portello, J. (2003). The mother-infant attachment process in adoptive families. *Canadian Journal of Counseling, 27,* 177–190.

Posner, M. I., & Dehaene, S. (1994). Attentional networks. *Trends in Neurosciences, 17*(2), 75–79.

Posner, M. I., & Petersen, S. E. (1990). The attention system of the human brain. *Annual Review of Neuroscience, 13,* 25–42.

Post, S. G. (2003). *Unlimited love: Altruism, compassion, and service*. Philadelphia: Templeton Foundation Press.

Postpartum Support International, http://www.postpartum.net/

Potok, C. (1978). *Wanderings: Chaim Potok's history of the Jews*. New York: Alfred Knopf.

Poulton, R., & Menzies, R. G. (2002). Non-associative fear acquisition: A review of the evidence from retrospective and longitudinal research. *Behaviour Research and Therapy, 40,* 127–149.

Powell, D. S., Batsche, C. J., Ferro, J., Fox, L., & Dunlap, G. (1997). A strengths-based approach in support of multi-risk families: Principles and issues. *Topics in Early Childhood Special Education, 17,* 1–26.

Power, S. (2002). *"A problem from hell": America and the age of genocide*. New York: Basic Books.

Powers, J. G. (1997). *Ancient weddings*. Retrieved from http://ablemedia.com/ctcweb/consortium/ancientweddings2.html

Powers, M. D. (Ed.). (2000). *Children with autism: A parent's guide* (2nd ed.). Bethesda, MD: Woodbine House.

Powers, M. D., & Poland, J. (2002). *Asperger syndrome and your child: A parent's guide*. New York: HarperResource.

Powers, S. W., Vannatta, K., Noll, R. B., Cool, V. A., & Stehbens, J. A. (1995). Leukemia and other childhood cancers. In M. C. Roberts (Ed.), *Handbook of pediatric psychology* (2nd ed., pp. 310–326). New York: Guilford.

Prager, K. J. (1995). *The psychology of intimacy*. New York: Guilford.

Praisner, C. L. (2003). Attitudes of elementary school principals toward the inclusion of students with disabilities. *Exceptional Children, 69*(2), 135–145.

Pratt, H. D. (2002). Neurodevelopmental issues in the assessment and treatment of deficits in attention, cognition, and learning during adolescence. *Adolescent Medicine: State of the Art Reviews, 13*(3), 579–598.

Pratt, H. D., & Greydanus, D. E. (2003). Violence: Current issues. *Pediatric Clinics of North America, 50*(5), 963–1003.

Pratt, M. W., Kerig, P., Cowan, P. A., & Cowan, C. P. (1988). Mothers and fathers teaching 3-year-olds: Authoritative parents and adult scaffolding of young children's learning. *Developmental Psychology, 24,* 832–839.

Pratt, M. W., & Norris, J. E. (1999). Moral development in maturity: Life-span perspectives on the processes of successful aging. In T. M. Hess (Ed.), *Social cognition and aging* (pp. 291–317). San Diego, CA: Academic Press.

Premack, D., & Woodruff, G. (1978). Does the chimpanzee have a theory of mind? *Behavioral and Brain Sciences, 4,* 515–526.

President's Council on Bioethics. (n.d.). *U.S. public policy and the biotechnologies that touch the beginnings of human life: A detailed overview*. Retrieved from http://bioethicsprint.bioethics.gov/background/biotechnology.html

Preston, S. H., Heuveline, P., & Guillot, M. (2001). *Demography: Measuring and modeling population processes*. Malden, MA: Blackwell.

Prevention and Relationship Enhancement Program, http://www.prepinc.com

Price, D. W., & Goodman, G. S. (1990). Visiting the wizard: Children's memory for a recurring event. *Child Development, 61,* 664–680.

Program for Appropriate Technology in Health. (1997). Infertility in developing countries. *Outlook, 15,* 1–6. Retrieved from http://www.path.org/files/e0115_3.pdf

Project PARA. (n.d.). *Lesson 4: Observation techniques.* Retrieved from http://www.para.unl.edu/para/Observation/Lesson4.html

Pronin, E., Puccio, C., & Ross, L. (2002). Understanding misunderstanding: Social psychological perspectives. In T. Gilovich, D. Griffin, & D. Kahneman (Eds.), *Heuristics and biases: The psychology of intuitive judgment.* Cambridge, UK: Cambridge University Press.

Prostate Cancer Foundation, http://www.prostatecancerfoundation.org/

Pruchno, R., & Rosenbaum, J. (2003). Social relationships in adulthood and old age. In R. M. Lerner, M. A. Easterbrooks, & J. Mistry (Eds.), *Handbook of psychology, Vol. 6: Developmental psychology* (pp. 487–509). Hoboken, NJ: Wiley.

Pruett, K. (1997). How men and children affect each other's development. *Zero to Three Journal, 18,* 3–11.

Prull, M. W., Gabrieli, J. D. E., & Bunge, S. A. (2000). Age-related changes in memory: A cognitive neuroscience perspective. In F. I. M. Craik & T. A. Salthouse (Eds.), *The handbook of aging and cognition* (2nd ed., pp. 91–153). Hillsdale, NJ: Erlbaum.

The Psi Cafe. (n.d.). *Developmental psychology.* Available from http://www.psy.pdx.edu/PsiCafe/Areas/Developmental/

The Psi Cafe. (n.d.). *Research in Psychology: Diagnosis and interpretation of stats.* Retrieved from http://www.psy.pdx.edu/PsiCafe/Research/Stats-Diag&Interp.htm

The Psi Cafe. (n.d.). *Research in psychology: Hypotheses and variables.* Retrieved from http://www.psy.pdx.edu/PsiCafe/Research/Hyp&Var.htm

Psybox Ltd. (n.d.). *Normal distribution.* Retrieved from http://www.psybox.com/web_dictionary/NormalDist.htm

The Psychological Corporation. (2002). *WAIS-III—WMS-III technical manual.* San Antonio, TX: Author.

Psychology Today. (n.d.). *Empty nest syndrome.* Retrieved from http://cms.psychologytoday.com/conditions/emptynest.html

Public Agenda. (2005). *Right to Die: Overview.* Retrieved from http://www.publicagenda.org/issues/overview.cfm?issue_type=right2die

Pueschel, S. M. (Ed.). (2001). *A parent's guide to Down syndrome* (Rev. ed.). Baltimore: Paul H. Brookes.

Pueschel, S. M., & Pueschel, J. K. (Eds.). (1992). *Biomedical concerns in persons with Down syndrome.* Baltimore: Paul H. Brookes.

Pulmonary Education and Research Foundation, http://www.perf2ndwind.org/html/breathing.html

Purves, D., Augustine, G. J., Fitzpatrick, D., Katz, L. C., LaMantia, A. S., McNamara, J. O., et al. (Eds.). (2001). *Neuroscience* (2nd ed.). Sunderland, MA: Sinauer Associates.

Putnam, R. D. (2000). *Bowling alone: The collapse and revival of American community.* New York: Simon & Schuster.

Putting Kids First. (n.d.). *Co parenting.* Retrieved from http://www.puttingkidsfirst.org/coparenting.html

Pyszczynski, T., Greenberg, J., Solomon, S., Arndt, J., & Schimel, J. (2004). Why do people need self-esteem? A theoretical and empirical review. *Psychological Bulletin, 130,* 435–468.

Queenan, J. (2002). *Balsamic dreams: A short but self-important history of the Baby Boomer generation.* New York: Picador.

Quinceanera Boutique. (n.d.). *Traditions.* Retrieved from http://www.quinceanera-boutique.com/quinceaneratradition.htm

Quinn, M. J., & Tomita, S. K. (1997). *Elder abuse and neglect: Causes, diagnosis, and intervention strategies* (2nd ed.). New York: Springer.

Quinsey, V. L., Skilling, T. A., Lalumière, M. L., & Craig, W. M. (2004). *Juvenile delinquency: Understanding the origins of individual differences.* Washington, DC: American Psychological Association.

Quittner, A., Espelage, D., Ievers-Landis, C., & Drotar, D. (2000). Measuring adherence to medical treatments in childhood chronic illness: Considering multiple methods and sources of information. *Journal of Clinical Psychology in Medical Settings, 7,* 41–54.

Rachman, S., & da Silva, P. (1978). Normal and abnormal obsessions. *Behaviour Research and Therapy, 16,* 233–248.

Rachman, S., & Shafran, R. (1998). Cognitive and behavioral features of obsessive-compulsive disorder. In R. P. Swinson, M. M. Antony, S. Rachman, & M. A. Richter (Eds.), *Obsessive-compulsive disorder: Theory, research, and treatment* (pp. 51–78). New York: Guilford.

Racik, P. (1972). Mode of cell migration to the superficial layers of fetal monkey neocortex. *Journal of Comparative Neurology, 145,* 61–83.

Rafael, T. (1995). *Perspectives on the Parents Anonymous National Network: 1994 Database survey analysis.* Claremont, CA: Parents Anonymous.

Rafael, T., & Pion-Berlin, L. (1999). *Parents Anonymous: Strengthening families.* Washington, DC: Office of Juvenile Justice and Delinquency Prevention.

Ragow-O'Brien, D., Hayslip, B., & Guarnaccia, C. (2000). The impact of hospice on attitudes toward funerals and subsequent bereavement adjustment. *Omega: Journal of Death and Dying, 41,* 291–305.

Raine, A. (2002). Biosocial studies of antisocial and violent behavior in children and adults: A review. *Journal of Abnormal Child Psychology, 30,* 311–326.

Raisman, G., & Field, P. (1973). A quantitative investigation of the development of collateral reinnervation after partial deafferentation of the septal nuclei. *Brain Research, 50,* 341–364.

Rakison, D. H., & Oakes, L. M. (Eds.). (2004). *Early category and concept development: Making sense of the blooming, buzzing confusion.* New York: Oxford University Press.

Ramachandran, V. (2000). *The reality club: Mirror neurons.* Retrieved from http://www.edge.org/discourse/mirror_neurons.html

Ramey, C. T., & Campbell, F. A. (1984). Preventive education for high-risk children: Cognitive consequences of the Carolina Abecedarian Project. *American Journal of Mental Deficiency, 88,* 515–523.

Ramey, C. T., & Campbell, F. A. (1991). Poverty, early childhood education, and academic competence: The Abecedarian experiment. In A. Huston (Ed.), *Children reared in poverty* (pp. 190–221). New York: Cambridge University Press.

Ramey, C. T., Campbell, F. A., Burchinal, M., Skinner, M. L., Gardner, D. M., & Ramey, S. L. (2000). Persistent effects of early intervention on high-risk children and their mothers. *Applied Developmental Science, 4,* 2–14.

Ramey, S. L., & Ramey, C. T. (1999). *Going to school: How to help your child succeed: A handbook for parents of children 3 to 8.* New York: Goddard Press.

Ramsey, P. S., & Goldenberg, R. L. (2000). Maternal infections and their consequences. In M.-L. Newell, & J. McIntyre (Eds.), *Congenital and perinatal infections: Prevention, diagnosis and treatment* (pp. 32–63). Cambridge, UK: Cambridge University Press.

Randall, B., & Wilson, A. S. D. (2003). The 2002 annual report of the Regional Infant and Child Mortality Committee. *Journal of Medicine, 56*(12), 505–509.

Rando, T. (1984). *Grief, dying, and death: Clinical interventions for caregivers.* Champaign, IL: Research Press.

Rando, T. (1991). *How to go on living when someone you love dies.* New York: Bantam Books.

Rao, S. M., Leo, G. J., Bernardin, L., & Unverzagt, F. (1991). Cognitive dysfunction in multiple sclerosis: I. Frequency, patterns, and prediction. *Neurology, 41,* 685–691.

Rapee, R. M. (2001). The development of generalized anxiety. In M. W. Vasey & M. R. Dadds (Eds.), *The developmental psychopathology of anxiety* (pp. 481–503). New York: Oxford University Press.

Rapp-Paglicci, L. A., Roberts, A. R., & Wodarski, J. S. (Eds.). (2002). *Handbook of violence.* New York: Wiley.

Rasmussen, S., & Eisen, J. L. (1991). Phenomenology of OCD: Clinical subtypes, heterogeneity and coexistence. In J. Zohar, T. Insel, & S. Rasmussen (Eds.), *The psychobiology of obsessive-compulsive disorder* (pp. 13–43). New York: Springer-Verlag.

Rasnake, L. K., Laube, E., Lewis, M., & Linscheid, T. R. (in press). Children's nutritional judgments: Relationship to eating attitudes and body image. *Health Communication.*

Rathus, S. A., Nevid, J. S., & Fichner-Rathus, L. (2000). *Human sexuality in a world of diversity* (4th ed.). Needham Heights, MA: Allyn & Bacon.

Ratner, C. (n.d.). *Activity as a key concept for cultural psychology.* Retrieved from http://www.humboldt1.com/~cr2/jaan.htm

Rauscher, F. H., Robinson, K. D., & Jens, J. J. (1998). Improved maze learning through early music exposure in rats. *Neurological Research, 20,* 427–432.

Rauscher, F. H., Shaw, G. L., & Ky, K. N. (1993). Music and spatial task performance. *Nature, 365,* 611.

Ray, S. (1999). *Upon this rock I will build my Church: St. Peter and the primacy of Rome in scripture and the early Church.* Fort Collins, CO: Ignatius Press.

Reach Out and Read National Center. (n.d.). *Developmental milestones of early literacy.* Retrieved from http://www.reachoutandread.org/downloads/RORmilestones_English.pdf

Rebello, P., Cummings, L., & Gardinier, M. (1995, April). *The United Nations Convention on the Rights of the Child: A call to child development professionals around the world.* Paper presented at the biennial meeting of the Society for Research in Child Development, Indianapolis, IN.

Reed, E. S. (1988). Applying the theory of action systems to the study of motor skills. In O. G. Meijer & K. Roth (Eds.), *Complex movement behavior: The motor-action controversy* (pp. 339–380). Amsterdam: Elsevier.

Reggio Emilia, http://www.reggiochildren.com/

REGGIO-L discussion list, http://ecap.crc.uiuc.edu/listserv/reggio-1.html

Regnier, V. (2002). *Design for assisted living: Guidelines for housing the physically and mentally frail.* New York: Wiley.

Reichle, E., Rayner, K., & Pollatsek, A. (2003). The E-Z Reader model of eye-movement control in reading: Comparison to other models. *Behavioral and Brain Sciences, 26,* 445–526.

Reid, J. B., Patterson, G. R., & Snyder, J. J. (Eds.). (2002). *Antisocial behavior in children and adolescents: A developmental analysis and the Oregon Model for Intervention.* Washington, DC: American Psychological Association.

Reilly, P. (2004). *Is it in your genes? The influence of genes on common disorders and diseases that affect you and your family.* Cold Spring Harbor, NY: Cold Spring Harbor Laboratory Press.

Reinforcement and punishment, http://www.psychology.uiowa.edu/Faculty/wasserman/Glossary/reinforcement.html

Reis, H. T., & Patrick, B. C. (1996). Attachment and intimacy: Component processes. In E. T. Higgins & A. W. Kruglanski (Eds.), *Social psychology: Handbook of basic principles* (pp. 523–563). New York: Guilford.

Reiss, S., & McNally, R. J. (1985). The expectancy model of fear. In S. Reiss & R. R. Bootzin (Eds.), *Theoretical issues in behavior therapy* (pp. 107–121). New York: Academic Press.

Rennison, C. (2001). *Bureau of Justice Statistics special report: Violent victimization and race, 1993–1998* (NCJ No. 176354). Retrieved from http://www.ojp.usdoj.gov/bjs/pub/pdf/vvr98.pdf

Renzulli, J. S. (1978). What makes giftedness? Re-examining a definition. *Phi Delta Kappan, 60,* 180–184.

Renzulli, J. S. (1986). The three-ring conception of giftedness: A developmental model for creative productivity. In R. J. Sternberg & J. E. Davidson (Eds.), *Conceptions of giftedness* (pp. 53–92). New York: Cambridge University Press.

Renzulli, J. S. (2002). Expanding the conception of giftedness to include co-cognitive traits and to promote social capital. *Phi Delta Kappan, 84*(1), 33–58.

Renzulli, J. S., & Reis, S. M. (1985). *The schoolwide enrichment model: A comprehensive plan for educational excellence.* Mansfield, CT: Creative Learning Press.

Rescorla, R. A. (1980). *Pavlovian second-order conditioning: Studies in associative learning.* New York: Wiley.

Resendes, R. (2005). *The celebration of the Quinceañera.* Retrieved from http://gomexico.about.com/cs/culture/a/quinceanera.htm

Resiliency in Action, http://www.resiliency.com

Resnick, H. S., Kilpatrick, D. G., Dansky, B. S., Saunders, B. E., & Best, C. L. (1993). Prevalence of civilian trauma and post-traumatic stress disorder in a representative national sample of women. *Journal of Consulting Psychology, 61,* 984–991.

Resnick, M. D., Bearman, P. S., Blum, R. W., Bauman, K. E., Harris, K. M., Jones, J., et al. (1997). Protecting adolescents from harm: Findings from the National Longitudinal Study on Adolescent Health. *Journal of the American Medical Association, 278,* 823–832.

Resnick, P. J. (1969). Child murder by parents: A psychiatric review of filicide. *American Journal of Psychiatry, 126,* 73–82.

Resnick, R. (2000). *The hidden disorder.* Washington, DC: American Psychological Association.

Resolve: The National Infertility Association, http://www.resolve.org/

Rest, J. (1986). *Moral development: Advances in research and theory.* New York: Praeger.

Rest, J. R. (1973). The hierarchical nature of moral judgment. *Journal of Personality, 41,* 86–109.

Rest, J. R. (1979). *Development in judging moral issues.* Minneapolis: University of Minnesota Press.

Rett Syndrome Research Foundation, http://rsrf.org

Reuter-Lorenz, P. A., & Miller, A. C. (1998). The cognitive neuroscience of human laterality: Lessons from the bisected brain. *Current Directions in Psychological Science, 7,* 15–20.

Revelle, W. (2004). *The personality project.* Retrieved from http://pmc.psych.nwu.edu/personality.html

Reynolds, P. P. (1997). The federal government's use of Title VI and Medicare to racially integrate hospitals in the United States, 1963 through 1967. *American Journal of Public Health, 87,* 1850–1858.

Rhoades, E. R. (2003). The health status of American Indian and Alaska Native males. *American Journal of Public Health, 93,* 774–778.

Rhodes, W., Layne, M., Johnson, P., & Hozik, L. (2002). *What America's users spend on illegal drugs 1988–1998.* Washington, DC: Office of National Drug Control Policy. Retrieved from http://www.whitehousedrugpolicy.gov/publications/drugfact/american_users_spend2002/

Rice, F. P. (1978). The period of adolescence. *The adolescent: Development, relationships and culture* (2nd ed., pp. 52–85). Boston: Allyn & Bacon.

Rice Virtual Lab in Statistics. (n.d.). *HyperStat online text-book.* Retrieved from http://davidmlane.com/hyperstat/index.html

Rich, A. (n.d.). *Compulsory heterosexuality and lesbian existence.* Retrieved from http://www.terry.uga.edu/~dawndba/4500compulsoryhet.htm

Rich, J. M., & DeVitis, J. L. (1994). *Theories of moral development* (2nd ed.). Springfield, IL: Charles C Thomas.

Richard E. Nisbett, http://umich.edu/~nisbett/research.html

Richards, J. E., & Rader, N. (1983), Affective, behavioral, and avoidance responses on the visual cliff: Effects of crawling onset age, crawling experience, and testing age. *Psychophysiology, 20,* 633–642.

Richards, S. (n.d.). *Ludwig Wittgenstein (1889–1951).* Retrieved from http://www.faithnet.org.uk/Philosophy/wittgenstein.htm

Ridley, M. (2003). *Nature via nurture: Genes, experience and what makes us human.* London: Fourth Estate.

Riegel, K. F. (1976). The dialectics of human development. *American Psychologist, 31,* 689–700.

Rimm, E. B., Willett, W. C., Hu, F. B., Sampson, L., Colditz, G. A., Manson, J. E., et al. (1998). Folate and vitamin B6 from diet and supplements in relation to risk of coronary heart disease among women. *Journal of the American Medical Association, 279,* 359.

Rimm-Kaufman, S. E., & Pianta, R. C. (2000). An ecological perspective on the transition to kindergarten: A theoretical framework to guide empirical research. *Journal of Applied Developmental Psychology, 21,* 491–511.

Rind, B., Tromovitch, P., & Bauserman, R. (1998). A meta-analytic examination of assumed properties of child sexual abuse using college samples. *Psychological Bulletin, 124,* 22–53.

Ritchie, W. C., & Bhatia, T. K. (1999). *Handbook of child language acquisition.* San Diego, CA: Academic Press.

Rizzolatti, G., Fogassi, L., & Gallese, V. (2001). Neurophysiological mechanisms underlying the understanding of imitation and action. *Nature Reviews/Neuroscience, 2,* 661–670.

Robbins, L. (1963). The accuracy of parental recall of aspects of child development and of child rearing practices. *Journal of Abnormal Social Psychology, 66,* 261–270.

Roberto, K.A., & Stroes, J. (1992). Grandchildren and grandparents: Roles, influences, and relationships. *International Journal of Aging and Human Development, 34,* 227–239.

Roberts, D. F., Foehr, U. G., Rideout, V. J., & Brodie, M. (1999). *Kids & media @ the new millennium.* Menlo Park, CA: Kaiser Family Foundation. Retrieved from http://www.kff.org/entmedia/1535-index.cfm

Roberts, D. F., Foehr, U. G., Rideout, V. J., & Brodie, M. (2004). *Kids and media in America: Patterns of use at the millennium.* New York: Cambridge University Press.

Roberts, M. C. (2003). *Handbook of pediatric psychology* (3rd ed.). New York: Guilford.

Roberts, M. C., Brown, K. J., Boles, R. E., Mashunkashey, J. O., & Mayes, S. (2003). Prevention of disease and injury in pediatric psychology. In M. C. Roberts (Ed.), *Handbook of pediatric psychology* (pp. 84–98). New York: Guilford.

Robin, A. L., & Foster, S. L. (1989). Negotiating parent-adolescent conflict. New York: Guilford.

Robinson, B. A. (n.d.). *Corporal punishment of children. Spanking: All points of view.* Retrieved from http://www.religioustolerance.org/spanking.htm

Rochat, P. (2001). *The infant's world.* London: Harvard University Press.

Roche, J. P. (1986). Premarital sex: Attitudes and behavior by dating stage. *Adolescence, 21,* 107–121.

Rock, E. E., Fessler, M. A., & Church, R. (1997). The concomitance of learning disabilities and emotional/behavioral disorders: A conceptual model. *Journal of Learning Disabilities, 30*(3), 245–263.

Rodgers, J. L., Cleveland, H. H., van den Oord, E., & Rowe, D. C. (2000). Resolving the debate over birth order, family size, and intelligence. *American Psychologist, 55,* 599–615.

Rodriguez Rust, P. (Ed.). (2000). *Bisexuality in the United States: A social science reader.* New York: Columbia University Press.

Roeckelein, J. E. (2002). *The psychology of humor: A reference guide and annotated bibliography.* Westport, CT: Greenwood Press.

Roediger, H. L., III. (1996). Memory illusions. *Journal of Memory and Language, 35,* 76–100.

Roehling, P. V., & Moen, P. (2003). *Dual earner couples.* Retrieved from http://www.bc.edu/bc_org/avp/wfnetwork/rft/wfpedia/wfpDECent.html

Roep, B. O. (2003). The role of T-cells in the pathogenesis of Type 1 diabetes: from cause to cure. *Diabetologia, 46,* 305–321.

Roepke, S., McAdams, L. A., Lindamer, L. A., Patterson, T. L., & Jeste, D. V. (2001). Personality profiles among normal aged individuals as measured by the NEO-PI-R. *Aging and Mental Health, 5*(2), 159–164.

Rogers, C. (1951). *Client-centered therapy.* New York: Houghton Mifflin.

Rogers, C. (1961). *On becoming a person.* Boston: Houghton Mifflin.

Rogers, C., Kirschenbaum, H., & Henderson, V. (1989). *The Carl Rogers reader.* Boston: Houghton Mifflin.

Rogers, K. B. (1998). Using current research to make good decisions about grouping. *National Association of Secondary School Principals Bulletin 82*(595), 38–46.

Rogoff, B. (1990). *Apprenticeship in thinking: Cognitive development in social context.* New York: Oxford University Press.

Rogoff, B. (2003). *The cultural nature of human development.* Oxford, UK: Oxford University Press.

Rogoff, B., & Morelli, G. (1989). Perspectives on children's development from cultural psychology. *American Psychologist, 44,* 343–348.

Rohrbeck, C. A., Ginsburg-Block, M. D., Fantuzzo, J. W., & Miller, T. R. (2002). Peer-assisted learning interventions with elementary school students: A meta-analytic review. *Journal of Educational Psychology, 94*(2), 240–257.

Roizen, N. J., & Patterson, D. (2003). Down syndrome. *The Lancet, 361,* 1281–1289.

Roleff, T. L. (1998). *Sex education (opposing viewpoints).* Berkeley: University of California Press.

Romans, S. E., Martin, J. M., Gendall, K., & Herbison, G. P. (2003). Age of menarche: The role of some psychosocial factors. *Psychological Medicine, 33,* 933–939.

Rooks, J. P. (1997). *Midwifery & childbirth in America.* Philadelphia: Temple University Press.

Rooks, J. P., Weatherby, N. L., Ernst, E. K., Stapleton, S., Rosen, D., & Rosenfield, A. (1998). Outcomes of care in birth centers: The national birth center study. *New England Journal of Medicine, 321*(26), 1804–1811.

Root, M. P. P. (1992). *Racially mixed people in America.* Newbury Park, CA: Sage.

Root, M. P. P. (1996). *The multiracial experience.* Thousand Oaks, CA: Sage.

Root, M. P. P. (2001). *Love's revolution: Interracial marriage.* Philadelphia: Temple University Press.

Roper, A. S. W. (2003). *Americans talk about illegal immigration.* Retrieved from http://www.npg.org/immpoll.html

Roque, H., Gillen-Goldstein, J., Funai, E., Young, B. K., & Lockwood, C. J. (2003). Perinatal outcomes in monoamniotic gestations. *Journal of Maternal Fetal Neonatal Medicine, 13*(6), 414–421.

Rose, E. (1999). *A mother's job: The history of day care, 1890–1960.* New York: Oxford University Press.

Rose, P. I. (Ed.). (1970). *Slavery and its aftermath: Americans from Africa.* Chicago: Aldine.

Rose, S. A., Feldman, J. F., & Jankowski, J. J. (2001). Attention and recognition memory in the 1st year of life: A longitudinal study of preterm and full-term infants. *Developmental Psychology, 37,* 539–549.

Rose, S. A., & Orlian, E. K. (2001). Visual information processing. In L. T. Singer & P. S. Zeskind, (Eds.), *Biobehavioral assessment of the infant* (pp. 274–292). New York: Guilford.

Roseberry-McKibbin, C. (1995). *Multicultural students with special language needs.* Oceanside, CA: Academic Communication Associates.

Rosen, J. (1995, January 22). Rewriting the end: Elisabeth Kübler-Ross. *New York Times Magazine,* pp. 22–25. Retrieved from http://www.elisabethkublerross.com/pages/books.html

Rosen, J. (2000). *Advocating for adolescent reproductive health: Addressing cultural sensitivities.* Research Triangle Park, NC: Family Health International. Available from http://www.fhi.org

Rosen, S. M. (1999). Evolution of attentional processes in the human organism. *Group Analysis, 32*(2), 243–253.

Rosenberg, R., & Schiller, G. (Directors). (1984). *Before Stonewall* [VHS Video]. First Run Features.

Rosenberg, S. D., Rosenberg, H. J., & Farrell M. P. (1999). The midlife crisis revisited. In S. L. Willis & J. D. Reid (Eds.), *Life in the middle: Psychological and social development in middle age.* San Diego, CA: Academic Press.

Rosenberger, P. H., & Miller, G. A. (1989). Comparing borderline definitions: DSM-III borderline and schizotypal personality disorders. *Journal of Abnormal Psychology, 98,* 161–169.

Rosenfeld, A. A., Pilowsky, D. J., Fine, P., Thorpe, M., Fein, E., Simms, M. D., et al. (1997). Foster care: An update. *Journal of the American Academy of Child and Adolescent Psychiatry, 36,* 448–457.

Rosenfeld, B. (2004). *Assisted suicide and the right to die: The interface of social science, public policy, and medical ethics.* Washington, DC: American Psychological Association Press.

Rosengren, K. S., Johnson, C. N., & Harris P. L. (Eds.). (2001). *Imagining the impossible: Magical, scientific, and religious thinking in children.* New York: Cambridge University Press.

Rosenthal, R. (1987). Pygmalion effects: Existence, magnitude, and social importance. *Educational Researcher, 16,* 37–41.

Rosenthal, R., & Jacobson, L. (1969). *Pygmalion in the classroom.* New York: Holt, Rinehart & Winston.

Rosenthal, R., & Lawson, R. (1964). A longitudinal study of the effects of experimenter bias on the operant learning of laboratory rats. *Journal of Psychiatric Research, 2,* 61–72.

Rosnow, R. L., & Rosenthal, R. (2001). *Beginning behavioral research: A conceptual primer* (4th ed.). Upper Saddle River, NJ: Prentice-Hall.

Ross, D. M. (2003). *Childhood bullying, teasing, and violence: What school personnel, other professionals, and parents can do* (2nd ed.). Alexandria, VA: American Counseling Association.

Ross, E. M. (2002). Evaluation and treatment of iron deficiency in adults. *Nutrition in Clinical Care, 5,* 220–224.

Ross, R. (1976). Pathogenesis of atherosclerosis. In E. Braunwald (Ed.), *Heart disease: A textbook of cardiovascular medicine* (pp. 1105–1125). Philadelphia: WB Saunders.

Rossetti, L. (1989). *High-risk infants: Identification, assessment and intervention.* Boston: College Hill Press.

Rossi, A. S., & Rossi, P. H. (1990). *Of human bonding: Parent-child relations across the life course.* New York: Aldine de Gruyter.

Rostosky, S. S. (2005). Adolescent romantic relations and sexual behavior: Theory, research, and practical implications. *Journal of Adolescent Research, 20,* 136–138.

Roth, W. M. (2003). *Toward an anthropology of graphing: Semiotic and activity-theoretic perspectives.* Dordrecht, Netherlands: Kluwer Academic.

Roth, W. M. (Ed.). (2004). Activity theory in education. *Mind, Culture, & Activity, 11*(special issue), 1–77.

Rothbart, M. K., & Bates, J. E. (1998). Temperament. In N. Eisenberg (Ed.) & W. Damon (Series Ed.), *Handbook of child psychology: Vol. 3: Social, emotional, and personality development* (5th ed., pp. 105–176). New York: Wiley.

Rothblum, E. D. (2000). Somewhere in Des Moines or San Antonio: Historical perspectives on lesbian, gay, and bisexual mental health. In R. Perez, K. DeBord, & K. Bieschke (Eds.), *Handbook of therapy with lesbians, gays, and bisexuals*

(pp. 57–79). Washington, DC: American Psychological Association.

Rotundo, E. A. (1993). *American manhood: Transformations in masculinity from the revolution to the modern era.* New York: Basic Books.

Rovee, C. K., & Rovee, D. T. (1969). Conjugate reinforcement of infant exploratory behavior. *Journal of the Experimental Analysis of Behavior, 8,* 33–39.

Rovee-Collier, C., & Barr, R. (2001). Infant learning and memory. In G. Bremner & A. Fogel (Eds.), *Blackwell handbook of infant development* (pp. 139–168). Malden, MA: Blackwell.

Rovee-Collier, C., & Barr, R. (2002). Infant cognition. In H. Pashler & J. Wixted (Eds.), *Stevens' handbook of experimental psychology* (pp. 693–791). New York: Wiley.

Rowe, D. C. (1994). *The limits of family influence: Genes, experience and behavior.* New York: Guilford.

Rowe, J. W., & Kahn, R. L. (1997). Successful aging. *Gerontologist, 37,* 433–440.

Rowe, J., & Kahn, R. (1999). *Successful aging.* New York: Dell.

Roy, P., Rutter, M., & Pickles, A. (2000). Institution care: Risk from family background or pattern of rearing? *Journal of Child Psychology and Psychiatry, 41,* 139–150.

Royal College of Psychiatrists. (n.d.). *Anxiety and phobias.* Retrieved from http://www.rcpsych.ac.uk/info/anxpho.htm

Royzman, E. B., Cassidy, K. W., & Baron, J. (2003). "I know, you know": Epistemic egocentrism in children and adults. *Review of General Psychology, 7,* 38–65.

Rozanski, A., Blumenthal, J. A., & Kaplan, J. (1999). Impact of psychological factors on the pathogenesis of cardiovascular disease and implications for therapy. *Circulation, 99,* 2192–2217.

Rozien, N. J. (2002). Down syndrome. In M. L. Batshaw (Ed.), *Children with disabilities* (5th ed., pp. 307–320). Baltimore: Paul H. Brookes.

Rozin, P., & Fallon, A. E. (1987). A perspective on disgust. *Psychological Review, 94,* 23–41.

Rozin, P., Haidt, J., & McCauley, C. (1999). Individual differences in disgust sensitivity: Comparisons and evaluations of paper-and-pencil versus behavioral measures. *Journal of Research in Personality, 33,* 330–351.

RTI International. (n.d.). *NICHD study of early child care and youth development.* Retrieved from http://secc.rti.org/home.cfm

Rubin, K. H., Bukowski, W., & Parker, J. G. (1998). Peer interactions, relationships, and groups. In W. Damon (Ed.-in-Chief) & N. Eisenberg (Ed.), *Handbook of child psychology. Vol. 3. Social, emotional, and personality development* (pp. 619–700). New York: Wiley.

Rubin, K. H., Fein, G. G., & Vandenberg, B. (1983). Play. In E. M. Hetherington (Ed.), *Handbook of child psychology: Vol. 4. Socialization, personality, and social development* (4th ed., pp. 693–744). New York: Wiley.

Ruble, D. N., & Martin, C. L. (1998). Gender development. In W. Damon (Series Ed.) & N. Eisenberg (Vol. Ed.),

Handbook of child psychology: Vol. 3. Social, emotional, and personality development (5th ed., pp. 933–1016). New York: Wiley.

Ruch, W. (Ed.). (1998). *The sense of humor: Explorations of a personality characteristic.* Berlin: Mouton de Gruyter.

Rudolph, F. (1962). *The American college and university.* New York: Vintage Books.

Ruf, D. L. (2003). *Use of the SB5 in the assessment of high abilities.* Itasca, IL: Riverside.

Rumack, C. M., Wilson, S., & Charboneau, W. (2004). *Diagnostic ultrasound.* New York: Elsevier Mosby.

Runco, M. A. (1999). Self-actualization and creativity. In M. A. Runco & S. Pritzker (Eds.), *Encyclopedia of creativity* (pp. 533–536). San Diego, CA: Academic Press.

Runco, M. A., Ebersole, P., & Mraz, W. (1991). Self-actualization and creativity. *Journal of Social Behavior and Personality, 6,* 161–167.

Runyan, C. (2003). Introduction: back to the future—revisiting Haddon's conceptualization of injury epidemiology and prevention. *Epidemiology Review, 25,* 60–64.

Rushton, C. H. (2001). Pediatric palliative care: Coming of age. In M. Z. Solomon, A. L. Romer, K. S. Heller, & D. E. Weissman (Eds.), *Innovations in end-of-life care: Practical strategies and international perspectives, Vol. 2.* (pp. 167–170). Larchmont, NY: Mary Ann Liebert.

Rushton, J. P. (1975). Generosity in children: Immediate and long term effects of modeling, preaching, and moral judgment. *Journal of Personality and Social Psychology, 31,* 459–466.

Russell, D. (1986). *The secret trauma: Incest in the lives of girls and women.* New York: Basic Books.

Russell, D. (1996). The UCLA Loneliness Scale (Version 3); Reliability, validity and factor structure. *Journal of Personality Assessment, 66,* 20–40.

Russell, J. (1999). Cognitive development as an executive process—in part: A homeopathic dose of Piaget. *Developmental Science, 2*(3), 247–295.

Rust, K. F., Wallace, L., & Qian, J. (2001). Sample design for the state assessment. In N. L. Allen, J. R. Donoghue, & T. L. Schoeps (Eds.), *The NAEP 1998 technical report.* Washington, DC: National Center for Educational Statistics.

Rutter, M., & Garmezy, N. (1983). Developmental psychopathology. In P. H. Mussen (Series Ed.) & E. M. Hetherington (Vol. Ed.), *Handbook of child psychology: Vol. 4. Socialization, personality and development* (pp. 775–911). New York: Wiley.

Rutter, M., Giller, H., & Hagell, A. (1998). *Antisocial behavior by young people.* Cambridge, UK: Cambridge University Press.

Rutter, M., & Rutter, M. (1992). *Developing minds: Challenge and continuity across the lifespan.* London: Penguin.

Rutter, M., & Sroufe, L. A. (2000). Developmental psychopathology: Concepts and challenges. *Development and Psychopathology, 12,* 265–296.

Ryder, M. (n.d.). *Activity theory.* Retrieved from http://carbon.cudenver.edu/~mryder/itc_data/activity.html

Saaman, R. A. (2000). The influences of race, ethnicity and poverty on the mental health of children. *Journal of Health Care for the Poor and Underserved, 11,* 100–110.

Saba, F. (2003). *Distance education: Foundations and fundamental concepts* [Editorial]. Available from http://www.distance-educator.com

Sabbatini, R. M. E. (n.d.). *Mapping the brain.* Retrieved from http://www.epub.org.br/cm/n03/tecnologia/eeg.htm

Sach, J. (2003). *The everything Buddhism book: Learn the ancient traditions and apply them to modern life.* Avon, MA: Adams Media.

Safer Child, Inc. (2003). *Toilet training.* Retrieved from http://www.saferchild.com/potty.htm

Sage, N. A. (2001). *Elements of a research study (part IV).* Retrieved from http://www.psy.pdx.edu/PsyTutor/Tutorials/Research/Elements/P4.htm

Sagrestano, L. M., Heavy, C. L., & Christensen, A. (1999). Perceived power and physical violence in marital conflict. *Journal of Social Issues, 55,* 65–79.

Sales, B. D., & Folkman, S. (2000). *Ethics in research with human participants.* Washington, DC: American Psychological Association.

Salkin, J. K. (1991). *For kids—Putting God on your guest list.* Woodstock, VT: Jewish Lights.

Salkind, N. J. (2004). *Introduction to theories of human development.* Thousand Oaks, CA: Sage.

Salkind, N. J. (2004). *Statistics for people who (think they) hate statistics.* Thousand Oaks, CA: Sage.

Salkind, N. J. (2005). *Exploring research* (6th ed.). Upper Saddle River, NJ: Prentice-Hall.

Sallis, J. F., Prochaska, J. J., & Taylor, W. C. (2000). A review of correlates of physical activity of children and adolescents. *Medicine and Science in Sports and Exercise, 32,* 963–975.

Salovey, P., & Mayer, J. D. (1990). Emotional intelligence. *Imagination, Cognition and Personality, 9*(3), 185–211.

Salthouse, T. A. (1991). *Theoretical perspectives on cognitive aging.* Hillside, NJ: Erlbaum.

Salthouse, T. A. (2004). What and when of cognitive aging. *Current Directions in Psychological Science, 13*(4), 140–144.

Saluja, G., Scott-Little, C., & Clifford, R. M. (2000). Readiness for school: A survey of state policies and definitions. *Early Childhood Research and Practice, 2*(2). Retrieved from http://ecrp.uiuc.edu/v2n2/saluja.html

Salzinger, K. (1980). The immediacy hypothesis in a theory of schizophrenia. In W. D. Spaulding & J. K. Cole (Eds.), *Nebraska symposium on motivation: Theories of schizophrenia and psychosis.* Lincoln: University of Nebraska Press.

Samaan, R. A. (2000). The influences of race, ethnicity, and poverty on the mental health of children. *Journal of Health Care for the Poor & Underserved, 11,* 100–110.

Samaritans, http://www.samaritans.org

Sameroff, A., & Haith, M. (1996). Interpreting developmental transitions. In A. Sameroff & M. Haith (Eds.), *The five to seven shift: The age of reason and responsibility* (pp. 4–15). Chicago: University of Chicago Press.

Sammons, W., & Lewis, J. (2001). Helping children survive divorce. *Contemporary Pediatrics, 18*(3), 103–114.

Sampson, R., Raudenbush, S., & Earls, F. (1997). Neighborhoods and violent crime: A multilevel study of collective efficacy. *Science, 277,* 918–924.

Sandbank, A. C. (1999). *Twin and triplet psychology.* London: Routledge.

Sanders, S. (n.d.). *Early childhood: The importance of developing fundamental motor skills.* Available from http://www.pecentral.org

Sani, F., & Bennett, M. (n.d.). *Developmental aspects of social identity.* Available from http://www.esrcsocietytoday.ac.uk/ESRCInfoCentre/index.aspx

Sansone, C., & Harackiewicz, J. (Eds.). (2000). *Intrinsic and extrinsic motivation: The search for optimal motivation.* San Diego, CA: Academic Press.

Santa, C., & Hayes, B. (Eds.). (1981). *Children's prose comprehension.* Newark, DE: International Reading Association.

Santor, D. A., Messervey, D., & Kusumakar, V. (2000). Measuring peer pressure, popularity, and conformity in adolescent boys and girls: Predicting school performance, sexual attitudes, and substance use. *Journal of Youth and Adolescence, 29,* 163–182.

Saracho, O. N., & Spodek, B. (1988). *Multiple perspectives on play in early childhood education.* Albany: State University of New York Press.

Sardar, Z., & Davies, M. W. (2004). *The no-nonsense guide to Islam.* Oxford, UK: New Internationalist Publications.

Sargent, L. T. (1994). The three faces of utopianism revisited. *Utopian Studies, 5,* 1–37.

Sarnat, H. B., & Flores-Sarnat, L. (2002). Role of Cajal-Retzius and subplate neurons in cerebral cortical development. *Seminar in Pediatric Neurology, 9,* 302–308.

Sass, H., Veatch, R. M., & Kimur, R. (1998). *Advance directives and surrogate decision making in health care: United States, Germany, and Japan.* Baltimore: Johns Hopkins University Press.

Sassler, S. (2004). The process of entering into cohabiting unions. *Journal of Marriage & the Family, 66,* 491–504.

Saterfiel and Associates. (2003). Employment testing and aptitude assessment products. Retrieved from http://www.employment-testing.com

Sattler, J. (2001). *Assessment of children: Cognitive applications* (4th ed.). San Diego, CA: Jerome M. Sattler.

Saunders, D. S. (1977). *An introduction to biological rhythms.* London: Blackie & Son.

Savickas, M. L. (1997). The spirit in career counseling: Fostering self-completion through work. In D. P. Bloch & L. J. Richmond (Eds.), *Connections between spirit and work in career development: New approaches and practical perspectives* (pp. 3–25). Palo Alto, CA: Davies-Black.

Saw, S.-M. (2003). A synopsis of the prevalence rates and environmental risk factors for myopia. *Clinical and Experimental Optometry, 86,* 289–294.

Saw, S.-M., Shih-Yen, E. C., Koh, A., & Tan, D. (2002). Interventions to retard myopia progression in children; an evidence-based update. *Ophthalmology, 109,* 415–427.

Sawchuk, C. N., Lohr, J. M., Westendorf, D. H., Meunier, S. A., & Tolin, D. F. (2002). Emotional responding to fearful and disgusting stimuli in specific phobics. *Behaviour Research and Therapy, 40,* 1031–1046.

Sax, G. (Ed.). (1997). *Principles of educational and psychological measurement and evaluation* (4th ed.). Belmont, CA: Wadsworth.

Scarr, S. (1996). How people make their own environments: Implications for parents and policy makers. *Psychology, Public Policy, and Law, 2,* 204–228.

Scarr, S., & McCartney, K. (1983). How people make their own environments: A theory of genotype environment effects. *Child Development, 54*(2), 424–435.

Schaal, B., Soussignan, R., & Marlier, L. (2003). Olfactory cognition at the start of life: The perinatal shaping of selective odor responsiveness. In C. Rouby, B. Schaal, D. Dubois, R. Gervais, & A. Holley (Eds.), *Olfaction, taste, and cognition* (pp. 421–440). Cambridge, UK: Cambridge University Press.

Schacht, J. (1964). *An introduction to Islamic law.* Oxford, UK: Clarendon.

Schachtman, T. R. (Ed.). (2004). Pavlovian conditioning: Basic associative processes. Special Issue. *International Journal of Comparative Psychology, 17*(2–3).

Schacter, D. L. (2000). *The seven sins of memory: How the mind forgets and remembers.* Boston: Houghton Mifflin.

Schaefer, C. E., & DiGeronimo, T. F. (1997). *Toilet training without tears* (Rev. ed.). New York: Signet.

Schaefer, E. S., & Bayley, N. (1963). Maternal behavior, child behavior, and their intercorrelations from infancy through adolescence. *Monographs of the Society for Research in Child Development, 28*(3), 1–127.

Schaie, K. W. (1965). A general model for the study of developmental problems. *Psychological Bulletin, 64,* 92–107.

Schaie, K. W. (1983). The Seattle Longitudinal Study: A twenty-one year investigation of psychometric intelligence. In K. W. Schaie (Ed.), *Longitudinal studies of adult personality development* (pp. 64–155). New York: Guilford.

Schaie, K. W. (1996). *Intellectual development in adulthood: The Seattle Longitudinal Study.* New York: Cambridge University Press.

Schaie, K. W. (2004). *Developmental influences on adult intelligence: The Seattle Longitudinal Study.* New York: Oxford University Press.

Schaie, K. W., & Schooler, C. (1998). *Impact of work on older adults.* New York: Springer.

Schaie, K. W., Willis, S. L., & Caskie, G. I. L. (2004). The Seattle Longitudinal Study: Relationship between personality and cognition. *Aging, Neuropsychology, and Cognition, 11,* 304–324.

Schank, R. (2000). *Coloring outside the lines.* New York: HarperCollins.

Scharf, M., Shulman, S., & Avigad-Spitz, L. (2005). Sibling relationships in emerging adulthood and in adolescence. *Journal of Adolescent Research. 20,* 64–90.

Scheibe, K. E. (1995). *Self studies: The psychology of self and identity.* Westport, CT: Praeger.

Scheidt, R. J., Humpherys, D. R., & Yorason, J. B. (1999). Successful aging: What's not to like? *Journal of Applied Gerontology, 18,* 277–282.

Schettler, T., Solomon, G., Valenti, M., & Huddle, A. (1999). *Generations at risk: Reproductive health and the environment.* Cambridge: MIT Press.

Schienle, A., Stark, R., & Vaitl, D. (2001). Evaluative conditioning: A possible explanation for the acquisition of disgust responses? *Learning and Motivation, 32,* 65–83.

Schiffman, S. S. (1997). Taste and smell losses in normal aging and disease. *Journal of the American Medical Association, 278,* 1357–1362.

Schindler, L. W. (n.d.). *Understanding the immune system.* Retrieved from http://rex.nci.nih.gov/behindthenews/uis/uisframe.htm

Schindler, R. A. (1999). Description of the Clarion Multi-Strategy Cochlear Implant. *Annals of Otology, Rhinology, and Laryngology, 108*(Suppl. 177, Part 2).

SCHIP, http://www.cms.hhs.gov/schip/consumers_default.asp

Schlinger, H. D. (1995). *A behavior analytic view of child development.* New York: Plenum.

Schmaling, K. B., Hernandez, D. V., & Giardino, N. D. (2003). Provider and patient adherence with asthma evaluation and treatment. In T. N. Wise (Series Ed.) & E. S. Brown (Vol. Ed.), *Advances in psychosomatic medicine: Vol. 24. Asthma: Social and psychological factors and psychosomatic syndromes* (pp. 98–114). Dallas, TX: Karger.

Schmidt, R. A., & Lee, T. D. (1999). *Motor control and learning: A behavioral emphasis* (3rd ed.). Champaign, IL: Human Kinetics.

Schonfeld, L. S. (2003). Behavior problems in assisted living facilities. *Journal of Applied Gerontology, 22*(4), 490–505.

Schopler, E., Reichler, R. J., Bashford, A., Lansing, M. D., & Marcus, L. M. (1990). *Psycho-Educational Profile–Revised (PEP-R).* Austin, TX: Pro-Ed.

Schroeder, C. S., & Gordon, B. N. (2002). Toileting: Training, enuresis, and encopresis. In *Assessment & treatment of childhood problems* (2nd ed., pp. 115–158). New York: Guilford.

Schroeder, D., Penner, L., Dovidio, J., & Piliavin, J. (1995). *The psychology of helping and altruism.* New York: McGraw-Hill.

Schuler, A., & Prizant, B. M. (1985). Echolalia. In E. Schopler & G. B. Mesibov (Eds.), *Communication problems in autism.* New York: Plenum.

Schull, W. J. (1995). *Effects of atomic radiation: A half-century from Hiroshima and Nagasaki.* New York: Wiley-Liss.

Schulman, K. (2000). *The high cost of childcare puts quality care out of reach for many families.* Washington, DC: Children's Defense Fund.

Schwartz, P. (1994). *Peer marriage: How love between equals really works.* New York: Free Press.

Schwartz-Kenney, B. M., McCauley, M., & Epstein, M. A. (Eds.). (2001). *Child abuse: A global view.* Westport, CT: Greenwood.

Schwartz-Nobel, L. (2002). *Hunger and malnutrition in America.* New York: HarperCollins.

Schweigert, W. A. (1994). *Research methods and statistics for psychology.* Pacific Grove, CA: Brooks/Cole.

Schweinhart, L. (2002, June). Lasting benefits of preschool programs. *Association of School Boards Journal, 189*(6).

Schweinhart, L. J., & Weikart, D. P. (1980). *Young children grow up: The effects of The Perry Preschool Program on youths through age 19.* Ypsilanti, MI: High/Scope Educational Research Foundation.

Schweinhart, L. J., & Weikart, D. P. (2002). The Perry Preschool Project: Significant benefits. *Journal of At-Risk Issues, 8*(1), 5–8.

Schwimmer, J. B., Burwinkle, T. M., & Varni, J. W. (2003). Health-related quality of life of severely obese children and adolescents. *Journal of the American Medical Association, 289,* 1813–1819.

Sclafani, J. D. (2004). Parenting and co-parenting issues related to divorce. *The educated parent: Making sense of the current literature.* Westport, CT: Praeger.

Scott, J. P. (1962). Critical periods in behavioral development. *Science, 138,* 949–958.

Scott, J. P. (Ed.). (1978). *Critical periods.* Stroudsberg, PA: Dowden, Hutchinson, & Ross.

Scott, W. D. (1915). The scientific selection of salesmen. *Advertising and Selling, 5,* 5–7.

Scragg, R. K. R., Mitchell, E. A., Stewart, A. W., Ford, R. P. K., Taylor, B. J., Hassall, I. B., et al. (1996). Infant room-sharing and prone sleep position in sudden infant death syndrome. *Lancet, 347,* 7–12.

Scribner, R., & Cohen, D. (2001, Fall). The effect of enforcement on merchant compliance with the minimum legal drinking age law. *Journal of Drug Issues, 31*(4), 857–866. Retrieved from http://www.findarticles.com/p/articles/mi_qa3733/is_200110/ai_n 8957561/pg_2

Sears, J. T. (1992). *Sexuality and the curriculum: The politics and practices of sexuality education.* New York: Teachers College Press.

Sears, R. (1941). Non-aggressive reactions to frustration. *Psychological Review, 48,* 343–346.

Sears, R. (1965). *Identification and child rearing.* Stanford, CA: Stanford University Press.

Sears, W., & Sears, M. (1993). The *baby book: Everything you need to know about your baby from birth to age two.* New York: Little, Brown.

Seattle Longitudinal Study, http://geron.psu.edu/sls

Segal, D. L., & Coolidge, F. L. (2003). Structured interviewing and DSM classification. In M. Hersen & S. Turner (Eds.), *Adult psychopathology and diagnosis* (4th ed., pp. 72–103). New York: Wiley.

Segal, D. L., & Coolidge, F. L. (2004). Objective assessment of personality and psychopathology: An overview. In

M. Hilsenroth, D. L. Segal (Eds.), & M. Hersen (Ed.-in-Chief), *Comprehensive handbook of psychological assessment, Vol. 2: Personality assessment* (pp. 3–13). New York: Wiley.

Segal, D. L., Hersen, M., & Van Hasselt, V. B. (1994). Reliability of the structured clinical interview for DSM-III R: An evaluative review. *Comprehensive Psychiatry, 35,* 316–327.

Segrave, K. (2001). *Age discrimination by employers.* Jefferson, NC: McFarland & Company.

Seigel, D. J., & Martzell, M. (2003). *Parenting from the inside out: How a deeper self-understanding can help you raise children who thrive.* New York: Tarcher/Putnam.

Seligman, M. (1990). *Learned optimism.* New York: Simon & Schuster.

Seligman, M. E. P. (2004). *Teaching hope.* Retrieved from http://www.psych.upenn.edu/seligman/teachinghope.htm

Seligman, M. E. P., Maier, S. F., & Solomon, R. L. (1971). Unpredictable and uncontrollable aversive events. In F. R. Brush (Ed.), *Aversive conditioning and learning.* New York: Academic Press.

Selman, R. (1980). The growth of interpersonal understanding: Developmental and clinical analyses. New York: Academic Press.

Senger, P. L. (1997). *Pathways to pregnancy and parturition.* Pullman, WA: Current Conceptions.

Serbin, L., & Karp, J. (2003). Intergenerational studies of parenting and the transfer of risk from parent to child. *Current Directions in Psychological Science, 12*(4), 138–142.

Serna, L., Nielsen, E., Lambros, K., & Forness, S. (2000). Primary prevention with children at risk for emotional and behavioral disorders: Data on a universal intervention for Head Start classrooms. *Behavioral Disorders, 26,* 70–84.

Serpell, J. A. (1996). *In the company of animals: A study of human-animal relationships.* Cambridge, UK: Cambridge University Press.

Serper, M., & Bergman, A. (2003). *Psychotic violence: Motives, methods, madness.* Madison, CT: International Universities Press/Psychosocial Press.

Serper, M., Bergman, A., Copersino, M., Chou, J., Richarme, D., & Cancro, R. (2000). Learning and memory impairment in cocaine-dependent and comorbid schizophrenia patients. *Psychiatry Research, 93,* 21–32.

Serper, M., & Chou, J. C.-Y. (1997). Novel neuroleptics improve schizophrenic patients attentional functioning. *CNS Spectrums, 46,* 22–26.

Serper, M., Chou, J. C.-Y., Allen, M., Czobor, P., & Cancro, R. (1999). Symptomatic overlap of cocaine intoxication and acute schizophrenia at emergency presentation. *Schizophrenia Bulletin, 25,* 387–394.

Sethi, A., & Hayslip, B. (2002). *Predictors of volunteer attrition in hospice.* Unpublished manuscript, University of North Texas, Denton, TX.

Severy, L. J., & Newcomer, S. (2005). Critical issues in contraceptive and STI acceptability research. *Journal of Social Issues, 61*(1), 45–65.

Severy, L. J., & Silver, S. E. (1993). Two reasonable people: Joint decision making in fertility regulation. In L. J. Severy (Ed.), *Advances in population: Psychosocial perspectives: Vol. 1.* London: Jessica Kingsley.

Severy, L. J., & Spieler, J. (2000). New methods of family planning: Implications for intimate behaviors. *Journal of Sex Research, 37,* 258–265.

Sewell, W. H. (1992). A theory of structure: Duality, agency and transformation. *American Journal of Sociology, 98,* 1–29.

Sex Scrolls. (2002). *A brief history of marriage.* Retrieved from http://www.sexscrolls.net/marriage.html

Sexuality Information and Education Council of the United States. (n.d.). *State profiles—A portrait of sexuality education and abstinence-only-until-marriage programs in the states.* Retrieved from http://www.siecus.org/policy/states/index.html

Sgroi, S. M. (Ed.). (1982). *Handbook of clinical intervention in child sexual abuse.* Lexington, MA: Lexington Books.

Sgroi, S. M. (1988). *Vulnerable populations: Evaluation and treatment of sexually abused children and adult survivors, Volume I.* New York: Free Press.

Shadish, W. R., Cook, T. D., & Campbell, D. T. (2002). *Experimental and quasi experimental designs for generalized causal inference.* Boston: Houghton-Mifflin.

Shafii, M., & Shafii, S. L. (Eds.). (2001). *School violence: Assessment, management, prevention.* Washington, DC: American Psychiatric Press.

Shanas, E. (1973). Family-kin networks and aging in cross-cultural perspective. *Journal of Marriage and the Family, 35,* 505–511.

Shantz, C. U. (1987). Conflicts between children. *Child Development, 58,* 283–305.

Shantz, C. U., & Hartup, W. W. (1992). *Conflict in child and adolescent development.* New York: Cambridge University Press.

Shapiro, V. B., Shapiro, J. R., & Paret, I. H. (2001). *Complex adoption and assisted reproductive technology.* New York: Guilford.

Sharma, L. (2001). Local factors in osteoarthritis. *Current Opinions in Rheumatology, 13,* 441–446.

Sharma, S. (2004). *Hypertension.* Retrieved from http://www.emedicine.com/med/topic1106.htm

Shatz, M. (1994). *A toddler's life: Becoming a person.* New York: Oxford University Press.

Shaughnessy, J. J., Zechmeister, E. B., & Zechmeister, J. S. (2003). *Research methods in psychology* (6th ed.). New York: McGraw-Hill.

Shavelson, R. J. (1996). *Statistical reasoning for the behavioral sciences* (3rd ed.). Needham Heights, MA: Allyn & Bacon.

Shaw, G. L. (2004). *Keeping Mozart in mind* (2nd ed.). San Diego, CA: Elsevier/Academic Press.

Shaywitz, S. (1996, November). Dyslexia. *Scientific American,* 98–104.

Shaywitz, S. (2003). *Overcoming dyslexia: A new and complete science-based program for reading problems at any level.* New York: Knopf.

Shea, M. P. (1996). *By what authority? An evangelical discovers Catholic tradition.* Huntington, IN: Our Sunday Visitor.

Sheffield, F. D. (1965). Relations between classical conditioning and instrumental learning. In W. F. Prokasy (Ed.), *Classical conditioning: A symposium* (pp. 302–322). New York: Appleton-Century-Crofts.

Sheiner, E., Levy, A., Feinstein, U., Hallak, M., & Mazor, M. (2002). Risk factors and outcome of failure to progress during the first stage of labor: A population-based study. *Acta Obstetrica et Gynecologia Scandinavica, 81,* 222–226.

Sheiner, E., Levy, A., Feinstein, U., Hershkovitz, R., Hallak, M., & Mazor, M. (2002). Obstetric risk factors for failure to progress in the first versus the second stage of labor. *Journal of Maternal and Fetal Neonatal Medicine, 11,* 409–413.

Sheiner, E., Levy, A., Katz, M., Hershkovitz, R., Leron, E., & Mazor, M. (2004). Gender does matter in perinatal medicine. *Fetal Diagnosis and Therapy, 19,* 366–369.

Shek, D. T. (1995). Gender differences in marital quality and well-being in Chinese married adults. *Sex Roles, 32,* 699–715.

Shek, D. T. (1995). Marital quality and psychological well-being of married adults in a Chinese context. *Sex Roles, 156,* 21–36.

Shek, D. T. (1996). Midlife crisis in Chinese men and women. *Journal of Psychology, 130,* 109–119.

Shek, D. T. (1997). Parent-child relationship and parental well-being of Chinese parents in Hong Kong. *International Journal of Intercultural Relations, 21,* 459–473.

Shelov, S. P. (Ed.-in-Chief) & Hanneman, R. E. (1998). *Caring for your baby and young child: Birth to age 5.* New York: Bantam.

Shepard, L. A., & Smith, M. L. (Eds.). (1989). *Flunking grades: Research and policies on retention.* London: Falmer.

Shepherd, G. M. (1994). *Neurobiology* (3rd ed.). New York: Oxford University Press.

Sherif, M., Harvey, O. J., White, F. J., Hood, W. R., & Sherif, C. W. (1961). *Intergroup conflict and cooperation: The Robbers' Cave Experiment.* Norman: University of Oklahoma Press.

Sherwin, B. B. (2003). Estrogen and cognitive functioning in women. *Endocrine Reviews, 24*(2), 133–151.

Shilts, R. (1987). *And the band played on: Politics, people and the AIDS epidemic.* New York: St. Martin's Press.

Shonkoff, J. P., & Phillips, D. A. (Eds.). (2000). Nurturing relationships. *From neurons to neighborhoods: The science of early childhood development* (pp. 225–266). Washington, DC: National Academies Press. Retrieved from http://www.nap.edu/books/0309069882/html

Shorris, E. (1992). *Latinos: A biography of the people.* New York: W. W. Norton.

Shorvon, S., Dreifuss, F., Fish, T., & Thomas, D. (1996). *The treatment of epilepsy.* Oxford, UK: Blackwell Science.

Showalter, S. E. (1998). Looking through different eyes: Beyond cultural diversity. In K. J. Doka & J. D. Davidson (Eds.), *Living with grief: Who we are, how we grieve* (pp. 71–82). Washington, DC: Hospice Foundation of America/Taylor & Francis.

Shreeve, J. (2004). *The genome wars.* New York: Knopf.

Shrimpton, R. (2003). Preventing low birthweight and reduction of child mortality. *Transactions of the Royal Society of Tropical Medicine and Hygiene, 97*(1), 39–42.

Shulman, D. (1997). *Co-parenting after divorce: How to raise happy, healthy children in two-home families.* Sherman Oaks, CA: WinnSpeed Press.

Shulman, S., & Kipnis, O. (2001). Adolescent romantic relationships: A look from the future. *Journal of Adolescence, 24,* 337–351.

The Shyness Institute, http://www.shyness.com

Sidman, M. (1960). *Tactics of scientific research: Evaluating experimental data in psychology.* Boston: Authors Cooperative.

Siegel, B. (1996). *The world of the autistic child: Understanding and treating autistic spectrum disorders.* New York: Oxford University Press.

Siegel, N. (2000). *Entwined lives: Twins and what they tell us about human behavior.* New York: Plume.

Siegler, I. C., Bastian, L. A., & Bosworth, H. B. (2001). Health, behavior and age. In A. Baum, T. A. Revenson, & J. E. Singer (Eds.), *Handbook of health psychology* (pp. 469–476). Mahwah, NJ: Erlbaum.

Siegler, R. (1996). *Emerging minds.* New York: Oxford University Press.

Siegler, R. (1998). *Children's thinking* (3rd ed.). Englewood Cliffs, NJ: Prentice-Hall.

Siegler, R., & Alibali, M. (2005). *Children's thinking.* Englewood Cliffs, NJ: Prentice-Hall.

Sign Writing, http://www.signwriting.org/

Silberman, M. (Ed.). (2003). *Violence and society: A reader.* Upper Saddle River, NJ: Prentice-Hall.

Silverman, P. R. (2000). *Never too young to know: Death in children's lives.* New York: Oxford University Press.

Silverstein, M., & Long, J. D. (1998). Trajectories of grandparents' perceived solidarity with adult grandchildren: A growth curve analysis over 23 years. *Journal of Marriage and the Family, 60,* 912–923.

Silverstein, M., & Schaie, K. W. (2005). *Annual review of gerontology and geriatrics: Focus on intergenerational relations across time and place.* New York: Springer.

Simkin, P., Whalley, J., & Keppler, A. (2001). *Pregnancy, childbirth, and the newborn, revised and updated: The complete guide.* Minnetonka, MN: Meadowbrook.

Simkin, S., Hawton, K., Whitehead, L., & Fagg, J. (1995). Media influence on parasuicide: A study of the effects of a television drama portrayal of paracetamol self-poisoning. *British Journal of Psychiatry, 167,* 754–759.

The Simon Foundation for Continence, http://www.simon foundation.org

Simonte, S. J., & Cunningham-Rundles, C. (2003). Update on primary immunodeficiency: Defects of lymphocytes. *Clinical Immunology, 109,* 109–118.

Sinclair, J., & Milner, D. (2005). On being Jewish: A qualitative study of identity among British Jews in emerging adulthood. *Journal of Adolescent Research, 20,* 91–117.

Singer, D. G., & Revenson, T. A. (1997). *A Piaget primer: How a child thinks.* (Rev. ed.). Madison, CT: International Universities Press.

Singer, D. G., & Singer, J. L. (1990). *The house of make-believe: Children's play and the developing imagination.* Cambridge, MA: Harvard University Press.

Singer, L. T., Minnes, S., Short, E., Arendt, R., Farkas, K., Lewis, B., et al. (2004). Cognitive outcomes of preschool children with prenatal cocaine exposure. *Journal of the American Medical Association, 291,* 2448–2456.

Singer, P. (1994). *Rethinking life and death: The collapse of our traditional ethics.* New York: St. Martin's Press.

Singer, R. N., Hausenblas, H. A., & Janelle, C. M. (2001). *Handbook of sport psychology* (2nd ed.). New York: Wiley.

Singer, T., Lindenberger, U., & Baltes, P. B. (2003). Plasticity of memory for new learning in very old age: A story of major loss? *Psychology and Aging, 18*(2), 306–317.

Singer, T., Verhaeghan, P., Ghisletta, P., Lindenberger, U., & Baltes, P. B. (2003). The fate of cognition in very old age: Six-year longitudinal findings in the Berlin Aging Study (BASE). *Psychology and Aging, 18*(2), 318–331.

Singh, D. (1995). Female judgment of male attractiveness and desirability for relationships: Role of waist to hip ratio and financial status. *Journal of Personality and Social Psychology, 69,* 1089–1101.

Singh, K. D. (1998). *The grace in dying: How we are transformed spiritually as we die.* New York: Harper Collins.

Single Parent Central, http://www.singleparentcentral.com/

Single Parents Association, http://singleparents.org

Siris, E. S., Bilezikian, J. P., Rubin, M. R., Black, D. M., Bockman, R. S., Bone, H. G., et al. (2003). Pins and plaster aren't enough: A call for the evaluation and treatment of patients with osteoporotic fractures. *Journal of Clinical Endocrinology and Metabolism, 88*(8), 3482–3486.

The Skeptic's Dictionary. (2005). *Science.* Retrieved from http://www.skepdic.com/science.html

Skinner, B. F. (1938). *The behavior of organisms: An experimental analysis.* New York: Appleton-Century.

Skinner, B. F. (1948/1976). *Walden two.* New York: Macmillan.

Skinner, B. F. (1953). *Science and human behavior.* New York: Macmillan.

Skinner, B. F. (1999). *Cumulative record* (Definitive ed., V. G. Laties & A. C. Catania, Eds.). Cambridge, MA: B. F. Skinner Foundation.

Skinner, E. A. (1996). A guide to constructs of control. *Journal of Personality and Social Psychology, 71,* 549–570.

Skinner, E. A., Wellborn, J. G., & Connell, J. P. (1990). What it takes to do well in school and whether I've got it: A process model of perceived control and children's engagement and achievement in school. *Journal of Educational Psychology, 82*(1), 22–32.

Skinner, J. D., Carruth, B. R., Bounds, W., & Ziegler, P. (2002). Children's food preferences: A longitudinal analysis. *Journal of the American Dietetic Association, 102,* 1638–1647.

Skoner, D. P. (2002). Outcome measures in childhood asthma. *Pediatrics, 109,* 393–398.

Skuse, D. H., Pickles, A., Wolke, D., & Reilly, S. (1994). Postnatal growth and mental development: Evidence for a "sensitive period." *Journal of Child Psychology and Psychiatry and Allied Disciplines, 35,* 521–545.

Slavin, R. E., Hurley, E. A., & Chamberlain, A. M. (2003). Cooperative learning and achievement: Theory and research. In W. M. Reynolds & G. E. Miller (Eds.), *Handbook of psychology: Vol. 7* (pp. 177–198). Hoboken, NJ: Wiley.

The Sleep Well, http://www.stanford.edu/~dement

Sleeping Like a Baby.net, http://www.tau.ac.il/~sadeh/baby/

Slikker, W., Jr., & Chang, L. W. (Eds.). (1998). *Handbook of developmental neurotoxicity.* New York: Academic Press.

Slotkin, T. A. (1998). Fetal nicotine or cocaine exposure: Which one is worse? *Journal of Pharmacology and Experimental Therapeutics, 285,* 931–945.

Small, M. F. (1998). *Our babies, ourselves: How biology and culture shape the way we parent.* New York: Anchor Books.

Smart Marriages, http://www.smartmarriages.com

Smiley, P. A., & Dweck, C. S. (1994). Individual differences in achievement goals among young children. *Child Development, 65,* 1723–1743.

Smith, D. (2003). *The older population in the United States: March 2002.* U.S. Census Bureau Current Population Reports, P20–546. Washington, DC: U.S. Government Printing Office.

Smith, D. V., & Margolskee, R. F. (2001, March). Making sense of taste. *Scientific American,* 32–39.

Smith, E. E., & Jonides, J. (1999). Neuroscience—Storage and executive processes in the frontal lobes. *Science, 283*(5408), 1657–1661.

Smith, E. E., Jonides J., & Koeppe R. A. (1996). Dissociating verbal and spatial working memory using PET. *Cerebral Cortex, 6,* 11–20.

Smith, E. J. (n.d.). *Introduction to EEG.* Retrieved from http://www.ebme.co.uk/arts/eegintro/

Smith, H. (2001). *Why religion matters.* New York: HarperCollins.

Smith, J., & Baltes, P. B. (1997). Profiles of psychological functioning in the old and oldest old. *Psychology and Aging, 12*(3), 458–472.

Smith, J., Borchelt, M., Maier, H., & Jopp, D. (2002). Health and well-being in the young old and oldest old. *Journal of Social Issues, 58*(4), 715–732.

Smith, P. K., & Hart, C. H. (Eds.). (2002). *Blackwell handbook of childhood social development.* Oxford, UK: Blackwell.

Smith, R. A., & Davis, S. F. (2004). *The psychologist as detective* (3rd ed.). Upper Saddle River, NJ: Prentice-Hall.

Smith, R. L. (1984). Human sperm competition. In R. L. Smith (Ed.), *Sperm competition and the evolution of animal mating systems* (pp. 601–659). New York: Academic Press.

Smith, S. E., & Willms, D. G. (Eds.). (1997). *Nurtured by knowledge: Learning to do participatory action-research.* New York: Apex Press.

Smith, T. W., & Ruiz, J. M. (2002). Psychosocial influences on the development and course of coronary heart disease: Current status and implications for research and practice. *Journal of Consulting and Clinical Psychology, 70,* 548–568.

Smith, W. J. (1997). *Forced exit: The slippery slope from assisted suicide to legalized murder.* New York: Random House.

Smock, P. J. (2000). Cohabitation in the United States: An appraisal of research themes, findings, and implications. *Annual Review of Sociology, 26,* 1–20.

Smock, T. K. (1999). *Physiological psychology: A neuroscience approach.* Upper Saddle River, NJ: Prentice-Hall.

Smokowski, P. R., Reynolds, A. J., & Bezruczko, N. (1999). Resilience and protective factors in adolescence: An autobiographical perspective from disadvantaged youth. *Journal of School Psychology, 37*(4), 425–448.

Smolensky, E., & Gootman, J. A. (Eds.). (2003). *Working families and growing kids: Caring for children and adolescents.* Washington, DC: National Academies Press.

Snarey, J., Reimer, J., & Kohlberg, L. (1984). The socio-moral development of Kibbutz adolescents: A longitudinal, cross-cultural study. *Developmental Psychology, 21,* 3–17.

Snelling, J. (1991). *The Buddhist handbook: A complete guide to Buddhist schools, teaching, practice, and history.* Rochester, VT: Inner Traditions.

Snow, R. E. (1976). Research on aptitude for learning: A progress report. *Review of Research in Education, 4,* 50–105.

Snow, R. E. (1978). Theory and method for research on aptitude processes. *Intelligence, 2,* 225–278.

Snow, R. E. (1980). Aptitude processes. In R. E. Snow, P-A. Federico, & W. E. Montague (Eds.), *Aptitude, learning, and instruction, Vol. 1: Cognitive process analyses of aptitude* (pp. 27–63). Hillsdale, NJ: Erlbaum.

Snow, R. E. (1981). Toward a theory of aptitude for learning: I. Fluid and crystallized abilities and their correlates. In M. P. Friedman, J. P. Das, & N. O'Connor (Eds.), *Intelligence and learning* (pp. 345–362). New York: Plenum.

Snow, R. E., Corno, L., & Jackson, D. (1996). Individual differences in affective and conative functions. In D. C. Berlinger & R. C. Calfee (Eds.), *Handbook of educational psychology* (pp. 243–310). New York: Macmillan.

Snow, R. E., & Lohman, D. F. (1989). Implications of cognitive psychology for educational measurement. In R. L. Linn (Ed.), *Educational measurement* (3rd ed., pp. 263–331). New York: American Council on Education/Macmillan.

Snyder, C. R. (1994). *The psychology of hope.* New York: The Free Press.

Snyder, C. R. (Ed.). (1999). *Coping: The psychology of what works.* New York: Oxford University Press.

Snyder, C. R. (2004). Home page. Retrieved from http://www.psych.ku.edu/faculty/rsnyder/

Snyder, C. R., Rand, K. L., & Sigmon, D. R. (2002). Hope theory: A member of the positive psychology family. In C. R. Snyder & S. J. Lopez (Eds.), *Handbook of positive psychology* (pp. 257–276). New York: Oxford University Press.

Snyder, C. R., Shorey, H. S., Cheavens, J., Pulvers, K. M., Adams, V. H., & Wiklund, C. (2002). Hope and academic success in college. *Journal of Educational Psychology, 94,* 820–826.

Snyder, H. (2000). *Juvenile arrests 1999.* Washington, DC: Office of Juvenile Justice and Delinquency Prevention.

Sober, E., & Wilson, D. S. (1998). *Unto others: The evolution and psychology of unselfish behavior.* Cambridge, MA: Harvard University Press.

Social Phobia/Social Anxiety Disorder Association, http://www.socialphobia.org/

Social Psychology Network, http://www.socialpsychology.org/

Social Security Administration, http://www.ssa.gov/history/lifeexpect.html

Social Security Online, http://www.ssa.gov

Social Security Online. (n.d.). *Separate program for abstinence education.* Retrieved from http://www.ssa.gov/OP_Home/ssact/title05/0510.htm

Socie, E. M., Wagner, S. A., & Hopkins, R. S. (1994). The relative effectiveness of sanctions applied to first-time drunken driving offenders. *American Journal of Preventive Medicine, 10*(2), 85–90.

Society for Assisted Reproductive Technology and the American Society for Reproductive Medicine. (n.d.). *Assisted reproductive technology in the United States: 1999 results generated by the American Society for Reproductive Medicine/Society for Assisted Reproductive Technology Registry.* Retrieved from http://www.asrm.org/Professionals/Fertility&Sterility/1999sartresults.pdf

Society for Judgment and Decision Making, http://www.sjdm.org/

Society for Menstrual Cycle Research, http://www.pop.psu.edu/smcr/

Society for Neuroscience, http://apu.sfn.org/

Society for Neuroscience Brain Briefings, http://web.sfn.org/content/Publications/BrainBriefings/index.html

Society for Neuroscience Brain Briefings. (1996, May). Brain imaging. Retrieved from http://web.sfn.org/content/Publications/BrainBriefings/brain_imaging.html

Society for Neuroscience. (2001, November). Myelin and spinal cord repair. Retrieved from http://web.sfn.org/content/Publications/BrainBriefings/brain_spinalcord.html

Society for Neuroscience. (n.d.). *Estrogen's influence on the brain.* Retrieved from http://web.sfn.org/content/Publications/BrainBriefings/estrogen.html

Society for Neuroscience. (n.d.). *Resource links: Neurotransmitters.* Retrieved from http://web.sfn.org/Template.cfm?Section=PublicResources&Template=/PublicResources/ResourceLink.cfm&subcat_id=101

Society for Research in Child Development, http://www.srcd.org

Society for Research in Child Development. (n.d.). *Ethical standards for research with children.* Retrieved from http://www.srcd.org/ethicalstandards.html

Society for Research on Adolescence, http://www.s-r-a.org/

Society for Research on Adolescence. (n.d.). *Emerging Adulthood Special Interest Group.* Retrieved from http://www.s-r-a.org/easig.html

Society for Research on Adolescence. (2002). *Websites related to emerging adulthood.* Retrieved from http://www.s-r-a.org/easigrelatedwebsites.html

Society for Women's Health Research. (n.d.). *Sex differences in cardio/cerebrovascular disease.* Retrieved from http://www.womenshealthresearch.org/hs/facts_cardio.htm

Soderquist, D. R. (2002). *Sensory processes.* Thousand Oaks, CA: Sage.

Soliday, E. (1998). Services and supports for foster caregivers: Research and recommendations. *Children's Services: Social Policy, Research, and Practice, 1,* 19–38.

Solomon, A. (2002). *The noonday demon.* New York: Scribner.

Solomon, J., & George, C. (1999). The measurement of attachment security in infancy and childhood. In J. Cassidy & P. Shaver (Eds.), *Handbook of attachment: Theory, research, and clinical applications* (pp. 287–318). New York: Guilford.

Solomon, L. (2001). Clinical features of osteoarthritis. In S. Ruddy, E. D. Harris, Jr., C. B. Sledge, R. C. Budd, & J. S. Sergent (Eds.), *Kelley's textbook of rheumatology* (6th ed.). Philadelphia: WB Saunders.

Sontag, S. (1979). The double standard of aging. In J. Williams (Ed.), *Psychology of women* (pp. 462–478). San Diego, CA: Academic Press.

Southern Poverty Law Center. (2004). *Teaching tolerance.* Retrieved from http://www.tolerance.org/teach/

Spahn, J. D., & Szefler, S. J. (2002). Childhood asthma: New insights into management. *Journal of Allergy and Clinical Immunology, 109,* 3–13.

Spandorfer, S. D. (2003). The impact of maternal age and ovarian age on fertility. *INCIID Insights, 1*(8). Retrieved from http://www.inciid.org/newsletter/october/2003/impactSpandorfer.html

Spanier, G. B. (1983). Married and unmarried cohabitation in the United States: 1980. *Journal of Marriage and the Family, 45,* 277–288.

Spanos, N. P. (1994). Multiple identity enactments and multiple personality disorder: A sociocognitive perspective. *Psychological Bulletin, 116,* 143–165.

Spaulding W. D., Reed, D., Sullivan, M., Richardson, C., & Weiler, M. (1999). Effects of cognitive treatment in psychiatric rehabilitation. *Schizophrenia Bulletin, 25,* 657–676.

Spearman, C. (1927). *The abilities of man: Their nature and measurement.* London: Macmillan.

Spearman, C. (1981). *The nature of "intelligence" and the principles of cognition.* New York: AMS Publishers. (Original work published 1923)

Spemann, H. (1938). *Embryonic development and induction.* New Haven, CT: Yale University Press.

Spence, J. T., & Buckner, C. (1995). Masculinity and femininity: Defining the undefinable. In P. J. Kalbfleisch & M. J. Cody (Eds.), *Gender, power, and communication in human relationships* (pp. 105–138). Hillsdale, NJ: Erlbaum.

Spence, J. T., & Buckner, C. E. (2000). Instrumental and expressive traits, trait stereotypes, and sexist attitudes: What do they signify? *Psychology of Women Quarterly, 24,* 44–62.

Spence, J. T., & Helmreich, R. L. (1978). *Masculinity and femininity: Their psychological dimensions, correlates and antecedents.* Austin: University of Texas Press.

Spence, J. T., Helmreich, R. L., & Stapp, J. (1974). The Personal Attributes Questionnaire: A measure of sex role stereotypes and masculinity–femininity. *JSAS Catalog of Selected Documents in Psychology, 4,* Ms. No. 617.

Spencer, P., Erting, C., & Marschark, M. (Eds.). (2000). *The deaf child in the family and at school.* Mahwah, NJ: Erlbaum.

Spitz, R. A. (1945). Hospitalism. In R. S. Eissler (Ed.), *The psychoanalytic study of the child (Vol. I).* New York: International Universities Press.

Spivack, G., & Shure, M. B. (1974). *Social adjustment of young children: A cognitive approach to solving real-life problems.* San Francisco: Jossey-Bass.

Spodek, B., & Saracho, O. (Eds.). (2005). *Handbook of research on the education of young children.* Mahwah, NJ: Erlbaum.

Squire, L. R., & Schacter, D. L. (2002). *Neuropsychology of memory.* New York: Guilford.

Sri Rahula, W. (1997). *What the Buddha taught.* London: Oneworld.

Sroufe, L. A. (1977). Wariness of strangers and the study of infant development. *Child Development, 48,* 731–746.

Sroufe, L. A. (1990). An organizational perspective on the self. In D. Cicchetti & M. Beeghly (Eds.), *Transitions from infancy to childhood: The self.* Chicago: University of Chicago Press.

Sroufe, L. A. (1995). *Emotional development: The organization of emotional life in the early years.* New York: Cambridge University Press.

St. Joseph's Covenant Keepers, http://www.dads.org/

St. Louis, K. (2001). *Living with stuttering.* Morgantown, WV: Populore.

Stack, D. M., & Muir, D. W. (1992). Adult tactile stimulation during face-to-face interactions modulates five-month-olds' affect and attention. *Child Development, 63,* 1509–1525.

Stanovich, K. (1980). Toward an interactive-compensatory model of individual differences in the development of reading fluency. *Reading Research Quarterly, 16,* 32–71.

Stanovich, P. J., & Jordan, A. (2002). Preparing general educators to teach in inclusive classrooms: Some food for thought. *Teacher Educator, 37*(3), 173–185.

Stanton, G. T. (2003, August 27). *Is marriage in jeopardy?* Retrieved from http://family.org/cforum/fosi/marriage/FAQs/a0026916.cfm

Stanton, J., & Simpson, A. (2002). Filicide: A review. *International Journal of Law and Psychiatry, 25*, 1–14.

Staples, R. (1995). Health among Afro-American males. In D. F. Sabo & D. F. Gordon (Eds.), *Research on men and masculinities series* (Vol. 8, pp. 121–138). Thousand Oaks, CA: Sage.

Starkweather, C. W. (1987). *Fluency and stuttering.* Englewood Cliffs, NJ: Prentice-Hall.

State University of Campinas, http://www.epub.org.br/cm/n14/experimento/lorenz/index-lorenz.html

State University of New York, Buffalo, Center for Children and Families. (n.d.). *What parents and teachers should know about ADHD.* Retrieved from http://ctadd.net/ctadd/PDFs_CTADD/What_Parents_Teachers.pdf

Stathis, G. M. (2000). The Safavids and the beginning of the modern Iranian nation and state. *Journal of the Utah Academy of Sciences, Arts and Letters, 77*, 275–284.

StatSoft, Inc. (n.d.). *Basic statistics: Correlations.* Retrieved from http://www.statsoft.com/textbook/stbasic.html

Stefan, S. (2002). *Hollow promises: Employment discrimination against people with mental disabilities.* Washington, DC: American Psychological Association.

Steil, J. M. (1997). Intimacy, emotion work and husbands' and wives' well-being. In J. M. Steil, *Marital equality: Its relationship to the well-being of husbands and wives* (pp. 73–89). Thousand Oaks, CA: Sage.

Stein, M., Keefer, C., & Kessler, D. (2004). Selective affective response to a parent in a 6 month old infant. *Journal of Developmental and Behavioral Pediatrics, 25*, 8–14.

Stein, S. J., & Book, H. E. (2000). *The EQ edge: Emotional intelligence and your success.* Toronto, Canada: Stoddart.

Steinauer, J. E., DePineres, T., Robert, A. M., Westfall, J., & Darney, P. (1997). Training family practice residents in abortion and other reproductive health care: A nationwide survey. *Family Planning Perspectives, 29*, 222–227.

Steinberg, L. (2002). *Adolescence.* Boston: McGraw-Hill.

Steinberg, L., Dornbusch, S., & Brown, B. (1992). Ethnic differences in adolescent achievement: An ecological perspective. *American Psychologist, 47*, 723–729.

Steinberg, M. (1947). *Basic Judaism.* New York: Harcourt.

Steitz, J. A. (1982). Locus of control as a life-span developmental process: Revision of the construct. *International Journal of Behavioral Development, 5*, 299–316.

Stepfamily Association of America, http://www.saafamilies.org

Stern, D. (1985). *The interpersonal world of the infant.* New York: Basic Books.

Stern, J.-M. (2004). *The cochlear implant—rejection of culture, or aid to improve hearing?* Retrieved from http://www.deaftoday.com/news/archives/003876.html

Stern, R. M., Ray, W. J., & Quigley, K. S. (2000). *Psychophysiological recording* (2nd ed.). New York: Oxford University Press.

Sternberg, R. J. (1977). Component processes in analogical reasoning. *Psychological Review, 84*, 353–378.

Sternberg, R. J. (1977). *Intelligence, information processing, and analogical reasoning: The componential analysis of human abilities.* Hillsdale, NJ: Erlbaum.

Sternberg, R. J. (1985). *Beyond IQ: A triarchic theory of human intelligence.* New York: Cambridge University Press.

Sternberg, R. J. (1986). A triarchic theory of intellectual giftedness. In R. J. Sternberg & J. E. Davidson (Eds.), *Conceptions of giftedness* (pp. 223–243). New York: Cambridge University Press.

Sternberg, R. J. (1997). *Successful intelligence.* New York: Plume.

Sternberg, R. J. (1997). *Thinking styles.* Cambridge, UK: Cambridge University Press.

Sternberg, R. J. (1998). *In search of the human mind.* Orlando, FL: Harcourt Brace.

Sternberg, R. J. (1999). *Cognitive psychology* (2nd ed.). Fort Worth, TX: Harcourt Brace.

Sternberg, R. J. (1999). *Handbook of creativity.* New York: Cambridge University Press.

Sternberg, R., & Grigorenko, E. L. (2000–2001). Guilford's structure of intellect model and model of creativity: Contributions and limitations. *Creativity Research Journal, 13*, 309–316.

Sternberg, R. J., Forsythe, G. B., Hedlund, J., Horvath, J. A., Wagner, R. K., Williams, W. M., et al. (2000). *Practical intelligence in everyday life.* New York: Cambridge University Press.

Sternberg, R. J., & Grigorenko, E. (2002). The theory of successful intelligence as a basis for gifted education. *Gifted Child Quarterly, 46*(4), 265–277.

Sternberg, R. J., Lautrey, J., & Lubart, T. I. (Eds.). (2003). *Models of intelligence: International perspectives.* Washington, DC: American Psychological Association.

Sternberg, R. J., & Lubart, T. I. (1996). Investing in creativity. *American Psychologist, 51*, 677–688.

Sterns, H., & Miklos, S. M. (1995). The aging worker in a changing environment: *Journal of Vocational Behavior, 47*(3), 248–268.

Stever, F. B. (1994). *The psychological development of children.* Pacific Grove, CA: Brooks/Cole.

Steward S. M., & Bond, M. H. (2002). A critical look at parenting research from mainstream: Problems uncovered while adapting Western research to non-Western cultures. *British Journal of Developmental Psychology, 20*, 379–392.

Stewart, A. E. (2004). Can knowledge of client birth order bias clinical judgment? *The Journal of Counseling & Development, 82*, 167–176.

Stewart, A. M., Webb, J., & Hewitt, D. A. (1958). A survey of childhood malignancies. *British Medical Journal, 1*, 1495–1508.

Stewart, E. A. (2003). *Exploring twins: Towards a social analysis of twinship.* New York: St. Martin's Press.

Stewart, S. E., Manion, I. G., & Davidson, S. (2002). Emergency management of the adolescent suicide attemptor: A review of the literature. *Journal of Adolescent Health, 30*(5), 312–325.

Stine, G. J. (2004). *AIDS update 2004.* Upper Saddle River, NJ: Prentice-Hall.

Stipek, D. (2002). At what age should children enter kindergarten? A question for policy makers and parents. *Social Policy Report, 16*(2).

Stockard, C. R. (1921). Developmental rate and structural expression: An experimental study of twins, 'double monsters' and single deformities, and the interaction among embryonic organs during their origin and development. *American Journal of Anatomy, 28,* 115–275.

Stockburger, D. W. (n.d.). *Hypothesis testing.* Retrieved from http://www.psychstat.smsu.edu/introbook/SBK18.htm

Stockes, B. (2000, November 29). Older Americans Act reauthorized: Provisions benefit tribal elders. *Indian Country Today, 20*(24), A6.

Stockman, J. (2001). Overview of the state of the art of Rh disease: History, current clinical management, and recent progress. *Journal of Pediatric Hematology/Oncology, 23*(6), 385–393.

Stone, B. A., Vargyas, J. M., & Ringler, G. E., Stein, A. L., & Marrs, R.P. (1999). Determinants of the outcome of intrauterine insemination: Analysis of outcomes of 9963 consecutive cycles. *American Journal of Obstetrics and Gynecology, 180,* 1522–1534.

Stone, S. M., & Pittman, S. (2003). *Therapy pets in special education classes.* Research Day for Regional Universities, University of Central Oklahoma, Edmond, OK.

Stop It Now! The Campaign to Prevent Child Sexual Abuse, http://www.stopitnow.com

Stoppard, M. (2000). *Conception, pregnancy, and birth.* New York: Dorling Kindersley.

Storfer, M. (1990). *Intelligence and giftedness: The contributions of heredity and environment.* San Francisco: Jossey-Bass.

Strain, P. S., & Odom, S. (in press). Innovations in the education of preschool children with severe handicaps. In R. H. Horner, L. M. Voeltz, & H. B. Fredericks (Eds.), *Education of learners with severe handicaps: Exemplary service strategies.*

Strassfeld, M. (1985). *The Jewish holidays.* New York: HarperCollins.

Stratov, I., DeRose, R., Purcell, D. F., & Kent, S. J. (2004). Vaccines and vaccine strategies against HIV. *Current Drug Targets, 5,* 71–88.

Stratton, K. R., Durch, J. S., & Lawrence R. S. (Eds.). (2000). *Vaccines for the 21st century: A tool for decisionmaking.* Washington, DC: National Academy Press.

Straus, M. A., & Donnelly, D. A. (2001). *Beating the devil out of them: Corporal punishment in American families and its effect on children.* New Brunswick, NJ: Transaction.

Straus, M. A., & Mouradian, V. E. (1998). Impulsive corporal punishment by mothers and antisocial behavior and impulsiveness of children. *Behavior Science and Law, 16,* 353–374.

Strauss, L. G., & Conti, P. S. (1991). The applications of pet in clinical oncology. *Journal of Nuclear Medicine, 32*(4), 623–648.

Strickland, B. R. (1989). Internal-external control expectancies: From contingency to creativity. *American Psychologist, 44,* 1–12.

Strike, P. C., & Steptoe, A. (2004). Psychosocial factors in the development of coronary artery disease. *Progress in Cardiovascular Disease, 46,* 337–347.

Strock, M. (2004). *Autism spectrum disorders (pervasive developmental disorders).* NIH Publication No. NIH-04-5511. Bethesda, MD: National Institute of Mental Health. Retrieved from http://www.nimh.nih.gov/publicat/autism.cfm

Stroebe, M. S., Hansson, R. O., Stroebe, W., & Schut, H. (Eds.). (2001). *Handbook of bereavement research: Consequences, coping, and care.* Washington, DC: American Psychological Association.

Stuckey, J. E. (1999). *The violence of literacy.* Portsmouth, NH: Boynton/Cook.

Students Against Drunk Driving (SADD), http://www.saddonline.com/

Studies in Moral Development and Education. (2002). *Moral development and moral education: An overview.* Retrieved from http://tigger.uic.edu/~lnucci/MoralEd/overview.html

Stuttering Foundation of America, http://www.stutteringhelp.org

The Stuttering Home Page, Minnesota State University, Mankato, http://www.stutteringhomepage.com

Styne, D. M. (2004). *Pediatric endocrinology.* Philadelphia: Lippincott Williams & Wilkins.

Suárez-Orozco, C., & Suárez-Orozco, M. M. (2001). *Children of immigration.* Cambridge, MA: Harvard University Press.

Substance Abuse and Mental Health Services Administration. (2003). Percent reporting alcohol use in the past year by age group and demographic characteristics: NSDUH (NHSDA), 1994–2002. *Results from the 2002 National Survey on Drug Use and Health: National findings.* DHHS Pub. No. (SMA) 03-3836. Retrieved from http://www.niaaa.nih.gov/databases/dkpat3.htm

Substance Abuse and Mental Health Services Administration. (2003). *Results from the 2002 National Survey on Drug Use and Health: National findings* (NHSDA Series H-22, DHHS Publication No. SMA 03-3836). Rockville, MD: Office of Applied Studies. Retrieved from http://www.oas.samhsa.gov/nhsda/2k2nsduh/Results/2k2Results.htm

The Substance Abuse and Mental Health Services Administration's National Mental Health Information Center. (n.d.). *Preparing youth for peer pressure.* Retrieved from http://www.mentalhealth.org/publications/allpubs/CA-0047/default.asp

Suderman, M., & Jaffe, P. G. (1999). *Child witnesses of domestic violence.* In R. T. Ammerman & M. Hersen (Eds.), *Assessment of family violence: A clinical and legal sourcebook* (pp. 342–366). New York: Wiley.

Sugarman, D. B., & Hotaling, G. T. (1991). Dating violence: A review of contextual and risk factors. In M. Pirog-Good & J. Stets (Eds.), *Dating violence: Young women in danger* (pp. 100–118). New York: Seal Press.

Sugarman, L. (2001). *Life-span development.* New York: Taylor & Francis.

Sugarman, S. D. (2003). Single parent families. In M. A. Mason, A. Skolnick, & S. D. Sugarman (Eds.), *All our families: New policies for a new century* (pp. 117–143). New York: Oxford University Press.

Suicide Awareness Voices of Education, http://www.save.org

Suicide Prevention Action Network, http://www.spanusa.org

Suinn, R. M. (2001). The terrible twos—anger and anxiety: Hazardous to your health. *American Psychologist, 56,* 27–36.

Suler, J. (2004). Computer and cyberspace addiction. *International Journal of Applied Psychoanalytic Studies, 1,* 359–362. Retrieved from http://www.rider.edu/users/suler/psycyber/cybaddict.html

Suler, J. R. (1990). Wandering in search of a sign: A contemporary version of the vision quest. *Journal of Humanistic Psychology, 30,* 73–88.

Sulik, K. K., & Bream, P. R., Jr. (n.d.). *Embryo images: Normal and abnormal mammalian development.* Retrieved from http://www.med.unc.edu/embryo_images/

Sullivan, A. (1997). *Same-sex marriage: Pro and con.* New York: Vintage.

Suls, J., & Greenwald, A. G. (Eds.). (1986). *Psychological perspectives on the self* (Vol. 3). Hillsdale, NJ: Erlbaum.

Sulzer-Azaroff, B., & Mayer, G. R. (1991). *Behavior analysis for lasting change.* Belmont, CA: Wadsworth.

Summit, R. C. (1983). The child sexual abuse accommodation syndrome. *Child Abuse & Neglect, 7,* 177–193.

Sumner, A. E., Chin, M. M., Abrahm, J. L., Berry, G. T., Gracely, E. J., Allen, R. H., et al. (1996). Elevated methylmalonic acid and total homocysteine levels show high prevalence of vitamin B12 deficiency after gastric surgery. *Annals of Internal Medicine, 124,* 469–476.

SUPPORT Principal Investigators. (1995). A controlled trial to improve care for seriously ill hospitalized patients: The study to understand prognoses and preferences for outcomes and risks of treatment (SUPPORT). *Journal of the American Medical Association, 274,* 1591–1598.

Survey and Program Areas, http://nces.ed.gov/surveys/Survey Groups.asp?group=showall

Susan G. Komen Breast Cancer Foundation, http://www.komen.org

Susman, E. J., Dorn, L. D., & Schiefelbein, V. (2003). Puberty, sexuality, and health. *Handbook of Psychology: Developmental Psychology, 6,* 295–324.

Suzman, R. M., Willis, D. P., & Manton, K. G. (1992). *The oldest old.* New York: Oxford University Press.

Swain, R. A. (2004). *Surface features of the adult brain.* Retrieved from http://www.uwm.edu/~rswain/class/SUM03/sum3.html

Swain, R. A., Harris, A. B., Wiener, E. C., Dutka, M. V., Morris, H. D., Theien, B. E., et al. (2003). Prolonged exercise induces angiogenesis and increases cerebral blood volume in primary motor cortex of the rat. *Neuroscience, 117,* 1037–1046.

Swanson, H. L. (2000). Issues facing the field of learning disabilities. *Learning Disability Quarterly, 23,* 37–50.

Swanson, H. L., Harris, K. R., & Graham, S. (Eds.). (2003). *Handbook of learning disabilities.* New York: Guilford.

Swarbrick, H. A. (2004). Orthokeratology (corneal refractive therapy): What is it and how does it work? *Eye & Contact Lens, 30,* 181–185.

Symanski, E. M., & Parker, R. M. (Eds.). (1996). *Work and disability: Issues and strategies in career development and job placement.* Austin, TX: Pro-Ed.

Szabó, Z. G. (n.d.). *Brief biography of Chomsky, Noam Avram (1928–).* Retrieved from http://www.people.cornell.edu/pages/zs15/Chomsky.pdf

Szinovacz, M. E. (2003). Retirement. *International encyclopedia of marriage and the family.* New York: Macmillan.

Tabachnick, B. G., & Fidell, L. S. (2001). *Computer-assisted research design and analysis.* Needham Heights, MA: Allyn & Bacon.

Tabachnick, B. G., & Fidell, L. S. (2001). *Using multivariate statistics* (4th ed.). Needham Heights, MA: Allyn & Bacon.

Takamura, J. C. (1999, August). Getting ready for the 21st century: The aging of America and the Older Americans Act. *Health & Social Work, 24*(3), 232–239.

Talaga, J. A., & Beehr, T. A. (1989). Retirement: A psychological perspective. In C. L. Cooper & I. T. Robertson (Eds.), *International review of industrial and organizational psychology* (pp. 185–211). New York: Wiley.

Talmi, A., & Harmon, R. J. (2003). Relationships between preterm infants and their parents. *Zero to Three, 24*(2), 13–20.

Tamis-LeMonda, C. S., & Cabrera, N. (Eds.). (2002). *Handbook of father involvement: Multidisciplinary perspectives.* Mahwah, NJ: Erlbaum.

Tan, D. T., Lam, D. S., Chua, W. H., Shu-Ping, D. F., Crockett, R. S., & Asian Pirenzepine Study Group. (2005). One-year multicenter, double-masked, placebo-controlled, parallel safety and efficacy study of 2% pirenzepine ophthalmic gel in children with myopia. *Ophthalmology, 112,* 84–91.

Tangney, J. P. (1998). How does guilt differ from shame? In J. Bybee (Ed.), *Guilt and children* (pp. 1–17). San Diego, CA: Academic Press.

Tangney, J. P., & Fischer, K. W. (Eds.). (1995). *The self-conscious emotions.* New York: Guilford.

Tanner, J. M. (1988). *History of the study of human growth.* New York: Academic Press.

Tanner, J. M. (1989). *Foetus into man* (Revised & enlarged). Cambridge, MA: Harvard University Press.

Tano, Y. (2002). Pathologic myopia: Where are we now? *American Journal of Ophthalmology, 134,* 645–660.

Tatara, T., & Kuzmeskus, L. (1997). *Summaries of statistical data on elder abuse in domestic settings for FY 95 and FY 96.* Washington, DC: National Center on Elder Abuse.

Tauber, R. T. (1997). *Self-fulfilling prophecy: A practical guide to its use in education.* Westport, CT: Praeger.

Taubes, G. (1998). As obesity rates rise, experts struggle to explain why. *Science, 280,* 1367–1368.

Taverner, W. J. (2002). *Taking sides: Clashing views on controversial issues in human sexuality.* Dubuque, IA: McGraw-Hill/Dushkin.

Taylor, A. (2002). *The handbook of family dispute resolution: Mediation theory and practice.* San Francisco: Jossey-Bass.

Taylor, D., Mitchell, E., Woods, N., Mariella, A., Berg, J., & Quinn, A. A. (2003). From menarche to menopause: New understanding of women's symptom experience [Abstract]. In *Abstracts of the 15th Conference of the Society for Menstrual Cycle Research.* Pittsburgh, PA: SMCR.

Taylor, E. (1999). James and Sigmund Freud: The future of psychology belongs to your work. *Psychological Science, 10*(6), 465–469.

Taylor, J., Gilligan, C. & Sullivan, A. (1995). *Between voice and silence: Women and girls, race and relationships.* Cambridge, MA: Harvard University Press.

Taylor, K., & Walton, S. (2001). Who is Norm? And what is he doing in my class? *Instructor, 110*(6), 18–19.

Taylor, M. (1999). *Imaginary companions and the children who create them.* New York: Oxford University Press.

Taylor, M., & Carlson, S. (1997). The relation between individual differences in fantasy and theory of mind. *Child Development, 68,* 436–455.

Taylor, R. L. (2002). Black American families. In R. L. Taylor (Ed.), *Minority families in the United States: A multicultural perspective* (3rd ed., pp. 20–47). Upper Saddle River, NJ: Prentice-Hall. Retrieved from http://www.ssc.wisc.edu/~rturley/Black%20Families.pdf

Taylor, S. (2002). Cognition in obsessive compulsive disorder: An overview. In R. O. Frost & G. Steketee (Eds.), *Cognitive approaches to obsessions and compulsions: Theory, assessment, and treatment* (pp. 1–12). Amsterdam: Elsevier.

Taylor, S. (in press). Dimensional and categorical models of OCD: A critical analysis. In J. S. Abramowitz & A. C. Houts (Eds.), *Handbook of controversial issues in obsessive-compulsive disorder.* New York: Kluwer.

Taylor, S. E. (2003). *Health psychology* (5th ed.). Boston: McGraw-Hill.

Tay-Sachs Disease Hub, http://www.genomelink.org/taysachs

Te Nijenjuis, J., Evers, A., & Jakko, M. P. (2000). Validity of the Differential Aptitude Test for the assessment of immigrant children. *Educational Psychology, 20,* 99–115.

Teachers College Record, http://www.tcrecord.org

Teachers of English to Speakers of Other Languages, http://www.tesol.org

Teaser, P. (2003). *A response to the abuse of vulnerable adults: The 2000 survey of Adult Protective Services.* Washington, DC: National Center on Elder Abuse.

Tedeschi, R., & Calhoun, L. (1995). *Trauma and transformation.* Thousand Oaks, CA: Sage.

Tellis, W. (1997, September). Application of a case study methodology. *The Qualitative Report* [On-line serial], *3*(3). Retrieved from http://www.nova.edu/ssss/QR/QR3–3/tellis2.html

Telushkin, J. (1991). *Jewish literacy.* New York: William Morrow.

Temple University Libraries (n.d.). *Urban Archives, Gray Panthers, Accession 835, Records, 1950s–mid 1990s. Part 1: Background and history.* Retrieved from http://www.library.temple.edu/urbana/gray-01.htm

Temple University Libraries. (n.d.). *Urban Archives, Gray Panthers, Accession 924, Records, 1970s–1990s.* Retrieved from http://www.library.temple.edu/urbana/gray-924.htm

Teresi, M. E. (2000). Iron deficiency and megaloblastic anemias. In E. T. Herfindal & D. R. Gourley (Eds.), *Textbook of therapeutics: Drug and disease management* (7th ed.). Hagerstown, MD: Lippincott, Williams & Wilkins.

Terman, L. M., & Miles, C. C. (1936). *Sex and personality: Studies in masculinity and femininity.* New York: McGraw-Hill.

Tesser, A., Felson, R. B., & Suls, J. M. (Eds.). (2000). *Psychological perspectives on self and identity.* Washington, DC: American Psychological Association.

Tesser, A., Stapel, D. A., & Wood, J. W. (Eds.). (2002). *Self and motivation: Emerging psychological perspectives.* Washington, DC: American Psychological Association.

Thalidomide Victims Association of Canada, http://www.thalidomide.ca

Tharp, R. G., & Gallimore, R. (1988). *Rousing minds to life: Teaching, learning, and schooling in social context.* New York: Cambridge University Press.

Thelen, E., Fisher, D. M., & Ridley-Johnson, R. (2002). The relationship between physical growth and a newborn reflex. *Infant Behavior and Development, 25,* 72–85.

Thelen, E., & Smith, L. B. (1994). *A dynamic systems approach to the development of cognition and action.* Cambridge: MIT Press.

Thelen, E., & Smith, L. B. (1997). Dynamic systems theories. In R. M. Lerner (Ed.), *Theoretical models of human development. Handbook of child psychology* (Vol. 1, 5th ed., pp. 563–634). New York: Wiley.

Thelen, E., & Ulrich, B. (1991). Hidden skills. *Monographs of the Society for Research in Child Development, 56* (No. 1, Serial No. 223). Chicago: University of Chicago Press.

Theoretical and clinical papers, psychoanalytic links, and other helpful information related to psychoanalytic developmental psychology, http://www.psychematters.com

Theory of Planned Behavior, http://www.people.umass.edu/aizen/tpb.html

Therrien, M., & Ramirez, R. R. (2001). *The Hispanic population in the United States: March 2000* (Current Population Reports, P20-535). Washington DC: U.S. Bureau of the Census.

Thomas, A., & Chess, S. (1977). *Temperament and development.* Oxford, UK: Brunner/Mazel.

Thomas, A., Chess, S., & Birch, H. G. (1968). *Temperament and behavior disorders in children.* New York: New York University Press.

Thomas, D., & Gaslin, T. (2001). "Camping up" self-esteem in children with hemophilia. *Issues in Comprehensive Pediatric Nursing, 24,* 253–263.

Thomas, R. M. (1999). *Comparing theories of child development.* Pacific Grove, CA: Wadsworth.

Thomas, R. M. (2000). *Comparing theories of child development* (5th ed.). Stanford, CT: Wadsworth.

Thompson, R., Jr., & Gustafson, K. (1996). *Adaptation to chronic childhood illness.* Washington, DC: American Psychological Association.

Thompson, R. A. (1994). The role of the father after divorce. In *The Future of Children, Vol. 4, No. 1: Children and divorce* (pp. 210–235). San Francisco: Center for the Future of Children.

Thompson, R. F., & Spencer, W. A. (1966). Habituation: A model phenomenon for the study of neuronal substrates of behavior. *Psychological Review, 73,* 16–43.

Thornton, J. E. (2002). Myths of aging or ageist stereotypes. *Educational Gerontology, 28,* 301–312.

Thurstone, L. L. (1973). *The nature of intelligence.* Westport, CT: Greenwood. (Original work published 1924)

Tiefer, L. (2000). The social construction and social effects of sex research: The sexological model of sexuality. In C. B. Travis & J. W. White (Eds.), *Sexuality, society, and feminism.* Washington, DC: American Psychological Association.

Tierney, L. M. (Ed.). (2005). *Current medical diagnosis and treatment* (44th ed.). New York: McGraw-Hill.

Timmerman, G. M., & Gregg, E. K. (2003). Dieting, perceived deprivation, and preoccupation with food. *Western Journal of Nursing Research, 25,* 405–418.

Tinbergen, N. (1951). *The study of instinct.* Oxford, UK: Clarendon.

Tinbergen, N. (1953). *The herring gull's world.* London: Collins.

Titchener, E. B. (1915). *A beginner's psychology.* New York: Macmillan.

Tjaden, P., & Thoennes, N. (1998, November). *Prevalence, incidence, and consequences of violence against women: Findings from the National Violence Against Women Survey.* Washington, DC: National Institute of Justice and Centers for Disease Control and Prevention Research in Brief.

Toga, A. W., & Thompson, P. M. (2003). Mapping brain asymmetry. *Nature Reviews Neuroscience, 4,* 37–48.

Tolman, C. W. (1994). *Psychology, society, and subjectivity: An introduction to German critical psychology.* New York: Routledge.

Tomasello, M. (2000). Culture and cognitive development. *Current Directions in Psychological Science, 9,* 37–40.

Tomasello, M., Kruger, A. C., & Ratner, H. H. (1993). Cultural learning. *Brain and Behavioral Sciences, 16,* 495–552.

Tomasello, M., Savage-Rumbaugh, S., & Kruger, A. C. (1993). Imitative learning of actions on objects by children, chimpanzees, and enculturated chimpanzees. *Child Development, 64,* 1688–1705.

Tomer, A. (2000). *Death attitudes and the older adult.* New York: Brunner Routledge.

Tonigan, J. S., Connors, G. J., & Miller, W. R. (2003). Participation and involvement in Alcoholics Anonymous. In T. Babor & F. K. Del Boca (Eds.), *Matching alcoholism treatments to client heterogeneity: The results of Project MATCH* (pp. 184–204). New York: Cambridge University Press.

Torgesen, J. K. (2004). *Catch them before they fall: Identification and assessment to prevent reading failure in young children.* Retrieved from http://www.ldonline.org/ld_indepth/reading/torgesen_catchthem.html

Tormey, R., Good, A., & MacKeough, C. (1995). *Post-methodology? New directions for research methodologies in the social sciences* [Web book]. Retrieved from http://www.iol.ie/~mazzoldi/toolsforchange/postmet/book.html

Torr, J. D. (2000). *Euthanasia: Opposing viewpoints.* San Diego, CA: Greenhaven.

Torrance Center for Creative Studies, http://jane.coe.uga.edu/torrance/index.html

Torrance, E. P. (1974). *Torrance tests of creative thinking.* Lexington, MA: Personal Press.

Torrey, E. F. (1998). *Out of the shadows: Confronting America's mental illness crisis.* New York: Wiley.

Torrey, E. F., Bowler, A. E., & Clark, K. (1997). Urban birth and residence as risk factors for psychoses: An analysis of 1880 data. *Schizophrenia Research, 25,* 69–76.

Touch Research Institute, http://www.miami.edu/touch-research/

Treatment Advocacy Center. (2004). *Hospital closures.* Retrieved from http://www.psychlaws.org/HospitalClosure/Index.htm

Tremblay, R. E. (2000). The development of aggressive behavior during childhood: What have we learned in the past century? *International Journal of Behavioral Development, 24,* 129–141.

Trigilio, J., & Brighenti, K. (2003). *Catholicism for dummies.* Hoboken, NJ: Wiley.

Triplet Connection, http://www.tripletconnection.org

Trivers, R. L. (1971). The evolution of reciprocal altruism. *Quarterly Review of Biology, 46,* 35–37.

Trochim, W. M. (2001). *The research methods knowledge base* (2nd ed.). Cincinnati, OH: Atomic Dog. Retrieved from http://trochim.human.cornell.edu/kb/quasiexp.htm

Trochim, W. M. (2002). *Experimental design.* Retrieved from http://trochim.human.cornell.edu/kb/desexper.htm

Trochim, W. M. (2002). *Research methods knowledge base.* Retrieved from http://www.socialresearchmethods.net/kb/index.htm

Trochim, W. M. K. (2002). *Nonprobability sampling.* Retrieved from http://trochim.human.cornell.edu/kb/sampnon.htm

Trochim, W. M. K. (2002). *Probability sampling.* Retrieved from http://trochim.human.cornell.edu/kb/sampprob.htm

Tronick, E. Z. (1995). Touch in mother-infant interaction. In T. M. Field (Ed.), *Touch in early development* (pp. 53–65). Mahwah, NJ: Erlbaum.

Trotter, A. (2004, April 14). Studies fault results of retention in Chicago. *Education Week.* Retrieved from http://www.edweek.org/ew/ewstory.cfm?slug=31Chicago.h23&keywords=retention

Tsiaras, A., & Werth, B. (2002). *From conception to birth: A life unfolds.* New York: Doubleday.

Tuason, M. T. (1992). *Five urban poor families with alcoholic fathers: A clinically descriptive and exploratory study.* Unpublished master's thesis, Ateneo de Manila University, Quezon City, Philippines.

Tudor, J. F. (1971). The development of class awareness in children. *Social Forces, 49,* 470–476.

Turiel, E. (1983). *The development of social knowledge.* Cambridge, UK: Cambridge University Press.

Turiel, E. (1998). The development of morality. In W. Damon & N. Eisenberg (Eds.), *Handbook of child psychology: Vol. 3. Social, emotional, and personality development* (5th ed., pp. 863–932). New York: Wiley.

Turk, D. C. (1996). Biopsychosocial perspectives on chronic pain. In R. J. Gatchel & D. C. Turk (Eds.), *Psychological approaches to pain management: A practitioner's handbook.* New York: Guilford.

Turk, D. C. (2001). Physiological and psychological bases of pain. In A. Baum, T. A. Revenson, & J. E. Singer (Eds.), *Handbook of health psychology* (pp. 117–137). Mahwah, NJ: Erlbaum.

Turkheimer, E., Haley, A., Waldron, M., D'Onofrio, B., & Gottesman, I. I. (2003). Socioeconomic status modifies heritability of IQ in young children. *Psychological Science, 14,* 623–628.

Turkkan, J. S. (1989). Classical contingency: The new hegemony. *Behavioral and Brain Sciences, 12,* 121–179.

Turnbull, R., Turnbull, A., Shank, M., & Smith, S. (2004). *Exceptional lives: Special education in today's schools* (4th ed.). Upper Saddle River, NJ: Prentice-Hall.

Turnbull, R., Turnbull, A., Shank, M., Smith, S., & Leal, D. (2001). Implementing IDEA's principles. In R. Turnbull, A. Turnbull, M. Shank, S. Smith, & D. Leal (Eds.), *Exceptional lives: Special education in today's schools* (3rd ed., pp. 40–71). Upper Saddle River, NJ: Prentice-Hall.

Turner, S. M., Beidel, D. C., Borden, J. W., Stanley, M. A., & Jacob, R. G. (1991). Social phobia: Axis I and II correlates. *Journal of Abnormal Psychology, 100,* 102–106.

Turner, S. M., & Hersen, M. (2003). *Adult psychopathology and diagnosis* (4th ed.). New York: Wiley.

Turone, F. (2004). Italy to pass new law on assisted reproduction. *British Medical Journal, 328,* 9.

Twenge, J. M. (1997). Changes in masculine and feminine traits over time: A meta-analysis. *Sex Roles. 36,* 305–325.

Twenge, J. M. (2001). Changes in women's assertiveness in response to status and roles: A cross-temporal meta-analysis, 1931–1993. *Journal of Personality and Social Psychology, 81,* 133–145.

20th Century History. (n.d.). *The Holocaust.* Retrieved from http://history1900s.about.com/library/holocaust/blholocaust.htm

Twin Stuff, http://www.twinstuff.com

Twins and Multiple Births Association, http://www.tamba.org

UCLA Healthcare. (2005). Memory disorders. *Patient Learning Series.* Available from http://www.healthcare.ucla.edu/periodicals

Uhlenberg, P. (1996). The burden of aging: A theoretical framework for understanding the shifting balance of care-giving and care receiving as cohorts age. *Gerontologist, 36,* 761–767.

UNAIDS. (2003). *AIDS epidemic update.* Retrieved from http://www.unaids.org

Understanding Vaccines (NIAID & NIH), http://www.niaid.nih.gov/publications/vaccine/pdf/undvacc.pdf

Ungerleider, L. G. (1995). Functional brain imaging studies of cortical mechanisms for memory. *Science, 270*(5237), 769–775.

UNICEF, http://www.unicef.org

UNICEF. (2001). *The state of the world's children.* New York: Author. Retrieved from http://www.unicef.org/sowc01

UNICEF. (n.d.). *Convention on the rights of a child.* Available from http://www.unicef.org/crc/crc.htm

United Cerebral Palsy. (2001). *Cerebral palsy—Facts and figures.* Retrieved from http://www.ucp.org/ucp_generaldoc.cfm/1/9/37/37–37/447

United Nations. (1998). *Revision of the world population estimates and projections.* Available from http://www.popin.org

United Nations. (1998). *United Nations principles for older persons.* Retrieved from http://www.un.org/esa/socdev/iyoppop.htm

University of Chicago, Division of Biological Sciences—Sleep, Chronobiology and Neuroendocrinology Center, http://www.sleep.uchicago.edu/index3.html?content=studies.html

University of Kansas, Circle of Inclusion Project, http://www.circleofinclusion.org/

University of Michigan Health System. (n.d.). *Weight-loss diets.* Retrieved from http://med.umich.edu/1libr/aha/aha_odiet_crs.htm

University of Minnesota, Center for Early Education and Development. (n.d.). *Attachment and bonding.* Retrieved from http://education.umn.edu/ceed/publications/earlyreport/winter91.htm

University of Phoenix, http://www.uophx.edu/

University of Pittsburgh Medical Center. (2005). *Alcoholism.* Retrieved from http://alcoholism.upmc.com

Urberg, K. A. (1999). Some thoughts on studying the influence of peers on children and adolescents. *Merrill-Palmer Quarterly, 45,* 1–12.

Urie Bronfenbrenner. (n.d.). Retrieved from http://people.cornell.edu/pages/ub11/index.html

Urofsky, M. I. (2000). *Lethal judgment: Assisted suicide and American law.* Lawrence: University Press of Kansas.

U.S. Bureau of the Census. (1989). *Projections of the population of the United States by age, sex, and race: 1988–2080, Current population reports: Population estimates and projections.* Series P-25, No. 1018. Washington, DC: U.S. Government Printing Office.

U.S. Bureau of the Census. (2001). *Overview of race and Hispanic origin* (Census 2000 Brief). Retrieved from http://www.census.gov/prod/2001pubs/c2kbr01-1.pdf

U.S. Bureau of the Census. (2002). *The Hispanic population in the United States: March 2002 (population characteristics).* P20-545. Washington, DC: Author.

U.S. Bureau of Justice Statistics. (n.d.). *Homicide trends in the U.S.: Infanticide.* Retrieved from http://www.ojp.usdoj.gov/bjs/Shomicide/tables/kidsagetab.htm

U.S. Census Bureau, http://www.census.gov

U.S. Census Bureau. (1996). *65+ in the United States.* Current Population Reports, Special Studies, P23-190. Washington, DC: U.S. Government Printing Office. Retrieved from http://www.census.gov/prod/1/pop/p23-190/p23-190.pdf

U.S. Census Bureau. (1999). *Historical census statistics on the foreign-born population of the United States: 1850 to 1990.* Retrieved from http://www.census.gov/population/www/documentation/twps0029/twps0029.html

U.S. Census Bureau. (2000). *The American Indian Population: 2000.* Retrieved from http://www.census.gov/population/www/socdemo/race/indian.html

U.S. Census Bureau. (2000). *Current population reports: America's families and living arrangements.* Retrieved from http://www.census.gov/population/www/socdemo/hh-fam.html

U.S. Census Bureau. (2000). *Poverty in the United States 2002.* Retrieved from http://www.census.gov/hhes/www/poverty02.html

U.S. Census Bureau. (2002). *America's families and living arrangements: March 2002* (Table FG5). Retrieved from http://www.census.gov/population/www/socdemo/hh-fam/cps2002.html

U.S. Census Bureau. (2003). *American community survey profile* [2003, Table PCT013]. Retrieved from http://www.census.gov/acs/www/index.html

U.S. Census Bureau. (2003). *Custodial mothers and fathers and their child support: 2001.* Washington, DC: Author.

U.S. Census Bureau. (2003). *Facts for features: American Indian and Alaska Native Heritage Month: November 2003.* Retrieved from http://www.census.gov/Press-Release/www/releases/archives/facts_for_features/001492.html

U.S. Census Bureau. (2003, September). *Poverty in the United States: 2002.* Washington, DC: Authors. Retrieved from http://www.census.gov/hhes/www/poverty02.html

U.S. Census Bureau, Population Division. (2004). Table 5: Annual estimates of the population by race alone or in combination and Hispanic or Latino origin for the United States and States: July 1, 2003 (SC-EST2003-05). Retrieved from http://www.census.gov/popest/states/asrh/ SC-EST200304.html

U.S. Charter Schools, http://www.uscharterschools.org/pub/uscs_docs/index.htm

U.S. Consumer Product Safety Commission, NEISS All Injury Program, http://www.cpsc.gov/LIBRARY/neiss.html

U.S. Department of Agriculture. (2000). *Nutrition and your health: Dietary guidelines for Americans* (5th ed.). Home and Garden Bulletin No. 232.

U.S. Department of Agriculture. (2002). *Nutrition education in FNS: A coordinated approach for promoting healthy behavior. A report to Congress.* Alexandria, VA: Food and Nutrition Service.

U.S. Department of Defense. (1985). *Black Americans in defense of our nation.* Retrieved from http://unx1.shsu.edu/~his_ncp/AfrAmer.html

U.S. Department of Education, http://www.ed.gov/index.jhtml

U.S. Department of Education. (1999). Assistance to states for the education of children with disabilities and the early intervention program for infants and toddlers with disabilities. *Federal Register, 64*(48), 12405–12454.

U.S. Department of Education (Sponsor). (2000, August). *Family literacy: An annotated bibliography.* Chapel Hill: University of North Carolina. Retrieved from http://www.lacnyc.org/resources/familylit/FL_bibliography.pdf

U.S. Department of Education. (2004). *A guide to the individualized education program.* Retrieved from http://www.ed.gov/parents/needs/speced/iepguide/index.html

U.S. Department of Education. (n.d.). *No Child Left Behind.* Retrieved from http://www.ed.gov/nclb/landing.jhtml

U.S. Department of Education. (n.d.). *Taking responsibility for ending social promotion: A guide for educators and state and local leaders.* Retrieved from http://www.ed.gov/pubs/socialpromotion/index.html

U.S. Department of Health and Human Services. (2000). *Administration on Developmental Disabilities, fiscal year 2000 annual report.* Washington, DC: Author.

U.S. Department of Health and Human Services. (2000). *HHS blueprint for action on breastfeeding.* Washington, DC: Office on Women's Health.

U.S. Department of Health and Human Services. (2001). *Youth violence: A report of the Surgeon General.* Rockville, MD: Author.

U.S. Department of Health and Human Services. (2002). *Child Health USA 2002.* Retrieved from http://mchb.hrsa.gov/chusa02/index.htm

U.S. Department of Health and Human Services. (2003). *Emerging practices in the prevention of child abuse and neglect.* Washington, DC: U.S. Government Printing Office.

U.S. Department of Health & Human Services. (2001). *Youth violence: A report of the Surgeon General.* Retrieved from http://www.surgeongeneral.gov/library/youthviolence/chapter1/sec1.html

U.S. Department of Health and Human Services, Administration for Children and Families, http://www.acf.hhs.gov/index.html

U.S. Department of Health and Human Services, Administration for Children and Families (n.d.). *AFCARS—Adoption and Foster Care Analysis and Reporting System.* Available from http://www.acf.hhs.gov/programs/cb/dis/afcars

U.S. Department of Health and Human Services, Administration for Children and Families (n.d.). *Children's Bureau fact sheets and reports/publications.* Retrieved from http://www.acf.hhs.gov/programs/cg/publications

U.S. Department of Health and Human Services, Administration for Children and Families—Head Start Bureau. (n.d.). *The statement of the advisory committee on services for families with infants and toddlers.* Retrieved from http://www.acf.hhs.gov/programs/hsb/research/infants_toddlers/research_rationale.htm

U.S. Department of Health and Human Services, Administration for Children and Families, Office of Child Support Enforcement. (n.d.). *State and local IV-D agencies on the WEB.* Retrieved from http://www.acf.hhs.gov/programs/cse/extinf.htm#exta

U.S. Department of Health and Human Services, Administration on Children, Youth and Families. (2002). *Eleven years of reporting child maltreatment 2000.* Washington, DC: U.S. Government Printing Office.

U.S. Department of Health and Human Services, Centers for Disease Control and Prevention, National Center for Chronic Disease Prevention and Health Promotion. (1996). *Physical activity and health: A report of the Surgeon General.* Atlanta, GA: Author.

U.S. Department of Health and Human Services, Centers for Disease Control and Prevention, National Center for Chronic Disease Prevention and Health Promotion. (2004). *The health consequences of smoking: A report of the Surgeon General.* Washington, DC: Office on Smoking and Health. Retrieved from http://www.cdc.gov/tobacco/sgr/sgr_2004/chapters.htm

U.S. Department of Health and Human Services, Centers for Disease Control and Prevention, National Center for Chronic Disease Prevention and Health Promotion. (n.d.). *Physical activity for everyone.* Available from http://www.cdc.gov/nccdphp/dnpa/physical/index.htm

U.S. Department of Health and Human Services. Children's Bureau, http://www.acf.hhs.gov/programs/cb/

U.S. Department of Health and Human Services, Health Resources and Services Administration, Maternal and Child Health Bureau. (2003). *Women's health USA 2003.* Rockville, MD: Author.

U.S. Department of Health and Human Services, National Center for Health Statistics. (1993). *Survey on child health.* Washington, DC: U.S. Government Printing Office.

U.S. Department of Health and Human Services, National Clearinghouse on Child Abuse & Neglect Information, http://nccanch.acf.hhs.gov/

U.S. Department of Justice. (2002). *A guide to disability rights laws.* Washington, DC: U.S. Government Printing Office.

U.S. Department of Justice. (n.d.). *Community relations service.* Retrieved from http://www.usdoj.gov/crs/

U.S. Department of Labor. (2002). *Fatal occupational injuries in the United States, 1995–1999: A chartbook.* Washington, DC: U.S. Bureau of Labor Statistics.

U.S. Department of State. (2003). *Immigrant visas issued to orphans coming to the U.S.* Retrieved from http://travel.state.gov/orphan_numbers.html

U.S. Drug Enforcement Administration, http://www.usdoj.gov/dea/

U.S. Environmental Protection Agency. (2004). *What you need to know about mercury in fish and shellfish.* Retrieved from http://www.epa.gov/waterscience/fishadvice/advice.html

U.S. Environmental Protection Agency. (n.d.). *Endocrine disruptor research initiative.* Retrieved from http://www.epa.gov/endocrine/

U.S. Environmental Protection Agency. (n.d.). *Pesticides.* Retrieved from http://www.epa.gov/pesticides/

U.S. Equal Employment Opportunity Commission. (2000). *Highlights of EEOC enforcement of the Americans with Disabilities Act: A preliminary status report, July 26, 1992, through March 31, 2000.* Available from http://www.eeoc.gov

U.S. Federal Glass Ceiling Commission. (1995). *Good for business: Making full use of the nation's human capital.* Washington, DC: Author.

U.S. Federal Glass Ceiling Commission. (1995). *A solid investment: Making full use of the nation's human capital.* Washington, DC: Author.

U.S. Living Will Registry, http://www.uslivingwillregistry.com

U.S. National Center for Health Statistics, http://www.cdc.gov/nchs/fastats/lifexpec.htm

U.S. National Library of Medicine. (n.d.). *Infantile reflexes.* Retrieved from http://www.nlm.nih.gov/medlineplus/ency/article/003292.htm

U.S. National Library of Medicine. (n.d.). *Pesticides.* Retrieved from http://www.nlm.nih.gov/medlineplus/pesticides.html

U.S. National Library of Medicine and National Institutes of Health. (2003). *Medical encyclopedia: Well-child visits.* Retrieved from http://www.nlm.hih.gov/medlineplus/ency/article/001928.htm

U.S. Preventive Task Force. (2002). Postmenopausal hormone replacement therapy for primary prevention of chronic conditions: Recommendations and rationale. *Annals of Internal Medicine, 137,* 834–839.

Uzgiris, I. C. (1981). Two functions of imitation during infancy. *International Journal of Behavioral Development, 4,* 1–12.

Vaillant, G. (2002). *Aging well: Surprising guideposts to a happier life from the landmark Harvard Study of Adult Development.* New York: Little, Brown.

Valsiner, J. (1998). The development of the concept of development: Historical and epistemological perspectives. In W. Damon (Editor-in-Chief) & Richard Lerner (Vol. Ed.), *Handbook of child psychology: Vol. 1. Theoretical models of human development* (5th ed., pp. 189–232). New York: Wiley.

van Beilen, M., Kiers, H., Bouma, A., van Zomeren, E., Withaar, F., Arends, J., et al. (2003). Cognitive deficits and social functioning in schizophrenia: A clinical perspective. *The Clinical Neuropsychologist, 17,* 507–514.

van Beusekom, I., & Iguchi, M. Y. (2001). *A review of recent advances in knowledge about methadone maintenance treatment.* Santa Monica, CA: Rand. Retrieved from http://www.rand.org/publications/MR/MR1396/

van der Veer, R., & Valsiner, J. (1991). *Understanding Vygotsky: A quest for synthesis.* Cambridge, MA: Blackwell.

Van Dijken, S. (1998). *John Bowlby: His early life. A biographical journey into the roots of attachment theory.* London/New York: Free Association Books.

Van Dyke, F. (n.d.). *A visual approach to deductive reasoning.* Retrieved from http://illuminations.nctm.org/lessonplans/9-12/reasoning/

Van Gundy, K., & Rebellon, C. J. (2002). *Revisiting the gateway hypothesis: The conditioning influences of employment, age, and use versus misuse.* Annual Meetings of the American Society of Criminology, Denver, CO.

van IJzendoorn, M. H. (1995). Adult attachment representations, parental responsiveness, and infant attachment: A metaanalysis on the predictive validity of the Adult

Attachment Interview. *Psychological Bulletin, 117,* 387–403.

van IJzendoorn, M. H., & Kroonenberg, P. M. (1988). Cross-cultural patterns of attachment: A meta-analysis of the strange situation. *Child Development, 58,* 147–156.

Van IJzendoorn, M. H., & Sagi, A. (1999). Cross-cultural patterns of attachment: Universal and contextual dimensions. In J. Cassidy & P. Shaver (Eds.), *Handbook of attachment.* New York: Guilford.

Van Kampen, M., De Weerdt, W., Van Poppel, H., De Ridder, D., Feys, H., & Baert, L. (2000). Effect of pelvic floor re-education on duration and degree of incontinence after radical prostatectomy: A randomized controlled trial. *Lancet, 355*(8), 98–102.

van Os, J., Hanssen, M., Bak, M., Bijl, R. V., & Vollebergh, W. (2003). Do urbanicity and familial liability coparticipate in causing psychosis? *American Journal of Psychiatry, 160,* 477–482.

Vande Kemp, H. (n.d.). *Diana Blumberg Baumrind.* Retrieved from http://www.psych.yorku.ca/femhop/Diana%20Baumrind .htm

Vannatta, K., & Gerhardt, C. (2003). Pediatric oncology: Psychosocial outcomes for children and families. In M. C. Roberts (Ed.), *Handbook of pediatric psychology* (3rd ed., pp. 342–357). New York: Guilford.

Varin, D., Crugnola, C. R., Molina, P., & Ripamonti, C. (1996). Sensitive periods in the development of attachment and the age of entry into day care. *European Journal of Psychology of Education, 11,* 215–229.

Vartanian, L. R. (2000). Revisiting the imaginary audience and personal fable constructs of adolescent egocentrism: A conceptual review. *Adolescence, 35,* 639–661.

Vartanian, L. R. (2001). Adolescents' reactions to hypothetical peer group conversations: Evidence for an imaginary audience? *Adolescence, 36,* 347–380.

Vasey, M. W., & Dadds, M. R. (Eds.). (2001). *The developmental psychopathology of anxiety.* New York: Oxford University Press.

The Vatican. (n.d.). *The Holy See.* Available from http://www .vatican.va/

Vaughan, A. (2004). *Contributions of temperament and joint attention to social competence, externalizing, and internalizing behavior in normally developing children.* Unpublished doctoral dissertation, University of Miami, Miami, FL.

Vaughn, C., & Leff, J. (1976). The measurement of expressed emotion in the families of psychiatric patients. *British Journal of Social and Clinical Psychology, 15,* 157–165.

Vaughn, S., Bos, C. S., & Schumm, J. S. (2003). *Teaching exceptional, diverse, and at-risk students in the general education classroom* (3rd ed.). Boston: Allyn & Bacon.

Vega, W. A. (1990). Hispanic families in the 1980's: A decade of research. *Journal of Marriage and Family, 52,* 1015–1024.

Velting, D. M., & Gould, M. S. (1997). Suicide contagion. In R. Maris, S. Canetto, & M. Silverman (Eds.), *Review of suicidology.* New York: Guilford.

Venezia, M., Messinger, D. S., Thorp, D., & Mundy, P. (2004). Timing changes: The development of anticipatory smiling. *Infancy, 6*(3), 397–406.

Ventura, S. J., Abma, J. C., Mosher, W. D., & Henshaw, S. (2004). Estimated pregnancy rates for the United States, 1990–2000: An update. *National Vital Statistics Reports, 52*(23).

Verbrugge, L. M. (1989). The twain meet: Empirical explanations of sex differences in health and mortality. *Journal of Health and Social Behavior, 30,* 282–304.

Vermeer, C., & Schurgers, L. J. (2000). A comprehensive review of vitamin K and vitamin K antagonists. *Hematology/Oncology Clinics of North America, 14,* 339.

Vernberg, E. M., & Varela, R. E. (2001). Posttraumatic stress disorder: A developmental perspective. In M. W. Vasey & M. R. Dadds (Eds.), *The developmental psychopathology of anxiety* (pp. 386–406). New York: Oxford University Press.

Vernon, P. A., & Jensen, A. R. (1984). Individual and group differences in intelligence and speed of information processing. *Personality & Individual Differences, 5,* 411–423.

Vernon, P. E. (1950/1961). *The structure of human abilities.* London: Methuen.

Veysey, L. R. (1965). *The emergence of the American university.* Chicago: University of Chicago Press.

Vidal Sassoon International Center for the Study of Antisemitism (SICSA), Hebrew University of Jerusalem, http://sicsa.huji.ac.il/

Vigil, J. D. (1998). *From Indians to Chicanos: The dynamics of Mexican American culture.* Prospect Heights, IL: Waveland Press.

Virginia Apgar, http://web.mit.edu/invent/iow/apgar.html

Virginia Apgar, http://www.apgar.net/virginia

The Visible Embryo, http://www.visembryo.com/

Vissing, Y. (2002). *Women without children: Nurturing lives.* Piscataway, NJ: Rutgers University Press.

Vitzhum, V. J. (2003). A number no greater than the sum of its parts: The use and abuse of heritability. *Human Biology, 75,* 539–558.

Volavka, J. (1999). The effects of clozapine on aggression and substance abuse in schizophrenic patients. *Journal of Clinical Psychiatry, 60*(Suppl. 12), 43–46.

Volpe, E. P. (1993). *Biology and human concerns* (4th ed.). Dubuque, IA: William C. Brown.

von Frisch, K. (1947). The dances of the honey bee. *Annual Report of the Board of Regents of the Smithsonian Institution* (Publication 3490, pp. 423–431). Washington, DC: U.S. Government Printing Office.

Von Karolyi, C., Ramos-Ford, V., & Gardner, H. (2003). Multiple intelligences: A perspective on giftedness. In N. Colangelo & G. A. Davis (Eds.), *Handbook of gifted education* (pp. 100–112). Boston: Allyn & Bacon.

von Senger, H. (Ed.). (1999). *Die List* [The cunning]. Frankfurt am Main, Germany: Suhrkamp.

Voneche, J. (2003). The changing structure of Piaget's thinking: Invariance and transformations. *Creativity Research Journal, 15*(1), 3–9.

Vulliamy, E. (1994). *Seasons in Hell: Understanding Bosnia's war.* London: Simon & Schuster.

Vygotsky, L. S. (1962). *Thought and language* (E. Hanfmann & G. Vakar, Eds. & Trans.). Cambridge: MIT Press. (Original work published 1934)

Vygotsky, L. S. (1978). *Mind in society: The development of higher mental processes* (M. Cole, V. John-Steiner, S. Scribner, & E. Souberman, Eds. & Trans.). Cambridge, MA: Harvard University Press. (Original work published 1930–1935)

Vygotsky, L. S., & Luria, A. R. (1993). *Studies on the history of behavior: Ape, primitive, and child* (V. I. Golod & J. E. Knox, Eds. & Trans.). Hillsdale, NJ: Erlbaum. (Original work published 1930)

Wadden, T. A., Brownell, K. D., & Foster, G. D. (2002). Obesity: Responding to the global epidemic. *Journal of Consulting and Clinical Psychology, 70,* 510–525.

Wade, C., & Tavris, C. (1990). *Psychology.* New York: HarperCollins.

Wade, P. (1999). *Practice agenda—technology 3rd question.* Washington, DC: American College Personnel Association [On-line]. Retrieved from http://www.acpa.nche.edu/tech3.htm

Wagner, T. H., & Hu, T. W. (1998). Economic costs of urinary incontinence in 1995. *Urology, 51*(3), 355–361.

Wainer, H. (1989). Eelworms, bullet holes, and Geraldine Ferraro: Some problems with statistical adjustment and some solutions. *Journal of Educational Statistics, 14,* 121–140.

Waisbren, S. E. (1999). Phenylketonuria. In S. Goldstein & C. R. Reynolds (Eds.), *Handbook of neurodevelopmental and genetic disorders in children* (pp. 433–458). New York: Guilford.

Waite, L. J., & Nielsen, M. (2001). The rise of the dual-earner family, 1963–1997. In R. Hertz & N. L. Marshall (Eds.), *Working families: The transformation of the American home.* Berkeley: University of California Press.

Waldrop, D. P., & Weber, J. A. (2001). Grandparents raising grandchildren: Families in transition. *Journal of Gerontological Social Work, 33*(2), 27–46.

Walker, H. M., Kavanagh, K., Stiller, B., Golly, A., Severson, H. H., & Feil, E. G. (1998). First step to success: An early intervention approach for preventing school antisocial behavior. *Journal of Emotional and Behavioral Disorders, 6,* 66–80.

Walker, H. M., Ramsey, E., & Gresham, F. M. (2004). *Antisocial behavior in school: Evidence-based practices* (2nd ed.). Belmont, CA: Wadsworth.

Walker, L. E. (1979). *The battered woman.* New York: Harper and Row.

Walker, L. E. (1984). *Battered woman syndrome.* New York: Springer-Verlag.

Walker, L. J. (1984). Sex differences in the development of moral reasoning: A critical review. *Child Development, 55,* 677–691.

Walker, L. J. (1989). A longitudinal study of moral reasoning. *Child Development, 60,* 157–166.

Wall, P. D. (2000). *Pain: The science of suffering.* New York: Columbia University Press.

Wallace, A. (1999). *The psychology of the Internet.* New York: Cambridge University Press.

Wallerstein, J., & Blakeslee, S. (1989). *Second chances: Men, women, and children a decade after divorce.* New York: Ticknor & Fields.

Wallerstein, J., & Blakeslee, S. (2003). *What about the kids?* New York: Hyperion.

Wallerstein, J., & Kelly, J. (1980). *Surviving the breakup.* New York: Basic Books.

Wallerstein, J., Lewis, J., & Blakeslee, S. (2000). *The unexpected legacy of divorce.* New York: Hyperion.

Wallman, J., & Winawer, J. (2004). Homeostasis of eye growth and the question of myopia. *Neuron, 43,* 447–468.

Wallston, K. A. (1992). Hocus-pocus, the focus isn't strictly on locus: Rotter's social learning theory modified for health. *Cognitive Therapy and Research, 16,* 183–199.

Walsh, F. (Ed.). (2003). *Normal family processes: Growing diversity and complexity* (3rd ed.). New York: Guilford.

Walsh, M. R. (1997). *Women, men, and gender: Ongoing debates.* New Haven, CT: Yale University Press.

Walsh, P. C., & Worthington, J. F. (2001). *Dr. Patrick Walsh's guide to surviving prostate cancer.* New York: Warner Books.

Walsh, W. B., & Osipow, S. H. (Eds.). (1994). *Career counseling for women.* Hillsdale, NJ: Erlbaum.

Walter, S., Morgan, M., & Walter, L. (1996). *Prepare for a literacy program.* Retrieved from http://www.sil.org/lingualinks/literacy/PrepareForALiteracyProgram/Index.htm

Wang, M. C., & Gordon, E. W. (1994). *Educational resilience in inner-city America: Challenges and prospects.* Hillsdale, NJ: Erlbaum.

Want, S. C., & Harris, P. L. (2000). Social learning: Compounding some problems and dissolving others. *Developmental Science, 5,* 39–41.

Ward, J., Hall, W., & Mattick, R. P. (1999). Role of maintenance treatment in opioid dependence. *The Lancet, 353,* 221–226.

Ward, T., Laws, D. R., & Hudson, S. M. (Eds.). (2003). *Sexual deviance: Issues and controversies.* Thousand Oaks, CA: Sage.

Wartner, U. B., Grossman, K., Freemer-Bombik, E., & Suess, G. (1994). Attachment patterns at age six in south Germany: Predictability from infancy and implications for preschool behavior. *Child Development, 65,* 1014–1027.

Waters, E., Hamilton, C. E., & Weinfield, N. S. (2000). The stability of attachment security from infancy to adulthood: General introduction. *Child Development, 71,* 684–689.

Waters, E., Merrick, S., Treboux, D., Crowell, J., & Albersheim, L. (2000). Attachment security in infancy and early adulthood: A twenty-year longitudinal study. *Child Development, 71,* 684–689.

Watson, D. (1989). Defining and describing whole language. *Elementary School Journal, 90,* 130–141.

Watson, J. B. (1913). Psychology as the behaviorist views it. *Psychological Review, 20,* 158–177.

Watson, J. B. (1930). *Behaviorism* (Rev. ed.). Chicago: University of Chicago Press.

Watson, L. C., Garrett, J. M., Sloane, P. D., Gruber-Baldini, A. L., & Zimmerman, S. (2003). Depression in assisted living: Results from a four-state study. *American Journal of Geriatric Psychiatry, 115,* 534–542.

WE MOVE. (2004). *Rett syndrome.* Retrieved from http://www.wemove.org/rett/

Weatherall, D. J., & Clegg, J. B. (2001). *The thalassaemia syndromes* (4th ed.). Oxford, UK: Blackwell.

Weaver, C. (1990). *Understanding whole language: From principle to practice.* Portsmouth, NH: Heinemann Educational Books.

Webb, M. (1997). *The good death: The new American search to reshape the end of life.* New York: Bantam.

Webb, W. B. (1992). *Sleep: The gentle tyrant.* Bolton: Anker.

WebMD, http://www.webmd.com

WebMD Health. (n.d.). *Coronary artery disease.* Retrieved from http://my.webmd.com/hw/heart_disease/hw112708.asp

WebMD Health. (n.d.). *Rh sensitization during pregnancy.* Retrieved from http://my.webmd.com/hw/being_pregnant/hw135945.asp?lastselectedguid={5FE84E90-BC77-4056A91C-9531713CA348}

Webster, A., Feiler, A., & Webster, V. (2003). Early intensive family intervention and evidence of effectiveness: Lessons from the South West Autism Programme. *Early Child Development and Care, 173*(4; Special Autism Issue), pp. 383–398.

Webster-Stratton, C., & Reid, M. J. (2003). The Incredible Years Parents, Teachers, and Children training series: A multifaceted treatment approach for young children with conduct problems. In A. E. Kazdin & J. R. Weisz (Eds.), *Evidence-based psychotherapies for children and adolescents.* (pp. 224–240). New York: Guilford.

Wechsler, D. (1974). *Wechsler Intelligence Scale for Children—Revised.* San Antonio, TX: The Psychological Corporation.

Wechsler, D. (2003). *WISC-IV technical and interpretive manual.* San Antonio, TX: The Psychological Corporation.

Wechsler, H., Lee, J. E., Kuo, M., Seibring, M., Nelson, T. F., & Lee, H. (2002). Trends in college binge drinking during a period of increased prevention efforts. *Journal of American College Health, 50*(5), 203–217.

Wedding, D., Horton, A. M., Jr., & Webster, D. (Eds.). (1986). *Neuropsychology handbook: Behavioral and clinical perspectives.* New York: Springer.

Weeks, J. (1985). *Sexuality and its discontents: Meanings, myths & modern sexualities.* London: Routledge & Kegan Paul.

Wehmeyer, M. L., & Patton, R. J. (2000). *Mental retardation in the 21st century.* Austin, TX: Pro-Ed.

Weich, T., & Sandberg, D. E. (2004). Diabetes mellitus, type 1. In T. H. Ollendick & C. S. Schroeder (Eds.), *Encyclopedia of clinical child and pediatric psychology.* New York: Kluwer Academic/Plenum.

Weinberg, M. S., Williams, C. J., & Pryor, D. W. (1994). *Dual attraction: Understanding bisexuality.* New York: Oxford University Press.

Weiner, B. (1985). An attributional theory of achievement motivation and emotion. *Psychological Review, 92,* 548–573.

Weiner, B. (1995). *Judgments of responsibility: Foundations of a theory of social action.* New York: Guilford.

Weiner, D. L. (2001). Pediatrics, inborn errors of metabolism. In G. Wilkes, R. Konop, W. Wolfram, J. Halamka, & W. K. Mallon (Eds.), *eMedicine world medical library.* Retrieved from http://www.emedicine.com/emerg/topic768.htm

Weinfield, N. S., Sroufe, L. A., Egeland, B., & Carlson, E. A. (1999). The nature of individual differences in infant-caregiver attachment. In J. Cassidy & P. Shaver (Eds.), *Handbook of attachment: Theory, research, and clinical applications* (pp. 68–98). New York: Guilford.

Weinraub, M., Horvath, D. L., & Gringlas, M. B. (2002). Single parenthood. In M. H. Bornstein (Ed.), *Handbook of parenting: Vol. 3: Being and becoming a parent* (2nd ed., pp. 109–140). Mahwah, NJ: Erlbaum.

Weinraub, M., & Lewis, M. (1977). The determinants of children's responses to separation. *Monographs of the Society for Research in Child Development, 42*(Serial No. 172), 1–127.

Weinshenker, B. G. (1994). Natural history of multiple sclerosis. *Annals of Neurology, 36*(Suppl.), 6–11.

Weisbuch, M., Beal, D., & O'Neal, E. C. (1999). How masculine ought I be? Men's masculinity and aggression. *Sex Roles, 40,* 583–592.

Weiser, F. X. (1958). *Handbook of Christian feasts and customs: The year of the Lord in liturgy and folklore.* New York: Harcourt, Brace, & World.

Weiss, A. (2000). The destruction of European Jewry, 1933–1945. In R. Rozett & S. Spector (Eds.), *Encyclopedia of the Holocaust* (pp. 45–55). New York: Facts on File.

Weiss, B. (2004). *When the doctor says Alzheimer's: Your caregiver's guide to Alzheimer's and dementia.* Bloomington, IN: AuthorHouse.

Weiss, J. (1996). *Ideology of death: Why the Holocaust happened in Germany.* Chicago: Ivan R. Dee.

Weiss, M. R. (2004). *Developmental sport and exercise psychology: A lifespan approach.* Morgantown, WV: Fitness Information Technology.

Weissbluth, M. (1984). *Crybabies. Coping with colic: What to do when baby won't stop crying!* New York: Berkley Books.

Welch, S. S. (2001). A review of the literature on the epidemiology of parasuicide in the general population. *Psychiatric Services, 52*(3), 368–375.

Wellcome Trust Human Genome, http://www.wellcome.ac.uk/en/genome/index.html

Weller, E. B., Weller, R. A., Stristad, M. A., Cain, S. E., & Bowes, J. M. (1988). Should children attend their parent's funeral? *Journal of American Academy of Child and Adolescent Psychiatry, 27,* 559–562.

Wellman, H., & Gellman, S. (1992). Cognitive development: Foundational theories of core domains. *Annual Review of Psychology, 43,* 337–375.

Wellman, H. M. (2002). Enlargement and constraint. In U. M. Staudinger & U. Lindenberger (Eds.), *Understanding human development: Dialogues with lifespan psychology.* Dordrecht, Netherlands: Kluwer.

Wellman, H. M., Cross, D., & Watson, J. (2001). Meta-analysis of theory-of-mind development: The truth about false belief. *Child Development, 72*(3), 655–684.

Wells, A., & Clark, D. M. (1997). Social phobia: A cognitive approach. In G. C. L. Davey (Ed.), *Phobias: A handbook of theory, research and treatment* (pp. 3–26). Chichester, UK: Wiley.

Wells, G. (1999). The zone of proximal development and its implications for learning and teaching. *Dialogic inquiry: Towards a sociocultural practice and theory of education.* New York: Cambridge University Press. Retrieved from http://tortoise.oise.utoronto.ca/~gwells/resources/ZPD.html

Welsh, M., & Pennington, B. (2000). Phenylketonuria. In K. O. Yeates, M. D. Ris, & H. G. Taylor (Eds.), *Pediatric neuropsychology: Research, theory, and practice. The science and practice of neuropsychology: A Guilford series* (pp. 275–299). New York: Guilford.

Welshons, W. V., Thayer, K. A., Judy, B. M., Taylor, J. A., Curran, E. M., & vom Saal, F. S. (2003). Large effects from small exposures. I. Mechanisms for endocrine-disrupting chemicals with estrogenic activity. *Environmental Health Perspectives, 111*(8), 994–1006.

Werner, E. E., & Smith, R. S. (1982). *Vulnerable but invincible: A study of resilient children.* New York: McGraw-Hill.

Werner, E. E., & Smith, R. S. (2001). *Journeys from childhood to midlife: Risk, resilience, and recovery.* Ithaca, NY: Cornell University Press.

Werner, H. (1957). The concept of development from a comparative and organismic point of view. In D. B. Harris (Ed.), *The concept of development* (pp. 125–148). Minneapolis: University of Minnesota Press.

Wertsch, J. V. (1985). *Vygotsky and the social formation of mind.* Cambridge, MA: Harvard University Press.

Wessel, M. A., Cobb, J. C., Jackson, E. B., Harris, G. S., & Detwiler, A. C. (1954). Paroxysmal fussing in infancy, sometimes called "colic." *Pediatrics, 14,* 421–434.

West Coast Analytical Service. (n.d.). *Methylmercury by IC-ICPMS.* Retrieved from http://www.wcas.com/tech/methylhg.htm

Westenberg, P. M., & Gjerde, P. F. (1999). Ego development during the transition from adolescence to young adulthood: A 9-year longitudinal study. *Journal of Research in Personality, 33,* 233–252.

Westinghouse Learning Corporation. (1969). *The impact of Head Start: An evaluation of the effects of Head Start on children's cognitive and affective development.* Washington, DC: Clearinghouse for Federal, Scientific, & Technical Information.

Wetherby, A., & Prizant, B. (2000). *Autism spectrum disorders: A transactional developmental perspective.* Baltimore: Paul H Brookes.

Wethington, E. (2000). Expecting stress: Americans and the "midlife crisis." *Motivation and Emotion, 24,* 85–103.

WGBH/NOVA Science Unit and Clear Blue Sky Productions. (n.d.). *Darwin.* Retrieved from http://www.pbs.org/wgbh/evolution/darwin/index.html

Whelehan, I. (1995). *Modern feminist thought: From the second wave to postfeminism.* New York: New York University Press.

Where in Africa did African Americans originate?, http://www.africanamericans.com/Origins.htm

Whipple, E. E., & Richey, C. A. (1997). Crossing the line from physical discipline to child abuse: How much is too much? *Child Abuse & Neglect, 21*(5), 431–444.

Whitaker, R. C., Wright, J. A., Pepe, M. S., Seidel, K. D., & Dietz, W. H. (1997). Predicting obesity in young adulthood from childhood and parental obesity. *New England Journal of Medicine, 337,* 869–873.

Whitbourne, S. K. (2005). *Adult development & aging: Biopsychosocial perspectives* (2nd ed.). Hoboken, NJ: Wiley.

White, J. W., Bondurant, B., & Travis, C. B. (2000). Social constructions of sexuality: Unpacking hidden meanings. In C. B. Travis & J. W. White (Eds.), *Sexuality, society, and feminism.* Washington, DC: American Psychological Association.

White, L. (1994). Stepfamilies over the life-course: Social support. In A. Booth & J. Dunn (Eds.), *Stepfamilies* (pp. 109–138). Mahwah, NJ: Erlbaum.

White, S. (1965). Evidence for a hierarchical arrangement of learning processes. In L. Lipsitt & C. Spiker (Eds.), *Advances in child development and behavior.* New York: Academic Press.

White, S. (1996). The child's entry into the "age of reason." In A. Sameroff & M. Haith (Eds.), *The five to seven shift: The age of reason and responsibility* (pp. 17–30). Chicago: University of Chicago Press.

White, S., & Vanneman, A. (2000). How does NAEP select schools and students? *Focus on NAEP, 4*(1). Retrieved from http://nces.ed.gov/pubs2000/2000459.pdf

White, S., & Vanneman, A. (2001). How does NAEP endure consistency in scoring? *Focus on NAEP, 4*(2). Retrieved from http://nces.ed.gov/pubs2000/2000490.pdf

Whitehead, M. B. (1989). *A mother's story.* New York: St. Martin's.

Whiteman, M. C., Deary, I. J., Lee, A. J., & Fowkes, F. G. R. (1997). Submissiveness and protection from coronary heart disease in the general population: Edinburgh Artery Study. *Lancet, 350,* 541–545.

Whitley, B. E., Jr. (1996). *Principles of research in behavioral science.* Mountain View, CA: Mayfield.

Widerstrom, A. H., Mowder, B. A., & Sandall, S. R. (1991). *At-risk and handicapped newborns and infants. Development, assessment and intervention.* Englewood Cliffs, NJ: Prentice-Hall.

Widow Net—Resources for Widows and Widowers, http://www.widownet.org

Wigfield, A., & Eccles, J. S. (Eds.). (2002). *Development of achievement motivation.* San Diego, CA: Academic Press.

Wiggins, J. S. (Ed.). (1996). *The five-factor model of personality: Theoretical perspectives.* New York: Guilford.

Wikipedia. (n.d.). *Donald Olding Hebb.* Retrieved from http://www.absoluteastronomy.com/encyclopedia/d/do/donald_olding_hebb.htm

Wilbur, R. B. (1987). *American Sign Language: Linguistic and applied dimensions* (2nd ed.). Boston: College-Hill Press.

Wildsoet, C. F. (1997). Active emmetropization—Evidence for its existence and ramifications for clinical practice. *Ophthalmic and Physiological Optics, 17,* 279–290.

Wilkin, C. S., & Powell, J. (n.d.). *Learning to live through loss: Helping children understand death.* Retrieved from http://www.nncc.org/Guidance/understand.death.html

Wilkinson, L., & Task Force on Statistical Inference. (1999). Statistical methods in psychology journals: Guidelines and explanations. *American Psychologist, 54,* 594–604. Retrieved from http://www.apa.org/journals/amp/amp 548594.html

Willett, W. C. (1994). Diet and health: What should we eat? *Science, 264,* 532–537.

Williams, D. R., & Williams, H. (1969). Automaintenance in the pigeon: Sustained pecking despite contingent non-reinforcement. *Journal of the Experimental Analysis of Behavior, 12,* 511–520.

Williams, D. S. (1972). Computer program organization induced from problem examples. In H. A. Simon & L. Siklossy (Eds.), *Representation and meaning: Experiments with information processing systems* (pp. 143–205). Englewood Cliffs, NJ: Prentice-Hall.

Williams, J. H. G., Whiten, A., Suddendorf, T., & Perrett, I. (2001). Imitation, mirror neurons and autism. *Neuroscience and Biobehavioural Review, 25,* 287–295. Retrieved from http://cogprints.ecs.soton.ac.uk/archive/00002613/

Williams, L. M., Morrow, B., Lansky, A., Beck, L. F., Barfield, W., Helms, K., et al. (2003). *Surveillance for selected maternal behaviors and experiences before, during, and after pregnancy: Pregnancy risk assessment monitoring system (PRAMS) 2000.* Washington, DC: Division of Reproductive Health, National Center for Chronic Disease Prevention and Health Promotion, Centers for Disease Control and Prevention.

Williams, R. H., Larsen, P. R., Kronenberg, H. M., Melmed, S., Polonsky, K. S., Wilson, J. D., et al. (2002). *Williams textbook of endocrinology.* Philadelphia: WB Saunders.

Williams, S. J., & Gruneberg, M. (2002). Memory failures in supermarket shoppers: Evidence for age and gender differences. *Cognitive Technology, 7,* 34–38.

Williamson, J. B., & Schneidman, E. S. (1995). *Death: Current perspectives.* Mountain View, CA: Mayfield.

Willis, D. J., Dobrec, A., & Sipes, D. S. B. (1992). Treating American Indian victims of abuse and neglect. In L. A. Vargas & J. D. Koss-Chioino (Eds.), *Working with culture: Psychotherapeutic interventions with ethnic minority children and adolescents* (pp. 276–299). San Francisco: Jossey-Bass.

Wilmes, D. (1998). *Parenting for prevention: How to raise a child to say no to alcohol/drug. For parents, teachers, and other concerned adults.* Minneapolis, MN: Hazelden.

Wilson, E. O. (2002). *The future of life.* New York: Knopf.

Wilson, J. F. (2003). *Biological foundations of human behavior.* Belmont, CA: Thomson Wadsworth.

Wilson, J. F. (2004). New treatments for growing scourge of brittle bones. *Annals of Internal Medicine, 140*(2), 153–156.

Wilson, W. (1997). *When work disappears: The world of the new urban poor.* New York: Alfred A. Knopf.

Wineburgh, A. L. (2000). Treatment of children with absent fathers. *Child and Adolescent Social Work Journal, 17,* 255–273.

Wing, L. (1981). Asperger's syndrome: A clinical account. *Psychological Medicine, 11,* 115–129.

Wingwood, G. M., & DiClemente, R. J. (Eds.). (2002). *Handbook of women's sexual and reproductive health.* New York: Kluwer Academic/Plenum.

Winner, E. (1996). *Gifted children: Myths and realities.* New York: Basic Books.

Winningham, R. G., Anunsen, R. A., Hanson, L., Laux, L., Kaus, K., & Reifers, A. (2004). MemAerobics: A cognitive intervention to improve memory ability and reduce depression in older adults. *Journal of Mental Health and Aging, 9*(3), 183–192.

Winsler, A., De León, J. R., Wallace, B., Carlton, M. P, & Willson-Quayle, A. (2003). Private speech in preschool children: Developmental stability and change, across-task consistency, and relations with classroom behavior. *Journal of Child Language, 30,* 583–608.

Wissow, L. S. (2002). Child discipline in the first three years of life. In N. Halfon, K. T. McLearn, & M. A. Schuster (Eds.), *Child rearing in America* (pp. 146–177). New York: Cambridge University Press.

Witkin, H. A., & Goodenough, D. R. (1981). *Cognitive styles: Essence and origins.* New York: International Universities Press.

Wodrich, D. (1999). *ADHD: What every parent wants to know* (2nd ed.). Baltimore: Paul H. Brookes.

Wohlfarth, T. (1997). Socioeconomic inequality and psychopathology: Are socioeconomic status and social class interchangeable? *Social Science and Medicine, 45,* 399–410.

Wolak, J., Mitchell, K., & Finkelhor, D. (2003, November). *Internet sex crimes against minors: The response of law enforcement.* Alexandria, VA: National Center for Missing & Exploited Children.

Wolf, A. W., Lozoff, B., Latz, S., & Paladetto, R. (1996). Parental theories in the management of young children's sleep in Japan, Italy, and the United States. In S. Harkness & C. Super (Eds.), *Parents' cultural belief systems: Their origins, expressions, and consequences* (pp. 364–384). New York: Guilford.

Wolf, T. H. (1973). *Alfred Binet.* Chicago: University of Chicago Press.

Wolfe, D. A., Crooks, C. V., Lee, V., McIntyre-Smith, A., & Jaffe, P. G. (2003). The effects of children's exposure to domestic violence: A meta-analysis and critique. *Clinical Child and Family Psychology Review, 6,* 171–187.

Wolfe, J. M. (1994). Guided search 2.0: A revised model of visual-search. *Psychonomic Bulletin & Review, 1*(2), 202–238.

Wolfe, J., Grier, H. E., Klar, N., Levin, S. B., Ellenbogen, J. M., Salem-Schatz, S., et al. (2000). Symptoms and suffering at the end of life in children with cancer. *New England Journal of Medicine, 342,* 326–333.

Wolfe, L. M. (n.d.). *Developmental research methods.* http://www.webster.edu/~woolflm/methods/devresearchmethods.html

Wolff, P. (1968). The serial organization of sucking in the young infant. *Pediatrics, 42*(6), 943–956.

Wolfgang, M. (1958). *Patterns in criminal homicide.* Philadelphia: University of Pennsylvania.

Wolfle, D. (1997). The reorganized American Psychological Association. *American Psychologist, 52,* 721–724.

Wolitski, R. J., Valdiserri, R. O., Denning, P. H., & Levine, W. C. (2001). Are we headed for a resurgence of the HIV epidemic among men who have sex with men? *American Journal of Public Health, 91,* 883–888.

Women's Health Initiative (WHI), http://www.nhlbi.nih.gov/whi/

Women's Intellectual Contributions to the Study of Mind and Society. (n.d.). *Carol Gilligan (1936–present).* Retrieved from http://www.webster.edu/~woolflm/gilligan.html

Women's Intellectual Contributions to the Study of Mind and Society. (n.d.). *Nancy Bayley.* Retrieved from http://www.webster.edu/~woolflm/bayley.html

Wong, A. S. L. (2000). *Kohlberg's stages explained and illustrated.* Retrieved from http://www.vtaide.com/png/Kohlberg.htm

Wong, W. Y., Thomas, C. M. G., Merkus, J. M. W. M., Zielhuis, G. A., & Steegers-Theunissen, R. P. M. (2000). Male factor subfertility: Possible causes and the impact of nutritional factors. *Fertility and Sterility, 73,* 435–442.

Woo, J. S. K. (n.d.). *A short history of the development of ultrasound in obstetrics and gynecology.* Retrieved from http://www.ob-ultrasound.net/history1.html

Wood, D. J., & Middleton, D. (1975). A study of assisted problem solving. *British Journal of Psychology, 66,* 181–191.

Wood, W., & Eagly, A. (2002). A cross-cultural analysis of the behavior of women and men: Implications for the origins of sex differences. *Psychological Bulletin, 128,* 699–727.

Woodcock, R. W., & Johnson, M. B. (1989). *Woodcock-Johnson Psycho-Educational Battery—Revised.* Chicago: Riverside.

Woodrow-Lafield, K. A. (1995). *Potential sponsorship by IRCA-legalized immigrants.* Washington, DC: U.S. Commission on Immigration Reform.

Woodrow-Lafield, K. A. (2001). Implications of immigration for apportionment. *Population Research and Policy Review, 20*(4), 267–289.

Woodrow Wilson School of Public and International Affairs at Princeton University and The Brookings Institution. (n.d.). *The future of children.* Available from http://www.futureofchildren.org/

Woody, C. D. (2004). Reflex learning. In G. Adelman & B. H. Smith (Eds.), *Encyclopedia of neuroscience* (3rd ed.). Amsterdam: Elsevier.

Woody, S. R., & Teachman, B. A. (2000). Intersection of disgust and fear: Normative and pathological views. *Clinical Psychology: Science and Practice, 7,* 291–311.

Woolf, L. M. (n.d.). *Developmental research methods.* Retrieved from http://www.webster.edu/~woolflm/methods/devresearchmethods.html

Woolfe, L. M. (n.d.). *Theoretical perspectives relevant to developmental psychology.* Retrieved from http://www.webster.edu/~woolflm/designs.html

Woolfolk, A. (2004). *Educational psychology* (9th ed.). Boston: Pearson.

Woollacott, M. H., & Jensen, J. L. (1996). Posture and locomotion. In H. Heuer & S. Keele (Eds.), *Handbook of perception and action* (Vol. 2, pp. 333–403). London: Academic Press.

Wootten, I. L. (n.d.). *Hetherington's groundbreaking work shows how families cope with divorce.* Retrieved from http://www.virginia.edu/insideuva/2000/09/hetherington.html

Worden, W. (1982) *Grief counselling and grief therapy,* New York: Springer.

WordIQ.com, list of firearms, http://www.wordiq.com/definition/List_of_firearms/

World Federation of Hemophilia. (2002). *Frequently asked questions.* Retrieved from http://www.wfh.org/ShowDoc.asp?Rubrique=28&Document=42

World Federation of Right to Die Societies, http://www.worldrtd.net/

World Health Organization (WHO), http://www.who.int/aboutwho

World Health Organization. (1991). *Infertility: A tabulation of available data on prevalence of primary and secondary infertility.* Geneva, Switzerland: Department of Reproductive Health and Research.

World Health Organization. (1997). *Programme on substance abuse, amphetamine-type stimulants.* Geneva: Division of Mental Health and Prevention of Substance Abuse.

World Health Organization. (2004). *Maternal mortality in 2000: Estimates developed by WHO, UNICEF and UNFPA.* Geneva: Department of Reproductive Health and Research.

World Health Organization InterNetwork Access to Research Initiative, http://www.healthinternetwork.org

World Health Organization, Ionizing Radiation, http://www.who.int/ionizing_radiation/en/

The World of Work. (n.d.). *History of work in Minnesota.* Retrieved from http://www.rb-29.net/graa/wowork/index.html

Worley, K., & Wolraich, M. (2003). Attention deficit hyperactivity disorder. In M. Wolraich (Ed.), *Disorders of learning and development* (3rd ed., pp. 311–327). Hamilton, Ontario: BC Decker.

Worthington-Roberts, B. (2004). *Human nutrition.* Retrieved from http://encarta.msn.com/text

Woznick, L. A., & Goodheart, C. D. (2002). *Living with childhood cancer: A practical guide to help families cope.* Washington, DC: American Psychological Association.

Wright, H. R., & Lack, L. C. (2004). The effect of different wavelengths of light in changing the phase of the melatonin circadian rhythm. In S. R. Pandi-Perumal & D. P. Cardinali (Eds.), *Melatonin: Biological basis of its function in health and disease.* Georgetown, TX: Landes Bioscience. Retrieved from http://www.eurekah.com/abstract.php?chapid=1467&bookid=110&catid=48

Wright, R. (1995). *The moral animal.* New York: Vintage.

Wrightslaw, http://www.wrightslaw.com

Wrightsman, L. S., Greene, E., Nietzel, M. T., & Fortune, W. H. (2002). *Psychology and the legal system* (5th ed.). Belmont, CA: Wadsworth.

Wrobel, G., Grotevant, H. D., Berge, J., Mendenhall, T., & McRoy, R. G. (2003). Contact in adoption: The experience of adoptive families in the USA. *Adoption & Fostering, 27*(1), 57–67.

Wrobel, G., Grotevant, H. D., & McRoy, R. G. (2004). Adolescent search for birthparents: Who moves forward? *Journal of Adolescent Research, 19*(1), 132–151.

Wyatt, R., Alexander, R., Egan, M., & Kirch, D. (1987). Schizophrenia, just the facts: What do we know, how well do we know it? *Schizophrenia Research, 1,* 3–18.

Wysocki, T., Greco, P., & Buckloh, L. M. (2003). Childhood diabetes in psychological context. In M. C. Roberts (Ed.), *Handbook of pediatric psychology* (3rd ed., pp. 304–320). New York: Guilford.

Xiridou, M., Geskus, R., de Wit, J., Coutinho, R., & Kretzschmar, M. (2003). The contribution of steady and casual partnerships to the incidence of HIV infection among homosexual men in Amsterdam. *AIDS, 17,* 1029–1038.

Xueqin Ma, G. (2002). *Ethnicity and substance abuse: Prevention and intervention.* Springfield, IL: Charles C Thomas.

Yahoo Health. (2001). *Developmental coordination disorder.* Retrieved from http://health.yahoo.com/health/centers/parenting/001533.html

Yale Child Study Center, Developmental Disabilities Clinic, http://info.med.yale.edu/chldstdy/autism/aspergers.html

Yale PACE Center, Center on Psychology of Abilities, Competencies, and Expertise, http://www.yale.edu/pace

Yamaguchi, K., & Kandel, D. B. (1984). Patterns of drug use from adolescence to young adulthood. II. Sequences and progression. *American Journal of Public Health, 74,* 668–672.

Yang, L. J. (2003). Combination of extinction and protective measures in the treatment of severely self-injurious behavior. *Behavioral Interventions, 18,* 109–121.

Yarrow, M. R., Scott, P. M., & Waxler, C. Z. (1973). Learning concern for others. *Developmental Psychology, 8,* 240–260.

Yawn, B. P., Wollan, P., Kurland, M., & Scanlon, P. (2002). A longitudinal study of the prevalence of asthma in a community population of school-age children. *Journal of Pediatrics, 140,* 576–581.

Yedida, M. J., & MacGregory, B. (2001). Confronting the prospect of dying: Reports of terminally ill patients. *Journal of Pain and Symptom Management, 22,* 807–819.

Yi, H., Williams, G. D., & Dufour, M. C. (2003). *Surveillance report #65: Trends in alcohol-related fatal traffic crashes, United States, 1977–2001.* Bethesda, MD: National Institute on Alcohol Abuse and Alcoholism, Division of Biometry and Epidemiology. Retrieved from http://www.niaaa.nih.gov/databases/crash01.htm

Yoshikawa, H. (1995). Long-term effects of early childhood programs on social outcomes and delinquency [Electronic version]. *The Future of the Children, 5*(3). Retrieved from http://www.futureofchildren.org/information2826/information_show.htm?doc_id=77676

Young, B. A. (2003). *Public high school dropouts and completers from the common core of data: School year 2000–01* (NCES No. 2004-310). Washington, DC: U.S. Department of Education. Retrieved from http://nces.ed.gov/pubsearch/pubsinfo.asp?pubid=2002382

Young, K. S. (1998). *Caught in the net.* New York: Wiley.

Young, M. L. (2000). *Working memory, language and reading.* Retrieved from http://www.brainconnection.com/topics/?main=fa/memory-language

Young, T. M., Martin, S. S., Young, M. E., & Ting, L. (2001, Summer). Internal poverty and teen pregnancy. *Adolescence, 36*(142), 289–304.

Youngblut, J. M., Brooten, D., Singer, L. T., Standing, T., Lee, H., & Rodgers, W. L. (2001). Effects of maternal employment and prematurity on child outcomes in single parent families. *Nursing Research, 50*(6), 346–355.

Youngkin, E. Q., & Davis, M. S. (2004). *Women's health: A primary care clinical guide* (3rd ed.). Upper Saddle River, NJ: Pearson/Prentice-Hall.

Youth Ambassadors for Peace. (n.d.). *UN Convention on the Rights of the Child.* Retrieved from http://www.freethechildren.org/peace/childrenandwar/uncrc.html

YouthNet, http://www.fhi.org/en/youth/youthnet

Yu, V. Y. (2003). Global, regional and national perinatal and neonatal mortality. *Journal of Perinatal Medicine, 31*(5), 376–379.

Zachary, L. J., & Daloz, L. A. (2000). *Mentor's guide: Facilitating effective learning.* San Francisco: Jossey-Bass.

Zajonc, R. B. (1976). Family configurations and intelligence. *Science, 192,* 227–236.

Zanna, M. P., & Rempel, J. K. (1988). Attitudes: A new look at an old concept. In D. Bar-Tal & A. W. Kruglanski (Eds.), *The social psychology of knowledge* (pp. 315–334). Cambridge, UK: Cambridge University Press.

Zarit, S. H., & Eggebeen, D. J. (2002). Parent-child relationships in adulthood and later years. In M. H. Bornstein (Ed.), *Handbook of parenting: Vol. 2. Children and parenting* (2nd ed.). Mahwah, NJ: Erlbaum.

Zartman, K. (2004). *Why we give: A family's struggle with schizophrenia*. Retrieved from http://www.narsad.org/dc/schizophrenia/featured.html

Zasloff, R. L., & Kidd, A. H. (1994). Loneliness and pet ownership among single women. *Psychological Reports, 75,* 747–752.

Zautra, A. (2003). *Emotions, stress, and health*. New York: Oxford University Press.

Zero to Three, http://www.zerotothree.org/

Zero to Three, for parents, http://www.zerotothree.org/ztt_parents.html

Zeskind, P. S., & Lester, B. M. (1978). Acoustic features and auditory perceptions of the cries of newborns with prenatal and perinatal complications. *Child Development, 49,* 580–589.

Zigler, E., & Muenchow, S. (1992). *Head Start: The inside story of America's most successful educational experiment*. New York: Basic Books.

Zigler, E., & Styfco, S. J. (2004). *The Head Start debates*. Baltimore: Paul H. Brookes Publishing.

Zigler, E. G., & Hall, N. W. (2000). *Child development and social policy: Theory and applications*. Boston: McGraw-Hill.

Zillmer, E. A., & Spiers, M. V. (2001). *Principles of neuropsychology*. Belmont, CA: Wadsworth.

Zimbardo, P. G., & Radl, S. L. (1999). *The shy child: Overcoming and preventing shyness from infancy to adulthood*. Cambridge, MA: Malor Books.

Zimmer-Gembeck, M. J. (2002). The development of romantic relationships and adaptations in the system of peer relationships. *Journal of Adolescent Health, 31*(Suppl. 6), 216–225.

Zimmer-Gembeck, M. J., Siebenbruner, J., & Collins, W. A. (2001). Diverse aspects of dating: Associations with psychosocial functioning from early to middle adolescence. *Journal of Adolescence, 24,* 313–336.

Zimmerman, B. (2000). *Lesbian histories and cultures: An encyclopedia*. New York: Garland.

Zimmerman, B., & McNaron, A. H. (Eds.). (1996). *The new lesbian studies: Into the twenty-first century*. New York: The Feminist Press.

Zimmerman, D. R. (1973). *Rh: The intimate history of a disease and its conquest*. New York: Macmillan.

Zimmerman, S., Scott, A. C., Park, N. S., Hall, S. A., Wetherby, M. M., Gruber-Baldini, A. L., et al. (2003). Social engagement and its relationship to service provision in residential care and assisted living. *Social Work Research, 27*(1), 6–18.

Zimmerman, S., Sloane, P. D., Eckert, J. K., & Lawton, M. P. (Eds.). (2001). *Assisted living: Needs, practices, and policies in residential care for the elderly*. Baltimore: Johns Hopkins University Press.

Zoba, W. M. (2000, March 6). Won't you be my neighbor? *Christianity Today*. Retrieved from http://www.christianitytoday.com/ct/2000/003/1.38.html

Zorrilla, L., Cannon, T., Kronenberg, S., Mednick, S., Schulsinger F., Parnas, J., et al. (1997). Structural brain abnormalities in schizophrenia: A family study. *Biological Psychiatry, 42,* 1080–1086.

Zucker, K. J., & Bradley, S. J. (1995). *Gender identity disorder and psychosexual problems in children and adolescents*. New York: Guilford.

Zuckerman, M. (1994). *Behavioral expressions and biosocial bases of sensation seeking*. New York: Cambridge University Press.

Zuckerman, M. (1999). *Vulnerability to psychopathology: A biosocial model*. Washington, DC: American Psychological Association.

Zuckerman, M. (2000). Are you a risk-taker? *Psychology Today,* Nov/Dec, 54–87.

Zuckerman, M., & Kuhlman, D. M. (2000). Personality and risk-taking: Common biosocial factors. *Journal of Personality, 68,* 999–1029.

Zuckerman, M., & Kuhlman, D. M. (n.d.). *Sensation seeking scale: Roads and traffic authority*. Retrieved from http://www.rta.nsw.gov.au/licensing/tests/driverqualificationtest/sensationseekingscale/

Zupan, Z. (2003). Perinatal mortality and morbidity in developing countries. A global view. *Medecine Tropicale (Marseilles), 63*(4–5), 366–368.

Zwick, R. (Ed.). (2004). *Rethinking the SAT: The future of standardized testing in university admissions*. New York: Routledge Farmer.

Index